Machine Learning for Algorithmic Trading

Second Edition

Predictive models to extract signals from market and alternative data for systematic trading strategies with Python

Stefan Jansen

Packt

BIRMINGHAM - MUMBAI

Machine Learning for Algorithmic Trading

Second Edition

Producer: Tushar Gupta

Acquisition Editor – Peer Reviews: Suresh Jain

Content Development Editor: Chris Nelson

Technical Editor: Aniket Shetty

Project Editor: Carol Lewis

Copy Editor: Safis Editing

Proofreader: Safis Editing

Indexer: Priyanka Dhadke

Presentation Designer: Pranit Padwal

First published: December 2018

Second edition: July 2020

Production reference: 2141020

Published by Packt Publishing Ltd.

Livery Place

35 Livery Street

Birmingham B3 2PB, UK.

ISBN 978-1-83702-709-5

www.packt.com

packt.com

Subscribe to our online digital library for full access to over 7,000 books and videos, as well as industry leading tools to help you plan your personal development and advance your career. For more information, please visit our website.

Why subscribe?

- Spend less time learning and more time coding with practical eBooks and Videos from over 4,000 industry professionals
- Learn better with Skill Plans built especially for you
- Get a free eBook or video every month
- Fully searchable for easy access to vital information
- Copy and paste, print, and bookmark content

Did you know that Packt offers eBook versions of every book published, with PDF and ePub files available? You can upgrade to the eBook version at www.Packt.com and as a print book customer, you are entitled to a discount on the eBook copy. Get in touch with us at customercare@packtpub.com for more details.

At www.Packt.com, you can also read a collection of free technical articles, sign up for a range of free newsletters, and receive exclusive discounts and offers on Packt books and eBooks.

Contributors

About the author

Stefan Jansen is the founder and CEO of Applied AI. He advises Fortune 500 companies, investment firms, and start-ups across industries on data and AI strategy, building data science teams, and developing end-to-end machine learning solutions for a broad range of business problems.

Before his current venture, he was a partner and managing director at an international investment firm, where he built the predictive analytics and investment research practice. He was also a senior executive at a global fintech company with operations in 15 markets, advised central banks in emerging markets, and consulted for the World Bank.

He holds master's degrees in computer science from Georgia Tech and in economics from Harvard and Free University Berlin, and a CFA charter. He has worked in six languages across Europe, Asia, and the Americas and taught data science at DataCamp and General Assembly.

This thorough revision of the first edition was only possible with the collaboration and support of my family, friends, and colleagues. I want to thank the team at Packt for responding to reader feedback and taking the project from start to finish. Chris Nelson was a thorough editor and provided constructive advice. I want to thank my clients for the opportunity to do such exciting work that often offered valuable inspiration for this book.

Most important, however, has been the unrelenting patience and support of Mariana. To her and Bastian, who make it all worthwhile, I dedicate this book.

About the reviewers

Prem Jebaseelan has about 20 years of experience in handling different financial data and enjoys the challenge of organizing, storing, retrieving, and analyzing large volumes of data. Prem has designed and implemented several enterprise-level solutions for front office trading strategies, middle office, and back office applications for funds, and has good experience in applying machine learning and AI-based solutions. Prem has an engineering degree.

Prem is currently the co-founder and CEO of Zentropy Technologies, a fintech company that specializes in creating machine learning based solutions in the financial domain. Prior to this, Prem worked in one of the leading hedge funds as a technology solutions provider.

I would like to thank all my previous employers who have helped me in developing real-world solutions that bring technology and finance together. I would specifically like to thank Dr Yves Hilpisch for our work together in the application of machine learning to real-world trading strategies.

Ramanathan Ramakrishnamoorthy is one of the co founders and directors at Zentropy Technologies. Ramanathan started his professional career with a leading hedge fund and in his latest position, he worked as a project manager responsible for building tools and technologies required by the middle and back office. At Zentropy, Ramanathan is primarily responsible for better understanding project requirements and converting them to technical specs. alongside executing them. Having a keen eye for subtle data patterns, Ramanathan also has a good understanding of the machine learning and data science domain, particularly with expertise in the time series analysis domain. Ramanathan's experience has primarily been around building trading systems, quant warehouses, and backtesting engines for capital markets.

Ramanathan is also an active core group member in the Hyderabad Python group. He leads some of the most important activities of the community, like organizing conferences, monthly meetups, and conducting Python sessions at colleges.

Table of Contents

Preface

If you are reading this, you are probably aware that **machine learning** (**ML**) **has become a strategic capability** in many industries, including the investment industry. The explosion of digital data closely related to the rise of ML is having a particularly powerful impact on investing, which already has a long history of using sophisticated models to process information. These trends are enabling **novel approaches to quantitative investment** and are boosting the demand for the application of data science to both discretionary and algorithmic trading strategies.

The **scope of trading across asset classes** is vast because it ranges from equities and government bonds to commodities and real estate. This implies that a very large range of new alternative data sources may be relevant above and beyond the market and fundamental data that used to be at the center of most analytical efforts in the past.

You also may have come across the insight that the successful application of ML or data science requires the **integration of statistical knowledge, computational skills, and domain expertise** at the individual or team level. In other words, it is essential to ask the right questions, identify and understand the data that may provide the answers, deploy a broad range of tools to obtain results, and interpret them in a way that leads to the right decisions.

Therefore, this book provides an integrated perspective on the application of ML to the domain of investment and trading. In this preface, we outline what you should expect, how we have organized the content to facilitate achieving our objectives, and what you need both to meet your goals and have fun in the process.

What to expect

This book aims to equip you with a strategic perspective, conceptual understanding, and practical tools to add value when applying ML to the trading and investment process. To this end, we cover ML as a key element in a process rather than a standalone exercise. Most importantly, we introduce an **end-to-end ML for trading (ML4T) workflow** that we apply to numerous use cases with relevant data and code examples.

The ML4T workflow starts with generating ideas and sourcing data and continues to extracting features, tuning ML models, and designing trading strategies that act on the models' predictive signals. It also includes simulating strategies on historical data using a backtesting engine and evaluating their performance.

First and foremost, the book demonstrates how you can extract signals from a diverse set of data sources and design trading strategies for different asset classes using a broad range of **supervised, unsupervised, and reinforcement learning algorithms**. In addition, it provides relevant mathematical and statistical background to facilitate tuning an algorithm and interpreting the results. Finally, it includes financial background to enable you to work with market and fundamental data, extract informative features, and manage the performance of a trading strategy.

The book emphasizes that investors can gain at least as much value from third-party data as other industries. As a consequence, it covers not only how to work with market and fundamental data but also how to source, evaluate, process, and model **alternative data sources** such as unstructured text and image data.

It should not be a surprise that **this book does not provide investment advice** or ready-made trading algorithms. On the contrary, it intends to communicate that ML faces many additional challenges in the trading domain, ranging from lower signal content to shorter time series that often make it harder to achieve robust results. In fact, we have included several examples that do not yield great results to avoid exaggerating the benefits of ML or understating the effort it takes to have a good idea, obtain the right data, engineer ingenious features, and design an effective strategy (with potentially attractive rewards).

Instead, you should find the book most useful as a guide to leveraging key ML algorithms to inform a trading strategy using a systematic workflow. To this end, we present a **framework that guides you through the ML4T process** of the following:

1. Sourcing, evaluating, and combining data for any investment objective
2. Designing and tuning ML models that extract predictive signals from the data
3. Developing and evaluating trading strategies based on the results

After reading this book, you will be able to begin designing and evaluating your own ML-based strategies and might want to consider participating in competitions or connecting to the API of an online broker and begin trading in the real world.

What's new in the second edition

This second edition emphasizes the end-to-end ML4T workflow, reflected in a new chapter on strategy backtesting (*Chapter 8, The ML4T Workflow – From Model to Strategy Backtesting*), a new appendix describing over 100 different alpha factors, and many new practical applications. We have also rewritten most of the existing content for clarity and readability.

The applications now use a broader range of data sources beyond daily US equity prices, including international stocks and ETFs, as well as minute-frequency equity data to demonstrate an intraday strategy. Also, there is now broader coverage of alternative data sources, including SEC filings for sentiment analysis and return forecasts, as well as satellite images to classify land use.

Furthermore, the book replicates several applications recently published in academic papers. *Chapter 18, CNNs for Financial Time Series and Satellite Images*, demonstrates how to apply convolutional neural networks to time series converted to image format for return predictions. *Chapter 20, Autoencoders for Conditional Risk Factors and Asset Pricing*, shows how to extract risk factors conditioned on stock characteristics for asset pricing using autoencoders. *Chapter 21, Generative Adversarial Networks for Synthetic Time-Series Data*, examines how to create synthetic training data using generative adversarial networks.

All applications now use the latest available (at the time of writing) software versions, such as pandas 1.0 and TensorFlow 2.2. There is also a customized version of Zipline that makes it easy to include machine learning model predictions when designing a trading strategy.

Who should read this book

You should find the book informative if you are an **analyst, data scientist, or ML engineer** with an understanding of financial markets and an interest in trading strategies. You should also find value as an investment professional who aims to leverage ML to make better decisions.

If your background is in software and ML, you may be able to just skim or skip some introductory material in this area. Similarly, if your expertise is in investment, you will likely be familiar with some, or all, of the financial context that we provide for those with different backgrounds.

The book assumes that you want to continue to learn about this very dynamic area. To this end, it includes numerous end-of-chapter academic references and additional resources linked in the `README` files for each chapter in the companion GitHub repository.

You should be comfortable using Python 3 and scientific computing libraries like NumPy, pandas, or SciPy and look forward to picking up numerous others along the way. Some experience with ML and scikit-learn would be helpful, but we briefly cover the basic workflow and reference various resources to fill gaps or dive deeper. Similarly, basic knowledge of finance and investment will make some terminology easier to follow.

What this book covers

This book provides a comprehensive introduction to how ML can add value to the design and execution of trading strategies. It is organized into four parts that cover different aspects of the data sourcing and strategy development process, as well as different solutions to various ML challenges.

Part 1 – Data, alpha factors, and portfolios

The first part covers fundamental aspects relevant across trading strategies that leverage machine learning. It focuses on the data that drives the ML algorithms and strategies discussed in this book, outlines how you can engineer features that capture the data's signal content, and explains how to optimize and evaluate the performance of a portfolio.

Chapter 1, Machine Learning for Trading – From Idea to Execution, summarizes how and why ML became important for trading, describes the investment process, and outlines how ML can add value.

Chapter 2, Market and Fundamental Data – Sources and Techniques, covers how to source and work with market data, including exchange-provided tick data, and reported financials. It also demonstrates access to numerous **open source data providers** that we will rely on throughout this book.

Chapter 3, Alternative Data for Finance – Categories and Use Cases, explains categories and criteria to assess the exploding number of **sources and providers**. It also demonstrates how to create alternative datasets by scraping websites, for example, to collect earnings call transcripts for use with **natural language processing** (**NLP**) and sentiment analysis, which we cover in the second part of the book.

Chapter 4, Financial Feature Engineering – How to Research Alpha Factors, presents the process of creating and evaluating data transformations that capture the predictive signal and shows how to measure factor performance. It also summarizes insights from research into risk factors that aim to explain alpha in financial markets otherwise deemed to be efficient. Furthermore, it demonstrates how to **engineer alpha factors** using Python libraries offline and introduces the **Zipline** and **Alphalens** libraries to backtest factors and evaluate their predictive power.

Chapter 5, Portfolio Optimization and Performance Evaluation, introduces how to manage, optimize, and evaluate a portfolio resulting from the execution of a strategy. It presents risk metrics and shows how to apply them using the Zipline and **pyfolio** libraries. It also introduces methods to **optimize a strategy from a portfolio risk perspective**.

Part 2 – ML for trading – Fundamentals

The second part illustrates how fundamental supervised and unsupervised learning algorithms can inform trading strategies in the context of an end-to-end workflow.

Chapter 6, The Machine Learning Process, sets the stage by outlining how to formulate, train, tune, and evaluate the predictive performance of ML models in a systematic way. It also addresses **domain-specific concerns**, such as using cross-validation with financial time series to select among alternative ML models.

Chapter 7, Linear Models – From Risk Factors to Return Forecasts, shows how to use **linear and logistic regression** for inference and prediction and how to use regularization to manage the risk of overfitting. It demonstrates how to **predict US equity returns** or the direction of their future movements and how to evaluate the signal content of these predictions using Alphalens.

Chapter 8, The ML4T Workflow – From Model to Strategy Backtesting, integrates the various building blocks of the ML4T workflow thus far discussed separately. It presents an end-to-end perspective on the process of designing, simulating, and evaluating a trading strategy driven by an ML algorithm. To this end, it demonstrates how to **backtest an ML-driven strategy** in a historical market context using the Python libraries backtrader and Zipline.

Chapter 9, Time-Series Models for Volatility Forecasts and Statistical Arbitrage, covers univariate and multivariate time series diagnostics and models, including vector autoregressive models as well as ARCH/GARCH models for volatility forecasts. It also introduces cointegration and shows how to use it for a **pairs trading strategy using a diverse set of exchange-traded funds (ETFs)**.

Chapter 10, Bayesian ML – Dynamic Sharpe Ratios and Pairs Trading, presents probabilistic models and how **Markov chain Monte Carlo** (**MCMC**) sampling and variational Bayes facilitate approximate inference. It also illustrates how to use **PyMC3** for probabilistic programming to gain deeper insights into **parameter and model uncertainty**, for example, when evaluating **portfolio performance**.

Chapter 11, Random Forests – A Long-Short Strategy for Japanese Stocks, shows how to build, train, and tune nonlinear tree-based models for insight and prediction. It introduces tree-based ensembles and shows how random forests use bootstrap aggregation to overcome some of the weaknesses of decision trees. We then proceed to develop and backtest a **long-short strategy for Japanese equities**.

Chapter 12, Boosting Your Trading Strategy, introduces gradient boosting and demonstrates how to use the libraries XGBoost, LightBGM, and CatBoost for high-performance training and prediction. It reviews how to tune the numerous hyperparameters and interpret the model using **SHapley Additive exPlanation** (**SHAP**) values before building and evaluating a strategy that trades US equities based on LightGBM return forecasts.

Chapter 13, Data-Driven Risk Factors and Asset Allocation with Unsupervised Learning, shows how to use dimensionality reduction and clustering for algorithmic trading. It uses principal and independent component analysis to extract data-driven risk factors and generate **eigenportfolios**. It presents several clustering techniques and demonstrates the use of hierarchical clustering for **asset allocation**.

Part 3 – Natural language processing

Part 3 focuses on text data and introduces state-of-the-art unsupervised learning techniques to extract high-quality signals from this key source of alternative data.

Chapter 14, *Text Data for Trading - Sentiment Analysis*, demonstrates how to convert text data into a numerical format and applies the classification algorithms from Part 2 for sentiment analysis to large datasets.

Chapter 15, *Topic Modeling - Summarizing Financial News*, uses unsupervised learning to extract topics that summarize a large number of documents and offer more effective ways to explore text data or use topics as features for a classification model. It demonstrates how to apply this technique to earnings call transcripts sourced in *Chapter 3* and to annual reports filed with the **Securities and Exchange Commission** (**SEC**).

Chapter 16, *Word Embeddings for Earnings Calls and SEC Filings*, uses neural networks to learn state-of-the-art language features in the form of word vectors that capture semantic context much better than traditional text features and represent a very promising avenue for extracting trading signals from text data.

Part 4 – Deep and reinforcement learning

Part 4 introduces deep learning and reinforcement learning.

Chapter 17, *Deep Learning for Trading*, introduces TensorFlow 2 and PyTorch, the most popular deep learning frameworks, which we will use throughout Part 4. It presents techniques for training and tuning, including regularization. It also builds and evaluates a **trading strategy for US equities**.

Chapter 18, *CNNs for Financial Time Series and Satellite Images*, covers **convolutional neural networks** (**CNNs**) that are very powerful for classification tasks with unstructured data at scale. We will introduce successful architectural designs, train a CNN on satellite data (for example, to predict economic activity), and use transfer learning to speed up training. We'll also replicate a recent idea to **convert financial time series into a two-dimensional image format** to leverage the built-in assumptions of CNNs.

Chapter 19, *RNNs for Multivariate Time Series and Sentiment Analysis*, shows how **recurrent neural networks** (**RNNs**) are useful for sequence-to-sequence modeling, including for univariate and multivariate time series to predict. It demonstrates how RNNs capture nonlinear patterns over longer periods using word embeddings introduced in *Chapter 16* to **predict returns based on the sentiment expressed in SEC filings**.

Chapter 20, *Autoencoders for Conditional Risk Factors and Asset Pricing*, covers autoencoders for the nonlinear compression of high-dimensional data. It implements a recent paper that uses a deep autoencoder to learn both risk factor returns and factor loadings from the data while conditioning the latter on asset characteristics. We'll create a large US equity dataset with metadata and generate predictive signals.

Chapter 21, Generative Adversarial Networks for Synthetic Time-Series Data, presents one of the most exciting advances in deep learning. **Generative adversarial networks** (**GANs**) are capable of learning to reproduce synthetic replicas of a target data type, such as images of celebrities. In addition to images, GANs have also been applied to time-series data. This chapter replicates a novel approach to generate synthetic stock price data that could be used to train an ML model or backtest a strategy, and also evaluate its quality.

Chapter 22, Deep Reinforcement Learning – Building a Trading Agent, presents how **reinforcement learning** (**RL**) permits the design and training of agents that learn to optimize decisions over time in response to their environment. You will see how to create a custom trading environment and build an agent that responds to market signals using OpenAI Gym.

Chapter 23, Conclusions and Next Steps, summarizes the lessons learned and outlines several steps you can take to continue learning and building your own trading strategies.

Appendix, Alpha Factor Library, lists almost 200 popular financial features, explains their rationale, and shows how to compute them. It also evaluates and compares their performance in predicting daily stock returns.

To get the most out of this book

In addition to the content summarized in the previous section, the hands-on nature of the book consists of over 160 Jupyter notebooks hosted on GitHub that demonstrate the use of ML for trading in practice on a broad range of data sources. This section describes how to use the GitHub repository, obtain the data used in the numerous examples, and set up the environment to run the code.

The GitHub repository

The book revolves around the application of ML algorithms to trading. The hands-on aspects are covered in Jupyter notebooks, hosted on GitHub, that illustrate many of the concepts and models in more detail. While the chapters aim to be self-contained, the code examples and results often take up too much space to include in their complete forms. Therefore, it is very important to view the notebooks that contain significant additional content while reading the chapter, even if you do not intend to run the code yourself.

The repository is organized so that each chapter has its own directory containing the relevant notebooks and a `README` file containing separate instructions where needed, as well as references and resources specific to the chapter's content. The relevant notebooks are identified throughout each chapter, as necessary. The repository also contains instructions on how to install the requisite libraries and obtain the data.

You can find the code files placed at: `https://github.com/PacktPublishing/Machine-Learning-for-Algorithmic-Trading-Second-Edition`.

Data sources

We will use freely available historical data from market, fundamental, and alternative sources. *Chapter 2* and *Chapter 3* cover characteristics and access to these data sources and introduce key providers that we will use throughout the book. The companion GitHub repository just described contains instructions on how to obtain or create some of the datasets that we will use throughout and includes some smaller datasets.

A few sample data sources that we will source and work with include, but are not limited to:

- Nasdaq ITCH order book data
- Electronic Data Gathering, Analysis, and Retrieval (EDGAR) SEC filings
- Earnings call transcripts from Seeking Alpha
- Quandl daily prices and other data points for over 3,000 US stocks
- International equity data from Stooq and using the yfinance library
- Various macro fundamental and benchmark data from the Federal Reserve
- Large Yelp business reviews and Twitter datasets
- EUROSAT satellite image data

Some of the data is large (several gigabytes), such as Nasdaq and SEC filings. The notebooks indicate when that is the case.

See the data directory in the root folder of the GitHub repository for instructions.

Anaconda and Docker images

The book requires Python 3.7 or higher and uses the Anaconda distribution. The book uses various conda environments for the four parts to cover a broad range of libraries while limiting dependencies and conflicts.

The installation directory in the GitHub repository contains detailed instructions. You can either use the provided Docker image to create a container with the necessary environments or use the `.yml` files to create them locally.

Download the example code files

You can download the example code files for this book from your account at `http://www.packtpub.com`. If you purchased this book elsewhere, you can visit `http://www.packtpub.com/support` and register to have the files emailed directly to you.

You can download the code files by following these steps:

1. Log in or register at `http://www.packtpub.com`.

2. Select the **SUPPORT** tab.
3. Click on **Code Downloads & Errata**.
4. Enter the name of the book in the **Search** box and follow the on-screen instructions.

Once the file is downloaded, please make sure that you unzip or extract the folder using the latest version of your preferred compression tool:

- WinRAR or 7-Zip for Windows
- Zipeg, iZip, or UnRarX for Mac
- 7-Zip or PeaZip for Linux

The code bundle for the book is also hosted on GitHub at `https://github.com/PacktPublishing/Machine-Learning-for-Algorithmic-Trading-Second-Edition`. We also have other code bundles from our rich catalog of books and videos available at `https://github.com/PacktPublishing/`. Check them out!

Download the color images

We also provide a PDF file that has color images of the screenshots/diagrams used in this book. You can download it here: `https://static.packt-cdn.com/downloads/9781839217715_ColorImages.pdf`.

Conventions used

There are a number of text conventions used throughout this book.

`CodeInText`: Indicates code words in text, database table names, folder names, filenames, file extensions, pathnames, dummy URLs, user input, and Twitter handles. For example, "The `compute_factors()` method creates a `MeanReversion` factor instance and creates long, short, and ranking pipeline columns."

A block of code is set as follows:

```
from pykalman import KalmanFilter
kf = KalmanFilter(transition_matrices = [1],
                  observation_matrices = [1],
                  initial_state_mean = 0,
                  initial_state_covariance = 1,
                  observation_covariance=1,
                  transition_covariance=.01)
```

Bold: Indicates a new term, an important word, or words that you see on the screen, for example, in menus or dialog boxes, also appear in the text like this. For example, "The **Python Algorithmic Trading Library** (**PyAlgoTrade**) focuses on backtesting and offers support for paper trading and live trading."

Informational notes appear like this.

Get in touch

Feedback from our readers is always welcome.

General feedback: Email `feedback@packtpub.com`, and mention the book's title in the subject of your message. If you have questions about any aspect of this book, please email us at `questions@packtpub.com`.

Errata: Although we have taken every care to ensure the accuracy of our content, mistakes do happen. If you have found a mistake in this book we would be grateful if you would report this to us. Please visit, `http://www.packtpub.com/submit-errata`, selecting your book, clicking on the Errata Submission Form link, and entering the details.

Piracy: If you come across any illegal copies of our works in any form on the Internet, we would be grateful if you would provide us with the location address or website name. Please contact us at `copyright@packtpub.com` with a link to the material.

If you are interested in becoming an author: If there is a topic that you have expertise in and you are interested in either writing or contributing to a book, please visit `http://authors.packtpub.com`.

Reviews

Please leave a review. Once you have read and used this book, why not leave a review on the site that you purchased it from? Potential readers can then see and use your unbiased opinion to make purchase decisions, we at Packt can understand what you think about our products, and our authors can see your feedback on their book. Thank you!

For more information about Packt, please visit packtpub.com.

Download a free PDF copy of this book

Thanks for purchasing this book!

Do you like to read on the go but are unable to carry your print books everywhere?
Is your eBook purchase not compatible with the device of your choice?

Don't worry, now with every Packt book you get a DRM-free PDF version of that book at no cost.

Read anywhere, any place, on any device. Search, copy, and paste code from your favorite technical books directly into your application.

The perks don't stop there, you can get exclusive access to discounts, newsletters, and great free content in your inbox daily

Follow these simple steps to get the benefits:

1. Scan the QR code or visit the link below

`https://packt.link/free-ebook/9781839217715`

2. Submit your proof of purchase
3. That's it! We'll send your free PDF and other benefits to your email directly

1

Machine Learning for Trading – From Idea to Execution

Algorithmic trading relies on computer programs that execute algorithms to automate some or all elements of a trading strategy. **Algorithms** are a sequence of steps or rules designed to achieve a goal. They can take many forms and facilitate optimization throughout the investment process, from idea generation to asset allocation, trade execution, and risk management.

Machine learning (**ML**) involves algorithms that learn rules or patterns from data to achieve a goal such as minimizing a prediction error. The examples in this book will illustrate how ML algorithms can extract information from data to support or automate key investment activities. These activities include observing the market and analyzing data to form expectations about the future and decide on placing buy or sell orders, as well as managing the resulting portfolio to produce attractive returns relative to the risk.

Ultimately, the goal of active investment management is to generate alpha, defined as portfolio returns in excess of the benchmark used for evaluation. The **fundamental law of active management** postulates that the key to generating alpha is having accurate return forecasts combined with the ability to act on these forecasts (Grinold 1989; Grinold and Kahn 2000).

This law defines the **information ratio** (**IR**) to express the value of active management as the ratio of the return difference between the portfolio and a benchmark to the volatility of those returns. It further approximates the IR as the product of the following:

- The **information coefficient** (**IC**), which measures the quality of forecasts as their rank correlation with outcomes
- The square root of the **breadth of a strategy** expressed as the number of independent bets on these forecasts

The competition of sophisticated investors in financial markets implies that making precise predictions to generate alpha requires superior information, either through access to better data, a superior ability to process it, or both.

This is where ML comes in: applications of **ML for trading** (**ML4T**) typically aim to make more efficient use of a rapidly diversifying range of data to produce both better and more actionable forecasts, thus improving the quality of investment decisions and results.

Historically, algorithmic trading used to be more narrowly defined as the automation of trade execution to minimize the costs offered by the sell-side. This book takes a more comprehensive perspective since the use of algorithms in general and ML in particular has come to impact a broader range of activities, from generating ideas and extracting signals from data to asset allocation, position-sizing, and testing and evaluating strategies.

This chapter looks at industry trends that have led to the emergence of ML as a source of competitive advantage in the investment industry. We will also look at where ML fits into the investment process to enable algorithmic trading strategies. More specifically, we will be covering the following topics:

- Key trends behind the rise of ML in the investment industry
- The design and execution of a trading strategy that leverages ML
- Popular use cases for ML in trading

> You can find links to additional resources and references in the README file for this chapter in the GitHub repository (`https://github.com/PacktPublishing/Machine-Learning-for-Algorithmic-Trading-Second-Edition`).

The rise of ML in the investment industry

The investment industry has evolved dramatically over the last several decades and continues to do so amid increased competition, technological advances, and a challenging economic environment. This section reviews key trends that have shaped the overall investment environment and the context for algorithmic trading and the use of ML more specifically.

The trends that have propelled algorithmic trading and ML to their current prominence include:

- Changes in the **market microstructure**, such as the spread of electronic trading and the integration of markets across asset classes and geographies
- The development of investment strategies framed in terms of **risk-factor exposure**, as opposed to asset classes
- The revolutions in **computing power**, **data generation and management**, and **statistical methods**, including breakthroughs in deep learning

- The **outperformance of the pioneers** in algorithmic trading relative to human, discretionary investors

In addition, the financial crises of 2001 and 2008 have affected how investors approach diversification and risk management. One outcome is the rise in low-cost **passive investment vehicles** in the form of **exchange-traded funds** (**ETFs**).

Amid low yields and low volatility following the 2008 crisis, which triggered large-scale asset purchases by leading central banks, cost-conscious investors shifted over $3.5 trillion from actively managed mutual funds into passively managed ETFs.

Competitive pressure is also reflected in **lower hedge fund fees**, which dropped from the traditional 2 percent annual management fee and 20 percent take of profits to an average of 1.48 percent and 17.4 percent, respectively, in 2017.

From electronic to high-frequency trading

Electronic trading has advanced dramatically in terms of capabilities, volume, coverage of asset classes, and geographies since networks started routing prices to computer terminals in the 1960s. Equity markets have been at the forefront of this trend worldwide. See Harris (2003) and Strumeyer (2017) for comprehensive coverage of relevant changes in financial markets; we will return to this topic when we cover how to work with market and fundamental data in the next chapter.

The 1997 order-handling rules by the SEC introduced competition to exchanges through **electronic communication networks** (**ECNs**). ECNs are automated **alternative trading systems** (**ATS**) that match buy-and-sell orders at specified prices, primarily for equities and currencies, and are registered as broker-dealers. It allows significant brokerages and individual traders in different geographic locations to trade directly without intermediaries, both on exchanges and after hours.

Dark pools are another type of private ATS that allows institutional investors to trade large orders without publicly revealing their information, contrary to how exchanges managed their order books prior to competition from ECNs. Dark pools do not publish pre-trade bids and offers, and trade prices only become public some time after execution. They have grown substantially since the mid-2000s to account for 40 percent of equities traded in the US due to concerns about adverse price movements of large orders and order front-running by high-frequency traders. They are often housed within large banks and are subject to SEC regulation.

With the rise of electronic trading, **algorithms for cost-effective execution** developed rapidly and adoption spread quickly from the sell-side to the buy-side and across asset classes. Automated trading emerged around 2000 as a sell-side tool aimed at cost-effective execution that broke down orders into smaller, sequenced chunks to limit their market impact. These tools spread to the buy side and became increasingly sophisticated by taking into account, for example, transaction costs and liquidity, as well as short-term price and volume forecasts.

Direct market access (**DMA**) gives a trader greater control over execution by allowing them to send orders directly to the exchange using the infrastructure and market participant identification of a broker who is a member of an exchange. Sponsored access removes pre-trade risk controls by the brokers and forms the basis for **high-frequency trading** (**HFT**).

HFT refers to automated trades in financial instruments that are executed with extremely low latency in the microsecond range and where participants hold positions for very short periods. The goal is to detect and exploit **inefficiencies in the market microstructure**, the institutional infrastructure of trading venues.

HFT has grown substantially over the past 10 years and is estimated to make up roughly 55 percent of trading volume in US equity markets and about 40 percent in European equity markets. HFT has also grown in futures markets to roughly 80 percent of foreign-exchange futures volumes and two-thirds of both interest rate and Treasury 10-year futures volumes (Miller 2016).

HFT strategies aim to earn small profits per trade using **passive or aggressive strategies**. Passive strategies include arbitrage trading to profit from very small price differentials for the same asset, or its derivatives, traded on different venues. Aggressive strategies include order anticipation or momentum ignition. Order anticipation, also known as liquidity detection, involves algorithms that submit small exploratory orders to detect hidden liquidity from large institutional investors and trade ahead of a large order to benefit from subsequent price movements. Momentum ignition implies an algorithm executing and canceling a series of orders to spoof other HFT algorithms into buying (or selling) more aggressively and benefit from the resulting price changes.

Regulators have expressed concern over the potential link between certain aggressive HFT strategies and **increased market fragility and volatility**, such as that experienced during the May 2010 Flash Crash, the October 2014 Treasury market volatility, and the sudden crash by over 1,000 points of the Dow Jones Industrial Average on August 24, 2015. At the same time, market liquidity has increased with trading volumes due to the presence of HFT, which has lowered overall transaction costs.

The combination of reduced trading volumes amid lower volatility and rising costs of technology and access to both data and trading venues has led to financial pressure. Aggregate HFT revenues from US stocks were estimated to have dropped beneath $1 billion in 2017 for the first time since 2008, down from $7.9 billion in 2009. This trend has led to **industry consolidation**, with various acquisitions by, for example, the largest listed proprietary trading firm, Virtu Financial, and shared infrastructure investments, such as the new Go West ultra-low latency route between Chicago and Tokyo. Simultaneously, start-ups such as Alpha Trading Labs are making HFT trading infrastructure and data available to democratize HFT by crowdsourcing algorithms in return for a share of the profits.

Factor investing and smart beta funds

The return provided by an asset is a function of the uncertainty or risk associated with the investment. An equity investment implies, for example, assuming a company's business risk, and a bond investment entails default risk. To the extent that **specific risk characteristics predict returns**, identifying and forecasting the behavior of these risk factors becomes a primary focus when designing an investment strategy. It yields valuable trading signals and is the key to superior active-management results. The industry's understanding of risk factors has evolved very substantially over time and has impacted how ML is used for trading. *Chapter 4, Financial Feature Engineering – How to Research Alpha Factors*, and *Chapter 5, Portfolio Optimization and Performance Evaluation*, will dive deeper into the practical applications of the concepts outlined here; see Ang (2014) for comprehensive coverage.

Modern portfolio theory (**MPT**) introduced the distinction between idiosyncratic and systematic sources of risk for a given asset. Idiosyncratic risk can be eliminated through diversification, but systematic risk cannot. In the early 1960s, the **capital asset pricing model** (**CAPM**) identified a single factor driving all asset returns: the return on the market portfolio in excess of T-bills. The market portfolio consisted of all tradable securities, weighted by their market value. The systematic exposure of an asset to the market is measured by **beta**, which is the correlation between the returns of the asset and the market portfolio.

The recognition that the risk of an asset does not depend on the asset in isolation, but rather how it moves relative to other assets and the market as a whole, was a major conceptual breakthrough. In other words, assets earn a **risk premium** based on their exposure to underlying, **common risks** experienced by all assets, not due to their specific, idiosyncratic characteristics.

Subsequently, academic research and industry experience have raised numerous critical questions regarding the CAPM prediction that an asset's risk premium depends only on its exposure to a single factor measured by the asset's beta. Instead, **numerous additional risk factors** have since been discovered. A factor is a quantifiable signal, attribute, or any variable that has historically correlated with future stock returns and is expected to remain correlated in the future.

These risk factors were labeled anomalies since they contradicted the **efficient market hypothesis** (**EMH**). The EMH maintains that market equilibrium would always price securities according to the CAPM so that no other factors should have predictive power (Malkiel 2003). The economic theory behind factors can be either rational, where factor risk premiums compensate for low returns during bad times, or behavioral, where agents fail to arbitrage away excess returns.

Well-known anomalies include the value, size, and momentum effects that help predict returns while controlling for the CAPM market factor. The **size effect** rests on small firms systematically outperforming large firms (Banz 1981; Reinganum 1981). The **value effect** (Basu et. al. 1981) states that firms with low valuation metrics outperform their counterparts with the opposite characteristics. It suggests that firms with low price multiples, such as the price-to-earnings or the price-to-book ratios, perform better than their more expensive peers (as suggested by the inventors of value investing, Benjamin Graham and David Dodd, and popularized by Warren Buffet).

The **momentum effect**, discovered in the late 1980s by, among others, Clifford Asness, the founding partner of AQR, states that stocks with good momentum, in terms of recent 6-12 month returns, have higher returns going forward than poor momentum stocks with similar market risk. Researchers also found that value and momentum factors explain returns for stocks outside the US, as well as for other asset classes, such as bonds, currencies, and commodities, and additional risk factors (Jegadeesh and Titman 1993; Asness, Moskowitz, and Pedersen 2013).

In fixed income, the value strategy is called **riding the yield curve** and is a form of the duration premium. In commodities, it is called the **roll return**, with a positive return for an upward-sloping futures curve and a negative return otherwise. In foreign exchange, the value strategy is called **carry**.

There is also an **illiquidity premium**. Securities that are more illiquid trade at low prices and have high average excess returns, relative to their more liquid counterparts. Bonds with a higher default risk tend to have higher returns on average, reflecting a credit risk premium. Since investors are willing to pay for insurance against high volatility when returns tend to crash, sellers of volatility protection in options markets tend to earn high returns.

Multifactor models define risks in broader and more diverse terms than just the market portfolio. In 1976, Stephen Ross proposed the **arbitrage pricing theory**, which asserted that investors are compensated for multiple systematic sources of risk that cannot be diversified away (Roll and Ross 1984). The three most important macro factors are growth, inflation, and volatility, in addition to productivity, demographic, and political risk. In 1993, Eugene Fama and Kenneth French combined the equity risk factors' size and value with a market factor into a single three-factor model that better explained cross-sectional stock returns. They later added a model that also included bond risk factors to simultaneously explain returns for both asset classes (Fama and French 1993; 2015).

A particularly attractive aspect of risk factors is their **low or negative correlation**. Value and momentum risk factors, for instance, are negatively correlated, reducing the risk and increasing risk-adjusted returns above and beyond the benefit implied by the risk factors. Furthermore, using leverage and long-short strategies, factor strategies can be combined into **market-neutral approaches**. The combination of long positions in securities exposed to positive risks with underweight or short positions in the securities exposed to negative risks allows for the collection of dynamic risk premiums.

As a result, the factors that explained returns above and beyond the CAPM were incorporated into investment styles that tilt portfolios in favor of one or more factors, and assets began to migrate into factor-based portfolios. The 2008 financial crisis underlined how asset-class labels could be highly misleading and create a false sense of diversification when investors do not look at the underlying factor risks, as asset classes came crashing down together.

Over the past several decades, quantitative factor investing has evolved from a simple approach based on two or three styles to **multifactor smart or exotic beta products**. Smart beta funds have crossed $1 trillion AUM in 2017, testifying to the popularity of the hybrid investment strategy that combines active and passive management. **Smart beta funds** take a passive strategy but modify it according to one or more factors, such as cheaper stocks or screening them according to dividend payouts, to generate better returns. This growth has coincided with increasing criticism of the high fees charged by traditional active managers as well as heightened scrutiny of their performance.

The ongoing discovery and successful forecasting of risk factors that, either individually or in combination with other risk factors, significantly impact future asset returns across asset classes is a key driver of the surge in ML in the investment industry and will be a key theme throughout this book.

Algorithmic pioneers outperform humans

The track record and growth of **assets under management** (**AUM**) of firms that spearheaded algorithmic trading has played a key role in generating investor interest and subsequent industry efforts to replicate their success. **Systematic funds differ from HFT** in that trades may be held significantly longer while seeking to exploit arbitrage opportunities as opposed to advantages from sheer speed.

Systematic strategies that mostly or exclusively rely on algorithmic decision-making were most famously introduced by mathematician James Simons, who founded **Renaissance Technologies** in 1982 and built it into the premier quant firm. Its secretive Medallion Fund, which is closed to outsiders, has earned an estimated annualized return of 35 percent since 1982.

D. E. Shaw, Citadel, and Two Sigma, three of the most prominent quantitative hedge funds that use systematic strategies based on algorithms, rose to the all-time top-20 performers for the first time in 2017, in terms of total dollars earned for investors, after fees, and since inception.

D. E. Shaw, founded in 1988 and with $50 billion in AUM in 2019, joined the list at number 3. Citadel, started in 1990 by Kenneth Griffin, manages $32 billion, and ranked 5. Two Sigma, started only in 2001 by D. E. Shaw alumni John Overdeck and David Siegel, has grown from $8 billion in AUM in 2011 to $60 billion in 2019. **Bridgewater**, started by Ray Dalio in 1975, had over $160 billion in AUM in 2019 and continues to lead due to its Pure Alpha fund, which also incorporates systematic strategies.

Similarly, on the Institutional Investors 2018 Hedge Fund 100 list, the four largest firms, and five of the top six firms, rely largely or completely on computers and trading algorithms to make investment decisions—and all of them have been growing their assets in an otherwise challenging environment. Several quantitatively focused firms climbed the ranks and, in some cases, grew their assets by double-digit percentages. Number 2-ranked **Applied Quantitative Research** (**AQR**) grew its hedge fund assets by 48 percent in 2017 and by 29 percent in 2018 to nearly $90 billion.

ML-driven funds attract $1 trillion in AUM

The familiar three revolutions in computing power, data availability, and statistical methods have made the adoption of systematic, data-driven strategies not only more compelling and cost-effective but a key source of competitive advantage.

As a result, algorithmic approaches are not only finding **wider application** in the hedge-fund industry that pioneered these strategies but across a broader range of asset managers and even passively managed vehicles such as ETFs. In particular, **predictive analytics** using ML and algorithmic automation play an increasingly prominent role in all steps of the investment process across asset classes, from idea generation and research to strategy formulation and portfolio construction, trade execution, and risk management.

Estimates of **industry size** vary because there is no objective definition of a quantitative or algorithmic fund. Many traditional hedge funds or even mutual funds and ETFs are introducing computer-driven strategies or integrating them into a discretionary environment in a human-plus-machine approach.

According to the *Economist*, in 2016, systematic funds became the largest driver of institutional trading in the US stock market (ignoring HFT, which mainly acts as a middleman). In 2019, they accounted for over 35 percent of institutional volume, up from just 18 percent in 2010; just 10% of trading is still due to traditional equity funds. Measured by the Russell 3000 index, the **value of US stocks** is around $31 trillion. The three types of **computer-managed funds**—index funds, ETFs, and quant funds—**run around 35 percent**, whereas human managers at traditional hedge funds and other mutual funds manage just 24 percent.

The market research firm Preqin estimates that almost 1,500 hedge funds make a majority of their trades with help from computer models. Quantitative hedge funds are now responsible for 27 percent of all US stock trades by investors, up from 14 percent in 2013. But many use data scientists—or quants—who, in turn, use machines to build large statistical models.

In recent years, however, funds have moved toward true ML, where artificially intelligent systems can analyze large amounts of data at speed and improve themselves through such analyses. Recent examples include Rebellion Research, Sentient, and Aidyia, which rely on evolutionary algorithms and deep learning to devise fully automatic **artificial intelligence** (**AI**)-driven investment platforms.

From the core hedge fund industry, the adoption of algorithmic strategies has spread to mutual funds and even passively managed EFTs in the form of smart beta funds, and to discretionary funds in the form of quantamental approaches.

The emergence of quantamental funds

Two distinct approaches have evolved in active investment management: **systematic (or quant)** and **discretionary investing**. Systematic approaches rely on algorithms for a repeatable and data-driven approach to identify investment opportunities across many securities. In contrast, a discretionary approach involves an in-depth analysis of the fundamentals of a smaller number of securities. These two approaches are becoming more similar as fundamental managers take more data science-driven approaches.

Even **fundamental traders** now arm themselves with quantitative techniques, accounting for $55 billion of systematic assets, according to Barclays. Agnostic to specific companies, quantitative funds trade based on patterns and dynamics across a wide swath of securities. Such quants accounted for about 17 percent of total hedge fund assets, as data compiled by Barclays in 2018 showed.

Point72, with $14 billion in assets, has been shifting about half of its portfolio managers to a human-plus-machine approach. Point72 is also investing tens of millions of dollars into a group that analyzes large amounts of alternative data and passes the results on to traders.

Investments in strategic capabilities

Three trends have boosted the use of data in algorithmic trading strategies and may further shift the investment industry from discretionary to quantitative styles:

- The exponential increase in the availability of digital data
- The increase in computing power and data storage capacity at a lower cost
- The advances in statistical methods for analyzing complex datasets

Rising investments in related capabilities—technology, data, and, most importantly, skilled humans—highlight how significant algorithmic trading using ML has become for competitive advantage, especially in light of the rising popularity of passive, indexed investment vehicles, such as ETFs, since the 2008 financial crisis.

Morgan Stanley noted that only 23 percent of its quant clients say they are not considering using or not already using ML, down from 44 percent in 2016. **Guggenheim Partners** built what it calls a supercomputing cluster for $1 million at the Lawrence Berkeley National Laboratory in California to help crunch numbers for Guggenheim's quant investment funds. Electricity for computers costs another $1 million per year.

AQR is a quantitative investment group that relies on academic research to identify and systematically trade factors that have, over time, proven to beat the broader market. The firm used to eschew the purely computer-powered strategies of quant peers such as Renaissance Technologies or DE Shaw. More recently, however, AQR has begun to seek profitable patterns in markets using ML to parse through novel datasets, such as satellite pictures of shadows cast by oil wells and tankers.

The leading firm **BlackRock**, with over $5 trillion in AUM, also bets on algorithms to beat discretionary fund managers by heavily investing in SAE, a systematic trading firm it acquired during the financial crisis. Franklin Templeton bought Random Forest Capital, a debt-focused, data-led investment company, for an undisclosed amount, hoping that its technology can support the wider asset manager.

ML and alternative data

Hedge funds have long looked for alpha through **informational advantage** and the ability to uncover new uncorrelated signals. Historically, this included things such as proprietary surveys of shoppers, or of voters ahead of elections or referendums.

Occasionally, the use of company insiders, doctors, and expert networks to expand knowledge of industry trends or companies crosses legal lines: a series of prosecutions of traders, portfolio managers, and analysts for using **insider information** after 2010 has shaken the industry.

In contrast, the informational advantage from exploiting conventional and alternative data sources using ML is not related to expert and industry networks or access to corporate management, but rather the ability to collect large quantities of very diverse data sources and analyze them in real time.

Conventional data includes economic statistics, trading data, or corporate reports. **Alternative data** is much broader and includes sources such as satellite images, credit card sales, sentiment analysis, mobile geolocation data, and website scraping, as well as the conversion of data generated in the ordinary course of business into valuable intelligence. It includes, in principle, **any data source containing (potential) trading signals**.

For instance, data from an insurance company on the sales of new car insurance policies captures not only the volumes of new car sales but can be broken down into brands or geographies. Many vendors scrape websites for valuable data, ranging from app downloads and user reviews to airline and hotel bookings. Social media sites can also be scraped for hints on consumer views and trends.

Typically, the datasets are large and require storage, access, and analysis using **scalable data solutions** for parallel processing, such as Hadoop and Spark. There are more than 1 billion websites with more than 10 trillion individual web pages, with 500 exabytes (or 500 billion gigabytes) of data, according to Deutsche Bank. And more than 100 million websites are added to the internet every year.

Real-time insights into a company's prospects, long before their results are released, can be gleaned from a decline in job listings on its website, the internal rating of its chief executive by employees on the recruitment site Glassdoor, or a dip in the average price of clothes on its website. Such information can be combined with satellite images of car parks and geolocation data from mobile phones that indicate how many people are visiting stores. On the other hand, strategic moves can be learned from a jump in job postings for specific functional areas or in certain geographies.

Among the most valuable sources is data that directly reveals consumer expenditures, with **credit card information** as a primary source. This data offers only a partial view of sales trends, but it can offer vital insights when combined with other data. Point72, for instance, at some point analyzed 80 million credit card transactions every day. We will explore the various sources, their use cases, and how to evaluate them in detail in *Chapter 3, Alternative Data for Finance – Categories and Use Cases*.

Investment groups have more than doubled their **spending on alternative sets** and data scientists in the past two years, as the asset management industry has tried to reinvigorate its fading fortunes. In December 2018, there were 375 alternative data providers listed on `alternativedata.org` (sponsored by provider Yipit).

Asset managers spent a total of $373 million on datasets and hiring new employees to parse them in 2017, up 60 percent from 2016, and will probably spend a total of $616 million this year, according to a survey of investors by `alternativedata.org`. It forecast that overall expenditures will climb to over $1 billion by 2020. Some estimates are even higher: Optimus, a consultancy, estimates that investors are spending about $5 billion per year on alternative data, and expects the industry to grow 30 percent per year over the coming years.

As competition for valuable data sources intensifies, exclusivity arrangements are a key feature of data-source contracts, to maintain an informational advantage. At the same time, privacy concerns are mounting, and regulators have begun to start looking at the currently largely unregulated data-provider industry.

Crowdsourcing trading algorithms

More recently, several algorithmic trading firms have begun to offer investment platforms that provide access to data and a programming environment to crowdsource risk factors that become part of an investment strategy or entire trading algorithms. Key examples include WorldQuant, Quantopian, and, most recently, Alpha Trading Labs (launched in 2018).

WorldQuant was spun out of Millennium Management (AUM: $41 billion) in 2007, for whom it manages around $5 billion. It employs hundreds of scientists and many more part-time workers around the world in its alpha factory, which organizes the investment process as a quantitative assembly line. This factory claims to have produced 4 million successfully tested alpha factors for inclusion in more complex trading strategies and is aiming for 100 million. Each alpha factor is an algorithm that seeks to predict a future asset price change. Other teams then combine alpha factors into strategies and strategies into portfolios, allocate funds between portfolios, and manage risk while avoiding strategies that cannibalize each other. See the *Appendix, Alpha Factor Library*, for dozens of examples of quantitative factors used at WorldQuant.

Designing and executing an ML-driven strategy

In this book, we demonstrate **how ML fits into the overall process of designing, executing, and evaluating a trading strategy**. To this end, we'll assume that an ML-based strategy is driven by data sources that contain predictive signals for the target universe and strategy, which, after suitable preprocessing and feature engineering, permit an ML model to predict asset returns or other strategy inputs. The model predictions, in turn, translate into buy or sell orders based on human discretion or automated rules, which in turn may be manually encoded or learned by another ML algorithm in an end-to-end approach.

Figure 1.1 depicts the key steps in this workflow, which also shapes the organization of this book:

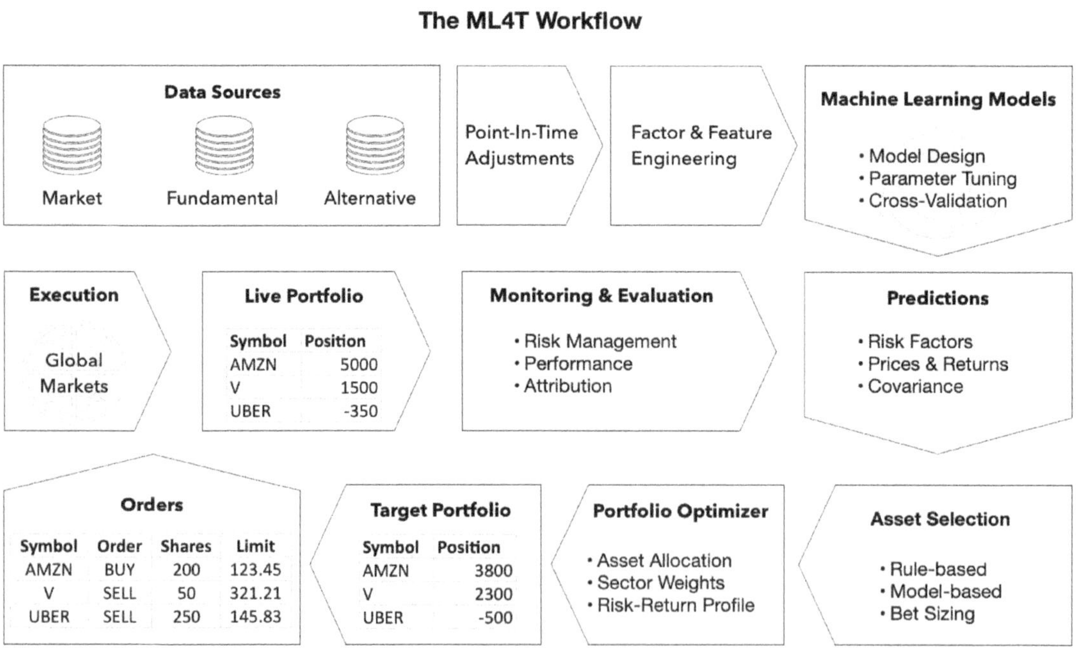

Figure 1.1: The ML4T workflow

Part 1 introduces important skills and techniques that apply across different strategies and ML use cases. These include the following:

- How to source and manage important data sources
- How to engineer informative features or alpha factors that extract signal content
- How to manage a portfolio and track strategy performance

Moreover, *Chapter 8, The ML4T Workflow – From Model to Strategy Backtesting*, in Part 2, covers strategy backtesting. We will briefly outline each of these areas before turning to relevant ML use cases, which make up the bulk of the book in Parts 2, 3, and 4.

Sourcing and managing data

The dramatic evolution of data availability in terms of volume, variety, and velocity is a key complement to the application of ML to trading, which in turn has boosted industry spending on the acquisition of new data sources. However, the proliferating supply of data requires careful selection and management to uncover the potential value, including the following steps:

1. Identify and evaluate market, fundamental, and alternative data sources containing alpha signals that do not decay too quickly.
2. Deploy or access a cloud-based scalable data infrastructure and analytical tools like Hadoop or Spark to facilitate fast, flexible data access.
3. Carefully manage and curate data to avoid look-ahead bias by adjusting it to the desired frequency on a point-in-time basis. This means that data should reflect only information available and known at the given time. ML algorithms trained on distorted historical data will almost certainly fail during live trading.

We will cover these aspects in practical detail in *Chapter 2, Market and Fundamental Data – Sources and Techniques*, and *Chapter 3, Alternative Data for Finance – Categories and Use Cases*.

From alpha factor research to portfolio management

Alpha factors are designed to extract signals from data to predict returns for a given investment universe over the trading horizon. A typical factor takes on a single value for each asset when evaluated at a given point in time, but it may combine one or several input variables or time periods. If you are already familiar with the ML workflow (see *Chapter 6, The Machine Learning Process*), you may view alpha factors as domain-specific features designed for a specific strategy. Working with alpha factors entails a research phase and an execution phase as outlined in *Figure 1.2*:

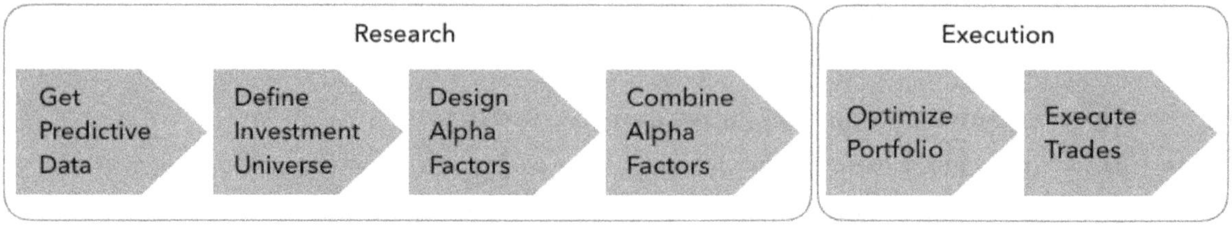

Figure 1.2: The alpha factor research process

The research phase

The **research phase** includes the design and evaluation of alpha factors. A **predictive factor** captures some aspect of a systematic relationship between a data source and an important strategy input like asset returns. Optimizing the predictive power requires creative feature engineering in the form of effective data transformations.

False discoveries due to **data mining** are a key risk that requires careful management. One way of reducing the risk is to focus the search process by following the guidance of decades of academic research that has produced several Nobel prizes. Many investors still prefer factors that align with theories about financial markets and investor behavior. Laying out these theories is beyond the scope of this book, but the references highlight avenues to dive deeper into this important framing aspect.

Validating the signal content of an alpha factor requires a **robust estimate of its predictive power** in a representative context. There are numerous methodological and practical pitfalls that undermine a reliable estimate. In addition to data mining and the failure to correct for multiple testing bias, these pitfalls include the use of data contaminated by survivorship or look-ahead bias, not reflecting realistic **Principal, Interest and Taxes** (**PIT**) information. *Chapter 4, Financial Feature Engineering – How to Research Alpha Factors,* discusses how to successfully manage this process.

The execution phase

During the **execution phase**, alpha factors emit signals that lead to buy or sell orders. The resulting portfolio holdings, in turn, have specific risk profiles that interact and contribute to the aggregate portfolio risk. Portfolio management involves optimizing position sizes to achieve a balance of return and risk of the portfolio that aligns with the investment objectives.

Chapter 5, Portfolio Optimization and Performance Evaluation, introduces key techniques and tools applicable to this phase of the trading strategy workflow, from portfolio optimization to performance measurement.

Strategy backtesting

Incorporating an investment idea into a real-life algorithmic strategy implies a significant risk that requires a **scientific approach**. Such an approach involves extensive empirical tests with the goal of rejecting the idea based on its performance in alternative out-of-sample market scenarios. Testing may involve simulated data to capture scenarios deemed possible but not reflected in historic data.

To obtain unbiased performance estimates for a candidate strategy, we need a **backtesting engine** that simulates its execution in a realistic manner. In addition to the potential biases introduced by the data or a flawed use of statistics, the backtesting engine needs to accurately represent the practical aspects of trade-signal evaluation, order placement, and execution in line with market conditions.

Chapter 8, The ML4T Workflow – From Model to Strategy Backtesting, shows how to use backtrader and Zipline and navigate the multiple methodological challenges and completes the introduction to the end-to-end ML4T workflow.

ML for trading – strategies and use cases

In practice, we apply ML to trading in the context of a specific strategy to meet a certain business goal. In this section, we briefly describe how trading strategies have evolved and diversified, and outline real-world examples of ML applications, highlighting how they relate to the content covered in this book.

The evolution of algorithmic strategies

Quantitative strategies have evolved and become more sophisticated in three waves:

1. In the 1980s and 1990s, signals often emerged from **academic research** and used a single or very few inputs derived from market and fundamental data. AQR, one of the largest quantitative hedge funds today, was founded in 1998 to implement such strategies at scale. These signals are now largely commoditized and available as ETF, such as basic mean-reversion strategies.
2. In the 2000s, **factor-based investing** proliferated based on the pioneering work by Eugene Fama and Kenneth French and others. Funds used algorithms to identify assets exposed to risk factors like value or momentum to seek arbitrage opportunities. Redemptions during the early days of the financial crisis triggered the quant quake of August 2007, which cascaded through the factor-based fund industry. These strategies are now also available as long-only smart beta funds that tilt portfolios according to a given set of risk factors.

3. The third era is driven by investments in **ML capabilities and alternative** data to generate profitable signals for repeatable trading strategies. Factor decay is a major challenge: the excess returns from new anomalies have been shown to drop by a quarter from discovery to publication, and by over 50 percent after publication due to competition and crowding.

Today, traders pursue a range of different objectives when using algorithms to execute rules:

- Trade execution algorithms that aim to achieve favorable pricing
- Short-term trades that aim to profit from small price movements, for example, due to arbitrage
- Behavioral strategies that aim to anticipate the behavior of other market participants
- Trading strategies based on absolute and relative price and return predictions

Trade-execution programs aim to limit the market impact of trades and range from the simple slicing of trades to match time-weighted or volume-weighted average pricing. Simple algorithms leverage historical patterns, whereas more sophisticated versions take into account transaction costs, implementation shortfall, or predicted price movements.

HFT funds most prominently rely on very short holding periods to benefit from minor price movements based on bid-ask or statistical arbitrage. **Behavioral algorithms** usually operate in lower-liquidity environments and aim to anticipate moves by a larger player with significant price impact, based, for example, on sniffing algorithms that generate insights into other market participants' strategies.

In this book, we will focus on strategies that trade based on expectations of relative price changes over various time horizons beyond the very short term, dominated by latency advantages, because they are both widely used and very suitable for the application of ML.

Use cases of ML for trading

ML is capable of extracting tradable signals from a wide range of market, fundamental, and alternative data and is thus applicable to strategies targeting a range of asset classes and investment horizons. More generally, however, it is a flexible tool to support or automate decisions with quantifiable goals and digital data relevant to achieving these goals. Therefore, it can be applied at several steps of the trading process. There are numerous use cases in different categories, including:

- Data mining to identify patterns, extract features, and generate insights
- Supervised learning to generate risk factors or alphas and create trade ideas
- The aggregation of individual signals into a strategy
- The allocation of assets according to risk profiles learned by an algorithm
- The testing and evaluation of strategies, including through the use of synthetic data
- The interactive, automated refinement of a strategy using reinforcement learning

We briefly highlight some of these applications and identify where we will demonstrate their use in later chapters.

Data mining for feature extraction and insights

The cost-effective evaluation of large, complex datasets requires the detection of signals at scale. There are several examples throughout the book:

- **Information theory** helps estimate a signal content of candidate features and is thus useful for extracting the most valuable inputs for an ML model. In *Chapter 4, Financial Feature Engineering – How to Research Alpha Factors,* we use mutual information to compare the potential values of individual features for a supervised learning algorithm to predict asset returns. Chapter 18 in De Prado (2018) estimates the information content of a price series as a basis for deciding between alternative trading strategies.
- **Unsupervised learning** provides a broad range of methods to identify structure in data to gain insights or help solve a downstream task. We provide several examples:
    - In *Chapter 13, Data-Driven Risk Factors and Asset Allocation with Unsupervised Learning,* we introduce clustering and dimensionality reduction to generate features from high-dimensional datasets.
    - In *Chapter 15, Topic Modeling – Summarizing Financial News,* we apply Bayesian probability models to summarize financial text data.
    - In *Chapter 20, Autoencoders for Conditional Risk Factors and Asset Pricing,* we use deep learning to extract nonlinear risk factors conditioned on asset characteristics and predict stock returns based on Kelly et al. (2020).
- **Model transparency** emphasizes model-specific ways to gain insights into the predictive power of individual variables and introduce a novel game-theoretic approach called **SHapley Additive exPlanations** (**SHAP**). We apply it to gradient boosting machines with a large number of input variables in *Chapter 12, Boosting Your Trading Strategy,* and the *Appendix, Alpha Factor Library.*

Supervised learning for alpha factor creation

The most familiar rationale for applying ML to trading is to obtain predictions of asset fundamentals, price movements, or market conditions. A strategy can leverage multiple ML algorithms that build on each other:

- **Downstream models** can generate signals at the portfolio level by integrating predictions about the prospects of individual assets, capital market expectations, and the correlation among securities.
- Alternatively, ML predictions can inform **discretionary trades** as in the quantamental approach outlined previously.

ML predictions can also **target specific risk factors**, such as value or volatility, or implement technical approaches, such as trend-following or mean reversion:

- In *Chapter 3, Alternative Data for Finance – Categories and Use Cases*, we illustrate how to work with fundamental data to create inputs to ML-driven valuation models.
- In *Chapter 14, Text Data for Trading – Sentiment Analysis*, *Chapter 15, Topic Modeling – Summarizing Financial News*, and *Chapter 16, Word Embeddings for Earnings Calls and SEC Filings*, we use alternative data on business reviews that can be used to project revenues for a company as an input for a valuation exercise.
- In *Chapter 9, Time-Series Models for Volatility Forecasts and Statistical Arbitrage*, we demonstrate how to forecast macro variables as inputs to market expectations and how to forecast risk factors such as volatility.
- In *Chapter 19, RNNs for Multivariate Time Series and Sentiment Analysis*, we introduce recurrent neural networks that achieve superior performance with nonlinear time series data.

Asset allocation

ML has been used to allocate portfolios based on decision-tree models that compute a hierarchical form of risk parity. As a result, risk characteristics are driven by patterns in asset prices rather than by asset classes and achieve superior risk-return characteristics.

In *Chapter 5, Portfolio Optimization and Performance Evaluation*, and *Chapter 13, Data-Driven Risk Factors and Asset Allocation with Unsupervised Learning*, we illustrate how hierarchical clustering extracts data-driven risk classes that better reflect correlation patterns than conventional asset class definition (see *Chapter 16* in De Prado 2018).

Testing trade ideas

Backtesting is a critical step to select successful algorithmic trading strategies. Cross-validation using synthetic data is a key ML technique to generate reliable out-of-sample results when combined with appropriate methods to correct for multiple testing. The time-series nature of financial data requires modifications to the standard approach to avoid look-ahead bias or otherwise contaminating the data used for training, validation, and testing. In addition, the limited availability of historical data has given rise to alternative approaches that use synthetic data.

We will demonstrate various methods to test ML models using market, fundamental, and alternative data sources that obtain sound estimates of out-of-sample errors.

In *Chapter 21, Generative Adversarial Networks for Synthetic Time-Series Data*, we present **generative adversarial networks** (**GANs**), which are capable of producing high-quality synthetic data.

Reinforcement learning

Trading takes place in a competitive, interactive marketplace. Reinforcement learning aims to train agents to learn a policy function based on rewards; it is often considered as one of the most promising areas in financial ML. See, for example, Hendricks and Wilcox (2014) and Nevmyvaka, Feng, and Kearns (2006) for applications to trade execution.

In *Chapter 22, Deep Reinforcement Learning - Building a Trading Agent*, we present key reinforcement algorithms like Q-learning to demonstrate the training of reinforcement learning algorithms for trading using OpenAI's Gym environment.

Summary

In this chapter, we reviewed key industry trends around algorithmic trading strategies, the emergence of alternative data, and the use of ML to exploit these new sources of informational advantage. Furthermore, we introduced key elements of the ML4T workflow and outlined important use cases of ML for trading in the context of different strategies.

In the next two chapters, we will take a closer look at the oil that fuels any algorithmic trading strategy—the market, fundamental, and alternative data sources—using ML.

2

Market and Fundamental Data – Sources and Techniques

Data has always been an essential driver of trading, and traders have long made efforts to gain an advantage from access to superior information. These efforts date back at least to the rumors that the House of Rothschild benefited handsomely from bond purchases upon advance news about the British victory at Waterloo, which was carried by pigeons across the channel.

Today, investments in faster data access take the shape of the Go West consortium of leading **high-frequency trading** (**HFT**) firms that connects the **Chicago Mercantile Exchange** (**CME**) with Tokyo. The round-trip latency between the CME and the **BATS** (**Better Alternative Trading System**) exchanges in New York has dropped to close to the theoretical limit of eight milliseconds as traders compete to exploit arbitrage opportunities. At the same time, regulators and exchanges have started to introduce speed bumps that slow down trading to limit the adverse effects on competition of uneven access to information.

Traditionally, investors mostly relied on **publicly available market and fundamental data**. Efforts to create or acquire private datasets, for example, through proprietary surveys, were limited. Conventional strategies focus on equity fundamentals and build financial models on reported financials, possibly combined with industry or macro data to project earnings per share and stock prices. Alternatively, they leverage **technical analysis** to extract signals from market data using indicators computed from price and volume information.

Machine learning (**ML**) algorithms promise to exploit market and fundamental data more efficiently than human-defined rules and heuristics, particularly when combined with **alternative data**, which is the topic of the next chapter. We will illustrate how to apply ML algorithms ranging from linear models to **recurrent neural networks** (**RNNs**) to market and fundamental data and generate tradeable signals.

This chapter introduces market and fundamental data sources and explains how they reflect the environment in which they are created. The details of the **trading environment** matter not only for the proper interpretation of market data but also for the design and execution of your strategy and the implementation of realistic backtesting simulations.

We also illustrate how to access and work with trading and financial statement data from various sources using Python.

In particular, this chapter will cover the following topics:

- How market data reflects the structure of the trading environment
- Working with trade and quote data at minute frequency
- Reconstructing an order book from tick data using Nasdaq ITCH
- Summarizing tick data using various types of bars
- Working with **eXtensible Business Reporting Language** (**XBRL**)-encoded electronic filings
- Parsing and combining market and fundamental data to create a **price-to-earnings** (**P/E**) series
- How to access various market and fundamental data sources using Python

> You can find the code samples for this chapter and links to additional resources in the corresponding directory of the GitHub repository. The notebooks include color versions of the images.

Market data reflects its environment

Market data is the product of how traders place orders for a financial instrument directly or through intermediaries on one of the numerous marketplaces, how they are processed, and how prices are set by matching demand and supply. As a result, the data reflects the institutional environment of trading venues, including the rules and regulations that govern orders, trade execution, and price formation. See Harris (2003) for a global overview and Jones (2018) for details on the U.S. market.

Algorithmic traders use algorithms, including ML, to analyze the flow of buy and sell orders and the resulting volume and price statistics to extract trade signals that capture insights into, for example, demand-supply dynamics or the behavior of certain market participants.

We will first review institutional features that impact the simulation of a trading strategy during a backtest before we start working with actual tick data created by one such environment, namely Nasdaq.

Market microstructure – the nuts and bolts

Market microstructure studies how the **institutional environment** affects the trading process and shapes outcomes like price discovery, bid-ask spreads and quotes, intraday trading behavior, and transaction costs (Madhavan 2000; 2002). It is one of the fastest-growing fields of financial research, propelled by the rapid development of algorithmic and electronic trading.

Today, hedge funds sponsor in-house analysts to track the rapidly evolving, complex details and ensure execution at the best possible market prices and design strategies that exploit market frictions. We will provide only a brief overview of these key concepts before we dive into the data generated by trading. The references contain several sources that treat this subject in great detail.

How to trade – different types of orders

Traders can place various types of buy or sell orders. Some orders guarantee immediate execution, while others may state a price threshold or other conditions that trigger execution. Orders are typically valid for the same trading day unless specified otherwise.

A *market order* is intended for immediate execution of the order upon arrival at the trading venue, at the price that prevails at that moment. In contrast, a *limit order* only executes if the market price is higher than the limit for a sell limit order, or lower than the limit for a buy limit order. A *stop order*, in turn, only becomes active when the market price rises above a specified price for a buy stop order, or falls below a specified price for a sell order. A *buy stop order* can be used to limit the losses of short sales. Stop orders may also have limits.

Numerous other conditions can be attached to orders. For example, *all or none orders* prevent partial execution; they are filled only if a specified number of shares is available and can be valid for a day or longer. They require special handling and are not visible to market participants. *Fill or kill orders* also prevent partial execution but cancel if not executed immediately. *Immediate or cancel orders* immediately buy or sell the number of shares that are available and cancel the remainder. *Not-held orders* allow the broker to decide on the time and price of execution. Finally, the market on *open/close orders* executes on or near the opening or closing of the market. Partial executions are allowed.

Where to trade – from exchanges to dark pools

Securities trade in highly organized and **regulated exchanges** or with varying degrees of formality in **over-the-counter** (**OTC**) markets. An exchange is a central marketplace where buyers and sellers compete for the lowest ask and highest bid, respectively. Exchange regulations typically impose listing and reporting requirements to create transparency and attract more traders and liquidity. OTC markets, such as the Best Market (OTCQX) or the Venture Market (OTCQB), often have lower regulatory barriers. As a result, they are suitable for a far broader range of securities, including bonds or **American Depositary Receipts** (**ADRs**; equity listed on a foreign exchange, for example, for Nestlé, S.A.).

Exchanges may rely on bilateral trading or centralized order-driven systems that match all buy and sell orders according to certain rules. Many exchanges use intermediaries that provide liquidity by making markets in certain securities. These **intermediaries** include dealers that act as principals on their own behalf and brokers that trade as agents on behalf of others. **Price formation** may occur through auctions, such as in the **New York Stock Exchange** (**NYSE**), where the highest bid and lowest offer are matched, or through dealers who buy from sellers and sell to buyers.

Back in the day, companies either registered and traded mostly on the NYSE, or they traded on OTC markets like Nasdaq. On the NYSE, a sole **specialist** intermediated trades of a given security. The specialist received buy and sell orders via a broker and tracked limit orders in a central order book. Limit orders were executed with a priority based on price and time. Buy market orders routed to the specialist transacted with the lowest ask (and sell market orders routed to the specialist transacted with the highest bid) in the limit order book, prioritizing earlier limit orders in the case of ties. Access to all orders in the central order book allowed the specialist to publish the best bid, ask prices, and set market prices based on the overall buy-sell imbalance.

On Nasdaq, multiple **market makers** facilitated stock trades. Each dealer provided their best bid and ask price to a central quotation system and stood ready to transact the specified number of shares at the specified prices. Traders would route their orders to the market maker with the best quote via their broker. The competition for orders made execution at fair prices very likely. Market makers ensured a fair and orderly market, provided liquidity, and disseminated prices like specialists but only had access to the orders routed to them as opposed to market-wide supply and demand. This fragmentation could create difficulties in identifying fair value market prices.

Today, **trading has fragmented**; instead of two principal venues in the US, there are more than thirteen displayed trading venues, including exchanges and (unregulated) **alternative trading systems** (**ATSs**) such as **electronic communication networks** (**ECNs**). Each reports trades to the consolidated tape, but at different latencies. To make matters more difficult, the rules of engagement for each venue differ with several different pricing and queuing models.

The following table lists some of the larger global exchanges and the trading volumes for the 12 months ending 03/2018 in various asset classes, including derivatives. Typically, a minority of financial instruments account for most trading:

Exchange	Stocks				
	Market cap (USD mn)	**# Listed companies**	**Volume/day (USD mn)**	**# Shares/ day ('000)**	**# Options / day ('000)**
NYSE	23,138,626	2,294	78,410	6,122	1,546
Nasdaq – US	10,375,718	2,968	65,026	7,131	2,609
Japan Exchange Group Inc.	6,287,739	3,618	28,397	3,361	1
Shanghai Stock Exchange	5,022,691	1,421	34,736	9,801	
Euronext	4,649,073	1,240	9,410	836	304
Hong Kong Exchanges and Clearing	4,443,082	2,186	12,031	1,174	516
LSE Group	3,986,413	2,622	10,398	1,011	
Shenzhen Stock Exchange	3,547,312	2,110	40,244	14,443	
Deutsche Boerse AG	2,339,092	506	7,825	475	
BSE India Limited	2,298,179	5,439	602	1,105	
National Stock Exchange of India Limited	2,273,286	1,952	5,092	10,355	
BATS Global Markets - US					1,243
Chicago Board Options Exchange					1,811
International Securities Exchange					1,204

The ATSs mentioned previously include dozens of **dark pools** that allow traders to execute anonymously. They are estimated to account for 40 percent of all U.S. stock trades in 2017, compared with an estimated 16 percent in 2010. Dark pools emerged in the 1980s when the SEC allowed brokers to match buyers and sellers of big blocks of shares. The rise of high-frequency electronic trading and the 2007 SEC Order Protection rule that intended to spur competition and cut transaction costs through transparency as part of **Regulation National Market System (Reg NMS)** drove the growth of dark pools, as traders aimed to avoid the visibility of large trades (Mamudi 2017). Reg NMS also established the **National Best Bid and Offer (NBBO)** mandate for brokers to route orders to venues that offer the best price.

Some ATSs are called dark pools because they do not broadcast pre-trade data, including the presence, price, and amount of buy and sell orders as traditional exchanges are required to do. However, dark pools report information about trades to the **Financial Industry**

Regulatory Authority (**FINRA**) after they occur. As a result, dark pools do not contribute to the process of price discovery until after trade execution but provide protection against various HFT strategies outlined in the first chapter.

In the next section, we will see how market data captures trading activity and reflect the institutional infrastructure in U.S. markets.

Working with high-frequency data

Two categories of market data cover the thousands of companies listed on U.S. exchanges that are traded under Reg NMS: the **consolidated feed** combines trade and quote data from each trading venue, whereas each individual exchange offers **proprietary products** with additional activity information for that particular venue.

In this section, we will first present proprietary order flow data provided by Nasdaq that represents the actual stream of orders, trades, and resulting prices as they occur on a tick-by-tick basis. Then, we will demonstrate how to regularize this continuous stream of data that arrives at irregular intervals into bars of a fixed duration. Finally, we will introduce AlgoSeek's equity minute bar data, which contains consolidated trade and quote information. In each case, we will illustrate how to work with the data using Python so that you can leverage these sources for your trading strategy.

How to work with Nasdaq order book data

The **primary source of market data** is the order book, which updates in real time throughout the day to reflect all trading activity. Exchanges typically offer this data as a real-time service for a fee; however, they may provide some historical data for free.

In the United States, stock markets provide quotes in three tiers, namely Level L1, L2, and L3, that offer increasingly granular information and capabilities:

- **Level 1 (L1)**: Real-time bid- and ask-price information, as available from numerous online sources.
- **Level 2 (L2)**: Adds information about bid and ask prices by specific market makers as well as the size and time of recent transactions for better insights into the liquidity of a given equity.
- **Level 3 (L3)**: Adds the ability to enter or change quotes, execute orders, and confirm trades and is available only to market makers and exchange member firms. Access to Level 3 quotes permits registered brokers to meet best execution requirements.

The trading activity is reflected in numerous **messages about orders** sent by market participants. These messages typically conform to the **electronic Financial Information eXchange** (**FIX**) communications protocol for the real-time exchange of securities transactions and market data or a native exchange protocol.

Communicating trades with the FIX protocol

Just like SWIFT is the message protocol for back-office (for example, in trade-settlement) messaging, the FIX protocol is the **de facto messaging standard** for communication before and during trade executions between exchanges, banks, brokers, clearing firms, and other market participants. Fidelity Investments and Salomon Brothers introduced FIX in 1992 to facilitate the electronic communication between broker-dealers and institutional clients who, until then, exchanged information over the phone.

It became popular in global equity markets before expanding into foreign exchange, fixed income and derivatives markets, and further into post-trade to support straight-through processing. Exchanges provide access to FIX messages as a real-time data feed that is **parsed by algorithmic traders** to track market activity and, for example, identify the footprint of market participants and anticipate their next move.

The sequence of messages allows for the **reconstruction of the order book**. The scale of transactions across numerous exchanges creates a large amount (~10 TB) of unstructured data that is challenging to process and, hence, can be a source of competitive advantage.

The FIX protocol, currently at version 5.0, is a free and open standard with a large community of affiliated industry professionals. It is self-describing, like the more recent XML, and a FIX session is supported by the underlying **Transmission Control Protocol (TCP)** layer. The community continually adds new functionality.

The protocol supports pipe-separated key-value pairs, as well as a **tag-based FIXML** syntax. A sample message that requests a server login would look as follows:

```
8=FIX.5.0|9=127|35=A|59=theBroker.123456|56=CSERVER|34=1|32=20180117-
08:03:04|57=TRADE|50=any_string|98=2|108=34|141=Y|553=12345|554=passw0
rd!|10=131|
```

There are a few open source FIX implementations in Python that can be used to formulate and parse FIX messages. The service provider Interactive Brokers offers a FIX-based **computer-to-computer interface (CTCI)** for automated trading (refer to the resources section for this chapter in the GitHub repository).

The Nasdaq TotalView-ITCH data feed

While FIX has a dominant market share, exchanges also offer native protocols. Nasdaq offers a TotalView-ITCH **direct data-feed protocol**, which allows subscribers to **track individual orders** for equity instruments from placement to execution or cancellation.

Historical records of this data flow permit the reconstruction of the order book that keeps track of the active limit orders for a specific security. The order book reveals the **market depth** throughout the day by listing the number of shares being bid or offered at each price point. It may also identify the market participant responsible for specific buy and sell orders unless they are placed anonymously. Market depth is a key indicator of liquidity and the **potential price impact** of sizable market orders.

In addition to matching market and limit orders, Nasdaq also operates **auctions or crosses** that execute a large number of trades at market opening and closing. Crosses are becoming more important as passive investing continues to grow and traders look for opportunities to execute larger blocks of stock. TotalView also disseminates the **Net Order Imbalance Indicator** (**NOII**) for Nasdaq opening and closing crosses and Nasdaq IPO/Halt Cross.

How to parse binary order messages

The ITCH v5.0 specification declares over 20 message types related to system events, stock characteristics, the placement and modification of limit orders, and trade execution. It also contains information about the net order imbalance before the open and closing cross.

Nasdaq offers samples of daily binary files for several months. The GitHub repository for this chapter contains a notebook, `parse_itch_order_flow_messages.ipynb`, that illustrates how to download and parse a sample file of ITCH messages. The notebook `rebuild_nasdaq_order_book.ipynb` then goes on to reconstruct both the executed trades and the order book for any given ticker.

The following table shows the frequency of the **most common message types** for the sample file date October 30, 2019:

Message type	Order book impact	Number of messages
A	New unattributed limit order	127,214,649
D	Order canceled	123,296,742
U	Order canceled and replaced	25,513,651
E	Full or partial execution; possibly multiple messages for the same original order	7,316,703
X	Modified after partial cancellation	3,568,735
F	Add attributed order	1,423,908
P	Trade message (non-cross)	1,525,363
C	Executed in whole or in part at a price different from the initial display price	129,729
Q	Cross trade message	17,775

For each message, the **specification** lays out the components and their respective length and data types:

Name	Offset	Length	Value	Notes
Message type	0	1	S	System event message.
Stock locate	1	2	Integer	Always 0.
Tracking number	3	2	Integer	Nasdaq internal tracking number.
Timestamp	5	6	Integer	The number of nanoseconds since midnight.

Order reference number	11	8	Integer	The unique reference number assigned to the new order at the time of receipt.
Buy/sell indicator	19	1	Alpha	The type of order being added: B = Buy Order, and S = Sell Order.
Shares	20	4	Integer	The total number of shares associated with the order being added to the book.
Stock	24	8	Alpha	Stock symbol, right - padded with spaces.
Price	32	4	Price (4)	The display price of the new order. Refer to *Data Types* in the specification for field processing notes.
Attribution	36	4	Alpha	The Nasdaq market participant identifier associated with the entered order.

Python provides the `struct` module to parse binary data using format strings that identify the message elements by indicating the length and type of the various components of the `byte` string as laid out in the specification.

Let's walk through the critical steps required to parse the trading messages and reconstruct the order book:

1. The ITCH parser relies on the message specifications provided in the file `message_types.xlsx` (refer to the notebook `parse_itch_order_flow_messages.ipynb` for details). It assembles format strings according to the `formats` dictionary:

```
formats = {
    ('integer', 2): 'H',  # int of length 2 => format string 'H'
    ('integer', 4): 'I',
    ('integer', 6): '6s', # int of length 6 => parse as string,
      convert later
    ('integer', 8): 'Q',
    ('alpha', 1)  : 's',
    ('alpha', 2)  : '2s',
    ('alpha', 4)  : '4s',
    ('alpha', 8)  : '8s',
    ('price_4', 4): 'I',
    ('price_8', 8): 'Q',
}
```

2. The parser translates the message specs into format strings and named tuples that capture the message content:

```
# Get ITCH specs and create formatting (type, length) tuples
specs = pd.read_csv('message_types.csv')
specs['formats'] = specs[['value', 'length']].apply(tuple,
                            axis=1).map(formats)
# Formatting for alpha fields
alpha_fields = specs[specs.value == 'alpha'].set_index('name')
alpha_msgs = alpha_fields.groupby('message_type')
alpha_formats = {k: v.to_dict() for k, v in alpha_msgs.formats}
alpha_length = {k: v.add(5).to_dict() for k, v in alpha_msgs.length}
# Generate message classes as named tuples and format strings
message_fields, fstring = {}, {}
for t, message in specs.groupby('message_type'):
    message_fields[t] = namedtuple(typename=t,
                                   field_names=message.name.tolist())
    fstring[t] = '>' + ''.join(message.formats.tolist())
```

3. Fields of the alpha type require postprocessing, as defined in the `format_alpha` function:

```
def format_alpha(mtype, data):
    """Process byte strings of type alpha"""

    for col in alpha_formats.get(mtype).keys():
        if mtype != 'R' and col == 'stock':
            data = data.drop(col, axis=1)
            continue
        data.loc[:, col] = (data.loc[:, col]
                            .str.decode("utf-8")
                            .str.strip())
        if encoding.get(col):
            data.loc[:, col] = data.loc[:, col].map(encoding.get(col))
    return data
```

The binary file for a single day contains over 300,000,000 messages that are worth over 9 GB. The script appends the parsed result iteratively to a file in the fast HDF5 format to avoid memory constraints. (Refer to the *Efficient data storage with pandas* section later in this chapter for more information on the HDF5 format.)

The following (simplified) code processes the binary file and produces the parsed orders stored by message type:

```
with (data_path / file_name).open('rb') as data:
    while True:
        message_size = int.from_bytes(data.read(2), byteorder='big',
                                      signed=False)
        message_type = data.read(1).decode('ascii')
        message_type_counter.update([message_type])
        record = data.read(message_size - 1)
        message = message_fields[message_type]._make(
            unpack(fstring[message_type], record))
        messages[message_type].append(message)

        # deal with system events like market open/close
        if message_type == 'S':
            timestamp = int.from_bytes(message.timestamp,
                                       byteorder='big')
            if message.event_code.decode('ascii') == 'C': # close
                store_messages(messages)
                break
```

Summarizing the trading activity for all 8,500 stocks

As expected, a small number of the 8,500-plus securities traded on this day account for most trades:

```
with pd.HDFStore(itch_store) as store:
    stocks = store['R'].loc[:, ['stock_locate', 'stock']]
    trades = (store['P'].append(
            store['Q'].rename(columns={'cross_price': 'price'}),
            sort=False).merge(stocks))
trades['value'] = trades.shares.mul(trades.price)
trades['value_share'] = trades.value.div(trades.value.sum())
trade_summary = (trades.groupby('stock').value_share
                 .sum().sort_values(ascending=False))
trade_summary.iloc[:50].plot.bar(figsize=(14, 6),
                                 color='darkblue',
                                 title='Share of Traded Value')
f = lambda y, _: '{:.0%}'.format(y)
plt.gca().yaxis.set_major_formatter(FuncFormatter(f))
```

Figure 2.1 shows the resulting plot:

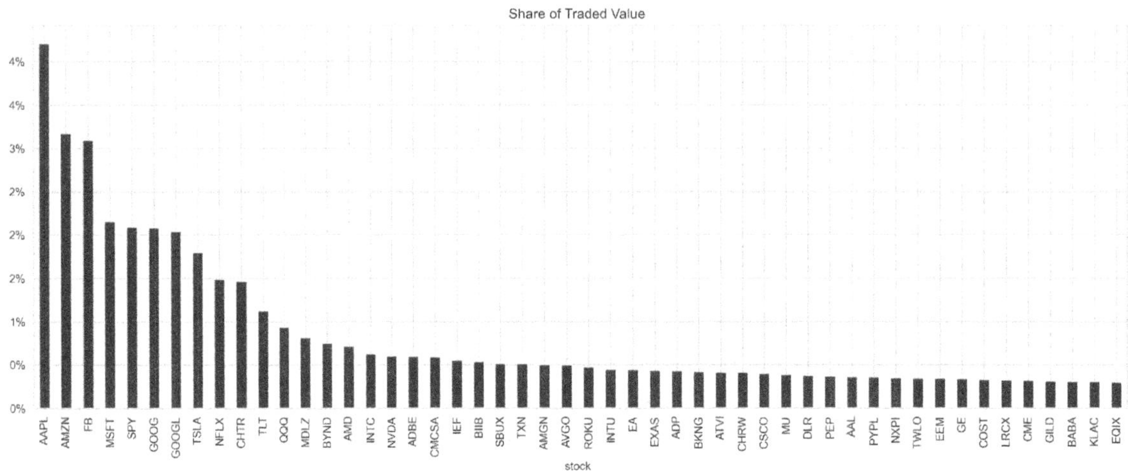

Figure 2.1: The share of traded value of the 50 most traded securities

How to reconstruct all trades and the order book

The parsed messages allow us to rebuild the order flow for the given day. The `'R'` message type contains a listing of all stocks traded during a given day, including information about **initial public offerings** (**IPOs**) and trading restrictions.

Throughout the day, new orders are added, and orders that are executed and canceled are removed from the order book. The proper accounting for messages that reference orders placed on a prior date would require tracking the order book over multiple days.

The `get_messages()` function illustrates how to collect the orders for a single stock that affects trading. (Refer to the ITCH specification for details about each message.) The code is slightly simplified; refer to the notebook `rebuild_nasdaq_order_book.ipynb` for further details:

```
def get_messages(date, stock=stock):
    """Collect trading messages for given stock"""
    with pd.HDFStore(itch_store) as store:
        stock_locate = store.select('R', where='stock =
                                    stock').stock_locate.iloc[0]
        target = 'stock_locate = stock_locate'
        data = {}
        # relevant message types
        messages = ['A', 'F', 'E', 'C', 'X', 'D', 'U', 'P', 'Q']
        for m in messages:
            data[m] = store.select(m,
              where=target).drop('stock_locate', axis=1).assign(type=m)
    order_cols = ['order_reference_number', 'buy_sell_indicator',
                  'shares', 'price']
    orders = pd.concat([data['A'], data['F']], sort=False,
```

```
                                ignore_index=True).loc[:, order_cols]
    for m in messages[2: -3]:
        data[m] = data[m].merge(orders, how='left')
    data['U'] = data['U'].merge(orders, how='left',
                                right_on='order_reference_number',
                                left_on='original_order_reference_number',
                                suffixes=['', '_replaced'])
    data['Q'].rename(columns={'cross_price': 'price'}, inplace=True)
    data['X']['shares'] = data['X']['cancelled_shares']
    data['X'] = data['X'].dropna(subset=['price'])
    data = pd.concat([data[m] for m in messages], ignore_index=True,
                      sort=False)
```

Reconstructing successful trades—that is, orders that were executed as opposed to those that were canceled from trade-related message types `C`, `E`, `P`, and `Q`—is relatively straightforward:

```
def get_trades(m):
    """Combine C, E, P and Q messages into trading records"""
    trade_dict = {'executed_shares': 'shares', 'execution_price': 'price'}
    cols = ['timestamp', 'executed_shares']
    trades = pd.concat([m.loc[m.type == 'E',
                              cols + ['price']].rename(columns=trade_dict),
                        m.loc[m.type == 'C',
                              cols + ['execution_price']]
                        .rename(columns=trade_dict),
                        m.loc[m.type == 'P', ['timestamp', 'price',
                                              'shares']],
                        m.loc[m.type == 'Q',
                              ['timestamp', 'price', 'shares']]
                        .assign(cross=1), ],
                       sort=False).dropna(subset=['price']).fillna(0)
    return trades.set_index('timestamp').sort_index().astype(int)
```

The order book keeps track of limit orders, and the various price levels for buy and sell orders constitute the depth of the order book. Reconstructing the order book for a given level of depth requires the following steps:

The `add_orders()` function accumulates sell orders in ascending order and buy orders in descending order for a given timestamp up to the desired level of depth:

```
def add_orders(orders, buysell, nlevels):
    new_order = []
    items = sorted(orders.copy().items())
    if buysell == 1:
        items = reversed(items)
    for i, (p, s) in enumerate(items, 1):
        new_order.append((p, s))
        if i == nlevels:
```

```
            break
    return orders, new_order
```

We iterate over all ITCH messages and process orders and their replacements as required by the specification:

```
for message in messages.itertuples():
    i = message[0]
    if np.isnan(message.buy_sell_indicator):
        continue
    message_counter.update(message.type)
    buysell = message.buy_sell_indicator
    price, shares = None, None
    if message.type in ['A', 'F', 'U']:
        price, shares = int(message.price), int(message.shares)
        current_orders[buysell].update({price: shares})
        current_orders[buysell], new_order =
          add_orders(current_orders[buysell], buysell, nlevels)
        order_book[buysell][message.timestamp] = new_order
    if message.type in ['E', 'C', 'X', 'D', 'U']:
        if message.type == 'U':
            if not np.isnan(message.shares_replaced):
                price = int(message.price_replaced)
                shares = -int(message.shares_replaced)
        else:
            if not np.isnan(message.price):
                price = int(message.price)
                shares = -int(message.shares)
        if price is not None:
            current_orders[buysell].update({price: shares})
            if current_orders[buysell][price] <= 0:
                current_orders[buysell].pop(price)
            current_orders[buysell], new_order =
              add_orders(current_orders[buysell], buysell, nlevels)
            order_book[buysell][message.timestamp] = new_order
```

Figure 2.2 highlights the depth of liquidity at any given point in time using different intensities that visualize the number of orders at different price levels. The left panel shows how the distribution of limit order prices was weighted toward buy orders at higher prices.

The right panel plots the evolution of limit orders and prices throughout the trading day: the dark line tracks the prices for executed trades during market hours, whereas the red and blue dots indicate individual limit orders on a per-minute basis (refer to the notebook for details):

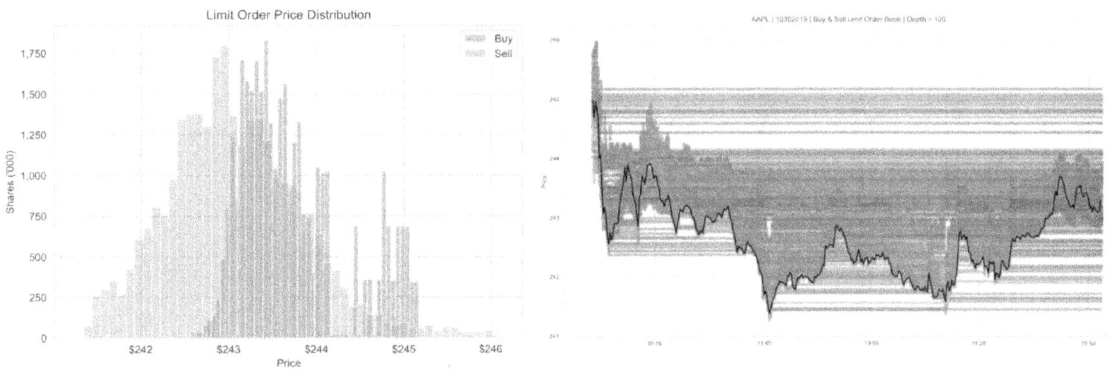

Figure 2.2: AAPL market liquidity according to the order book

From ticks to bars – how to regularize market data

The trade data is indexed by nanoseconds, arrives at irregular intervals, and is very noisy. The **bid-ask bounce**, for instance, causes the price to oscillate between the bid and ask prices when trade initiation alternates between buy and sell market orders. To improve the noise-signal ratio and the statistical properties of the price series, we need to resample and regularize the tick data by aggregating the trading activity.

We typically collect the **open (first), high, low, and closing (last) price and volume** (jointly abbreviated as **OHLCV**) for the aggregated period, alongside the **volume-weighted average price** (**VWAP**) and the timestamp associated with the data.

Refer to the `normalize_tick_data.ipynb` notebook in the folder for this chapter on GitHub for additional details.

The raw material – tick bars

The following code generates a plot of the raw tick price and volume data for AAPL:

```
stock, date = 'AAPL', '20191030'
title = '{} | {}'.format(stock, pd.to_datetime(date).date()
with pd.HDFStore(itch_store) as store:
    sys_events = store['S'].set_index('event_code') # system events
    sys_events.timestamp = sys_events.timestamp.add(pd.to_datetime(date)).
dt.time
    market_open = sys_events.loc['Q', 'timestamp']
    market_close = sys_events.loc['M', 'timestamp']
with pd.HDFStore(stock_store) as store:
    trades = store['{}/trades'.format(stock)].reset_index()
trades = trades[trades.cross == 0] # excluding data from open/close crossings
trades.price = trades.price.mul(1e-4) # format price
```

```
trades = trades[trades.cross == 0]    # exclude crossing trades
trades = trades.between_time(market_open, market_close) # market hours only
tick_bars = trades.set_index('timestamp')
tick_bars.index = tick_bars.index.time
tick_bars.price.plot(figsize=(10, 5), title=title), lw=1)
```

Figure 2.3 displays the resulting plot:

Figure 2.3: Tick bars

The tick returns are far from normally distributed, as evidenced by the low p-value of `scipy.stats.normaltest`:

```
from scipy.stats import normaltest
normaltest(tick_bars.price.pct_change().dropna())
NormaltestResult(statistic=62408.76562431228, pvalue=0.0)
```

Plain-vanilla denoising – time bars

Time bars involve trade aggregation by period. The following code gets the data for the time bars:

```
def get_bar_stats(agg_trades):
    vwap = agg_trades.apply(lambda x: np.average(x.price,
           weights=x.shares)).to_frame('vwap')
    ohlc = agg_trades.price.ohlc()
    vol = agg_trades.shares.sum().to_frame('vol')
    txn = agg_trades.shares.size().to_frame('txn')
    return pd.concat([ohlc, vwap, vol, txn], axis=1)
resampled = trades.groupby(pd.Grouper(freq='1Min'))
time_bars = get_bar_stats(resampled)
```

We can display the result as a price-volume chart:

```
def price_volume(df, price='vwap', vol='vol', suptitle=title, fname=None):
    fig, axes = plt.subplots(nrows=2, sharex=True, figsize=(15, 8))
    axes[0].plot(df.index, df[price])
    axes[1].bar(df.index, df[vol], width=1 / (len(df.index)),
                color='r')
    xfmt = mpl.dates.DateFormatter('%H:%M')
    axes[1].xaxis.set_major_locator(mpl.dates.HourLocator(interval=3))
    axes[1].xaxis.set_major_formatter(xfmt)
    axes[1].get_xaxis().set_tick_params(which='major', pad=25)
    axes[0].set_title('Price', fontsize=14)
    axes[1].set_title('Volume', fontsize=14)
    fig.autofmt_xdate()
    fig.suptitle(suptitle)
    fig.tight_layout()
    plt.subplots_adjust(top=0.9)
price_volume(time_bars)
```

The preceding code produces *Figure 2.4*:

Figure 2.4: Time bars

Alternatively, we can represent the data as a candlestick chart using the Bokeh plotting library:

```
resampled = trades.groupby(pd.Grouper(freq='5Min')) # 5 Min bars for better
print
df = get_bar_stats(resampled)
increase = df.close > df.open
decrease = df.open > df.close
w = 2.5 * 60 * 1000 # 2.5 min in ms
WIDGETS = "pan, wheel_zoom, box_zoom, reset, save"
p = figure(x_axis_type='datetime', tools=WIDGETS, plot_width=1500,
          title = "AAPL Candlestick")
p.xaxis.major_label_orientation = pi/4
p.grid.grid_line_alpha=0.4
p.segment(df.index, df.high, df.index, df.low, color="black")
p.vbar(df.index[increase], w, df.open[increase], df.close[increase],
       fill_color="#D5E1DD", line_color="black")
p.vbar(df.index[decrease], w, df.open[decrease], df.close[decrease],
       fill_color="#F2583E", line_color="black")
show(p)
```

This produces the plot in *Figure 2.5*:

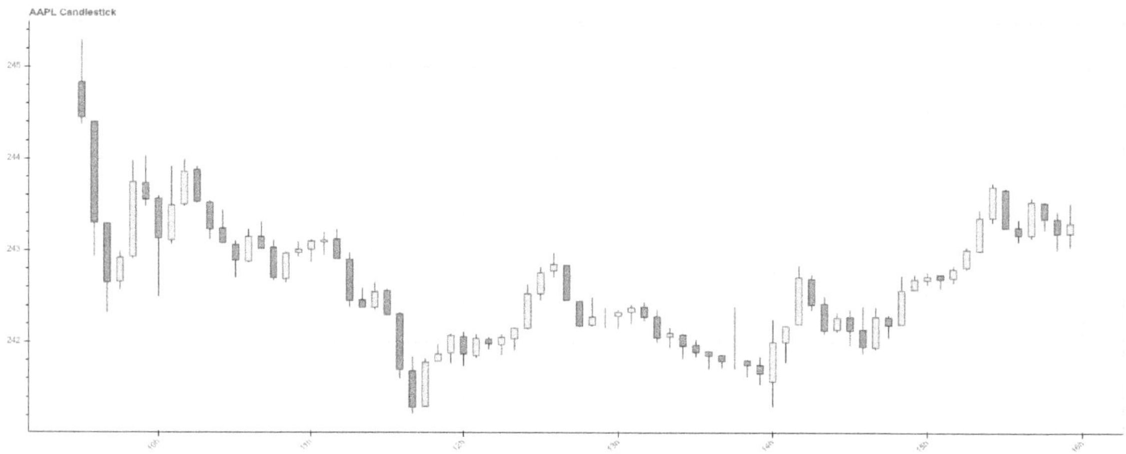

Figure 2.5: Bokeh candlestick plot

Accounting for order fragmentation – volume bars

Time bars smooth some of the noise contained in the raw tick data but may fail to account for the fragmentation of orders. Execution-focused algorithmic trading may aim to match the **volume-weighted average price (VWAP)** over a given period. This will divide a single order into multiple trades and place orders according to historical patterns. Time bars would treat the same order differently, even though no new information has arrived in the market.

Volume bars offer an alternative by aggregating trade data according to volume. We can accomplish this as follows:

```
min_per_trading_day = 60 * 7.5
trades_per_min = trades.shares.sum() / min_per_trading_day
trades['cumul_vol'] = trades.shares.cumsum()
df = trades.reset_index()

by_vol = (df.groupby(df.cumul_vol.
                     div(trades_per_min)
                     .round().astype(int)))

vol_bars = pd.concat([by_vol.timestamp.last().to_frame('timestamp'),
                      get_bar_stats(by_vol)], axis=1)
price_volume(vol_bars.set_index('timestamp'))
```

We get the plot in *Figure 2.6* for the preceding code:

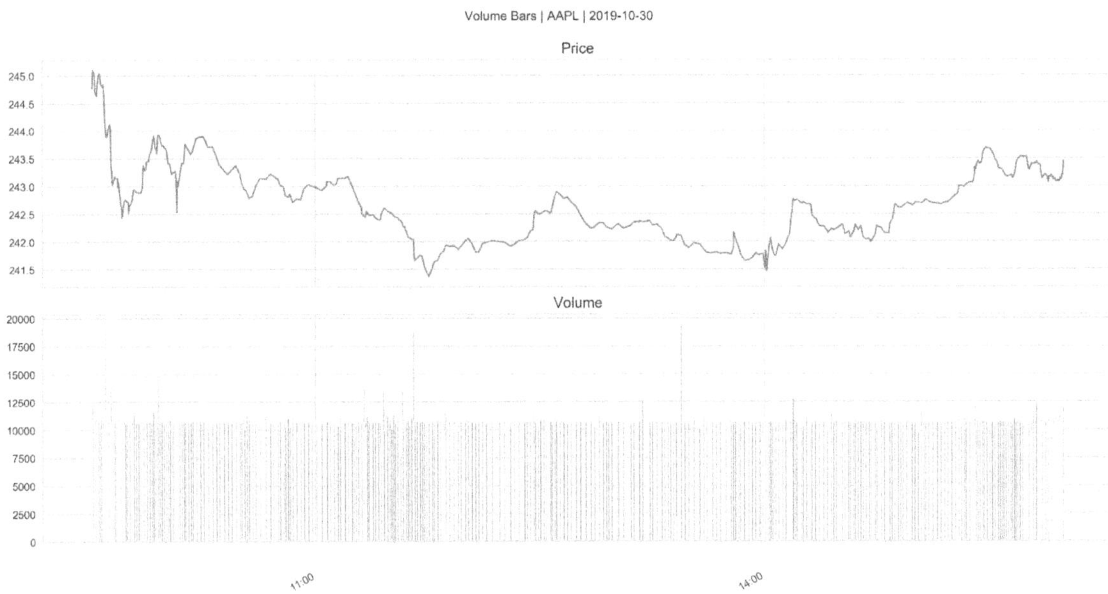

Figure 2.6: Volume bars

Accounting for price changes – dollar bars

When asset prices change significantly, or after stock splits, the value of a given amount of shares changes. Volume bars do not correctly reflect this and can hamper the comparison of trading behavior for different periods that reflect such changes. In these cases, the volume bar method should be adjusted to utilize the product of shares and prices to produce dollar bars.

The following code shows the computation for dollar bars:

```
value_per_min = trades.shares.mul(trades.price).sum()/(60*7.5) # min per
trading day
trades['cumul_val'] = trades.shares.mul(trades.price).cumsum()
df = trades.reset_index()
by_value = df.groupby(df.cumul_val.div(value_per_min).round().astype(int))
dollar_bars = pd.concat([by_value.timestamp.last().to_frame('timestamp'),
get_bar_stats(by_value)], axis=1)
price_volume(dollar_bars.set_index('timestamp'),
             suptitle=f'Dollar Bars | {stock} | {pd.to_datetime(date).
date()}')
```

The plot looks quite similar to the volume bar since the price has been fairly stable throughout the day:

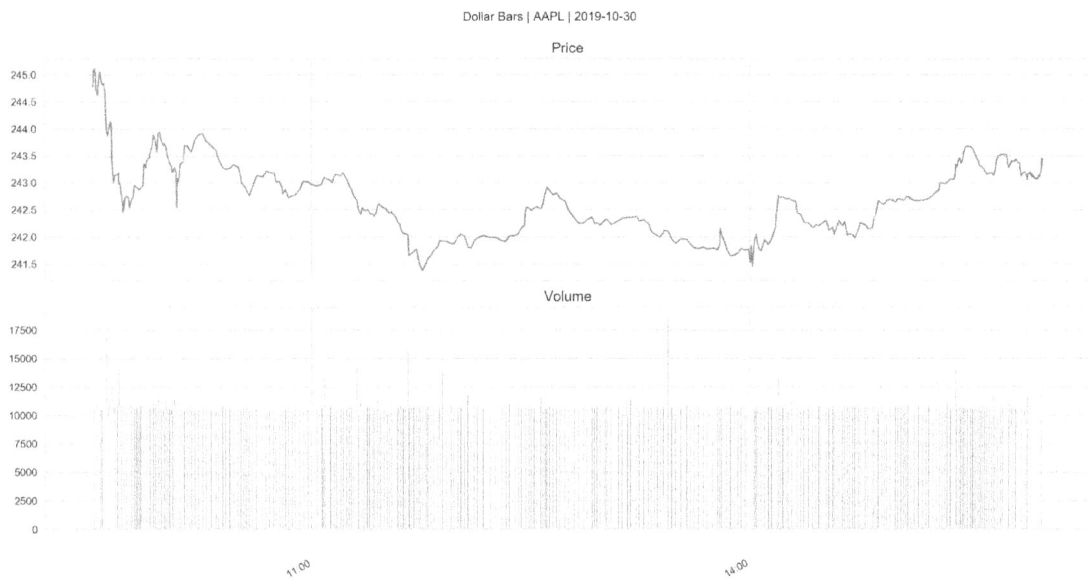

Figure 2.7: Dollar bars

AlgoSeek minute bars – equity quote and trade data

AlgoSeek provides historical intraday data of the quality previously available only to institutional investors. The AlgoSeek Equity bars provide very detailed intraday quote and trade data in a user-friendly format, which is aimed at making it easy to design and backtest intraday ML-driven strategies. As we will see, the data includes not only OHLCV information but also information on the bid-ask spread and the number of ticks with up and down price moves, among others.

AlgoSeek has been so kind as to provide samples of minute bar data for the Nasdaq 100 stocks from 2013-2017 for demonstration purposes and will make a subset of this data available to readers of this book.

In this section, we will present the available trade and quote information and show how to process the raw data. In later chapters, we will demonstrate how you can use this data for ML-driven intraday strategies.

From the consolidated feed to minute bars

AlgoSeek minute bars are based on data provided by the **Securities Information Processor** (**SIP**), which manages the consolidated feed mentioned at the beginning of this section. You can view the documentation at `https://www.algoseek.com/samples/`.

The SIP aggregates the best bid and offers quotes from each exchange, as well as the resulting trades and prices. Exchanges are prohibited by law from sending their quotes and trades to direct feeds before sending them to the SIP. Given the fragmented nature of U.S. equity trading, the consolidated feed provides a convenient snapshot of the current state of the market.

More importantly, the SIP acts as the benchmark used by regulators to determine the **National Best Bid and Offer** (**NBBO**) according to Reg NMS. The OHLC bar quote prices are based on the NBBO, and each bid or ask quote price refers to an NBBO price.

Every exchange publishes its top-of-book price and the number of shares available at that price. The NBBO changes when a published quote improves the NBBO. Bid/ask quotes persist until there is a change due to trade, price improvement, or the cancelation of the latest bid or ask. While historical OHLC bars are often based on trades during the bar period, NBBO bid/ask quotes may be carried forward from the previous bar until there is a new NBBO event.

AlgoSeek bars cover the whole trading day, from the opening of the first exchange until the closing of the last exchange. Bars outside regular market hours normally exhibit limited activity. Trading hours, in Eastern Time, are:

- Premarket: Approximately 04:00:00 (this varies by exchange) to 09:29:59
- Market: 09:30:00 to 16:00:00
- Extended hours: 16:00:01 to 20:00:00

Quote and trade data fields

The minute bar data contains up to 54 fields. There are eight fields for the **open**, **high**, **low**, and **close** elements of the bar, namely:

- The timestamp for the bar and the corresponding trade
- The price and the size for the prevailing bid-ask quote and the relevant trade

There are also 14 data points with **volume information** for the bar period:

- The number of shares and corresponding trades
- The trade volumes at or below the bid, between the bid quote and the midpoint, at the midpoint, between the midpoint and the ask quote, and at or above the ask, as well as for crosses
- The number of shares traded with upticks or downticks, that is, when the price rose or fell, as well as when the price did not change, differentiated by the previous direction of price movement

The AlgoSeek data also contains the number of shares **reported to FINRA** and processed internally at broker-dealers, by dark pools, or OTC. These trades represent volume that is hidden or not publicly available until after the fact.

Finally, the data includes the **volume-weighted average price** (**VWAP**) and minimum and maximum bid-ask spread for the bar period.

How to process AlgoSeek intraday data

In this section, we'll process the AlgoSeek sample data. The `data` directory on GitHub contains instructions on how to download that data from AlgoSeek.

The minute bar data comes in four versions: with and without quote information, and with or without FINRA's reported volume. There is one zipped folder per day, containing one CSV file per ticker.

The following code example extracts the trade-only minute bar data into daily `.parquet` files:

```
directories = [Path(d) for d in ['1min_trades']]
target = directory / 'parquet'
for zipped_file in directory.glob('*/**/*.zip'):
    fname = zipped_file.stem
    print('\t', fname)
    zf = ZipFile(zipped_file)
    files = zf.namelist()
    data = (pd.concat([pd.read_csv(zf.open(f),
                                   parse_dates=[['Date',
                                                 'TimeBarStart']])
                       for f in files],
                      ignore_index=True)
            .rename(columns=lambda x: x.lower())
            .rename(columns={'date_timebarstart': 'date_time'})
            .set_index(['ticker', 'date_time']))
    data.to_parquet(target / (fname + '.parquet'))
```

We can combine the `parquet` files into a single piece of HDF5 storage as follows, yielding 53.8 million records that consume 3.2 GB of memory and covering 5 years and 100 stocks:

```
path = Path('1min_trades/parquet')
df = pd.concat([pd.read_parquet(f) for f in path.glob('*.parquet')]).
dropna(how='all', axis=1)
df.columns = ['open', 'high', 'low', 'close', 'trades', 'volume', 'vwap']
df.to_hdf('data.h5', '1min_trades')

print(df.info(null_counts=True))
MultiIndex: 53864194 entries, (AAL, 2014-12-22 07:05:00) to (YHOO, 2017-06-16
19:59:00)
Data columns (total 7 columns):
open      53864194 non-null float64
high      53864194 non-null float64
Low       53864194 non-null float64
close     53864194 non-null float64
trades    53864194 non-null int64
volume    53864194 non-null int64
vwap      53852029 non-null float64
```

We can use `plotly` to quickly create an interactive candlestick plot for one day of AAPL data to view in a browser:

```
idx = pd.IndexSlice
with pd.HDFStore('data.h5') as store:
    print(store.info())
    df = (store['1min_trades']
          .loc[idx['AAPL', '2017-12-29'], :]
          .reset_index())

fig = go.Figure(data=go.Ohlc(x=df.date_time,
                             open=df.open,
                             high=df.high,
                             low=df.low,
                             close=df.close))
```

Figure 2.8 shows the resulting static image:

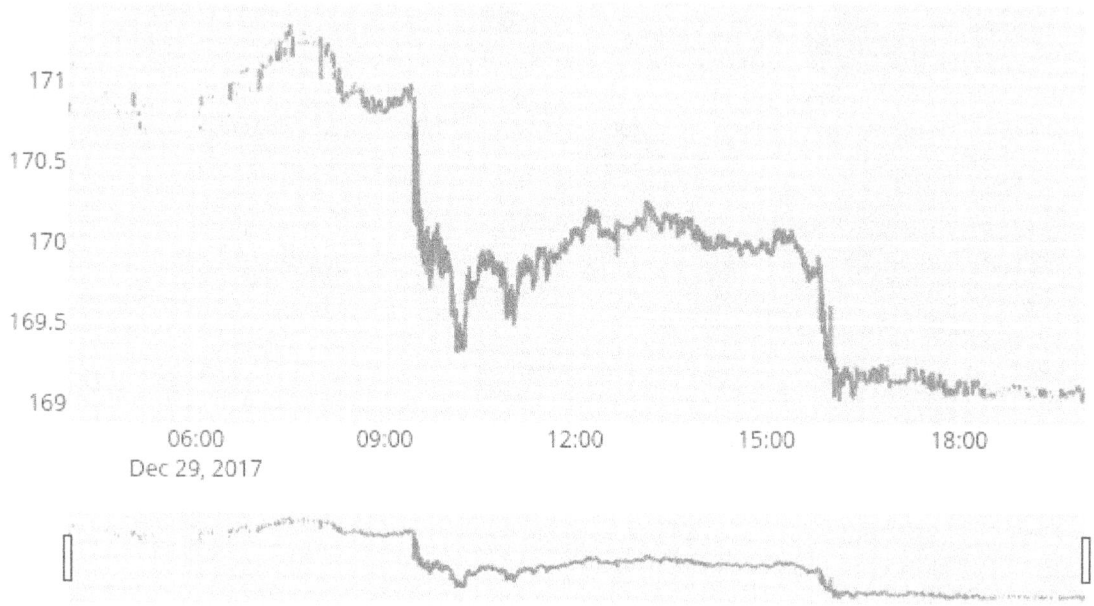

Figure 2.8: Plotly candlestick plot

AlgoSeek also provides adjustment factors to correct pricing and volumes for stock splits, dividends, and other corporate actions.

API access to market data

There are several options you can use to access market data via an API using Python. We will first present a few sources built into the pandas library and the `yfinance` tool that facilitates the downloading of end-of-day market data and recent fundamental data from Yahoo! Finance.

Then we will briefly introduce the trading platform Quantopian, the data provider Quandl, and the Zipline backtesting library that we will use later in the book, as well as listing several additional options to access various types of market data. The directory `data_providers` on GitHub contains several notebooks that illustrate the usage of these options.

Remote data access using pandas

The pandas library enables access to data displayed on websites using the `read_html` function and access to the API endpoints of various data providers through the related `pandas-datareader` library.

Reading HTML tables

Downloading the content of one or more HTML tables, such as for the constituents of the S&P 500 index from Wikipedia, works as follows:

```
sp_url = 'https://en.wikipedia.org/wiki/List_of_S%26P_500_companies'
sp = pd.read_html(sp_url, header=0)[0] # returns a list for each table
sp.info()
RangeIndex: 505 entries, 0 to 504
Data columns (total 9 columns):
Symbol                    505 non-null object
Security                  505 non-null object
SEC filings               505 non-null object
GICS Sector               505 non-null object
GICS Sub Industry         505 non-null object
Headquarters Location     505 non-null object
Date first added          408 non-null object
CIK                       505 non-null int64
Founded                   234 non-null object
```

pandas-datareader for market data

pandas used to facilitate access to data provider APIs directly, but this functionality has moved to the `pandas-datareader` library (refer to the `README` for links to the documentation).

The stability of the APIs varies with provider policies and continues to change. Please consult the documentation for up-to-date information. As of December 2019, at version 0.8.1, the following sources are available:

Source	Scope	Comment
Tiingo	Historical end-of-day prices on equities, mutual funds, and ETF.	Free registration for the API key. Free accounts can access only 500 symbols.
Investor Exchange (IEX)	Historical stock prices are available if traded on IEX.	Requires an API key from IEX Cloud Console.
Alpha Vantage	Historical equity data for daily, weekly, and monthly frequencies, 20+ years, and the past 3-5 days of intraday data. It also has FOREX and sector performance data.	
Quandl	Free data sources as listed on their website.	
Fama/French	Risk factor portfolio returns.	Used in *Chapter 7, Linear Models – From Risk Factors to Return Forecasts.*
TSP Fund Data	Mutual fund prices.	

Nasdaq	Latest metadata on traded tickers.	
Stooq Index Data	Some equity indices are not available from elsewhere due to licensing issues.	
MOEX	Moscow Exchange historical data.	

The access and retrieval of data follow a similar API for all sources, as illustrated for Yahoo! Finance:

```
import pandas_datareader.data as web
from datetime import datetime
start = '2014'              # accepts strings
end = datetime(2017, 5, 24) # or datetime objects
yahoo= web.DataReader('FB', 'yahoo', start=start, end=end)
yahoo.info()
DatetimeIndex: 856 entries, 2014-01-02 to 2017-05-25
Data columns (total 6 columns):
High         856 non-null float64
Low          856 non-null float64
Open         856 non-null float64
Close        856 non-null float64
Volume       856 non-null int64
Adj Close    856 non-null float64
dtypes: float64(5), int64(1)
```

yfinance – scraping data from Yahoo! Finance

`yfinance` aims to provide a reliable and fast way to download historical market data from Yahoo! Finance. The library was originally named `fix-yahoo-finance`. The usage of this library is very straightforward; the notebook `yfinance_demo` illustrates the library's capabilities.

How to download end-of-day and intraday prices

The `Ticker` object permits the downloading of various data points scraped from Yahoo's website:

```
import yfinance as yf
symbol = 'MSFT'
ticker = yf.Ticker(symbol)
```

The `.history` method obtains historical prices for various periods, from one day to the maximum available, and at different frequencies, whereas intraday is only available for the last several days. To download adjusted OHLCV data at a one-minute frequency and corporate actions, use:

```
data = ticker.history(period='5d',
                      interval='1m',
                      actions=True,
                      auto_adjust=True)
data.info()
DatetimeIndex: 1747 entries, 2019-11-22 09:30:00-05:00 to 2019-11-29
13:00:00-05:00
Data columns (total 7 columns):
Open            1747 non-null float64
High            1747 non-null float64
Low             1747 non-null float64
Close           1747 non-null float64
Volume          1747 non-null int64
Dividends       1747 non-null int64
Stock Splits    1747 non-null int64
```

The notebook also illustrates how to access quarterly and annual financial statements, sustainability scores, analyst recommendations, and upcoming earnings dates.

How to download the option chain and prices

yfinance also provides access to the option expiration dates and prices and other information for various contracts. Using the `ticker` instance from the previous example, we get the expiration dates using:

```
ticker.options
('2019-12-05', '2019-12-12', '2019-12-19',..)
```

For any of these dates, we can access the option chain and view details for the various put/call contracts as follows:

```
options = ticker.option_chain('2019-12-05')
options.calls.info()
Data columns (total 14 columns):
contractSymbol       35 non-null object
lastTradeDate        35 non-null datetime64[ns]
strike               35 non-null float64
lastPrice            35 non-null float64
bid                  35 non-null float64
ask                  35 non-null float64
change               35 non-null float64
percentChange        35 non-null float64
volume               34 non-null float64
openInterest         35 non-null int64
impliedVolatility    35 non-null float64
inTheMoney           35 non-null bool
contractSize         35 non-null object
currency             35 non-null object
```

The library also permits the use of proxy servers to prevent rate limiting and facilitates the bulk downloading of multiple tickers. The notebook demonstrates the usage of these features as well.

Quantopian

Quantopian is an investment firm that offers a research platform to crowd-source trading algorithms. Registration is free, and members can research trading ideas using a broad variety of data sources. It also offers an environment to backtest the algorithm against historical data, as well as to forward-test it out of sample with live data. It awards investment allocations for top-performing algorithms whose authors are entitled to a 10 percent (at the time of writing) profit share.

The Quantopian research platform consists of a Jupyter Notebook environment for research and development for alpha-factor research and performance analysis. There is also an **interactive development environment** (**IDE**) for coding algorithmic strategies and backtesting the result using historical data since 2002 with minute-bar frequency.

Users can also simulate algorithms with live data, which is known as *paper trading*. Quantopian provides various market datasets, including U.S. equity and futures price and volume data at a one-minute frequency, and U.S. equity corporate fundamentals, and it also integrates numerous alternative datasets.

We will dive into the Quantopian platform in much more detail in *Chapter 4, Financial Feature Engineering - How to Research Alpha Factors*, and rely on its functionality throughout the book, so feel free to open an account right away. (Refer to the GitHub repository for more details.)

Zipline

Zipline is the algorithmic trading library that powers the Quantopian backtesting and live-trading platform. It is also available offline to develop a strategy using a limited number of free data bundles that can be ingested and used to test the performance of trading ideas before porting the result to the online Quantopian platform for paper and live trading.

Zipline requires a custom environment—view the instructions at the beginning of the notebook `zipline_data_demo.ipynb` The following code illustrates how Zipline permits us to access daily stock data for a range of companies. You can run Zipline scripts in the Jupyter Notebook using the magic function of the same name.

First, you need to initialize the context with the desired security symbols. We'll also use a counter variable. Then, Zipline calls `handle_data`, where we use the `data.history()` method to look back a single period and append the data for the last day to a `.csv` file:

```
%load_ext zipline
%%zipline --start 2010-1-1 --end 2018-1-1 --data-frequency daily
from zipline.api import order_target, record, symbol
def initialize(context):
    context.i = 0
    context.assets = [symbol('FB'), symbol('GOOG'), symbol('AMZN')]

def handle_data(context, data):
    df = data.history(context.assets, fields=['price', 'volume'],
                      bar_count=1, frequency="1d")
    df = df.to_frame().reset_index()

    if context.i == 0:
        df.columns = ['date', 'asset', 'price', 'volume']
        df.to_csv('stock_data.csv', index=False)
    else:
        df.to_csv('stock_data.csv', index=False, mode='a', header=None)
    context.i += 1
df = pd.read_csv('stock_data.csv')
df.date = pd.to_datetime(df.date)
df.set_index('date').groupby('asset').price.plot(lw=2, legend=True,
       figsize=(14, 6));
```

We get the following plot for the preceding code:

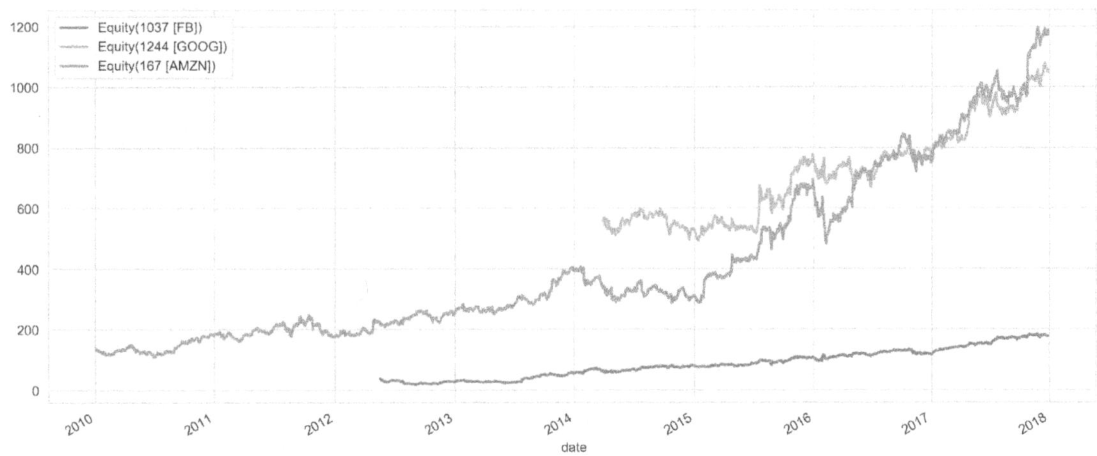

Figure 2.9: Zipline data access

We will explore the capabilities of Zipline, and especially the online Quantopian platform, in more detail in the coming chapters.

Quandl

Quandl provides a broad range of data sources, both free and as a subscription, using a Python API. Register and obtain a free API key to make more than 50 calls per day. Quandl data covers multiple asset classes beyond equities and includes FX, fixed income, indexes, futures and options, and commodities.

API usage is straightforward, well-documented, and flexible, with numerous methods beyond single-series downloads, for example, including bulk downloads or metadata searches.

The following call obtains oil prices from 1986 onward, as quoted by the U.S. Department of Energy:

```
import quandl
oil = quandl.get('EIA/PET_RWTC_D').squeeze()
oil.plot(lw=2, title='WTI Crude Oil Price')
```

We get this plot for the preceding code:

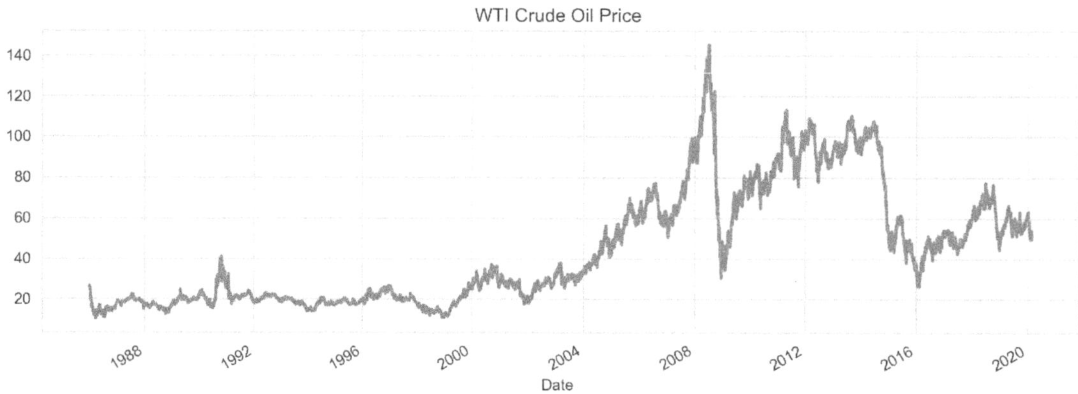

Figure 2.10: Quandl oil price example

Other market data providers

A broad variety of providers offer market data for various asset classes. Examples in relevant categories include:

- Exchanges derive a growing share of their revenues from an ever-broader range of data services, typically using a subscription.
- Bloomberg and Thomson Reuters have long been the leading data aggregators with a combined share of over 55 percent in the $28.5 billion financial data market. Smaller rivals, such as FactSet, are growing or emerging, such as money.net, Quandl, Trading Economics, and Barchart.
- Specialist data providers abound. One example is LOBSTER, which aggregates Nasdaq order-book data in real time.

- Free data providers include Alpha Vantage, which offers Python APIs for real-time equity, FX, and cryptocurrency market data, as well as technical indicators.
- Crowd-sourced investment firms that provide research platforms with data access include, in addition to Quantopian, Alpha Trading Labs, launched in March 2018, which provides HFT infrastructure and data.

How to work with fundamental data

Fundamental data pertains to the economic drivers that determine the value of securities. The nature of the data depends on the asset class:

- For equities and corporate credit, it includes corporate financials, as well as industry and economy-wide data.
- For government bonds, it includes international macro data and foreign exchange.
- For commodities, it includes asset-specific supply-and-demand determinants, such as weather data for crops.

We will focus on equity fundamentals for the U.S., where data is easier to access. There are some 13,000+ public companies worldwide that generate 2 million pages of annual reports and more than 30,000 hours of earnings calls. In algorithmic trading, fundamental data and features engineered from this data may be used to derive trading signals directly, for example, as value indicators, and are an essential input for predictive models, including ML models.

Financial statement data

The Securities and Exchange Commission (SEC) requires U.S. issuers—that is, listed companies and securities, including mutual funds—to file three quarterly financial statements (Form 10-Q) and one annual report (Form 10-K), in addition to various other regulatory filing requirements.

Since the early 1990s, the SEC made these filings available through its **Electronic Data Gathering, Analysis, and Retrieval** (**EDGAR**) system. They constitute the primary data source for the fundamental analysis of equity and other securities, such as corporate credit, where the value depends on the business prospects and financial health of the issuer.

Automated processing – XBRL

Automated analysis of regulatory filings has become much easier since the SEC introduced **XBRL**, which is a free, open, and global standard for the electronic representation and exchange of business reports. XBRL is based on XML; it relies on taxonomies that define the meaning of the elements of a report and map to tags that highlight the corresponding information in the electronic version of the report. One such taxonomy represents the U.S. **Generally Accepted Accounting Principles** (**GAAP**).

The SEC introduced voluntary XBRL filings in 2005 in response to accounting scandals before requiring this format for all filers as of 2009, and it continues to expand the mandatory coverage to other regulatory filings. The SEC maintains a website that lists the current taxonomies that shape the content of different filings and can be used to extract specific items.

The following datasets provide information extracted from EX-101 attachments submitted to the commission in a flattened data format to assist users in consuming data for analysis. The data reflects selected information from the XBRL-tagged financial statements. It currently includes numeric data from the quarterly and annual financial statements, as well as certain additional fields, for example, **Standard Industrial Classification** (**SIC**).

There are several avenues to track and access fundamental data reported to the SEC:

- As part of the EDGAR **Public Dissemination Service** (**PDS**), electronic feeds of accepted filings are available for a fee.
- The SEC updates the RSS feeds, which list the structured disclosure submissions, every 10 minutes.
- There are public index files for the retrieval of all filings through FTP for automated processing.
- The financial statement (and notes) datasets contain parsed XBRL data from all financial statements and the accompanying notes.

The SEC also publishes log files containing the internet search traffic for EDGAR filings through SEC.gov, albeit with a six month delay.

Building a fundamental data time series

The scope of the data in the financial statement and notes datasets consists of numeric data extracted from the primary financial statements (balance sheet, income statement, cash flows, changes in equity, and comprehensive income) and footnotes on those statements. The available data is from as early as 2009.

Extracting the financial statements and notes dataset

The following code downloads and extracts all historical filings contained in the **financial statement and notes** (**FSN**) datasets for the given range of quarters (refer to `edgar_xbrl.ipynb` for additional details):

```
SEC_URL = 'https://www.sec.gov/files/dera/data/financial-statement-and-notes-data-sets/'
first_year, this_year, this_quarter = 2014, 2018, 3
past_years = range(2014, this_year)
filing_periods = [(y, q) for y in past_years for q in range(1, 5)]
filing_periods.extend([(this_year, q) for q in range(1, this_quarter +
                                                      1)])
for i, (yr, qtr) in enumerate(filing_periods, 1):
    filing = f'{yr}q{qtr}_notes.zip'
    path = data_path / f'{yr}_{qtr}' / 'source'
    response = requests.get(SEC_URL + filing).content
    with ZipFile(BytesIO(response)) as zip_file:
        for file in zip_file.namelist():
            local_file = path / file
            with local_file.open('wb') as output:
                for line in zip_file.open(file).readlines():
                    output.write(line)
```

The data is fairly large, and to enable faster access than the original text files permit, it is better to convert the text files into a binary, Parquet columnar format (refer to the *Efficient data storage with pandas* section later in this chapter for a performance comparison of various data-storage options that are compatible with pandas DataFrames):

```
for f in data_path.glob('**/*.tsv'):
    file_name = f.stem  + '.parquet'
    path = Path(f.parents[1]) / 'parquet'
    df = pd.read_csv(f, sep='\t', encoding='latin1', low_memory=False)
    df.to_parquet(path / file_name)
```

For each quarter, the FSN data is organized into eight file sets that contain information about submissions, numbers, taxonomy tags, presentation, and more. Each dataset consists of rows and fields and is provided as a tab-delimited text file:

File	Dataset	Description
SUB	Submission	Identifies each XBRL submission by company, form, date, and so on
TAG	Tag	Defines and explains each taxonomy tag
DIM	Dimension	Adds detail to numeric and plain text data
NUM	Numeric	One row for each distinct data point in filing
TXT	Plain text	Contains all non-numeric XBRL fields
REN	Rendering	Information for rendering on the SEC website
PRE	Presentation	Details of tag and number presentation in primary statements
CAL	Calculation	Shows the arithmetic relationships among tags

Retrieving all quarterly Apple filings

The submission dataset contains the unique identifiers required to retrieve the filings: the **Central Index Key** (**CIK**) and the **Accession Number** (**adsh**). The following shows some of the information about Apple's 2018Q1 10-Q filing:

```
apple = sub[sub.name == 'APPLE INC'].T.dropna().squeeze()
key_cols = ['name', 'adsh', 'cik', 'name', 'sic', 'countryba',
            'stprba', 'cityba', 'zipba', 'bas1', 'form', 'period',
            'fy', 'fp', 'filed']
apple.loc[key_cols]
name                        APPLE INC
adsh                        0000320193-18-000070
cik                         320193
name                        APPLE INC
sic                         3571
countryba                   US
stprba                      CA
cityba                      CUPERTINO
zipba                       95014
bas1                        ONE APPLE PARK WAY
form                        10-Q
period                      20180331
fy                          2018
fp                          Q2
filed                      20180502
```

Using the CIK, we can identify all of the historical quarterly filings available for Apple and combine this information to obtain 26 10-Q forms and 9 annual 10-K forms:

```
aapl_subs = pd.DataFrame()
for sub in data_path.glob('**/sub.parquet'):
    sub = pd.read_parquet(sub)
    aapl_sub = sub[(sub.cik.astype(int) == apple.cik) &
                   (sub.form.isin(['10-Q', '10-K']))]
    aapl_subs = pd.concat([aapl_subs, aapl_sub])
aapl_subs.form.value_counts()
10-Q    15
10-K     4
```

With the accession number for each filing, we can now rely on the taxonomies to select the appropriate XBRL tags (listed in the `TAG` file) from the `NUM` and `TXT` files to obtain the numerical or textual/footnote data points of interest.

First, let's extract all of the numerical data that is available from the 19 Apple filings:

```
aapl_nums = pd.DataFrame()
for num in data_path.glob('**/num.parquet'):
    num = pd.read_parquet(num).drop('dimh', axis=1)
    aapl_num = num[num.adsh.isin(aapl_subs.adsh)]
    aapl_nums = pd.concat([aapl_nums, aapl_num])
aapl_nums.ddate = pd.to_datetime(aapl_nums.ddate, format='%Y%m%d')
aapl_nums.shape
(28281, 16)
```

Building a price/earnings time series

In total, the 9 years of filing history provide us with over 28,000 numerical values. We can select a useful field, such as **earnings per diluted share** (**EPS**), that we can combine with market data to calculate the popular **price-to-earnings** (**P/E**) valuation ratio.

We do need to take into account, however, that Apple split its stock by 7:1 on June 4, 2014, and adjust the earnings per share values before the split to make the earnings comparable to the price data, which, in its *adjusted* form, accounts for these changes. The following code block shows you how to adjust the earnings data:

```
field = 'EarningsPerShareDiluted'
stock_split = 7
split_date = pd.to_datetime('20140604')
# Filter by tag; keep only values measuring 1 quarter
eps = aapl_nums[(aapl_nums.tag == 'EarningsPerShareDiluted')
                & (aapl_nums.qtrs == 1)].drop('tag', axis=1)
# Keep only most recent data point from each filing
eps = eps.groupby('adsh').apply(lambda x: x.nlargest(n=1, columns=['ddate']))
# Adjust earnings prior to stock split downward
eps.loc[eps.ddate < split_date,'value'] = eps.loc[eps.ddate <
        split_date, 'value'].div(7)
eps = eps[['ddate', 'value']].set_index('ddate').squeeze()
# create trailing 12-months eps from quarterly data
eps = eps.rolling(4, min_periods=4).sum().dropna()
```

We can use Quandl to obtain Apple stock price data since 2009:

```
import pandas_datareader.data as web
symbol = 'AAPL.US'
aapl_stock = web.DataReader(symbol, 'quandl', start=eps.index.min())
aapl_stock = aapl_stock.resample('D').last() # ensure dates align with
                                               eps data
```

Now we have the data to compute the trailing 12-month P/E ratio for the entire period:

```
pe = aapl_stock.AdjClose.to_frame('price').join(eps.to_frame('eps'))
pe = pe.fillna(method='ffill').dropna()
pe['P/E Ratio'] = pe.price.div(pe.eps)
axes = pe.plot(subplots=True, figsize=(16,8), legend=False, lw=2);
```

We get the following plot from the preceding code:

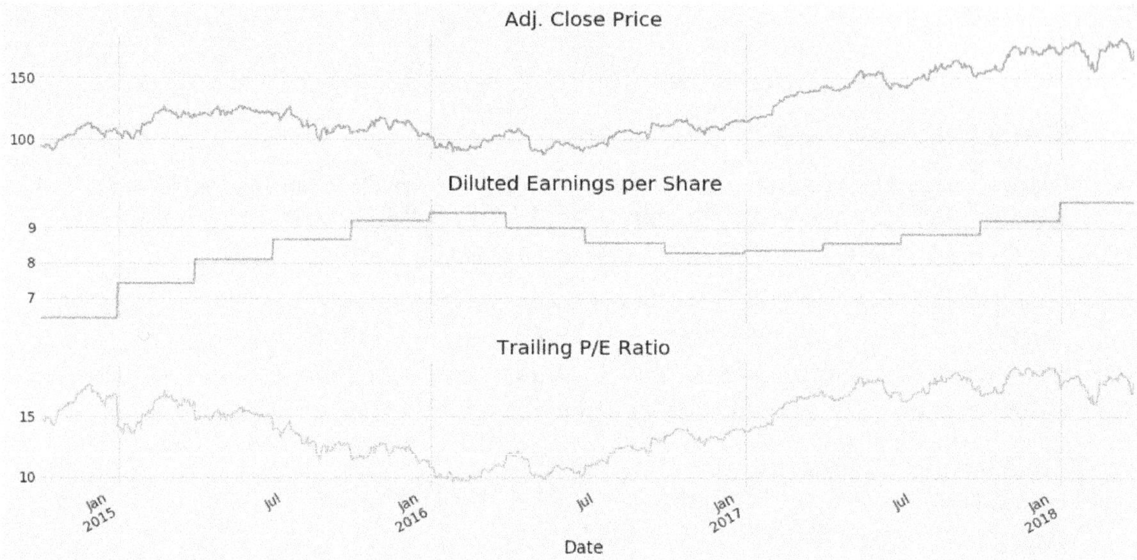

Figure 2.11: Trailing P/E ratio from EDGAR filings

Other fundamental data sources

There are numerous other sources for fundamental data. Many are accessible using the `pandas_datareader` module that was introduced earlier. Additional data is available from certain organizations directly, such as the IMF, the World Bank, or major national statistical agencies around the world (refer to the *references* section on GitHub).

pandas-datareader – macro and industry data

The `pandas-datareader` library facilitates access according to the conventions introduced at the end of the preceding section on market data. It covers APIs for numerous global fundamental macro- and industry-data sources, including the following:

- Kenneth French's data library: Market data on portfolios capturing returns on key risk factors like size, value, and momentum factors, disaggregated by industry (refer to *Chapter 4, Financial Feature Engineering – How to Research Alpha Factors*)
- St. Louis FED (FRED): Federal Reserve data on the U.S. economy and financial markets
- World Bank: Global database on long-term, lower-frequency economic and social development and demographics

- OECD: Similar to the World Bank data for OECD countries
- Enigma: Various datasets, including alternative sources
- Eurostat: EU-focused economic, social, and demographic data

Efficient data storage with pandas

We'll be using many different datasets in this book, and it's worth comparing the main formats for efficiency and performance. In particular, we'll compare the following:

- **CSV**: Comma-separated, standard flat text file format.
- **HDF5**: Hierarchical data format, developed initially at the National Center for Supercomputing Applications. It is a fast and scalable storage format for numerical data, available in pandas using the PyTables library.
- **Parquet**: Part of the Apache Hadoop ecosystem, a binary, columnar storage format that provides efficient data compression and encoding and has been developed by Cloudera and Twitter. It is available for pandas through the pyarrow library, led by Wes McKinney, the original author of pandas.

The `storage_benchmark.ipynb` notebook compares the performance of the preceding libraries using a test DataFrame that can be configured to contain numerical or text data, or both. For the HDF5 library, we test both the fixed and table formats. The table format allows for queries and can be appended to.

The following charts illustrate the read and write performance for 100,000 rows with either 1,000 columns of random floats and 1,000 columns of a random 10-character string, or just 2,000 float columns (on a log scale):

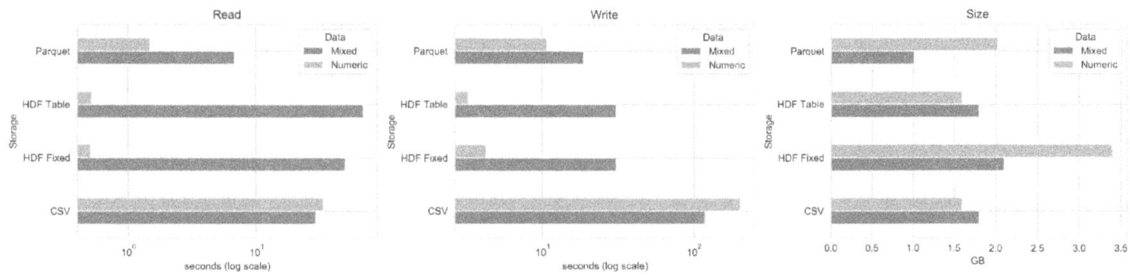

Figure 2.12: Storage benchmarks

The left panel shows that, for purely numerical data, the HDF5 format performs best by far, and the table format also shares with CSV the smallest memory footprint at 1.6 GB. The `fixed` format uses twice as much space, while the `parquet` format uses 2 GB.

For a mix of numerical and text data, Parquet is the best choice for read and write operations. HDF5 has an advantage with *read* in relation to CSV, but it is slower with *write* because it pickles text data.

The notebook illustrates how to configure, test, and collect the timing using the `%%timeit` cell magic and, at the same time, demonstrates the usage of the related pandas commands that are required to use these storage formats.

Summary

This chapter introduced the market and fundamental data sources that form the backbone of most trading strategies. You learned about the various ways to access this data and how to preprocess the raw information so that you can begin extracting trading signals using the ML techniques that we will be introducing shortly.

In the next chapter, before moving on to the design and evaluation of trading strategies and the use of ML models, we need to cover alternative datasets that have emerged in recent years and have been a significant driver of the popularity of ML for algorithmic trading.

3

Alternative Data for Finance – Categories and Use Cases

The previous chapter covered working with market and fundamental data, which have been the traditional drivers of trading strategies. In this chapter, we'll fast-forward to the recent emergence of a broad range of much more diverse data sources as fuel for discretionary and algorithmic strategies. Their heterogeneity and novelty have inspired the label of alternative data and created a rapidly growing provider and service industry.

Behind this trend is a familiar story: propelled by the explosive growth of the internet and mobile networks, digital data continues to grow exponentially amid advances in the technology to process, store, and analyze new data sources. The exponential growth in the availability of and ability to manage more diverse digital data, in turn, has been a critical force behind the dramatic performance improvements of **machine learning** (**ML**) that are driving innovation across industries, including the investment industry.

The scale of the data revolution is extraordinary: the past 2 years alone have witnessed the creation of 90 percent of all data that exists in the world today, and by 2020, each of the 7.7 billion people worldwide is expected to produce 1.7 MB of new information every second of every day. On the other hand, back in 2012, only 0.5 percent of all data was ever analyzed and used, whereas 33 percent is deemed to have value by 2020. The gap between data availability and usage is likely to narrow quickly as global investments in analytics are set to rise beyond $210 billion by 2020, while the value creation potential is a multiple higher.

This chapter explains how individuals, business processes, and sensors produce **alternative data**. It also provides a framework to navigate and evaluate the proliferating supply of alternative data for investment purposes. It demonstrates the workflow, from acquisition to preprocessing and storage, using Python for data obtained through web scraping to set the stage for the application of ML. It concludes by providing examples of sources, providers, and applications.

This chapter will cover the following topics:

- Which new sources of information have been unleashed by the alternative data revolution
- How individuals, business processes, and sensors generate alternative data
- Evaluating the burgeoning supply of alternative data used for algorithmic trading
- Working with alternative data in Python, such as by scraping the internet
- Important categories and providers of alternative data

> You can find the code samples for this chapter and links to additional resources in the corresponding directory of the GitHub repository. The notebooks include color versions of the images.

The alternative data revolution

The data deluge driven by digitization, networking, and plummeting storage costs has led to profound qualitative changes in the nature of information available for predictive analytics, often summarized by the five Vs:

- **Volume**: The amount of data generated, collected, and stored is orders of magnitude larger as the byproduct of online and offline activity, transactions, records, and other sources. Volumes continue to grow with the capacity for analysis and storage.
- **Velocity**: Data is generated, transferred, and processed to become available near, or at, real-time speed.
- **Variety**: Data is organized in formats no longer limited to structured, tabular forms, such as CSV files or relational database tables. Instead, new sources produce semi-structured formats, such as JSON or HTML, and unstructured content, including raw text, "images"? and audio or video data, adding new challenges to render data suitable for ML algorithms.
- **Veracity**: The diversity of sources and formats makes it much more difficult to validate the reliability of the data's information content.
- **Value**: Determining the value of new datasets can be much more time- and resource-consuming, as well as more uncertain than before.

For algorithmic trading, new data sources offer an informational advantage if they provide access to information unavailable from traditional sources or provide access sooner. Following global trends, the investment industry is rapidly expanding beyond market and fundamental data to alternative sources to reap alpha through an informational edge. Annual spending on data, technological capabilities, and related talent is expected to increase from the current $3 billion by 12.8 percent annually through 2020.

Today, investors can access macro or company-specific data in real time that, historically, has been available only at a much lower frequency. Use cases for new data sources include the following:

- **Online price data** on a representative set of goods and services can be used to measure inflation.
- The number of **store visits or purchases** permits real-time estimates of company - or industry-specific sales or economic activity.
- **Satellite images** can reveal agricultural yields, or activity at mines or on oil rigs before this information is available elsewhere.

As the standardization and adoption of big datasets advances, the information contained in conventional data will likely lose most of its predictive value.

Furthermore, the capability to process and integrate diverse datasets and apply ML allows for complex insights. In the past, quantitative approaches relied on simple heuristics to rank companies using historical data for metrics such as the price-to-book ratio, whereas ML algorithms synthesize new metrics and learn and adapt such rules while taking into account evolving market data. These insights create new opportunities to capture classic investment themes such as value, momentum, quality, and sentiment:

- **Momentum**: ML can identify asset exposures to market price movements, industry sentiment, or economic factors.
- **Value**: Algorithms can analyze large amounts of economic and industry-specific structured and unstructured data, beyond financial statements, to predict the intrinsic value of a company.
- **Quality**: The sophisticated analysis of integrated data allows for the evaluation of customer or employee reviews, e-commerce, or app traffic to identify gains in market share or other underlying earnings quality drivers.
- **Sentiment**: The real-time processing and interpretation of news and social media content permits ML algorithms to both rapidly detect emerging sentiment and synthesize information from diverse sources into a more coherent big picture.

In practice, however, data containing valuable signals is often not freely available and is typically produced for purposes other than trading. As a result, alternative datasets require thorough evaluation, costly acquisition, careful management, and sophisticated analysis to extract tradable signals.

Sources of alternative data

Alternative datasets are generated by many sources but can be classified at a high level as predominantly produced by:

- **Individuals** who post on social media, review products, or use search engines
- **Businesses** that record commercial transactions (in particular, credit card payments) or capture supply-chain activity as intermediaries
- **Sensors** that, among many other things, capture economic activity through images from satellites or security cameras, or through movement patterns such as cell phone towers

The nature of alternative data continues to evolve rapidly as new data sources become available and sources previously labeled "alternative" become part of the mainstream. The **Baltic Dry Index** (**BDI**), for instance, assembles data from several hundred shipping companies to approximate the supply/demand of dry bulk carriers and is now available on the Bloomberg Terminal.

Alternative data includes raw data as well as data that is aggregated or has been processed in some form to add value. For instance, some providers aim to extract tradeable signals, such as sentiment scores. We will address the various types of providers in *Chapter 4, Financial Feature Engineering – How to Research Alpha Factors*.

Alternative data sources differ in crucial respects that determine their value or signal content for algorithmic trading strategies. We will address these aspects in the next section after looking at the main sources in this one.

Individuals

Individuals automatically create electronic data through online activities, as well as through their offline activity as the latter is captured electronically and often linked to online identities. Data generated by individuals is frequently unstructured in text, image, or video formats, disseminated through multiple platforms, and includes:

- Social media posts, such as opinions or reactions on general-purpose sites such as Twitter, Facebook, or LinkedIn, or business-review sites such as Glassdoor or Yelp
- E-commerce activity that reflects an interest in or the perception of products on sites like Amazon or Wayfair
- Search engine activity using platforms such as Google or Bing
- Mobile app usage, downloads, and reviews
- Personal data such as messaging traffic

The analysis of social media sentiment has become very popular because it can be applied to individual stocks, industry baskets, or market indices. The most common source is Twitter, followed by various news vendors and blog sites. Supply is competitive, and prices are lower because it is often obtained through increasingly commoditized web scraping. Reliable social media datasets that include blogs, tweets, or videos have typically less than 5 years of history, given how recently consumers have adopted these tools at scale. Search history, in contrast, is available from 2004.

Business processes

Businesses and public entities produce and collect many valuable sources of alternative data. Data that results from business processes often has more structure than that generated by individuals. It is very effective as a leading indicator for activity that is otherwise available at a much lower frequency.

Data generated by business processes includes:

- Payment card transaction data possibly available for purchase from processors and financial institutions
- Company exhaust data produced by ordinary digitized activity or record-keeping, such as banking records, cashier scanner data, or supply chain orders
- Trade flow and market microstructure data (such as L2 and L3 order book data, illustrated by the NASDAQ ITCH tick data example in *Chapter 2, Market and Fundamental Data – Sources and Techniques*)
- Company payments monitored by credit rating agencies or financial institutions to assess liquidity and creditworthiness

Credit card transactions and company exhaust data, such as point-of-sale data, are among the most reliable and predictive datasets. Credit card data is available with around 10 years of history and, at different lags, almost up to real time, while corporate earnings are reported quarterly with a 2.5-week lag. The time horizon and reporting lag for company exhaust data varies widely, depending on the source. Market microstructure datasets have over 15 years of history compared to sell-side flow data, which typically has fewer than 5 years of consistent history.

Sensors

Networked sensors embedded in a broad range of devices are among the most rapidly growing data sources, driven by the proliferation of smartphones and the reduction in the cost of satellite technologies.

This category of alternative data is typically very unstructured and often significantly larger in volume than data generated by individuals or business processes, and it poses much tougher processing challenges. Key alternative data sources in this category include:

- Satellite imaging to monitor economic activity, such as construction, shipping, or commodity supply
- Geolocation data to track traffic in retail stores, such as using volunteered smartphone data, or on transport routes, such as on ships or trucks
- Cameras positioned at a location of interest
- Weather and pollution sensors

The **Internet of Things** (**IoT**) will further accelerate the large-scale collection of this type of alternative data by embedding networked microprocessors into personal and commercial electronic devices, such as home appliances, public spaces, and industrial production processes.

Sensor-based alternative data that contains satellite images, mobile app usage, or cellular-location tracking is typically available with a 3- to 4-year history.

Satellites

The resources and timelines required to launch a geospatial imaging satellite have dropped dramatically; instead of tens of millions of dollars and years of preparation, the cost has fallen to around $100,000 to place a small satellite as a secondary payload into a low Earth orbit. Hence, companies can obtain much higher-frequency coverage (currently about daily) of specific locations using entire fleets of satellites.

Use cases include monitoring economic activity that can be captured using aerial coverage, such as agricultural and mineral production and shipments, or the construction of commercial or residential buildings or ships; industrial incidents, such as fires; or car and foot traffic at locations of interest. Related sensor data is contributed by drones that are used in agriculture to monitor crops using infrared light.

Several challenges often need to be addressed before satellite image data can be reliably used in ML models. In addition to substantial preprocessing, these include accounting for weather conditions such as cloud cover and seasonal effects around holidays. Satellites may also offer only irregular coverage of specific locations that could affect the quality of the predictive signals.

Geolocation data

Geolocation data is another rapidly growing category of alternative data generated by sensors. A familiar source is smartphones, with which individuals voluntarily share their geographic location through an application, or from wireless signals such as GPS, CDMA, or Wi-Fi that measure foot traffic around places of interest, such as stores, restaurants, or event venues.

Furthermore, an increasing number of airports, shopping malls, and retail stores have installed sensors that track the number and movements of customers. While the original motivation to deploy these sensors was often to measure the impact of marketing activity, the resulting data can also be used to estimate foot traffic or sales. Sensors to capture geolocation data include 3D stereo video and thermal imaging, which lowers privacy concerns but works well with moving objects. There are also sensors attached to ceilings, as well as pressure-sensitive mats. Some providers use multiple sensors in combination, including vision, audio, and cellphone location, for a comprehensive account of the shopper journey, which includes not only the count and duration of visits, but extends to the conversion and measurement of repeat visits.

Criteria for evaluating alternative data

The ultimate objective of alternative data is to provide an informational advantage in the competitive search for trading signals that produce alpha, namely positive, uncorrelated investment returns. In practice, the signals extracted from alternative datasets can be used on a standalone basis or combined with other signals as part of a quantitative strategy. Independent usage is viable if the Sharpe ratio generated by a strategy based on a single dataset is sufficiently high, but that is rare in practice. (See *Chapter 4, Financial Feature Engineering – How to Research Alpha Factors*, for details on signal measurement and evaluation.)

Quant firms are building libraries of alpha factors that may be weak signals individually but can produce attractive returns in combination. As highlighted in *Chapter 1, Machine Learning for Trading – From Idea to Execution*, investment factors should be based on a fundamental and economic rationale; otherwise, they are more likely the result of overfitting to historical data than persisting and generating alpha on new data.

Signal decay due to competition is a serious concern, and as the alternative data ecosystem evolves, it is unlikely that many datasets will retain meaningful Sharpe ratio signals. Effective strategies to extend the half-life of the signal content of an alternative dataset include exclusivity agreements, or a focus on datasets that pose processing challenges to raise the barriers to entry.

An alternative dataset can be evaluated based on the quality of its signal content, qualitative aspects of the data, and various technical aspects.

Quality of the signal content

The signal content can be evaluated with respect to the target asset class, the investment style, the relation to conventional risk premiums, and most importantly, its alpha content.

Asset classes

Most alternative datasets contain information directly relevant to equities and commodities. Interesting datasets targeting investments in real estate have also multiplied after Zillow successfully pioneered price estimates in 2006.

Alternative data on corporate credit is growing as alternative sources for monitoring corporate payments, including for smaller businesses, are being developed. Data on fixed income and around interest-rate projections is a more recent phenomenon but continues to increase as more product sales and price information are being harvested at scale.

Investment style

The majority of datasets focus on specific sectors and stocks, and as such, naturally appeal to long-short equity investors. As the scale and scope of alternative data collection continues to rise, alternative data will likely also become relevant to investors in macro themes, such as consumer credit, activity in emerging markets, and commodity trends.

Some alternative datasets that reflect broader economic activity or consumer sentiment can be used as proxies for traditional measures of market risk. In contrast, signals that capture news may be more relevant to high-frequency traders that use quantitative strategies over a brief time horizon.

Risk premiums

Some alternative datasets, such as credit card payments or social media sentiment, have been shown to produce signals that have a low correlation (lower than 5 percent) with traditional risk premiums in equity markets, such as value, momentum, and quality of volatility. As a result, combining signals derived from such alternative data with an algorithmic trading strategy based on traditional risk factors can be an important building block toward a more diversified risk premiums portfolio.

Alpha content and quality

The signal strength required to justify the investment in an alternative dataset naturally depends on its costs, and alternative data prices vary widely. Data that scores social sentiment can be acquired for a few thousand dollars or less, while the cost of a dataset on comprehensive and timely credit card payments can cost several million per year.

We will explore in detail how to evaluate trading strategies driven by alternative data using historical data, so-called *backtests*, to estimate the amount of alpha contained in a dataset. In isolated cases, a dataset may contain sufficient alpha signal to drive a strategy on a standalone basis, but more typical is the combined use of various alternative and other sources of data. In these cases, a dataset permits the extraction of weak signals that produce a small positive Sharpe ratio that would not receive a capital allocation on its own but can deliver a portfolio-level strategy when integrated with similar other signals. This is not guaranteed, however, as there are also many alternative datasets that do not contain any alpha content.

Besides evaluating a dataset's alpha content, it is also important to assess to which extent a signal is incremental or orthogonal—that is, unique to a dataset or already captured by other data—and in the latter case, compare the costs for this type of signal.

Finally, it is essential to evaluate the potential capacity of a strategy that relies on a given, that is, the amount of capital that can be allocated without undermining its success. This is because a capacity limit will make it more difficult to recover the cost of the data.

Quality of the data

The quality of a dataset is another important criterion because it impacts the effort required to analyze and monetize it, and the reliability of the predictive signal it contains. Quality aspects include the data frequency and the length of its available history, the reliability or accuracy of the information it contains, the extent to which it complies with current or potential future regulations, and how exclusive its use is.

Legal and reputational risks

The use of alternative datasets may carry legal or reputational risks, especially when they include the following items:

- **Material non-public information** (**MNPI**), because it implies an infringement of insider trading regulations
- **Personally identifiable information** (**PII**), primarily since the European Union has enacted the **General Data Protection Regulation** (**GDPR**)

Accordingly, legal and compliance requirements need a thorough review. There could also be conflicts of interest when the provider of the data is also a market participant that is actively trading based on the dataset.

Exclusivity

The likelihood that an alternative dataset contains a signal that is sufficiently predictive to drive a strategy on a standalone basis, with a high Sharpe ratio for a meaningful period, is inversely related to its availability and ease of processing. In other words, the more exclusive and harder to process the data, the better the chances that a dataset with alpha content can drive a strategy without suffering rapid signal decay.

Public fundamental data that provides standard financial ratios contains little alpha and is not attractive for a standalone strategy, but it may help diversify a portfolio of risk factors. Large, complex datasets will take more time to be absorbed by the market, and new datasets continue to emerge on a frequent basis. Hence, it is essential to assess how familiar other investors already are with a dataset, and whether the provider is the best source for this type of information.

Additional benefits to exclusivity or being an early adopter of a new dataset may arise when a business just begins to sell exhaust data that it generated for other purposes. This is because it may be possible to influence how the data is collected or curated, or to negotiate conditions that limit access for competitors at least for a certain time period.

Time horizon

A more extensive history is highly desirable to test the predictive power of a dataset in different scenarios. The availability varies greatly between several months and several decades, and has important implications for the scope of the trading strategy that can be built and tested based on the data. We mentioned some ranges for time horizons for different datasets when introducing the main types of sources.

Frequency

The frequency of the data determines how often new information becomes available and how differentiated a predictive signal can be over a given period. It also impacts the time horizon of the investment strategy and ranges from intra-day to daily, weekly, or an even lower frequency.

Reliability

Naturally, the degree to which the data accurately reflects what it intends to measure or how well this can be verified is of significant concern and should be validated by means of a thorough audit. This applies to both raw and processed data, where the methodology used to extract or aggregate information needs to be analyzed, taking into account the cost-benefit ratio for the proposed acquisition.

Technical aspects

Technical aspects concern the latency, or delay of reporting, and the format in which the data is made available.

Latency

Data providers often provide resources in batches, and a delay can result from how the data is collected, subsequent processing and transmission, as well as regulatory or legal constraints.

Format

The data is made available in a broad range of formats, depending on the source. Processed data will be in user-friendly formats and easily integrated into existing systems or queries via a robust API. On the other end of the spectrum are voluminous data sources, such as video, audio, or image data, or a proprietary format, that require more skills to prepare for analysis, but also provide higher barriers to entry for potential competitors.

The market for alternative data

The investment industry spent an estimated $2-3 billion on data services in 2018, and this number is expected to grow at a double-digit rate per year in line with other industries. This expenditure includes the acquisition of alternative data, investments in related technology, and the hiring of qualified talent.

A survey by Ernst & Young shows significant adoption of alternative data in 2017; 43 percent of funds were using scraped web data, for instance, and almost 30 percent were experimenting with satellite data (see *Figure 3.1*). Based on the experience so far, fund managers considered scraped web data and credit card data to be most insightful, in contrast to geolocation and satellite data, which around 25 percent considered to be less informative:

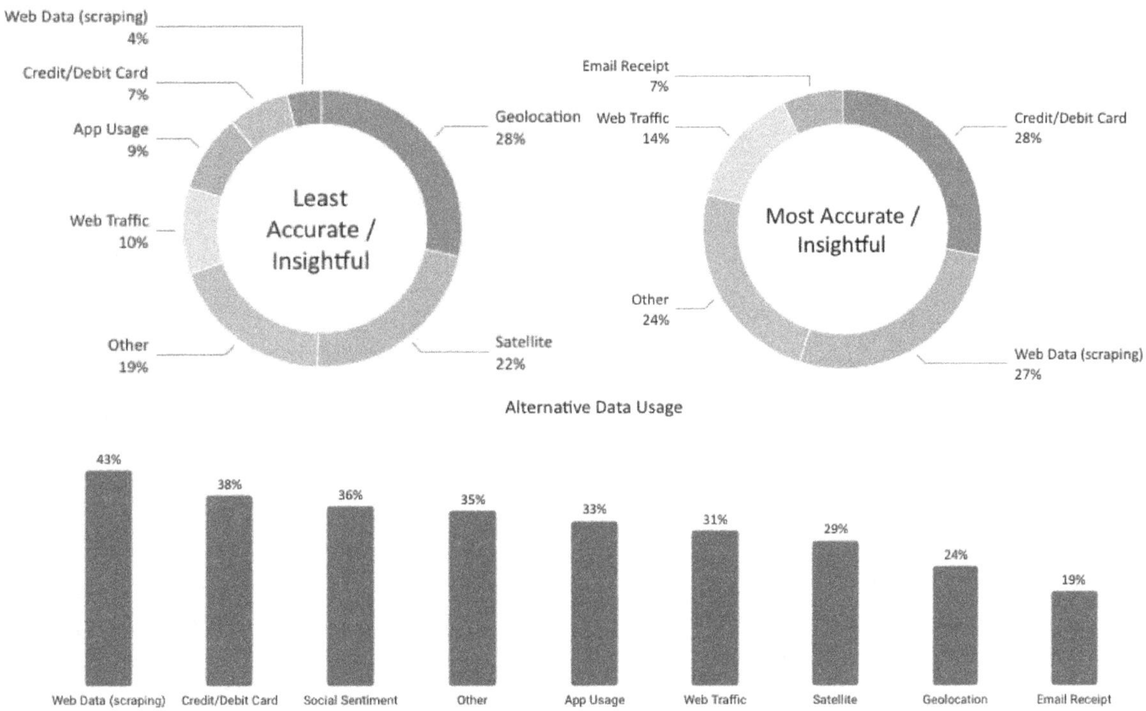

Figure 3.1: Usefulness and usage of alternative data (Source: Ernst & Young, 2017)

Reflecting the rapid growth of this new industry, the market for alternative data providers is quite fragmented. J.P. Morgan lists over 500 specialized data firms, while `AlternativeData.org` lists over 300. Providers play numerous roles, including intermediaries such as consultants, aggregators, and tech solutions; sell-side supports deliver data in various formats, ranging from raw to semi-processed data or some form of a signal extracted from one or more sources.

We will highlight the size of the main categories and profile a few prominent examples to illustrate their diversity.

Data providers and use cases

`AlternativeData.org` (supported by the provider YipitData) lists several categories that can serve as a rough proxy for activity in various data-provider segments. Social sentiment analysis is by far the largest category, while satellite and geolocation data have been growing rapidly in recent years:

Product category	**# Providers**
Social sentiment	48
Satellite	26
Geolocation	22
Web data and traffic	22
Infrastructure and interfaces	20
Consultants	18
Credit and debit card usage	14
Data brokers	10
Public data	10
App usage	7
Email and consumer receipts	6
Sell side	6
Weather	4
Other	87

The following brief examples aim to illustrate the broad range of service providers and potential use cases.

Social sentiment data

Social sentiment analysis is most closely associated with Twitter data. Gnip was an early social-media aggregator that provided data from numerous sites using an API and was acquired by Twitter in 2014 for $134 million. Search engines are another source that became prominent when researchers published, in *Nature*, that investment strategies based on Google Trends for terms such as debt could be used for a profitable trading strategy over an extended period (Preis, Moat, and Stanley 2013).

Dataminr

Dataminr was founded in 2009 and provides social-sentiment and news analysis based on an exclusive agreement with Twitter. The company is one of the larger alternative providers and raised an additional $391 million in funding in June 2018, led by Fidelity, at a $1.6 billion valuation, bringing total funding to $569 billion. It emphasizes real-time signals extracted from social media feeds using machine learning and serves a wide range of clients, including not only buy - and sell-side investment firms, but also news organizations and the public sector.

StockTwits

StockTwits is a social network and micro-blogging platform where several hundred thousand investment professionals share information and trading ideas in the form of StockTwits. These are viewed by a large audience across the financial web and social media platforms. This data can be exploited because it may reflect investor sentiment or itself drive trades that, in turn, impact prices. Nasseri, Tucker, and de Cesare (2015) built a trading strategy on selected features.

RavenPack

RavenPack analyzes a large amount of diverse, unstructured, text-based data to produce structured indicators, including sentiment scores, that aim to deliver information relevant to investors. The underlying data sources range from premium newswires and regulatory information to press releases and over 19,000 web publications. J.P. Morgan tested a long-short sovereign bond and equity strategies based on sentiment scores and achieved positive results, with a low correlation to conventional risk premiums (Kolanovic and Krishnamachari, 2017).

Satellite data

RS Metrics, founded in 2010, triangulates geospatial data from satellites, drones, and airplanes with a focus on metals and commodities, as well as real estate and industrial applications. The company offers signals, predictive analytics, alerts, and end-user applications based on its own high-resolution satellites. Use cases include the estimation of retail traffic at certain chains or commercial real estate, as well as the production and storage of certain common metals or employment at related production locations.

Geolocation data

Advan, founded in 2015, serves hedge fund clients with signals derived from mobile phone traffic data, targeting 1,600 tickers across various sectors in the US and EU. The company collects data using apps that install geolocation codes on smartphones with explicit user consent and track location using several channels (such as Wi-Fi, Bluetooth, and cellular signal) for enhanced accuracy. The use cases include estimates of customer traffic at physical store locations, which, in turn, can be used as input to models that predict the top-line revenues of traded companies.

Email receipt data

Eagle Alpha provides, among other services, data on a large set of online transactions using email receipts, covering over 5,000 retailers, including SKU-level transaction data categorized into 53 product groups. J.P. Morgan analyzed a time series dataset, covering 2013-16, that covered a constant group of users active throughout the entire sample period. The dataset contained the total aggregate spend, number of orders, and number of unique buyers per period (Kolanovic and Krishnamachari, 2017).

Working with alternative data

We will illustrate the acquisition of alternative data using web scraping, targeting first OpenTable restaurant data, and then move on to earnings call transcripts hosted by Seeking Alpha.

Scraping OpenTable data

Typical sources of alternative data are review websites such as Glassdoor or Yelp, which convey insider insights using employee comments or guest reviews. Clearly, user-contributed content does not capture a representative view, but rather is subject to severe selection biases. We'll look at Yelp reviews in *Chapter 14, Text Data for Trading – Sentiment Analysis*, for example, and find many more very positive and negative ratings on the five-star scale than you might expect. Nonetheless, this data can be valuable input for ML models that aim to predict a business's prospects or market value relative to competitors or over time to obtain trading signals.

The data needs to be extracted from the HTML source, barring any legal obstacles. To illustrate the web scraping tools that Python offers, we'll retrieve information on restaurant bookings from OpenTable. Data of this nature can be used to forecast economic activity by geography, real estate prices, or restaurant chain revenues.

Parsing data from HTML with Requests and BeautifulSoup

In this section, we will request and parse HTML source code. We will be using the Requests library to make **Hypertext Transfer Protocol** (**HTTP**) requests and retrieve the HTML source code. Then, we'll rely on the Beautiful Soup library, which makes it easy to parse the HTML markup code and extract the text content we are interested in.

We will, however, encounter a common obstacle: websites may request certain information from the server only after initial page-load using JavaScript. As a result, a direct HTTP request will not be successful. To sidestep this type of protection, we will use a headless browser that retrieves the website content as a browser would:

```
from bs4 import BeautifulSoup
import requests
# set and request url; extract source code
url = https://www.opentable.com/new-york-restaurant-listings
html = requests.get(url)
html.text[:500]
' <!DOCTYPE html><html lang="en"><head><meta charset="utf-8"/><meta
http-equiv="X-UA-Compatible" content="IE=9; IE=8; IE=7; IE=EDGE"/>
<title>Restaurant Reservation Availability</title> <meta name="robots"
content="noindex" > </meta> <link rel="shortcut icon" href="//components.
otstatic.com/components/favicon/1.0.4/favicon/favicon.ico" type="image/
x-icon"/><link rel="icon" href="//components.otstatic.com/components/
favicon/1.0.4/favicon/favicon-16.png" sizes="16x16"/><link rel='
```

Now, we can use Beautiful Soup to parse the HTML content, and then look for all span tags with the class associated with the restaurant names that we obtain by inspecting the source code, `rest-row-name-text` (see the GitHub repository for linked instructions to examine website source code):

```
# parse raw html => soup object
soup = BeautifulSoup(html.text, 'html.parser')
# for each span tag, print out text => restaurant name
for entry in soup.find_all(name='span', attrs={'class':'rest-row-name-text'}):
    print(entry.text)
Wade Coves
Alley
Dolorem Maggio
Islands
...
```

Once you have identified the page elements of interest, Beautiful Soup makes it easy to retrieve the contained text. If you want to get the price category for each restaurant, for example, you can use:

```
# get the number of dollars signs for each restaurant
for entry in soup.find_all('div', {'class':'rest-row-pricing'}):
    price = entry.find('i').text
```

When you try to get the number of bookings, however, you just get an empty list because the site uses JavaScript code to request this information after the initial loading is complete:

```
soup.find_all('div', {'class':'booking'})
[]
```

This is precisely the challenge we mentioned earlier—rather than sending all content to the browser as a static page that can be easily parsed, JavaScript loads critical pieces dynamically. To obtain this content, we need to execute the JavaScript just like a browser—that's what Selenium is for.

Introducing Selenium – using browser automation

We will use the browser automation tool Selenium to operate a headless Firefox browser that will parse the HTML content for us.

The following code opens the Firefox browser:

```
from selenium import webdriver
# create a driver called Firefox
driver = webdriver.Firefox()
```

Let's close the browser:

```
# close it
driver.close()
```

Now, we retrieve the HTML source code, including the parts loaded dynamically, with Selenium and Firefox. To this end, we provide the URL to our driver and then use its `page_source` attribute to get the full-page content, as displayed in the browser.

From here on, we can fall back on Beautiful Soup to parse the HTML, as follows:

```
import time, re
# visit the opentable listing page
driver = webdriver.Firefox()
driver.get(url)
time.sleep(1) # wait 1 second
# retrieve the html source
html = driver.page_source
html = BeautifulSoup(html, "lxml")
for booking in html.find_all('div', {'class': 'booking'}):
    match = re.search(r'\d+', booking.text)
    if match:
        print(match.group())
```

Building a dataset of restaurant bookings and ratings

Now, you only need to combine all the interesting elements from the website to create a feature that you could use in a model to predict economic activity in geographic regions, or foot traffic in specific neighborhoods.

With Selenium, you can follow the links to the next pages and quickly build a dataset of over 10,000 restaurants in NYC, which you could then update periodically to track a time series.

First, we set up a function that parses the content of the pages that we plan on crawling, using the familiar Beautiful Soup parse syntax:

```
def parse_html(html):
    data, item = pd.DataFrame(), {}
    soup = BeautifulSoup(html, 'lxml')
    for i, resto in enumerate(soup.find_all('div',
                                           class_='rest-row-info')):
        item['name'] = resto.find('span',
                                  class_='rest-row-name-text').text
        booking = resto.find('div', class_='booking')
        item['bookings'] = re.search('\d+', booking.text).group() \
            if booking else 'NA'
        rating = resto.find('div', class_='star-rating-score')
        item['rating'] = float(rating['aria-label'].split()[0]) \
            if rating else 'NA'
        reviews = resto.find('span', class_='underline-hover')
        item['reviews'] = int(re.search('\d+', reviews.text).group()) \
            if reviews else 'NA'
        item['price'] = int(resto.find('div', class_='rest-row-pricing')
                            .find('i').text.count('$'))
        cuisine_class = 'rest-row-meta--cuisine rest-row-meta-text
sfx1388addContent'
        item['cuisine'] = resto.find('span', class_=cuisine_class).text
        location_class = 'rest-row-meta--location rest-row-meta-text
sfx1388addContent'
        item['location'] = resto.find('span', class_=location_class).text
        data[i] = pd.Series(item)
    return data.T
```

Then, we start a headless browser that continues to click on the **Next** button for us and captures the results displayed on each page:

```
restaurants = pd.DataFrame()
driver = webdriver.Firefox()
url = https://www.opentable.com/new-york-restaurant-listings
driver.get(url)
while True:
    sleep(1)
    new_data = parse_html(driver.page_source)
    if new_data.empty:
        break
    restaurants = pd.concat([restaurants, new_data], ignore_index=True)
    print(len(restaurants))
    driver.find_element_by_link_text('Next').click()
driver.close()
```

A sample run in early 2020 yields location, cuisine, and price category information on 10,000 restaurants. Furthermore, there are same-day booking figures for around 1,750 restaurants (on a Monday), as well as ratings and reviews for around 3,500 establishments.

Figure 3.2 shows a quick summary: the left panel displays the breakdown by price category for the top 10 locations with the most restaurants. The central panel suggests that ratings are better, on average, for more expensive restaurants, and the right panel highlights that better - rated restaurants receive more bookings. Tracking this information over time could be informative, for example, with respect to consumer sentiment, location preferences, or specific restaurant chains:

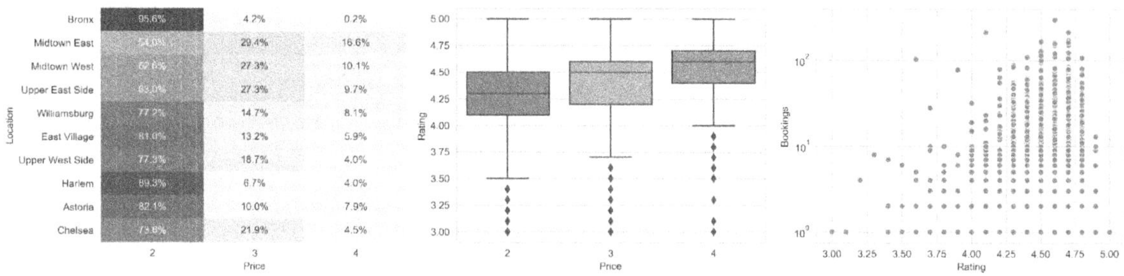

Figure 3.2: OpenTable data summary

Websites continue to change, so this code may stop working at some point. To update our bot, we need to identify the changes to the site navigation, such as new class or ID names, and correct the parser accordingly.

Taking automation one step further with Scrapy and Splash

Scrapy is a powerful library used to build bots that follow links, retrieve the content, and store the parsed result in a structured way. In combination with the Splash headless browser, it can also interpret JavaScript and becomes an efficient alternative to Selenium.

You can run the spider using the `scrapy crawl opentable` command in the `01_opentable` directory, where the results are logged to `spider.log`:

```
from opentable.items import OpentableItem
from scrapy import Spider
from scrapy_splash import SplashRequest
class OpenTableSpider(Spider):
    name = 'opentable'
    start_urls = ['https://www.opentable.com/new-york-restaurant-
                  listings']
    def start_requests(self):
        for url in self.start_urls:
            yield SplashRequest(url=url,
                                callback=self.parse,
                                endpoint='render.html',
```

```
                                    args={'wait': 1},
                                    )
    def parse(self, response):
        item = OpentableItem()
        for resto in response.css('div.rest-row-info'):
            item['name'] = resto.css('span.rest-row-name-
                                       text::text').extract()
            item['bookings'] =
                  resto.css('div.booking::text').re(r'\d+')
            item['rating'] = resto.css('div.all-
                  stars::attr(style)').re_first('\d+')
            item['reviews'] = resto.css('span.star-rating-text--review-
                                          text::text').re_first(r'\d+')
            item['price'] = len(resto.css('div.rest-row-pricing >
                                i::text').re('\$'))
            item['cuisine'] = resto.css('span.rest-row-meta—
                                          cuisine::text').extract()
            item['location'] = resto.css('span.rest-row-meta—
                                  location::text').extract()
            yield item
```

There are numerous ways to extract information from this data beyond the reviews and bookings of individual restaurants or chains.

We could further collect and geo-encode the restaurants' addresses, for instance, to link the restaurants' physical location to other areas of interest, such as popular retail spots or neighborhoods to gain insights into particular aspects of economic activity. As mentioned previously, such data will be most valuable in combination with other information.

Scraping and parsing earnings call transcripts

Textual data is an essential alternative data source. One example of textual information is the transcripts of earnings calls, where executives do not only present the latest financial results, but also respond to questions by financial analysts. Investors utilize transcripts to evaluate changes in sentiment, emphasis on particular topics, or style of communication.

We will illustrate the scraping and parsing of earnings call transcripts from the popular trading website `www.seekingalpha.com`. As in the OpenTable example, we'll use Selenium to access the HTML code and Beautiful Soup to parse the content. To this end, we begin by instantiating a Selenium `webdriver` instance for the Firefox browser:

```
from urllib.parse import urljoin
from bs4 import BeautifulSoup
from furl import furl
from selenium import webdriver
transcript_path = Path('transcripts')
SA_URL = 'https://seekingalpha.com/'
TRANSCRIPT = re.compile('Earnings Call Transcript')
next_page = True
page = 1
driver = webdriver.Firefox()
```

Then, we iterate over the transcript pages, creating the URLs based on the navigation logic we obtained from inspecting the website. As long as we find relevant hyperlinks to additional transcripts, we access the webdriver's `page_source` attribute and call the `parse_html` function to extract the content:

```
while next_page:
    url = f'{SA_URL}/earnings/earnings-call-transcripts/{page}'
    driver.get(urljoin(SA_URL, url))
    response = driver.page_source
    page += 1
    soup = BeautifulSoup(response, 'lxml')
    links = soup.find_all(name='a', string=TRANSCRIPT)
    if len(links) == 0:
        next_page = False
    else:
        for link in links:
            transcript_url = link.attrs.get('href')
            article_url = furl(urljoin(SA_URL,
                           transcript_url)).add({'part': 'single'})
            driver.get(article_url.url)
            html = driver.page_source
            meta, participants, content = parse_html(html)
            meta['link'] = link
driver.close()
```

To collect structured data from the unstructured transcripts, we can use regular expressions in addition to Beautiful Soup.

They allow us to collect detailed information not only about the earnings call company and timing, but also about who was present and attribute the statements to analysts and company representatives:

```
def parse_html(html):
    date_pattern = re.compile(r'(\d{2})-(\d{2})-(\d{2})')
    quarter_pattern = re.compile(r'(\bQ\d\b)')
    soup = BeautifulSoup(html, 'lxml')
    meta, participants, content = {}, [], []
    h1 = soup.find('h1', itemprop='headline').text
    meta['company'] = h1[:h1.find('(')].strip()
    meta['symbol'] = h1[h1.find('(') + 1:h1.find(')')]
    title = soup.find('div', class_='title').text
    match = date_pattern.search(title)
    if match:
        m, d, y = match.groups()
        meta['month'] = int(m)
        meta['day'] = int(d)
        meta['year'] = int(y)
    match = quarter_pattern.search(title)
    if match:
        meta['quarter'] = match.group(0)
    qa = 0
    speaker_types = ['Executives', 'Analysts']
    for header in [p.parent for p in soup.find_all('strong')]:
        text = header.text.strip()
        if text.lower().startswith('copyright'):
            continue
        elif text.lower().startswith('question-and'):
            qa = 1
            continue
        elif any([type in text for type in speaker_types]):
            for participant in header.find_next_siblings('p'):
                if participant.find('strong'):
                    break
                else:
                    participants.append([text, participant.text])
        else:
            p = []
            for participant in header.find_next_siblings('p'):
                if participant.find('strong'):
                    break
                else:
                    p.append(participant.text)
            content.append([header.text, qa, '\n'.join(p)])
    return meta, participants, content
```

We'll store the result in several `.csv` files for easy access when we use ML to process natural language in *Chapters 14-16*:

```
def store_result(meta, participants, content):
    path = transcript_path / 'parsed' / meta['symbol']
    pd.DataFrame(content, columns=['speaker', 'q&a',
              'content']).to_csv(path / 'content.csv', index=False)
    pd.DataFrame(participants, columns=['type', 'name']).to_csv(path /
                 'participants.csv', index=False)
    pd.Series(meta).to_csv(path / 'earnings.csv')
```

See the `README` in the GitHub repository for additional details and references for further resources to learn how to develop web scraping applications.

Summary

In this chapter, we introduced new sources of alternative data made available as a result of the big data revolution, including individuals, business processes, and sensors, such as satellites or GPS location devices. We presented a framework to evaluate alternative datasets from an investment perspective and laid out key categories and providers to help you navigate this vast and quickly expanding area that provides critical inputs for algorithmic trading strategies that use ML.

We also explored powerful Python tools you can use to collect your own datasets at scale. We did this so that you can potentially work on getting your private informational edge as an algorithmic trader using web scraping.

We will now proceed, in the following chapter, to the design and evaluation of alpha factors that produce trading signals and look at how to combine them in a portfolio context.

4

Financial Feature Engineering – How to Research Alpha Factors

Algorithmic trading strategies are driven by signals that indicate when to buy or sell assets to generate superior returns relative to a benchmark, such as an index. The portion of an asset's return that is not explained by exposure to this benchmark is called **alpha**, and hence the signals that aim to produce such uncorrelated returns are also called **alpha factors**.

If you are already familiar with ML, you may know that feature engineering is a key ingredient for successful predictions. This is no different in trading. Investment, however, is particularly rich in decades of research into how markets work, and which features may work better than others to explain or predict price movements as a result. This chapter provides an overview as a starting point for your own search for alpha factors.

This chapter also presents key tools that facilitate computing and testing alpha factors. We will highlight how the NumPy, pandas, and TA-Lib libraries facilitate the manipulation of data and present popular smoothing techniques like the wavelets and the Kalman filter, which help reduce noise in data.

We will also preview how you can use the trading simulator Zipline to evaluate the predictive performance of (traditional) alpha factors. We will discuss key alpha factor metrics like the information coefficient and factor turnover. An in-depth introduction to backtesting trading strategies that use machine learning follows in *Chapter 6, The Machine Learning Process*, which covers the ML4T workflow that we will use throughout this book to evaluate trading strategies.

In particular, this chapter will address the following topics:

- Which categories of factors exist, why they work, and how to measure them
- Creating alpha factors using NumPy, pandas, and TA-Lib
- How to denoise data using wavelets and the Kalman filter
- Using Zipline offline and on Quantopian to test individual and multiple alpha factors
- How to use Alphalens to evaluate predictive performance and turnover using, among other metrics, the **information coefficient** (IC)

> You can find the code samples for this chapter and links to additional resources in the corresponding directory of the GitHub repository. The notebooks include color versions of the images. The *Appendix, Alpha Factor Library*, contains additional information on financial feature engineering, including more than 100 worked examples that you can leverage for your own strategy..

Alpha factors in practice – from data to signals

Alpha factors are transformations of raw data that aim to predict asset price movements. They are designed to **capture risks that drive asset returns**. A factor may combine one or several inputs, but outputs a single value for each asset, every time the strategy evaluates the factor to obtain a signal. Trade decisions may rely on relative factor values across assets or patterns for a single asset.

The design, evaluation, and combination of alpha factors are critical steps during the research phase of the algorithmic trading strategy workflow, which is displayed in *Figure 4.1*:

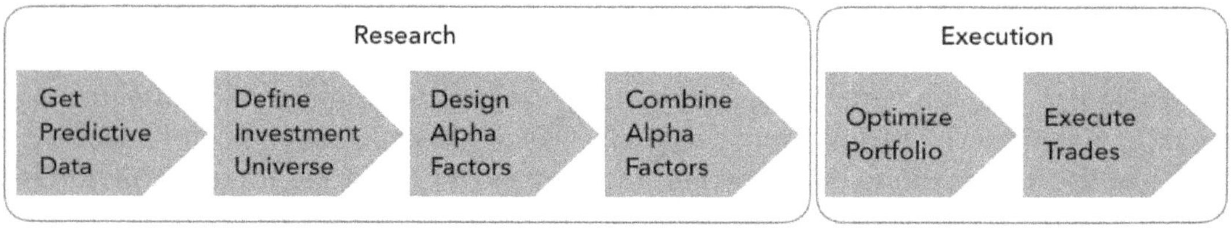

Figure 4.1: Alpha factor research and execution workflow

This chapter focuses on the research phase; the next chapter covers the execution phase. The remainder of this book will then focus on how to leverage ML to learn new factors from data and effectively aggregate the signals from multiple alpha factors.

Alpha factors are transformations of market, fundamental, and alternative data that contain predictive signals. Some factors describe fundamental, economy-wide variables such as growth, inflation, volatility, productivity, and demographic risk. Other factors represent investment styles, such as value or growth, and momentum investing that can be traded and are thus priced by the market. There are also factors that explain price movements based on the economics or institutional setting of financial markets, or investor behavior, including known biases of this behavior.

The economic theory behind factors can be **rational** so that factors have high returns over the long run to compensate for their low returns during bad times. It can also be **behavioral**, where factor risk premiums result from the possibly biased, or not entirely rational, behavior of agents that is not arbitraged away.

There is a constant search for and discovery of new factors that may better capture known or reflect new drivers of returns. Jason Hsu, the co-founder of Research Affiliates, which manages close to $200 billion, identified some 250 factors that had been published with empirical evidence in reputable journals by 2015. He estimated that this number was likely to increase by 40 factors per year.

To avoid false discoveries and ensure a factor delivers consistent results, it should have a meaningful **economic intuition** based on the various established factor categories like momentum, value, volatility, or quality and their rationales, which we'll outline in the next section. This makes it more plausible that the factor reflects risks for which the market would compensate.

Alpha factors result from transforming raw market, fundamental, or alternative data using simple arithmetic, such as absolute or relative changes of a variable over time, ratios between data series, or aggregations over a time window like a simple or exponential moving average. They also include metrics that have emerged from the technical analysis of price and volume patterns, such as the **relative strength index** of demand versus supply and numerous metrics familiar from the fundamental analysis of securities. Kakushadze (2016) lists the formulas for 101 alpha factors, 80 percent of which were used in production at the WorldQuant hedge fund at the time of writing.

Historically, trading strategies applied simple ranking heuristics, value thresholds, or quantile cutoffs to one or several alpha factors computed across multiple securities in the investment universe. Examples include the value investing approach popularized in one of Warren Buffet's favorite books, *Security Analysis*, by Graham and Dodd (1934), which relies on metrics like the book-to-market ratio.

Modern research into alpha factors that predict above-market returns has been led by Eugene Fama (who won the 2013 Nobel Prize in Economics) and Kenneth French, who provided evidence on the size and value factors (1993). This work led to the three- and five-factor models, which we will discuss in *Chapter 7, Linear Models – From Risk Factors to Return Forecasts*, using daily data on factor returns provided by the authors on their website. An excellent, more recent, overview of modern factor investing has been written by Andrew Ang (2014), who heads this discipline at BlackRock, which manages close to $7 trillion.

As we will see throughout this book, ML has proven quite effective in learning to extract signals directly from a more diverse and much larger set of input data without using prescribed formulas. As we will also see, however, alpha factors remain useful inputs for an ML model that combines their information content in a more optimal way than manually set rules.

As a result, algorithmic trading strategies today leverage a large number of signals, many of which may be weak individually but can yield reliable predictions when combined with other model-driven or traditional factors by an ML algorithm.

Building on decades of factor research

In an idealized world, risk factors should be independent of each other, yield positive risk premia, and form a complete set that spans all dimensions of risk and explains the systematic risks for assets in a given class. In practice, these requirements hold only approximately, and there are important correlations between different factors. For instance, momentum is often stronger among smaller firms (Hou, Xue, and Zhang, 2015). We will show how to derive synthetic, data-driven risk factors using unsupervised learning—in particular, principal and independent component analysis —in *Chapter 13, Data-Driven Risk Factors and Asset Allocation with Unsupervised Learning*.

In this section, we will review a few key factor categories prominent in financial research and trading applications, explain their economic rationale, and present metrics typically used to capture these drivers of returns.

In the next section, we will demonstrate how to implement some of these factors using NumPy and pandas, use the TA-Lib library for technical analysis, and demonstrate how to evaluate factors using the Zipline backtesting library. We will also highlight some factors built into Zipline that are available on the Quantopian platform.

Momentum and sentiment – the trend is your friend

Momentum investing is among the most well-established factor strategies, underpinned by quantitative evidence since Jegadeesh and Titman (1993) for the US equity market. It follows the adage: *the trend is your friend or let your winners run*. Momentum factors are designed to go long on assets that have performed well, while going short on assets with poor performance over a certain period. Clifford Asness, the founder of the $200 billion hedge fund AQR, presented evidence for momentum effects across eight different asset classes and markets much more recently (Asness, Moskowitz, and Pedersen, 2013).

The premise of strategies using this factor is that **asset prices exhibit a trend**, reflected in positive serial correlation. Such price momentum defies the hypothesis of efficient markets, which states that past price returns alone cannot predict future performance. Despite theoretical arguments to the contrary, price momentum strategies have produced positive returns across asset classes and are an important part of many trading strategies.

The chart in *Figure 4.2* shows the historical performance of portfolios formed based on their exposure to various alpha factors (using data from the Fama-French website). The factor **winner minus loser** (**WML**) represents the difference in performance between portfolios containing US stocks in the top and bottom three deciles, respectively, of the prior 2-12 months of returns:

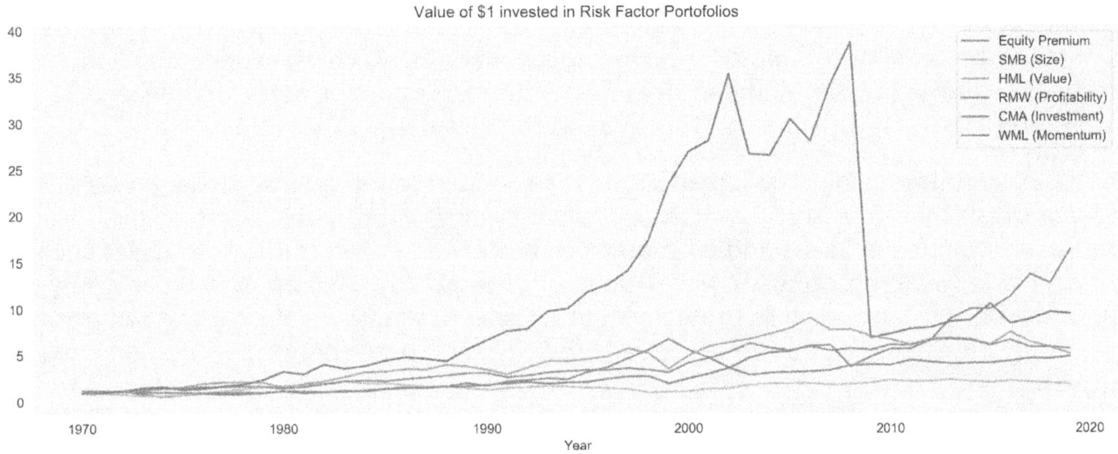

Figure 4.2: Returns on various risk factors

The momentum factor dramatically outperformed other prominent risk factors up to the 2008 crisis. The other factors include the **high-minus-low** (**HML**) value factor, the **robust-minus-weak** (**RMW**) profitability factor, and the **conservative-minus-aggressive** (**CMA**) investment factor. The equity premium is the difference between the market return (for example, the S&P 500) and the risk-free rate.

Why might momentum and sentiment drive excess returns?

Reasons for the momentum effect point to investor behavior, persistent supply and demand imbalances, a positive feedback loop between risk assets and the economy, or the market microstructure.

The **behavioral rationale** reflects the biases of underreaction (Hong, Lim, and Stein, 2000) and over-reaction (Barberis, Shleifer, and Vishny, 1998) to market news as investors process new information at different speeds. After an initial under-reaction to news, investors often extrapolate past behavior and create price momentum. The technology stocks rally during the late 90s market bubble was an extreme example. A fear and greed psychology also motivates investors to increase exposure to winning assets and continue selling losing assets (Jegadeesh and Titman, 2011).

Momentum can also have **fundamental drivers** such as a positive feedback loop between risk assets and the economy. Economic growth boosts equities, and the resulting wealth effect feeds back into the economy through higher spending, again fueling growth. Positive feedback between prices and the economy often extends momentum in equities and credit to longer horizons than for bonds, FOEX, and commodities, where negative feedback creates reversals, requiring a much shorter investment horizon. Another cause of momentum can be persistent demand-supply imbalances due to market frictions. One example is the delay of commodity production in adjusting to changing demand. Oil production may lag higher demand from a booming economy for years, and persistent supply shortages can trigger and support upward price momentum (Novy-Marx, 2015).

Over shorter, intraday horizons, **market microstructure** effects can also create price momentum as investors implement strategies that mimic their biases. For example, the trading wisdom to cut losses and let profits run has investors use trading strategies such as stop-loss, **constant proportion portfolio insurance** (**CPPI**), dynamical delta hedging, or option-based strategies such as protective puts. These strategies create momentum because they imply an advance commitment to sell when an asset underperforms and buy when it outperforms.

Similarly, risk parity strategies (see the next chapter) tend to buy low-volatility assets that often exhibit positive performance and sell high-volatility assets that often have had negative performance (see the *Volatility and size anomalies* section later in this chapter). The automatic rebalancing of portfolios using these strategies tends to reinforce price momentum.

How to measure momentum and sentiment

Momentum factors are typically derived from changes in price time series by identifying trends and patterns. They can be constructed based on absolute or relative return by comparing a cross-section of assets or analyzing an asset's time series, within or across traditional asset classes, and at different time horizons.

A few popular illustrative indicators are listed in the following table (see the *Appendix* for formulas):

Factor	Description
Relative strength index (RSI)	RSI compares the magnitude of recent price changes across stocks to identify stocks as overbought or oversold. A high RSI (usually above 70) indicates overbought and a low RSI (typically below 30) indicates oversold. It first computes the average price change for a given number (often 14) of prior trading days with rising prices Δ_p^{up} and falling prices Δ_p^{down}, respectively, to compute $\text{RSI} = 100 - \frac{100}{1 + \frac{\Delta_p^{up}}{\Delta_p^{down}}}$.

Price momentum	This factor computes the total return for a given number of prior trading days. In academic literature, it is common to use the last 12 months except for the most recent month due to a short-term reversal effect that's frequently observed. However, shorter periods have also been widely used.
12-month price momentum volume adjustment	The indicator normalizes the total return over the previous 12 months by dividing it by the standard deviation of these returns.
Price acceleration	Price acceleration calculates the gradient of the price trend (adjusted for volatility) using linear regression on daily prices for a longer and a shorter period, for example, 1 year and 3 months of trading days, and compares the change in the slope as a measure of price acceleration.
Percent off 52-week high	This factor uses the percent difference between the most recent and the highest price for the last 52 weeks.

Additional sentiment indicators include the following metrics; inputs like analyst estimates can be obtained from data providers like Quandl or Bloomberg, among others:

Factor	Description
Earnings estimates count	This metric ranks stocks by the number of consensus estimates as a proxy for analyst coverage and information uncertainty. A higher value is more desirable.
N-month change in recommendation	This factor ranks stocks by the change in consensus recommendation over the prior *N* month, where improvements are desirable (regardless of whether they have moved from strong sell to sell or buy to strong buy and so on).
12-month change in shares outstanding	This factor measures the change in a company's split-adjusted share count over the last 12 months, where a negative change implies share buybacks and is desirable because it signals that management views the stock as cheap relative to its intrinsic and, hence, future value.
6-month change in target price	The metric tracks the 6-month change in mean analyst target price. A higher positive change is naturally more desirable.
Net earnings revisions	This factor expresses the difference between upward and downward revisions to earnings estimates as a percentage of the total number of revisions.
Short interest to shares outstanding	This measure is the percentage of shares outstanding currently being sold short, that is, sold by an investor who has borrowed the share and needs to repurchase it at a later day while speculating that its price will fall. Hence, a high level of short interest indicates negative sentiment and is expected to signal poor performance going forward.

There are also numerous data providers that aim to offer sentiment indicators constructed from social media, such as Twitter. We will create our own sentiment indicators using **natural language processing** in Part 3 of this book.

Value factors – hunting fundamental bargains

Stocks with low prices relative to their fundamental value tend to deliver returns in excess of a capitalization-weighted benchmark. Value factors reflect this correlation and are designed to send buy signals for undervalued assets that are relatively cheap and sell signals for overvalued assets. Hence, at the core of any value strategy is a model that estimates the asset's fair or fundamental value. Fair value can be defined as an absolute price level, a spread relative to other assets, or a range in which an asset should trade.

Relative value strategies

Value strategies rely on the mean-reversion of prices to the asset's fair value. They assume that prices only temporarily move away from fair value due to behavioral effects like overreaction or herding, or liquidity effects such as temporary market impact or long-term supply/demand friction. Value factors often exhibit properties opposite to those of momentum factors because they rely on mean-reversion. For equities, the opposite of value stocks is growth stocks that have a high valuation due to growth expectations.

Value factors enable a broad array of systematic strategies, including fundamental and market valuation and cross-asset relative value. They are often collectively labeled **statistical arbitrage** (**StatArb**) strategies, implemented as market-neutral long/short portfolios without exposure to other traditional or alternative risk factors.

Fundamental value strategies

Fundamental value strategies derive fair asset values from economic and fundamental indicators that depend on the target asset class. In fixed income, currencies, and commodities, indicators include levels and changes in the capital account balance, economic activity, inflation, or fund flows. For equities and corporate credit, value factors go back to Graham and Dodd's previously mentioned *Security Analysis*. Equity value approaches compare a stock price to fundamental metrics such as book value, top-line sales, bottom-line earnings, or various cash-flow metrics.

Market value strategies

Market value strategies use statistical or machine learning models to identify mispricing due to inefficiencies in liquidity provision. Statistical and index arbitrage are prominent examples that capture the reversion of temporary market impacts over short time horizons. (We will cover pairs trading in *Chapter 9, Time-Series Models for Volatility Forecasts and Statistical Arbitrage*). Over longer time horizons, market value trades also leverage seasonal effects in equities and commodities.

Cross-asset relative value strategies

Cross-asset relative value strategies focus on mispricing across asset classes. For example, convertible bond arbitrage involves trades on the relative value between the bond that can be turned into equity and the underlying stock of a single company. Relative value strategies also include trades between credit and equity volatility, using credit signals to trade equities or trades between commodities and related equities.

Why do value factors help predict returns?

There are both rational and behavioral explanations for the existence of the **value effect**, defined as the excess return on a portfolio of value stocks relative to a portfolio of growth stocks, where the former have a low market value and the latter have a high market value relative to fundamentals. We will cite a few prominent examples from a wealth of research (see, for example, Fama and French, 1998, and Asness, Moskowitz, and Pedersen, 2013).

In the **rational, efficient markets view**, the value premium compensates for higher real or perceived risks. Researchers have presented evidence that value firms have less flexibility to adapt to the unfavorable economic environments than leaner and more flexible growth companies, or that value stock risks relate to high financial leverage and more uncertain future earnings. Value and small-cap portfolios have also been shown to be more sensitive to macro shocks than growth and large-cap portfolios (Lakonishok, Shleifer, and Vishny, 1994).

From a **behavioral perspective**, the value premium can be explained by loss aversion and mental accounting biases. Investors may be less concerned about losses on assets with a strong recent performance due to the cushions offered by prior gains. This loss aversion bias induces investors to perceive the stock as less risky than before and discount its future cash flows at a lower rate. Conversely, poor recent performance may lead investors to raise the asset's discount rate.

These **differential return expectations** can produce a value premium: growth stocks with a high price multiple relative to fundamentals have done well in the past, but investors will require a lower average return going forward due to their biased perception of lower risks, while the inverse is true for value stocks.

How to capture value effects

A large number of valuation proxies are computed from fundamental data. These factors can be combined as inputs into a machine learning valuation model to predict asset prices. The following examples apply to equities, and we will see how some of these factors are used in the following chapters:

Factor	Description
Cash flow yield	The ratio divides the operational cash flow per share by the share price. A higher ratio implies better cash returns for shareholders (if paid out using dividends or share buybacks or profitably reinvested in the business).
Free cash flow yield	The ratio divides the free cash flow per share, which reflects the amount of cash available for distribution after necessary expenses and investments, by the share price. Higher and growing free cash flow yield is commonly viewed as a signal of outperformance.
Cash flow return on invested capital (CFROIC)	CFROIC measures a company's cash flow profitability. It divides operating cash flow by invested capital, defined as total debt plus net assets. A higher return means the business has more cash for a given amount of invested capital, generating more value for shareholders.

Cash flow to total assets	This ratio divides operational cash flow by total assets and indicates how much cash a company can generate relative to its assets, where a higher ratio is better, as with CFROIC.
Free cash flow to enterprise value	This ratio measures the free cash flow that a company generates relative to its enterprise value, measured as the combined value of equity and debt. The debt and equity values can be taken from the balance sheet, but market values often provide a more accurate picture assuming the corresponding assets are actively traded.
EBITDA to enterprise value	This ratio measures a company's **earnings before interest, taxes, depreciation, and amortization** (**EBITDA**), which is a proxy for cash flow relative to its enterprise value.
Earnings yield	This ratio divides the sum of earnings for the past 12 months by the last market (close) price.
Earnings yield 1-year forward	Instead of using historical earnings, this ratio divides the average of earnings forecasted by stock analyst for the next 12 months by the last price.
PEG ratio	The **price/earnings to growth** (**PEG**) ratio divides a stock's **price-to-earnings** (**P/E**) ratio by the earnings growth rate for a given period. The ratio adjusts the price paid for a dollar of earnings (measured by the P/E ratio) by the company's earnings growth.
P/E 1-year forward relative to the sector	Forecasts the P/E ratio relative to the corresponding sector P/E. It aims to alleviate the sector bias of the generic P/E ratio by accounting for sector differences in valuation.
Sales yield	The ratio measures the valuation of a stock relative to its ability to generate revenues. All else being equal, stocks with higher historical sales to price ratios are expected to outperform.
Sales yield forward	The forward sales-to-price ratio uses analyst sales forecast, combined to a (weighted) average.
Book value yield	The ratio divides the historical book value by the share price.
Dividend yield	The current annualized dividend divided by the last close price. Discounted cash flow valuation assumes a company's market value equates to the present value of its future cash flows.

Chapter 2, Market and Fundamental Data – Sources and Techniques, discussed how you can source the fundamental data used to compute these metrics from company filings.

Volatility and size anomalies

The **size effect** is among the older risk factors and relates to the excess performance of stocks with a low market capitalization (see *Figure 4.2* at the beginning of this section). More recently, the **low-volatility factor** has been shown to capture excess returns on stocks with below-average volatility, beta, or idiosyncratic risk. Stocks with a larger market capitalization tend to have lower volatility so that the traditional size factor is often combined with the more recent volatility factor.

The low volatility anomaly is an empirical puzzle that is at odds with the basic principles of finance. The **capital asset pricing model (CAPM)** and other asset pricing models assert that higher risk should earn higher returns (as we will discuss in detail in the next chapter), but in numerous markets and over extended periods, the opposite has been true, with less risky assets outperforming their riskier peers.

Figure 4.3 plots a rolling mean of the S&P 500 returns of 1990-2019 against the VIX index, which measures the implied volatility of at-the-money options on the S&P 100. It illustrates how stock returns and this measure of volatility have moved inversely with a negative correlation of -.54 over this period. In addition to this aggregate effect, there is also evidence that stocks with a greater sensitivity to changes in the VIX perform worse (Ang et al. 2006):

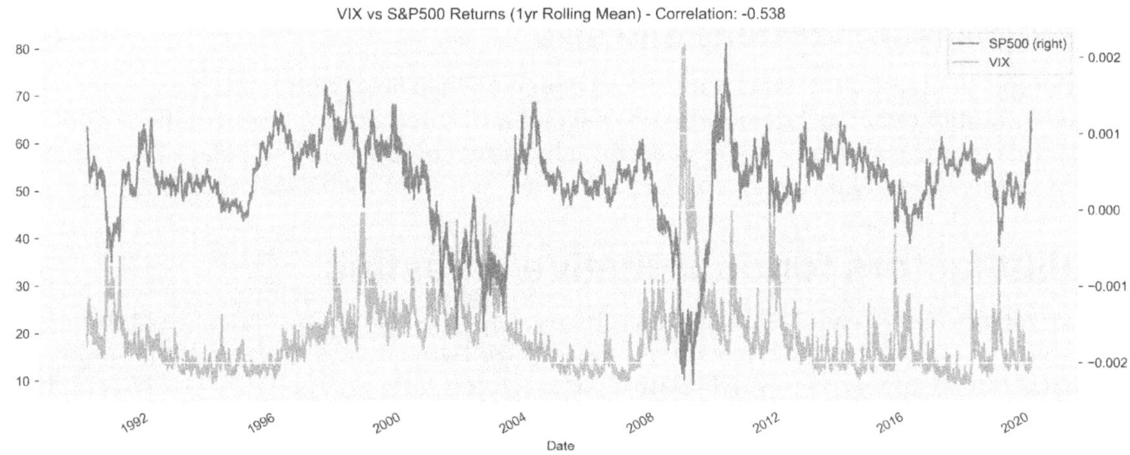

Figure 4.3: Correlation between the VIX and the S&P 500

Why do volatility and size predict returns?

The low volatility anomaly contradicts the hypothesis of efficient markets and the CAPM assumptions. Several behavioral explanations have been advanced to explain its existence.

The **lottery effect** builds on empirical evidence that individuals take on bets that resemble lottery tickets with a small expected loss but a large potential win, even though this large win may have a fairly low probability. If investors perceive that the risk-return profile of a low price, volatile stock is like a lottery ticket, then it could be an attractive bet. As a result, investors may overpay for high-volatility stocks and underpay for low-volatility stocks due to their biased preferences.

The **representativeness bias** suggests that investors extrapolate the success of a few, well-publicized volatile stocks to all volatile stocks while ignoring the speculative nature of such stocks.

Investors may also be **overconfident** in their ability to forecast the future, and their differences in opinions are higher for volatile stocks with more uncertain outcomes. Since it is easier to express a positive view by going long—that is, owning an asset—than a negative view by going short, optimists may outnumber pessimists and keep driving up the price of volatile stocks, resulting in lower returns.

Furthermore, investors behave differently during bull markets and crises. During bull markets, the dispersion of betas is much lower so that low-volatility stocks do not underperform much, if at all, whereas during crises, investors seek or keep low-volatility stocks and the beta dispersion increases. As a result, lower volatility assets and portfolios do better over the long term.

How to measure volatility and size

Metrics used to identify low-volatility stocks cover a broad spectrum, with realized volatility (standard deviation) on one end and forecast (implied) volatility and correlations on the other end. Some operationalize low volatility as low beta. The evidence in favor of the volatility anomaly appears robust for different metrics (Ang, 2014).

Quality factors for quantitative investing

Quality factors aim to capture the excess returns reaped by companies that are highly profitable, operationally efficient, safe, stable, and well-governed—in short, high quality. The markets also appear to reward relative earnings certainty and penalize stocks with high earnings volatility.

A portfolio tilt toward businesses with high quality has been long advocated by stock pickers that rely on fundamental analysis, but it is a relatively new phenomenon in quantitative investments. The main challenge is how to define the quality factor consistently and objectively using quantitative indicators, given the subjective nature of quality.

Strategies based on standalone quality factors tend to perform in a counter-cyclical way as investors pay a premium to minimize downside risks and drive up valuations. For this reason, quality factors are often combined with other risk factors in a multi-factor strategy, most frequently with value to produce the quality at a reasonable price strategy.

Long-short quality factors tend to have negative market beta because they are long quality stocks that are also low volatility, and short more volatile, low-quality stocks. Hence, quality factors are often positively correlated with low volatility and momentum factors, and negatively correlated with value and broad market exposure.

Why quality matters

Quality factors may signal outperformance because superior fundamentals such as sustained profitability, steady growth in cash flow, prudent leveraging, a low need for capital market financing, or low financial risk underpin the demand for equity shares and support the price of such companies in the long run. From a corporate finance perspective, a quality company often manages its capital carefully and reduces the risk of over-leveraging or over-capitalization.

A behavioral explanation suggests that investors under-react to information about quality, similar to the rationale for momentum, where investors chase winners and sell losers.

Another argument for quality premia is a herding argument, similar to growth stocks. Fund managers may find it easier to justify buying a company with strong fundamentals, even when it is getting expensive, rather than a more volatile (risky) value stock.

How to measure asset quality

Quality factors rely on metrics computed from the balance sheet and income statement, which indicate profitability reflected in high profit or cash flow margins, operating efficiency, financial strength, and competitiveness more broadly because it implies the ability to sustain a profitability position over time.

Hence, quality has been measured using gross profitability (which has been recently added to the Fama–French factor model; see *Chapter 7, Linear Models – From Risk Factors to Return Forecasts*), return on invested capital, low earnings volatility, or a combination of various profitability, earnings quality, and leverage metrics, with some options listed in the following table.

Earnings management is mainly exercised by manipulating accruals. Hence, the size of accruals is often used as a proxy for earnings quality: higher total accruals relative to assets make low earnings quality more likely. However, this is not unambiguous as accruals can reflect earnings manipulation just as well as accounting estimates of future business growth:

Factor	Description
Asset turnover	This factor measures how efficiently a company uses its assets, which require capital, to produce revenue and is calculated by dividing sales by total assets. A higher turnover is better.
Asset turnover 12-month change	This factor measures a change in management's efficiency in using assets to produce revenue over the last year. Stocks with the highest level of efficiency improvements are typically expected to outperform.
Current ratio	The current ratio is a liquidity metric that measures a company's ability to pay short-term obligations. It compares a company's current assets to its current liabilities, and a higher current ratio is better from a quality perspective.
Interest coverage	This factor measures how easily a company will be able to pay interest on its debt. It is calculated by dividing a company's **earnings before interest and taxes** (**EBIT**) by its interest expense. A higher ratio is desirable.

Leverage	A firm with significantly more debt than equity is considered to be highly leveraged. The debt-to-equity ratio is typically inversely related to prospects, with lower leverage being better.
Payout ratio	The share of earnings paid out in dividends to shareholders. Stocks with higher payout ratios are ranked higher.
Return on equity (ROE)	ROE is computed as the ratio of net income to shareholders' equity. Equities with higher historical returns on equity are ranked higher.

Equipped with a high-level categorization of alpha factors that have been shown to be associated with abnormal returns to varying degrees, we'll now start developing our own financial features from market, fundamental, and alternative data.

Engineering alpha factors that predict returns

Based on a conceptual understanding of key factor categories, their rationale, and popular metrics, a key task is to identify new factors that may better capture the risks embodied by the return drivers laid out previously, or to find new ones. In either case, it will be important to compare the performance of innovative factors to that of known factors to identify incremental signal gains.

Key tools that facilitate the transformation of data into factors include the Python libraries for numerical computing, NumPy and pandas, as well as the Python wrapper around the specialized library for technical analysis, TA-Lib. Alternatives include the expression alphas developed in Zura Kakushadze's 2016 paper, *101 Formulaic Alphas*, and implemented by the alphatools library. In addition, the Quantopian platform provides a large number of built-in factors to speed up the research process.

To apply one or more factors to an investment universe, we can use the Zipline backtesting library (which also includes some built-in factors) and evaluate their performance using the Alphalens library using metrics discussed in the following section.

How to engineer factors using pandas and NumPy

NumPy and pandas are the key tools for custom factor computations. This section demonstrates how they can be used to quickly compute the transformations that yield various alpha factors. If you are not familiar with these libraries, in particular pandas, which we will use throughout this book, please see the `README` for this chapter in the GitHub repo for links to documentation and tutorials.

The notebook `feature_engineering.ipynb` in the `alpha_factors_in_practice` directory contains examples of how to create various factors. The notebook uses data generated by the `create_data.ipynb` notebook in the `data` folder in the root directory of the GitHub repo, which is stored in HDF5 format for faster access. See the notebook `storage_benchmarks.ipynb` in the directory for *Chapter 2*, in the GitHub repo for a comparison of parquet, HDF5, and CSV storage formats for pandas DataFrames.

The NumPy library for scientific computing was created by Travis Oliphant in 2005 by integrating the older Numeric and Numarray libraries that had been developed since the mid-1990s. It is organized in a high-performance *n*-dimensional array data structure called `ndarray`, which enables functionality comparable to MATLAB.

The pandas library emerged in 2008 when Wes McKinney was working at AQR Capital Management. It provides the DataFrame data structure, which is based on NumPy's `ndarray`, but allows for more user-friendly data manipulation with label-based indexing. It includes a wide array of computational tools particularly well-suited to financial data, including rich time-series operations with automatic date alignment, which we will explore here.

The following sections illustrate some steps in transforming raw stock price data into selected factors. See the notebook `feature_engineering.ipynb` for additional detail and visualizations that we have omitted here to save some space. See the resources listed in the `README` for this chapter on GitHub for links to the documentation and tutorials on how to use pandas and NumPy.

Loading, slicing, and reshaping the data

After loading the Quandl Wiki stock price data on US equities, we select the 2000-18 time slice by applying `pd.IndexSlice` to `pd.MultiIndex`, which contains timestamp and ticker information. We then select and unpivot the adjusted close price column using the `.stack()` method to convert the DataFrame into wide format, with tickers in the columns and timestamps in the rows:

```
idx = pd.IndexSlice
with pd.HDFStore('../../data/assets.h5') as store:
    prices = (store['quandl/wiki/prices']
              .loc[idx['2000':'2018', :], 'adj_close']
              .unstack('ticker'))

prices.info()
DatetimeIndex: 4706 entries, 2000-01-03 to 2018-03-27
Columns: 3199 entries, A to ZUMZ
```

Resampling – from daily to monthly frequency

To reduce training time and experiment with strategies for longer time horizons, we convert the business-daily data into month-end frequency using the available adjusted close price:

```
monthly_prices = prices.resample('M').last()
```

How to compute returns for multiple historical periods

To capture time-series dynamics like momentum patterns, we compute historical multi-period returns using the `pct_change(n_periods)` method, where `n_periods` identifies the number of lags. We then convert the wide result back into long format using `.stack()`, use `.pipe()` to apply the `.clip()` method to the resulting DataFrame, and winsorize returns at the [1%, 99%] levels; that is, we cap outliers at these percentiles.

Finally, we normalize returns using the geometric average. After using `.swaplevel()` to change the order of the `MultiIndex` levels, we obtain the compounded monthly returns over six different periods, ranging from 1 to 12 months:

```
outlier_cutoff = 0.01
data = pd.DataFrame()
lags = [1, 2, 3, 6, 9, 12]
for lag in lags:
    data[f'return_{lag}m'] = (monthly_prices
                              .pct_change(lag)
                              .stack()
                              .pipe(lambda x:
                                    x.clip(lower=x.quantile(outlier_cutoff),
                                           upper=x.quantile(1-outlier_cutoff)))
                              .add(1)
                              .pow(1/lag)
                              .sub(1)
                              )
data = data.swaplevel().dropna()
data.info()
MultiIndex: 521806 entries, (A, 2001-01-31 00:00:00) to (ZUMZ, 2018-03-
                                31 00:00:00)
Data columns (total 6 columns):
return_1m 521806 non-null float64
return_2m 521806 non-null float64
return_3m 521806 non-null float64
return_6m 521806 non-null float64
return_9m 521806 non-null float64
return_12m 521806 non-null float6
```

We can use these results to compute momentum factors based on the difference between returns over longer periods and the most recent monthly return, as well as for the difference between 3- and 12-month returns, as follows:

```
for lag in [2,3,6,9,12]:
    data[f'momentum_{lag}'] = data[f'return_{lag}m'].sub(data.return_1m)
data[f'momentum_3_12'] = data[f'return_12m'].sub(data.return_3m)
```

Using lagged returns and different holding periods

To use lagged values as input variables or features associated with the current observations, we use the `.shift()` method to move historical returns up to the current period:

```
for t in range(1, 7):
    data[f'return_1m_t-{t}'] = data.groupby(level='ticker').return_1m.
shift(t)
```

Similarly, to compute returns for various holding periods, we use the normalized period returns computed previously and shift them back to align them with the current financial features:

```
for t in [1,2,3,6,12]:
    data[f'target_{t}m'] = (data.groupby(level='ticker')
                            [f'return_{t}m'].shift(-t))
```

The notebook also demonstrates how to compute various descriptive statistics for the different return series and visualize their correlation using the seaborn library.

Computing factor betas

We will introduce the Fama-French data to estimate the exposure of assets to common risk factors using linear regression in *Chapter 7, Linear Models - From Risk Factors to Return Forecasts*. The five Fama-French factors, namely market risk, size, value, operating profitability, and investment, have been shown empirically to explain asset returns. They are commonly used to assess the exposure of a portfolio to well-known drivers of risk and returns, where the unexplained portion is then attributed to the manager's idiosyncratic skill. Hence, it is natural to include past factor exposures as financial features in models that aim to predict future returns.

We can access the historical factor returns using the pandas-datareader and estimate historical exposures using the `PandasRollingOLS` rolling linear regression functionality in the pyfinance library, as follows:

```
factors = ['Mkt-RF', 'SMB', 'HML', 'RMW', 'CMA']
factor_data = web.DataReader('F-F_Research_Data_5_Factors_2x3',
              'famafrench', start='2000')[0].drop('RF', axis=1)
factor_data.index = factor_data.index.to_timestamp()
factor_data = factor_data.resample('M').last().div(100)
factor_data.index.name = 'date'
factor_data = factor_data.join(data['return_1m']).sort_index()
T = 24
betas = (factor_data
         .groupby(level='ticker', group_keys=False)
         .apply(lambda x: PandasRollingOLS(window=min(T, x.shape[0]-1), y=x.
return_1m, x=x.drop('return_1m', axis=1)).beta))
```

As mentioned previously, we will explore both the Fama-French factor model and linear regression in *Chapter 7, Linear Models – From Risk Factors to Return Forecasts*, in more detail. See the notebook `feature_engineering.ipynb` for additional examples, including the computation of lagged and forward returns.

How to add momentum factors

We can use the 1-month and 3-month results to compute simple momentum factors. The following code example shows how to compute the difference between returns over longer periods and the most recent monthly return, as well as for the difference between 3- and 12-month returns:

```
for lag in [2,3,6,9,12]:
    data[f'momentum_{lag}'] = data[f'return_{lag}m'].sub(data.return_1m)
data[f'momentum_3_12'] = data[f'return_12m'].sub(data.return_3m)
```

Adding time indicators to capture seasonal effects

Basic factors also include seasonal anomalies like the January effect, which has been observed to cause higher returns for stocks during this month, possibly for tax reasons. This and other seasonal effects can be modeled through indicator variables that represent specific time periods such as the year and/or the month. These can be generated as follows:

```
dates = data.index.get_level_values('date')
data['year'] = dates.year
data['month'] = dates.month
```

How to create lagged return features

If you want to use lagged returns, that is, returns from previous periods as input variables or features to train a model that learns return patterns to predict future returns, you can use the `.shift()` method to move historical returns up to the current period. The following example moves the returns for the periods 1 to 6 months ago up by the corresponding lag so that they are associated with the observation for the current month:

```
for t in range(1, 7):
    data[f'return_1m_t-{t}'] = data.groupby(level='ticker').return_1m.shift(t)
```

How to create forward returns

Similarly, you can create forward returns for the current period, that is, returns that will occur in the future, using `.shift()` with a negative period (assuming your data is sorted in ascending order):

```
for t in [1,2,3,6,12]:
    data[f'target_{t}m'] = (data.groupby(level='ticker')
                              [f'return_{t}m'].shift(-t))
```

We will use forward returns when we train ML models starting in *Chapter 6, The Machine Learning Process.*

How to use TA-Lib to create technical alpha factors

TA-Lib is an open source library written in C++ with a Python interface that is widely used by trading software developers. It contains standardized implementations of over 200 popular indicators for technical analysis; that is, these indicators only use market data, namely price and volume information.

TA-Lib is compatible with pandas and NumPy, rendering its usage very straightforward. The following examples demonstrate how to compute two popular indicators.

Bollinger Bands consist of a **simple moving average** (**SMA**) surrounded by bands two rolling standard deviations below and above the SMA. It was introduced for the visualization of potential overbought/oversold conditions when the price dipped outside the two bands on the upper or lower side, respectively. The inventor, John Bollinger, actually recommended a trading system of 22 rules that generate trade signals.

We can compute the Bollinger Bands and, for comparison, the **relative strength index** described earlier in this section on popular alpha factors as follows.

We load the adjusted close for a single stock—in this case, AAPL:

```
with pd.HDFStore(DATA_STORE) as store:
    data = (store['quandl/wiki/prices']
            .loc[idx['2007':'2010', 'AAPL'],
                 ['adj_open', 'adj_high', 'adj_low', 'adj_close',
                  'adj_volume']]
            .unstack('ticker')
            .swaplevel(axis=1)
            .loc[:, 'AAPL']
            .rename(columns=lambda x: x.replace('adj_', '')))
```

Then, we pass the one-dimensional `pd.Series` through the relevant TA-Lib functions:

```
from talib import RSI, BBANDS
up, mid, low = BBANDS(data.close, timeperiod=21, nbdevup=2, nbdevdn=2,
                      matype=0)
rsi = RSI(adj_close, timeperiod=14)
```

Then, we collect the results in a DataFrame and plot the Bollinger Bands with the AAPL stock price and the RSI with the 30/70 lines, which suggest long/short opportunities:

```
data = pd.DataFrame({'AAPL': data.close, 'BB Up': up, 'BB Mid': mid,
                     'BB down': low, 'RSI': rsi})
fig, axes= plt.subplots(nrows=2, figsize=(15, 8))
data.drop('RSI', axis=1).plot(ax=axes[0], lw=1, title='Bollinger Bands')
data['RSI'].plot(ax=axes[1], lw=1, title='Relative Strength Index')
axes[1].axhline(70, lw=1, ls='--', c='k')
axes[1].axhline(30, lw=1, ls='--', c='k')
```

The result, shown in *Figure 4.4*, is rather mixed—both indicators suggested overbought conditions during the early post-crisis recovery when the price continued to rise:

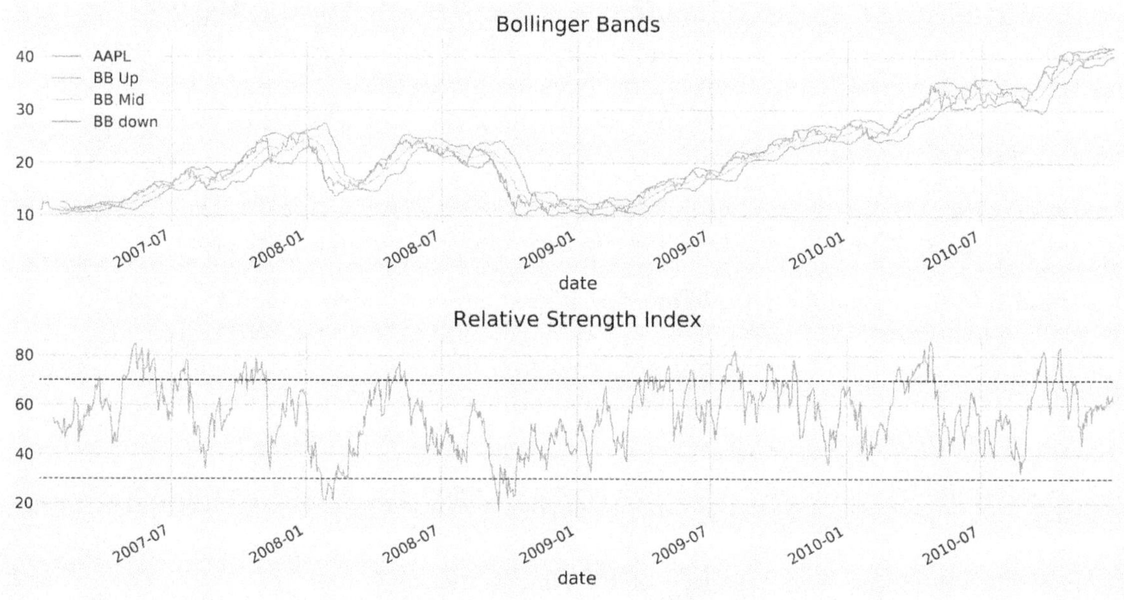

Figure 4.4: Bollinger Bands and relative strength index

Denoising alpha factors with the Kalman filter

The concept of **noise in data** relates to the domain of signal processing, which aims to retrieve the correct information from a signal sent, for example, through the air in the form of electromagnetic waves. As the waves move through space, environmental interference can be added to the originally pure signal in the form of noise, making it necessary to separate the two once received.

The Kalman filter was introduced in 1960 and has become very popular for many applications that require processing noisy data because it permits more accurate estimates of the underlying signal.

This technique is widely used to track objects in computer vision, to support the localization and navigation of aircraft and spaceships, and to control robotic motion based on noisy sensor data, besides its use in time series analysis.

Noise is used similarly in data science, finance, and other domains, implying that the raw data contains useful information, for instance, in terms of trading signals, that needs to be extracted and separated from irrelevant, extraneous information. Clearly, the fact that we do not know the true signal can make this separation rather challenging at times.

We will first review how the Kalman filter works and which assumptions it makes to achieve its objectives. Then, we will demonstrate how to apply it to financial data using the pykalman library.

How does the Kalman filter work?

The Kalman filter is a dynamic linear model of sequential data like a time series that adapts to new information as it arrives. Rather than using a fixed-size window like a moving average or a given set of weights like an exponential moving average, it incorporates new data into its estimates of the current value of the time series based on a probabilistic model.

More specifically, the Kalman filter is a probabilistic model of a sequence of observations $z_1, z_2, \ldots, z_T$ and a corresponding sequence of hidden states $x_1, x_2, \ldots, x_T$ (with the notation used by the pykalman library that we will demonstrate here). This can be represented by the following graph:

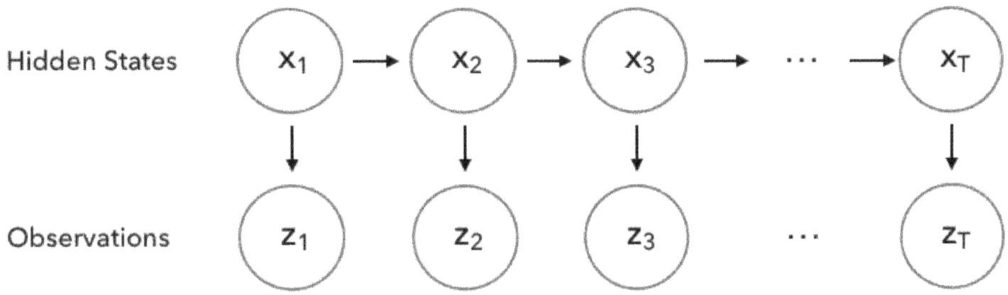

Figure 4.5: Kalman filter as a graphical model

Technically speaking, the Kalman filter takes a Bayesian approach that propagates the posterior distribution of the state variables x given their measurements z over time (see *Chapter 10, Bayesian ML – Dynamic Sharpe Ratios and Pairs Trading,* for more details on Bayesian inference). We can also view it as an unsupervised algorithm for tracking a single object in a continuous state space, where we will take the object to be, for example, the value of or returns on a security, or an alpha factor (see *Chapter 13, Data-Driven Risk Factors and Asset Allocation with Unsupervised Learning*).

To recover the hidden states from a sequence of observations that may become available in real time, the algorithm iterates between two steps:

1. **Prediction step**: Estimate the current state of the process.
2. **Measurement step**: Use noisy observations to update its estimate by averaging the information from both steps in a way that weighs more certain estimates higher.

The basic idea behind the algorithm is as follows: certain assumptions about a dynamic system and a history of corresponding measurements will allow us to estimate the system's state in a way that maximizes the probability of the previous measurements.

To achieve its objective of recovering the hidden state, the Kalman filter makes the following assumptions:

- The system that we are modeling behaves in a linear fashion.
- The hidden state process is a Markov chain so that the current hidden state x_t depends only on the most recent prior hidden state x_{t-1}.
- Measurements are subject to Gaussian, uncorrelated noise with constant covariance.

As a result, the Kalman filter is similar to a hidden Markov model, except that the state space of the latent variables is continuous, and both hidden and observed variables have normal distributions, denoted as $\mathcal{N}(\mu, \sigma)$ with mean μ and standard

In mathematical terms, the key components of the model (and corresponding parameters in the pykalman implementation) are:

- The initial hidden state has a normal distribution: $x_0 \sim \mathcal{N}(\mu_0, \Sigma_0)$ with `initial_state_mean`, μ and `initial_state_covariance`, Σ.
- The hidden state x_{t+1} is an affine transformation of x_t with `transition_matrix` A, `transition_offset` b, and added Gaussian noise with `transition_covariance` Q: $x_{t+1} = A_t x_t + b_t + \epsilon_{t+1}^1, \ \epsilon_t^1 \sim \mathcal{N}(0, Q)$.
- The observation z_t is an affine transformation of the hidden state x_t with `observation_matrix` C, `observation_offset` d, and added Gaussian noise with `observation_covariance` R: $z_t = C_t x_t + d_t + \epsilon_t^2, \ \epsilon_t^2 \sim \mathcal{N}(0, R)$.

Among the advantages of a Kalman filter is that it flexibly adapts to non-stationary data with changing distributional characteristics (see *Chapter 9, Time-Series Models for Volatility Forecasts and Statistical Arbitrage*, for more details on stationarity).

Key disadvantages are the assumptions of linearity and Gaussian noise that financial data often violate. To address these shortcomings, the Kalman filter has been extended to systems with nonlinear dynamics in the form of the extended and the unscented Kalman filters. The particle filter is an alternative approach that uses sampling-based Monte Carlo approaches to estimate non-normal distributions.

How to apply a Kalman filter using pykalman

The Kalman filter is particularly useful for rolling estimates of data values or model parameters that change over time. This is because it adapts its estimates at every time step based on new observations and tends to weigh recent observations more heavily.

Except for conventional moving averages, the Kalman filter does not require us to specify the length of a window used for the estimate. Rather, we start out with our estimate of the mean and covariance of the hidden state and let the Kalman filter correct our estimates based on periodic observations. The code examples for this section are in the notebook `kalman_filter_and_wavelets.ipynb`.

The following code example shows how to apply the Kalman filter to smoothen the S&P 500 stock price series for the 2008-09 period:

```
with pd.HDFStore(DATA_STORE) as store:
    sp500 = store['sp500/stooq'].loc['2008': '2009', 'close']
```

We initialize the `KalmanFilter` with unit covariance matrices and zero means (see the pykalman documentation for advice on dealing with the challenges of choosing appropriate initial values):

```
from pykalman import KalmanFilter
kf = KalmanFilter(transition_matrices = [1],
                  observation_matrices = [1],
                  initial_state_mean = 0,
                  initial_state_covariance = 1,
                  observation_covariance=1,
                  transition_covariance=.01)
```

Then, we run the `filter` method to trigger the forward algorithm, which iteratively estimates the hidden state, that is, the mean of the time series:

```
state_means, _ = kf.filter(sp500)
```

Finally, we add moving averages for comparison and plot the result:

```
sp500_smoothed = sp500.to_frame('close')
sp500_smoothed['Kalman Filter'] = state_means
for months in [1, 2, 3]:
    sp500_smoothed[f'MA ({months}m)'] = (sp500.rolling(window=months * 21)
                                         .mean())
ax = sp500_smoothed.plot(title='Kalman Filter vs Moving Average',
                         figsize=(14, 6), lw=1, rot=0)
```

The resulting plot in *Figure 4.6* shows that the Kalman filter performs similarly to a 1-month moving average but is more sensitive to changes in the behavior of the time series:

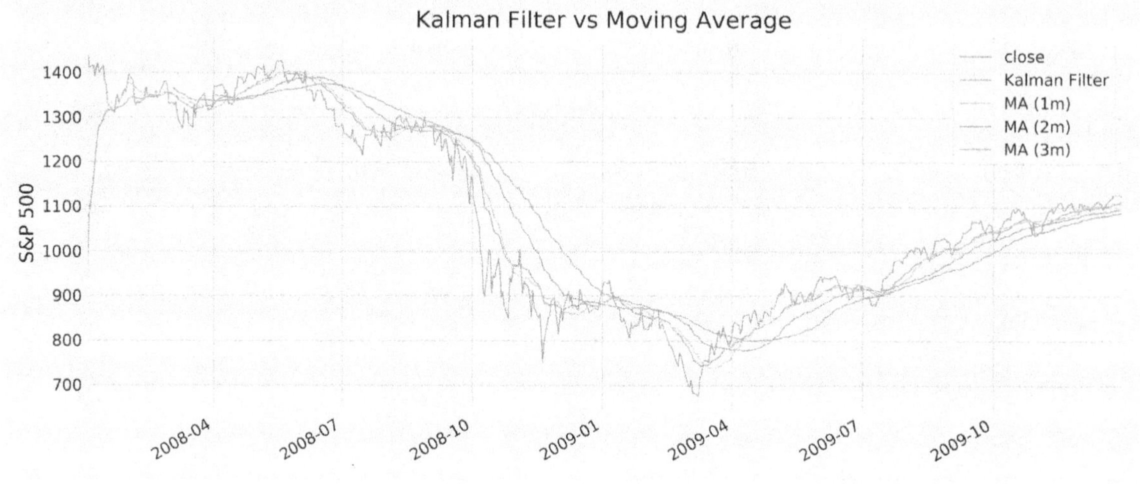

Figure 4.6: Kalman filter versus moving average

How to preprocess your noisy signals using wavelets

Wavelets are related to Fourier analysis, which combines sine and cosine waves at different frequencies to approximate noisy signals. While Fourier analysis is particularly useful to translate signals from the time to the frequency domain, wavelets are useful for filtering out specific patterns that may occur at different scales, which, in turn, may correspond to a frequency range.

Wavelets are functions or wave-like patterns that decompose a discrete or continuous-time signal into components of different scales. A wavelet transform, in turn, represents a function using wavelets as scaled and translated copies of a finite-length waveform. This transform has advantages over Fourier transforms for functions with discontinuities and sharp peaks, and to approximate non-periodic or non-stationary signals.

To denoise a signal, you can use wavelet shrinkage and thresholding methods. First, you choose a specific wavelet pattern to decompose a dataset. The wavelet transform yields coefficients that correspond to details in the dataset.

The idea of thresholding is simply to omit all coefficients below a particular cutoff, assuming that they represent minor details that are not necessary to represent the true signal. These remaining coefficients are then used in an inverse wavelet transformation to reconstruct the (denoised) dataset.

We'll now use the pywavelets library to apply wavelets to noisy stock data. The following code example illustrates how to denoise the S&P 500 returns using a forward and inverse wavelet transform with a Daubechies 6 wavelet and different threshold values.

First, we generate daily S&P 500 returns for the 2008-09 period:

```
signal = (pd.read_hdf(DATA_STORE, 'sp500/stooq')
          .loc['2008': '2009']
          .close.pct_change()
          .dropna())
```

Then, we select one of the Daubechies wavelets from the numerous built-in wavelet functions:

```
import pywt
pywt.families(short=False)
['Haar', 'Daubechies', 'Symlets', 'Coiflets', 'Biorthogonal', 'Reverse
biorthogonal', 'Discrete Meyer (FIR Approximation)', 'Gaussian', 'Mexican
hat wavelet', 'Morlet wavelet', 'Complex Gaussian wavelets', 'Shannon
wavelets', 'Frequency B-Spline wavelets', 'Complex Morlet wavelets']
```

The Daubechies 6 wavelet is defined by a scaling function ψ and the wavelet function φ itself (see the PyWavelet documentation for details and the accompanying notebook `kalman_filter_and_wavelets.ipynb` for plots of all built-in wavelet functions):

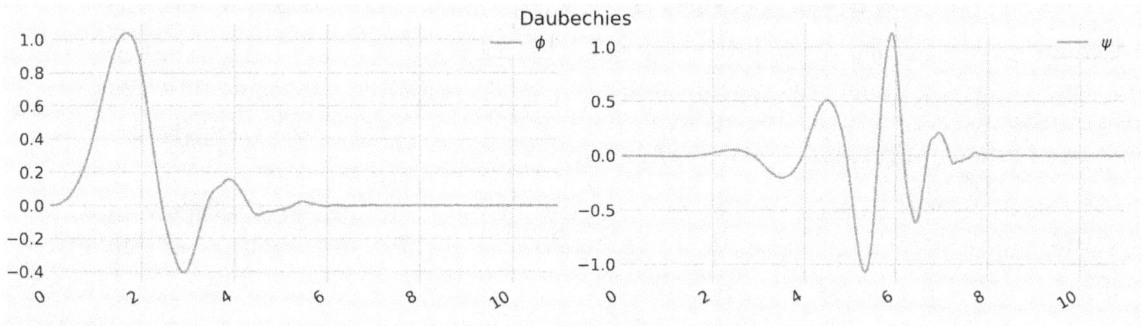

Figure 4.7: Daubechies wavelets

Given a wavelet function, we first decompose the return signal using the `.wavedec` function, which yields the coefficients for the wavelet transform. Next, we filter out all coefficients above a given threshold and then reconstruct the signal using only those coefficients using the inverse transform `.waverec`:

```
wavelet = "db6"
for i, scale in enumerate([.1, .5]):

    coefficients = pywt.wavedec(signal, wavelet, mode='per')
    coefficients[1:] = [pywt.threshold(i, value=scale*signal.max(),
mode='soft') for i in coefficients[1:]]
    reconstructed_signal = pywt.waverec(coefficients, wavelet, mode='per')
    signal.plot(color="b", alpha=0.5, label='original signal', lw=2,
                title=f'Threshold Scale: {scale:.1f}', ax=axes[i])
    pd.Series(reconstructed_signal, index=signal.index).plot(c='k',
label='DWT smoothing}', linewidth=1, ax=axes[i])
```

The notebook shows how to apply this denoising technique with different thresholds, and the resulting plot, shown in *Figure 4.8*, clearly shows how a higher threshold value yields a significantly smoother series:

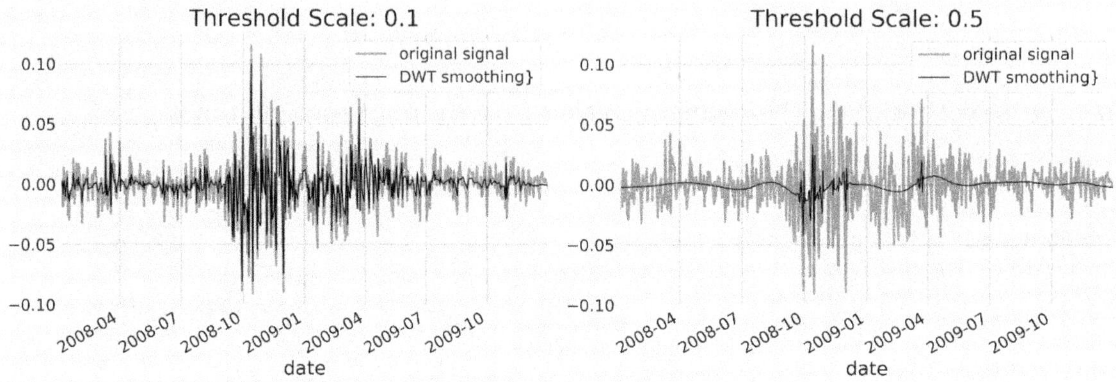

Figure 4.8: Wavelet denoising with different thresholds

From signals to trades – Zipline for backtests

The open source library Zipline is an event-driven backtesting system. It generates market events to simulate the reactions of an algorithmic trading strategy and tracks its performance. A particularly important feature is that it provides the algorithm with historical point-in-time data that avoids look-ahead bias.

The library has been popularized by the crowd-sourced quantitative investment fund Quantopian, which uses it in production to facilitate algorithm development and live-trading.

In this section, we'll provide a brief demonstration of its basic functionality. *Chapter 8, The ML4T Workflow – From Model to Strategy Backtesting*, contains a more detailed introduction to prepare us for more complex use cases.

How to backtest a single-factor strategy

You can use Zipline offline in conjunction with data bundles to research and evaluate alpha factors. When using it on the Quantopian platform, you will get access to a wider set of fundamental and alternative data. We will also demonstrate the Quantopian research environment in this chapter, and the backtesting IDE in the next chapter. The code for this section is in the `01_factor_research_evaluation` sub-directory of the GitHub repo folder for this chapter, including installation instructions and an environment tailored to Zipline's dependencies.

For installation, please see the instructions in this chapter's `README` on GitHub. After installation and before executing the first algorithm, you need to ingest a data bundle that, by default, consists of Quandl's community-maintained data on stock prices, dividends, and splits for 3,000 US publicly traded companies.

You need a Quandl API key to run the following code, which stores the data in your `home` folder under `~/.zipline/data/<bundle>`:

```
$ QUANDL_API_KEY=<yourkey> zipline ingest [-b <bundle>]
```

A single alpha factor from market data

We are first going to illustrate the Zipline alpha factor research workflow in an offline environment. In particular, we will develop and test a simple mean-reversion factor that measures how much recent performance has deviated from the historical average.

Short-term reversal is a common strategy that takes advantage of the weakly predictive pattern that stock prices are likely to revert back to a rolling mean over horizons from less than 1 minute to 1 month. See the notebook `single_factor_zipline.ipynb` for details.

To this end, the factor computes the *z*-score for the last monthly return relative to the rolling monthly returns over the last year. At this point, we will not place any orders to simply illustrate the implementation of a `CustomFactor` and record the results during the simulation.

Zipline includes numerous built-in factors for many common operations (see the *Quantopian* documentation linked on GitHub for details). While this is often convenient and sufficient, in other cases, we want to transform our available data differently. For this purpose, Zipline provides the `CustomFactor` class, which offers a lot of flexibility for us to specify a wide range of calculations. It does this using the various features available for the cross-section of securities and custom lookback periods using NumPy.

To this end, after some basic settings, `MeanReversion` subclasses `CustomFactor` and defines a `compute()` method. It creates default inputs of monthly returns over an also default year-long window so that the `monthly_return` variable will have 252 rows and one column for each security in the Quandl dataset on a given day.

The `compute_factors()` method creates a `MeanReversion` factor instance and creates long, short, and ranking pipeline columns. The former two contain Boolean values that can be used to place orders, and the latter reflects that overall ranking to evaluate the overall factor performance. Furthermore, it uses the built-in `AverageDollarVolume` factor to limit the computation to more liquid stocks:

```
from zipline.api import attach_pipeline, pipeline_output, record
from zipline.pipeline import Pipeline, CustomFactor
from zipline.pipeline.factors import Returns, AverageDollarVolume
from zipline import run_algorithm
MONTH, YEAR = 21, 252
N_LONGS = N_SHORTS = 25
VOL_SCREEN = 1000
class MeanReversion(CustomFactor):
    """Compute ratio of latest monthly return to 12m average,
       normalized by std dev of monthly returns"""
    inputs = [Returns(window_length=MONTH)]
```

```
    window_length = YEAR
    def compute(self, today, assets, out, monthly_returns):
        df = pd.DataFrame(monthly_returns)
        out[:] = df.iloc[-1].sub(df.mean()).div(df.std())

def compute_factors():
    """Create factor pipeline incl. mean reversion,
        filtered by 30d Dollar Volume; capture factor ranks"""
    mean_reversion = MeanReversion()
    dollar_volume = AverageDollarVolume(window_length=30)
    return Pipeline(columns={'longs'  : mean_reversion.bottom(N_LONGS),
                             'shorts' : mean_reversion.top(N_SHORTS),
                             'ranking':
                          mean_reversion.rank(ascending=False)},
                          screen=dollar_volume.top(VOL_SCREEN))
```

The result will allow us to place long and short orders. In the next chapter, we will learn how to build a portfolio by choosing a rebalancing period and adjusting portfolio holdings as new signals arrive.

The `initialize()` method registers the `compute_factors()` pipeline, and the `before_trading_start()` method ensures the pipeline runs on a daily basis. The `record()` function adds the pipeline's ranking column, as well as the current asset prices, to the performance DataFrame returned by the `run_algorithm()` function:

```
def initialize(context):
    """Setup: register pipeline, schedule rebalancing,
        and set trading params"""
    attach_pipeline(compute_factors(), 'factor_pipeline')
def before_trading_start(context, data):
    """Run factor pipeline"""
    context.factor_data = pipeline_output('factor_pipeline')
    record(factor_data=context.factor_data.ranking)
    assets = context.factor_data.index
    record(prices=data.current(assets, 'price'))
```

Finally, define the `start` and `end` Timestamp objects in UTC terms, set a capital base, and execute `run_algorithm()` with references to the key execution methods. The performance DataFrame contains nested data, for example, the prices column consists of a `pd.Series` for each cell. Hence, subsequent data access is easier when stored in pickle format:

```
start, end = pd.Timestamp('2015-01-01', tz='UTC'), pd.Timestamp('2018-
             01-01', tz='UTC')
capital_base = 1e7
performance = run_algorithm(start=start,
                            end=end,
                            initialize=initialize,
                            before_trading_start=before_trading_start,
                            capital_base=capital_base)
performance.to_pickle('single_factor.pickle')
```

We will use the factor and pricing data stored in the `performance` DataFrame to evaluate the factor performance for various holding periods in the next section, but first, we'll take a look at how to create more complex signals by combining several alpha factors from a diverse set of data sources on the Quantopian platform.

Built-in Quantopian factors

The accompanying notebook `factor_library_quantopian.ipynb` contains numerous example factors that are either provided by the Quantopian platform or computed from data sources available using the research API from a Jupyter Notebook.

There are built-in factors that can be used in combination with quantitative Python libraries—in particular, NumPy and pandas—to derive more complex factors from a broad range of relevant data sources such as US equity prices, Morningstar fundamentals, and investor sentiment.

For instance, the price-to-sales ratio is available as part of the Morningstar fundamentals dataset. It can be used as part of a pipeline that will be further described as we introduce the Zipline library.

Combining factors from diverse data sources

The Quantopian research environment is tailored to the rapid testing of predictive alpha factors. The process is very similar because it builds on Zipline but offers much richer access to data sources. The following code sample illustrates how to compute alpha factors not only from market data, as done previously, but also from fundamental and alternative data. See the notebook `multiple_factors_quantopian_research.ipynb` for details.

Quantopian provides several hundred Morningstar fundamental variables for free and also includes Stocktwits signals as an example of an alternative data source. There are also custom universe definitions such as `QTradableStocksUS`, which applies several filters to limit the backtest universe to stocks that were likely tradeable under realistic market conditions:

```
from quantopian.research import run_pipeline
from quantopian.pipeline import Pipeline
from quantopian.pipeline.data.builtin import USEquityPricing
from quantopian.pipeline.data.morningstar import income_statement,
    operation_ratios, balance_sheet
from quantopian.pipeline.data.psychsignal import stocktwits
from quantopian.pipeline.factors import CustomFactor,
    SimpleMovingAverage, Returns
from quantopian.pipeline.filters import QTradableStocksUS
```

We will use a custom `AggregateFundamentals` class to use the last reported fundamental data point. This aims to address the fact that fundamentals are reported quarterly, and Quantopian does not currently provide an easy way to aggregate historical data, say, to obtain the sum of the last four quarters, on a rolling basis:

```
class AggregateFundamentals(CustomFactor):
    def compute(self, today, assets, out, inputs):
        out[:] = inputs[0]
```

We will again use the custom `MeanReversion` factor from the preceding code. We will also compute several other factors for the given universe definition using the `rank()` method's `mask` parameter:

```
def compute_factors():
    universe = QTradableStocksUS()
    profitability = (AggregateFundamentals(inputs=
                     [income_statement.gross_profit],
                                          window_length=YEAR) /
                     balance_sheet.total_assets.latest).rank(mask=universe)
    roic = operation_ratios.roic.latest.rank(mask=universe)
    ebitda_yield = (AggregateFundamentals(inputs=
                              [income_statement.ebitda],
                                         window_length=YEAR) /
                    USEquityPricing.close.latest).rank(mask=universe)
    mean_reversion = MeanReversion().rank(mask=universe)
    price_momentum = Returns(window_length=QTR).rank(mask=universe)
    sentiment = SimpleMovingAverage(inputs=[stocktwits.bull_minus_bear],
                                    window_length=5).rank(mask=universe)
    factor = profitability + roic + ebitda_yield + mean_reversion +
             price_momentum + sentiment
    return Pipeline(
            columns={'Profitability'      : profitability,
                     'ROIC'                : roic,
                     'EBITDA Yield'        : ebitda_yield,
```

```
                "Mean Reversion (1M)": mean_reversion,
                'Sentiment'          : sentiment,
                "Price Momentum (3M)": price_momentum,
                'Alpha Factor'       : factor})
```

This algorithm simply averages how the six individual factors rank each asset to combine their information. This is a fairly naive method that does not account for the relative importance and incremental information each factor may provide when predicting future returns. The ML algorithms of the following chapters will allow us to do exactly this, using the same backtesting framework.

Execution also relies on `run_algorithm()`, but the `return` DataFrame on the Quantopian platform only contains the factor values created by the `Pipeline`. This is convenient because this data format can be used as input for Alphalens, the library that's used for the evaluation of the predictive performance of alpha factors.

> **Using TA-Lib with Zipline**
>
> The TA-Lib library includes numerous technical factors. A Python implementation is available for local use, for example, with Zipline and Alphalens, and it is also available on the Quantopian platform. The notebook also illustrates several technical indicators available using TA-Lib.

Separating signal from noise with Alphalens

Quantopian has open sourced the Python Alphalens library for the performance analysis of predictive stock factors. It integrates well with the Zipline backtesting library and the portfolio performance and risk analysis library pyfolio, which we will explore in the next chapter.

Alphalens facilitates the analysis of the predictive power of alpha factors concerning the:

- Correlation of the signals with subsequent returns
- Profitability of an equal or factor-weighted portfolio based on a (subset of) the signals
- Turnover of factors to indicate the potential trading costs
- Factor performance during specific events
- Breakdowns of the preceding by sector

The analysis can be conducted using tearsheets or individual computations and plots. The tearsheets are illustrated in the online repository to save some space.

Creating forward returns and factor quantiles

To utilize Alphalens, we need to provide two inputs:

- Signals for a universe of assets, like those returned by the ranks of the `MeanReversion` factor
- The forward returns that we would earn by investing in an asset for a given holding period

See the notebook `06_performance_eval_alphalens.ipynb` for details.

We will recover the prices from the `single_factor.pickle` file as follows (and proceed in the same way for `factor_data`; see the notebook):

```
performance = pd.read_pickle('single_factor.pickle')
prices = pd.concat([df.to_frame(d) for d, df in performance.prices.
items()],axis=1).T
prices.columns = [re.findall(r"\[(.+)\]", str(col))[0] for col in
                  prices.columns]
prices.index = prices.index.normalize()
prices.info()
<class 'pandas.core.frame.DataFrame'>
DatetimeIndex: 755 entries, 2015-01-02 to 2017-12-29
Columns: 1661 entries, A to ZTS
dtypes: float64(1661)
```

We can generate the Alphalens input data, namely the factor signal and forward returns described previously, in the required format from the Zipline output using the `get_clean_factor_and_forward_returns` utility function. This function returns the signal quintiles and the forward returns for the given holding periods:

```
HOLDING_PERIODS = (5, 10, 21, 42)
QUANTILES = 5
alphalens_data = get_clean_factor_and_forward_returns(factor=factor_data,
                                          prices=prices,
                                          periods=HOLDING_PERIODS,
                                          quantiles=QUANTILES)
Dropped 14.5% entries from factor data: 14.5% in forward returns computation
and 0.0% in binning phase (set max_loss=0 to see potentially suppressed
Exceptions). max_loss is 35.0%, not exceeded: OK!
```

The `alphalens_data` DataFrame contains the returns on an investment in the given asset on a given date for the indicated holding period, as well as the factor value—that is, the asset's `MeanReversion` ranking on that date and the corresponding quantile value:

date	asset	5D	10D	21D	42D	factor	factor_quantile
1/2/2015	A	-1.87%	-1.11%	-4.61%	5.28%	2618	4
	AAL	-0.06%	-8.03%	-9.63%	-10.39%	1088	2
	AAP	-1.32%	0.23%	-1.63%	-2.39%	791	1
	AAPL	-2.82%	-0.07%	8.51%	18.07%	2917	5
	ABBV	-1.88%	-0.20%	-7.88%	-8.24%	2952	5

The forward returns and the signal quantiles are the basis for evaluating the predictive power of the signal. Typically, a factor should deliver markedly different returns for distinct quantiles, such as negative returns for the bottom quintile of the factor values and positive returns for the top quantile.

Predictive performance by factor quantiles

As a first step, we would like to visualize the average period return by factor quantile. We can use the built-in function `mean_return_by_quantile` from the performance module and `plot_quantile_returns_bar` from the plotting module:

```
from alphalens.performance import mean_return_by_quantile
from alphalens.plotting import plot_quantile_returns_bar
mean_return_by_q, std_err = mean_return_by_quantile(alphalens_data)
plot_quantile_returns_bar(mean_return_by_q);
```

The result is a bar chart that breaks down the mean of the forward returns for the four different holding periods based on the quintile of the factor signal.

As you can see in *Figure 4.9*, the bottom quintiles yielded markedly more negative results than the top quintiles, except for the longest holding period:

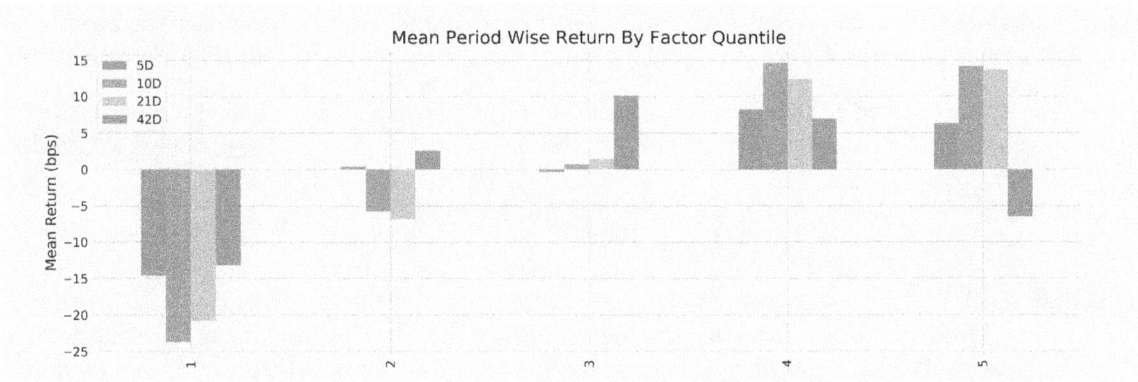

Figure 4.9: Mean period return by factor quantile

The **10D** holding period provides slightly better results for the first and fourth quartiles on average across the trading period.

We would also like to see the performance over time of investments driven by each of the signal quintiles. To this end, we calculate daily as opposed to average returns for the **5D** holding period. Alphalens adjusts the period returns to account for the mismatch between daily signals and a longer holding period (for details, see the Alphalens documentation):

```
from alphalens.plotting import plot_cumulative_returns_by_quantile
mean_return_by_q_daily, std_err =
     mean_return_by_quantile(alphalens_data, by_date=True)
plot_cumulative_returns_by_quantile(mean_return_by_q_daily['5D'],
     period='5D');
```

The resulting line plot in *Figure 4.10* shows that, for most of this 3-year period, the top two quintiles significantly outperformed the bottom two quintiles. However, as suggested by the previous plot, the signals by the fourth quintile produced slightly better performance than those by the top quintile due to their relative performance during 2017:

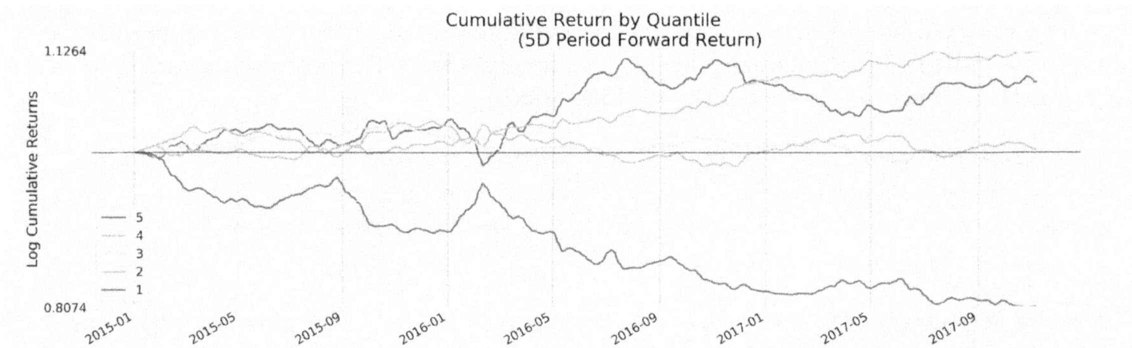

Figure 4.10: Cumulative return by quantile for a 5-day holding period

A factor that is useful for a trading strategy shows the preceding pattern, where cumulative returns develop along clearly distinct paths, because this allows for a long-short strategy with lower capital requirements and, correspondingly, lower exposure to the overall market.

However, we also need to take the dispersion of period returns into account, rather than just the averages. To this end, we can rely on the built-in `plot_quantile_returns_violin`:

```
from alphalens.plotting import plot_quantile_returns_violin
plot_quantile_returns_violin(mean_return_by_q_daily);
```

This distributional plot, shown in *Figure 4.11*, highlights that the range of daily returns is fairly wide. Despite different means, the separation of the distributions is very limited so that, on any given day, the differences in performance between the different quintiles may be rather limited:

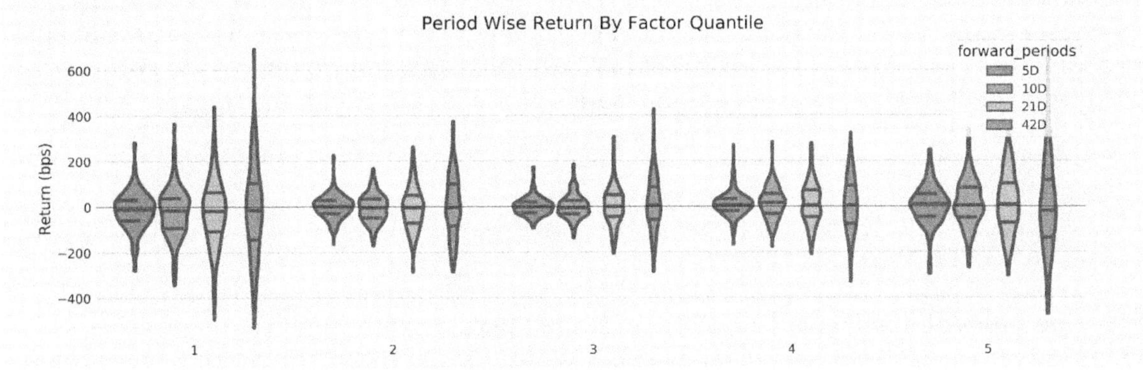

Figure 4.11: Distribution of the period-wise return by factor quintile

While we focus on the evaluation of a single alpha factor, we are simplifying things by ignoring practical issues related to trade execution that we will relax when we address proper backtesting in the next chapter. Some of these include:

- The transaction costs of trading
- Slippage, or the difference between the price at decision and trade execution, for example, due to the market impact

The information coefficient

Most of this book is about the design of alpha factors using ML models. ML is about optimizing some predictive objective, and in this section, we will introduce the key metrics used to measure the performance of an alpha factor. We will define **alpha** as *the average return in excess of a benchmark.*

This leads to the **information ratio (IR)**, which measures the average excess return per unit of risk taken by dividing alpha by the tracking risk. When the benchmark is the risk-free rate, the IR corresponds to the well-known Sharpe ratio, and we will highlight crucial statistical measurement issues that arise in the typical case when returns are not normally distributed. We will also explain the fundamental law of active management, which breaks the IR down into a combination of forecasting skill and a strategy's ability to effectively leverage these forecasting skills.

The goal of alpha factors is the accurate directional prediction of future returns. Hence, a natural performance measure is the correlation between an alpha factor's predictions and the forward returns of the target assets.

It is better to use the non-parametric Spearman rank correlation coefficient, which measures how well the relationship between two variables can be described using a monotonic function, as opposed to the Pearson correlation, which measures the strength of a linear relationship.

We can obtain the **information coefficient** (**IC**) using Alphalens, which relies on `scipy.stats.spearmanr` under the hood (see the repo for an example of how to use `scipy` directly to obtain *p*-values). The `factor_information_coefficient` function computes the period-wise correlation and `plot_ic_ts` creates a time-series plot with a 1-month moving average:

```
from alphalens.performance import factor_information_coefficient
from alphalens.plotting import plot_ic_ts
ic = factor_information_coefficient(alphalens_data)
plot_ic_ts(ic[['5D']])
```

The time series plot in *Figure 4.12* shows extended periods with significantly positive moving average IC. An IC of 0.05 or even 0.1 allows for significant outperformance if there are sufficient opportunities to apply this forecasting skill, as the fundamental law of active management will illustrate:

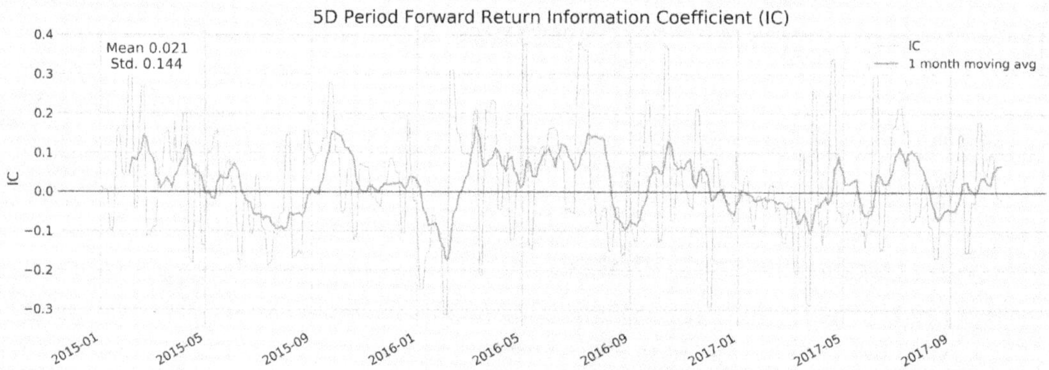

Figure 4.12: Moving average of the IC for 5-day horizon

A plot of the annual mean IC highlights how the factor's performance was historically uneven:

```
ic = factor_information_coefficient(alphalens_data)
ic_by_year = ic.resample('A').mean()
ic_by_year.index = ic_by_year.index.year
ic_by_year.plot.bar(figsize=(14, 6))
```

This produces the chart shown in *Figure 4.13*:

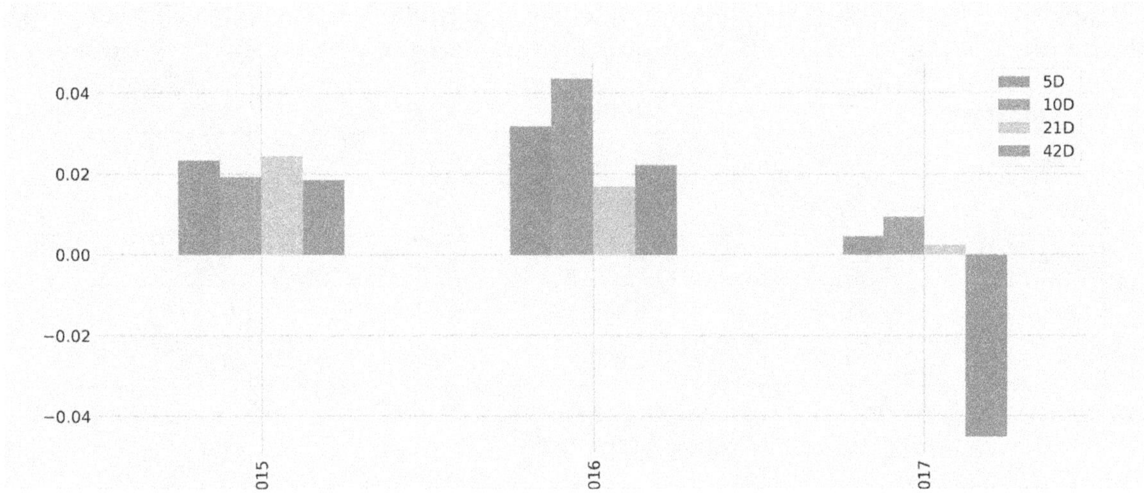

Figure 4.13: IC by year

An information coefficient below 0.05, as in this case, is low but significant and can produce positive residual returns relative to a benchmark, as we will see in the next section. The command `create_summary_tear_sheet(alphalens_data)` creates IC summary statistics.

The risk-adjusted IC results from dividing the mean IC by the standard deviation of the IC, which is also subjected to a two-sided *t*-test with the null hypothesis *IC = 0* using `scipy.stats.ttest_1samp`:

	5D	10D	21D	42D
IC mean	0.021	0.025	0.015	0.001
IC std.	0.144	0.13	0.12	0.12
Risk-adjusted IC	0.145	0.191	0.127	0.01
t-stat (IC)	3.861	5.107	3.396	0.266
p-value (IC)	0	0	0.001	0.79
IC skew	0.384	0.251	0.115	0.134
IC kurtosis	0.019	-0.584	-0.353	-0.494

Factor turnover

Factor turnover measures how frequently the assets associated with a given quantile change, that is, how many trades are required to adjust a portfolio to the sequence of signals. More specifically, it measures the share of assets currently in a factor quantile that was not in that quantile in the last period. The following table is produced by this command:

```
create_turnover_tear_sheet(alphalens_data)
```

The share of assets that were to join a quintile-based portfolio is fairly high, suggesting that the trading costs pose a challenge to reaping the benefits from the predictive performance:

Mean turnover	5D	10D	21D	42D
Quantile 1	0.587	0.826	0.828	0.41
Quantile 2	0.737	0.801	0.81	0.644
Quantile 3	0.764	0.803	0.808	0.679
Quantile 4	0.737	0.803	0.808	0.641
Quantile 5	0.565	0.802	0.809	0.393

An alternative view on factor turnover is the correlation of the asset rank due to the factor over various holding periods, also part of the tear sheet:

	5D	10D	21D	42D
Mean factor rank autocorrelation	0.713	0.454	-0.011	-0.016

Generally, more stability is preferable to keep trading costs manageable.

Alpha factor resources

The research process requires designing and selecting alpha factors with respect to the predictive power of their signals. An algorithmic trading strategy will typically build on multiple alpha factors that send signals for each asset. These factors may be aggregated using an ML model to optimize how the various signals translate into decisions about the timing and sizing of individual positions, as we will see in subsequent chapters.

Alternative algorithmic trading libraries

Additional open source Python libraries for algorithmic trading and data collection include the following (see GitHub for links):

- **QuantConnect** is a competitor to Quantopian.
- **WorldQuant** offers online competition and recruits community contributors to a crowd-sourced hedge fund.
- **Alpha Trading Labs** offers an s high-frequency focused testing infrastructure with a business model similar to Quantopian.
- The **Python Algorithmic Trading Library** (**PyAlgoTrade**) focuses on backtesting and offers support for paper trading and live trading. It allows you to evaluate an idea for a trading strategy with historical data and aims to do so with minimal effort.

- **pybacktest** is a vectorized backtesting framework that uses pandas and aims to be compact, simple, and fast. (The project is currently on hold.)
- **ultrafinance** is an older project that combines real-time financial data collection and the analysis and backtesting of trading strategies.
- **Trading with Python** offers courses and a collection of functions and classes for quantitative trading.
- **Interactive Brokers** offers a Python API for live trading on their platform.

Summary

In this chapter, we introduced a range of alpha factors that have been used by professional investors to design and evaluate strategies for decades. We laid out how they work and illustrated some of the economic mechanisms believed to drive their performance. We did this because a solid understanding of how factors produce excess returns helps innovate new factors.

We also presented several tools that you can use to generate your own factors from various data sources and demonstrated how the Kalman filter and wavelets allow us to smoothen noisy data in the hope of retrieving a clearer signal.

Finally, we provided a glimpse of the Zipline library for the event-driven simulation of a trading algorithm, both offline and on the Quantopian online platform. You saw how to implement a simple mean reversion factor and how to combine multiple factors in a simple way to drive a basic strategy. We also looked at the Alphalens library, which permits the evaluation of the predictive performance and trading turnover of signals.

The portfolio construction process, in turn, takes a broader perspective and is aims at the optimal sizing of positions from a risk and return perspective. In the next chapter, *Portfolio Optimization and Strategy Evaluation*, we will turn to various strategies to balance risk and returns in a portfolio process. We will also look in more detail at the challenges of backtesting trading strategies on a limited set of historical data, as well as how to address these challenges.

5

Portfolio Optimization and Performance Evaluation

Alpha factors generate signals that an algorithmic strategy translates into trades, which, in turn, produce long and short positions. The returns and risk of the resulting portfolio determine the success of the strategy.

To test a strategy prior to implementation under market conditions, we need to simulate the trades that the algorithm would make and verify their performance. Strategy evaluation includes backtesting against historical data to optimize the strategy's parameters and forward-testing to validate the in-sample performance against new, out-of-sample data. The goal is to avoid false discoveries from tailoring a strategy to specific past circumstances.

In a portfolio context, positive asset returns can offset negative price movements. Positive price changes for one asset are more likely to offset losses on another, the lower the correlation between the two positions is. Based on how portfolio risk depends on the positions' covariance, Harry Markowitz developed the theory behind modern portfolio management based on diversification in 1952. The result is mean-variance optimization, which selects weights for a given set of assets to minimize risk, measured as the standard deviation of returns for a given expected return.

The **capital asset pricing model** (**CAPM**) introduces a risk premium, measured as the expected return in excess of a risk-free investment, as an equilibrium reward for holding an asset. This reward compensates for the exposure to a single risk factor—the market—that is systematic as opposed to idiosyncratic to the asset and thus cannot be diversified away.

Risk management has evolved to become more sophisticated as additional risk factors and more granular choices for exposure have emerged. The Kelly criterion is a popular approach to dynamic portfolio optimization, which is the choice of a sequence of positions over time; it was famously adapted from its original application in gambling to the stock market by Edward Thorp in 1968.

As a result, there are several approaches to optimize portfolios, including the application of **machine learning** (**ML**) to learn hierarchical relationships among assets, and to treat their holdings as complements or substitutes with respect to the portfolio risk profile.

In this chapter, we will cover the following topics:

- How to measure portfolio risk and return
- Managing portfolio weights using mean-variance optimization and alternatives
- Using machine learning to optimize asset allocation in a portfolio context
- Simulating trades and create a portfolio based on alpha factors using Zipline
- How to evaluate portfolio performance using pyfolio

> You can find the code samples for this chapter and links to additional resources in the corresponding directory of the GitHub repository. The notebooks include color versions of the images..

How to measure portfolio performance

To evaluate and compare different strategies or to improve an existing strategy, we need metrics that reflect their performance with respect to our objectives. In investment and trading, the most common objectives are the return and the risk of the investment portfolio.

Typically, these metrics are compared to a benchmark that represents alternative investment opportunities, such as a summary of the investment universe like the S&P 500 for US equities or the risk-free interest rate for fixed income assets.

There are several metrics to evaluate these objectives. In this section, we will review the most common measures for comparing portfolio results. These measures will be useful when we look at different approaches to optimize portfolio performance, simulate the interaction of a strategy with the market using Zipline, and compute relevant performance metrics using the pyfolio library in later sections.

We'll use some simple notation: let R be the time series of one-period simple portfolio returns, $R=(r_1, ..., r_T)$, from dates 1 to T, and $R^f=(r^f_1, ..., r^f_T)$ be the matching time series of risk-free rates, so that $R_e=R-R_f=(r_1-r^f_1,..., r_T-r^f_T)$ is the excess return.

Capturing risk-return trade-offs in a single number

The return and risk objectives imply a trade-off: taking more risk may yield higher returns in some circumstances, but also implies greater downside. To compare how different strategies navigate this trade-off, ratios that compute a measure of return per unit of risk are very popular. We'll discuss the Sharpe ratio and the information ratio in turn.

The Sharpe ratio

The ex ante **Sharpe ratio** (**SR**) compares the portfolio's expected excess return to the volatility of this excess return, measured by its standard deviation. It measures the compensation as the average excess return per unit of risk taken:

$$\mu \equiv E(R_t)$$
$$\sigma_{R^e}^2 \equiv \text{Var}(R - R^f)$$
$$\text{SR} \equiv \frac{\mu - R_f}{\sigma_{R^e}}$$

Expected returns and volatilities are not observable, but can be estimated as follows from historical data:

$$\hat{\mu}_{R^e} = \frac{1}{T}\sum_{t=1}^{T} r_t^e$$
$$\hat{\sigma}_{R^e}^2 = \frac{1}{T}\sum_{t=1}^{T}(r_t^e - \hat{\mu}_{R^e})^2$$
$$\text{SR} \equiv \frac{\hat{\mu}_{R^e} - R_f}{\hat{\sigma}_{R^e}^2}$$

Unless the risk-free rate is volatile (as in emerging markets), the standard deviation of excess and raw returns will be similar.

For **independently and identically distributed** (**IID**) returns, the distribution of the SR estimator for tests of statistical significance follows from the application of the **central limit theorem** (**CLT**), according to large-sample statistical theory, to $\hat{\mu}$ and $\hat{\sigma}^2$. The CLT implies that sums of IID random variables like $\hat{\mu}$ and $\hat{\sigma}^2$ converge to the normal distribution.

When you need to compare SR for different frequencies, say for monthly and annual data, you can multiply the higher frequency SR by the square root of the number of the corresponding period contained in the lower frequency. To convert a monthly SR into an annual SR, multiply by $\sqrt{12}$, and from daily to monthly multiply by $\sqrt{12}$.

However, financial returns often violate the IID assumption. Andrew Lo has derived the necessary adjustments to the distribution and the time aggregation for returns that are stationary but autocorrelated. This is important because the time-series properties of investment strategies (for example, mean reversion, momentum, and other forms of serial correlation) can have a non-trivial impact on the SR estimator itself, especially when annualizing the SR from higher-frequency data (Lo, 2002).

The information ratio

The **information ratio** (**IR**) is similar to the Sharpe ratio but uses a benchmark rather than the risk-free rate. The benchmark is usually chosen to represent the available investment universe such as the S&P 500 for a portfolio on large-cap US equities.

Hence, the IR measures the excess return of the portfolio, also called alpha, relative to the tracking error, which is the deviation of the portfolio returns from the benchmark returns, that is:

$$\text{IR} = \frac{\text{Alpha}}{\text{Tracking Error}}$$

The IR has also been used to explain how excess returns depend on a manager's skill and the nature of her strategy, as we will see next.

The fundamental law of active management

> *"Diversification is protection against ignorance. It makes little sense if you know what you are doing."*
>
> *– Warren Buffet*

It's a curious fact that **Renaissance Technologies** (**RenTec**), the top-performing quant fund founded by Jim Simons, which we mentioned in *Chapter 1, Machine Learning for Trading – From Idea to Execution*, has produced similar returns as Warren Buffet, despite extremely different approaches. Warren Buffet's investment firm Berkshire Hathaway holds some 100-150 stocks for fairly long periods, whereas RenTec may execute 100,000 trades per day. How can we compare these distinct strategies?

A high IR reflects an attractive out-performance of the benchmark relative to the additional risk taken. The **Fundamental Law of Active Management** explains how such a result can be achieved: it approximates the IR as the product of the **information coefficient** (**IC**) and the breadth of the strategy.

As discussed in the previous chapter, the IC measures the rank correlation between return forecasts, like those implied by an alpha factor, and the actual forward returns. Hence, it is a measure of the forecasting skill of the manager. The breadth of the strategy is measured by the independent number of bets (that is, trades) an investor makes in a given time period, and thus represents the ability to apply the forecasting skills.

The Fundamental Law states that the IR, also known as the **appraisal risk** (Treynor and Black), is the product of both values. In other words, it summarizes the importance to play both often (high breadth) and to play well (high IC):

$$\text{IR} \sim \text{IC} * \sqrt{\text{breadth}}$$

This framework has been extended to include the **transfer coefficient** (**TC**) to reflect portfolio constraints as an additional factor (for example, on short-selling) that may limit the information ratio below a level otherwise achievable given IC or strategy breadth. The TC proxies the efficiency with which the manager translates insights into portfolio bets: if there are no constraints, the TC would simply equal one; but if the manager does not short stocks even though forecasts suggests they should, the TC will be less than one and reduce the IC (Clarke et al., 2002).

The Fundamental Law is important because it highlights the key drivers of outperformance: both accurate predictions and the ability to make independent forecasts and act on these forecasts matter.

In practice, managers with a broad set of investment decisions can achieve significant risk-adjusted excess returns with information coefficients between 0.05 and 0.15, as illustrated by the following simulation:

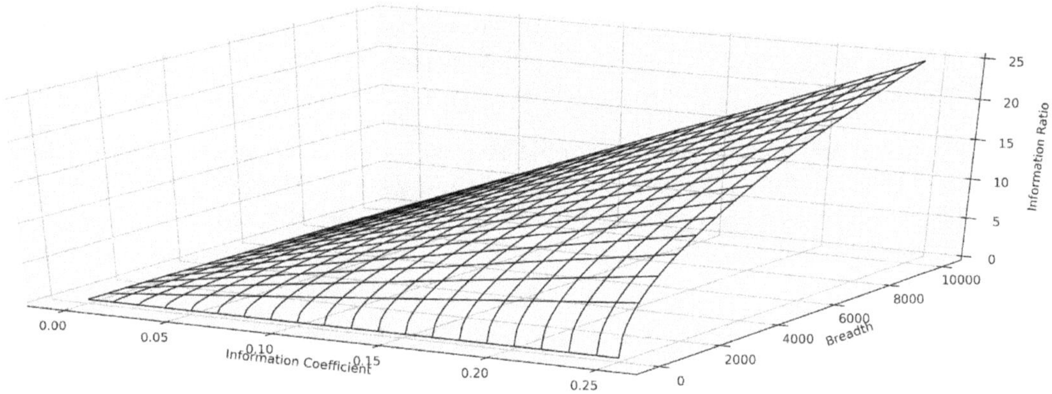

Figure 5.1: Information ratios for different values of breadth and information coefficient

In practice, estimating the breadth of a strategy is difficult, given the cross-sectional and time-series correlation among forecasts. You should view the Fundamental Law and its extensions as a useful analytical framework for thinking about how to improve your risk-adjusted portfolio performance. We'll look at techniques for doing so in practice next.

How to manage portfolio risk and return

Portfolio management aims to pick and size positions in financial instruments that achieve the desired risk-return trade-off regarding a benchmark. As a portfolio manager, in each period, you select positions that optimize diversification to reduce risks while achieving a target return. Across periods, these positions may require rebalancing to account for changes in weights resulting from price movements to achieve or maintain a target risk profile.

The evolution of modern portfolio management

Diversification permits us to reduce risks for a given expected return by exploiting how imperfect correlation allows for one asset's gains to make up for another asset's losses. Harry Markowitz invented **modern portfolio theory** (**MPT**) in 1952 and provided the mathematical tools to optimize diversification by choosing appropriate portfolio weights.

Markowitz showed how portfolio risk, measured as the standard deviation of portfolio returns, depends on the covariance among the returns of all assets and their relative weights. This relationship implies the existence of an **efficient frontier** of portfolios that maximizes portfolio returns given a maximal level of portfolio risk.

However, mean-variance frontiers are highly sensitive to the estimates of the inputs required for their calculation, namely expected returns, volatilities, and correlations. In practice, mean-variance portfolios that constrain these inputs to reduce sampling errors have performed much better. These constrained special cases include equal-weighted, minimum-variance, and risk-parity portfolios.

The **capital asset pricing model** (**CAPM**) is an asset valuation model that builds on the MPT risk-return relationship. It introduces the concept of a risk premium that an investor can expect in market equilibrium for holding a risky asset; the premium compensates for the time value of money and the exposure to overall market risk that cannot be eliminated through diversification (as opposed to the idiosyncratic risk of specific assets).

The economic rationale for **non-diversifiable risk** includes, for example, macro drivers of the business risks affecting all equity returns or bond defaults. Hence, an asset's expected return, $E[r_i]$, is the sum of the risk-free interest rate, r_f, and a risk premium proportional to the asset's exposure to the expected excess return of the market portfolio, r_m, over the risk-free rate:

$$E[r_i] = \alpha_i + r_f + \beta_i(E[r_m] - r_f)$$

In theory, the **market portfolio** contains all investable assets and, in equilibrium, will be held by all rational investors. In practice, a broad value-weighted index approximates the market, for example, the S&P 500 for US equity investments.

β_i measures the exposure of asset, i, to the excess returns of the market portfolio. If the CAPM is valid, the intercept component, α_i, should be zero. In reality, the CAPM assumptions are often not met, and alpha captures the returns left unexplained by exposure to the broad market.

As discussed in the previous chapter, over time, research uncovered **non-traditional sources of risk premiums**, such as the momentum or the equity value effects that explained some of the original alpha. Economic rationales, such as behavioral biases of under- or overreaction by investors to new information, justify risk premiums for exposure to these alternative risk factors.

These factors evolved into investment styles designed to capture these **alternative betas** that became tradable in the form of specialized index funds. Similarly, risk management now aims to control the exposure of numerous sources of risk beyond the market portfolio.

After isolating contributions from these alternative risk premiums, true alpha becomes limited to idiosyncratic asset returns and the manager's ability to time risk exposures.

The **efficient market hypothesis** (**EMH**) has been refined over the past several decades to rectify many of the original shortcomings of the CAPM, including imperfect information and the costs associated with transactions, financing, and agency. Many behavioral biases have the same effect, and some frictions are modeled as behavioral biases.

Modern portfolio theory and practice have evolved significantly over the last several decades. We will introduce several approaches:

- Mean-variance optimization, and its shortcomings
- Alternatives such as minimum-risk and $1/n$ allocation
- Risk parity approaches
- Risk factor approaches

Mean-variance optimization

Modern portfolio theory solves for the optimal portfolio weights to minimize volatility for a given expected return or maximize returns for a given level of volatility. The key requisite inputs are expected asset returns, standard deviations, and the covariance matrix.

How it works

Diversification works because the variance of portfolio returns depends on the covariance of the assets. It can be reduced below the weighted average of the asset variances by including assets with less than perfect correlation.

In particular, given a vector, ω, of portfolio weights and the covariance matrix, Σ, the portfolio variance, σ_{PF}, is defined as:

$$\sigma_{\text{PF}} = \omega^T \Sigma \omega$$

Markowitz showed that the problem of maximizing the expected portfolio return subject to a target risk has an equivalent dual representation of minimizing portfolio risk, subject to a target expected return level, μ_{PF}. Hence, the optimization problem becomes:

$$\begin{aligned} \min_{\omega} \quad & \sigma_{\text{PF}}^2 = \omega^T \Sigma \omega \\ \text{s.t.} \quad & \omega^T \mu = \sigma_{\text{PF}} \\ & \|\omega\| = 1 \end{aligned}$$

Finding the efficient frontier in Python

We can calculate an efficient frontier using `scipy.optimize.minimize` and the historical estimates for asset returns, standard deviations, and the covariance matrix. SciPy 's `minimize` function implements a range of constrained and unconstrained optimization algorithms for scalar functions that output a single number from one or more input variables (see the SciPy documentation for more details). The code can be found in the `strategy_evaluation` subfolder of the repository for this chapter and implements the following sequence of steps:

First, the simulation generates random weights using the Dirichlet distribution and computes the mean, standard deviation, and SR for each sample portfolio using the historical return data:

```
def simulate_portfolios(mean_ret, cov, rf_rate=rf_rate, short=True):
    alpha = np.full(shape=n_assets, fill_value=.05)
    weights = dirichlet(alpha=alpha, size=NUM_PF)
    if short:
        weights *= choice([-1, 1], size=weights.shape)

    returns = weights @ mean_ret.values + 1
    returns = returns ** periods_per_year - 1
    std = (weights @ monthly_returns.T).std(1)
    std *= np.sqrt(periods_per_year)
    sharpe = (returns - rf_rate) / std
    return pd.DataFrame({'Annualized Standard Deviation': std,
                         'Annualized Returns': returns,
                         'Sharpe Ratio': sharpe}), weights
```

Next, we set up the quadratic optimization problem to solve for the minimum standard deviation for a given return or the maximum SR. To this end, we define the functions that measure the key performance metrics:

```
def portfolio_std(wt, rt=None, cov=None):
    """Annualized PF standard deviation"""
    return np.sqrt(wt @ cov @ wt * periods_per_year)

def portfolio_returns(wt, rt=None, cov=None):
    """Annualized PF returns"""
    return (wt @ rt + 1) ** periods_per_year - 1

def portfolio_performance(wt, rt, cov):
    """Annualized PF returns & standard deviation"""
    r = portfolio_returns(wt, rt=rt)
    sd = portfolio_std(wt, cov=cov)
    return r, sd
```

Next, we define a target function that represents the negative SR for scipy's `minimize` function to optimize, given the constraints that the weights are bounded by, [0, 1], and sum to one in absolute terms:

```
def neg_sharpe_ratio(weights, mean_ret, cov):
    r, sd = portfolio_performance(weights, mean_ret, cov)
    return -(r - rf_rate) / sd

weight_constraint = {'type': 'eq',
                     'fun': lambda x: np.sum(np.abs(x)) - 1}

def max_sharpe_ratio(mean_ret, cov, short=False):
    return minimize(fun=neg_sharpe_ratio,
                    x0=x0,
                    args=(mean_ret, cov),
                    method='SLSQP',
                    bounds=((-1 if short else 0, 1),) * n_assets,
                    constraints=weight_constraint,
                    options={'tol':1e-10, 'maxiter':1e4})
```

Then, we compute the efficient frontier by iterating over a range of target returns and solving for the corresponding minimum variance portfolios. To this end, we formulate the optimization problem using the constraints on portfolio risk and return as a function of the weights, as follows:

```
def min_vol_target(mean_ret, cov, target, short=False):
    def ret_(wt):
        return portfolio_returns(wt, mean_ret)
    constraints = [{'type': 'eq', 'fun': lambda x: ret_(x) - target},
                    weight_constraint]
    bounds = ((-1 if short else 0, 1),) * n_assets
    return minimize(portfolio_std, x0=x0, args=(mean_ret, cov),
                    method='SLSQP', bounds=bounds,
                    constraints=constraints,
                    options={'tol': 1e-10, 'maxiter': 1e4})
```

The solution requires iterating over ranges of acceptable values to identify optimal risk-return combinations:

```
def efficient_frontier(mean_ret, cov, ret_range):
    return [min_vol_target(mean_ret, cov, ret) for ret in ret_range]
```

The simulation yields a subset of the feasible portfolios, and the efficient frontier identifies the optimal in-sample return-risk combinations that were achievable given historic data.

Figure 5.2 shows the result, including the minimum variance portfolio, the portfolio that maximizes the SR, and several portfolios produced by alternative optimization strategies that we'll discuss in the following sections:

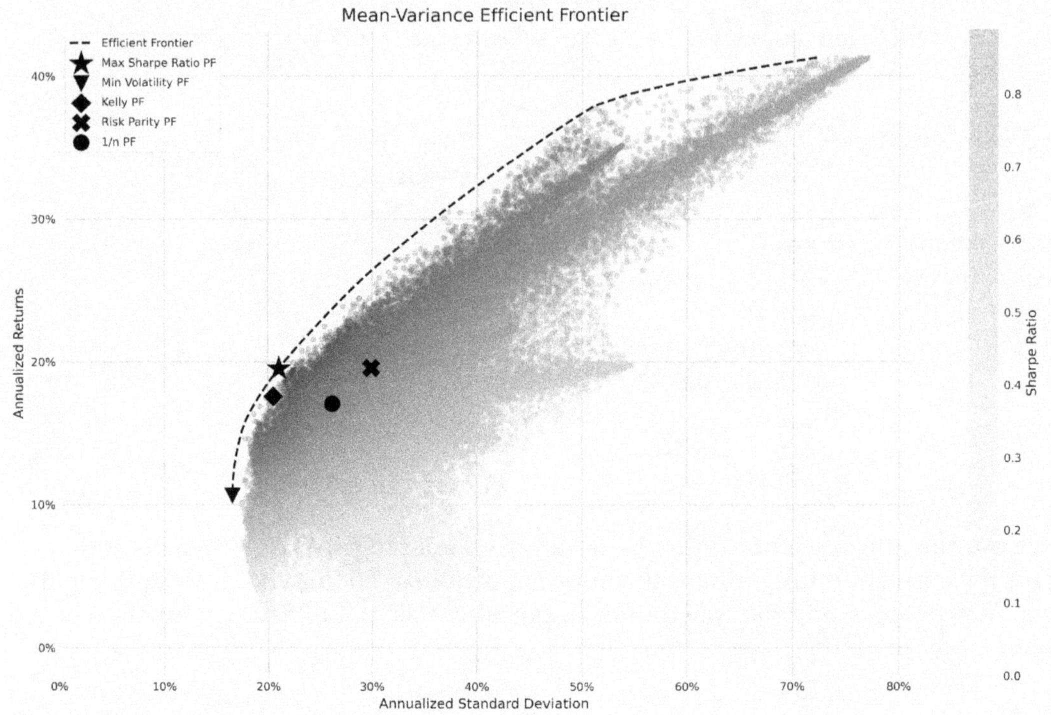

Figure 5.2: The efficient frontier and different optimized portfolios

The portfolio optimization can be run at every evaluation step of the trading strategy to optimize the positions.

Challenges and shortcomings

The preceding mean-variance frontier estimation illustrates **in-sample**, that is, **backward-looking** optimization. In practice, portfolio optimization requires forward-looking inputs and outputs. However, expected returns are notoriously difficult to estimate accurately. It is best viewed as a starting point and benchmark for numerous improvements.

The covariance matrix can be estimated somewhat more reliably, which has given rise to several alternative approaches. However, covariance matrices with correlated assets pose computational challenges since the optimization problem requires inverting the matrix. The high condition number induces numerical instability, which in turn gives rise to the **Markovitz curse**: the more diversification is required (by correlated investment opportunities), the more unreliable the weights produced by the algorithm.

Many investors prefer to use portfolio-optimization techniques with less onerous input requirements. We will now introduce several alternatives that aim to address these shortcomings, including a more recent approach based on machine learning.

Alternatives to mean-variance optimization

The challenges with accurate inputs for the mean-variance optimization problem have led to the adoption of several practical alternatives that constrain the mean, the variance, or both, or omit return estimates that are more challenging, such as the risk parity approach, which we'll discuss later in this section.

The 1/N portfolio

Simple portfolios provide useful benchmarks to gauge the added value of complex models that generate the risk of overfitting. The simplest strategy—an **equally-weighted portfolio**—has been shown to be one of the best performers.

Famously, de Miguel, Garlappi, and Uppal (2009) compared the out-of-sample performance of portfolios produced by various mean-variance optimizers, including robust Bayesian estimators, portfolio constraints, and optimal combinations of portfolios, to the simple 1/N rule. They found that the 1/N portfolio produced a higher Sharpe ratio than the alternatives on various datasets, explained by the high cost of estimation errors that often outweighs the benefits of sophisticated optimization out of sample.

More specifically, they found that the estimation window required for the sample-based mean-variance strategy and its extensions to outperform the 1/N benchmark is around 3,000 months for a portfolio with 25 assets and about 6,000 months for a portfolio with 50 assets.

The 1/N portfolio is also included in *Figure 5.2* in the previous section.

The minimum-variance portfolio

Another alternative is the **global minimum-variance** (**GMV**) portfolio, which prioritizes the minimization of risk. It is shown in *Figure 5.2* and can be calculated, as follows, by minimizing the portfolio standard deviation using the mean-variance framework:

```
def min_vol(mean_ret, cov, short=False):
    return minimize(fun=portfolio_std,
                    x0=x0,
                    args=(mean_ret, cov),
                    method='SLSQP',
                    bounds=bounds = ((-1 if short else 0, 1),) *
                          n_assets,
                          constraints=weight_constraint,
                          options={'tol': 1e-10, 'maxiter': 1e4})
```

The corresponding minimum volatility portfolio lies on the efficient frontier, as shown previously in *Figure 5.2*.

Global Portfolio Optimization – the Black-Litterman approach

The **Global Portfolio Optimization** approach of Black and Litterman (1992) combines economic models with statistical learning. It is popular because it generates estimates of expected returns that are plausible in many situations.

The technique assumes that the market is a mean-variance portfolio, as implied by the CAPM equilibrium model. It builds on the fact that the observed market capitalization can be considered as optimal weights assigned to each security by the market. Market weights reflect market prices that, in turn, embody the market's expectations of future returns.

The approach can thus reverse-engineer the unobservable future expected returns from the assumption that the market is close enough to equilibrium, as defined by the CAPM. Investors can adjust these estimates to their own beliefs using a shrinkage estimator. The model can be interpreted as a Bayesian approach to portfolio optimization. We will introduce Bayesian methods in *Chapter 10, Bayesian ML – Dynamic Sharpe Ratios and Pairs Trading Strategies*.

How to size your bets – the Kelly criterion

The **Kelly criterion** has a long history in gambling because it provides guidance on how much to stake on each bet in an (infinite) sequence of bets with varying (but favorable) odds to maximize terminal wealth. It was published in a 1956 paper, *A New Interpretation of the Information Rate*, by John Kelly, who was a colleague of Claude Shannon's at Bell Labs. He was intrigued by bets placed on candidates at the new quiz show "The $64,000 Question," where a viewer on the west coast used the three-hour delay to obtain insider information about the winners.

Kelly drew a connection to Shannon's information theory to solve for the bet that is optimal for long-term capital growth when the odds are favorable, but uncertainty remains. His rule maximizes logarithmic wealth as a function of the odds of success of each game and includes implicit bankruptcy protection since *log(0)* is negative infinity so that a Kelly gambler would naturally avoid losing everything.

The optimal size of a bet

Kelly began by analyzing games with a binary win-lose outcome. The key variables are:

- b: The odds defining the amount won for a $1 bet. Odds = 5/1 implies a $5 gain if the bet wins, plus recovery of the $1 capital.
- p: The probability defining the likelihood of a favorable outcome.
- f: The share of the current capital to bet.
- V: The value of the capital as a result of betting.

The Kelly criterion aims to maximize the value's growth rate, G, of infinitely repeated bets:

$$G = \lim_{N\to\infty} \frac{1}{N} \log \frac{V_N}{V_0}$$

When W and L are the numbers of wins and losses, then:

$$\begin{aligned} V_N &= (1 + b * f)^W (1 - f)^L V_0 && \Rightarrow \\ G &= \lim_{N\to\infty} \left[\frac{W}{N} \log(1 + \text{odds} * \text{share}) + \frac{L}{N} \log(1 - f) \right] && \Leftrightarrow \\ &= p \log(1 + b * f) + (1 - p) \log(1 - f) \end{aligned}$$

We can maximize the rate of growth G by maximizing G with respect to f, as illustrated using SymPy, as follows (you can find this in the `kelly_rule` notebook):

```
from sympy import symbols, solve, log, diff
share, odds, probability = symbols('share odds probability')
Value = probability * log(1 + odds * share) + (1 - probability) * log(1
     - share)
solve(diff(Value, share), share)
[(odds*probability + probability - 1)/odds]
```

We arrive at the optimal share of capital to bet:

$$\text{Kelly Criterion:} \quad f^* = \frac{b * p + p - 1}{b}$$

Optimal investment – single asset

In a financial market context, both outcomes and alternatives are more complex, but the Kelly criterion logic does still apply. It was made popular by Ed Thorp, who first applied it profitably to gambling (described in the book *Beat the Dealer*) and later started the successful hedge fund Princeton/Newport Partners.

With continuous outcomes, the growth rate of capital is defined by an integrate over the probability distribution of the different returns that can be optimized numerically:

$$\begin{aligned} E[G] &= \int \log(1 * fr) P(r) dr \quad \Leftrightarrow \\ \frac{d}{df} E[G] &= \int_{-\infty}^{+\infty} \frac{r}{1 * fr} P(r) dr = 0 \end{aligned}$$

We can solve this expression for the optimal f^* using the `scipy.optimize` module. The `quad` function computes the value of a definite integral between two values a and b using FORTRAN's QUADPACK library (hence its name). It returns the value of the integral and an error estimate:

```
def norm_integral(f, m, st):
    val, er = quad(lambda s: np.log(1+f*s)*norm.pdf(s, m, st), m-3*st,
                   m+3*st)
    return -val

def norm_dev_integral(f, m, st):
    val, er = quad(lambda s: (s/(1+f*s))*norm.pdf(s, m, st), m-3*st,
                   m+3*st)
    return val
m = .058
s = .216

# Option 1: minimize the expectation integral
sol = minimize_scalar(norm_integral, args=(
              m, s), bounds=[0., 2.], method='bounded')
print('Optimal Kelly fraction: {:.4f}'.format(sol.x))
Optimal Kelly fraction: 1.1974
```

Optimal investment – multiple assets

We will use an example with various equities. E. Chan (2008) illustrates how to arrive at a multi-asset application of the Kelly criterion, and that the result is equivalent to the (potentially levered) maximum Sharpe ratio portfolio from the mean-variance optimization.

The computation involves the dot product of the precision matrix, which is the inverse of the covariance matrix, and the return matrix:

```
mean_returns = monthly_returns.mean()
cov_matrix = monthly_returns.cov()
precision_matrix = pd.DataFrame(inv(cov_matrix), index=stocks,
columns=stocks)
kelly_wt = precision_matrix.dot(mean_returns).values
```

The Kelly portfolio is also shown in the previous efficient frontier diagram (after normalization so that the sum of the absolute weights equals one). Many investors prefer to reduce the Kelly weights to reduce the strategy's volatility, and Half-Kelly has become particularly popular.

Risk parity

The fact that the previous 15 years have been characterized by two major crises in the global equity markets, a consistently upwardly sloping yield curve, and a general decline in interest rates, made risk parity look like a particularly compelling option. Many institutions carved out strategic allocations to risk parity to further diversify their portfolios.

A simple implementation of risk parity allocates assets according to the inverse of their variances, ignoring correlations and, in particular, return forecasts:

```
var = monthly_returns.var()
risk_parity_weights = var / var.sum()
```

The risk parity portfolio is also shown in the efficient frontier diagram at the beginning of this section.

Risk factor investment

An alternative framework for estimating input is to work down to the underlying determinants, or factors, that drive the risk and returns of assets. If we understand how the factors influence returns, and we understand the factors, we will be able to construct more robust portfolios.

The concept of factor investing looks beyond asset class labels. It looks to the underlying factor risks that we discussed in the previous chapter on alpha factors to maximize the benefits of diversification. Rather than distinguishing investment vehicles by labels such as hedge funds or private equity, factor investing aims to identify distinct risk-return profiles based on differences in exposure to fundamental risk factors (Ang 2014).

The naive approach to mean-variance investing plugs (artificial) groupings as distinct asset classes into a mean-variance optimizer. Factor investing recognizes that such groupings share many of the same factor risks as traditional asset classes. Diversification benefits can be overstated, as investors discovered during the 2008 crisis when correlations among risky asset classes increased due to exposure to the same underlying factor risks.

In *Chapter 7, Linear Models – From Risk Factors to Return Forecasts*, we will show how to measure the exposure of a portfolio to various risk factors so that you can either adjust the positions to tune your factor exposure, or hedge accordingly.

Hierarchical risk parity

Mean-variance optimization is very sensitive to the estimates of expected returns and the covariance of these returns. The covariance matrix inversion also becomes more challenging and less accurate when returns are highly correlated, as is often the case in practice.
The result has been called the Markowitz curse: when diversification is more important because investments are correlated, conventional portfolio optimizers will likely produce an unstable solution. The benefits of diversification can be more than offset by mistaken estimates. As discussed, even naive, equally weighted portfolios can beat mean-variance and risk-based optimization out of sample.

More robust approaches have incorporated additional constraints (Clarke et al., 2002) or Bayesian priors (Black and Litterman, 1992), or used shrinkage estimators to make the precision matrix more numerically stable (Ledoit and Wolf, 2003), available in scikit-learn (`http://scikit-learn.org/stable/modules/generated/sklearn.covariance.LedoitWolf.html`).

Hierarchical risk parity (**HRP**), in contrast, leverages unsupervised machine learning to achieve superior out-of-sample portfolio allocations. A recent innovation in portfolio optimization leverages graph theory and hierarchical clustering to construct a portfolio in three steps (Lopez de Prado, 2015):

1. Define a distance metric so that correlated assets are close to each other, and apply single-linkage clustering to identify hierarchical relationships.
2. Use the hierarchical correlation structure to quasi-diagonalize the covariance matrix.
3. Apply top-down inverse-variance weighting using a recursive bisectional search to treat clustered assets as complements, rather than substitutes, in portfolio construction and to reduce the number of degrees of freedom.

A related method to construct **hierarchical clustering portfolios** (**HCP**) was presented by Raffinot (2016). Conceptually, complex systems such as financial markets tend to have a structure and are often organized in a hierarchical way, while the interaction among elements in the hierarchy shapes the dynamics of the system. Correlation matrices also lack the notion of hierarchy, which allows weights to vary freely and in potentially unintended ways.

Both HRP and HCP have been tested by JP Morgan (2012) on various equity universes. The HRP, in particular, produced equal or superior risk-adjusted returns and Sharpe ratios compared to naive diversification, the maximum-diversified portfolios, or GMV portfolios.

We will present the Python implementation in *Chapter 13, Data-Driven Risk Factors and Asset Allocation with Unsupervised Learning*.

Trading and managing portfolios with Zipline

In the previous chapter, we introduced Zipline to simulate the computation of alpha factors from trailing market, fundamental, and alternative data for a cross-section of stocks. In this section, we will start acting on the signals emitted by alpha factors. We'll do this by submitting buy and sell orders so we can enter long and short positions or rebalance the portfolio to adjust our holdings to the most recent trade signals.

We will postpone optimizing the portfolio weights until later in this chapter and, for now, just assign positions of equal value to each holding. As mentioned in the previous chapter, an in-depth introduction to the testing and evaluation of strategies that include ML models will follow in *Chapter 6, The Machine Learning Process*.

Scheduling signal generation and trade execution

We will use the custom MeanReversion factor developed in the previous chapter (see the implementation in 01_backtest_with_trades.ipynb).

The Pipeline created by the compute_factors() method returns a table with columns containing the 50 longs and shorts. It selects the equities according to the largest negative and positive deviations, respectively, of their last monthly return from the annual average, normalized by the standard deviation:

```
def compute_factors():
    """Create factor pipeline incl. mean reversion,
        filtered by 30d Dollar Volume; capture factor ranks"""
    mean_reversion = MeanReversion()
    dollar_volume = AverageDollarVolume(window_length=30)
    return Pipeline(columns={'longs'   : mean_reversion.bottom(N_LONGS),
                             'shorts'  : mean_reversion.top(N_SHORTS),
                             'ranking': mean_reversion.rank(ascending=False)},
                    screen=dollar_volume.top(VOL_SCREEN))
```

It also limited the universe to the 1,000 stocks with the highest average trading volume over the last 30 trading days. before_trading_start() ensures the daily execution of the Pipeline and the recording of the results, including the current prices:

```
def before_trading_start(context, data):
    """Run factor pipeline"""
    context.factor_data = pipeline_output('factor_pipeline')
    record(factor_data=context.factor_data.ranking)
    assets = context.factor_data.index
    record(prices=data.current(assets, 'price'))
```

The new rebalance() method submits trade orders to the exec_trades() method for the assets flagged for long and short positions by the Pipeline with equal positive and negative weights. It also divests any current holdings that are no longer included in the factor signals:

```
def exec_trades(data, assets, target_percent):
    """Place orders for assets using target portfolio percentage"""
    for asset in assets:
        if data.can_trade(asset) and not get_open_orders(asset):
            order_target_percent(asset, target_percent)
```

```
def rebalance(context, data):
    """Compute long, short and obsolete holdings; place trade orders"""
    factor_data = context.factor_data
    assets = factor_data.index
    longs = assets[factor_data.longs]
    shorts = assets[factor_data.shorts]
    divest = context.portfolio.positions.keys() - longs.union(shorts)
    exec_trades(data, assets=divest, target_percent=0)
    exec_trades(data, assets=longs, target_percent=1 / N_LONGS if N_LONGS
                else 0)
    exec_trades(data, assets=shorts, target_percent=-1 / N_SHORTS if N_SHORTS
                else 0)
```

The `rebalance()` method runs according to `date_rules` and `time_rules` set by the `schedule_function()` utility at the beginning of the week, right after `market_open`, as stipulated by the built-in `US_EQUITIES` calendar (see the Zipline documentation for details on rules).

You can also specify a trade commission both in relative terms and as a minimum amount. There is also an option to define slippage, which is the cost of an adverse change in price between trade decision and execution:

```
def initialize(context):
    """Setup: register pipeline, schedule rebalancing,
        and set trading params"""
    attach_pipeline(compute_factors(), 'factor_pipeline')
    schedule_function(rebalance,
                      date_rules.week_start(),
                      time_rules.market_open(),
                      calendar=calendars.US_EQUITIES)
    set_commission(us_equities=commission.PerShare(cost=0.00075,
                                                   min_trade_cost=.01))
    set_slippage(us_equities=slippage.VolumeShareSlippage(volume_
limit=0.0025, price_impact=0.01))
```

The algorithm continues to execute after calling the `run_algorithm()` function and returns the same backtest performance `DataFrame` that we saw in the previous chapter.

Implementing mean-variance portfolio optimization

We demonstrated in the previous section how to find the efficient frontier using `scipy.optimize`. In this section, we will leverage the PyPortfolioOpt library, which offers portfolio optimization (using SciPy under the hood), including efficient frontier techniques and more recent shrinkage approaches that regularize the covariance matrix (see *Chapter 7, Linear Models – From Risk Factors to Return Forecasts,* on shrinkage for linear regression). The code example lives in `02_backtest_with_pf_optimization.ipynb`.

We'll use the same setup with 50 long and short positions derived from the `MeanReversion` factor ranking. The `rebalance()` function receives the suggested long and short positions and passes each subset on to a new `optimize_weights()` function to obtain dictionaries with `asset: target_percent` pairs:

```
def rebalance(context, data):
    """Compute long, short and obsolete holdings; place orders"""

    factor_data = context.factor_data
    assets = factor_data.index

    longs = assets[factor_data.longs]
    shorts = assets[factor_data.shorts]

    divest = context.portfolio.positions.keys() - longs.union(shorts)
    exec_trades(data, positions={asset: 0 for asset in divest})

    # get price history
    prices = data.history(assets, fields='price',
                          bar_count=252+1, # 1 yr of returns
                          frequency='1d')


    if len(longs) > 0:
        long_weights = optimize_weights(prices.loc[:, longs])
        exec_trades(data, positions=long_weights)
    if len(shorts) > 0:
        short_weights = optimize_weights(prices.loc[:, shorts], short=True)
        exec_trades(data, positions=short_weights)
```

The `optimize_weights()` function uses the `EfficientFrontier` object, provided by PyPortfolioOpt, to find the weights that maximize the Sharpe ratio based on the last year of returns and the covariance matrix, both of which the library also computes:

```
def optimize_weights(prices, short=False):
    returns = expected_returns.mean_historical_return(prices=prices,
                                                      frequency=252)
    cov = risk_models.sample_cov(prices=prices, frequency=252)

    # get weights that maximize the Sharpe ratio
    ef = EfficientFrontier(expected_returns=returns,
                           cov_matrix=cov,
                           weight_bounds=(0, 1),
                           gamma=0)

    weights = ef.max_sharpe()
    if short:
```

```
            return {asset: -weight for asset, weight in ef.clean_weights().
items()}
        else:
            return ef.clean_weights()
```

It returns normalized weights that sum to 1, set to negative values for the short positions.

Figure 5.3 shows that, for this particular set of strategies and time frame, the mean-variance optimized portfolio performs significantly better:

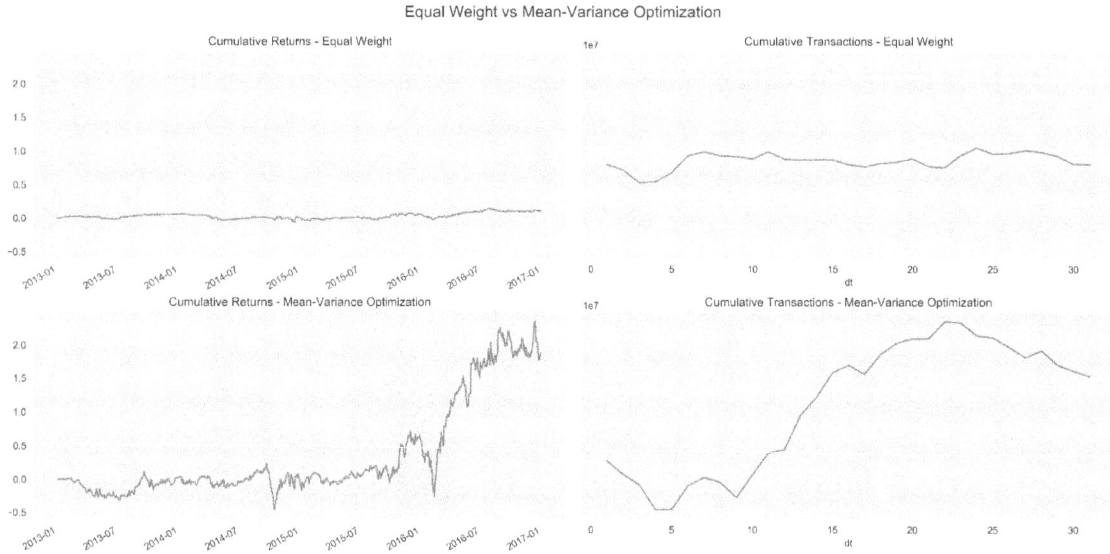

Figure 5.3: Mean-variance vs equal-weighted portfolio performance

PyPortfolioOpt also finds the minimum volatility portfolio. More generally speaking, this example illustrates how you can add logic to tweak portfolio weights using the methods presented in the previous section, or any other of your choosing.

We will now turn to common measures of portfolio return and risk, and how to compute them using the pyfolio library.

Measuring backtest performance with pyfolio

Pyfolio facilitates the analysis of portfolio performance, both in and out of sample using a rich set of metrics and visualizations. It produces tear sheets that cover the analysis of returns, positions, and transactions, as well as event risk during periods of market stress using several built-in scenarios. It also includes Bayesian out-of-sample performance analysis.

Pyfolio relies on portfolio returns and position data and can also take into account the transaction costs and slippage losses of trading activity. It uses the empyrical library, which can also be used on a standalone basis to compute performance metrics.

Creating the returns and benchmark inputs

The library is part of the Quantopian ecosystem and is compatible with Zipline and Alphalens. We will first demonstrate how to generate the requisite inputs from Alphalens and then show how to extract them from a Zipline backtest performance `DataFrame`. The code samples for this section are in the notebook `03_pyfolio_demo.ipynb`.

Getting pyfolio input from Alphalens

Pyfolio also integrates with Alphalens directly and permits the creation of pyfolio input data using `create_pyfolio_input`:

```
from alphalens.performance import create_pyfolio_input
qmin, qmax = factor_data.factor_quantile.min(),
             factor_data.factor_quantile.max()
input_data = create_pyfolio_input(alphalens_data,
                                  period='1D',
                                  capital=100000,
                                  long_short=False,
                                  equal_weight=False,
                                  quantiles=[1, 5],
                                  benchmark_period='1D')
returns, positions, benchmark = input_data
```

There are two options to specify how portfolio weights will be generated:

- `long_short`: If `False`, weights will correspond to factor values divided by their absolute value so that negative factor values generate short positions. If `True`, factor values are first demeaned so that long and short positions cancel each other out, and the portfolio is market neutral.
- `equal_weight`: If `True` and `long_short` is `True`, assets will be split into two equal-sized groups, with the top/bottom half making up long/short positions.

Long-short portfolios can also be created for groups if `factor_data` includes, for example, sector information for each asset.

Getting pyfolio input from a Zipline backtest

The result of a Zipline backtest can also be converted into the required pyfolio input using `extract_rets_pos_txn_from_zipline`:

```
returns, positions, transactions =
         extract_rets_pos_txn_from_zipline(backtest)
```

Walk-forward testing – out-of-sample returns

Testing a trading strategy involves back- and forward testing. The former involves historical data and often refers to the sample period used to fine-tune alpha factor parameters. Forward-testing simulates the strategy on new market data to validate that it performs well out of sample and is not too closely tailored to specific historical circumstances.

Pyfolio allows for the designation of an out-of-sample period to simulate walk-forward testing. There are numerous aspects to take into account when testing a strategy to obtain statistically reliable results. We will address this in more detail in *Chapter 8, The ML4T Workflow – From Model to Strategy Backtesting*.

The `plot_rolling_returns` function displays cumulative in- and out-of-sample returns against a user-defined benchmark (we are using the S&P 500). Pyfolio computes cumulative returns as the product of simple returns after adding 1 to each:

```
from pyfolio.plotting import plot_rolling_returns
plot_rolling_returns(returns=returns,
                     factor_returns=benchmark_rets,
                     live_start_date='2016-01-01',
                     cone_std=(1.0, 1.5, 2.0))
```

The plot in *Figure 5.4* includes a cone that shows expanding confidence intervals to indicate when out-of-sample returns appear unlikely, given random-walk assumptions. Here, our toy strategy did not perform particularly well against the S&P 500 benchmark during the simulated 2016 out-of-sample period:

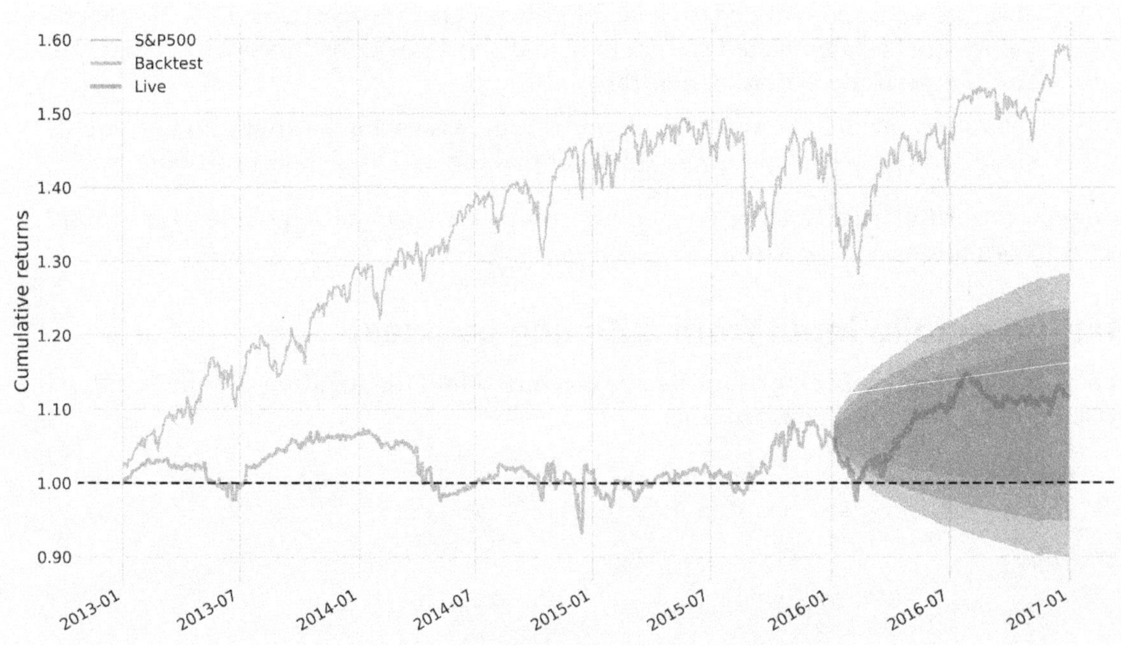

Figure 5.4: Pyfolio cumulative performance plot

Summary performance statistics

Pyfolio offers several analytic functions and plots. The `perf_stats` summary displays the annual and cumulative returns, volatility, skew, and kurtosis of returns and the SR.

The following additional metrics (which can also be calculated individually) are most important:

- **Max drawdown**: Highest percentage loss from the previous peak
- **Calmar ratio**: Annual portfolio return relative to maximal drawdown
- **Omega ratio**: Probability-weighted ratio of gains versus losses for a return target, zero per default
- **Sortino ratio**: Excess return relative to downside standard deviation
- **Tail ratio**: Size of the right tail (gains, the absolute value of the 95th percentile) relative to the size of the left tail (losses, absolute value of the 5th percentile)
- **Daily value at risk (VaR)**: Loss corresponding to a return two standard deviations below the daily mean
- **Alpha**: Portfolio return unexplained by the benchmark return
- **Beta**: Exposure to the benchmark

The `plot_perf_stats` function bootstraps estimates of parameter variability and displays the result as a box plot:

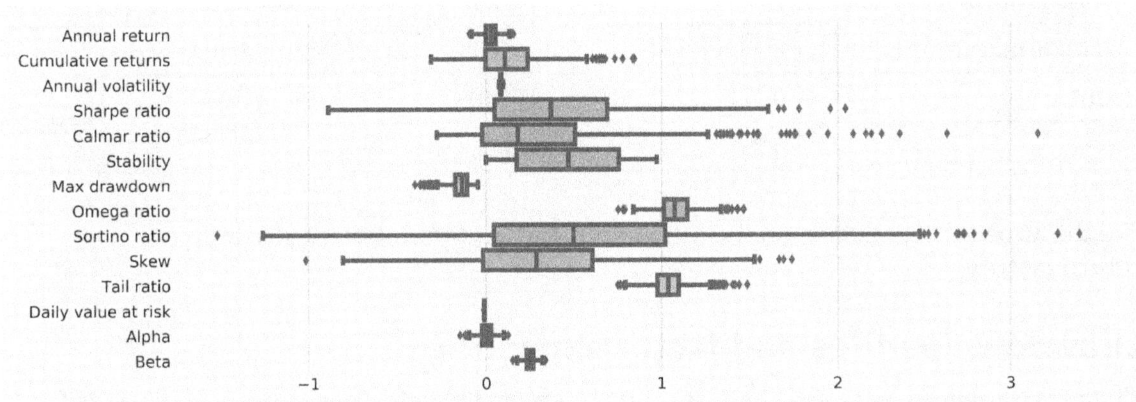

Figure 5.5: Pyfolio performance statistic plot

The `show_perf_stats` function computes numerous metrics for the entire period, as well as separately, for in- and out-of-sample periods:

```
from pyfolio.timeseries import show_perf_stats
show_perf_stats(returns=returns,
                factor_returns=benchmark_rets,
                positions=positions,
                transactions=transactions,
                live_start_date=oos_date)
```

For the simulated long-short portfolio derived from the `MeanReversion` factor, we obtain the following performance statistics:

Metric	All	In-sample	Out-of-sample
Annual return	2.80%	2.10%	4.70%
Cumulative returns	11.60%	6.60%	4.70%
Annual volatility	8.50%	8.80%	7.60%
Sharpe ratio	0.37	0.29	0.64
Calmar ratio	0.21	0.16	0.57
Stability	0.26	0.01	0.67
Max drawdown	-13.10%	-13.10%	-8.30%
Omega ratio	1.07	1.06	1.11
Sortino ratio	0.54	0.42	0.96
Skew	0.33	0.35	0.25
Kurtosis	7.2	8.04	2
Tail ratio	1.04	1.06	1.01
Daily value at risk	-1.10%	-1.10%	-0.90%
Gross leverage	0.69	0.68	0.72
Daily turnover	8.10%	8.00%	8.40%
Alpha	0	-0.01	0.03
Beta	0.25	0.27	0.17

See the appendix for details on the calculation and interpretation of portfolio risk and return metrics.

Drawdown periods and factor exposure

The `plot_drawdown_periods(returns)` function plots the principal drawdown periods for the portfolio, and several other plotting functions show the rolling SR and rolling factor exposures to the market beta or the Fama-French size, growth, and momentum factors:

```
fig, ax = plt.subplots(nrows=2, ncols=2, figsize=(16, 10))
axes = ax.flatten()
plot_drawdown_periods(returns=returns, ax=axes[0])
plot_rolling_beta(returns=returns, factor_returns=benchmark_rets,
                  ax=axes[1])
plot_drawdown_underwater(returns=returns, ax=axes[2])
plot_rolling_sharpe(returns=returns)
```

The plots in *Figure 5.6*, which highlights a subset of the visualization contained in the various tear sheets, illustrate how pyfolio allows us to drill down into the performance characteristics and gives us exposure to fundamental drivers of risk and returns:

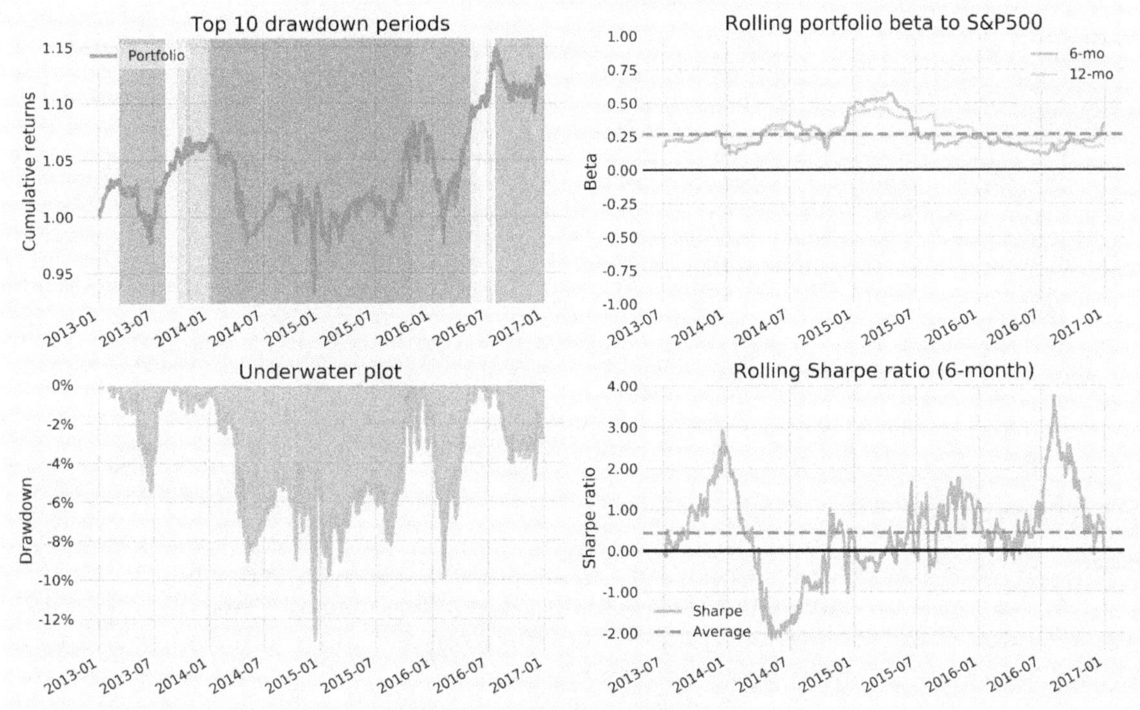

Figure 5.6: Various pyfolio plots of performance over time

Modeling event risk

Pyfolio also includes timelines for various events that you can use to compare the performance of a portfolio to a benchmark during this period. Pyfolio uses the S&P 500 by default, but you can also provide benchmark returns of your choice. The following example compares the performance to the S&P 500 during the fall 2015 selloff, following the Brexit vote:

```
interesting_times = extract_interesting_date_ranges(returns=returns)
interesting_times['Fall2015'].to_frame('pf') \
  .join(benchmark_rets) \
  .add(1).cumprod().sub(1) \
  .plot(lw=2, figsize=(14, 6), title='Post-Brexit Turmoil')
```

Figure 5.7 shows the resulting plot:

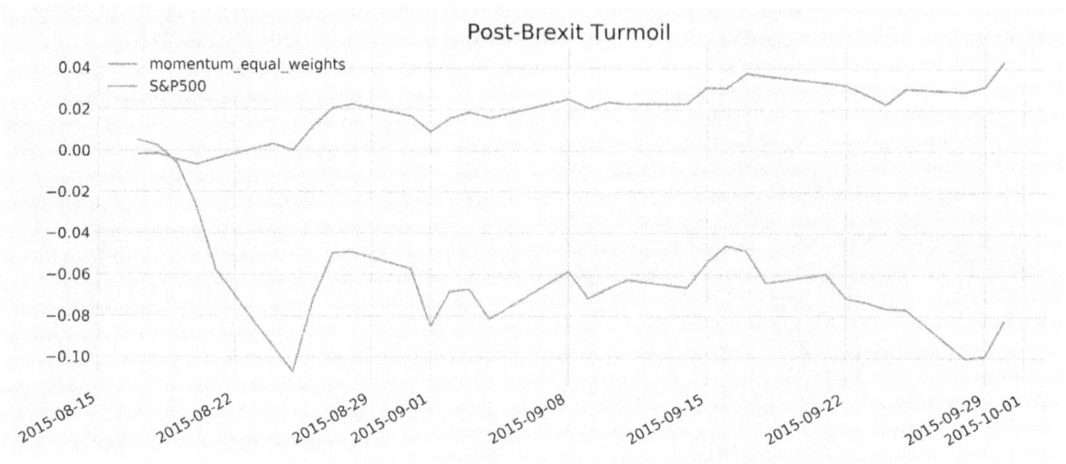

Figure 5.7: Pyfolio event risk analysis

Summary

In this chapter, we covered the important topic of portfolio management, which involves the combination of investment positions with the objective of managing risk-return trade-offs. We introduced pyfolio to compute and visualize key risk and return metrics, as well as to compare the performance of various algorithms.

We saw how important accurate predictions are for optimizing portfolio weights and maximizing diversification benefits. We also explored how machine learning can facilitate more effective portfolio construction by learning hierarchical relationships from the asset-returns covariance matrix.

We will now move on to the second part of this book, which focuses on the use of machine learning models. These models will produce more accurate predictions by making more effective use of more diverse information. They do this to capture more complex patterns than the simpler alpha factors that were most prominent so far.

We will begin by training, testing, and tuning linear models for regression and classification using cross-validation to achieve robust out-of-sample performance. We will also embed these models within the framework for defining and backtesting algorithmic trading strategies, which we covered in the previous two chapters.

6

The Machine Learning Process

This chapter starts Part 2 of this book, where we'll illustrate how you can use a range of supervised and unsupervised **machine learning** (**ML**) models for trading. We will explain each model's assumptions and use cases before we demonstrate relevant applications using various Python libraries. The categories of models that we will cover in Parts 2-4 include:

- Linear models for the regression and classification of cross-section, time series, and panel data
- Generalized additive models, including nonlinear tree-based models, such as decision trees
- Ensemble models, including random forest and gradient-boosting machines
- Unsupervised linear and nonlinear methods for dimensionality reduction and clustering
- Neural network models, including recurrent and convolutional architectures
- Reinforcement learning models

We will apply these models to the market, fundamental, and alternative data sources introduced in the first part of this book. We will build on the material covered so far by demonstrating how to embed these models in a trading strategy that translates model signals into trades, how to optimize portfolio, and how to evaluate strategy performance.

There are several aspects that many of these models and their applications have in common. This chapter covers these common aspects so that we can focus on model-specific usage in the following chapters. They include the overarching goal of learning a functional relationship from data by optimizing an objective or loss function. They also include the closely related methods of measuring model performance.

We'll distinguish between unsupervised and supervised learning and outline use cases for algorithmic trading. We'll contrast supervised regression and classification problems and the use of supervised learning for statistical inference of relationships between input and output data, along with its use for the prediction of future outputs.

We'll also illustrate how prediction errors are due to the model's bias or variance, or because of a high noise-to-signal ratio in the data. Most importantly, we'll present methods to diagnose sources of errors like overfitting and improve your model's performance.

In this chapter, we will cover the following topics relevant to applying the ML workflow in practice:

- How supervised and unsupervised learning from data works
- Training and evaluating supervised learning models for regression and classification tasks
- How the bias-variance trade-off impacts predictive performance
- How to diagnose and address prediction errors due to overfitting
- Using cross-validation to optimize hyperparameters with a focus on time-series data
- Why financial data requires additional attention when testing out-of-sample

If you are already quite familiar with ML, feel free to skip ahead and dive right into learning how to use ML models to produce and combine alpha factors for an algorithmic trading strategy. This chapter's directory in the GitHub repository contains the code examples and lists additional resources.

How machine learning from data works

Many definitions of ML revolve around the automated detection of meaningful patterns in data. Two prominent examples include:

- AI pioneer **Arthur Samuelson** defined ML in 1959 as a subfield of computer science that gives computers the ability to learn without being explicitly programmed.
- **Tom Mitchell**, one of the current leaders in the field, pinned down a well-posed learning problem more specifically in 1998: a computer program learns from experience with respect to a task and a performance measure of whether the performance of the task improves with experience (Mitchell 1997).

Experience is presented to an algorithm in the form of training data. The principal difference from previous attempts of building machines that solve problems is that the rules that an algorithm uses to make decisions are learned from the data, as opposed to being programmed by humans as was the case, for example, for expert systems prominent in the 1980s.

Recommended textbooks that cover a wide range of algorithms and general applications include James et al (2013), Hastie, Tibshirani, and Friedman (2009), Bishop (2006), and Mitchell (1997).

The challenge – matching the algorithm to the task

The key challenge of automated learning is to identify patterns in the training data that are meaningful when generalizing the model's learning to new data. There are a large number of potential patterns that a model could identify, while the training data only constitutes a sample of the larger set of phenomena that the algorithm may encounter when performing the task in the future.

The infinite number of functions that could have generated the observed outputs from the given input makes the search process for the true function impossible, without restricting the eligible set of candidates. The types of patterns that an algorithm is capable of learning are limited by the size of its **hypothesis space** that contains the functions it can possibly represent. It is also limited by the amount of information provided by the sample data.

The size of the hypothesis space varies significantly between algorithms, as we will see in the following chapters. On the one hand, this limitation enables a successful search, and on the other hand, it implies an inductive bias that may lead to poor performance when the algorithm generalizes from the training sample to new data.

Hence, the key challenge becomes how to choose a model with a hypothesis space large enough to contain a solution to the learning problem, yet small enough to ensure reliable learning and generalization given the size of the training data. With more informative data, a model with a larger hypothesis space has a better chance of being successful.

The **no-free-lunch theorem** states that there is no universal learning algorithm. Instead, a learner's hypothesis space has to be tailored to a specific task using prior knowledge about the task domain in order for the search for meaningful patterns that generalize well to succeed (Gómez and Rojas 2015).

We will pay close attention to the assumptions that a model makes about data relationships for a specific task throughout this chapter and emphasize the importance of matching these assumptions with empirical evidence gleaned from data exploration.

There are several categories of machine learning tasks that differ by purpose, available information, and, consequently, the learning process itself. The main categories are supervised, unsupervised, and reinforcement learning, and we will review their key differences next.

Supervised learning – teaching by example

Supervised learning is the most commonly used type of ML. We will dedicate most of the chapters in this book to applications in this category. The term *supervised* implies the presence of an outcome variable that guides the learning process—that is, it teaches the algorithm the correct solution to the task at hand. Supervised learning aims to capture a functional input-output relationship from individual samples that reflect this relationship and to apply its learning by making valid statements about new data.

Depending on the field, the output variable is also interchangeably called the label, target, or outcome, as well as the endogenous or left-hand side variable. We will use y_i for outcome observations $i = 1, ..., N$, or y for a (column) vector of outcomes. Some tasks come with several outcomes and are called **multilabel problems**.

The input data for a supervised learning problem is also known as features, as well as exogenous or right-hand side variables. We use x_i for a vector of features with observations $i = 1, ..., N$, or X in matrix notation, where each column contains a feature and each row an observation.

The solution to a supervised learning problem is a function $\hat{f}(X)$ that represents what the model learned about the input-output relationship from the sample and approximates the true relationship, represented by $y \approx \hat{f}(X)$. This function can potentially be used to infer statistical associations or even causal relationships among variables of interest beyond the sample, or it can be used to predict outputs for new input data.

The task of learning an input-outcome relationship from data that permits accurate predictions of outcomes for new inputs faces important trade-offs. More complex models have more moving parts that are capable of representing more nuanced relationships. However, they are also more likely to learn random noise particular to the training sample, as opposed to a systematic signal that represents a general pattern. When this happens, we say the model is **overfitting** to the training data. In addition, complex models may also be more difficult to inspect, making it more difficult to understand the nature of the learned relationship or the drivers of specific predictions.

Overly simple models, on the other hand, will miss complex signals and deliver biased results. This trade-off is known as the **bias-variance trade-off** in supervised learning, but conceptually, this also applies to the other forms of ML where too simple or too complex models may perform poorly beyond the training data.

Unsupervised learning – uncovering useful patterns

When solving an **unsupervised learning** problem, we only observe the features and have no measurements of the outcome. Instead of predicting future outcomes or inferring relationships among variables, unsupervised algorithms aim to identify structure in the input that permits a new representation of the information contained in the data.

Frequently, the measure of success is the contribution of the result to the solution of some other problem. This includes identifying commonalities, or clusters, among observations, or transforming features to obtain a compressed summary that captures relevant information.

The key challenge is that unsupervised algorithms have to accomplish their mission without the guidance provided by outcome information. As a consequence, we are often unable to evaluate the result against a ground truth as in the supervised case, and its quality may be in the eye of the beholder. However, sometimes, we can evaluate its contribution to a downstream task, for example when dimensionality reduction enables better predictions.

There are numerous approaches, from well-established cluster algorithms to cutting-edge deep learning models, and several relevant use cases for our purposes.

Use cases – from risk management to text processing

There are numerous trading use cases for unsupervised learning that we will cover in later chapters:

- Grouping securities with similar risk and return characteristics (see **hierarchical risk parity** in *Chapter 13, Data-Driven Risk Factors and Asset Allocation with Unsupervised Learning*)
- Finding a small number of risk factors driving the performance of a much larger number of securities using **principal component analysis** (*Chapter 13, Data-Driven Risk Factors and Asset Allocation with Unsupervised Learning*) or **autoencoders** (*Chapter 19, RNN for Multivariate Time Series and Sentiment Analysis*)
- Identifying latent topics in a body of documents (for example, earnings call transcripts) that comprise the most important aspects of those documents (*Chapter 14, Text Data for Trading – Sentiment Analysis*)

At a high level, these applications rely on methods to identify clusters and methods to reduce the dimensionality of the data.

Cluster algorithms – seeking similar observations

Cluster algorithms apply a concept of similarity to identify observations or data attributes that contain comparable information. They summarize a dataset by assigning a large number of data points to a smaller number of clusters. They do this so that the cluster members are more closely related to each other than to members of other clusters.

Cluster algorithms differ in what they assume about how the various groupings were generated and what makes them alike. As a result, they tend to produce alternative types of clusters and should thus be selected based on the characteristics of the data. Some prominent examples are:

- **K-means clustering**: Data points belong to one of the *k* clusters of equal size that take an elliptical form.
- **Gaussian mixture models**: Data points have been generated by any of the various multivariate normal distributions.
- **Density-based clusters**: Clusters are of arbitrary shape and defined only by the existence of a minimum number of nearby data points.
- **Hierarchical clusters**: Data points belong to various supersets of groups that are formed by successively merging smaller clusters.

Dimensionality reduction – compressing information

Dimensionality reduction produces new data that captures the most important information contained in the source data. Rather than grouping data into clusters while retaining the original data, these algorithms transform the data with the goal of using fewer features to represent the original information.

Algorithms differ with respect to how they transform data and, thus, the nature of the resulting compressed dataset, as shown in the following list:

- **Principal component analysis (PCA)**: Finds the linear transformation that captures most of the variance in the existing dataset
- **Manifold learning**: Identifies a nonlinear transformation that yields a lower-dimensional representation of the data
- **Autoencoders**: Uses a neural network to compress data nonlinearly with minimal loss of information

We will dive deeper into these unsupervised learning models in several of the following chapters, including important applications to **natural language processing** (**NLP**) in the form of topic modeling and Word2vec feature extraction.

Reinforcement learning – learning by trial and error

Reinforcement learning (**RL**) is the third type of ML. It centers on an agent that needs to pick an action at each time step, based on information provided by the environment. The agent could be a self-driving car, a program playing a board game or a video game, or a trading strategy operating in a certain security market. You find an excellent introduction in *Sutton and Barto (2018)*.

The agent aims to choose the action that yields the highest reward over time, based on a set of observations that describes the current state of the environment. It is both dynamic and interactive: the stream of positive and negative rewards impacts the algorithm's learning, and actions taken now may influence both the environment and future rewards.

The agent needs to take action right from start and learns in an "online" fashion, one example at a time as it goes along. The learning process follows a trial-and-error approach. This is because the agent needs to manage the trade-off between exploiting a course of action that has yielded a certain reward in the past and exploring new actions that may increase the reward in the future. RL algorithms optimize the agent's learning using dynamical systems theory and, in particular, the optimal control of Markov decision processes with incomplete information.

RL differs from supervised learning, where the training data lays out both the context and the correct decision for the algorithm. It is tailored to interactive settings where the outcomes only become available over time and learning must proceed in a continuous fashion as the agent acquires new experience.

However, some of the most notable progress in **artificial intelligence** (**AI**) involves RL, which uses deep learning to approximate functional relationships between actions, environments, and future rewards. It also differs from unsupervised learning because feedback on the actions will be available, albeit with a delay.

RL is particularly suitable for algorithmic trading because the model of a return-maximizing agent in an uncertain, dynamic environment has much in common with an investor or a trading strategy that interacts with financial markets. We will introduce RL approaches to building an algorithmic trading strategy in *Chapter 21, Generative Adversarial Networks for Synthetic Time-Series Data.*

The machine learning workflow

Developing an ML solution for an algorithmic trading strategy requires a systematic approach to maximize the chances of success while economizing on resources. It is also very important to make the process transparent and replicable in order to facilitate collaboration, maintenance, and later refinements.

The following chart outlines the key steps, from problem definition to the deployment of a predictive solution:

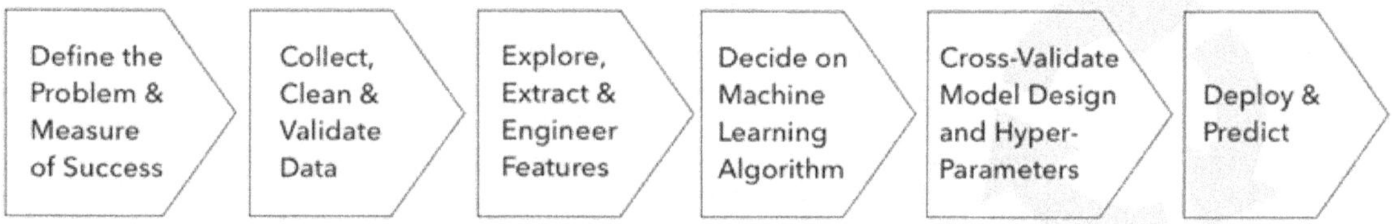

Figure 6.1: Key steps of the machine learning workflow

The process is iterative throughout, and the effort required at different stages will vary according to the project. Generally, however, this process should include the following steps:

1. Frame the problem, identify a target metric, and define success.
2. Source, clean, and validate the data.
3. Understand your data and generate informative features.
4. Pick one or more machine learning algorithms suitable for your data.
5. Train, test, and tune your models.
6. Use your model to solve the original problem.

We will walk through these steps in the following sections using a simple example to illustrate some of the key points.

Basic walkthrough – k-nearest neighbors

The `machine_learning_workflow.ipynb` notebook in this chapter's folder of this book's GitHub repository contains several examples that illustrate the machine learning workflow using a dataset of house prices.

We will use the fairly straightforward **k-nearest neighbors** (**KNN**) algorithm, which allows us to tackle both regression and classification problems. In its default scikit-learn implementation, it identifies the *k* nearest data points (based on the Euclidean distance) to make a prediction. It predicts the most frequent class among the neighbors or the average outcome in the classification or regression case, respectively.

The `README` for this chapter on GitHub links to additional resources; see Bhatia and Vandana (2010) for a brief survey.

Framing the problem – from goals to metrics

The starting point for any machine learning project is the use case it ultimately aims to address. Sometimes, this goal will be statistical inference in order to identify an association or even a causal relationship between variables. Most frequently, however, the goal will be the prediction of an outcome to yield a trading signal.

Both inference and prediction tasks rely on metrics to evaluate how well a model achieves its objective. Due to their prominence in practice, we will focus on common objective functions and the corresponding error metrics for predictive models.

We distinguish prediction tasks by the nature of the output: a continuous output variable poses a **regression** problem, a categorical variable implies **classification**, and the special case of ordered categorical variables represents a **ranking** problem.

You can often frame a given problem in different ways. The task at hand may be how to efficiently combine several alpha factors. You could frame this task as a regression problem that aims to predict returns, a binary classification problem that aims to predict the direction of future price movements, or a multiclass problem that aims to assign stocks to various performance classes such as return quintiles.

In the following section, we will introduce these objectives and look at how to measure and interpret related error metrics.

Prediction versus inference

The functional relationship produced by a supervised learning algorithm can be used for inference—that is, to gain insights into how the outcomes are generated. Alternatively, you can use it to predict outputs for unknown inputs.

For algorithmic trading, we can use inference to estimate the statistical association of the returns of an asset with a risk factor. This implies, for instance, assessing how likely this observation is due to noise, as opposed to an actual influence of the risk factor. Prediction, in turn, can be used to forecast the risk factor, which can help predict the asset return and price and be translated into a trading signal.

Statistical inference is about drawing conclusions from sample data about the parameters of the underlying probability distribution or the population. Potential conclusions include hypothesis tests about the characteristics of the distribution of an individual variable, or the existence or strength of numerical relationships among variables. They also include the point or interval estimates of metrics.

Inference depends on the assumptions about the process that originally generated the data. We will review these assumptions and the tools that are used for inference with linear models where they are well established. More complex models make fewer assumptions about the structural relationship between input and output. Instead, they approach the task of function approximation with fewer restrictions, while treating the data-generating process as a black box.

These models, including decision trees, ensemble models, and neural networks, have gained in popularity because they often outperform on prediction tasks. However, we will see that there have been numerous recent efforts to increase the transparency of complex models. Random forests, for example, have recently gained a framework for statistical inference (Wager and Athey 2019).

Causal inference – correlation does not imply causation

Causal inference aims to identify relationships where certain input values imply certain outputs—for example, a certain constellation of macro variables causing the price of a given asset to move in a certain way, while assuming all other variables remain constant.

Statistical inference about relationships among two or more variables produces measures of correlation. Correlation can only be interpreted as a causal relationship when several other conditions are met—for example, when alternative explanations or reverse causality has been ruled out.

Meeting these conditions requires an experimental setting where all relevant variables of interest can be fully controlled to isolate causal relationships. Alternatively, quasi-experimental settings expose units of observations to changes in inputs in a randomized way. It does this to rule out that other observable or unobservable features are responsible for the observed effects of the change in the environment.

These conditions are rarely met, so inferential conclusions need to be treated with care. The same applies to the performance of predictive models that also rely on the statistical association between features and outputs, which may change with other factors that are not part of the model.

The non-parametric nature of the KNN model does not lend itself well to inference, so we'll postpone this step in the workflow until we encounter linear models in *Chapter 7, Linear Models – From Risk Factors to Return Forecasts*.

Regression – popular loss functions and error metrics

Regression problems aim to predict a continuous variable. The **root-mean-square error (RMSE)** is the most popular loss function and error metric, not least because it is differentiable. The loss is symmetric, but larger errors weigh more in the calculation. Using the square root has the advantage that we can measure the error in the units of the target variable.

The **root-mean-square of the log of the error (RMSLE)** is appropriate when the target is subject to exponential growth. Its asymmetric penalty weighs negative errors less than positive errors. You can also log-transform the target prior to training the model and then use the RMSE, as we'll do in the example later in this section.

The **mean of the absolute errors (MAE)** and **median of the absolute errors (MedAE)** are symmetric but do not give more weight to larger errors. The MedAE is robust to outliers.

The **explained variance score** computes the proportion of the target variance that the model accounts for and varies between 0 and 1. The **R2 score** is also called the coefficient of determination and yields the same outcome if the mean of the residuals is 0, but can differ otherwise. In particular, it can be negative when calculated on out-of-sample data (or for a linear regression without intercept).

The following table defines the formulas used for calculation and the corresponding scikit-learn function that can be imported from the metrics module. The `scoring` parameter is used in combination with automated train-test functions (such as `cross_val_score` and `GridSearchCV`), which we'll will introduce later in this section, and which are illustrated in the accompanying notebook:

Name	Formula	scikit-learn function	Scoring parameter
Mean squared error	$\frac{1}{N}\sum_{i=1}^{N}(y_i - \hat{y}_i)^2$	`mean_squared_error`	`neg_mean_squared_error`
Mean squared log error	$\frac{1}{N}\sum_{i=1}^{N}(\ln(1+y_i) - \ln(1+\hat{y}_i))^2$	`mean_squared_log_error`	`neg_mean_squared_log_error`
Mean absolute error	$\frac{1}{N}\sum_{i=1}^{N}\lvert y_i - \hat{y}_i\rvert$	`mean_absolute_error`	`neg_mean_absolute_error`
Median absolute error	$\text{median}(\lvert y_1 - \hat{y}_1\rvert, \ldots, \lvert y_N - \hat{y}_N$	`median_absolute_error`	`neg_median_absolute_error`
Explained variance	$1 - \frac{(y - \hat{y})}{(y)}$	`explained_variance_score`	`explained_variance`
R^2 score	$1 - \frac{\sum_{i=1}^{N}(y_i - \hat{y}_i)^2}{\sum_{i=1}^{N}(y_i - \bar{y}_i)^2}$	`r2_score`	`r2`

Figure 6.2 shows the various error metrics for the house price regression that we'll compute in the notebook:

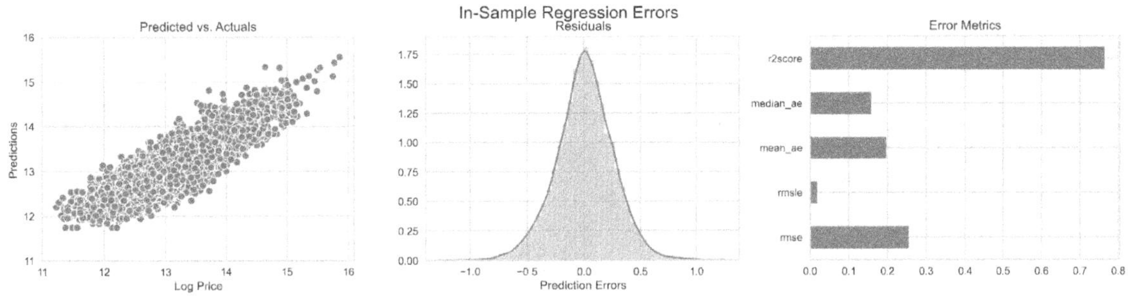

Figure 6.2: In-sample regression errors

The `sklearn` function also supports multilabel evaluation—that is, assigning multiple outcome values to a single observation; see the documentation referenced on GitHub for more details.

Classification – making sense of the confusion matrix

Classification problems have categorical outcome variables. Most predictors will output a score to indicate whether an observation belongs to a certain class. In the second step, these scores are then translated into actual predictions using a threshold value.

In the binary case, with a positive and a negative class label, the score typically varies between zero and one or is normalized accordingly. Once the scores are converted into predictions of one class or the other, there can be four outcomes, since each of the two classes can be either correctly or incorrectly predicted. With more than two classes, there can be more cases if you differentiate between the several potential mistakes.

All error metrics are computed from the breakdown of predictions across the four fields of the 2×2 confusion matrix that associates actual and predicted classes.

The metrics listed in the following table, such as accuracy, evaluate a model for a given threshold:

		Actual (Truth)	
		Positive	**Negative**
Prediction	**Positive**	True Positive (TP)	False Positive (FP)
	Negative	False Negative (FN)	True Negative (TN)

$$\text{Accuracy} = \frac{\text{\# Correct Predictions}}{\text{\# Cases}} = \frac{TP + TN}{TP + FP + TN + FN}$$

$$\text{True Positive Rate (Sensitivity, Recall)} = \frac{\text{\# Correct Positive Predictions}}{\text{\# Positive Cases}} = \frac{TP}{TP + FN}$$

$$\text{False Negative Rate (Miss Rate)} = 1 - \text{True Positive Rate}$$

$$\text{True Negative Rate (Specificity)} = \frac{\text{\# Correct Negative Predictions}}{\text{\# Negative Cases}} = \frac{TN}{TN + FP}$$

$$\text{False Positive Rate (Fall-Out)} = 1 - \text{True Negative Rate}$$

Figure 6.3: Confusion matrix and related error metrics

The classifier usually doesn't output calibrated probabilities. Instead, the threshold used to distinguish positive from negative cases is itself a decision variable that should be optimized, taking into account the costs and benefits of correct and incorrect predictions.

All things equal, a lower threshold tends to imply more positive predictions, with a potentially rising false positive rate, whereas for a higher threshold, the opposite is likely to be true.

Receiver operating characteristics the area under the curve

The **receiver operating characteristics** (**ROC**) curve allows us to visualize, compare, and select classifiers based on their performance. It computes the pairs of **true positive rates** (**TPR**) and **false positive rates** (**FPR**) that result from using all predicted scores as a threshold to produce class predictions. It visualizes these pairs inside a square with unit side length.

Random predictions (weighted to take into account class imbalance), on average, yield equal TPR and FPR that appear on the diagonal, which becomes the benchmark case. Since an underperforming classifier would benefit from relabeling the predictions, this benchmark also becomes the minimum.

The **area under the curve** (**AUC**) is defined as the area under the ROC plot that varies between 0.5 and the maximum of 1. It is a summary measure of how well the classifier's scores are able to rank data points with respect to their class membership. More specifically, the AUC of a classifier has the important statistical property of representing the probability that the classifier will rank a randomly chosen positive instance higher than a randomly chosen negative instance, which is equivalent to the Wilcoxon ranking test (Fawcett 2006). In addition, the AUC has the benefit of not being sensitive to class imbalances.

Precision-recall curves – zooming in on one class

When predictions for one of the classes are of particular interest, precision and recall curves visualize the trade-off between these error metrics for different thresholds. Both measures evaluate the quality of predictions for a particular class. The following list shows how they are applied to the positive class:

- **Recall** measures the share of actual positive class members that a classifier predicts as positive for a given threshold. It originates from information retrieval and measures the share of relevant documents successfully identified by a search algorithm.
- **Precision**, in contrast, measures the share of positive predictions that are correct.

Recall typically increases with a lower threshold, but precision may decrease. Precision-recall curves visualize the attainable combinations and allow for the optimization of the threshold, given the costs and benefits of missing a lot of relevant cases or producing lower-quality predictions.

The **F1 score** is a harmonic mean of precision and recall for a given threshold, and can be used to numerically optimize the threshold, all while taking into account the relative weights that these two metrics should assume.

Figure 6.4 illustrates the ROC curve and corresponding AUC, alongside the precision-recall curve and the F1 score, which, using equal weights for precision and recall, yields an optimal threshold of 0.37. The chart has been taken from the accompanying notebook, where you can find the code for the KNN classifier that operates on binarized housing prices:

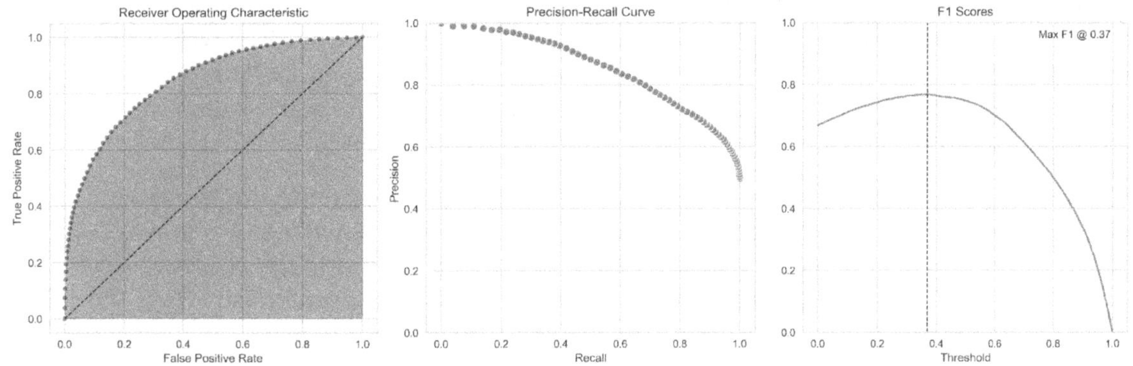

Figure 6.4: Receiver-Operating Characteristics, Precision-Recall Curve, and F1 Scores charts

Collecting and preparing the data

We already addressed important aspects of how to source market, fundamental, and alternative data in *Chapter 2, Market and Fundamental Data – Sources and Techniques*, and *Chapter 3, Alternative Data for Finance – Categories and Use Cases*. We will continue to work with various examples of these sources as we illustrate the application of the various models.

In addition to market and fundamental data, we will also acquire and transform text data as we explore natural language processing and image data when we look at image processing and recognition. Besides obtaining, cleaning, and validating the data, we may need to assign labels such as sentiment for news articles or timestamps to align it with trading data typically available in a time-series format.

It is also important to store it in a format that enables quick exploration and iteration. We recommend the HDF and parquet formats (see *Chapter 2, Market and Fundamental Data – Sources and Techniques*). For data that does not fit into memory and requires distributed processing on several machines, Apache Spark is often the best solution for interactive analysis and machine learning.

Exploring, extracting, and engineering features

Understanding the distribution of individual variables and the relationships among outcomes and features is the basis for picking a suitable algorithm. This typically starts with **visualizations** such as scatter plots, as illustrated in the accompanying notebook and shown in *Figure 6.5*:

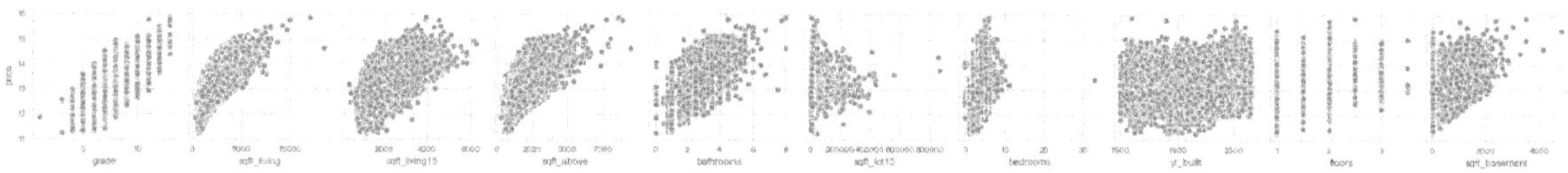

Figure 6.5: Pairwise scatter plots of outcome and features

It also includes **numerical evaluations** ranging from linear metrics like correlation to nonlinear statistics, such as the Spearman rank correlation coefficient that we encountered when we introduced the information coefficient in *Chapter 4, Financial Feature Engineering – How to Research Alpha Factors*. There are also information-theoretic measures, such as mutual information, which we'll illustrate in the next subsection.

A systematic exploratory analysis is also the basis of what is often the single most important ingredient of a successful predictive model: the **engineering of features** that extract information contained in the data, but which are not necessarily accessible to the algorithm in their raw form. Feature engineering benefits from domain expertise, the application of statistics and information theory, and creativity.

It relies on smart data transformations that effectively tease out the systematic relationship between input and output data. There are many choices that include outlier detection and treatment, functional transformations, and the combination of several variables, including unsupervised learning. We will illustrate examples throughout, but will emphasize that this central aspect of the ML workflow is best learned through experience. Kaggle is a great place to learn from other data scientists who share their experiences with the community.

Using information theory to evaluate features

The **mutual information** (**MI**) between a feature and the outcome is a measure of the mutual dependence between the two variables. It extends the notion of correlation to nonlinear relationships. More specifically, it quantifies the information obtained about one random variable through the other random variable.

The concept of MI is closely related to the fundamental notion of entropy of a random variable. Entropy quantifies the amount of information contained in a random variable. Formally, the mutual information—$I(X, Y)$—of two random variables, X and Y, is defined as the following:

$$I(X,Y) = \int_Y \int_X p(x,y) \log\left(\frac{p(x,y)}{p(x)p(y)}\right)$$

The sklearn function implements `feature_selection.mutual_info_regression`, which computes the mutual information between all features and a continuous outcome to select the features that are most likely to contain predictive information. There is also a classification version (see the sklearn documentation for more details). The `mutual_information.ipynb` notebook contains an application for the financial data we created in *Chapter 4, Financial Feature Engineering – How to Research Alpha Factors.*

Selecting an ML algorithm

The remainder of this book will introduce several model families, ranging from linear models, which make fairly strong assumptions about the nature of the functional relationship between input and output variables, to deep neural networks, which make very few assumptions. As mentioned in the introductory section, fewer assumptions will require more data with significant information about the relationship so that the learning process can be successful.

We will outline the key assumptions and how to test them where applicable as we introduce these models.

Design and tune the model

The ML process includes steps to diagnose and manage model complexity based on estimates of the model's generalization error. An important goal of the ML process is to obtain an unbiased estimate of this error using a statistically sound and efficient procedure. Key to managing the model design and tuning process is an understanding of how the bias-variance tradeoff relates to under- and overfitting.

The bias-variance trade-off

The prediction errors of an ML model can be broken down into reducible and irreducible parts. The irreducible part is due to random variation (noise) in the data due to, for example, the absence of relevant variables, natural variation, or measurement errors. The reducible part of the generalization error, in turn, can be broken down into errors due to **bias** and **variance**.

Both result from discrepancies between the true functional relationship and the assumptions made by the machine learning algorithm, as detailed in the following list:

- **Error due to bias**: The hypothesis is too simple to capture the complexity of the true functional relationship. As a result, whenever the model attempts to learn the true function, it makes systematic mistakes and, on average, the predictions will be similarly biased. This is also called *underfitting*.
- **Error due to variance**: The algorithm is overly complex in view of the true relationship. Instead of capturing the true relationship, it overfits the data and extracts patterns from the noise. As a result, it learns different functional relationships from each sample, and out-of-sample predictions will vary widely.

Underfitting versus overfitting – a visual example

Figure 6.6 illustrates overfitting by measuring the in-sample error of approximations of a *sine* function by increasingly complex polynomials. More specifically, we draw a random sample with some added noise (n = 30) to learn a polynomial of varying complexity (see the code in the notebook, `bias_variance.ipynb`). The model predicts new data points, and we capture the mean-squared error for these predictions.

The left-hand panel of *Figure 6.6* shows a polynomial of degree 1; a straight line clearly underfits the true function. However, the estimated line will not differ dramatically from one sample drawn from the true function to the next.

The middle panel shows that a degree 5 polynomial approximates the true relationship reasonably well on the interval from about $-\pi$ until 2π. On the other hand, a polynomial of degree 15 fits the small sample almost perfectly, but provides a poor estimate of the true relationship: it overfits to the random variation in the sample data points, and the learned function will vary strongly as a function of the sample:

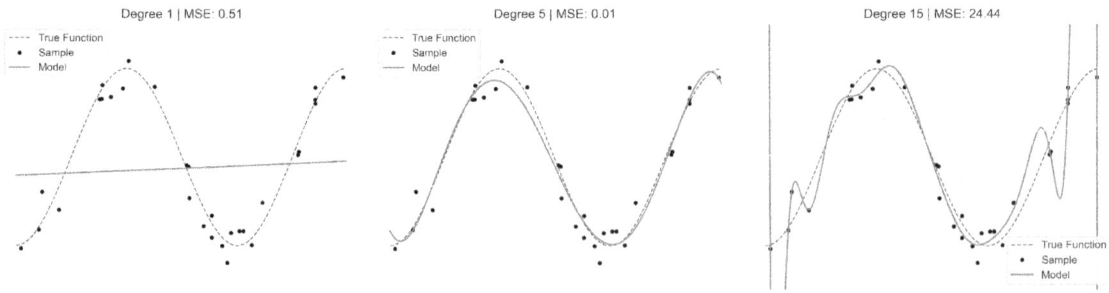

Figure 6.6: A visual example of overfitting with polynomials

How to manage the bias-variance trade-off

To further illustrate the impact of overfitting versus underfitting, we'll try to learn a Taylor series approximation of the *sine* function of the ninth degree with some added noise. *Figure 6.7* shows the in- and-out-of-sample errors and the out-of-sample predictions for polynomials that underfit, overfit, and provide an approximately correct level of flexibility with degrees 1, 15, and 9, respectively, to 100 random samples of the true function.

The left-hand panel shows the distribution of the errors that result from subtracting the true function values from the predictions. The high bias but low variance of an underfit polynomial of degree 1 compares to the low bias but exceedingly high variance of the errors for an overfitting polynomial of degree 15. The underfit polynomial produces a straight line with a poor in-sample fit that is significantly off-target out of sample. The overfit model shows the best fit in-sample with the smallest dispersion of errors, but the price is a large variance out-of-sample. The appropriate model that matches the functional form of the true model performs, on average, by far the best on out-of-sample data.

The right-hand panel of *Figure 6.7* shows the actual predictions rather than the errors to visualize the different types of fit in practice:

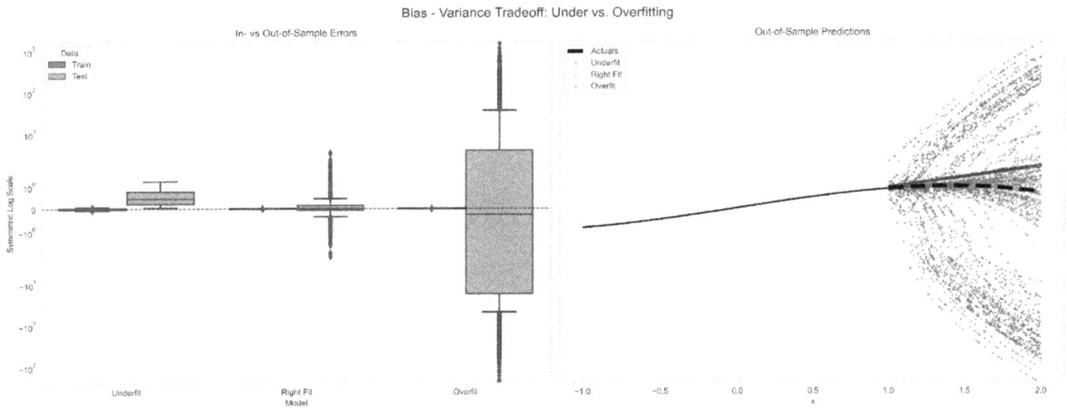

Figure 6.7: Errors and out-of-sample predictions for polynomials of different degrees

Learning curves

A learning curve plots the evolution of train and test errors against the size of the dataset used to learn the functional relationship. It helps to diagnose the bias-variance trade-off for a given model, and also answer the question of whether increasing the sample size might improve predictive performance. A model with a high bias will have a high but similar training error, both in-sample and out-of-sample. An overfit model will have a very low training but much higher test errors.

Figure 6.8 shows how the out-of-sample error for the overfitted model declines as the sample size increases, suggesting that it may benefit from additional data or tools to limit the model's complexity, such as regularization. Regularization adds data-driven constraints to the model's complexity; we'll introduce this technique in *Chapter 7, Linear Models – From Risk Factors to Return Forecasts.*

Underfit models, in contrast, require either more features or need to increase their capacity to capture the true relationship:

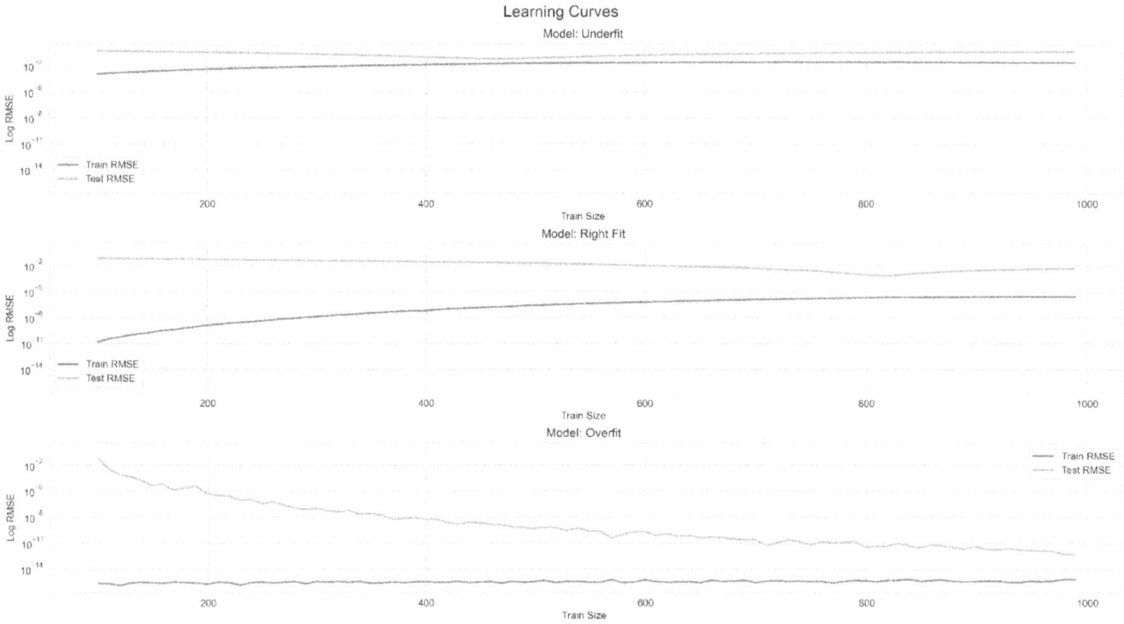

Figure 6.8: Learning curves and bias-variance tradeoff

How to select a model using cross-validation

There are usually several candidate models for your use case, and the task of choosing one of them is known as the **model selection problem**. The goal is to identify the model that will produce the lowest prediction error when given new data.

A good choice requires an unbiased estimate of this generalization error, which, in turn, requires testing the model on data that was not part of model training. Otherwise, the model would have already been able to peek at the "solution" and learn something about the prediction task ahead of time that will inflate its performance.

To avoid this, we only use part of the available data to train the model and set aside another part of the data to validate its performance. The resulting estimate of the model's prediction error on new data will only be unbiased if absolutely no information about the validation set leaks into the training set, as shown in *Figure 6.9*:

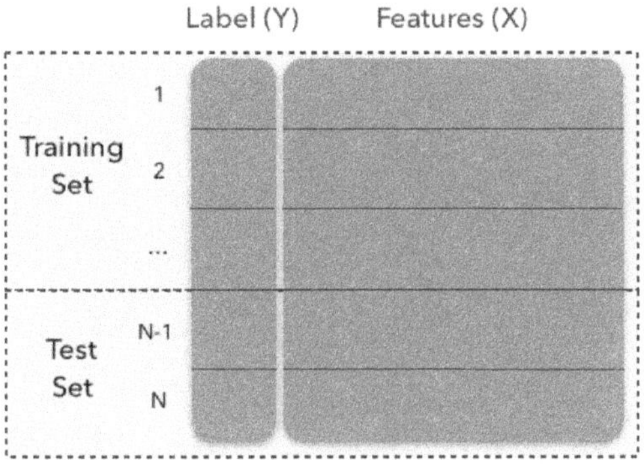

Figure 6.9: Training and test set

Cross-validation (**CV**) is a popular strategy for model selection. The main idea behind CV is to split the data one or several times. This is done so that each split is used once as a validation set and the remainder as a training set: part of the data (the training sample) is used to train the algorithm, and the remaining part (the validation sample) is used to estimate the algorithm's predictive performance. Then, CV selects the algorithm with the smallest estimated error or risk.

Several methods can be used to split the available data. They differ in terms of the amount of data used for training, the variance of the error estimates, the computational intensity, and whether structural aspects of the data are taken into account when splitting the data, such as maintaining the ratio between class labels.

While the data-splitting heuristic is very general, a key assumption of CV is that the data is **independently and identically distributed** (**IID**). In the following section and throughout this book, we will emphasize that **time-series data** requires a different approach because it usually does not meet this assumption. Moreover, we need to ensure that splits respect the temporal order to avoid **lookahead bias**. We'll do this by including some information from the future that we aim to predict in the historical training set.

Model selection often involves hyperparameter tuning, which may result in many CV iterations. The resulting validation score of the best-performing model will be subject to **multiple testing bias**, which reflects the sampling noise inherent in the CV process. As a result, it is no longer a good estimate of the generalization error. For an unbiased estimate of the error rate, we have to estimate the score from a fresh dataset.

For this reason, we use a three-way split of the data, as shown in *Figure 6.10*: one part is used in cross-validation and is repeatedly split into a training and validation set. The remainder is set aside as a hold-out set that is only used once after, cross-validation is complete to generate an unbiased test error estimate.

We will illustrate this method as we start building ML models in the next chapter:

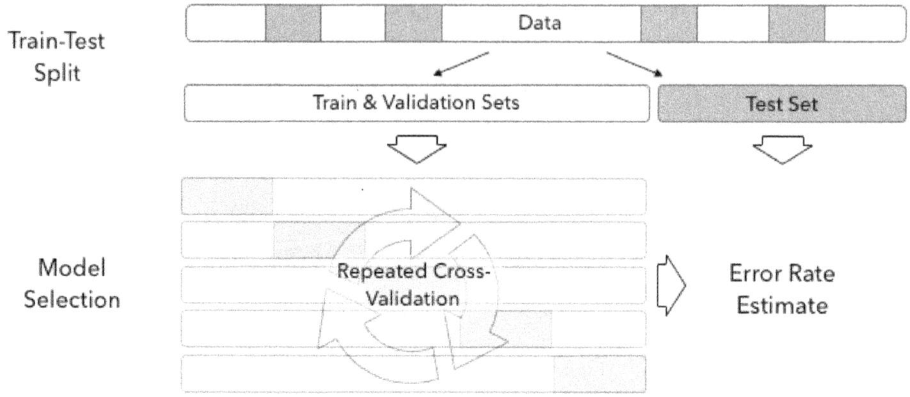

Figure 6.10: Train, validation, and hold-out test set

How to implement cross-validation in Python

We will illustrate various options for splitting data into training and test sets. We'll do this by showing how the indices of a mock dataset with 10 observations are assigned to the train and test set (see `cross_validation.py` for details), as shown in following code:

```
data = list(range(1, 11))
[1, 2, 3, 4, 5, 6, 7, 8, 9, 10]
```

Scikit-learn's CV functionality, which we'll demonstrate in this section, can be imported from `sklearn.model_selection`.

For a single split of your data into a training and a test set, use `train_test_split`, where the `shuffle` parameter, by default, ensures the randomized selection of observations. You can ensure replicability by seeding the random number generator by setting `random_state`. There is also a `stratify` parameter, which ensures for a classification problem that the train and test sets will contain approximately the same proportion of each class. The result looks as follows:

```
train_test_split(data, train_size=.8)
[[8, 7, 4, 10, 1, 3, 5, 2], [6, 9]]
```

In this case, we train a model using all data except row numbers `6` and `9`, which will be used to generate predictions and measure the errors given on the known labels. This method is useful for quick evaluation but is sensitive to the split, and the standard error of the performance measure estimate will be higher.

KFold iterator

The `KFold` iterator produces several disjunct splits and assigns each of these splits once to the validation set, as shown in the following code:

```
kf = KFold(n_splits=5)
for train, validate in kf.split(data):
    print(train, validate)
[2 3 4 5 6 7 8 9] [0 1]
[0 1 4 5 6 7 8 9] [2 3]
[0 1 2 3 6 7 8 9] [4 5]
[0 1 2 3 4 5 8 9] [6 7]
[0 1 2 3 4 5 6 7] [8 9]
```

In addition to the number of splits, most CV objects take a `shuffle` argument that ensures randomization. To render results reproducible, set the `random_state` as follows:

```
kf = KFold(n_splits=5, shuffle=True, random_state=42)
for train, validate in kf.split(data):
    print(train, validate)
[0 2 3 4 5 6 7 9] [1 8]
[1 2 3 4 6 7 8 9] [0 5]
[0 1 3 4 5 6 8 9] [2 7]
[0 1 2 3 5 6 7 8] [4 9]
[0 1 2 4 5 7 8 9] [3 6]
```

Leave-one-out CV

The original CV implementation used a **leave-one-out method** that used each observation once as the validation set, as shown in the following code:

```
loo = LeaveOneOut()
for train, validate in loo.split(data):
    print(train, validate)
[1 2 3 4 5 6 7 8 9] [0]
[0 2 3 4 5 6 7 8 9] [1]
...
[0 1 2 3 4 5 6 7 9] [8]
[0 1 2 3 4 5 6 7 8] [9]
```

This maximizes the number of models that are trained, which increases computational costs. While the validation sets do not overlap, the overlap of training sets is maximized, driving up the correlation of models and their prediction errors. As a result, the variance of the prediction error is higher for a model with a larger number of folds.

Leave-P-Out CV

A similar version to leave-one-out CV is **leave-P-out CV**, which generates all possible combinations of `p` data rows, as shown in the following code:

```
lpo = LeavePOut(p=2)
for train, validate in lpo.split(data):
    print(train, validate)
[2 3 4 5 6 7 8 9] [0 1]
[1 3 4 5 6 7 8 9] [0 2]
...
[0 1 2 3 4 5 6 8] [7 9]
[0 1 2 3 4 5 6 7] [8 9]
```

ShuffleSplit

The `ShuffleSplit` class creates independent splits with potentially overlapping validation sets, as shown in the following code:

```
ss = ShuffleSplit(n_splits=3, test_size=2, random_state=42)
for train, validate in ss.split(data):
    print(train, validate)
[4 9 1 6 7 3 0 5] [2 8]
[1 2 9 8 0 6 7 4] [3 5]
[8 4 5 1 0 6 9 7] [2 3]
```

Challenges with cross-validation in finance

A key assumption for the cross-validation methods discussed so far is the IID distribution of the samples available for training.

For financial data, this is often not the case. On the contrary, financial data is neither independently nor identically distributed because of serial correlation and time-varying standard deviation, also known as **heteroskedasticity** (see *Chapter 7, Linear Models – From Risk Factors to Return Forecasts,* and *Chapter 9, Time Series Models for Volatility Forecasts and Statistical Arbitrage,* for more details). `TimeSeriesSplit` in the `sklearn.model_selection` module aims to address the linear order of time-series data.

Time series cross-validation with scikit-learn

The time-series nature of the data implies that cross-validation produces a situation where data from the future will be used to predict data from the past. This is unrealistic at best and data snooping at worst, to the extent that future data reflects past events.

To address time dependency, the `TimeSeriesSplit` object implements a walk-forward test with an expanding training set, where subsequent training sets are supersets of past training sets, as shown in the following code:

```
tscv = TimeSeriesSplit(n_splits=5)
```

```
for train, validate in tscv.split(data):
    print(train, validate)
[0 1 2 3 4] [5]
[0 1 2 3 4 5] [6]
[0 1 2 3 4 5 6] [7]
[0 1 2 3 4 5 6 7] [8]
[0 1 2 3 4 5 6 7 8] [9]
```

You can use the `max_train_size` parameter to implement walk-forward cross-validation, where the size of the training set remains constant over time, similar to how Zipline tests a trading algorithm. Scikit-learn facilitates the design of custom cross-validation methods using **subclassing**, which we will implement in the following chapters.

Purging, embargoing, and combinatorial CV

For financial data, labels are often derived from overlapping data points because returns are computed from prices across multiple periods. In the context of trading strategies, the result of a model's prediction, which may imply taking a position in an asset, can only be known later when this decision is evaluated—for example, when a position is closed out.

The risks include the leakage of information from the test into the training set, which would very likely artificially inflate performance. We need to address this risk by ensuring that all data is point-in-time—that is, truly available and known at the time it is used as the input for a model. For example, financial disclosures may refer to a certain time period but only become available later. If we include this information too early, our model might do much better in hindsight than it would have under realistic circumstances.

Marcos Lopez de Prado, one of the leading practitioners and academics in the field, has proposed several methods to address these challenges in his book, *Advances in Financial Machine Learning* (2018). Techniques to adapt cross-validation to the context of financial data and trading include:

- **Purging**: Eliminate training data points where the evaluation occurs after the prediction of a point-in-time data point in the validation set to avoid look-ahead bias.
- **Embargoing**: Further eliminate training samples that follow a test period.
- **Combinatorial cross-validation**: Walk-forward CV severely limits the historical paths that can be tested. Instead, given T observations, compute all possible train/test splits for $N<T$ groups that each maintain their order, and purge and embargo potentially overlapping groups. Then, train the model on all combinations of $N-k$ groups while testing the model on the remaining k groups. The result is a much larger number of possible historical paths.

Prado's *Advances in Financial Machine Learning* contains sample code to implement these approaches; the code is also available via the new Python library, timeseriescv.

Parameter tuning with scikit-learn and Yellowbrick

Model selection typically involves repeated cross-validation of the out-of-sample performance of models using different algorithms (such as linear regression and random forest) or different configurations. Different configurations may involve changes to hyperparameters or the inclusion or exclusion of different variables.

The Yellowbrick library extends the scikit-learn API to generate diagnostic visualization tools to facilitate the model-selection process. These tools can be used to investigate relationships among features, analyze classification or regression errors, monitor cluster algorithm performance, inspect the characteristics of text data, and help with model selection. We will demonstrate validation and learning curves that provide valuable information during the parameter-tuning phase—see the `machine_learning_workflow.ipynb` notebook for implementation details.

Validation curves – plotting the impact of hyperparameters

Validation curves (see the left-hand panel in *Figure 6.11*) visualize the impact of a single hyperparameter on a model's cross-validation performance. This is useful to determine whether the model underfits or overfits the given dataset.

In our example of `KNeighborsRegressor`, which only has a single hyperparameter, the number of neighbors is *k*. Note that model complexity increases as the number of neighbors drop because the model can now make predictions for more distinct areas in the feature space.

We can see that the model underfits for values of *k* above 20. The validation error drops as we reduce the number of neighbors and make our model more complex. For values below 20, the model begins to overfit as training and validation errors diverge and average out-of-sample performance quickly deteriorates:

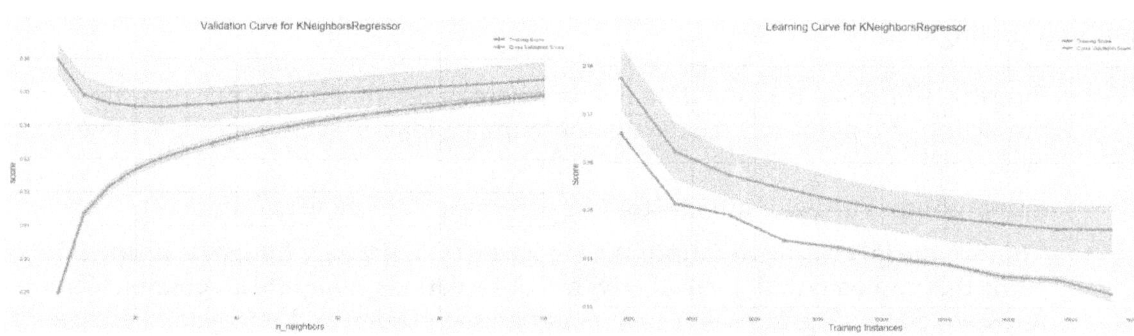

Figure 6.11: Validation and learning curves

Learning curves – diagnosing the bias-variance trade-off

The learning curve (see the right-hand panel of *Figure 6.11* for our house price regression example) helps determine whether a model's cross-validation performance would benefit from additional data, and whether the prediction errors are more driven by bias or by variance.

More data is unlikely to improve performance if training and cross-validation scores converge. At this point, it is important to evaluate whether the model performance meets expectations, determined by a human benchmark. If this is not the case, then you should modify the model's hyperparameter settings to better capture the relationship between the features and the outcome, or choose a different algorithm with a higher capacity to capture complexity.

In addition, the variation of train and test errors shown by the shaded confidence intervals provides clues about the bias and variance sources of the prediction error. Variability around the cross-validation error is evidence of variance, whereas variability for the training set suggests bias, depending on the size of the training error.

In our example, the cross-validation performance has continued to drop, but the incremental improvements have shrunk, and the errors have plateaued, so there are unlikely to be many benefits from a larger training set. On the other hand, the data is showing substantial variance given the range of validation errors compared to that shown for the training errors.

Parameter tuning using GridSearchCV and pipeline

Since hyperparameter tuning is a key ingredient of the machine learning workflow, there are tools to automate this process. The scikit-learn library includes a `GridSearchCV` interface that cross-validates all combinations of parameters in parallel, captures the result, and automatically trains the model using the parameter setting that performed best during cross-validation on the full dataset.

In practice, the training and validation set often requires some processing prior to cross-validation. Scikit-learn offers the `Pipeline` to also automate any feature-processing steps while using `GridSearchCV`.

You can look at the implementation examples in the included `machine_learning_workflow.ipynb` notebook to see these tools in action.

Summary

In this chapter, we introduced the challenge of learning from data and looked at supervised, unsupervised, and reinforcement models as the principal forms of learning that we will study in this book to build algorithmic trading strategies. We discussed the need for supervised learning algorithms to make assumptions about the functional relationships that they attempt to learn. They do this to limit the search space while incurring an inductive bias that may lead to excessive generalization errors.

We presented key aspects of the machine learning workflow, introduced the most common error metrics for regression and classification models, explained the bias-variance trade-off, and illustrated the various tools for managing the model selection process using cross-validation.

In the following chapter, we will dive into linear models for regression and classification to develop our first algorithmic trading strategies that use machine learning.

7

Linear Models – From Risk Factors to Return Forecasts

The family of linear models represents one of the most useful hypothesis classes. Many learning algorithms that are widely applied in algorithmic trading rely on linear predictors because they can be efficiently trained, are relatively robust to noisy financial data, and have strong links to the theory of finance. Linear predictors are also intuitive, easy to interpret, and often fit the data reasonably well or at least provide a good baseline.

Linear regression has been known for over 200 years, since Legendre and Gauss applied it to astronomy and began to analyze its statistical properties. Numerous extensions have since adapted the linear regression model and the baseline **ordinary least squares** (**OLS**) method to learn its parameters:

- **Generalized linear models** (**GLM**) expand the scope of applications by allowing for response variables that imply an error distribution other than the normal distribution. GLMs include the probit or logistic models for **categorical response variables** that appear in classification problems.
- More **robust estimation methods** enable statistical inference where the data violates baseline assumptions due to, for example, correlation over time or across observations. This is often the case with panel data that contains repeated observations on the same units, such as historical returns on a universe of assets.
- **Shrinkage methods** aim to improve the predictive performance of linear models. They use a complexity penalty that biases the coefficients learned by the model, with the goal of reducing the model's variance and improving out-of-sample predictive performance.

In practice, linear models are applied to regression and classification problems with the goals of inference and prediction. Numerous asset pricing models have been developed by academic and industry researchers that leverage linear regression. Applications include the identification of significant factors that drive asset returns for better risk and performance management, as well as the prediction of returns over various time horizons. Classification problems, on the other hand, include directional price forecasts.

In this chapter, we will cover the following topics:

- How linear regression works and which assumptions it makes
- Training and diagnosing linear regression models
- Using linear regression to predict stock returns
- Use regularization to improve predictive performance
- How logistic regression works
- Converting a regression into a classification problem

> You can find the code samples for this chapter and links to additional resources in the corresponding directory of the GitHub repository. The notebooks include color versions of the images.

From inference to prediction

As the name suggests, linear regression models assume that the output is the result of a linear combination of the inputs. The model also assumes a random error that allows for each observation to deviate from the expected linear relationship. The reasons that the model does not perfectly describe the relationship between inputs and output in a deterministic way include, for example, missing variables, measurement, or data collection issues.

If we want to draw statistical conclusions about the true (but not observed) linear relationship in the population based on the regression parameters estimated from the sample, we need to add assumptions about the statistical nature of these errors. The baseline regression model makes the strong assumption that the distribution of the errors is identical across observations. It also assumes that errors are independent of each other—in other words, knowing one error does not help to forecast the next error. The assumption of **independent and identically distributed** (**IID**) errors implies that their covariance matrix is the identity matrix multiplied by a constant representing the error variance.

These assumptions guarantee that the OLS method delivers estimates that are not only unbiased but also efficient, which means that OLS estimates achieve the lowest sampling error among all linear learning algorithms. However, these assumptions are rarely met in practice.

In finance, we often encounter panel data with repeated observations on a given cross section. The attempt to estimate the systematic exposure of a universe of assets to a set of risk factors over time typically reveals correlation along the time axis, in the cross-sectional dimension, or both. Hence, alternative learning algorithms have emerged that assume error covariance matrices that are more complex than multiples of the identity matrix.

On the other hand, methods that learn biased parameters for a linear model may yield estimates with lower variance and, hence, improve their predictive performance. Shrinkage methods reduce the model's complexity by applying regularization, which adds a penalty term to the linear objective function.

This penalty is positively related to the absolute size of the coefficients so that they are shrunk relative to the baseline case. Larger coefficients imply a more complex model that reacts more strongly to variations in the inputs. When properly calibrated, the penalty can limit the growth of the model's coefficients beyond what is optimal from a bias-variance perspective.

First, we will introduce the baseline techniques for cross-section and panel data for linear models, as well as important enhancements that produce accurate estimates when key assumptions are violated. We will then illustrate these methods by estimating factor models that are ubiquitous in the development of algorithmic trading strategies. Finally, we will turn our attention to how shrinkage methods apply regularization and demonstrate how to use them to predict asset returns and generate trading signals.

The baseline model – multiple linear regression

We will begin with the model's specification and objective function, the methods we can use to learn its parameters, and the statistical assumptions that allow the inference and diagnostics of these assumptions. Then, we will present extensions that we can use to adapt the model to situations that violate these assumptions. Useful references for additional background include *Wooldridge* (*2002* and *2008*).

How to formulate the model

The multiple regression model defines a linear functional relationship between one continuous outcome variable and p input variables that can be of any type but may require preprocessing. Multivariate regression, in contrast, refers to the regression of multiple outputs on multiple input variables.

In the population, the linear regression model has the following form for a single instance of the output y, an input vector $\mathbf{X}^T = [x_1,, x_p]$, and the error ϵ:

$$y = f(\mathrm{x}) + \epsilon = \beta_0 + \beta_1 x_1 \ldots + \beta_p x_p + \epsilon = \beta_0 + \sum_{j=1}^{p} \beta_j x_j + \epsilon$$

The interpretation of the coefficients is straightforward: the value of a coefficient β_i is the partial, average effect of the variable x_i on the output, holding all other variables constant.

We can also write the model more compactly in matrix form. In this case, y is a vector of N output observations, X is the design matrix with N rows of observations on the p variables plus a column of 1s for the intercept, and β is the vector containing the $P = p+1$ coefficients:

$$\underset{(N \times 1)}{\boldsymbol{y}} = \underset{(N \times P)}{\boldsymbol{X}}\underset{(P \times 1)}{\boldsymbol{\beta}} + \underset{(N \times 1)}{\boldsymbol{\epsilon}}$$

The model is linear in its p +1 parameters but can represent nonlinear relationships if we choose or transform variables accordingly, for example, by including a polynomial basis expansion or logarithmic terms. You can also use categorical variables with dummy encoding, and include interactions between variables by creating new inputs of the form $x_i x_j$.

To complete the formulation of the model from a statistical point of view so that we can test hypotheses about its parameters, we need to make specific assumptions about the error term. We'll do this after introducing the most important methods to learn the parameters.

How to train the model

There are several methods we can use to learn the model parameters from the data: **ordinary least squares** (OLS), **maximum likelihood estimation** (MLE), and **stochastic gradient descent** (SGD). We will present each method in turn.

Ordinary least squares – how to fit a hyperplane to the data

The method of least squares is the original method that learns the parameters of the hyperplane that best approximates the output from the input data. As the name suggests, it takes the best approximation to minimize the sum of the squared distances between the output value and the hyperplane represented by the model.

The difference between the model's prediction and the actual outcome for a given data point is the **residual** (whereas the deviation of the true model from the true output in the population is called **error**). Hence, in formal terms, the least-squares estimation method chooses the coefficient vector to minimize the **residual sum of squares** (**RSS**):

$$\begin{aligned}\mathrm{RSS}(\boldsymbol{\beta}) &= \sum_{i=1}^{N} \epsilon_i^2 \\ &= \sum_{i=1}^{N} (y_i - f(x_i))^2 \\ &= \sum_{i=1}^{N} \left(y_i - \beta_0 - \sum_{j=1}^{p} x_{ij}\beta_j \right)^2 \\ &= (\boldsymbol{y} - \boldsymbol{X}\beta)^T(\boldsymbol{y} - \boldsymbol{X}\beta)\end{aligned}$$

Thus, the least-squares coefficients β^{LS} are computed as:

$$\underset{\beta^{LS}}{\operatorname{argmin}} \ \mathrm{RSS}(\boldsymbol{\beta}) = (y - \boldsymbol{X}\beta)^T(y - \boldsymbol{X}\beta)$$

The optimal parameter vector that minimizes the RSS results from setting the derivatives with respect to $\boldsymbol{\beta}$ of the preceding expression to zero. Assuming X has full column rank, which requires that the input variables are not linearly dependent, it is thus invertible, and we obtain a unique solution, as follows:

$$\hat{\beta} = (\boldsymbol{X}^T X)^{-1} \boldsymbol{X}^T \boldsymbol{y}$$

When y and X have means of zero, which can be achieved by subtracting their respective means, $\boldsymbol{\beta}$ represents the ratio of the covariance between the inputs and the outputs $\boldsymbol{X}^T\boldsymbol{y}$ and the output variance $\boldsymbol{X}^T\boldsymbol{X}$

There is also a geometric interpretation: the coefficients that minimize RSS ensure that the vector of residuals $\boldsymbol{y}-\hat{\boldsymbol{y}}$ is orthogonal to the subspace of $\mathbb{R}^P$ spanned by the P columns of X, and the estimates $\hat{y}$ are orthogonal projections into that subspace.

Maximum likelihood estimation

MLE is an important general method used to estimate the parameters of a statistical model. It relies on the likelihood function, which computes how likely it is to observe the sample of outputs when given the input data as a function of the model parameters. The likelihood differs from probabilities in that it is not normalized to a range from 0 to 1.

We can set up the likelihood function for the multiple linear regression example by assuming a distribution for the error term, such as the standard normal distribution:

$$\epsilon_i \sim N(0,1) \quad \forall\, i = 1, \dots, n$$

This allows us to compute the conditional probability of observing a given output y_i given the corresponding input vector x_i and the parameters $\boldsymbol{\beta}$, $p(y_i|\boldsymbol{x}_i, \boldsymbol{\beta})$:

$$p(y_i|\boldsymbol{x}_i, \boldsymbol{\beta}) = \frac{1}{\sigma\sqrt{2\pi}} e^{-\frac{\epsilon_i^2}{2\sigma}} = \frac{1}{\sigma\sqrt{2\pi}} e^{-\frac{(y_i - x_i\beta)^2}{2\sigma}}$$

Assuming the output values are conditionally independent, given the inputs, the likelihood of the sample is proportional to the product of the conditional probabilities of the individual output data points. Since it is easier to work with sums than with products, we apply the logarithm to obtain the **log-likelihood function**:

$$\log \mathcal{L}(\boldsymbol{y}, \boldsymbol{x}, \boldsymbol{\beta}) = \sum_{i=1}^{n} \frac{1}{\sigma\sqrt{2\pi}} e^{-\frac{(y_i - x_i\beta)^2}{2\sigma}}$$

The goal of MLE is to choose the model parameters that maximize the probability of the observed output sample, taking the inputs as given. Hence, the MLE parameter estimate results from maximizing the log-likelihood function:

$$\beta_{\text{MLE}} = \underset{\beta}{\operatorname{argmin}} \quad \mathcal{L}$$

Due to the assumption of normally distributed errors, maximizing the log-likelihood function produces the same parameter solution as least squares. This is because the only expression that depends on the parameters is the squared residual in the exponent.

For other distributional assumptions and models, MLE will produce different results, as we will see in the last section on binary classification, where the outcome follows a Bernoulli distribution. Furthermore, MLE is a more general estimation method because, in many cases, the least-squares method is not applicable, as we will see later for logistic regression.

Gradient descent

Gradient descent is a general-purpose optimization algorithm that will find stationary points of smooth functions. The solution will be a global optimum if the objective function is convex. Variations of gradient descent are widely used in training complex neural networks, but also to compute solutions for MLE problems.

The algorithm uses the gradient of the objective function. The gradient contains the partial derivatives of the objective with respect to the parameters. These derivatives indicate how much the objective changes for an infinitesimal (infinitely small) step in the direction of the corresponding parameters. It turns out that the maximal change of the function value results from a step in the direction of the gradient itself.

Figure 7.1 sketches the process for a single variable x and a convex function $f(x)$, where we are looking for the minimum, x_0 . Where the function has a negative slope, gradient descent increases the target value for x_0, and decreases the values otherwise:

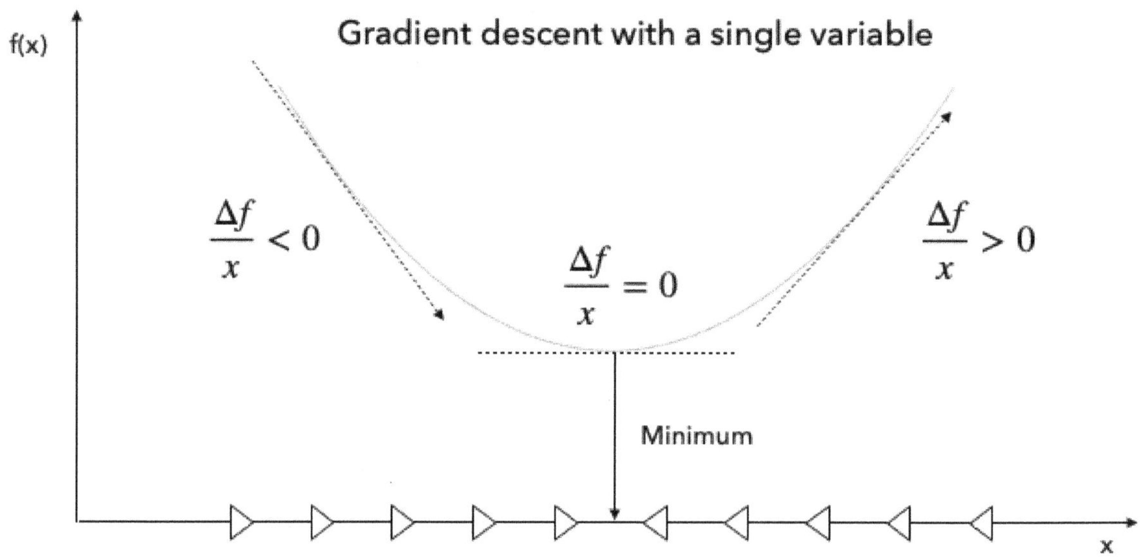

Figure 7.1: Gradient descent

When we minimize a function that describes, for example, the cost of a prediction error, the algorithm computes the gradient for the current parameter values using the training data. Then, it modifies each parameter in proportion to the negative value of its corresponding gradient component. As a result, the objective function will assume a lower value and move the parameters closer to the solution. The optimization stops when the gradient becomes small, and the parameter values change very little.

The size of these steps is determined by the learning rate, which is a critical parameter that may require tuning. Many implementations include the option for this learning rate to gradually decrease with the number of iterations. Depending on the size of the data, the algorithm may iterate many times over the entire dataset. Each such iteration is called an **epoch**. The number of epochs and the tolerance used to stop further iterations are additional hyperparameters you can tune.

Stochastic gradient descent randomly selects a data point and computes the gradient for this data point, as opposed to an average over a larger sample to achieve a speedup. There are also batch versions that use a certain number of data points for each step.

The Gauss–Markov theorem

To assess the statistical properties of the model and run inference, we need to make assumptions about the residuals that represent the part of the input data the model is unable to correctly fit or "explain."

The **Gauss–Markov theorem** (**GMT**) defines the assumptions required for OLS to produce unbiased estimates of the model parameters $\boldsymbol{\beta}$, and for these estimates to have the lowest standard error among all linear models for cross-sectional data.

The baseline multiple regression model makes the following GMT assumptions (Wooldridge 2008):

- In the population, linearity holds so that $y = \beta_0 + \beta_1 x_x + \cdots + \beta_k x_x + \epsilon$, where $\boldsymbol{\beta}_{\mathrm{i}}$ are unknown but constant and $\boldsymbol{\epsilon}$ is a random error.
- The data for the input variables $x_1, \ldots, x_k$ is a random sample from the population.
- No perfect collinearity—there are no exact linear relationships among the input variables.
- The error $\boldsymbol{\epsilon}$ has a conditional mean of zero given any of the inputs: $E[\epsilon_1, \ldots, x_k] = 0$.
- Homoskedasticity—the error term ϵ has constant variance given the inputs: $E[\epsilon|x_1, \ldots, x_k] = \sigma^2$

The fourth assumption implies that no missing variable exists that is correlated with any of the input variables.

Under the first four assumptions (GMT 1-4), the OLS method delivers unbiased estimates. Including an irrelevant variable does not bias the intercept and slope estimates, but omitting a relevant variable will result in biased parameter estimates.

Under GMT 1-4, OLS is then also consistent: as the sample size increases, the estimates converge to the true value as the standard errors become arbitrary. The converse is, unfortunately, also true: if the conditional expectation of the error is not zero because the model misses a relevant variable or the functional form is wrong (for example, quadratic or log terms are missing), then all parameter estimates are biased. If the error is correlated with any of the input variables, then OLS is also not consistent and adding more data will not remove the bias.

If we add the fifth assumption, then OLS also produces the **best linear unbiased estimates (BLUE)**. Best means that the estimates have the lowest standard error among all linear estimators. Hence, if the five assumptions hold and the goal is statistical inference, then the OLS estimates are the way to go. If the goal, however, is to predict, then we will see that other estimators exist that trade some bias for a lower variance to achieve superior predictive performance in many settings.

Now that we have introduced the basic OLS assumptions, we can take a look at inference in small and large samples.

How to conduct statistical inference

Inference in the linear regression context aims to draw conclusions from the sample data about the true relationship in the population. This includes testing hypotheses about the significance of the overall relationship or the values of particular coefficients, as well as estimates of confidence intervals.

The key ingredient for statistical inference is a test statistic with a known distribution, typically computed from a quantity of interest like a regression coefficient. We can formulate a null hypothesis about this statistic and compute the probability of observing the actual value for this statistic, given the sample under the assumption that the hypothesis is correct. This probability is commonly referred to as the **p-value**: if it drops below a significance threshold (typically 5 percent), then we reject the hypothesis because it makes the value that we observed for the test statistic in the sample very unlikely. On the flip side, the p-value reflects the probability that we are wrong in rejecting what is, in fact, a correct hypothesis.

In addition to the five GMT assumptions, the **classical linear model** assumes **normality**—that the population error is normally distributed and independent of the input variables. This strong assumption implies that the output variable is normally distributed, conditional on the input variables. It allows for the derivation of the exact distribution of the coefficients, which, in turn, implies exact distributions of the test statistics that are needed for exact hypotheses tests in small samples. This assumption often fails in practice—asset returns, for instance, are not normally distributed.

Fortunately, however, the test statistics used under normality are also approximately valid when normality does not hold. More specifically, the following distributional characteristics of the test statistics hold approximately under GMT assumptions 1-5 and exactly when normality holds:

- The parameter estimates follow a multivariate normal distribution: $\hat{\beta} \sim N(\beta, (\boldsymbol{X}^T\boldsymbol{X})^{-1}\sigma$.
- Under GMT 1-5, the parameter estimates are unbiased, and we can get an unbiased estimate of σ, the constant error variance, using $\hat{\sigma} = \frac{1}{N-p-1}\sum_{i=1}^{N}(y_i - \hat{y}_i)^2$.
- The **t-statistic for a hypothesis test about an individual coefficient** β_j is $t_j = \frac{\hat{\beta}_j}{\hat{\sigma}\sqrt{v_j}} \sim t_{N-p-1}$ and follows a *t* distribution with *N-p*-1 degrees of freedom, where v_j is the *j*'s element of the diagonal of $(X^TX)^{-1}$.
- The *t* distribution converges to the normal distribution. Since the 97.5 quantile of the normal distribution is about 1.96, a useful rule of thumb for a **95 percent confidence interval around a parameter estimate** is $\hat{\beta} \pm 2 \cdot \mathrm{se}(\hat{\beta})$, where *se* means **standard error**. An interval that includes zero implies that we can't reject the null hypothesis that the true parameter is zero and, hence, irrelevant for the model.
- The F-statistic allows for tests of restrictions on several parameters, including whether the entire regression is significant. It measures the change (reduction) in the RSS that results from additional variables.
- Finally, the **Lagrange multiplier** (**LM**) test is an alternative to the F-test for testing multiple restrictions.

How to diagnose and remedy problems

Diagnostics validate the model assumptions and help us prevent wrong conclusions when interpreting the result and conducting statistical inference. They include goodness of fit measures and various tests of the assumptions about the error term, including how closely the residuals match a normal distribution.

Furthermore, diagnostics evaluate whether the residual variance is indeed constant or exhibits heteroskedasticity (covered later in this section). They also test if the errors are conditionally uncorrelated or exhibit serial correlation, that is, if knowing one error helps to predict consecutive errors.

In addition to conducting the following diagnostic tests, you should always visually inspect the residuals. This helps to detect whether they reflect systematic patterns, as opposed to random noise that suggests the model is missing one or more factors that drive the outcome.

Goodness of fit

Goodness-of-fit measures assess how well a model explains the variation in the outcome. They help to evaluate the quality of the model specification, for instance, when selecting among different model designs.

Goodness-of-fit metrics differ in how they measure the fit. Here, we will focus on in-sample metrics; we will use out-of-sample testing and cross-validation when we focus on predictive models in the next section.

Prominent goodness-of-fit measures include the **(adjusted) R2**, which should be maximized and is based on the least-squares estimate:

- R^2 measures the share of the variation in the outcome data explained by the model and is computed as $R^2 = 1 - \frac{\text{RSS}}{\text{TSS}}$, where TSS is the sum of squared deviations of the outcome from its mean. It also corresponds to the squared correlation coefficient between the actual outcome values and those estimated by the model. The implicit goal is to maximize R^2. However, it never decreases as we add more variables. One of the shortcomings of R^2, therefore, is that it encourages overfitting.
- The adjusted R^2 penalizes R^2 for adding more variables; each additional variable needs to reduce the RSS significantly to produce better goodness of fit.

Alternatively, the **Akaike information criterion** (**AIC**) and the **Bayesian information criterion** (**BIC**) are to be minimized and are based on the maximum-likelihood estimate:

- $\text{AIC} = -2\log(\mathcal{L}^*) + 2k$, where $\mathcal{L}^*$ is the value of the maximized likelihood function and k is the number of parameters.
- $\text{BIC} = -2\log(\mathcal{L}^*) + \log(N)k$, where N is the sample size.

Both metrics penalize for complexity. BIC imposes a higher penalty, so it might underfit relative to AIC and vice versa.

Conceptually, AIC aims to find the model that best describes an unknown data-generating process, whereas BIC tries to find the best model among the set of candidates. In practice, both criteria can be used jointly to guide model selection when the goal is an in-sample fit; otherwise, cross-validation and selection based on estimates of generalization error are preferable.

Heteroskedasticity

GMT assumption 5 requires the residual covariance to take the shape $\Sigma = \sigma^2\boldsymbol{I}$, that is, a diagonal matrix with entries equal to the constant variance of the error term. **Heteroskedasticity** occurs when the residual variance is not constant but differs across observations. If the residual variance is positively correlated with an input variable, that is, when errors are larger for input values that are far from their mean, then OLS standard error estimates will be too low; consequently, the t-statistic will be inflated, leading to false discoveries of relationships where none actually exist.

Diagnostics starts with a visual inspection of the residuals. Systematic patterns in the (supposedly random) residuals suggest statistical tests of the null hypothesis that errors are homoscedastic against various alternatives. These tests include the Breusch–Pagan and White tests.

There are several ways to correct OLS estimates for heteroskedasticity:

- **Robust standard errors** (sometimes called *White standard errors*) take heteroskedasticity into account when computing the error variance using a so-called **sandwich estimator**.
- **Clustered standard errors** assume that there are distinct groups in your data that are homoscedastic, but the error variance differs between groups. These groups could be different asset classes or equities from different industries.

Several alternatives to OLS estimate the error covariance matrix using different assumptions when $\Sigma \neq \sigma^2 \boldsymbol{I}$. The following are available in `statsmodels`:

- **Weighted least squares (WLS)**: For heteroskedastic errors where the covariance matrix has only diagonal entries, as for OLS, but now the entries are allowed to vary.
- **Feasible generalized least squares (GLSAR)**: For autocorrelated errors that follow an autoregressive AR(p) process (see *Chapter 9*, *Time-Series Models for Volatility Forecasts and Statistical Arbitrage*).
- **Generalized least squares (GLS)**: For arbitrary covariance matrix structure; yields efficient and unbiased estimates in the presence of heteroskedasticity or serial correlation.

Serial correlation

Serial correlation means that consecutive residuals produced by linear regression are correlated, which violates the fourth GMT assumption. Positive serial correlation implies that the standard errors are underestimated and that the t-statistics will be inflated, leading to false discoveries if ignored. However, there are procedures to correct for serial correlation when calculating standard errors.

The **Durbin–Watson statistic** diagnoses serial correlation. It tests the hypothesis that the OLS residuals are not autocorrelated against the alternative that they follow an autoregressive process (which we will explore in the next chapter). The test statistic ranges from 0 to 4; values near 2 indicate non-autocorrelation, lower values suggest positive autocorrelation, and higher values indicate negative autocorrelation. The exact threshold values depend on the number of parameters and observations and need to be looked up in tables.

Multicollinearity

Multicollinearity occurs when two or more independent variables are highly correlated. This poses several challenges:

- It is difficult to determine which factors influence the dependent variable.
- The individual p-values can be misleading—a p-value can be high, even if the variable is, in fact, important.
- The confidence intervals for the regression coefficients will be too wide, possibly even including zero. This complicates the determination of an independent variable's effect on the outcome.

There is no formal or theory-based solution that corrects for multicollinearity. Instead, try to remove one or more of the correlated input variables, or increase the sample size.

How to run linear regression in practice

The accompanying notebook, `linear_regression_intro.ipynb`, illustrates a simple and then a multiple linear regression, the latter using both OLS and gradient descent. For the multiple regression, we generate two random input variables x_1 and x_2 that range from -50 to +50, and an outcome variable that's calculated as a linear combination of the inputs, plus random Gaussian noise, to meet the normality assumption GMT 6:

$$y = 50 + x_1 + 3x_2 + \epsilon, \quad \epsilon \sim N(0,50)$$

OLS with statsmodels

We use `statsmodels` to estimate a multiple regression model that accurately reflects the data-generating process, as follows:

```
import statsmodels.api as sm
X_ols = sm.add_constant(X)
model = sm.OLS(y, X_ols).fit()
model.summary()
```

This yields the following OLS Regression Results summary:

```
                            OLS Regression Results
==============================================================================
Dep. Variable:                      Y   R-squared:                       0.791
Model:                            OLS   Adj. R-squared:                  0.790
Method:                 Least Squares   F-statistic:                     1176.
Date:                Thu, 14 Nov 2019   Prob (F-statistic):          4.33e-212
Time:                        18:58:15   Log-Likelihood:                -3309.2
No. Observations:                 625   AIC:                             6624.
Df Residuals:                     622   BIC:                             6638.
Df Model:                           2
Covariance Type:            nonrobust
==============================================================================
                 coef    std err          t      P>|t|      [0.025      0.975]
------------------------------------------------------------------------------
const         53.2923      1.934     27.561      0.000      49.495      57.089
X_1            0.9904      0.064     15.390      0.000       0.864       1.117
X_2            2.9600      0.064     45.996      0.000       2.834       3.086
==============================================================================
Omnibus:                        0.267   Durbin-Watson:                   2.148
Prob(Omnibus):                  0.875   Jarque-Bera (JB):                0.149
Skew:                           0.014   Prob(JB):                        0.928
Kurtosis:                       3.071   Cond. No.                         30.0
==============================================================================

Warnings:
[1] Standard Errors assume that the covariance matrix of the errors is correctly specified.
```

Figure 7.2: OLS Regression Results summary

The upper part of the summary displays the dataset characteristics—namely, the estimation method and the number of observations and parameters—and indicates that standard error estimates do not account for heteroskedasticity. The middle panel shows the coefficient values that closely reflect the artificial data-generating process. We can confirm that the estimates displayed in the middle of the summary result can be obtained using the OLS formula derived previously:

```
beta = np.linalg.inv(X_ols.T.dot(X_ols)).dot(X_ols.T.dot(y))
pd.Series(beta, index=X_ols.columns)
const   53.29
X_1      0.99
X_2      2.96
```

The following code visualizes how the model fitted by the model to the randomly generated data points:

```
three_dee = plt.figure(figsize=(15, 5)).gca(projection='3d')
three_dee.scatter(data.X_1, data.X_2, data.Y, c='g')
data['y-hat'] = model.predict()
to_plot = data.set_index(['X_1', 'X_2']).unstack().loc[:, 'y-hat']
three_dee.plot_surface(X_1, X_2, to_plot.values, color='black', alpha=0.2,
linewidth=1, antialiased=True)
for _, row in data.iterrows():
    plt.plot((row.X_1, row.X_1), (row.X_2, row.X_2), (row.Y, row['y-hat']),
             'k-');
three_dee.set_xlabel('$X_1$');three_dee.set_ylabel('$X_2$');three_dee.set_
zlabel('$Y, \hat{Y}$')
```

Figure 7.3 displays the resulting hyperplane and original data points:

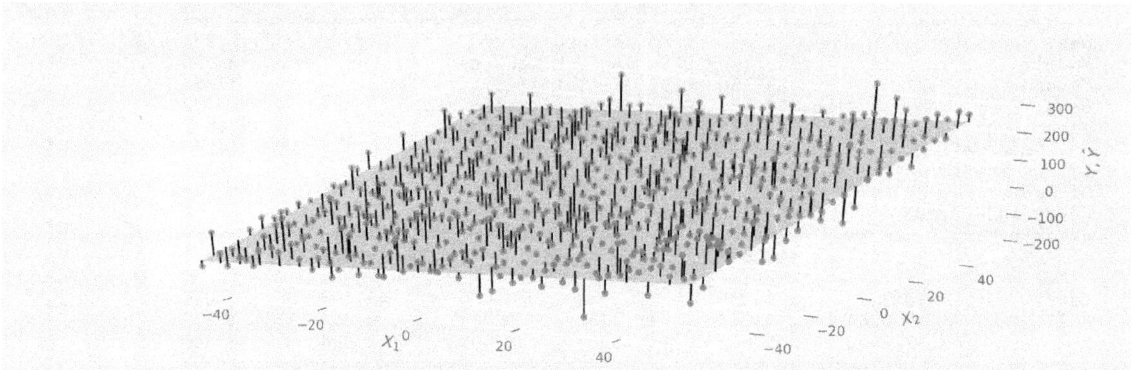

Figure 7.3: Regression hyperplane

The upper right part of the panel displays the goodness-of-fit measures we just discussed, alongside the F-test, which rejects the hypothesis that all coefficients are zero and irrelevant. Similarly, the t-statistics indicate that intercept and both slope coefficients are, unsurprisingly, highly significant.

The bottom part of the summary contains the residual diagnostics. The left panel displays skew and kurtosis, which are used to test the normality hypothesis. Both the Omnibus and the Jarque–Bera tests fail to reject the null hypothesis that the residuals are normally distributed. The Durbin–Watson statistic tests for serial correlation in the residuals and has a value near 2, which, given two parameters and 625 observations, fails to reject the hypothesis of no serial correlation, as outlined in the previous section on this topic.

Lastly, the condition number provides evidence about multicollinearity: it is the ratio of the square roots of the largest and the smallest eigenvalue of the design matrix that contains the input data. A value above 30 suggests that the regression may have significant multicollinearity.

`statsmodels` includes additional diagnostic tests that are linked in the notebook.

Stochastic gradient descent with sklearn

The sklearn library includes an `SGDRegressor` model in its `linear_models` module. To learn the parameters for the same model using this method, we need to standardize the data because the gradient is sensitive to the scale.

We use the `StandardScaler()` for this purpose: it computes the mean and the standard deviation for each input variable during the fit step, and then subtracts the mean and divides by the standard deviation during the transform step, which we can conveniently conduct in a single `fit_transform()` command:

```
scaler = StandardScaler()
X_ = scaler.fit_transform(X)
```

Then, we instantiate `SGDRegressor` using the default values except for a `random_state` setting to facilitate replication:

```
sgd = SGDRegressor(loss='squared_loss',
                   fit_intercept=True,
                   shuffle=True, # shuffle data for better estimates
                   random_state=42,
                   learning_rate='invscaling', # reduce rate over time
                   eta0=0.01, # parameters for learning rate path
                   power_t=0.25)
```

Now, we can fit the `sgd` model, create the in-sample predictions for both the OLS and the `sgd` models, and compute the root mean squared error for each:

```
sgd.fit(X=X_, y=y)
resids = pd.DataFrame({'sgd': y - sgd.predict(X_),
                       'ols': y - model.predict(sm.add_constant(X))})
resids.pow(2).sum().div(len(y)).pow(.5)
ols   48.22
sgd   48.22
```

As expected, both models yield the same result. We will now take on a more ambitious project using linear regression to estimate a multi-factor asset pricing model.

How to build a linear factor model

Algorithmic trading strategies use factor models to quantify the relationship between the return of an asset and the sources of risk that are the main drivers of these returns. Each factor risk carries a premium, and the total asset return can be expected to correspond to a weighted average of these risk premia.

There are several practical applications of factor models across the portfolio management process, from construction and asset selection to risk management and performance evaluation. The importance of factor models continues to grow as common risk factors are now tradeable:

- A summary of the returns of many assets, by a much smaller number of factors, reduces the amount of data required to estimate the covariance matrix when optimizing a portfolio.
- An estimate of the exposure of an asset or a portfolio to these factors allows for the management of the resulting risk, for instance, by entering suitable hedges when risk factors are themselves traded or can be proxied.
- A factor model also permits the assessment of the incremental signal content of new alpha factors.

- A factor model can also help assess whether a manager's performance, relative to a benchmark, is indeed due to skillful asset selection and market timing, or if the performance can instead be explained by portfolio tilts toward known return drivers. These drivers can, today, be replicated as low-cost, passively managed funds that do not incur active management fees.

The following examples apply to equities, but risk factors have been identified for all asset classes (Ang 2014).

From the CAPM to the Fama–French factor models

Risk factors have been a key ingredient to quantitative models since the **capital asset pricing model** (**CAPM**) explained the expected returns of all N assets $r_i, \; i = 1, \ldots, N$ using their respective exposure β_i to a single factor, the expected excess return of the overall market over the risk-free rate r_f. The CAPM model takes the following linear form:

$$E[r_i] = \alpha_i + r_f + \beta_i(E[r_m] - r_f$$

This differs from the classic fundamental analysis, à la Dodd and Graham, where returns depend on firm characteristics. The rationale is that, in the aggregate, investors cannot eliminate this so-called systematic risk through diversification. Hence, in equilibrium, they require compensation for holding an asset commensurate with its systematic risk. The model implies that, given efficient markets where prices immediately reflect all public information, there should be no superior risk-adjusted returns. In other words, the value of α should be zero.

Empirical tests of the model use linear regression and have consistently failed, for example, by identifying anomalies in the form of superior risk-adjusted returns that do not depend on overall market exposure, such as higher returns for smaller firms (Goyal 2012).

These failures have prompted a lively debate about whether the efficient markets or the single factor aspect of the joint hypothesis is to blame. It turns out that both premises are probably wrong:

- Joseph Stiglitz earned the 2001 Nobel Prize in economics in part for showing that markets are generally not perfectly efficient: if markets are efficient, there is no value in collecting data because this information is already reflected in prices. However, if there is no incentive to gather information, it is hard to see how it should be already reflected in prices.
- On the other hand, theoretical and empirical improvements of the CAPM suggest that additional factors help explain some of the anomalies mentioned previously, which result in various multi-factor models.

Stephen Ross proposed the **arbitrage pricing theory** (**APT**) in 1976 as an alternative that allows for several risk factors while eschewing market efficiency. In contrast to the CAPM, it assumes that opportunities for superior returns due to mispricing may exist but will quickly be arbitraged away. The theory does not specify the factors, but research suggests that the most important are changes in inflation and industrial production, as well as changes in risk premia or the term structure of interest rates.

Kenneth French and Eugene Fama (who won the 2013 Nobel Prize) identified additional risk factors that depend on firm characteristics and are widely used today. In 1993, the Fama–French three-factor model added the relative size and value of firms to the single CAPM source of risk. In 2015, the five-factor model further expanded the set to include firm profitability and level of investment, which had been shown to be significant in the intervening years. In addition, many factor models include a price momentum factor.

The Fama–French risk factors are computed as the return difference on diversified portfolios with high or low values, according to metrics that reflect a given risk factor. These returns are obtained by sorting stocks according to these metrics and then going long stocks above a certain percentile, while shorting stocks below a certain percentile. The metrics associated with the risk factors are defined as follows:

- **Size**: **Market equity** (**ME**)
- **Value**: **Book value of equity** (**BE**) divided by ME
- **Operating profitability (OP)**: Revenue minus cost of goods sold/assets
- **Investment**: Investment/assets

There are also unsupervised learning techniques for the data-driven discovery of risk factors that use factors and principal component analysis. We will explore this in *Chapter 13, Data-Driven Risk Factors and Asset Allocation with Unsupervised Learning*.

Obtaining the risk factors

Fama and French make updated risk factors and research portfolio data available through their website, and you can use the `pandas_datareader` library to obtain the data. For this application, refer to the `fama_macbeth.ipynb` notebook for the following code examples and additional detail.

In particular, we will be using the five Fama–French factors that result from sorting stocks, first into three size groups and then into two, for each of the remaining three firm-specific factors. Hence, the factors involve three sets of value-weighted portfolios formed as 3 × 2 sorts on size and book-to-market, size and operating profitability, and size and investment. The risk factor values computed as the average returns of the **portfolios** (**PF**) are outlined in the following table:

Concept	Label	Name	Risk factor calculation
Size	SMB	Small minus big	Nine small stock PF minus nine large stock PF.
Value	HML	High minus low	Two value PF minus two growth (with low BE/ ME value) PF.
Profitability	RMW	Robust minus weak	Two robust OP PF minus two weak OP PF.
Investment	CMA	Conservative minus aggressive	Two conservative investment portfolios, minus two aggressive investment portfolios.
Market	Rm-Rf	Excess return on the market	Value-weight return of all firms incorporated in and listed on major US exchanges with good data, minus the one-month Treasury bill rate.

We will use returns at a monthly frequency that we will obtain for the period 2010–2017, as follows:

```
import pandas_datareader.data as web
ff_factor = 'F-F_Research_Data_5_Factors_2x3'
ff_factor_data = web.DataReader(ff_factor, 'famafrench', start='2010',
                                end='2017-12')[0]
ff_factor_data.info()
PeriodIndex: 96 entries, 2010-01 to 2017-12
Freq: M
Data columns (total 6 columns):
Mkt-RF 96 non-null float64
SMB    96 non-null float64
HML    96 non-null float64
RMW    96 non-null float64
CMA    96 non-null float64
RF     96 non-null float64
```

Fama and French also made numerous portfolios available that we can use to illustrate the estimation of the factor exposures, as well as the value of the risk premia available in the market for a given time period. We will use a panel of the 17 industry portfolios at a monthly frequency. We will subtract the risk-free rate from the returns because the factor model works with excess returns:

```
ff_portfolio = '17_Industry_Portfolios'
ff_portfolio_data = web.DataReader(ff_portfolio, 'famafrench', start='2010',
                                   end='2017-12')[0]
ff_portfolio_data = ff_portfolio_data.sub(ff_factor_data.RF, axis=0)
ff_factor_data = ff_factor_data.drop('RF', axis=1)
ff_portfolio_data.info()
PeriodIndex: 96 entries, 2010-01 to 2017-12
Freq: M
Data columns (total 17 columns):
Food     96 non-null float64
```

```
Mines     96 non-null float64
Oil       96 non-null float64
...
Rtail     96 non-null float64
Finan     96 non-null float64
Other     96 non-null float64
```

We will now build a linear factor model based on this panel data using a method that addresses the failure of some basic linear regression assumptions.

Fama–Macbeth regression

Given data on risk factors and portfolio returns, it is useful to estimate the portfolio's exposure to these returns to learn how much they drive the portfolio's returns. It is also of interest to understand the premium that the market pays for the exposure to a given factor, that is, how much taking this risk is worth. The risk premium then permits to estimate the return for any portfolio provide we know or can assume its factor exposure.

More formally, we will have i=1, ..., N asset or portfolio returns over t=1, ..., T periods, and each asset's excess period return will be denoted. The goal is to test whether the j=1, ..., M factors explain the excess returns and the risk premium associated with each factor. In our case, we have N=17 portfolios and M=5 factors, each with 96 periods of data.

Factor models are estimated for many stocks in a given period. Inference problems will likely arise in such cross-sectional regressions because the fundamental assumptions of classical linear regression may not hold. Potential violations include measurement errors, covariation of residuals due to heteroskedasticity and serial correlation, and multicollinearity (Fama and MacBeth 1973).

To address the inference problem caused by the correlation of the residuals, Fama and MacBeth proposed a two-step methodology for a cross-sectional regression of returns on factors. The two-stage Fama–Macbeth regression is designed to estimate the premium rewarded for the exposure to a particular risk factor by the market. The two stages consist of:

- First stage: N time-series regression, one for each asset or portfolio, of its excess returns on the factors to estimate the factor loadings. In matrix form, for each asset:

$$\underset{T\times 1}{\boldsymbol{r}_i} = \underset{T\times(m+1)}{\boldsymbol{F}}\underset{(m+1)\times 1}{\boldsymbol{\beta}_i} + \underset{T\times 1}{\boldsymbol{\epsilon}_i}$$

- Second stage: T cross-sectional regression, one for each time period, to estimate the risk premium. In matrix form, we obtain a vector of risk premia for each period:

$$\underset{N\times(M+1)}{\boldsymbol{r}_t} = \underset{N\times(M+1)}{\widehat{\boldsymbol{\beta}}}\underset{(M+1)\times 1}{\boldsymbol{\lambda}_t}$$

Now, we can compute the factor risk premia as the time average and get a t-statistic to assess their individual significance, using the assumption that the risk premia estimates are independent over time:

$$t = \frac{\lambda_j}{\sigma(\lambda_j)/\sqrt{(T)}}$$

If we had a very large and representative data sample on traded risk factors, we could use the sample mean as a risk premium estimate. However, we typically do not have a sufficiently long history to, and the margin of error around the sample mean could be quite large. The Fama-Macbeth methodology leverages the covariance of the factors with other assets to determine the factor premia.

The second moment of asset returns is easier to estimate than the first moment, and obtaining more granular data improves estimation considerably, which is not true of mean estimation.

We can implement the first stage to obtain the 17 factor loading estimates as follows:

```
betas = []
for industry in ff_portfolio_data:
    step1 = OLS(endog=ff_portfolio_data.loc[ff_factor_data.index, industry],
                exog=add_constant(ff_factor_data)).fit()
    betas.append(step1.params.drop('const'))
betas = pd.DataFrame(betas,
                     columns=ff_factor_data.columns,
                     index=ff_portfolio_data.columns)
betas.info()
Index: 17 entries, Food  to Other
Data columns (total 5 columns):
Mkt-RF    17 non-null float64
SMB       17 non-null float64
HML       17 non-null float64
RMW       17 non-null float64
CMA       17 non-null float64
```

For the second stage, we run 96 regressions of the period returns for the cross section of portfolios on the factor loadings:

```
lambdas = []
for period in ff_portfolio_data.index:
    step2 = OLS(endog=ff_portfolio_data.loc[period, betas.index],
                exog=betas).fit()
    lambdas.append(step2.params)
lambdas = pd.DataFrame(lambdas,
                       index=ff_portfolio_data.index,
                       columns=betas.columns.tolist())
lambdas.info()
```

```
PeriodIndex: 96 entries, 2010-01 to 2017-12
Freq: M
Data columns (total 5 columns):
Mkt-RF      96 non-null float64
SMB         96 non-null float64
HML         96 non-null float64
RMW         96 non-null float64
CMA         96 non-null float64
```

Finally, we compute the average for the 96 periods to obtain our factor risk premium estimates:

```
lambdas.mean()
Mkt-RF      1.243632
SMB        -0.004863
HML        -0.688167
RMW        -0.237317
CMA        -0.318075
RF         -0.013280
```

The linearmodels library extends `statsmodels` with various models for panel data and also implements the two-stage Fama-MacBeth procedure:

```
model = LinearFactorModel(portfolios=ff_portfolio_data,
                          factors=ff_factor_data)
res = model.fit()
```

This provides us with the same result:

```
                     LinearFactorModel Estimation Summary
================================================================================
No. Test Portfolios:                 17   R-squared:                      0.6944
No. Factors:                          6   J-statistic:                    19.501
No. Observations:                    95   P-value                         0.0527
Date:                  Thu, Nov 14 2019   Distribution:                 chi2(11)
Time:                          19:34:04
Cov. Estimator:                  robust

                            Risk Premia Estimates
==============================================================================
             Parameter  Std. Err.     T-stat    P-value   Lower CI   Upper CI
------------------------------------------------------------------------------
Mkt-RF          1.2436     0.3928     3.1662     0.0015     0.4738     2.0135
SMB            -0.0049     0.6993    -0.0070     0.9945    -1.3754     1.3657
HML            -0.6882     0.5360    -1.2838     0.1992    -1.7388     0.3625
RMW            -0.2373     0.6729    -0.3527     0.7243    -1.5562     1.0815
CMA            -0.3181     0.4633    -0.6865     0.4924    -1.2261     0.5900
RF             -0.0133     0.0132    -1.0026     0.3161    -0.0392     0.0127
==============================================================================

Covariance estimator:
HeteroskedasticCovariance
See full_summary for complete results
```

Figure 7.4: LinearFactorModel estimation summary

The accompanying notebook illustrates the use of categorical variables by using industry dummies when estimating risk premia for a larger panel of individual stocks.

Regularizing linear regression using shrinkage

The least-squares method to train a linear regression model will produce the best linear and unbiased coefficient estimates when the Gauss–Markov assumptions are met. Variations like GLS fare similarly well, even when OLS assumptions about the error covariance matrix are violated. However, there are estimators that produce biased coefficients to reduce the variance and achieve a lower generalization error overall (Hastie, Tibshirani, and Friedman 2009).

When a linear regression model contains many correlated variables, their coefficients will be poorly determined. This is because the effect of a large positive coefficient on the RSS can be canceled by a similarly large negative coefficient on a correlated variable. As a result, the risk of prediction errors due to high variance increases because this wiggle room for the coefficients makes the model more likely to overfit to the sample.

How to hedge against overfitting

One popular technique to control overfitting is that of **regularization**, which involves the addition of a penalty term to the error function to discourage the coefficients from reaching large values. In other words, size constraints on the coefficients can alleviate the potentially negative impact on out-of-sample predictions. We will encounter regularization methods for all models since overfitting is such a pervasive problem.

In this section, we will introduce shrinkage methods that address two motivations to improve on the approaches to linear models discussed so far:

- **Prediction accuracy**: The low bias but high variance of least-squares estimates suggests that the generalization error could be reduced by shrinking or setting some coefficients to zero, thereby trading off a slightly higher bias for a reduction in the variance of the model.
- **Interpretation**: A large number of predictors may complicate the interpretation or communication of the big picture of the results. It may be preferable to sacrifice some detail to limit the model to a smaller subset of parameters with the strongest effects.

Shrinkage models restrict the regression coefficients by imposing a penalty on their size. They achieve this goal by adding a term $S(\boldsymbol{\beta})$ to the objective function. This term implies that the coefficients of a shrinkage model minimize the RSS, plus a penalty that is positively related to the (absolute) size of the coefficients.

The added penalty thus turns the linear regression coefficients into the solution to a constrained minimization problem that, in general, takes the following Lagrangian form:

$$\begin{aligned}\hat{\boldsymbol{\beta}}^S &= \underset{\beta^S}{\operatorname{argmin}} \sum_{i=1}^{N} \left[\left(y_i - \beta_0 - \sum_{j=1}^{p} \beta_j x_j \right)^2 + \lambda S(\boldsymbol{\beta}) \right] \\ &= \underset{\beta^S}{\operatorname{argmin}}\, \boldsymbol{y} - \boldsymbol{X\beta} - \lambda S(\boldsymbol{\beta})\end{aligned}$$

The regularization parameter λ determines the size of the penalty effect, that is, the strength of the regularization. As soon as λ is positive, the coefficients will differ from the unconstrained least squared parameters, which implies a biased estimate. You should choose hyperparameter λ adaptively via cross-validation to minimize an estimate of the expected prediction error. We will illustrate how to do so in the next section.

Shrinkage models differ by how they calculate the penalty, that is, the functional form of S. The most common versions are the **ridge regression**, which uses the sum of the squared coefficients, and the **lasso model**, which bases the penalty on the sum of the absolute values of the coefficients.

Elastic net regression, which is not explicitly covered here, uses a combination of both. Scikit-learn includes an implementation that works very similarly to the examples we will demonstrate here.

How ridge regression works

Ridge regression shrinks the regression coefficients by adding a penalty to the objective function that equals the sum of the squared coefficients, which in turn corresponds to the L2 norm of the coefficient vector (Hoerl and Kennard 1970):

$$S(\boldsymbol{\beta}) = \sum_{i=1}^{p} \beta_i^2 = \|\boldsymbol{\beta}\|^2$$

Hence, the ridge coefficients are defined as:

$$\begin{aligned}\widehat{\boldsymbol{\beta}}^{\text{Ridge}} &= \underset{\boldsymbol{\beta}^{\text{Ridge}}}{\operatorname{argmin}} \sum_{i=1}^{N} \left[\left(y_i - \beta_0 - \sum_{j=1}^{p} \beta_j x_j \right)^2 + \lambda \sum_{j=1}^{p} \boldsymbol{\beta}_j^2 \right] \\ &= \underset{\boldsymbol{\beta}^{\text{Ridge}}}{\operatorname{argmin}} (\boldsymbol{y} - \boldsymbol{X\beta})^T (\boldsymbol{y} - \boldsymbol{X\beta}) + \lambda \boldsymbol{\beta}^T \boldsymbol{\beta}\end{aligned}$$

The intercept β_0 has been excluded from the penalty to make the procedure independent of the origin chosen for the output variable—otherwise, adding a constant to all output values would change all slope parameters, as opposed to a parallel shift.

It is important to standardize the inputs by subtracting from each input the corresponding mean and dividing the result by the input's standard deviation. This is because the ridge solution is sensitive to the scale of the inputs. There is also a closed solution for the ridge estimator that resembles the OLS case:

$$\widehat{\boldsymbol{\beta}}^{\text{Ridge}} = (\boldsymbol{X}^T \boldsymbol{X} + \lambda I)^{-1} \boldsymbol{X}^T \boldsymbol{y}$$

The solution adds the scaled identity matrix λI to X^TX before inversion, which guarantees that the problem is non-singular, even if X^TX does not have full rank. This was one of the motivations for using this estimator when it was originally introduced.

The ridge penalty results in the proportional shrinkage of all parameters. In the case of orthonormal inputs, the ridge estimates are just a scaled version of the least-squares estimates, that is:

$$\hat{\boldsymbol{\beta}}^{\text{Ridge}} = \frac{\hat{\boldsymbol{\beta}}^{\text{LS}}}{1+\lambda}$$

Using the **singular value decomposition** (**SVD**) of the input matrix X, we can gain insight into how the shrinkage affects inputs in the more common case where they are not orthonormal. The SVD of a centered matrix represents the principal components of a matrix (see *Chapter 13, Data-Driven Risk Factors and Asset Allocation with Unsupervised Learning*) that capture uncorrelated directions in the column space of the data in descending order of variance.

Ridge regression shrinks the coefficients relative to the alignment of input variables with the directions in the data that exhibit most variance. More specifically, it shrinks those coefficients the most that represent inputs aligned with the principal components that capture less variance. Hence, the assumption that's implicit in ridge regression is that the directions in the data that vary the most will be most influential or most reliable when predicting the output.

How lasso regression works

The lasso (Hastie, Tibshirani, and Wainwright 2015), known as basis pursuit in signal processing, also shrinks the coefficients by adding a penalty to the sum of squares of the residuals, but the lasso penalty has a slightly different effect. The lasso penalty is the sum of the absolute values of the coefficient vector, which corresponds to its L1 norm. Hence, the lasso estimate is defined by:

$$\begin{aligned}\hat{\boldsymbol{\beta}}^{\text{Lasso}} &= \underset{\boldsymbol{\beta}^{\text{Lasso}}}{\text{argmin}} \sum_{i=1}^{N}\left[\left(y_i - \beta_0 - \sum_{j=1}^{p}\beta_j x_j\right)^2 + \lambda\sum_{j=1}^{p}|\beta_j|\right] \\ &= \underset{\boldsymbol{\beta}^{\text{Lasso}}}{\text{argmin}} (\boldsymbol{y}-\boldsymbol{X\beta})^T(\boldsymbol{y}-\boldsymbol{X\beta}) + \lambda\boldsymbol{\beta}|\end{aligned}$$

Similar to ridge regression, the inputs need to be standardized. The lasso penalty makes the solution nonlinear, and there is no closed-form expression for the coefficients, as in ridge regression. Instead, the lasso solution is a quadratic programming problem, and there are efficient algorithms that compute the entire path of coefficients, which results in different values of λ with the same computational cost as ridge regression.

The lasso penalty had the effect of gradually reducing some coefficients to zero as the regularization increases. For this reason, the lasso can be used for the continuous selection of a subset of features.

Let's now move on and put the various linear regression models to practical use and generate predictive stock trading signals.

How to predict returns with linear regression

In this section, we will use linear regression with and without shrinkage to predict returns and generate trading signals.

First, we need to create the model inputs and outputs. To this end, we'll create features along the lines we discussed in *Chapter 4, Financial Feature Engineering – How to Research Alpha Factors*, as well as forward returns for various time horizons, which we will use as outcomes for the models.

Then, we will apply the linear regression models discussed in the previous section to illustrate their usage with `statsmodels` and sklearn and evaluate their predictive performance. In the next chapter, we will use the results to develop a trading strategy and demonstrate the end-to-end process of backtesting a strategy driven by a machine learning model.

Preparing model features and forward returns

To prepare the data for our predictive model, we need to:

- Select a universe of equities and a time horizon
- Build and transform alpha factors that we will use as features
- Calculate forward returns that we aim to predict
- And (potentially) clean our data

The notebook `preparing_the_model_data.ipynb` contains the code examples for this section.

Creating the investment universe

We will use daily equity data from the Quandl Wiki US Stock Prices dataset for the years 2013 to 2017. See the instructions in the `data` directory in the root folder of the GitHub repository for this book on how to obtain the data.

We start by loading the daily (adjusted) **open, high, low, close, and volume** (OHLCV) prices and metadata, which includes sector information. Use the path to `DATA_STORE`, where you originally saved the Quandl Wiki data:

```
START = '2013-01-01'
END = '2017-12-31'
idx = pd.IndexSlice # to select from pd.MultiIndex
DATA_STORE = '../data/assets.h5'
with pd.HDFStore(DATA_STORE) as store:
```

```
    prices = (store['quandl/wiki/prices']
              .loc[idx[START:END, :],
                   ['adj_open', 'adj_close', 'adj_low',
                    'adj_high', 'adj_volume']]
              .rename(columns=lambda x: x.replace('adj_', ''))
              .swaplevel()
              .sort_index())
    stocks = (store['us_equities/stocks']
              .loc[:, ['marketcap', 'ipoyear', 'sector']])
```

We remove tickers that do not have at least 2 years of data:

```
MONTH = 21
YEAR = 12 * MONTH
min_obs = 2 * YEAR
nobs = prices.groupby(level='ticker').size()
keep = nobs[nobs > min_obs].index
prices = prices.loc[idx[keep, :], :]
```

Next, we clean up the sector names and ensure that we only use equities with both price and sector information:

```
stocks = stocks[~stocks.index.duplicated() & stocks.sector.notnull()]
# clean up sector names
stocks.sector = stocks.sector.str.lower().str.replace(' ', '_')
stocks.index.name = 'ticker'
shared = (prices.index.get_level_values('ticker').unique()
          .intersection(stocks.index))
stocks = stocks.loc[shared, :]
prices = prices.loc[idx[shared, :], :]
```

For now, we are left with 2,265 tickers with daily price data for at least 2 years. First, there's the `prices` DataFrame:

```
prices.info(null_counts=True)
MultiIndex: 2748774 entries, (A, 2013-01-02) to (ZUMZ, 2017-12-29)
Data columns (total 5 columns):
open      2748774 non-null float64
close     2748774 non-null float64
low       2748774 non-null float64
high      2748774 non-null float64
volume    2748774 non-null float64
memory usage: 115.5+ MB
```

Next, there's the `stocks` DataFrame:

```
stocks.info()
Index: 2224 entries, A to ZUMZ
Data columns (total 3 columns):
marketcap    2222 non-null float64
ipoyear      962 non-null float64
sector       2224 non-null object
memory usage: 69.5+ KB
```

We will use a 21-day rolling average of the (adjusted) dollar volume traded to select the most liquid stocks for our model. Limiting the number of stocks also has the benefit of reducing training and backtesting time; excluding stocks with low dollar volumes can also reduce the noise of price data.

The computation requires us to multiply the daily close price with the corresponding volume and then apply a rolling mean to each ticker using `.groupby()`, as follows:

```
prices['dollar_vol'] = prices.loc[:, 'close'].mul(prices.loc[:, 'volume'],
axis=0)
prices['dollar_vol'] = (prices
                        .groupby('ticker',
                                 group_keys=False,
                                 as_index=False)
                        .dollar_vol
                        .rolling(window=21)
                        .mean()
                        .reset_index(level=0, drop=True))
```

We then use this value to rank stocks for each date so that we can select, for example, the 100 most-traded stocks for a given date:

```
prices['dollar_vol_rank'] = (prices
                             .groupby('date')
                             .dollar_vol
                             .rank(ascending=False))
```

Selecting and computing alpha factors using TA-Lib

We will create a few momentum and volatility factors using TA-Lib, as described in *Chapter 4, Financial Feature Engineering – How to Research Alpha Factors.*

First, we add the **relative strength index** (**RSI**), as follows:

```
prices['rsi'] = prices.groupby(level='ticker').close.apply(RSI)
```

A quick evaluation shows that, for the 100 most-traded stocks, the mean and median 5-day forward returns are indeed decreasing in the RSI values, grouped to reflect the commonly 30/70 buy/sell thresholds:

```
(prices[prices.dollar_vol_rank<100]
 .groupby('rsi_signal')['target_5d'].describe())
```

rsi_signal	count	Mean	std	min	25%	50%	75%	max
(0, 30]	4,154	0.12%	1.01%	-5.45%	-0.34%	0.11%	0.62%	4.61%
(30, 70]	107,329	0.05%	0.76%	-16.48%	-0.30%	0.06%	0.42%	7.57%
(70, 100]	10,598	0.00%	0.63%	-8.79%	-0.28%	0.01%	0.31%	5.86%

Then, we compute **Bollinger Bands**. The TA-Lib `BBANDS` function returns three values so that we set up a function that returns a `DataFrame` with the higher and lower bands for use with `groupby()` and `apply()`:

```
def compute_bb(close):
    high, mid, low = BBANDS(close)
    return pd.DataFrame({'bb_high': high, 'bb_low': low}, index=close.index)

prices = (prices.join(prices
                      .groupby(level='ticker')
                      .close
                      .apply(compute_bb)))
```

We take the percentage difference between the stock price and the upper or lower Bollinger Band and take logs to compress the distribution. The goal is to reflect the current value, relative to the recent volatility trend:

```
prices['bb_high'] = prices.bb_high.sub(prices.close).div(prices.bb_high).
apply(np.log1p)
prices['bb_low'] = prices.close.sub(prices.bb_low).div(prices.close).
apply(np.log1p)
```

Next, we compute the **average true range** (**ATR**), which takes three inputs, namely, the high, low, and close prices. We standardize the result to make the metric more comparable across stocks:

```
def compute_atr(stock_data):
    df = ATR(stock_data.high, stock_data.low,
             stock_data.close, timeperiod=14)
    return df.sub(df.mean()).div(df.std())
prices['atr'] = (prices.groupby('ticker', group_keys=False)
                 .apply(compute_atr))
```

Finally, we generate the **moving average convergence/divergence** (**MACD**) indicator, which reflects the difference between a shorter and a longer-term exponential moving average:

```
def compute_macd close:
   macd = MACD(close)[0]
    return (macd - np.mean(macd))/np.std(macd)

prices['macd'] = (prices
                  .groupby('ticker', group_keys=False)
                  .close
                  .apply(lambda x: MACD(x)[0]))
```

Adding lagged returns

To capture the price trend for various historical lags, we compute the corresponding returns and transform the result into the daily geometric mean. We'll use lags for 1 day; 1 and 1 weeks; and 1, 2, and 3 months. We'll also winsorize the returns by clipping the values at the 0.01st and 99.99th percentile:

```
q = 0.0001
lags = [1, 5, 10, 21, 42, 63]
for lag in lags:
    prices[f'return_{lag}d'] = (prices.groupby(level='ticker').close
                                .pct_change(lag)
                                .pipe(lambda x: x.clip(lower=x.quantile(q),
                                                       upper=x.quantile(1 - q)
                                                       ))
                                .add(1)
                                .pow(1 / lag)
                                .sub(1)
                                )
```

We then shift the daily, (bi-)weekly, and monthly returns to use them as features for the current observations. In other words, in addition to the latest returns for these periods, we also use the prior five results. For example, we shift the weekly returns for the prior 5 weeks so that they align with the current observations and can be used to predict the current forward return:

```
for t in [1, 2, 3, 4, 5]:
    for lag in [1, 5, 10, 21]:
        prices[f'return_{lag}d_lag{t}'] = (prices.groupby(level='ticker')
                                           [f'return_{lag}d'].shift(t * lag))
```

Generating target forward returns

We will test predictions for various lookahead periods. The goal is to identify the holding period that produces the best predictive accuracy, as measured by the **information coefficient** (IC).

More specifically, we shift returns for time horizon t back by t days to use them as forward returns. For instance, we shift the 5-day return from t_0 to t_5 back by 5 days so that this value becomes the model target for t_0. We can generate daily, (bi-)weekly, and monthly forward returns as follows:

```
for t in [1, 5, 10, 21]:
    prices[f'target_{t}d'] = prices.groupby(level='ticker')[f'return_{t}d'].
shift(-t)
```

Dummy encoding of categorical variables

We need to convert any categorical variable into a numeric format so that the linear regression can process it. For this purpose, we will use a dummy encoding that creates individual columns for each category level and flags the presence of this level in the original categorical column with an entry of 1, and 0 otherwise. The pandas function `get_dummies()` automates dummy encoding. It detects and properly converts columns of type objects, as illustrated here. If you need dummy variables for columns containing integers, for instance, you can identify them using the keyword columns:

```
df = pd.DataFrame({'categories': ['A','B', 'C']})
  categories
0          A
1          B
2          C
pd.get_dummies(df)
   categories_A  categories_B  categories_C
0             1             0             0
1             0             1             0
2             0             0             1
```

When converting all categories into dummy variables and estimating the model with an intercept (as you typically would), you inadvertently create multicollinearity: the matrix now contains redundant information, no longer has full rank, and instead becomes singular.

It is simple to avoid this by removing one of the new indicator columns. The coefficient on the missing category level will now be captured by the intercept (which is always 1, including when every remaining category dummy is 0).

Use the `drop_first` keyword to correct the dummy variables accordingly:

```
pd.get_dummies(df, drop_first=True)
   categories_B  categories_C
0             0             0
1             1             0
2             0             1
```

To capture seasonal effects and changing market conditions, we create time indictor variables for the year and month:

```
prices['year'] = prices.index.get_level_values('date').year
prices['month'] = prices.index.get_level_values('date').month
```

Then, we combine our price data with the sector information and create dummy variables for the time and sector categories:

```
prices = prices.join(stocks[['sector']])
prices = pd.get_dummies(prices,
                        columns=['year', 'month', 'sector'],
                        prefix=['year', 'month', ''],
                        prefix_sep=['_', '_', ''],
                        drop_first=True)
```

We obtain some 50 features as a result that we can now use with the various regression models discussed in the previous section.

Linear OLS regression using statsmodels

In this section, we will demonstrate how to run statistical inference with stock return data using `statsmodels` and interpret the results. The notebook `04_statistical_inference_of_stock_returns_with_statsmodels.ipynb` contains the code examples for this section.

Selecting the relevant universe

Based on our ranked rolling average of the dollar volume, we select the top 100 stocks for any given trading day in our sample:

```
data = data[data.dollar_vol_rank<100]
```

We then create our outcome variables and features, as follows:

```
y = data.filter(like='target')
X = data.drop(y.columns, axis=1)
```

Estimating the vanilla OLS regression

We can estimate a linear regression model using OLS with `statsmodels`, as demonstrated previously. We select a forward return, for example, for a 5-day holding period, and fit the model accordingly:

```
target = 'target_5d'
model = OLS(endog=y[target], exog=add_constant(X))
trained_model = model.fit()
trained_model.summary()
```

Diagnostic statistics

You can view the full summary output in the notebook. We will omit it here to save some space, given the large number of features, and only display the diagnostic statistics:

```
==============================================================================
Omnibus:                    33104.830   Durbin-Watson:                   0.436
Prob(Omnibus):                  0.000   Jarque-Bera (JB):          1211101.670
Skew:                          -0.780   Prob(JB):                         0.00
Kurtosis:                      19.205   Cond. No.                         79.8
==============================================================================
```

The diagnostic statistics show a low p-value for the Jarque-Bera statistic, suggesting that the residuals are not normally distributed: they exhibit negative skew and high kurtosis. The left panel of *Figure 7.5* plots the residual distribution versus the normal distribution and highlights this shortcoming. In practice, this implies that the model is making more large errors than "normal":

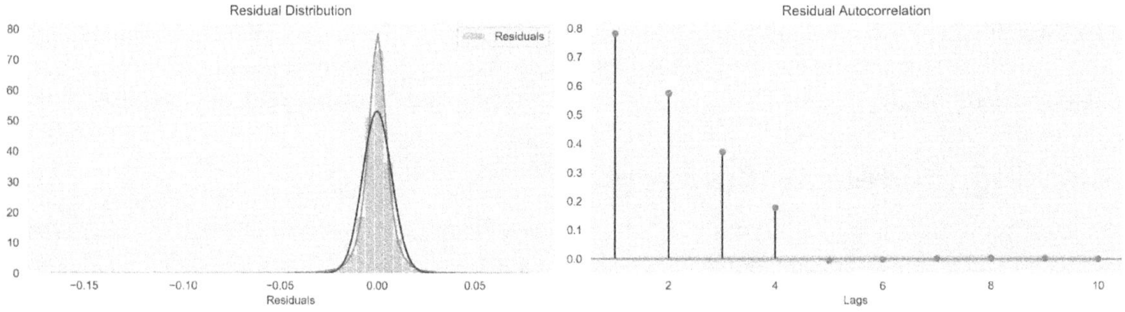

Figure 7.5: Residual distribution and autocorrelation plots

Furthermore, the Durbin-Watson statistic is low at 0.43 so that we comfortably reject the null hypothesis of "no autocorrelation" at the 5 percent level. Hence, the residuals are likely positively correlated. The right panel of the preceding figure plots the autocorrelation coefficients for the first 10 lags, pointing to a significant positive correlation up to lag 4. This result is due to the overlap in our outcomes: we are predicting 5-day returns for each day so that outcomes for consecutive days contain four identical returns.

If our goal were to understand which factors are significantly associated with forward returns, we would need to rerun the regression using robust standard errors (a parameter in statsmodels' `.fit()` method) or use a different method altogether, such as a panel model that allows for more complex error covariance.

Linear regression using scikit-learn

Since sklearn is tailored toward prediction, we will evaluate the linear regression model based on its predictive performance using cross-validation. You can find the code samples for this section in the notebook `05_predicting_stock_returns_with_linear_regression.ipynb`.

Selecting features and targets

We will select the universe for our experiment, as we did previously in the OLS case, limiting tickers to the 100 most traded in terms of the dollar value on any given date. The sample still contains 5 years of data from 2013-2017.

Cross-validating the model

Our data consists of numerous time series, one for each security. As discussed in *Chapter 6, The Machine Learning Process*, sequential data like time series requires careful cross-validation to be set up so that we do not inadvertently introduce look-ahead bias or leakage.

We can achieve this using the `MultipleTimeSeriesCV` class that we introduced in *Chapter 6, The Machine Learning Process*. We initialize it with the desired lengths for the train and test periods, the number of test periods that we would like to run, and the number of periods in our forecasting horizon. The `split()` method returns a generator yielding pairs of train and test indices, which we can then use to select outcomes and features. The number of pairs depends on the parameter `n_splits`.

The test periods do not overlap and are located at the end of the period available in the data. After a test period is used, it becomes part of the training data that rolls forward and remains constant in size.

We will test this using 63 trading days, or 3 months, to train the model and then predict 1-day returns for the following 10 days. As a result, we can use around 75 10-day splits during the 3 years, starting in 2015. We will begin by defining the basic parameters and data structures, as follows:

```
train_period_length = 63
test_period_length = 10
n_splits = int(3 * YEAR/test_period_length)
lookahead =1
cv = MultipleTimeSeriesCV(n_splits=n_splits,
                          test_period_length=test_period_length,
                          lookahead=lookahead,
                          train_period_length=train_period_length)
```

The cross-validation loop iterates over the train and test indices provided by `TimeSeriesCV`, selects features and outcomes, trains the model, and predicts the returns for the test features. We also capture the root mean squared error and the Spearman rank correlation between the actual and predicted values:

```
target = f'target_{lookahead}d'
lr_predictions, lr_scores = [], []
lr = LinearRegression()
for i, (train_idx, test_idx) in enumerate(cv.split(X), 1):
    X_train, y_train, = X.iloc[train_idx], y[target].iloc[train_idx]
    X_test, y_test = X.iloc[test_idx], y[target].iloc[test_idx]
    lr.fit(X=X_train, y=y_train)
    y_pred = lr.predict(X_test)

    preds_by_day = (y_test.to_frame('actuals').assign(predicted=y_pred)
                    .groupby(level='date'))
    ic = preds_by_day.apply(lambda x: spearmanr(x.predicted,
                                                x.actuals)[0] * 100)
    rmese = preds_by_day.apply(lambda x: np.sqrt(
                               mean_squared_error(x.predicted, x.actuals)))
    scores = pd.concat([ic.to_frame('ic'), rmse.to_frame('rmse')], axis=1)

    lr_scores.append(scores)
    lr_predictions.append(preds)
```

The cross-validation process takes 2 seconds. We'll evaluate the results in the next section.

Evaluating the results – information coefficient and RMSE

We have captured 3 years of daily test predictions for our universe. To evaluate the model's predictive performance, we can compute the information coefficient for each trading day, as well as for the entire period by pooling all forecasts.

The left panel of *Figure 7.6* (see the code in the notebook) shows the distribution of the rank correlation coefficients computed for each day and displays their mean and median, which are close to 1.95 and 2.56, respectively.

The figure's right panel shows a scatterplot of the predicted and actual 1-day returns across all test periods. The seaborn `jointplot` estimates a robust regression that assigns lower weights to outliers and shows a small positive relationship. The rank correlation of actual and predicted returns for the entire 3-year test period is positive but low at 0.017 and statistically significant:

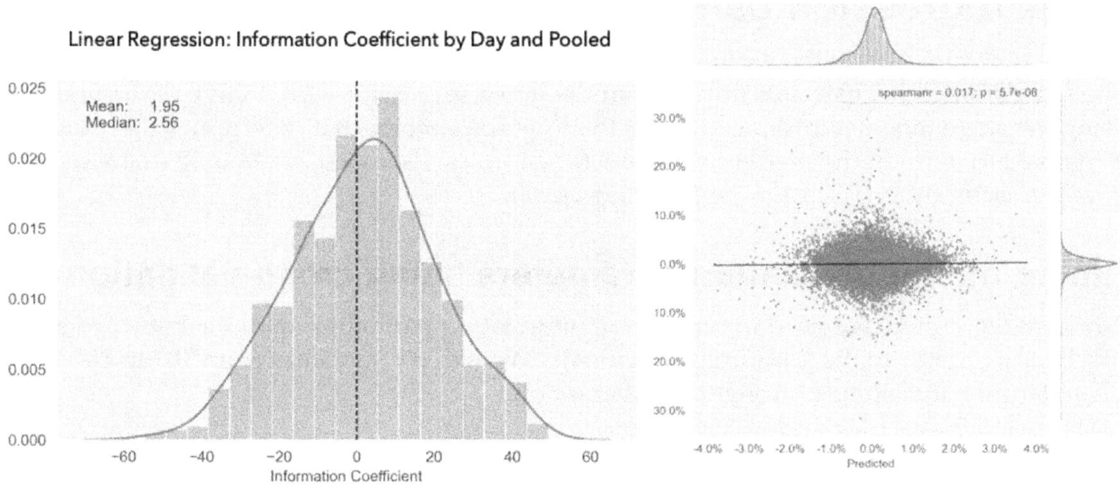

Figure 7.6: Daily and pooled IC for linear regression

In addition, we can track how predictions performed in terms of the IC on a daily basis. *Figure 7.7* displays a 21-day rolling average for both the daily information coefficient and the RMSE, as well as their respective means for the validation period. This perspective highlights that the small positive IC for the entire period hides substantial variation that ranges from -10 to +10:

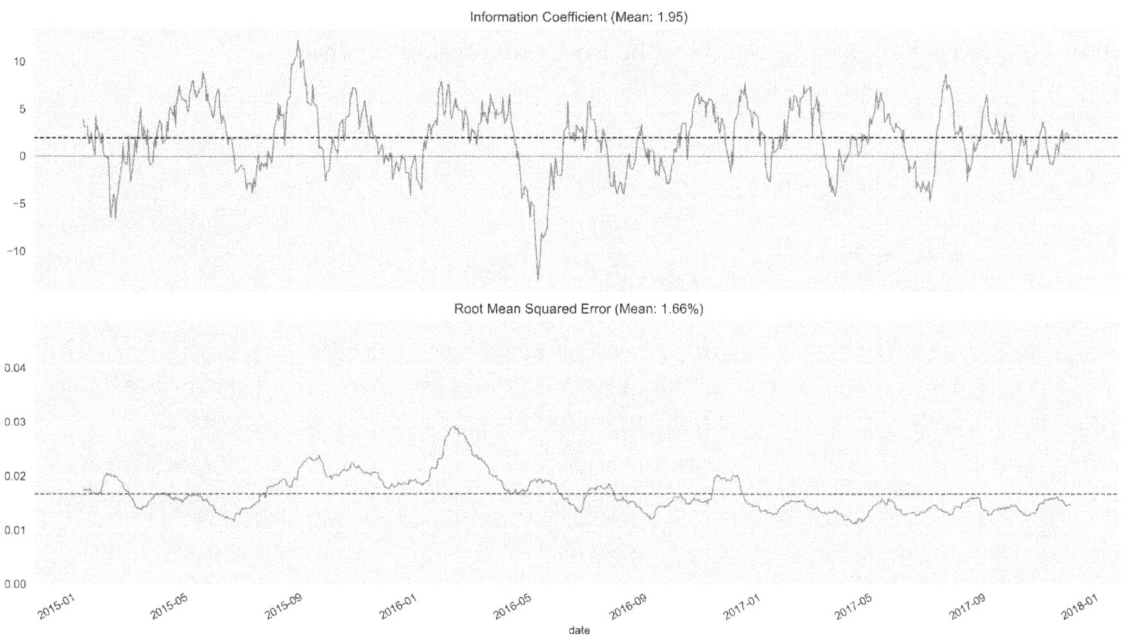

Figure 7.7: 21-day rolling average for the daily IC and RMSE for the linear regression model

Ridge regression using scikit-learn

We will now move on to the regularized ridge model, which we will use to evaluate whether parameter constraints improve on the linear regression's predictive performance. Using the ridge model allows us to select the hyperparameter that determines the weight of the penalty term in the model's objective function, as discussed previously in the section *Shrinkage methods: regularization for linear regression*.

Tuning the regularization parameters using cross-validation

For ridge regression, we need to tune the regularization parameter with the keyword `alpha`, which corresponds to the λ we used previously. We will try 18 values from 10^{-4} to 10^{4}, where larger values imply stronger regularization:

```
ridge_alphas = np.logspace(-4, 4, 9)
ridge_alphas = sorted(list(ridge_alphas) + list(ridge_alphas * 5))
```

We will apply the same cross-validation parameters as in the linear regression case, training for 3 months to predict 10 days of daily returns.

The scale sensitivity of the ridge penalty requires us to standardize the inputs using `StandardScaler`. Note that we always learn the mean and the standard deviation from the training set using the `.fit_transform()` method and then apply these learned parameters to the test set using the `.transform()` method. To automate the preprocessing, we create a `Pipeline`, as illustrated in the following code example. We also collect the ridge coefficients. Otherwise, cross-validation resembles the linear regression process:

```
for alpha in ridge_alphas:
    model = Ridge(alpha=alpha,
                  fit_intercept=False,
                  random_state=42)
    pipe = Pipeline([
        ('scaler', StandardScaler()),
        ('model', model)])
    for i, (train_idx, test_idx) in enumerate(cv.split(X), 1):
        X_train, y_train = X.iloc[train_idx], y[target].iloc[train_idx]
        X_test, y_test = X.iloc[test_idx], y[target].iloc[test_idx]

        pipe.fit(X=X_train, y=y_train)
        y_pred = pipe.predict(X_test)
```

```
    preds = y_test.to_frame('actuals').assign(predicted=y_pred)
    preds_by_day = preds.groupby(level='date')
    scores = pd.concat([preds_by_day.apply(lambda x:
                                  spearmanr(x.predicted,
                                            x.actuals)[0] * 100)
                        .to_frame('ic'),
                        preds_by_day.apply(lambda x: np.sqrt(
                                            mean_squared_error(
                                            y_pred=x.predicted,
                                            y_true=x.actuals)))
                        .to_frame('rmse')], axis=1)

    ridge_scores.append(scores.assign(alpha=alpha))
    ridge_predictions.append(preds.assign(alpha=alpha))
    coeffs.append(pipe.named_steps['model'].coef_)
```

Cross-validation results and ridge coefficient paths

We can now plot the IC for each hyperparameter value to visualize how it evolves as the regularization increases. The results show that we get the highest mean and median IC value for $\lambda = 100$.

For these levels of regularization, the right panel of *Figure 7.8* shows that the coefficients have been slightly shrunk compared to the (almost) unconstrained model with $\lambda = 10^{-4}$:

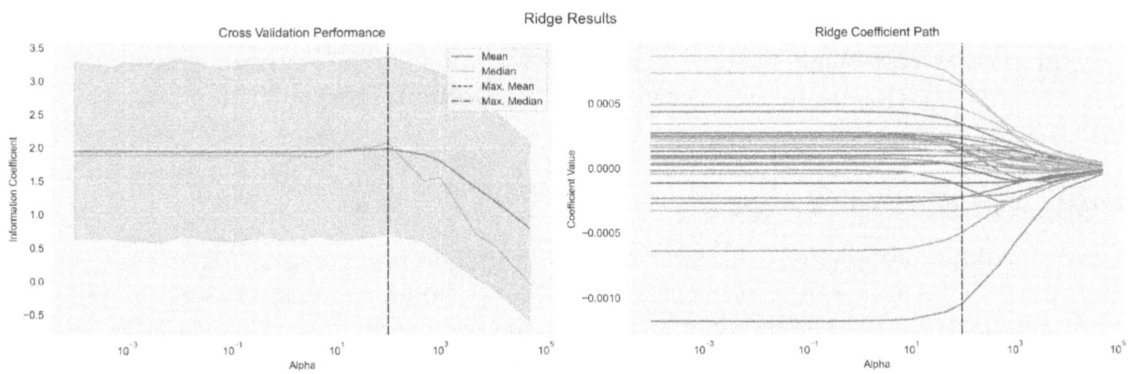

Figure 7.8: Ridge regression cross-validation results

The left panel of the figure shows that the predictive accuracy increases only slightly in terms of the mean and median IC values for optimal regularization values.

Top 10 coefficients

The standardization of the coefficients allows us to draw conclusions about their relative importance by comparing their absolute magnitude. *Figure 7.9* displays the 10 most relevant coefficients for regularization using $\lambda = 100$, averaged over all trained models:

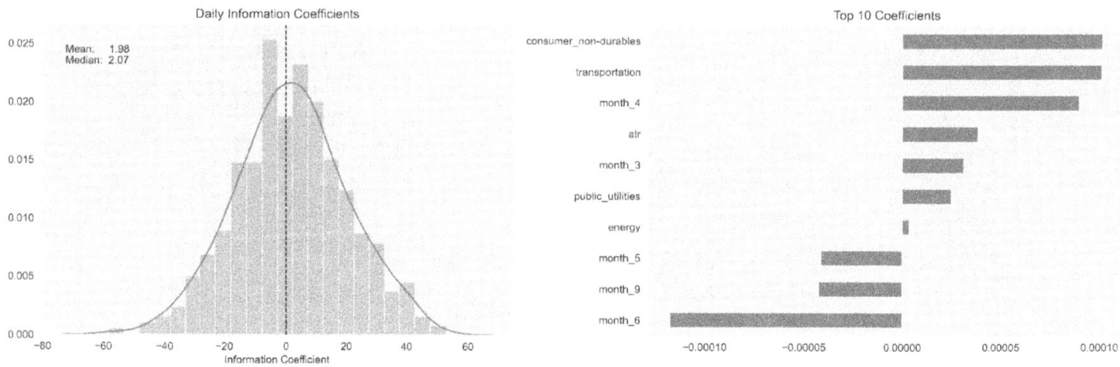

Figure 7.9: Daily IC distribution and most important coefficients

For this simple model and sample period, lagged monthly returns and various sector indicators played the most important role.

Lasso regression using sklearn

The lasso implementation looks very similar to the ridge model we just ran. The main difference is that lasso needs to arrive at a solution using iterative coordinate descent, whereas ridge regression can rely on a closed-form solution. This can lead to longer training times.

Cross-validating the lasso model

The cross-validation code only differs with respect to the `Pipeline` setup. The `Lasso` object lets you set the tolerance and the maximum number of iterations it uses to determine whether it has converged or should abort, respectively. You can also rely on a `warm_start` so that the next training starts from the last optimal coefficient values. Please refer to the sklearn documentation and the notebook for additional detail.

We will use eight `alpha` values in the range 10^{-10} to 10^{-3}:

```
lasso_alphas = np.logspace(-10, -3, 8)
for alpha in lasso_alphas:
    model = Lasso(alpha=alpha,
                  fit_intercept=False,
                  random_state=42,
                  tol=1e-4,
                  max_iter=1000,
```

```
                    warm_start=True,
                    selection='random')

pipe = Pipeline([
    ('scaler', StandardScaler()),
    ('model', model)])
```

Evaluating the results – IC and lasso path

As we did previously, we can plot the average information coefficient for all test sets used during cross-validation. We can see once more that regularization improves the IC over the unconstrained model, delivering the best out-of-sample result at a level of $\lambda = 10^{-4}$.

The optimal regularization value is different from ridge regression because the penalty consists of the sum of the absolute, not the squared values of the relatively small coefficient values. We can also see in *Figure 7.10* that for this regularization level, the coefficients have been similarly shrunk, as in the ridge regression case:

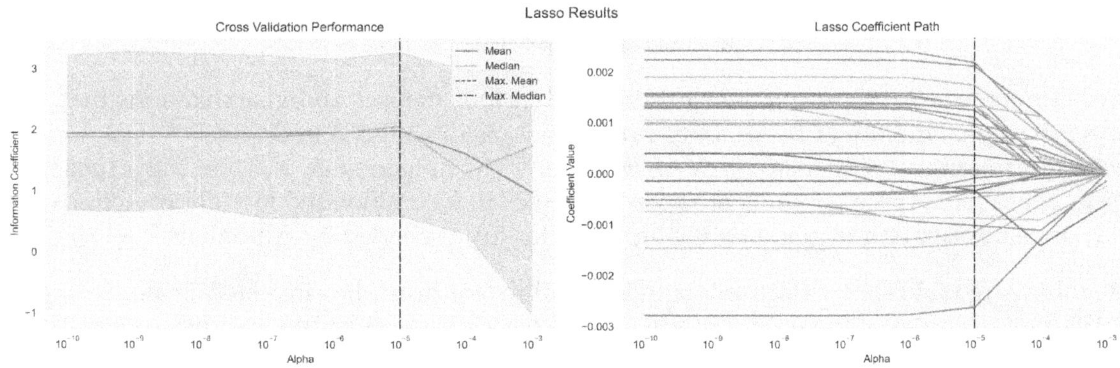

Figure 7.10: Lasso cross-validation results

The mean and median IC coefficients are slightly higher for lasso regression in this case, and the best-performing models use, on average, a different set of coefficients:

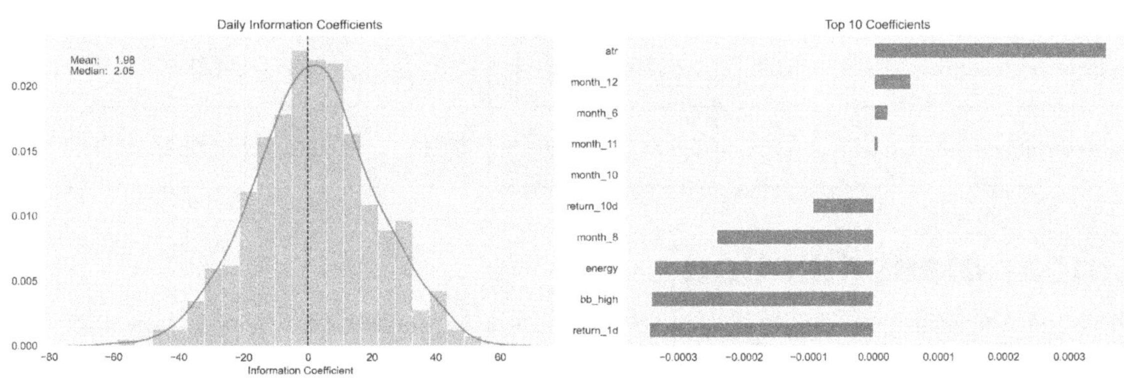

Figure 7.11: Lasso daily IC distribution and top 10 coefficients

Comparing the quality of the predictive signals

In sum, ridge and lasso regression often produce similar results. Ridge regression often computes faster, but lasso regression also offers continuous feature subset selection by gradually reducing coefficients to zero, hence eliminating features.

In this particular setting, lasso regression produces the best mean and median IC values, as displayed in *Figure 7.12*:

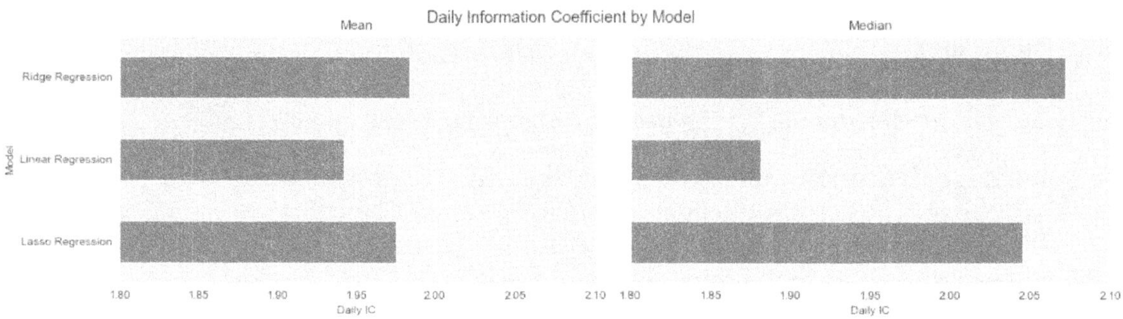

Figure 7.12: Mean and median daily IC for the three models

Furthermore, we can use Alphalens to compute various metrics and visualizations that reflect the signal quality of the model's predictions, as introduced in *Chapter 4, Financial Feature Engineering – How to Research Alpha Factors*. The notebook `06_evaluating_signals_using_alphalens.ipynb` contains the code examples that combine the model predictions with price information to generate the alpha factor input needed by Alphalens.

The following table shows the alpha and beta values for portfolios invested in, according to different quintiles of the model predictions. In this simple example, the differences in performance are very small:

Metric	**Alpha**					**Beta**			
Model	**1D**	**5D**	**10D**	**21D**		**1D**	**5D**	**10D**	**21D**
Linear regression	0.03	0.02	0.007	0.004		-0.012	-0.081	-0.059	0.019
Ridge regression	0.029	0.022	0.012	0.008		-0.01	-0.083	-0.060	0.021
Lasso regression	0.03	0.021	0.009	0.006		-0.011	-0.081	-0.057	0.02

Linear classification

The linear regression model discussed so far assumes a quantitative response variable. In this section, we will focus on approaches to modeling qualitative output variables for inference and prediction, a process that is known as **classification** and that occurs even more frequently than regression in practice.

Predicting a qualitative response for a data point is called classifying that observation because it involves assigning the observation to a category, or class. In practice, classification methods often predict probabilities for each of the categories of a qualitative variable and then use this probability to decide on the proper classification.

We could approach this classification problem by ignoring the fact that the output variable assumes discrete values, and then applying the linear regression model to try to predict a categorical output using multiple input variables. However, it is easy to construct examples where this method performs very poorly. Furthermore, it doesn't make intuitive sense for the model to produce values larger than 1 or smaller than 0 when we know that $y \in [0,1]$.

There are many different classification techniques, or classifiers, that are available to predict a qualitative response. In this section, we will introduce the widely used logistic regression, which is closely related to linear regression. We will address more complex methods in the following chapters on generalized additive models, which includes decision trees and random forests, as well as gradient boosting machines and neural networks.

The logistic regression model

The logistic regression model arises from the desire to model the probabilities of the output classes, given a function that is linear in x, just like the linear regression model, while at the same time ensuring that they sum to one and remain in [0, 1], as we would expect from probabilities.

In this section, we will introduce the objective and functional form of the logistic regression model and describe the training method. We will then illustrate how to use logistic regression for statistical inference with macro data using `statsmodels`, as well as how to predict price movements using the regularized logistic regression implemented by sklearn.

The objective function

To illustrate the **objective function**, we'll use the output variable y, which takes on the value 1 if a stock return is positive over a given time horizon d, and 0 otherwise:

$$y_t = \begin{cases} 1 & r_{t+d} > 0 \\ 0 & \text{otherwise} \end{cases}$$

We could easily extend y to three categories, where 0 and 2 reflect negative and positive price moves beyond a certain threshold, and 1 otherwise.

Rather than modeling the output variable y directly, logistic regression models the probability that y belongs to either of the categories, given a vector of alpha factors or features x_t. In other words, logistic regression models the probability that the stock price goes up, depending on the values of the variables included in the model:

$$P(\boldsymbol{x}_t) = P_r(y_t = 1|\boldsymbol{x}_t$$

The logistic function

To prevent the model from producing values outside the [0, 1] interval, we must model $p(x)$ using a function that only gives outputs between 0 and 1 over the entire domain of x. The **logistic function** meets this requirement and always produces an S-shaped curve and so, regardless of the value of x, we will obtain a prediction that makes sense in probability terms:

$$p(x) = \frac{e^{\beta_0 + \sum_{i=1}^{p} \beta_i x_i}}{1 + e^{\beta_0 + \sum_{i=1}^{p} \beta_i x_i}} = \frac{e^{x\boldsymbol{\beta}}}{1 + e^{x\boldsymbol{\beta}}}$$

Here, the vector x includes a 1 for the intercept captured by the first component of $\boldsymbol{\beta}$, $\boldsymbol{\beta}_0$. We can transform this expression to isolate the part that looks like a linear regression to arrive at:

$$\underbrace{\frac{p(\boldsymbol{x})}{1 - p(\boldsymbol{x})}}_{\text{odds}} = e^{\beta_0 + \sum_{i=1}^{p} \beta_i} \Leftrightarrow \underbrace{\log\left(\frac{p(\boldsymbol{x})}{1 - p(\boldsymbol{x})}\right)}_{\text{logit}} = \beta_0 + \sum_{i=1}^{p} \beta_i$$

The quantity $p(x)/[1-p(x)]$ is called the **odds**, an alternative way to express probabilities that may be familiar from gambling. This can take on any value odds between 0 and ∞, where low values also imply low probabilities and high values imply high probabilities.

The logit is also called **log-odds** (since it is the logarithm of the odds). Hence, logistic regression represents a logit that is linear in x and looks a lot like the preceding linear regression.

Maximum likelihood estimation

The coefficient vector $\boldsymbol{\beta}$ must be estimated using the available training data. Although we could use (nonlinear) least squares to fit the logistic regression model, the more general method of maximum likelihood is preferred, since it has better statistical properties. As we have just discussed, the basic intuition behind using maximum likelihood to fit a logistic regression model is to seek estimates for $\boldsymbol{\beta}$ such that the predicted probability $\hat{p}$ corresponds as closely as possible to the actual outcome. In other words, we try to find $\hat{\beta}$ such that these estimates yield a number close to 1 for all cases where the stock price went up, and a number close to 0 otherwise. More formally, we are seeking to maximize the likelihood function:

$$\max_{\beta} \mathcal{L}(\boldsymbol{\beta}) = \prod_{i:y_i=1} p(\boldsymbol{x}_i) \prod_{i':y_{i'}=0} (1 - p(\boldsymbol{x}_{i'}))$$

It is easier to work with sums than with products, so let's take logs on both sides to get the log-likelihood function and the corresponding definition of the logistic regression coefficients:

$$\boldsymbol{\beta}^{\text{ML}} = \operatorname{argmax} \log \mathcal{L}(\boldsymbol{\beta}) = \sum_{i=1}^{N} (y_i \log p(\boldsymbol{x}_i, \boldsymbol{\beta}) + (1 - y_i \log(1 - p(\boldsymbol{x}_i, \boldsymbol{\beta}))))$$

To maximize this equation, we set the derivatives of $\mathcal{L}$ with respect to $\boldsymbol{\beta}$ to zero. This yields $p+1$ so-called score equations, which are nonlinear in the parameters and can be solved using iterative numerical methods.

How to conduct inference with statsmodels

We will illustrate how to use logistic regression with `statsmodels` based on a simple built-in dataset containing quarterly US macro data from 1959 to 2009 (see the notebook `logistic_regression_macro_data` for details).

The variables and their transformations are listed in the following table:

Variable	Description	Transformation
`realgdp`	Real gross domestic product	Annual Growth Rate
`realcons`	Real personal consumption expenditures	Annual Growth Rate
`realinv`	Real gross private domestic investment	Annual Growth Rate
`realgovt`	Real federal expenditures and gross investment	Annual Growth Rate
`realdpi`	Real private disposable income	Annual Growth Rate
`m1`	M1 nominal money stock	Annual Growth Rate
`tbilrate`	Monthly Treasury bill rate	Level
`unemp`	Seasonally adjusted unemployment rate (%)	Level
`infl`	Inflation rate	Level
`realint`	Real interest rate	Level

To obtain a binary target variable, we compute the 20-quarter rolling average of the annual growth rate of quarterly real GDP. We then assign 1 if the current growth exceeds the moving average and 0 otherwise. Finally, we shift the indicator variables to align the next quarter's outcome with the current quarter.

We use an intercept and convert the quarter values into dummy variables and train the logistic regression model, as follows:

```
import statsmodels.api as sm
data = pd.get_dummies(data.drop(drop_cols, axis=1), columns=['quarter'],
drop_first=True).dropna()
model = sm.Logit(data.target, sm.add_constant(data.drop('target', axis=1)))
result = model.fit()
result.summary()
```

This produces the following summary for our model, which shows 198 observations and 13 variables, including an intercept:

```
                           Logit Regression Results
==============================================================================
Dep. Variable:                 target   No. Observations:                  198
Model:                          Logit   Df Residuals:                      185
Method:                           MLE   Df Model:                           12
Date:                Mon, 10 Sep 2018   Pseudo R-squ.:                  0.5022
Time:                        20:27:53   Log-Likelihood:                -67.907
converged:                       True   LL-Null:                       -136.42
                                        LLR p-value:                 2.375e-23
==============================================================================
                 coef    std err          z      P>|z|      [0.025      0.975]
------------------------------------------------------------------------------
const         -8.5881      1.908     -4.502      0.000     -12.327      -4.849
realcons     130.1446     26.633      4.887      0.000      77.945     182.344
realinv       18.8414      4.053      4.648      0.000      10.897      26.786
realgovt     -19.0318      6.010     -3.166      0.002     -30.812      -7.252
realdpi      -52.2473     19.912     -2.624      0.009     -91.275     -13.220
m1            -1.3462      6.177     -0.218      0.827     -13.453      10.761
tbilrate      60.8607     44.350      1.372      0.170     -26.063     147.784
unemp          0.9487      0.249      3.818      0.000       0.462       1.436
infl         -60.9647     44.362     -1.374      0.169    -147.913      25.984
realint      -61.0453     44.359     -1.376      0.169    -147.987      25.896
quarter_2      0.1128      0.618      0.182      0.855      -1.099       1.325
quarter_3     -0.1991      0.609     -0.327      0.744      -1.393       0.995
quarter_4      0.0007      0.608      0.001      0.999      -1.191       1.192
==============================================================================
```

Figure 7.13: Logit regression results

The summary indicates that the model has been trained using maximum likelihood and provides the maximized value of the log-likelihood function at -67.9.

The LL-Null value of -136.42 is the result of the maximized log-likelihood function when only an intercept is included. It forms the basis for the **pseudo-R2 statistic** and the **log-likelihood ratio (LLR)** test.

The pseudo-R^2 statistic is a substitute for the familiar R^2 available under least squares. It is computed based on the ratio of the maximized log-likelihood function for the null model m_0 and the full model m_1, as follows:

$$\rho^2 = 1 - \frac{\log \mathcal{L}(m_1^*)}{\log \mathcal{L}(m_0^*)}$$

The values vary from 0 (when the model does not improve the likelihood) to 1, where the model fits perfectly and the log-likelihood is maximized at 0. Consequently, higher values indicate a better fit.

The LLR test generally compares a more restricted model and is computed as:

$$\text{LLR} = -2\log(\mathcal{L}(m_0^*)/\mathcal{L}(m_1^*)) = 2(\log \mathcal{L}(m_1^*) - \log \mathcal{L}(m_0^*))$$

The null hypothesis is that the restricted model performs better, but the low p-value suggests that we can reject this hypothesis and prefer the full model over the null model. This is similar to the F-test for linear regression (where we can also use the LLR test when we estimate the model using MLE).

The z-statistic plays the same role as the t-statistic in the linear regression output and is equally computed as the ratio of the coefficient estimate and its standard error. The p-values also indicate the probability of observing the test statistic, assuming the null hypothesis $H_0 : \beta = 0$ that the population coefficient is zero. We can reject this hypothesis for the `intercept`, `realcons`, `realinv`, `realgovt`, `realdpi`, and `unemp`.

Predicting price movements with logistic regression

The lasso L1 penalty and the ridge L2 penalty can both be used with logistic regression. They have the same shrinkage effect that we have just discussed, and the lasso can again be used for variable selection with any linear regression model.

Just as with linear regression, it is important to standardize the input variables as the regularized models are scale sensitive. The regularization hyperparameter also requires tuning using cross-validation, as in the case of linear regression.

How to convert a regression into a classification problem

We will continue with the price prediction example, but now we will binarize the outcome variable so that it takes on the value 1 whenever the 1-day return is positive and 0 otherwise (see the notebook `predicting_price_movements_with_logistic_regression.ipynb` for the code examples given in this section):

```
target = 'target_1d'
y['label'] = (y[target] > 0).astype(int)
```

The outcomes are slightly unbalanced, with more positive than negative moves:

```
y.label.value_counts()
1    56443
0    53220
```

With this new categorical outcome variable, we can now train a logistic regression using the default L2 regularization.

Cross-validating the logistic regression hyperparameters

For logistic regression, the regularization is formulated inversely to linear regression: higher values for λ imply less regularization and vice versa.

We will cross-validate 11 options for the regularization hyperparameter using our custom `TimeSeriesCV`, as follows:

```
n_splits = 4*252
cv = TimeSeriesCV(n_splits=n_splits,
                  test_period_length=1,
                  train_period_length=252)
Cs = np.logspace(-5, 5, 11)
```

The `train-test` loop now uses sklearn's `LogisticRegression` and computes the `roc_auc_score` (see the notebook for details):

```
for C in Cs:
    model = LogisticRegression(C=C, fit_intercept=True)

    pipe = Pipeline([
        ('scaler', StandardScaler()),
        ('model', model)])
    for i, (train_idx, test_idx) in enumerate(cv.split(X), 1):
        X_train, y_train, = X.iloc[train_idx], y.label.iloc[train_idx]
        pipe.fit(X=X_train, y=y_train)
        X_test, y_test = X.iloc[test_idx], y.label.iloc[test_idx]
        y_score = pipe.predict_proba(X_test)[:, 1]
        auc = roc_auc_score(y_score=y_score, y_true=y_test)
```

In addition, we can also compute the IC based on the predicted probabilities and the actual returns:

```
        actuals = y[target].iloc[test_idx]
        ic, pval = spearmanr(y_score, actuals)
```

Evaluating the results using AUC and IC

We can again plot the AUC result for the range of hyperparameter values. In *Figure 7.14*, the left panel shows that the best median AUC results for *C*=0.1, whereas the best mean AUC corresponds to $C=10^{-3}$. The right panel displays the distribution of the information coefficients for the model with $C=10^{4}$. This also highlights that we obtain somewhat higher values for the mean and the median compared to the regression models shown previously:

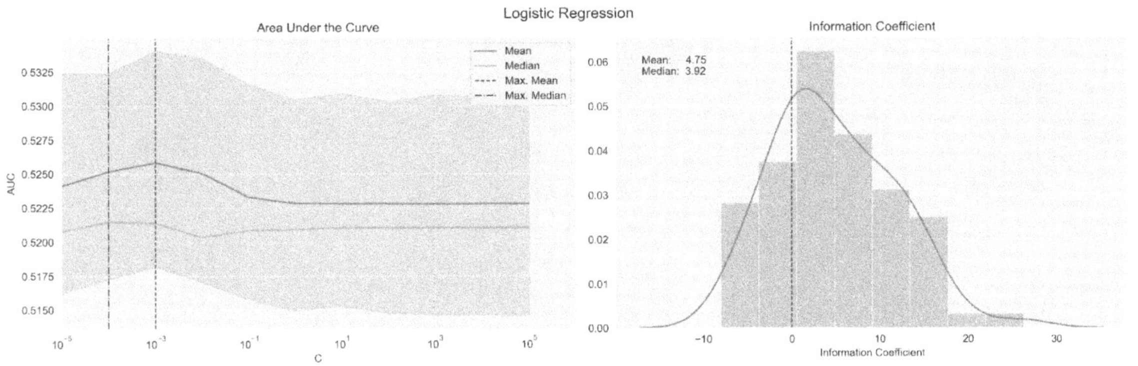

Figure 7.14: Logistic regression

In the next chapter, we will use the predictions produced by these basic models to generate signals for trading strategies and demonstrate how to backtest their performance.

Summary

In this chapter, we introduced the first of our machine learning models using the important baseline case of linear models for regression and classification. We explored the formulation of the objective functions for both tasks, learned about various training methods, and learned how to use the model for both inference and prediction.

We applied these new machine learning techniques to estimate linear factor models that are very useful to manage risks, assess new alpha factors, and attribute performance. We also applied linear regression and classification to accomplish the first predictive task of predicting stock returns in absolute and directional terms.

In the next chapter, we will put together what we have covered so far in the form of the machine learning for trading workflow. This process starts with sourcing and preparing the data about a specific investment universe and the computation of useful features, continues with the design and evaluation of machine learning models to extract actionable signals from these features, and culminates in the simulated execution and evaluation of a strategy that translates these signals into optimized portfolios.

8

The ML4T Workflow – From Model to Strategy Backtesting

Now, it's time to **integrate the various building blocks** of the **machine learning for trading** (**ML4T**) workflow that we have so far discussed separately. The goal of this chapter is to present an end-to-end perspective of the process of designing, simulating, and evaluating a trading strategy driven by an ML algorithm. To this end, we will demonstrate in more detail how to backtest an ML-driven strategy in a historical market context using the Python libraries backtrader and Zipline.

The **ultimate objective of the ML4T workflow** is to gather evidence from historical data. This helps us decide whether to deploy a candidate strategy in a live market and put financial resources at risk. This process builds on the skills you developed in the previous chapters because it relies on your ability to:

- Work with a diverse set of data sources to engineer informative factors
- Design ML models that generate predictive signals to inform your trading strategy
- Optimize the resulting portfolio from a risk-return perspective

A realistic simulation of your strategy also needs to faithfully represent how security markets operate and how trades are executed. Therefore, the institutional details of exchanges, such as which order types are available and how prices are determined, also matter when you design a backtest or evaluate whether a backtesting engine includes the requisite features for accurate performance measurements. Finally, there are several methodological aspects that require attention to avoid biased results and false discoveries that will lead to poor investment decisions.

More specifically, after working through this chapter, you will be able to:

- Plan and implement end-to-end strategy backtesting
- Understand and avoid critical pitfalls when implementing backtests
- Discuss the advantages and disadvantages of vectorized versus event-driven backtesting engines
- Identify and evaluate the key components of an event-driven backtester
- Design and execute the ML4T workflow using data sources at both minute and daily frequencies, with ML models trained separately or as part of the backtest
- Use Zipline and backtrader

> You can find the code samples for this chapter and links to additional resources in the corresponding directory of the GitHub repository. The notebooks include color versions of the images.

How to backtest an ML-driven strategy

In a nutshell, the ML4T workflow, illustrated in *Figure 8.1*, is about backtesting a trading strategy that leverages machine learning to generate trading signals, select and size positions, or optimize the execution of trades. It involves the following steps, with a specific investment universe and horizon in mind:

1. Source and prepare market, fundamental, and alternative data
2. Engineer predictive alpha factors and features
3. Design, tune, and evaluate ML models to generate trading signals
4. Decide on trades based on these signals, for example, by applying rules
5. Size individual positions in the portfolio context
6. Simulate the resulting trades triggered using historical market data
7. Evaluate how the resulting positions would have performed

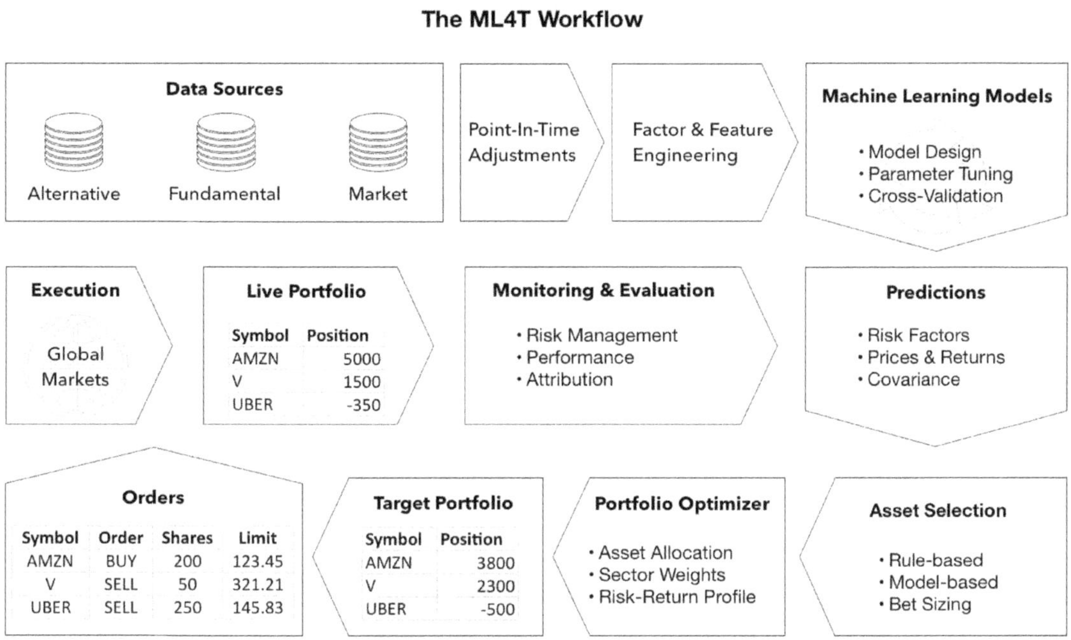

Figure 8.1: The ML4T workflow

When we discussed the ML process in *Chapter 6, The Machine Learning Process*, we emphasized that the model's learning should generalize well to new applications. In other words, the predictions of an ML model trained on a given set of data should perform equally well when provided new input data. Similarly, the (relative) **backtest performance of a strategy should be indicative of future market performance**.

Before we take a look at how backtesting engines run historical simulations, we need to review several methodological challenges. Failing to properly address them will render results unreliable and lead to poor decisions about the strategy's live implementation.

Backtesting pitfalls and how to avoid them

Backtesting simulates an algorithmic strategy based on historical data, with the goal of producing performance results that generalize to new market conditions. In addition to the generic uncertainty around predictions in the context of ever-changing markets, several implementation aspects can bias the results and increase the risk of mistaking in-sample performance for patterns that will hold out-of-sample.

These aspects are under our control and include the selection and preparation of data, unrealistic assumptions about the trading environment, and the flawed application and interpretation of statistical tests. The risks of false backtest discoveries multiply with increasing computing power, bigger datasets, and more complex algorithms that facilitate the misidentification of apparent signals in a noisy sample.

In this section, we will outline the most serious and common methodological mistakes. Please refer to the literature on multiple testing for further detail, in particular, a series of articles by Marcos Lopez de Prado collected in *Advances in Financial Machine Learning (2018)*. We will also introduce the deflated **Sharpe ratio** (**SR**), which illustrates how to adjust metrics that result from repeated trials when using the same set of financial data for your analysis.

Getting the data right

Data issues that undermine the validity of a backtest include **look-ahead bias**, **survivorship bias**, **outlier control**, as well as the **selection of the sample period**. We will address each of these in turn.

Look-ahead bias – use only point-in-time data

At the heart of an algorithmic strategy are trading rules that trigger actions based on data. Look-ahead bias emerges when we develop or evaluate trading rules **using historical information before it was known or available**. The resulting performance measures will be misleading and not representative of the future when data availability differs during live strategy execution.

A common cause of this bias is the failure to account for corrections or restatements of reported financials after their initial publication. Stock splits or reverse splits can also generate look-ahead bias. For example, when computing the earnings yield, **earnings-per-share** (**EPS**) data is usually reported on a quarterly basis, whereas market prices are available at a much higher frequency. Therefore, adjusted EPS and price data need to be synchronized, taking into account when the available data was, in fact, released to market participants.

The **solution** involves the careful validation of the timestamps of all data that enters a backtest. We need to guarantee that conclusions are based only on point-in-time data that does not inadvertently include information from the future. High-quality data providers ensure that these criteria are met. When point-in-time data is not available, we need to make (conservative) assumptions about the lag in reporting.

Survivorship bias – track your historical universe

Survivorship bias arises when the backtest data contains only securities that are currently active while **omitting assets that have disappeared** over time, due to, for example, bankruptcy, delisting, or acquisition. Securities that are no longer part of the investment universe often did not perform well, and failing to include these cases positively skew the backtest result.

The **solution**, naturally, is to verify that datasets include all securities available over time, as opposed to only those that are still available when running the test. In a way, this is another way of ensuring the data is truly point-in-time.

Outlier control – do not exclude realistic extremes

Data preparation typically includes some treatment of outliers such as winsorizing, or clipping, extreme values. The challenge is to **identify outliers that are truly not representative** of the period under analysis, as opposed to any extreme values that are an integral part of the market environment at that time. Many market models assume normally distributed data when extreme values are observed more frequently, as suggested by fat-tailed distributions.

The **solution** involves a careful analysis of outliers with respect to the probability of extreme values occurring and adjusting the strategy parameters to this reality.

Sample period – try to represent relevant future scenarios

A backtest will not yield representative results that generalize to the future if the sample data does not **reflect the current (and likely future) environment**. A poorly chosen sample data might lack relevant market regime aspects, for example, in terms of volatility or volumes, fail to include enough data points, or contain too many or too few extreme historical events.

The **solution** involves using sample periods that include important market phenomena or generating synthetic data that reflects the relevant market characteristics.

Getting the simulation right

Practical issues related to the implementation of the historical simulation include:

- Failure to **mark to market** to accurately reflect market prices and account for drawdowns
- **Unrealistic assumptions** about the availability, cost, or market impact of trades
- Incorrect **timing of signals and trade execution**

Let's see how to identify and address each of these issues.

Mark-to-market performance – track risks over time

A strategy needs to **meet investment objectives and constraints at all times**. If it performs well over the course of the backtest but leads to unacceptable losses or volatility over time, this will (obviously) not be practical. Portfolio managers need to track and report the value of their positions, called mark to market, on a regular basis and possibly in real time.

The solution involves plotting performance over time or calculating (rolling) risk metrics, such as the **value at risk (VaR)** or the Sortino ratio.

Transaction costs – assume a realistic trading environment

Markets do not permit the execution of all trades at all times or at the targeted price. A backtest that assumes **trades that may not actually be available** or would have occurred at less favorable terms will produce biased results.

Practical shortcomings include a strategy that assumes short sales when there may be no counterparty, or one that underestimates the market impact of trades (slippage) that are large or deal in less liquid assets, or the costs that arise due to broker fees.

The **solution** includes a limitation to a liquid universe and/or realistic parameter assumptions for trading and slippage costs. This also safeguards against misleading conclusions from unstable factor signals that decay fast and produce a high portfolio turnover.

Timing of decisions – properly sequence signals and trades

Similar to look-ahead bias, the simulation could make **unrealistic assumptions about when it receives and trades on signals**. For instance, signals may be computed from close prices when trades are only available at the next open, with possibly quite different prices. When we evaluate performance using the close price, the backtest results will not represent realistic future outcomes.

The **solution** involves careful orchestration of the sequence of signal arrival, trade execution, and performance evaluation.

Getting the statistics right

The most prominent challenge when backtesting validity, including published results, is the discovery of spurious patterns due to multiple testing. Selecting a strategy based on the tests of different candidates on the same data will bias the choice. This is because a positive outcome is more likely caused by the stochastic nature of the performance measure itself. In other words, the strategy overfits the test sample, producing deceptively positive results that are unlikely to generalize to future data that's encountered during live trading.

Hence, backtest performance is only informative if the number of trials is reported to allow for an assessment of the risk of selection bias. This is rarely the case in practical or academic research, inviting doubts about the validity of many published claims.

Furthermore, the risk of backtest overfitting does not only arise from running numerous tests but also affects strategies designed based on prior knowledge of what works and doesn't. Since the risks include the knowledge of backtests run by others on the same data, backtest-overfitting is very hard to avoid in practice.

Proposed **solutions** include prioritizing tests that can be justified using investment or economic theory, rather than arbitrary data-mining efforts. It also implies testing in a variety of contexts and scenarios, including possibly on synthetic data.

The minimum backtest length and the deflated SR

Marcos Lopez de Prado (`http://www.quantresearch.info/`) has published extensively on the risks of backtesting and how to detect or avoid it. This includes an online simulator of backtest-overfitting (`http://datagrid.lbl.gov/backtest/`, *Bailey, et al. 2015*).

Another result includes an estimate of the minimum length of the backtest period that an investor should require to avoid selecting a strategy that achieves a certain SR for a given number of in-sample trials, but has an expected out-of-sample SR of zero. The result implies that, for example, 2 years of daily backtesting data does not support conclusions about more than seven strategies. 5 years of data expands this number to 45 strategy variations. See *Bailey, Borwein, and Prado (2016)* for implementation details.

Bailey and Prado (2014) also derived a deflated SR to compute the probability that the SR is statistically significant while controlling for the inflationary effect of multiple testing, non-normal returns, and shorter sample lengths. (See the `multiple_testing` subdirectory for the Python implementation of `deflated_sharpe_ratio.py` and references for the derivation of the related formulas.)

Optimal stopping for backtests

In addition to limiting backtests to strategies that can be justified on theoretical grounds as opposed to mere data-mining exercises, an important question is when to stop running additional tests.

One way to answer this question relies on the solution to the **secretary problem** from the optimal stopping theory. This problem assumes we are selecting an applicant based on interview results and need to decide whether to hold an additional interview or choose the most recent candidate. In this context, the optimal rule is to always reject the first n/e candidates and then select the first candidate that surpasses all the previous options. Using this rule results in a $1/e$ probability of selecting the best candidate, irrespective of the size n of the candidate pool.

Translating this rule directly to the backtest context produces the following **recommendation**: test a random sample of $1/e$ (roughly 37 percent) of reasonable strategies and record their performance. Then, continue with the tests until a strategy outperforms those tested before. This rule applies to tests of several alternatives, with the goal of choosing a near-best as soon as possible while minimizing the risk of a false positive. See the resources listed on GitHub for additional information.

How a backtesting engine works

Put simply, a backtesting engine iterates over historical prices (and other data), passes the current values to your algorithm, receives orders in return, and keeps track of the resulting positions and their value.

In practice, there are numerous requirements for creating a realistic and robust simulation of the ML4T workflow that was depicted in *Figure 8.1* at the beginning of this chapter. The difference between vectorized and event-driven approaches illustrates how the faithful reproduction of the actual trading environment adds significant complexity.

Vectorized versus event-driven backtesting

A vectorized backtest is the most basic way to evaluate a strategy. It simply multiplies a signal vector that represents the target position size with a vector of returns for the investment horizon to compute the period performance.

Let's illustrate the vectorized approach using the daily return predictions that we created using ridge regression in the previous chapter. Using a few simple technical factors, we predicted the returns for the next day for the 100 stocks with the highest recent dollar trading volume (see *Chapter 7, Linear Models – From Risk Factors to Return Forecasts*, for details).

We'll transform the predictions into signals for a very simple strategy: on any given trading day, we will go long on the 10 highest positive predictions and go short on the lowest 10 negative predictions. If there are fewer positive or negative predictions, we'll hold fewer long or short positions. The notebook `vectorized_backtest` contains the following code example, and the script `data.py` creates the input data stored in `backtest.h5`.

First, we load the data for our strategy, as well as S&P 500 prices (which we convert into daily returns) to benchmark the performance:

```
sp500 = web.DataReader('SP500', 'fred', '2014', '2018').pct_change()

data = pd.read_hdf('00_data/backtest.h5', 'data')
data.info()
MultiIndex: 187758 entries, ('AAL', Timestamp('2014-12-09 00:00:00')) to
('ZTS', Timestamp('2017-11-30 00:00:00'))
Data columns (total 6 columns):
 #   Column     Non-Null Count   Dtype
---  ------     --------------   -----
 0   predicted  74044 non-null   float64
 1   open       187758 non-null  float64
 2   high       187758 non-null  float64
 3   low        187758 non-null  float64
 4   close      187758 non-null  float64
 5   volume     187758 non-null  float64
```

The data combines daily return predictions and OHLCV market data for 253 distinct stocks over the 2014-17 period, with 100 equities for each day. Now, we can compute the daily forward returns and convert these and the predictions into wide format, with one ticker per column:

```
daily_returns = data.open.unstack('ticker').sort_index().pct_change()
fwd_returns = daily_returns.shift(-1)
predictions = data.predicted.unstack('ticker')
```

The next step is to select positive and negative predictions, rank them in descending and ascending fashion, and create long and short signals using an integer mask that identifies the top 10 on each side with identifies the predictions outside the top 10 with a one, and a zero:

```
long_signals = (predictions.where(predictions>0).rank(axis=1,
ascending=False) > 10).astype(int)
short_signals = (predictions.where(predictions<0).rank(axis=1) > 10).
astype(int)
```

We can then multiply the binary DataFrames with the forward returns (using their negative inverse for the shorts) to get the daily performance of each position, assuming equal-sized investments. The daily average of these returns corresponds to the performance of equal-weighted long and short portfolios, and the sum reflects the overall return of a market-neutral long-short strategy:

```
long_returns = long_signals.mul(fwd_returns).mean(axis=1)
short_returns = short_signals.mul(-fwd_returns).mean(axis=1)
strategy = long_returns.add(short_returns).to_frame('strategy')
```

When we compare the results, as shown in *Figure 8.2*, our strategy performed well compared to the S&P 500 for the first 2 years of the period – that is, until the benchmark catches up and our strategy underperforms during 2017.

The strategy returns are also less volatile with a standard deviation of 0.002 compared to 0.008 for the S&P 500; the correlation is low and negative at -0.093:

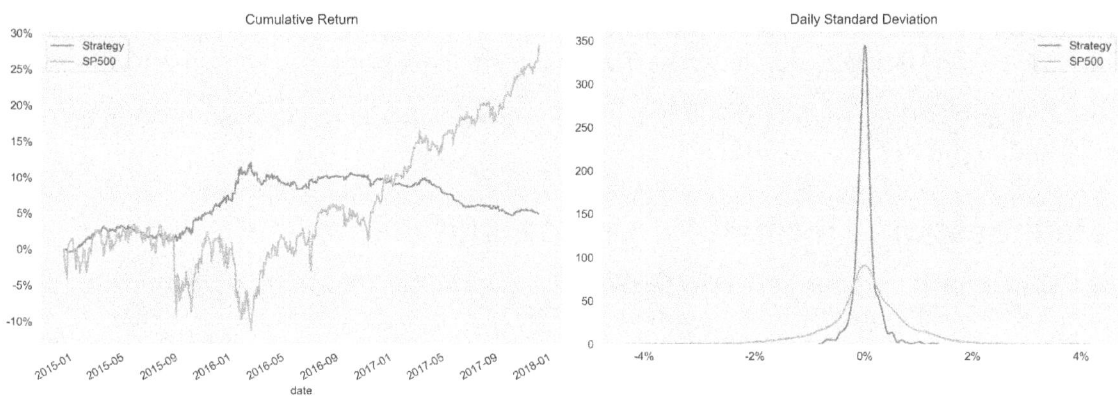

Figure 8.2: Vectorized backtest results

While this approach permits a quick back-of-the-envelope evaluation, it misses important features of a robust, realistic, and user-friendly backtest engine; for example:

- We need to manually align the timestamps of predictions and returns (using pandas' built-in capabilities) and do not have any safeguards against inadvertent look-ahead bias.

- There is no explicit position sizing and representation of the trading process that accounts for costs and other market realities, or an accounting system that tracks positions and their performance.
- There is also no performance measurement other than what we compute after the fact, and risk management rules like stop-loss are difficult to simulate.

That's where event-driven backtesting comes in. An event-driven backtesting engine explicitly simulates the time dimension of the trading environment and imposes significantly more structure on the simulation. This includes the use of historical calendars that define when trades can be made and when quotes are available. The enforcement of timestamps also helps to avoid look-ahead bias and other implementation errors mentioned in the previous section (but there is no guarantee).

Generally, event-driven systems aim to capture the actions and constraints encountered by a strategy more closely and, ideally, can readily be converted into a live trading engine that submits actual orders.

Key implementation aspects

The requirements for a realistic simulation may be met by a **single platform** that supports all steps of the process in an end-to-end fashion, or by **multiple tools** that each specialize in different aspects.

For instance, you could handle the design and testing of ML models that generate signals using generic ML libraries like scikit-learn, or others that we will encounter in this book, and feed the model outputs into a separate backtesting engine. Alternatively, you could run the entire ML4T workflow end-to-end on a single platform like Quantopian or QuantConnect.

The following sections highlight key items and implementation details that need to be addressed to put this process into action.

Data ingestion – format, frequency, and timing

The first step in the process concerns the sources of data. Traditionally, algorithmic trading strategies focused on market data, namely the OHLCV price and volume data that we discussed in *Chapter 2, Market and Fundamental Data – Sources and Techniques*. Today, data sources are more diverse and raise the question of how many different **storage formats and data types** to support, and whether to use a proprietary or custom format or rely on third-party or open source formats.

Another aspect is the **frequency of data sources** that can be used and whether sources at different frequencies can be combined. Common options in increasing order of computational complexity and memory and storage requirements include daily, minute, and tick frequency. Intermediate frequencies are also possible. Algorithmic strategies tend to perform better at higher frequencies, even though quantamental investors are gaining ground, as discussed in *Chapter 1, Machine Learning for Trading – From Idea to Execution*. Regardless, institutional investors will certainly require tick frequency.

Finally, data ingestion should also address **point-in-time constraints** to avoid look-ahead bias, as outlined in the previous section. The use of trading calendars helps limit data to legitimate dates and times; adjustments to reflect corporate actions like stock splits and dividends or restatements that impact prices revealed at specific times need to be made prior to ingestion.

Factor engineering – built-in factors versus libraries

To facilitate the engineering of alpha factors for use in ML models, many backtesting engines include computational tools suitable for numerous standard transformations like moving averages and various technical indicators. A key advantage of **built-in factor engineering** is the easy conversion of the backtesting pipeline into a live trading engine that applies the same computations to the input data.

The **numerical Python libraries** (pandas, NumPy, TA-Lib) presented in *Chapter 4, Financial Feature Engineering - How to Research Alpha Factors,* are an alternative to **pre-compute factors**. This can be efficient when the goal is to reuse factors in various backtests that amortize the computational cost.

ML models, predictions, and signals

As mentioned earlier, the ML workflow discussed in *Chapter 6, The Machine Learning Process,* can be embedded in an end-to-end platform that integrates the model design and evaluation part into the backtesting process. While convenient, this is also costly because model training becomes part of the backtest when the goal is perhaps to fine-tune trading rules.

Similar to factor engineering, you can decouple these aspects and design, train, and evaluate ML models using generic libraries for this purpose, and also provide the relevant predictions as inputs to the backtester. We will mostly use this approach in this book because it makes the exposition more concise and less repetitive.

Trading rules and execution

A realistic strategy simulation requires a faithful representation of the trading environment. This includes access to relevant exchanges, the availability of the various order types discussed in *Chapter 2, Market and Fundamental Data - Sources and Techniques,* and the accounting for transaction costs. Costs include broker commissions, bid-ask spreads, and slippage, giving us the difference between the target execution price and the price that's eventually obtained. It is also important to ensure trades execute with delays that reflect liquidity and operating hours.

Performance evaluation

Finally, a backtesting platform needs to facilitate performance evaluation. It can provide standard metrics derived from its accounting of transactions, or provide an output of the metrics that can be used with a library like **pyfolio** that's suitable for this purpose.

In the next two sections, we will explore two of the most popular backtesting libraries, namely backtrader and Zipline.

backtrader – a flexible tool for local backtests

backtrader is a popular, flexible, and user-friendly Python library for local backtests with great documentation, developed since 2015 by Daniel Rodriguez. In addition to a large and active community of individual traders, there are several banks and trading houses that use backtrader to prototype and test new strategies before porting them to a production-ready platform using, for example, Java. You can also use backtrader for live trading with several brokers of your choice (see the backtrader documentation and *Chapter 23, Conclusions and Next Steps*).

We'll first summarize the key concepts of backtrader to clarify the big picture of the backtesting workflow on this platform, and then demonstrate its usage for a strategy driven by ML predictions.

Key concepts of backtrader's Cerebro architecture

backtrader's **Cerebro** (Spanish for "brain") architecture represents the key components of the backtesting workflow as (extensible) Python objects. These objects interact to facilitate processing input data and the computation of factors, formulate and execute a strategy, receive and execute orders, and track and measure performance. A Cerebro instance orchestrates the overall process from collecting inputs, executing the backtest bar by bar, and providing results.

The library uses conventions for these interactions that allow you to omit some detail and streamline the backtesting setup. I highly recommend browsing the documentation to dive deeper if you plan on using backtrader to develop your own strategies.

Figure 8.3 outlines the key elements in the Cerebro architecture, and the following subsections summarize their most important functionalities:

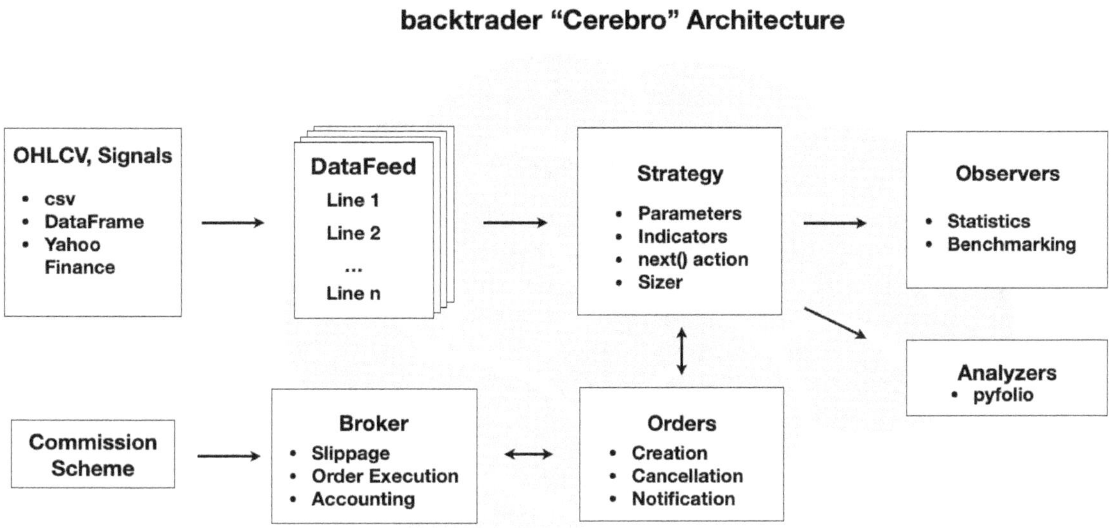

Figure 8.3: The backtrader Cerebro architecture

Data feeds, lines, and indicators

Data feeds are the raw material for a strategy and contain information about individual securities, such as OHLCV market data with a timestamp for each observation, but you can customize the available fields. backtrader can ingest data from various sources, including CSV files and pandas DataFrames, and from online sources like Yahoo Finance. There are also extensions you can use to connect to online trading platforms like Interactive Brokers to ingest live data and execute transactions. The compatibility with DataFrame objects implies that you can load data from accessible by pandas, ranging from databases to HDF5 files. (See the demonstration in the *How to use backtrader in practice* section; also, see the *I/O* section of the pandas documentation.)

Once loaded, we add the data feeds to a Cerebro instance, which, in turn, makes it available to one or more strategies in the order received. Your strategy's trading logic can access each data feed by name (for example, the ticker) or sequence number and retrieve the current and past values of any field of the data feed. Each field is called a **line**.

backtrader comes with over 130 common technical **indicators** that allow you to compute new values from lines or other indicators for each data feed to drive your strategy. You can also use standard Python **operations** to derive new values. Usage is fairly straightforward and well explained in the documentation.

From data and signals to trades – strategy

The **Strategy** object contains your trading logic that places orders based on data feed information that the Cerebro instance presents at every bar during backtest execution. You can easily test variations by configuring a Strategy to accept arbitrary parameters that you define when adding an instance of your Strategy to your Cerebro.

For every bar of a backtest, the Cerebro instance calls either the `.prenext()` or `.next()` method of your Strategy instance. The role of `.prenext()` is to address bars that do not yet have complete data for all feeds, for example, before there are enough periods to compute an indicator like a built-in moving average or if there is otherwise missing data. The default is to do nothing, but you can add trading logic of your choice or call `next()` if your main Strategy is designed to handle missing values (see the *How to use backtrader in practice* section).

You can also use backtrader without defining an explicit Strategy and instead use a simplified Signals interface. The Strategy API gives you more control and flexibility, though; see the backtrader documentation for details on how to use the Signals API.

A Strategy outputs orders: let's see how backtrader handles these next.

Commissions instead of commission schemes

Once your Strategy has evaluated current and past data points at each bar, it needs to decide which orders to place. backtrader lets you create several standard **order** types that Cerebro passes to a Broker instance for execution and provides a notification of the result at each bar.

You can use the Strategy methods `buy()` and `sell()` to place market, close, and limit orders, as well as stop and stop-limit orders. Execution works as follows:

- **Market order**: Fills at the next open bar
- **Close order**: Fills at the next close bar
- **Limit order**: Executes only if a price threshold is met (for example, only buy up to a certain price) during an (optional) period of validity
- **Stop order**: Becomes a market order if the price reaches a given threshold
- **Stop limit order**: Becomes a limit order once the stop is triggered

In practice, stop orders differ from limit orders because they cannot be seen by the market prior to the price trigger. backtrader also provides target orders that compute the required size, taking into account the current position to achieve a certain portfolio allocation in terms of the number of shares, the value of the position, or the percentage of portfolio value. Furthermore, there are **bracket orders** that combine, for a long order, a buy with two limit sell orders that activate as the buy executes. Should one of the sell orders fill or cancel, the other sell order also cancels.

The **Broker** handles order execution, tracks the portfolio, cash value, and notifications and implements transaction costs like commission and slippage. The Broker may reject trades if there is not enough cash; it can be important to sequence buys and sells to ensure liquidity. backtrader also has a `cheat_on_open` feature that permits looking ahead to the next bar, to avoid rejected trades due to adverse price moves by the next bar. This feature will, of course, bias your results.

In addition to **commission schemes** like a fixed or percentage amount of the absolute transaction value, you can implement your own logic, as demonstrated later, for a flat fee per share.

Making it all happen – Cerebro

The Cerebro control system synchronizes the data feeds based on the bars represented by their timestamp, and runs the trading logic and broker actions on an event-by-event basis accordingly. backtrader does not impose any restrictions on the frequency or the trading calendar and can use multiple time frames in parallel.

It also vectorizes the calculation for indicators if it can preload source data. There are several options you can use to optimize operations from a memory perspective (see the Cerebro documentation for details).

How to use backtrader in practice

We are going to demonstrate backtrader using the daily return predictions from the ridge regression from *Chapter 7*, *Linear Models – From Risk Factors to Return Forecasts*, as we did for the vectorized backtest earlier in this chapter. We will create the Cerebro instance, load the data, formulate and add the Strategy, run the backtest, and review the results.

The notebook `backtesting_with_backtrader` contains the following code examples and some additional details.

How to load price and other data

We need to ensure that we have price information for all the dates on which we would like to buy or sell stocks, not only for the days with predictions. To load data from a pandas DataFrame, we subclass backtrader's `PandasData` class to define the fields that we will provide:

```
class SignalData(PandasData):
    """
    Define pandas DataFrame structure
    """
    cols = OHLCV + ['predicted']

    # create lines
    lines = tuple(cols)

    # define parameters
    params = {c: -1 for c in cols}
    params.update({'datetime': None})
    params = tuple(params.items())
```

We then instantiate a `Cerebro` class and use the `SignalData` class to add one data feed for each ticker in our dataset that we load from HDF5:

```
cerebro = bt.Cerebro()  # create a "Cerebro" instance
idx = pd.IndexSlice
data = pd.read_hdf('00_data/backtest.h5', 'data').sort_index()
tickers = data.index.get_level_values(0).unique()

for ticker in tickers:
    df = data.loc[idx[ticker, :], :].droplevel('ticker', axis=0)
    df.index.name = 'datetime'
    bt_data = SignalData(dataname=df)
    cerebro.adddata(bt_data, name=ticker)
```

Now, we are ready to define our Strategy.

How to formulate the trading logic

Our `MLStrategy` subclasses backtrader's `Strategy` class and defines parameters that we can use to modify its behavior. We also create a log file to create a record of the transactions:

```
class MLStrategy(bt.Strategy):
    params = (('n_positions', 10),
              ('min_positions', 5),
              ('verbose', False),
              ('log_file', 'backtest.csv'))
```

```
    def log(self, txt, dt=None):
        """ Logger for the strategy"""
        dt = dt or self.datas[0].datetime.datetime(0)
        with Path(self.p.log_file).open('a') as f:
            log_writer = csv.writer(f)
            log_writer.writerow([dt.isoformat()] + txt.split(','))
```

The core of the strategy resides in the `.next()` method. We go long/short on the `n_position` stocks with the highest positive/lowest negative forecast, as long as there are at least `min_positions` positions. We always sell any existing positions that do not appear in the new long and short lists and use `order_target_percent` to build equal-weights positions in the new targets (log statements are omitted to save some space):

```
    def prenext(self):
        self.next()

    def next(self):
        today = self.datas[0].datetime.date()
        positions = [d._name for d, pos in self.getpositions().items() if pos]
        up, down = {}, {}
        missing = not_missing = 0
        for data in self.datas:
            if data.datetime.date() == today:
                if data.predicted[0] > 0:
                    up[data._name] = data.predicted[0]
                elif data.predicted[0] < 0:
                    down[data._name] = data.predicted[0]

        # sort dictionaries ascending/descending by value
        # returns list of tuples
        shorts = sorted(down, key=down.get)[:self.p.n_positions]
        longs = sorted(up, key=up.get, reverse=True)[:self.p.n_positions]
        n_shorts, n_longs = len(shorts), len(longs)
        # only take positions if at least min_n longs and shorts
        if n_shorts < self.p.min_positions or n_longs < self.p.min_positions:
            longs, shorts = [], []
        for ticker in positions:
            if ticker not in longs + shorts:
                self.order_target_percent(data=ticker, target=0)
         short_target = -1 / max(self.p.n_positions, n_short)
        long_target = 1 / max(self.p.top_positions, n_longs)
        for ticker in shorts:
            self.order_target_percent(data=ticker, target=short_target)
        for ticker in longs:
            self.order_target_percent(data=ticker, target=long_target)
```

Now, we need to configure our `Cerebro` instance and add our `Strategy`.

How to configure the Cerebro instance

We use a custom commission scheme that assumes we pay a fixed amount of $0.02 per share that we buy or sell:

```
class FixedCommisionScheme(bt.CommInfoBase):
    """
    Simple fixed commission scheme for demo
    """
    params = (
        ('commission', .02),
        ('stocklike', True),
        ('commtype', bt.CommInfoBase.COMM_FIXED),
    )

    def _getcommission(self, size, price, pseudoexec):
        return abs(size) * self.p.commission
```

Then, we define our starting cash amount and configure the broker accordingly:

```
cash = 10000
cerebro.broker.setcash(cash)
comminfo = FixedCommisionScheme()
cerebro.broker.addcommissioninfo(comminfo)
```

Now, all that's missing is adding the `MLStrategy` to our `Cerebro` instance, providing parameters for the desired number of positions and the minimum number of long/shorts. We'll also add a pyfolio analyzer so we can view the performance tearsheets we presented in *Chapter 5, Portfolio Optimization and Performance Evaluation*:

```
cerebro.addanalyzer(bt.analyzers.PyFolio, _name='pyfolio')
cerebro.addstrategy(MLStrategy, n_positions=10, min_positions=5,
                    verbose=True, log_file='bt_log.csv')
results = cerebro.run()
ending_value = cerebro.broker.getvalue()

f'Final Portfolio Value: {ending_value:,.2f}'
Final Portfolio Value: 10,502.32
```

The backtest uses 869 trading days and takes around 45 seconds to run. The following figure shows the cumulative return and the evolution of the portfolio value, as well as the daily value of long and short positions.

Performance looks somewhat similar to the preceding vectorized test, with outperformance relative to the S&P 500 benchmark during the first half and poor performance thereafter.

The `backtesting_with_backtrader` notebook contains the complete pyfolio results:

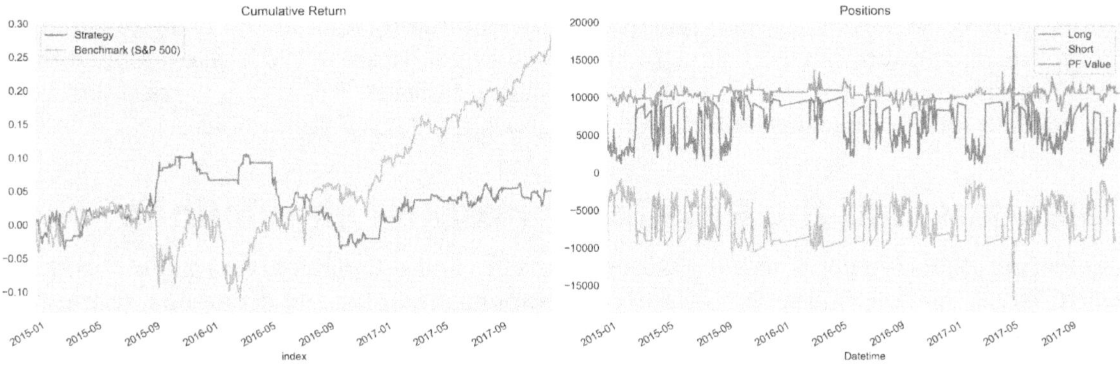

Figure 8.4: backtrader results

backtrader summary and next steps

backtrader is a very straightforward yet flexible and performant backtesting engine for local backtesting. You can load any dataset at the frequency you desire from a broad range of sources due to pandas compatibility. `Strategy` lets you define arbitrary trading logic; you just need to ensure you access the distinct data feeds as needed. It also integrates well with pyfolio for quick yet comprehensive performance evaluation.

In the demonstration, we applied our trading logic to predictions from a pre-trained model. We can also train a model during backtesting because we can access data prior to the current bar. Often, however, it is more efficient to decouple model training from strategy selection and avoid duplicating model training.

One of the reasons for backtrader's popularity is the ability to use it for live trading with a broker of your choosing. The community is very lively, and code to connect to brokers or additional data sources, including for cryptocurrencies, is readily available online.

Zipline – scalable backtesting by Quantopian

The backtesting engine Zipline powers Quantopian's online research, backtesting, and live (paper) trading platform. As a hedge fund, Quantopian aims to identify robust algorithms that outperform, subject to its risk management criteria. To this end, they use competitions to select the best strategies and allocate capital to share profits with the winners.

Quantopian first released Zipline in 2012 as version 0.5, and the latest version, 1.3, dates from July 2018. Zipline works well with its sister libraries Alphalens, pyfolio, and empyrical that we introduced in *Chapter 4, Financial Feature Engineering – How to Research Alpha Factors* and *Chapter 5, Portfolio Optimization and Performance Evaluation*, and integrates well with NumPy, pandas, and numeric libraries, but may not always support the latest version.

Zipline is designed to operate at the scale of thousands of securities, and each can be associated with a large number of indicators. It imposes more structure on the backtesting process than backtrader to ensure data quality by eliminating look-ahead bias, for example, and optimize computational efficiency while executing a backtest. We'll take a look at the key concepts and elements of the architecture, shown in *Figure 8.5*, before we demonstrate how to use Zipline to backtest ML-driven models on the data of your choice.

Calendars and the Pipeline for robust simulations

Key features that contribute to the goals of scalability and reliability are data bundles that store OHLCV market data with on-the-fly adjustments for splits and dividends, trading calendars that reflect operating hours of exchanges around the world, and the powerful Pipeline API (see the following diagram). We will discuss their usage in the following sections to complement the brief Zipline introduction we gave in earlier chapters:

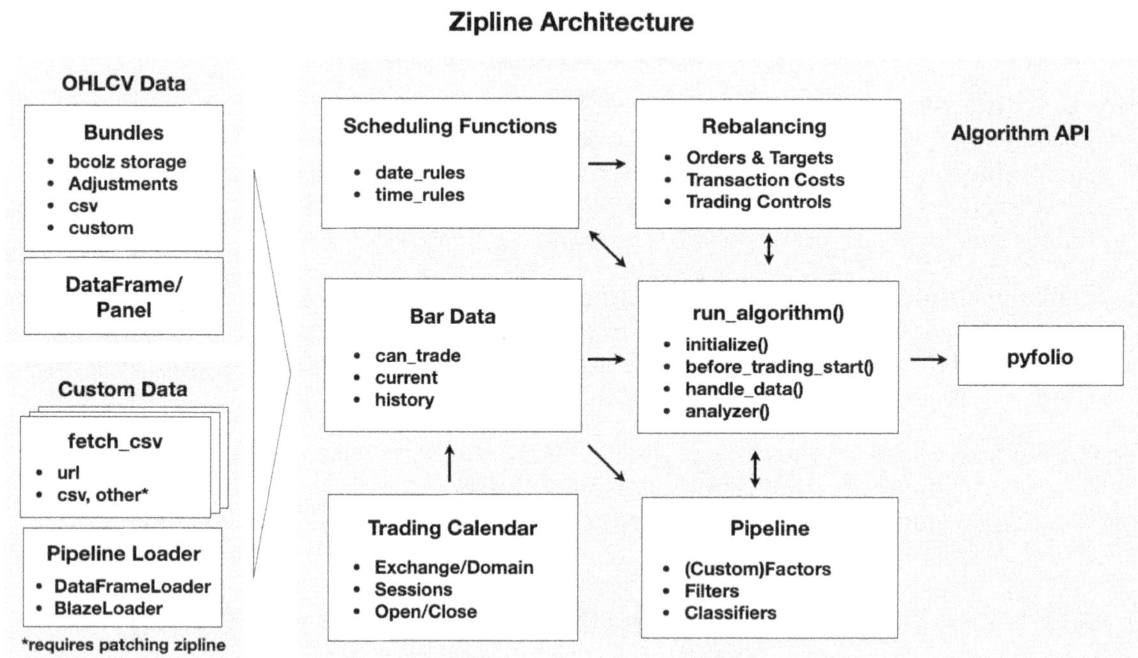

Figure 8.5: The Zipline architecture

Bundles – point-in-time data with on-the-fly adjustments

The principal data store is a **bundle** that resides on disk in compressed, columnar bcolz format for efficient retrieval, combined with metadata stored in an SQLite database. Bundles are designed to contain only OHLCV data and are limited to daily and minute frequency. A great feature is that bundles store split and dividend information, and Zipline computes **point-in-time adjustments**, depending on the time period you pick for your backtest.

Zipline relies on the **TradingCalendar** library (also maintained by Quantopian) for operational details on exchanges around the world, such as time zone, market open and closing times, or holidays. Data sources have domains (for now, these are countries) and need to conform to the assigned exchange calendar. Quantopian is actively developing support for international securities, and these features may evolve.

After installation, the command `zipline ingest -b bundle` lets you install the Quandl Wiki dataset (daily frequency) right away. The result ends up in the `.zipline` directory, which, by default, resides in your home folder. In addition, you can design your own bundles, as we'll see.

In addition to bundles, you can provide OHCLV data to an algorithm as a pandas DataFrame or Panel. (Panel is recently deprecated, but Zipline is a few pandas versions behind.) However, bundles are more convenient and efficient.

A shortcoming of bundles is that they do not let you store data other than price and volume information. However, two alternatives let you accomplish this: the `fetch_csv()` function downloads DataFrames from a URL and was designed for other Quandl data sources, for example, fundamentals. Zipline reasonably expects the data to refer to the same securities for which you have provided OHCLV data and aligns the bars accordingly. It's very easy to patch the library to load a local CSV or HDF5 using pandas, and the GitHub repository provides some guidance on how to do so.

In addition, `DataFrameLoader` and `BlazeLoader` permit you to feed additional attributes to a Pipeline (see the `DataFrameLoader` demo later in this chapter). `BlazeLoader` can interface with numerous sources, including databases. However, since the Pipeline API is limited to daily data, `fetch_csv()` will be critical to adding features at a minute frequency, as we will do in later chapters.

The Algorithm API – backtests on a schedule

The `TradingAlgorithm` class implements the Zipline Algorithm API and operates on `BarData` that has been aligned with a given trading calendar. After the initial setup, the backtest runs for a specified period and executes its trading logic as specific events occur. These events are driven by the daily or minutely trading frequency, but you can also schedule arbitrary functions to evaluate signals, place orders, and rebalance your portfolio, or log information about the ongoing simulation.

You can execute an algorithm from the command line, in a Jupyter Notebook, or by using the `run_algorithm()` method of the underlying `TradingAlgorithm` class. The algorithm requires an `initialize()` method that is called once when the simulation starts. It keeps state through a context dictionary and receives actionable information through a data variable containing point-in-time current and historical data.

You can add properties to the context dictionary, which is available to all other `TradingAlgorithm` methods, or register pipelines that perform more complex data processing, such as computing alpha factors and filtering securities accordingly.

Algorithm execution occurs through optional methods that are either scheduled automatically by Zipline or at user-defined intervals. The method `before_trading_start()` is called daily before the market opens and primarily serves to identify a set of securities the algorithm may trade during the day. The method `handle_data()` is called at the given trading frequency, for example, every minute.

Upon completion, the algorithm returns a DataFrame containing portfolio performance metrics if there were any trades, as well as user-defined metrics. As demonstrated in *Chapter 5, Portfolio Optimization and Performance Evaluation*, the output is compatible with pyfolio so that you can quickly create performance tearsheets.

Known issues

Zipline currently requires the presence of Treasury curves and the S&P 500 returns for benchmarking (`https://github.com/quantopian/zipline/issues/2480`). The latter relies on the IEX API, which now requires registration to obtain a key. It is easy to patch Zipline to circumvent this and download data from the Federal Reserve, for instance. The GitHub repository describes how to go about this. Alternatively, you can move the SPY returns provided in `zipline/resources/market_data/SPY_benchmark.csv` to your `.zipline` folder, which usually lives in your home directory, unless you changed its location.

Live trading (`https://github.com/zipline-live/zipline`) your own systems is only available with Interactive Brokers and is not fully supported by Quantopian.

Ingesting your own bundles with minute data

We will use the NASDAQ100 2013-17 sample provided by AlgoSeek that we introduced in *Chapter 2, Market and Fundamental Data – Sources and Techniques,* to demonstrate how to write your own custom bundle. There are four steps:

1. Divide your OHCLV data into one file per ticker and store metadata and split and dividend adjustments.
2. Write a script to pass the result to an `ingest()` function, which, in turn, takes care of writing the bundle to bcolz and SQLite format.
3. Register the bundle in an extension.py script that lives in your `.zipline` directory in your home folder, and symlink the data sources.
4. For AlgoSeek data, we also provide a custom TradingCalendar because it includes trading activity outside NYSE market hours.

The directory `custom_bundles` contains the code examples for this section.

Getting your data ready to be bundled

In *Chapter 2, Market and Fundamental Data – Sources and Techniques*, we parsed the daily files containing the AlgoSeek NASDAQ 100 OHLCV data to obtain a time series for each ticker. We will use this result because Zipline also stores each security individually.

In addition, we obtain equity metadata using the pandas DataReader `get_nasdaq_symbols()` function. Finally, since the Quandl Wiki data covers the NASDAQ 100 tickers for the relevant period, we extract the split and dividend adjustments from that bundle's SQLite database.

The result is an HDF5 store containing price and volume data on some 135 tickers, as well as the corresponding meta and adjustment data. The script `algoseek_preprocessing.py` illustrates this process.

Writing your custom bundle ingest function

The Zipline documentation outlines the required parameters for an `ingest()` function, which kicks off the I/O process, but does not provide a lot of practical detail. The script `algoseek_1min_trades.py` shows how to get this part to work for minute data.

There is a `load_equities()` function that provides the metadata, a `ticker_generator()` function that feeds symbols to a `data_generator()`, which, in turn, loads and format each symbol's market data, and an `algoseek_to_bundle()` function, which integrates all the pieces and returns the desired `ingest()` function.

Time zone alignment matters because Zipline translates all data series to UTC; we add US/Eastern time zone information to the OHCLV data and convert it to UTC. To facilitate execution, we create symlinks for this script and the `algoseek.h5` data in the `custom_data` folder in the `.zipline` directory, which we'll add to the `PATH` in the next step so Zipline can find this information.

Registering your bundle

Before we can run `zipline ingest -b algoseek`, we need to register our custom bundle so Zipline knows what we are talking about. To this end, we'll add the following lines to an `extension.py` script in the `.zipline` file, which you may have to create first, alongside some inputs and settings (see the `extension.py` example).

The registration itself is fairly straightforward but highlights a few important details. First, Zipline needs to be able to import the `algoseek_to_bundle()` function, so its location needs to be on the search path, for example, by using `sys.path.append()`. Second, we reference a custom calendar that we will create and register in the next step. Third, we need to inform Zipline that our trading days are longer than the default 6 and a half hours of NYSE days to avoid misalignments:

```
register('algoseek',
        algoseek_to_bundle(),
        calendar_name='AlgoSeek',
        minutes_per_day=960
        )
```

Creating and registering a custom TradingCalendar

As mentioned previously, Quantopian also provides a TradingCalendar library to support trading around the world. The package contains numerous examples, and it is fairly straightforward to subclass one of the examples. Based on the NYSE calendar, we only need to override the open/close times and change the name:

```
class AlgoSeekCalendar(XNYSExchangeCalendar):
    """
    A calendar for trading assets before and after market hours

    Open Time: 4AM, US/Eastern
    Close Time: 19:59PM, US/Eastern
    """

    @property
    def name(self):
        return "AlgoSeek"

    @property
    def open_time(self):
        return time(4, 0)

    @property
    def close_time(self):
        return time(19, 59)
```

We put the definition into `extension.py` and add the following registration:

```
register_calendar(
        'AlgoSeek',
        AlgoSeekCalendar())
```

And now, we can refer to this trading calendar to ensure a backtest includes off-market hour activity.

The Pipeline API – backtesting an ML signal

The Pipeline API facilitates the definition and computation of alpha factors for a cross-section of securities from historical data. Pipeline significantly improves efficiency because it optimizes computations over the entire backtest period, rather than tackling each event separately. In other words, it continues to follow an event-driven architecture but vectorizes the computation of factors where possible.

A pipeline uses factors, filters, and classifiers classes to define computations that produce columns in a table with point-in-time values for a set of securities. Factors take one or more input arrays of historical bar data and produce one or more outputs for each security. There are numerous built-in factors, and you can also design your own `CustomFactor` computations.

The following diagram depicts how loading the data using `DataFrameLoader`, computing the predictive `MLSignal` using the Pipeline API, and various scheduled activities integrate with the overall trading algorithm that's executed via the `run_algorithm()` function. We'll go over the details and the corresponding code in this section:

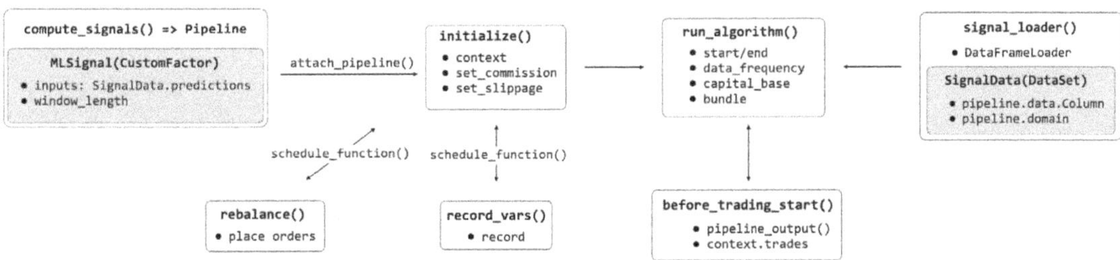

Figure 8.6: ML signal backtest using Zipline's Pipeline API

You need to register your pipeline with the `initialize()` method and execute it at each time step or on a custom schedule. Zipline provides numerous built-in computations, such as moving averages or Bollinger Bands, that can be used to quickly compute standard factors, but it also allows for the creation of custom factors, as we will illustrate next.

Most importantly, the Pipeline API renders alpha factor research modular because it separates the alpha factor computation from the remainder of the algorithm, including the placement and execution of trade orders and the bookkeeping of portfolio holdings, values, and so on.

We'll now illustrate how to load the lasso model daily return predictions, together with price data for our universe, into a pipeline and use a `CustomFactor` to select the top and bottom 10 predictions as long and short positions, respectively. The notebook `backtesting_with_zipline` contains the following code examples.

Our goal is to combine the daily return predictions with the OHCLV data from our Quandl bundle, and then to go long on up to 10 equities with the highest predicted returns and short on those with the lowest predicted returns, requiring at least five stocks on either side, similar to the backtrader example above.

Enabling the DataFrameLoader for our Pipeline

First, we load our predictions for the 2015-17 period and extract the Zipline IDs for the ~250 stocks in our universe during this period using the `bundle.asset_finder.lookup_symbols()` method, as shown in the following code:

```
def load_predictions(bundle):
    predictions = pd.read_hdf('../00_data/backtest.h5', 'data')
[['predicted']].dropna()
    tickers = predictions.index.get_level_values(0).unique().tolist()

    assets = bundle.asset_finder.lookup_symbols(tickers, as_of_date=None)
    predicted_sids = pd.Int64Index([asset.sid for asset in assets])
    ticker_map = dict(zip(tickers, predicted_sids))
    return (predictions
            .unstack('ticker')
            .rename(columns=ticker_map)
            .predicted
            .tz_localize('UTC')), assets

bundle_data = bundles.load('quandl')
predictions, assets = load_predictions(bundle_data)
```

To make the predictions available to the Pipeline API, we need to define a `Column` with a suitable data type for a `DataSet` with an appropriate `domain`, like so:

```
class SignalData(DataSet):
    predictions = Column(dtype=float)
    domain = US_EQUITIES
```

While the bundle's OHLCV data can rely on the built-in `USEquityPricingLoader`, we need to define our own `DataFrameLoader`, as follows:

```
signal_loader = {SignalData.predictions:
                     DataFrameLoader(SignalData.predictions, predictions)}
```

In fact, we need to slightly modify the Zipline library's source code to bypass the assumption that we will only load price data. To this end, we add a `custom_loader` parameter to the `run_algorithm` method and ensure that this loader is used when the pipeline needs one of SignalData's `Column` instances.

Creating a pipeline with a custom ML factor

Our pipeline is going to have two Boolean columns that identify the assets we would like to trade as long and short positions. To get there, we first define a `CustomFactor` called `MLSignal` that just receives the current return predictions. The motivation is to allow us to use some of the convenient `Factor` methods designed to rank and filter securities:

```
class MLSignal(CustomFactor):
    """Converting signals to Factor
        so we can rank and filter in Pipeline"""
    inputs = [SignalData.predictions]
    window_length = 1

    def compute(self, today, assets, out, preds):
        out[:] = preds
```

Now, we can set up our actual pipeline by instantiating `CustomFactor`, which requires no arguments other than the defaults provided. We combine its `top()` and `bottom()` methods with a filter to select the highest positive and lowest negative predictions:

```
def compute_signals():
    signals = MLSignal()
    return Pipeline(columns={
        'longs' : signals.top(N_LONGS, mask=signals > 0),
        'shorts': signals.bottom(N_SHORTS, mask=signals < 0)},
            screen=StaticAssets(assets))
```

The next step is to initialize our algorithm by defining a few context variables, setting transaction cost parameters, performing schedule rebalancing and logging, and attaching our pipeline:

```
def initialize(context):
    """
    Called once at the start of the algorithm.
    """
    context.n_longs = N_LONGS
    context.n_shorts = N_SHORTS
    context.min_positions = MIN_POSITIONS
    context.universe = assets

    set_slippage(slippage.FixedSlippage(spread=0.00))
    set_commission(commission.PerShare(cost=0, min_trade_cost=0))
```

```
    schedule_function(rebalance,
                      date_rules.every_day(),
                      time_rules.market_open(hours=1, minutes=30))

    schedule_function(record_vars,
                      date_rules.every_day(),
                      time_rules.market_close())

    pipeline = compute_signals()
    attach_pipeline(pipeline, 'signals')
```

Every day before the market opens, we run our pipeline to obtain the latest predictions:

```
def before_trading_start(context, data):
    """
    Called every day before market open.
    """
    output = pipeline_output('signals')
    context.trades = (output['longs'].astype(int)
                      .append(output['shorts'].astype(int).mul(-1))
                      .reset_index()
                      .drop_duplicates()
                      .set_index('index')
                      .squeeze())
```

After the market opens, we place orders for our long and short targets and close all other positions:

```
def rebalance(context, data):
    """
    Execute orders according to schedule_function() date & time rules.
    """
    trades = defaultdict(list)

    for stock, trade in context.trades.items():
        if not trade:
            order_target(stock, 0)
        else:
            trades[trade].append(stock)
    context.longs, context.shorts = len(trades[1]), len(trades[-1])
    if context.longs > context.min_positions and context.shorts > context.
min_positions:
        for stock in trades[-1]:
            order_target_percent(stock, -1 / context.shorts)
        for stock in trades[1]:
            order_target_percent(stock, 1 / context.longs)
```

Now, we are ready to execute our backtest and pass the results to pyfolio:

```
results = run_algorithm(start=start_date,
                        end=end_date,
                        initialize=initialize,
                        before_trading_start=before_trading_start,
                        capital_base=1e6,
                        data_frequency='daily',
                        bundle='quandl',
                        custom_loader=signal_loader) # need to modify zipline
returns, positions, transactions = pf.utils.extract_rets_pos_txn_from_
zipline(results)
```

Figure 8.7 shows the plots for the strategy's cumulative returns (left panel) and the rolling Sharpe ratio, which are comparable to the previous backtrader example.

The backtest only takes around half the time, though:

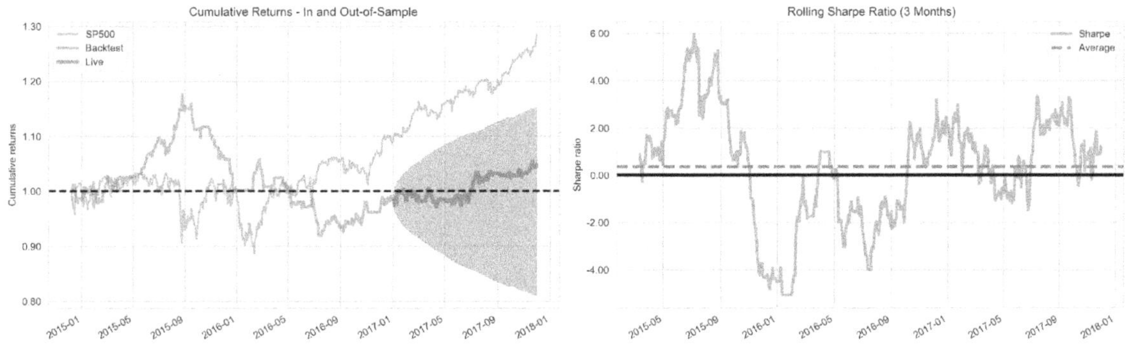

Figure 8.7: Zipline backtest results

The notebook `backtesting_with_zipline` contains the full pyfolio tearsheet with additional metrics and plots.

How to train a model during the backtest

We can also integrate the model training into our backtest. You can find the code for the following end-to-end example of our ML4T workflow in the `ml4t_with_zipline` notebook:

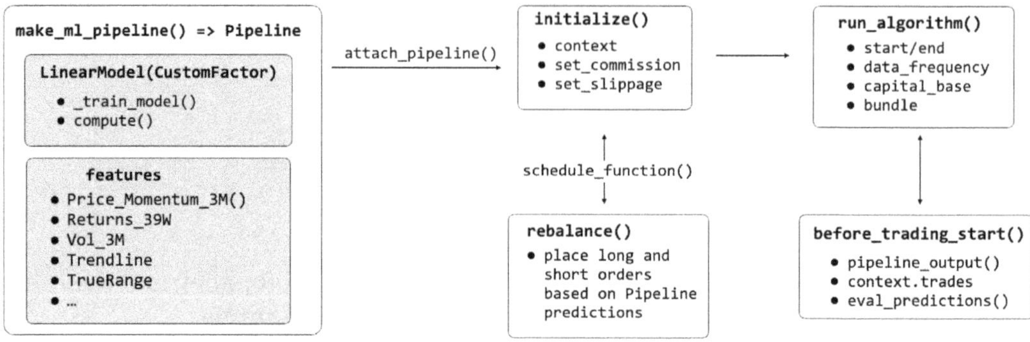

Figure 8.8: Flowchart of Zipline backtest with model training

The goal is to roughly replicate the ridge regression daily return predictions we used earlier and generated in *Chapter 7, Linear Models – From Risk Factors to Return Forecasts*. We will, however, use a few additional pipeline factors to illustrate their usage. The principal new element is a `CustomFactor` that receives features and returns them as inputs to train a model and produce predictions.

Preparing the features – how to define pipeline factors

To create a **pipeline factor**, we need one or more input variables, a `window_length` that indicates the number of most recent data points for each input and security, and the computation we want to conduct.

A linear price trend that we estimate using linear regression (see *Chapter 7, Linear Models – From Risk Factors to Return Forecasts*) works as follows: we use the 252 latest close prices to compute the regression coefficient on a linear time trend:

```
class Trendline(CustomFactor):
    # Linear 12-month price trend regression
    inputs = [USEquityPricing.close]
    window_length = 252

    def compute(self, today, assets, out, close):
        X = np.arange(self.window_length).reshape(-1, 1).astype(float)
        X -= X.mean()
        Y = close - np.nanmean(close, axis=0)
        out[:] = (X.T @ Y / np.var(X)) / self.window_length
```

We will use 10 custom and built-in factors as features for our model to capture risk factors like momentum and volatility (see notebook `ml4t_with_zipline` for details). Next, we'll come up with a `CustomFactor` that trains our model.

How to design a custom ML factor

Our `CustomFactor`, called `ML`, will have `StandardScaler` and a **stochastic gradient descent** (**SGD**) implementation of ridge regression as instance attributes, and we will train the model 3 days a week:

```
class LinearModel(CustomFactor):
    """Obtain model predictions"""
    train_on_weekday = [0, 2, 4]

    def __init__(self, *args, **kwargs):
        super().__init__(self, *args, **kwargs)

        self._scaler = StandardScaler()
        self._model = SGDRegressor(penalty='L2')
        self._trained = False
```

The `compute` method generates predictions (addressing potential missing values), but first checks if the model should be trained:

```
    def _maybe_train_model(self, today, returns, inputs):
        if (today.weekday() in self.train_on_weekday) or not self._trained:
            self._train_model(today, returns, inputs)

    def compute(self, today, assets, out, returns, *inputs):
        self._maybe_train_model(today, returns, inputs)

        # Predict most recent feature values
        X = np.dstack(inputs)[-1]
        missing = np.any(np.isnan(X), axis=1)
        X[missing, :] = 0
        X = self._scaler.transform(X)
        preds = self._model.predict(X)
        out[:] = np.where(missing, np.nan, preds)
```

The `_train_model` method is the centerpiece of the puzzle. It shifts the returns and aligns the resulting forward returns with the factor features, removing missing values in the process. It scales the remaining data points and trains the linear `SGDRegressor`:

```
    def _train_model(self, today, returns, inputs):

        scaler = self._scaler
        model = self._model

        shift_by = N_FORWARD_DAYS + 1
        outcome = returns[shift_by:].flatten()
        features = np.dstack(inputs)[:-shift_by]
```

```
        n_days, n_stocks, n_features = features.shape
        features = features.reshape(-1, n_features)
        features = features[~np.isnan(outcome)]
        outcome = outcome[~np.isnan(outcome)]
        outcome = outcome[np.all(~np.isnan(features), axis=1)]
        features = features[np.all(~np.isnan(features), axis=1)]
        features = scaler.fit_transform(features)

        model.fit(X=features, y=outcome)
        self._trained = True
```

The `make_ml_pipeline()` function preprocesses and combines the outcome, feature, and model parts into a pipeline with a column for predictions:

```
def make_ml_pipeline(universe, window_length=21, n_forward_days=5):
    pipeline_columns = OrderedDict()

    # ensure that returns is the first input
    pipeline_columns['Returns'] = Returns(inputs=[USEquityPricing.open],
                                          mask=universe,
                                          window_length=n_forward_days + 1)

    # convert factors to ranks; append to pipeline
    pipeline_columns.update({k: v.rank(mask=universe)
                             for k, v in features.items()})

    # Create ML pipeline factor.
    # window_length = length of the training period
    pipeline_columns['predictions'] = LinearModel(
        inputs=pipeline_columns.values(),
        window_length=window_length + n_forward_days,
        mask=universe)

    return Pipeline(screen=universe, columns=pipeline_columns)
```

Tracking model performance during a backtest

We obtain new predictions using the `before_trading_start()` function, which runs every morning before the market opens:

```
def before_trading_start(context, data):
    output = pipeline_output('ml_model')
    context.predicted_returns = output['predictions']
    context.predicted_returns.index.rename(['date', 'equity'], inplace=True)

    evaluate_predictions(output, context)
```

`evaluate_predictions` does exactly this: it tracks the past predictions of our model and evaluates them once returns for the relevant time horizon materialize (in our example, the next day):

```
def evaluate_predictions(output, context):
    # Look at past predictions to evaluate model performance out-of-sample
    # A day has passed, shift days and drop old ones
    context.past_predictions = {
        k - 1: v for k, v in context.past_predictions.items() if k > 0}

    if 0 in context.past_predictions:
        # Use today's forward returns to evaluate predictions
        returns, predictions = (output['Returns'].dropna()
                                .align(context.past_predictions[0].dropna(),
                                       join='inner'))
        if len(returns) > 0 and len(predictions) > 0:
            context.ic = spearmanr(returns, predictions)[0]
            context.rmse = np.sqrt(
                mean_squared_error(returns, predictions))
            context.mae = mean_absolute_error(returns, predictions)

            long_rets = returns[predictions > 0].mean()
            short_rets = returns[predictions < 0].mean()
            context.returns_spread_bps = (
                long_rets - short_rets) * 10000

    # Store current predictions
    context.past_predictions[N_FORWARD_DAYS] = context.predicted_returns
```

We also record the evaluation on a daily basis so we can review it after the backtest:

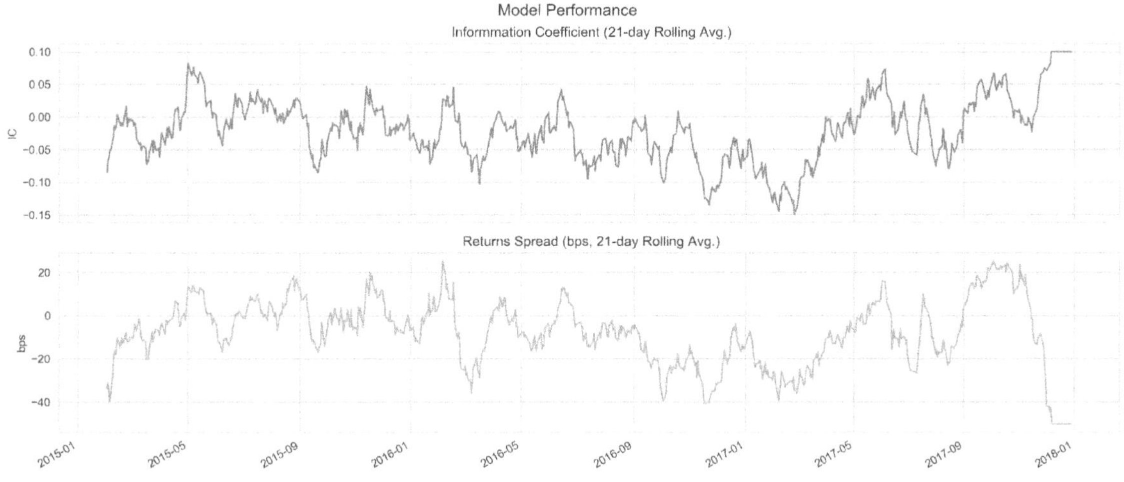

Figure 8.9: Model out-of-sample performance

The following plots summarize the backtest performance in terms of the cumulative returns and the rolling SR. The results have improved relative to the previous example (due to a different feature set), yet the model still underperforms the benchmark since mid-2016:

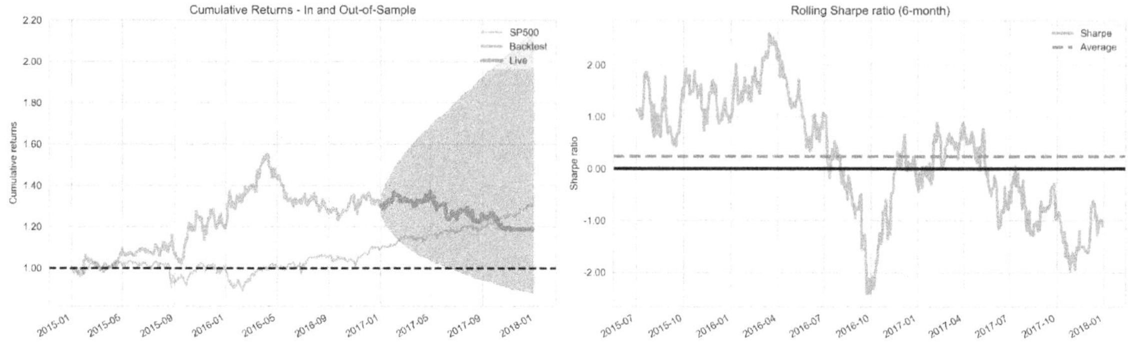

Figure 8.10: Zipline backtest performance with model training

Please see the notebook for additional details on how we define a universe, run the backtest, and rebalance and analyze the results using pyfolio.

Instead of how to use

The notebook `ml4t_quantopian` contains an example of how to backtest a strategy that uses a simple ML model in the Quantopian research environment. The key benefit of using Zipline in the Quantopian cloud is access to many additional datasets, including fundamental and alternative data. See the notebook for more details on the various factors that we can derive in this context.

Summary

In this chapter, we took a much closer look at how backtesting works, what challenges there are, and how to manage them. We demonstrated how to use the two popular backtesting libraries, backtrader and Zipline.

Most importantly, however, we walked through the end-to-end process of designing and testing an ML model, showed you how to implement trading logic that acts on the signals provided by the model's predictions, and saw how to conduct and evaluate backtests. Now, we are ready to continue exploring a much broader and more sophisticated array of ML models than the linear regressions we started with.

The next chapter will cover how to incorporate the time dimension into our models.

9

Time-Series Models for Volatility Forecasts and Statistical Arbitrage

In *Chapter 7, Linear Models – From Risk Factors to Asset Return Forecasts*, we introduced linear models for inference and prediction, starting with static models for a contemporaneous relationship with cross-sectional inputs that have an immediate effect on the output. We presented the **ordinary least squares** (**OLS**) learning algorithm, and saw that it produces unbiased coefficients for a correctly specified model with residuals that are not correlated with the input variables. Adding the assumption that the residuals have constant variance guarantees that OLS produces the smallest mean squared prediction error among unbiased estimators.

We also encountered panel data that had both cross-sectional and time-series dimensions, when we learned how the Fama-Macbeth regressions estimate the value of risk factors over time and across assets. However, the relationship between returns across time is typically fairly low, so this procedure could largely ignore the time dimension.

Furthermore, we covered the regularized ridge and lasso regression models, which produce biased coefficient estimates but can reduce the mean squared prediction error. These predictive models took a more dynamic perspective and combined historical returns with other inputs to predict forward returns.

In this chapter, we will build dynamic linear models to explicitly represent time and include variables observed at specific intervals or lags. A key characteristic of time-series data is their sequential order: rather than random samples of individual observations, as in the case of cross-sectional data, our data is a single realization of a stochastic process that we cannot repeat.

Our goal is to identify systematic patterns in time series that help us predict how the time series will behave in the future. More specifically, we will focus on models that extract signals from a historical sequence of the output and, optionally, other contemporaneous or lagged input variables to predict future values of the output. For example, we might try to predict future returns for a stock using past returns, combined with historical returns of a benchmark or macroeconomic variables. We will focus on linear time-series models before turning to nonlinear models like recurrent or convolutional neural networks in Part 4.

Time-series models are very popular given the time dimension inherent to trading. Key applications include the prediction of asset returns and volatility, as well as the identification of the co-movements of asset price series. Time-series data is likely to become more prevalent as an ever-broader array of connected devices collects regular measurements with potential signal content.

We will first introduce the tools we can use to diagnose time-series characteristics and to extract features that capture potential patterns. Then, we will cover how to diagnose and achieve time-series stationarity. Next, we will introduce univariate and multivariate time-series models and apply them in order to forecast macro data and volatility patterns. We will conclude with the concept of cointegration and how to apply it to develop a pairs trading strategy.

In particular, we will cover the following topics:

- How to use time-series analysis to prepare and inform the modeling process
- Estimating and diagnosing univariate autoregressive and moving-average models
- Building **autoregressive conditional heteroskedasticity** (ARCH) models to predict volatility
- How to build multivariate vector autoregressive models
- Using cointegration to develop a pairs trading strategy

> You can find the code samples for this chapter and links to additional resources in the corresponding directory of the GitHub repository. The notebooks include color versions of the images. For a thorough introduction to the topics of this chapter from an investment perspective, see Tsay (2005) and Fabozzi, Focardi, and Kolm (2010).

Tools for diagnostics and feature extraction

A time series is a sequence of values separated by discrete intervals that are typically even spaced (except for missing values). A time series is often modeled as a stochastic process consisting of a collection of random variables, $y(t_1), \ldots, y(t_T)$, with one variable for each point in time, $t_i, i = 1, \ldots, T$. A univariate time series consists of a single value, y, at each point in time, whereas a multivariate time series consists of several observations that can be represented by a vector.

The number of periods, $\Delta t = t_i - t_j$, between distinct points in time, t_i, t_j, is called **lag**, with T-1 distinct lags for each time series. Just as relationships between different variables at a given point in time is key for cross-sectional models, relationships between data points separated by a given lag are fundamental to analyzing and exploiting patterns in time series.

For cross-sectional models, we distinguished between input and output variables, or target and predictors, with the labels y and x, respectively. In a time-series context, some or all of the lagged values $y_{t-1}, y_{t-2}, \ldots, y_{t_T}$ of the outcome y play the role of the input or x values in the cross-section context.

A time series is called **white noise** if it is a sequence of **independent and identically distributed** (IID) random variables, ϵ_t, with finite mean and variance. In particular, the series is called a **Gaussian white noise** if the random variables are normally distributed with a mean of zero and a constant variance of σ.

A time series is linear if it can be written as a weighted sum of past disturbances, ϵ_t, that are also called innovations and are here assumed to represent white noise, and the mean of the series, μ:

$$y_t = \mu + \sum_{i=0}^{\infty} a_i \epsilon_{t-i}, \quad a_0 = 1, \epsilon \sim \mathrm{i.i.d}$$

A key goal of time-series analysis is to understand the dynamic behavior that is driven by the coefficients, a_i. The analysis of time series offers methods tailored to this type of data with the goal of extracting useful patterns that, in turn, help us build predictive models.

We will introduce the most important tools for this purpose, including the decomposition into key systematic elements, the analysis of autocorrelation, and rolling window statistics such as moving averages.

For most of the examples in this chapter, we will work with data provided by the Federal Reserve that you can access using pandas-datareader, which we introduced in *Chapter 2, Market and Fundamental Data – Sources and Techniques*. The code examples for this section are available in the notebook `tsa_and_stationarity`.

How to decompose time-series patterns

Time-series data typically contains a mix of patterns that can be decomposed into several components. In particular, a time series often combines systematic components like trend, seasonality, and cycles with unsystematic noise. These components can be modeled as a linear combination (for example, when fluctuations do not depend on the level of the series) or in a nonlinear, multiplicative form.

Based on the model assumptions, they can also be split up automatically. Statsmodels includes a simple method to split the time series into separate trend, seasonal, and residual components using moving averages. We can apply it to monthly data on industrial manufacturing that contain both a strong trend component and a seasonality component, as follows:

```
import statsmodels.tsa.api as tsa
industrial_production = web.DataReader('IPGMFN', 'fred', '1988', '2017-12').
squeeze()
components = tsa.seasonal_decompose(industrial_production, model='additive')
ts = (industrial_production.to_frame('Original')
      .assign(Trend=components.trend)
      .assign(Seasonality=components.seasonal)
      .assign(Residual=components.resid))
ts.plot(subplots=True, figsize=(14, 8));
```

Figure 9.1 shows the resulting charts that display the additive components. The residual component would be the focus of subsequent modeling efforts, assuming that the trend and seasonality components are more deterministic and amenable to simple extrapolation:

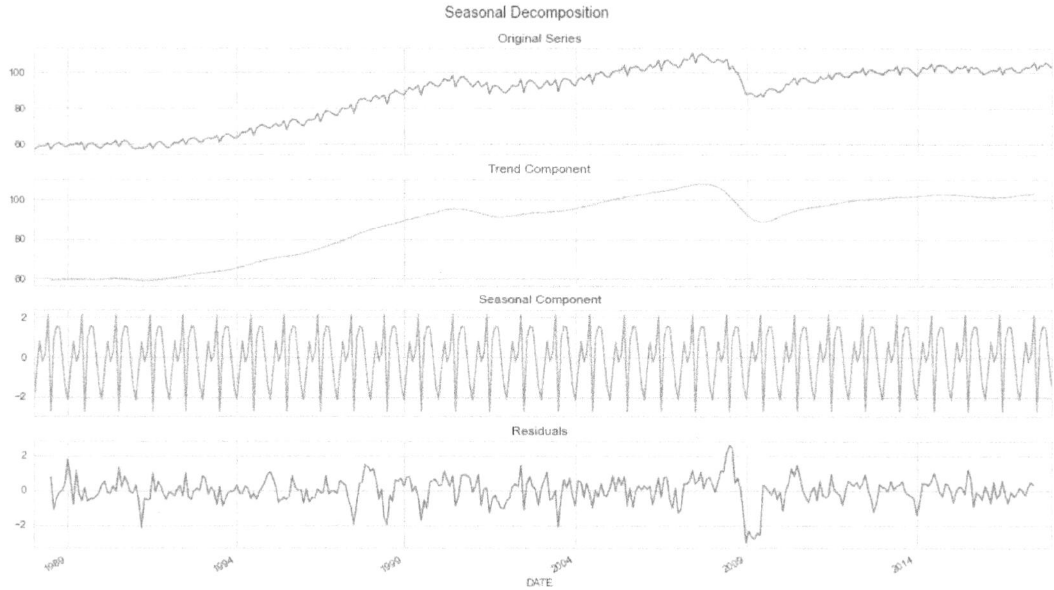

Figure 9.1: Time-series decomposition into trend, seasonality, and residuals

There are more sophisticated model-based approaches—see, for example, *Chapter 6, The Machine Learning Process,* in Hyndman and Athanasopoulos (2018).

Rolling window statistics and moving averages

Given the sequential ordering of time-series data, it is natural to compute familiar descriptive statistics for periods of a given length. The goal is to detect whether the series is stable or changes over time and obtain a smoothed representation that captures systematic aspects while filtering out the noise.

Rolling window statistics serve this process: they produce a new time series where each data point represents a summary statistic computed for a certain period of the original data. Moving averages are the most familiar example. The original data points can enter the computation with weights that are equal or, for example, emphasize more recent data points. Exponential moving averages recursively compute weights that decay for data points further in the past. The new data points are typically a summary of all preceding data points, but they can also be computed from a surrounding window.

The pandas library includes rolling or expanding windows and allows for various weight distributions. In a second step, you can apply computations to each set of data captured by a window. These computations include built-in functions for individual series, such as the mean or the sum, and the correlation or covariance for several series, as well as user-defined functions.

We used this functionality to engineer features in *Chapter 4, Financial Feature Engineering - How to Research Alpha Factors*, and *Chapter 7, Linear Models - From Risk Factors to Return Forecasts*, for example. The moving average and exponential smoothing examples in the following section will also apply these tools.

Early forecasting models included **moving-average models** with exponential weights called **exponential smoothing models**. We will encounter moving averages again as key building blocks for linear time series. Forecasts that rely on exponential smoothing methods use weighted averages of past observations, where the weights decay exponentially as the observations get older. Hence, a more recent observation receives a higher associated weight. These methods are popular for time series that do not have very complicated or abrupt patterns.

How to measure autocorrelation

Autocorrelation (also called *serial correlation*) adapts the concept of correlation to the time-series context: just as the correlation coefficient measures the strength of a linear relationship between two variables, the **autocorrelation coefficient**, ρ_k, measures the extent of a linear relationship between time-series values separated by a given lag, k:

$$\rho_k = \frac{\sum_{t=k+1}^{T}(y_t - \bar{y})(y_{t-k} - \bar{y})}{\sum_{t=1}^{T}(y_t - \bar{y})^2}$$

Hence, we can calculate one autocorrelation coefficient for each of the T-1 lags in a time series of length T. The **autocorrelation function** (**ACF**) computes the correlation coefficients as a function of the lag.

The autocorrelation for a lag larger than 1 (that is, between observations more than one timestep apart) reflects both the direct correlation between these observations and the indirect influence of the intervening data points. The **partial autocorrelation** removes this influence and only measures the linear dependence between data points at the given lag distance, T. Removing means using the residuals of a linear regression with the outcome x_t and the lagged values $x_{t-1}, x_{t-2}, \ldots, x_{T-1}$ as features (also known as an $AR(T\text{-}1)$ model, which we'll discuss in the next section on univariate time-series models). The **partial autocorrelation function** (**PACF**) provides all the correlations that result once the effects of a correlation at shorter lags have been removed, as described previously.

There are also algorithms that estimate the partial autocorrelation from the sample autocorrelation based on the exact theoretical relationship between the PACF and the ACF.

A **correlogram** is simply a plot of the ACF or PACF for sequential lags, k=0,1,...,n. It allows us to inspect the correlation structure across lags at one glance (see *Figure 9.3* for an example). The main usage of correlograms is to detect any autocorrelation after the removal of a deterministic trend or seasonality. Both the ACF and the PACF are key diagnostic tools for the design of linear time-series models, and we will review examples of ACF and PACF plots in the following section on time-series transformations.

How to diagnose and achieve stationarity

The statistical properties, such as the mean, variance, or autocorrelation, of a **stationary time series** are independent of the period—that is, they don't change over time. Thus, **stationarity** implies that a time series does not have a trend or seasonal effects. Furthermore, it requires that descriptive statistics, such as the mean or the standard deviation, when computed for different rolling windows, are constant or do not change significantly over time. A stationary time series reverts to its mean, and the deviations have a constant amplitude, while short-term movements are always alike in a statistical sense.

More formally, **strict stationarity** requires the joint distribution of any subset of time-series observations to be independent of time with respect to all moments. So, in addition to the mean and variance, higher moments such as skew and kurtosis also need to be constant, irrespective of the lag between different observations. In most applications, such as most time-series models in this chapter that we can use to model asset returns, we limit stationarity to first and second moments so that the time series is covariance stationary with constant mean, variance, and autocorrelation. However, we abandon this assumption when building modeling volatility and explicitly assume the variance to change over time in predictable ways.

Note that we specifically allow for **dependence between output values at different lags**, just like we want the input data for linear regression to be correlated with the outcome. Stationarity implies that these relationships are stable. Stationarity is a key assumption of classical statistical models. The following two subsections introduce transformations that can help make a time series stationary, as well as how to address the special case of a stochastic trend caused by a unit root.

Transforming a time series to achieve stationarity

To satisfy the stationarity assumption of many time-series models, we need to transform the original series, often in several steps. Common transformations include the (natural) **logarithm** to convert an exponential growth pattern into a linear trend and stabilize the variance. **Deflation** implies dividing a time series by another series that causes trending behavior, for example, dividing a nominal series by a price index to convert it into a real measure.

A series is **trend-stationary** if it reverts to a stable long-run linear trend. It can often be made stationary by fitting a trend line using linear regression and using the residuals. This implies including the time index as an independent variable in a linear regression model, possibly combined with logging or deflating.

In many cases, detrending is not sufficient to make the series stationary. Instead, we need to transform the original data into a series of **period-to-period and/or season-to-season differences**. In other words, we use the result of subtracting neighboring data points or values at seasonal lags from each other. Note that when such differencing is applied to a log-transformed series, the results represent instantaneous growth rates or returns in a financial context.

If a univariate series becomes stationary after differencing d times, it is said to be integrated of the order of d, or simply integrated if d=1. This behavior is due to unit roots, which we will explain next.

Handling instead of how to handle

Unit roots pose a particular problem for determining the transformation that will render a time series stationary. We will first explain the concept of a unit root before discussing diagnostics tests and solutions.

On unit roots and random walks

Time series are often modeled as stochastic processes of the following autoregressive form so that the current value is a weighted sum of past values, plus a random disturbance:

$$y_t = a_1 y_{t-1} + a_2 y_{t-2} + \ldots + a_p y_{t-p} + \epsilon_t$$

We will explore these models in more detail as the AR building block for ARIMA models in the next section on univariate time-series models. Such a process has a characteristic equation of the following form:

$$m^p - m^{p-1}a_1 - m^{p-2}a_2 - \ldots - a_p = 0$$

If one of the (up to) p roots of this polynomial equals 1, then the process is said to have a **unit root**. It will be non-stationary but will not necessarily have a trend. If the remaining roots of the characteristic equation are less than 1 in absolute terms, the first difference of the process will be stationary, and the **process is integrated of order 1 or I(1)**. With additional roots larger than 1 in absolute terms, the order of integration is higher and additional differencing will be required.

In practice, time series of interest rates or asset prices are often not stationary because there isn't a price level to which the series reverts. The most prominent example of a non-stationary series is the random walk. Given a time series of prices p_t with starting price p_0(for example, a stock's IPO price) and a white-noise disturbance ϵ_t, then a random walk satisfies the following autoregressive relationship:

$$p_t = p_{t-1} + \epsilon_t = \sum_{s-0}^{t} \epsilon_s + p_0$$

Repeated substitution shows that the current value, p_t, is the sum of all prior disturbances or innovations, ϵ_t, and the initial price, p_0. If the equation includes a constant term, then the random walk is said to have **drift**.

The random walk is thus an **autoregressive stochastic process** of the following form:

$$y_t = a_1 y_{t-1} + \epsilon_t, \quad a_1 = 1$$

It has the characteristic equation $m - a_1 = 0$ with a unit root and is both non-stationary and integrated of order 1. On the one hand, given the IID nature of ε, the variance of the time series equals $t\sigma^2$, which is **not second-order stationary**, and implies that, in principle, the series could assume any value over time. On the other hand, taking the **first difference**, $\Delta p_t = p_t - p_{t-1}$, leaves $\Delta p_t = \varepsilon_t$, which is **stationary**, given the statistical assumption about ε.

The defining characteristic of a non-stationary series with a unit-root is **long memory**: since current values are the sum of past disturbances, large innovations persist for much longer than for a mean-reverting, stationary series.

How to diagnose a unit root

Statistical unit root tests are a common way to determine objectively whether (additional) differencing is necessary. These are statistical hypothesis tests of stationarity that are designed to determine whether differencing is required.

The **augmented Dickey-Fuller test** (**ADF test**) evaluates the null hypothesis that a time-series sample has a unit root against the alternative of stationarity. It regresses the differenced time series on a time trend, the first lag, and all lagged differences, and computes a test statistic from the value of the coefficient on the lagged time-series value. `statsmodels` makes it easy to implement (see the notebook `tsa_and_stationarity`).

Formally, the ADF test for a time series, y_t, runs the linear regression where α is a constant, β is a coefficient on a time trend, and p refers to the number of lags used in the model:

$$\Delta y_t = \alpha + \beta t + \gamma y_{t-1} + \delta_1 \Delta y_{t-1} + \ldots + \delta_{p-1} \Delta y_{t-p+1} + \epsilon_t$$

The constraint $\alpha = \beta = 0$ implies a random walk, whereas only $\beta = 0$ implies a random walk with drift. The lag order is usually decided using the **Akaike information criterion** (**AIC**) and **Bayesian information criterion** (**BIC**) information criteria introduced in *Chapter 7, Linear Models – From Risk Factors to Return Forecasts.*

The ADF test statistic uses the sample coefficient γ, which, under the null hypothesis of unit-root non-stationarity, equals zero and is negative otherwise. It intends to demonstrate that, for an integrated series, the lagged series value should not provide useful information in predicting the first difference above and beyond lagged differences.

How to remove unit roots and work with the resulting series

In addition to using the difference between neighboring data points to remove a constant pattern of change, we can apply **seasonal differencing** to remove patterns of seasonal change. This involves taking the difference of values at a lag distance that represents the length of the seasonal pattern. For monthly data, this usually involves differences at lag 12, and for quarterly data, it involves differences at lag 4 to remove both seasonality and linear trend.

Identifying the correct transformation and, in particular, the appropriate number and lags for differencing is not always clear-cut. Some **heuristics** have been suggested, which can be summarized as follows:

- Lag-1 autocorrelation close to zero or negative, or autocorrelation generally small and patternless: there is no need for higher-order differencing
- Positive autocorrelations up to 10+ lags: the series probably needs higher-order differencing
- Lag-1 autocorrelation < -0.5: the series may be over-differenced
- Slightly over- or under-differencing can be corrected with AR or MA terms (see the next section on univariate time-series models)

Some authors recommend fractional differencing as a more flexible approach to rendering an integrated series stationary, and may be able to keep more information or signal than simple or seasonal differences at discrete intervals. See, for example, *Chapter 5, Portfolio Optimization and Performance Evaluation,* in Marcos Lopez de Prado (2018).

Time-series transformations in practice

The charts in *Figure 9.2* shows time series for the NASDAQ stock index and industrial production for the 30 years through 2017 in their original form, as well as the transformed versions after applying the logarithm and subsequently applying the first and seasonal differences (at lag 12), respectively.

The charts also display the ADF p-value, which allows us to reject the hypothesis of unit-root non-stationarity after all transformations in both cases:

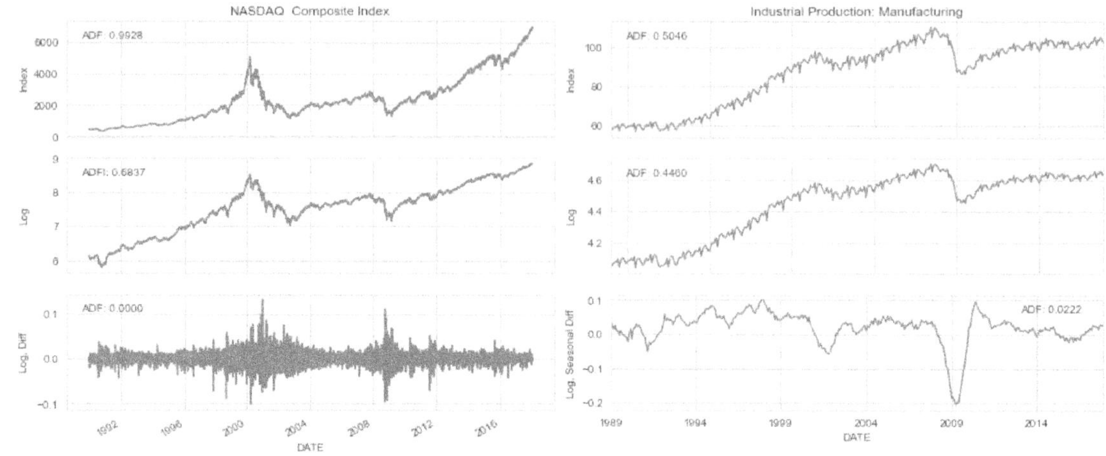

Figure 9.2: Time-series transformations and unit-root test results

We can further analyze the relevant time-series characteristics for the transformed series using a Q-Q plot that compares the quantiles of the distribution of the time-series observation to the quantiles of the normal distribution and the correlograms based on the ACF and PACF.

For the NASDAQ plots in *Figure 9.3*, we can see that while there is no trend, the variance is not constant but rather shows clustered spikes around periods of market turmoil in the late 1980s, 2001, and 2008. The Q-Q plot highlights the fat tails of the distribution with extreme values that are more frequent than the normal distribution would suggest.

The ACF and the PACF show similar patterns, with autocorrelation at several lags appearing to be significant:

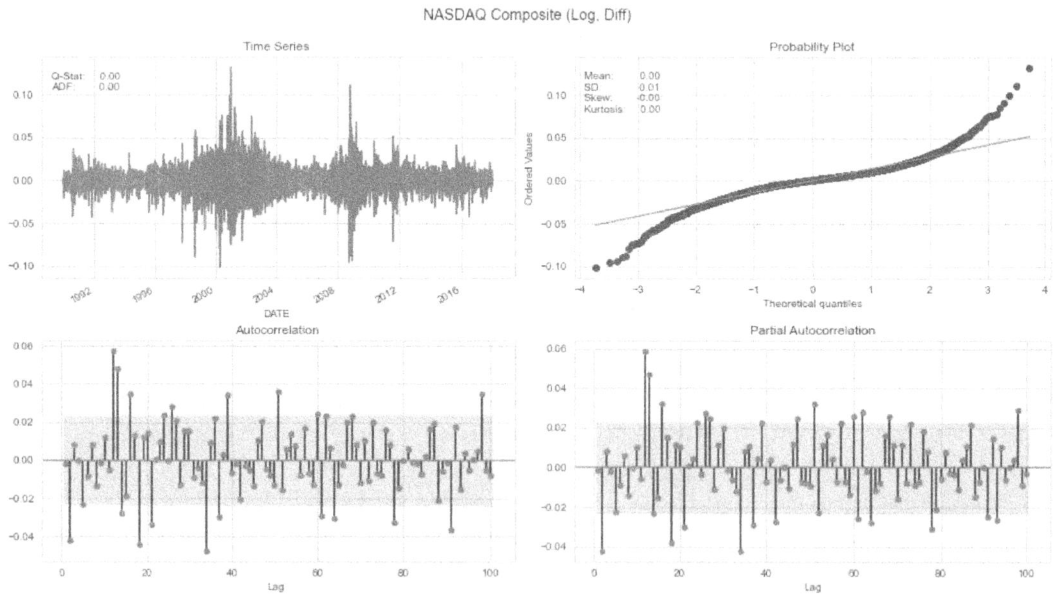

Figure 9.3: Descriptive statistics for transformed NASDAQ Composite index

For the monthly time series on industrial manufacturing production, we can see a large negative outlier following the 2008 crisis, as well as the corresponding skew in the Q-Q plot (see *Figure 9.4*). The autocorrelation is much higher than for the NASDAQ returns and declines smoothly. The PACF shows distinct positive autocorrelation patterns at lags 1 and 13 and significant negative coefficients at lags 3 and 4:

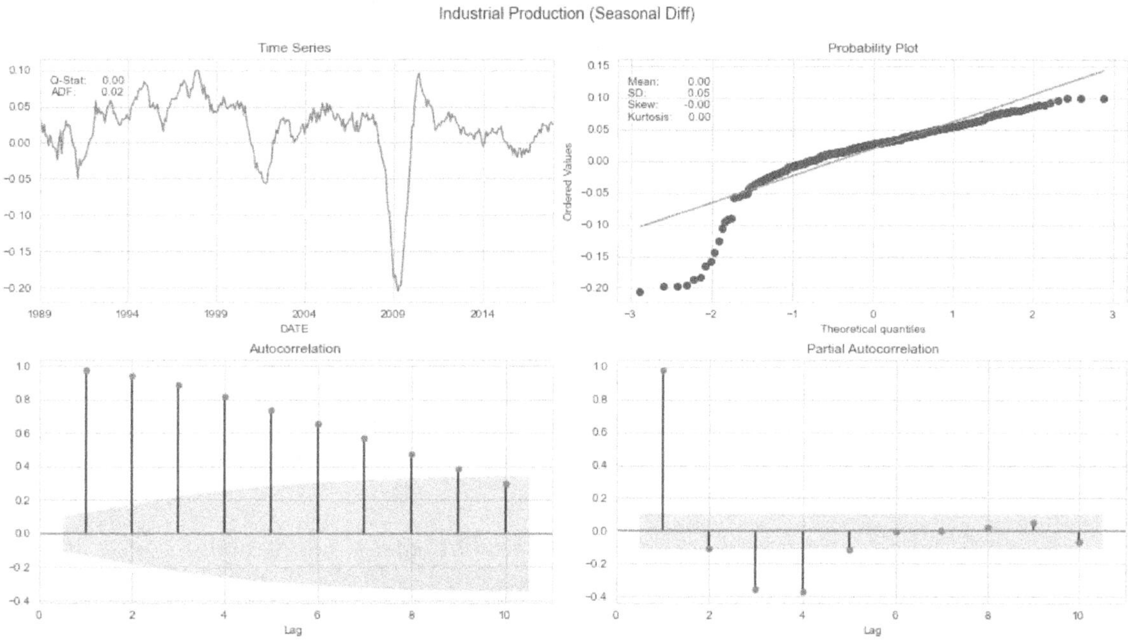

Figure 9.4: Descriptive statistics for transformed industrial production data

Univariate time-series models

Multiple linear-regression models expressed the variable of interest as a linear combination of the inputs, plus a random disturbance. In contrast, univariate time-series models relate the current value of the time series to a linear combination of lagged values of the series, current noise, and possibly past noise terms.

While exponential smoothing models are based on a description of the trend and seasonality in the data, **ARIMA models aim to describe the autocorrelations in the data**. ARIMA(p, d, q) models require stationarity and leverage two building blocks:

- **Autoregressive** (**AR**) terms consisting of p lagged values of the time series
- **Moving average** (**MA**) terms that contain q lagged disturbances

The **I** stands for *integrated* because the model can account for unit-root non-stationarity by differentiating the series d times. The term autoregression underlines that ARIMA models imply a regression of the time series on its own values.

We will introduce the ARIMA building blocks, AR and MA models, and explain how to combine them in **autoregressive moving-average** (**ARMA**) models that may account for series integration as ARIMA models or include exogenous variables as **AR(I)MAX** models. Furthermore, we will illustrate how to include seasonal AR and MA terms to extend the toolbox so that it also includes **SARMAX** models.

How to build autoregressive models

An AR model of order p aims to capture the linear dependence between time-series values at different lags and can be written as follows:

$$\text{AR}(p):\ y_t = \emptyset_0 + \emptyset_1 y_{t-1} + \emptyset_2 y_{t-2} + \ldots + \emptyset_p y_{t-p} + \epsilon_t,\quad \epsilon \sim \text{i. i. d}$$

This closely resembles a multiple linear regression on lagged values of y_t. This model has the following characteristic equation:

$$1 - \emptyset_1 x - \emptyset_2 x^2 - \ldots - \emptyset_p x^p = 0$$

The inverses of the solution to this polynomial of degree p in x are the characteristic roots, and the AR(p) process is stationary if all roots are less than 1 in absolute terms, and unstable otherwise. For a stationary series, multistep forecasts will converge to the mean of the series.

We can estimate the model parameters with the familiar least squares method using the p+1, ..., T observations to ensure there is data for each lagged term and the outcome.

How to identify the number of lags

In practice, the challenge consists of deciding on the appropriate order p of lagged terms. The time-series analysis tools for serial correlation, which we discussed in the *How to measure autocorrelation* section, play a key role in making this decision.

More specifically, a visual inspection of the correlogram often provides helpful clues:

- The **ACF** estimates the autocorrelation between observations at different lags, which, in turn, results from both direct and indirect linear dependence. Hence, if an AR model of order k is the correct model, the ACF will show a significant serial correlation up to lag k and, due to the inertia caused by the indirect effects of the linear relationship, will extend to subsequent lags until it eventually trails off as the effect weakens.
- The **PACF**, in turn, only measures the direct linear relationship between observations a given lag apart so that it will not reflect correlation for lags beyond k.

How to diagnose model fit

If the model properly captures the linear dependence across lags, then the residuals should resemble white noise, and the ACF should highlight the absence of significant autocorrelation coefficients.

In addition to a residual plot, the **Ljung-Box Q-statistic** allows us to test the hypothesis that the residual series follows white noise. The null hypothesis is that all m serial correlation coefficients are zero against the alternative that some coefficients are not. The test statistic is computed from the sample autocorrelation coefficients $\rho_k$for different lags k and follows a X^2 distribution:

$$Q(m) = T(T+2)\sum_{t=1}^{m}\frac{\rho_l^2}{T-l}$$

As we will see, statsmodels provides information about the significance of coefficients for different lags, and insignificant coefficients should be removed. If the Q-statistic rejects the null hypothesis of no autocorrelation, you should consider additional AR terms.

How to build moving-average models

An MA(q) model uses q past disturbances rather than lagged values of the time series in a regression-like model, as follows:

$$\text{MA}(q):\ y_t = c + \epsilon_t + \theta_1\epsilon_{t-1} + \theta_2\epsilon_{t-2} + \ldots + \theta_p\epsilon_{t-p},\ \ \epsilon \sim \text{i.i.d}$$

Since we do not observe the white-noise disturbance values, ϵ_t, MA(q) is not a regression model like the ones we have seen so far. Rather than using least squares, MA(q) models are estimated using **maximum likelihood** (**MLE**), alternatively initializing or estimating the disturbances at the beginning of the series and then recursively and iteratively computing the remainder.

The MA(q) model gets its name from representing each value of y_t as a weighted moving average of the past q innovations. In other words, current estimates represent a correction relative to past errors made by the model. The use of moving averages in MA(q) models differs from that of exponential smoothing, or the estimation of seasonal time-series components, because an MA(q) model aims to forecast future values, as opposed to denoising or estimating the trend cycle of past values.

MA(q) processes are always stationary because they are the weighted sum of white noise variables that are, themselves, stationary.

How to identify the number of lags

A time series generated by an MA(q) process is driven by the residuals of the prior q model predictions. Hence, the ACF for the MA(q) process will show significant coefficients for values up to lag q and then decline sharply because this is how the model assumes the series values have been generated.

Note how this differs from the AR case we just described, where the PACF would show a similar pattern.

The relationship between the AR and MA models

An AR(p) model can always be expressed as an MA(∞) process using repeated substitution, as in the random walk example in the *How to handle stochastic trends caused by unit roots* section.

When the coefficients of the MA(q) process meet certain size constraints, it also becomes invertible and can be expressed as an AR(∞) process (see Tsay, 2005, for details).

How to build ARIMA models and extensions

Autoregressive integrated moving-average—ARIMA(p, d, q)—models combine AR(p) and MA(q) processes to leverage the complementarity of these building blocks and simplify model development. They do this using a more compact form and reducing the number of parameters, in turn reducing the risk of overfitting.

The models also take care of eliminating unit-root non-stationarity by using the dth difference of the time-series values. An ARIMA(p, 1, q) model is the same as using an ARMA(p, q) model with the first differences of the series. Using y' to denote the original series after non-seasonal differencing d times, the ARIMA(p, d, q) model is simply:

$$\begin{aligned} \text{ARIMA}(p,d,q): \quad y'_t &= \text{AR}(p) + \text{MA}(q) \\ &= \phi_0 + \phi_1 y'_{t-1} + \ldots + \phi_p y'_{t-p} + \epsilon_t + \theta_1 \epsilon_{t-1} + \ldots + \theta_q \epsilon_{t-q}, \quad \epsilon \sim \text{i.i.d.} \end{aligned}$$

ARIMA models are also estimated using MLE. Depending on the implementation, higher-order models may generally subsume lower-order models.

For example, up to version 0.11, statsmodels includes all lower-order p and q terms and does not permit removing coefficients for lags below the highest value. In this case, higher-order models will always fit better. Be careful not to overfit your model to the data by using too many terms. The most recent version, which is 0.11 at the time of writing, added an experimental new ARIMA model with more flexible configuration options.

How to model differenced series

There are also guidelines for designing the univariate times-series models when using data:

- A model without differencing assumes that the original series is stationary, including mean-reverting. It normally includes a constant term to allow for a non-zero mean.
- A model with one order of differencing assumes that the original series has a constant trend and should thus include a constant term.
- A model with two orders of differencing assumes that the original series has a time-varying trend and should not include a constant.

How to identify the number of AR and MA terms

Since AR(p) and MA(q) terms interact, the information provided by the ACF and PACF is no longer reliable and can only be used as a starting point.

Traditionally, the AIC and BIC information criteria have been used to rely on in-sample fit when selecting the model design. Alternatively, we can rely on out-of-sample tests to cross-validate multiple parameter choices.

The following summary provides some guidance on how to choose the model order in the case of considering AR and MA models in isolation:

- The lag beyond which the PACF cuts off is the indicated number of AR terms. If the PACF of the differenced series cuts off sharply and/or the lag-1 autocorrelation is positive, add one or more AR terms.
- The lag beyond which the ACF cuts off is the indicated number of MA terms. If the ACF of the differenced series displays a sharp cutoff and/or the lag-1 autocorrelation is negative, consider adding an MA term to the model.
- AR and MA terms may cancel out each other's effects, so always try to reduce the number of AR and MA terms by 1 if your model contains both to avoid overfitting, especially if the more complex model requires more than 10 iterations to converge.
- If the AR coefficients sum to nearly one and suggest a unit root in the AR part of the model, eliminate one AR term and difference the model once (more).
- If the MA coefficients sum to nearly one and suggest a unit root in the MA part of the model, eliminate one MA term and reduce the order of differencing by one.
- Unstable long-term forecasts suggest there may be a unit root in the AR or MA part of the model.

Adding features – ARMAX

An **autoregressive moving-average model with exogenous inputs** (**ARMAX**) model adds input variables or covariate on the right-hand side of the ARMA time-series model (assuming the series is stationary, so we can skip differencing):

$$\begin{aligned}\text{ARIMA}(p,d,q): \quad y_t &= \beta x_t + \text{AR}(p) + \text{MA}(q)\\ &= \beta x_t + \phi_0 + \phi_1 y_{t-1} + \dots + \phi_p y_{t-p} + \epsilon_t + \theta_1 \epsilon_{t-1} + \dots + \theta_q \epsilon_{t-q}, \quad \epsilon \sim \text{i.i.d.}\end{aligned}$$

This resembles a linear regression model but is quite difficult to interpret. This is because the effect of β on y_t is not the effect of an increase in x_t by one unit as in linear regression. Instead, the presence of lagged values of y_t on the right-hand side of the equation implies that the coefficient can only be interpreted, given the lagged values of the response variable, which is hardly intuitive.

Adding seasonal differencing – SARIMAX

For time series with seasonal effects, we can include AR and MA terms that capture the seasonality's periodicity. For instance, when using monthly data and the seasonal effect length is 1 year, the seasonal AR and MA terms would reflect this particular lag length.

The ARIMAX(p, d, q) model then becomes a SARIMAX(p, d, q) × (P, D, Q) model, which is a bit more complicated to write out, but the statsmodels documentation (see link on GitHub) provides this information in detail.

We will now build a seasonal ARMA model using macro-data to illustrate its implementation.

How to forecast macro fundamentals

We will build a SARIMAX model for monthly data on an industrial production time series for the 1988-2017 period. As illustrated in the first section on analytical tools, the data has been log-transformed, and we are using seasonal (lag-12) differences. We estimate the model for a range of both ordinary and conventional AR and MA parameters using a rolling window of 10 years of training data, and evaluate the **root mean square error** (**RMSE**) of the 1-step-ahead forecast, as shown in the following simplified code (see the notebook `arima_models` for details):

```
for p1 in range(4):                # AR order
    for q1 in range(4):            # MA order
        for p2 in range(3):        # seasonal AR order
            for q2 in range(3):    # seasonal MA order
                y_pred = []
                for i, T in enumerate(range(train_size, len(data))):
                    train_set = data.iloc[T - train_size:T]
                    model = tsa.SARIMAX(endog=train_set, # model specification
                                        order=(p1, 0, q1),
                                        seasonal_order=(p2, 0, q2, 12)).fit()
                    preds.iloc[i, 1] = model.forecast(steps=1)[0]
                mse = mean_squared_error(preds.y_true, preds.y_pred)
                results[(p1, q1, p2, q2)] = [np.sqrt(mse),
                    preds.y_true.sub(preds.y_pred).std(),
                    np.mean(aic)]
```

We also collect the AIC and BIC criteria, which show a very high rank correlation coefficient of 0.94, with BIC favoring models with slightly fewer parameters than AIC. The best five models by RMSE are:

```
                RMSE         AIC         BIC
p1 q1 p2 q2
2  3  1  0   0.009323 -772.247023 -752.734581
3  2  1  0   0.009467 -768.844028 -749.331586
2  2  1  0   0.009540 -770.904835 -754.179884
   3  0  0   0.009773 -760.248885 -743.523935
   2  0  0   0.009986 -758.775827 -744.838368
```

We reestimate a SARIMA(2, 0 ,3) × (1, 0, 0) model, as follows:

```
best_model = tsa.SARIMAX(endog=industrial_production_log_diff, order=(2, 0,
                                                                        3),
                         seasonal_order=(1, 0, 0, 12)).fit()
print(best_model.summary())
```

We obtain the following summary:

```
                                 Statespace Model Results
==========================================================================================
Dep. Variable:                           IPGMFN   No. Observations:                   348
Model:             SARIMAX(2, 0, 3)x(1, 0, 0, 12)   Log Likelihood                1139.719
Date:                          Sat, 22 Sep 2018   AIC                          -2265.438
Time:                                  17:48:17   BIC                          -2238.472
Sample:                              01-01-1989   HQIC                         -2254.702
                                   - 12-01-2017
Covariance Type:                            opg
==============================================================================
                 coef    std err          z      P>|z|      [0.025      0.975]
------------------------------------------------------------------------------
ar.L1          1.4934      0.104     14.351      0.000       1.289       1.697
ar.L2         -0.5159      0.102     -5.083      0.000      -0.715      -0.317
ma.L1         -0.5499      0.114     -4.813      0.000      -0.774      -0.326
ma.L2          0.2872      0.062      4.662      0.000       0.166       0.408
ma.L3          0.1815      0.070      2.589      0.010       0.044       0.319
ar.S.L12      -0.4486      0.047     -9.533      0.000      -0.541      -0.356
sigma2      8.141e-05   5.65e-06     14.399      0.000    7.03e-05    9.25e-05
===================================================================================
Ljung-Box (Q):                       61.58   Jarque-Bera (JB):                 9.97
Prob(Q):                              0.02   Prob(JB):                         0.01
Heteroskedasticity (H):               1.07   Skew:                            -0.20
Prob(H) (two-sided):                  0.71   Kurtosis:                         3.73
===================================================================================

Warnings:
[1] Covariance matrix calculated using the outer product of gradients (complex-step).
```

Figure 9.5: SARMAX model results

The coefficients are significant, and the Q-statistic rejects the hypothesis of further autocorrelation. The correlogram similarly indicates that we have successfully eliminated the series' autocorrelation:

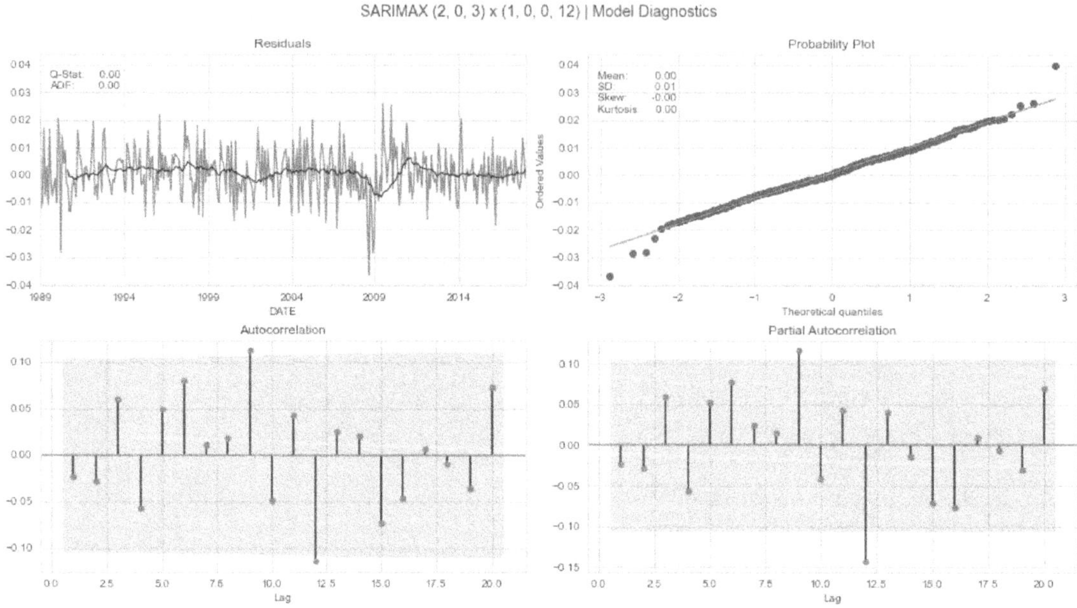

Figure 9.6: SARIMAX model diagnostics

How to use time-series models to forecast volatility

A particularly important application for univariate time-series models in finance is the prediction of volatility. This is because it is usually not constant over time, with bouts of volatility clustering together. Changes in variance create challenges for time-series forecasting using the classical ARIMA models that assume stationarity. To address this challenge, we will now model volatility so that we can predict changes in variance.

Heteroskedasticity is the technical term for changes in a variable's variance. The ARCH model expresses the variance of the error term as a function of the errors in previous periods. More specifically, it assumes that the error variance follows an AR(p) model.

The **generalized autoregressive conditional heteroskedasticity** (**GARCH**) model broadens the scope of ARCH to allow for ARMA models. Time-series forecasting often combines ARIMA models for the expected mean and ARCH/GARCH models for the expected variance of a time series. The 2003 Nobel Prize in Economics was awarded to Robert Engle and Clive Granger for developing this class of models. The former also runs the Volatility Lab at New York University's Stern School (`vlab.stern.nyu.edu`), which has numerous online examples and tools concerning the models we will discuss.

The ARCH model

The ARCH(p) model is simply an AR(p) model that's applied to the variance of the residuals of a time-series model, which makes this variance at time t conditional on lagged observations of the variance.

More specifically, the error terms, ε_t, are residuals of a linear model, such as ARIMA, on the original time series and are split into a time-dependent standard deviation, σ_t, and a disturbance, z_t, as follows:

$$\begin{aligned} \text{ARCH}(p): \quad \text{var}(x_t) &= \sigma_t^2 \\ &= \omega + \alpha_1 \epsilon_{t-1}^2 + \cdots + \alpha_p \epsilon_{t-p}^2 \\ \epsilon_t &= \sigma_t z_t \\ z_t &\sim \text{i.i.d.} \end{aligned}$$

An ARCH(p) model can be estimated using OLS. Engle proposed a method to identify the appropriate ARCH order using the Lagrange multiplier test, which corresponds to the F-test of the hypothesis that all coefficients in linear regression are zero (see *Chapter 7, Linear Models – From Risk Factors to Return Forecasts*).

A key **strength** of the ARCH model is that it produces volatility estimates with positive excess kurtosis — that is, fat tails relative to the normal distribution — which, in turn, is in line with empirical observations about returns. **Weaknesses** include the assumption of the same effect for positive and negative volatility shocks, whereas asset prices tend to respond differently. It also does not explain the variations in volatility and is likely to overpredict volatility because they respond slowly to large, isolated shocks to the return series.

For a properly specified ARCH model, the standardized residuals (divided by the model estimate for the period of standard deviation) should resemble white noise and can be subjected to a Ljung-Box Q test.

Generalizing ARCH – the GARCH model

The ARCH model is relatively simple but often requires many parameters to capture the volatility patterns of an asset-return series. The GARCH model applies to a log-return series, r_t, with disturbances, $\epsilon_t = r_t - \mu$, that follow a GARCH(p, q) model if:

$$\epsilon_t = \sigma_t z_t, \quad \sigma_t^2 = \omega + \sum_{i=1}^{p} \alpha_i \epsilon_{t-i}^2 + \sum_{j=1}^{q} \beta_i \sigma_{t-j}^2, \quad z_t \sim \text{i. i. d}$$

The GARCH(p, q) model assumes an ARMA(p, q) model for the variance of the error term, ε_t.

Similar to ARCH models, the tail distribution of a GARCH(1,1) process is heavier than that of a normal distribution. The model encounters the same weaknesses as the ARCH model. For instance, it responds equally to positive and negative shocks.

To configure the lag order for ARCH and GARCH models, use the squared residuals of the time series trained to predict the mean of the original series. The residuals are zero-centered so that their squares are also the variance. Then, inspect the ACF and PACF plots of the squared residuals to identify autocorrelation patterns in the variance of the time series.

How to build a model that forecasts volatility

The development of a volatility model for an asset-return series consists of four steps:

1. Build an ARMA time-series model for the financial time series based on the serial dependence revealed by the ACF and PACF
2. Test the residuals of the model for ARCH/GARCH effects, again relying on the ACF and PACF for the series of the squared residual
3. Specify a volatility model if serial correlation effects are significant, and jointly estimate the mean and volatility equations
4. Check the fitted model carefully and refine it if necessary

When applying volatility forecasting to return series, the serial dependence may be limited so that a constant mean may be used instead of an ARMA model.

The `arch` library (see link to the documentation on GitHub) provides several options to estimate volatility-forecasting models. You can model the expected mean as a constant, as an AR(p) model, as discussed in the *How to build autoregressive models*, section or as more recent **heterogeneous autoregressive processes** (**HAR**), which use daily (1 day), weekly (5 days), and monthly (22 days) lags to capture the trading frequencies of short-, medium-, and long-term investors.

The mean models can be jointly defined and estimated with several conditional heteroskedasticity models that include, in addition to ARCH and GARCH, the **exponential GARCH** (**EGARCH**) model, which allows for asymmetric effects between positive and negative returns, and the **heterogeneous ARCH** (**HARCH**) model, which complements the HAR mean model.

We will use daily NASDAQ returns from 2000-2020 to demonstrate the usage of a GARCH model (see the notebook `arch_garch_models` for details):

```
nasdaq = web.DataReader('NASDAQCOM', 'fred', '2000', '2020').squeeze()
nasdaq_returns = np.log(nasdaq).diff().dropna().mul(100) # rescale to
facilitate optimization
```

The rescaled daily return series exhibits only limited autocorrelation, but the squared deviations from the mean do have substantial memory reflected in the slowly decaying ACF and the PACF, which are high for the first two and cut off only after the first six lags:

```
plot_correlogram(nasdaq_returns.sub(nasdaq_returns.mean()).pow(2), lags=120,
                 title='NASDAQ Daily Volatility')
```

The function `plot_correlogram` produces the following output:

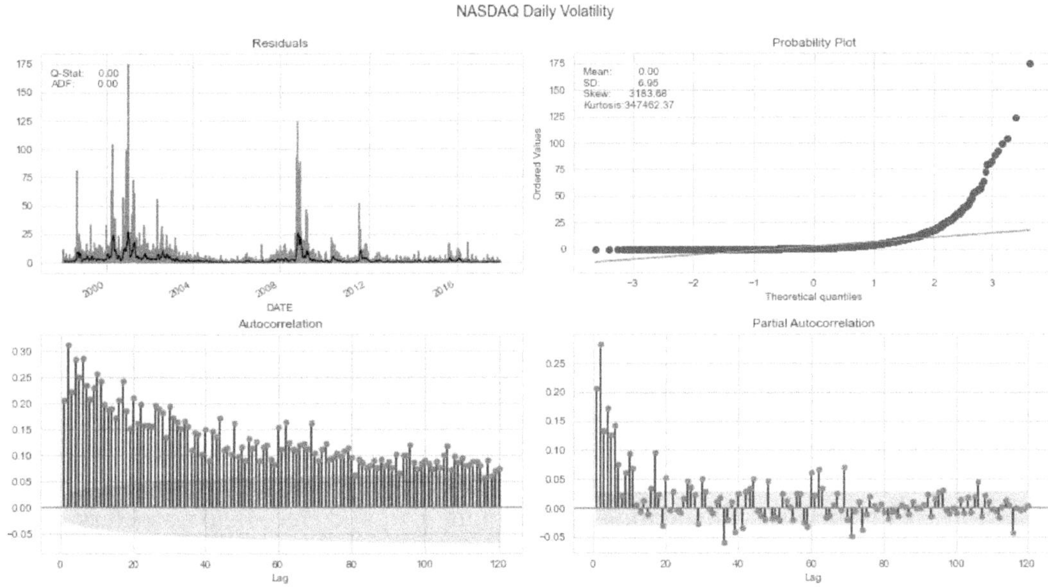

Figure 9.7: Daily NASDAQ composite volatility

Hence, we can estimate a GARCH model to capture the linear relationship of past volatilities. We will use rolling 10-year windows to estimate a GARCH(p, q) model with p and q ranging from 1-4 to generate one-step out-of-sample forecasts.

We then compare the RMSE of the predicted volatility relative to the actual squared deviation of the return from its mean to identify the most predictive model. We are using winsorized data to limit the impact of extreme return values being reflected in the very high positive skew of the volatility:

```
trainsize = 10 * 252  # 10 years
data = nasdaq_returns.clip(lower=nasdaq_returns.quantile(.05),
                           upper=nasdaq_returns.quantile(.95))
T = len(nasdaq_returns)
results = {}
for p in range(1, 5):
    for q in range(1, 5):
        print(f'{p} | {q}')
        result = []
        for s, t in enumerate(range(trainsize, T-1)):
            train_set = data.iloc[s: t]
            test_set = data.iloc[t+1]  # 1-step ahead forecast
            model = arch_model(y=train_set, p=p, q=q).fit(disp='off')
            forecast = model.forecast(horizon=1)
            mu = forecast.mean.iloc[-1, 0]
            var = forecast.variance.iloc[-1, 0]
            result.append([(test_set-mu)**2, var])
```

```
        df = pd.DataFrame(result, columns=['y_true', 'y_pred'])
        results[(p, q)] = np.sqrt(mean_squared_error(df.y_true, df.y_pred))
```

The GARCH(2, 2) model achieves the lowest RMSE (same value as GARCH(4, 2) but with fewer parameters), so we go ahead and estimate this model to inspect the summary:

```
am = ConstantMean(nasdaq_returns.clip(lower=nasdaq_returns.quantile(.05),
                                      upper=nasdaq_returns.quantile(.95)))
am.volatility = GARCH(2, 0, 2)
am.distribution = Normal()
best_model = am.fit(update_freq=5)
print(best_model.summary())
```

The output shows the maximized log-likelihood, as well as the AIC and BIC criteria, which are commonly minimized when selecting models based on in-sample performance (see *Chapter 7, Linear Models – From Risk Factors to Return Forecasts*). It also displays the result for the mean model, which, in this case, is just a constant estimate, as well as the GARCH parameters for the constant omega, the AR parameters, α, and the MA parameters, β, all of which are statistically significant:

```
                     Constant Mean - GARCH Model Results
==============================================================================
Dep. Variable:                NASDAQCOM   R-squared:                      -0.001
Mean Model:               Constant Mean   Adj. R-squared:                 -0.001
Vol Model:                        GARCH   Log-Likelihood:               -7244.08
Distribution:                    Normal   AIC:                           14500.2
Method:              Maximum Likelihood   BIC:                           14539.1
                                          No. Observations:                 4851
Date:                  Thu, Apr 16 2020   Df Residuals:                     4845
Time:                          22:41:39   Df Model:                            6
                                 Mean Model
============================================================================
                 coef    std err          t       P>|t|      95.0% Conf. Int.
----------------------------------------------------------------------------
mu             0.0526  1.416e-02      3.714  2.043e-04 [2.484e-02,8.036e-02]
                              Volatility Model
============================================================================
                 coef    std err          t       P>|t|      95.0% Conf. Int.
----------------------------------------------------------------------------
omega          0.0270  1.047e-02      2.574  1.005e-02 [6.430e-03,4.748e-02]
alpha[1]       0.0350  1.581e-02      2.215  2.678e-02 [4.027e-03,6.601e-02]
alpha[2]       0.0581  3.943e-02      1.473      0.141 [-1.919e-02,  0.135]
beta[1]        0.8675      0.535      1.622      0.105    [ -0.181,  1.916]
beta[2]        0.0179      0.495  3.618e-02      0.971    [ -0.952,  0.987]
============================================================================

Covariance estimator: robust
```

Figure 9.8: GARCH Model results

Let's now explore models for multiple time series and the concept of cointegration, which will enable a new trading strategy.

Multivariate time-series models

Multivariate time-series models are designed to capture the dynamic of multiple time series simultaneously and leverage dependencies across these series for more reliable predictions. The most comprehensive introduction to this subject is Lütkepohl (2005).

Systems of equations

Univariate time-series models, like the ARMA approach we just discussed, are limited to statistical relationships between a target variable and its lagged values or lagged disturbances and exogenous series, in the case of ARMAX. In contrast, multivariate time-series models also allow for lagged values of other time series to affect the target. This effect applies to all series, resulting in complex interactions, as illustrated in the following diagram:

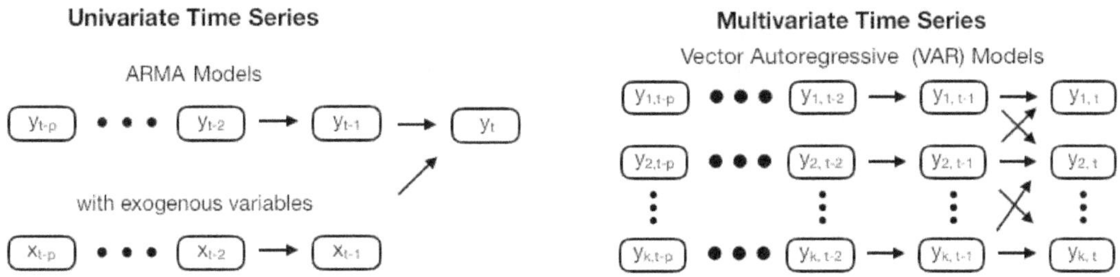

Figure 9.9: Interactions in univariate and multivariate time-series models

In addition to potentially better forecasting, multivariate time series are also used to gain insights into cross-series dependencies. For example, in economics, multivariate time series are used to understand how policy changes to one variable, such as an interest rate, may affect other variables over different horizons.

The **impulse-response** function produced by the multivariate model serves this purpose and allows us to simulate how one variable responds to a sudden change in other variables. The concept of **Granger causality** analyzes whether one variable is useful in forecasting another (in the least-squares sense). Furthermore, multivariate time-series models allow for a decomposition of the prediction error variance to analyze how other series contribute.

The vector autoregressive (VAR) model

We will see how the **vector autoregressive VAR(p) model** extends the AR(p) model to k series by creating a system of k equations, where each contains p lagged values of all k series. In the simplest case, a VAR(1) model for k=2 takes the following form:

$$\begin{aligned} y_{1,t} &= c_1 + \alpha_{1,1} y_{1,t-1} + \alpha_{1,2} y_{2,t-1} + \epsilon_{1,t} \\ y_{2,t} &= c_2 + \alpha_{2,1} y_{1,t-1} + \alpha_{2,2} y_{2,t-1} + \epsilon_{2,t} \end{aligned}$$

This model can be expressed somewhat more concisely in **matrix form**:

$$\begin{bmatrix} y_{1,t} \\ y_{2,t} \end{bmatrix} = \begin{bmatrix} c_1 \\ c_2 \end{bmatrix} + \begin{bmatrix} a_{1,1} & a_{1,2} \\ a_{2,1} & a_{2,2} \end{bmatrix} \begin{bmatrix} y_{1,t-1} \\ y_{2,t-2} \end{bmatrix} + \begin{bmatrix} \epsilon_{1,t} \\ \epsilon_{2,t} \end{bmatrix}$$

The **coefficients** on the lagged values of the output provide information about the dynamics of the series itself, whereas the cross-variable coefficients offer some insight into the interactions across the series. This notation extends to k time series and order p, as follows:

$$\underset{k\times 1}{\boldsymbol{y_t}} = \underset{k\times 1}{\boldsymbol{c}} + \underset{k\times k}{\boldsymbol{A_1}}\,\underset{k\times 1}{\boldsymbol{y_{t-1}}} + \ldots + \underset{k\times k}{\boldsymbol{A_p}}\,\underset{k\times 1}{\boldsymbol{y_{t-p}}} + \underset{k\times 1}{\boldsymbol{\epsilon_t}}$$

VAR(p) models also require **stationarity** so that the initial steps from univariate time-series modeling carry over. First, explore the series and determine the necessary transformations. Then, apply the augmented Dickey-Fuller test to verify that the stationarity criterion is met for each series and apply further transformations otherwise. It can be estimated with an OLS conditional on initial information or with MLE, which is the equivalent for normally distributed errors but not otherwise.

If some or all of the k series are unit-root non-stationary, they may be **cointegrated** (see the next section). This extension of the unit root concept to multiple time series means that a linear combination of two or more series is stationary and, hence, mean-reverting.

The VAR model is not equipped to handle this case without differencing; instead, use the **vector error correction model (VECM**, Johansen and Juselius 1990). We will further explore cointegration because, if present and assumed to persist, it can be leveraged for a pairs-trading strategy.

The **determination of the lag order** also takes its cues from the ACF and PACF for each series, but is constrained by the fact that the same lag order applies to all series. After model estimation, **residual diagnostics** also call for a result resembling white noise, and model selection can use in-sample information criteria or, if the goal is to use the model for prediction, out-of-sample predictive performance to cross-validate alternative model designs.

As mentioned in the univariate case, predictions of the original time series require us to reverse the transformations applied to make a series stationary before training the model.

Using the VAR model for macro forecasts

We will extend the univariate example of using a single time series of monthly data on industrial production and add a monthly time series on consumer sentiment, both of which are provided by the Federal Reserve's data service. We will use the familiar pandas-datareader library to retrieve data from 1970 through 2017:

```
df = web.DataReader(['UMCSENT', 'IPGMFN'],
                    'fred', '1970', '2017-12').dropna()
df.columns = ['sentiment', 'ip']
```

Log-transforming the industrial production series and seasonal differencing using a lag of 12 for both series yields stationary results:

```
df_transformed = pd.DataFrame({'ip': np.log(df.ip).diff(12),
                               'sentiment': df.sentiment.diff(12)}).dropna()
test_unit_root(df_transformed) # see notebook for details and additional
plots
          p-value
ip         0.0003
sentiment  0.0000
```

This leaves us with the following series:

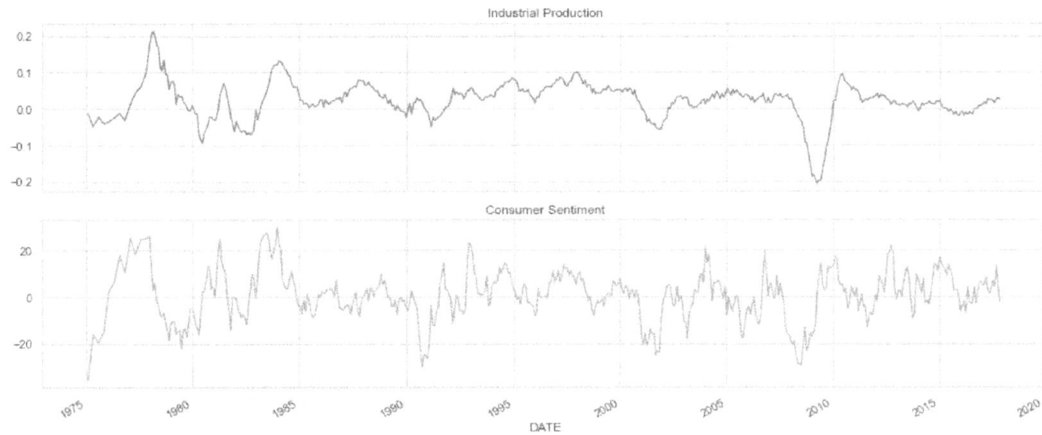

Figure 9.10: Transformed time series: industrial production and consumer sentiment

To limit the size of the output, we will just estimate a VAR(1) model using the statsmodels `VARMAX` implementation (which allows for optional exogenous variables) with a constant trend using the first 480 observations:

```
model = VARMAX(df_transformed.loc[:'2017'], order=(1,1),
               trend='c').fit(maxiter=1000)
```

This produces the following summary:

```
                           Statespace Model Results
==================================================================================
Dep. Variable:        ['ip', 'sentiment']   No. Observations:                  468
Model:                         VARMA(1,1)   Log Likelihood                 -71.870
                              + intercept   AIC                            169.741
Date:                    Thu, 16 Apr 2020   BIC                            223.671
Time:                            22:55:23   HQIC                           190.962
Sample:                                 0
                                    - 468
Covariance Type:                      opg
===================================================================================
Ljung-Box (Q):                 127.93, 161.51   Jarque-Bera (JB):       128.70, 17.04
Prob(Q):                           0.00, 0.00   Prob(JB):                  0.00, 0.00
Heteroskedasticity (H):            0.48, 1.10   Skew:                      0.19, 0.21
Prob(H) (two-sided):               0.00, 0.57   Kurtosis:                  5.54, 3.83
                          Results for equation ip
===================================================================================
                        coef    std err          z      P>|z|      [0.025      0.975]
-----------------------------------------------------------------------------------
intercept             0.0015      0.001      2.401      0.016       0.000       0.003
L1.ip                 0.9284      0.010     93.628      0.000       0.909       0.948
L1.sentiment          0.0006   6.03e-05     10.059      0.000       0.000       0.001
L1.e(ip)              0.0116      0.037      0.311      0.756      -0.062       0.085
L1.e(sentiment) -9.925e-05      0.000     -0.814      0.415      -0.000       0.000
                       Results for equation sentiment
===================================================================================
                        coef    std err          z      P>|z|      [0.025      0.975]
-----------------------------------------------------------------------------------
intercept             0.3374      0.279      1.208      0.227      -0.210       0.885
L1.ip               -14.3677      5.450     -2.636      0.008     -25.049      -3.687
L1.sentiment          0.8801      0.023     37.598      0.000       0.834       0.926
L1.e(ip)             39.6834     18.798      2.111      0.035       2.839      76.528
L1.e(sentiment)       0.0509      0.052      0.983      0.326      -0.051       0.152
                            Error covariance matrix
============================================================================================
                              coef    std err          z      P>|z|      [0.025      0.975]
--------------------------------------------------------------------------------------------
sqrt.var.ip                 0.0129      0.000     40.298      0.000       0.012       0.014
sqrt.cov.ip.sentiment       0.0368      0.231      0.159      0.873      -0.416       0.489
sqrt.var.sentiment          5.2738      0.148     35.519      0.000       4.983       5.565
============================================================================================

Warnings:
[1] Covariance matrix calculated using the outer product of gradients (complex-step).
```

Figure 9.11: VAR(1) model results

The output contains the coefficients for both time-series equations, as outlined in the preceding VAR(1) illustration. statsmodels provides diagnostic plots to check whether the residuals meet the white noise assumptions. This is not exactly the case in this simple example because the variance does not appear to be constant (upper left) and the quantile plot shows differences in the distribution, namely fat tails (lower left):

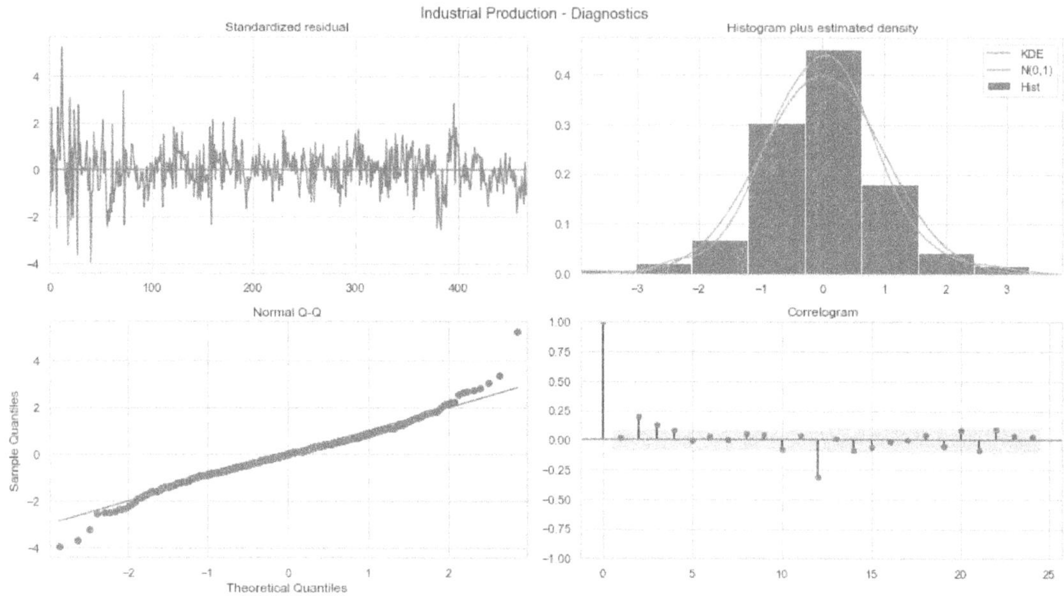

Figure 9.12: statsmodels VAR model diagnostic plot

You can generate out-of-sample predictions as follows:

```
preds = model.predict(start=480, end=len(df_transformed)-1)
```

The following visualization of actual and predicted values shows how the prediction lags the actual values and does not capture nonlinear, out-of-sample patterns well:

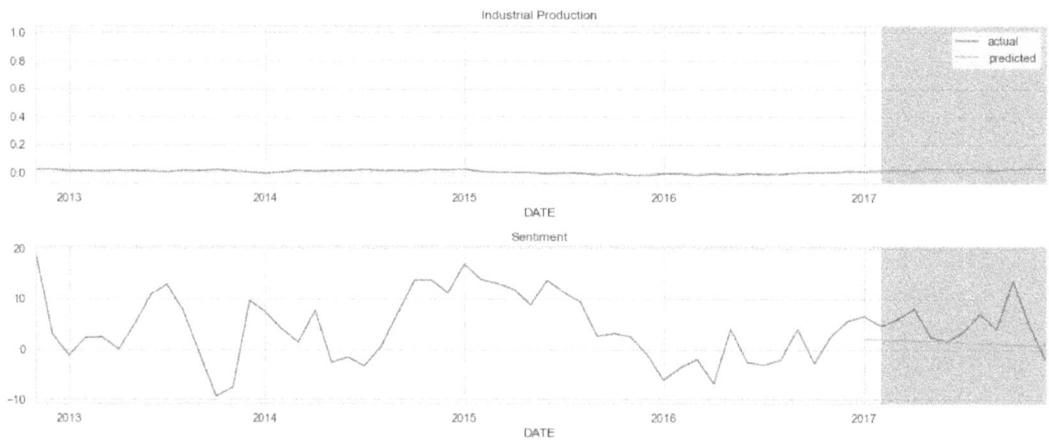

Figure 9.13: VAR model predictions versus actuals

Cointegration – time series with a shared trend

We briefly mentioned cointegration in the previous section on multivariate time-series models. Let's now explain this concept and how to diagnose its presence in more detail before leveraging it for a statistical arbitrage trading strategy.

We have seen how a time series can have a unit root that creates a stochastic trend and makes the time series highly persistent. When we use such an integrated time series in their original, rather than in differenced, form as a feature in a linear regression model, its relationship with the outcome will often appear statistically significant, even though it is not. This phenomenon is called spurious regression (for details, see *Chapter 18, CNNs for Financial Time Series and Satellite Images*, in Wooldridge, 2008). Therefore, the recommended solution is to difference the time series so they become stationary before using them in a model.

However, there is an exception when there are cointegration relationships between the outcome and one or more input variables. To understand the concept of cointegration, let's first remember that the residuals of a regression model are a linear combination of the inputs and the output series.

Usually, the residuals of the regression of one integrated time series on one or more such series yields non-stationary residuals that are also integrated, and thus behave like a random walk. However, for some time series, this is not the case: the regression produces coefficients that yield a linear combination of the time series in the form of the residuals that are stationary, even though the individual series are not. Such time series are *cointegrated.*

A non-technical example is that of a drunken man on a random walk accompanied by his dog (on a leash). Both trajectories are non-stationary but cointegrated because the dog will occasionally revert to his owner. In the trading context, arbitrage constraints imply cointegration between spot and futures prices.

In other words, a **linear combination of two or more cointegrated series has a stable mean** to which this linear combination reverts. This also applies when the individual series are integrated of a higher order and the linear combination reduces the overall order of integration.

Cointegration differs from correlation: two series can be highly correlated but need not be cointegrated. For example, if two growing series are constant multiples of each other, their correlation will be high, but any linear combination will also grow rather than revert to a stable mean.

Cointegration is very useful: if two or more asset price series tend to revert to a common mean, we can leverage deviations from the trend because they should imply future price moves in the opposite direction. The mathematics behind cointegration is more involved, so we will only focus on the practical aspects; for an in-depth treatment, see Lütkepohl (2005).

In this section, we will address how we can identify pairs with such a long-term stationary relationship, estimate the expected time for any disequilibrium to correct, and how to utilize these tools to implement and backtest a long-short pairs trading strategy.

There are two approaches to testing for cointegration:

- The Engle-Granger two-step method
- The Johansen test

We'll discuss each in turn before we show how they help identify cointegrated securities that tend to revert to a common trend, a fact that we can leverage for a statistical arbitrage strategy.

The Engle-Granger two-step method

The **Engle-Granger method** is used to identify cointegration relationships between two series. It involves both of the following:

1. Regressing one series on another to estimate the stationary long-term relationship
2. Applying an ADF unit-root test to the regression residual

The null hypothesis is that the residuals have a unit root and are integrated; if we can reject it, then we assume that the residuals are stationary and, thus, the series are cointegrated (Engle and Granger 1987).

A key benefit of this approach is that the regression coefficient represents the multiplier that renders the combination stationary, that is, mean-reverting. Unfortunately, the test results will differ, depending on which variable we consider independent, so that we try both ways and then pick the relation with the more negative test statistic that has the lower p-value.

Another downside is that this test is limited to pairwise relationships. The more complex Johansen procedure can identify significant cointegration among up to a dozen time series.

The Johansen likelihood-ratio test

The **Johansen procedure**, in contrast, tests the restrictions imposed by cointegration on a VAR model, as discussed in the previous section. More specifically, after subtracting the target vector from both sides of a generic VAR(*p*) model, we obtain the **error correction model** (**ECM**) formulation:

$$\Delta \boldsymbol{y}_t = \boldsymbol{c} + \boldsymbol{\Pi} \boldsymbol{y}_{t-1} + \boldsymbol{\Gamma}_1 \Delta \boldsymbol{y}_{t-1} + \ldots + \boldsymbol{\Gamma}_p \Delta \boldsymbol{y}_{t-p} + \boldsymbol{\epsilon}_t$$

The resulting modified VAR(*p*) equation has only one vector term in levels (y_{t-1}) that is not expressed as a difference using the Δ operator. The nature of cointegration depends on the rank of the coefficient matrix Π of this term (Johansen 1991).

While this equation appears structurally similar to the ADF test setup, there are now several potential constellations of common trends because there are multiple series involved. To identify the number of cointegration relationships, the Johansen test successively tests for an increasing rank of Π, starting at 0 (no cointegration). We will explore the application to the case of two series in the following section.

Gonzalo and Lee (1998) discuss practical challenges due to misspecified model dynamics and other implementation aspects, including how to combine both test procedures that we will rely on for our sample statistical arbitrage strategy in the next section.

Statistical arbitrage with cointegration

Statistical arbitrage refers to strategies that employ some statistical model or method to take advantage of what appears to be relative mispricing of assets, while maintaining a level of market neutrality.

Pairs trading is a conceptually straightforward strategy that has been employed by algorithmic traders since at least the mid-eighties (Gatev, Goetzmann, and Rouwenhorst 2006). The goal is to find two assets whose prices have historically moved together, track the spread (the difference between their prices), and, once the spread widens, buy the loser that has dropped below the common trend and short the winner. If the relationship persists, the long and/or the short leg will deliver profits as prices converge and the positions are closed.

This approach extends to a multivariate context by forming baskets from multiple securities and trading one asset against a basket of two baskets against each other.

In practice, the strategy requires two steps:

1. **Formation phase**: Identify securities that have a long-term mean-reverting relationship. Ideally, the spread should have a high variance to allow for frequent profitable trades while reliably reverting to the common trend.
2. **Trading phase**: Trigger entry and exit trading rules as price movements cause the spread to diverge and converge.

Several approaches to the formation and trading phases have emerged from increasingly active research in this area, across multiple asset classes, over the last several years. The next subsection outlines the key differences before we dive into an example application.

How to select and trade comoving asset pairs

A recent comprehensive survey of pairs trading strategies (Krauss 2017) identified four different methodologies, plus a number of other more recent approaches, including ML-based forecasts:

- **Distance approach**: The oldest and most-studied method identifies candidate pairs with distance metrics like correlation and uses non-parametric thresholds like Bollinger Bands to trigger entry and exit trades. Its computational simplicity allows for large-scale applications with demonstrated profitability across markets and asset classes for extended periods of time since Gatev, et al. (2006). However, performance has decayed more recently.
- **Cointegration approach**: As outlined previously, this approach relies on an econometric model of a long-term relationship among two or more variables, and allows for statistical tests that promise more reliability than simple distance metrics. Examples in this category use the Engle-Granger and Johansen procedures to identify pairs and baskets of securities, as well as simpler heuristics that aim to capture the concept (Vidyamurthy 2004). Trading rules often resemble the simple thresholds used with distance metrics.
- **Time-series approach**: With a focus on the trading phase, strategies in this category aim to model the spread as a mean-reverting stochastic process and optimize entry and exit rules accordingly (Elliott, Hoek, and Malcolm 2005). It assumes promising pairs have already been identified.
- **Stochastic control approach**: Similar to the time-series approach, the goal is to optimize trading rules using stochastic control theory to find value and policy functions to arrive at an optimal portfolio (Liu and Timmermann 2013). We will address this type of approach in *Chapter 21, Generative Adversarial Networks for Synthetic Time-Series Data*.
- **Other approaches**: Besides pair identification based on unsupervised learning like principal component analysis (see *Chapter 13, Data-Driven Risk Factors and Asset Allocation with Unsupervised Learning*) and statistical models like copulas (Patton 2012), machine learning has become popular more recently to identify pairs based on their relative price or return forecasts (Huck 2019). We will cover several ML algorithms that can be used for this purpose and illustrate corresponding multivariate pairs trading strategies in the coming chapters.

This summary of the various approaches offers barely a glimpse at the flexibility afforded by the design of a pairs trading strategy. In addition to higher-level questions about pair selection and trading rule logic, there are **numerous parameters** that we need **to define for implementation**. These parameters include the following:

- Investment universe to screen for potential pairs or baskets
- Length of the formation period
- Strength of the relationship used to pick tradeable candidates
- Degree of deviation from and convergence to their common means to trigger entry or exit trades or to adjust existing positions as spreads fluctuate

Pairs trading in practice

The **distance approach** identifies pairs using the correlation of (normalized) asset prices or their returns, and is simple and orders of magnitude less computationally intensive than cointegration tests. The notebook `cointegration_test` illustrates this for a sample of ~150 stocks with 4 years of daily data: it takes ~30ms to compute the correlation with the returns of an ETF, compared to 18 seconds for a suite of cointegration tests (using statsmodels) – 600x slower.

The **speed advantage** is particularly valuable. This is because the number of potential pairs is the product of the number of candidates to be considered on either side so that evaluating combinations of 100 stocks and 100 ETFs requires comparing 10,000 tests (we'll discuss the challenge of multiple testing bias later).

On the other hand, distance metrics do not necessarily select the most profitable pairs: correlation is maximized for perfect co-movement, which, in turn, eliminates actual trading opportunities. Empirical studies confirm that the volatility of the price spread of cointegrated pairs is almost twice as high as the volatility of the price spread of distance pairs (Huck and Afawubo 2015).

To balance the **tradeoff between computational cost and the quality of the resulting pairs**, Krauss (2017) recommends a procedure that combines both approaches based on his literature review:

1. Select pairs with a stable spread that shows little drift to reduce the number of candidates
2. Test the remaining pairs with the highest spread variance for cointegration

This process aims to select cointegrated pairs with lower divergence risk while ensuring more volatile spreads that, in turn, generate higher profit opportunities.

A large number of tests introduce **data snooping bias**, as discussed in *Chapter 6, The Machine Learning Process*: multiple testing is likely to increase the number of false positives that mistakenly reject the null hypothesis of no cointegration. While statistical significance may not be necessary for profitable trading (Chan 2008), a study of commodity pairs (Cummins and Bucca 2012) shows that controlling the familywise error rate to improve the tests' power, according to Romano and Wolf (2010), can lead to better performance.

In the following subsection, we'll take a closer look at how predictive various heuristics for the degree of comovement of asset prices are for the result of cointegration tests.

The example code uses a sample of 172 stocks and 138 ETFs traded on the NYSE and NASDAQ, with daily data from 2010 - 2019 provided by Stooq.

The securities represent the largest average dollar volume over the sample period in their respective class; highly correlated and stationary assets have been removed. See the notebook `create_datasets` in the `data` folder of the GitHub repository for instructions on how to obtain the data, and the notebook `cointegration_tests` for the relevant code and additional preprocessing and exploratory details.

Distance-based heuristics to find cointegrated pairs

`compute_pair_metrics()` computes the following distance metrics for over 23,000 pairs of stocks and **Exchange Traded Funds** (**ETFs**) for 2010-14 and 2015-19:

- The **drift of the spread**, defined as a linear regression of a time trend on the spread
- The **spread's volatility**
- The **correlations** between the normalized price series and between their returns

Low drift and volatility, as well as high correlation, are simple proxies for cointegration.

To evaluate the predictive power of these heuristics, we also run **Engle-Granger and Johansen cointegration** tests using statsmodels for the preceding pairs. This takes place in the loop in the second half of `compute_pair_metrics()`.

We first estimate the optimal number of lags that we need to specify for the Johansen test. For both tests, we assume that the cointegrated series (the spread) may have an intercept different from zero but no trend:

```
def compute_pair_metrics(security, candidates):
    security = security.div(security.iloc[0])
    ticker = security.name
    candidates = candidates.div(candidates.iloc[0])

    # compute heuristics
    spreads = candidates.sub(security, axis=0)
    n, m = spreads.shape
    X = np.ones(shape=(n, 2))
    X[:, 1] = np.arange(1, n + 1)
    drift = ((np.linalg.inv(X.T @ X) @ X.T @ spreads).iloc[1]
             .to_frame('drift'))
    vol = spreads.std().to_frame('vol')
    corr_ret = (candidates.pct_change()
                .corrwith(security.pct_change())
                .to_frame('corr_ret'))
    corr = candidates.corrwith(security).to_frame('corr')
    metrics = drift.join(vol).join(corr).join(corr_ret).assign(n=n)
    tests = []

    # compute cointegration tests
    for candidate, prices in candidates.items():
        df = pd.DataFrame({'s1': security, 's2': prices})
        var = VAR(df)
        lags = var.select_order() # select VAR order
        k_ar_diff = lags.selected_orders['aic']
```

```
        # Johansen Test with constant Term and estd. Lag order
        cj0 = coint_johansen(df, det_order=0, k_ar_diff=k_ar_diff)
        # Engle-Granger Tests
        t1, p1 = coint(security, prices, trend='c')[:2]
        t2, p2 = coint(prices, security, trend='c')[:2]
        tests.append([ticker, candidate, t1, p1, t2, p2,
                      k_ar_diff, *cj0.lr1])

    return metrics.join(tests)
```

To check for the **significance of the cointegration tests**, we compare the Johansen trace statistic for rank 0 and 1 to their respective critical values and obtain the Engle-Granger p-value.

We follow the recommendation by Gonzalo and Lee (1998), mentioned at the end of the previous section, to apply both tests and accept pairs where they agree. The authors suggest additional due diligence in case of disagreement, which we are going to skip:

```
spreads['trace_sig'] = ((spreads.trace0 > trace0_cv) &
                        (spreads.trace1 > trace1_cv)).astype(int)
spreads['eg_sig'] = (spreads.p < .05).astype(int)
```

For the over 46,000 pairs across both sample periods, the Johansen test considers 3.2 percent of the relationships as significant, while the Engle-Granger considers 6.5 percent. They agree on 366 pairs (0.79 percent).

How well do the heuristics predict significant cointegration?

When we compare the distributions of the heuristics for series that are cointegrated according to both tests with the remainder that is not, volatility and drift are indeed lower (in absolute terms). *Figure 9.14* shows that the picture is less clear for the two correlation measures:

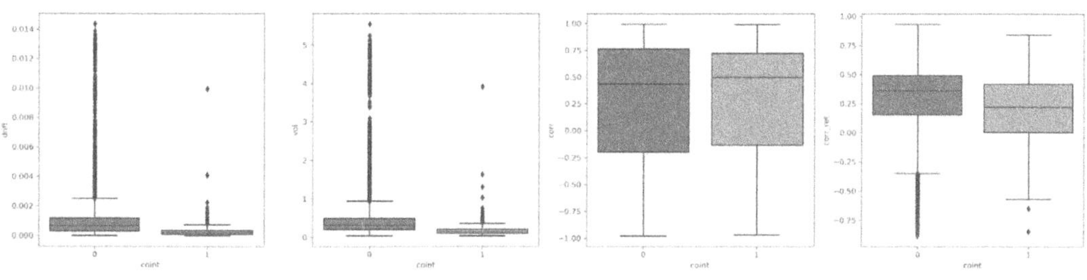

Figure 9.14: The distribution of heuristics, broken down by the significance of both cointegration tests

To evaluate the predictive accuracy of the heuristics, we first run a logistic regression model with these features to predict significant cointegration. It achieves an **area-under-the-curve** (**AUC**) cross-validation score of 0.815; excluding the correlation metrics, it still scores 0.804. A decision tree does slightly better at AUC=0.821, with or without the correlation features.

Not least due to the strong class imbalance, there are large numbers of false positives: correctly identifying 80 percent of the 366 cointegrated pairs implies over 16,500 false positives, but eliminates almost 30,000 of the candidates. See the notebook `cointegration_tests` for additional detail.

The **key takeaway** is that distance heuristics can help screen a large universe more efficiently, but this comes at a cost of missing some cointegrated pairs and still requires substantial testing.

Preparing the strategy backtest

In this section, we are going to implement a statistical arbitrage strategy based on cointegration for the sample of stocks and ETFs and the 2017-2019 period. Some aspects are simplified to streamline the presentation. See the notebook `statistical_arbitrage_with_cointegrated_pairs` for the code examples and additional detail.

We first generate and store the cointegration tests for all candidate pairs and the resulting trading signals. Then, we backtest a strategy based on these signals, given the computational intensity of the process.

Precomputing the cointegration tests

First, we run quarterly cointegration tests over a 2-year lookback period on each of the 23,000 potential pairs, Then, we select pairs where both the Johansen and the Engle-Granger tests agree for trading. We should exclude assets that are stationary during the lookback period, but we eliminated assets that are stationary for the entire period, so we skip this step to simplify it.

This procedure follows the steps outlined previously; please see the notebook for details.

Figure 9.15 shows the original stock and ETF series of the two different pairs selected for trading; note the clear presence of a common trend over the sample period:

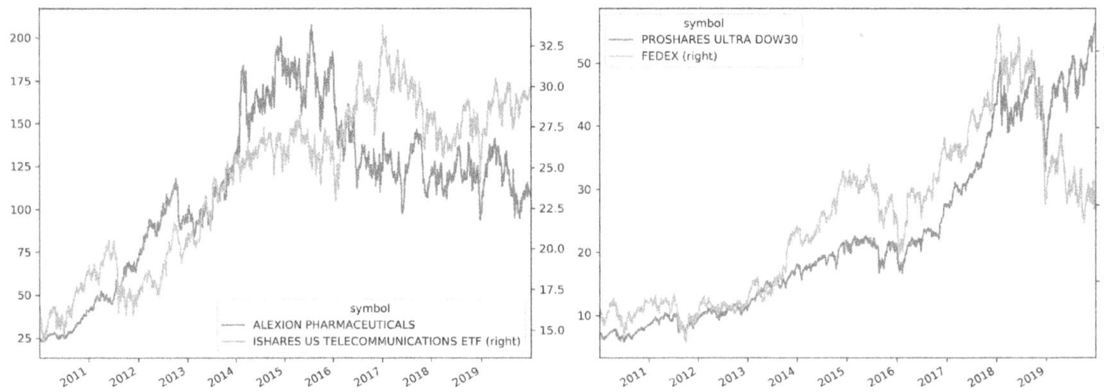

Figure 9.15: Price series for two selected pairs over the sample period

Getting entry and exit trades

Now, we can compute the spread for each candidate pair based on a rolling hedge ratio. We also calculate a **Bollinger Band** because we will consider moves of the spread larger than two rolling standard deviations away from its moving average as **long and short entry signals**, and crossings of the moving average in reverse as exit signals.

Smoothing prices with the Kalman filter

To this end, we first apply a rolling **Kalman filter** (**KF**) to remove some noise, as demonstrated in *Chapter 4, Financial Feature Engineering – How to Research Alpha Factors*:

```
def KFSmoother(prices):
    """Estimate rolling mean"""

    kf = KalmanFilter(transition_matrices=np.eye(1),
                      observation_matrices=np.eye(1),
                      initial_state_mean=0,
                      initial_state_covariance=1,
                      observation_covariance=1,
                      transition_covariance=.05)

    state_means, _ = kf.filter(prices.values)
    return pd.Series(state_means.flatten(),
                     index=prices.index)
```

Computing the rolling hedge ratio using the Kalman filter

To obtain a dynamic hedge ratio, we use the KF for rolling linear regression, as follows:

```
def KFHedgeRatio(x, y):
    """Estimate Hedge Ratio"""
    delta = 1e-3
    trans_cov = delta / (1 - delta) * np.eye(2)
    obs_mat = np.expand_dims(np.vstack([[x], [np.ones(len(x))]]).T, axis=1)

    kf = KalmanFilter(n_dim_obs=1, n_dim_state=2,
                      initial_state_mean=[0, 0],
                      initial_state_covariance=np.ones((2, 2)),
                      transition_matrices=np.eye(2),
                      observation_matrices=obs_mat,
                      observation_covariance=2,
                      transition_covariance=trans_cov)

    state_means, _ = kf.filter(y.values)
    return -state_means
```

Estimating the half-life of mean reversion

If we view the spread as a mean-reverting stochastic process in continuous time, we can model it as an Ornstein-Uhlenbeck process. The benefit of this perspective is that we gain a formula for the half-life of mean reversion, as an approximation of the time required for the spread to converge again after a deviation (see *Chapter 2, Market and Fundamental Data - Sources and Techniques,* in Chan 2013 for details):

```
def estimate_half_life(spread):
    X = spread.shift().iloc[1:].to_frame().assign(const=1)
    y = spread.diff().iloc[1:]
    beta = (np.linalg.inv(X.T@X)@X.T@y).iloc[0]
    halflife = int(round(-np.log(2) / beta, 0))
    return max(halflife, 1)
```

Computing spread and Bollinger Bands

The following function orchestrates the preceding computations and expresses the spread as a z-score that captures deviations from the moving average with a window equal to two half-lives in terms of the rolling standard deviations:

```
def get_spread(candidates, prices):
    pairs, half_lives = [], []

    periods = pd.DatetimeIndex(sorted(candidates.test_end.unique()))
    start = time()
    for p, test_end in enumerate(periods, 1):
        start_iteration = time()
        period_candidates = candidates.loc[candidates.test_end == test_end,
                                           ['y', 'x']]
        trading_start = test_end + pd.DateOffset(days=1)
        t = trading_start - pd.DateOffset(years=2)
        T = trading_start + pd.DateOffset(months=6) - pd.DateOffset(days=1)
        max_window = len(prices.loc[t: test_end].index)
        print(test_end.date(), len(period_candidates))
        for i, (y, x) in enumerate(zip(period_candidates.y,
                                       period_candidates.x), 1):
            pair = prices.loc[t: T, [y, x]]
            pair['hedge_ratio'] = KFHedgeRatio(
                y=KFSmoother(prices.loc[t: T, y]),
                x=KFSmoother(prices.loc[t: T, x]))[:, 0]
            pair['spread'] = pair[y].add(pair[x].mul(pair.hedge_ratio))
            half_life = estimate_half_life(pair.spread.loc[t: test_end])

            spread = pair.spread.rolling(window=min(2 * half_life,
                                                    max_window))
            pair['z_score'] = pair.spread.sub(spread.mean()).div(spread.
```

```
std())
            pairs.append(pair.loc[trading_start: T].assign(s1=y, s2=x, 
period=p, pair=i).drop([x, y], axis=1))

            half_lives.append([test_end, y, x, half_life])
    return pairs, half_lives
```

Getting entry and exit dates for long and short positions

Finally, we use the set of z-scores to derive trading signals:

1. We enter a long (short) position if the z-score is below (above) two, which implies the spread has moved two rolling standard deviations below (above) the moving average
2. We exit trades when the spread crosses the moving average again

We derive rules on a quarterly basis for the set of pairs that passed the cointegration tests during the prior lookback period but allow pairs to exit during the subsequent 3 months.

We again simplify this by dropping pairs that do not close during this 6-month period. Alternatively, we could have handled this using the stop-loss risk management that we included in the strategy (see the next section on backtesting):

```
def get_trades(data):
    pair_trades = []
    for i, ((period, s1, s2), pair) in enumerate(
             data.groupby(['period', 's1', 's2']), 1):
        if i % 100 == 0:
            print(i)

        first3m = pair.first('3M').index
        last3m = pair.last('3M').index

        entry = pair.z_score.abs() > 2
        entry = ((entry.shift() != entry)
                 .mul(np.sign(pair.z_score))
                 .fillna(0)
                 .astype(int)
                 .sub(2))

        exit = (np.sign(pair.z_score.shift().fillna(method='bfill'))
                != np.sign(pair.z_score)).astype(int) - 1

        trades = (entry[entry != -2].append(exit[exit == 0])
                  .to_frame('side')
                  .sort_values(['date', 'side'])
                  .squeeze())
```

```
        trades.loc[trades < 0] += 2
        trades = trades[trades.abs().shift() != trades.abs()]
        window = trades.loc[first3m.min():first3m.max()]
        extra = trades.loc[last3m.min():last3m.max()]
        n = len(trades)

        if window.iloc[0] == 0:
            if n > 1:
                print('shift')
                window = window.iloc[1:]
        if window.iloc[-1] != 0:
            extra_exits = extra[extra == 0].head(1)
            if extra_exits.empty:
                continue
            else:
                window = window.append(extra_exits)

        trades = (pair[['s1', 's2', 'hedge_ratio', 'period', 'pair']]
                  .join(window. to_frame('side'), how='right'))
        trades.loc[trades.side == 0, 'hedge_ratio'] = np.nan
        trades.hedge_ratio = trades.hedge_ratio.ffill()
        pair_trades.append(trades)
    return pair_trades
```

Backtesting the strategy using backtrader

Now, we are ready to formulate our strategy on our backtesting platform, execute it, and evaluate the results. To do so, we need to track our pairs, in addition to individual portfolio positions, and monitor the spread of active and inactive pairs to apply our trading rules.

Tracking pairs with a custom DataClass

To account for active pairs, we define a `dataclass` (introduced in Python 3.7—see the Python documentation for details). This data structure, called `Pair`, allows us to store the pair components, their number of shares, and the hedge ratio, and compute the current spread and the return, among other things. See a simplified version in the following code:

```
@dataclass
class Pair:
    period: int
    s1: str
    s2: str
    size1: float
    size2: float
    long: bool
    hr: float
```

```
    p1: float
    p2: float
    entry_date: date = None
    exit_date: date = None
    entry_spread: float = np.nan
    exit_spread: float = np.nan

    def compute_spread(self, p1, p2):
        return p1 * self.size1 + p2 * self.size2

    def compute_spread_return(self, p1, p2):
        current_spread = self.compute_spread(p1, p2)
        delta = self.entry_spread - current_spread
        return (delta / (np.sign(self.entry_spread) *
                         self.entry_spread))
```

Running and evaluating the strategy

Key implementation aspects include:

- The daily exit from pairs that have either triggered the exit rule or exceeded a given negative return
- The opening of new long and short positions for pairs whose spreads triggered entry signals
- In addition, we adjust positions to account for the varying number of pairs

The code for the strategy itself takes up too much space to display here; see the notebook `pairs_trading_backtest` for details.

Figure 9.16 shows that, at least for the 2017-2019 period, this simplified strategy had its moments (note that we availed ourselves of some lookahead bias and ignored transaction costs).

Under these lax assumptions, it underperformed the S&P 500 at the beginning and end of the period and was otherwise roughly in line (left panel). It yields an alpha of 0.08 and a negative beta of -0.14 (right panel), with an average Sharpe ratio of 0.75 and a Sortino ratio of 1.05 (central panel):

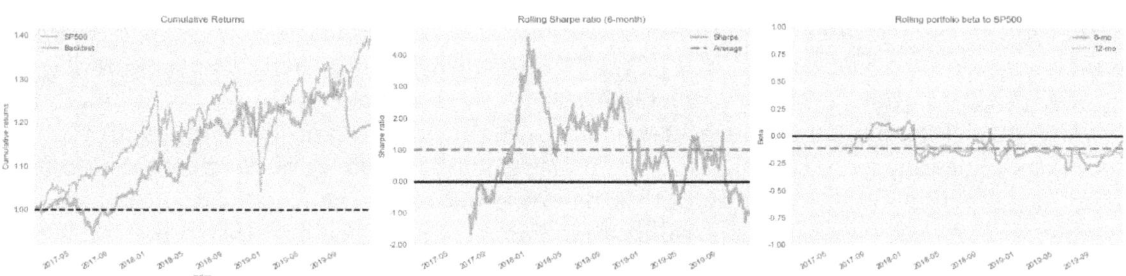

Figure 9.16: Strategy performance metrics

While we should take these performance metrics with a grain of salt, the strategy demonstrates the anatomy of a statistical arbitrage based on cointegration in the form of pairs trading. Let's take a look at a few steps you could take to build on this framework to produce better performance.

Extensions – how to do better

Cointegration is a very useful concept to identify pairs or groups of stocks that tend to move in unison. Compared to the statistical sophistication of cointegration, we used very simple and static trading rules; the computation on a quarterly basis also distorts the strategy, as the patterns of long and short holdings show (see notebook).

To be successful, you will, at a minimum, need to screen a larger universe and optimize several of the parameters, including the trading rules. Moreover, risk management should account for concentrated positions that arise when certain assets appear relatively often on the same side of a traded pair.

You could also operate with baskets as opposed to individual pairs; however, to address the growing number of candidates, you would likely need to constrain the composition of the baskets.

As mentioned in the *Pairs trading – statistical arbitrage with cointegration* section, there are alternatives that aim to predict price movements. In the following chapters, we will explore various machine learning models that aim to predict the absolute size or the direction of price movements for a given investment universe and horizon. Using these forecasts as long and short entry signals is a natural extension or alternative to the pairs trading framework that we studied in this section.

Summary

In this chapter, we explored linear time-series models for the univariate case of individual series, as well as multivariate models for several interacting series. We encountered applications that predict macro fundamentals, models that forecast asset or portfolio volatility with widespread use in risk management, and multivariate VAR models that capture the dynamics of multiple macro series. We also looked at the concept of cointegration, which underpins the popular pair-trading strategy.

Similar to *Chapter 7, Linear Models – From Risk Factors to Return Forecasts*, we saw how linear models impose a lot of structure, that is, they make strong assumptions that potentially require transformations and extensive testing to verify that these assumptions are met. If they are, model-training and interpretation are straightforward, and the models provide a good baseline that more complex models may be able to improve on. In the next two chapters, we will see two examples of this, namely random forests and gradient boosting models, and we will encounter several more in *Part 4*, which is on deep learning.

10

Bayesian ML – Dynamic Sharpe Ratios and Pairs Trading

In this chapter, we will introduce Bayesian approaches to **machine learning** (**ML**) and how their different perspective on uncertainty adds value when developing and evaluating trading strategies.

Bayesian statistics allows us to quantify uncertainty about future events and refine our estimates in a principled way as new information arrives. This dynamic approach adapts well to the evolving nature of financial markets. It is particularly useful when there are fewer relevant data and we require methods that systematically integrate prior knowledge or assumptions.

We will see that Bayesian approaches to machine learning allow for richer insights into the uncertainty around statistical metrics, parameter estimates, and predictions. The applications range from more granular risk management to dynamic updates of predictive models that incorporate changes in the market environment. The Black-Litterman approach to asset allocation (see *Chapter 5, Portfolio Optimization and Performance Evaluation*) can be interpreted as a Bayesian model. It computes the expected return of an asset as an average of the market equilibrium and the investor's views, weighted by each asset's volatility, cross-asset correlations, and the confidence in each forecast.

More specifically, in this chapter, we will cover:

- How Bayesian statistics apply to ML
- Probabilistic programming with PyMC3
- Defining and training ML models using PyMC3
- How to run state-of-the-art sampling methods to conduct approximate inference
- Bayesian ML applications to compute dynamic Sharpe ratios, dynamic pairs trading hedge ratios, and estimate stochastic volatility

> You can find the code samples for this chapter and links to additional resources in the corresponding directory of the GitHub repository. The notebooks include color versions of the images.

How Bayesian machine learning works

Classical statistics is said to follow the frequentist approach because it interprets probability as the relative frequency of an event over the long run, that is, after observing a large number of trials. In the context of probabilities, an event is a combination of one or more elementary outcomes of an experiment, such as any of six equal results in rolls of two dice or an asset price dropping by 10 percent or more on a given day).

Bayesian statistics, in contrast, views probability as a measure of the confidence or belief in the occurrence of an event. The Bayesian perspective, thus, leaves more room for subjective views and differences in opinions than the frequentist interpretation. This difference is most striking for events that do not happen often enough to arrive at an objective measure of long-term frequency.

Put differently, frequentist statistics assumes that data is a random sample from a population and aims to identify the fixed parameters that generated the data. Bayesian statistics, in turn, takes the data as given and considers the parameters to be random variables with a distribution that can be inferred from data. As a result, frequentist approaches require at least as many data points as there are parameters to be estimated. Bayesian approaches, on the other hand, are compatible with smaller datasets, and well suited for online learning from one sample at a time.

The Bayesian view is very useful for many real-world events that are rare or unique, at least in important respects. Examples include the outcome of the next election or the question of whether the markets will crash within 3 months. In each case, there is both relevant historical data as well as unique circumstances that unfold as the event approaches.

We will first introduce Bayes' theorem, which crystallizes the concept of updating beliefs by combining prior assumptions with new empirical evidence, and compare the resulting parameter estimates with their frequentist counterparts. We will then demonstrate two approaches to Bayesian statistical inference, namely conjugate priors and approximate inference, which produce insights into the posterior distribution of latent (that is, unobserved) parameters, such as the expected value:

- **Conjugate priors** facilitate the updating process by providing a closed-form solution that allows us to precisely compute the solution. However, such exact, analytical methods are not always available.
- **Approximate inference** simulates the distribution that results from combining assumptions and data and uses samples from this distribution to compute statistical insights.

How to update assumptions from empirical evidence

> *"When the facts change, I change my mind. What do you do, sir?"*
>
> *– John Maynard Keynes*

The theorem that Reverend Thomas Bayes came up with, over 250 years ago, uses fundamental probability theory to prescribe how probabilities or beliefs should change as relevant new information arrives. The preceding Keynes quotation captures that spirit. It relies on the conditional and total probability and the chain rule; see Bishop (2006) and Gelman et al. (2013) for an introduction and more.

The probabilistic belief concerns a single parameter or a vector of parameters θ (also: hypotheses). Each parameter can be discrete or continuous. θ could be a one-dimensional statistic like the (discrete) mode of a categorical variable or a (continuous) mean, or a higher dimensional set of values like a covariance matrix or the weights of a deep neural network.

A key difference to frequentist statistics is that Bayesian assumptions are expressed as probability distributions rather than parameter values. Consequently, while frequentist inference focuses on point estimates, Bayesian inference yields probability distributions.

Bayes' theorem updates the beliefs about the parameters of interest by computing the **posterior probability distribution** from the following inputs, as shown in *Figure 10.1*:

- The **prior** distribution indicates how likely we consider each possible hypothesis.
- The **likelihood function** outputs the probability of observing a dataset when given certain values for the parameters θ, that is, for a specific hypothesis.
- The **evidence** measures how likely the observed data is, given all possible hypotheses. Hence, it is the same for all parameter values and serves to normalize the numerator.

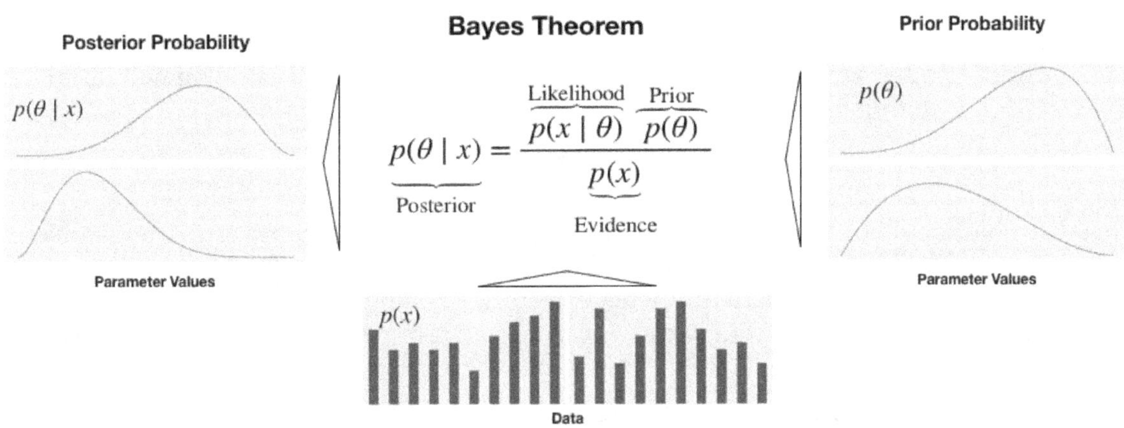

Figure 10.1: How evidence updates the prior to the posterior probability distribution

The posterior is the product of prior and likelihood, divided by the evidence. Thus, it reflects the probability distribution of the hypothesis, updated by taking into account both prior assumptions and the data. Viewed differently, the posterior probability results from applying the chain rule, which, in turn, factorizes the joint distribution of data and parameters.

With higher-dimensional, continuous variables, the formulation becomes more complex and involves (multiple) integrals. Also, an alternative formulation uses odds to express the posterior odds as the product of the prior odds, times the likelihood ratio (see Gelman et al. 2013).

Exact inference – maximum a posteriori estimation

Practical applications of Bayes' rule to exactly compute posterior probabilities are quite limited. This is because the computation of the evidence term in the denominator is quite challenging. The evidence reflects the probability of the observed data over all possible parameter values. It is also called the *marginal likelihood* because it requires "marginalizing out" the parameters' distribution by adding or integrating over their distribution. This is generally only possible in simple cases with a small number of discrete parameters that assume very few values.

Maximum a posteriori probability (**MAP**) estimation leverages the fact that the evidence is a constant factor that scales the posterior to meet the requirements for a probability distribution. Since the evidence does not depend on θ, the posterior distribution is proportional to the product of the likelihood and the prior. Hence, MAP estimation chooses the value of θ that maximizes the posterior given the observed data and the prior belief, that is, the mode of the posterior.

The MAP approach contrasts with the **Maximum Likelihood Estimation** (**MLE**) of parameters that define a **probability distribution**. MLE picks the parameter value θ that maximizes the likelihood function for the observed training data.

A look at the definitions highlights that **MAP differs from MLE by including the prior distribution**. In other words, unless the prior is a constant, the MAP estimate will differ from its MLE counterpart:

$$\theta_{\text{MLE}} = \arg\max_{\theta} P(X|\theta)$$

The MLE solution tends to reflect the frequentist notion that probability estimates should reflect observed ratios. On the other hand, the impact of the prior on the MAP estimate often corresponds to adding data that reflects the prior assumptions to the MLE. For example, a strong prior that a coin is biased can be incorporated in the MLE context by adding skewed trial data.

Prior distributions are a critical ingredient to Bayesian models. We will now introduce some convenient choices that facilitate analytical inference.

How to select priors

The prior should reflect knowledge about the distribution of the parameters because it influences the MAP estimate. If a prior is not known with certainty, we need to make a choice, often from several reasonable options. In general, it is good practice to justify the prior and check for robustness by testing whether alternatives lead to the same conclusion.

There are several types of priors:

- **Objective** priors maximize the impact of the data on the posterior. If the parameter distribution is unknown, we can select an uninformative prior like a uniform distribution, also called a *flat prior*, over a relevant range of parameter values.
- In contrast, **subjective** priors aim to incorporate information external to the model into the estimate. In the Black-Litterman context, the investor's belief about an asset's future return would be an example of a subjective prior.
- An **empirical** prior combines Bayesian and frequentist methods and uses historical data to eliminate subjectivity, for example, by estimating various moments to fit a standard distribution. Using some historical average of daily returns rather than a belief about future returns would be an example of a simple empirical prior.

In the context of an ML model, the prior can be viewed as a regularizer because it limits the values that the posterior can assume. Parameters that have zero prior probability, for instance, are not part of the posterior distribution. Generally, more good data allows for stronger conclusions and reduces the influence of the prior.

How to keep inference simple – conjugate priors

A prior distribution is conjugate with respect to the likelihood when the resulting posterior is of the same class or family of distributions as the prior, except for different parameters. For example, when both the prior and the likelihood are normally distributed, then the posterior is also normally distributed.

The conjugacy of prior and likelihood implies a **closed-form solution for the posterior** that facilitates the update process and avoids the need to use numerical methods to approximate the posterior. Moreover, the resulting posterior can be used as the prior for the next update step.

Let's illustrate this process using a binary classification example for stock price movements.

Dynamic probability estimates of asset price moves

When the data consists of binary Bernoulli random variables with a certain success probability for a positive outcome, the number of successes in repeated trials follows a binomial distribution. The conjugate prior is the beta distribution with support over the interval [0, 1] and two shape parameters to model arbitrary prior distributions over the success probability. Hence, the posterior distribution is also a beta distribution that we can derive by directly updating the parameters.

We will collect samples of different sizes of **binarized daily S&P 500 returns**, where the positive outcome is a price increase. Starting from an uninformative prior that allocates equal probability to each possible success probability in the interval [0, 1], we compute the posterior for different evidence samples.

The following code sample shows that the update consists of simply adding the observed numbers of success and failure to the parameters of the prior distribution to obtain the posterior:

```
n_days = [0, 1, 3, 5, 10, 25, 50, 100, 500]
outcomes = sp500_binary.sample(n_days[-1])
p = np.linspace(0, 1, 100)

# uniform (uninformative) prior
a = b = 1
for i, days in enumerate(n_days):
    up = outcomes.iloc[:days].sum()
    down = days - up
    update = stats.beta.pdf(p, a + up , b + down)
```

The resulting posterior distributions have been plotted in the following image. They illustrate the evolution from a uniform prior that views all success probabilities as equally likely to an increasingly peaked distribution.

After 500 samples, the probability is concentrated near the actual probability of a positive move at 54.7 percent from 2010 to 2017. It also shows the small differences between MLE and MAP estimates, where the latter tends to be pulled slightly toward the expected value of the uniform prior:

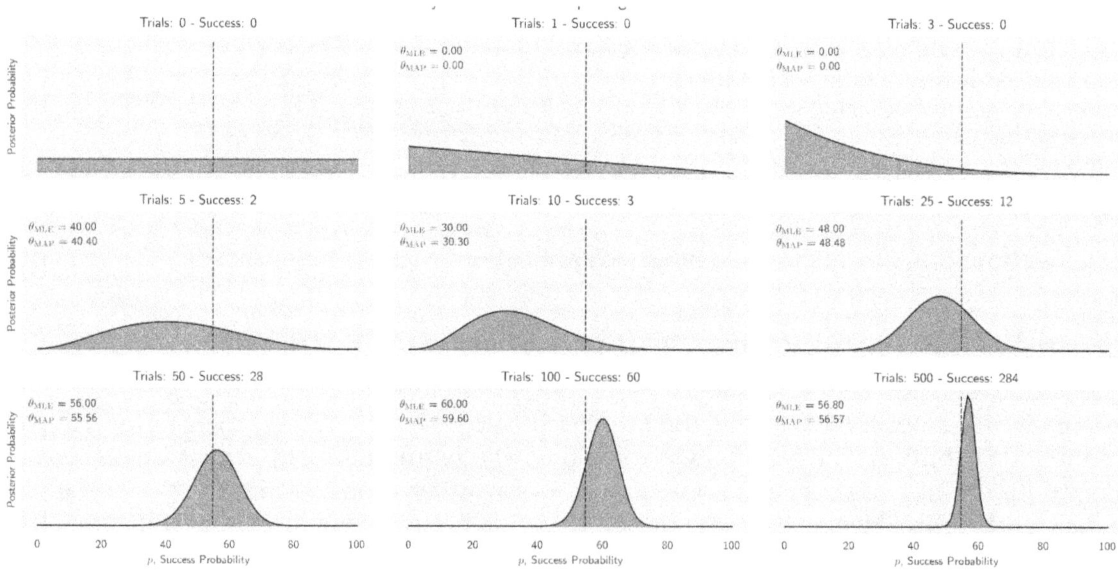

Figure 10.2: Posterior distributions of the probability that the S&P 500 goes up the next day after up to 500 updates

In practice, the use of conjugate priors is limited to low-dimensional cases. In addition, the simplified MAP approach avoids computing the evidence term but has a key shortcoming, even when it is available: it does not return a distribution so that we can derive a measure of uncertainty or use it as a prior. Hence, we need to resort to an approximate rather than exact inference using numerical methods and stochastic simulations, which we will introduce next.

Deterministic and stochastic approximate inference

For most models of practical relevance, it will not be possible to derive the exact posterior distribution analytically and compute expected values for the latent parameters. The model may have too many parameters, or the posterior distribution may be too complex for an analytical solution:

- For **continuous variables**, the integrals may not have closed-form solutions, while the dimensionality of the space and the complexity of the integrand may prohibit numerical integration.
- For **discrete variables**, the marginalizations involve summing over all possible configurations of the hidden variables, and though this is always possible in principle, we often find in practice that there may be exponentially many hidden states that render this calculation prohibitively expensive.

Although for some applications the posterior distribution over unobserved parameters will be of interest, most often, it is primarily required to evaluate expectations, for example, to make predictions. In such situations, we can rely on approximate inference, which includes stochastic and deterministic approaches:

- **Stochastic** techniques based on **Markov chain Monte Carlo** (**MCMC**) sampling have popularized the use of Bayesian methods across many domains. They generally have the property to converge to the exact result. In practice, sampling methods can be computationally demanding and are often limited to small-scale problems.
- **Deterministic** methods called **variational inference** or **variational Bayes** are based on analytical approximations to the posterior distribution and can scale well to large applications. They make simplifying assumptions, for example, that the posterior factorizes in a particular way or it has a specific parametric form, such as a Gaussian. Hence, they do not generate exact results and can be used as complements to sampling methods.

We will outline both approaches in the following two sections.

Markov chain MonteCarlo sampling

Sampling is about drawing samples $X=(x_1, \ldots, x_n)$ from a given distribution $p(x)$. Assuming the samples are independent, the law of large numbers ensures that for a growing number of samples, the fraction of a given instance x_i in the sample (for the discrete case) corresponds to its probability $p(x=x_i)$. In the continuous case, the analogous reasoning applies to a given region of the sample space. Hence, averages over samples can be used as unbiased estimators of the expected values of parameters of the distribution.

A practical challenge consists of ensuring independent sampling because the distribution is unknown. Dependent samples may still be unbiased, but tend to increase the variance of the estimate, so that more samples will be needed for an equally precise estimate as for independent samples.

Sampling from a multivariate distribution is computationally demanding as the number of states increases exponentially with the number of dimensions. Numerous algorithms facilitate the process; we will introduce a few popular variations of MCMC-based methods here.

A **Markov chain** is a dynamic stochastic model that describes a random walk over a set of states connected by transition probabilities. The Markov property stipulates that the process has no memory and that the next step only depends on the current state. In other words, this depends on whether the present, past, and future are independent, that is, information about past states does not help to predict the future beyond what we know from the present.

Monte Carlo methods rely on repeated random sampling to approximate results that may be deterministic but that do not permit an exact analytic solution. It was developed during the Manhattan Project to estimate energy at the atomic level and received its enduring code name to ensure secrecy.

Many algorithms apply the Monte Carlo method to a Markov chain and generally proceed as follows:

1. Start at the current position
2. Draw a new position from a proposal distribution
3. Evaluate the probability of the new position in light of data and prior distributions
    a. If sufficiently likely, move to the new position
    b. Otherwise, remain at the current position
4. Repeat from *step 1*
5. After a given number of iterations, return all accepted positions

MCMC methods aim to identify and explore interesting regions of the posterior that concentrate significant probability density. The memoryless process is said to converge when it consistently moves through nearby high-probability states of the posterior where the acceptance rate increases. A key challenge is to balance the need for random exploration of the sample space with the risk of reducing the acceptance rate.

The initial steps of the process are likely more reflective of the starting position than the posterior, and are typically discarded as *burn-in* **samples**. A key MCMC property is that the process should "forget" about its initial position after a certain (but unknown) number of iterations.

The remaining samples are called the **trace** of the process. Assuming convergence, the relative frequency of samples approximates the posterior and can be used to compute expected values based on the law of large numbers.

As already indicated, the precision of the estimate depends on the serial correlation of the samples collected by the random walk, each of which, by design, depends only on the previous state. Higher correlation limits the effective exploration of the posterior and needs to be subjected to diagnostic tests.

General techniques to design such a Markov chain include Gibbs sampling, the Metropolis-Hastings algorithm, and more recent Hamiltonian MCMC methods, which tend to perform better.

Gibbs sampling

Gibbs sampling simplifies multivariate sampling to a sequence of one-dimensional draws. From some starting point, it iteratively holds n-1 variables constant while sampling the nth variable. It incorporates this sample and repeats it.

The algorithm is very simple and easy to implement but produces highly correlated samples that slow down convergence. The sequential nature also prevents parallelization. See Casella and George (1992) for a detailed description and explanation.

Metropolis-Hastings sampling

The Metropolis-Hastings algorithm randomly proposes new locations based on its current state. It does so to effectively explore the sample space and reduce the correlation of samples relative to Gibbs sampling. To ensure that it samples from the posterior, it evaluates the proposal using the product of prior and likelihood, which is proportional to the posterior. It accepts with a probability that depends on the result relative to the corresponding value for the current sample.

A key benefit of the proposal evaluation method is that it works with a proportional rather than an exact evaluation of the posterior. However, it can take a long time to converge. This is because the random movements that are not related to the posterior can reduce the acceptance rate so that a large number of steps produces only a small number of (potentially correlated) samples. The acceptance rate can be tuned by reducing the variance of the proposal distribution, but the resulting smaller steps imply less exploration. See Chib and Greenberg (1995) for a detailed, introductory exposition of the algorithm.

Hamiltonian Monte Carlo – going NUTS

Hamiltonian Monte Carlo (**HMC**) is a hybrid method that leverages the first-order derivative information of the gradient of the likelihood. With this, it proposes new states for exploration and overcomes some of the MCMC challenges. In addition, it incorporates momentum to efficiently "jump around" the posterior. As a result, it converges faster to a high-dimensional target distribution than simpler random walk Metropolis or Gibbs sampling. See Betancourt (2018) for a comprehensive conceptual introduction.

The **No U-Turn Sampler** (**NUTS**, Hoffman and Gelman 2011) is a self-tuning HMC extension that adaptively regulates the size and number of moves around the posterior before selecting a proposal. It works well on high-dimensional and complex posterior distributions, and allows many complex models to be fit without specialized knowledge about the fitting algorithm itself. As we will see in the next section, it is the default sampler in **PyMC3**.

Variational inference and automatic differentiation

Variational inference (**VI**) is an ML method that approximates probability densities through optimization. In the Bayesian context, it approximates the posterior distribution, as follows:

1. Select a parametrized family of probability distributions
2. Find the member of this family closest to the target, as measured by Kullback-Leibler divergence

Compared to MCMC, variational Bayes tends to converge faster and scales better to large data. While MCMC approximates the posterior with samples from the chain that will eventually converge arbitrarily close to the target, variational algorithms approximate the posterior with the result of the optimization that is not guaranteed to coincide with the target.

Variational inference is better suited for large datasets, for example, hundreds of millions of text documents, so we can quickly explore many models. In contrast, MCMC will deliver more accurate results on smaller datasets or when time and computational resources pose fewer constraints. For example, MCMC would be a good choice if you had spent 20 years collecting a small but expensive dataset, are confident that your model is appropriate, and you require precise inferences. See Salimans, Kingma, and Welling (2015) for a more detailed comparison.

The downside of variational inference is the need for model-specific derivations and the implementation of a tailored optimization routine, which slows down widespread adoption.

The recent **Automatic Differentiation Variational Inference** (**ADVI**) algorithm automates this process so that the user only specifies the model, expressed as a program, and ADVI automatically generates a corresponding variational algorithm (see the references on GitHub for implementation details).

We will see that **PyMC3 supports various variational inference techniques**, including ADVI.

Probabilistic programming with PyMC3

Probabilistic programming provides a language to describe and fit probability distributions so that we can design, encode, and automatically estimate and evaluate complex models. It aims to abstract away some of the computational and analytical complexity to allow us to focus on the conceptually more straightforward and intuitive aspects of Bayesian reasoning and inference.

The field has become quite dynamic since new languages emerged after Uber open sourced Pyro (based on PyTorch). Google, more recently, added a probability module to TensorFlow.

As a result, the practical relevance and use of Bayesian methods in ML will likely increase to generate insights into uncertainty and, in particular, for use cases that require transparent rather than black-box models.

In this section, we will introduce the popular **PyMC3** library, which implements advanced MCMC sampling and variational inference for ML models using Python. Together with **Stan** (named after Stanislaw Ulam, who invented the Monte Carlo method, and developed by Andrew Gelman at Columbia University since 2012), PyMC3 is the most popular probabilistic programming language.

Bayesian machine learning with Theano

PyMC3 was released in January 2017 to add Hamiltonian MC methods to the Metropolis-Hastings sampler used in PyMC2 (released 2012). PyMC3 uses Theano as its computational backend for dynamic C compilation and automatic differentiation. Theano is a matrix-focused and GPU-enabled optimization library developed at Yoshua Bengio's **Montreal Institute for Learning Algorithms** (**MILA**), which inspired TensorFlow. MILA recently ceased to further develop Theano due to the success of newer deep learning libraries (see *Chapter 16*, *Word Embeddings for Earnings Calls and SEC Filings*, for details).

> PyMC4, released in alpha in December 2019, uses TensorFlow instead of Theano and aims to limit the impact on the API (see the link to the repository on GitHub).

The PyMC3 workflow – predicting a recession

PyMC3 aims for intuitive and readable, yet powerful, syntax that reflects how statisticians describe models. The modeling process generally follows these three steps:

1. Encode a probability model by defining:
    a. The prior distributions that quantify knowledge and uncertainty about latent variables
    b. The likelihood function that conditions the parameters on observed data

2. Analyze the posterior using one of the options described in the previous section:
    a. Obtain a point estimate using MAP inference
    b. Sample from the posterior using MCMC methods
    c. Approximate the posterior using variational Bayes
3. Check your model using various diagnostic tools
4. Generate predictions

The resulting model can be used for inference to gain detailed insights into parameter values, as well as to predict outcomes for new data points.

We will illustrate this workflow using a simple logistic regression to model the prediction of a recession (see the notebook `pymc3_workflow`). Subsequently, we will use PyMC3 to compute and compare Bayesian Sharpe ratios, estimate dynamic pairs trading ratios, and implement Bayesian linear time-series models.

The data – leading recession indicators

We will use a small and simple dataset so we can focus on the workflow. We will use the **Federal Reserve's Economic Data** (**FRED**) service (see *Chapter 2, Market and Fundamental Data – Sources and Techniques*) to download the US recession dates, as defined by the **National Bureau of Economic Research** (**NBER**). We will also source four variables that are commonly used to predict the onset of a recession (Kelley 2019) and available via FRED, namely:

- **The long-term spread of the treasury yield curve**, defined as the difference between the 10-year and the 3-month Treasury yields
- The University of Michigan's **consumer sentiment** indicator
- The **National Financial Conditions Index** (**NFCI**)
- The NFCI **nonfinancial leverage** subindex

The recession dates are identified on a quarterly basis; we will resample all series' frequency to monthly frequency to obtain some 457 observations from 1982-2019. If a quarter is labeled as a recession, we consider all months in that quarter as such.

We will build a model that intends to answer the question: **will the US economy be in recession x months into the future?** In other words, we do not focus on predicting only the first month of a recession; this limits the imbalance to 48 recessionary months.

To this end, we need to pick a lead time; plenty of research has been conducted into a suitable time horizon for various leading indicators: the yield curve tends to send signals up to 24 months ahead of a recession; the NFCI indicators tend to have a shorter lead time (see Kelley, 2019).

The following table largely confirms this experience: it displays the mutual information (see *Chapter 6*, *The Machine Learning Process*) between the binary recession variable and the four leading indicators for horizons from 1-24 months:

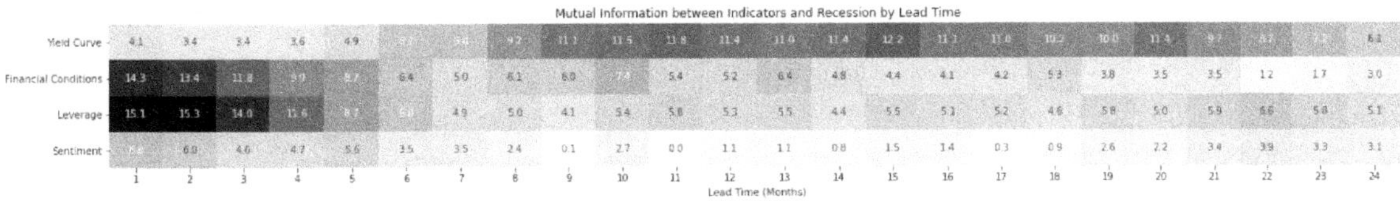

Figure 10.3: Mutual information between recession and leading indicators for horizons from 1-24 months

To strike a balance between the shorter horizon for the NFCI indicators and the yield curve, we will pick 12 months as our prediction horizon. The following plots are for the distribution of each indicator, broken down by recession status:

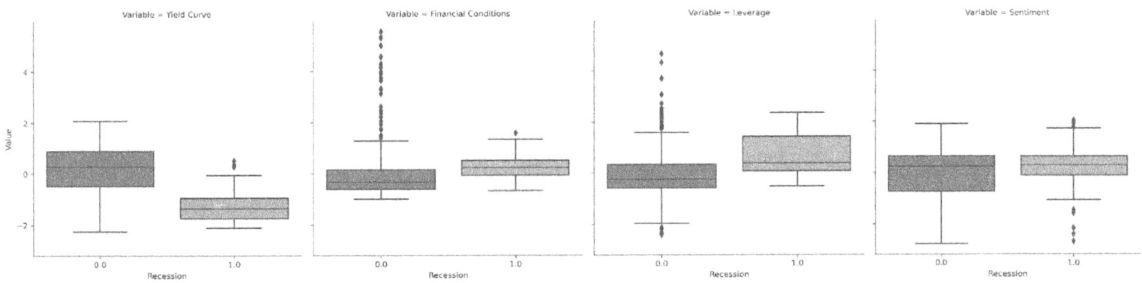

Figure 10.4: Leading indicator distributions by recession status

This shows that recessions tend to be associated with a negative long-term spread of the treasury yield curve, also known as an **inverted yield curve**, when short-term interest rates rise above long-term rates. The NFCI indicators behave as we would expect; the sentiment indicator appears to have the weakest association.

Model definition – Bayesian logistic regression

As discussed in *Chapter 6*, *The Machine Learning Process*, logistic regression estimates a linear relationship between a set of features and a binary outcome, mediated by a sigmoid function to ensure the model produces probabilities. The frequentist approach resulted in point estimates for the parameters that measure the influence of each feature on the probability that a data point belongs to the positive class, with confidence intervals based on assumptions about the parameter distribution.

In contrast, Bayesian logistic regression estimates the posterior distribution over the parameters itself. The posterior allows for more robust estimates of what is called a **Bayesian credible interval** for each parameter, with the benefit of more transparency about the model's uncertainty.

A probabilistic program consists of **observed and unobserved random variables** (**RVs**). As discussed previously, we define the observed RVs via likelihood distributions and unobserved RVs via prior distributions. PyMC3 includes numerous probability distributions for this purpose.

The PyMC3 library makes it very straightforward to perform approximate Bayesian inference for logistic regression. Logistic regression models the probability that the economy will be in recession 12 months after month *i* based on *k* features, as outlined on the left side of the following figure:

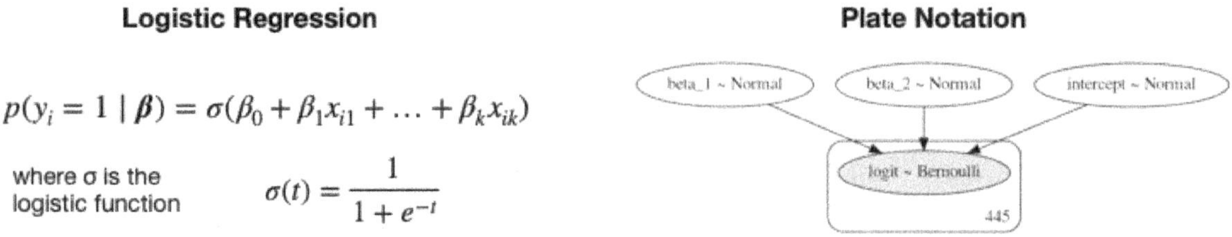

Figure 10.5: Bayesian logistic regression

We will use the context manager `with` to define a `manual_logistic_model` that we can refer to later as a probabilistic model:

1. The RVs for the unobserved parameters for intercept and two features are expressed using uninformative priors, These assume normal distributions with a mean of 0 and a standard deviation of 100.
2. The likelihood combines the parameters with the data according to the specification of the logistic regression.
3. The outcome is modeled as a Bernoulli RV with the success probability given by the likelihood:

```
with pm.Model() as manual_logistic_model:
    # coefficients as rvs with uninformative priors
    intercept = pm.Normal('intercept', 0, sd=100)
    beta_1 = pm.Normal('beta_1', 0, sd=100)
    beta_2 = pm.Normal('beta_2', 0, sd=100)

    # Likelihood transforms rvs into probabilities p(y=1)
    # according to logistic regression model.
    likelihood = pm.invlogit(intercept +
                             beta_1 * data.yield_curve +
                             beta_2 * data.leverage)

    # Outcome as Bernoulli rv with success probability
    # given by sigmoid function conditioned on actual data
    pm.Bernoulli(name='logit',
                 p=likelihood,
                 observed=data.recession)
```

Model visualization and plate notation

The command `pm.model_to_graphviz(manual_logistic_model)` produces the plate notation displayed on the right in *Figure 10.5*. It shows the unobserved parameters as light ovals and the observed elements as dark ovals. The rectangle indicates the number of repetitions of the observed model element implied by the data that are included in the model definition.

The generalized linear models module

PyMC3 includes numerous common models so that we can limit the manual specification for custom applications.

The following code defines the same logistic regression as a member of the **Generalized Linear Models** (**GLM**) family. It does so using the formula format inspired by the statistical language R and is ported to Python by the patsy library:

```
with pm.Model() as logistic_model:
    pm.glm.GLM.from_formula(recession ~ yield_curve + leverage,
                            data,
                            family=pm.glm.families.Binomial())
```

Exact MAP inference

We obtain point MAP estimates for the three parameters using the just-defined model's `.find_MAP()` method. As expected, a lower spread value increases the recession probability, as does higher leverage (but to a lesser extent):

```
with logistic_model:
    map_estimate = pm.find_MAP()
print_map(map_estimate)
Intercept     -4.892884
yield_curve   -3.032943
leverage       1.534055
```

PyMC3 solves the optimization problem of finding the posterior point with the highest density using the quasi-Newton **Broyden-Fletcher-Goldfarb-Shanno** (**BFGS**) algorithm, but offers several alternatives provided by the SciPy library.

The MAP point estimates are identical to the corresponding `statsmodels` coefficients (see the notebook `pymc3_workflow`).

Approximate inference – MCMC

If we are only interested in point estimates for the model parameters, then for this simple model, the MAP estimate would be sufficient. More complex, custom probabilistic models require sampling techniques to obtain a posterior probability for the parameters.

We will use the model with all its variables to illustrate MCMC inference:

```
formula = 'recession ~ yield_curve + leverage + financial_conditions +
sentiment'

with pm.Model() as logistic_model:
    pm.glm.GLM.from_formula(formula=formula,
                            data=data,
                            family=pm.glm.families.Binomial())

# note that pymc3 uses y for the outcome
logistic_model.basic_RVs
[Intercept, yield_curve, leverage, financial_conditions, sentiment, y]
```

Note that variables measured on very different scales can slow down the sampling process. Hence, we first apply the `scale()` function provided by scikit-learn to standardize all features.

Once we have defined our model like this with the new formula, we are ready to perform inference to approximate the posterior distribution. MCMC sampling algorithms are available through the `pm.sample()` function.

By default, PyMC3 automatically selects the most efficient sampler and initializes the sampling process for efficient convergence. For a continuous model, PyMC3 chooses the NUTS sampler discussed in the previous section. It also runs variational inference via ADVI to find good starting parameters for the sampler. One among several alternatives is to use the MAP estimate.

To see what convergence looks like, we first draw only 100 samples after tuning the sampler for 1,000 iterations. These will be discarded. The sampling process can be parallelized for multiple chains using the `cores` argument (except when using GPU):

```
with logistic_model:
    trace = pm.sample(draws=100,
                      tune=1000,
                      init='adapt_diag',
                      chains=4,
                      cores=4,
                      random_seed=42)
```

The resulting `trace` contains the sampled values for each RV. We can inspect the posterior distribution of the chains using the `plot_traces()` function:

```
plot_traces(trace, burnin=0)
```

Figure 10.6 shows both the sample distribution and their values over time for the first two features and the intercept (see the notebook for the full output). At this point, the sampling process has not converged since for each of the features, the four traces yield quite different results; the numbers shown vertically in the left five panels are the averages of the modes of the distributions generated by the four traces:

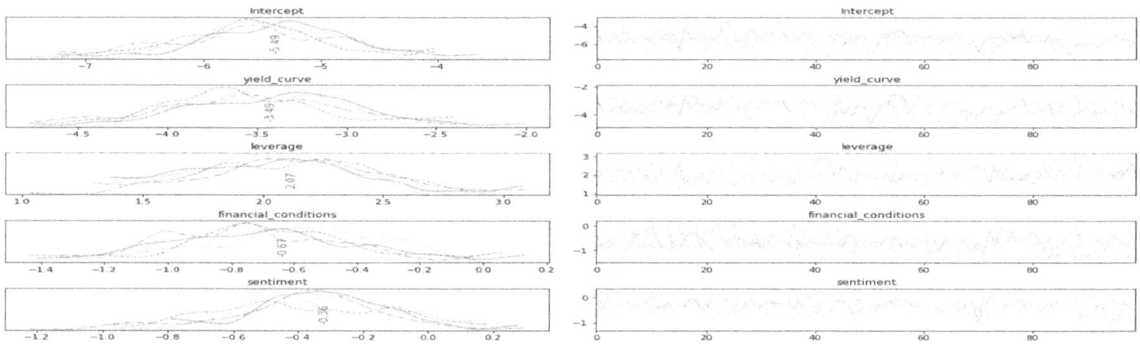

Figure 10.6: Traces after 100 samples

We can continue sampling by providing the trace of a prior run as input. After an additional 20,000 samples, we observe a much different picture, as shown in the following figure. This shows how the sampling process is now much closer to convergence. Also, note that the initial coefficient point estimates were relatively close to the current values:

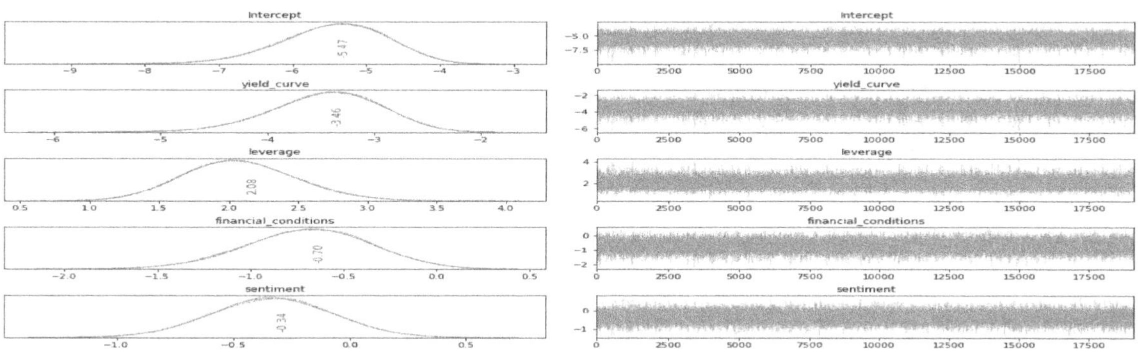

Figure 10.7: Traces after an additional 50,000 samples

We can compute the **credible intervals**, the Bayesian counterpart of confidence intervals, as percentiles of the trace. The resulting boundaries reflect our confidence about the range of the parameter value for a given probability threshold, as opposed to the number of times the parameter will be within this range for a large number of trials. *Figure 10.8* shows the credible intervals for the variables' yield curve and leverage, expressed in terms of the odds ratio that results from raising *e* to the power of the coefficient value (see *Chapter 7*, *Linear Models – From Risk Factors to Return Forecasts*).

See the notebook `pymc3_workflow` for the implementation:

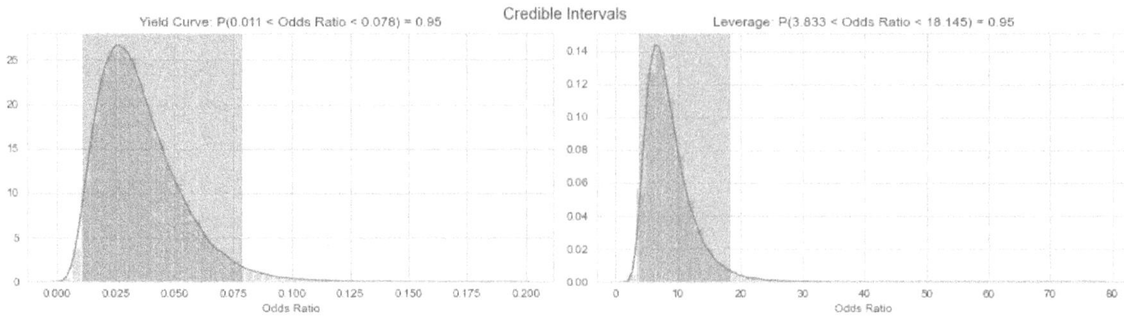

Figure 10.8: Credible intervals for yield curve and leverage

Approximate inference – variational Bayes

The interface for variational inference is very similar to the MCMC implementation. We just use `fit()` instead of the `sample()` function, with the option to include an early stopping `CheckParametersConvergence` callback if the distribution-fitting process converges up to a given tolerance:

```
with logistic_model:
    callback = CheckParametersConvergence(diff='absolute')
    approx = pm.fit(n=100000,
                    callbacks=[callback])
```

We can draw samples from the approximated distribution to obtain a trace object, as we did previously for the MCMC sampler:

```
trace_advi = approx.sample(10000)
```

Inspection of the trace summary shows that the results are slightly less accurate.

Model diagnostics

Bayesian model diagnostics includes validating that the sampling process has converged and consistently samples from high-probability areas of the posterior, as well as confirming that the model represents the data well.

Convergence

We can visualize the samples over time and their distributions to check the quality of the results. The charts shown in the following image show the posterior distributions after an initial 100 and an additional 200,000 samples, respectively, and illustrate how convergence implies that multiple chains identify the same distribution:

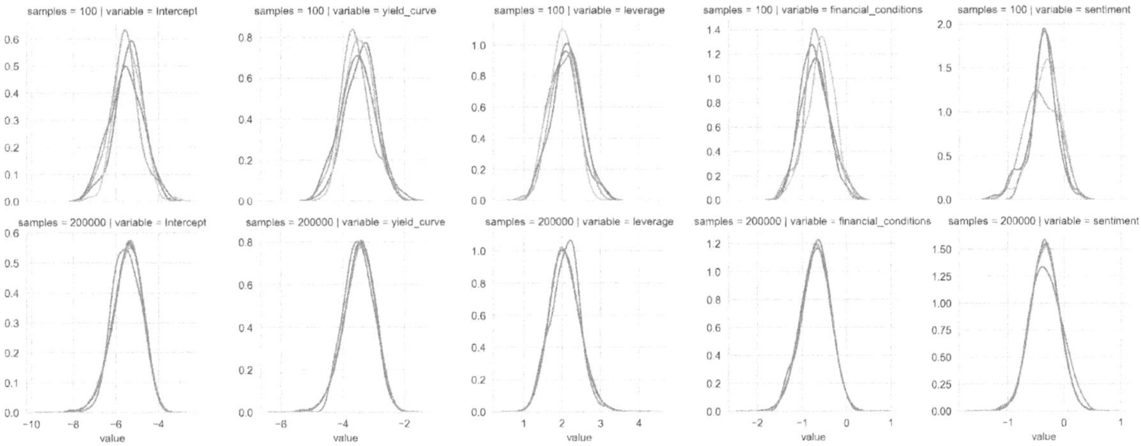

Figure 10.9: Traces after 400 and after over 200,000 samples

PyMC3 produces various summary statistics for a sampler. These are available as individual functions in the stats module, or by providing a trace to the function `pm.summary()`.

The following table includes the (separately computed) statsmodels logit coefficients in the first column to show that, in this simple case, both models slightly agree because the sample mean does not match the coefficients. This is likely due to the high degree of quasi-separation: the yield curve's high predictability allows for the perfect prediction of 17 percent of the data points, which, in turn, leads to poorly defined MLE estimates for the logistic regression (see the statsmodels output in the notebook for more information):

Parameters	statsmodels	PyMC3					
	Coefficients	Mean	SD	HPD 3%	HPD 97%	Effective Samples	R hat
Intercept	-5.22	-5.47	0.71	-6.82	-4.17	68,142	1.00
yield_curve	-3.30	-3.47	0.51	-4.44	-2.55	70,479	1.00
leverage	1.98	2.08	0.40	1.34	2.83	72,639	1.00
financial_ conditions	-0.65	-0.70	0.33	-1.33	-0.07	91,104	1.00
sentiment	-0.33	-0.34	0.26	-0.82	0.15	106,751	1.00

The remaining columns contain the **highest posterior density** (HPD) estimate for the minimum width credible interval, the Bayesian version of a confidence interval, which, here, is computed at the 95 percent level. The `n_eff` statistic summarizes the number of effective (not rejected) samples resulting from the ~100,000 draws.

R-hat, also known as the **Gelman-Rubin statistic**, checks convergence by comparing the variance between chains to the variance within each chain. If the sampler converged, these variances should be identical, that is, the chains should look similar. Hence, the statistic should be near 1.

For high-dimensional models with many variables, it becomes cumbersome to inspect numerous traces. When using NUTS, the energy plot helps us assess problems of convergence. It summarizes how efficiently the random process explores the posterior. The plot shows the energy and the energy transition matrix, which should be well matched, as in the example shown in the right-hand panel of the following image:

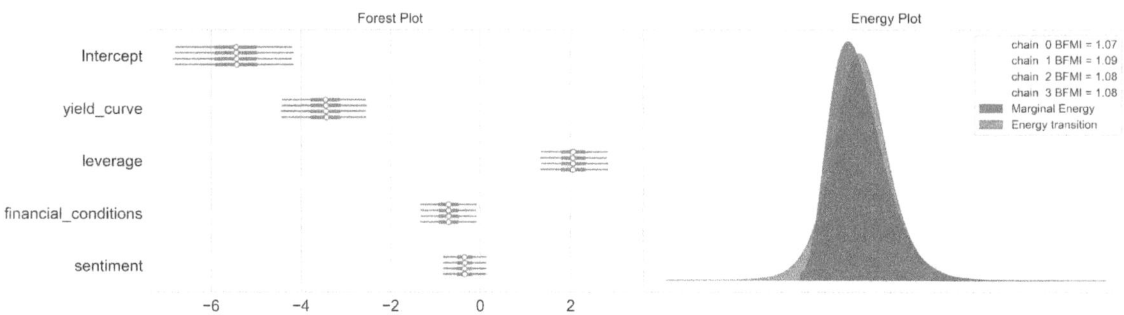

Figure 10.10: Forest and energy plot

Posterior predictive checks

Posterior predictive checks (**PPCs**) are very useful for examining how well a model fits the data. They do so by generating data from the model using parameters from draws from the posterior. We use the function `pm.sample_ppc` for this purpose and obtain n samples for each observation (the GLM module automatically names the outcome `'y'`):

```
ppc = pm.sample_ppc(trace_NUTS, samples=500, model=logistic_model)
ppc['y'].shape
(500, 445)
```

We can evaluate the in-sample fit using the area under the receiver-operating characteristic curve (AUC, see *Chapter 6, The Machine Learning Process*) score to, for example, compare different models:

```
roc_auc_score(y_score=np.mean(ppc['y'], axis=0),
              y_true=data.income)
0.9483627204030226
```

The result is fairly high at almost 0.95.

How to generate predictions

Predictions use Theano's *shared variables* to replace the training data with test data before running posterior predictive checks. To allow for visualization and to simplify the exposition, we use the yield curve variable as the only predictor and ignore the time-series nature of our data.

Instead, we create the train and test sets using scikit-learn's basic `train_test_split()` function, stratified by the outcome, to maintain the class imbalance:

```
X = data[['yield_curve']]
labels = X.columns
y = data.recession
X_train, X_test, y_train, y_test = train_test_split(X, y,
                                                    test_size=0.2,
                                                    random_state=42,
                                                    stratify=y)
```

We then create a shared variable for that training set, which we replace with the test set in the next step. Note that we need to use NumPy arrays and provide a list of column labels:

```
X_shared = theano.shared(X_train.values)
with pm.Model() as logistic_model_pred:
    pm.glm.GLM(x=X_shared, labels=labels,
               y=y_train, family=pm.glm.families.Binomial())
```

We then run the sampler, as we did previously:

```
with logistic_model_pred:
    pred_trace = pm.sample(draws=10000,
                           tune=1000,
                           chains=2,
                           cores=2,
                           init='adapt_diag')
```

Now, we substitute the test data for the train data on the shared variable and apply the `pm.sample_ppc` function to the resulting `trace`:

```
X_shared.set_value(X_test)
ppc = pm.sample_ppc(pred_trace,
                    model=logistic_model_pred,
                    samples=100)
y_score = np.mean(ppc['y'], axis=0)
roc_auc_score(y_score=np.mean(ppc['y'], axis=0),
              y_true=y_test)
0.8386
```

The AUC score for this simple model is 0.86. Clearly, it is much easier to predict the same recession for another month if the training set already includes examples of this recession from nearby months. Keep in mind that we are using this model for demonstration purposes only.

Figure 10.11 plots the predictions that were sampled from the 100 Monte Carlo chain and the uncertainty surrounding them, as well as the actual binary outcomes and the logistic curve corresponding to the model predictions:

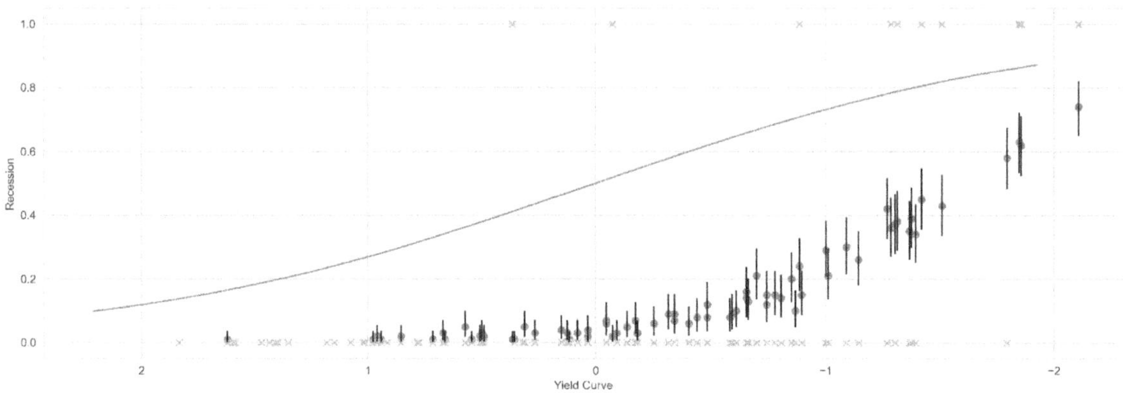

Figure 10.11: Single-variable model predictions

Summary and key takeaways

We have built a simple logistic regression model to predict the probability that the US economy will be in recession in 12 months using four leading indicators. For this simple model, we could get exact MAP estimates of the coefficient values, which we could then use to parameterize the model and make predictions.

However, more complex, custom probability models will not allow for this shortcut, and MAP estimates also do not generate insight into the posterior distribution beyond the point estimate. For this reason, we demonstrated how to run approximate inference using PyMC3. The results illustrated how we learn about the posterior distribution for each of the model parameters, but also showed that even for a small model, the computational cost increases considerably compared to statsmodels MLE estimates. Nonetheless, for sophisticated probabilistic models, sampling-based solutions are the only way to learn about the data.

We will now proceed to illustrate how to apply Bayesian analysis to some trading-related use cases.

Bayesian ML for trading

Now that we are familiar with the Bayesian approach to ML and probabilistic programming with PyMC3, let's explore a few relevant trading-related applications, namely:

- Modeling the Sharpe ratio as a probabilistic model for more insightful performance comparison
- Computing pairs trading hedge ratios using Bayesian linear regression
- Analyzing linear time series models from a Bayesian perspective

Thomas Wiecki, one of the main PyMC3 authors who also leads Data Science at Quantopian, has created several examples that the following sections follow and build on. The PyMC3 documentation has many additional tutorials (see GitHub for links).

Bayesian Sharpe ratio for performance comparison

In this section, we will illustrate:

- How to define the **Sharpe Ratio** (**SR**) as a probabilistic model using PyMC3
- How to compare its posterior distributions for different return series

The Bayesian estimation for two series offers very rich insights because it provides the complete distributions of the credible values for the effect size, the group SR means and their difference, as well as standard deviations and their difference. The Python implementation is due to Thomas Wiecki and was inspired by the R package BEST (Meredith and Kruschke, 2018).

Relevant use cases of a Bayesian SR include the analysis of differences between alternative strategies, or between a strategy's in-sample return and its out-of-sample return (see the notebook `bayesian_sharpe_ratio` for details). The Bayesian SR is also part of pyfolio's Bayesian tearsheet.

Defining a custom probability model

To model the SR as a probabilistic model, we need the priors about the distribution of returns and the parameters that govern this distribution. The Student t distribution exhibits fat tails relative to the normal distribution for low **degrees of freedom** (**DF**), and is a reasonable choice to capture this aspect of returns.

We thus need to **model the three parameters of this distribution**, namely the mean and standard deviation of returns, and the DF. We'll assume normal and uniform distributions for the mean and the standard deviation, respectively, and an exponential distribution for the DF with a sufficiently low expected value to ensure fat tails.

The returns are based on these probabilistic inputs, and the annualized SR results from the standard computation, ignoring a risk-free rate (using daily returns). We will provide AMZN stock returns from 2010-2018 as input (see the notebook for more on data preparation):

```
mean_prior = data.stock.mean()
std_prior = data.stock.std()
std_low = std_prior / 1000
std_high = std_prior * 1000

with pm.Model() as sharpe_model:
    mean = pm.Normal('mean', mu=mean_prior, sd=std_prior)
    std = pm.Uniform('std', lower=std_low, upper=std_high)
    nu = pm.Exponential('nu_minus_two', 1 / 29, testval=4) + 2
    returns = pm.StudentT('returns', nu=nu, mu=mean, sd=std,
observed=data.stock)

    sharpe = returns.distribution.mean / returns.distribution.variance **
.5 * np.sqrt(252)
    pm.Deterministic('sharpe', sharpe)
```

The plate notation, which we introduced in the previous section on the PyMC3 workflow, visualizes the three parameters and their relationships, along with the returns and the number of observations we provided in the following diagram:

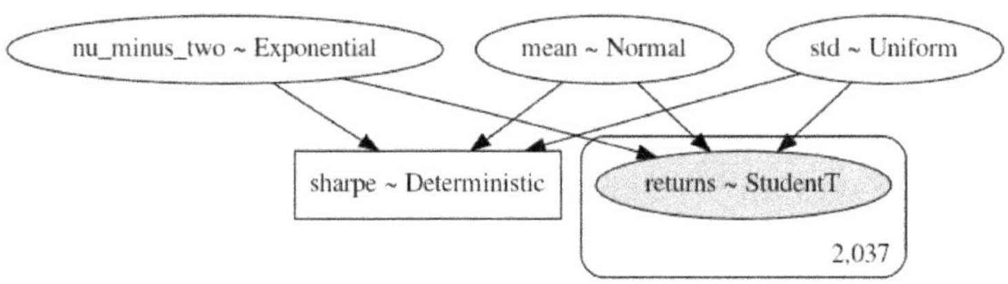

Figure 10.12: The Bayesian SR in plate notation

We then run the MCMC sampling process we introduced in the previous section (see the notebook `bayesian_sharpe_ratio` for the implementation details that follow the familiar workflow). After some 25,000 samples for each of four chains, we obtain the posterior distributions for the model parameters as follows, with the results appearing in the following plots:

```
plot_posterior(data=trace);
```

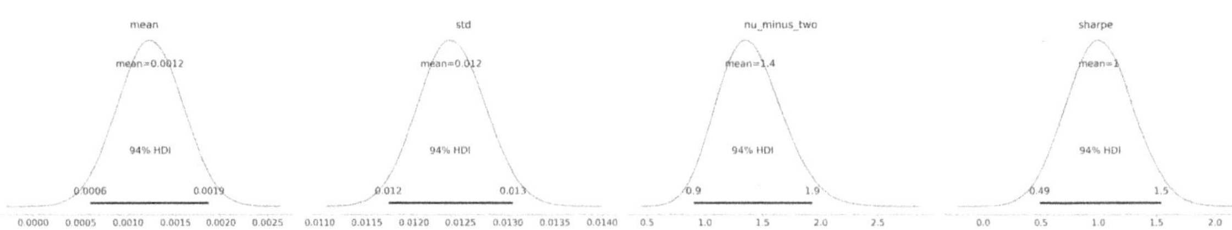

Figure 10.13: The posterior distribution for the model parameters

Now that we know how to evaluate the SR for a single asset or portfolio, let's see how we can compare the performance of two different return series using the Bayesian SR.

Comparing the performance of two return series

To compare the performance of two return series, we will model each group's SR separately and compute the effect size as the difference between the volatility-adjusted returns. The corresponding probability model, displayed in the following diagram, is naturally larger because it includes two SRs, plus their difference:

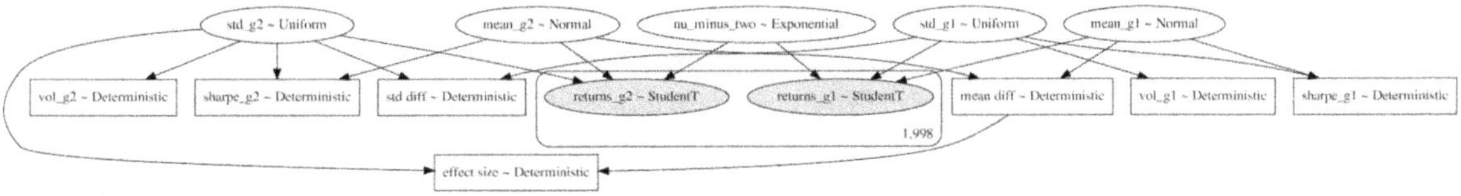

Figure 10.14: The difference between two Bayesian SRs in plate notation

Once we have defined the model, we run it through the MCMC sampling process to obtain the posterior distribution for its parameters. We use 2,037 daily returns for the AMZN stock 2010-2018 and compare it with S&P 500 returns for the same period. We could use the returns on any of our strategy backtests instead of the AMZN returns.

Visualizing the traces reveals granular performance insights into the distributions of each metric, as illustrated by the various plots in *Figure 10.15*:

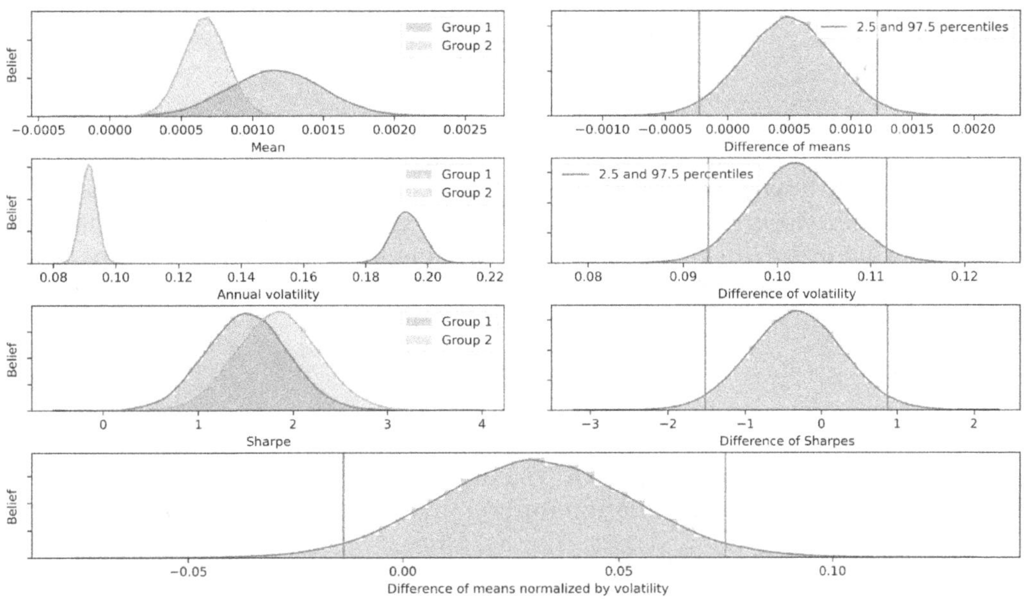

Figure 10.15: The posterior distributions for the differences between two Bayesian SRs

The most important metric is the difference between the two SRs in the bottom panel. Given the full posterior distribution, it is straightforward to visualize or compute the probability that one return series is superior from an SR perspective.

Bayesian rolling regression for pairs trading

In the previous chapter, we introduced pairs trading as a popular trading strategy that relies on the cointegration of two or more assets. Given such assets, we need to estimate the hedging ratio to decide on the relative magnitude of long and short positions. A basic approach uses linear regression. You can find the code for this section in the notebook `rolling_regression`, which follows Thomas Wiecki's rolling regression example (see the link to the PyMC3 tutorials on GitHub).

A popular example of pairs trading candidates is ETF GLD, which reflects the gold price and a gold mining stock like GFI. We source the close price data using yfinance for the 2004-2020 period. The left panel of *Figure 10.16* shows the historical price series, while the right panel shows a scatter plot of historical prices, where the hue indicates the time dimension to highlight how the correlation appears to have been evolving. **Note that we should be using the returns**, as we did in *Chapter 9, Time-Series Models for Volatility Forecasts and Statistical Arbitrage*, to compute the hedge ratio; however, using the prices series creates more striking visualizations. The modeling process itself remains unaffected:

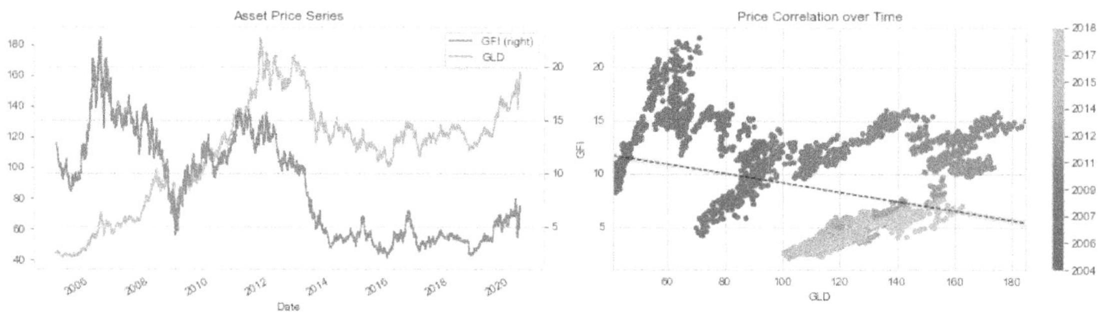

Figure 10.16: Price series and correlation over time of two pairs of trading candidates

We want to illustrate how a rolling Bayesian linear regression can track changes in the relationship between the prices of the two assets over time. The main idea is to incorporate the time dimension into a linear regression by allowing for changes in the regression coefficients. Specifically, we will assume that intercept and slope follow a random walk through time:

$$\alpha_t \sim N(\alpha_{t-1}, \sigma_\alpha^2)$$
$$\beta_t \sim N(\beta_{t-1}, \sigma_\beta^2)$$

We specify `model_randomwalk` using PyMC3's built-in `pm.GaussianRandomWalk` process. It requires us to define a standard deviation for both intercept alpha and slope beta:

```
model_randomwalk = pm.Model()
with model_randomwalk:
    sigma_alpha = pm.Exponential('sigma_alpha', 50.)
    alpha = pm.GaussianRandomWalk('alpha',
                                  sd=sigma_alpha,
                                  shape=len(prices))
```

```
    sigma_beta = pm.Exponential('sigma_beta', 50.)
    beta = pm.GaussianRandomWalk('beta',
                                 sd=sigma_beta,
                                 shape=len(prices))
```

Given the specification of the probabilistic model, we will now define the regression and connect it to the input data:

```
with model_randomwalk:
    # Define regression
    regression = alpha + beta * prices_normed.GLD
    # Assume prices are normally distributed
    # Get mean from regression.
    sd = pm.HalfNormal('sd', sd=.1)
    likelihood = pm.Normal('y',
                           mu=regression,
                           sd=sd,
                           observed=prices_normed.GFI)
```

Now, we can run our MCMC sampler to generate the posterior distribution for the model parameters:

```
with model_randomwalk:
    trace_rw = pm.sample(tune=2000,
                         cores=4,
                         draws=200,
                         nuts_kwargs=dict(target_accept=.9))
```

Figure 10.17 depicts how the intercept and slope coefficients have changed over the years, underlining the evolving correlations:

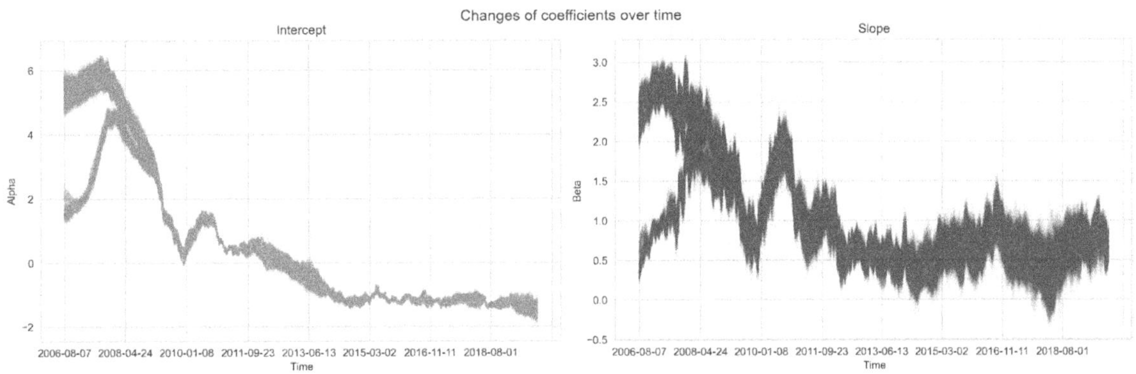

Figure 10.17: Changes in intercept and slope coefficients over time

Using the dynamic regression coefficients, we can now visualize how the hedge ratio suggested by the rolling regression would have changed over the years using this Bayesian approach, which models the coefficients as a random walk.

The following plot combines the prices series and the regression lines, where the hue once again indicates the timeline (view this in the notebook for the color output):

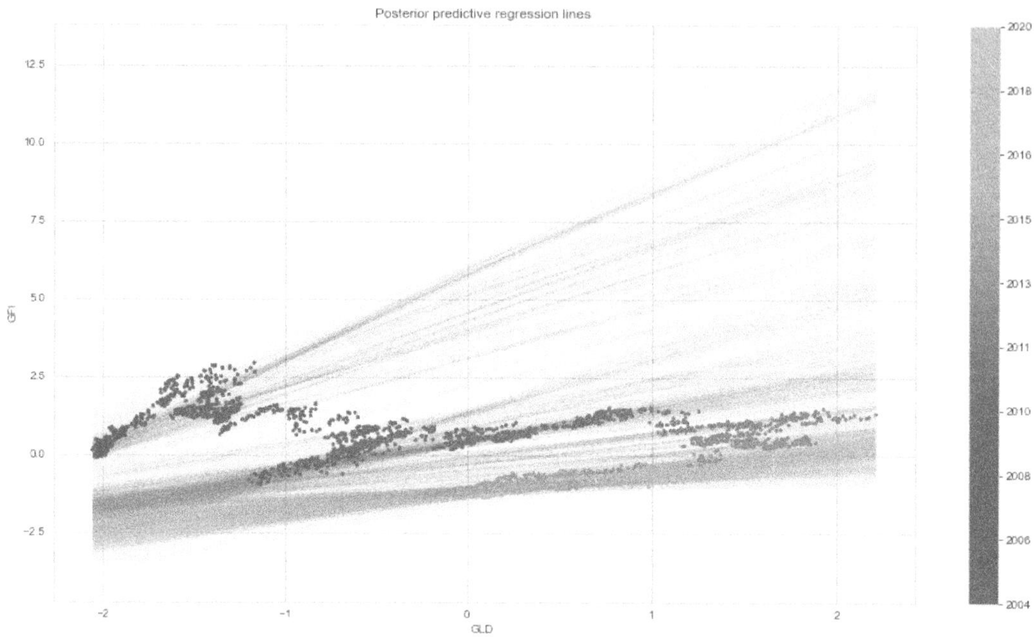

Figure 10.18: Rolling regression lines and price series

For our last example, we'll implement a Bayesian stochastic volatility model.

Stochastic volatility models

As discussed in the previous chapter, asset prices have time-varying volatility. In some periods, returns are highly variable, while in others, they are very stable. We covered ARCH/GARCH models that approach this challenge from a classical linear regression perspective in *Chapter 9, Time-Series Models for Volatility Forecasts and Statistical Arbitrage*.

Bayesian stochastic volatility models capture this volatility phenomenon with a latent volatility variable, modeled as a stochastic process. The No-U-Turn Sampler was introduced using such a model (Hoffman, et al. 2011), and the notebook `stochastic_volatility` illustrates this use case with daily data for the S&P 500 after 2000. *Figure 10.19* shows several volatility clusters throughout the period:

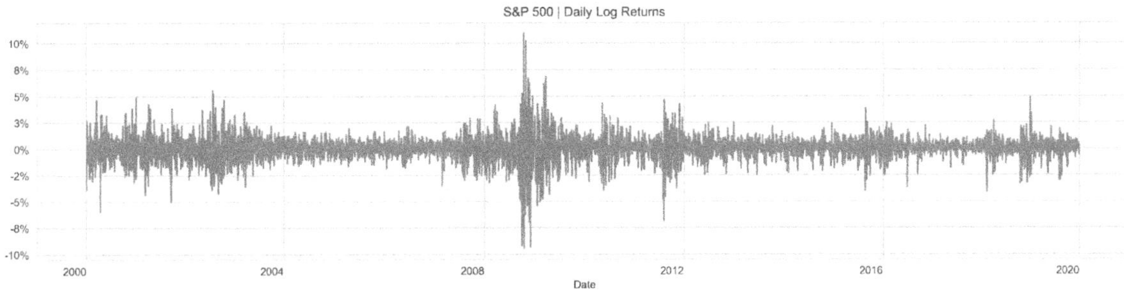

Figure 10.19: Daily S&P 500 log returns

The probabilistic model specifies that the log returns follow a t-distribution, which has fat tails, as also generally observed for asset returns. The t-distribution is governed by the parameter ν, which represents the DF. It is also called the normality parameter because the t-distribution approaches the normal distribution as ν increases. This parameter is assumed to have an exponential distribution with parameter $\lambda = 0.1$.

Furthermore, the log returns are assumed to have mean zero, while the standard deviation follows a random walk with a standard deviation that also has an exponential distribution:

$$\nu \sim \text{Exponential}(.1)$$
$$\sigma \sim \text{Exponential}(50)$$

$$s_i \sim \text{Normal}(s_{i-1}, \sigma^{-2})$$

$$\log(r_i) \sim t(\nu, 0, \exp(-2s_i))$$

We implement this model in PyMC3 as follows to mirror its probabilistic specification, using log returns to match the model:

```
prices = pd.read_hdf('../data/assets.h5', key='sp500/prices').loc['2000':,
                                                                   'Close']
log_returns = np.log(prices).diff().dropna()

with pm.Model() as model:
    step_size = pm.Exponential('sigma', 50.)
    s = GaussianRandomWalk('s', sd=step_size,
                           shape=len(log_returns))
    nu = pm.Exponential('nu', .1)
    r = pm.StudentT('r', nu=nu,
                    lam=pm.math.exp(-2*s),
                    observed=log_returns)
```

Next, we draw 5,000 NUTS samples after a burn-in period of 2,000 samples, using a higher acceptance rate than the default of 0.8, as recommended for problematic posteriors by the PyMC3 docs (see the appropriate links on GitHub):

```
with model:
    trace = pm.sample(tune=2000,
                      draws=5000,
                      nuts_kwargs=dict(target_accept=.9))
```

```
Auto-assigning NUTS sampler...
Initializing NUTS using jitter+adapt_diag...
Multiprocess sampling (4 chains in 4 jobs)
NUTS: [nu, s, sigma]
Sampling 4 chains, 0 divergences: 100%|██████████| 28000/28000 [27:46<00:00,
16.80draws/s]
The estimated number of effective samples is smaller than 200 for some
parameters.
```

After 28,000 total samples for the four chains, the trace plot in the following image confirms that the sampling process has converged:

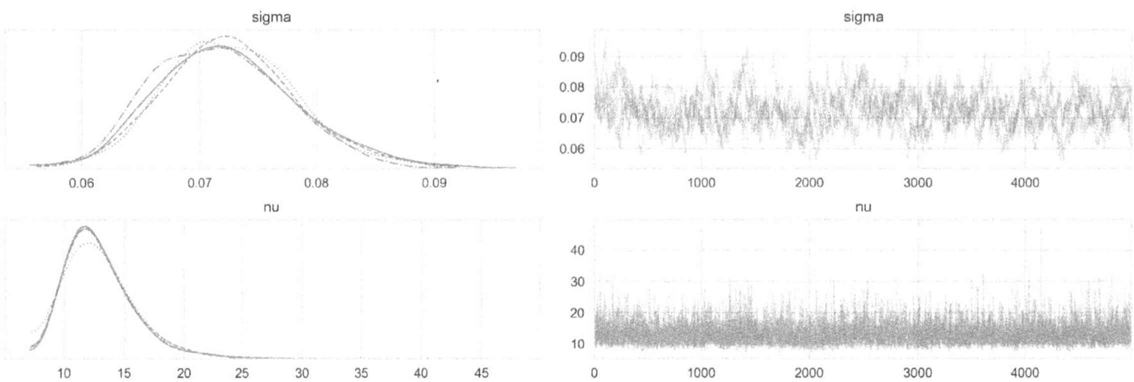

Figure 10.20: Trace plot for the stochastic volatility model

When we plot the samples against the S&P 500 returns in *Figure 10.21*, we see that this simple stochastic volatility model tracks the volatility clusters fairly well:

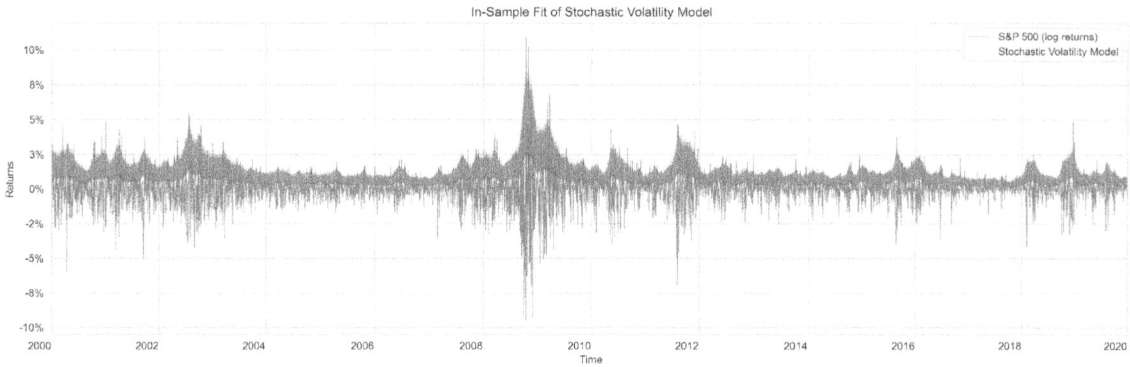

Figure 10.21: Model

Keep in mind that this represents the in-sample fit. As a next step, you should try to evaluate the predictive accuracy. We covered how to make predictions in the previous subsection on rolling linear regression and used time-series cross validation in several previous chapters, which provides you with all the tools you need for this purpose!

Summary

In this chapter, we explored Bayesian approaches to machine learning. We saw that they have several advantages, including the ability to encode prior knowledge or opinions, deeper insights into the uncertainty surrounding model estimates and predictions, and suitability for online learning, where each training sample incrementally impacts the model's prediction.

We learned to apply the Bayesian workflow from model specification to estimation, diagnostics, and prediction using PyMC3 and explored several relevant applications. We will encounter more Bayesian models in *Chapter 14*, *Text Data for Trading – Sentiment Analysis*, where we'll discuss natural language processing and topic modeling, and in *Chapter 20*, *Autoencoders for Conditional Risk Factors and Asset Pricing*, where we'll introduce variational autoencoders.

The next chapter introduces nonlinear, tree-based models, namely decision trees, and shows how to combine multiple models into an ensemble of trees to create a random forest.

11

Random Forests – A Long-Short Strategy for Japanese Stocks

In this chapter, we will learn how to use two new classes of machine learning models for trading: **decision trees** and **random forests**. We will see how decision trees learn rules from data that encode nonlinear relationships between the input and the output variables. We will illustrate how to train a decision tree and use it for prediction with regression and classification problems, visualize and interpret the rules learned by the model, and tune the model's hyperparameters to optimize the bias-variance trade-off and prevent overfitting.

Decision trees are not only important standalone models but are also frequently used as components in other models. In the second part of this chapter, we will introduce ensemble models that combine multiple individual models to produce a single aggregate prediction with lower prediction-error variance.

We will illustrate **bootstrap aggregation**, often called *bagging*, as one of several methods to randomize the construction of individual models and reduce the correlation of the prediction errors made by an ensemble's components. We will illustrate how bagging effectively reduces the variance and learn how to configure, train, and tune random forests. We will see how random forests, as an ensemble of a (potentially large) number of decision trees, can dramatically reduce prediction errors, at the expense of some loss in interpretation.

Then, we will proceed and build a long-short trading strategy that uses a random forest to generate profitable signals for large-cap Japanese equities over the last 3 years. We will source and prepare the stock price data, tune the hyperparameters of a random forest model, and backtest trading rules based on the model's signals. The resulting long-short strategy uses machine learning rather than the cointegration relationship we saw in *Chapter 9, Time-Series Models for Volatility Forecasts and Statistical Arbitrage*, to identify and trade baskets of securities whose prices will likely move in opposite directions over a given investment horizon.

In short, after reading this chapter, you will be able to:

- Use decision trees for regression and classification
- Gain insights from decision trees and visualize the rules learned from the data
- Understand why ensemble models tend to deliver superior results
- Use bootstrap aggregation to address the overfitting challenges of decision trees
- Train, tune, and interpret random forests
- Employ a random forest to design and evaluate a profitable trading strategy

> You can find the code samples for this chapter and links to additional resources in the corresponding directory of the GitHub repository. The notebooks include color versions of the images.

Decision trees – learning rules from data

A decision tree is a machine learning algorithm that predicts the value of a target variable based on **decision rules learned from data**. The algorithm can be applied to both regression and classification problems by changing the objective function that governs how the tree learns the rules.

We will discuss how decision trees use rules to make predictions, how to train them to predict (continuous) returns as well as (categorical) directions of price movements, and how to interpret, visualize, and tune them effectively. See Rokach and Maimon (2008) and Hastie, Tibshirani, and Friedman (2009) for additional details and further background information.

How trees learn and apply decision rules

The **linear models** we studied in *Chapter 7, Linear Models – From Risk Factors to Return Forecasts*, and *Chapter 9, Time-Series Models for Volatility Forecasts and Statistical Arbitrage*, learn a set of parameters to predict the outcome using a linear combination of the input variables, possibly after being transformed by an S-shaped link function, in the case of logistic regression.

Decision trees take a different approach: they learn and sequentially apply a set of rules that split data points into subsets and then make one prediction for each subset. The predictions are based on the outcome values for the subset of training samples that result from the application of a given sequence of rules. **Classification trees** predict a probability estimated from the relative class frequencies or the value of the majority class directly, whereas **regression trees** compute prediction from the mean of the outcome values for the available data points.

Each of these rules relies on one particular feature and uses a threshold to split the samples into two groups, with values either below or above the threshold for this feature. A **binary tree** naturally represents the logic of the model: the root is the starting point for all samples, nodes represent the application of the decision rules, and the data moves along the edges as it is split into smaller subsets until it arrives at a leaf node, where the model makes a prediction.

For a linear model, the parameter values allow an interpretation of the impact of the input variables on the output and the model's prediction. In contrast, for a decision tree, the various possible paths from the root to the leaves determine how the features and their values lead to specific decisions by the model. As a consequence, decision trees are **capable of capturing interdependence** among features that linear models cannot capture "out of the box."

The following diagram highlights how the model learns a rule. During training, the algorithm scans the features and, for each feature, seeks to find a cutoff that splits the data to minimize the loss that results from predictions made. It does so using the subsets that would result from the split, weighted by the number of samples in each subset:

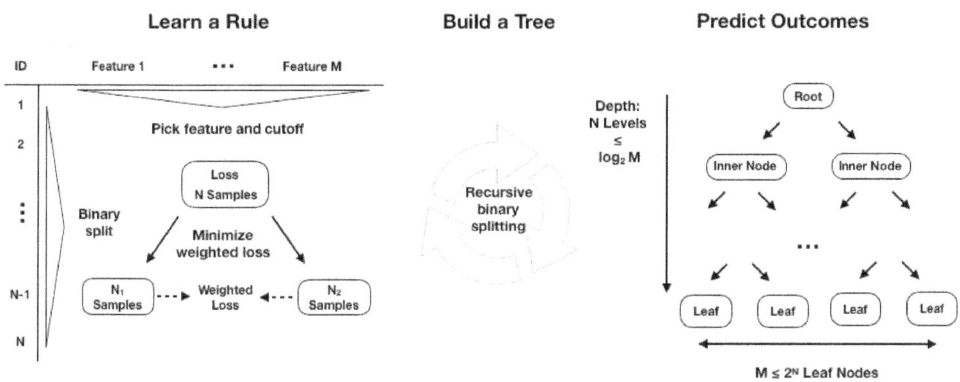

Figure 11.1: How a decision tree learns rules from data

To build an entire tree during training, the learning algorithm repeats this process of dividing the feature space, that is, the set of possible values for the p input variables, X_1, X_2, ..., X_p, into mutually-exclusive and collectively exhaustive regions, each represented by a leaf node. Unfortunately, the algorithm will not be able to evaluate every possible partition of the feature space, given the explosive number of possible combinations of sequences of features and thresholds. Tree-based learning takes a **top-down, greedy approach**, known as **recursive binary splitting**, to overcome this computational limitation.

This process is recursive because it uses subsets of data resulting from prior splits. It is top-down because it begins at the root node of the tree, where all observations still belong to a single region, and then successively creates two new branches of the tree by adding one more split to the predictor space. It is greedy because the algorithm picks the best rule in the form of a feature-threshold combination based on the immediate impact on the objective function, rather than looking ahead and evaluating the loss several steps ahead. We will return to the splitting logic in the more specific context of regression and classification trees because this represents the major difference between them.

The number of training samples continues to shrink as recursive splits add new nodes to the tree. If rules split the samples evenly, resulting in a perfectly balanced tree with an equal number of children for every node, then there would be 2^n nodes at level n, each containing a corresponding fraction of the total number of observations. In practice, this is unlikely, so the number of samples along some branches may diminish rapidly, and trees tend to grow to different levels of depth along different paths.

Recursive splitting would continue until each leaf node contains only a single sample and the training error has been reduced to zero. We will introduce several methods to limit splits and prevent this natural tendency of decision trees to produce extreme overfitting.

To arrive at a **prediction** for a new observation, the model uses the rules that it inferred during training to decide which leaf node the data point should be assigned to, and then uses the mean (for regression) or the mode (for classification) of the training observations in the corresponding region of the feature space. A smaller number of training samples in a given region of the feature space, that is, in a given leaf node, reduces the confidence in the prediction and may reflect overfitting.

Decision trees in practice

In this section, we will illustrate how to use tree-based models to gain insight and make predictions. To demonstrate regression trees, we predict returns, and for the classification case, we return to the example of positive and negative asset price moves. The code examples for this section are in the notebook `decision_trees`, unless stated otherwise.

The data – monthly stock returns and features

We will select a subset of the Quandl US equity dataset covering the period 2006-2017 and follow a process similar to our first feature engineering example in *Chapter 4, Financial Feature Engineering – How to Research Alpha Factors*. We will compute monthly returns and 25 (hopefully) predictive features for the 500 most-traded stocks based on the 5-year moving average of their dollar volume, yielding 56,756 observations. The features include:

- **Historical returns** for the past 1, 3, 6, and 12 months.
- **Momentum indicators** that relate the most recent 1- or 3-month returns to those for longer horizons.
- **Technical indicators** designed to capture volatility like the (normalized) average true range (NATR and ATR) and momentum like the **relative strength index** (**RSI**).
- **Factor loadings** for the five Fama-French factors based on rolling OLS regressions.
- **Categorical variables** for year and month, as well as sector.

Figure 11.2 displays the mutual information between these features and the monthly returns we use for regression (left panel) and their binarized classification counterpart, which represents positive or negative price moves for the same period. It shows that, on a univariate basis, there appear to be substantial differences in the signal content regarding both outcomes across the features.

More details can be found in the `data_prep` notebook in the GitHub repository for this chapter. The decision tree models in this chapter are not equipped to handle missing or categorical variables, so we will drop the former and apply dummy encoding (see *Chapter 4, Financial Feature Engineering – How to Research Alpha Factors* and *Chapter 6, The Machine Learning Process*) to the categorical sector variable:

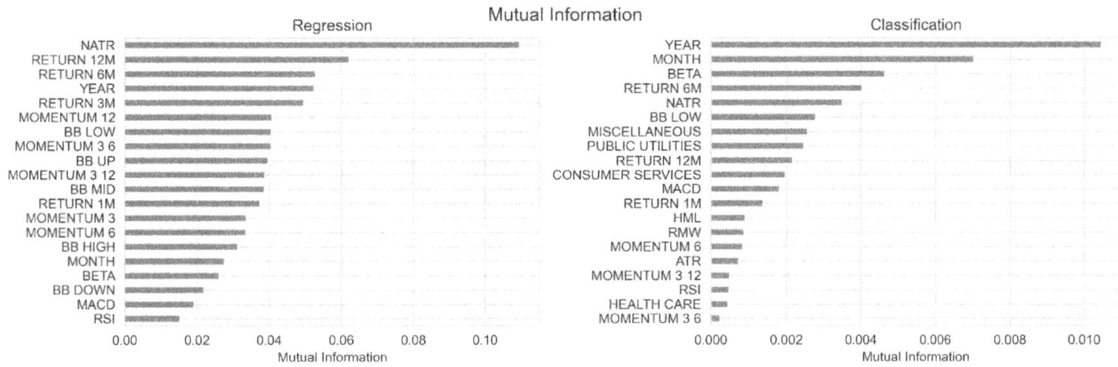

Figure 11.2: Mutual information for features and returns or price move direction

Building a regression tree with time-series data

Regression trees make predictions based on the mean outcome value for the training samples assigned to a given node, and typically rely on the mean-squared error to select optimal rules during recursive binary splitting.

Given a training set, the algorithm iterates over the p predictors, X_1, X_2, ..., X_p, and n possible cutpoints, s_1, s_2, ..., s_n, to find an optimal combination. The optimal rule splits the feature space into two regions, $\{X \mid X_i < s_j\}$ and $\{X \mid X_i > s_j\}$, with values for the X_i feature either below or above the s_j threshold, so that predictions based on the training subsets maximize the reduction of the squared residuals relative to the current node.

Let's start with a simplified example to facilitate visualization and also demonstrate how we can use time-series data with a decision tree. We will only use 2 months of lagged returns to predict the following month, in the vein of an AR(2) model from the previous chapter:

$$r_t = f(r_{t-1}, r_{t-2})$$

Using scikit-learn, configuring and training a regression tree is very straightforward:

```
from sklearn.tree import DecisionTreeRegressor
# configure regression tree
regression_tree = DecisionTreeRegressor(criterion='mse',
                                        max_depth=6,
                                        min_samples_leaf=50)


# Create training data
y = data.target
X = data.drop(target, axis=1)
X2 = X.loc[:, ['t-1', 't-2']]
# fit model
regression_tree.fit(X=X2, y=y)
# fit OLS model
ols_model = sm.OLS(endog=y, exog=sm.add_constant(X2)).fit()
```

The OLS summary and a visualization of the first two levels of the decision tree reveal the striking differences between the models (see *Figure 11.3*). The OLS model provides three parameters for the intercepts and the two features in line with the linear assumption this model makes about the function.

In contrast, the regression tree chart displays, for each node of the first two levels, the feature and threshold used to split the data (note that features can be used repeatedly), as well as the current value of the **mean-squared error** (**MSE**), the number of samples, and the predicted value based on these training samples. Also, note that training the decision tree takes 58 milliseconds compared to 66 microseconds for the linear regression. While both models run fast with only two features, the difference is a factor of 1,000:

```
                            OLS Regression Results
==============================================================================
Dep. Variable:                      y   R-squared:                       0.001
Model:                            OLS   Adj. R-squared:                  0.001
Method:                 Least Squares   F-statistic:                     39.02
Date:                Wed, 22 Apr 2020   Prob (F-statistic):           1.17e-17
Time:                        19:18:07   Log-Likelihood:                 56967.
No. Observations:               56186   AIC:                        -1.139e+05
Df Residuals:                   56183   BIC:                        -1.139e+05
Df Model:                           2
Covariance Type:            nonrobust
==============================================================================
                 coef    std err          t      P>|t|      [0.025      0.975]
------------------------------------------------------------------------------
const          0.0088      0.000     23.412      0.000       0.008       0.009
t-1            0.0327      0.004      7.761      0.000       0.024       0.041
t-2           -0.0187      0.004     -4.437      0.000      -0.027      -0.010
==============================================================================
Omnibus:                     2103.126   Durbin-Watson:                   1.999
Prob(Omnibus):                  0.000   Jarque-Bera (JB):             6483.607
Skew:                           0.018   Prob(JB):                         0.00
Kurtosis:                       4.664   Cond. No.                         11.5
==============================================================================
```

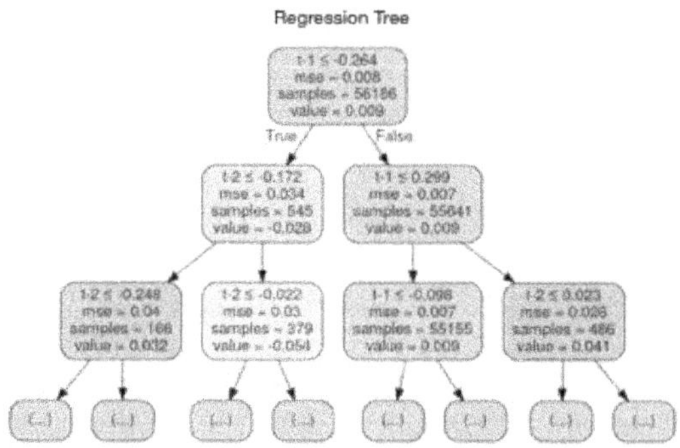

Figure 11.3: OLS results and regression tree

The tree chart also highlights the uneven distribution of samples across the nodes as the numbers vary between 545 and 55,000 samples after the first splits.

To further illustrate the different assumptions about the functional form of the relationships between the input variables and the output, we can visualize the current return predictions as a function of the feature space, that is, as a function of the range of values for the lagged returns. The following image shows the current monthly return as a function of returns one and two periods ago for linear regression (left panel) and the regression tree:

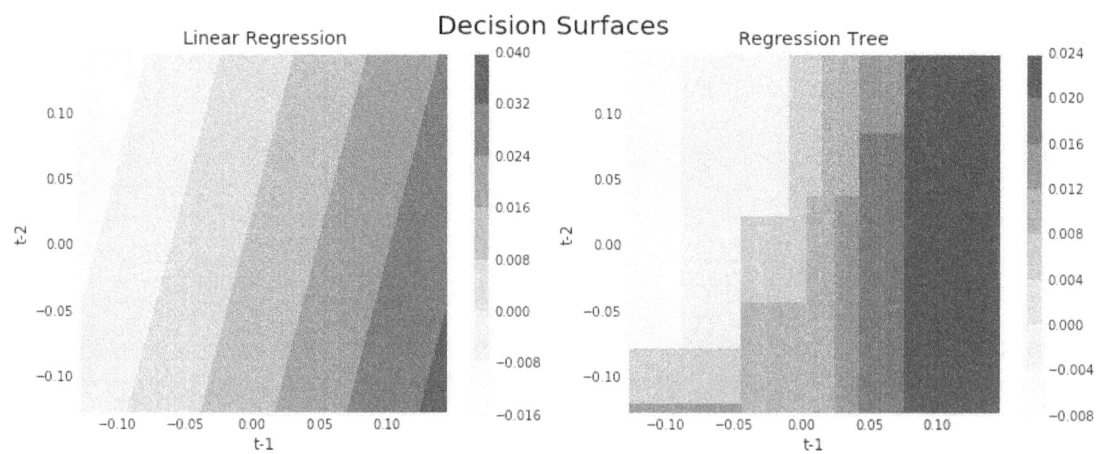

Figure 11.4: Decision surfaces for linear regression and the regression tree

The linear regression model result on the left-hand side underlines the linearity of the relationship between lagged and current returns, whereas the regression tree chart on the right illustrates the nonlinear relationship encoded in the recursive partitioning of the feature space.

Building a classification tree

A classification tree works just like the regression version, except that the categorical nature of the outcome requires a different approach to making predictions and measuring the loss. While a regression tree predicts the response for an observation assigned to a leaf node using the mean outcome of the associated training samples, a classification tree uses the mode, that is, the most common class among the training samples in the relevant region. A classification tree can also generate probabilistic predictions based on relative class frequencies.

How to optimize for node purity

When growing a classification tree, we also use recursive binary splitting, but instead of evaluating the quality of a decision rule using the reduction of the mean-squared error, we can use the **classification error rate**, which is simply the fraction of the training samples in a given (leaf) node that do not belong to the most common class.

However, the alternative measures, either **Gini impurity** or **cross-entropy**, are preferred because they are more sensitive to node purity than the classification error rate, as you can see in *Figure 11.5*. **Node purity** refers to the extent of the preponderance of a single class in a node. A node that only contains samples with outcomes belonging to a single class is pure and implies successful classification for this particular region of the feature space.

Let's see how to compute these measures for a classification outcome with K categories 0,1,..., K-1 (with K=2, in the binary case). For a given node m, let p_{mk} be the proportion of samples from the kth class:

$$\text{Gini impurity} = \sum_k p_{mk}(1 - p_{mk})$$

$$\text{cross entropy} = -\sum_k p_{mk}\, log(p_{mk})$$

The following plot shows that both the Gini impurity and cross-entropy measures are maximized over the [0, 1] interval when the class proportions are even, or 0.5 in the binary case. Both measures decline when the class proportions approach zero or one and the child nodes tend toward purity as a result of a split. At the same time, they imply a higher penalty for node impurity than the classification error rate:

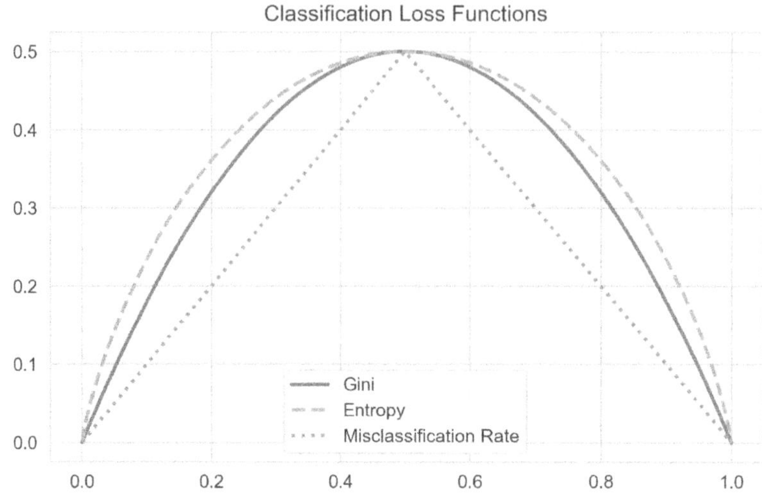

Figure 11.5: Classification loss functions

Note that cross-entropy takes almost 20 times as long to compute as the Gini measure (see the notebook for details).

How to train a classification tree

We will now train, visualize, and evaluate a classification tree with up to five consecutive splits using 80 percent of the samples for training to predict the remaining 20 percent. We will take a shortcut here to simplify the illustration and use the built-in `train_test_split`, which does not protect against lookahead bias, as the custom `MultipleTimeSeriesCV` iterator we introduced in *Chapter 6, The Machine Learning Process* and will use later in this chapter.

The tree configuration implies up to 2^5=32 leaf nodes that, on average, in the balanced case, would contain over 1,400 of the training samples. Take a look at the following code:

```
# randomize train-test split
X_train, X_test, y_train, y_test = train_test_split(X, y_binary, test_
size=0.2, random_state=42)
# configure & train tree learner

clf = DecisionTreeClassifier(criterion='gini',
                             max_depth=5,
                             random_state=42)
clf.fit(X=X_train, y=y_train)
# Output:
DecisionTreeClassifier(class_weight=None, criterion='gini', max_depth=5,
            max_features=None, max_leaf_nodes=None,

            min_impurity_decrease=0.0, min_impurity_split=None,
            min_samples_leaf=1, min_samples_split=2,
```

```
            min_weight_fraction_leaf=0.0, presort=False, random_state=42,
            splitter='best')
```

The output after training the model displays all the `DecisionTreeClassifier` parameters. We will address these in more detail in the *Hyperparameter tuning* section.

Visualizing a decision tree

You can visualize the tree using the Graphviz library (see GitHub for installation instructions) because scikit-learn can output a description of the tree using the DOT language used by that library. You can configure the output to include feature and class labels and limit the number of levels to keep the chart readable, as follows:

```
dot_data = export_graphviz(classifier,
                           out_file=None, # save to file and convert to png
                           feature_names=X.columns,
                           class_names=['Down', 'Up'],
                           max_depth=3,
                           filled=True,
                           rounded=True,
                           special_characters=True)
graphviz.Source(dot_data)
```

The following diagram shows how the model uses different features and indicates the split rules for both continuous and categorical (dummy) variables. Under the label value for each node, the chart shows the number of samples from each class and, under the label class, the most common class (there were more up months during the sample period):

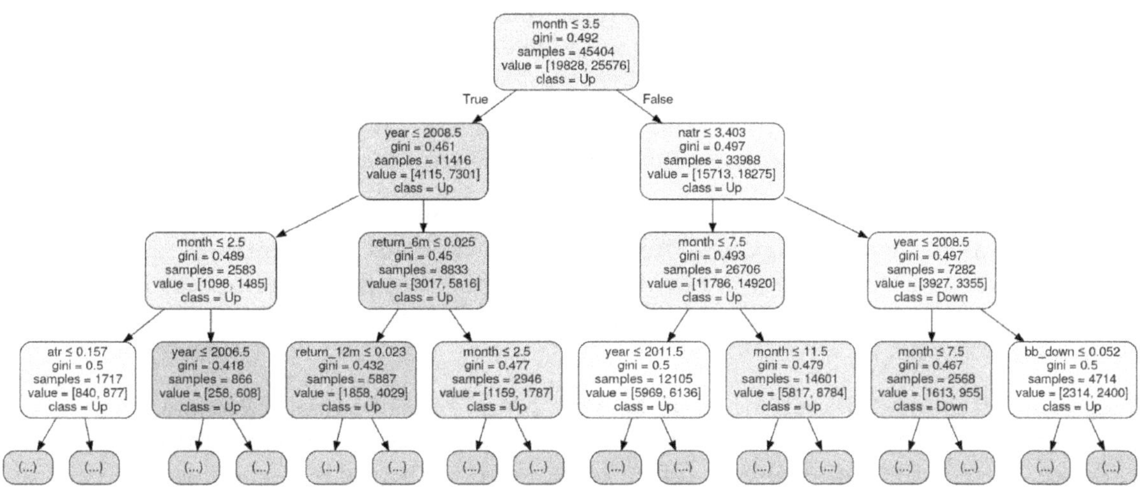

Figure 11.6: Visualization of a classification tree

Evaluating decision tree predictions

To evaluate the predictive accuracy of our first classification tree, we will use our test set to generate predicted class probabilities, as follows:

```
# only keep probabilities for pos. class
y_score = classifier.predict_proba(X=X_test)[:, 1]
```

The `.predict_proba()` method produces one probability for each class. In the binary class, these probabilities are complementary and sum to 1, so we only need the value for the positive class. To evaluate the generalization error, we will use the area under the curve based on the receiver-operating characteristic, which we introduced in *Chapter 6, The Machine Learning Process*. The result indicates a significant improvement above and beyond the baseline value of 0.5 for a random prediction (but keep in mind that the cross-validation method here does not respect the time-series nature of the data):

```
roc_auc_score(y_score=y_score, y_true=y_test)
0.6341
```

Overfitting and regularization

Decision trees have a strong tendency to overfit, especially when a dataset has a large number of features relative to the number of samples. As discussed in previous chapters, overfitting increases the prediction error because the model does not only learn the signal contained in the training data, but also the noise.

There are multiple ways to **address the risk of overfitting**, including:

- **Dimensionality reduction** (see *Chapter 13, Data-Driven Risk Factors and Asset Allocation with Unsupervised Learning*) improves the feature-to-sample ratio by representing the existing features with fewer, more informative, and less noisy features.
- **Ensemble models**, such as random forests, combine multiple trees while randomizing the tree construction, as we will see in the second part of this chapter.

Decision trees provide several regularization hyperparameters to limit the growth of a tree and the associated complexity. While every split increases the number of nodes, it also reduces the number of samples available per node to support a prediction. For each additional level, twice the number of samples is needed to populate the new nodes with the same sample density.

Tree pruning is an additional tool to reduce the complexity of a tree. It does so by eliminating nodes or entire parts of a tree that add little value but increase the model's variance. Cost-complexity-pruning, for instance, starts with a large tree and recursively reduces its size by replacing nodes with leaves, essentially running the tree construction in reverse. The various steps produce a sequence of trees that can then be compared using cross-validation to select the ideal size.

How to regularize a decision tree

The following table lists the key parameters available for this purpose in the scikit-learn decision tree implementation. After introducing the most important parameters, we will illustrate how to use cross-validation to optimize the hyperparameter settings with respect to the bias-variance trade-off and lower prediction errors:

Parameter	Description	Default	Options
`max_depth`	The maximum number of levels: split the nodes until `max_depth` has been reached. All leaves are pure or contain fewer samples than `min_samples_split`.	None	int
`max_features`	Number of features to consider for a split.	None	None: all features `int`: # features `float`: fraction `auto`, `sqrt`: sqrt(`n_features`) `log2`: log2(`n_features`)
`max_leaf_nodes`	Split nodes until creating this many leaves.	None	None: unlimited `int`
`min_impurity_decrease`	Split node if impurity decreases by at least this value.	0	`float`
`min_samples_leaf`	A split will only be considered if there are at least `min_samples_leaf` training samples in each of the left and right branches.	1	`int`; `float` (as a percent of *N*)
`min_samples_split`	The minimum number of samples required to split an internal node.	2	`int`; `float` (percent of *N*)
`min_weight_fraction_leaf`	The minimum weighted fraction of the sum total of all sample weights needed at a leaf node. Samples have equal weight unless `sample_weight` is provided in the fit method.	0	

The `max_depth` parameter imposes a hard limit on the number of consecutive splits and represents the most straightforward way to cap the growth of a tree.

The `min_samples_split` and `min_samples_leaf` parameters are alternative, data-driven ways to limit the growth of a tree. Rather than imposing a hard limit on the number of consecutive splits, these parameters control the minimum number of samples required to further split the data. The latter guarantees a certain number of samples per leaf, while the former can create very small leaves if a split results in a very uneven distribution. Small parameter values facilitate overfitting, while a high number may prevent the tree from learning the signal in the data. The default values are often quite low, and you should use cross-validation to explore a range of potential values. You can also use a float to indicate a percentage, as opposed to an absolute number.

The scikit-learn documentation contains additional details about how to use the various parameters for different use cases; see the resources linked on GitHub for more information.

Decision tree pruning

Recursive binary-splitting will likely produce good predictions on the training set but tends to overfit the data and produce poor generalization performance. This is because it leads to overly complex trees, which are reflected in a large number of leaf nodes, or partitioning of the feature space. Fewer splits and leaf nodes imply an overall smaller tree and often lead to better predictive performance, as well as interpretability.

One approach to limit the number of leaf nodes is to avoid further splits unless they yield significant improvements in the objective metric. The downside of this strategy, however, is that sometimes, splits that result in small improvements enable more valuable splits later as the composition of the samples keeps changing.

Tree pruning, in contrast, starts by growing a very large tree before removing or pruning nodes to reduce the large tree to a less complex and overfit subtree. Cost-complexity-pruning generates a sequence of subtrees by adding a penalty for adding leaf nodes to the tree model and a regularization parameter, similar to the lasso and ridge linear-regression models, that modulates the impact of the penalty. Applied to the large tree, an increasing penalty will automatically produce a sequence of subtrees. Cross-validation of the regularization parameter can be used to identify the optimal, pruned subtree.

This method was introduced in scikit-learn version 0.22; see Esposito et al. (1997) for a survey of how various methods work and perform.

Hyperparameter tuning

Decision trees offer an array of hyperparameters to control and tune the training result. Cross-validation is the most important tool to obtain an unbiased estimate of the generalization error, which, in turn, permits an informed choice among the various configuration options. scikit-learn offers several tools to facilitate the process of cross-validating numerous parameter settings, namely the `GridSearchCV` convenience class, which we will illustrate in the next section. Learning curves also allow diagnostics that evaluate potential benefits of collecting additional data to reduce the generalization error.

Using GridsearchCV with a custom metric

As highlighted in *Chapter 6, The Machine Learning Process*, scikit-learn provides a method to define ranges of values for multiple hyperparameters. It automates the process of cross-validating the various combinations of these parameter values to identify the optimal configuration. Let's walk through the process of automatically tuning your model.

The first step is to instantiate a model object and define a dictionary where the keywords name the hyperparameters, and the values list the parameter settings to be tested:

```
reg_tree = DecisionTreeRegressor(random_state=42)
param_grid = {'max_depth': [2, 3, 4, 5, 6, 7, 8, 10, 12, 15],
              'min_samples_leaf': [5, 25, 50, 100],
              'max_features': ['sqrt', 'auto']}
```

Then, instantiate the `GridSearchCV` object, providing the estimator object and parameter grid, as well as a scoring method and cross-validation choice, to the initialization method.

We set our custom `MultipleTimeSeriesSplit` class to train the model for 60 months, or 5 years, of data and to validate performance using the subsequent 6 months, repeating the process over 10 folds to cover an out-of-sample period of 5 years:

```
cv = MultipleTimeSeriesCV(n_splits=10,
                          train_period_length=60,
                          test_period_length=6,
                          lookahead=1)
```

We use the `roc_auc` metric to score the classifier, and define a custom information coefficient (IC) metric using scikit-learn's `make_scorer` function for the regression model:

```
def rank_correl(y, y_pred):
    return spearmanr(y, y_pred)[0]
ic = make_scorer(rank_correl)
```

We can parallelize the search using the `n_jobs` parameter and automatically obtain a trained model that uses the optimal hyperparameters by setting `refit=True`.

With all the settings in place, we can fit `GridSearchCV` just like any other model:

```
gridsearch_reg = GridSearchCV(estimator=reg_tree,
                          param_grid=param_grid,
                          scoring=ic,
                          n_jobs=-1,
                          cv=cv,  # custom MultipleTimeSeriesSplit
                          refit=True,
                          return_train_score=True)
gridsearch_reg.fit(X=X, y=y)
```

The training process produces some new attributes for our `GridSearchCV` object, most importantly the information about the optimal settings and the best cross-validation score (now using the proper setup, which avoids lookahead bias).

The following table lists the parameters and scores for the best regression and classification model, respectively. With a shallower tree and more regularized leaf nodes, the regression tree achieves an IC of 0.083, while the classifier's AUC score is 0.525:

Parameter	Regression	Classification
max_depth	6	12
max_features	sqrt	sqrt
min_samples_leaf	50	5
Score	0.0829	0.5250

The automation is quite convenient, but we also would like to inspect how the performance evolves for different parameter values. Upon completion of this process, the `GridSearchCV` object makes detailed cross-validation results available so that we can gain more insights.

How to inspect the tree structure

The notebook also illustrates how to run cross-validation more manually to obtain custom tree attributes, such as the total number of nodes or leaf nodes associated with certain hyperparameter settings. The following function accesses the internal `.tree_ attribute` to retrieve information about the total node count, as well as how many of these nodes are leaf nodes:

```
def get_leaves_count(tree):
    t = tree.tree_
    n = t.node_count
    leaves = len([i for i in range(t.node_count) if t.children_left[i]== -1])
    return leaves
```

We can combine this information with the train and test scores to gain detailed knowledge about the model behavior throughout the cross-validation process, as follows:

```
train_scores, val_scores, leaves = {}, {}, {}
for max_depth in range(1, 26):
    print(max_depth, end=' ', flush=True)
    clf = DecisionTreeClassifier(criterion='gini',
                                 max_depth=max_depth,
                                 min_samples_leaf=10,
                                 max_features='auto',
                                 random_state=42)
    train_scores[max_depth], val_scores[max_depth] = [], []
    leaves[max_depth] = []
    for train_idx, test_idx in cv.split(X):
        X_train, = X.iloc[train_idx],
```

```
    y_train  = y_binary.iloc[train_ idx]
    X_test, y_test = X.iloc[test_idx], y_binary.iloc[test_idx]
    clf.fit(X=X_train, y=y_train)
    train_pred = clf.predict_proba(X=X_train)[:, 1]
    train_score = roc_auc_score(y_score=train_pred, y_true=y_train)
    train_scores[max_depth].append(train_score)
    test_pred = clf.predict_proba(X=X_test)[:, 1]
    val_score = roc_auc_score(y_score=test_pred, y_true=y_test)
    val_scores[max_depth].append(val_score)
    leaves[max_depth].append(get_leaves_count(clf))
```

The following plot displays how the number of leaf nodes increases with the depth of the tree. Due to the sample size of each cross-validation fold containing 60 months with around 500 data points each, the number of leaf nodes is limited to around 3,000 when limiting the number of `min_samples_leaf` to 10 samples:

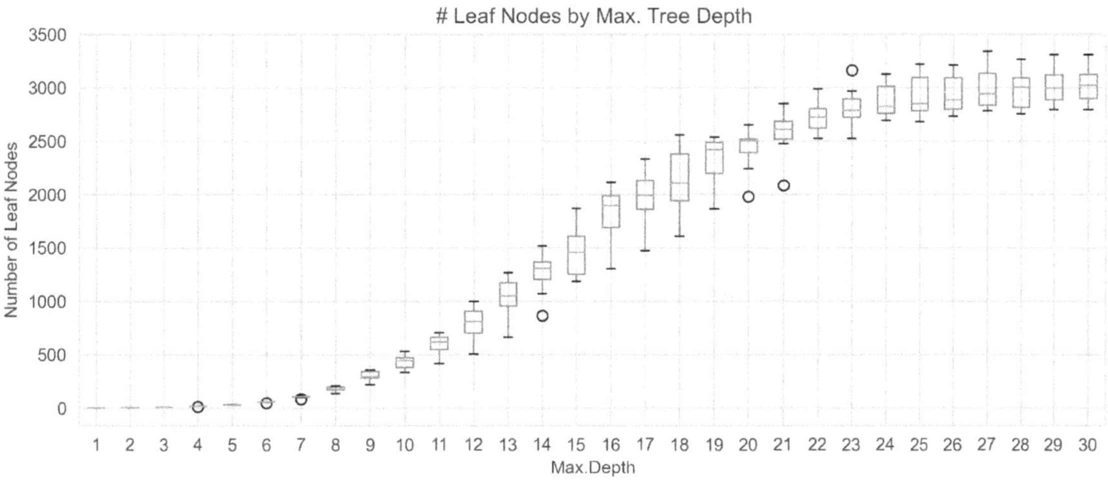

Figure 11.7: Visualization of a classification tree

Comparing regression and classification performance

To take a closer look at the performance of the models, we will show the cross-validation performance for various levels of depth, while maintaining the other parameter settings that produced the best grid search results. *Figure 11.8* displays the train and the validation scores and highlights the degree of overfitting for deeper trees. This is because the training scores steadily increase, whereas validation performance remains flat or decreases.

Note that, for the classification tree, the grid search suggested 12 levels for the best predictive accuracy. However, the plot shows similar AUC scores for less complex trees, with three or seven levels. We would prefer a shallower tree that promises comparable generalization performance while reducing the risk of overfitting:

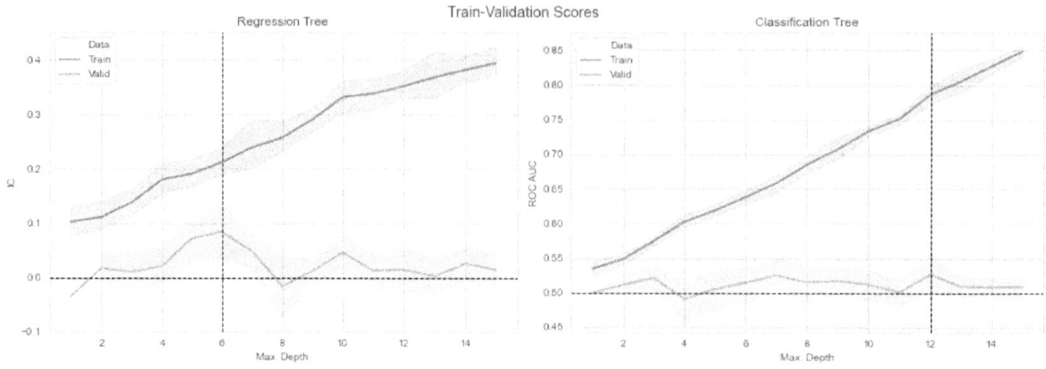

Figure 11.8: Train and validation scores for both models

Diagnosing training set size with learning curves

A **learning curve** is a useful tool that displays how the validation and training scores evolve as the number of training samples increases.

The purpose of the learning curve is to find out whether and how much the model would benefit from using more data during training. It also helps to diagnose whether the model's generalization error is more likely driven by bias or variance.

If the training score meets performance expectations and the validation score exhibits significant improvement as the training sample grows, training for a longer lookback period or obtaining more data might add value. If, on the other hand, both the validation and the training score converge to a similarly poor value, despite an increasing training set size, the error is more likely due to bias, and additional training data is unlikely to help.

The following image depicts the learning curves for the best regression and classification models:

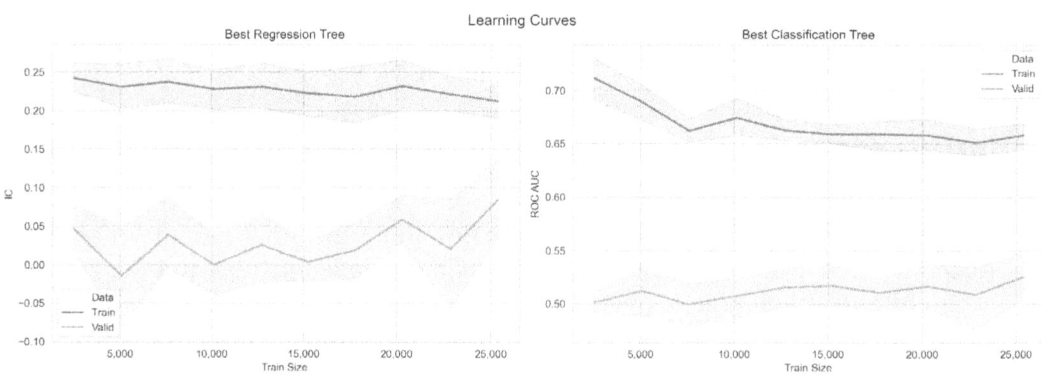

Figure 11.9: Learning curves for the best version of each model

Especially for the regression model, the validation performance improves with a larger training set. This suggests that a longer training period may yield better results. Try it yourself to see if it works!

Gaining insight from feature importance

Decision trees can not only be visualized to inspect the decision path for a given feature, but can also summarize the contribution of each feature to the rules learned by the model to fit the training data.

Feature importance captures how much the splits produced by each feature help optimize the model's metric used to evaluate the split quality, which in our case is the Gini impurity. A feature's importance is computed as the (normalized) total reduction of this metric and takes into account the number of samples affected by a split. Hence, features used earlier in the tree where the nodes tend to contain more samples are typically considered of higher importance.

Figure 11.10 shows the plots for feature importance for the top 15 features of each model. Note how the order of features differs from the univariate evaluation based on the mutual information scores given at the beginning of this section. Clearly, the ability of decision trees to capture interdependencies, such as between time periods and other features, can alter the value of each feature:

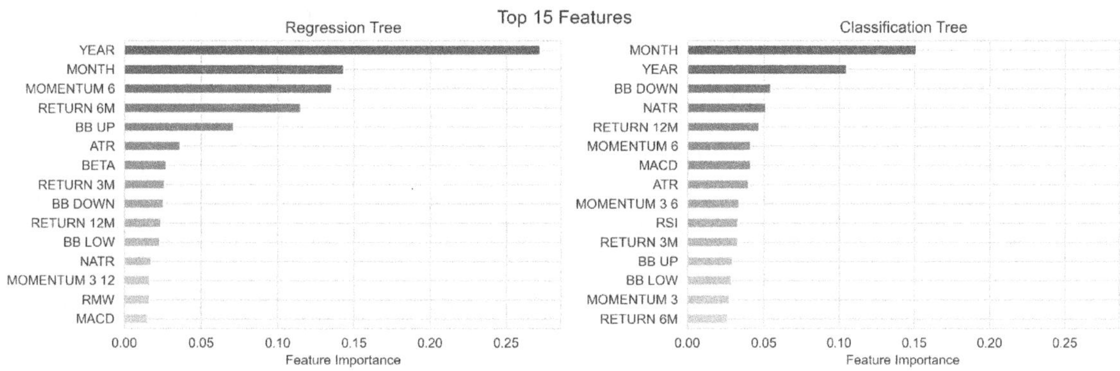

Figure 11.10: Feature importance for the best regression and classification models

Strengths and weaknesses of decision trees

Regression and classification trees approach making predictions very differently from the linear models we have explored in the previous chapters. How do you **decide which model is more suitable** for the problem at hand? Consider the following:

- If the relationship between the outcome and the features is approximately linear (or can be transformed accordingly), then linear regression will likely outperform a more complex method, such as a decision tree that does not exploit this linear structure.
- If the relationship appears highly nonlinear and more complex, decision trees will likely outperform the classical models. Keep in mind that the complexity of the relationship needs to be systematic or "real," rather than driven by noise, which leads more complex models to overfit.

Several **advantages** have made decision trees very popular:

- They are fairly straightforward to understand and to interpret, not least because they can be easily visualized and are thus more accessible to a non-technical audience. Decision trees are also referred to as white-box models, given the high degree of transparency about how they arrive at a prediction. Black-box models, such as ensembles and neural networks, may deliver better prediction accuracy, but the decision logic is often much more challenging to understand and interpret.
- Decision trees require less data preparation than models that make stronger assumptions about the data or are more sensitive to outliers and require data standardization (such as regularized regression).
- Some decision tree implementations handle categorical input, do not require the creation of dummy variables (improving memory efficiency), and can work with missing values, as we will see in *Chapter 12, Boosting Your Trading Strategy*, but this is not the case for scikit-learn.
- Prediction is fast because it is logarithmic in the number of leaf nodes (unless the tree becomes extremely unbalanced).
- It is possible to validate the model using statistical tests and account for its reliability (see the references for more details).

Decision trees also have several key **disadvantages**:

- Decision trees have a built-in tendency to overfit to the training set and produce a high generalization error. The key steps to address this weakness are pruning and regularization using the early-stopping criteria that limits tree growth, as outlined in this section.
- Decision trees are also sensitive to unbalanced class weights and may produce biased trees. One option is to oversample the underrepresented classes or undersample the more frequent class. It is typically better, though, to use class weights and directly adjust the objective function.
- The high variance of decision trees is tied to their ability to closely adapt to a training set. As a result, minor variations in the data can produce wide swings in the tree's structure and, consequently, the model's predictions. A key prevention mechanism is the use of an ensemble of randomized decision trees that have low bias and produce uncorrelated prediction errors.
- The greedy approach to decision-tree learning optimizes local criteria that reduce the prediction error at the current node and do not guarantee a globally optimal outcome. Again, ensembles consisting of randomized trees help to mitigate this problem.

We will now turn to the ensemble method of mitigating the risk of overfitting that's inherent when using decision trees.

Random forests – making trees more reliable

Decision trees are not only useful for their transparency and interpretability. They are also fundamental building blocks for more powerful ensemble models that combine many individual trees, while randomly varying their design to address the overfitting problems we just discussed.

Why ensemble models perform better

Ensemble learning involves combining several machine learning models into a single new model that aims to make better predictions than any individual model. More specifically, an ensemble integrates the predictions of several base estimators, trained using one or more learning algorithms, to reduce the generalization error that these models produce on their own.

For ensemble learning to achieve this goal, **the individual models must be**:

- **Accurate**: Outperform a naive baseline (such as the sample mean or class proportions)
- **Independent**: Predictions are generated differently to produce different errors

Ensemble methods are among the most successful machine learning algorithms, in particular for standard numerical data. Large ensembles are very successful in machine learning competitions and may consist of many distinct individual models that have been combined by hand or using another machine learning algorithm.

There are several disadvantages to combining predictions made by different models. These include reduced interpretability and higher complexity and cost of training, prediction, and model maintenance. As a result, in practice (outside of competitions), the small gains in accuracy from large-scale ensembling may not be worth the added costs.

There are two groups of ensemble methods that are typically distinguished between, depending on how they optimize the constituent models and then integrate the results for a single ensemble prediction:

- **Averaging methods** train several base estimators independently and then average their predictions. If the base models are not biased and make different prediction errors that are not highly correlated, then the combined prediction may have lower variance and can be more reliable. This resembles the construction of a portfolio from assets with uncorrelated returns to reduce the volatility without sacrificing the return.
- **Boosting methods**, in contrast, train base estimators sequentially with the specific goal of reducing the bias of the combined estimator. The motivation is to combine several weak models into a powerful ensemble.

We will focus on automatic averaging methods in the remainder of this chapter and boosting methods in *Chapter 12, Boosting Your Trading Strategy*.

Bootstrap aggregation

We saw that decision trees are likely to make poor predictions due to high variance, which implies that the tree structure is quite sensitive to the available training sample. We have also seen that a model with low variance, such as linear regression, produces similar estimates, despite different training samples, as long as there are sufficient samples given the number of features.

For a given a set of independent observations, each with a variance of σ^2, the standard error of the sample mean is given by $\sigma/\sqrt{n}$. In other words, averaging over a larger set of observations reduces the variance. A natural way to reduce the variance of a model and its generalization error would, thus, be to collect many training sets from the population, train a different model on each dataset, and average the resulting predictions.

In practice, we do not typically have the luxury of many different training sets. This is where **bagging**, short for **bootstrap aggregation**, comes in. Bagging is a general-purpose method that's used to reduce the variance of a machine learning model, which is particularly useful and popular when applied to decision trees.

We will first explain how this technique mitigates overfitting and then show how to apply it to decision trees.

How bagging lowers model variance

Bagging refers to the aggregation of bootstrap samples, which are random samples with replacement. Such a random sample has the same number of observations as the original dataset but may contain duplicates due to replacement.

Bagging increases predictive accuracy but decreases model interpretability because it's no longer possible to visualize the tree to understand the importance of each feature. As an ensemble algorithm, bagging methods train a given number of base estimators on these bootstrapped samples and then aggregate their predictions into a final ensemble prediction.

Bagging reduces the variance of the base estimators to reduce their generalization error by:

1. Randomizing how each tree is grown
2. Averaging their predictions

It is often a straightforward approach to improve on a given model without the need to change the underlying algorithm. This technique works best with **complex models that have low bias and high variance**, such as deep decision trees, because its goal is to limit overfitting. Boosting methods, in contrast, work best with weak models, such as shallow decision trees.

There are several bagging methods that differ by the random sampling process they apply to the training set:

- **Pasting** draws random samples from the training data without replacement, whereas bagging samples with replacement.

- **Random subspaces** randomly sample from the features (that is, the columns) without replacement.
- **Random patches** train base estimators by randomly sampling both observations and features.

Bagged decision trees

To apply bagging to decision trees, we create bootstrap samples from our training data by repeatedly sampling with replacement. Then, we train one decision tree on each of these samples and create an ensemble prediction by averaging over the predictions of the different trees. You can find the code for this example in the notebook `bagged_decision_trees`, unless otherwise noted.

Bagged decision trees are usually grown large, that is, they have many levels and leaf nodes and are not pruned so that each tree has a low bias but high variance. The effect of averaging their predictions then aims to reduce their variance. Bagging has been shown to substantially improve predictive performance by constructing ensembles that combine hundreds or even thousands of trees trained on bootstrap samples.

To illustrate the effect of bagging on the variance of a regression tree, we can use the `BaggingRegressor` meta-estimator provided by scikit-learn. It trains a user-defined base estimator based on parameters that specify the sampling strategy:

- `max_samples` and `max_features` control the size of the subsets drawn from the rows and the columns, respectively.
- `bootstrap` and `bootstrap_features` determine whether each of these samples is drawn with or without replacement.

The following example uses an exponential function to generate training samples for a single `DecisionTreeRegressor` and a `BaggingRegressor` ensemble that consists of 10 trees, each grown 10 levels deep. Both models are trained on the random samples and predict outcomes for the actual function with added noise.

Since we know the true function, we can decompose the mean-squared error into bias, variance, and noise, and compare the relative size of these components for both models according to the following breakdown:

$$E\left[y_0 - \hat{f}(x_0)\right]^2 = \mathrm{Var}\left(\hat{f}(x_0)\right) + \left[\mathrm{Bias}\left(\hat{f}(x_0)\right)\right]^2 + Var(\epsilon)$$

We will draw 100 random samples of 250 training and 500 test observations each to train each model and collect the predictions:

```
noise = .5  # noise relative to std(y)
noise = y.std() * noise
X_test = choice(x, size=test_size, replace=False)
max_depth = 10
n_estimators=10
tree = DecisionTreeRegressor(max_depth=max_depth)
```

```
bagged_tree = BaggingRegressor(base_estimator=tree, n_estimators=n_
estimators)
learners = {'Decision Tree': tree, 'Bagging Regressor': bagged_tree}
predictions = {k: pd.DataFrame() for k, v in learners.items()}
for i in range(reps):
    X_train = choice(x, train_size)
    y_train = f(X_train) + normal(scale=noise, size=train_size)
    for label, learner in learners.items():
        learner.fit(X=X_train.reshape(-1, 1), y=y_train)
        preds = pd.DataFrame({i: learner.predict(X_test.reshape(-1, 1))},
                             index=X_test)
        predictions[label] = pd.concat([predictions[label], preds], axis=1)
```

For each model, the plots in *Figure 11.11* show:

- The mean prediction and a band of two standard deviations around the mean (upper panel)
- The bias-variance-noise breakdown based on the values for the true function (bottom panel)

We find that the variance of the predictions of the individual decision tree (left side) is almost twice as high as that for the small ensemble of 10 bagged trees, based on bootstrapped samples:

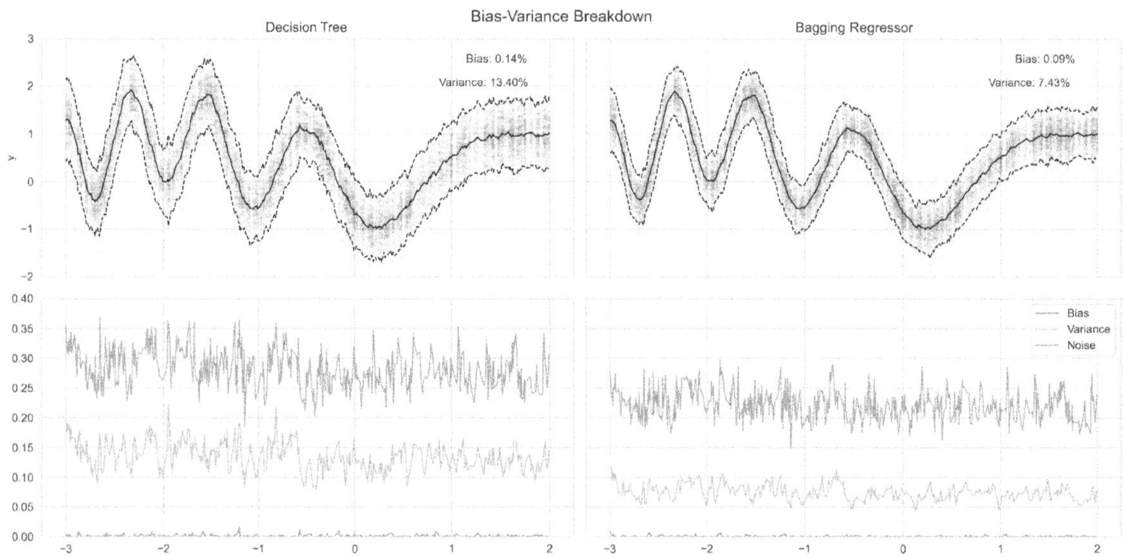

Figure 11.11: Bias-variance breakdown for individual and bagged decision trees

See the notebook `bagged_decision_trees` for implementation details.

How to build a random forest

The random forest algorithm builds on the randomization introduced by bagging to further reduce variance and improve predictive performance.

In addition to training each ensemble member on bootstrapped training data, random forests also randomly sample from the features used in the model (without replacement). Depending on the implementation, the random samples can be drawn for each tree or each split. As a result, the algorithm faces different options when learning new rules, either at the level of a tree or for each split.

The **sample size for the features** differs between regression and classification trees:

- For **classification**, the sample size is typically the square root of the number of features.
- For **regression**, it can be anywhere from one-third to all features and should be selected based on cross-validation.

The following diagram illustrates how random forests randomize the training of individual trees and then aggregate their predictions into an ensemble prediction:

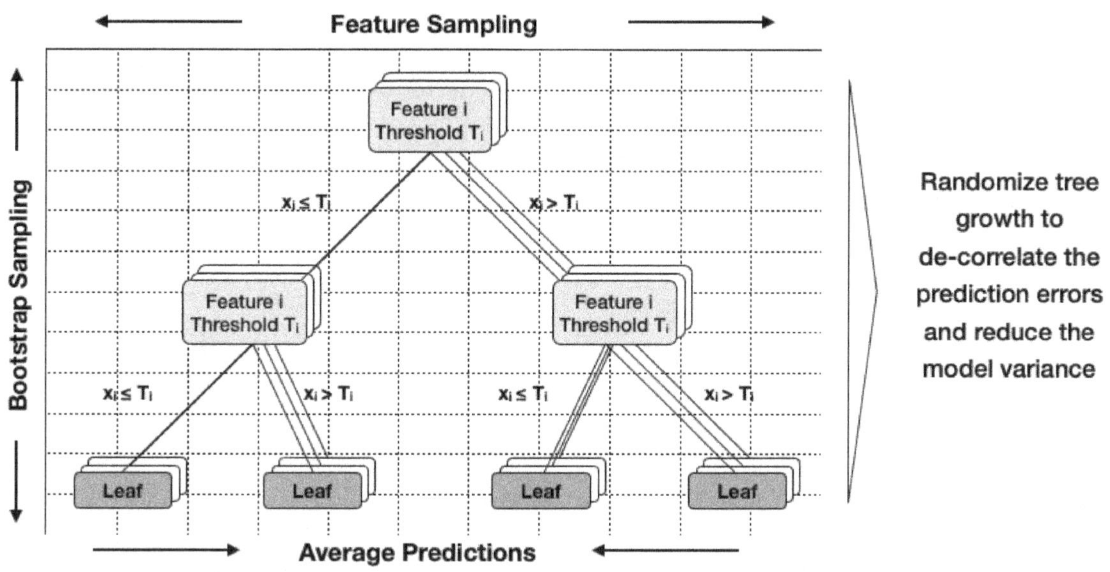

Figure 11.12: How a random forest grows individual trees

The goal of randomizing the features in addition to the training observations is to further **decorrelate the prediction errors** of the individual trees. All features are not created equal, and a small number of highly relevant features will be selected much more frequently and earlier in the tree-construction process, making decision trees more alike across the ensemble. However, the less the generalization errors of individual trees correlate, the more the overall variance will be reduced.

How to train and tune a random forest

The key configuration parameters include the various hyperparameters for the individual decision trees introduced in the *How to tune the hyperparameters* section. The following table lists additional options for the two `RandomForest` classes:

Keyword	Default	Description
`bootstrap`	`TRUE`	Bootstrap samples during training
`n_estimators`	`10`	Number of trees in the forest
`oob_score`	`FALSE`	Uses out-of-bag samples to estimate the R2 on unseen data

The `bootstrap` parameter activates the bagging algorithm just described. Bagging, in turn, enables the computation of the out-of-bag score (`oob_score`), which estimates the generalization accuracy from samples not included in the bootstrap sample used to train a given tree (see the *Out-of-bag testing* section).

The parameter `n_estimators` defines the number of trees to be grown as part of the forest. Larger forests perform better, but also take more time to build. It is important to monitor the cross-validation error as the number of base learners grows. The goal is to identify when the rising cost of training an additional tree outweighs the benefit of reducing the validation error, or when the latter starts to increase again.

The `max_features` parameter controls the size of the randomly selected feature subsets available when learning a new decision rule and to split a node. A lower value reduces the correlation of the trees and, thus, the ensemble's variance, but may also increase the bias. As pointed out at the beginning of this section, good starting values are the number of training features for regression problems and the square root of this number for classification problems, but will depend on the relationships among features and should be optimized using cross-validation.

Random forests are designed to contain deep fully-grown trees, which can be created using `max_depth=None` and `min_samples_split=2`. However, these values are not necessarily optimal, especially for high-dimensional data with many samples and, consequently, potentially very deep trees that can become very computationally, and memory, intensive.

The `RandomForest` class provided by scikit-learn supports parallel training and prediction by setting the `n_jobs` parameter to the k number of jobs to run on different cores. The `-1` value uses all available cores. The overhead of interprocess communication may limit the speedup from being linear so that k jobs may take more than $1/k$ the time of a single job. Nonetheless, the speedup is often quite significant for large forests or deep individual trees that may take a meaningful amount of time to train when the data is large, and split evaluation becomes costly.

As always, the best parameter configuration should be identified using cross-validation. The following steps illustrate the process. The code for this example is in the notebook `random_forest_tuning`.

We will use `GridSearchCV` to identify an optimal set of parameters for an ensemble of classification trees:

```
rf_clf = RandomForestClassifier(n_estimators=100,
                                criterion='gini',
                                max_depth=None,
                                min_samples_split=2,
                                min_samples_leaf=1,
                                min_weight_fraction_leaf=0.0,
                                max_features='auto',
                                max_leaf_nodes=None,
                                min_impurity_decrease=0.0,
                                min_impurity_split=None,
                                bootstrap=True, oob_score=False,
                                n_jobs=-1, random_state=42)
```

We use the same 10-fold custom cross-validation as in the decision tree example previously and populate the parameter grid with values for the key configuration settings:

```
cv = MultipleTimeSeriesCV(n_splits=10, train_period_length=60,
                          test_period_length=6, lookahead=1)

clf = RandomForestClassifier(random_state=42, n_jobs=-1)
param_grid = {'n_estimators': [50, 100, 250],
              'max_depth': [5, 15, None],
              'min_samples_leaf': [5, 25, 100]}
```

Configure `GridSearchCV` using the preceding as input:

```
gridsearch_clf = GridSearchCV(estimator=clf,
                              param_grid=param_grid,
                              scoring='roc_auc',
                              n_jobs=-1,
                              cv=cv,
                              refit=True,
                              return_train_score=True,
                              verbose=1)
```

We run our grid search as before and find the following result for the best-performing regression and classification models. A random forest regression model does better with shallower trees compared to the classifier but otherwise uses the same settings:

Parameter	Regression	Classification
max_depth	5	15
min_samples_leaf	5	5
n_estimators	100	100
Score	0.0435	0.5205

However, both models underperform their individual decision tree counterparts, highlighting that more complex models do not necessarily outperform simpler approaches, especially when the data is noisy and the risk of overfitting is high.

Feature importance for random forests

A random forest ensemble may contain hundreds of individual trees, but it is still possible to obtain an overall summary measure of feature importance from bagged models.

For a given feature, the **importance score** is the total reduction in the objective function's value due to splits on this feature and is averaged over all trees. Since the objective function takes into account how many features are affected by a split, features used near the top of a tree will get higher scores due to the larger number of observations contained in the smaller number of available nodes. By averaging over many trees grown in a randomized fashion, the feature importance estimate loses some variance and becomes more accurate.

The score is measured in terms of the mean-squared error for regression trees and the Gini impurity or entropy for classification trees. scikit-learn further normalizes feature importance so that it sums up to 1. Feature importance thus computed is also popular for feature selection as an alternative to the mutual information measures we saw in *Chapter 6, The Machine Learning Process* (see `SelectFromModel` in the `sklearn.feature_selection` module).

Figure 11.13 shows the values for the top 15 features for both models. The regression model relies much more on time periods than the better-performing decision tree:

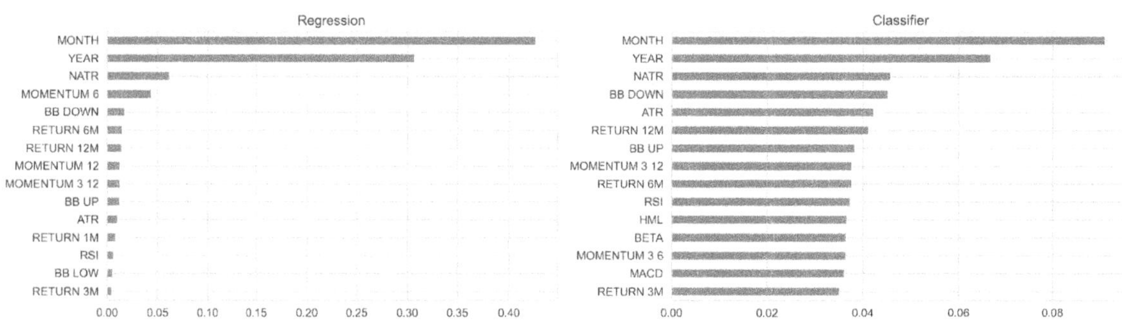

Figure 11.13: Random forest feature importance

Out-of-bag testing

Random forests offer the benefit of built-in cross-validation because individual trees are trained on bootstrapped versions of the training data. As a result, each tree uses, on average, only two-thirds of the available observations. To see why, consider that a bootstrap sample has the same size, n, as the original sample, and each observation has the same probability, $1/n$, to be drawn. Hence, the probability of not entering a bootstrap sample at all is $(1-1/n)n$, which converges (quickly) to $1/e$, or roughly one third.

This remaining one-third of the observations that are not included in the training set is used to grow a bagged tree called **out-of-bag (OOB)** observations, and can serve as a validation set. Just as with cross-validation, we predict the response for an OOB sample for each tree built without this observation, and then average the predicted responses (if regression is the goal) or take a majority vote or predicted probability (if classification is the goal) for a single ensemble prediction for each OOB sample. These predictions produce an unbiased estimate of the generalization error, which is conveniently computed during training.

The resulting OOB error is a valid estimate of the generalization error for this observation. This is because the prediction is produced using decision rules learned in the absence of this observation. Once the random forest is sufficiently large, the OOB error closely approximates the leave-one-out cross-validation error. The OOB approach to estimate the test error is very efficient for large datasets where cross-validation can be computationally costly.

However, the same caveats apply as for cross-validation: you need to take care to avoid a lookahead bias that would ensue if OOB observations could be selected *out-of-order*. In practice, this makes it very difficult to use OOB testing with time-series data, where the validation set needs to be selected subject to the sequential nature of the data.

Pros and cons of random forests

Bagged ensemble models have both advantages and disadvantages.

The **advantages** of random forests include:

- Depending on the use case, a random forest can perform on par with the best supervised learning algorithms.
- Random forests provide a reliable feature importance estimate.
- They offer efficient estimates of the test error without incurring the cost of repeated model training associated with cross-validation.

On the other hand, the **disadvantages** of random forests include:

- An ensemble model is inherently less interpretable than an individual decision tree.
- Training a large number of deep trees can have high computational costs (but can be parallelized) and use a lot of memory.
- Predictions are slower, which may create challenges for applications that require low latency.

Let's now take a look at how we can use a random forest for a trading strategy.

Long-short signals for Japanese stocks

In *Chapter 9*, *Time-Series Models for Volatility Forecasts and Statistical Arbitrage*, we used cointegration tests to identify pairs of stocks with a long-term equilibrium relationship in the form of a common trend to which their prices revert.

In this chapter, we will use the predictions of a machine learning model to identify assets that are likely to go up or down so we can enter market-neutral long and short positions, accordingly. The approach is similar to our initial trading strategy that used linear regression in *Chapter 7, Linear Models – From Risk Factors to Return Forecasts*, and *Chapter 8, The ML4T Workflow – From Model to Strategy Backtesting*.

Instead of the scikit-learn random forest implementation, we will use the LightGBM package, which has been primarily designed for gradient boosting. One of several advantages is LightGBM's ability to efficiently encode categorical variables as numeric features rather than using one-hot dummy encoding (Fisher 1958). We'll provide a more detailed introduction in the next chapter, but the code samples should be easy to follow as the logic is similar to the scikit-learn version.

The data – Japanese equities

We are going to design a strategy for a universe of Japanese stocks, using data provided by Stooq, a Polish data provider that currently offers interesting datasets for various asset classes, markets, and frequencies, which we also relied upon in *Chapter 9, Time-Series Models for Volatility Forecasts and Statistical Arbitrage*.

While there is little transparency regarding the sourcing and quality of the data, it has the powerful advantage of currently being free of charge. In other words, we get to experiment with data on stocks, bonds, commodities, and FX at daily, hourly, and 5-minute frequencies, but should take the results with a large grain of salt.

The `create_datasets` notebook in the data directory of this book's GitHub repository contains instructions for downloading the data and storing them in HDF5 format. For this example, we are using price data on some 3,000 Japanese stocks for the 2010-2019 period. The last 2 years will serve as the out-of-sample test period, while the prior years will serve as our cross-validation sample for model selection.

Please refer to the notebook `japanese_equity_features` for the code samples in this section. We remove tickers with more than five consecutive missing values and only keep the 1,000 most-traded stocks.

The features – lagged returns and technical indicators

We'll keep it relatively simple and combine historical returns for 1, 5, 10, 21, and 63 trading days with several technical indicators provided by TA-Lib (see *Chapter 4, Financial Feature Engineering – How to Research Alpha Factors*).

More specifically, we compute for each stock:

- **Percentage price oscillator** (**PPO**): A normalized version of the **moving average convergence/divergence** (**MACD**) indicator that measures the difference between the 14-day and the 26-day exponential moving average to capture differences in momentum across assets.

- **Normalized average true range** (**NATR**): Measures price volatility in a way that can be compared across assets.
- **Relative strength index** (**RSI**): Another popular momentum indicator (see *Chapter 4, Financial Feature Engineering – How to Research Alpha Factors* for details).
- **Bollinger Bands**: Ratios of the moving average to the moving standard deviations used to identify opportunities for mean reversion.

We will also include markers for the time periods year, month, and weekday, and rank stocks on a scale from 1 to 20 with respect to their latest return for each of the six intervals on each trading day.

The outcomes – forward returns for different horizons

To test the predictive ability of a random forest given these features, we generate forward returns for the same intervals up to 21 trading days (1 month).

The leads and lags implied by the historical and forward returns cause some loss of data that increases with the investment horizon. We end up with 2.3 million observations on 18 features and 4 outcomes for 941 stocks.

The ML4T workflow with LightGBM

We will now embark on selecting a random forest model that produces tradeable signals. Several studies have done so successfully; see, for instance, Krauss, Do, and Huck (2017) and Rasekhschaffe and Jones (2019) and the resources referenced there.

We will use the fast and memory-efficient LightGBM implementation that's open sourced by Microsoft and most popular for gradient boosting, which is the topic of the next chapter, where we will take a closer look at the various LightGBM features.

We will begin by discussing key experimental design decisions, then build and evaluate a predictive model whose signals will drive the trading strategy that we will design and evaluate in the final step. Please refer to the notebook `random_forest_return_signals` for the code samples in this section, unless otherwise stated.

From universe selection to hyperparameter tuning

To develop a trading strategy that uses a machine learning model, we need to make several decisions on the scope and design of the model, including:

- **Lookback period**: How many historical trading days to use for training
- **Lookahead period**: How many days into the future to predict returns
- **Test period**: For how many consecutive days to make predictions with the same model
- **Hyperparameters**: Which parameters and configurations to evaluate
- **Ensembling**: Whether to rely on a single model or some combination of multiple models

To evaluate the options of interest, we also need to select a **universe** and **time period** for cross-validation, as well as an out-of-sample test period and universe. More specifically, we cross-validate several options for the period up to 2017 on a subset of our sample of Japanese stocks.

Once we've settled on a model, we'll define trading rules and backtest the strategy that uses the signals of our model **out-of-sample** over the last 2 years on the complete universe to validate its performance.

For the time-series cross-validation, we'll rely on the `MultipleTimeSeriesCV` that we developed in *Chapter 7*, *Linear Models – From Risk Factors to Return Forecasts*, to parameterize the length of the training and test period while avoiding lookahead bias. This custom CV class permits us to:

- Train the model on a consecutive sample containing `train_length` days for each ticker.
- Validate its performance during a subsequent period containing `test_length` days and `lookahead` number of days, apart from the training period, to avoid data leakage.
- Repeat for a given number of `n_splits` while rolling the train and validation periods forward for `test_length` number of days each time.

We'll work on the model selection step in this section and on strategy backtesting in the following one.

Sampling tickers to speed up cross-validation

Training a random forest takes quite a bit longer than linear regression and depends on the configuration, where the number of trees and their depth are the main drivers.

To keep our experiments manageable, we'll select the 250 most-traded stocks over the 2010-17 period to evaluate the performance of different outcomes and model configurations, as follows:

```
DATA_DIR = Path('..', 'data')
prices = (pd.read_hdf(DATA_DIR / 'assets.h5', 'stooq/jp/tse/stocks/prices')
          .loc[idx[:, '2010': '2017'], :])

dollar_vol = prices.close.mul(prices.volume)
dollar_vol_rank = dollar_vol.groupby(level='date').rank(ascending=False)
universe = dollar_vol_rank.groupby(level='symbol').mean().nsmallest(250).index
```

Defining lookback, lookahead, and roll-forward periods

Running our strategy requires training models on a rolling basis, using a certain number of trading days (the lookback period) from our universe to learn the model parameters and predict the outcome for a certain number of future days. In our example, we'll consider 63, 126, 252, 756, and 1,260 trading days for training while rolling forward and predicting for 5, 21, or 63 days during each iteration.

We will pair the parameters in a list for easy iteration and optional sampling and/or shuffling, as follows:

```
train_lengths = [1260, 756, 252, 126, 63]
test_lengths = [5, 21, 63]

test_params = list(product(train_lengths, test_lengths))
n = len(test_params)
test_param_sample = np.random.choice(list(range(n)),
                                     size=int(n),
                                     replace=False)
test_params = [test_params[i] for i in test_param_sample]
```

Hyperparameter tuning with LightGBM

The LightGBM model accepts a large number of parameters, as the documentation explains in detail (see `https://lightgbm.readthedocs.io/` and the next chapter). For our purposes, we just need to enable the random forest algorithm by defining `boosting_type`, setting `bagging_freq` to a positive number, and setting `objective` to `regression`:

```
base_params = dict(boosting_type='rf',
                   objective='regression',
                   bagging_freq=1)
```

Next, we select the hyperparameters most likely to affect the predictive accuracy, namely:

- The number of trees to grow for the model (`num_boost_round`)
- The share of rows (`bagging_fraction`) and columns (`feature_fraction`) used for bagging
- The minimum number of samples required in a leaf (`min_data_in_leaf`) to control for overfitting

Another benefit of LightGBM is that we can evaluate a trained model for a subset of its trees (or continue training after a certain number of evaluations), which allows us to test multiple `num_iteration` values during a single training session.

Alternatively, you can enable `early_stopping` to interrupt training when the loss metric for a validation set no longer improves. However, the cross-validation performance estimates will be biased upward as the model uses information on the outcome that will not be available under realistic circumstances.

We'll use the following values for the hyperparameters, which control the bagging method and tree growth:

```
bagging_fraction_opts = [.5, .75, .95]
feature_fraction_opts = [.75, .95]
min_data_in_leaf_opts = [250, 500, 1000]

cv_params = list(product(bagging_fraction_opts,
                         feature_fraction_opts,
                         min_data_in_leaf_opts))
n_cv_params = len(cv_params)
```

Cross-validating signals over various horizons

To evaluate a model for a given set of hyperparameters, we will generate predictions using the lookback, lookahead, and roll-forward periods.

First, we will identify categorical variables because LightGBM does not require one-hot encoding; instead, it sorts the categories according to the outcome, which delivers better results for regression trees, according to Fisher (1958). We'll create variables to identify different periods:

```
categoricals = ['year', 'weekday', 'month']
for feature in categoricals:
    data[feature] = pd.factorize(data[feature], sort=True)[0]
```

To this end, we will create the binary LightGBM Dataset and configure `MultipleTimeSeriesCV` using the given `train_length` and `test_length`, which determine the number of splits for our 2-year validation period:

```
for train_length, test_length in test_params:
    n_splits = int(2 * YEAR / test_length)
    cv = MultipleTimeSeriesCV(n_splits=n_splits,
                              test_period_length=test_length,
                              lookahead=lookahead,
                              train_period_length=train_length)

    label = label_dict[lookahead]
    outcome_data = data.loc[:, features + [label]].dropna()

    lgb_data = lgb.Dataset(data=outcome_data.drop(label, axis=1),
                           label=outcome_data[label],
                           categorical_feature=categoricals,
                           free_raw_data=False)
```

Next, we take the following steps:

1. Select the hyperparameters for this iteration.
2. Slice the binary LightGM Dataset we just created into train and test sets.

3. Train the model.
4. Generate predictions for the validation set for a range of num_iteration settings:

```
for p, (bagging_fraction, feature_fraction, min_data_in_leaf) \
        in enumerate(cv_params_):
    params = base_params.copy()
    params.update(dict(bagging_fraction=bagging_fraction,
                       feature_fraction=feature_fraction,
                       min_data_in_leaf=min_data_in_leaf))

    start = time()
    cv_preds, nrounds = [], []
    for i, (train_idx, test_idx) in \
            enumerate(cv.split(X=outcome_data)):
        lgb_train = lgb_data.subset(train_idx.tolist()).construct()
        lgb_test = lgb_data.subset(test_idx.tolist()).construct()

        model = lgb.train(params=params,
                          train_set=lgb_train,
                          num_boost_round=num_boost_round,
                          verbose_eval=False)

        test_set = outcome_data.iloc[test_idx, :]
        X_test = test_set.loc[:, model.feature_name()]
        y_test = test_set.loc[:, label]
        y_pred = {str(n): model.predict(X_test, num_iteration=n)
                  for n in num_iterations}
        cv_preds.append(y_test.to_frame('y_test')
                        .assign(**y_pred).assign(i=i))
        nrounds.append(model.best_iteration)
```

5. To evaluate the validation performance, we compute the IC for the complete set of predictions, as well as on a daily basis, for a range of numbers of iterations:

```
df = [by_day.apply(lambda x: spearmanr(x.y_test,
                                       x[str(n)])[0]).to_frame(n)
      for n in num_iterations]
ic_by_day = pd.concat(df, axis=1)

daily_ic.append(ic_by_day.assign(bagging_fraction=bagging_fraction,
                                 feature_fraction=feature_fraction,
                                 min_data_in_leaf=min_data_in_leaf))

cv_ic = [spearmanr(cv_preds.y_test, cv_preds[str(n)])[0]
         for n in num_iterations]
ic.append([bagging_fraction, feature_fraction,
           min_data_in_leaf, lookahead] + cv_ic)
```

Now, we need to assess the signal content of the predictions to select a model for our trading strategy.

Analyzing cross-validation performance

First, we'll take a look at the distribution of the IC for the various train and test windows, as well as prediction horizons across all hyperparameter settings. Then, we'll take a closer look at the impact of the hyperparameter settings on the model's predictive accuracy.

IC for different lookback, roll-forward, and lookahead periods

The following image illustrates the distribution and quantiles of the daily mean IC for four prediction horizons and five training windows, as well as the best-performing 21-day test window. Unfortunately, it does not yield conclusive insights into whether shorter or longer windows do better, but rather illustrates the degree of noise in the data due to the range of model configurations we tested and the resulting lack of consistency in outcomes:

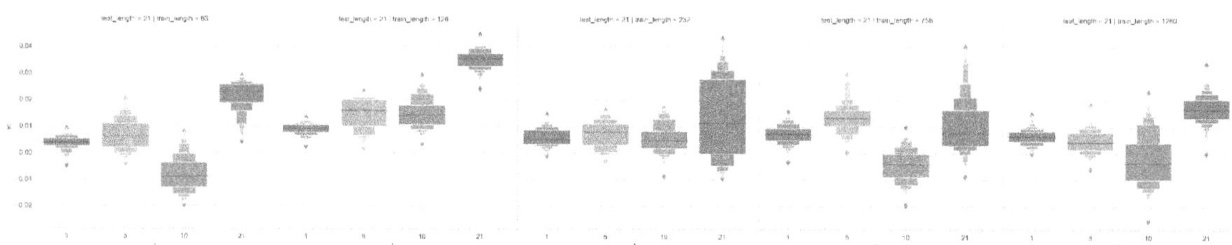

Figure 11.14: Distribution of the daily mean information coefficient for various model configurations

OLS regression of random forest configuration parameters

To understand in more detail how the parameters of our experiment affect the outcome, we can run an OLS regression of these parameters on the daily mean IC. *Figure 11.15* shows the coefficients and confidence intervals for the 1- and 5-day lookahead periods.

All variables are one-hot encoded and can be interpreted relative to the smallest category of each that is captured by the constant. The results differ across the horizons; the longest training period works best for the 1-day prediction but yields the worst performance for 5 days, with no clear patterns. Longer training appears to improve the 1-day model up to a certain point, but this is less clear for the 5-day model. The only somewhat consistent result seems to suggest a lower bagging fraction and higher minimum sample settings:

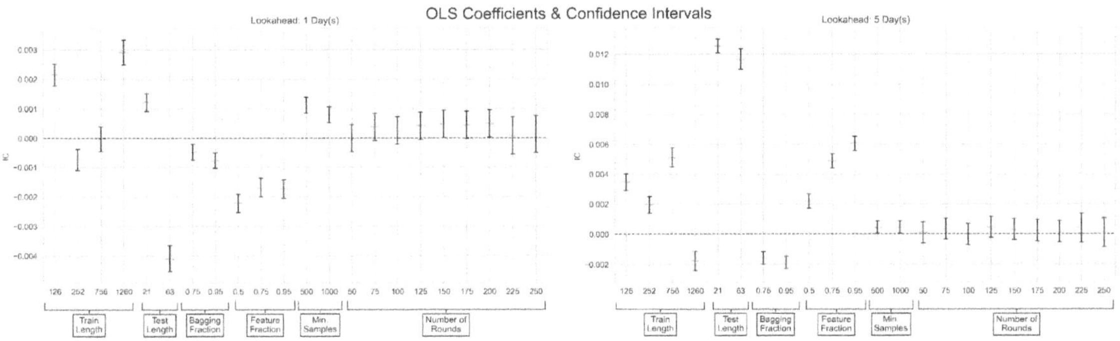

Figure 11.15: OLS coefficients and confidence intervals for the various random forest configuration parameters

Ensembling forecasts – signal analysis using Alphalens

Ultimately, we care about the signal content of the model predictions regarding our investment universe and holding period. To this end, we'll evaluate the return spread produced by equal-weighted portfolios invested in different quantiles of the predicted returns using Alphalens.

As discussed in *Chapter 4, Financial Feature Engineering – How to Research Alpha Factors*, Alphalens computes and visualizes various metrics that summarize the predictive performance of an Alpha Factor. The notebook `alphalens_signals_quality` illustrates how to combine the model predictions with price data in the appropriate format using the utility function `get_clean_factor_and_forward_returns`.

To address some of the noise inherent in the CV predictions, we select the top three 1-day models according to their mean daily IC and average their results.

When we provide the resulting signal to Alphalens, we find the following for a 1-day holding period:

- Annualized alpha of 0.081 and beta of 0.083
- A mean period-wise spread between top and bottom quintile returns of 5.16 basis points

The following image visualizes the mean period-wise returns by factor quintile and the cumulative daily forward returns associated with the stocks in each quintile:

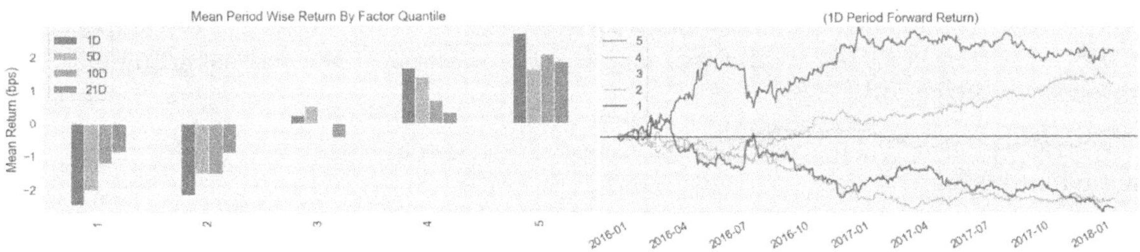

Figure 11.16: Alphalens factor signal evaluation

The preceding image shows that the 1-day ahead predictions appear to contain useful trading signals over a short horizon based on the return spread of the top and bottom quintiles. We'll now move on and develop and backtest a strategy that uses predictions generated by the top ten 1-day lookahead models that produced the results shown here for the validation period.

The strategy – backtest with Zipline

To design and backtest a trading strategy using Zipline, we need to generate predictions for our universe for the test period, ingest the Japanese equity data and load the signal into Zipline, set up a pipeline, and define rebalancing rules to trigger trades accordingly.

Ingesting Japanese Equities into Zipline

We follow the process described in *Chapter 8, The ML4T Workflow - From Model to Strategy Backtesting*, to convert our Stooq equity OHLCV data into a Zipline bundle. The directory `custom_bundle` contains the preprocessing module that creates the asset IDs and metadata, defines an ingest function that does the heavy lifting, and registers the bundle with an extension.

The folder contains a `README` with additional instructions.

Running an in- and out-of-sample strategy backtest

The notebook `random_forest_return_signals` shows how to select the hyperparameters that produced the best validation IC performance and generate forecasts accordingly.

We will use our 1-day model predictions and apply some simple logic: we will enter long and short positions for the 25 assets with the highest positive and lowest negative predicted returns. We will trade every day, as long as there are at least 15 candidates on either side, and close out all positions that are not among the current top forecasts.

This time, we will also include a small trading commission of $0.05 per share but will not use slippage since we are trading the most liquid Japanese stocks with a relatively modest capital base.

The results – evaluation with pyfolio

The left panel shown in *Figure 11.17* shows the in-sample (2016-17) and out-of-sample (2018-19) performance of the strategy relative to the Nikkei 225, which was mostly flat throughout the period.

The strategy earns 10.4 percent for in-sample and 5.5 percent for out-of-sample on an annualized basis.

The right panel shows the 3-month rolling Sharpe ratio, which reaches 0.96 in-sample and 0.61 out-of-sample:

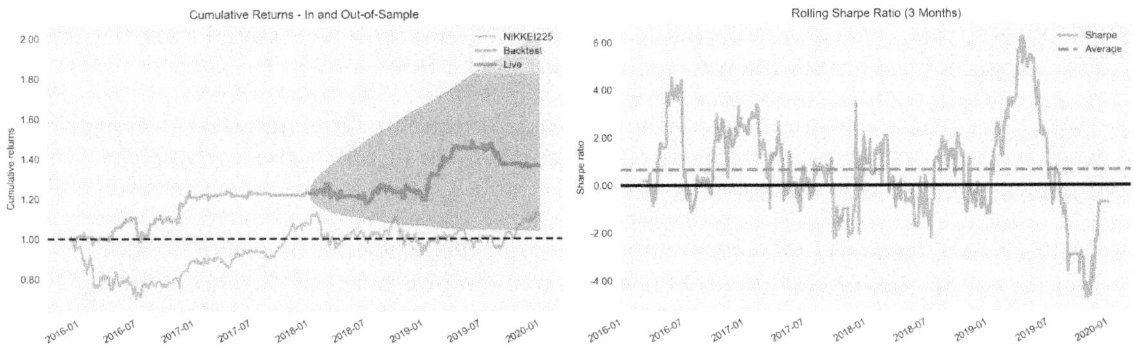

Figure 11.17: Pyfolio strategy evaluation

The overall performance statistics highlight cumulative returns of 36.6 percent after the (low) transaction costs of $0.05 cent per share, implying an out-of-sample alpha of 0.06 and a beta of 0.08 (relative to the NIKKEI 225). The maximum drawdown was 11.0 percent in-sample and 8.7 percent out-of-sample:

	All	In-sample	Out-of-sample
# Months	48	25	23
Annual return	8.00%	10.40%	5.50%
Cumulative returns	36.60%	22.80%	11.20%
Annual volatility	10.20%	10.90%	9.60%
Sharpe ratio	0.8	0.96	0.61
Calmar ratio	0.72	0.94	0.63
Stability	0.82	0.82	0.64
Max drawdown	-11.00%	-11.00%	-8.70%
Sortino ratio	1.26	1.53	0.95
Daily value at risk	-1.30%	-1.30%	-1.20%
Alpha	0.08	0.11	0.06
Beta	0.06	0.04	0.08

The pyfolio tearsheets contain lots of additional details regarding exposure, risk profile, and other aspects.

Summary

In this chapter, we learned about a new class of model capable of capturing a non-linear relationship, in contrast to the classical linear models we had explored so far. We saw how decision trees learn rules to partition the feature space into regions that yield predictions, and thus segment the input data into specific regions.

Decision trees are very useful because they provide unique insights into the relationships between features and target variables, and we saw how to visualize the sequence of decision rules encoded in the tree structure.

Unfortunately, a decision tree is prone to overfitting. We learned that ensemble models and the bootstrap aggregation method manage to overcome some of the shortcomings of decision trees and render them useful as components of much more powerful composite models.

In the next chapter, we will explore another ensemble model, boosting, which has come to be considered one of the most important machine learning algorithms.

12

Boosting Your Trading Strategy

In the previous chapter, we saw how **random forests** improve on the predictions of a decision tree by combining many trees into an ensemble. The key to reducing the high variance of an individual tree is the use of **bagging**, short for **bootstrap aggregation**, which introduces randomness into the process of growing individual trees. More specifically, bagging samples from the data with replacements so that each tree is trained on a different but equal-sized random subset, with some observations repeating. In addition, a random forest randomly selects a subset of the features so that both the rows and the columns of the training set for each tree are random versions of the original data. The ensemble then generates predictions by averaging over the outputs of the individual trees.

Individual random forest trees are usually grown deep to ensure low bias while relying on the randomized training process to produce different, uncorrelated prediction errors that have a lower variance when aggregated than individual tree predictions. In other words, the randomized training aims to decorrelate (think *diversify*) the errors of individual trees. It does this so that the ensemble is less susceptible to overfitting, has a lower variance, and thus generalizes better to new data.

This chapter explores **boosting**, an alternative ensemble algorithm for decision trees that often produces even better results. The key difference is that boosting modifies the training data for each new tree based on the cumulative errors made by the model so far. In contrast to random forests that train many trees independently using samples of the training set, boosting proceeds sequentially using reweighted versions of the data. State-of-the-art boosting implementations also adopt the randomization strategies of random forests.

Over the last three decades, boosting has become one of the most successful **machine learning** (**ML**) algorithms, dominating many ML competitions for structured, tabular data (as opposed to high-dimensional image or speech data with a more complex input-out relationship where deep learning excels). We will show how boosting works, introduce several high-performance implementations, and apply boosting to **high-frequency data** and backtest an **intraday trading strategy**.

More specifically, after reading this chapter, you will be able to:

- Understand how boosting differs from bagging and how gradient boosting evolved from adaptive boosting.
- Design and tune adaptive boosting and gradient boosting models with scikit-learn.
- Build, tune, and evaluate gradient boosting models on large datasets using the state-of-the-art implementations XGBoost, LightGBM, and CatBoost.
- Interpret and gain insights from gradient boosting models.
- Use boosting with high-frequency data to design an intraday strategy.

> You can find the code samples for this chapter and links to additional resources in the corresponding directory of the GitHub repository. The notebooks include color versions of the images.

Getting started – adaptive boosting

Like bagging, boosting is an ensemble learning algorithm that combines base learners (typically decision trees) into an ensemble. Boosting was initially developed for classification problems, but can also be used for regression, and has been called one of the most potent learning ideas introduced in the last 20 years (Hastie, Tibshirani, and Friedman 2009). Like bagging, it is a general method or metamethod that can be applied to many statistical learning methods.

The motivation behind boosting was to find a method that **combines** the outputs of **many weak models**, where "weak" means they perform only slightly better than a random guess, into a highly **accurate, boosted joint prediction** (Schapire and Freund 2012).

In general, boosting learns an additive hypothesis, H_M, of a form similar to linear regression. However, each of the m= 1,..., M elements of the summation is a weak base learner, called h_t, which itself requires training. The following formula summarizes this approach:

$$H_M(x) = \sum_{m=1}^{M} \underbrace{h_t(x)}_{\text{weak learner}}$$

As discussed in the previous chapter, bagging trains base learners on different random samples of the data. Boosting, in contrast, proceeds sequentially by training the base learners on data that it repeatedly modifies to reflect the cumulative learning. The goal is to ensure that the next base learner compensates for the shortcomings of the current ensemble. We will see in this chapter that boosting algorithms differ in how they define shortcomings. The ensemble makes predictions using a weighted average of the predictions of the weak models.

The first boosting algorithm that came with a mathematical proof that it enhances the performance of weak learners was developed by Robert Schapire and Yoav Freund around 1990. In 1997, a practical solution for classification problems emerged in the form of the **adaptive boosting** (**AdaBoost**) algorithm, which won the Göedel Prize in 2003 (Freund and Schapire 1997). About another 5 years later, this algorithm was extended to arbitrary objective functions when Leo Breiman (who invented random forests) connected the approach to gradient descent, and Jerome Friedman came up with **gradient boosting** in 1999 (Friedman 2001).

Numerous optimized implementations, such as XGBoost, LightGBM, and CatBoost, which we will look at later in this chapter, have emerged in recent years and firmly established gradient boosting as the go-to solution for structured data. In the following sections, we'll briefly introduce AdaBoost and then focus on the gradient boosting model, as well as the three state-of-the-art implementations of this very powerful and flexible algorithm we just mentioned.

The AdaBoost algorithm

When it emerged in the 1990s, AdaBoost was the first ensemble algorithm to iteratively adapt to the cumulative learning progress when fitting an additional ensemble member. In particular, AdaBoost changed the weights on the training data to reflect the cumulative errors of the current ensemble on the training set, before fitting a new, weak learner. AdaBoost was the most accurate classification algorithm at the time, and Leo Breiman referred to it as the best off-the-shelf classifier in the world at the 1996 NIPS conference (Hastie, Tibshirani, and Friedman 2009).

Over the subsequent decades, the algorithm had a large impact on machine learning because it provided theoretical performance guarantees. These guarantees only require sufficient data and a weak learner that reliably predicts just better than a random guess. As a result of this adaptive method that learns in stages, the development of an accurate ML model no longer required accurate performance over the entire feature space. Instead, the design of a model could focus on finding weak learners that just outperformed a coin flip using a small subset of the features.

In contrast to bagging, which builds ensembles of very large trees to reduce bias, AdaBoost grows shallow trees as weak learners, often producing superior accuracy with stumps—that is, trees formed by a single split. The algorithm starts with an equally weighted training set and then successively alters the sample distribution. After each iteration, AdaBoost increases the weights of incorrectly classified observations and reduces the weights of correctly predicted samples so that subsequent weak learners focus more on particularly difficult cases. Once trained, the new decision tree is incorporated into the ensemble with a weight that reflects its contribution to reducing the training error.

The AdaBoost algorithm for an ensemble of base learners, $h_m(x)$, $m=1, \ldots, M$, that predicts discrete classes, $y \in [-1, 1]$, and N training observations can be summarized as follows:

1. Initialize sample weights $w_i=1/N$ for observations $i=1, \ldots, N$.
2. For each base classifier, h_m, $m=1, \ldots, M$, do the following:
    1. Fit $h_m(x)$ to the training data, weighted by w_i.
    2. Compute the base learner's weighted error rate ε_m on the training set.

3. Compute the base learner's ensemble weight α_m as a function of its error rate, as shown in the following formula:

$$\alpha_m = \log\left(\frac{1-\varepsilon_m}{\varepsilon_m}\right)$$

4. Update the weights for misclassified samples according to $w_i * exp(\alpha_m)$

3. Predict the positive class when the weighted sum of the ensemble members is positive, and negative otherwise, as shown in the following formula:

$$H(x) = \text{sign}\left(\sum_{m=1}^{M} \underbrace{\alpha_m h_m(x)}_{\text{weighted weak learner}}\right)$$

AdaBoost has many practical **advantages**, including ease of implementation and fast computation, and can be combined with any method for identifying weak learners. Apart from the size of the ensemble, there are no hyperparameters that require tuning. AdaBoost is also useful for identifying outliers because the samples that receive the highest weights are those that are consistently misclassified and inherently ambiguous, which is also typical for outliers.

There are also **disadvantages**: the performance of AdaBoost on a given dataset depends on the ability of the weak learner to adequately capture the relationship between features and outcome. As the theory suggests, boosting will not perform well when there is insufficient data, or when the complexity of the ensemble members is not a good match for the complexity of the data. It can also be susceptible to noise in the data.

See Schapire and Freund (2012) for a thorough introduction and review of boosting algorithms.

Using AdaBoost to predict monthly price moves

As part of its ensemble module, scikit-learn provides an `AdaBoostClassifier` implementation that supports two or more classes. The code examples for this section are in the notebook `boosting_baseline`, which compares the performance of various algorithms with a dummy classifier that always predicts the most frequent class.

We need to first define a `base_estimator` as a template for all ensemble members and then configure the ensemble itself. We'll use the default `DecisionTreeClassifier` with `max_depth=1` — that is, a stump with a single split. Alternatives include any other model from linear or logistic regression to a neural network that conforms to the scikit-learn interface (see the documentation). However, decision trees are by far the most common in practice.

The complexity of `base_estimator` is a key tuning parameter because it depends on the nature of the data. As demonstrated in the previous chapter, changes to `max_depth` should be combined with appropriate regularization constraints using adjustments to, for example, `min_samples_split`, as shown in the following code:

```
base_estimator = DecisionTreeClassifier(criterion='gini',
                                        splitter='best',
                                        max_depth=1,
```

```
                                min_samples_split=2,
                                min_samples_leaf=20,
                                min_weight_fraction_leaf=0.0,
                                max_features=None,
                                random_state=None,
                                max_leaf_nodes=None,
                                min_impurity_decrease=0.0,
                                min_impurity_split=None)
```

In the second step, we'll design the ensemble. The `n_estimators` parameter controls the number of weak learners, and `learning_rate` determines the contribution of each weak learner, as shown in the following code. By default, weak learners are decision tree stumps:

```
ada_clf = AdaBoostClassifier(base_estimator=base_estimator,
                             n_estimators=100,
                             learning_rate=1.0,
                             algorithm='SAMME.R',
                             random_state=42)
```

The main tuning parameters that are responsible for good results are `n_estimators` and the `base_estimator` complexity. This is because the depth of the tree controls the extent of the interaction among the features.

We will cross-validate the AdaBoost ensemble using the custom `OneStepTimeSeriesSplit`, a simplified version of the more flexible `MultipleTimeSeriesCV` (see *Chapter 6*, *The Machine Learning Process*). It implements a 12-fold rolling time-series split to predict 1 month ahead for the last 12 months in the sample, using all available prior data for training, as shown in the following code:

```
cv = OneStepTimeSeriesSplit(n_splits=12, test_period_length=1, shuffle=True)
def run_cv(clf, X=X_dummies, y=y, metrics=metrics, cv=cv, fit_params=None):
    return cross_validate(estimator=clf,
                          X=X,
                          y=y,
                          scoring=list(metrics.keys()),
                          cv=cv,
                          return_train_score=True,
                          n_jobs=-1,                    # use all cores
                          verbose=1,
                          fit_params=fit_params)
```

The validation results show a weighted accuracy of 0.5068, an AUC score of 0.5348, and precision and recall values of 0.547 and 0.576, respectively, implying an F1 score of 0.467. This is marginally below a random forest with default settings that achieves a validation AUC of 0.5358. *Figure 12.1* shows the distribution of the various metrics for the 12 train and test folds as a boxplot (note that the random forest perfectly fits the training set):

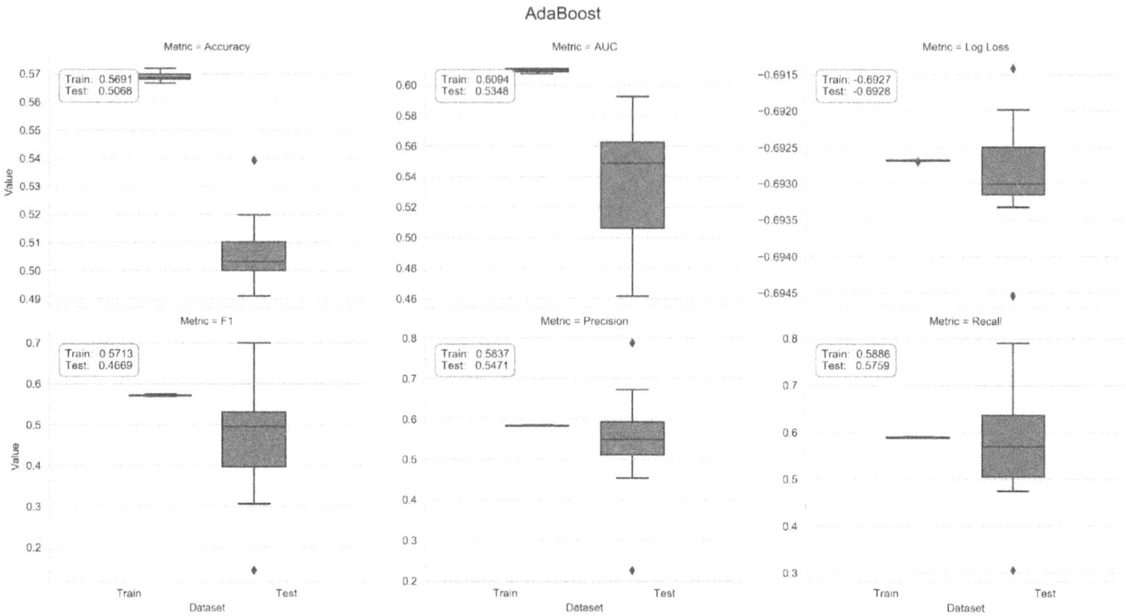

Figure 12.1: AdaBoost cross-validation performance

See the companion notebook for additional details on the code to cross-validate and process the results.

Gradient boosting – ensembles for most tasks

AdaBoost can also be interpreted as a stagewise forward approach to minimizing an exponential loss function for a binary outcome, $y \in [-1, 1]$, that identifies a new base learner, h_m, at each iteration, m, with the corresponding weight, α_m, and adds it to the ensemble, as shown in the following formula:

$$\underset{\alpha,h}{\operatorname{argmin}} \sum_{i=1}^{N} \exp\left(\underbrace{-y_i(f_{m-1}(x_i))}_{\text{current ensemble}} + \underbrace{\alpha_m h_m(x_i)}_{\text{new member}}\right)$$

This interpretation of AdaBoost as a gradient descent algorithm that minimizes a particular loss function, namely exponential loss, was only discovered several years after its original publication.

Gradient boosting leverages this insight and **applies the boosting method to a much wider range of loss functions**. The method enables the design of machine learning algorithms to solve any regression, classification, or ranking problem, as long as it can be formulated using a loss function that is differentiable and thus has a gradient. Common example loss functions for different tasks include:

- **Regression**: The mean-squared and absolute loss
- **Classification**: Cross-entropy
- **Learning to rank**: Lambda rank loss

We covered regression and classification loss functions in *Chapter 6, The Machine Learning Process*; learning to rank is outside the scope of this book, but see Nakamoto (2011) for an introduction and Chen et al. (2009) for details on ranking loss.

The flexibility to customize this general method to many specific prediction tasks is essential to boosting's popularity. Gradient boosting is also not limited to weak learners and often achieves the best performance with decision trees several levels deep.

The main idea behind the resulting **gradient boosting machines** (**GBMs**) algorithm is training the base learners to learn the negative gradient of the current loss function of the ensemble. As a result, each addition to the ensemble directly contributes to reducing the overall training error, given the errors made by prior ensemble members. Since each new member represents a new function of the data, gradient boosting is also said to optimize over the functions h_m in an additive fashion.

In short, the algorithm successively fits weak learners h_m, such as decision trees, to the negative gradient of the loss function that is evaluated for the current ensemble, as shown in the following formula:

$$H_m(x) = \underbrace{H_{m-1}(x)}_{\text{current ensemble}} + \underbrace{\gamma_m h_m(x)}_{\text{new member}} = H_{m-1}(x) + \underset{\gamma,h}{\operatorname{argmin}} \sum_{i=1}^{N} \underbrace{L(y_i, H_{m-1}(x_i) + h(x))}_{\text{loss function}}$$

In other words, at a given iteration m, the algorithm computes the gradient of the current loss for each observation and then fits a regression tree to these pseudo-residuals. In a second step, it identifies an optimal prediction for each leaf node that minimizes the incremental loss due to adding this new learner to the ensemble.

This differs from standalone decision trees and random forests, where the prediction depends on the outcomes for the training samples assigned to a terminal node, namely their average, in the case of regression, or the frequency of the positive class for binary classification. The focus on the gradient of the loss function also implies that gradient boosting uses regression trees to learn both regression and classification rules because the gradient is always a continuous function.

The final ensemble model makes predictions based on the weighted sum of the predictions of the individual decision trees, each of which has been trained to minimize the ensemble loss, given the prior prediction for a given set of feature values, as shown in the following diagram:

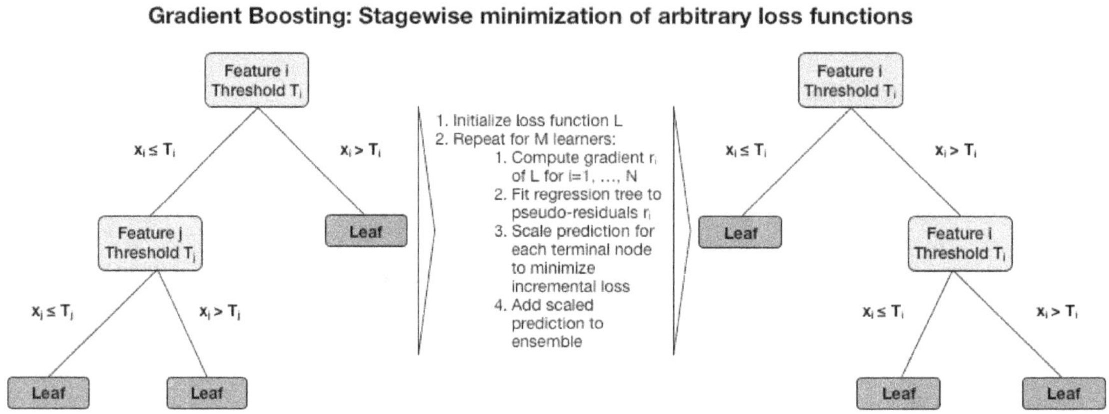

Figure 12.2: The gradient boosting algorithm

Gradient boosting trees have produced **state-of-the-art performance on many classification**, **regression**, and **ranking benchmarks**. They are probably the most popular ensemble learning algorithms as standalone predictors in a diverse set of ML competitions, as well as in real-world production pipelines, for example, to predict click-through rates for online ads.

The success of gradient boosting is based on its ability to learn complex functional relationships in an incremental fashion. However, the flexibility of this algorithm requires the careful management of the **risk of overfitting** by tuning **hyperparameters** that constrain the model's tendency to learn noise, as opposed to the signal, in the training data.

We will introduce the key mechanisms to control the complexity of a gradient boosting tree model, and then illustrate model tuning using the sklearn implementation.

How to train and tune GBM models

Boosting has often demonstrated **remarkable resilience to overfitting**, despite significant growth of the ensemble and, thus, the complexity of the model. The combination of very low and decreasing training error with non-increasing validation error is often associated with improved confidence in the predictions: as boosting continues to grow the ensemble with the goal of improving predictions for the most challenging cases, it adjusts the decision boundary to maximize the distance, or margin, of the data points.

However, overfitting certainly happens, and the **two key drivers of gradient boosting performance** are the size of the ensemble and the complexity of its constituent decision trees.

The control of the **complexity of decision trees** aims to avoid learning highly specific rules that typically imply a very small number of samples in leaf nodes. We covered the most effective constraints used to limit the ability of a decision tree to overfit to the training data in the previous chapter. They include minimum thresholds for:

- The number of samples to either split a node or accept it as a terminal node.
- The improvement in node quality, as measured by the purity or entropy for classification, or mean-squared error for regression, to further grow the tree.

In addition to directly controlling the size of the ensemble, there are various regularization techniques, such as **shrinkage**, that we encountered in the context of the ridge and lasso linear regression models in *Chapter 7, Linear Models – From Risk Factors to Return Forecasts*. Furthermore, the randomization techniques used in the context of random forests are also commonly applied to gradient boosting machines.

Ensemble size and early stopping

Each boosting iteration aims to reduce the training loss, increasing the risk of overfitting for a large ensemble. Cross-validation is the best approach to find the optimal ensemble size that minimizes the generalization error.

Since the ensemble size needs to be specified before training, it is useful to monitor the performance on the validation set and abort the training process when, for a given number of iterations, the validation error no longer decreases. This technique is called **early stopping** and is frequently used for models that require a large number of iterations and are prone to overfitting, including deep neural networks.

Keep in mind that using early stopping with the same validation set for a large number of trials will also lead to overfitting, but just for the particular validation set rather than the training set. It is best to avoid running a large number of experiments when developing a trading strategy as the risk of **false discoveries** increases significantly. In any case, keep a **hold-out test set** to obtain an unbiased estimate of the generalization error.

Shrinkage and learning rate

Shrinkage techniques apply a penalty for increased model complexity to the model's loss function. For boosting ensembles, shrinkage can be applied by **scaling the contribution of each new ensemble member down** by a factor between 0 and 1. This factor is called the **learning rate** of the boosting ensemble. Reducing the learning rate increases shrinkage because it lowers the contribution of each new decision tree to the ensemble.

The learning rate has the opposite effect of the ensemble size, which tends to increase for lower learning rates. Lower learning rates coupled with larger ensembles have been found to reduce the test error, in particular for regression and probability estimation. Large numbers of iterations are computationally more expensive but often feasible with fast, state-of-the-art implementations as long as the individual trees remain shallow.

Depending on the implementation, you can also use **adaptive learning rates** that adjust to the number of iterations, typically lowering the impact of trees added later in the process. We will see some examples later in this chapter.

Subsampling and stochastic gradient boosting

As discussed in detail in the previous chapter, bootstrap averaging (bagging) improves the performance of an otherwise noisy classifier.

Stochastic gradient boosting samples the training data without replacement at each iteration to grow the next tree (whereas bagging uses sampling with replacement). The benefit is lower computational effort due to the smaller sample and often better accuracy, but subsampling should be combined with shrinkage.

As you can see, the number of hyperparameters keeps increasing, which drives up the number of potential combinations. As a result, the risk of false positives increases when choosing the best model from a large number of trials based on a limited amount of training data. The best approach is to proceed sequentially and select parameter values individually or use combinations of subsets of low cardinality.

How to use gradient boosting with sklearn

The ensemble module of sklearn contains an implementation of gradient boosting trees for regression and classification, both binary and multiclass. The following `GradientBoostingClassifier` initialization code illustrates the key tuning parameters. The notebook `sklearn_gbm_tuning` contains the code examples for this section. More recently (version 0.21), scikit-learn introduced a much faster, yet still experimental, `HistGradientBoostingClassifier` inspired by the implementations in the following section.

The available loss functions include the exponential loss that leads to the AdaBoost algorithm and the deviance that corresponds to the logistic regression for probabilistic outputs. The `friedman_mse` node quality measure is a variation on the mean-squared error, which includes an improvement score (see the scikit-learn documentation linked on GitHub), as shown in the following code:

```
# deviance = logistic reg; exponential: AdaBoost
gb_clf = GradientBoostingClassifier(loss='deviance',
# shrinks the contribution of each tree
                                    learning_rate=0.1,
# number of boosting stages
                                    n_estimators=100,
# fraction of samples used t fit base learners
                                    subsample=1.0,
# measures the quality of a split
                                    criterion='friedman_mse',
                                    min_samples_split=2,
                                    min_samples_leaf=1,
# min. fraction of sum of weights
                                    min_weight_fraction_leaf=0.0,
```

```
# opt value depends on interaction
                                 max_depth=3,
                                 min_impurity_decrease=0.0,
                                 min_impurity_split=None,
                                 max_features=None,
                                 max_leaf_nodes=None,
                                 warm_start=False,
                                 presort='auto',
                                 validation_fraction=0.1,
                                 tol=0.0001)
```

Similar to `AdaBoostClassifier`, this model cannot handle missing values. We'll again use 12-fold cross-validation to obtain errors for classifying the directional return for rolling 1-month holding periods, as shown in the following code:

```
gb_cv_result = run_cv(gb_clf, y=y_clean, X=X_dummies_clean)
gb_result = stack_results(gb_cv_result)
```

We parse and plot the result to find a slight improvement—using default parameter values—over both `AdaBoostClassifier` and the random forest as the test AUC increases to 0.537. *Figure 12.3* shows boxplots for the various loss metrics we are tracking:

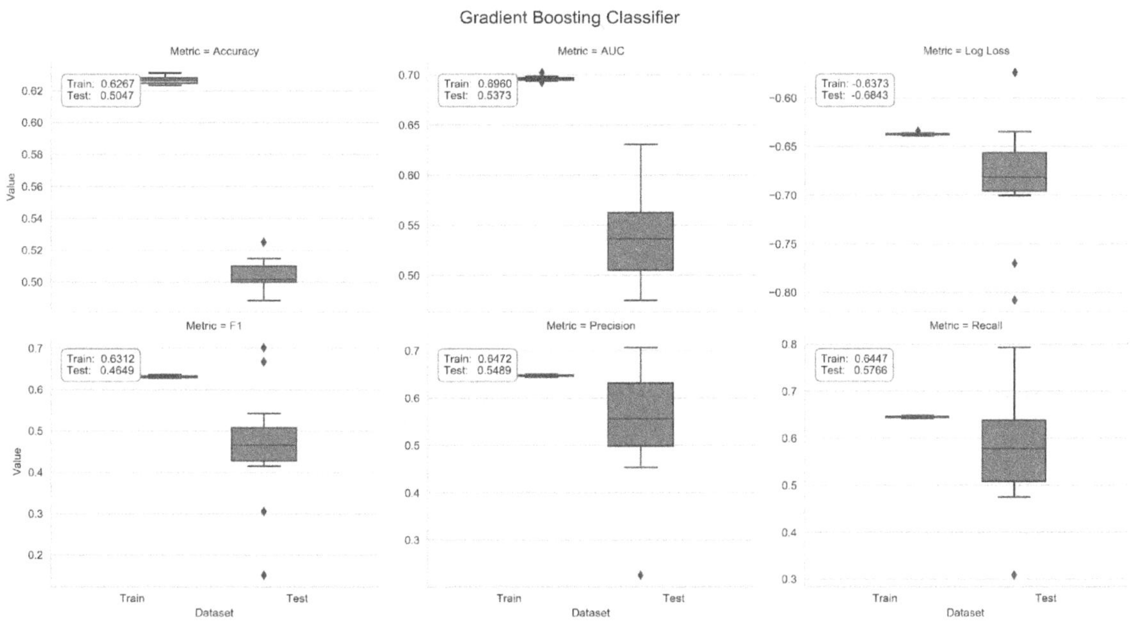

Figure 12.3: Cross-validation performance of the scikit-learn gradient boosting classifier

How to tune parameters with GridSearchCV

The `GridSearchCV` class in the `model_selection` module facilitates the systematic evaluation of all combinations of the hyperparameter values that we would like to test. In the following code, we will illustrate this functionality for seven tuning parameters, which, when defined, will result in a total of $24 \times 32 \times 4 = 576$ different model configurations:

```
cv = OneStepTimeSeriesSplit(n_splits=12)
param_grid = dict(
        n_estimators=[100, 300],
        learning_rate=[.01, .1, .2],
        max_depth=list(range(3, 13, 3)),
        subsample=[.8, 1],
        min_samples_split=[10, 50],
        min_impurity_decrease=[0, .01],
        max_features=['sqrt', .8, 1])
```

The `.fit()` method executes the cross-validation using the custom `OneStepTimeSeriesSplit` and the `roc_auc` score to evaluate the 12 folds. Sklearn lets us persist the result, as it would for any other model, using the `joblib` pickle implementation, as shown in the following code:

```
gs = GridSearchCV(gb_clf,
                  param_grid,
                  cv=cv,
                  scoring='roc_auc',
                  verbose=3,
                  n_jobs=-1,
                  return_train_score=True)
gs.fit(X=X, y=y)
# persist result using joblib for more efficient storage of large numpy arrays
joblib.dump(gs, 'gbm_gridsearch.joblib')
```

The `GridSearchCV` object has several additional attributes, after completion, that we can access after loading the pickled result. We can use them to learn which hyperparameter combination performed best and its average cross-validation AUC score, which results in a modest improvement over the default values. This is shown in the following code:

```
pd.Series(gridsearch_result.best_params_)
learning_rate              0.01
max_depth                  9.00
max_features               1.00
min_impurity_decrease      0.01
min_samples_split         50.00
n_estimators             300.00
subsample                  1.00

gridsearch_result.best_score_
0.5569
```

Parameter impact on test scores

The `GridSearchCV` result stores the average cross-validation scores so that we can analyze how different hyperparameter settings affect the outcome.

The six seaborn swarm plots in the right panel of *Figure 12.4* show the distribution of AUC test scores for all hyperparameter values. In this case, the highest AUC test scores required a low `learning_rate` and a large value for `max_features`. Some parameter settings, such as a low `learning_rate`, produce a wide range of outcomes that depend on the complementary settings of other parameters:

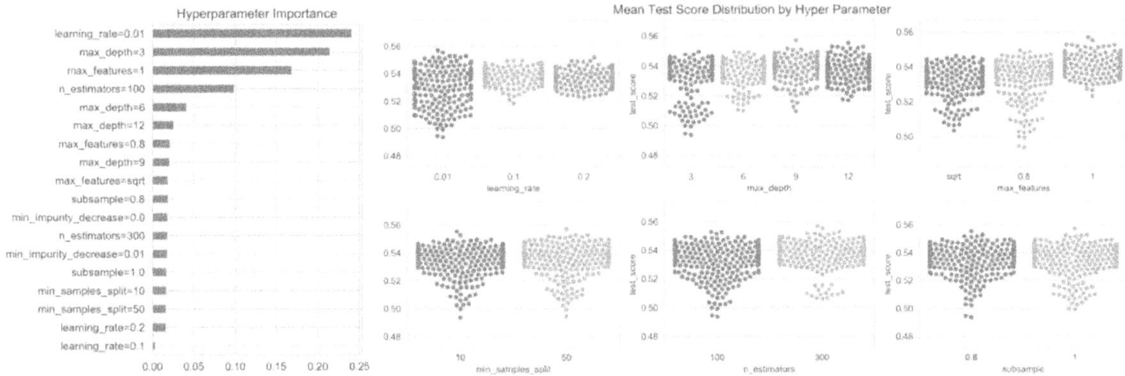

Figure 12.4: Hyperparameter impact for the scikit-learn gradient boosting model

We will now explore how hyperparameter settings jointly affect the cross-validation performance. To gain insight into how parameter settings interact, we can train a `DecisionTreeRegressor` with the mean CV AUC as the outcome and the parameter settings, encoded in one-hot or dummy format (see the notebook for details). The tree structure highlights that using all features (`max_features=1`), a low `learning_rate`, and a `max_depth` above three led to the best results, as shown in the following diagram:

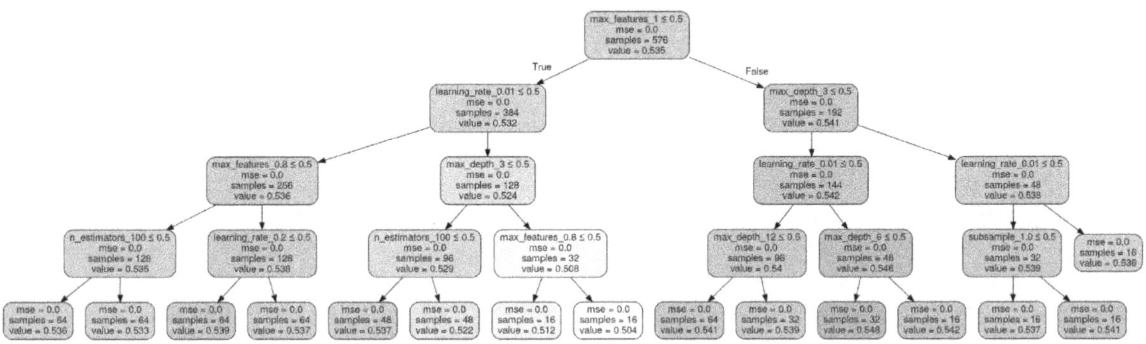

Figure 12.5: Impact of the gradient boosting model hyperparameter settings on test performance

The bar chart in the left panel of *Figure 12.4* displays the influence of the hyperparameter settings in producing different outcomes, measured by their feature importance for a decision tree that has grown to its maximum depth. Naturally, the features that appear near the top of the tree also accumulate the highest importance scores.

How to test on the holdout set

Finally, we would like to evaluate the best model's performance on the holdout set that we excluded from the `GridSearchCV` exercise. It contains the last 7 months of the sample period (through February 2018; see the notebook for details).

We obtain a generalization performance estimate based on the AUC score of 0.5381 for the first month of the hold-out period using the following code example:

```
idx = pd.IndexSlice
auc = {}
for i, test_date in enumerate(test_dates):
    test_data = test_feature_data.loc[idx[:, test_date], :]
    preds = best_model.predict(test_data)
    auc[i] = roc_auc_score(y_true=test_target.loc[test_data.index], y_
score=preds)
auc = pd.Series(auc)
```

The downside of the sklearn gradient boosting implementation is the **limited training speed**, which makes it difficult to try out different hyperparameter settings quickly. In the next section, we will see that several optimized implementations have emerged over the last few years that significantly reduce the time required to train even large-scale models, and have greatly contributed to a broader scope for applications of this highly effective algorithm.

Using XGBoost, LightGBM, and CatBoost

Over the last few years, several new gradient boosting implementations have used various innovations that accelerate training, improve resource efficiency, and allow the algorithm to scale to very large datasets. The new implementations and their sources are as follows:

- **XGBoost**: Started in 2014 by T. Chen during his Ph.D. (T. Chen and Guestrin 2016)
- **LightGBM**: Released in January 2017 by Microsoft (Ke et al. 2017)
- **CatBoost**: Released in April 2017 by Yandex (Prokhorenkova et al. 2019)

These innovations address specific challenges of training a gradient boosting model (see this chapter's `README` file on GitHub for links to the documentation). The XGBoost implementation was the first new implementation to gain popularity: among the 29 winning solutions published by Kaggle in 2015, 17 solutions used XGBoost. Eight of these solely relied on XGBoost, while the others combined XGBoost with neural networks.

We will first introduce the key innovations that have emerged over time and subsequently converged (so that most features are available for all implementations), before illustrating their implementation.

How algorithmic innovations boost performance

Random forests can be trained in parallel by growing individual trees on independent bootstrap samples. The **sequential approach of gradient boosting**, in contrast, slows down training, which, in turn, complicates experimentation with the large number of hyperparameters that need to be adapted to the nature of the task and the dataset.

To add a tree to the ensemble, the algorithm minimizes the prediction error with respect to the negative gradient of the loss function, similar to a conventional gradient descent optimizer. The **computational cost during training is thus proportional to the time it takes to evaluate potential split points** for each feature.

Second-order loss function approximation

The most important algorithmic innovations lower the cost of evaluating the loss function by using an approximation that relies on second-order derivatives, resembling Newton's method to find stationary points. As a result, scoring potential splits becomes much faster.

As discussed, a gradient boosting ensemble H_M is trained incrementally to minimize the sum of the prediction error and the regularization penalty. Denoting the prediction of the outcome y_i by the ensemble after step m as $\hat{y}_i(m)$, as a differentiable convex loss function that measures the difference between the outcome and the prediction, and Ω as a penalty that increases with the complexity of the ensemble H_M. The incremental hypothesis h_m aims to minimize the following objective L:

$$\mathcal{L}^{(m)} = \sum_{i=1}^{n} \underbrace{l\left(y_i, \hat{y}_i^{(m)}\right)}_{\text{Loss at step m}} + \sum_{i=1}^{t} \underbrace{\Omega(H_m)}_{\text{Regularization}} = \sum_{i=1}^{n} l\left(y_i, \hat{y}_i^{(m-1)} + \underbrace{h_m(x_i)}_{\text{additional tree}}\right) + \Omega(H_m)$$

The regularization penalty helps to avoid overfitting by favoring a model that uses simple yet predictive regression trees. In the case of XGBoost, for example, the penalty for a regression tree h depends on the number of leaves per tree T, the regression tree scores for each terminal node w, and the hyperparameters γ and λ. This is summarized in the following formula:

$$\Omega(h) = \gamma T + \frac{1}{2}\lambda||w||^2$$

Therefore, at each step, the algorithm greedily adds the hypothesis h_m that most improves the regularized objective. The second-order approximation of a loss function, based on a Taylor expansion, speeds up the evaluation of the objective, as summarized in the following formula:

$$\mathcal{L}^{(m)} \simeq \sum_{i=1}^{n} \left[g_i f_m(x_i) + \frac{1}{2} h_i f_m^2(x_i)\right] + \Omega\left(h_m\right)$$

Here, g_i is the first-order gradient of the loss function before adding the new learner for a given feature value, and h_i is the corresponding second-order gradient (or Hessian) value, as shown in the following formulas:

$$g_i = \partial_{\hat{y}_i^{(m-1)}} l\left(y_i, \hat{y}_i^{(m-1)}\right)$$

$$h_i = \partial^2_{\hat{y}_i^{(m-1)}} l\left(y_i, \hat{y}_i^{(m-1)}\right)$$

The XGBoost algorithm was the first open source algorithm to leverage this approximation of the loss function to compute the optimal leaf scores for a given tree structure and the corresponding value of the loss function. The score consists of the ratio of the sums of the gradient and Hessian for the samples in a terminal node. It uses this value to score the information gain that would result from a split, similar to the node impurity measures we saw in the previous chapter, but applicable to arbitrary loss functions. See Chen and Guestrin (2016) for the detailed derivation.

Simplified split-finding algorithms

The original gradient boosting implementation by sklearn finds the optimal split that enumerates all options for continuous features. This **exact greedy algorithm** is computationally very demanding due to the potentially very large number of split options for each feature. This approach faces additional challenges when the data does not fit in memory or when training in a distributed setting on multiple machines.

An **approximate split-finding** algorithm reduces the number of split points by assigning feature values to a user-determined set of bins, which can also greatly reduce the memory requirements during training. This is because only a single value needs to be stored for each bin. XGBoost introduced a **quantile sketch** algorithm that divides weighted training samples into percentile bins to achieve a uniform distribution. XGBoost also introduced the ability to handle sparse data caused by missing values, frequent zero-gradient statistics, and one-hot encoding, and can learn an optimal default direction for a given split. As a result, the algorithm only needs to evaluate non-missing values.

In contrast, LightGBM uses **gradient-based one-side sampling** (**GOSS**) to exclude a significant proportion of samples with small gradients, and only uses the remainder to estimate the information gain and select a split value accordingly. Samples with larger gradients require more training and tend to contribute more to the information gain.

LightGBM also uses exclusive feature bundling to combine features that are mutually exclusive, in that they rarely take nonzero values simultaneously, to reduce the number of features. As a result, LightGBM was the fastest implementation when released and still often performs best.

Depth-wise versus leaf-wise growth

LightGBM differs from XGBoost and CatBoost in how it prioritizes which nodes to split. LightGBM decides on splits leaf-wise, that is, it splits the leaf node that maximizes the information gain, even when this leads to unbalanced trees. In contrast, XGBoost and CatBoost expand all nodes depth-wise and first split all nodes at a given level of depth, before adding more levels. The two approaches expand nodes in a different order and will produce different results except for complete trees. The following diagram illustrates these two approaches:

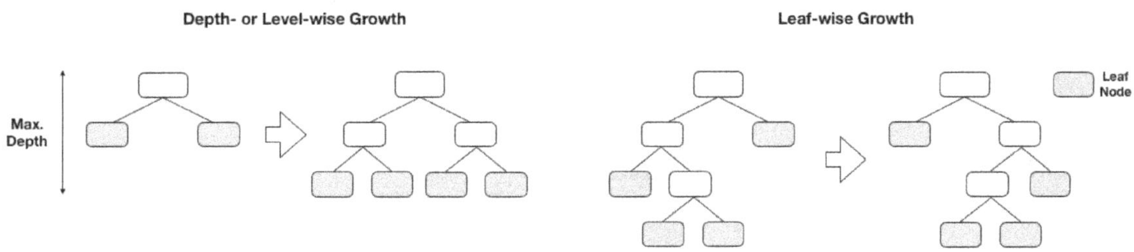

Figure 12.6: Depth-wise vs leaf-wise growth

LightGBM's leaf-wise splits tend to increase model complexity and may speed up convergence, but also increase the risk of overfitting. A tree grown depth-wise with n levels has up to 2^n terminal nodes, whereas a leaf-wise tree with 2^n leaves can have significantly more levels and contain correspondingly fewer samples in some leaves. Hence, tuning LightGBM's `num_leaves` setting requires extra caution, and the library allows us to control `max_depth` at the same time to avoid undue node imbalance. More recent versions of LightGBM also offer depth-wise tree growth.

GPU-based training

All new implementations support training and prediction on one or more GPUs to achieve significant speedups. They are compatible with current CUDA-enabled GPUs. Installation requirements vary and are evolving quickly. The XGBoost and CatBoost implementations work for several current versions, but LightGBM may require local compilation (see GitHub for links to the documentation).

The speedups depend on the library and the type of the data, and they range from low, single-digit multiples to factors of several dozen. Activation of the GPU only requires the change of a task parameter and no other hyperparameter modifications.

DART – dropout for additive regression trees

Rashmi and Gilad-Bachrach (2015) proposed a new model to train gradient boosting trees to address a problem they labeled **over-specialization**: trees added during later iterations tend only to affect the prediction of a few instances, while making a minor contribution to the remaining instances. However, the model's out-of-sample performance can suffer, and it may become over-sensitive to the contributions of a small number of trees.

The new algorithms employ dropouts that have been successfully used for learning more accurate deep neural networks, where they mute a random fraction of the neural connections during training. As a result, nodes in higher layers cannot rely on a few connections to pass the information needed for the prediction. This method has made a significant contribution to the success of deep neural networks for many tasks and has also been used with other learning techniques, such as logistic regression.

DART, or **dropout for additive regression trees**, operates at the level of trees and mutes complete trees as opposed to individual features. The goal is for trees in the ensemble generated using DART to contribute more evenly toward the final prediction. In some cases, this has been shown to produce more accurate predictions for ranking, regression, and classification tasks. The approach was first implemented in LightGBM and is also available for XGBoost.

Treatment of categorical features

The CatBoost and LightGBM implementations handle categorical variables directly without the need for dummy encoding.

The CatBoost implementation (which is named for its treatment of categorical features) includes several options to handle such features, in addition to automatic one-hot encoding. It assigns either the categories of individual features or combinations of categories for several features to numerical values. In other words, CatBoost can create new categorical features from combinations of existing features. The numerical values associated with the category levels of individual features or combinations of features depend on their relationship with the outcome value. In the classification case, this is related to the probability of observing the positive class, computed cumulatively over the sample, based on a prior, and with a smoothing factor. See the CatBoost documentation for more detailed numerical examples.

The LightGBM implementation groups the levels of the categorical features to maximize homogeneity (or minimize variance) within groups with respect to the outcome values. The XGBoost implementation does not handle categorical features directly and requires one-hot (or dummy) encoding.

Additional features and optimizations

XGBoost optimizes computation in several respects to enable multithreading. Most importantly, it keeps data in memory in compressed column blocks, where each column is sorted by the corresponding feature value. It computes this input data layout once before training and reuses it throughout to amortize the up-front cost. As a result, the search for split statistics over columns becomes a linear scan of quantiles that can be done in parallel and supports column subsampling.

The subsequently released LightGBM and CatBoost libraries built on these innovations, and LightGBM further accelerated training through optimized threading and reduced memory usage. Because of their open source nature, libraries have tended to converge over time.

XGBoost also supports **monotonicity constraints**. These constraints ensure that the values for a given feature are only positively or negatively related to the outcome over its entire range. They are useful to incorporate external assumptions about the model that are known to be true.

A long-short trading strategy with boosting

In this section, we'll design, implement, and evaluate a trading strategy for US equities driven by daily return forecasts produced by gradient boosting models. We'll use the Quandl Wiki data to engineer a few simple features (see the notebook `preparing_the_model_data` for details), select a model while using 2015/16 as validation period, and run an out-of-sample test for 2017.

As in the previous examples, we'll lay out a framework and build a specific example that you can adapt to run your own experiments. There are numerous aspects that you can vary, from the asset class and investment universe to more granular aspects like the features, holding period, or trading rules. See, for example, the Alpha Factor Library in the *Appendix* for numerous additional features.

We'll keep the trading strategy simple and only use a single ML signal; a real-life application will likely use multiple signals from different sources, such as complementary ML models trained on different datasets or with different lookahead or lookback periods. It would also use sophisticated risk management, from simple stop-loss to value-at-risk analysis.

Generating signals with LightGBM and CatBoost

XGBoost, LightGBM, and CatBoost offer interfaces for multiple languages, including Python, and have both a scikit-learn interface that is compatible with other scikit-learn features, such as `GridSearchCV` and their own methods to train and predict gradient boosting models. The notebook `boosting_baseline.ipynb` that we used in the first two sections of this chapter illustrates the scikit-learn interface for each library. The notebook compares the predictive performance and running times of various libraries. It does so by training boosting models to predict monthly US equity returns for the 2001-2018 range with the features we created in *Chapter 4, Financial Feature Engineering – How to Research Alpha Factors*.

The left panel of the following image displays the predictive accuracy of the forecasts of 1-month stock price movements using default settings for all implementations, measured in terms of the mean AUC resulting from 12-fold cross-validation:

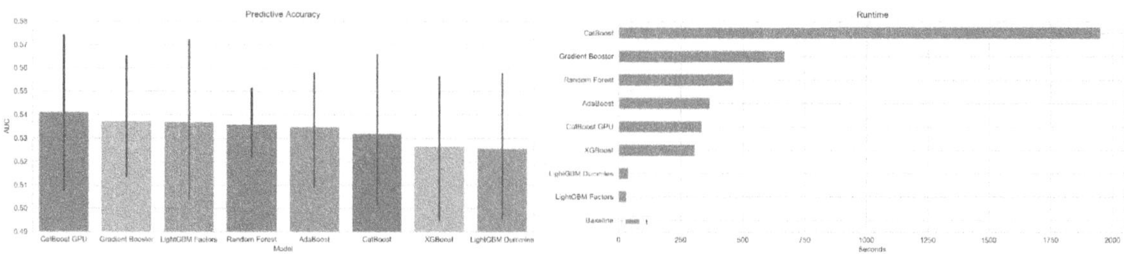

Figure 12.7: Predictive performance and runtimes of the various gradient boosting models

The **predictive performance** varies from 0.525 to 0.541. This may look like a small range but with the random benchmark AUC at 0.5, the worst-performing model improves on the benchmark by 5 percent while the best does so by 8 percent, which, in turn, is a relative rise of 60 percent. CatBoost with GPUs and LightGBM (using integer-encoded categorical variables) perform best, underlining the benefits of converting categorical into numerical variables outlined previously.

The **running time** for the experiment varies much more significantly than the predictive performance. LightGBM is 10x faster on this dataset than either XGBoost or CatBoost (using GPU) while delivering very similar predictive performance. Due to this large speed advantage and because GPU is not available to everyone, we'll focus on LightGBM but also illustrate how to use CatBoost; XGBoost works very similarly to both.

Working with LightGBM and CatBoost models entails:

1. Creating library-specific binary data formats
2. Configuring and tuning various hyperparameters
3. Evaluating the results

We will describe these steps in the following sections. The notebook `trading_signals_with_lightgbm_and_catboost` contains the code examples for this subsection, unless otherwise noted.

From Python to C++ – creating binary data formats

LightGBM and CatBoost are written in C++ and translate Python objects, like a pandas DataFrame, into binary data formats before precomputing feature statistics to accelerate the search for split points, as described in the previous section. The result can be persisted to accelerate the start of subsequent training.

We'll subset the dataset mentioned in the preceding section through the end of 2016 to cross-validate several model configurations for various lookback and lookahead windows, as well as different roll-forward periods and hyperparameters. Our approach to model selection will be similar to the one we used in the previous chapter and uses the custom `MultipleTimeSeriesCV` introduced in *Chapter 7, Linear Models – From Risk Factors to Return Forecasts.*

We select the train and validation sets, identify labels and features, and integer-encode categorical variables with values starting at zero, as expected by LightGBM (not necessary as long as the category codes have values less than 2^{32}, but avoids a warning):

```
data = (pd.read_hdf('data.h5', 'model_data')
            .sort_index()
            .loc[idx[:, :'2016'], :])
labels = sorted(data.filter(like='fwd').columns)
features = data.columns.difference(labels).tolist()

categoricals = ['year', 'weekday', 'month']
for feature in categoricals:
    data[feature] = pd.factorize(data[feature], sort=True)[0]
```

The notebook example iterates over many configurations, optionally using random samples to speed up model selection using a diverse subset. The goal is to identify the most impactful parameters without trying every possible combination.

To do so, we create the binary `Dataset` objects. For LightGBM, this looks as follows:

```
import lightgbm as lgb
outcome_data = data.loc[:, features + [label]].dropna()
lgb_data = lgb.Dataset(data=outcome_data.drop(label, axis=1),
                       label=outcome_data[label],
                       categorical_feature=categoricals,
                       free_raw_data=False)
```

The CatBoost data structure is called `Pool` and works similarly:

```
cat_cols_idx = [outcome_data.columns.get_loc(c) for c in categoricals]
catboost_data = Pool(label=outcome_data[label],
                     data=outcome_data.drop(label, axis=1),
                     cat_features=cat_cols_idx)
```

For both libraries, we identify the categorical variables for conversion into numerical variables based on outcome information, as described in the previous section. The CatBoost implementation needs feature columns to be identified using indices rather than labels.

We can simply slice the binary datasets using the train and validation set indices provided by `MultipleTimeSeriesCV` during cross-validation as follows, combining both examples into one snippet:

```
for i, (train_idx, test_idx) in enumerate(cv.split(X=outcome_data)):
   lgb_train = lgb_data.subset(train_idx.tolist()).construct()
   train_set = catboost_data.slice(train_idx.tolist())
```

How to tune hyperparameters

LightGBM and CatBoost implementations come with numerous hyperparameters that permit fine-grained control. Each library has parameter settings to:

- Specify the task objective and learning algorithm
- Design the base learners
- Apply various regularization techniques
- Handle early stopping during training
- Enable the use of GPU or parallelization on CPU

The documentation for each library details the various parameters. Since they implement variations of the same algorithms, parameters may refer to the same concept but have different names across libraries. The GitHub repository lists resources that clarify which XGBoost and LightGBM parameters have a comparable effect.

Objectives and loss functions

The libraries support several boosting algorithms, including gradient boosting for trees and linear base learners, as well as DART for LightGBM and XGBoost. LightGBM also supports the GOSS algorithm, which we described previously, as well as random forests.

The appeal of gradient boosting consists of the efficient support of arbitrary differentiable loss functions, and each library offers various options for regression, classification, and ranking tasks. In addition to the chosen loss function, additional evaluation metrics can be used to monitor performance during training and cross-validation.

Learning parameters

Gradient boosting models typically use decision trees to capture feature interaction, and the size of individual trees is the most important tuning parameter. XGBoost and CatBoost set the `max_depth` default to 6. In contrast, LightGBM uses a default `num_leaves` value of 31, which corresponds to five levels for a balanced tree, but imposes no constraints on the number of levels. To avoid overfitting, `num_leaves` should be lower than 2^{max_depth}. For example, for a well-performing `max_depth` value of 7, you would set `num_leaves` to 70–80 rather than 2^7=128, or directly constrain `max_depth`.

The number of trees or boosting iterations defines the overall size of the ensemble. All libraries support `early_stopping` to abort training once the loss functions register no further improvements during a given number of iterations. As a result, it is often most efficient to set a large number of iterations and stop training based on the predictive performance on a validation set. However, keep in mind that the validation error will be biased upward due to the implied lookahead bias.

The libraries also permit the use of custom loss metrics to track train and validation performance and execute `early_stopping`. The notebook illustrates how to code the **information coefficient** (IC) for LightGBM and CatBoost. However, we will not rely on `early_stopping` for our experiments to avoid said bias.

Regularization

All libraries implement the regularization strategies for base learners, such as minimum values for the number of samples or the minimum information gain required for splits and leaf nodes.

They also support regularization at the ensemble level using shrinkage, which is implemented via a learning rate that constrains the contribution of new trees. It is also possible to implement an adaptive learning rate via callback functions that lower the learning rate as the training progresses, as has been successfully used in the context of neural networks. Furthermore, the gradient boosting loss function can be constrained using L1 or L2 regularization, similar to the ridge and lasso regression models, for example, by increasing the penalty for adding more trees.

The libraries also allow for the use of bagging or column subsampling to randomize tree growth for random forests and decorrelate prediction errors to reduce overall variance. The quantization of features for approximate split finding adds larger bins as an additional option to protect against overfitting.

Randomized grid search

To explore the hyperparameter space, we specify values for key parameters that we would like to test in combination. The sklearn library supports `RandomizedSearchCV` to cross-validate a subset of parameter combinations that are sampled randomly from specified distributions. We will implement a custom version that allows us to monitor performance so we can abort the search process once we're satisfied with the result, rather than specifying a set number of iterations beforehand.

To this end, we specify options for the relevant hyperparameters of each library, generate all combinations using the Cartesian product generator provided by the itertools library, and shuffle the result.

In the case of LightGBM, we focus on the learning rate, the maximum size of the trees, the randomization of the feature space during training, and the minimum number of data points required for a split. This results in the following code, where we randomly select half of the configurations:

```
learning_rate_ops = [.01, .1, .3]
max_depths = [2, 3, 5, 7]
num_leaves_opts = [2 ** i for i in max_depths]
feature_fraction_opts = [.3, .6, .95]
min_data_in_leaf_opts = [250, 500, 1000]

cv_params = list(product(learning_rate_ops,
                         num_leaves_opts,
                         feature_fraction_opts,
                         min_data_in_leaf_opts))
n_params = len(cv_params)
```

```
# randomly sample 50%
cvp = np.random.choice(list(range(n_params)),
                       size=int(n_params / 2),
                       replace=False)
cv_params_ = [cv_params[i] for i in cvp]
```

Now, we are mostly good to go: during each iteration, we create a `MultipleTimeSeriesCV` instance based on the `lookahead`, `train_period_length`, and `test_period_length` parameters, and cross-validate the selected hyperparameters accordingly over a 2-year period.

Note that we generate validation predictions for a range of ensemble sizes so that we can infer the optimal number of iterations:

```
num_iterations = [10, 25, 50, 75] + list(range(100, 501, 50))
num_boost_round = num_iterations[-1]

for lookahead, train_length, test_length in test_params:
   n_splits = int(2 * YEAR / test_length)
   cv = MultipleTimeSeriesCV(n_splits=n_splits,
                             lookahead=lookahead,
                             test_period_length=test_length,
                             train_period_length=train_length)
   for p, param_vals in enumerate(cv_params_):
       for i, (train_idx, test_idx) in enumerate(cv.split(X=outcome_data)):
           lgb_train = lgb_data.subset(train_idx.tolist()).construct()
           model = lgb.train(params=params,
                             train_set=lgb_train,
                             num_boost_round=num_boost_round,
                             verbose_eval=False)

           test_set = outcome_data.iloc[test_idx, :]
           X_test = test_set.loc[:, model.feature_name()]
           y_test = test_set.loc[:, label]
           y_pred = {str(n): model.predict(X_test, num_iteration=n) for n in
num_iterations}
```

Please see the notebook `trading_signals_with_lightgbm_and_catboost` for additional details, including how to log results and compute and capture various metrics that we need for the evaluation of the results, to which we'll turn to next.

How to evaluate the results

Now that cross-validation of numerous configurations has produced a large number of results, we need to evaluate the predictive performance to identify the model that generates the most reliable and profitable signals for our prospective trading strategy. The notebook `evaluate_trading_signals` contains the code examples for this section.

We produced a larger number of LightGBM models because it runs an order of magnitude faster than CatBoost and will demonstrate some evaluation strategies accordingly.

Cross-validation results – LightGBM versus CatBoost

First, we compare the predictive performance of the models produced by the two libraries across all configurations in terms of their validation IC, both across the entire validation period and averaged over daily forecasts.

The following image shows that that LightGBM performs (slightly) better than CatBoost, especially for longer horizons. This is not an entirely fair comparison because we ran more configurations for LightGBM, which also, unsurprisingly, shows a wider dispersion of outcomes:

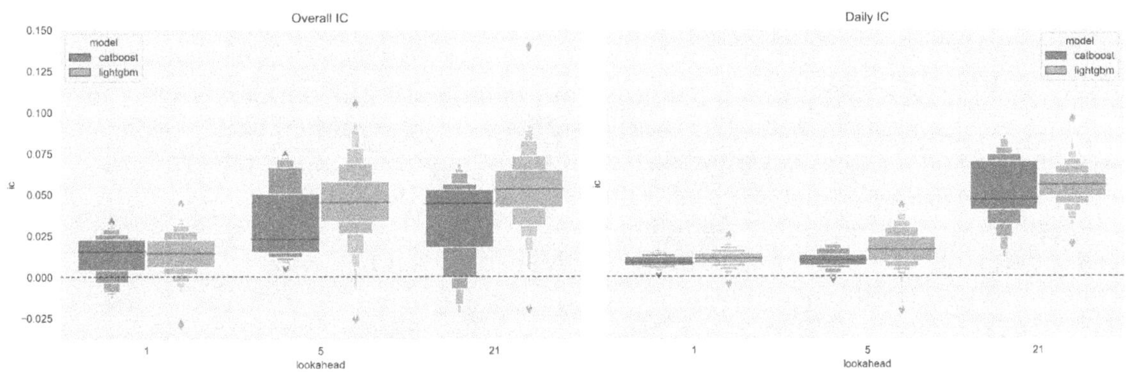

Figure 12.8: Overall and daily IC for the LightGBM and CatBoost models over three prediction horizons

Regardless, we will focus on LightGBM results; see the notebooks `trading_signals_with_lightgbm_and_catboost` and `evaluate_trading_signals` for more details on CatBoost or to run your own experiments.

In view of the substantial dispersion across model results, let's take a closer look at the best-performing parameter settings.

Best-performing parameter settings

The top-performing LightGBM models uses the following parameters for the three different prediction horizons (see the notebook for details):

Lookahead	Learning Rate	# Leaves	Feature Fraction	Min. Data in Leaf	Daily Average		Overall	
					IC	# Rounds	IC	# Rounds
1	0.3	4	95%	1,000	1.70	75	4.41	50
1	0.3	4	95%	250	1.34	250	4.36	25
1	0.3	4	95%	1,000	1.70	75	4.30	75
5	0.1	8	95%	1,000	3.95	300	10.46	300
5	0.3	4	95%	1,000	3.43	150	10.32	50

5	0.3	4	95%	1,000	3.43	150	10.24	150
21	0.1	8	60%	500	5.84	25	13.97	10
21	0.1	32	60%	250	5.89	50	11.59	10
21	0.1	4	60%	250	7.33	75	11.40	10

Note that shallow trees produce the best overall IC across the three prediction horizons. Longer training over 4.5 years also produced better results.

Hyperparameter impact – linear regression

Next, we'd like to understand if there's a systematic, statistical relationship between the hyperparameters and the outcomes across daily predictions. To this end, we will run a linear regression using the various LightGBM hyperparameter settings as dummy variables and the daily validation IC as the outcome.

The chart in *Figure 12.9* shows the coefficient estimates and their confidence intervals for 1- and 21-day forecast horizons. For the shorter horizon, a longer lookback period, a higher learning rate, and deeper trees (more leaf nodes) have a positive impact. For the longer horizon, the picture is a little less clear: shorter trees do better, but the lookback period is not significant. A higher feature sampling rate also helps. In both cases, a larger ensemble does better. Note that these results apply to this specific example only.

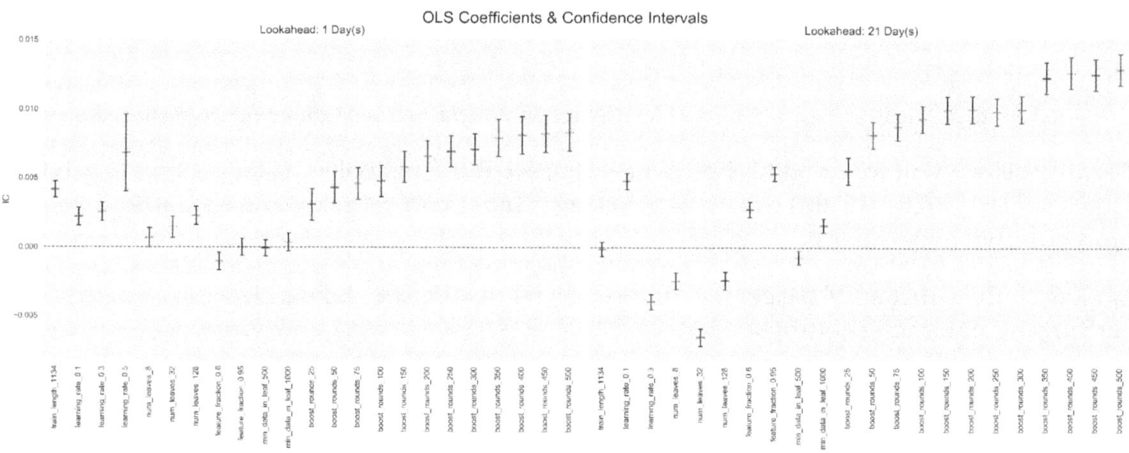

Figure 12.9: Coefficient estimates and their confidence intervals for different forecast horizons

Use IC instead of information coefficient

We average the top five models and provide the corresponding prices to Alphalens, in order to compute the mean period-wise return earned on an equal-weighted portfolio invested in the daily factor quintiles for various holding periods:

Metric	Holding Period			
	1D	5D	10D	21D
Mean Period Wise Spread (bps)	12.1654	6.9514	4.9465	4.4079
Ann. alpha	0.1759	0.0776	0.0446	0.0374
beta	0.0891	0.1516	0.1919	0.1983

We find a 12 bps spread between the top and the bottom quintile, which implies an annual alpha of 0.176 while the beta is low at 0.089 (see *Figure 12.10*):

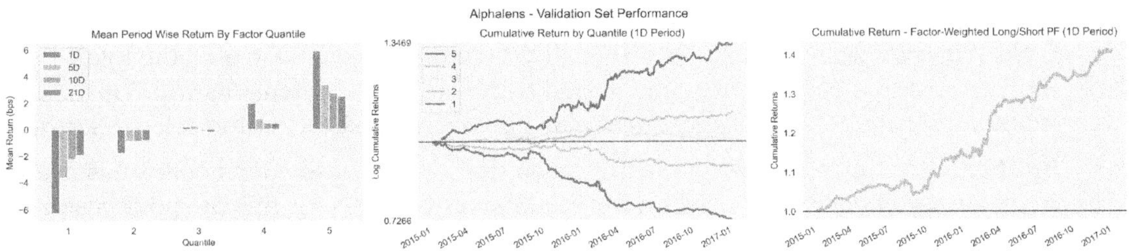

Figure 12.10: Average and cumulative returns by factor quantile

The following charts show the quarterly rolling IC for the 1-day and the 21-day forecasts over the 2-year validation period for the best-performing models:

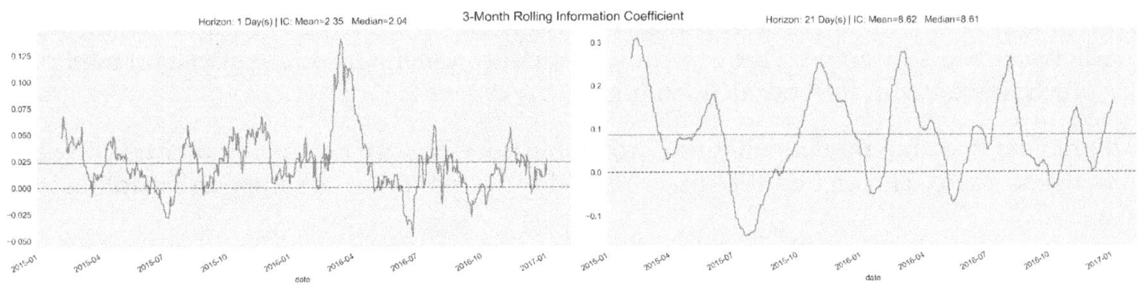

Figure 12.11: Rolling IC for 1-day and 21-day return forecasts

The average IC is 2.35 and 8.52 for the shorter and the longer horizon models, respectively, and remain positive for the large majority of days in the sample.

We'll now take a look at how to gain additional insight into how the model works before we select our models, generate predictions, define a trading strategy, and evaluate their performance.

Inside the black box – interpreting GBM results

Understanding why a model predicts a certain outcome is very important for several reasons, including trust, actionability, accountability, and debugging. Insights into the nonlinear relationship between features and the outcome uncovered by the model, as well as interactions among features, are also of value when the goal is to learn more about the underlying drivers of the phenomenon under study.

A common approach to gaining insights into the predictions made by tree ensemble methods, such as gradient boosting or random forest models, is to attribute feature importance values to each input variable. These feature importance values can be computed on an individual basis for a single prediction or globally for an entire dataset (that is, for all samples) to gain a higher-level perspective of how the model makes predictions.

The code examples for this section are in the notebook `model_interpretation`.

Feature importance

There are three primary ways to compute global feature importance values:

- **Gain**: This classic approach, introduced by Leo Breiman in 1984, uses the total reduction of loss or impurity contributed by all splits for a given feature. The motivation is largely heuristic, but it is a commonly used method to select features.
- **Split count**: This is an alternative approach that counts how often a feature is used to make a split decision, based on the selection of features for this purpose based on the resultant information gain.
- **Permutation**: This approach randomly permutes the feature values in a test set and measures how much the model's error changes, assuming that an important feature should create a large increase in the prediction error. Different permutation choices lead to alternative implementations of this basic approach.

Individualized feature importance values that compute the relevance of features for a single prediction are less common. This is because available model-agnostic explanation methods are much slower than tree-specific methods.

All gradient boosting implementations provide feature-importance scores after training as a model attribute. The LightGBM library provides two versions, as shown in the following list:

- **gain**: Contribution of a feature to reducing the loss
- **split**: The number of times the feature was used

These values are available using the trained model's `.feature_importance()` method with the corresponding `importance_type` parameter. For the best-performing LightGBM model, the results for the 20 most important features are as shown in *Figure 12.12*:

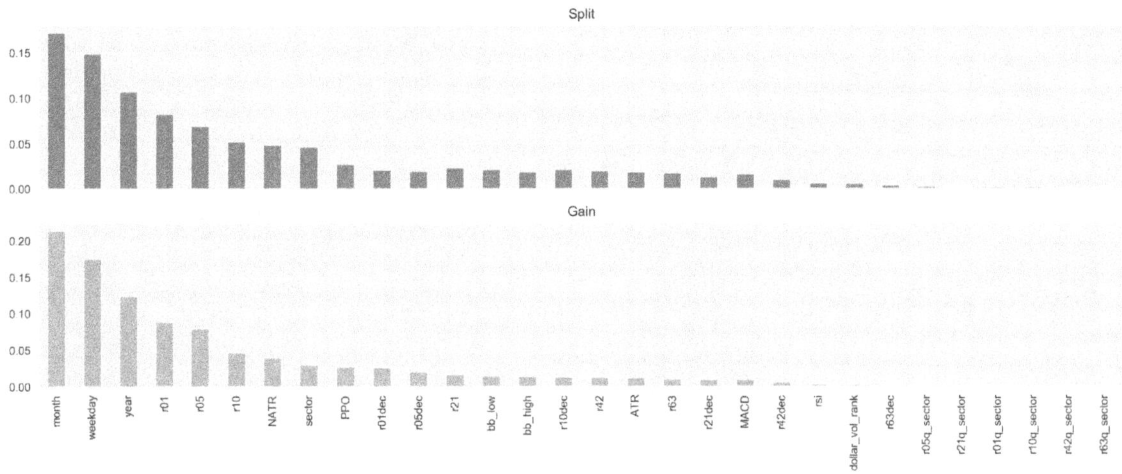

Figure 12.12: LightGBM feature importance

The time period indicators dominate, followed by the latest returns, the normalized ATR, the sector dummy, and the momentum indicator (see the notebook for implementation details).

Partial dependence plots

In addition to the summary contribution of individual features to the model's prediction, partial dependence plots visualize the relationship between the target variable and a set of features. The nonlinear nature of gradient boosting trees causes this relationship to depend on the values of all other features. Hence, we will marginalize these features out. By doing so, we can interpret the partial dependence as the expected target response.

We can visualize partial dependence only for individual features or feature pairs. The latter results in contour plots that show how combinations of feature values produce different predicted probabilities, as shown in the following code:

```
fig, axes = plot_partial_dependence(estimator=best_model,
                                    X=X,
                                    features=['return_12m', 'return_6m',
                                              'CMA', ('return_12m',
                                                      'return_6m')],
                                    percentiles=(0.01, 0.99),
                                    n_jobs=-1,
                                    n_cols=2,
                                    grid_resolution=250)
```

After some additional formatting (see the companion notebook), we obtain the results shown in *Figure 12.13*:

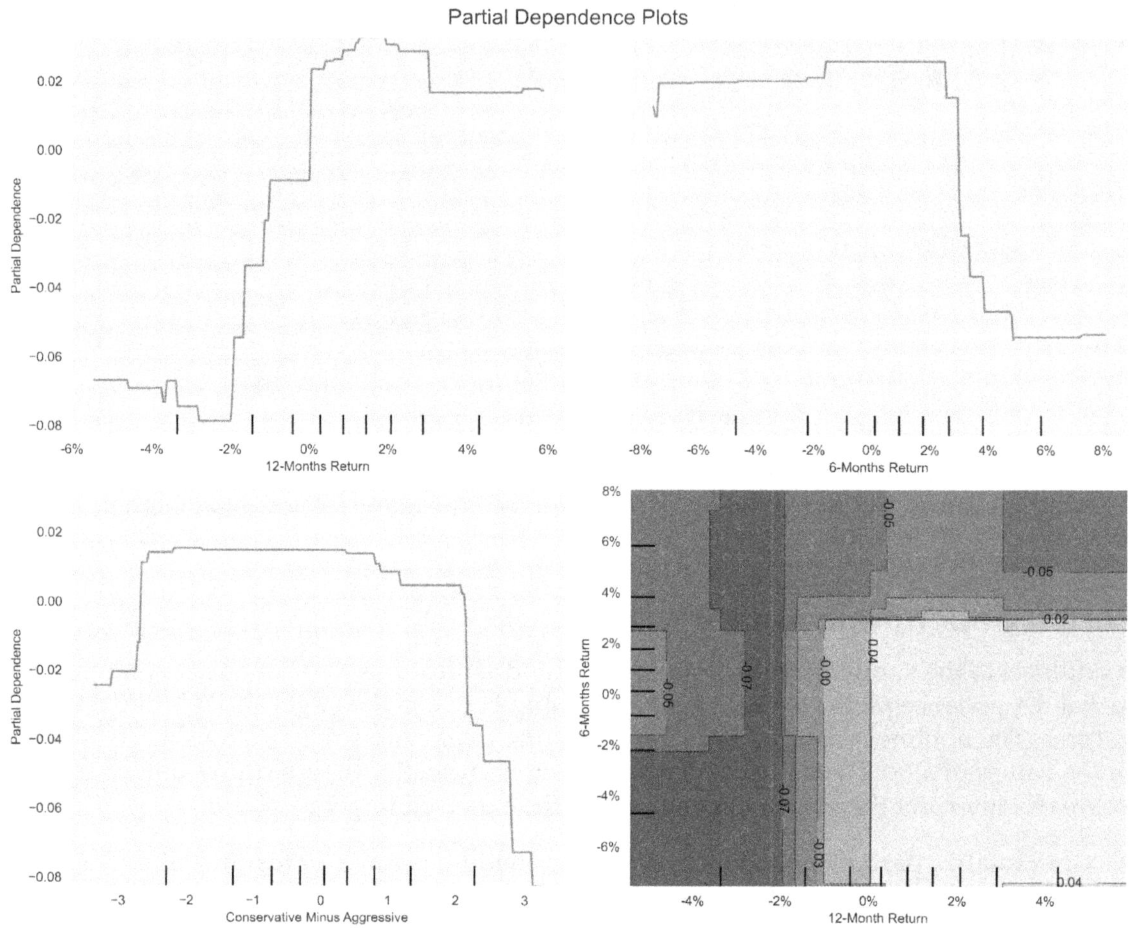

Figure 12.13: Partial dependence plots for scikit-learn GradientBoostingClassifier

The lower-right plot shows the dependence of the probability of a positive return over the next month, given the range of values for lagged 12-month and 6-month returns, after eliminating outliers at the [1%, 99%] percentiles. The `month_9` variable is a dummy variable, hence the step-function-like plot. We can also visualize the dependency in 3D, as shown in the following code:

```
targets = ['return_12m', 'return_6m']
pdp, axes = partial_dependence(estimator=gb_clf,
                               features=targets,
                               X=X_,
                               grid_resolution=100)
XX, YY = np.meshgrid(axes[0], axes[1])
Z = pdp[0].reshape(list(map(np.size, axes))).T
fig = plt.figure(figsize=(14, 8))
```

```
ax = Axes3D(fig)
surf = ax.plot_surface(XX, YY, Z,
                       rstride=1,
                       cstride=1,
                       cmap=plt.cm.BuPu,
                       edgecolor='k')
ax.set_xlabel(' '.join(targets[0].split('_')).capitalize())
ax.set_ylabel(' '.join(targets[1].split('_')).capitalize())
ax.set_zlabel('Partial Dependence')
ax.view_init(elev=22, azim=30)
```

This produces the following 3D plot of the partial dependence of the 1-month return direction on lagged 6-month and 12-months returns:

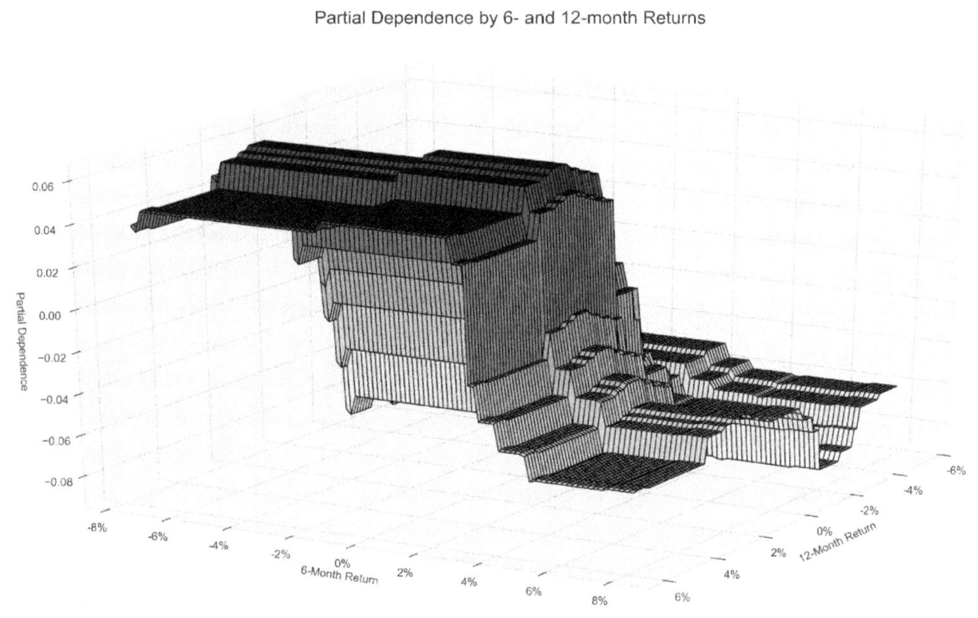

Figure 12.14: Partial dependence as a 3D plot

SHapley Additive exPlanations

At the 2017 NIPS conference, Scott Lundberg and Su-In Lee, from the University of Washington, presented a new and more accurate approach to explaining the contribution of individual features to the output of tree ensemble models called **SHapley Additive exPlanations**, or **SHAP** values.

This new algorithm departs from the observation that feature-attribution methods for tree ensembles, such as the ones we looked at earlier, are inconsistent—that is, a change in a model that increases the impact of a feature on the output can lower the importance values for this feature (see the references on GitHub for detailed illustrations of this).

SHAP values unify ideas from collaborative game theory and local explanations, and have been shown to be theoretically optimal, consistent, and locally accurate based on expectations. Most importantly, Lundberg and Lee have developed an algorithm that manages to reduce the complexity of computing these model-agnostic, additive feature-attribution methods from $O(TLDM)$ to $O(TLD^2)$, where T and M are the number of trees and features, respectively, and D and L are the maximum depth and number of leaves across the trees. This important innovation permits the explanation of predictions from previously intractable models with thousands of trees and features in a fraction of a second. An open source implementation became available in late 2017 and is compatible with XGBoost, LightGBM, CatBoost, and sklearn tree models.

Shapley values originated in game theory as a technique for assigning a value to each player in a collaborative game that reflects their contribution to the team's success. SHAP values are an adaptation of the game theory concept to tree-based models and are calculated for each feature and each sample. They measure how a feature contributes to the model output for a given observation. For this reason, SHAP values provide differentiated insights into how the impact of a feature varies across samples, which is important, given the role of interaction effects in these nonlinear models.

How to summarize SHAP values by feature

To get a high-level overview of the feature importance across a number of samples, there are two ways to plot the SHAP values: a simple average across all samples that resembles the global feature-importance measures computed previously (as shown in the left-hand panel of *Figure 12.15*), or a scatterplot to display the impact of every feature for every sample (as shown in the right-hand panel of the figure). They are very straightforward to produce using a trained model from a compatible library and matching input data, as shown in the following code:

```
# Load JS visualization code to notebook
shap.initjs()
# explain the model's predictions using SHAP values
explainer = shap.TreeExplainer(model)
shap_values = explainer.shap_values(X_test)
shap.summary_plot(shap_values, X_test, show=False)
```

The scatterplot sorts features by their total SHAP values across all samples and then shows how each feature impacts the model output, as measured by the SHAP value, as a function of the feature's value, represented by its color, where red represents high values and blue represents low values relative to the feature's range:

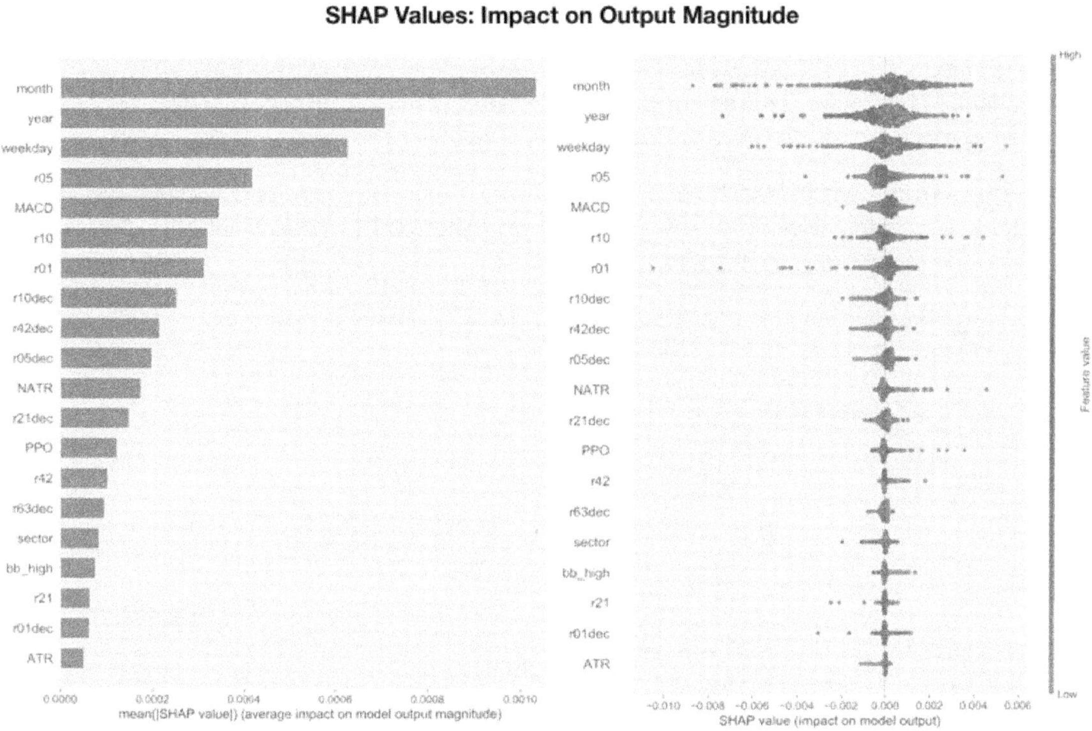

Figure 12.15: SHAP summary plots

There are some interesting differences compared to the conventional feature importance shown in *Figure 12.12*; namely, the MACD indicator turns out more important, as well as the relative return measures.

How to use force plots to explain a prediction

The force plot in the following image shows the **cumulative impact of various features and their values** on the model output, which in this case was 0.6, quite a bit higher than the base value of 0.13 (the average model output over the provided dataset). Features highlighted in red with arrows pointing to the right increase the output. The month being October is the most important feature and increases the output from 0.338 to 0.537, whereas the year being 2017 reduces the output.

Hence, we obtain a detailed breakdown of how the model arrived at a specific prediction, as shown in the following plot:

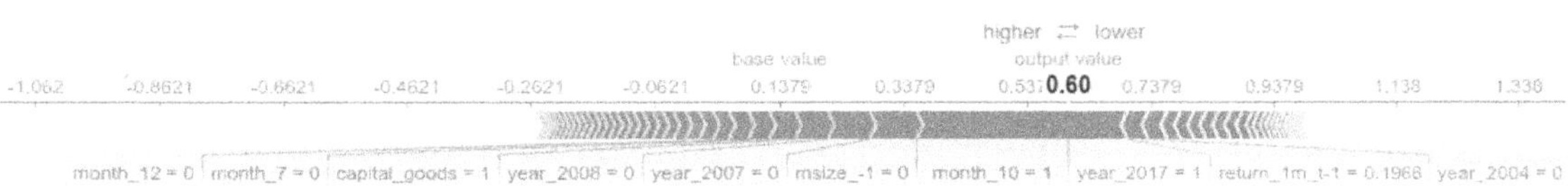

Figure 12.16: SHAP force plot

We can also compute **force plots for multiple data points** or predictions at a time and use a **clustered visualization** to gain insights into how prevalent certain influence patterns are across the dataset. The following plot shows the force plots for the first 1,000 observations rotated by 90 degrees, stacked horizontally, and ordered by the impact of different features on the outcome for the given observation.

The implementation uses hierarchical agglomerative clustering of data points on the feature SHAP values to identify these patterns, and displays the result interactively for exploratory analysis (see the notebook), as shown in the following code:

```
shap.force_plot(explainer.expected_value, shap_values[:1000,:],
                X_test.iloc[:1000])
```

This produces the following output:

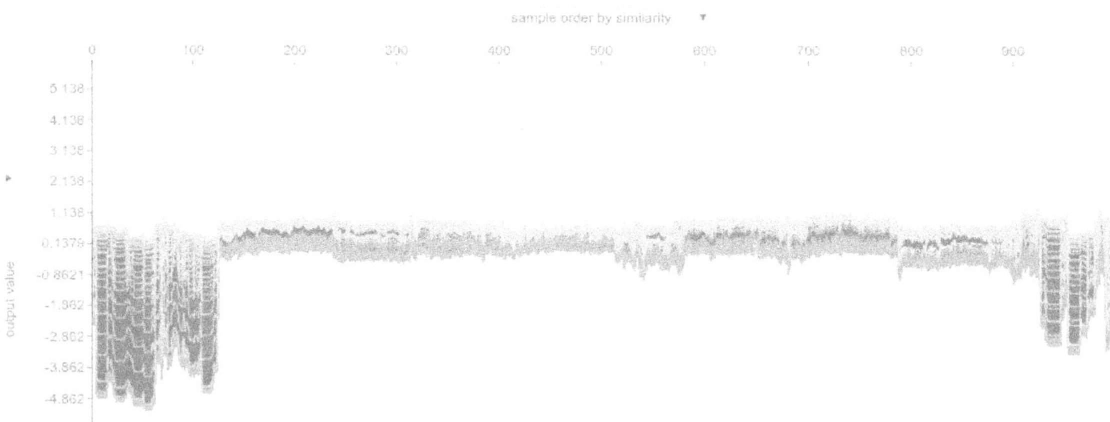

Figure 12.17: SHAP clustered force plot

How to analyze feature interaction

Lastly, SHAP values allow us to gain additional insights into the interaction effects between different features by separating these interactions from the main effects. `shap.dependence_plot` can be defined as follows:

```
shap.dependence_plot(ind='r01',
                     shap_values=shap_values,
                     features=X,
                     interaction_index='r05',
                     title='Interaction between 1- and 5-Day Returns')
```

It displays how different values for 1-month returns (on the x-axis) affect the outcome (SHAP value on the y-axis), differentiated by 3-month returns (see the following plot):

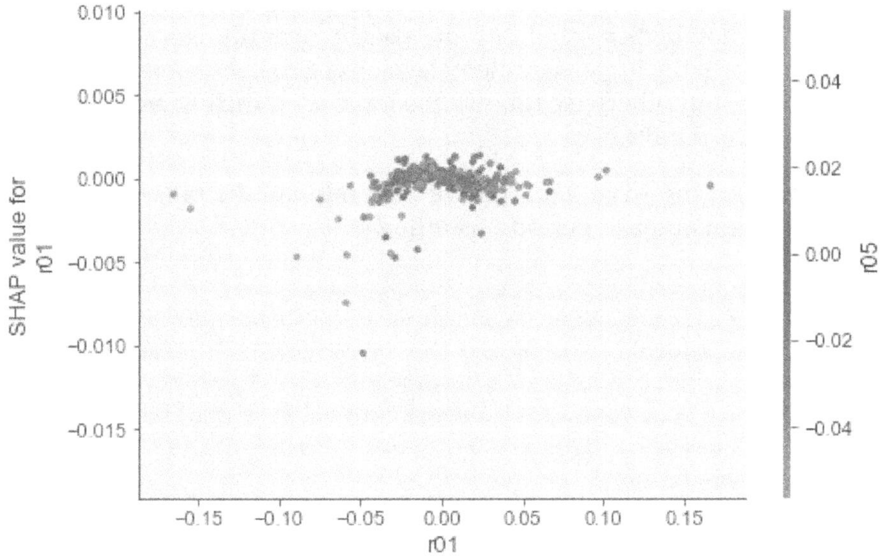

Figure 12.18: SHAP interaction plot

SHAP values provide granular feature attribution at the level of each individual prediction and enable much richer inspection of complex models through (interactive) visualization. The SHAP summary dot plot displayed earlier in this section (*Figure 12.15*) offers much more differentiated insights than a global feature-importance bar chart. Force plots of individual clustered predictions allow more detailed analysis, while SHAP dependence plots capture interaction effects and, as a result, provide more accurate and detailed results than partial dependence plots.

The limitations of SHAP values, as with any current feature-importance measure, concern the attribution of the influence of variables that are highly correlated because their similar impact can be broken down in arbitrary ways.

Backtesting a strategy based on a boosting ensemble

In this section, we'll use Zipline to evaluate the performance of a long-short strategy that enters 25 long and 25 short positions based on a daily return forecast signal. To this end, we'll select the best-performing models, generate forecasts, and design trading rules that act on these predictions.

Based on our evaluation of the cross-validation results, we'll select one or several models to generate signals for a new out-of-sample period. For this example, we'll combine predictions for the best 10 LightGBM models to reduce variance for the 1-day forecast horizon based on its solid mean quantile spread computed by Alphalens.

We just need to obtain the parameter settings for the best-performing models and then train accordingly. The notebook `making_out_of_sample_predictions` contains the requisite code. Model training uses the hyperparameter settings of the best-performing models and data for the test period, but otherwise follows the logic used during cross-validation very closely, so we'll omit the details here.

In the notebook `backtesting_with_zipline`, we've combined the predictions of the top 10 models for the validation and test periods, as follows:

```
def load_predictions(bundle):
    predictions = (pd.read_hdf('predictions.h5', 'train/01')
                   .append(pd.read_hdf('predictions.h5', 'test/01')
                   .drop('y_test', axis=1)))
    predictions = (predictions.loc[~predictions.index.duplicated()]
                   .iloc[:, :10]
                   .mean(1)
                   .sort_index()
                   .dropna()
                  .to_frame('prediction'))
```

We'll use the custom ML factor that we introduced in *Chapter 8, The ML4T Workflow – From Model to Strategy Backtesting*, to import the predictions and make it accessible in a pipeline.

We'll execute `Pipeline` from the beginning of the validation period to the end of the test period. *Figure 12.19* shows (unsurprisingly) solid in-sample performance with annual returns of 27.3 percent, compared to 8.0 percent out-of-sample. The right panel of the image shows the cumulative returns relative to the S&P 500:

Metric	All	In-sample	Out-of-sample
Annual return	20.60%	27.30%	8.00%
Cumulative returns	75.00%	62.20%	7.90%
Annual volatility	19.40%	21.40%	14.40%
Sharpe ratio	1.06	1.24	0.61
Max drawdown	-17.60%	-17.60%	-9.80%
Sortino ratio	1.69	2.01	0.87
Skew	0.86	0.95	-0.16
Kurtosis	8.61	7.94	3.07
Daily value at risk	-2.40%	-2.60%	-1.80%
Daily turnover	115.10%	108.60%	127.30%
Alpha	0.18	0.25	0.05
Beta	0.24	0.24	0.22

The Sharpe ratio is 1.24 in-sample and 0.61 out-of-sample; the right panel shows the quarterly rolling value. Alpha is 0.25 in-sample versus 0.05 out-of-sample, with beta values of 0.24 and 0.22, respectively. The worst drawdown leads to losses of 17.59 percent in the second half of 2015:

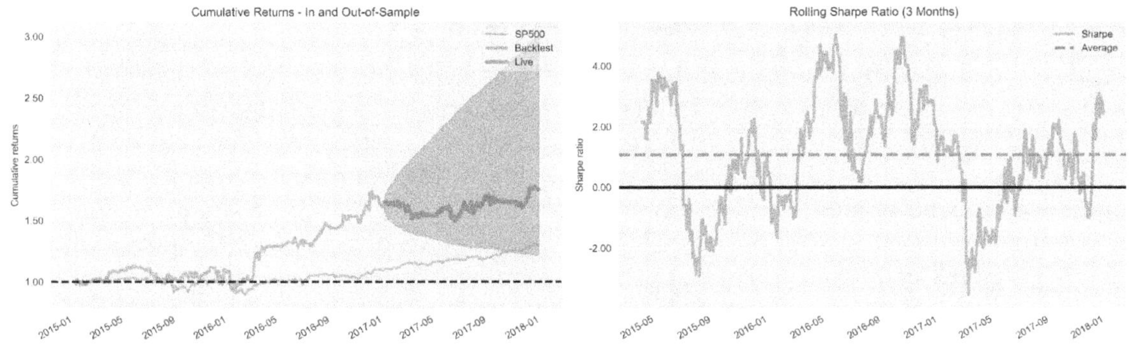

Figure 12.19: Strategy performance—cumulative returns and rolling Sharpe ratio

Long trades are slightly more profitable than short trades, which lose on average:

Summary stats	**All trades**	**Short trades**	**Long trades**
Total number of round_trips	22,352	11,631	10,721
Percent profitable	50.0%	48.0%	51.0%
Winning round_trips	11,131	5,616	5,515
Losing round_trips	11,023	5,935	5,088
Even round_trips	198	80	118

Lessons learned and next steps

Overall, we can see that despite using only market data in a highly liquid environment, the gradient boosting models manage to deliver predictions that are significantly better than random guesses. Clearly, profits are anything but guaranteed, not least since we made very generous assumptions regarding transaction costs (note the high turnover).

However, there are several ways to improve on this basic framework, that is, by varying parameters from more general and strategic to more specific and tactical aspects, such as:

1. Try a different investment universe (for example, fewer liquid stocks or other assets).
2. Be creative about adding complementary data sources.
3. Engineer more sophisticated features.
4. Vary the experiment setup using, for example, longer or shorter holding and lookback periods.
5. Come up with more interesting trading rules and use several rather than a single ML signal.

Hopefully, these suggestions inspire you to build on the template we laid out and come up with an effective ML-driven trading strategy!

Boosting for an intraday strategy

We introduced **high-frequency trading** (**HFT**) in *Chapter 1, Machine Learning for Trading – From Idea to Execution*, as a key trend that accelerated the adoption of algorithmic strategies. There is no objective definition of HFT that pins down the properties of the activities it encompasses, including holding periods, order types (for example, passive versus aggressive), and strategies (momentum or reversion, directional or liquidity provision, and so on). However, most of the more technical treatments of HFT seem to agree that the data driving HFT activity tends to be the most granular available. Typically, this would be microstructure data directly from the exchanges such as the NASDAQ ITCH data that we introduced in *Chapter 2, Market and Fundamental Data – Sources and Techniques*, to demonstrate how it details every order placed, every execution, and every cancelation, and thus permits the reconstruction of the full limit order book, at least for equities and except for certain hidden orders.

The application of ML to HFT includes the optimization of trade execution both on official exchanges and in dark pools. ML can also be used to generate trading signals, as we will show in this section; see also Kearns and Nevmyvaka (2013) for additional details and examples of how ML can add value in the HFT context.

This section uses the **AlgoSeek NASDAQ 100 dataset** from the Consolidated Feed produced by the Securities Information Processor. The data includes information on the National Best Bid and Offer quotes and trade prices at **minute bar frequency**. It also contains some features on the price dynamic, such as the number of trades at the bid or ask price, or those following positive and negative price moves at the tick level (see *Chapter 2, Market and Fundamental Data – Sources and Techniques*, for additional background and the download and preprocessing instructions in the data directory in the GitHub repository).

We'll first describe how we can engineer features for this dataset, then train a gradient boosting model to predict the volume-weighted average price for the next minute, and then evaluate the quality of the resulting trading signals.

Engineering features for high-frequency data

The dataset that AlgoSeek generously made available for this book contains over 50 variables on 100 tickers for any given day at minute frequency for the period 2013-2017. The data also covers pre-market and after-hours trading, but we'll limit this example to official market hours to the 390 minutes from 9:30 a.m. to 4:00 p.m. to somewhat restrict the size of the data, as well as to avoid having to deal with periods of irregular trading activity. See the notebook `intraday_features` for the code examples in this section.

We'll select 12 variables with over 51 million observations as raw material to create features for an ML model. This will aim predict the 1-min forward return for the volume-weighted average price:

```
MultiIndex: 51242505 entries, ('AAL', Timestamp('2014-12-22 09:30:00')) to
('YHOO', Timestamp('2017-06-16 16:00:00'))
```

```
Data columns (total 12 columns):
 #   Column  Non-Null Count     Dtype
---  ------  --------------     -----
 0   first   51242500 non-null  float64
 1   high    51242500 non-null  float64
 2   low     51242500 non-null  float64
 3   last    51242500 non-null  float64
 4   price   49242369 non-null  float64
 5   volume  51242505 non-null  int64
 6   up      51242505 non-null  int64
 7   down    51242505 non-null  int64
 8   rup     51242505 non-null  int64
 9   rdown   51242505 non-null  int64
 10  atask   51242505 non-null  int64
 11  atbid   51242505 non-null  int64
dtypes: float64(5), int64(7)
memory usage: 6.1+ GB
```

Due to the large memory footprint of the data, we only create 20 simple features, namely:

- The lagged returns for each of the last 10 minutes.
- The number of shares traded with upticks and downticks during a bar, divided by the total number of shares.
- The number of shares traded where the trade price is the same (repeated) following and upticks or downticks during a bar, divided by the total number of shares.
- The difference between the number of shares traded at the ask versus the bid price, divided by total volume during the bar.
- Several technical indicators, including the Balance of Power, the Commodity Channel Index, and the Stochastic RSI (see the *Appendix, Alpha Factor Library*, for details).

We'll make sure that we shift the data to avoid lookahead bias, as exemplified by the computation of the Money Flow Index, which uses the TA-Lib implementation:

```
data['MFI'] = (by_ticker
               .apply(lambda x: talib.MFI(x.high,
                                          x.low,
                                          x['last'],
                                          x.volume,
                                          timeperiod=14)
                      .shift()))
```

The following graph shows a standalone evaluation of the individual features' predictive content using their rank correlation with the 1-minute forward returns. It reveals that the recent lagged returns are presumably the most informative variables:

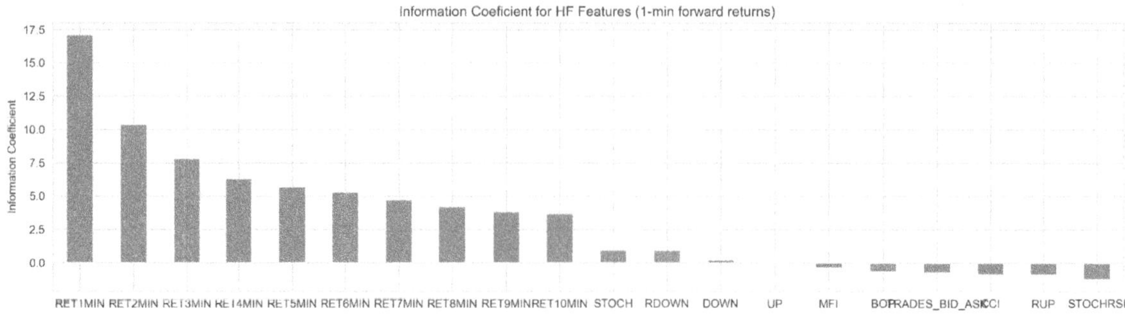

Figure 12.20: Information coefficient for high-frequency features

We can now proceed to train a gradient boosting model using these features.

Minute-frequency signals with LightGBM

To generate predictive signals for our HFT strategy, we'll train a LightGBM boosting model to predict the 1-min forward returns. The model receives 12 months of minute data during training the model and generates out-of-sample forecasts for the subsequent 21 trading days. We'll repeat this for 24 train-test splits to cover the last 2 years of our 5-year sample.

The training process follows the preceding LightGBM example closely; see the notebook `intraday_model` for the implementation details.

One key difference is the adaptation of the custom `MultipleTimeSeriesCV` to minute frequency; we'll be referencing the `date_time` level of `MultiIndex` (see notebook for implementation). We compute the lengths of the train and test periods based on 390 observations per ticker and day as follows:

```
DAY = 390   # minutes; 6.5 hrs (9:30 - 15:59)
MONTH = 21  # trading days
n_splits = 24

cv = MultipleTimeSeriesCV(n_splits=n_splits,
                          lookahead=1,
                          test_period_length=MONTH * DAY,
                          train_period_length=12 * MONTH * DAY,
                          date_idx='date_time')
```

The large data size significantly drives up training time, so we use default settings but set the number to trees per ensemble to 250. We track the IC on the test set using the following `ic_lgbm()` custom metric definition that we pass to the model's `.train()` method.

The custom metric receives the model prediction and the binary training dataset, which we can use to compute any metric of interest; note that we set `is_higher_better` to `True` since the model minimizes loss functions by default (see the LightGBM documentation for additional information):

```
def ic_lgbm(preds, train_data):
    """Custom IC eval metric for lightgbm"""
    is_higher_better = True
    return 'ic', spearmanr(preds, train_data.get_label())[0], is_higher_
better

model = lgb.train(params=params,
                  train_set=lgb_train,
                  valid_sets=[lgb_train, lgb_test],
                  feval=ic_lgbm,
                  num_boost_round=num_boost_round,
                  early_stopping_rounds=50,
                  verbose_eval=50)
```

At 250 iterations, the validation IC is still improving for most folds, so our results are not optimal, but training already takes several hours this way. Let's now take a look at the predictive content of the signals generated by our model.

Evaluating the trading signal quality

Now, we would like to know how accurate the model's out-of-sample predictions are, and whether they could be the basis for a profitable trading strategy.

First, we compute the IC, both for all predictions and on a daily basis, as follows:

```
ic = spearmanr(cv_preds.y_test, cv_preds.y_pred)[0]

by_day = cv_preds.groupby(cv_preds.index.get_level_values('date_time').date)
ic_by_day = by_day.apply(lambda x: spearmanr(x.y_test, x.y_pred)[0])
daily_ic_mean = ic_by_day.mean()
daily_ic_median = ic_by_day.median()
```

For the 2 years of rolling out-of-sample tests, we obtain a statistically significant, positive 1.90. On a daily basis, the mean IC is 1.98 and the median IC equals 1.91.

These results clearly suggest that the predictions contain meaningful information about the direction and size of short-term price movements that we could use for a trading strategy.

Next, we calculate the average and cumulative forward returns for each decile of the predictions:

```
dates = cv_preds.index.get_level_values('date_time').date
cv_preds['decile'] = (cv_preds.groupby(dates, group_keys=False)
min_ret_by_decile = cv_preds.groupby(['date_time', 'decile']).y_test.mean()
                      .apply(lambda x: pd.qcut(x.y_pred, q=10))))
```

```
cumulative_ret_by_decile = (min_ret_by_decile
                            .unstack('decile')
                            .add(1)
                            .cumprod()
                            .sub(1))
```

Figure 12.21 displays the results. The left panel shows the average 1-min return per decile and indicates an average spread of 0.5 basis points per minute. The right panel shows the cumulative return of an equal-weighted portfolio invested in each decile, suggesting that—before transaction costs—a long-short strategy appears attractive:

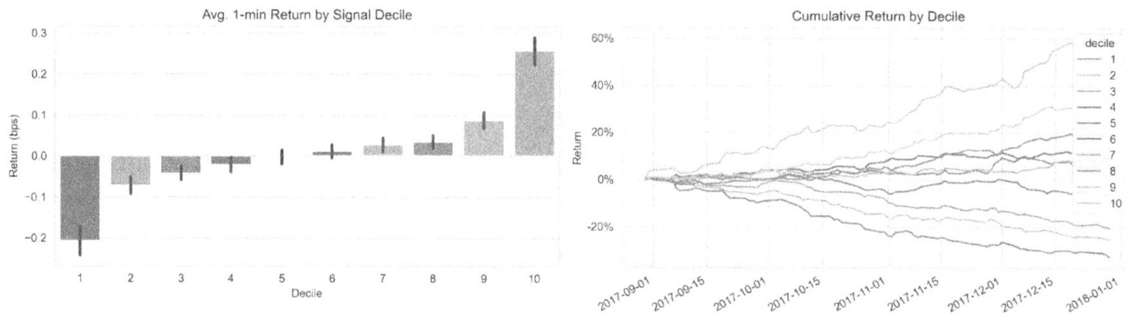

Figure 12.21: Average 1-min returns and cumulative returns by decile

The backtest with minute data is quite time-consuming, so we've omitted this step; however, feel free to experiment with Zipline or backtrader to evaluate this strategy under more realistic assumptions regarding transaction costs or using proper risk controls.

Summary

In this chapter, we explored the gradient boosting algorithm, which is used to build ensembles in a sequential manner, adding a shallow decision tree that only uses a very small number of features to improve on the predictions that have been made. We saw how gradient boosting trees can be very flexibly applied to a broad range of loss functions, as well as offer many opportunities to tune the model to a given dataset and learning task.

Recent implementations have greatly facilitated the use of gradient boosting. They've done this by accelerating the training process and offering more consistent and detailed insights into the importance of features and the drivers of individual predictions.

Finally, we developed a simple trading strategy driven by an ensemble of gradient boosting models that was actually profitable, at least before significant trading costs. We also saw how to use gradient boosting with high-frequency data.

In the next chapter, we will turn to Bayesian approaches to machine learning.

13

Data-Driven Risk Factors and Asset Allocation with Unsupervised Learning

Chapter 6, The Machine Learning Process, introduced how unsupervised learning adds value by uncovering structures in data without the need for an outcome variable to guide the search process. This contrasts with supervised learning, which was the focus of the last several chapters: instead of predicting future outcomes, unsupervised learning aims to learn an informative representation of the data that helps explore new data, discover useful insights, or solve some other task more effectively.

Dimensionality reduction and clustering are the main tasks for unsupervised learning:

- **Dimensionality reduction** transforms the existing features into a new, smaller set while minimizing the loss of information. Algorithms differ by how they measure the loss of information, whether they apply linear or nonlinear transformations or which constraints they impose on the new feature set.
- **Clustering algorithms** identify and group similar observations or features instead of identifying new features. Algorithms differ in how they define the similarity of observations and their assumptions about the resulting groups.

These unsupervised algorithms are useful when a **dataset does not contain an outcome**. For instance, we may want to extract tradeable information from a large body of financial reports or news articles. In *Chapter 14, Text Data for Trading – Sentiment Analysis*, we'll use topic modeling to discover hidden themes that allow us to explore and summarize content more effectively, and identify meaningful relationships that can help us to derive signals.

The algorithms are also useful when we want to **extract information independently from an outcome**. For example, rather than using third-party industry classifications, clustering allows us to identify synthetic groupings based on the attributes of assets useful for our purposes, such as returns over a certain time horizon, exposure to risk factors, or similar fundamentals. In this chapter, we will learn how to use clustering to manage portfolio risks by identifying hierarchical relationships among asset returns.

More specifically, after reading this chapter, you will understand:

- How **principal component analysis** (**PCA**) and **independent component analysis** (**ICA**) perform linear dimensionality reduction
- Identifying data-driven risk factors and eigenportfolios from asset returns using PCA
- Effectively visualizing nonlinear, high-dimensional data using manifold learning
- Using T-SNE and UMAP to explore high-dimensional image data
- How k-means, hierarchical, and density-based clustering algorithms work
- Using agglomerative clustering to build robust portfolios with hierarchical risk parity

> You can find the code samples for this chapter and links to additional resources in the corresponding directory of the GitHub repository. The notebooks include color versions of the images.

Dimensionality reduction

In linear algebra terms, the features of a dataset create a **vector space** whose dimensionality corresponds to the number of linearly independent rows or columns, whichever is larger. Two columns are linearly dependent when they are perfectly correlated so that one can be computed from the other using the linear operations of addition and multiplication.

In other words, they are parallel vectors that represent the same direction rather than different ones in the data and thus only constitute a single dimension. Similarly, if one variable is a linear combination of several others, then it is an element of the vector space created by those columns and does not add a new dimension of its own.

The number of dimensions of a dataset matters because each new dimension can add a signal concerning an outcome. However, there is also a downside known as the **curse of dimensionality**: as the number of independent features grows while the number of observations remains constant, the average distance between data points also grows, and the density of the feature space drops exponentially, with dramatic implications for **machine learning** (**ML**). **Prediction becomes much harder** when observations are more distant, that is, different from each other. Alternative data sources, like text and images, typically are of high dimensionality, but they generally affect models that rely on a large number of features. The next section addresses the resulting challenges.

Dimensionality reduction seeks to **represent the data more efficiently** by using fewer features. To this end, algorithms project the data to a lower-dimensional space while discarding any variation that is not informative, or by identifying a lower-dimensional subspace or manifold on or near to where the data lives.

A **manifold** is a space that locally resembles Euclidean space. One-dimensional manifolds include a line or a circle, but not the visual representation of the number eight due to the crossing point.

The manifold hypothesis maintains that high-dimensional data often resides in a lower-dimensional space, which, if identified, permits a faithful representation of the data in this subspace. Refer to Fefferman, Mitter, and Narayanan (2016) for background information and the description of an algorithm that tests this hypothesis.

Dimensionality reduction, therefore, compresses the data by finding a different, smaller set of variables that capture what matters most in the original features to minimize the loss of information. Compression helps counter the curse of dimensionality, economizes on memory, and permits the visualization of salient aspects of higher-dimensional data that is otherwise very difficult to explore.

Dimensionality reduction algorithms differ by the constraints they impose on the new variables and how they aim to minimize the loss of information (see Burges 2010 for an excellent overview):

- **Linear algorithms** like PCA and ICA constrain the new variables to be linear combinations of the original features; for example, hyperplanes in a lower-dimensional space. Whereas PCA requires the new features to be uncorrelated, ICA goes further and imposes statistical independence, implying the absence of both linear and nonlinear relationships.
- **Nonlinear algorithms** are not restricted to hyperplanes and can capture a more complex structure in the data. However, given the infinite number of options, the algorithms still need to make assumptions in order to arrive at a solution. Later in this section, we will explain how **t-distributed Stochastic Neighbor Embedding** (**t-SNE**) and **Uniform Manifold Approximation and Projection** (**UMAP**) are very useful to visualize higher-dimensional data. *Figure 13.1* illustrates how manifold learning identifies a two-dimensional subspace in the three-dimensional feature space. (The notebook `manifold_learning` illustrates the use of additional algorithms, including local linear embedding.)

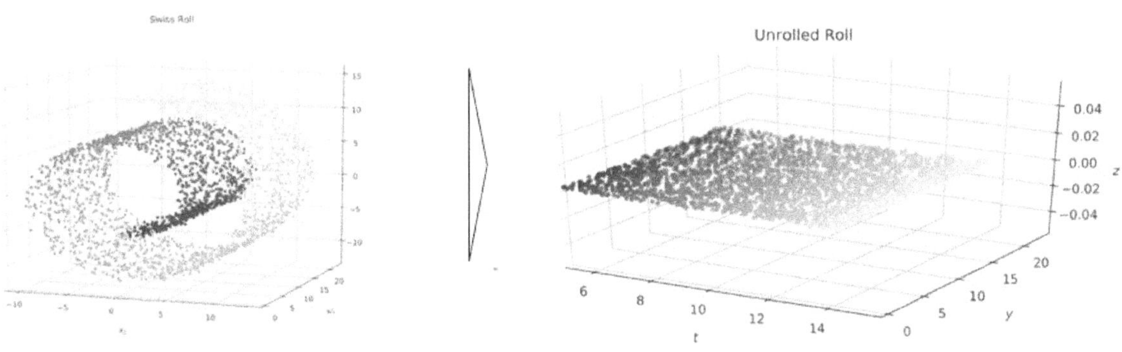

Figure 13.1: Nonlinear dimensionality reduction

The curse of dimensionality

An increase in the number of dimensions of a dataset means that there are more entries in the vector of features that represents each observation in the corresponding Euclidean space.

We measure the distance in a vector space using the Euclidean distance, also known as the L^2 norm, which we applied to the vector of linear regression coefficients to train a regularized ridge regression.

The Euclidean distance between two n-dimensional vectors with Cartesian coordinates $p = (p_1, p_2, ..., p_n)$ and $q = (q_1, q_2, ..., q_n)$ is computed using the familiar formula developed by Pythagoras:

$$d(p, q) = \sqrt{\sum_{i=1}^{n} (p_i - q_i)^2}$$

Therefore, each new dimension adds a non-negative term to the sum so that the distance increases with the number of dimensions for distinct vectors. In other words, as the number of features grows for a given number of observations, the feature space becomes increasingly sparse, that is, less dense or emptier. On the flip side, the lower data density requires more observations to keep the average distance between the data points the same.

Figure 13.2 illustrates the exponential growth in the number of data points needed to maintain the average distance among observations as the number of dimensions increases. 10 points uniformly distributed on a line correspond to 10^2 points in two dimensions and 10^3 points in three dimensions in order to keep the density constant.

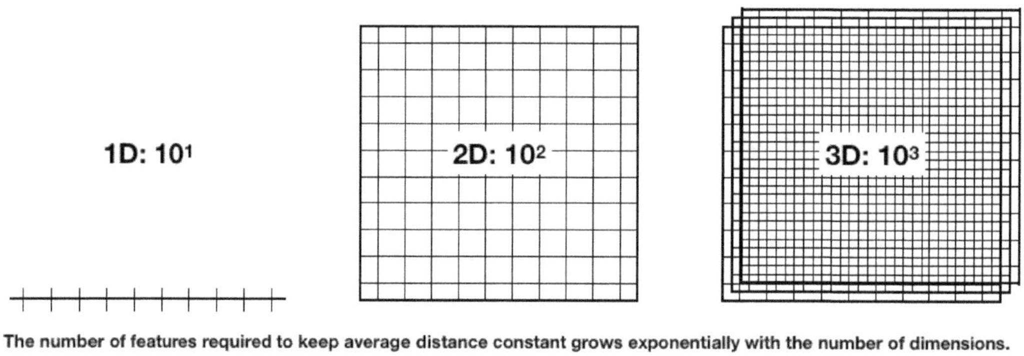

Figure 13.2: The number of features required to keep the average distance constant grows exponentially with the number of dimensions

The notebook `the_curse_of_dimensionality` in the GitHub repository folder for this section simulates how the average and minimum distances between data points increase as the number of dimensions grows (see *Figure 13.3*).

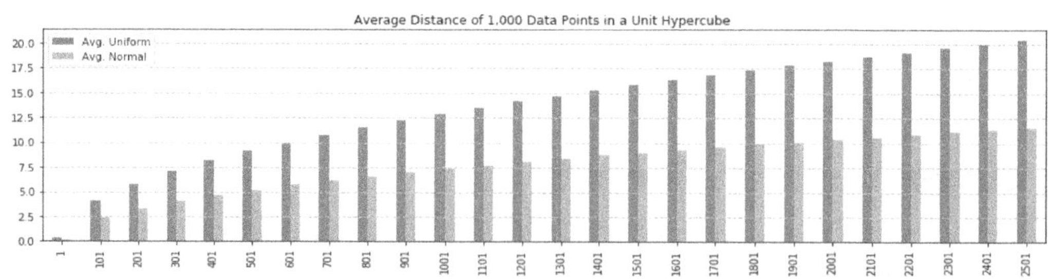

Figure 13.3: Average distance of 1,000 data points in a unit hypercube

The **simulation** randomly samples up to 2,500 features in the range [0, 1] from an uncorrelated uniform or a correlated normal distribution. The average distance between data points increases to over 11 times the unitary feature range for the normal distribution, and to over 20 times in the (extreme) case of an uncorrelated uniform distribution.

When the **distance between observations** grows, supervised ML becomes more difficult because predictions for new samples are less likely to be based on learning from similar training features. Put simply, the number of possible unique rows grows exponentially as the number of features increases, making it much harder to efficiently sample the space. Similarly, the complexity of the functions learned by flexible algorithms that make fewer assumptions about the actual relationship grows exponentially with the number of dimensions.

Flexible algorithms include the tree-based models we saw in *Chapter 11, Random Forests – A Long-Short Strategy for Japanese Stocks*, and *Chapter 12, Boosting Your Trading Strategy*. They also include the deep neural networks that we will cover later in the book, starting with *Chapter 16, Word Embeddings for Earnings Calls and SEC Filings*. The variance of these algorithms increases as **more dimensions add opportunities to overfit** to noise, resulting in poor generalization performance.

Dimensionality reduction leverages the fact that, in practice, features are often correlated or exhibit little variation. If so, it can compress data without losing much of the signal and complements the use of regularization to manage prediction error due to variance and model complexity.

The critical question that we take on in the following section then becomes: what are the best ways to find a lower-dimensional representation of the data?

Linear dimensionality reduction

Linear dimensionality reduction algorithms compute linear combinations that **translate**, **rotate**, and **rescale the original features** to capture significant variations in the data, subject to constraints on the characteristics of the new features.

PCA, invented in 1901 by Karl Pearson, finds new features that reflect directions of maximal variance in the data while being mutually uncorrelated. ICA, in contrast, originated in signal processing in the 1980s with the goal of separating different signals while imposing the stronger constraint of statistical independence.

This section introduces these two algorithms and then illustrates how to apply PCA to asset returns in order to learn risk factors from the data, and build so-called eigenportfolios for systematic trading strategies.

Principal component analysis

PCA finds linear combinations of the existing features and uses these principal components to represent the original data. The number of components is a hyperparameter that determines the target dimensionality and can be, at most, equal to the lesser of the number of rows or columns.

PCA aims to capture most of the variance in the data to make it easy to recover the original features and ensures that each component adds information. It reduces dimensionality by projecting the original data into the principal component space.

The PCA algorithm works by identifying a sequence of components, each of which aligns with the direction of maximum variance in the data after accounting for variation captured by previously computed components. The sequential optimization ensures that new components are not correlated with existing components and produces an orthogonal basis for a vector space.

This new basis is a rotation of the original basis, such that the new axes point in the direction of successively decreasing variance. The decline in the amount of variance of the original data explained by each principal component reflects the extent of correlation among the original features. In other words, the share of components that captures, for example, 95 percent of the original variation provides insight into the linearly independent information in the original data.

Visualizing PCA in 2D

Figure 13.4 illustrates several aspects of PCA for a two-dimensional random dataset (refer to the notebook `pca_key_ideas`):

- The left panel shows how the first and second principal components align with the **directions of maximum variance** while being orthogonal.
- The central panel shows how the first principal component minimizes the **reconstruction error**, measured as the sum of the distances between the data points and the new axis.
- The right panel illustrates **supervised OLS** (refer to *Chapter 7, Linear Models – From Risk Factors to Return Forecasts*), which approximates the outcome (x_2) by a line computed from the single feature x_1. The vertical lines highlight how OLS minimizes the distance along the outcome axis, whereas PCA minimizes the distances that are orthogonal to the hyperplane.

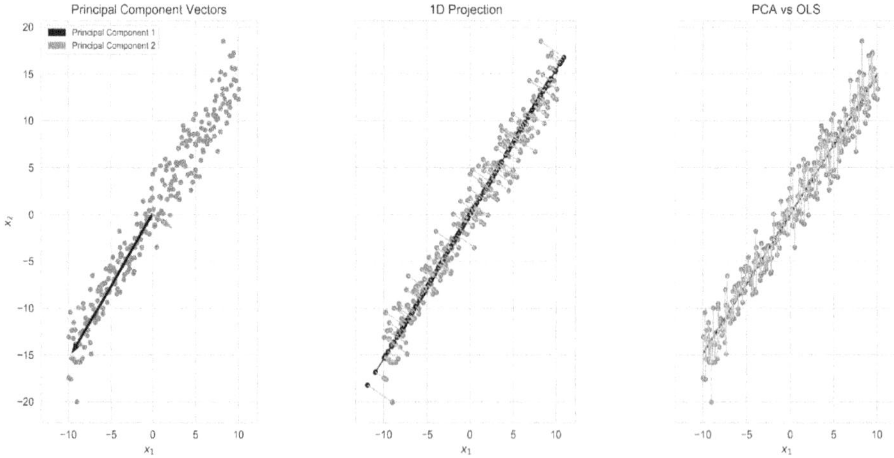

Figure 13.4: PCA in 2D from various perspectives

Key assumptions made by PCA

PCA makes several assumptions that are important to keep in mind. These include:

- High variance implies a high signal-to-noise ratio.
- The data is standardized so that the variance is comparable across features.
- Linear transformations capture the relevant aspects of the data.
- Higher-order statistics beyond the first and second moments do not matter, which implies that the data has a normal distribution.

The emphasis on the first and second moments aligns with standard risk/return metrics, but the normality assumption may conflict with the characteristics of market data. Market data often exhibits skew or kurtosis (fat tails) that differ from those of the normal distribution and will not be taken into account by PCA.

How the PCA algorithm works

The algorithm finds vectors to create a hyperplane of target dimensionality that minimizes the reconstruction error, measured as the sum of the squared distances of the data points to the plane. As illustrated previously, this goal corresponds to finding a sequence of vectors that align with directions of maximum retained variance given the other components, while ensuring all principal components are mutually orthogonal.

In practice, the algorithm solves the problem either by computing the eigenvectors of the covariance matrix or by using the **singular value decomposition** (**SVD**).

We illustrate the computation using a randomly generated three-dimensional ellipse with 100 data points, as shown in the left panel of *Figure 13.5*, including the two-dimensional hyperplane defined by the first two principal components. (Refer to the notebook `the_math_behind_pca` for the code samples in the following three sections.)

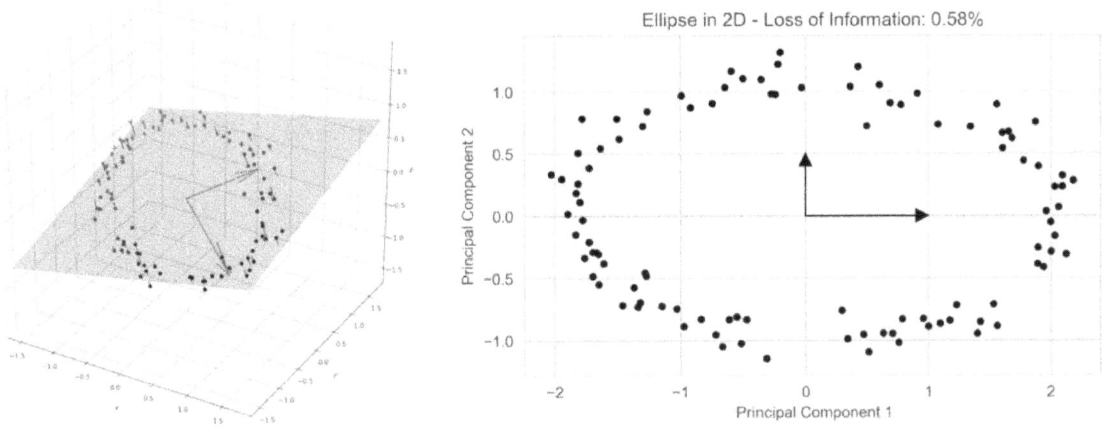

Figure 13.5: Visual representation of dimensionality reduction from 3D to 2D

PCA based on the covariance matrix

We first compute the principal components using the square covariance matrix with the pairwise sample covariances for the features x_i, x_j, $i, j = 1, ..., n$ as entries in row i and column j:

$$cov_{i,j} = \frac{\sum_{k=1}^{N}(x_{ik} - \bar{x}_i)\left(x_{jk} - \bar{x}_j\right)}{N - 1}$$

For a square matrix M of n dimension, we define the eigenvectors ω_i and eigenvalues λ_i, i=1, ..., n as follows:

$$Mw_i = \lambda_i w_i$$

Therefore, we can represent the matrix M using eigenvectors and eigenvalues, where W is a matrix that contains the eigenvectors as column vectors, and L is a matrix that contains λ_i as diagonal entries (and 0s otherwise). We define the **eigendecomposition** as:

$$M = WLW^{-1}$$

Using NumPy, we implement this as follows, where the pandas DataFrame data contains the 100 data points of the ellipse:

```
# compute covariance matrix:
cov = np.cov(data.T) # expects variables in rows by default
cov.shape
(3, 3)
```

Next, we calculate the eigenvectors and eigenvalues of the covariance matrix. The eigenvectors contain the principal components (where the sign is arbitrary):

```
eigen_values, eigen_vectors = eig(cov)
eigen_vectors

array([[ 0.71409739, -0.66929454, -0.20520656],
       [-0.70000234, -0.68597301, -0.1985894 ],
       [ 0.00785136, -0.28545725,  0.95835928]])
```

We can compare the result with the result obtained from sklearn and find that they match in absolute terms:

```
pca = PCA()
pca.fit(data)
C = pca.components_.T # columns = principal components
C
array([[ 0.71409739,  0.66929454,  0.20520656],
       [-0.70000234,  0.68597301,  0.1985894 ],
       [ 0.00785136,  0.28545725, -0.95835928]])

np.allclose(np.abs(C), np.abs(eigen_vectors))
True
```

We can also **verify the eigendecomposition**, starting with the diagonal matrix *L* that contains the eigenvalues:

```
# eigenvalue matrix
ev = np.zeros((3, 3))
np.fill_diagonal(ev, eigen_values)
ev # diagonal matrix

array([[1.92923132, 0.        , 0.        ],
       [0.        , 0.55811089, 0.        ],
       [0.        , 0.        , 0.00581353]])
```

We find that the result does indeed hold:

```
decomposition = eigen_vectors.dot(ev).dot(inv(eigen_vectors))
np.allclose(cov, decomposition)
```

PCA using the singular value decomposition

Next, we'll take a look at the alternative computation using the SVD. This algorithm is slower when the number of observations is greater than the number of features (which is the typical case) but yields better **numerical stability**, especially when some of the features are strongly correlated (which is often the reason to use PCA in the first place).

SVD generalizes the eigendecomposition that we just applied to the square and symmetric covariance matrix to the more general case of *m* x *n* rectangular matrices. It has the form shown at the center of the following figure. The diagonal values of Σ are the singular values, and the transpose of *V** contains the principal components as column vectors.

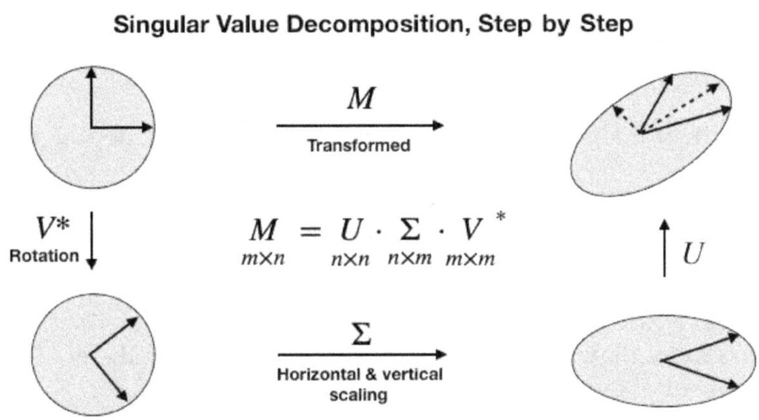

Figure 13.6: The SVD decomposed

In this case, we need to make sure our data is centered with mean zero (the computation of the covariance earlier took care of this):

```
n_features = data.shape[1]
data_ = data - data.mean(axis=0)
```

Using the centered data, we compute the SVD:

```
U, s, Vt = svd(data_)
U.shape, s.shape, Vt.shape
((100, 100), (3,), (3, 3))
```

We can convert the vector s, which contains only singular values, into an *n* x *m* matrix and show that the decomposition works:

```
S = np.zeros_like(data_)
S[:n_features, :n_features] = np.diag(s)
S.shape
(100, 3)
```

We find that the decomposition does indeed reproduce the standardized data:

```
np.allclose(data_, U.dot(S).dot(Vt))
True
```

Lastly, we confirm that the columns of the transpose of V^* contain the principal components:

```
np.allclose(np.abs(C), np.abs(Vt.T))
```

In the next section, we will demonstrate how sklearn implements PCA.

PCA with sklearn

The `sklearn.decomposition.PCA` implementation follows the standard API based on the `fit()` and `transform()` methods that compute the desired number of principal components and project the data into the component space, respectively. The convenience method `fit_transform()` accomplishes this in a single step.

PCA offers three different algorithms that can be specified using the `svd_solver` parameter:

- **full** computes the exact SVD using the LAPACK solver provided by scipy.
- **arpack** runs a truncated version suitable for computing less than the full number of components.
- **randomized** uses a sampling-based algorithm that is more efficient when the dataset has more than 500 observations and features, and the goal is to compute less than 80 percent of the components.
- **auto** also randomizes where it is most efficient; otherwise, it uses the full SVD.

Please view the references on GitHub for algorithmic implementation details.

Other key configuration parameters of the PCA object are:

- **n_components**: Compute all principal components by passing `None` (the default), or limit the number to `int`. For `svd_solver=full`, there are two additional options: a `float` in the interval [0, 1] computes the number of components required to retain the corresponding share of the variance in the data, and the option `mle` estimates the number of dimensions using the maximum likelihood.
- **whiten**: If `True`, it standardizes the component vectors to unit variance, which, in some cases, can be useful in a predictive model (the default is `False`).

To compute the first two principal components of the three-dimensional ellipsis and project the data into the new space, use `fit_transform()`:

```
pca2 = PCA(n_components=2)
projected_data  = pca2.fit_transform(data)
projected_data.shape
(100, 2)
```

The explained variance of the first two components is very close to 100 percent:

```
pca2.explained_variance_ratio_
array([0.77381099, 0.22385721])
```

Figure 13.5 shows the projection of the data into the new two-dimensional space.

Independent component analysis

ICA is another linear algorithm that identifies a new basis to represent the original data but pursues a different objective than PCA. Refer to Hyvärinen and Oja (2000) for a detailed introduction.

ICA emerged in signal processing, and the problem it aims to solve is called **blind source separation**. It is typically framed as the cocktail party problem, where a given number of guests are speaking at the same time so that a single microphone records overlapping signals. ICA assumes there are as many different microphones as there are speakers, each placed at different locations so that they record a different mix of signals. ICA then aims to recover the individual signals from these different recordings.

In other words, there are n original signals and an unknown square mixing matrix A that produces an n-dimensional set of m observations so that

$$\underset{n \times m}{X} = \underset{n \times n}{A} \quad \underset{n \times m}{s}$$

The goal is to find the matrix $W = A^{-1}$ that untangles the mixed signals to recover the sources.

The ability to uniquely determine the matrix W hinges on the non-Gaussian distribution of the data. Otherwise, W could be rotated arbitrarily given the multivariate normal distribution's symmetry under rotation. Furthermore, ICA assumes the mixed signal is the sum of its components and is, therefore, unable to identify Gaussian components because their sum is also normally distributed.

ICA assumptions

ICA makes the following critical assumptions:

- The sources of the signals are statistically independent
- Linear transformations are sufficient to capture the relevant information
- The independent components do not have a normal distribution
- The mixing matrix *A* can be inverted

ICA also requires the data to be centered and whitened, that is, to be mutually uncorrelated with unit variance. Preprocessing the data using PCA, as outlined earlier, achieves the required transformations.

The ICA algorithm

`FastICA`, used by sklearn, is a fixed-point algorithm that uses higher-order statistics to recover the independent sources. In particular, it maximizes the distance to a normal distribution for each component as a proxy for independence.

An alternative algorithm called `InfoMax` minimizes the mutual information between components as a measure of statistical independence.

ICA with sklearn

The ICA implementation by sklearn uses the same interface as PCA, so there is little to add. Note that there is no measure of explained variance because ICA does not compute components successively. Instead, each component aims to capture the independent aspects of the data.

Manifold learning – nonlinear dimensionality reduction

Linear dimensionality reduction projects the original data onto a lower-dimensional hyperplane that aligns with informative directions in the data. The focus on linear transformations simplifies the computation and echoes common financial metrics, such as PCA's goal to capture the maximum variance.

However, linear approaches will naturally ignore signals reflected in nonlinear relationships in the data. Such relationships are very important in alternative datasets containing, for example, image or text data. Detecting such relationships during exploratory analysis can provide important clues about the data's potential signal content.

In contrast, the **manifold hypothesis** emphasizes that high-dimensional data often lies on or near a lower-dimensional nonlinear manifold that is embedded in the higher-dimensional space. The two-dimensional Swiss roll displayed in *Figure 13.1* (at the beginning of this chapter) illustrates such a topological structure. Manifold learning aims to find the manifold of intrinsic dimensionality and then represent the data in this subspace. A simplified example uses a road as a one-dimensional manifold in a three-dimensional space and identifies data points using house numbers as local coordinates.

Several techniques approximate a lower-dimensional manifold. One example is **locally linear embedding** (**LLE**), which was invented by Lawrence Saul and Sam Roweis (2000) and used to "unroll" the Swiss roll shown in *Figure 13.1* (view the examples in the `manifold_learning_lle` notebook).

For each data point, LLE identifies a given number of nearest neighbors and computes weights that represent each point as a linear combination of its neighbors. It finds a lower-dimensional embedding by linearly projecting each neighborhood on global internal coordinates on the lower-dimensional manifold and can be thought of as a sequence of PCA applications.

Visualization requires that the reduction is at least three dimensions, possibly below the intrinsic dimensionality, and poses the **challenge of faithfully representing both the local and global structure**. This challenge relates to the curse of dimensionality; that is, while the volume of a sphere expands exponentially with the number of dimensions, the lower-dimensional space available to represent high-dimensional data is much more limited. For instance, in 12 dimensions, there can be 13 equidistant points; however, in two dimensions, there can only be 3 that form a triangle with sides of equal length. Therefore, accurately reflecting the distance of one point to its high-dimensional neighbors in lower dimensions risks distorting the relationships among all other points. The result is the **crowding problem**: to maintain global distances, local points may need to be placed too closely together.

The next two sections cover techniques that have allowed us to make progress in addressing the crowding problem for the visualization of complex datasets. We will use the fashion MNIST dataset, which is a more sophisticated alternative to the classic handwritten digit MNIST benchmark data used for computer vision. It contains 60,000 training and 10,000 test images of fashion objects in 10 classes (take a look at the sample images in the notebook `manifold_learning_intro`). The goal of a manifold learning algorithm for this data is to detect whether the classes lie on distinct manifolds to facilitate their recognition and differentiation.

t-distributed Stochastic Neighbor Embedding

t-SNE is an award-winning algorithm, developed by Laurens van der Maaten and Geoff Hinton in 2008, to detect patterns in high-dimensional data. It takes a probabilistic, nonlinear approach to locate data on several different but related low-dimensional manifolds. The algorithm emphasizes keeping similar points together in low dimensions as opposed to maintaining the distance between points that are apart in high dimensions, which results from algorithms like PCA that minimize squared distances.

The algorithm proceeds by **converting high-dimensional distances into (conditional) probabilities**, where high probabilities imply low distance and reflect the likelihood of sampling two points based on similarity. It accomplishes this by, first, positioning a normal distribution over each point and computing the density for a point and each neighbor, where the `perplexity` parameter controls the effective number of neighbors. In the second step, it arranges points in low dimensions and uses similarly computed low-dimensional probabilities to match the high-dimensional distribution. It measures the difference between the distributions using the Kullback-Leibler divergence, which puts a high penalty on misplacing similar points in low dimensions.

The low-dimensional probabilities use a Student's t-distribution with one degree of freedom because it has fatter tails that reduce the penalty of misplacing points that are more distant in high dimensions to manage the crowding problem.

The upper panels in *Figure 13.7* show how t-SNE is able to differentiate between the FashionMNIST image classes. A higher perplexity value increases the number of neighbors used to compute the local structure and gradually results in more emphasis on global relationships. (Refer to the repository for a high-resolution color version of this figure.)

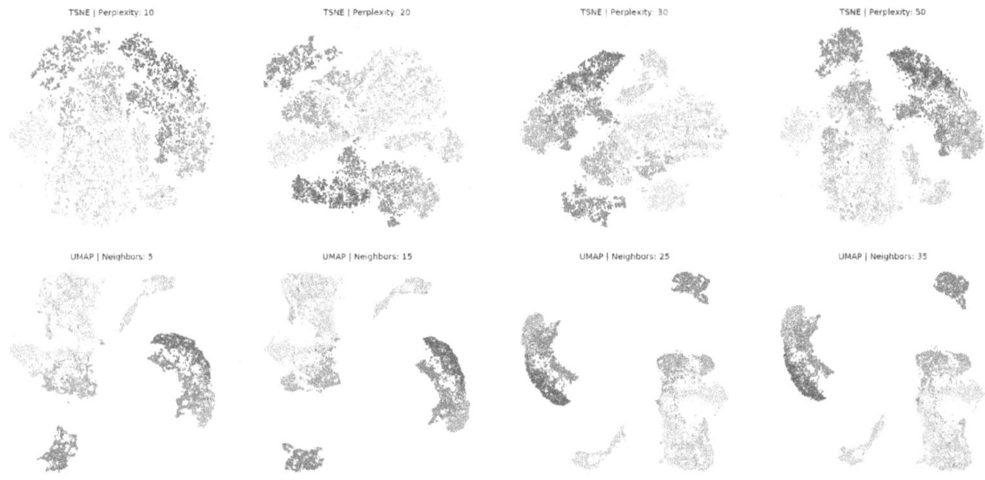

Figure 13.7: t-SNE and UMAP visualization of Fashion MNIST image data for different hyperparameters

t-SNE is the current state of the art in high-dimensional data visualization. Weaknesses include the computational complexity that scales quadratically in the number n of points because it evaluates all pairwise distances, but a subsequent tree-based implementation has reduced the cost to $n \log n$.

Unfortunately, t-SNE does not facilitate the projection of new data points into the low-dimensional space. The compressed output is not a very useful input for distance- or density-based cluster algorithms because t-SNE treats small and large distances differently.

Uniform Manifold Approximation and Projection

UMAP is a more recent algorithm for visualization and general dimensionality reduction. It assumes the data is uniformly distributed on a locally connected manifold and looks for the closest low-dimensional equivalent using fuzzy topology. It uses a `neighbors` parameter, which impacts the result in a similar way to `perplexity` in the preceding section.

It is faster and hence scales better to large datasets than t-SNE and sometimes preserves the global structure better than t-SNE. It can also work with different distance functions, including cosine similarity, which is used to measure the distance between word count vectors.

The preceding figure illustrates how UMAP does indeed move the different clusters further apart, whereas t-SNE provides more granular insight into the local structure.

The notebook also contains interactive Plotly visualizations for each of the algorithms that permit the exploration of the labels and identify which objects are placed close to each other.

PCA for trading

PCA is useful for algorithmic trading in several respects, including:

- The data-driven derivation of risk factors by applying PCA to asset returns
- The construction of uncorrelated portfolios based on the principal components of the correlation matrix of asset returns

We will illustrate both of these applications in this section.

Data-driven risk factors

In *Chapter 7, Linear Models – From Risk Factors to Return Forecasts*, we explored **risk factor models** used in quantitative finance to capture the main drivers of returns. These models explain differences in returns on assets based on their exposure to systematic risk factors and the rewards associated with these factors. In particular, we explored the **Fama-French approach**, which specifies factors based on prior knowledge about the empirical behavior of average returns, treats these factors as observable, and then estimates risk model coefficients using linear regression.

An alternative approach treats risk factors as **latent variables** and uses factor analytic techniques like PCA to simultaneously learn the factors from data and estimate how they drive returns. In this section, we will demonstrate how this method derives factors in a purely statistical or data-driven way with the advantage of not requiring ex ante knowledge of the behavior of asset returns (see the notebook `pca_and_risk_factor_models` for more details).

Preparing the data – top 350 US stocks

We will use the Quandl stock price data and select the daily adjusted close prices of the 500 stocks with the largest market capitalization and data for the 2010-2018 period. We will then compute the daily returns as follows:

```
idx = pd.IndexSlice
with pd.HDFStore('../../data/assets.h5') as store:
    stocks = store['us_equities/stocks'].marketcap.nlargest(500)
    returns = (store['quandl/wiki/prices']
               .loc[idx['2010': '2018', stocks.index], 'adj_close']
               .unstack('ticker')
               .pct_change())
```

We obtain 351 stocks and returns for over 2,000 trading days:

```
returns.info()
DatetimeIndex: 2072 entries, 2010-01-04 to 2018-03-27
Columns: 351 entries, A to ZTS
```

PCA is sensitive to outliers, so we winsorize the data at the 2.5 percent and 97.5 percent quantiles, respectively:

PCA does not permit missing data, so we will remove any stocks that do not have data for at least 95 percent of the time period. Then, in a second step, we will remove trading days that do not have observations on at least 95 percent of the remaining stocks:

```
returns = returns.dropna(thresh=int(returns.shape[0] * .95), axis=1)
returns = returns.dropna(thresh=int(returns.shape[1] * .95))
```

We are left with 315 equity return series covering a similar period:

```
returns.info()
DatetimeIndex: 2071 entries, 2010-01-05 to 2018-03-27
Columns: 315 entries, A to LYB
```

We impute any remaining missing values using the average return for any given trading day:

```
daily_avg = returns.mean(1)
returns = returns.apply(lambda x: x.fillna(daily_avg))
```

Running PCA to identify the key return drivers

Now we are ready to fit the principal components model to the asset returns using default parameters to compute all of the components using the full SVD algorithm:

```
pca = PCA(n_components='mle')
pca.fit(returns)
```

We find that the most important factor explains around 55 percent of the daily return variation. The dominant factor is usually interpreted as "the market," whereas the remaining factors can be interpreted as industry or style factors in line with our discussions in *Chapter 5, Portfolio Optimization and Performance Evaluation*, and *Chapter 7, Linear Models – From Risk Factors to Return Forecasts*, depending on the results of a closer inspection (please refer to the next example).

The plot on the right of *Figure 13.8* shows the cumulative explained variance and indicates that around 10 factors explain 60 percent of the returns of this cross-section of stocks.

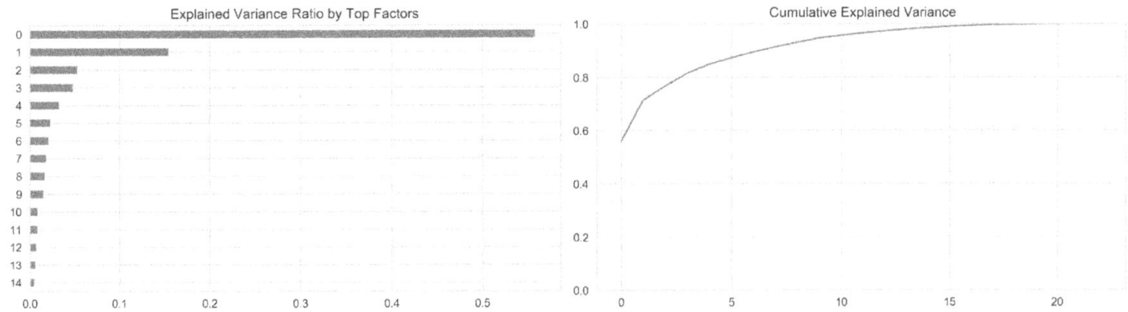

Figure 13.8: (Cumulative) explained return variance by PCA-based risk factors

The notebook contains a **simulation** for a broader cross-section of stocks and the longer 2000-2018 time period. It finds that, on average, the first three components explained 40 percent, 10 percent, and 5 percent of 500 randomly selected stocks, as shown in *Figure 13.9*:

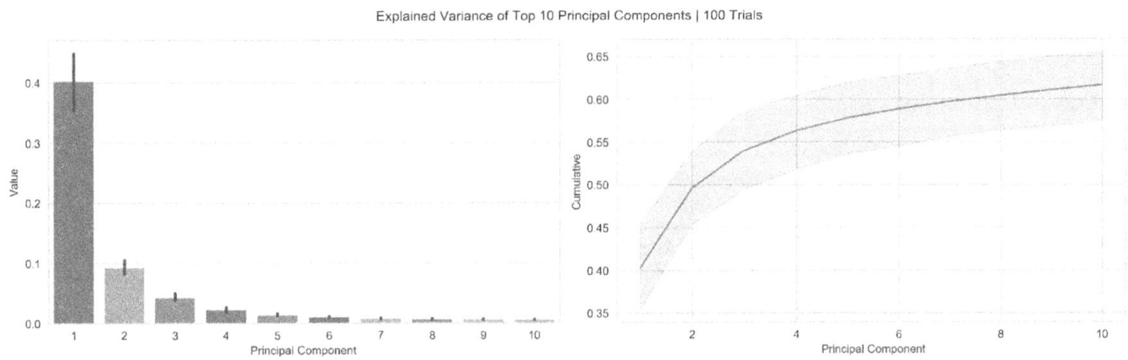

Figure 13.9: Explained variance of the top 10 principal components—100 trials

The cumulative plot shows a typical "elbow" pattern that can help to identify a suitable target dimensionality as the number of components beyond which additional components add less incremental value.

We can select the top two principal components to verify that they are indeed uncorrelated:

```
risk_factors = pd.DataFrame(pca.transform(returns)[:, :2],
                            columns=['Principal Component 1',
                                     'Principal Component 2'],
                            index=returns.index)
(risk_factors['Principal Component 1']
.corr(risk_factors['Principal Component 2']))
7.773256996252084e-15
```

Moreover, we can plot the time series to highlight how each factor captures different volatility patterns, as shown in the following figure:

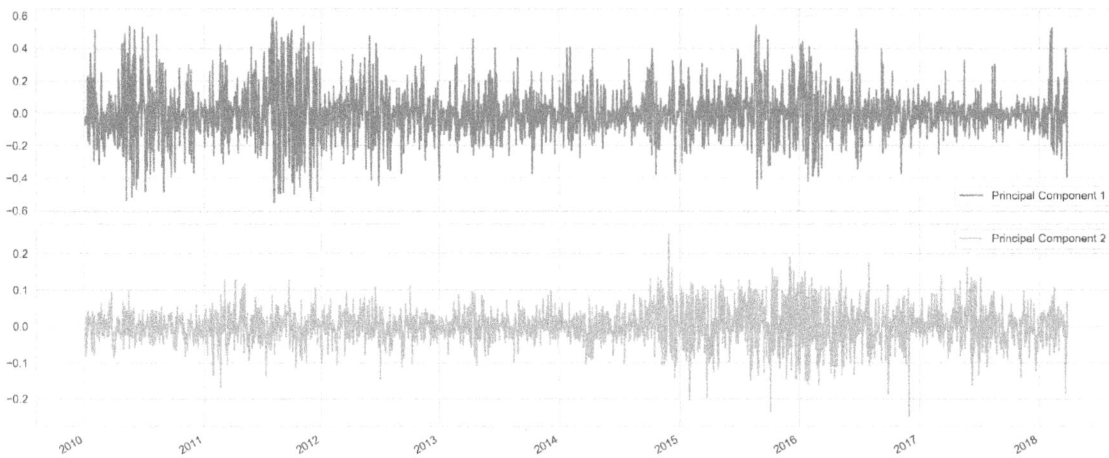

Figure 13.10: Return volatility patterns captured by the first two principal components

A risk factor model would employ a subset of the principal components as features to predict future returns, similar to our approach in *Chapter 7*, *Linear Models – From Risk Factors to Return Forecasts*.

Eigenportfolios

Another application of PCA involves the covariance matrix of the normalized returns. The principal components of the correlation matrix capture most of the covariation among assets in descending order and are mutually uncorrelated. Moreover, we can use standardized principal components as portfolio weights. You can find the code example for this section in the notebook `pca_and_eigen_portfolios`.

Let's use the 30 largest stocks with data for the 2010-2018 period to facilitate the exposition:

```
idx = pd.IndexSlice
with pd.HDFStore('../../data/assets.h5') as store:
    stocks = store['us_equities/stocks'].marketcap.nlargest(30)
    returns = (store['quandl/wiki/prices']
               .loc[idx['2010': '2018', stocks.index], 'adj_close']
               .unstack('ticker')
               .pct_change())
```

We again winsorize and also normalize the returns:

```
normed_returns = scale(returns
                       .clip(lower=returns.quantile(q=.025),
                             upper=returns.quantile(q=.975),
                             axis=1)
                       .apply(lambda x: x.sub(x.mean()).div(x.std())))
```

After dropping assets and trading days like in the previous example, we are left with 23 assets and over 2,000 trading days. We compute the return covariance and estimate all of the principal components to find that the two largest explain 55.9 percent and 15.5 percent of the covariation, respectively:

```
cov = returns.cov()
pca = PCA()
pca.fit(cov)
pd.Series(pca.explained_variance_ratio_).head()
0    55.91%
1    15.52%
2    5.36%
3    4.85%
4    3.32%
```

Next, we select and normalize the four largest components so that they sum to 1, and we can use them as weights for portfolios that we can compare to an EW portfolio formed from all of the stocks:

```
top4 = pd.DataFrame(pca.components_[:4], columns=cov.columns)
eigen_portfolios = top4.div(top4.sum(1), axis=0)
eigen_portfolios.index = [f'Portfolio {i}' for i in range(1, 5)]
```

The weights show distinct emphasis, as you can see in *Figure 13.11*. For example, Portfolio 3 puts large weights on Mastercard and Visa, the two payment processors in the sample, whereas Portfolio 2 has more exposure to technology companies:

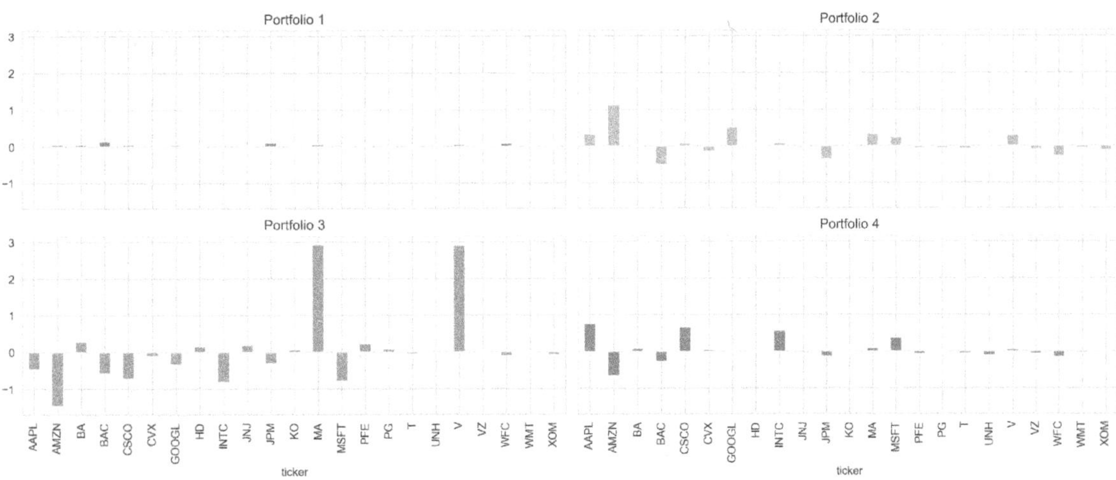

Figure 13.11: Eigenportfolio weights

When comparing the performance of each portfolio over the sample period to "the market" consisting of our small sample, we find that Portfolio 1 performs very similarly, whereas the other portfolios capture different return patterns (see *Figure 13.12*).

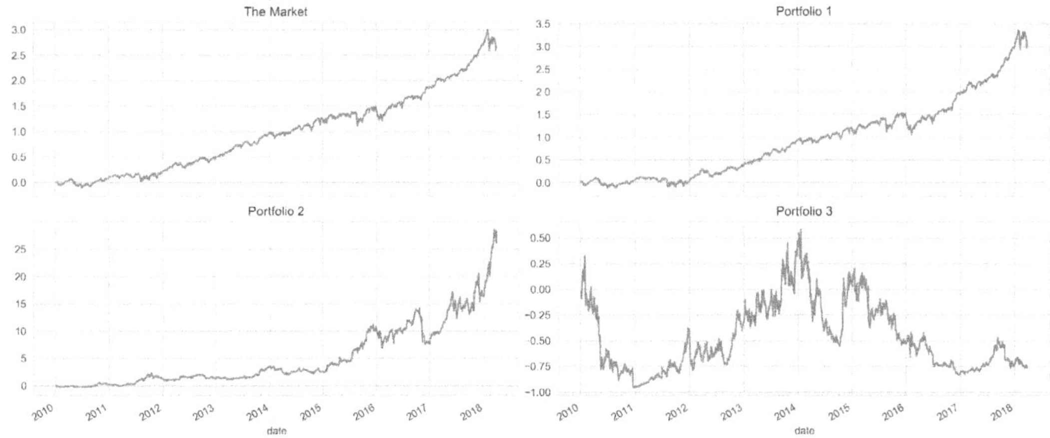

Figure 13.12: Cumulative eigenportfolio returns

Clustering

Both clustering and dimensionality reduction summarize the data. As we have just discussed, dimensionality reduction compresses the data by representing it using new, fewer features that capture the most relevant information. Clustering algorithms, in contrast, assign existing observations to subgroups that consist of similar data points.

Clustering can serve to better understand the data through the lens of categories learned from continuous variables. It also permits you to automatically categorize new objects according to the learned criteria. Examples of related applications include hierarchical taxonomies, medical diagnostics, and customer segmentation. Alternatively, clusters can be used to represent groups as prototypes, using, for example, the midpoint of a cluster as the best representatives of learned grouping. An example application includes image compression.

Clustering algorithms differ with respect to their strategy of identifying groupings:

- **Combinatorial** algorithms select the most coherent of different groupings of observations.
- **Probabilistic** modeling estimates distributions that most likely generated the clusters.
- **Hierarchical clustering** finds a sequence of nested clusters that optimizes coherence at any given stage.

Algorithms also differ by the notion of what constitutes a useful collection of objects that needs to match the data characteristics, domain, and goal of the applications. Types of groupings include:

- Clearly separated groups of various shapes
- Prototype- or center-based, compact clusters
- Density-based clusters of arbitrary shape
- Connectivity- or graph-based clusters

Important additional aspects of a clustering algorithm include whether it:

- Requires exclusive cluster membership
- Makes hard, that is, binary, or soft, probabilistic assignments
- Is complete and assigns all data points to clusters

The following sections introduce key algorithms, including **k-means**, **hierarchical**, and **density-based clustering**, as well as **Gaussian mixture models** (**GMMs**). The notebook `clustering_algos` compares the performance of these algorithms on different, labeled datasets to highlight strengths and weaknesses. It uses mutual information (refer to *Chapter 6, The Machine Learning Process*) to measure the congruence of cluster assignments and labels.

k-means clustering

k-means is the most well-known clustering algorithm, and it was first proposed by Stuart Lloyd at Bell Labs in 1957. It finds *k* centroids and assigns each data point to exactly one cluster with the goal of minimizing the within-cluster variance (called *inertia*). It typically uses the Euclidean distance, but other metrics can also be used. k-means assumes that clusters are spherical and of equal size and ignores the covariance among features.

Assigning observations to clusters

The problem is computationally difficult (NP-hard) because there are k^N ways to partition the N observations into k clusters. The standard iterative algorithm delivers a local optimum for a given k and proceeds as follows:

1. Randomly define k cluster centers and assign points to the nearest centroid
2. Repeat:
    1. For each cluster, compute the centroid as the average of the features
    2. Assign each observation to the closest centroid
3. Convergence: assignments (or within-cluster variation) don't change

The notebook `kmeans_implementation` shows you how to code the algorithm using Python. It visualizes the algorithm's iterative optimization and demonstrates how the resulting centroids partition the feature space into areas called Voronoi that delineate the clusters. The result is optimal for the given initialization, but alternative starting positions will produce different results. Therefore, we compute multiple clusterings from different initial values and select the solution that minimizes within-cluster variance.

k-means requires continuous or one-hot encoded categorical variables. Distance metrics are typically sensitive to scale, making it necessary to standardize features to ensure they have equal weight.

The **strengths** of k-means include its wide range of applicability, fast convergence, and linear scalability to large data while producing clusters of even size. The **weaknesses** include the need to tune the hyperparameter *k*, no guarantee of finding a global optimum, the restrictive assumption that clusters are spheres, and features not being correlated. It is also sensitive to outliers.

Evaluating cluster quality

Cluster quality metrics help select from among alternative clustering results. The notebook `kmeans_evaluation` illustrates the following options.

The **k-means objective** function suggests we compare the evolution of the inertia or within-cluster variance. Initially, additional centroids decrease the inertia sharply because new clusters improve the overall fit. Once an appropriate number of clusters has been found (assuming it exists), new centroids reduce the **within-cluster variance** by much less, as they tend to split natural groupings.

Therefore, when k-means finds a good cluster representation of the data, the **inertia** tends to follow an elbow-shaped path similar to the explained variance ratio for PCA (take a look at the notebook for implementation details).

The **silhouette coefficient** provides a more detailed picture of cluster quality. It answers the question: how far are the points in the nearest cluster relative to the points in the assigned cluster? To this end, it compares the mean intra-cluster distance a to the mean distance of the nearest cluster b and computes the following score s:

$$s = \frac{b - a}{\max(a,\ b)} \in [-1, 1]$$

The score can vary between -1 and 1, but negative values are unlikely in practice because they imply that the majority of points are assigned to the wrong cluster. A useful visualization of the silhouette score compares the values for each data point to the global average because it highlights the coherence of each cluster relative to the global configuration. The rule of thumb is to avoid clusters with mean scores below the average for all samples.

Figure 13.13 shows an excerpt from the silhouette plot for three and four clusters, where the former highlights the poor fit of cluster 1 by subpar contributions to the global silhouette score, whereas all of the four clusters have some values that exhibit above-average scores.

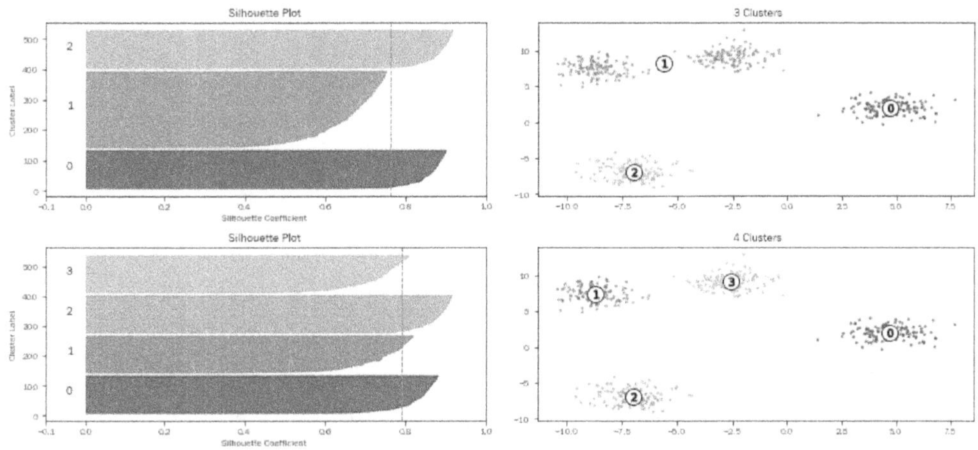

Figure 13.13: Silhouette plots for three and four clusters

In sum, given the usually unsupervised nature, it is necessary to vary the hyperparameters of the cluster algorithms and evaluate the different results. It is also important to calibrate the scale of the features, particularly when some should be given a higher weight and thus be measured on a larger scale. Finally, to validate the robustness of the results, use subsets of data to identify whether particular cluster patterns emerge consistently.

Hierarchical clustering

Hierarchical clustering avoids the need to specify a target number of clusters because it assumes that data can successively be merged into increasingly dissimilar clusters. It does not pursue a global objective but decides incrementally how to produce a sequence of nested clusters that range from a single cluster to clusters consisting of the individual data points.

Different strategies and dissimilarity measures

There are two approaches to hierarchical clustering:

1. **Agglomerative clustering** proceeds bottom-up, sequentially merging two of the remaining groups based on similarity.
2. **Divisive clustering** works top-down and sequentially splits the remaining clusters to produce the most distinct subgroups.

Both groups produce *N*-1 hierarchical levels and facilitate the selection of clustering at the level that best partitions data into homogenous groups. We will focus on the more common agglomerative clustering approach.

The agglomerative clustering algorithm departs from the individual data points and computes a similarity matrix containing all mutual distances. It then takes *N*-1 steps until there are no more distinct clusters and, each time, updates the similarity matrix to substitute elements that have been merged by the new cluster so that the matrix progressively shrinks.

While hierarchical clustering does not have hyperparameters like k-means, the **measure of dissimilarity** between clusters (as opposed to individual data points) has an important impact on the clustering result. The options differ as follows:

- **Single-link**: Distance between the nearest neighbors of two clusters
- **Complete link**: Maximum distance between the respective cluster members
- **Ward's method**: Minimize within-cluster variance
- **Group average**: Uses the cluster midpoint as a reference distance

Visualization – dendrograms

Hierarchical clustering provides insight into degrees of similarity among observations as it continues to merge data. A significant change in the similarity metric from one merge to the next suggests that a natural clustering existed prior to this point.

The **dendrogram** visualizes the successive merges as a binary tree, displaying the individual data points as leaves and the final merge as the root of the tree. It also shows how the similarity monotonically decreases from the bottom to the top. Therefore, it is natural to select a clustering by cutting the dendrogram. Refer to the notebook `hierarchical_clustering` for implementation details.

Figure 13.14 illustrates the dendrogram for the classic Iris dataset with four classes and three features using the four different distance metrics introduced in the preceding section. It evaluates the fit of the hierarchical clustering using the **cophenetic correlation** coefficient that compares the pairwise distances among points and the cluster similarity metric at which a pairwise merge occurred. A coefficient of 1 implies that closer points always merge earlier.

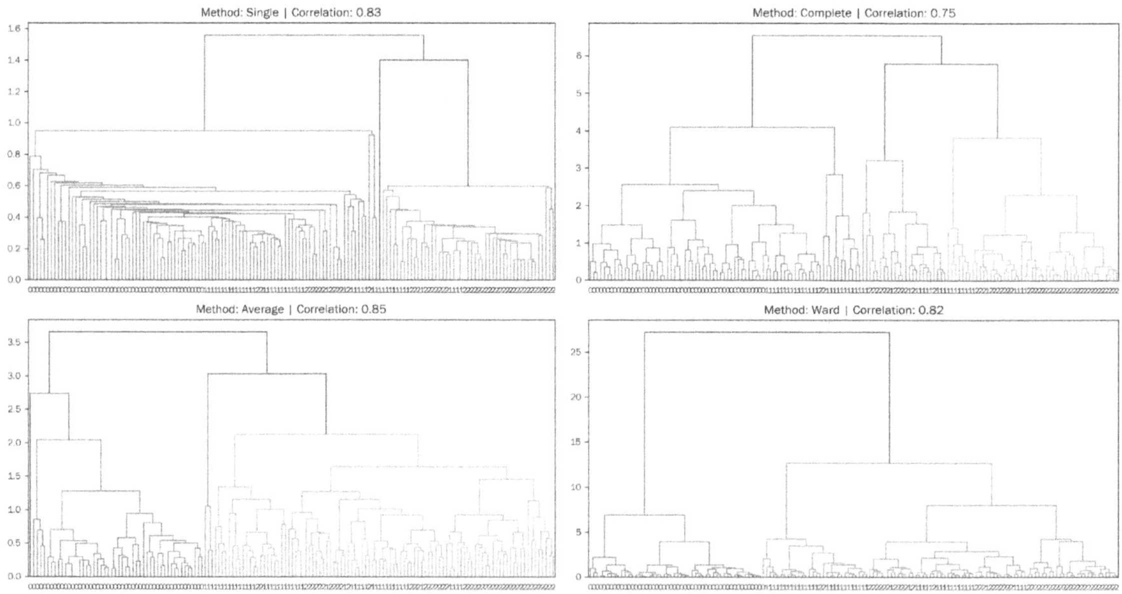

Figure 13.14: Dendrograms and cophenetic correlation for different dissimilarity measures

Different linkage methods produce different dendrogram "looks" so that we cannot use this visualization to compare results across methods. In addition, the Ward method, which minimizes the within-cluster variance, may not properly reflect the change in variance from one level to the next. Instead, the dendrogram can reflect the total within-cluster variance at different levels, which may be misleading. Alternative quality metrics are more appropriate, such as the **cophenetic correlation** or measures like **inertia** if aligned with the overall goal.

The **strengths** of hierarchical clustering include:

- The algorithm does not need the specific number of clusters but, instead, provides insight about potential clustering by means of an intuitive visualization.
- It produces a hierarchy of clusters that can serve as a taxonomy.
- It can be combined with k-means to reduce the number of items at the start of the agglomerative process.

On the other hand, its **weaknesses** include:

- The high cost in terms of computation and memory due to the numerous similarity matrix updates.
- All merges are final so that it does not achieve the global optimum.
- The curse of dimensionality leads to difficulties with noisy, high-dimensional data.

Density-based clustering

Density-based clustering algorithms assign cluster membership based on proximity to other cluster members. They pursue the goal of identifying dense regions of arbitrary shapes and sizes. They do not require the specification of a certain number of clusters but instead rely on parameters that define the size of a neighborhood and a density threshold.

We'll outline the two popular algorithms: DBSCAN and its newer hierarchical refinement. Refer to the notebook `density_based_clustering` for the relevant code samples and the link in this chapter's `README` on GitHub to a Quantopian example by Jonathan Larking that uses DBSCAN for a pairs trading strategy.

DBSCAN

Density-based spatial clustering of applications with noise (**DBSCAN**) was developed in 1996 and awarded the KDD Test of Time award at the 2014 KDD conference because of the attention it has received in theory and practice.

It aims to identify core and non-core samples, where the former extend a cluster and the latter are part of a cluster but do not have sufficient nearby neighbors to further grow the cluster. Other samples are outliers and are not assigned to any cluster.

It uses a parameter `eps` for the radius of the neighborhood and `min_samples` for the number of members required for core samples. It is deterministic and exclusive and has difficulties with clusters of different density and high-dimensional data. It can be challenging to tune the parameters to the requisite density, especially as it is often not constant.

Hierarchical DBSCAN

Hierarchical DBSCAN (HDBSCAN) is a more recent development that assumes clusters are islands of potentially differing density to overcome the DBSCAN challenges just mentioned. It also aims to identify the core and non-core samples. It uses the parameters `min_cluster_size` and `min_samples` to select a neighborhood and extend a cluster. The algorithm iterates over multiple `eps` values and chooses the most stable clustering. In addition to identifying clusters of varying density, it provides insight into the density and hierarchical structure of the data.

Figure 13.15 shows how DBSCAN and HDBSCAN, respectively, are able to identify clusters that differ in shape significantly from those discovered by k-means, for example. The selection of the clustering algorithm is a function of the structure of your data; refer to the pairs trading strategy that was referenced earlier in this section for a practical example.

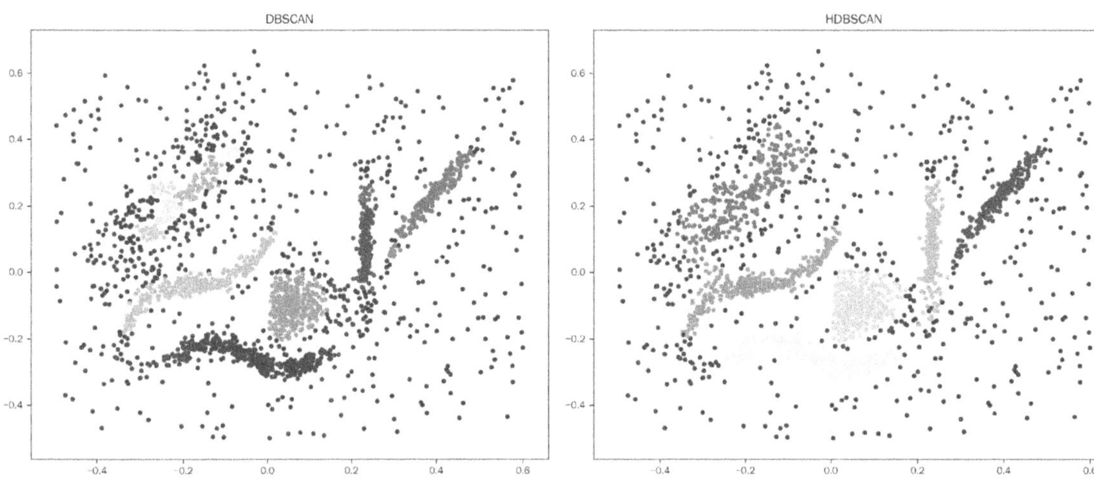

Figure 13.15: Comparing the DBSCAN and HDBSCAN clustering algorithms

Gaussian mixture models

GMMs are generative models that assume the data has been generated by a mix of various multivariate normal distributions. The algorithm aims to estimate the mean and covariance matrices of these distributions.

A GMM generalizes the k-means algorithm: it adds covariance among features so that clusters can be ellipsoids rather than spheres, while the centroids are represented by the means of each distribution. The GMM algorithm performs soft assignments because each point has a probability of being a member of any cluster.

The notebook gaussian_mixture_models demonstrates the implementation and visualizes the resulting cluster. You are likely to prefer GMM over other clustering algorithms when the k-means assumption of spherical clusters is too constraining; GMM often needs fewer clusters to produce a good fit given its greater flexibility. The GMM algorithm is also preferable when you need a generative model; because GMM estimates the probability distributions that generated the samples, it is easy to generate new samples based on the result.

Hierarchical clustering for optimal portfolios

In *Chapter 5, Portfolio Optimization and Performance Evaluation*, we discussed several methods that aim to choose portfolio weights for a given set of assets to optimize the risk and return profile of the resulting portfolio. These included the mean-variance optimization of Markowitz's modern portfolio theory, the Kelly criterion, and risk parity. In this section, we cover **hierarchical risk parity** (**HRP**), a more recent innovation (Prado 2016) that leverages hierarchical clustering to assign position sizes to assets based on the risk characteristics of subgroups.

We will first present how HRP works and then compare its performance against alternatives using a long-only strategy driven by the gradient boosting models we developed in the last chapter.

How hierarchical risk parity works

The key ideas of hierarchical risk parity are to do the following:

- Use hierarchical clustering of the covariance matrix to group assets with a similar correlation structure together
- Reduce the number of degrees of freedom by only considering similar assets as substitutes when constructing the portfolio

Refer to the notebook and Python files in the subfolder hierarchical_risk_parity for implementation details.

The first step is to compute a distance matrix that represents proximity for correlated assets and meets distance metric requirements. The resulting matrix becomes an input to the SciPy hierarchical clustering function that computes the successive clusters using one of several available methods, as discussed previously in this chapter.

```
def get_distance_matrix(corr):
    """Compute distance matrix from correlation;
        0 <= d[i,j] <= 1"""
    return np.sqrt((1 - corr) / 2)

distance_matrix = get_distance_matrix(corr)
linkage_matrix = linkage(squareform(distance_matrix), 'single')
```

The `linkage_matrix` can be used as input to the `sns.clustermap` function to visualize the resulting hierarchical clustering. The dendrogram displayed by seaborn shows how individual assets and clusters of assets merged based on their relative distances (see the left panel of *Figure 13.16*).

```
clustergrid = sns.clustermap(distance_matrix,
                             method='single',
                             row_linkage=linkage_matrix,
                             col_linkage=linkage_matrix,
                             cmap=cmap, center=0)

sorted_idx = clustergrid.dendrogram_row.reordered_ind
sorted_tickers = corr.index[sorted_idx].tolist()
```

Compared to a `seaborn.heatmap` of the original correlation matrix, there is now significantly more structure in the sorted data (the right panel) compared to the original correlation matrix displayed in the central panel.

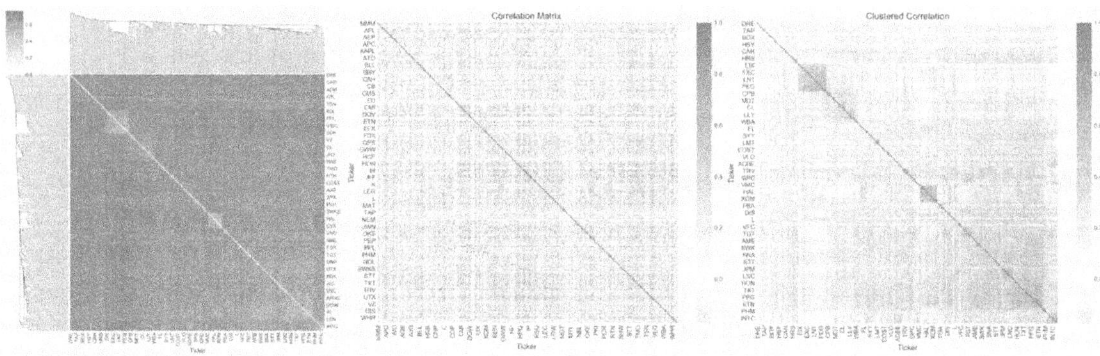

Figure 13.16: Original and clustered correlation matrix

Using the tickers sorted according to the hierarchy induced by the clustering algorithm, HRP now proceeds to compute a top-down inverse-variance allocation that successively adjusts weights depending on the variance of the subclusters further down the tree.

```
def get_inverse_var_pf(cov):
    """Compute the inverse-variance portfolio"""
    ivp = 1 / np.diag(cov)
    return ivp / ivp.sum()

def get_cluster_var(cov, cluster_items):
    """Compute variance per cluster"""
    cov_ = cov.loc[cluster_items, cluster_items]  # matrix slice
    w_ = get_inverse_var_pf(cov_)
    return (w_ @ cov_ @ w_).item()
```

To this end, the algorithm uses a bisectional search to allocate the variance of a cluster to its elements based on their relative riskiness.

```
def get_hrp_allocation(cov, tickers):
    """Compute top-down HRP weights"""
    weights = pd.Series(1, index=tickers)
    clusters = [tickers] # initialize one cluster with all assets

    while len(clusters) > 0:
        # run bisectional search:
        clusters = [c[start:stop] for c in clusters
                    for start, stop in ((0, int(len(c) / 2)),
                                        (int(len(c) / 2), len(c)))
                    if len(c) > 1]
        for i in range(0, len(clusters), 2):  # parse in pairs
            cluster0 = clusters[i]
            cluster1 = clusters[i + 1]

            cluster0_var = get_cluster_var(cov, cluster0)
            cluster1_var = get_cluster_var(cov, cluster1)

            weight_scaler = 1 - cluster0_var / (cluster0_var + cluster1_var)
            weights[cluster0] *= weight_scaler
            weights[cluster1] *= 1 - weight_scaler
    return weights
```

The resulting portfolio allocation produces weights that sum to 1 and reflect the structure present in the correlation matrix (refer to the notebook for details).

Backtesting HRP using an ML trading strategy

Now that we know how HRP works, we would like to test how it performs in practice compared to some alternatives, namely a simple equal-weighted portfolio and a mean-variance optimized portfolio. You can find the code samples for this section and additional details and analyses in the notebook `pf_optimization_with_hrp_zipline_benchmark`.

To this end, we'll build on the gradient boosting models developed in the last chapter. We will backtest a strategy for 2015-2017 with a universe of the 1,000 most liquid US stocks. The strategy relies on the model predictions to enter long positions in the 25 stocks with the highest positive return prediction for the next day. On a daily basis, we rebalance our holdings so that the weights for our target positions match the values suggested by HRP.

Ensembling the gradient boosting model predictions

We begin by averaging the predictions of the 10 models that performed best during the 2015-16 cross-validation period (refer to *Chapter 12, Boosting Your Trading Strategy*, for details), as shown in the following code excerpt:

```
def load_predictions(bundle):
    path = Path('../../12_gradient_boosting_machines/data')
    predictions = (pd.read_hdf(path / 'predictions.h5', 'lgb/train/01')
                   .append(pd.read_hdf(path / 'predictions.h5', 'lgb/
test/01').drop('y_test', axis=1)))
    predictions = (predictions.loc[~predictions.index.duplicated()]
                   .iloc[:, :10]
                   .mean(1)
                   .sort_index()
                   .dropna()
                  .to_frame('prediction'))
```

On a daily basis, we obtain the model predictions and select the top 25 tickers. If there are at least 20 tickers with positive forecasts, we enter the long positions and close all of the other holdings:

```
def before_trading_start(context, data):
    """
    Called every day before market open.
    """
    output = pipeline_output('signals')['longs'].astype(int)
    context.longs = output[output!=0].index
    if len(context.longs) < MIN_POSITIONS:
        context.divest = set(context.portfolio.positions.keys())
    else:
        context.divest = context.portfolio.positions.keys() - context.longs
```

Using PyPortfolioOpt to compute HRP weights

PyPortfolioOpt, which we used in *Chapter 5, Portfolio Optimization and Performance Evaluation*, to compute mean-variance optimized weights, also implements HRP. We'll run it as part of the scheduled rebalancing that takes place every morning. It needs the return history for the target assets and returns a dictionary of ticker-weight pairs that we use to place orders:

```
def rebalance_hierarchical_risk_parity(context, data):
    """Execute orders according to schedule_function()"""
    for symbol, open_orders in get_open_orders().items():
        for open_order in open_orders:
            cancel_order(open_order)
    for asset in context.divest:
        order_target(asset, target=0)
```

```
    if len(context.longs) > context.min_positions:
        returns = (data.history(context.longs, fields='price',
                                bar_count=252+1, # for 1 year of returns
                                frequency='1d')
                   .pct_change()
                   .dropna(how='all'))
        hrp_weights = HRPOpt(returns=returns).hrp_portfolio()
        for asset, target in hrp_weights.items():
            order_target_percent(asset=asset, target=target)
```

Markowitz rebalancing follows a similar process, as outlined in *Chapter 5, Portfolio Optimization and Performance Evaluation*, and is included in the notebook.

Performance comparison with pyfolio

The following charts show the cumulative returns for the in- and out-of-sample (with respect to the ML model selection process) of the **equal-weighted** (**EW**), the HRP, and the **mean-variance** (**MV**) optimized portfolios.

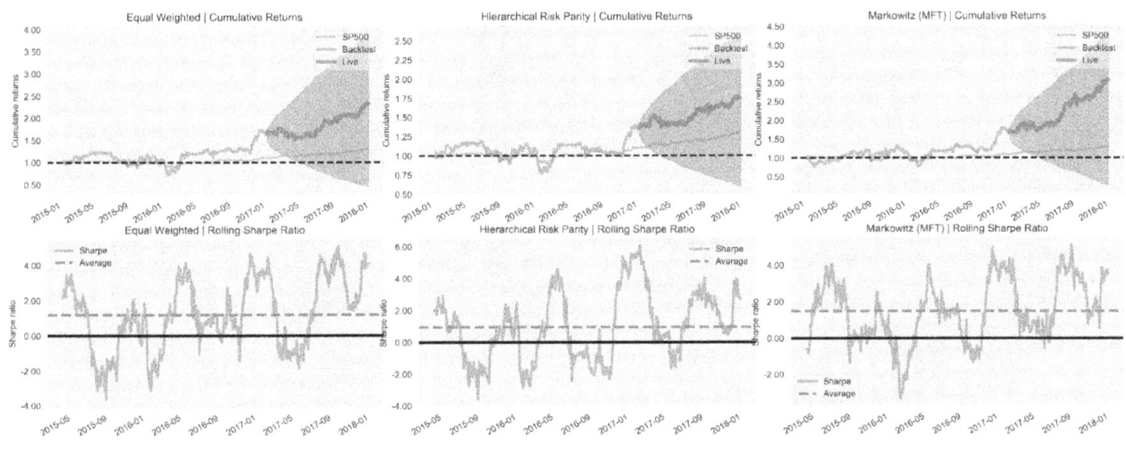

Figure 13.17: Cumulative returns for the different portfolios

The cumulative returns are 207.3 percent for MV, 133 percent for EW, and 75.1 percent for HRP. The Sharpe ratios are 1.16, 1.01, and 0.83, respectively. Alpha returns are 0.28 for MV, 0.16 for EW, and 0.16 for HRP, with betas of 1.77, 1.87, and 1.67, respectively.

Therefore, it turns out that, in this particular context, the often-criticized MV approach does best, while HRP comes up last. However, be aware that the results are quite sensitive to the number of stocks traded, the time period, and other factors.

Try it out for yourself, and learn which technique performs best under the circumstances most relevant for you!

Summary

In this chapter, we explored unsupervised learning methods that allow us to extract valuable signals from our data without relying on the help of outcome information provided by labels.

We learned how to use linear dimensionality reduction methods like PCA and ICA to extract uncorrelated or independent components from data that can serve as risk factors or portfolio weights. We also covered advanced nonlinear manifold learning techniques that produce state-of-the-art visualizations of complex, alternative datasets. In the second part of the chapter, we covered several clustering methods that produce data-driven groupings under various assumptions. These groupings can be useful, for example, to construct portfolios that apply risk-parity principles to assets that have been clustered hierarchically.

In the next three chapters, we will learn about various machine learning techniques for a key source of alternative data, namely natural language processing for text documents.

14

Text Data for Trading – Sentiment Analysis

This is the first of three chapters dedicated to extracting signals for algorithmic trading strategies from text data using **natural language processing** (**NLP**) and **machine learning** (**ML**).

Text data is very rich in content but highly unstructured, so it requires more preprocessing to enable an ML algorithm to extract relevant information. A key challenge consists of converting text into a numerical format without losing its meaning. We will cover several techniques capable of capturing the nuances of language so that they can be used as input for ML algorithms.

In this chapter, we will introduce fundamental **feature extraction** techniques that focus on individual semantic units, that is, words or short groups of words called **tokens**. We will show how to represent documents as vectors of token counts by creating a document-term matrix and then proceed to use it as input for **news classification** and **sentiment analysis**. We will also introduce the naive Bayes algorithm, which is popular for this purpose.

In the following two chapters, we build on these techniques and use ML algorithms such as topic modeling and word-vector embeddings to capture the information contained in a broader context.

In particular in this chapter, we will cover the following:

- What the fundamental NLP workflow looks like
- How to build a multilingual feature extraction pipeline using spaCy and TextBlob
- Performing NLP tasks such as **part-of-speech** (**POS**) tagging or named entity recognition
- Converting tokens to numbers using the document-term matrix
- Classifying text using the naive Bayes model
- How to perform sentiment analysis

> You can find the code samples for this chapter and links to additional resources in the corresponding directory of the GitHub repository. The notebooks include color versions of the images.

ML with text data – from language to features

Text data can be extremely valuable given how much information humans communicate and store using natural language. The diverse set of data sources relevant to financial investments range from formal documents like company statements, contracts, and patents, to news, opinion, and analyst research or commentary, to various types of social media postings or messages.

Numerous and diverse text data samples are available online to explore the use of NLP algorithms, many of which are listed among the resources included in this chapter's `README` file on GitHub. For a comprehensive introduction, see Jurafsky and Martin (2008).

To realize the potential value of text data, we'll introduce the specialized NLP techniques and the most effective Python libraries, outline key challenges particular to working with language data, introduce critical elements of the NLP workflow, and highlight NLP applications relevant for algorithmic trading.

Key challenges of working with text data

The conversion of unstructured text into a machine-readable format requires careful preprocessing to preserve the valuable semantic aspects of the data. How humans comprehend the content of language is not fully understood and improving machines' ability to understand language remains an area of very active research.

NLP is particularly challenging because the effective use of text data for ML requires an understanding of the inner workings of language as well as knowledge about the world to which it refers. Key challenges include the following:

- Ambiguity due to **polysemy**, that is, a word or phrase having different meanings depending on context ("Local High School Dropouts Cut in Half")
- The nonstandard and **evolving use** of language, especially on social media
- The use of **idioms** like "throw in the towel"
- Tricky **entity names** like "Where is A Bug's Life playing?"
- Knowledge of the world: "Mary and Sue are sisters" versus "Mary and Sue are mothers"

The NLP workflow

A key goal for using ML from text data for algorithmic trading is to extract signals from documents. A document is an individual sample from a relevant text data source, for example, a company report, a headline, a news article, or a tweet. A corpus, in turn, is a collection of documents.

Figure 14.1 lays out the **key steps** to convert documents into a dataset that can be used to train a supervised ML algorithm capable of making actionable predictions:

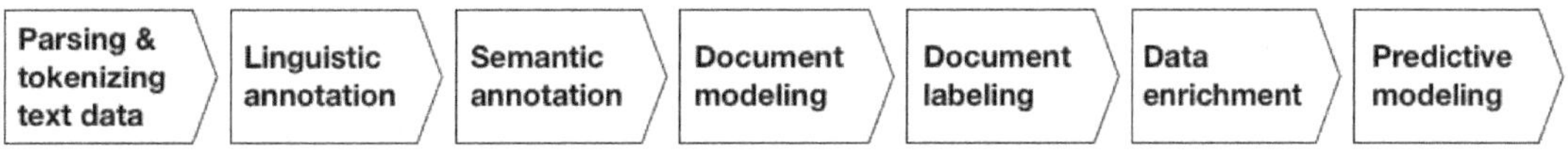

Figure 14.1: The NLP workflow

Fundamental techniques extract text features as isolated semantic units called tokens and use rules and dictionaries to annotate them with linguistic and semantic information. The bag-of-words model uses token frequency to model documents as token vectors, which leads to the document-term matrix that is frequently used for text classification, retrieval, or summarization.

Advanced approaches rely on ML to refine basic features such as tokens and produce richer document models. These include topic models that reflect the joint usage of tokens across documents and word-vector models that aim to capture the context of token usage.

We will review key decisions at each step of the workflow and the related tradeoffs in more detail before illustrating their implementation using the spaCy library in the next section. The following table summarizes the key tasks of an NLP pipeline:

Feature	Description
Tokenization	Segment text into words, punctuation marks, and so on.
Part-of-speech tagging	Assign word types to tokens, such as a verb or noun.
Dependency parsing	Label syntactic token dependencies, like subject <=> object.
Stemming and lemmatization	Assign the base forms of words: "was" => "be", "rats" => "rat".
Sentence boundary detection	Find and segment individual sentences.
Named entity recognition	Label "real-world" objects, such as people, companies, or locations.
Similarity	Evaluate the similarity of words, text spans, and documents.

Parsing and tokenizing text data – selecting the vocabulary

A token is an instance of a sequence of characters in a given document and is considered a semantic unit. The vocabulary is the set of tokens contained in a corpus deemed relevant for further processing; tokens not in the vocabulary will be ignored.

The **goal**, of course, is to extract tokens that most accurately reflect the document's meaning. The **key tradeoff** at this step is the choice of a larger vocabulary to better reflect the text source at the expense of more features and higher model complexity (discussed as the *curse of dimensionality* in *Chapter 13, Data-Driven Risk Factors and Asset Allocation with Unsupervised Learning*).

Basic choices in this regard concern the treatment of punctuation and capitalization, the use of spelling correction, and whether to exclude very frequent so-called "stop words" (such as "and" or "the") as meaningless noise.

In addition, we need to decide whether to include groupings of *n* individual tokens called ***n*-grams** as semantic units (an individual token is also called *unigram*). An example of a two-gram (or *bigram*) is "New York", whereas "New York City" is a three-gram (or *trigram*). The decision can rely on dictionaries or a comparison of the relative frequencies of the individual and joint usage. There are more unique combinations of tokens than unigrams, hence adding *n*-grams will drive up the number of features and risks adding noise unless filtered for by frequency.

Linguistic annotation – relationships among tokens

Linguistic annotations include the application of **syntactic and grammatical rules** to identify the boundary of a sentence despite ambiguous punctuation, and a token's role and relationships in a sentence for POS tagging and dependency parsing. It also permits the identification of common root forms for stemming and lemmatization to group together related words.

The following are some key concepts related to annotations:

- **Stemming** uses simple rules to remove common endings such as *s*, *ly*, *ing*, or *ed* from a token and reduce it to its stem or root form.
- **Lemmatization** uses more sophisticated rules to derive the canonical root (**lemma**) of a word. It can detect irregular common roots such as "better" and "best" and more effectively condenses the vocabulary but is slower than stemming. Both approaches simplify the vocabulary at the expense of semantic nuances.
- **POS** annotations help disambiguate tokens based on their function (for example, when a verb and noun have the same form), which increases the vocabulary but may capture meaningful distinctions.
- **Dependency parsing** identifies hierarchical relationships among tokens and is commonly used for translation. It is important for interactive applications that require more advanced language understanding, such as chatbots.

Semantic annotation – from entities to knowledge graphs

Named-entity recognition (**NER**) aims at identifying tokens that represent objects of interest, such as persons, countries, or companies. It can be further developed into a **knowledge graph** that captures semantic and hierarchical relationships among such entities. It is a critical ingredient for applications that, for example, aim at predicting the impact of news events on sentiment.

Labeling – assigning outcomes for predictive modeling

Many NLP applications learn to predict outcomes based on meaningful information extracted from the text. Supervised learning requires labels to teach the algorithm the true input-output relationship. With text data, establishing this relationship may be challenging and require explicit data modeling and collection.

Examples include decisions on how to quantify the sentiment implicit in a text document such as an email, transcribed interview, or tweet with respect to a new domain, or which aspects of a research document or news report should be assigned a specific outcome.

Applications

The use of ML with text data for trading relies on extracting meaningful information in the form of features that help predict future price movements. Applications range from the exploitation of the short-term market impact of news to the longer-term fundamental analysis of the drivers of asset valuation. Examples include the following:

- The evaluation of product review sentiment to assess a company's competitive position or industry trends
- The detection of anomalies in credit contracts to predict the probability or impact of a default
- The prediction of news impact in terms of direction, magnitude, and affected entities

JP Morgan, for instance, developed a predictive model based on 250,000 analyst reports that outperformed several benchmark indices and produced uncorrelated signals relative to sentiment factors formed from consensus EPS and recommendation changes.

From text to tokens – the NLP pipeline

In this section, we will demonstrate how to construct an NLP pipeline using the open-source Python library spaCy. The textacy library builds on spaCy and provides easy access to spaCy attributes and additional functionality.

Refer to the notebook `nlp_pipeline_with_spaCy` for the following code samples, installation instruction, and additional details.

NLP pipeline with spaCy and textacy

spaCy is a widely used Python library with a comprehensive feature set for fast text processing in multiple languages. The usage of the tokenization and annotation engines requires the installation of language models. The features we will use in this chapter only require the small models; the larger models also include word vectors that we will cover in *Chapter 16, Word Embeddings for Earnings Calls and SEC Filings*.

With the library installed and linked, we can instantiate a spaCy language model and then apply it to the document. The result is a `Doc` object that tokenizes the text and processes it according to configurable pipeline components that by default consist of a tagger, a parser, and a named-entity recognizer:

```
nlp = spacy.load('en')
nlp.pipe_names
['tagger', 'parser', 'ner']
```

Let's illustrate the pipeline using a simple sentence:

```
sample_text = 'Apple is looking at buying U.K. startup for $1 billion'
doc = nlp(sample_text)
```

Parsing, tokenizing, and annotating a sentence

The parsed document content is iterable, and each element has numerous attributes produced by the processing pipeline. The next sample illustrates how to access the following attributes:

- `.text`: The original word text
- `.lemma_`: The word root
- `.pos_`: A basic POS tag
- `.tag_`: The detailed POS tag
- `.dep_`: The syntactic relationship or dependency between tokens
- `.shape_`: The shape of the word, in terms of capitalization, punctuation, and digits
- `.is alpha`: Checks whether the token is alphanumeric
- `.is stop`: Checks whether the token is on a list of common words for the given language

We iterate over each token and assign its attributes to a `pd.DataFrame`:

```
pd.DataFrame([[t.text, t.lemma_, t.pos_, t.tag_, t.dep_, t.shape_,
               t.is_alpha, t.is_stop]
              for t in doc],
             columns=['text', 'lemma', 'pos', 'tag', 'dep', 'shape',
                      'is_alpha', is_stop'])
```

This produces the following result:

text	lemma	pos	tag	dep	shape	is_alpha	is_stop
Apple	apple	PROPN	NNP	nsubj	Xxxxx	TRUE	FALSE
is	be	VERB	VBZ	aux	xx	TRUE	TRUE
looking	look	VERB	VBG	ROOT	xxxx	TRUE	FALSE
at	at	ADP	IN	prep	xx	TRUE	TRUE
buying	buy	VERB	VBG	pcomp	xxxx	TRUE	FALSE
U.K.	u.k.	PROPN	NNP	compound	X.X.	FALSE	FALSE
startup	startup	NOUN	NN	dobj	xxxx	TRUE	FALSE
for	for	ADP	IN	prep	xxx	TRUE	TRUE
$	$	SYM	$	quantmod	$	FALSE	FALSE
1	1	NUM	CD	compound	d	FALSE	FALSE
billion	billion	NUM	CD	pobj	xxxx	TRUE	FALSE

We can visualize the syntactic dependency in a browser or notebook using the following:

```
displacy.render(doc, style='dep', options=options, jupyter=True)
```

The preceding code allows us to obtain a dependency tree like the following one:

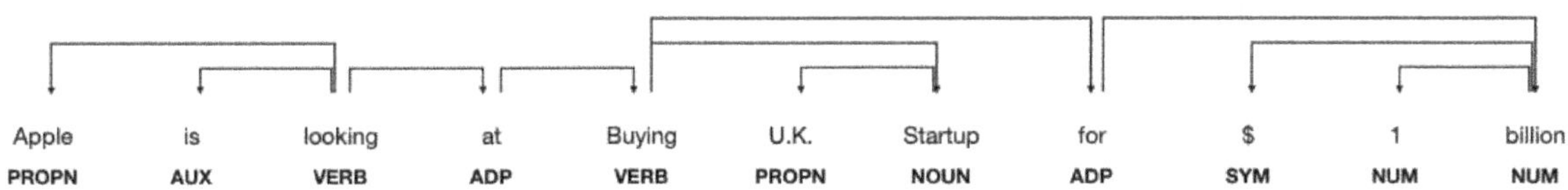

Figure 14.2: spaCy dependency tree

We can get additional insight into the meaning of attributes using `spacy.explain()`, such as the following, for example:

```
spacy.explain("VBZ")
verb, 3rd person singular present
```

Batch-processing documents

We will now read a larger set of 2,225 BBC News articles (see GitHub for the data source details) that belong to five categories and are stored in individual text files. We do the following:

1. Call the `.glob()` method of the `pathlib` module's `Path` object.
2. Iterate over the resulting list of paths.
3. Read all lines of the news article excluding the heading in the first line.
4. Append the cleaned result to a list:

```
files = Path('..', 'data', 'bbc').glob('**/*.txt')
bbc_articles = []
```

```
    for i, file in enumerate(sorted(list(files))):
        with file.open(encoding='latin1') as f:
            lines = f.readlines()
            body = ' '.join([l.strip() for l in lines[1:]]).strip()
            bbc_articles.append(body)
    len(bbc_articles)
    2225
```

Sentence boundary detection

We will illustrate sentence detection by calling the NLP object on the first of the articles:

```
doc = nlp(bbc_articles[0])
type(doc)
spacy.tokens.doc.Doc
```

spaCy computes sentence boundaries from the syntactic parse tree so that punctuation and capitalization play an important but not decisive role. As a result, boundaries will coincide with clause boundaries, even for poorly punctuated text.

We can access the parsed sentences using the `.sents` attribute:

```
sentences = [s for s in doc.sents]
sentences[:3]
[Quarterly profits at US media giant TimeWarner jumped 76% to $1.13bn (Â£600m)
for the three months to December, from $639m year-earlier.  ,
 The firm, which is now one of the biggest investors in Google, benefited from
sales of high-speed internet connections and higher advert sales.,
 TimeWarner said fourth quarter sales rose 2% to $11.1bn from $10.9bn.]
```

Named entity recognition

spaCy enables named entity recognition using the `.ent_type_` attribute:

```
for t in sentences[0]:
    if t.ent_type_:
        print('{} | {} | {}'.format(t.text, t.ent_type_, spacy.explain(t.
ent_type_)))
Quarterly | DATE | Absolute or relative dates or periods
US | GPE | Countries, cities, states
TimeWarner | ORG | Companies, agencies, institutions, etc.
```

Textacy makes access to the named entities that appear in the first article easy:

```
entities = [e.text for e in entities(doc)]
pd.Series(entities).value_counts().head()
TimeWarner         7
AOL                5
```

```
fourth quarter    3
year-earlier      2
one               2
```

N-grams

N-grams combine *n* consecutive tokens. This can be useful for the bag-of-words model because, depending on the textual context, treating (for example) "data scientist" as a single token may be more meaningful than the two distinct tokens "data" and "scientist".

Textacy makes it easy to view the `ngrams` of a given length `n` occurring at least `min_freq` times:

```
pd.Series([n.text for n in ngrams(doc, n=2, min_freq=2)]).value_counts()
fourth quarter     3
quarter profits    2
Time Warner        2
company said       2
AOL Europe         2
```

spaCy's streaming API

To pass a larger number of documents through the processing pipeline, we can use spaCy's streaming API as follows:

```
iter_texts = (bbc_articles[i] for i in range(len(bbc_articles)))
for i, doc in enumerate(nlp.pipe(iter_texts, batch_size=50, n_threads=8)):
    assert doc.is_parsed
```

Multi-language NLP

spaCy includes trained language models for English, German, Spanish, Portuguese, French, Italian, and Dutch, as well as a multi-language model for named-entity recognition. Cross-language usage is straightforward since the API does not change.

We will illustrate the Spanish language model using a parallel corpus of TED talk subtitles (see the GitHub repo for data source references). For this purpose, we instantiate both language models:

```
model = {}
for language in ['en', 'es']:
    model[language] = spacy.load(language)
```

We read small corresponding text samples in each model:

```
text = {}
path = Path('../data/TED')
for language in ['en', 'es']:
```

```
    file_name = path /  'TED2013_sample.{}'.format(language)
    text[language] = file_name.read_text()
```

Sentence boundary detection uses the same logic but finds a different breakdown:

```
parsed, sentences = {}, {}
for language in ['en', 'es']:
    parsed[language] = model[language](text[language])
    sentences[language] = list(parsed[language].sents)
    print('Sentences:', language, len(sentences[language]))
Sentences: en 22
Sentences: es 22
```

POS tagging also works in the same way:

```
pos = {}
for language in ['en', 'es']:
    pos[language] = pd.DataFrame([[t.text, t.pos_, spacy.explain(t.pos_)]
                                  for t in sentences[language][0]],
                                 columns=['Token', 'POS Tag', 'Meaning'])
pd.concat([pos['en'], pos['es']], axis=1).head()
```

This produces the following table:

Token	POS Tag	Meaning	Token	POS Tag	Meaning
There	ADV	adverb	Existe	VERB	verb
s	VERB	verb	una	DET	determiner
a	DET	determiner	estrecha	ADJ	adjective
tight	ADJ	adjective	y	CONJ	conjunction
and	CCONJ	coordinating conjunction	sorprendente	ADJ	adjective

The next section illustrates how to use the parsed and annotated tokens to build a document-term matrix that can be used for text classification.

NLP with TextBlob

TextBlob is a Python library that provides a simple API for common NLP tasks and builds on the **Natural Language Toolkit** (**NLTK**) and the Pattern web mining libraries. TextBlob facilitates POS tagging, noun phrase extraction, sentiment analysis, classification, and translation, among others.

To illustrate the use of TextBlob, we sample a BBC Sport article with the headline "Robinson ready for difficult task". Similar to spaCy and other libraries, the first step is to pass the document through a pipeline represented by the `TextBlob` object to assign the annotations required for various tasks (see the notebook `nlp_with_textblob`):

```
from textblob import TextBlob
article = docs.sample(1).squeeze()
parsed_body = TextBlob(article.body)
```

Stemming

To perform stemming, we instantiate the `SnowballStemmer` from the NTLK library, call its `.stem()` method on each token, and display tokens that were modified as a result:

```
from nltk.stem.snowball import SnowballStemmer
stemmer = SnowballStemmer('english')
[(word, stemmer.stem(word)) for i, word in enumerate(parsed_body.words)
 if word.lower() != stemmer.stem(parsed_body.words[i])]
[('Manchester', 'manchest'),
 ('United', 'unit'),
 ('reduced', 'reduc'),
 ('points', 'point'),
 ('scrappy', 'scrappi')
```

Sentiment polarity and subjectivity

TextBlob provides polarity and subjectivity estimates for parsed documents using dictionaries provided by the Pattern library. These dictionaries lexicon-map adjectives frequently found in product reviews to sentiment polarity scores, ranging from -1 to +1 (negative ↔ positive) and a similar subjectivity score (objective ↔ subjective).

The `.sentiment` attribute provides the average for each score over the relevant tokens, whereas the `.sentiment_assessments` attribute lists the underlying values for each token (see the notebook):

```
parsed_body.sentiment
Sentiment(polarity=0.088031914893617, subjectivity=0.46456433637284694)
```

Counting tokens – the document-term matrix

In this section, we first introduce how the bag-of-words model converts text data into a numeric vector space representations. The goal is to approximate document similarity by their distance in that space. We then proceed to illustrate how to create a document-term matrix using the sklearn library.

The bag-of-words model

The bag-of-words model represents a document based on the frequency of the terms or tokens it contains. Each document becomes a vector with one entry for each token in the vocabulary that reflects the token's relevance to the document.

Creating the document-term matrix

The document-term matrix is straightforward to compute given the vocabulary. However, it is also a crude simplification because it abstracts from word order and grammatical relationships. Nonetheless, it often achieves good results in text classification quickly and, thus, provides a very useful starting point.

The left panel of *Figure 14.3* illustrates how this document model converts text data into a matrix with numerical entries where each row corresponds to a document and each column to a token in the vocabulary. The resulting matrix is usually both very high-dimensional and sparse, that is, it contains many zero entries because most documents only contain a small fraction of the overall vocabulary.

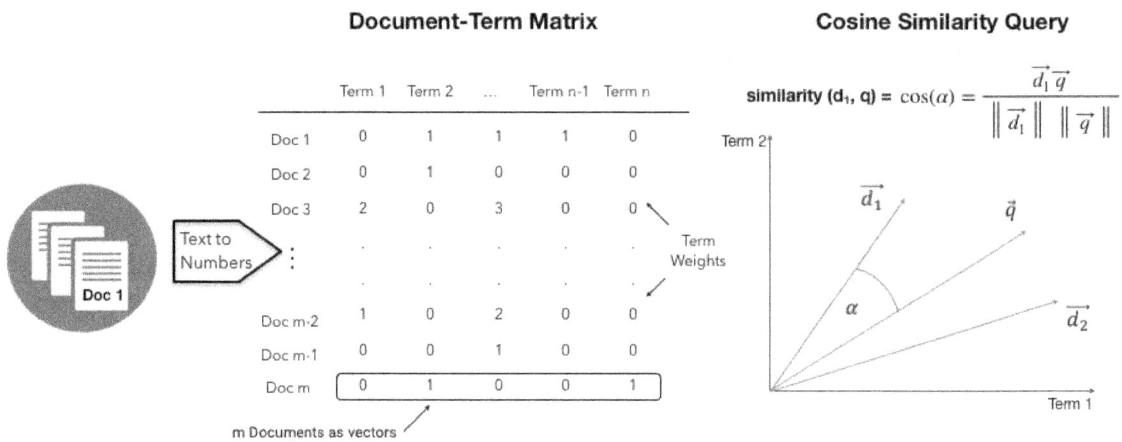

Figure 14.3: Document-term matrix and cosine similarity

There are several ways to weigh a token's vector entry to capture its relevance to the document. We will illustrate how to use sklearn to use binary flags that indicate presence or absence, counts, and weighted counts that account for differences in term frequencies across all documents in the corpus.

Measuring the similarity of documents

The representation of documents as word vectors assigns to each document a location in the vector space created by the vocabulary. Interpreting the vector entries as Cartesian coordinates in this space, we can use the angle between two vectors to measure their similarity because vectors that point in the same direction contain the same terms with the same frequency weights.

The right panel of the preceding figure illustrates—simplified in two dimensions—the calculation of the distance between a document represented by a vector d_1 and a query vector (either a set of search terms or another document) represented by the vector q.

The **cosine similarity** equals the cosine of the angle between the two vectors. It translates the size of the angle into a number in the range [0, 1] since all vector entries are non-negative token weights. A value of 1 implies that both documents are identical with respect to their token weights, whereas a value of 0 implies that the two documents only contain distinct tokens.

As shown in the figure, the cosine of the angle is equal to the dot product of the vectors, that is, the sum product of their coordinates, divided by the product of the lengths, measured by the Euclidean norms, of each vector.

Document-term matrix with scikit-learn

The scikit-learn preprocessing module offers two tools to create a document-term matrix. `CountVectorizer` uses binary or absolute counts to measure the **term frequency** (**TF**) *tf(d, t)* for each document *d* and token *t*.

`TfidfVectorizer`, by contrast, weighs the (absolute) term frequency by the **inverse document frequency** (**IDF**). As a result, a term that appears in more documents will receive a lower weight than a token with the same frequency for a given document but with a lower frequency across all documents. More specifically, using the default settings, the *tf-idf(d, t)* entries for the document-term matrix are computed as *tf-idf(d, t) = tf(d, t)* x *idf(t)* with:

$$\text{idf}(t) = \log\frac{1 + n_d}{1 + \text{df}(d, t)} + 1$$

where n_d is the number of documents and *df(d, t)* the document frequency of term *t*. The resulting TF-IDF vectors for each document are normalized with respect to their absolute or squared totals (see the sklearn documentation for details). The TF-IDF measure was originally used in information retrieval to rank search engine results and has subsequently proven useful for text classification and clustering.

Both tools use the same interface and perform tokenization and further optional preprocessing of a list of documents before vectorizing the text by generating token counts to populate the document-term matrix.

Key parameters that affect the size of the vocabulary include the following:

- `stop_words`: Uses a built-in or user-provided list of (frequent) words to exclude
- `ngram_range`: Includes *n*-grams in a range of *n* defined by a tuple of (n_{min}, n_{max})
- `lowercase`: Converts characters accordingly (the default is `True`)
- `min_df`/`max_df`: Ignores words that appear in less/more (`int`) or are present in a smaller/larger share of documents (if `float` [0.0,1.0])
- `max_features`: Limits the number of tokens in vocabulary accordingly
- `binary`: Sets non-zero counts to 1 (`True`)

See the notebook `document_term_matrix` for the following code samples and additional details. We are again using the 2,225 BBC news articles for illustration.

Using CountVectorizer

The notebook contains an interactive visualization that explores the impact of the `min_df` and `max_df` settings on the size of the vocabulary. We read the articles into a DataFrame, set `CountVectorizer` to produce binary flags and use all tokens, and call its `.fit_transform()` method to produce a document-term matrix:

```
binary_vectorizer = CountVectorizer(max_df=1.0,
                                    min_df=1,
                                    binary=True)
binary_dtm = binary_vectorizer.fit_transform(docs.body)
<2225x29275 sparse matrix of type '<class 'numpy.int64'>'
   with 445870 stored elements in Compressed Sparse Row format>
```

The output is a `scipy.sparse` matrix in row format that efficiently stores a small share (<0.7 percent) of the 445,870 non-zero entries in the 2,225 (document) rows and 29,275 (token) columns.

Visualizing the vocabulary distribution

The visualization in *Figure 14.4* shows that requiring tokens to appear in at least 1 percent and less than 50 percent of documents restricts the vocabulary to around 10 percent of the almost 30,000 tokens.

This leaves a mode of slightly over 100 unique tokens per document, as shown in the left panel of the following plot. The right panel shows the document frequency histogram for the remaining tokens:

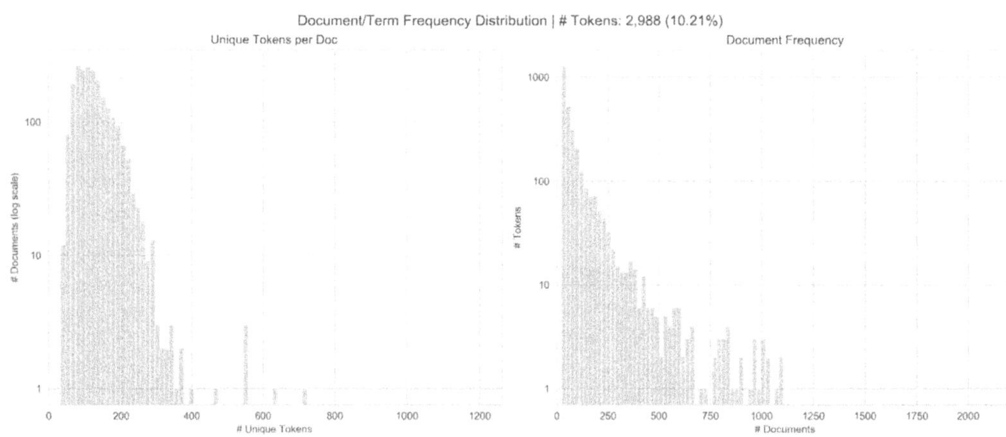

Figure 14.4: The distributions of unique tokens and number of tokens per document

Finding the most similar documents

`CountVectorizer` result lets us find the most similar documents using the `pdist()` functions for pairwise distances provided by the `scipy.spatial.distance` module. It returns a condensed distance matrix with entries corresponding to the upper triangle of a square matrix. We use `np.triu_indices()` to translate the index that minimizes the distance to the row and column indices that in turn correspond to the closest token vectors:

```
m = binary_dtm.todense()        # pdist does not accept sparse format
pairwise_distances = pdist(m, metric='cosine')
closest = np.argmin(pairwise_distances)  # index that minimizes distance
rows, cols = np.triu_indices(n_docs)      # get row-col indices
rows[closest], cols[closest]
(6, 245)
```

Articles 6 and 245 are closest by cosine similarity, due to the fact that they share 38 tokens out of a combined vocabulary of 303 (see notebook). The following table summarizes these two articles and demonstrates the limited ability of similarity measures based on word counts to identify deeper semantic similarity:

	Article 6	**Article 245**
Topic	Business	Business
Heading	Jobs growth still slow in the US	Ebbers 'aware' of WorldCom fraud
Body	The US created fewer jobs than expected in January, but a fall in jobseekers pushed the unemployment rate to its lowest level in three years. According to Labor Department figures, US firms added only 146,000 jobs in January.	Former WorldCom boss Bernie Ebbers was directly involved in the $11bn financial fraud at the firm, his closest associate has told a US court. Giving evidence in the criminal trial of Mr Ebbers, ex-finance chief Scott Sullivan implicated his colleague in the accounting scandal at the firm.

Both `CountVectorizer` and `TfidfVectorizer` can be used with spaCy, for example, to perform lemmatization and exclude certain characters during tokenization:

```
nlp = spacy.load('en')
def tokenizer(doc):
    return [w.lemma_ for w in nlp(doc)
                if not w.is_punct | w.is_space]
vectorizer = CountVectorizer(tokenizer=tokenizer, binary=True)
doc_term_matrix = vectorizer.fit_transform(docs.body)
```

See the notebook for additional detail and more examples.

TfidfTransformer and TfidfVectorizer

`TfidfTransformer` computes the TF-IDF weights from a document-term matrix of token counts like the one produced by `CountVectorizer`.

`TfidfVectorizer` performs both computations in a single step. It adds a few parameters to the `CountVectorizer` API that controls the smoothing behavior.

The TFIDF computation works as follows for a small text sample:

```
sample_docs = ['call you tomorrow',
               'Call me a taxi',
               'please call me... PLEASE!']
```

We compute the term frequency as before:

```
vectorizer = CountVectorizer()
tf_dtm = vectorizer.fit_transform(sample_docs).todense()
tokens = vectorizer.get_feature_names()
term_frequency = pd.DataFrame(data=tf_dtm,
                              columns=tokens)

  call  me  please  taxi  tomorrow  you
0    1   0       0     0         1    1
1    1   1       0     1         0    0
2    1   1       2     0         0    0
```

The document frequency is the number of documents containing the token:

```
vectorizer = CountVectorizer(binary=True)
df_dtm = vectorizer.fit_transform(sample_docs).todense().sum(axis=0)
document_frequency = pd.DataFrame(data=df_dtm,
                                  columns=tokens)
   call  me  please  taxi  tomorrow  you
0     3   2       1     1         1    1
```

The TF-IDF weights are the ratio of these values:

```
tfidf = pd.DataFrame(data=tf_dtm/df_dtm, columns=tokens)
   call   me please  taxi  tomorrow  you
0  0.33 0.00   0.00  0.00      1.00 1.00
1  0.33 0.50   0.00  1.00      0.00 0.00
2  0.33 0.50   2.00  0.00      0.00 0.00
```

The effect of smoothing

To avoid zero division, `TfidfVectorizer` uses smoothing for document and term frequencies:

- `smooth_idf`: Adds one to document frequency, as if an extra document contained every token in the vocabulary, to prevent zero divisions
- `sublinear_tf`: Applies sublinear tf scaling, that is, replaces tf with 1 + log(tf)

In combination with normed weights, the results differ slightly:

```
vect = TfidfVectorizer(smooth_idf=True,
                       norm='l2',  # squared weights sum to 1 by document
                       sublinear_tf=False,  # if True, use 1+log(tf)
                       binary=False)
pd.DataFrame(vect.fit_transform(sample_docs).todense(),
            columns=vect.get_feature_names())
   call   me  please  taxi  tomorrow  you
0  0.39 0.00    0.00  0.00      0.65 0.65
1  0.43 0.55    0.00  0.72      0.00 0.00
2  0.27 0.34    0.90  0.00      0.00 0.00
```

Summarizing news articles using TfidfVectorizer

Due to their ability to assign meaningful token weights, TF-IDF vectors are also used to summarize text data. For example, Reddit's `autotldr` function is based on a similar algorithm. See the notebook for an example using the BBC articles.

Key lessons instead of lessons learned

The large number of techniques and options to process natural language for use in ML models corresponds to the complex nature of this highly unstructured data source. The engineering of good language features is both challenging and rewarding, and arguably the most important step in unlocking the semantic value hidden in text data.

In practice, experience helps to select transformations that remove the noise rather than the signal, but it will likely remain necessary to cross-validate and compare the performance of different combinations of preprocessing choices.

NLP for trading

Once text data has been converted into numerical features using the NLP techniques discussed in the previous sections, text classification works just like any other classification task.

In this section, we will apply these preprocessing techniques to news articles, product reviews, and Twitter data and teach various classifiers to predict discrete news categories, review scores, and sentiment polarity.

First, we will introduce the naive Bayes model, a probabilistic classification algorithm that works well with the text features produced by a bag-of-words model.

The code samples for this section are in the notebook `news_text_classification`.

The naive Bayes classifier

The naive Bayes algorithm is very popular for text classification because its low computational cost and memory requirements facilitate training on very large, high-dimensional datasets. Its predictive performance can compete with more complex models, provides a good baseline, and is best known for successful spam detection.

The model relies on Bayes' theorem and the assumption that the various features are independent of each other given the outcome class. In other words, for a given outcome, knowing the value of one feature (for example, the presence of a token in a document) does not provide any information about the value of another feature.

Bayes' theorem refresher

Bayes' theorem expresses the conditional probability of one event (for example, that an email is spam as opposed to benign "ham") given another event (for example, that the email contains certain words) as follows:

$$\underbrace{P(\text{is spam} \mid \text{has words})}_{\text{Posterior}} = \frac{\overbrace{P(\text{has words} \mid \text{is spam})}^{\text{Likelihood}}\overbrace{P(\text{is spam})}^{\text{Prior}}}{\underbrace{P(\text{has words})}_{\text{Evidence}}} \%0$$

The **posterior** probability that an email is in fact spam given that it contains certain words depends on the interplay of three factors:

- The **prior** probability that an email is spam
- The **likelihood** of encountering these words in a spam email
- The **evidence**, that is, the probability of seeing these words in an email

To compute the posterior, we can ignore the evidence because it is the same for all outcomes (spam versus ham), and the unconditional prior may be easy to compute.

However, the likelihood poses insurmountable challenges for a reasonably sized vocabulary and a real-world corpus of emails. The reason is the combinatorial explosion of the words that did or did not appear jointly in different documents that prevent the evaluation required to compute a probability table and assign a value to the likelihood.

The conditional independence assumption

The key assumption to make the model both tractable and earn it the name *naive* is that the features are independent conditional on the outcome. To illustrate, let's classify an email with the three words "Send money now" so that Bayes' theorem becomes the following:

$$P(\text{spam} \mid \text{send money now}) = \frac{P(\text{send money now} \mid \text{spam}) \times P(\text{spam})}{P(\text{send money now})}$$

Formally, the assumption that the three words are conditionally independent means that the probability of observing "send" is not affected by the presence of the other terms given that the mail is spam, that is, $P(\text{send} \mid \text{money, now, spam}) = P(\text{send} \mid \text{spam})$. As a result, we can simplify the likelihood function:

$$P(\text{spam} \mid \text{send money now}) = \frac{P(\text{send} \mid \text{spam}) \times P(\text{money} \mid \text{spam}) \times P(\text{now} \mid \text{spam}) \times P(\text{spam})}{P(\text{send money now})}$$

Using the "naive" conditional independence assumption, each term in the numerator is straightforward to compute as relative frequencies from the training data. The denominator is constant across classes and can be ignored when posterior probabilities need to be compared rather than calibrated. The prior probability becomes less relevant as the number of factors, that is, features, increases.

In sum, the advantages of the naive Bayes model are fast training and prediction because the number of parameters is proportional to the number of features, and their estimation has a closed-form solution (based on training data frequencies) rather than expensive iterative optimization. It is also intuitive and somewhat interpretable, does not require hyperparameter tuning and is relatively robust to irrelevant features given sufficient signal.

However, when the independence assumption does not hold and text classification depends on combinations of features, or features are correlated, the model will perform poorly.

Classifying news articles

We start with an illustration of the naive Bayes model for news article classification using the BBC articles that we read before to obtain a `DataFrame` with 2,225 articles from five categories:

```
<class 'pandas.core.frame.DataFrame'>
RangeIndex: 2225 entries, 0 to 2224
Data columns (total 3 columns):
topic      2225 non-null object
heading    2225 non-null object
body       2225 non-null object
```

To train and evaluate a multinomial naive Bayes classifier, we split the data into the default 75:25 train-test set ratio, ensuring that the test set classes closely mirror the train set:

```
y = pd.factorize(docs.topic)[0] # create integer class values
X = docs.body
X_train, X_test, y_train, y_test = train_test_split(X, y, random_state=1,
                                                    stratify=y)
```

We proceed to learn the vocabulary from the training set and transform both datasets using `CountVectorizer` with default settings to obtain almost 26,000 features:

```
vectorizer = CountVectorizer()
X_train_dtm = vectorizer.fit_transform(X_train)
X_test_dtm = vectorizer.transform(X_test)
X_train_dtm.shape, X_test_dtm.shape
((1668, 25919), (557, 25919))
```

Training and prediction follow the standard sklearn fit/predict interface:

```
nb = MultinomialNB()
nb.fit(X_train_dtm, y_train)
y_pred_class = nb.predict(X_test_dtm)
```

We evaluate the multiclass predictions using `accuracy` to find the default classifier achieved an accuracy of almost 98 percent:

```
accuracy_score(y_test, y_pred_class)
0.97666068222621
```

Sentiment analysis with Twitter and Yelp data

Sentiment analysis is one of the most popular uses of NLP and ML for trading because positive or negative perspectives on assets or other price drivers are likely to impact returns.

Generally, modeling approaches to sentiment analysis rely on dictionaries (as does the TextBlob library) or models trained on outcomes for a specific domain. The latter is often preferable because it permits more targeted labeling, for example, by tying text features to subsequent price changes rather than indirect sentiment scores.

We will illustrate ML for sentiment analysis using a Twitter dataset with binary polarity labels and a large Yelp business review dataset with a five-point outcome scale.

Binary sentiment classification with Twitter data

We use a dataset that contains 1.6 million training and 350 test tweets from 2009 with algorithmically assigned binary positive and negative sentiment scores that are fairly evenly split (see the notebook for more detailed data exploration).

Multinomial naive Bayes

We create a document-term matrix with 934 tokens as follows:

```
vectorizer = CountVectorizer(min_df=.001, max_df=.8, stop_words='english')
train_dtm = vectorizer.fit_transform(train.text)
<1566668x934 sparse matrix of type '<class 'numpy.int64'>'
    with 6332930 stored elements in Compressed Sparse Row format>
```

We then train the `MultinomialNB` classifier as before and predict the test set:

```
nb = MultinomialNB()
nb.fit(train_dtm, train.polarity)
predicted_polarity = nb.predict(test_dtm)
```

The result has over 77.5 percent accuracy:

```
accuracy_score(test.polarity, predicted_polarity)
0.7768361581920904
```

Comparison with TextBlob sentiment scores

We also obtain TextBlob sentiment scores for the tweets and note (see the left panel in *Figure 14.5*) that positive test tweets receive a significantly higher sentiment estimate. We then use the `MultinomialNB` model's `.predict_proba()` method to compute predicted probabilities and compare both models using the respective area **under the curve**, or **AUC**, that we introduced in *Chapter 6, The Machine Learning Process* (see the right panel in *Figure 14.5*).

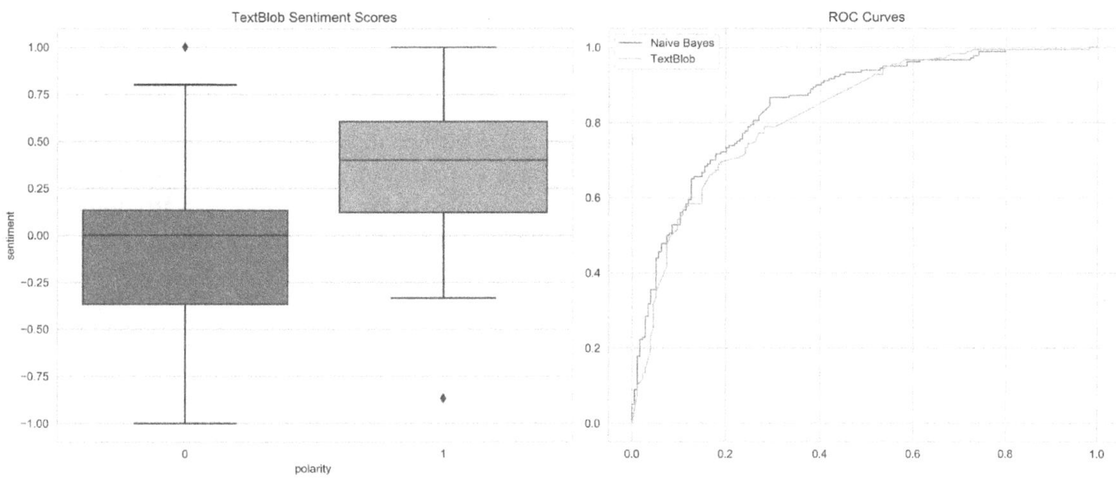

Figure 14.5: Accuracy of custom versus generic sentiment scores

The custom naive Bayes model outperforms TextBlob in this case, achieving a test AUC of 0.848 compared to 0.825 for TextBlob.

Multiclass sentiment analysis with Yelp business reviews

Finally, we apply sentiment analysis to the significantly larger Yelp business review dataset with five outcome classes (see the notebook `sentiment_analysis_yelp` for code and additional details).

The data consists of several files with information on the business, the user, the review, and other aspects that Yelp provides to encourage data science innovation.

We will use around six million reviews produced over the 2010-2018 period (see the notebook for details). The following figure shows the number of reviews and the average number of stars per year, as well as the star distribution across all reviews.

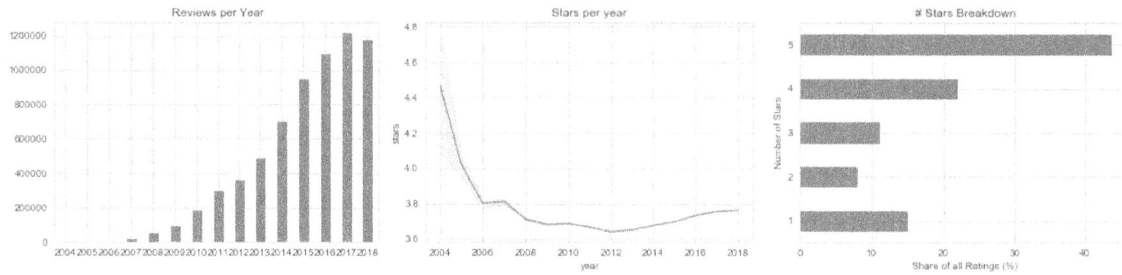

Figure 14.6: Basic exploratory analysis of Yelp reviews

We will train various models on a 10 percent sample of the data through 2017 and use the 2018 reviews as the test set. In addition to the text features resulting from the review texts, we will also use other information submitted with the review about the given user.

Combining text and numerical features

The dataset contains various numerical features (see notebook for implementation details).

The vectorizers produce `scipy.sparse` matrices. To combine the vectorized text data with other features, we need to first convert these to sparse matrices as well; many sklearn objects and other libraries such as LightGBM can handle these very memory-efficient data structures. Converting the sparse matrix to a dense NumPy array risks memory overflow.

Most variables are categorical, so we use one-hot encoding since we have a fairly large dataset to accommodate the increase in features.

We convert the encoded numerical features and combine them with the document-term matrix:

```
train_numeric = sparse.csr_matrix(train_dummies.astype(np.uint))
train_dtm_numeric = sparse.hstack((train_dtm, train_numeric))
```

Benchmark accuracy

Using the most frequent number of stars (=5) to predict the test set achieves an accuracy close to 52 percent:

```
test['predicted'] = train.stars.mode().iloc[0]
accuracy_score(test.stars, test.predicted)
0.5196950594793454
```

Multinomial naive Bayes model

Next, we train a naive Bayes classifier using a document-term matrix produced by `CountVectorizer` with default settings.

```
nb = MultinomialNB()
nb.fit(train_dtm,train.stars)
predicted_stars = nb.predict(test_dtm)
```

The prediction produces 64.7 percent accuracy on the test set, a 24.4 percent improvement over the benchmark:

```
accuracy_score(test.stars, predicted_stars)
0.6465164206691094
```

Training with the combination of text and other features improves the test accuracy to 0.671.

Logistic regression

In *Chapter 7, Linear Models – From Risk Factors to Return Forecasts,* we introduced binary logistic regression. sklearn also implements a multiclass model with a multinomial and a one-versus-all training option, where the latter trains a binary model for each class while considering all other classes as the negative class. The multinomial option is much faster and more accurate than the one-versus-all implementation.

We evaluate a range of values for the regularization parameter `C` to identify the best performing model, using the `lbfgs` solver as follows (see the sklearn documentation for details):

```
def evaluate_model(model, X_train, X_test, name, store=False):
    start = time()
    model.fit(X_train, train.stars)
    runtime[name] = time() - start
    predictions[name] = model.predict(X_test)
    accuracy[result] = accuracy_score(test.stars, predictions[result])
    if store:
        joblib.dump(model, f'results/{result}.joblib')

Cs = np.logspace(-5, 5, 11)
for C in Cs:
    model = LogisticRegression(C=C, multi_class='multinomial',
solver='lbfgs')
    evaluate_model(model, train_dtm, test_dtm, result, store=True)
```

Figure 14.7 shows the plots of the validation results.

Multiclass gradient boosting with LightGBM

For comparison, we also train a LightGBM gradient boosting tree ensemble with default settings and a `multiclass` objective:

```
param = {'objective':'multiclass', 'num_class': 5}
booster = lgb.train(params=param,
```

```
                       train_set=lgb_train,
                       num_boost_round=500,
                       early_stopping_rounds=20,
                       valid_sets=[lgb_train, lgb_test])
```

Predictive performance

Figure 14.7 displays the accuracy of each model for the combined data. The right panel plots the validation performance for the logistic regression models for both datasets and different levels of regularization.

Multinomial logistic regression performs best with a test accuracy slightly above 74 percent. Naive Bayes performs significantly worse. The default LightGBM settings did not improve over the linear model with an accuracy of 0.736. However, we could tune the hyperparameters of the gradient boosting model and may well see performance improvements that put it at least on par with logistic regression. Either way, the result serves as a reminder not to discount simple, regularized models as they may deliver not only good results, but also do so quickly.

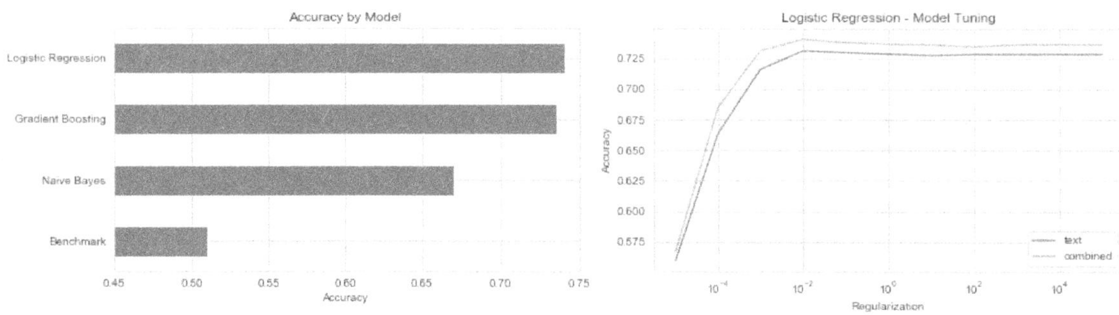

Figure 14.7: Test performance on combined data (all models, left) and for logistic regression with varying regularization

Summary

In this chapter, we explored numerous techniques and options to process unstructured data with the goal of extracting semantically meaningful numerical features for use in ML models.

We covered the basic tokenization and annotation pipeline and illustrated its implementation for multiple languages using spaCy and TextBlob. We built on these results to build a document model based on the bag-of-words model to represent documents as numerical vectors. We learned how to refine the preprocessing pipeline and then used the vectorized text data for classification and sentiment analysis.

We have two more chapters on alternative text data. In the next chapter, we will learn how to summarize texts using unsupervised learning to identify latent topics. Then, in *Chapter 16*, *Word Embeddings for Earnings Calls and SEC Filings*, we will learn how to represent words as vectors that reflect the context of word usage, a technique that has been used very successfully to provide richer text features for various classification tasks.

15

Topic Modeling – Summarizing Financial News

In the last chapter, we used the **bag-of-words** (**BOW**) model to convert unstructured text data into a numerical format. This model abstracts from word order and represents documents as word vectors, where each entry represents the relevance of a token to the document. The resulting **document-term matrix** (**DTM**)—or transposed as the term-document matrix—is useful for comparing documents to each other or a query vector for similarity based on their token content and, therefore, finding the proverbial needle in a haystack. It provides informative features to classify documents, such as in our sentiment analysis examples.

However, this document model produces both high-dimensional data and very sparse data, yet it does little to summarize the content or get closer to understanding what it is about. In this chapter, we will use **unsupervised machine learning** to extract hidden themes from documents using **topic modeling**. These themes can produce detailed insights into a large body of documents in an automated way. They are very useful in order to understand the haystack itself and allow us to tag documents based on their affinity with the various topics.

Topic models generate sophisticated, interpretable text features that can be a first step toward extracting trading signals from large collections of documents. They speed up the review of documents, help identify and cluster similar documents, and support predictive modeling.

Applications include the unsupervised discovery of potentially insightful themes in company disclosures or earnings call transcripts, customer reviews, or contracts. Furthermore, the document-topic associations facilitate the labeling by assigning, for example, sentiment metrics or, more directly, subsequent relevant asset returns.

More specifically, after reading this chapter, you'll understand:

- How topic modeling has evolved, what it achieves, and why it matters
- Reducing the dimensionality of the DTM using **latent semantic indexing** (**LSI**)
- Extracting topics with **probabilistic latent semantic analysis** (**pLSA**)
- How **latent Dirichlet allocation** (**LDA**) improves pLSA to become the most popular topic model
- Visualizing and evaluating topic modeling results
- Running LDA using sklearn and Gensim
- How to apply topic modeling to collections of earnings calls and financial news articles

> You can find the code samples for this chapter and links to additional resources in the corresponding directory of the GitHub repository. The notebooks include color versions of the images.

Learning latent topics – Goals and approaches

Topic modeling discovers hidden themes that capture semantic information beyond individual words in a body of documents. It aims to address a key challenge for a machine learning algorithm that learns from text data by transcending the lexical level of "what actually has been written" to the semantic level of "what was intended." The resulting topics can be used to annotate documents based on their association with various topics.

In practical terms, topic models automatically **summarize large collections of documents** to facilitate organization and management as well as search and recommendations. At the same time, it enables the understanding of documents to the extent that humans can interpret the descriptions of topics.

Topic models also mitigate the **curse of dimensionality** that often plagues the BOW model; representing documents with high-dimensional, sparse vectors can make similarity measures noisy, lead to inaccurate distance measurements, and result in the overfitting of text classification models.

Moreover, the BOW model loses context as well as semantic information since it ignores word order. It is also unable to capture synonymy (where several words have the same meaning) or polysemy (where one word has several meanings). As a result of the latter, document retrieval or similarity search may miss the point when the documents are not indexed by the terms used to search or compare.

These shortcomings of the BOW model prompt the question: how can we learn meaningful topics from data that facilitate a more productive interaction with documentary data?

Initial attempts by topic models to improve on the vector space model (developed in the mid-1970s) applied linear algebra to reduce the dimensionality of the DTM. This approach is similar to the algorithm that we discussed as principal component analysis in *Chapter 13, Data-Driven Risk Factors and Asset Allocation with Unsupervised Learning*. While effective, it is difficult to evaluate the results of these models without a benchmark model. In response, probabilistic models have emerged that assume an explicit document generation process and provide algorithms to reverse engineer this process and recover the underlying topics.

The following table highlights key milestones in the model evolution, which we will address in more detail in the following sections:

Model	Year	Description
Latent semantic indexing (LSI)	1988	Captures the semantic document-term relationship by reducing the dimensionality of the word space
Probabilistic latent semantic analysis (pLSA)	1999	Reverse engineers a generative process that assumes words generate a topic and documents as a mix of topics
Latent Dirichlet allocation (LDA)	2003	Adds a generative process for documents: a three-level hierarchical Bayesian model

Latent semantic indexing

Latent semantic indexing (**LSI**)—also called **latent semantic analysis** (**LSA**)—set out to improve the results of queries that omitted relevant documents containing synonyms of query terms (Dumais et al. 1988). Its goal was to model the relationships between documents and terms so that it could predict that a term should be associated with a document, even though, because of the variability in word use, no such association was observed.

LSI uses linear algebra to find a given number k of latent topics by decomposing the DTM. More specifically, it uses the **singular value decomposition** (**SVD**) to find the best lower-rank DTM approximation using k singular values and vectors. In other words, LSI builds on some of the dimensionality reduction techniques we encountered in *Chapter 13, Data-Driven Risk Factors and Asset Allocation with Unsupervised Learning*. The authors also experimented with hierarchical clustering but found it too restrictive for this purpose.

In this context, SVD identifies a set of uncorrelated indexing variables or factors that represent each term and document by its vector of factor values. *Figure 15.1* illustrates how SVD decomposes the DTM into three matrices: two matrices that contain orthogonal singular vectors and a diagonal matrix with singular values that serve as scaling factors.

Assuming some correlation in the input DTM, singular values decay in value. Therefore, selecting the T-largest singular values yields a lower-dimensional approximation of the original DTM that loses relatively little information. In the compressed version, the rows or columns that had N items only have $T < N$ entries.

The LSI decomposition of the DTM can be interpreted as shown in *Figure 15.1*:

- The first M × T matrix represents the relationships between documents and topics.
- The diagonal matrix scales the topics by their corpus strength.
- The third matrix models the term-topic relationship.

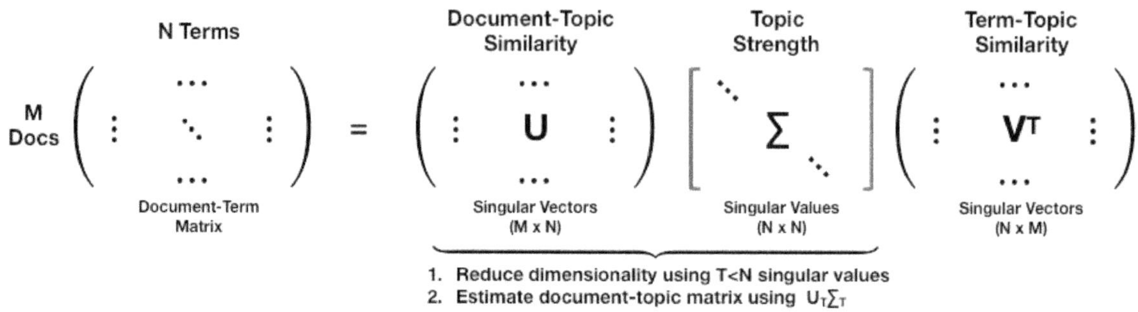

Figure 15.1: LSI and the SVD

The rows of the matrix produced by multiplying the first two matrices $U_T\Sigma_T$ correspond to the locations of the original documents projected into the latent topic space.

How to implement LSI using sklearn

We will illustrate LSI using the BBC articles data that we introduced in the last chapter because they are small enough for quick training and allow us to compare topic assignments with category labels. Refer to the notebook `latent_semantic_indexing` for additional implementation details.

We begin by loading the documents and creating a train and (stratified) test set with 50 articles. Then, we vectorize the data using `TfidfVectorizer` to obtain weighted DTM counts and filter out words that appear in less than 1 percent or more than 25 percent of the documents, as well as generic stopwords, to obtain a vocabulary of around 2,900 words:

```
vectorizer = TfidfVectorizer(max_df=.25, min_df=.01,
                             stop_words='english',
                             binary=False)
train_dtm = vectorizer.fit_transform(train_docs.article)
test_dtm = vectorizer.transform(test_docs.article)
```

We use scikit-learn's `TruncatedSVD` class, which only computes the *k*-largest singular values, to reduce the dimensionality of the DTM. The deterministic `arpack` algorithm delivers an exact solution, but the default "randomized" implementation is more efficient for large matrices.

We compute five topics to match the five categories, which explain only 5.4 percent of the total DTM variance, so a larger number of topics would be reasonable:

```
svd = TruncatedSVD(n_components=5, n_iter=5, random_state=42)
svd.fit(train_dtm)
svd.explained_variance_ratio_.sum()
0.05382357286057269
```

LSI identifies a new orthogonal basis for the DTM that reduces the rank to the number of desired topics. The `.transform()` method of the trained `svd` object projects the documents into the new topic space. This space results from reducing the dimensionality of the document vectors and corresponds to the $U_T\Sigma_T$ transformation illustrated earlier in this section:

```
train_doc_topics = svd.transform(train_dtm)
train_doc_topics.shape
(2175, 5)
```

We can sample an article to view its location in the topic space. We draw a "Politics" article that is most (positively) associated with topics 1 and 2:

```
i = randint(0, len(train_docs))
train_docs.iloc[i, :2].append(pd.Series(doc_topics[i], index=topic_labels))
Category                                    Politics
Heading     What the election should really be about?
Topic 1                                         0.33
Topic 2                                         0.18
Topic 3                                         0.12
Topic 4                                         0.02
Topic 5                                         0.06
```

The topic assignments for this sample align with the average topic weights for each category illustrated in *Figure 15.2* ("Politics" is the rightmost bar). They illustrate how LSI expresses the *k* topics as directions in a *k*-dimensional space (the notebook includes a projection of the average topic assignments per category into two-dimensional space).

Each category is clearly defined, and the test assignments match with train assignments. However, the weights are both positive and negative, making it more difficult to interpret the topics.

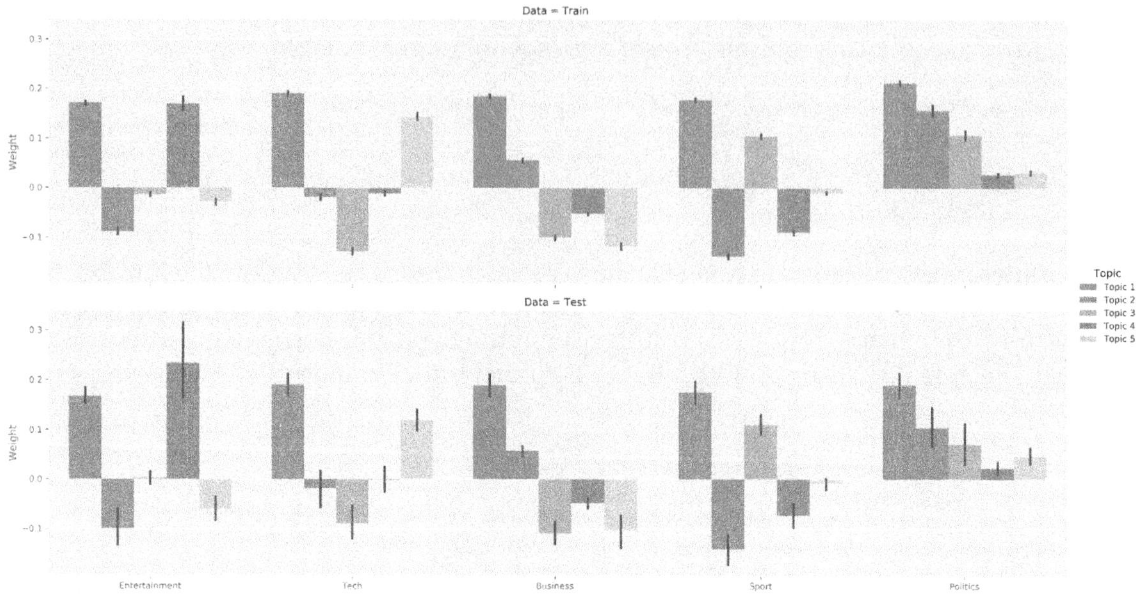

Figure 15.2: LSI topic weights for train and test data

We can also display the words that are most closely associated with each topic (in absolute terms). The topics appear to capture some semantic information but are not clearly differentiated (refer to *Figure 15.3*).

Figure 15.3: Top 10 words per LSI topic

Strengths and limitations

The strengths of LSI include the removal of noise and the mitigation of the curse of dimensionality. It also captures some semantic aspects, like synonymy, and clusters both documents and terms via their topic associations. Furthermore, it does not require knowledge of the document language, and both information retrieval queries and document comparisons are easy to do.

However, the results of LSI are difficult to interpret because topics are word vectors with both positive and negative entries. In addition, there is no underlying model that would permit the evaluation of fit or provide guidance when selecting the number of dimensions or topics to use.

Probabilistic latent semantic analysis

Probabilistic latent semantic analysis (pLSA) takes a **statistical perspective** on LSI/LSA and creates a generative model to address the lack of theoretical underpinnings of LSA (Hofmann 2001).

pLSA explicitly models the probability word w appearing in document d, as described by the DTM as a mixture of conditionally independent multinomial distributions that involve topics t.

There are both **symmetric and asymmetric formulations** of how word-document co-occurrences come about. The former assumes that both words and documents are generated by the latent topic class. In contrast, the asymmetric model assumes that topics are selected given the document, and words result in a second step given the topic.

$$P(w,d) = \underbrace{\sum_t P(d|t)P(w|t)}_{\text{symmetric}} = \underbrace{P(d)\sum_t P(t|d)P(w|t)}_{\text{asymmetric}}$$

The number of topics is a **hyperparameter** chosen prior to training and is not learned from the data.

The **plate notation** in *Figure 15.4* describes the statistical dependencies in a probabilistic model. More specifically, it encodes the relationship just described for the asymmetric model. Each rectangle represents multiple items: the outer block stands for M documents, while the inner shaded rectangle symbolizes N words for each document. We only observe the documents and their content; the model infers the hidden or latent topic distribution:

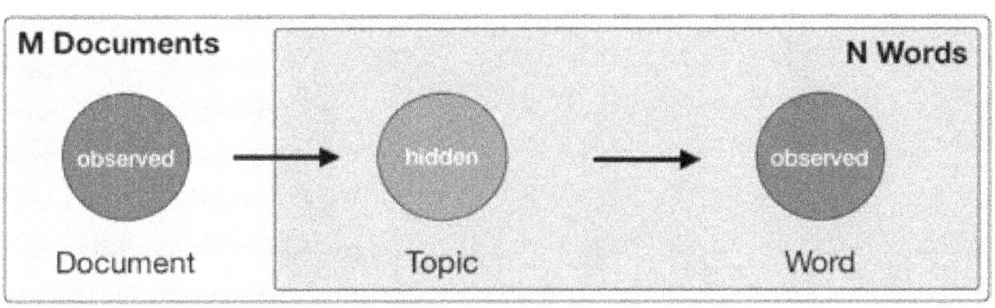

Figure 15.4: The statistical dependencies modeled by pLSA in plate notation

Let's now take a look at how we can implement this model in practice.

How to implement pLSA using sklearn

pLSA is equivalent to **non-negative matrix factorization** (**NMF**) using a Kullback-Leibler divergence objective (view the references on GitHub). Therefore, we can use the `sklearn.decomposition.NMF` class to implement this model following the LSI example.

Using the same train-test split of the DTM produced by `TfidfVectorizer`, we fit pLSA like so:

```
nmf = NMF(n_components=n_components,
          random_state=42,
          solver='mu',
          beta_loss='kullback-leibler',
          max_iter=1000)
nmf.fit(train_dtm)
```

We get a measure of the reconstruction error that is a substitute for the explained variance measure from earlier:

```
nmf.reconstruction_err_
316.2609400385988
```

Due to its probabilistic nature, pLSA produces only positive topic weights that result in more straightforward topic-category relationships for the test and training sets, as shown in *Figure 15.5*:

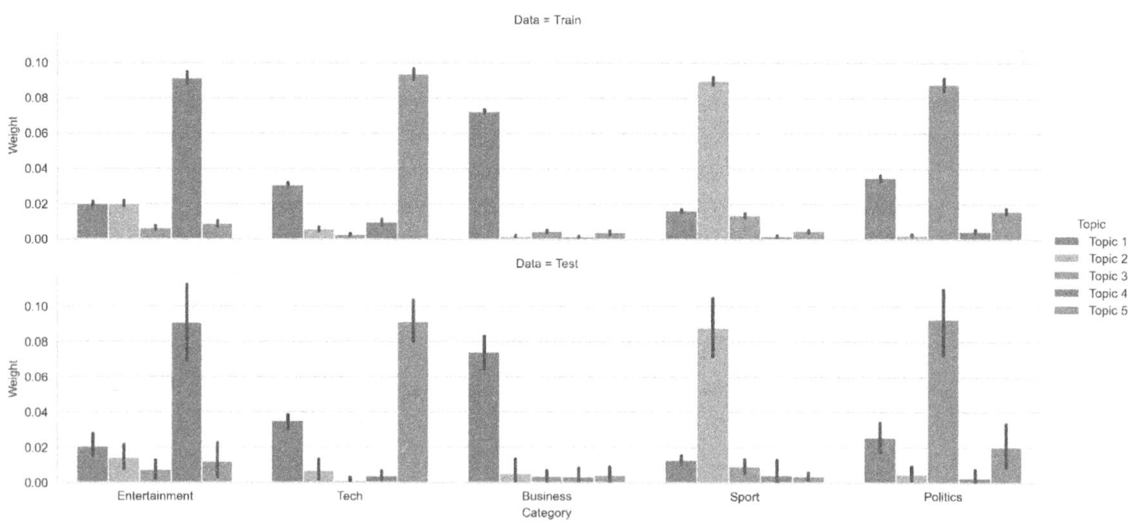

Figure 15.5: pLSA weights by topic for train and test data

We also note that the word lists that describe each topic begin to make more sense; for example, the "Entertainment" category is most directly associated with Topic 4, which includes the words "film," "star," and so forth, as you can see in *Figure 15.6*:

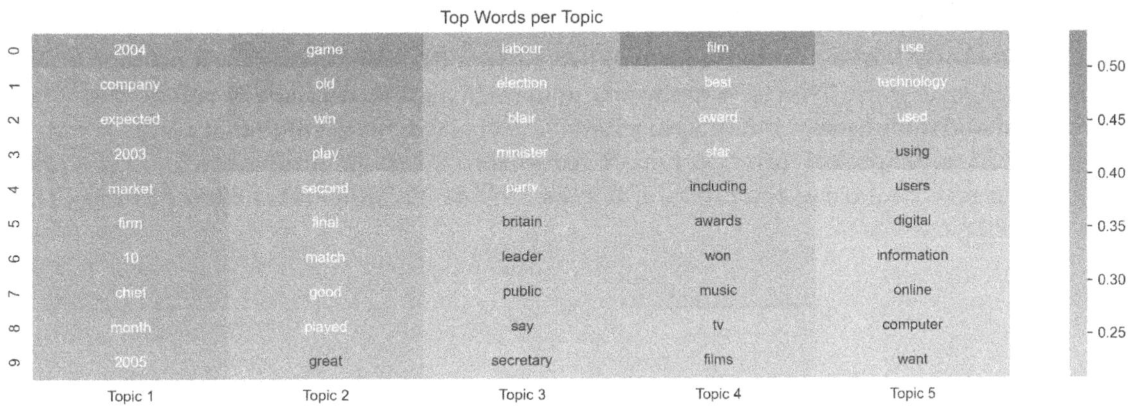

Figure 15.6: Top words per topic for pLSA

Strengths and limitations

The benefit of using a probability model is that we can now compare the performance of different models by evaluating the probability they assign to new documents given the parameters learned during training. It also means that the results have a clear probabilistic interpretation. In addition, pLSA captures more semantic information, including polysemy.

On the other hand, pLSA increases the computational complexity compared to LSI, and the algorithm may only yield a local as opposed to a global maximum. Finally, it does not yield a generative model for new documents because it takes them as given.

Latent Dirichlet allocation

Latent Dirichlet allocation (**LDA**) extends pLSA by adding a generative process for topics (Blei, Ng, and Jordan 2003). It is the most popular topic model because it tends to produce meaningful topics that humans can relate to, can assign topics to new documents, and is extensible. Variants of LDA models can include metadata, like authors or image data, or learn hierarchical topics.

How LDA works

LDA is a **hierarchical Bayesian model** that assumes topics are probability distributions over words, and documents are distributions over topics. More specifically, the model assumes that topics follow a sparse Dirichlet distribution, which implies that documents reflect only a small set of topics, and topics use only a limited number of terms frequently.

The Dirichlet distribution

The Dirichlet distribution produces probability vectors that can be used as a discrete probability distribution. That is, it randomly generates a given number of values that are positive and sum to one. It has a parameter α of positive real value that controls the concentration of the probabilities. Values closer to zero mean that only a few values will be positive and receive most of the probability mass. *Figure 15.7* illustrates three draws of size 10 for $\alpha = 0.1$:

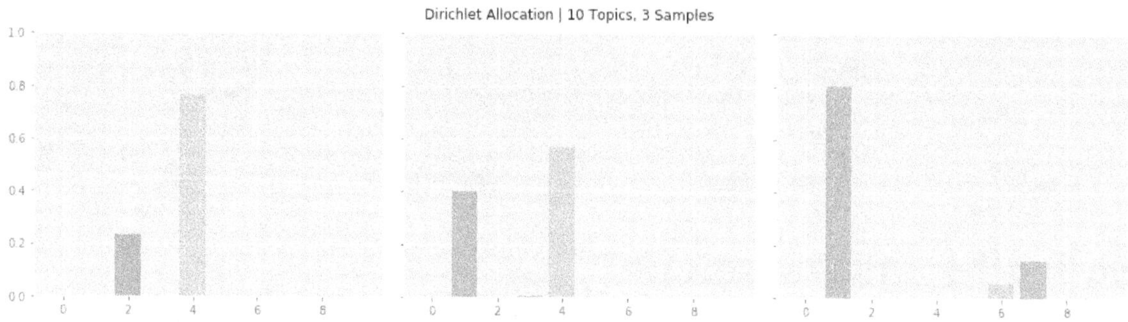

Figure 15.7: Three draws from the Dirichlet distribution

The notebook `dirichlet_distribution` contains a simulation that lets you experiment with different parameter values.

The generative model

The LDA topic model assumes the following generative process when an author adds an article to a body of documents:

1. Randomly mix a small subset of topics with proportions defined by the Dirichlet probabilities.
2. For each word in the text, select one of the topics according to the document-topic probabilities.
3. Select a word from the topic's word list according to the topic-word probabilities.

As a result, the article content depends on the weight of each topic and the terms that make up each topic. The Dirichlet distribution governs the selection of topics for documents and words for topics. It encodes the idea that a document only covers a few topics, while each topic uses only a small number of words frequently.

The **plate notation** for the LDA model in *Figure 15.8* summarizes these relationships and highlights the key model parameters:

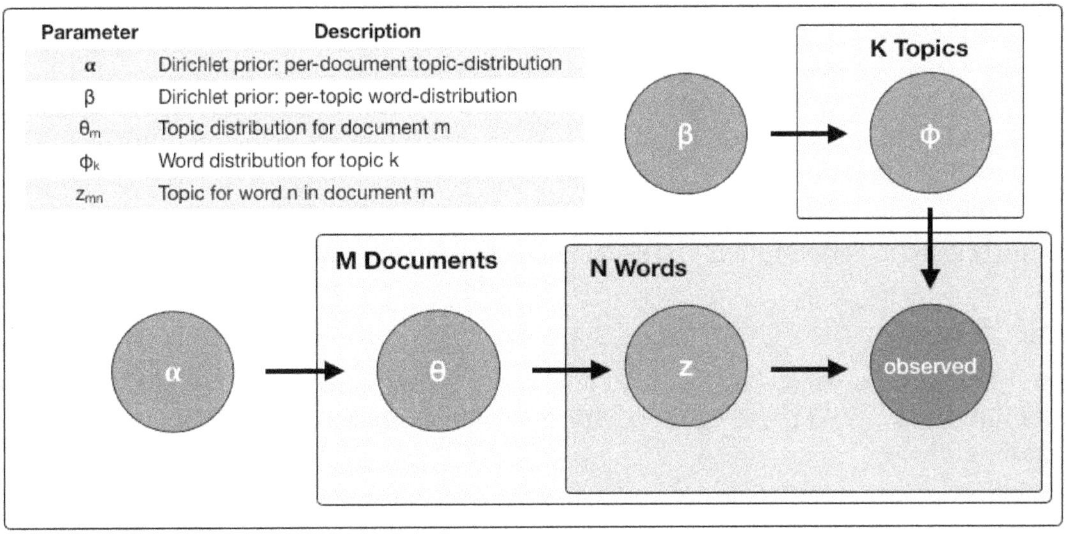

Figure 15.8: The statistical dependencies of the LDA model in plate notation

Reverse engineering the process

The generative process is clearly fictional but turns out to be useful because it permits the recovery of the various distributions. The LDA algorithm reverse engineers the work of the imaginary author and arrives at a summary of the document-topic-word relationships that concisely describes:

- The percentage contribution of each topic to a document
- The probabilistic association of each word with a topic

LDA solves the **Bayesian inference** problem of recovering the distributions from the body of documents and the words they contain by reverse engineering the assumed content generation process. The original paper by Blei et al. (2003) uses **variational Bayes** (**VB**) to approximate the posterior distribution. Alternatives include Gibbs sampling and expectation propagation. We will illustrate, shortly, the implementations by the sklearn and Gensim libraries.

How to evaluate LDA topics

Unsupervised topic models do not guarantee that the result will be meaningful or interpretable, and there is no objective metric to assess the quality of the result as in supervised learning. Human topic evaluation is considered the gold standard, but it is potentially expensive and not readily available at scale.

Two options to evaluate results more objectively include **perplexity**, which evaluates the model on unseen documents, and **topic coherence** metrics, which aim to evaluate the semantic quality of the uncovered patterns.

Perplexity

Perplexity, when applied to LDA, measures how well the topic-word probability distribution recovered by the model predicts a sample of unseen text documents. It is based on the entropy *H*(*p*) of this distribution *p* and is computed with respect to the set of tokens *w*:

$$2^{h(p)} = 2^{-\sum_w p(w) \log_2 p(w)}$$

Measures closer to zero imply the distribution is better at predicting the sample.

Topic coherence

Topic coherence measures the semantic consistency of the topic model results, that is, whether humans would perceive the words and their probabilities associated with topics as meaningful.

To this end, it scores each topic by measuring the degree of semantic similarity between the words most relevant to the topic. More specifically, coherence measures are based on the probability of observing the set of words *W* that defines a topic together.

There are two measures of coherence that have been designed for LDA and are shown to align with human judgments of topic quality, namely the UMass and the UCI metrics.

The UCI metric (Stevens et al. 2012) defines a word pair's score to be the sum of the **pointwise mutual information** (**PMI**) between two distinct pairs of (top) topic words w_i, w_j $\in w$ and a smoothing factor $\mathcal{E}$:

$$\text{coherence}_{\text{UCI}} = \sum_{(w_i, w_j) \in W} \log \frac{p(w_i, w_j) + \epsilon}{p(w_i) p(w_j)}$$

The probabilities are computed from word co-occurrence frequencies in a sliding window over an external corpus like Wikipedia so that this metric can be thought of as an external comparison to semantic ground truth.

In contrast, the UMass metric (Mimno et al. 2011) uses the co-occurrences in a number of documents *D* from the training corpus to compute a coherence score:

$$\text{coherence}_{\text{UMass}} = \sum_{(w_i, w_j) \in W} \log \frac{D(w_i, w_j) + \epsilon}{D(w_j)}$$

Rather than comparing the model result to extrinsic ground truth, this measure reflects intrinsic coherence. Both measures have been evaluated to align well with human judgment (Röder, Both, and Hinneburg 2015). In both cases, values closer to zero imply that a topic is more coherent.

How to implement LDA using sklearn

We will use the BBC data as before and train an LDA model using sklearn's `decomposition.LatentDirichletAllocation` class with five topics (refer to the sklearn documentation for details on the parameters and the notebook `lda_with_sklearn` for implementation details):

```
lda_opt = LatentDirichletAllocation(n_components=5,
                                    n_jobs=-1,
                                    max_iter=500,
                                    learning_method='batch',
                                    evaluate_every=5,
                                    verbose=1,
                                    random_state=42)
ldat.fit(train_dtm)
LatentDirichletAllocation(batch_size=128, doc_topic_prior=None,
             evaluate_every=5, learning_decay=0.7, learning_method='batch',
             learning_offset=10.0, max_doc_update_iter=100, max_iter=500,
             mean_change_tol=0.001, n_components=5, n_jobs=-1,
             n_topics=None, perp_tol=0.1, random_state=42,
             topic_word_prior=None, total_samples=1000000.0, verbose=1)
```

The model tracks the in-sample perplexity during training and stops iterating once this measure stops improving. We can persist and load the result as usual with sklearn objects:

```
joblib.dump(lda, model_path / 'lda_opt.pkl')
lda_opt = joblib.load(model_path / 'lda_opt.pkl')
```

How to visualize LDA results using pyLDAvis

Topic visualization facilitates the evaluation of topic quality using human judgment. pyLDAvis is a Python port of LDAvis, developed in R and `D3.js` (Sievert and Shirley 2014). We will introduce the key concepts; each LDA application notebook contains examples.

pyLDAvis displays the global relationships among topics while also facilitating their semantic evaluation by inspecting the terms most closely associated with each individual topic and, inversely, the topics associated with each term. It also addresses the challenge that terms that are frequent in a corpus tend to dominate the distribution over words that define a topic.

To this end, LDAVis introduces the **relevance** r of term w to topic t. The relevance produces a flexible ranking of terms by topic, by computing a weighted average of two metrics:

- The degree of association of topic t with term w, expressed as the conditional probability $p(w \mid t)$
- The saliency, or lift, which measures how the frequency of term w for the topic t, $p(w \mid t)$, compares to its overall frequency across all documents, $p(w)$

More specifically, we can compute the relevance *r* for a term *w* and a topic *t* given a user-defined weight $0 \leq \lambda \leq$, like the following:

$$r(w, t \mid \lambda) = \lambda \log(p(w|t)) + (1 - \lambda) \log \frac{p(w|t)}{p(w)}$$

The tool allows the user to interactively change λ to adjust the relevance, which updates the ranking of terms. User studies have found $\lambda = 0.6$ to produce the most plausible results.

How to implement LDA using Gensim

Gensim is a specialized **natural language processing** (**NLP**) library with a fast LDA implementation and many additional features. We will also use it in the next chapter on word vectors (refer to the notebook `lda_with_gensim` for details and the installation directory for related instructions).

We convert the DTM produced by sklearn's `CountVectorizer` or `TfIdfVectorizer` into Gensim data structures as follows:

```
train_corpus = Sparse2Corpus(train_dtm, documents_columns=False)
test_corpus = Sparse2Corpus(test_dtm, documents_columns=False)
id2word = pd.Series(vectorizer.get_feature_names()).to_dict()
```

Gensim's LDA algorithm includes numerous settings:

```
LdaModel(corpus=None,
       num_topics=100,
       id2word=None,
       distributed=False,
       chunksize=2000,  # No of doc per training chunk.
       passes=1,        # No of passes through corpus during training
       update_every=1,  # No of docs to be iterated through per update
       alpha='symmetric',
       eta=None,        # a-priori belief on word probability
       decay=0.5,      # % of lambda forgotten when new doc is examined
       offset=1.0,    # controls slow down of first few iterations.
       eval_every=10,  # how often estimate log perplexity (costly)
       iterations=50,  # Max. of iterations through the corpus
       gamma_threshold=0.001, # Min. change in gamma to continue
       minimum_probability=0.01, # Filter topics with lower probability
       random_state=None,
       ns_conf=None,
       minimum_phi_value=0.01, # lower bound on term probabilities
       per_word_topics=False,  #  Compute most word-topic probabilities
       callbacks=None,
       dtype=<class 'numpy.float32'>)
```

Gensim also provides an `LdaMulticore` model for parallel training that may speed up training using Python's multiprocessing features for parallel computation.

Model training just requires instantiating `LdaModel`, as follows:

```
lda_gensim = LdaModel(corpus=train_corpus,
                      num_topics=5,
                      id2word=id2word)
```

Gensim evaluates topic coherence, as introduced in the previous section, and shows the most important words per topic:

```
coherence = lda_gensim.top_topics(corpus=train_corpus, coherence='u_mass')
```

We can display the results as follows:

```
topic_coherence = []
topic_words = pd.DataFrame()
for t in range(len(coherence)):
    label = topic_labels[t]
    topic_coherence.append(coherence[t][1])
    df = pd.DataFrame(coherence[t][0], columns=[(label, 'prob'),
                                                (label, 'term')])
    df[(label, 'prob')] = df[(label, 'prob')].apply(
                            lambda x: '{:.2%}'.format(x))
    topic_words = pd.concat([topic_words, df], axis=1)

topic_words.columns = pd.MultiIndex.from_tuples(topic_words.columns)
pd.set_option('expand_frame_repr', False)
print(topic_words.head())
```

This shows the following top words for each topic:

Topic 1		**Topic 2**		**Topic 3**		**Topic 4**		**Topic 5**	
Probability	**Term**	**Probability**	**Term**	**Probability**	**Term**	**Probability**	**Term**	**Probability**	**Term**
0.55%	online	0.90%	best	1.04%	mobile	0.64%	market	0.94%	labour
0.51%	site	0.87%	game	0.98%	phone	0.53%	growth	0.72%	blair
0.46%	game	0.62%	play	0.51%	music	0.52%	sales	0.72%	brown
0.45%	net	0.61%	won	0.48%	film	0.49%	economy	0.65%	election
0.44%	used	0.56%	win	0.48%	use	0.45%	prices	0.57%	united

The left panel of *Figure 15.9* displays the topic coherence scores, which highlight the decay of topic quality (at least, in part, due to the relatively small dataset):

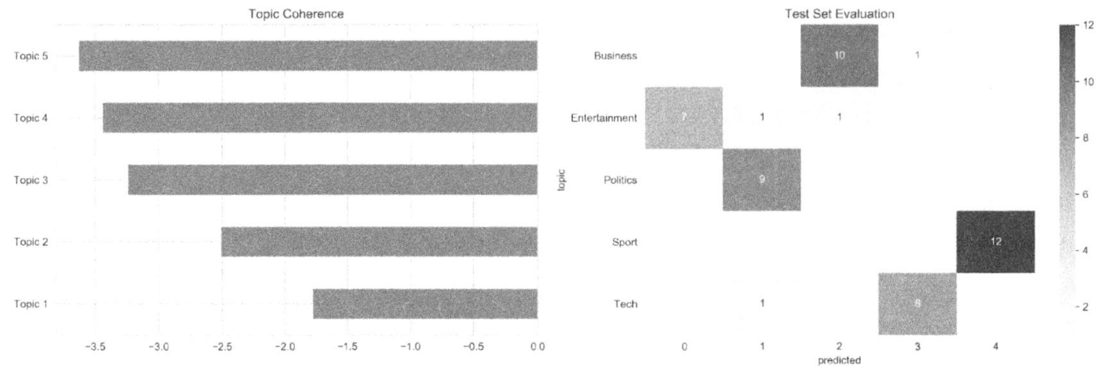

Figure 15.9: Topic coherence and test set assignments

The right panel displays the evaluation of our test set of 50 articles with our trained model. The model makes four mistakes for an accuracy of 92 percent.

Modeling topics discussed in earnings calls

In *Chapter 3, Alternative Data for Finance – Categories and Use Cases*, we learned how to scrape earnings call data from the SeekingAlpha site. In this section, we will illustrate topic modeling using this source. I'm using a sample of some 700 earnings call transcripts between 2018 and 2019. This is a fairly small dataset; for a practical application, we would need a larger dataset.

The directory `earnings_calls` contains several files with the code examples used in this section. Refer to the notebook `lda_earnings_calls` for details on loading, exploring, and preprocessing the data, as well as training and evaluating individual models, and the `run_experiments.py` file for the experiments described next.

Data preprocessing

The transcripts consist of individual statements by company representatives, an operator, and a Q&A session with analysts. We will treat each of these statements as separate documents, ignoring operator statements, to obtain 32,047 items with mean and median word counts of 137 and 62, respectively:

```
documents = []
for transcript in earnings_path.iterdir():
    content = pd.read_csv(transcript / 'content.csv')
    documents.extend(content.loc[(content.speaker!='Operator') & (content.
content.str.len() > 5), 'content'].tolist())
len(documents)
32047
```

We use spaCy to preprocess these documents, as illustrated in *Chapter 13, Data-Driven Risk Factors and Asset Allocation with Unsupervised Learning*, (refer to the notebook), and store the cleaned and lemmatized text as a new text file.

Exploration of the most common tokens, as shown in *Figure 15.10*, reveals domain-specific stopwords like "year" and "quarter" that we remove in a second step, where we also filter out statements with fewer than 10 words so that some 22,582 remain.

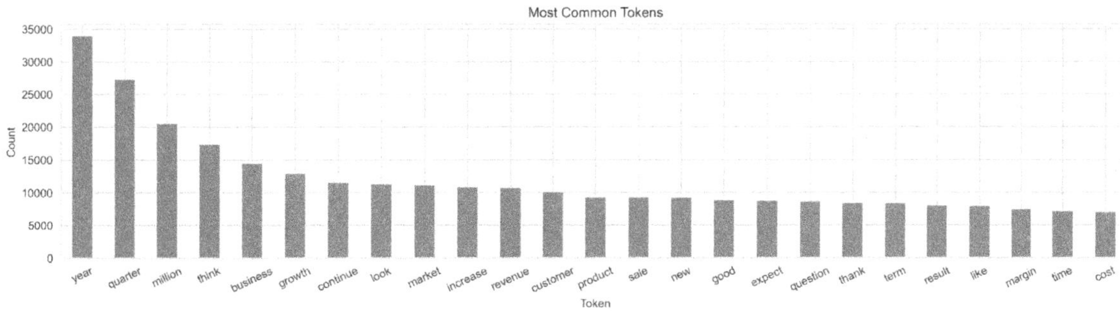

Figure 15.10: Most common earnings call tokens

Model training and evaluation

For illustration, we create a DTM containing terms appearing in between 0.5 and 25 percent of documents that results in 1,529 features. Now we proceed to train a 15-topic model using 25 passes over the corpus. This takes a bit over two minutes on a 4-core i7.

The top 10 words per topic, as shown in *Figure 15.11*, identify several distinct themes that range from obvious financial information to clinical trials (Topic 5), China and tariff issues (Topic 9), and technology issues (Topic 11).

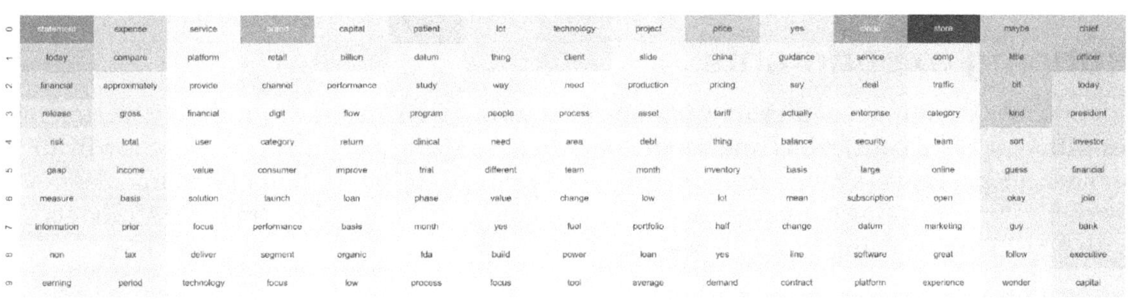

Figure 15.11: Most important words for earnings call topics

Using pyLDAvis' relevance metric with a 0.6 weighting of unconditional frequency relative to lift, topic definitions become more intuitive, as illustrated in *Figure 15.12* for Topic 7 about China and the trade wars:

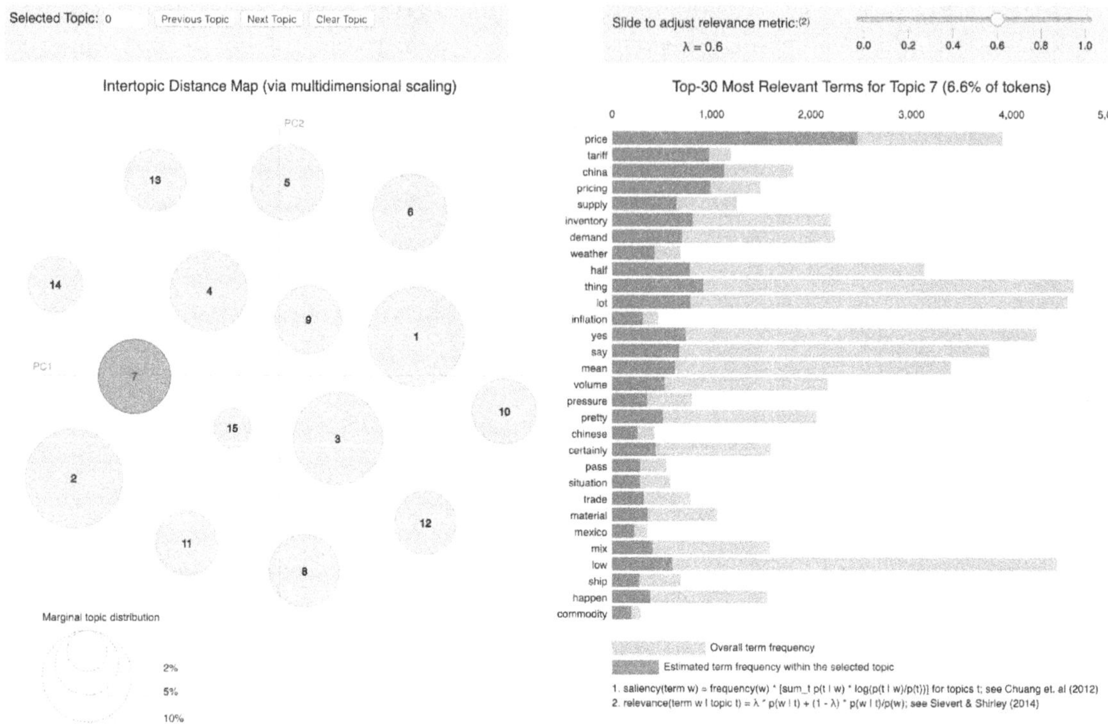

Figure 15.12: pyLDAVis' interactive topic explorer

The notebook also illustrates how you can look up documents by their topic association. In this case, an analyst can review relevant statements for nuances, use sentiment analysis to further process the topic-specific text data, or assign labels derived from market prices.

Running experiments

To illustrate the impact of different parameter settings, we run a few hundred experiments for different DTM constraints and model parameters. More specifically, we let the `min_df` and `max_df` parameters range from 50-500 words and 10 to 100 percent of documents, respectively, using alternatively binary and absolute counts. We then train LDA models with 3 to 50 topics, using 1 and 25 passes over the corpus.

The chart in *Figure 15.13* illustrates the results in terms of topic coherence (higher is better) and perplexity (lower is better). Coherence drops after 25-30 topics, and perplexity similarly increases.

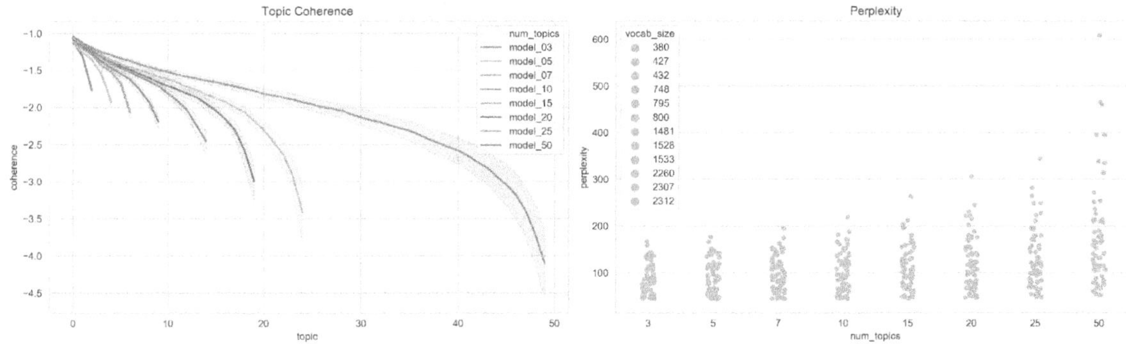

Figure 15.13: Impact of LDA hyperparameter settings on topic quality

The notebook includes regression results that quantify the relationships between parameters and outcomes. We generally get better results using absolute counts and a smaller vocabulary.

Topic modeling for with financial news

The notebook `lda_financial_news` contains an example of LDA applied to a subset of over 306,000 financial news articles from the first five months of 2018. The datasets have been posted on Kaggle, and the articles have been sourced from CNBC, Reuters, the Wall Street Journal, and more. The notebook contains download instructions.

We select the most relevant 120,000 articles based on their section titles with a total of 54 million tokens for an average word count of 429 words per article. To prepare the data for the LDA model, we rely on spaCy to remove numbers and punctuation and lemmatize the results.

Figure 15.14 highlights the remaining most frequent tokens and the article length distribution with a median length of 231 tokens; the 90th percentile is 642 words.

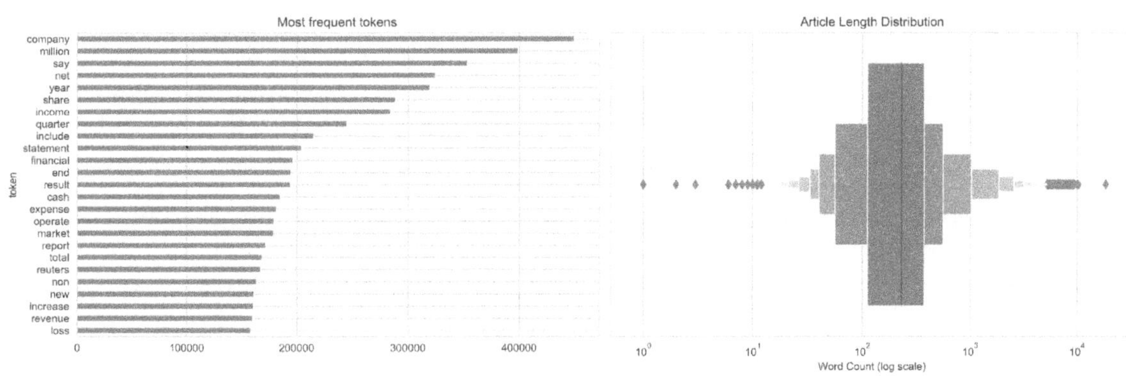

Figure 15.14: Corpus statistics for financial news data

In *Figure 15.15*, we show results for one model using a vocabulary of 3,570 tokens based on `min_df=0.005` and `max_df=0.1`, with a single pass to avoid the length training time for 15 topics. We can use the `top_topics` attribute of the trained `LdaModel` to obtain the most likely words for each topic (refer to the notebook for more details).

Figure 15.15: Top 15 words for financial news topics

The topics outline several issues relevant to the time period, including Brexit (Topic 8), North Korea (Topic 4), and Tesla (Topic 14).

Gensim provides a `LdaMultiCore` implementation that allows for parallel training using Python's multiprocessing module and improves performance by 50 percent when using four workers. More workers do not further reduce training time, though, due to I/O bottlenecks.

Summary

In this chapter, we explored the use of topic modeling to gain insights into the content of a large collection of documents. We covered latent semantic indexing that uses dimensionality reduction of the DTM to project documents into a latent topic space. While effective in addressing the curse of dimensionality caused by high-dimensional word vectors, it does not capture much semantic information. Probabilistic models make explicit assumptions about the interplay of documents, topics, and words that allow algorithms to reverse engineer the document generation process and evaluate the model fit on new documents. We learned that LDA is capable of extracting plausible topics that allow us to gain a high-level understanding of large amounts of text in an automated way, while also identifying relevant documents in a targeted way.

In the next chapter, we will learn how to train neural networks that embed individual words in a high-dimensional vector space that captures important semantic information and allows us to use the resulting word vectors as high-quality text features.

16

Word Embeddings for Earnings Calls and SEC Filings

In the two previous chapters, we converted text data into a numerical format using the **bag-of-words model**. The result is sparse, fixed-length vectors that represent documents in high-dimensional word space. This allows the similarity of documents to be evaluated and creates features to train a model with a view to classifying a document's content or rating the sentiment expressed in it. However, these vectors ignore the context in which a term is used so that two sentences containing the same words in a different order would be encoded by the same vector, even if their meaning is quite different.

This chapter introduces an alternative class of algorithms that use **neural networks** to learn a vector representation of individual semantic units like a word or a paragraph. These vectors are dense rather than sparse, have a few hundred real-valued entries, and are called **embeddings** because they assign each semantic unit a location in a continuous vector space. They result from training a model to **predict tokens from their context** so that similar usage implies a similar embedding vector. Moreover, the embeddings encode semantic aspects like relationships among words by means of their relative location. As a result, they are powerful features for deep learning models for solving tasks that require semantic information, such as machine translation, question answering, or maintaining a dialogue.

To develop a **trading strategy based on text data**, we are usually interested in the meaning of documents rather than individual tokens. For example, we might want to create a dataset that uses features representing a tweet or a news article with sentiment information (refer to *Chapter 14*, *Text Data for Trading – Sentiment Analysis*), or an asset's return for a given horizon after publication. Although the bag-of-words model loses plenty of information when encoding text data, it has the advantage of representing an entire document. However, word embeddings have been further developed to represent more than individual tokens. Examples include the **doc2vec** extension, which resorts to weighting word embeddings. More recently, the **attention** mechanism emerged to produce more context-sensitive sentence representations, resulting in **transformer** architectures such as the **BERT** family of models that has dramatically improved performance on numerous natural language tasks.

More specifically, after working through this chapter and the companion notebooks, you will know about the following:

- What word embeddings are, how they work, and why they capture semantic information
- How to obtain and use pretrained word vectors
- Which network architectures are most effective at training word2vec models
- How to train a word2vec model using Keras, Gensim, and TensorFlow
- Visualizing and evaluating the quality of word vectors
- How to train a word2vec model on SEC filings to predict stock price moves
- How doc2vec extends word2vec and can be used for sentiment analysis
- Why the transformer's attention mechanism had such an impact on natural language processing
- How to fine-tune pretrained BERT models on financial data and extract high-quality embeddings

You can find the code examples and links to additional resources in the GitHub directory for this chapter. This chapter uses neural networks and deep learning; if unfamiliar, you may want to first read *Chapter 17, Deep Learning for Trading,* which introduces key concepts and libraries.

How word embeddings encode semantics

The bag-of-words model represents documents as sparse, high-dimensional vectors that reflect the tokens they contain. Word embeddings represent tokens as dense, lower-dimensional vectors so that the relative location of words reflects how they are used in context. They embody the **distributional hypothesis** from linguistics that claims words are best defined by the company they keep.

Word vectors are capable of capturing numerous semantic aspects; not only are synonyms assigned nearby embeddings, but words can have multiple degrees of similarity. For example, the word "driver" could be similar to "motorist" or to "factor." Furthermore, embeddings encode relationships among pairs of words like analogies (*Tokyo is to Japan* what *Paris is to France*, or *went is to go* what *saw is to see*), as we will illustrate later in this section.

Embeddings result from training a neural network to predict words from their context or vice versa. In this section, we will introduce how these models work and present successful approaches, including word2vec, doc2vec, and the more recent transformer family of models.

How neural language models learn usage in context

Word embeddings result from training a shallow neural network to predict a word given its context. Whereas traditional language models define context as the words preceding the target, word embedding models use the words contained in a symmetric window surrounding the target. In contrast, the bag-of-words model uses the entire document as context and relies on (weighted) counts to capture the co-occurrence of words.

Earlier neural language models used included nonlinear hidden layers that increased the computational complexity. **word2vec**, introduced by Mikolov, Sutskever, et al. (2013) and its extensions simplified the architecture to enable training on large datasets. The Wikipedia corpus, for example, contains over 2 billion tokens. (Refer to *Chapter 17, Deep Learning for Trading*, for additional details on feedforward networks.)

word2vec – scalable word and phrase embeddings

A word2vec model is a two-layer neural net that takes a text corpus as input and outputs a set of embedding vectors for words in that corpus. There are two different architectures, shown in the following diagram, to efficiently learn word vectors using shallow neural networks (Mikolov, Chen, et al., 2013):

- The **continuous-bag-of-words** (**CBOW**) model predicts the target word using the average of the context word vectors as input so that their order does not matter. CBOW trains faster and tends to be slightly more accurate for frequent terms, but pays less attention to infrequent words.
- The **skip-gram** (**SG**) model, in contrast, uses the target word to predict words sampled from the context. It works well with small datasets and finds good representations even for rare words or phrases.

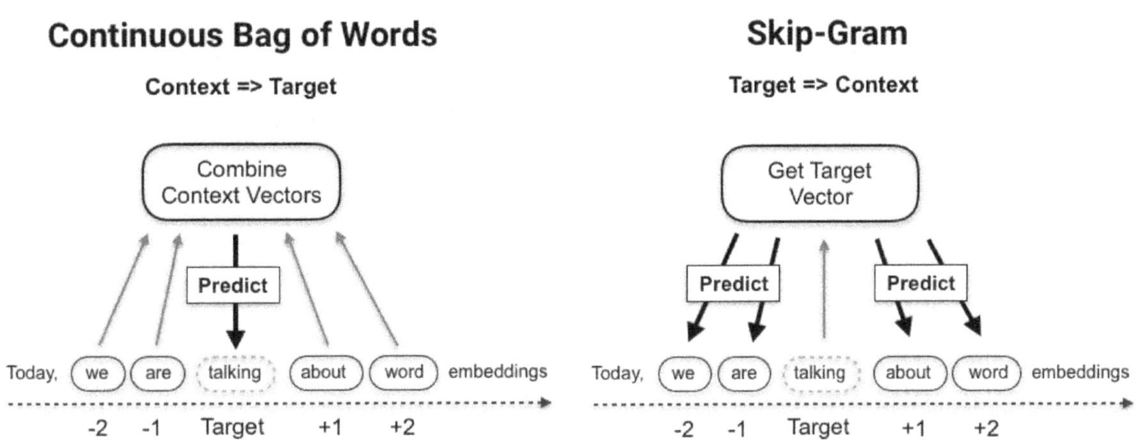

Figure 16.1: Continuous-bag-of-words versus skip-gram processing logic

The model receives an embedding vector as input and computes the dot product with another embedding vector. Note that, assuming normed vectors, the dot product is maximized (in absolute terms) when vectors are equal, and minimized when they are orthogonal.

During training, the **backpropagation algorithm** adjusts the embedding weights in response to the loss computed by an objective function based on classification errors. We will see in the next section how word2vec computes the loss.

Training proceeds by sliding the **context window** over the documents, typically segmented into sentences. Each complete iteration over the corpus is called an **epoch**. Depending on the data, several dozen epochs may be necessary for vector quality to converge.

The skip-gram model implicitly factorizes a word-context matrix that contains the pointwise mutual information of the respective word and context pairs (Levy and Goldberg, 2014).

Model objective – simplifying the softmax

Word2vec models aim to predict a single word out of a potentially very large vocabulary. Neural networks often use the softmax function as an output unit in the final layer to implement the multiclass objective because it maps an arbitrary number of real values to an equal number of probabilities. The softmax function is defined as follows, where h refers to the embedding and v to the input vectors, and c is the context of word w:

$$p(w|c) = \frac{\exp\left(h^{\mathrm{T}} v'_w\right)}{\sum_{w_i \in V} \exp\left(h^{\mathrm{T}} v'_{w_i}\right)}$$

However, the softmax complexity scales with the number of classes because the denominator requires computing the dot product for all words in the vocabulary to standardize the probabilities. Word2vec gains efficiency by using a modified version of the softmax or sampling-based approximations:

- The **hierarchical softmax** organizes the vocabulary as a binary tree with words as leaf nodes. The unique path to each node can be used to compute the word probability (Morin and Bengio, 2005).
- **Noise contrastive estimation** (**NCE**) samples out-of-context "noise words" and approximates the multiclass task by a binary classification problem. The NCE derivative approaches the softmax gradient as the number of samples increases, but as few as 25 samples can yield convergence similar to the softmax 45 times faster (Mnih and Kavukcuoglu, 2013).
- **Negative sampling** (**NEG**) omits the noise word samples to approximate NCE and directly maximizes the probability of the target word. Hence, NEG optimizes the semantic quality of embedding vectors (similar vectors for similar usage) rather than the accuracy on a test set. It may, however, produce poorer representations for infrequent words than the hierarchical softmax objective (Mikolov et al., 2013).

Automating phrase detection

Preprocessing typically involves phrase detection, that is, the identification of tokens that are commonly used together and should receive a single vector representation (for example, New York City; refer to the discussion of n-grams in *Chapter 13, Data-Driven Risk Factors and Asset Allocation with Unsupervised Learning*).

The original word2vec authors (Mikolov et al., 2013) use a simple lift scoring method that identifies two words w_i, w_j as a bigram if their joint occurrence exceeds a given threshold relative to each word's individual appearance, corrected by a discount factor, δ:

$$\text{score}(w_i, w_j) = \frac{\text{count}(w_i, w_j) - \delta}{\text{count}(w_i)\text{count}(w_j)}$$

The scorer can be applied repeatedly to identify successively longer phrases.

An alternative is the normalized pointwise mutual information score, which is more accurate, but also more costly to compute. It uses the relative word frequency $P(w)$ and varies between +1 and -1:

$$\text{NPMI} = \frac{\ln\left(P(w_i, w_j)/P(w_i)P(w_j)\right)}{-\ln\left(P(w_i, w_j)\right)}$$

Evaluating embeddings using semantic arithmetic

The bag-of-words model creates document vectors that reflect the presence and relevance of tokens to the document. As discussed in *Chapter 15, Topic Modeling – Summarizing Financial News*, **latent semantic analysis** reduces the dimensionality of these vectors and identifies what can be interpreted as latent concepts in the process. **Latent Dirichlet allocation** represents both documents and terms as vectors that contain the weights of latent topics.

The word and phrase vectors produced by word2vec do not have an explicit meaning. However, the **embeddings encode similar usage as proximity** in the latent space created by the model. The embeddings also capture semantic relationships so that analogies can be expressed by adding and subtracting word vectors.

Figure 16.2 shows how the vector that points from "Paris" to "France" (which measures the difference between their embedding vectors) reflects the "capital of" relationship. The analogous relationship between London and the UK corresponds to the same vector: the embedding for the term "UK" is very close to the location obtained by adding the "capital of" vector to the embedding for the term "London":

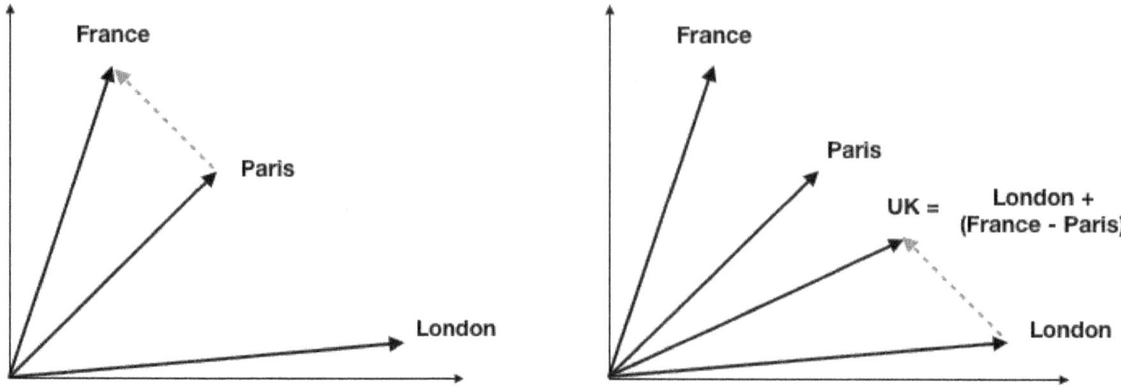

Figure 16.2: Embedding vector arithmetic

Just as words can be used in different contexts, they can be related to other words in different ways, and these relationships correspond to different directions in the latent space. Accordingly, there are several types of analogies that the embeddings should reflect if the training data permits.

The word2vec authors provide a list of over 25,000 relationships in 14 categories spanning aspects of geography, grammar and syntax, and family relationships to evaluate the quality of embedding vectors. As illustrated in the preceding diagram, the test validates that the target word "UK" is closest to the result of adding the vector that represents an analogous relationship "Paris: France" to the target's complement "London".

The following table shows the number of samples and illustrates some of the analogy categories. The test checks how close the embedding for *d* is to the location determined by *c + (b-a)*. Refer to the `evaluating_embeddings` notebook for implementation details.

Category	# Samples	a	b	c	d
Capital-Country	506	athens	greece	baghdad	iraq
City-State	4,242	chicago	illinois	houston	texas
Past Tense	1,560	dancing	danced	decreasing	decreased
Plural	1,332	banana	bananas	bird	birds
Comparative	1,332	bad	worse	big	bigger
Opposite	812	acceptable	unacceptable	aware	unaware
Superlative	1,122	bad	worst	big	biggest
Plural (Verbs)	870	decrease	decreases	describe	describes
Currency	866	algeria	dinar	angola	kwanza
Family	506	boy	girl	brother	sister

Similar to other unsupervised learning techniques, the goal of learning embedding vectors is to generate features for other tasks, such as text classification or sentiment analysis. There are a couple of options to obtain embedding vectors for a given corpus of documents:

- Use pretrained embeddings learned from a generic large corpus like Wikipedia or Google News
- Train your own model using documents that reflect a domain of interest

The less generic and more specialized the content of the subsequent text modeling task, the more preferable the second approach. However, quality word embeddings are data-hungry and require informative documents containing hundreds of millions of words.

We will first look at how you can use pretrained vectors and then demonstrate examples of how to build your own word2vec models using financial news and SEC filings data.

How to use pretrained word vectors

There are several sources for pretrained word embeddings. Popular options include Stanford's GloVE and spaCy's built-in vectors (refer to the `using_pretrained_vectors` notebook for details). In this section, we will focus on GloVe.

GloVe – Global vectors for word representation

GloVe (*Global Vectors for Word Representation*, Pennington, Socher, and Manning, 2014) is an unsupervised algorithm developed at the Stanford NLP lab that learns vector representations for words from aggregated global word-word co-occurrence statistics (see resources linked on GitHub). Vectors pretrained on the following web-scale sources are available:

- **Common Crawl** with 42 billion or 840 billion tokens and a vocabulary or 1.9 million or 2.2 million tokens
- **Wikipedia** 2014 + Gigaword 5 with 6 billion tokens and a vocabulary of 400,000 tokens
- **Twitter** using 2 billion tweets, 27 billion tokens, and a vocabulary of 1.2 million tokens

We can use Gensim to convert the vector text files using `glove2word2vec` and then load them into the `KeyedVector` object:

```
from gensim.models import Word2Vec, KeyedVectors
from gensim.scripts.glove2word2vec import glove2word2vec

glove2word2vec(glove_input_file=glove_file, word2vec_output_file=w2v_file)
model = KeyedVectors.load_word2vec_format(w2v_file, binary=False)
```

Gensim uses the **word2vec analogy tests** described in the previous section using text files made available by the authors to evaluate word vectors. For this purpose, the library has the `wv.accuracy` function, which we use to pass the path to the analogy file, indicate whether the word vectors are in binary format, and whether we want to ignore the case. We can also restrict the vocabulary to the most frequent to speed up testing:

```
accuracy = model.wv.accuracy(analogies_path,
                             restrict_vocab=300000,
                             case_insensitive=True)
```

The word vectors trained on the Wikipedia corpus cover all analogies and achieve an overall accuracy of 75.44 percent with some variation across categories:

Category	# Samples	Accuracy
Capital-Country	506	94.86%
Capitals RoW	8,372	96.46%
City-State	4,242	60.00%
Currency	752	17.42%
Family	506	88.14%
Nationality	1,640	92.50%
Adjective-Adverb	992	22.58%

Category	# Samples	Accuracy
Comparative	1,332	88.21%
Opposite	756	28.57%
Superlative	1,056	74.62%
Present-Participle	1,056	69.98%
Past Tense	1,560	61.15%
Plural	1,332	78.08%
Plural Verbs	870	58.51%

Figure 16.3 compares the performance for the three GloVe sources for the 100,000 most common tokens. It shows that Common Crawl vectors, which cover about 80 percent of the analogies, achieve slightly higher accuracy at 78 percent. The Twitter vectors cover only 25 percent, with 56.4 percent accuracy:

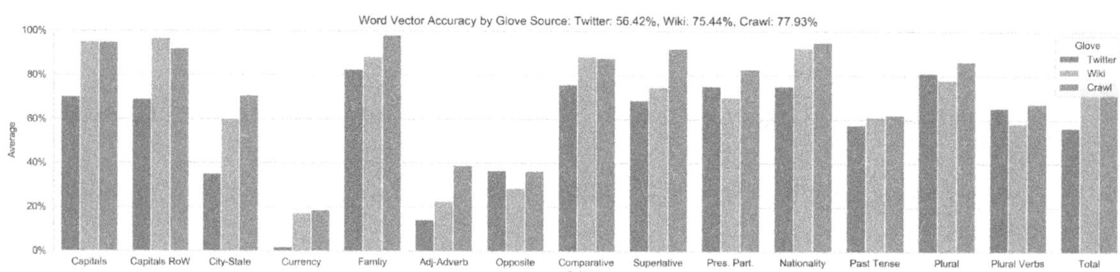

Figure 16.3: GloVe accuracy on word2vec analogies

Figure 16.4 projects the 300-dimensional embeddings of the most closely related analogies for a word2vec model trained on the Wikipedia corpus with over 2 billion tokens into two dimensions using PCA. A test of over 24,400 analogies from the following categories achieved an accuracy of over 73.5 percent:

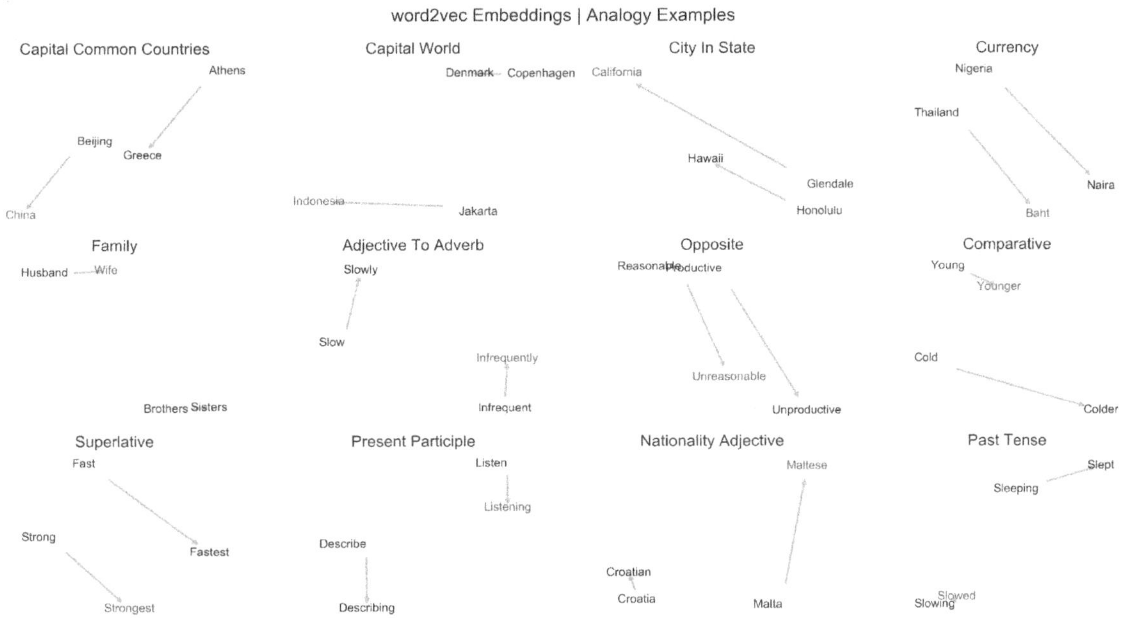

Figure 16.4: 2D visualization of selected analogy embeddings

Custom embeddings for financial news

Many tasks require embeddings of domain-specific vocabulary that models pretrained on a generic corpus may not be able to capture. Standard word2vec models are not able to assign vectors to out-of-vocabulary words and instead use a default vector that reduces their predictive value.

For example, when working with **industry-specific documents**, the vocabulary or its usage may change over time as new technologies or products emerge. As a result, the embeddings need to evolve as well. In addition, documents like corporate earnings releases use nuanced language that GloVe vectors pretrained on Wikipedia articles are unlikely to properly reflect.

In this section, we will train and evaluate domain-specific embeddings using financial news. We'll first show how to preprocess the data for this task, then demonstrate how the skip-gram architecture outlined in the first section works, and finally visualize the results. We also will introduce alternative, faster training methods.

Preprocessing – sentence detection and n-grams

To illustrate the word2vec network architecture, we'll use the financial news dataset with over 125,000 relevant articles that we introduced in *Chapter 15, Topic Modeling – Summarizing Financial News*, on topic modeling. We'll load the data as outlined in the `lda_financial_news.ipynb` notebook in that chapter. The `financial_news_preprocessing.ipynb` notebook contains the code samples for this section.

We use spaCy's built-in **sentence boundary detection** to split each article into sentences, remove less informative items, such as numbers and punctuation, and keep the result if it is between 6 and 99 tokens long:

```
def clean_doc(d):
    doc = []
    for sent in d.sents:
        s = [t.text.lower() for t in sent if not
        any([t.is_digit, not t.is_alpha, t.is_punct, t.is_space])]
        if len(s) > 5 or len(sent) < 100:
            doc.append(' '.join(s))
    return doc

nlp = English()
sentencizer = nlp.create_pipe("sentencizer")
nlp.add_pipe(sentencizer)

clean_articles = []
iter_articles = (article for article in articles)
for i, doc in enumerate(nlp.pipe(iter_articles, batch_size=100, n_process=8),
1):
    clean_articles.extend(clean_doc(doc))
```

We end up with 2.43 million sentences that, on average, contain 15 tokens.

Next, we create n-grams to capture composite terms. Gensim lets us identify n-grams based on the relative frequency of joint versus individual occurrence of the components. The `Phrases` module scores the tokens, and the `Phraser` class transforms the text data accordingly.

It transforms our list of sentences into a new dataset that we can write to file as follows:

```
sentences = LineSentence((data_path / f'articles_clean.txt').as_posix())
phrases = Phrases(sentences=sentences,
                  min_count=10,  # ignore terms with a lower count
                  threshold=0.5,  # only phrases with higher score
                  delimiter=b'_',  # how to join ngram tokens
                  scoring='npmi')  # alternative: default
grams = Phraser(phrases)
sentences = grams[sentences]

with (data_path / f'articles_ngrams.txt').open('w') as f:
        for sentence in sentences:
            f.write(' '.join(sentence) + '\n')
```

The notebook illustrates how we can repeat this process using the 2-gram file as input to create 3-grams. We end up with some 25,000 2-grams and 15,000 3- or 4-grams. Inspecting the result shows that the highest-scoring terms are names of companies or individuals, suggesting that we might want to tighten our initial cleaning criteria. Refer to the notebook for additional details on the dataset.

The skip-gram architecture in TensorFlow 2

In this section, we will illustrate how to build a word2vec model using the Keras interface of TensorFlow 2 that we will introduce in much more detail in the next chapter. The `financial_news_word2vec_tensorflow` notebook contains the code samples and additional implementation details.

We start by tokenizing the documents and assigning a unique ID to each item in the vocabulary. First, we sample a subset of the sentences created in the previous section to limit the training time:

```
SAMPLE_SIZE=.5
sentences = file_path.read_text().split('\n')
words = ' '.join(np.random.choice(sentences, size=int(SAMLE_SIZE* l
en(sentences)), replace=False)).split()
```

We require at least 10 occurrences in the corpus, keep a vocabulary of 31,300 tokens, and begin with the following steps:

1. Extract the top *n* most common words to learn embeddings.
2. Index these *n* words with unique integers.
3. Create an `{index: word}` dictionary.
4. Replace the *n* words with their index, and a dummy value `'UNK'` elsewhere:

```
# Get (token, count) tuples for tokens meeting MIN_FREQ
MIN_FREQ = 10
token_counts = [t for t in Counter(words).most_common() if t[1] >=
MIN_FREQ]
tokens, counts = list(zip(*token_counts))

# create id-token dicts & reverse dicts
id_to_token = pd.Series(tokens, index=range(1, len(tokens) + 1)).to_
dict()
id_to_token.update({0: 'UNK'})
token_to_id = {t:i for i, t in id_to_token.items()}
data = [token_to_id.get(word, 0) for word in words]
```

We end up with 17.4 million tokens and a vocabulary of close to 60,000 tokens, including up to 3-grams. The vocabulary covers around 72.5 percent of the analogies.

Noise-contrastive estimation – creating validation samples

Keras includes a `make_sampling_table` method that allows us to create a training set as pairs of context and noise words with corresponding labels, sampled according to their corpus frequencies. A lower factor increases the probability of selecting less frequent tokens; a chart in the notebook shows that the value of 0.1 limits sampling to the top 10,000 tokens:

```
SAMPLING_FACTOR =  1e-4
sampling_table = make_sampling_table(vocab_size,
                                     sampling_factor=SAMPLING_FACTOR)
```

Generating target-context word pairs

To train our model, we need pairs of tokens where one represents the target and the other is selected from the surrounding context window, as shown previously in the right panel of *Figure 16.1*. We can use Keras' `skipgrams()` function as follows:

```
pairs, labels = skipgrams(sequence=data,
                          vocabulary_size=vocab_size,
                          window_size=WINDOW_SIZE,
                          sampling_table=sampling_table,
                          negative_samples=1.0,
                          shuffle=True)
```

The result is 120.4 million context-target pairs, evenly split between positive and negative samples. The negative samples are generated according to the `sampling_table` probabilities we created in the previous step. The first five target and context word IDs with their matching labels appear as follows:

```
pd.DataFrame({'target': target_word[:5],
              'context': context_word[:5],
              'label': labels[:5]})
```

```
   target  context  label
0   30867     2117      1
1     196      359      1
2   17960    32467      0
3     314     1721      1
4   28387     7811      0
```

Creating the word2vec model layers

The word2vec model contains the following:

- An input layer that receives the two scalar values representing the target-context pair
- A shared embedding layer that computes the dot product of the vector for the target and context word
- A sigmoid output layer

The **input layer** has two components, one for each element of the target-context pair:

```
input_target = Input((1,), name='target_input')
input_context = Input((1,), name='context_input')
```

The **shared embedding layer** contains one vector for each element of the vocabulary that is selected according to the index of the target and context tokens, respectively:

```
embedding = Embedding(input_dim=vocab_size,
                      output_dim=EMBEDDING_SIZE,
                      input_length=1,
                      name='embedding_layer')
target = embedding(input_target)
target = Reshape((EMBEDDING_SIZE, 1), name='target_embedding')(target)

context = embedding(input_context)
context = Reshape((EMBEDDING_SIZE, 1), name='context_embedding')(context)
```

The **output layer** measures the similarity of the two embedding vectors by their dot product and transforms the result using the `sigmoid` function that we encountered when discussing logistic regression in *Chapter 7, Linear Models – From Risk Factors to Return Forecasts*:

```
# similarity measure
dot_product = Dot(axes=1)([target, context])
dot_product = Reshape((1,), name='similarity')(dot_product)
output = Dense(units=1, activation='sigmoid', name='output')(dot_product)
```

This skip-gram model contains a 200-dimensional embedding layer that will assume different values for each vocabulary item. As a result, we end up with 59,617 x 200 trainable parameters, plus two for the sigmoid output.

In each iteration, the model computes the dot product of the context and the target embedding vectors, passes the result through the sigmoid to produce a probability, and adjusts the embedding based on the gradient of the loss.

Visualizing embeddings using TensorBoard

TensorBoard is a visualization tool that permits the projection of the embedding vectors into two or three dimensions to explore the word and phrase locations. After loading the embedding metadata file we created (refer to the notebook), you can also search for specific terms to view and explore its neighbors, projected into two or three dimensions using UMAP, t-SNE, or PCA (refer to *Chapter 13, Data-Driven Risk Factors and Asset Allocation with Unsupervised Learning*). Refer to the notebook for a higher-resolution color version of the following screenshot:

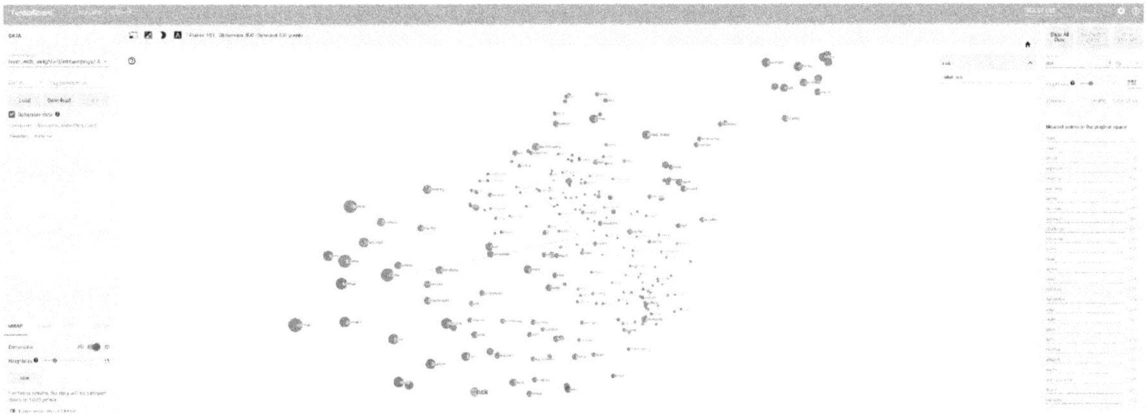

Figure 16.5: 3D embeddings and metadata visualization

How to train embeddings faster with Gensim

The TensorFlow implementation is very transparent in terms of its architecture, but it is not particularly fast. The **natural language processing** (**NLP**) library Gensim, which we also used for topic modeling in the last chapter, offers better performance and more closely resembles the C-based word2vec implementation provided by the original authors.

Usage is very straightforward. We first create a sentence generator that just takes the name of the file we produced in the preprocessing step as input (we'll work with 3-grams again):

```
sentence_path = data_path / FILE_NAME
sentences = LineSentence(str(sentence_path))
```

In a second step, we configure the word2vec model with the familiar parameters concerning the sizes of the embedding vector and the context window, the minimum token frequency, and the number of negative samples, among others:

```
model = Word2Vec(sentences,
                 sg=1, # set to 1 for skip-gram; CBOW otherwise
                 size=300,
                 window=5,
                 min_count=20,
                 negative=15,
                 workers=8,
                 iter=EPOCHS,
                 alpha=0.05)
```

One epoch of training takes a bit over 2 minutes on a modern 4-core i7 processor.

We can persist both the model and the word vectors, or just the word vectors, as follows:

```
# persist model
model.save(str(gensim_path / 'word2vec.model'))
# persist word vectors
model.wv.save(str(gensim_path / 'word_vectors.bin'))
```

We can validate model performance and continue training until we are satisfied with the results like so:

```
model.train(sentences, epochs=1, total_examples=model.corpus_count)
```

In this case, training for six additional epochs yields the best results with an accuracy of 41.75 percent across all analogies covered by the vocabulary. The left panel of *Figure 16.6* shows the correct/incorrect predictions and accuracy breakdown per category.

Gensim also allows us to evaluate custom semantic algebra. We can check the popular `"woman"+"king"-"man" ~ "queen"` example as follows:

```
most_sim = best_model.wv.most_similar(positive=['woman', 'king'],
negative=['man'], topn=10)
```

The right panel of the figure shows that "queen" is the third token, right after "monarch" and the less obvious "lewis", followed by several royalties:

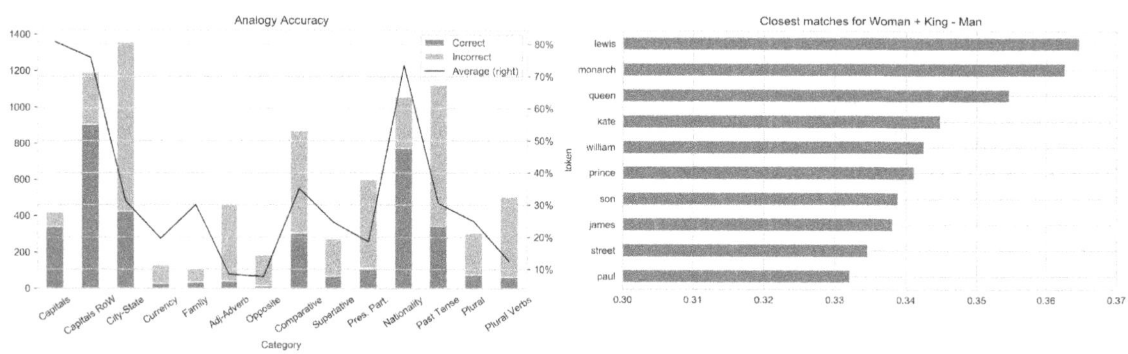

Figure 16.6: Analogy accuracy by category and for a specific example

We can also evaluate the tokens most similar to a given target to gain a better understanding of the embedding characteristics. We randomly select based on log corpus frequency:

```
counter = Counter(sentence_path.read_text().split())
most_common = pd.DataFrame(counter.most_common(), columns=['token', 'count'])
most_common['p'] = np.log(most_common['count'])/np.log(most_common['count']).
sum()similars = pd.DataFrame()
for token in np.random.choice(most_common.token, size=10, p=most_common.p):
    similars[token] = [s[0] for s in best_model.wv.most_similar(token)]
```

The following table exemplifies the results that include several n-grams:

Target	Closest Match				
	0	1	2	3	4
profiles	profile	users	political_ consultancy_ cambridge_ analytica	sophisticated	facebook
divestments	divestitures	acquisitions	takeovers	bayer	consolidation
readiness	training	military	command	air_force	preparations
arsenal	nuclear_ weapons	russia	ballistic_missile	weapons	hezbollah
supply_ disruptions	disruptions	raw_material	disruption	prices	downturn

We will now proceed to develop an application more closely related to real-life trading using SEC filings.

word2vec for trading with SEC filings

In this section, we will learn word and phrase vectors from annual SEC filings using Gensim to illustrate the potential value of word embeddings for algorithmic trading. In the following sections, we will combine these vectors as features with price returns to train neural networks to predict equity prices from the content of security filings.

In particular, we will use a dataset containing over **22,000 10-K annual reports** from the period **2013-2016** that are filed by over 6,500 listed companies and contain both financial information and management commentary (see *Chapter 2, Market and Fundamental Data – Sources and Techniques*).

For about 3,000 companies corresponding to 11,000 filings, we have stock prices to label the data for predictive modeling. (See data source details and download instructions and preprocessing code samples in the `sec_preprocessing` notebook in the `sec-filings` folder.)

Preprocessing – sentence detection and n-grams

Each filing is a separate text file, and a master index contains filing metadata. We extract the most informative sections, namely:

- Item 1 and 1A: Business and Risk Factors
- Item 7: Management's Discussion
- Item 7a: Disclosures about Market Risks

The `sec_preprocessing` notebook shows how to parse and tokenize the text using spaCy, similar to the approach in *Chapter 14*. We do not lemmatize the tokens to preserve nuances of word usage.

Automatic phrase detection

As in the previous section, we use Gensim to detect phrases that consist of multiple tokens, or n-grams. The notebook shows that the most frequent bigrams include `common_stock`, `united_states`, `cash_flows`, `real_estate`, and `interest_rates`.

We end up with a vocabulary of slightly over 201,000 tokens with a median frequency of 7, suggesting substantial noise that we can remove by increasing the minimum frequency when training our word2vec model.

Labeling filings with returns to predict earnings surprises

The dataset comes with a list of tickers and filing dates associated with the 10,000 documents. We can use this information to select stock prices for a certain period surrounding the filing publication. The goal would be to train a model that uses word vectors for a given filing as input to predict post-filing returns.

The following code example shows how to label individual filings with the 1-month return for the period after filing:

```
with pd.HDFStore(DATA_FOLDER / 'assets.h5') as store:
    prices = store['quandl/wiki/prices'].adj_close

sec = pd.read_csv('sec_path/filing_index.csv').rename(columns=str.lower)
sec.date_filed = pd.to_datetime(sec.date_filed)
sec = sec.loc[sec.ticker.isin(prices.columns), ['ticker', 'date_filed']]
price_data = []
```

```
for ticker, date in sec.values.tolist():
    target = date + relativedelta(months=1)
    s = prices.loc[date: target, ticker]
    price_data.append(s.iloc[-1] / s.iloc[0] - 1)

df = pd.DataFrame(price_data,
                  columns=['returns'],
                  index=sec.index)
```

We will come back to this when we work with deep learning architectures in the following chapters.

Model training

The `gensim.models.word2vec` class implements the skip-gram and CBOW architectures introduced previously. The notebook `word2vec` contains additional implementation details.

To facilitate memory-efficient text ingestion, the `LineSentence` class creates a generator from individual sentences contained in the text file provided:

```
sentence_path = Path('data', 'ngrams', f'ngrams_2.txt')
sentences = LineSentence(sentence_path)
```

The `Word2Vec` class offers the configuration options introduced earlier in this chapter:

```
model = Word2Vec(sentences,
                 sg=1,          # 1=skip-gram; otherwise CBOW
                 hs=0,          # hier. softmax if 1, neg. sampling if 0
                 size=300,      # Vector dimensionality
                 window=3,      # Max dist. btw target and context word
                 min_count=50,  # Ignore words with lower frequency
                 negative=10,   # noise word count for negative sampling
                 workers=8,     # no threads
                 iter=1,        # no epochs = iterations over corpus
                 alpha=0.025,   # initial learning rate
                 min_alpha=0.0001 # final learning rate
                )
```

The notebook shows how to persist and reload models to continue training, or how to store the embedding vectors separately, for example, for use in machine learning models.

Model evaluation

Basic functionality includes identifying similar words:

```
sims=model.wv.most_similar(positive=['iphone'], restrict_vocab=15000)
                  term   similarity
0                 ipad     0.795460
1              android     0.694014
2           smartphone     0.665732
```

We can also validate individual analogies using positive and negative contributions accordingly:

```
model.wv.most_similar(positive=['france', 'london'],
                      negative=['paris'],
                      restrict_vocab=15000)

             term  similarity
0  united_kingdom    0.606630
1         germany    0.585644
2     netherlands    0.578868
```

Performance impact of parameter settings

We can use the analogies to evaluate the impact of different parameter settings. The following results stand out (refer to the detailed results in the `models` folder):

- Negative sampling outperforms the hierarchical softmax, while also training faster.
- The skip-gram architecture outperforms CBOW.
- Different `min_count` settings have a smaller impact; the midpoint of 50 performs best.

Further experiments with the best-performing skip-gram model using negative sampling and a `min_count` of 50 show the following:

- Context windows smaller than 5 reduce performance.
- A higher negative sampling rate improves performance at the expense of slower training.
- Larger vectors improve performance, with a `size` of 600 yielding the best accuracy at 38.5 percent.

Sentiment analysis using doc2vec embeddings

Text classification requires combining multiple word embeddings. A common approach is to average the embedding vectors for each word in the document. This uses information from all embeddings and effectively uses vector addition to arrive at a different location point in the embedding space. However, relevant information about the order of words is lost.

In contrast, the document embedding model, doc2vec, developed by the word2vec authors shortly after publishing their original contribution, produces embeddings for pieces of text like a paragraph or a product review directly. Similar to word2vec, there are also two flavors of doc2vec:

- The **distributed bag of words** (**DBOW**) model corresponds to the word2vec CBOW model. The document vectors result from training a network on the synthetic task of predicting a target word based on both the context word vectors and the document's doc vector.
- The **distributed memory** (**DM**) model corresponds to the word2wec skip-gram architecture. The doc vectors result from training a neural net to predict a target word using the full document's doc vector.

Gensim's `Doc2Vec` class implements this algorithm. We'll illustrate the use of doc2vec by applying it to the Yelp sentiment dataset that we introduced in *Chapter 14*. To speed up training, we limit the data to a stratified random sample of 0.5 million Yelp reviews with their associated star ratings. The `doc2vec_yelp_sentiment` notebook contains the code examples for this section.

Creating doc2vec input from Yelp sentiment data

We load the combined Yelp dataset containing 6 million reviews, as created in *Chapter 14, Text Data for Trading – Sentiment Analysis*, and sample 100,000 reviews for each star rating:

```
df = pd.read_parquet('data_path / 'user_reviews.parquet').loc[:, ['stars',
                                                                    'text']]
stars = range(1, 6)
sample = pd.concat([df[df.stars==s].sample(n=100000) for s in stars])
```

We use nltk's `RegexpTokenizer` for simple and quick text cleaning:

```
tokenizer = RegexpTokenizer(r'\w+')
stopword_set = set(stopwords.words('english'))

def clean(review):
    tokens = tokenizer.tokenize(review)
    return ' '.join([t for t in tokens if t not in stopword_set])
sample.text = sample.text.str.lower().apply(clean)
```

After we filter out reviews shorter than 10 tokens, we are left with 485,825 samples. The left panel of *Figure 16.6* shows the distribution of the number of tokens per review.

The `gensim.models.Doc2Vec` class processes documents in the `TaggedDocument` format that contains the tokenized documents alongside a unique tag that permits the document vectors to be accessed after training:

```
sample = pd.read_parquet('yelp_sample.parquet')
sentences = []
for i, (stars, text) in df.iterrows():
    sentences.append(TaggedDocument(words=text.split(), tags=[i]))
```

Training a doc2vec model

The training interface works in a similar fashion to word2vec and also allows continued training and persistence:

```
model = Doc2Vec(documents=sentences,
                dm=1,           # 1=distributed memory, 0=dist.BOW
                epochs=5,
                size=300,       # vector size
                window=5,       # max. distance betw. target and context
                min_count=50,   # ignore tokens w. lower frequency
                negative=5,     # negative training samples
                dm_concat=0,    # 1=concatenate vectors, 0=sum
                dbow_words=0,   # 1=train word vectors as well
                workers=4)

model.save((results_path / 'sample.model').as_posix())
```

We can query the *n* terms most similar to a given token as a quick way to evaluate the resulting word vectors as follows:

```
model.most_similar('good')
```

The right panel of *Figure 16.7* displays the returned tokens and their similarity:

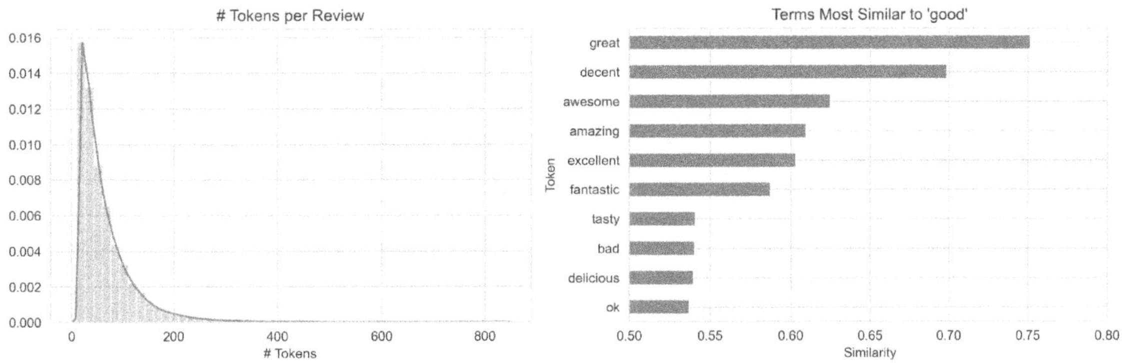

Figure 16.7: Histogram of the number of tokens per review (left) and terms most similar to the token 'good'

Training a classifier with document vectors

Now, we can access the document vectors to create features for a sentiment classifier:

```
y = sample.stars.sub(1)
X = np.zeros(shape=(len(y), size)) # size=300
for i in range(len(sample)):
    X[i] = model.docvecs[i]

X.shape
(485825, 300)
```

We create training and test sets as usual:

```
X_train, X_test, y_train, y_test = train_test_split(X, y,
                                                    test_size=0.2,
                                                    random_state=42,
                                                    stratify=y)
```

Now, we proceed to train a `RandomForestClassifier`, a LightGBM gradient boosting model, and a multinomial logistic regression. We use 500 trees for the random forest:

```
rf = RandomForestClassifier(n_jobs=-1, n_estimators=500)
rf.fit(X_train, y_train)
rf_pred = rf.predict(X_test)
```

We use early stopping with the LightGBM classifier, but it runs for the full 5,000 rounds because it continues to improve its validation performance:

```
train_data = lgb.Dataset(data=X_train, label=y_train)
test_data = train_data.create_valid(X_test, label=y_test)
params = {'objective': 'multiclass',
          'num_classes': 5}
lgb_model = lgb.train(params=params,
                      train_set=train_data,
                      num_boost_round=5000,
                      valid_sets=[train_data, test_data],
                      early_stopping_rounds=25,
                      verbose_eval=50)
# generate multiclass predictions
lgb_pred = np.argmax(lgb_model.predict(X_test), axis=1)
```

Finally, we build a multinomial logistic regression model as follows:

```
lr = LogisticRegression(multi_class='multinomial', solver='lbfgs',
                        class_weight='balanced')
lr.fit(X_train, y_train)
lr_pred = lr.predict(X_test)
```

When we compute the accuracy for each model on the validation set, gradient boosting performs significantly better at 62.24 percent. *Figure 16.8* shows the confusion matrix and accuracy for each model:

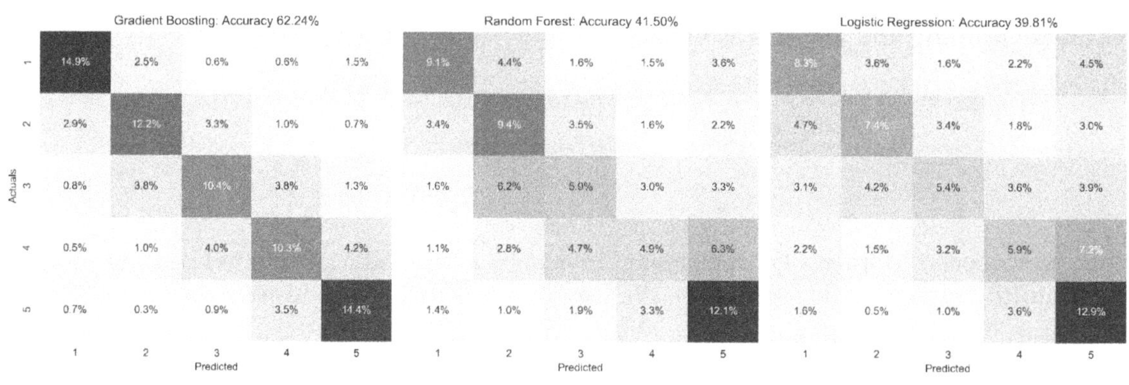

Figure 16.8: Confusion matrix and test accuracy for alternative models

The sentiment classification result in *Chapter 14, Text Data for Trading – Sentiment Analysis*, produced better accuracy for LightGBM (73.6 percent), but we used the full dataset and included additional features. You may want to test whether increasing the sample size or tuning the model parameters makes doc2vec perform equally well.

Lessons learned and next steps

This example applied sentiment analysis using doc2vec to **product reviews rather than financial documents**. We selected product reviews because it is very difficult to find financial text data that is large enough for training word embeddings from scratch and also has useful sentiment labels or sufficient information for us to assign them labels, such as asset returns, ourselves.

While product reviews allow us to demonstrate the workflow, we need to keep in mind **important structural differences**: product reviews are often short, informal, and specific to one particular object. Many financial documents, in contrast, are longer, more formal, and the target object may or may not be clearly identified. Financial news articles could concern multiple targets, and while corporate disclosures may have a clear source, they may also discuss competitors. An analyst report, for instance, may also discuss both positive and negative aspects of the same object or topic.

In short, the interpretation of sentiment expressed in financial documents often requires a more sophisticated, nuanced, and granular approach that builds up an understanding of the content's meaning from different aspects. Decision makers also often care to understand how a model arrives at its conclusion.

These challenges have not yet been solved and remain an area of very active research, complicated not least by the scarcity of suitable data sources. However, recent breakthroughs that significantly boosted performance on various NLP tasks since 2018 suggest that financial sentiment analysis may also become more robust in the coming years. We will turn to these innovations next.

New frontiers – pretrained transformer models

Word2vec and GloVe embeddings capture more semantic information than the bag-of-words approach. However, they allow only a single fixed-length representation of each token that does not differentiate between context-specific usages. To address unsolved problems such as multiple meanings for the same word, called **polysemy**, several new models have emerged that build on the **attention mechanism** designed to learn more contextualized word embeddings (Vaswani et al., 2017). The key characteristics of these models are as follows:

- The use of **bidirectional language models** that process text both left-to-right and right-to-left for a richer context representation
- The use of **semi-supervised pretraining** on a large generic corpus to learn universal language aspects in the form of embeddings and network weights that can be used and fine-tuned for specific tasks (a form of **transfer learning** that we will discuss in more detail in *Chapter 18, CNNs for Financial Time Series and Satellite Images*)

In this section, we briefly describe the attention mechanism, outline how the recent transformer models—starting with **Bidirectional Encoder Representation from Transformers** (**BERT**)—use it to improve performance on key NLP tasks, reference several sources for pretrained language models, and explain how to use them for financial sentiment analysis.

Attention is all you need

The **attention mechanism** explicitly models the relationships between words in a sentence to better incorporate the context. It was first applied to machine translation (Bahdanau, Cho, and Bengio, 2016), but has since become integral to neural language models for a wide variety of tasks.

Until 2017, **recurrent neural networks** (**RNNs**), which sequentially process text left-to-right or right-to-left, represented the state of the art for NLP tasks like translation. Google, for example, has employed such a model in production since late 2016. Sequential processing implies several steps to semantically connect words at distant locations and precludes parallel processing, which greatly speeds up computation on modern, specialized hardware like GPUs. (For more information on RNNs, refer to *Chapter 19, RNNs for Multivariate Time Series and Sentiment Analysis*.)

In contrast, the **Transformer** model, introduced in the seminal paper *Attention is all you need* (Vaswani et al., 2017), requires only a constant number of steps to identify semantically related words. It relies on a self-attention mechanism that captures links between all words in a sentence, regardless of their relative position. The model learns the representation of a word by assigning an attention score to every other word in the sentence that determines how much each of the other words should contribute to the representation. These scores then inform a weighted average of all words' representations, which is fed into a fully connected network to generate a new representation for the target word.

The Transformer model uses an encoder-decoder architecture with several layers, each of which uses several attention mechanisms (called **heads**) in parallel. It yielded large performance improvements on various translation tasks and, more importantly, inspired a wave of new research into neural language models addressing a broader range of tasks. The resources linked on GitHub contain various excellent visual explanations of how the attention mechanism works, so we won't go into more detail here.

BERT – towards a more universal language model

In 2018, Google released the **BERT** model, which stands for **Bidirectional Encoder Representations from Transformers** (Devlin et al., 2019). In a major breakthrough for NLP research, it achieved groundbreaking results on eleven natural language understanding tasks, ranging from question answering and named entity recognition to paraphrasing and sentiment analysis, as measured by the **General Language Understanding Evaluation (GLUE)** benchmark (see GitHub for links to task descriptions and a leaderboard).

The new ideas introduced by BERT unleashed a flurry of new research that produced dozens of improvements that soon surpassed non-expert humans on the GLUE tasks and led to the more challenging **SuperGLUE** benchmark designed by DeepMind (Wang et al., 2019). As a result, 2018 is now considered a turning point for NLP research; both Google Search and Microsoft's Bing are now using variations of BERT to interpret user queries and provide more accurate results.

We will briefly outline BERT's key innovations and provide indications on how to get started using it and its subsequent enhancements with one of several open source libraries providing pretrained models.

Key innovations – deeper attention and pretraining

The BERT model builds on **two key ideas**, namely, the **transformer architecture** described in the previous section and **unsupervised pretraining** so that it doesn't need to be trained from scratch for each new task; rather, its weights are fine-tuned:

- BERT takes the **attention mechanism** to a new (deeper) level by using 12 or 24 layers, depending on the architecture, each with 12 or 16 attention heads. This results in up to 24 × 16 = 384 attention mechanisms to learn context-specific embeddings.
- BERT uses **unsupervised, bidirectional pretraining** to learn its weights in advance on two tasks: **masked language modeling** (predicting a missing word given the left and right context) and **next sentence prediction** (predicting whether one sentence follows another).

Context-free models such as word2vec or GloVe generate a single embedding for each word in the vocabulary: the word "bank" would have the same context-free representation in "bank account" and "bank of the river." In contrast, BERT learns to represent each word based on the other words in the sentence. As a **bidirectional model**, BERT is able to represent the word "bank" in the sentence "I accessed the bank account," not only based on "I accessed the" as a unidirectional contextual model, but also based on "account."

BERT and its successors can be **pretrained on a generic corpus** like Wikipedia before adapting its final layers to a specific task and **fine-tuning its weights**. As a result, you can use large-scale, state-of-the-art models with billions of parameters, while only incurring a few hours rather than days or weeks of training costs. Several libraries offer such pretrained models that you can build on to develop a custom sentiment classifier for your dataset of choice.

Using pretrained state-of-the-art models

The recent NLP breakthroughs described in this section have shown how to acquire linguistic knowledge from unlabeled text with networks large enough to represent the long tail of rare usage phenomena. The resulting Transformer architectures make fewer assumptions about word order and context; instead, they learn a much more subtle understanding of language from very large amounts of data, using hundreds of millions or even billions of parameters.

We will highlight several libraries that make pretrained networks, as well as excellent Python tutorials available.

The Hugging Face Transformers library

Hugging Face is a US start-up developing chatbot applications designed to offer personalized AI-powered communication. It raised $15 million in late 2019 to further develop its very successful open source NLP library, Transformers.

The library provides general-purpose architectures for natural language understanding and generation with more than 32 pretrained models in more than 100 languages and deep interoperability between TensorFlow 2 and PyTorch. It has excellent documentation.

The spacy-transformers library includes wrappers to facilitate the inclusion of the pretrained transformer models in a spaCy pipeline. Refer to the reference links on GitHub for more information.

AllenNLP

AllenNLP is built and maintained by the Allen Institute for AI, started by Microsoft cofounder Paul Allen, in close collaboration with researchers at the University of Washington. It has been designed as a research library for developing state-of-the-art deep learning models on a wide variety of linguistic tasks, built on PyTorch.

It offers solutions for key tasks from question answering to sentence annotation, including reading comprehension, named entity recognition, and sentiment analysis. A pretrained **RoBERTa** model (a more robust version of BERT; Liu et al., 2019) achieves over 95 percent accuracy on the Stanford sentiment treebank and can be used with just a few lines of code (see links to the documentation on GitHub).

Trading on text data – lessons learned and next steps

As highlighted at the end of the section *Sentiment analysis using doc2vec embeddings*, there are important structural characteristics of financial documents that often complicate their interpretation and undermine simple dictionary-based methods.

In a recent survey of financial sentiment analysis, Man, Luo, and Lin (2019) found that most existing approaches only identify high-level polarities, such as positive, negative, or neutral. However, practical applications that lead to real decisions typically require a more nuanced and transparent analysis. In addition, the lack of large financial text datasets with relevant labels limits the potential for using traditional machine learning methods or neural networks for sentiment analysis.

The pretraining approach just described, which, in principle, yields a deeper understanding of textual information, thus offers substantial promise. However, most applied research using transformers has focused on NLP tasks such as translation, question answering, logic, or dialog systems. Applications in relation to financial data are still in their infancy (see, for example, Araci 2019). This is likely to change soon given the availability of pretrained models and their potential to extract more valuable information from financial text data.

Summary

In this chapter, we discussed a new way of generating text features that use shallow neural networks for unsupervised machine learning. We saw how the resulting word embeddings capture interesting semantic aspects beyond the meaning of individual tokens by capturing some of the context in which they are used. We also covered how to evaluate the quality of word vectors using analogies and linear algebra.

We used Keras to build the network architecture that produces these features and applied the more performant Gensim implementation to financial news and SEC filings. Despite the relatively small datasets, the word2vec embeddings did capture meaningful relationships. We also demonstrated how appropriate labeling with stock price data can form the basis for supervised learning.

We applied the doc2vec algorithm, which produces a document rather than token vectors, to build a sentiment classifier based on Yelp business reviews. While this is unlikely to yield tradeable signals, it illustrates the process of how to extract features from relevant text data and train a model to predict an outcome that may be informative for a trading strategy.

Finally, we outlined recent research breakthroughs that promise to yield more powerful natural language models due to the availability of pretrained architectures that only require fine-tuning. Applications to financial data, however, are still at the research frontier.

In the next chapter, we will dive into the final part of this book, which covers how various deep learning architectures can be useful for algorithmic trading.

17
Deep Learning for Trading

This chapter kicks off Part 4, which covers how several **deep learning** (**DL**) modeling techniques can be useful for investment and trading. DL has achieved numerous **breakthroughs in many domains**, ranging from image and speech recognition to robotics and intelligent agents that have drawn widespread attention and revived large-scale research into **artificial intelligence** (**AI**). The expectations are high that the rapid development will continue and many more solutions to difficult practical problems will emerge.

In this chapter, we will present **feedforward neural networks** to introduce key elements of working with neural networks relevant to the various DL architectures covered in the following chapters. More specifically, we will demonstrate how to train large models efficiently using the **backpropagation algorithm** and manage the risks of overfitting. We will also show how to use the popular TensorFlow 2 and PyTorch frameworks, which we will leverage throughout Part 4.

Finally, we will develop, backtest, and evaluate a trading strategy based on signals generated by a deep feedforward neural network. We will design and tune the neural network and analyze how key hyperparameter choices affect its performance.

In summary, after reading this chapter and reviewing the accompanying notebooks, you will know about:

- How DL solves AI challenges in complex domains
- Key innovations that have propelled DL to its current popularity
- How feedforward networks learn representations from data
- Designing and training deep **neural networks** (**NNs**) in Python
- Implementing deep NNs using Keras, TensorFlow, and PyTorch
- Building and tuning a deep NN to predict asset returns
- Designing and backtesting a trading strategy based on deep NN signals

In the following chapters, we will build on this foundation to design various architectures suitable for different investment applications with a particular focus on alternative text and image data.

These include **recurrent neural networks** (**RNNs**) tailored to sequential data such as time series or natural language, and **convolutional neural networks** (**CNNs**), which are particularly well suited to image data but can also be used with time-series data. We will also cover deep unsupervised learning, including autoencoders and **generative adversarial networks** (**GANs**) as well as reinforcement learning to train agents that interactively learn from their environment.

> You can find the code samples for this chapter and links to additional resources in the corresponding directory of the GitHub repository. The notebooks include color versions of the images.

Deep learning – what's new and why it matters

The **machine learning** (**ML**) algorithms covered in *Part 2* work well on a wide variety of important problems, including on text data, as demonstrated in *Part 3*. They have been less successful, however, in solving central AI problems such as recognizing speech or classifying objects in images. These limitations have motivated the development of DL, and the recent DL breakthroughs have greatly contributed to a resurgence of interest in AI. For a comprehensive introduction that includes and expands on many of the points in this section, see Goodfellow, Bengio, and Courville (2016), or for a much shorter version, see LeCun, Bengio, and Hinton (2015).

In this section, we outline how DL overcomes many of the limitations of other ML algorithms. These limitations particularly constrain performance on high-dimensional and unstructured data that requires sophisticated efforts to extract informative features.

The ML techniques we covered in *Parts 2* and *3* are best suited for processing structured data with well-defined features. We saw, for example, how to convert text data into tabular data using the document-text matrix in *Chapter 14, Text Data for Trading – Sentiment Analysis*. DL overcomes the **challenge of designing informative features**, possibly by hand, by learning a representation of the data that better captures its characteristics with respect to the outcome.

More specifically, we'll see how DL learns a **hierarchical representation of the data**, and why this approach works well for high-dimensional, unstructured data. We will describe how NNs employ a multilayered, deep architecture to compose a set of nested functions and discover a hierarchical structure. These functions compute successive and increasingly abstract representations of the data in each layer based on the learning of the previous layer. We will also look at how the backpropagation algorithm adjusts the network parameters so that these representations best meet the model's objective.

We will also briefly outline how DL fits into the evolution of AI and the diverse set of approaches that aim to achieve the current goals of AI.

Hierarchical features tame high-dimensional data

As discussed throughout *Part 2*, the key challenge of supervised learning is to generalize from training data to new samples. Generalization becomes exponentially more difficult as the dimensionality of the data increases. We encountered the root causes of these difficulties as the curse of dimensionality in *Chapter 13, Data-Driven Risk Factors and Asset Allocation with Unsupervised Learning*.

One aspect of this curse is that volume grows exponentially with the number of dimensions: for a hypercube with edge length 10, volume increases from 10^3 to 10^4 as its dimensionality increases from three to four. Conversely, the **data density for a given sample size drops exponentially**. In other words, the number of observations required to maintain a certain density grows exponentially.

Another aspect is that functional relationships between the features and the output can become more complex when they are allowed to vary across a growing number of dimensions. As discussed in *Chapter 6, The Machine Learning Process*, ML algorithms struggle to learn **arbitrary functions in a high-dimensional space** because the number of candidates grows exponentially while the density of the data available to infer the relationship drops simultaneously. To mitigate this problem, algorithms hypothesize that the target function belongs to a certain class and impose constraints on the search for the optimal solution within that class for the problem at hand.

Furthermore, algorithms typically assume that the output at a new point should be similar to the output at nearby training points. This prior **assumption of smoothness** or local constancy posits that the learned function will not change much in a small region, as illustrated by the k-nearest neighbor algorithm (see *Chapter 6, The Machine Learning Process*). However, as data density drops exponentially with a growing number of dimensions, the distance between training samples naturally rises. The notion of nearby training examples thus becomes less meaningful as the potential complexity of the target function increases.

For traditional ML algorithms, the number of parameters and required training samples is generally proportional to the number of regions in the input space that the algorithm is able to distinguish. DL is designed to overcome the challenges of learning an exponential number of regions from a limited number of training points by assuming that a hierarchy of features generates the data.

DL as representation learning

Many AI tasks like image or speech recognition require knowledge about the world. One of the key challenges is to encode this knowledge so a computer can utilize it. For decades, the development of ML systems required considerable domain expertise to transform the raw data (such as image pixels) into an internal representation that a learning algorithm could use to detect or classify patterns.

Similarly, how much value an ML algorithm adds to a trading strategy depends greatly on our ability to engineer features that represent the predictive information in the data so that the algorithm can process it. Ideally, the features capture independent drivers of the outcome, as discussed in *Chapter 4, Financial Feature Engineering – How to Research Alpha Factors*, and throughout *Parts 2* and *3* when designing and evaluating factors that capture trading signals.

Rather than relying on hand-designed features, representation learning allows an ML algorithm to automatically discover the representation of the data most useful for detecting or classifying patterns. DL combines this technique with specific assumptions about the nature of the features. See Bengio, Courville, and Vincent (2013) for additional information.

How DL extracts hierarchical features from data

The core idea behind DL is that a multi-level hierarchy of features has generated the data. Consequently, a DL model encodes the prior belief that the target function is composed of a nested set of simpler functions. This assumption permits an exponential gain in the number of regions that can be distinguished for a given number of training samples.

In other words, DL is a representation learning method that extracts a hierarchy of concepts from the data. It learns this hierarchical representation by **composing simple but non-linear functions** that successively transform the representation of one level (starting with the input data) into a new representation at a higher, slightly more abstract level. By combining enough of these transformations, DL is able to learn very complex functions.

Applied to a **classification task**, for example, higher levels of representation tend to amplify the aspects of the data most helpful for discriminating objects while suppressing irrelevant sources of variation. As we will see in more detail in *Chapter 18, CNNs for Financial Time Series and Satellite Images*, raw image data is just a two- or three-dimensional array of pixel values. The first layer of representation typically learns features that focus on the presence or absence of edges at particular orientations and locations. The second layer often learns motifs that depend on particular edge arrangements, regardless of small variations in their positions. The following layer may assemble motifs to represent parts of relevant objects, and subsequent layers would detect objects as combinations of these parts.

The **key breakthrough of DL** is that a general-purpose learning algorithm can extract hierarchical features suitable for modeling high-dimensional, unstructured data in a way that is infinitely more scalable than human engineering. It is thus no surprise that the rise of DL parallels the large-scale availability of unstructured image or text data. To the extent that these data sources also figure prominently among alternative data, DL has become highly relevant for algorithmic trading.

Good and bad news – the universal approximation theorem

The **universal approximation theorem** formalizes the ability of NNs to capture arbitrary relationships between input and output data. George Cybenko (1989) demonstrated that single-layer NNs using sigmoid activation functions can represent any continuous function on a closed and bounded subset of `Rn`. Kurt Hornik (1991) further showed that it is not the specific shape of the activation function but rather the **multilayered architecture** that enables the hierarchical feature representation, which in turn allows NNs to approximate universal functions.

However, the theorem does not help us identify the network architecture required to represent a specific target function. We will see in the last section of this chapter that there are numerous parameters to optimize, including the network's width and depth, the number of connections between neurons, and the type of activation functions.

Furthermore, the ability to represent arbitrary functions does not imply that a network can actually learn the parameters for a given function. It took over two decades for backpropagation, the most popular learning algorithm for NNs to become effective at scale. Unfortunately, given the highly nonlinear nature of the optimization problem, there is no guarantee that it will find the absolute best rather than just a relatively good solution.

How DL relates to ML and AI

AI has a long history, going back at least to the 1950s as an academic field and much longer as a subject of human inquiry, but has experienced several waves of ebbing and flowing enthusiasm since (see Nilsson, 2009, for an in-depth survey). ML is an important subfield with a long history in related disciplines such as statistics and became prominent in the 1980s. As we have just discussed, and as depicted in *Figure 17.1*, DL is a form of representation learning and is itself a subfield of ML.

The initial goal of AI was to achieve **general AI**, conceived as the ability to solve problems considered to require human-level intelligence, and to reason and draw logical conclusions about the world and automatically improve itself. AI applications that do not involve ML include knowledge bases that encode information about the world, combined with languages for logical operations.

Historically, much AI effort went into developing **rule-based systems** that aimed to capture expert knowledge and decision-making rules, but hard-coding these rules frequently failed due to excessive complexity. In contrast, ML implies a **probabilistic approach** that learns rules from data and aims at circumventing the limitations of human-designed rule-based systems. It also involves a shift to narrower, task-specific objectives.

The following figure sketches the relationship between the various AI subfields, outlines their goals, and highlights their relevance on a timeline.

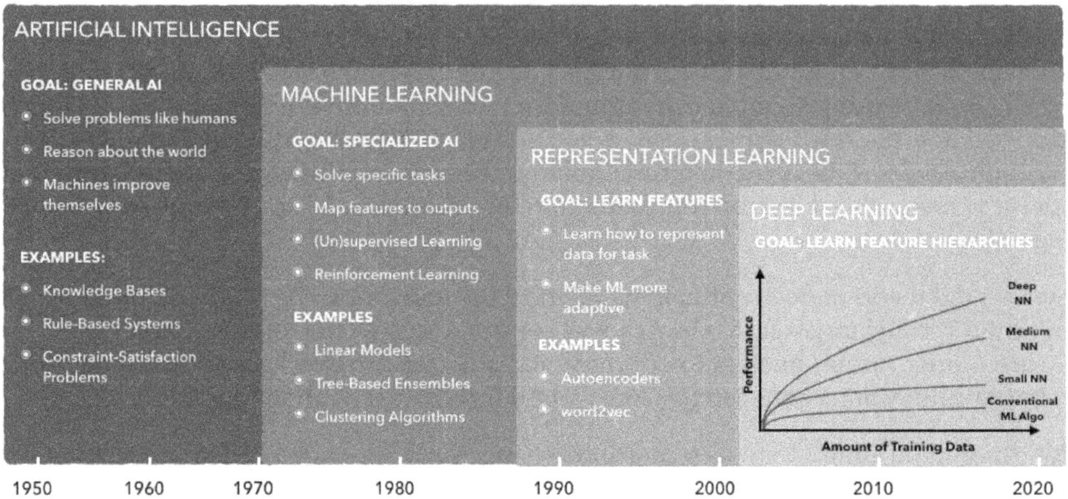

Figure 17.1: AI timeline and subfields

In the next section, we will see how to actually build a neural network.

Designing an NN

DL relies on **NNs**, which consist of a few key building blocks, which in turn can be configured in a multitude of ways. In this section, we introduce how NNs work and illustrate their most important components used to design different architectures.

(Artificial) NNs were originally inspired by biological models of learning like the human brain, either in an attempt to mimic how it works and achieve similar success, or to gain a better understanding through simulation. Current NN research draws less on neuroscience, not least since our understanding of the brain has not yet reached a sufficient level of granularity. Another constraint is overall size: even if the number of neurons used in NNs continued to double every year since their inception in the 1950s, they would only reach the scale of the human brain around 2050.

We will also explain how **backpropagation**, often simply called **backprop**, uses gradient information (the value of the partial derivative of the cost function with respect to a parameter) to adjust all neural network parameters based on training errors. The composition of various nonlinear modules implies that the optimization of the objective function can be quite challenging. We also introduce refinements of backpropagation that aim to accelerate the learning process.

A simple feedforward neural network architecture

In this section, we introduce **feedforward NNs**, which are based on the **multilayer perceptron** (**MLP**) and consist of one or more hidden layers that connect the input to the output layer. In feedforward NNs, information only flows from input to output, such that they can be represented as directed acyclic graphs, as in the following figure. In contrast, **recurrent neural networks** (**RNNs**; see *Chapter 19, RNNs for Multivariate Time Series and Sentiment Analysis*) include loops from the output back to the input to track or memorize past patterns and events.

We will first describe the feedforward NN architecture and how to implement it using NumPy. Then we will explain how backpropagation learns the NN weights and implement it in Python to train a binary classification network that produces perfect results even though the classes are not linearly separable. See the notebook `build_and_train_feedforward_nn` for implementation details.

A feedforward NN consists of several **layers**, each of which receives a sample of input data and produces an output. The **chain of transformations** starts with the input layer, which passes the source data to one of several internal or hidden layers, and ends with the output layer, which computes a result for comparison with the sample's output value.

The hidden and output layers consist of nodes or neurons. Nodes of a **fully connected** or dense layer connect to some or all nodes of the previous layer. The network architecture can be summarized by its depth, measured by the number of hidden layers, or the width and the number of nodes of each layer.

Each connection has a **weight** used to compute a linear combination of the input values. A layer may also have a **bias** node that always outputs a 1 and is used by the nodes in the subsequent layer, like a constant in linear regression. The goal of the training phase is to learn values for these weights that optimize the network's predictive performance.

Each node of the hidden layers computes the **dot product** of the weights and the output of the previous layer. An **activation function** transforms the result, which becomes the input to the subsequent layer. This transformation is typically nonlinear (like the sigmoid function used for logistic regression; see *Chapter 7, Linear Models – From Risk Factors to Return Forecasts,* on linear models) so that the network can learn nonlinear relationships; we'll discuss common activation functions in the next section. The output layer computes the linear combination of the output of the last hidden layer with its weights and uses an activation function that matches the type of ML problem.

The computation of the network output from the inputs thus flows through a chain of nested functions and is called **forward propagation**. *Figure 17.2* illustrates a single-layer feedforward NN with a two-dimensional input vector, a hidden layer of width three, and two nodes in the output layer. This architecture is simple enough, so we can still easily graph it yet illustrate the key concepts.

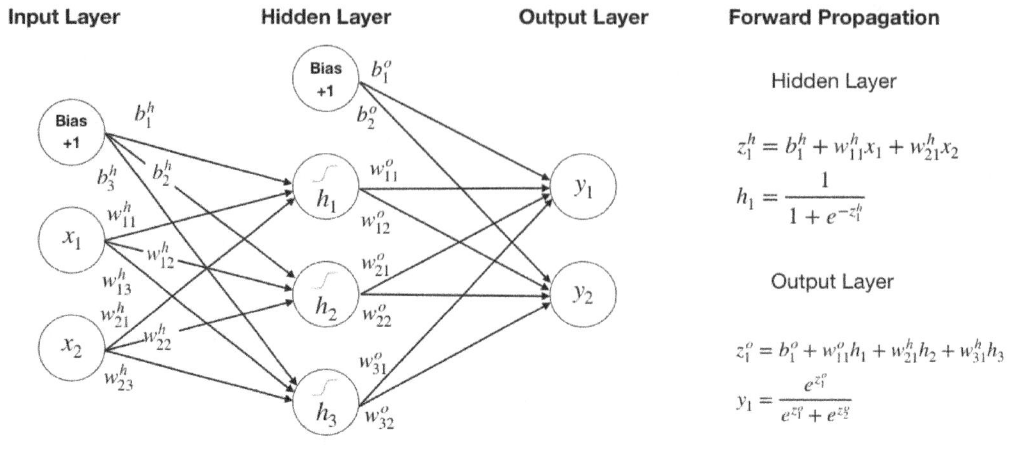

Figure 17.2: A feedforward architecture with one hidden layer

The **network graph** shows that each of the three hidden layer nodes (not counting the bias) has three weights, one for the input layer bias and two for each of the two input variables. Similarly, each output layer node has four weights to compute the product sum or dot product of the hidden layer bias and activations. In total, there are 17 parameters to be learned.

The **forward propagation** panel on the right of the figure lists the computations for an example node at the hidden and output layers, *h* and *o*, respectively. The first node in the hidden layer applies the sigmoid function to the linear combination *z* of its weights and inputs akin to logistic regression. The hidden layer thus runs three logistic regressions in parallel, while the backpropagation algorithm ensures that their parameters will most likely differ to best inform subsequent layers.

The output layer uses a **softmax** activation function (see *Chapter 6, The Machine Learning Process*) that generalizes the logistic sigmoid function to multiple classes. It adjusts the dot product of the hidden layer output with its weight to represent probabilities for the classes (only two in this case to simplify the presentation).

The forward propagation can also be expressed as nested functions, where *h* again represents the hidden layer and *o* the output layer to produce the NN estimate of the output: $\hat{y} = o(h(x))$.

Key design choices

Some NN design choices resemble those for other supervised learning models. For example, the output is dictated by the type of the ML problem such as regression, classification, or ranking. Given the output, we need to select a cost function to measure prediction success and failure, and an algorithm that optimizes the network parameters to minimize the cost.

NN-specific choices include the numbers of layers and nodes per layer, the connections between nodes of different layers, and the type of activation functions.

A key concern is **training efficiency**: the functional form of activations can facilitate or hinder the flow of the gradient information available to the backpropagation algorithm that adjusts the weights in response to training errors. Functions with flat regions for large input value ranges have a very low gradient and can impede training progress when parameter values get stuck in such a range.

Some architectures add **skip connections** that establish direct links beyond neighboring layers to facilitate the flow of gradient information. On the other hand, the deliberate omission of connections can reduce the number of parameters to limit the network's capacity and possibly lower the generalization error, while also cutting the computational cost.

Hidden units and activation functions

Several nonlinear activation functions besides the sigmoid function have been used successfully. Their design remains an area of research because they are the key element that allows the NN to learn nonlinear relationships. They also have a critical impact on the training process because their derivatives determine how errors translate into weight adjustments.

A very popular activation function is the **rectified linear unit** (**ReLU**). The activation is computed as $g(z) = \max(0, z)$ for a given activation z, resulting in a functional form similar to the payoff for a call option. The derivative is constant whenever the unit is active. ReLUs are usually combined with an affine input transformation that requires the presence of a bias node. Their discovery has greatly improved the performance of feedforward networks compared to sigmoid units, and they are often recommended as the default. There are several ReLU extensions that aim to address the limitations of ReLU to learn via gradient descent when they are not active and their gradient is zero (Goodfellow, Bengio, and Courville, 2016).

Another alternative to the logistic function σ is the **hyperbolic tangent function tanh**, which produces output values in the ranges [-1, 1]. They are closely related because $\tanh(z) = 2\sigma(2z) - 1$. Both functions suffer from saturation because their gradient becomes very small for very low and high input values. However, tanh often performs better because it more closely resembles the identity function so that for small activation values, the network behaves more like a linear model, which in turn facilitates training.

Output units and cost functions

The choice of NN output format and cost function depends on the type of supervised learning problem:

- **Regression problems** use a linear output unit that computes the dot product of its weights with the final hidden layer activations, typically in conjunction with mean squared error cost
- **Binary classification** uses sigmoid output units to model a Bernoulli distribution just like logistic regression with hidden activations as input
- **Multiclass problems** rely on softmax units that generalize the logistic sigmoid and model a discrete distribution over more than two classes, as demonstrated earlier

Binary and multiclass problems typically use cross-entropy loss, which significantly improves training efficacy compared to mean squared error (see *Chapter 6, The Machine Learning Process*, for additional information on loss functions).

How to regularize deep NNs

The downside of the capacity of NNs to approximate arbitrary functions is the greatly increased risk of overfitting. The best **protection against overfitting** is to train the model on a larger dataset. Data augmentation, such as creating slightly modified versions of images, is a powerful alternative approach. The generation of synthetic financial training data for this purpose is an active research area that we will address in *Chapter 20, Autoencoders for Conditional Risk Factors and Asset Pricing* (see, for example, Fu et al. 2019).

As an alternative or complement to obtaining more data, regularization can help mitigate the risk of overfitting. For all models discussed so far in this book, there is some form of regularization that modifies the learning algorithm to reduce its generalization error without negatively affecting its training error. Examples include the penalties added to the ridge and lasso regression objectives and the split or depth constraints used with decision trees and tree-based ensemble models.

Frequently, regularization takes the form of a soft constraint on the parameter values that trades off some additional bias for lower variance. A common practical finding is that the model with the lowest generalization error is not the model with the exact right size of parameters, but rather a larger model that has been well regularized. Popular NN regularization techniques that can be used in combination include parameter norm penalties, early stopping, and dropout.

Parameter norm penalties

We encountered **parameter norm penalties** for lasso and ridge regression as **L1 and L2 regularization**, respectively, in *Chapter 7, Linear Models – From Risk Factors to Return Forecasts*. In the NN context, parameter norm penalties similarly modify the objective function by adding a term that represents the L1 or L2 norm of the parameters, weighted by a hyperparameter that requires tuning. For NN, the bias parameters are usually not constrained, only the weights.

L1 regularization can produce sparse parameter estimates by reducing weights all the way to zero. L2 regularization, in contrast, preserves directions along which the parameters significantly reduce the cost function. Penalties or hyperparameter values can vary across layers, but the added tuning complexity quickly becomes prohibitive.

Early stopping

We encountered **early stopping** as a regularization technique in *Chapter 12, Boosting Your Trading Strategy*. It is perhaps the most common NN regularization method because it is both effective and simple to use: it monitors the model's performance on a validation set and stops training when the performance ceases to improve for a certain number of observations to prevent overfitting.

Early stopping can be viewed as **efficient hyperparameter selection** that automatically determines the correct amount of regularization, whereas parameter penalties require hyperparameter tuning to identify the ideal weight decay. Just be careful to avoid **lookahead bias**: backtest results will be exceedingly positive when early stopping uses out-of-sample data that would not be available during a real-life implementation of the strategy.

Dropout

Dropout refers to the randomized omission of individual units with a given probability during forward or backward propagation. As a result, these omitted units do not contribute to the training error or receive updates.

The technique is computationally inexpensive and does not constrain the choice of model or training procedure. While more iterations are necessary to achieve the same amount of learning, each iteration is faster due to the lower computational cost. Dropout reduces the risk of overfitting by preventing units from compensating for mistakes made by other units during the training process.

Training faster – optimizations for deep learning

Backprop refers to the computation of the gradient of the cost function with respect to the internal parameter we wish to update and the use of this information to update the parameter values. The gradient is useful because it indicates the direction of parameter change that causes the maximal increase in the cost function. Hence, adjusting the parameters according to the negative gradient produces an optimal cost reduction, at least for a region very close to the observed samples. See Ruder (2017) for an excellent overview of key gradient descent optimization algorithms.

Training deep NNs can be time-consuming due to the nonconvex objective function and the potentially large number of parameters. Several challenges can significantly delay convergence, find a poor optimum, or cause oscillations or divergence from the target:

- **Local minima** can prevent convergence to a global optimum and cause poor performance
- **Flat regions with low gradients** that are not a local minimum can also prevent convergence while most likely being distant from the global optimum
- **Steep regions with high gradients** resulting from multiplying several large weights can cause excessive adjustments
- Deep architectures or long-term dependencies in an RNN require the multiplication of many weights during backpropagation, leading to **vanishing gradients** so that at least parts of the NN receive few or no updates

Several algorithms have been developed to address some of these challenges, namely variations of stochastic gradient descent and approaches that use adaptive learning rates. There is no single best algorithm, although adaptive learning rates have shown some promise.

Stochastic gradient descent

Gradient descent iteratively adjusts these parameters using the gradient information. For a given parameter θ, the basic gradient descent rule adjusts the value by the negative gradient of the loss function with respect to this parameter, multiplied by a learning rate η:

$$\theta = \theta - \underbrace{\eta}_{\text{Learning Rate}} \cdot \underbrace{\nabla_\theta J(\theta)}_{\text{Gradient}}$$

The gradient can be evaluated for all training data, a randomized batch of data, or individual observations (called online learning). Random samples give rise to **stochastic gradient descent** (**SGD**), which often leads to faster convergence if random samples are an unbiased estimate of the gradient direction throughout the training process.

However, there are numerous challenges: it can be difficult to define a learning rate or a rate schedule that facilitates efficient convergence ex ante—too low a rate prolongs the process, and too high a rate can lead to repeated overshooting and oscillation around or even divergence from a minimum. Furthermore, the same learning rate may not be adequate for all parameters, that is, in all directions of change.

Momentum

A popular refinement of basic gradient descent adds momentum to **accelerate the convergence to a local minimum**. Illustrations of momentum often use the example of a local optimum at the center of an elongated ravine (while in practice the dimensionality would be much higher than three). It implies a minimum inside a deep and narrow canyon with very steep walls that have a large gradient on one side and a much gentler slope towards a local minimum at the bottom of this region on the other side. Gradient descent naturally follows the steep gradient and will make repeated adjustments up and down the walls of the canyons with much slower movements towards the minimum.

Momentum aims to address such a situation by **tracking recent directions** and adjusting the parameters by a weighted average of the most recent gradient and the currently computed value. It uses a momentum term γ to weigh the contribution of the latest adjustment to this iteration's update v_t:

$$v_t = \gamma v_{t-1} + \eta \nabla_\theta J(\theta)$$

Nesterov momentum is a simple change to normal momentum. Here, the gradient term is not computed at the current parameter space position θ_t but instead from an intermediate position. The goal is to correct for the momentum term overshooting or pointing in the wrong direction (Sutskever et al. 2013).

Adaptive learning rates

The choice of the appropriate learning rate is very challenging as highlighted in the previous subsection on stochastic gradient descent. At the same time, it is one of the most important parameters that strongly impacts training time and generalization performance.

While momentum addresses some of the issues with learning rates, it does so at the expense of introducing another hyperparameter, the **momentum rate**. Several algorithms aim to adapt the learning rate throughout the training process based on gradient information.

AdaGrad

AdaGrad accumulates all historical, parameter-specific gradient information and continues to rescale the learning rate inversely proportional to the squared cumulative gradient for a given parameter. The goal is to slow down changes for parameters that have already changed a lot and to encourage adjustments for those that haven't.

AdaGrad is designed to perform well on convex functions and has had a mixed performance in a DL context because it can reduce the learning rate too quickly based on early gradient information.

RMSProp

RMSProp modifies AdaGrad to use an exponentially weighted average of the cumulative gradient information. The goal is to put more emphasis on recent gradients. It also introduces a new hyperparameter that controls the length of the moving average.

RMSProp is a popular algorithm that often performs well, provided by the various libraries that we will introduce later and routinely used in practice.

Adam

Adam stands for **adaptive moment derivation** and combines aspects of RMSProp with Momentum. It is considered fairly robust and often used as the default optimization algorithm (Kingma and Ba, 2014).

Adam has several hyperparameters with recommended default values that may benefit from some tuning:

- **alpha**: The learning rate or step size determines how much weights are updated so that larger (smaller) values speed up (slow down) learning before the rate is updated; many libraries use the 0.001 default
- **beta$_1$**: The exponential decay rate for the first moment estimates; typically set to 0.9
- **beta$_2$**. The exponential decay rate for the second-moment estimates; usually set to 0.999
- **epsilon**: A very small number to prevent division by zero; often set to 1e-8

Summary – how to tune key hyperparameters

Hyperparameter optimization aims at **tuning the capacity of the model** so that it matches the complexity of the relationship between the input of the data. Excess capacity makes overfitting likely and requires either more data that introduces additional information into the learning process, reducing the size of the model, or more aggressive use of the various regularization tools just described.

The **principal diagnostic tool** is the behavior of training and validation error described in *Chapter 6, The Machine Learning Process*: if the validation error worsens while the training error continues to drop, the model is overfitting because its capacity is too high. On the other hand, if performance falls short of expectations, increasing the size of the model may be called for.

The most important aspect of parameter optimization is the architecture itself as it largely determines the number of parameters: other things being equal, more or wider hidden layers increase the capacity. As mentioned before, the best performance is often associated with models that have excess capacity but are well regularized using mechanisms like dropout or L1/L2 penalties.

In addition to **balancing model size and regularization**, it is important to tune the **learning rate** because it can undermine the optimization process and reduce the effective model capacity. The adaptive optimization algorithms offer a good starting point as described for Adam, the most popular option.

A neural network from scratch in Python

To gain a better understanding of how NNs work, we will formulate the single-layer architecture and forward propagation computations displayed in *Figure 17.2* using matrix algebra and implement it using NumPy. You can find the code samples in the notebook `build_and_train_feedforward_nn`.

The input layer

The architecture shown in *Figure 17.2* is designed for two-dimensional input data X that represents two different classes Y. In matrix form, both X and Y are of shape $N \times 2$:

$$X = \begin{bmatrix} x_{11} & x_{12} \\ \vdots & \vdots \\ x_{N1} & x_{N2} \end{bmatrix} \qquad Y = \begin{bmatrix} y_{11} & y_{12} \\ \vdots & \vdots \\ y_{N1} & y_{N2} \end{bmatrix}$$

We will generate 50,000 random binary samples in the form of two concentric circles with different radius using scikit-learn's `make_circles` function so that the classes are not linearly separable:

```
N = 50000
factor = 0.1
noise = 0.1

X, y = make_circles(n_samples=N, shuffle=True,
                    factor=factor, noise=noise)
```

We then convert the one-dimensional output into a two-dimensional array:

```
Y = np.zeros((N, 2))
for c in [0, 1]:
    Y[y == c, c] = 1
'Shape of: X: (50000, 2) | Y: (50000, 2) | y: (50000,)'
```

Figure 17.3 shows a scatterplot of the data that is clearly not linearly separable:

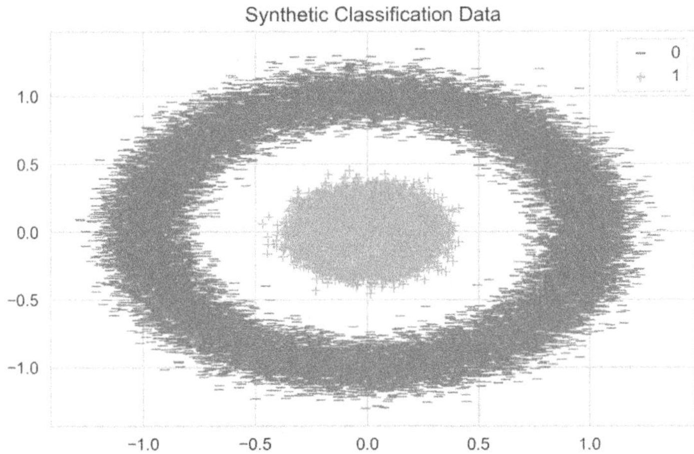

Figure 17.3: Synthetic data for binary classification

The hidden layer

The hidden layer h projects the two-dimensional input into a three-dimensional space using the weights W^h and translates the result by the bias vector b^h. To perform this affine transformation, the hidden layer weights are represented by a 2 × 3 matrix W^h, and the hidden layer bias vector by a three-dimensional vector:

$$\underset{2\times 3}{\mathbf{W}^h} = \begin{bmatrix} w^h{}_{11} & w^h{}_{12} & w^h{}_{13} \\ w^h{}_{21} & w^h{}_{22} & w^h{}_{23} \end{bmatrix} \quad \underset{1\times 3}{\mathbf{b}^h} \begin{bmatrix} b^h{}_1 & b^h{}_2 & b^h{}_3 \end{bmatrix}$$

The hidden layer activations H result from the application of the sigmoid function to the dot product of the input data and the weights after adding the bias vector:

$$\underset{N\times 3}{\mathbf{H}} = \sigma(\mathrm{X}\cdot\mathrm{W}^h + b^h) = \frac{1}{1+e^{-(\mathrm{X}\cdot\mathrm{W}^h+b^h)}} = \begin{bmatrix} h_{11} & h_{12} & h_{13} \\ \vdots & \vdots & \vdots \\ h_{N1} & h_{N2} & h_{N3} \end{bmatrix}$$

To implement the hidden layer using NumPy, we first define the `logistic` sigmoid function:

```
def logistic(z):
    """Logistic function."""
    return 1 / (1 + np.exp(-z))
```

We then define a function that computes the hidden layer activations as a function of the relevant inputs, weights, and bias values:

```
def hidden_layer(input_data, weights, bias):
    """Compute hidden activations"""
    return logistic(input_data @ weights + bias)
```

The output layer

The output layer compresses the three-dimensional hidden layer activations H back to two dimensions using a 3×2 weight matrix W^o and a two-dimensional bias vector $\mathbf{b}^o$:

$$\underset{3\times 2}{\mathbf{W}^o} = \begin{bmatrix} \mathrm{w}^o{}_{11} & \mathrm{w}^o{}_{12} \\ \mathrm{w}^o{}_{21} & \mathrm{w}^o{}_{22} \\ \mathrm{w}^o{}_{31} & \mathrm{w}^o{}_{32} \end{bmatrix} \qquad \underset{1\times 2}{\mathbf{b}^o} = [\mathrm{b}^o{}_1 \quad \mathrm{b}^o{}_2]$$

The linear combination of the hidden layer outputs results in an $N \times 2$ matrix $\mathbf{Z}^o$:

$$\underset{N\times 2}{\mathbf{Z}^o} = \underset{N\times 3}{\mathbf{H}} \cdot \underset{3\times 2}{\mathbf{W}^o} + \underset{1\times 2}{\mathbf{b}^o}$$

The output layer activations are computed by the softmax function ς that normalizes the $\mathbf{Z}^o$ to conform to the conventions used for discrete probability distributions:

$$\underset{N\times 2}{\mathbf{Y}} = \varsigma(\mathbf{H} \cdot \mathbf{W}^o + \mathbf{b}^o) = \begin{bmatrix} y_{11} & y_{12} \\ \vdots & \vdots \\ y_{n1} & y_{n2} \end{bmatrix}$$

We create a softmax function in Python as follows:

```
def softmax(z):
    """Softmax function"""
    return np.exp(z) / np.sum(np.exp(z), axis=1, keepdims=True)
```

As defined here, the output layer activations depend on the hidden layer activations and the output layer weights and biases:

```
def output_layer(hidden_activations, weights, bias):
    """Compute the output y_hat"""
    return softmax(hidden_activations @ weights + bias)
```

Now we have all the components we need to integrate the layers and compute the NN output directly from the input.

Forward propagation

The `forward_prop` function combines the previous operations to yield the output activations from the input data as a function of weights and biases:

```
def forward_prop(data, hidden_weights, hidden_bias, output_weights, output_
bias):
    """Neural network as function."""
    hidden_activations = hidden_layer(data, hidden_weights, hidden_bias)
    return output_layer(hidden_activations, output_weights, output_bias)
```

The `predict` function produces the binary class predictions given weights, biases, and input data:

```
def predict(data, hidden_weights, hidden_bias, output_weights, output_bias):
    """Predicts class 0 or 1"""
    y_pred_proba = forward_prop(data,
                                hidden_weights,
                                hidden_bias,
                                output_weights,
                                output_bias)
    return np.around(y_pred_proba)
```

The cross-entropy cost function

The final piece is the cost function to evaluate the NN output based on the given label. The cost function J uses the cross-entropy loss ξ, which sums the deviations of the predictions for each class c from the actual outcome:

$$J(\mathbf{Y}, \hat{\mathbf{Y}}) = \sum_{i=1}^{n} \xi(y_i, \hat{y}_i) = -\sum_{i=1}^{N} \sum_{i=c}^{C} y_{ic} \cdot log(\hat{y}_{ic})$$

It takes the following form in Python:

```
def loss(y_hat, y_true):
    """Cross-entropy"""
    return - (y_true * np.log(y_hat)).sum()
```

How to implement backprop using Python

To update the NN weights and bias values using backprop, we need to compute the gradient of the cost function. The gradient represents the partial derivative of the cost function with respect to the target parameter.

How to compute the gradient

The NN composes a set of nested functions as highlighted earlier. Hence, the gradient of the loss function with respect to internal, hidden parameters is computed using the chain rule of calculus.

For scalar values, given the functions $z = h(x)$ and $y = o(h(x)) = o\ (z)$, we compute the derivative of y with respect to x using the chain rule as follows:

$$\frac{dy}{dx} = \frac{dy}{dz}\frac{dz}{dx}$$

For vectors, with $z \in R^m$ and $x \in R^n$ so that the hidden layer h maps from R^n to R^m and $z = h(x)$ and $y = o\ (z)$, we get:

$$\frac{\partial y}{\partial x_i} = \sum_j \frac{\partial y}{\partial z_j}\frac{\partial z_j}{\partial x_i}$$

We can express this more concisely using matrix notation using the $m \times n$ Jacobian matrix of h:

$$m \times n\frac{dz}{dx}$$

which contains the partial derivatives for each of the m components of z with respect to each of the n inputs x. The gradient ∇ of y with respect to x contains all partial derivatives and can thus be written as:

$$\nabla_{\mathbf{x}} y = \left(\frac{dz}{dx}\right)^T \nabla_{\mathbf{z}} y$$

The loss function gradient

The derivative of the cross-entropy loss function J with respect to each output layer activation $i = 1, ..., N$ is a very simple expression (see the notebook for details), shown below on the left for scalar values and on the right in matrix notation:

$$\frac{\partial J}{\partial {z_i}^0} = \hat{y}_i - y_i \qquad \nabla_{\mathbf{z}^0} J = \hat{\mathbf{Y}} - \mathbf{Y} = \delta^0$$

We define `loss_gradient` function accordingly:

```
def loss_gradient(y_hat, y_true):
    """output layer gradient"""
    return y_hat - y_true
```

The output layer gradients

To propagate the update back to the output layer weights, we use the gradient of the loss function J with respect to the weight matrix:

$$\frac{\partial J}{\partial \mathbf{W}^0} = H^T \cdot \left(\hat{\mathbf{Y}} - \mathbf{Y}\right) = H^T \cdot \delta^0$$

and for the bias:

$$\frac{\partial J}{\partial \mathbf{b}^0} = \frac{\partial J}{\partial Y}\frac{\partial Y}{\partial Z^0}\frac{\partial Z^0}{\partial \mathbf{b}^0} = \sum_{i=1}^{N} 1 \cdot (\hat{\mathbf{y}}_i - \mathbf{y}_i) = \sum_{i=1}^{N} \delta_i^{\ 0}$$

We can now define `output_weight_gradient` and `output_bias_gradient` accordingly, both taking the loss gradient δ^0 as input:

```
def output_weight_gradient(H, loss_grad):
    """Gradients for the output layer weights"""
    return  H.T @ loss_grad

def output_bias_gradient(loss_grad):
    """Gradients for the output layer bias"""
    return np.sum(loss_grad, axis=0, keepdims=True)
```

The hidden layer gradients

The gradient of the loss function with respect to the hidden layer values computes as follows, where $\circ$ refers to the element-wise matrix product:

$$\nabla_{\mathbf{Z}^h} J = \mathbf{H} \circ (1 - \mathbf{H}) \circ [\delta_0 \cdot (\mathbf{W}^0)^T] = \delta_h$$

We define a `hidden_layer_gradient` function to encode this result:

```
def hidden_layer_gradient(H, out_weights, loss_grad):
    """Error at the hidden layer.
    H * (1-H) * (E . Wo^T)"""
    return H * (1 - H) * (loss_grad @ out_weights.T)
```

The gradients for hidden layer weights and biases are:

$$\nabla_{\mathbf{W}^h} J = \mathbf{X}^T \cdot \delta^h \qquad \nabla_{\mathbf{b}^h} J = \sum_{j=1}^{N} \delta_{hj}$$

The corresponding functions are:

```
def hidden_weight_gradient(X, hidden_layer_grad):
    """Gradient for the weight parameters at the hidden layer"""
    return X.T @ hidden_layer_grad

def hidden_bias_gradient(hidden_layer_grad):
    """Gradient for the bias parameters at the output layer"""
    return np.sum(hidden_layer_grad, axis=0, keepdims=True)
```

Putting it all together

To prepare for the training of our network, we create a function that combines the previous gradient definition and computes the relevant weight and bias updates from the training data and labels, and the current weight and bias values:

```
def compute_gradients(X, y_true, w_h, b_h, w_o, b_o):
    """Evaluate gradients for parameter updates"""

    # Compute hidden and output layer activations
    hidden_activations = hidden_layer(X, w_h, b_h)
    y_hat = output_layer(hidden_activations, w_o, b_o)

    # Compute the output layer gradients
    loss_grad = loss_gradient(y_hat, y_true)
    out_weight_grad = output_weight_gradient(hidden_activations, loss_grad)
    out_bias_grad = output_bias_gradient(loss_grad)
    # Compute the hidden layer gradients
    hidden_layer_grad = hidden_layer_gradient(hidden_activations,
                                              w_o, loss_grad)
    hidden_weight_grad = hidden_weight_gradient(X, hidden_layer_grad)
    hidden_bias_grad = hidden_bias_gradient(hidden_layer_grad)

    return [hidden_weight_grad, hidden_bias_grad, out_weight_grad, out_bias_grad]
```

Testing the gradients

The notebook contains a test function that compares the gradient derived previously analytically using multivariate calculus to a numerical estimate that we obtain by slightly perturbing individual parameters. The test function validates that the resulting change in output value is similar to the change estimated by the analytical gradient.

Implementing momentum updates using Python

To incorporate momentum into the parameter updates, define an `update_momentum` function that combines the results of the `compute_gradients` function we just used with the most recent momentum updates for each parameter matrix:

```
def update_momentum(X, y_true, param_list, Ms, momentum_term, learning_rate):
    """Compute updates with momentum."""
    gradients = compute_gradients(X, y_true, *param_list)
    return [momentum_term * momentum - learning_rate * grads
            for momentum, grads in zip(Ms, gradients)]
```

The `update_params` function performs the actual updates:

```
def update_params(param_list, Ms):
    """Update the parameters."""
    return [P + M for P, M in zip(param_list, Ms)]
```

Training the network

To train the network, we first randomly initialize all network parameters using a standard normal distribution (see the notebook). For a given number of iterations or epochs, we run momentum updates and compute the training loss as follows:

```
def train_network(iterations=1000, lr=.01, mf=.1):
    # Initialize weights and biases
    param_list = list(initialize_weights())

    # Momentum Matrices = [MWh, Mbh, MWo, Mbo]
    Ms = [np.zeros_like(M) for M in param_list]

    train_loss = [loss(forward_prop(X, *param_list), Y)]
    for i in range(iterations):
        # Update the moments and the parameters
        Ms = update_momentum(X, Y, param_list, Ms, mf, lr)
        param_list = update_params(param_list, Ms)
        train_loss.append(loss(forward_prop(X, *param_list), Y))

    return param_list, train_loss
```

Figure 17.4 plots the training loss over 50,000 iterations for 50,000 training samples with a momentum term of 0.5 and a learning rate of 1e-4. It shows that it takes over 5,000 iterations for the loss to start to decline but then does so very fast. We have not used SGD, which would have likely accelerated convergence significantly.

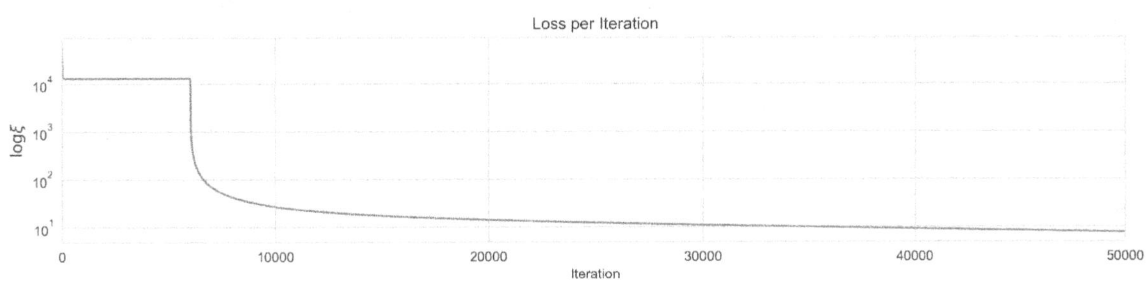

Figure 17.4: Training loss per iteration

The plots in *Figure 17.5* show the function learned by the neural network with a three-dimensional hidden layer from two-dimensional data with two classes that are not linearly separable. The left panel displays the source data and the decision boundary that misclassifies very few data points and would further improve with continued training.

The center panel shows the representation of the input data learned by the hidden layer. The network learns weights so that the projection of the input from two to three dimensions enables the linear separation of the two classes. The right plot shows how the output layer implements the linear separation in the form of a cutoff value of 0.5 in the output dimension:

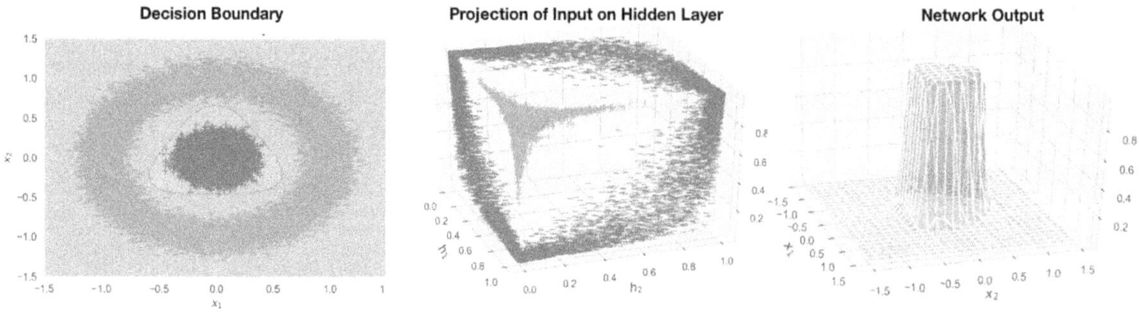

Figure 17.5: Visualizing the function learned by the neural network

To **sum up**: we have seen how a very simple network with a single hidden layer with three nodes and a total of 17 parameters is able to learn how to solve a nonlinear classification problem using backprop and gradient descent with momentum.

We will next review how to use popular DL libraries that facilitate the design and fast training of complex architectures while using sophisticated techniques to prevent overfitting and evaluate the results.

Popular deep learning libraries

Currently, the most popular DL libraries are TensorFlow (supported by Google), Keras (led by Francois Chollet, now at Google), and PyTorch (supported by Facebook). Development is very active with PyTorch at version 1.4 and TensorFlow at 2.2 as of March 2020. TensorFlow 2.0 adopted Keras as its main interface, effectively combining both libraries into one.

All libraries provide the design choices, regularization methods, and backprop optimizations we discussed previously in this chapter. They also facilitate fast training on one or several **graphics processing units** (**GPUs**). The libraries differ slightly in their focus with TensorFlow originally designed for deployment in production and prevalent in the industry, while PyTorch has been popular among academic researchers; however, the interfaces are gradually converging.

We will illustrate the use of TensorFlow and PyTorch using the same network architecture and dataset as in the previous section.

Leveraging GPU acceleration

DL is very computationally intensive, and good results often require large datasets. As a result, model training and evaluation can become rather time-consuming. GPUs are highly optimized for the matrix operations required by deep learning models and tend to have more processing power, rendering speedups of 10x or more not uncommon.

All popular deep learning libraries support the use of a GPU, and some also allow for parallel training on multiple GPUs. The most common types of GPU are produced by NVIDIA, and configuration requires installation and setup of the CUDA environment. The process continues to evolve and can be somewhat challenging depending on your computational environment.

A more straightforward way to leverage GPU is via the Docker virtualization platform. There are numerous images available that you can run in a local container managed by Docker that circumvents many of the driver and version conflicts that you may otherwise encounter. TensorFlow provides Docker images on its website that can also be used with Keras.

See GitHub for references and related instructions in the DL notebooks and the installation directory.

How to use TensorFlow 2

TensorFlow became the leading deep learning library shortly after its release in September 2015, one year before PyTorch. TensorFlow 2 simplified the API that had grown increasingly complex over time by making the Keras API its principal interface.

Keras was designed as a high-level API to accelerate the iterative workflow of designing and training deep neural networks with computational backends like TensorFlow, Theano, or CNTK. It has been integrated into TensorFlow in 2017. You can also combine code from both libraries to leverage Keras' high-level abstractions as well as customized TensorFlow graph operations.

In addition, TensorFlow adopts **eager execution**. Previously, you needed to define a complete computational graph for compilation into optimized operations. Running the compiled graph required the configuration of a session and the provision of the requisite data. Under eager execution, you can run TensorFlow operations on a line-by-line basis just like common Python code.

Keras supports both a slightly simpler Sequential API and a more flexible Functional API. We will introduce the former at this point and use the Functional API in more complex examples in the following chapters.

To create a model, we just need to instantiate a `Sequential` object and provide a list with the sequence of standard layers and their configurations, including the number of units, type of activation function, or name.

The first hidden layer needs information about the number of features in the matrix it receives from the input layer via the `input_shape` argument. In our simple case, there are just two. Keras infers the number of rows it needs to process during training, through the `batch_size` argument that we will pass to the `fit` method later in this section. TensorFlow infers the sizes of the inputs received by other layers from the previous layer's `units` argument:

```
from tensorflow.keras.models import Sequential
from tensorflow.keras.layers import Dense, Activation
```

```
model = Sequential([
    Dense(units=3, input_shape=(2,), name='hidden'),
    Activation('sigmoid', name='logistic'),
    Dense(2, name='output'),
    Activation('softmax', name='softmax'),
])
```

The Keras API provides numerous standard building blocks, including recurrent and convolutional layers, various options for regularization, a range of loss functions and optimizers, and also preprocessing, visualization, and logging (see the link to the TensorFlow documentation on GitHub for reference). It is also extensible.

The model's `summary` method produces a concise description of the network architecture, including a list of the layer types and shapes and the number of parameters:

```
model.summary()

Layer (type)                 Output Shape              Param #
=================================================================
hidden (Dense)               (None, 3)                 9
_________________________________________________________________
logistic (Activation)        (None, 3)                 0
_________________________________________________________________
output (Dense)               (None, 2)                 8
_________________________________________________________________
softmax (Activation)         (None, 2)                 0
=================================================================
Total params: 17
Trainable params: 17
Non-trainable params: 0
```

Next, we compile the Sequential model to configure the learning process. To this end, we define the optimizer, the loss function, and one or several performance metrics to monitor during training:

```
model.compile(optimizer='rmsprop',
              loss='binary_crossentropy',
              metrics=['accuracy'])
```

Keras uses callbacks to enable certain functionality during training, such as logging information for interactive display in TensorBoard (see the next section):

```
tb_callback = TensorBoard(log_dir='./tensorboard',
                          histogram_freq=1,
                          write_graph=True,
                          write_images=True)
```

To train the model, we call its `fit` method and pass several parameters in addition to the training data:

```
model.fit(X, Y,
          epochs=25,
          validation_split=.2,
          batch_size=128,
          verbose=1,
          callbacks=[tb_callback])
```

See the notebook for a visualization of the decision boundary that resembles the result from our earlier manual network implementation. The training with TensorFlow runs orders of magnitude faster, though.

How to use TensorBoard

TensorBoard is a great suite of visualization tools that comes with TensorFlow. It includes visualization tools to simplify the understanding, debugging, and optimization of NNs.

You can use it to visualize the computational graph, plot various execution and performance metrics, and even visualize image data processed by the network. It also permits comparisons of different training runs.

When you run the `how_to_use_tensorflow` notebook, with TensorFlow installed, you can launch TensorBoard from the command line:

```
tensorboard --logdir=/full_path_to_your_logs ## e.g. ./tensorboard
```

Alternatively, you can use it within your notebook by first loading the extension and then starting TensorBoard similarly by referencing the `log` directory:

```
%load_ext tensorboard
%tensorboard --logdir tensorboard/
```

For starters, the visualizations include train and validation metrics (see the left panel of *Figure 17.6*).

In addition, you can view histograms of the weights and biases over various epochs (right panel of Figure 17.6; epochs evolve from back to front). This is useful because it allows you to monitor whether backpropagation succeeds in adjusting the weights as learning progresses and whether they are converging.

The values of weights should change from their initialization values over the course of several epochs and eventually stabilize:

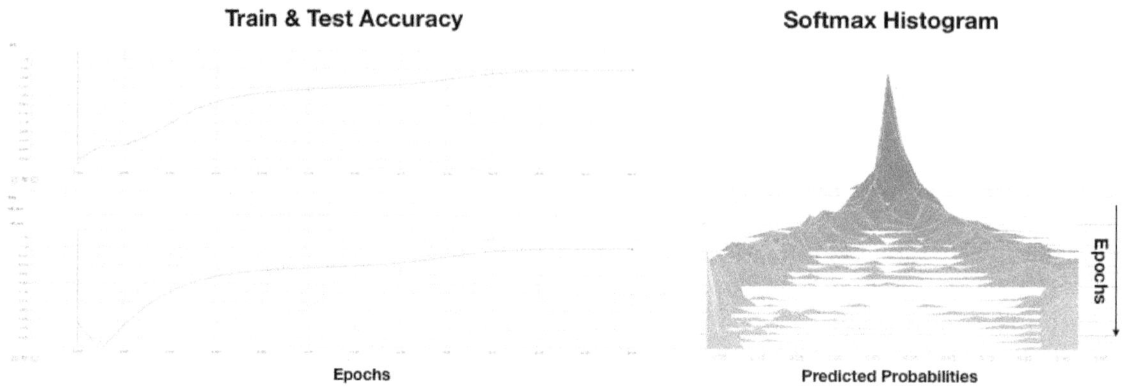

Figure 17.6: TensorBoard learning process visualization

TensorBoard also lets you display and interactively explore the computational graph of your network, drilling down from the high-level structure to the underlying operations by clicking on the various nodes. The visualization for our simple example architecture (see the notebook) already includes numerous components but is very useful when debugging. For further reference, see the links on GitHub to more detailed tutorials.

How to use PyTorch 1.4

PyTorch was developed at the **Facebook AI Research** (**FAIR**) group led by Yann LeCunn, and the first alpha version released in September 2016. It provides deep integration with Python libraries like NumPy that can be used to extend its functionality, strong GPU acceleration, and automatic differentiation using its autograd system. It provides more granular control than Keras through a lower-level API and is mainly used as a deep learning research platform but can also replace NumPy while enabling GPU computation.

It employs eager execution, in contrast to the static computation graphs used by, for example, Theano or TensorFlow. Rather than initially defining and compiling a network for fast but static execution, it relies on its autograd package for automatic differentiation of tensor operations; that is, it computes gradients "on the fly" so that network structures can be partially modified more easily. This is called **define-by-run**, meaning that backpropagation is defined by how your code runs, which in turn implies that every single iteration can be different. The PyTorch documentation provides a detailed tutorial on this.

The resulting flexibility combined with an intuitive Python-first interface and speed of execution has contributed to its rapid rise in popularity and led to the development of numerous supporting libraries that extend its functionality.

Let's see how PyTorch and autograd work by implementing our simple network architecture (see the `how_to_use_pytorch` notebook for details).

How to create a PyTorch DataLoader

We begin by converting the NumPy or pandas input data to `torch` tensors. Conversion from and to NumPy is very straightforward:

```
import torch
X_tensor = torch.from_numpy(X)
y_tensor = torch.from_numpy(y)

X_tensor.shape, y_tensor.shape
(torch.Size([50000, 2]), torch.Size([50000]))
```

We can use these PyTorch tensors to instantiate first a `TensorDataset` and, in a second step, a `DataLoader` that includes information about `batch_size`:

```
import torch.utils.data as utils

dataset = utils.TensorDataset(X_tensor,y_tensor)
dataloader = utils.DataLoader(dataset,
                              batch_size=batch_size,
                              shuffle=True)
```

How to define the neural network architecture

PyTorch defines an NN architecture using the `Net()` class. The central element is the `forward` function. autograd automatically defines the corresponding `backward` function that computes the gradients.

Any legal tensor operation is fair game for the `forward` function, providing a log of design flexibility. In our simple case, we just link the tensor through functional input-output relations after initializing their attributes:

```
import torch.nn as nn

class Net(nn.Module):
    def __init__(self, input_size, hidden_size, num_classes):
        super(Net, self).__init__()  # Inherited from nn.Module
        self.fc1 = nn.Linear(input_size, hidden_size)
        self.logistic = nn.LogSigmoid()
        self.fc2 = nn.Linear(hidden_size, num_classes)
        self.softmax = nn.Softmax(dim=1)

    def forward(self, x):
        """Forward pass: stacking each layer together"""
        out = self.fc1(x)
        out = self.logistic(out)
        out = self.fc2(out)
        out = self.softmax(out)
        return out
```

We then instantiate a `Net()` object and can inspect the architecture as follows:

```
net = Net(input_size, hidden_size, num_classes)
net
Net(
  (fc1): Linear(in_features=2, out_features=3, bias=True)
  (logistic): LogSigmoid()
  (fc2): Linear(in_features=3, out_features=2, bias=True)
  (softmax): Softmax()
)
```

To illustrate eager execution, we can also inspect the initialized parameters in the first tensor:

```
list(net.parameters())[0]
Parameter containing:
tensor([[ 0.3008, -0.2117],
        [-0.5846, -0.1690],
        [-0.6639,  0.1887]], requires_grad=True)
```

To enable GPU processing, you can use `net.cuda()`. See the PyTorch documentation for placing tensors on CPU and/or one or more GPU units.

We also need to define a loss function and the optimizer, using some of the built-in options:

```
criterion = nn.CrossEntropyLoss()
optimizer = torch.optim.Adam(net.parameters(), lr=learning_rate)
```

How to train the model

Model training consists of an outer loop for each epoch, that is, each pass over the training data, and an inner loop over the batches produced by the `DataLoader`. That executes the forward and backward passes of the learning algorithm. Some care needs to be taken to adjust data types to the requirements of the various objects and functions; for example, labels need to be integers and the features should be of type `float`:

```
for epoch in range(num_epochs):
    print(epoch)
    for i, (features, label) in enumerate(dataloader):

        features = Variable(features.float())
        label = Variable(label.long())

        # Initialize the hidden weights
        optimizer.zero_grad()

        # Forward pass: compute output given features
        outputs = net(features)
```

```
        # Compute the Loss
        loss = criterion(outputs, label)
        # Backward pass: compute the gradients
        loss.backward()
        # Update the weights
        optimizer.step()
```

The notebook also contains an example that uses the `livelossplot` package to plot losses throughout the training process as provided by Keras out of the box.

How to evaluate the model predictions

To obtain predictions from our trained model, we pass it feature data and convert the prediction to a NumPy array. We get softmax probabilities for each of the two classes:

```
test_value = Variable(torch.from_numpy(X)).float()
prediction = net(test_value).data.numpy()
Prediction.shape
(50000, 2)
```

From here on, we can proceed as before to compute loss metrics or visualize the result that again reproduces a version of the decision boundary we found earlier.

Alternative options

The huge interest in DL has led to the development of several competing libraries that facilitate the design and training of NNs. The most prominent include the following examples (also see references on GitHub).

Apache MXNet

MXNet, incubated at the Apache Foundation, is an open source DL software framework used to train and deploy deep NNs. It focuses on scalability and fast model training. They included the Gluon high-level interface to make it easy to prototype, train, and deploy DL models. MXNet has been picked by Amazon for deep learning on AWS.

Microsoft Cognitive Toolkit (CNTK)

The Cognitive Toolkit, previously known as CNTK, is Microsoft's contribution to the deep learning library collection. It describes an NN as a series of computational steps via a directed graph, similar to TensorFlow. In this directed graph, leaf nodes represent input values or network parameters, while other nodes represent matrix operations upon their inputs. CNTK allows users to build and combine popular model architectures ranging from deep feedforward NNs, convolutional networks, and recurrent networks (RNNs/LSTMs).

Fastai

The fastai library aims to simplify training NNs that are fast and accurate using modern best practices. These practices have emerged from research into DL at the company that makes both the software and accompanying courses available for free. Fastai includes support for models that process image, text, tabular, and collaborative filtering data.

Optimizing an NN for a long-short strategy

In practice, we need to explore variations for the design options for the NN architecture and how we train it from those we outlined previously because we can never be sure from the outset which configuration best suits the data. In this section, we will explore various architectures for a simple feedforward NN to predict daily stock returns using the dataset developed in *Chapter 12* (see the notebook `preparing_the_model_data` in the GitHub directory for that chapter).

To this end, we will define a function that returns a TensorFlow model based on several architectural input parameters and cross-validate alternative designs using the `MultipleTimeSeriesCV` we introduced in *Chapter 7, Linear Models – From Risk Factors to Return Forecasts*. To assess the signal quality of the model predictions, we build a simple ranking-based long-short strategy based on an ensemble of the models that perform best during the in-sample cross-validation period. To limit the risk of false discoveries, we then evaluate the performance of this strategy for an out-of-sample test period.

See the `optimizing_a_NN_architecture_for_trading` notebook for details.

Engineering features to predict daily stock returns

To develop our trading strategy, we use the daily stock returns for 995 US stocks for the eight-year period from 2010 to 2017. We will use the features developed in *Chapter 12, Boosting Your Trading Strategy* that include volatility and momentum factors, as well as lagged returns with cross-sectional and sectoral rankings. We load the data as follows:

```
data = pd.read_hdf('../12_gradient_boosting_machines/data/data.h5',
                   'model_data').dropna()
outcomes = data.filter(like='fwd').columns.tolist()
lookahead = 1
outcome= f'r{lookahead:02}_fwd'
X = data.loc[idx[:, :'2017'], :].drop(outcomes, axis=1)
y = data.loc[idx[:, :'2017'], outcome]
```

Defining an NN architecture framework

To automate the generation of our TensorFlow model, we create a function that constructs and compiles the model based on arguments that can later be passed during cross-validation iterations.

The following `make_model` function illustrates how to flexibly define various architectural elements for the search process. The `dense_layers` argument defines both the depth and width of the network as a list of integers. We also use `dropout` for regularization, expressed as a float in the range [0, 1] to define the probability that a given unit will be excluded from a training iteration:

```
def make_model(dense_layers, activation, dropout):
    '''Creates a multi-layer perceptron model

    dense_layers: List of layer sizes; one number per layer
    '''

    model = Sequential()
    for i, layer_size in enumerate(dense_layers, 1):
        if i == 1:
            model.add(Dense(layer_size, input_dim=X_cv.shape[1]))
            model.add(Activation(activation))
        else:
            model.add(Dense(layer_size))
            model.add(Activation(activation))
    model.add(Dropout(dropout))
    model.add(Dense(1))

    model.compile(loss='mean_squared_error',
                  optimizer='Adam')

    return model
```

Now we can turn to the cross-validation process to evaluate various NN architectures.

Cross-validating design options to tune the NN

We use the `MultipleTimeSeriesCV` to split the data into rolling training and validation sets comprising of 24 * 12 months of data, while keeping the final 12 * 21 days of data (starting November 30, 2016) as a holdout test. We train each model for 48 21-day periods and evaluate its results over 3 21-day periods, implying 12 splits for cross-validation and test periods combined:

```
n_splits = 12
train_period_length=21 * 12 * 4
test_period_length=21 * 3
cv = MultipleTimeSeriesCV(n_splits=n_splits,
                          train_period_length=train_period_length,
                          test_period_length=test_period_length,
                          lookahead=lookahead)
```

Next, we define a set of configurations for cross-validation. These include several options for two hidden layers and dropout probabilities; we'll only use tanh activations because a trial run did not suggest significant differences compared to ReLU. (We could also try out different optimizers. but I recommend you do not run this experiment, to limit what is already a computationally intensive effort):

```
dense_layer_opts = [(16, 8), (32, 16), (32, 32), (64, 32)]
dropout_opts = [0, .1, .2]

param_grid = list(product(dense_layer_opts, activation_opts, dropout_opts))
np.random.shuffle(param_grid)
len(param_grid)
12
```

To run the cross-validation, we define a function that produces the train and validation data based on the integer indices produced by the `MultipleTimeSeriesCV` as follows:

```
def get_train_valid_data(X, y, train_idx, test_idx):
    x_train, y_train = X.iloc[train_idx, :], y.iloc[train_idx]
    x_val, y_val = X.iloc[test_idx, :], y.iloc[test_idx]
    return x_train, y_train, x_val, y_val
```

During cross-validation, we train a model using one set of parameters from the previously defined grid for 20 epochs. After each epoch, we store a `checkpoint` that contains the learned weights that we can reload to quickly generate predictions for the best configuration without retraining.

After each epoch, we compute and store the **information coefficient** (**IC**) for the validation set by day:

```
ic = []
scaler = StandardScaler()
for params in param_grid:
    dense_layers, activation, dropout = params
    for batch_size in [64, 256]:
        checkpoint_path = checkpoint_dir / str(dense_layers) / activation /
                          str(dropout) / str(batch_size)
        for fold, (train_idx, test_idx) in enumerate(cv.split(X_cv)):
            x_train, y_train, x_val, y_val = get_train_valid_data(X_cv, y_cv,
                                             train_idx, test_idx)
            x_train = scaler.fit_transform(x_train)
            x_val = scaler.transform(x_val)
            preds = y_val.to_frame('actual')
            r = pd.DataFrame(index=y_val.groupby(level='date').size().index)
            model = make_model(dense_layers, activation, dropout)
            for epoch in range(20):
                model.fit(x_train, y_train,
```

```
                        batch_size=batch_size,
                        epochs=1, validation_data=(x_val, y_val))
            model.save_weights(
                (checkpoint_path / f'ckpt_{fold}_{epoch}').as_posix())
            preds[epoch] = model.predict(x_val).squeeze()
            r[epoch] = preds.groupby(level='date').apply(lambda x:
spearmanr(x.actual, x[epoch])[0]).to_frame(epoch)
        ic.append(r.assign(dense_layers=str(dense_layers),
                           activation=activation,
                           dropout=dropout,
                           batch_size=batch_size,
                           fold=fold))
```

With an NVIDIA GTX 1080 GPU, 20 epochs takes a bit over one hour with batches of 64 samples, and around 20 minutes with 256 samples.

Evaluating the predictive performance

Let's first take a look at the five models that achieved the highest median daily IC during the cross-validation period. The following code computes these values:

```
dates = sorted(ic.index.unique())
cv_period = 24 * 21
cv_dates = dates[:cv_period]
ic_cv = ic.loc[cv_dates]

(ic_cv.drop('fold', axis=1).groupby(params).median().stack()
 .to_frame('ic').reset_index().rename(columns={'level_3': 'epoch'})
 .nlargest(n=5, columns='ic'))
```

The resulting table shows that the architectures using 32 units in both layers and 16/8 in the first/second layer, respectively, performed best. These models also use `dropout` and were trained with batch sizes of 64 samples with the given number of epochs for all folds. The median IC values vary between 0.0236 and 0.0246:

Dense Layers	Dropout	Batch Size	Epoch	IC
(32, 32)	0.1	64	7	0.0246
(16, 8)	0.2	64	14	0.0241
(16, 8)	0.1	64	3	0.0238
(32, 32)	0.1	64	10	0.0237
(16, 8)	0.2	256	3	0.0236

Next, we'll take a look at how the parameter choices impact the predictive performance.

First, we visualize the daily information coefficient (averaged per fold) for different configurations by epoch to understand how the duration of training affects the predictive accuracy. The plots in *Figure 17.7*, however, highlight few conclusive patterns; the IC varies little across models and not particularly systematically across epochs:

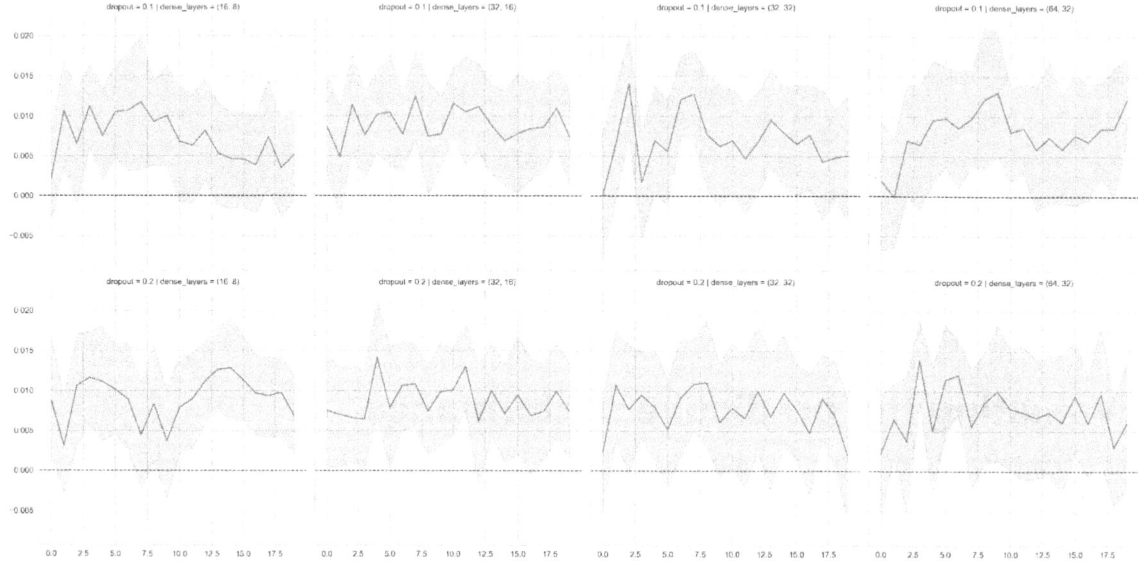

Figure 17.7: Information coefficients for various model configurations

For more statistically robust insights, we run a linear regression using **ordinary least squares (OLS)** (see *Chapter 7, Linear Models – From Risk Factors to Return Forecasts*) using dummy variables for the layer, dropout, and batch size choices as well as for each epoch:

```
data = pd.melt(ic, id_vars=params, var_name='epoch', value_name='ic')
data = pd.get_dummies(data, columns=['epoch'] + params, drop_first=True)
model = sm.OLS(endog=data.ic, exog=sm.add_constant(data.drop('ic', axis=1)))
```

The chart in *Figure 17.8* plots the confidence interval for each regression coefficient; if it does not include zero, then the coefficient is significant at the five percent level. The IC values on the y-axis reflect the differential from the constant (0.0027, p-value: 0.017) that represents the sample average over the configuration excluded while dropping one category of each dummy variable.

Across all configurations, batch size 256 and a dropout of 0.2 made significant (but small) positive contributions to performance. Similarly, training for seven epochs yielded slightly superior results. The regression is overall significant according to the F statistic but has a very low R2 value close to zero, underlining the high degree of noise in the data relative to the signal conveyed by the parameter choices.

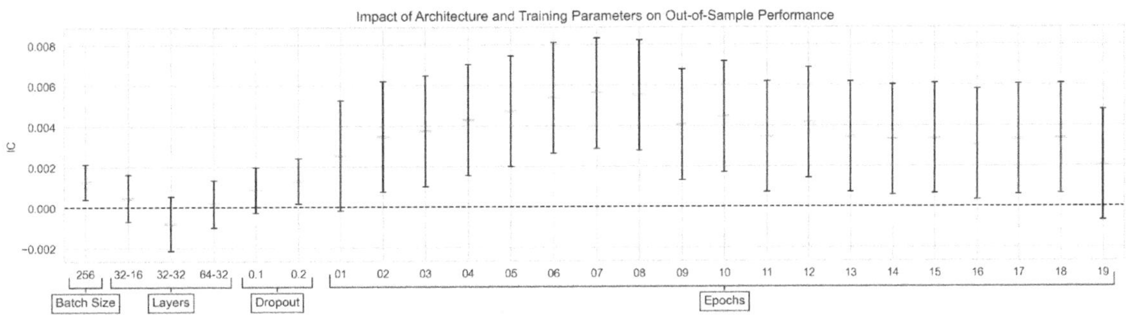

Figure 17.8: OLS coefficients and confidence intervals

Backtesting a strategy based on ensembled signals

To translate our NN model into a trading strategy, we generate predictions, evaluate their signal quality, create rules that define how to trade on these predictions, and backtest the performance of a strategy that implements these rules. See the notebook `backtesting_with_zipline` for the code examples in this section.

Ensembling predictions to produce tradeable signals

To reduce the variance of the predictions and hedge against in-sample overfitting, we combine the predictions of the best three models listed in the table in the previous section and average the result.

To this end, we define the following `generate_predictions()` function, which receives the model parameters as inputs, loads the weights for the models for the desired epoch, and creates forecasts for the cross-validation and out-of-sample periods (showing only the essentials here to save some space):

```
def generate_predictions(dense_layers, activation, dropout,
                         batch_size, epoch):
    checkpoint_dir = Path('logs')
    checkpoint_path = checkpoint_dir / dense_layers / activation /
                      str(dropout) / str(batch_size)

    for fold, (train_idx, test_idx) in enumerate(cv.split(X_cv)):
        x_train, y_train, x_val, y_val = get_train_valid_data(X_cv, y_cv,
                                                              train_idx,
                                                              test_idx)
        x_val = scaler.fit(x_train).transform(x_val)
        model = make_model(dense_layers, activation, dropout, input_dim)
```

```
        status = model.load_weights(
            (checkpoint_path / f'ckpt_{fold}_{epoch}').as_posix())
        status.expect_partial()
        predictions.append(pd.Series(model.predict(x_val).squeeze(),
                                     index=y_val.index))
    return pd.concat(predictions)
```

We store the results for evaluation with Alphalens and a Zipline backtest.

Evaluating signal quality using Alphalens

To gain some insight into the signal content of the ensembled model predictions, we use Alphalens to compute the return differences for investments into five equal-weighted portfolios differentiated by the forecast quantiles (see *Figure 17.9*). The spread between the top and the bottom quintile equals around 8 bps for a one-day holding period, which implies an alpha of 0.094 and a beta of 0.107:

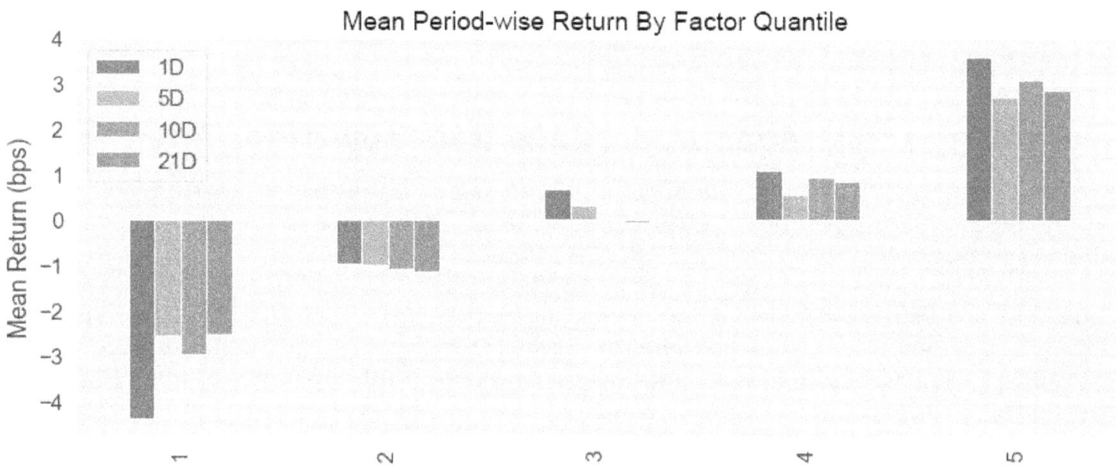

Figure 17.9: Signal quality evaluation

Backtesting the strategy using Zipline

Based on the Alphalens analysis, our strategy will enter long and short positions for the 50 stocks with the highest positive and lowest negative predicted returns, respectively, as long as there are at least 10 options on either side. The strategy trades every day.

The charts in *Figure 17.10* show that the strategy performs well in- and out-of-sample (before transaction costs):

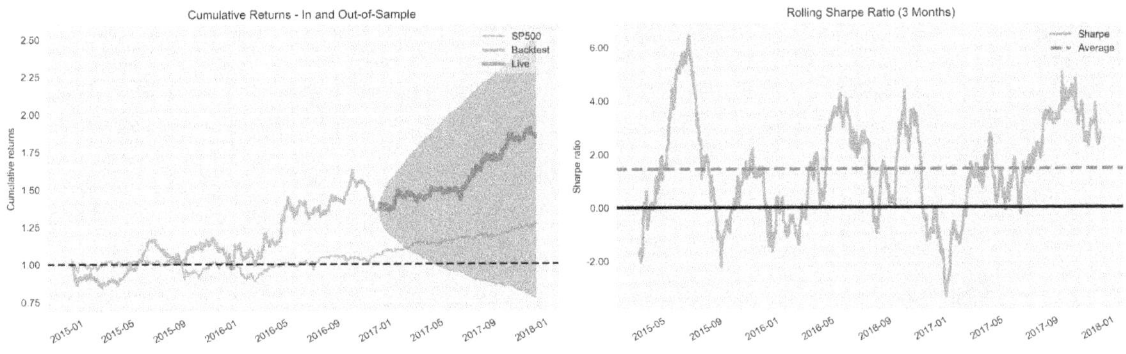

Figure 17.10: In- and out-of-sample backtest performance

It produces annualized returns of 22.8 percent over the 36-month period, 16.5 percent for the 24 in-sample months, and 35.7 percent for the 12 out-of-sample months. The Sharpe ratio is 0.72 in-sample and 2.15 out-of-sample, delivering an alpha of 0.18 (0.29) and a beta of 0.24 (0.16) in/out of sample.

How to further improve the results

The relatively simple architecture yields some promising results. To further improve performance, you can first and foremost add new features and more data to the model.

Alternatively, you can use more sophisticated architectures, including RNNs and CNNs, which are well suited to sequential data, whereas vanilla feedforward NNs are not designed to capture the ordered nature of the features.

We will turn to these specialized architectures in the following chapter.

Summary

In this chapter, we introduced DL as a form of representation learning that extracts hierarchical features from high-dimensional, unstructured data. We saw how to design, train, and regularize feedforward neural networks using NumPy. We demonstrated how to use the popular DL libraries PyTorch and TensorFlow that are suitable for use cases from rapid prototyping to production deployments.

Most importantly, we designed and tuned an NN using TensorFlow and were able to generate tradeable signals that delivered attractive returns during both the in-sample and out-of-sample periods.

In the next chapter, we will explore CNNs, which are particularly well suited for image data but are also well-suited for sequential data.

18

CNNs for Financial Time Series and Satellite Images

In this chapter, we introduce the first of several specialized deep learning architectures that we will cover in *Part 4*. Deep **convolutional neural networks** (**CNNs**) have enabled superhuman performance in various computer vision tasks such as classifying images and video and detecting and recognizing objects in images. CNNs can also extract signals from time-series data that shares certain characteristics with image data and have been successfully applied to speech recognition (Abdel-Hamid et al. 2014). Moreover, they have been shown to deliver state-of-the-art performance on time-series classification across various domains (Ismail Fawaz et al. 2019).

CNNs are named after a linear algebra operation called a **convolution** that replaces the general matrix multiplication typical of feedforward networks (discussed in the last chapter) in at least one of their layers. We will show how convolutions work and why they are particularly well suited to data with a certain regular structure typically found in images but also present in time series.

Research into **CNN architectures** has proceeded very rapidly, and new architectures that improve benchmark performance continue to emerge. We will describe a set of building blocks consistently used by successful applications. We will also demonstrate how **transfer learning** can speed up learning by using pretrained weights for CNN layers closer to the input while fine-tuning the final layers to a specific task. We will also illustrate how to use CNNs for the specific computer vision task of **object detection**.

CNNs can help build a **trading strategy** by generating signals from images or (multiple) time-series data:

- **Satellite data** may signal future commodity trends, including the supply of certain crops or raw materials via aerial images of agricultural areas, mines, or transport networks like oil tankers. **Surveillance camera** footage, for example, from shopping malls, could be used to track and predict consumer activity.

- **Time-series data** encompasses a very broad range of data sources and CNNs have been shown to deliver high-quality classification results by exploiting their structural similarity with images.

We will create a trading strategy based on predictions of a CNN that uses time-series data that's been deliberately formatted like images and demonstrate how to build a CNN to classify satellite images.

More specifically, in this chapter, you will learn about the following:

- How CNNs employ several building blocks to efficiently model grid-like data
- Training, tuning, and regularizing CNNs for images and time-series data using TensorFlow
- Using transfer learning to streamline CNNs, even with less data
- Designing a trading strategy using return predictions by a CNN trained on time-series data formatted like images
- How to classify satellite images

> You can find the code samples for this chapter and links to additional resources in the corresponding directory of the GitHub repository. The notebooks include color versions of the images.

How CNNs learn to model grid-like data

CNNs are conceptually similar to feedforward **neural networks** (**NNs**): they consist of units with parameters called weights and biases, and the training process adjusts these parameters to optimize the network's output for a given input according to a loss function. They are most commonly used for classification. Each unit uses its parameters to apply a linear operation to the input data or activations received from other units, typically followed by a nonlinear transformation.

The overall network models a **differentiable function** that maps raw data, such as image pixels, to class probabilities using an output activation function like softmax. CNNs use an objective function such as cross-entropy loss to measure the quality of the output with a single metric. They also rely on the gradients of the loss with respect to the network parameter to learn via backpropagation.

Feedforward NNs with fully connected layers do not scale well to high-dimensional image data with a large number of pixel values. Even the low-resolution images included in the CIFAR-10 dataset that we'll use in the next section contain 32×32 pixels with up to 256 different color values represented by 8 bits each. With three channels, for example, for the red, green, and blue channels of the RGB color model, a single unit in a fully connected input layer implies $32 \times 32 \times 3=3,072$ weights. A more standard resolution of 640×480 pixels already yields closer to 1 million weights for a single input unit. Deep architectures with several layers of meaningful width quickly lead to an exploding number of parameters that make overfitting during training all but certain.

A fully connected feedforward NN makes no assumptions about the local structure of the input data so that arbitrarily reordering the features has no impact on the training result. By contrast, CNNs make the **key assumption** that the **data has a grid-like topology** and that the **local structure matters**. In other words, they encode the assumption that the input has a structure typically found in image data: pixels form a two-dimensional grid, possibly with several channels to represent the components of the color signal. Furthermore, the values of nearby pixels are likely more relevant to detect key features such as edges and corners than faraway data points. Naturally, initial CNN applications such as handwriting recognition focused on image data.

Over time, however, researchers recognized **similar characteristics in time-series data**, broadening the scope for the productive use of CNNs. Time-series data consists of measurements at regular intervals that create a one-dimensional grid along the time axis, such as the lagged returns for a given ticker. There can also be a second dimension with additional features for this ticker and the same time periods. Finally, we could represent additional tickers using the third dimension.

A common CNN use case beyond images includes audio data, either in a one-dimensional waveform in the time domain or, after a Fourier transform, as a two-dimensional spectrum in the frequency domain. CNNs also play a key role in AlphaGo, the first algorithm to win a game of Go against humans, where they evaluated different positions on the grid-like board.

The most important element to encode the **assumption of a grid-like topology** is the **convolution** operation that gives CNNs their name, combined with **pooling**. We will see that the specific assumptions about the functional relationship between input and output data imply that CNNs need far fewer parameters and compute more efficiently.

In this section, we will explain how convolution and pooling layers learn filters that extract local features and why these operations are particularly suitable for data with the structure just described. State-of-the-art CNNs combine many of these basic building blocks to achieve the layered representation learning described in the previous chapter. We conclude by describing key architectural innovations over the last decade that saw enormous performance improvements.

From hand-coding to learning filters from data

For image data, this local structure has traditionally motivated the development of hand-coded filters that extract such patterns for the use as features in **machine learning** (**ML**) models.

Figure 18.1 displays the effect of simple filters designed to detect certain edges. The notebook `filter_example.ipynb` illustrates how to use hand-coded filters in a convolutional network and visualizes the resulting transformation of the image. The filters are simple [-1, 1] patterns arranged in a 2 × 2 matrix, shown in the upper right of the figure. Below each filter, its effects are shown; they are a bit subtle and will be easier to spot in the accompanying notebook.

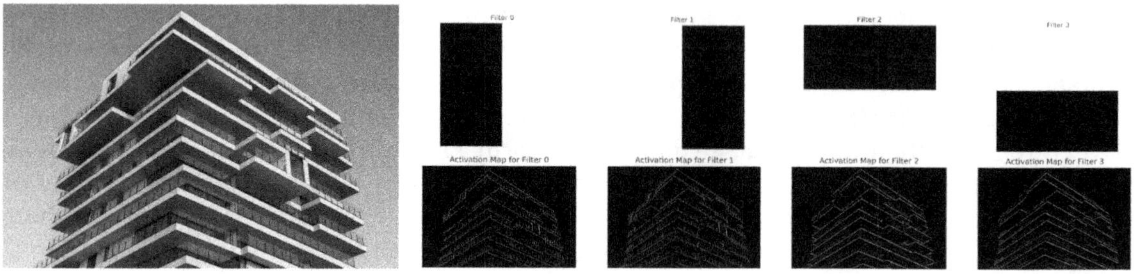

Figure 18.1: The result of basic edge filters applied to an image

Convolutional layers, by contrast, are designed to learn such local feature representations from the data. A key insight is to restrict their input, called the **receptive field**, to a small area of the input so it captures basic pixel constellations that reflect common patterns like edges or corners. Such patterns may occur anywhere in an image, though, so CNNs also need to recognize similar patterns in different locations and possibly with small variations.

Subsequent layers then learn to synthesize these local features to detect **higher-order features**. The linked resources on GitHub include examples of how to visualize the filters learned by a deep CNN using some of the deep architectures that we present in the next section on reference architectures.

How the elements of a convolutional layer operate

Convolutional layers integrate **three architectural ideas** that enable the learning of feature representations that are to some degree invariant to shifts, changes in scale, and distortion:

- Sparse rather than dense connectivity
- Weight sharing
- Spatial or temporal downsampling

Moreover, convolutional layers allow for inputs of variable size. We will walk through a typical convolutional layer and describe each of these ideas in turn.

Figure 18.2 outlines the set of operations that typically takes place in a three-dimensional convolutional layer, assuming image data is input with the three dimensions of height, width, and depth, or the number of channels. The range of pixel values depends on the bit representation, for example, [0, 255] for 8 bits. Alternatively, the width axis could represent time, the height different features, and the channels could capture observations on distinct objects such as tickers.

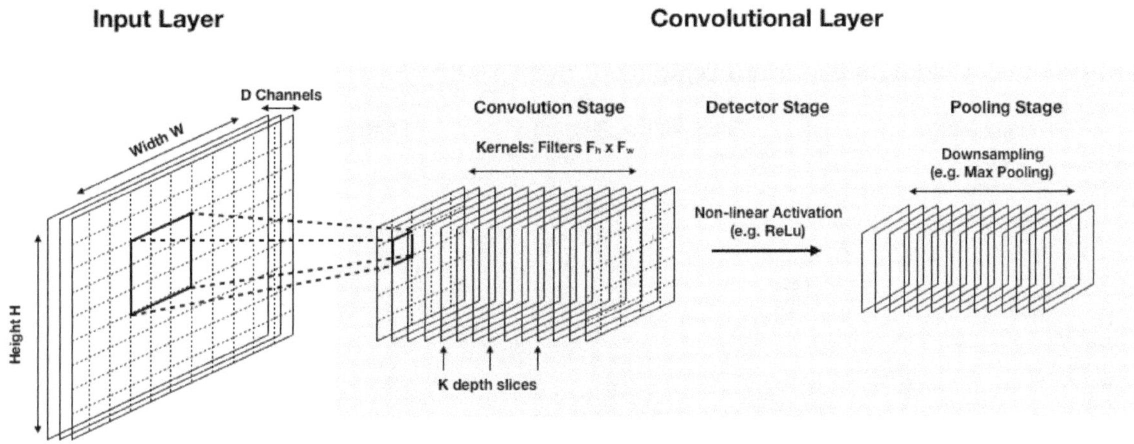

Figure 18.2: Typical operations in a two-dimensional convolutional layer

Successive computations process the input through the convolutional, detector, and pooling stages that we describe in the next three sections. In the example depicted in *Figure 18.2*, the convolutional layer receives three-dimensional input and produces an output of the same dimensionality.

State-of-the-art CNNs are composed of several such layers of varying sizes that are either stacked on top of each other or operate in parallel on different branches. With each layer, the network can detect higher-level, more abstract features.

The convolution stage – extracting local features

The first stage applies a filter, also called the **kernel**, to overlapping patches of the input image. The filter is a matrix of a much smaller size than the input so that its receptive field is limited to a few contiguous values such as pixels or time-series values. As a result, it focuses on local patterns and dramatically reduces the number of parameters and computations relative to a fully connected layer.

A complete convolutional layer has several **feature maps** organized as depth slices (depicted in *Figure 18.2*) so that each layer can extract multiple features.

From filters to feature maps

While scanning the input, the kernel is convolved with each input segment covered by its receptive field. The convolution operation is simply the dot product between the filter weights and the values of the matching input area after both have been reshaped to vectors. Each convolution thus produces a single number, and the entire scan yields a feature map. Since the dot product is maximized for identical vectors, the feature map indicates the degree of activation for each input region.

Figure 18.3 illustrates the result of the scan of a 5 × 5 input using a 3 × 3 filter with given values, and how the activation in the upper-right corner of the feature map results from the dot product of the flattened input region and the kernel:

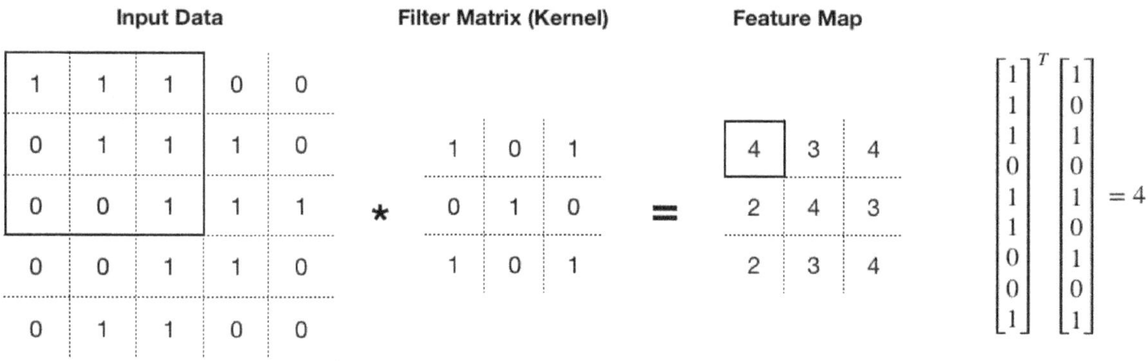

Figure 18.3: From convolutions to a feature map

The most important aspect is that the **filter values are the parameters** of the convolutional layers, **learned from the data** during training to minimize the chosen loss function. In other words, CNNs learn useful feature representations by finding kernel values that activate input patterns that are most useful for the task at hand.

How to scan the input – strides and padding

The **stride** defines the step size used for scanning the input, that is, the number of pixels to shift horizontally and vertically. Smaller strides scan more (overlapping) areas but are computationally more expensive. Four options are commonly used when the filter does not fit the input perfectly and partially crosses the image boundary during the scan:

- **Valid convolution**: Discards scans where the image and filter do not perfectly match
- **Same convolution**: Zero-pads the input to produce a feature map of equal size
- **Full convolution**: Zero-pads the input so that each pixel is scanned an equal number of times, including pixels at the border (to avoid oversampling pixels closer to the center)
- **Causal**: Zero-pads the input only on the left so that the output does not depend on an input from a later period; maintains the temporal order for time-series data

The choices depend on the nature of the data and where useful features are most likely located. In combination with the number of depth slices, they determine the output size of the convolution stage. The Stanford lecture notes by Andrew Karpathy (see GitHub) contain helpful examples using NumPy.

Parameter sharing for robust features and fast computation

The location of salient features may vary due to distortion or shifts. Furthermore, elementary feature detectors are likely useful across the entire image. CNNs encode these assumptions by sharing or tying the weights for the filter in a given depth slice.

As a result, each depth slice specializes in a certain pattern and the number of parameters is further reduced. Weight sharing works less well, however, when images are spatially centered and key patterns are less likely to be uniformly distributed across the input area.

The detector stage – adding nonlinearity

The feature maps are usually passed through a nonlinear transformation. The **rectified linear unit** (**ReLU**) that we encountered in the last chapter is a common function for this purpose. ReLUs replace negative activations element-wise by zero and mitigate the risk of vanishing gradients found in other activation functions such as tanh (see *Chapter 17*, *Deep Learning for Trading*).

A popular alternative is the **softplus function**:

$$f(x) = \ln(1 + e^x)$$

In contrast to ReLU, it has a derivative everywhere, namely the sigmoid function that we used for logistic regression (see *Chapter 7*, *Linear Models – From Risk Factors to Return Forecasts*).

The pooling stage – downsampling the feature maps

The last stage of the convolutional layer may downsample the feature map's input representation to do the following:

- Reduce its dimensionality and prevent overfitting
- Lower the computational cost
- Enable basic translation invariance

This assumes that the precise location of the features is not only less important for identifying a pattern but can even be harmful because it will likely vary for different instances of the target. Pooling lowers the spatial resolution of the feature map as a simple way to render the location information less precise. However, this step is optional and many architectures use pooling only for some layers or not at all.

A common pooling operation is **max pooling**, which uses only the maximum activation value from (typically) non-overlapping subregions. For a small 4×4 feature map, for instance, 2×2 max pooling outputs the maximum for each of the four non-overlapping 2×2 areas. Less common pooling operators use the average or the median. Pooling does not add or learn new parameters but the size of the input window and possibly the stride are additional hyperparameters.

The evolution of CNN architectures – key innovations

Several CNN architectures have pushed performance boundaries over the past two decades by introducing important innovations. Predictive performance growth accelerated dramatically with the arrival of big data in the form of ImageNet (Fei-Fei 2015) with 14 million images assigned to 20,000 classes by humans via Amazon's Mechanical Turk. The **ImageNet Large Scale Visual Recognition Challenge** (**ILSVRC**) became the focal point of CNN progress around a slightly smaller set of 1.2 million images from 1,000 classes.

It is useful to be familiar with the **reference architectures** dominating these competitions for practical reasons. As we will see in the next section on working with CNNs for image data, they offer a good starting point for standard tasks. Moreover, **transfer learning** allows us to address many computer vision tasks by building on a successful architecture with pretrained weights. Transfer learning not only speeds up architecture selection and training but also enables successful applications on much smaller datasets.

In addition, many publications refer to these architectures, and they often serve as a basis for networks tailored to segmentation or localization tasks. We will further describe some landmark architectures in the section on image classification and transfer learning.

Performance breakthroughs and network size

The left side of *Figure 18.4* plots the top-1 accuracy against the computational cost of a variety of network architectures. It suggests a positive relationship between the number of parameters and performance, but also shows that the marginal benefit of more parameters declines and that architectural design and innovation also matter.

The right side plots the top-1 accuracy per parameter for all networks. Several new architectures target use cases on less powerful devices such as mobile phones. While they do not achieve state-of-the-art performance, they have found much more efficient implementations. See the resources on GitHub for more details on these architectures and the analysis behind these charts.

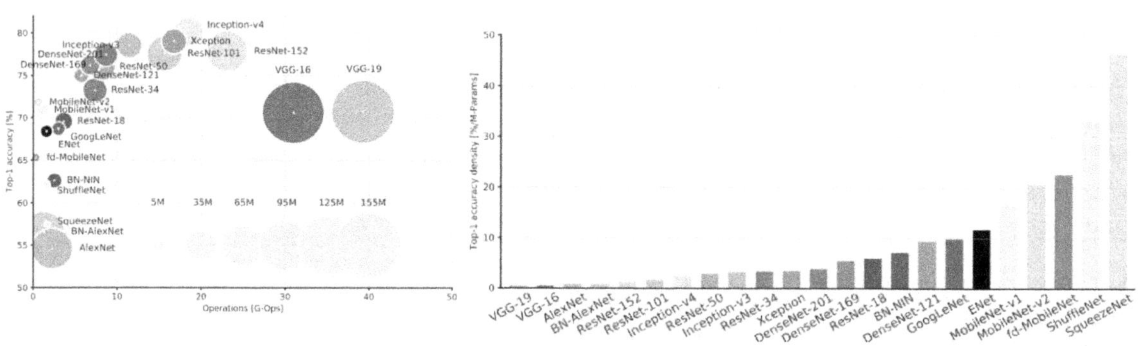

Figure 18.4: Predictive performance and computational complexity

Lessons learned

Some of the lessons learned from 20 years of CNN architecture developments, especially since 2012, include the following:

- **Smaller convolutional** filters perform better (possibly except at the first layer) because several small filters can substitute for a larger filter at a lower computational cost.
- **1 × 1 convolutions** reduce the dimensionality of feature maps so that the network can learn a larger number overall.
- **Skip connections** are able to create multiple paths through the network and enable the training of much higher-capacity CNNs.

CNNs for satellite images and object detection

In this section, we demonstrate how to solve key computer vision tasks such as image classification and object detection. As mentioned in the introduction and in *Chapter 3, Alternative Data for Finance – Categories and Use Cases*, image data can inform a trading strategy by providing clues about future trends, changing fundamentals, or specific events relevant to a target asset class or investment universe. Popular examples include exploiting satellite images for clues about the supply of agricultural commodities, consumer and economic activity, or the status of manufacturing or raw material supply chains. Specific tasks might include the following, for example:

- **Image classification**: Identifying whether cultivated land for certain crops is expanding, or predicting harvest quality and quantities
- **Object detection**: Counting the number of oil tankers on a certain transport route or the number of cars in a parking lot, or identifying the locations of shoppers in a mall

In this section, we'll demonstrate how to design CNNs to automate the extraction of such information, both from scratch using popular architectures and via transfer learning that fine-tunes pretrained weights to a given task. We'll also demonstrate how to detect objects in a given scene.

We will introduce key CNN architectures for these tasks, explain why they work well, and show how to train them using TensorFlow 2. We will also demonstrate how to source pretrained weights and fine-tune time. Unfortunately, satellite images with information directly relevant for a trading strategy are very costly to obtain and are not readily available. We will, however, demonstrate how to work with the EuroSat dataset to build a classifier that identifies different land uses. This brief introduction to CNNs for computer vision aims to demonstrate how to approach common tasks that you will likely need to tackle when aiming to design a trading strategy based on images relevant to the investment universe of your choice.

All the libraries we introduced in the last chapter provide support for convolutional layers; we'll focus on the Keras interface of TensorFlow 2. We are first going to illustrate the LeNet5 architecture using the MNIST handwritten digit dataset. Next, we'll demonstrate the use of data augmentation with AlexNet on CIFAR-10, a simplified version of the original ImageNet. Then we'll continue with transfer learning based on state-of-the-art architectures before we apply what we've learned to actual satellite images. We conclude with an example of object detection in real-life scenes.

LeNet5 – The first CNN with industrial applications

Yann LeCun, now the Director of AI Research at Facebook, was a leading pioneer in CNN development. In 1998, after several iterations starting in the 1980s, LeNet5 became the first modern CNN used in real-world applications that introduced several architectural elements still relevant today.

LeNet5 was published in a very instructive paper, *Gradient-Based Learning Applied to Document Recognition* (LeCun et al. 1989), that laid out many of the central concepts. Most importantly, it promoted the insight that convolutions with learnable filters are effective at extracting related features at multiple locations with few parameters. Given the limited computational resources at the time, efficiency was of paramount importance.

LeNet5 was designed to recognize the handwriting on checks and was used by several banks. It established a new benchmark for classification accuracy, with a result of 99.2 percent on the MNIST handwritten digit dataset. It consists of three convolutional layers, each containing a nonlinear tanh transformation, a pooling operation, and a fully connected output layer. Throughout the convolutional layers, the number of feature maps increases while their dimensions decrease. It has a total of 60,850 trainable parameters (Lecun et al. 1998).

"Hello World" for CNNs – handwritten digit classification

In this section, we'll implement a slightly simplified version of LeNet5 to demonstrate how to build a CNN using a TensorFlow implementation. The original MNIST dataset contains 60,000 grayscale images in 28 × 28 pixel resolution, each containing a single handwritten digit from 0 to 9. A good alternative is the more challenging but structurally similar Fashion MNIST dataset that we encountered in *Chapter 13, Data-Driven Risk Factors and Asset Allocation with Unsupervised Learning*. See the `digit_classification_with_lenet5` notebook for implementation details.

We can load it in Keras out of the box:

```
from tensorflow.keras.datasets import mnist
(X_train, y_train), (X_test, y_test) = mnist.load_data()
X_train.shape, X_test.shape
((60000, 28, 28), (10000, 28, 28))
```

Figure 18.5 shows the first ten images in the dataset and highlights significant variation among instances of the same digit. On the right, it shows how the pixel values for an individual image range from 0 to 255:

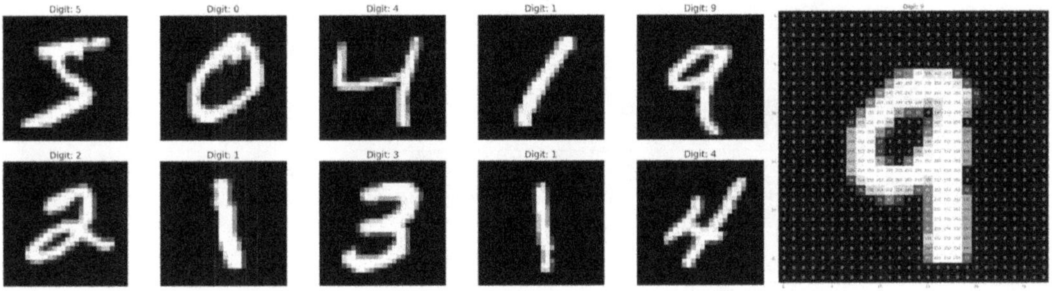

Figure 18.5: MNIST sample images

We rescale the pixel values to the range [0, 1] to normalize the training data and facilitate the backpropagation process and convert the data to 32-bit floats, which reduce memory requirements and computational cost while providing sufficient precision for our use case:

```
X_train = X_train.astype('float32')/255
X_test = X_test.astype('float32')/255
```

Defining the LeNet5 architecture

We can define a simplified version of LeNet5 that omits the original final layer containing radial basis functions as follows, using the default "valid" padding and single-step strides unless defined otherwise:

```
lenet5 = Sequential([
    Conv2D(filters=6, kernel_size=5, activation='relu',
           input_shape=(28, 28, 1), name='CONV1'),
    AveragePooling2D(pool_size=(2, 2), strides=(1, 1),
                     padding='valid', name='POOL1'),
    Conv2D(filters=16, kernel_size=(5, 5), activation='tanh', name='CONV2'),
    AveragePooling2D(pool_size=(2, 2), strides=(2, 2), name='POOL2'),
    Conv2D(filters=120, kernel_size=(5, 5), activation='tanh', name='CONV3'),
    Flatten(name='FLAT'),
    Dense(units=84, activation='tanh', name='FC6'),
    Dense(units=10, activation='softmax', name='FC7')
])
```

The summary indicates that the model thus defined has over 300,000 parameters:

```
Layer (type)                 Output Shape              Param #
CONV1 (Conv2D)               (None, 24, 24, 6)         156
POOL1 (AveragePooling2D)     (None, 23, 23, 6)         0
CONV2 (Conv2D)               (None, 19, 19, 16)        2416
_________________________________________________________________
POOL2 (AveragePooling2D)     (None, 9, 9, 16)          0
_________________________________________________________________
CONV3 (Conv2D)               (None, 5, 5, 120)         48120
```

```
_________________________________________________________________
FLAT (Flatten)               (None, 3000)              0
_________________________________________________________________
FC6 (Dense)                  (None, 84)                252084
_________________________________________________________________
FC7 (Dense)                  (None, 10)                850
=================================================================
Total params: 303,626
Trainable params: 303,626
```

We compile with `sparse_crossentropy_loss`, which accepts integers rather than one-hot-encoded labels and the original stochastic gradient optimizer:

```
lenet5.compile(loss='sparse_categorical_crossentropy',
               optimizer='SGD',
               metrics=['accuracy'])
```

Training and evaluating the model

Now we are ready to train the model. The model expects four-dimensional input, so we reshape accordingly. We use the standard batch size of 32 and an 80:20 train-validation split. Furthermore, we leverage checkpointing to store the model weights if the validation error improves, and make sure the dataset is randomly shuffled. We also define an `early_stopping` callback to interrupt training once the validation accuracy no longer improves for 20 iterations:

```
lenet_history = lenet5.fit(X_train.reshape(-1, 28, 28, 1),
                           y_train,
                           batch_size=32,
                           epochs=100,
                           validation_split=0.2, # use 0 to train on all data
                           callbacks=[checkpointer, early_stopping],
                           verbose=1,
                           shuffle=True)
```

The training history records the last improvement after 81 epochs that take around 4 minutes on a single GPU. The test accuracy of this sample run is 99.09 percent, almost exactly the same result as for the original LeNet5:

```
accuracy = lenet5.evaluate(X_test.reshape(-1, 28, 28, 1), y_test, verbose=0)
[1]
print('Test accuracy: {:.2%}'.format(accuracy))
Test accuracy: 99.09%
```

For comparison, a simple two-layer feedforward network achieves "only" 97.04 percent test accuracy (see the notebook). The LeNet5 improvement on MNIST is, in fact, modest. Non-neural methods have also achieved classification accuracies greater than or equal to 99 percent, including K-nearest neighbors and support vector machines. CNNs really shine with more challenging datasets as we will see next.

AlexNet – reigniting deep learning research

AlexNet, developed by Alex Krizhevsky, Ilya Sutskever, and Geoff Hinton at the University of Toronto, dramatically reduced the error rate and significantly outperformed the runner-up at the 2012 ILSVRC, achieving a top-5 error of 16 percent versus 26 percent (Krizhevsky, Sutskever, and Hinton 2012). This breakthrough triggered a renaissance in ML research and put deep learning for computer vision firmly on the global technology map.

The AlexNet architecture is similar to LeNet, but much deeper and wider. It is often credited with discovering **the importance of depth** with around 60 million parameters, exceeding LeNet5 by a factor of 1,000, a testament to increased computing power, especially the use of GPUs, and much larger datasets.

It included convolutions stacked on top of each other rather than combining each convolution with a pooling stage, and successfully used dropout for regularization and ReLU for efficient nonlinear transformations. It also employed data augmentation to increase the number of training samples, added weight decay, and used a more efficient implementation of convolutions. It also accelerated training by distributing the network over two GPUs.

The notebook `image_classification_with_alexnet.ipynb` has a slightly simplified version of AlexNet tailored to the CIFAR-10 dataset that contains 60,000 images from 10 of the original 1,000 classes. It has been compressed to a 32 × 32 pixel resolution from the original 224 × 224, but still has three color channels.

See the notebook `image_classification_with_alexnet` for implementation details; we will skip over some repetitive steps here.

Preprocessing CIFAR-10 data using image augmentation

CIFAR-10 can also be downloaded using TensorFlow's Keras interface, and we rescale the pixel values and one-hot encode the ten class labels as we did with MNIST in the previous section.

We first train a two-layer feedforward network on 50,000 training samples for 45 epochs to achieve a test accuracy of 45.78 percent. We also experiment with a three-layer convolutional net with over 528,000 parameters that achieves 74.51 percent test accuracy (see the notebook).

A common trick to enhance performance is to artificially increase the size of the training set by creating synthetic data. This involves randomly shifting or horizontally flipping the image or introducing noise into the image. TensorFlow includes an `ImageDataGenerator` class for this purpose. We can configure it and fit the training data as follows:

```
from tensorflow.keras.preprocessing.image import ImageDataGenerator
datagen = ImageDataGenerator(
    width_shift_range=0.1,   # randomly horizontal shift
    height_shift_range=0.1,  # randomly vertical shift
    horizontal_flip=True)    # randomly horizontal flip
datagen.fit(X_train)
```

The result shows how the augmented images (in low 32×32 resolution) have been altered in various ways as expected:

Figure 18.6: Original and augmented samples

The test accuracy for the three-layer CNN improves modestly to 76.71 percent after training on the larger, augmented data.

Defining the model architecture

We need to adapt the AlexNet architecture to the lower dimensionality of CIFAR-10 images relative to the ImageNet samples used in the competition. To this end, we use the original number of filters but make them smaller (see the notebook for implementation details).

The summary (see the notebook) shows the five convolutional layers followed by two fully connected layers with frequent use of batch normalization, for a total of 21.5 million parameters.

Comparing AlexNet performance

In addition to AlexNet, we trained a 2-layer feedforward NN and a 3-layer CNN, the latter with and without image augmentation. After 100 epochs (with early stopping if the validation accuracy does not improve for 20 rounds), we obtain the cross-validation trajectories and test accuracy for the four models, as displayed in *Figure 18.7*:

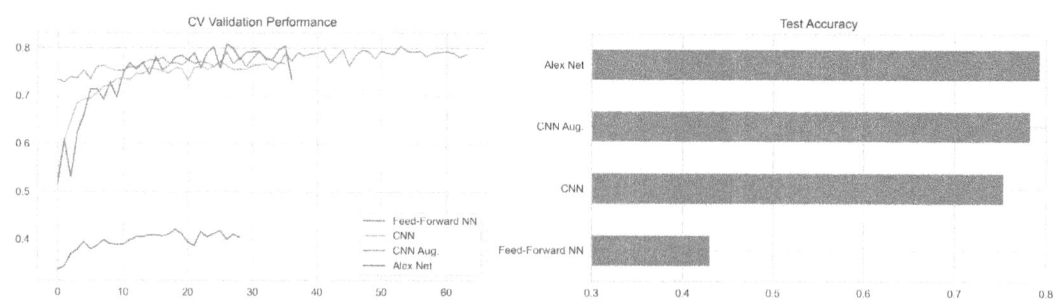

Figure 18.7: Validation performance and test accuracy on CIFAR-10

AlexNet achieves the highest test accuracy with 79.33 percent after some 35 epochs, closely followed by the shallower CNN with augmented images at 78.29 percent that trains for longer due to the larger dataset. The feedforward NN performs much worse than on MNIST on this more complex dataset, with a test accuracy of 43.05 percent.

Transfer learning – faster training with less data

In practice, sometimes we do not have enough data to train a CNN from scratch with random initialization. **Transfer learning** is an ML technique that repurposes a model trained on one set of data for another task. Naturally, it works if the learning from the first task carries over to the task of interest. If successful, it can lead to better performance and faster training that requires less labeled data than training a neural network from scratch on the target task.

Alternative approaches to transfer learning

The transfer learning approach to CNN relies on pretraining on a very large dataset like ImageNet. The goal is for the convolutional filters to extract a feature representation that generalizes to new images. In a second step, it leverages the result to either initialize and retrain a new CNN or use it as input to a new network that tackles the task of interest.

As discussed, CNN architectures typically use a sequence of convolutional layers to detect hierarchical patterns, adding one or more fully connected layers to map the convolutional activations to the outcome classes or values. The output of the last convolutional layer that feeds into the fully connected part is called the bottleneck features. We can use the **bottleneck features** of a pretrained network as inputs into a new fully connected network, usually after applying a ReLU activation function.

In other words, we freeze the convolutional layers and **replace the dense part of the network**. An additional benefit is that we can then use inputs of different sizes because it is the dense layers that constrain the input size.

Alternatively, we can use the bottleneck features as **inputs into a different machine learning algorithm**. In the AlexNet architecture, for instance, the bottleneck layer computes a vector with 4,096 entries for each 224 × 224 input image. We then use this vector as features for a new model.

We also can go a step further and not only replace and retrain the final layers using new data but also **fine-tune the weights of the pretrained CNN**. To achieve this, we continue training, either only for later layers while freezing the weights of some earlier layers, or for all layers. The motivation is presumably to preserve more generic patterns learned by lower layers, such as edge or color blob detectors, while allowing later layers of the CNN to adapt to the details of a new task. ImageNet, for example, contains a wide variety of dog breeds, which may lead to feature representations specifically useful for differentiating between these classes.

Building on state-of-the-art architectures

Transfer learning permits us to leverage top-performing architectures without incurring the potentially fairly GPU- and data-intensive training. We briefly outline the key characteristics of a few additional popular architectures that are popular starting points.

VGGNet – more depth and smaller filters

The runner-up in ILSVRC 2014 was developed by Oxford University's Visual Geometry Group (VGG, Simonyan 2015). It demonstrated the effectiveness of **much smaller** 3 × 3 **convolutional filters** combined in sequence and reinforced the importance of depth for strong performance. VGG16 contains 16 convolutional and fully connected layers that only perform 3 × 3 convolutions and 2 × 2 pooling (see *Figure 18.5*).

VGG16 has **140 million parameters** that increase the computational costs of training and inference as well as the memory requirements. However, most parameters are in the fully connected layers that were since discovered not to be essential so that removing them greatly reduces the number of parameters without negatively impacting performance.

GoogLeNet – fewer parameters through Inception

Christian Szegedy at Google reduced the computational costs using more efficient CNN implementations to facilitate practical applications at scale. The resulting GoogLeNet (Szegedy et al. 2015) won the ILSVRC 2014 with only 4 million parameters due to the **Inception module**, compared to AlexNet's 60 million and VGG16's 140 million.

The Inception module builds on the **network-in-network concept** that uses 1 × 1 convolutions to compress a deep stack of convolutional filters and thus reduce the cost of computation. The module uses parallel 1 × 1, 3 × 3, and 5 × 5 filters, combining the latter two with 1 × 1 convolutions to reduce the dimensionality of the filters passed in by the previous layer.

In addition, it uses average pooling instead of fully connected layers on top of the convolutional layers to eliminate many of the less impactful parameters. There have been several enhanced versions, most recently Inception-v4.

ResNet – shortcut connections beyond human performance

The **residual network (ResNet)** architecture was developed at Microsoft and won the ILSVRC 2015. It pushed the top-5 error to 3.7 percent, below the level of human performance on this task of around 5 percent (He et al. 2015).

It introduces identity shortcut connections that skip several layers and overcome some of the challenges of training deep networks, enabling the use of hundreds or even over a thousand layers. It also heavily uses batch normalization, which was shown to allow higher learning rates and be more forgiving about weight initialization. The architecture also omits the fully connected final layers.

As mentioned in the last chapter, the training of deep networks faces the notorious vanishing gradient challenge: as the gradient propagates to earlier layers, repeated multiplication of small weights risks shrinking the gradient toward zero. Hence, increasing depth may limit learning.

The shortcut connection that skips two or more layers has become one of the most popular developments in CNN architectures and triggered numerous research efforts to refine and explain its performance. See the references on GitHub for additional information.

Transfer learning with VGG16 in practice

Modern CNNs can take weeks to train on multiple GPUs on ImageNet, but fortunately, many researchers share their final weights. TensorFlow 2, for example, contains pretrained models for several of the reference architectures discussed previously, namely VGG16 and its larger version, VGG19, ResNet50, InceptionV3, and InceptionResNetV2, as well as MobileNet, DenseNet, NASNet, and MobileNetV2.

How to extract bottleneck features

The notebook `bottleneck_features.ipynb` illustrates how to download the pretrained VGG16 model, either with the final layers to generate predictions or without the final layers, as illustrated in *Figure 18.8*, to extract the outputs produced by the bottleneck features:

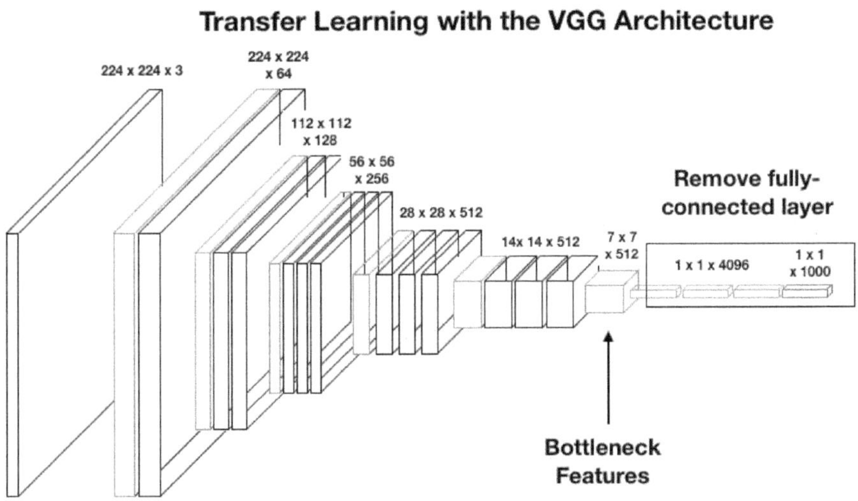

Figure 18.8: The VGG16 architecture

TensorFlow 2 makes it very straightforward to download and use pretrained models:

```
from tensorflow.keras.applications.vgg16 import VGG16
vgg16 = VGG16()
vgg16.summary()
Layer (type)                 Output Shape              Param #
input_1 (InputLayer)         (None, 224, 224, 3)       0
… several layers omitted...
```

```
block5_conv4 (Conv2D)        (None, 14, 14, 512)       2359808
_________________________________________________________________
block5_pool (MaxPooling2D)   (None, 7, 7, 512)         0
_________________________________________________________________
flatten (Flatten)           (None, 25088)             0
fc1 (Dense)                  (None, 4096)              102764544
fc2 (Dense)                  (None, 4096)              16781312
predictions (Dense)          (None, 1000)              4097000
Total params: 138,357,544
Trainable params: 138,357,544
```

You can use this model for predictions like any other Keras model: we pass in seven sample images and obtain class probabilities for each of the 1,000 ImageNet categories:

```
y_pred = vgg16.predict(img_input)
Y_pred.shape
(7, 1000)
```

To exclude the fully connected layers, just add the keyword `include_top=False`. Predictions are now output by the final convolutional layer `block5_pool` and match this layer's shape:

```
vgg16 = VGG16(include_top=False)
vgg16.predict(img_input).shape
(7, 7, 7, 512)
```

By omitting the fully connected layers and keeping only the convolutional modules, we are no longer forced to use a fixed input size for the model such as the original 224 × 224 ImageNet format. Instead, we can adapt the model to arbitrary input sizes.

How to fine-tune a pretrained model

We will demonstrate how to freeze some or all of the layers of a pretrained model and continue training using a new fully-connected set of layers and data with a different format (see the notebook `transfer_learning.ipynb` for code examples, adapted from a TensorFlow 2 tutorial).

We use the VGG16 weights, pretrained on ImageNet with TensorFlow's built-in cats versus dogs images (see the notebook on how to source the dataset).

Preprocessing resizes all images to 160 × 160 pixels. We indicate the new input size as we instantiate the pretrained VGG16 instance and then freeze all weights:

```
vgg16 = VGG16(input_shape=IMG_SHAPE, include_top=False, weights='imagenet')
vgg16.trainable = False
vgg16.summary()
Layer (type)                 Output Shape              Param #
... omitted layers...
block5_conv3 (Conv2D)        (None, 10, 10, 512)       2359808
block5_pool (MaxPooling2D)   (None, 5, 5, 512)         0
```

```
Total params: 14,714,688
Trainable params: 0
Non-trainable params: 14,714,688
```

The shape of the model output for 32 sample images now matches that of the last convolutional layer in the headless model:

```
feature_batch = vgg16(image_batch)
Feature_batch.shape
TensorShape([32, 5, 5, 512])
```

We can append new layers to the headless model using either the Sequential or the Functional API. For the Sequential API, adding `GlobalAveragePooling2D`, `Dense`, and `Dropout` layers works as follows:

```
global_average_layer = GlobalAveragePooling2D()
dense_layer = Dense(64, activation='relu')
dropout = Dropout(0.5)
prediction_layer = Dense(1, activation='sigmoid')
seq_model = tf.keras.Sequential([vgg16,
                                 global_average_layer,
                                 dense_layer,
                                 dropout,
                                 prediction_layer])
seq_model.compile(loss = tf.keras.losses.BinaryCrossentropy(from logits=True),
                  optimizer = 'Adam',
                  metrics=["accuracy"])
```

We set `from_logits=True` for the `BinaryCrossentropy` loss because the model provides a linear output. The summary shows how the new model combines the pretrained VGG16 convolutional layers and the new final layers:

```
seq_model.summary()
Layer (type)                 Output Shape              Param #
vgg16 (Model)                (None, 5, 5, 512)         14714688
global_average_pooling2d (Gl (None, 512)               0
dense_7 (Dense)              (None, 64)                32832
dropout_3 (Dropout)          (None, 64)                0
dense_8 (Dense)              (None, 1)                 65
Total params: 14,747,585
Trainable params: 11,831,937
Non-trainable params: 2,915,648
```

See the notebook for the Functional API version.

Prior to training the new final layer, the pretrained VGG16 delivers a validation accuracy of 48.75 percent. Now we proceed to train the model for 10 epochs as follows, adjusting only the final layer weights:

```
history = transfer_model.fit(train_batches,
                             epochs=initial_epochs,
                             validation_data=validation_batches)
```

10 epochs boost validation accuracy above 94 percent. To fine-tune the model, we can unfreeze the VGG16 models and continue training. Note that you should only do so after training the new final layers: randomly initialized classification layers will likely produce large gradient updates that can eliminate the pretraining results.

To unfreeze parts of the model, we select a layer, after which we set the weights to `trainable`; in this case, layer 12 of the total 19 layers in the VGG16 architecture:

```
vgg16.trainable = True
len(vgg16.layers)
19
# Fine-tune from this layer onward
start_fine_tuning_at = 12
# Freeze all the layers before the 'fine_tune_at' layer
for layer in vgg16.layers[:start_fine_tuning_at]:
    layer.trainable =  False
```

Now just recompile the model and continue training for up to 50 epochs using early stopping, starting in epoch 10 as follows:

```
fine_tune_epochs = 50
total_epochs = initial_epochs + fine_tune_epochs
history_fine_tune = transfer_model.fit(train_batches,
                                       epochs=total_epochs,
                                       initial_epoch=history.epoch[-1],
                                       validation_data=validation_batches,
                                       callbacks=[early_stopping])
```

Figure 18.9 shows how the validation accuracy increases substantially, reaching 97.89 percent after another 22 epochs:

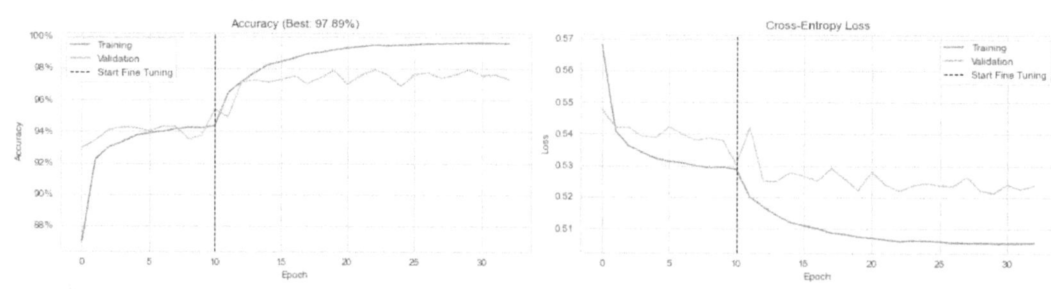

Figure 18.9: Cross-validation performance: accuracy and cross-entropy loss

Transfer learning is an important technique when training data is limited as is very often the case in practice. While cats and dogs are unlikely to produce tradeable signals, transfer learning could certainly help improve the accuracy of predictions on a relevant alternative dataset, such as the satellite images that we'll tackle next.

Classifying satellite images with transfer learning

Satellite images figure prominently among alternative data (see *Chapter 3, Alternative Data for Finance – Categories and Use Cases*). For instance, commodity traders may rely on satellite images to predict the supply of certain crops or resources by monitoring, activity on farms, at mining sites, or oil tanker traffic.

The EuroSat dataset

To illustrate working with this type of data, we load the EuroSat dataset included in the TensorFlow 2 datasets (Helber et al. 2019). The EuroSat dataset includes around 27,000 images in 64 × 64 format that represent 10 different types of land uses. *Figure 18.10* displays an example for each label:

Figure 18.10: Ten types of land use contained in the dataset

A time series of similar data could be used to track the relative sizes of cultivated, industrial, and residential areas or the status of specific crops to predict harvest quantities or quality, for example, for wine.

Fine-tuning a very deep CNN – DenseNet201

Huang et al. (2018) developed a new architecture dubbed **densely connected** based on the insight that CNNs can be deeper, more accurate, and more efficient to train if they contain shorter connections between layers close to the input and those close to the output.

One architecture, labeled **DenseNet201**, connects each layer to every other layer in a feedforward fashion. It uses the feature maps of all preceding layers as inputs, while each layer's own feature maps become inputs into all subsequent layers.

We download the DenseNet201 architecture from `tensorflow.keras.applications` and replace its final layers with the following dense layers interspersed with batch normalization to mitigate exploding or vanishing gradients in this very deep network with over 700 layers:

```
Layer (type)                 Output Shape              Param #
densenet201 (Model)          (None, 1920)              18321984
batch_normalization (BatchNo (None, 1920)              7680
dense (Dense)                (None, 2048)              3934208
batch_normalization_1 (Batch (None, 2048)              8192
dense_1 (Dense)              (None, 2048)              4196352
batch_normalization_2 (Batch (None, 2048)              8192
dense_2 (Dense)              (None, 2048)              4196352
batch_normalization_3 (Batch (None, 2048)              8192
dense_3 (Dense)              (None, 2048)              4196352
batch_normalization_4 (Batch (None, 2048)              8192
dense_4 (Dense)              (None, 10)                20490
Total params: 34,906,186
Trainable params: 34,656,906
Non-trainable params: 249,280
```

Model training and results evaluation

We use 10 percent of the training images for validation purposes and achieve the best out-of-sample classification accuracy of 97.96 percent after 10 epochs. This exceeds the performance cited in the original paper for the best-performing ResNet-50 architecture with a 90-10 split.

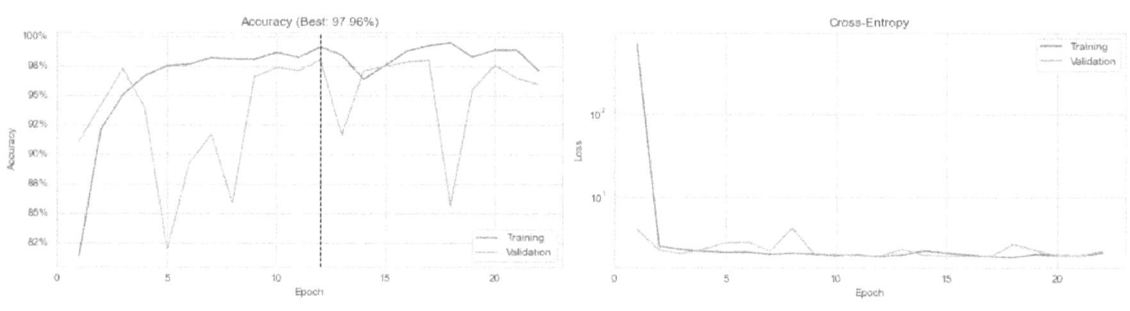

Figure 18.11: Cross-validation performance

There would likely be additional performance gains from augmenting the relatively small training set.

Object detection and segmentation

Image classification is a fundamental computer vision task that requires labeling an image based on certain objects it contains. Many practical applications, including investment and trading strategies, require additional information:

- The **object detection** task requires not only the identification but also the spatial location of all objects of interest, typically using bounding boxes. Several algorithms have been developed to overcome the inefficiency of brute-force sliding-window approaches, including region proposal methods (R-CNN; see for example Ren et al. 2015) and the **You Only Look Once** (**YOLO**) real-time object detection algorithm (Redmon 2016).
- The **object segmentation** task goes a step further and requires a class label and an outline of every object in the input image. This may be useful to count objects such as oil tankers, individuals, or cars in an image and evaluate a level of activity.
- **Semantic segmentation**, also called scene parsing, makes dense predictions to assign a class label to each pixel in the image. As a result, the image is divided into semantic regions and each pixel is assigned to its enclosing object or region.

Object detection requires the ability to distinguish between several classes of objects and to decide how many and which of these objects are present in an image.

Object detection in practice

A prominent example is Ian Goodfellow's identification of house numbers from Google's **Street View House Numbers** (**SVHN**) dataset (Goodfellow 2014). It requires the model to identify the following:

- How many of up to five digits make up the house number
- The correct digit for each component
- The proper order of the constituent digits

We will show how to preprocess the irregularly shaped source images, adapt the VGG16 architecture to produce multiple outputs, and train the final layer, before fine-tuning the pretrained weights to address the task.

Preprocessing the source images

The notebook `svhn_preprocessing.ipynb` contains code to produce a simplified, cropped dataset that uses bounding box information to create regularly shaped 32×32 images containing the digits; the original images are of arbitrary shape (Netzer 2011).

Figure 18.12: Cropped sample images of the SVHN dataset

The SVHN dataset contains house numbers with up to five digits and uses the class 10 if a digit is not present. However, since there are very few examples with five digits, we limit the images to those including up to four digits only.

Transfer learning with a custom final layer

The notebook `svhn_object_detection.ipynb` illustrates how to apply transfer learning to a deep CNN based on the VGG16 architecture, as outlined in the previous section. We will describe how to create new final layers that produce several outputs to meet the three SVHN task objectives, including one prediction of how many digits are present, and one for the value of each digit in the order they appear.

The best-performing architecture on the original dataset has eight convolutional layers and two final fully connected layers. We will use **transfer learning**, departing from the VGG16 architecture. As before, we import the VGG16 network pretrained on ImageNet weights, remove the layers after the convolutional blocks, freeze the weights, and create new dense and predictive layers as follows using the Functional API:

```
vgg16 = VGG16(input_shape=IMG_SHAPE, include_top=False, weights='imagenet')
vgg16.trainable = False
x = vgg16.output
x = Flatten()(x)
x = BatchNormalization()(x)
x = Dense(256)(x)
x = BatchNormalization()(x)
x = Activation('relu')(x)
x = Dense(128)(x)
x = BatchNormalization()(x)
x = Activation('relu')(x)
n_digits = Dense(SEQ_LENGTH, activation='softmax', name='n_digits')(x)
digit1 = Dense(N_CLASSES-1, activation='softmax', name='d1')(x)
digit2 = Dense(N_CLASSES, activation='softmax', name='d2')(x)
digit3 = Dense(N_CLASSES, activation='softmax', name='d3')(x)
digit4 = Dense(N_CLASSES, activation='softmax', name='d4')(x)
predictions = Concatenate()([n_digits, digit1, digit2, digit3, digit4])
```

The prediction layer combines the four-class output for the number of digits `n_digits` with four outputs that predict which digit is present at that position.

Creating a custom loss function and evaluation metrics

The custom output requires us to define a loss function that captures how well the model is meeting its objective. We would also like to measure accuracy in a way that reflects predictive accuracy tailored to the specific labels.

For the custom loss, we average the cross-entropy over the five categorical outputs, namely the number of digits and their respective values:

```
def weighted_entropy(y_true, y_pred):
    cce = tf.keras.losses.SparseCategoricalCrossentropy()
    n_digits = y_pred[:, :SEQ_LENGTH]
    digits = {}
    for digit, (start, end) in digit_pos.items():
        digits[digit] = y_pred[:, start:end]
    return (cce(y_true[:, 0], n_digits) +
            cce(y_true[:, 1], digits[1]) +
            cce(y_true[:, 2], digits[2]) +
            cce(y_true[:, 3], digits[3]) +
            cce(y_true[:, 4], digits[4])) / 5
```

To measure predictive accuracy, we compare the five predictions with the corresponding label values and average the share of correct matches over the batch of samples:

```
def weighted_accuracy(y_true, y_pred):
    n_digits_pred = K.argmax(y_pred[:, :SEQ_LENGTH], axis=1)

    digit_preds = {}
    for digit, (start, end) in digit_pos.items():
        digit_preds[digit] = K.argmax(y_pred[:, start:end], axis=1)
    preds = tf.dtypes.cast(tf.stack((n_digits_pred,
                                     digit_preds[1],
                                     digit_preds[2],
                                     digit_preds[3],
                                     digit_preds[4]), axis=1), tf.float32)

    return K.mean(K.sum(tf.dtypes.cast(K.equal(y_true, preds), tf.int64),
axis=1) / 5)
```

Finally, we integrate the base and final layers and compile the model with the custom loss and accuracy metric as follows:

```
model = Model(inputs=vgg16.input, outputs=predictions)
model.compile(optimizer='adam',
              loss=weighted_entropy,
              metrics=[weighted_accuracy])
```

Fine-tuning the VGG16 weights and final layer

We train the new final layers for 14 periods and continue fine-tuning all VGG16 weights, as in the previous section, for another 23 epochs (using early stopping in both cases).

The following charts show the training and validation accuracy and the loss over the entire training period. As we unfreeze the VGG16 weights after the initial training period, the accuracy drops and then improves, achieving a validation performance of 94.52 percent:

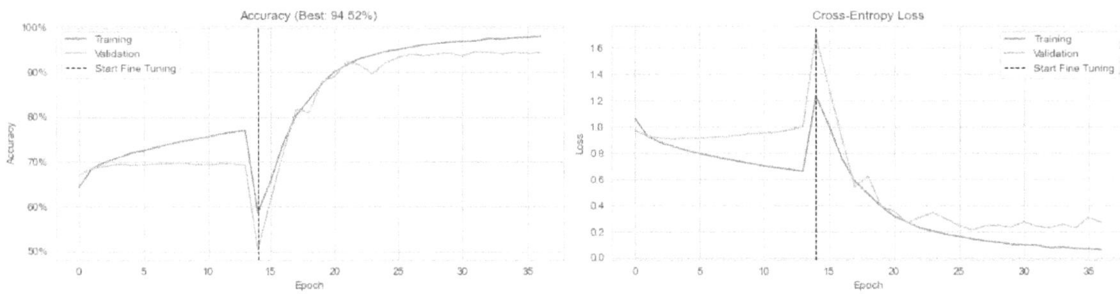

Figure 18.13: Cross-validation performance

See the notebook for additional implementation details and an evaluation of the results.

Lessons learned

We can achieve decent levels of accuracy using only the small training set. However, state-of-the-art performance achieves an error rate of only 1.02 percent (`https://benchmarks.ai/svhn`). To get closer, the most important step is to increase the amount of training data.

There are two easy ways to accomplish this: we can include the larger number of samples included in the **extra** dataset, and we can use image augmentation (see the *AlexNet: reigniting deep learning research* section). The currently best-performing approach relies heavily on augmentation learned from data (Cubuk 2019).

CNNs for time-series data – predicting returns

CNNs were originally developed to process image data and have achieved superhuman performance on various computer vision tasks. As discussed in the first section, time-series data has a grid-like structure similar to that of images, and CNNs have been successfully applied to one-, two- and three-dimensional representations of temporal data.

The application of CNNs to time series will most likely bear fruit if the data meets the model's key assumption that local patterns or relationships help predict the outcome. In the time-series context, local patterns could be autocorrelation or similar non-linear relationships at relevant intervals. Along the second and third dimensions, local patterns imply systematic relationships among different components of a multivariate series or among these series for different tickers. Since locality matters, it is important that the data is organized accordingly, in contrast to feed-forward networks where shuffling the elements of any dimension does not negatively affect the learning process.

In this section, we provide a relatively simple example using a one-dimensional convolution to model an autoregressive process (see *Chapter 9, Time-Series Models for Volatility Forecasts and Statistical Arbitrage*) that predicts future returns based on lagged returns. Then we replicate a recent research paper that achieved good results by formatting multivariate time-series data like images to predict returns. We will also develop and test a trading strategy based on the signals contained in the predictions.

An autoregressive CNN with 1D convolutions

We will introduce the time series use case for CNN using a univariate autoregressive asset return model. More specifically, the model receives the most recent 12 months of returns and uses a single layer of one-dimensional convolutions to predict the subsequent month.

The requisite steps are as follows:

1. Creating the rolling 12 months of lagged returns and corresponding outcomes
2. Defining the model architecture
3. Training the model and evaluating the results

In the following sections, we'll describe each step in turn; the notebook `time_series_prediction` contains the code samples for this section.

Preprocessing the data

First, we'll select the adjusted close price for all Quandl Wiki stocks since 2000 as follows:

```
prices = (pd.read_hdf('../data/assets.h5', 'quandl/wiki/prices')
          .adj_close
          .unstack().loc['2000':])
prices.info()
DatetimeIndex: 2896 entries, 2007-01-01 to 2018-03-27
Columns: 3199 entries, A to ZUMZ
```

Next, we resample the price data to month-end frequency, compute returns, and set monthly returns over 100 percent to missing as they likely represent data errors. Then we drop tickers with missing observations, retaining 1,511 stocks with 215 observations each:

```
returns = (prices
           .resample('M')
           .last()
           .pct_change()
           .dropna(how='all')
           .loc['2000': '2017']
           .dropna(axis=1)
           .sort_index(ascending=False))

# remove outliers likely representing data errors
returns = returns.where(returns<1).dropna(axis=1)
returns.info()
DatetimeIndex: 215 entries, 2017-12-31 to 2000-02-29
Columns: 1511 entries, A to ZQK
```

To create the rolling series of 12 lagged monthly returns with their corresponding outcome, we iterate over rolling 13-month slices and append the transpose of each slice to a list after assigning the outcome date to the index. After completing the loop, we concatenate the DataFrames in the list as follows:

```
n = len(returns)
nlags = 12
lags = list(range(1, nlags + 1))
cnn_data = []
for i in range(n-nlags-1):
    df = returns.iloc[i:i+nlags+1]        # select outcome and lags
    date = df.index.max()                 # use outcome date
    cnn_data.append(df.reset_index(drop=True) # append transposed series
                    .transpose()
                    .assign(date=date)
                    .set_index('date', append=True)
                    .sort_index(1, ascending=True))
```

```
cnn_data = (pd.concat(cnn_data)
            .rename(columns={0: 'label'})
            .sort_index())
```

We end up with over 305,000 pairs of outcomes and lagged returns for the 2001-2017 period:

```
cnn_data.info(null_counts=True)
MultiIndex: 305222 entries, ('A', Timestamp('2001-03-31 00:00:00')) to
                            ('ZQK', Timestamp('2017-12-31 00:00:00'))
Data columns (total 13 columns):
...
```

When we compute the information coefficient for each lagged return and the outcome, we find that only lag 5 is not statistically significant:

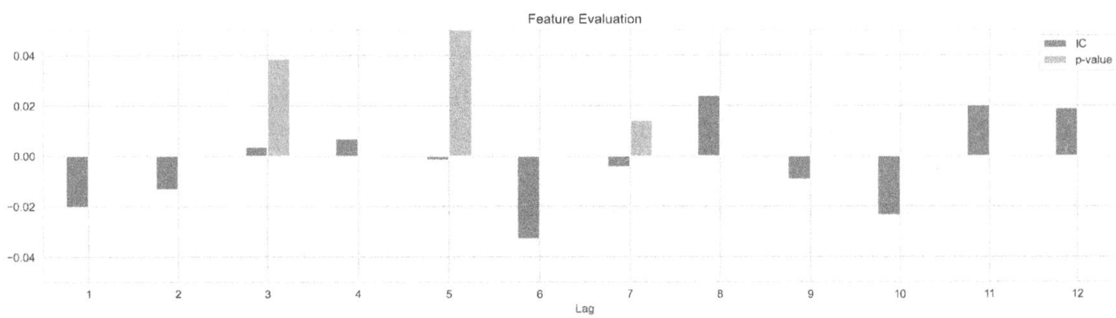

Figure 18.14: Information coefficient with respect to forward return by lag

Defining the model architecture

Now we'll define the model architecture using TensorFlow's Keras interface. We combine a one-dimensional convolutional layer with max pooling and batch normalization to produce a real-valued scalar output:

```
model = Sequential([Conv1D(filters=32,
                           kernel_size=4,
                           activation='relu',
                           padding='causal',
                           input_shape=(12, 1),
                           use_bias=True,
                           kernel_regularizer=regularizers.l1_l2(l1=1e-5,
                                                                  l2=1e-5)),
                    MaxPooling1D(pool_size=4),
                    Flatten(),
                    BatchNormalization(),
                    Dense(1, activation='linear')])
```

The one-dimensional convolution computes the sliding dot product of a (regularized) vector of length 4 with each input sequence of length 12, using causal padding to maintain the temporal order (see the *How to scan the input: strides and padding* section). The resulting 32 feature maps have the same length, 12, as the input that max pooling in groups of size 4 reduces to 32 vectors of length 3.

The model outputs the weighted average plus the bias of the flattened and normalized single vector of length 96, and has 449 trainable parameters:

```
Layer (type)                 Output Shape              Param #
conv1d (Conv1D)              (None, 12, 32)            160
max_pooling1d (MaxPooling1D) (None, 3, 32)             0
flatten (Flatten)           (None, 96)               0
batch_normalization (BatchNo (None, 96)                384
dense (Dense)                (None, 1)                 97
Total params: 641
Trainable params: 449
Non-trainable params: 192
```

The notebook wraps the model generation and subsequent compilation into a `get_model()` function that parametrizes the model configuration to facilitate experimentation.

Model training and performance evaluation

We train the model on five years of data for each ticker to predict the first month after this period and repeat this procedure 36 times using the `MultipleTimeSeriesCV` we developed in *Chapter 7, Linear Models – From Risk Factors to Return Forecasts*. See the notebook for the training loop that follows the pattern demonstrated in the previous chapter.

We use early stopping after five epochs to simplify the exposition, resulting in a positive bias so that the results have only illustrative character. Training length varies from 1 to 27 epochs, with a median of 5 epochs, which demonstrates that the model can often only learn very limited amounts of systematic information from the past returns. Thus cherry-picking the results yields a cumulative average information coefficient of around 4, as shown in *Figure 18.15*:

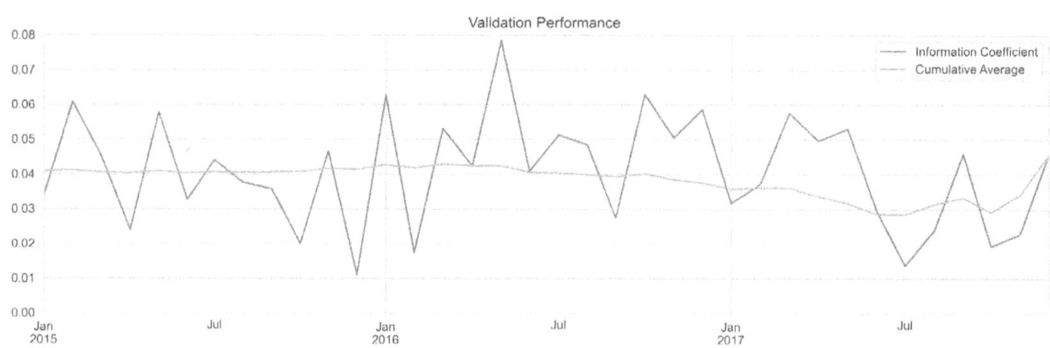

Figure 18.15: (Biased) out-of-sample information coefficients for best epochs

We'll now proceed to a more complex example of using CNNs for multiple time-series data.

CNN-TA – clustering time series in 2D format

To exploit the grid-like structure of time-series data, we can use CNN architectures for univariate and multivariate time series. In the latter case, we consider different time series as channels, similar to the different color signals.

An alternative approach converts a time series of alpha factors into a two-dimensional format to leverage the ability of CNNs to detect local patterns. Sezer and Ozbayoglu (2018) propose **CNN-TA**, which computes 15 technical indicators for different intervals and uses hierarchical clustering (see *Chapter 13, Data-Driven Risk Factors and Asset Allocation with Unsupervised Learning*) to locate indicators that behave similarly close to each other in a two-dimensional grid.

The authors train a CNN similar to the CIFAR-10 example we used earlier to predict whether to buy, hold, or sell an asset on a given day. They compare the CNN performance to "buy-and-hold" and other models and find that it outperforms all alternatives using daily price series for Dow 30 stocks and the nine most-traded ETFs over the 2007-2017 time period.

In this section, we experiment with this approach using daily US equity price data and demonstrate how to compute and convert a similar set of indicators into image format. Then we train a CNN to predict daily returns and evaluate a simple long-short strategy based on the resulting signals.

Creating technical indicators at different intervals

We first select a universe of the 500 most-traded US stocks from the Quandl Wiki dataset by dollar volume for rolling five-year periods for 2007-2017. See the notebook `engineer_cnn_features.ipynb` for the code examples in this section and some additional implementation details.

Our features consist of 15 technical indicators and risk factors that we compute for 15 different intervals and then arrange them in a 15 × 15 grid. The following table lists some of the technical indicators; in addition, we follow the authors in using the following metrics (see the *Appendix* for additional information):

- **Weighted and exponential moving averages** (**WMA** and **EMA**) of the close price
- **Rate of change** (**ROC**) of the close price
- **Chande Momentum Oscillator** (**CMO**)
- **Chaikin A/D Oscillators** (**ADOSC**)
- **Average Directional Movement Index** (**ADX**)

Indicator	Name	Formula
Relative Strength Index (RSI)	Oscillates in [0, 100] range; below 30: oversold, over 70: overbought	See Chapter 4
Williams %R	Momentum-based in [-100, 0] range, below -80: oversold, above -20: overbought	$R = \frac{\max(\textbf{high}) - \textbf{close}}{\max(\textbf{high}) - \min(\textbf{low})}$
Bollinger Bands	20-day moving average plus/minus daily standard deviation; prices above/below these bands indicate overbought/sold	See chapter 4.
Normalized Average True Range (NATR)	Avg. true range: max of current high-low, current high-prev.close or absolute of prev. close - current low, averaged over t days.	$\textbf{NATR} = \frac{\textbf{ATR}(t)}{\textbf{Close}}$
Percentage Price Oscillator (PPO)	Momentum: compares two exponential moving averages (EMA) in percentage terms	$\textbf{PPO} = \frac{\textbf{EMA}_{12} - \textbf{EMA}_{26}}{\textbf{EMA}_{26}}$
Commodity Channel Index (CCI)	Momentum-based: difference between current and simple moving average (SMA) of the historical average price, normalized by their mean difference	$p^{\textbf{hist}} = \sum_{t=1}^{P} (\textbf{high} + \textbf{low} + \textbf{close})/3$ $\textbf{CCI} = \frac{p^{\textbf{hist}} - \textbf{SMA}(p^{\textbf{hist}})}{0.15 \times \sum_{t=1}^{P} (\lvert p^{\textbf{hist}} - \textbf{SMA}(p^{\textbf{hist}})\rvert)/P}$

Figure 8.16: Technical indicators

For each indicator, we vary the time period from 6 to 20 to obtain 15 distinct measurements. For example, the following code example computes the **relative strength index (RSI)**:

```
T = list(range(6, 21))
for t in T:
    universe[f'{t:02}_RSI'] = universe.groupby(level='symbol').close.
apply(RSI, timeperiod=t)
```

For the **Normalized Average True Range** (**NATR**) that requires several inputs, the computation works as follows:

```
for t in T:
    universe[f'{t:02}_NATR'] = universe.groupby(
                         level='symbol', group_keys=False).apply(
                         lambda x: NATR(x.high, x.low, x.close, timeperiod=t))
```

See the TA-Lib documentation for further details.

Computing rolling factor betas for different horizons

We also use **five Fama-French risk factors** (**Fama** and French, 2015; see *Chapter 4, Financial Feature Engineering – How to Research Alpha Factors*). They reflect the sensitivity of a stock's returns to factors consistently demonstrated to impact equity returns. We capture these factors by computing the coefficients of a rolling OLS regression of a stock's daily returns on the returns of portfolios designed to reflect the underlying drivers:

- **Equity risk premium**: Value-weighted returns of US stocks minus the 1-month US Treasury bill rate
- **Size (SMB)**: Returns of stocks categorized as **Small** (by market cap) **Minus** those of **Big equities**

- **Value (HML)**: Returns of stocks with **High** book-to-market value **Minus** those with a **Low value**
- **Investment (CMA)**: Returns differences for companies with **Conservative** investment expenditures **Minus** those with **Aggressive spending**
- **Profitability (RMW)**: Similarly, return differences for stocks with **Robust** profitability **Minus** that with a **Weak** metric.

We source the data from Kenneth French's data library using `pandas_datareader` (see *Chapter 4, Financial Feature Engineering – How to Research Alpha Factors*):

```
import pandas_datareader.data as web
factor_data = (web.DataReader('F-F_Research_Data_5_Factors_2x3_daily',
                              'famafrench', start=START)[0])
```

Next, we apply statsmodels' `RollingOLS()` to run regressions over windowed periods of different lengths, ranging from 15 to 90 days. We set the `params_only` parameter on the `.fit()` method to speed up computation and capture the coefficients using the `.params` attribute of the fitted `factor_model`:

```
factors = [Mkt-RF, 'SMB', 'HML', 'RMW', 'CMA']
windows = list(range(15, 90, 5))
for window in windows:
    betas = []
    for symbol, data in universe.groupby(level='symbol'):
        model_data = data[[ret]].merge(factor_data, on='date').dropna()
        model_data[ret] -= model_data.RF
        rolling_ols = RollingOLS(endog=model_data[ret],
                                 exog=sm.add_constant(model_data[factors]),
                                                      window=window)
        factor_model = rolling_ols.fit(params_only=True).params.drop('const',
                                                                      axis=1)
        result = factor_model.assign(symbol=symbol).set_index('symbol',
                                                              append=True)
        betas.append(result)
    betas = pd.concat(betas).rename(columns=lambda x: f'{window:02}_{x}')
    universe = universe.join(betas)
```

Features selecting based on mutual information

The next step is to select the 15 most relevant features from the 20 candidates to fill the 15×15 input grid. The code examples for the following steps are in the notebook `convert_cnn_features_to_image_format`.

To this end, we estimate the mutual information for each indicator and the 15 intervals with respect to our target, the one-day forward returns. As discussed in *Chapter 4, Financial Feature Engineering – How to Research Alpha Factors*, scikit-learn provides the `mutual_info_regression()` function that makes this straightforward, albeit time-consuming and memory-intensive. To accelerate the process, we randomly sample 100,000 observations:

```
df = features.join(targets[target]).dropna().sample(n=100000)
X = df.drop(target, axis=1)
y = df[target]
mi[t] = pd.Series(mutual_info_regression(X=X, y=y), index=X.columns)
```

The left panel in *Figure 18.16* shows the mutual information, averaged across the 15 intervals for each indicator. NATR, PPO, and Bollinger Bands are most important from this metric's perspective:

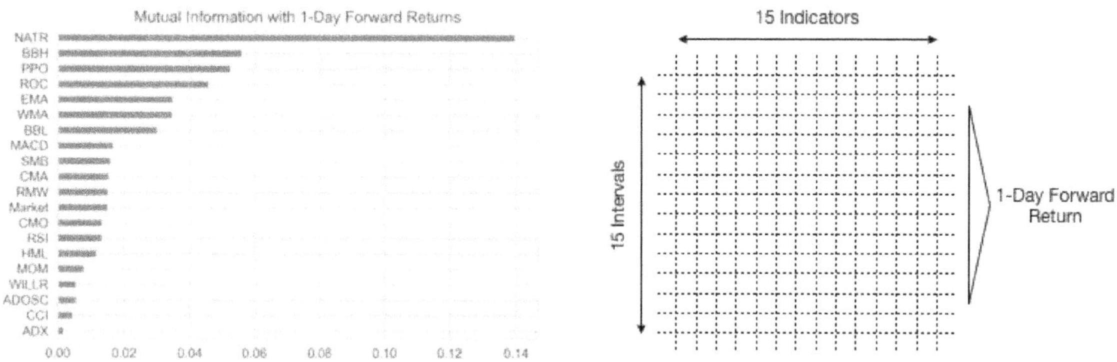

Figure 18.17: Mutual information and two-dimensional grid layout for time series

Hierarchical feature clustering

The right panel in *Figure 18.16* sketches the 15 X 15 two-dimensional feature grid that we will feed into our CNN. As discussed in the first section of this chapter, CNNs rely on the locality of relevant patterns that is typically found in images where nearby pixels are closely related and changes from one pixel to the next are often gradual.

To organize our indicators in a similar fashion, we will follow Sezer and Ozbayoglu's approach of applying hierarchical clustering. The goal is to identify features that behave similarly and order the columns and the rows of the grid accordingly.

We can build on SciPy's `pairwise_distance()`, `linkage()`, and `dendrogram()` functions that we introduced in *Chapter 13, Data-Driven Risk Factors and Asset Allocation with Unsupervised Learning* alongside other forms of clustering. We create a helper function that standardizes the input column-wise to avoid distorting distances among features due to differences in scale, and use the Ward criterion that merges clusters to minimize variance. The function returns the order of the leaf nodes in the dendrogram that in turn displays the successive formation of larger clusters:

```
def cluster_features(data, labels, ax, title):
    data = StandardScaler().fit_transform(data)
    pairwise_distance = pdist(data)
    Z = linkage(data, 'ward')
    dend = dendrogram(Z,
                      labels=labels,
                      orientation='top',
                      leaf_rotation=0.,
                      leaf_font_size=8.,
                      ax=ax)
    return dend['ivl']
```

To obtain the optimized order of technical indicators in the columns and the different intervals in the rows, we use NumPy's `.reshape()` method to ensure that the dimension we would like to cluster appears in the columns of the two-dimensional array we pass to `cluster_features()`:

```
labels = sorted(best_features)
col_order = cluster_features(features.dropna().values.reshape(-1, 15).T,
                             labels)

labels = list(range(1, 16))
row_order = cluster_features(
    features.dropna().values.reshape(-1, 15, 15).transpose((0, 2, 1)).
reshape(-1, 15).T, labels)
```

Figure 18.18 shows the dendrograms for both the row and column features:

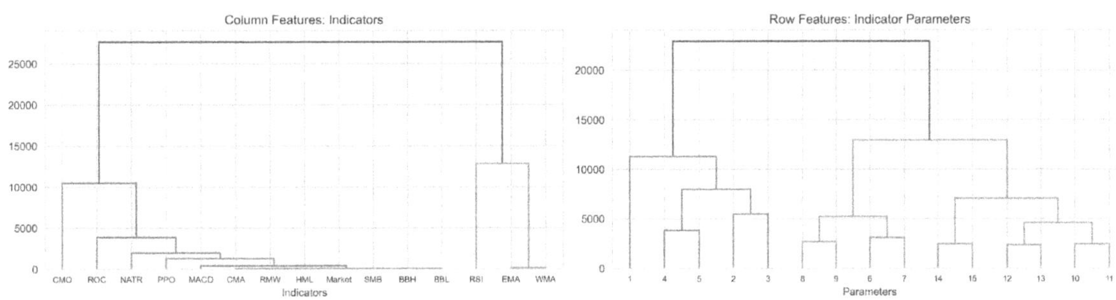

Figure 18.18: Dendrograms for row and column features

We reorder the features accordingly and store the result as inputs for the CNN that we will create in the next step.

Creating and training a convolutional neural network

Now we are ready to design, train, and evaluate a CNN following the steps outlined in the previous section. The notebook `cnn_for_trading.ipynb` contains the relevant code examples.

We again closely follow the authors in creating a CNN with 2 convolutional layers with kernel size 3 and 16 and 32 filters, respectively, followed by a max pooling layer of size 2. We flatten the output of the last stack of filters and connect the resulting 1,568 outputs to a dense layer of size 32, applying 25 and 50 percent dropout probability to the incoming and outcoming connections to mitigate overfitting. The following table summarizes the CNN structure that contains 55,041 trainable parameters:

```
Layer (type)                 Output Shape             Param #
CONV1 (Conv2D)               (None, 15, 15, 16)       160
CONV2 (Conv2D)               (None, 15, 15, 32)       4640
POOL1 (MaxPooling2D)         (None, 7, 7, 32)         0
DROP1 (Dropout)              (None, 7, 7, 32)         0
FLAT1 (Flatten)              (None, 1568)             0
FC1 (Dense)                  (None, 32)               50208
DROP2 (Dropout)              (None, 32)               0
FC2 (Dense)                  (None, 1)                33
Total params: 55,041
Trainable params: 55,041
Non-trainable params: 0
```

We cross-validate the model with the `MutipleTimeSeriesCV` train and validation set index generator introduced in *Chapter 7, Linear Models – From Risk Factors to Return Forecasts*. We provide 5 years of trading days during the training period in batches of 64 random samples and validate using the subsequent 3 months, covering the years 2014-2017.

We scale the features to the range [-1, 1] and again use NumPy's `.reshape()` method to create the requisite N × 15 × 15 × 1 format:

```
def get_train_valid_data(X, y, train_idx, test_idx):
    x_train, y_train = X.iloc[train_idx, :], y.iloc[train_idx]
    x_val, y_val = X.iloc[test_idx, :], y.iloc[test_idx]
    scaler = MinMaxScaler(feature_range=(-1, 1))
    x_train = scaler.fit_transform(x_train)
    x_val = scaler.transform(x_val)
    return (x_train.reshape(-1, size, size, 1), y_train,
            x_val.reshape(-1, size, size, 1), y_val)
```

Training and validation follow the process laid out in *Chapter 17, Deep Learning for Trading*, relying on checkpointing to store weights after each epoch and generate predictions for the best-performing iterations without the need for costly retraining.

To evaluate the model's predictive accuracy, we compute the daily **information coefficient (IC)** for the validation set like so:

```
checkpoint_path = Path('models', 'cnn_ts')
for fold, (train_idx, test_idx) in enumerate(cv.split(features)):
    X_train, y_train, X_val, y_val = get_train_valid_data(features, target,
train_idx, test_idx)
```

```
    preds = y_val.to_frame('actual')
    r = pd.DataFrame(index=y_val.index.unique(level='date')).sort_index()
    model = make_model(filter1=16, act1='relu', filter2=32,
                       act2='relu', do1=.25, do2=.5, dense=32)
    for epoch in range(n_epochs):
        model.fit(X_train, y_train,
                  batch_size=batch_size,
                  validation_data=(X_val, y_val),
                  epochs=1, verbose=0, shuffle=True)
        model.save_weights(
            (checkpoint_path / f'ckpt_{fold}_{epoch}').as_posix())
        preds[epoch] = model.predict(X_val).squeeze()
        r[epoch] = preds.groupby(level='date').apply(
            lambda x: spearmanr(x.actual, x[epoch])[0]).to_frame(epoch)
```

We train the model for up to 10 epochs using **stochastic gradient descent** with **Nesterov** momentum (see *Chapter 17*, *Deep Learning for Trading*) and find that the best performing epochs, 8 and 9, achieve a (low) daily average IC of around 0.009.

Assembling the best models to generate tradeable signals

To reduce the variance of the test-period forecasts, we generate and average the predictions for the 3 models that perform best during cross-validation, which here correspond to training for 4, 8, and 9 epochs. As in the previous time-series example, the relatively short training period underscores that the amount of signals in financial time series is low compared to the systematic information contained in, for example, image data.

The `generate_predictions()` function reloads the model weights and returns the forecasts for the target period:

```
def generate_predictions(epoch):
    predictions = []
    for fold, (train_idx, test_idx) in enumerate(cv.split(features)):
        X_train, y_train, X_val, y_val = get_train_valid_data(
            features, target, train_idx, test_idx)
        preds = y_val.to_frame('actual')
        model = make_model(filter1=16, act1='relu', filter2=32,
                           act2='relu', do1=.25, do2=.5, dense=32)
        status = model.load_weights(
            (checkpoint_path / f'ckpt_{fold}_{epoch}').as_posix())
        status.expect_partial()
        predictions.append(pd.Series(model.predict(X_val).squeeze(),
                                     index=y_val.index))
    return pd.concat(predictions)

preds = {}
for i, epoch in enumerate(ic.drop('fold', axis=1).mean().nlargest(3).index):
    preds[i] = generate_predictions(epoch)
```

We store the predictions and proceed to backtest a trading strategy based on these daily return forecasts.

Backtesting a long-short trading strategy

To get a sense of the signal quality, we compute the spread between equally weighted portfolios invested in stocks selected according to the signal quintiles using Alphalens (see *Chapter 4, Financial Feature Engineering – How to Research Alpha Factors*).

Figure 18.19 shows that for a one-day investment horizon, this naive strategy would have earned a bit over four basis points per day during the 2013-2017 period:

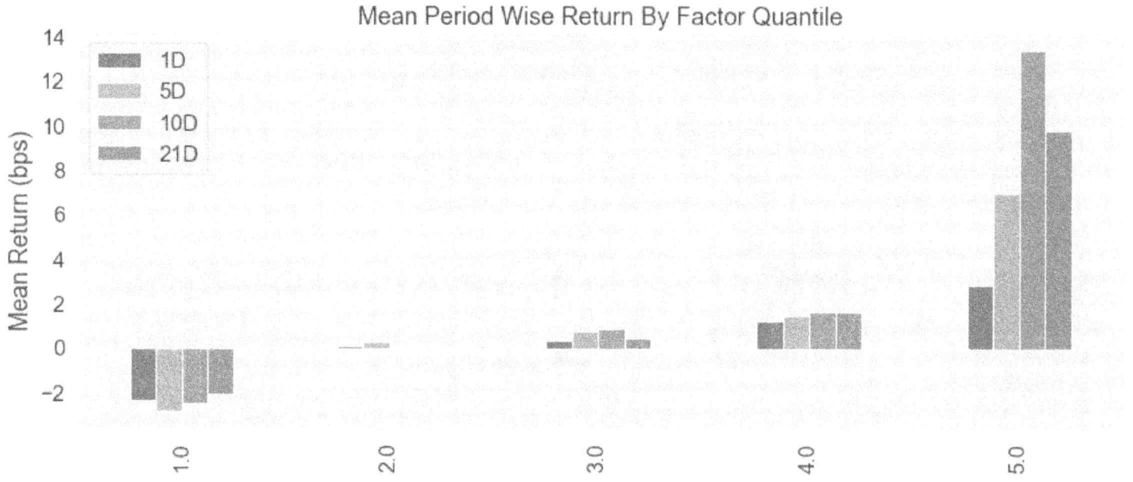

Figure 18.19: Alphalens signal quality evaluation

We translate this slightly encouraging result into a simple strategy that enters long (short) positions for the 25 stocks with the highest (lowest) return forecasts, trading on a daily basis. *Figure 18.20* shows that this strategy is competitive with the S&P 500 benchmark over much of the backtesting period (left panel), resulting in a 35.6 percent cumulative return and a Sharpe ratio of 0.53 (before transaction costs; right panel)

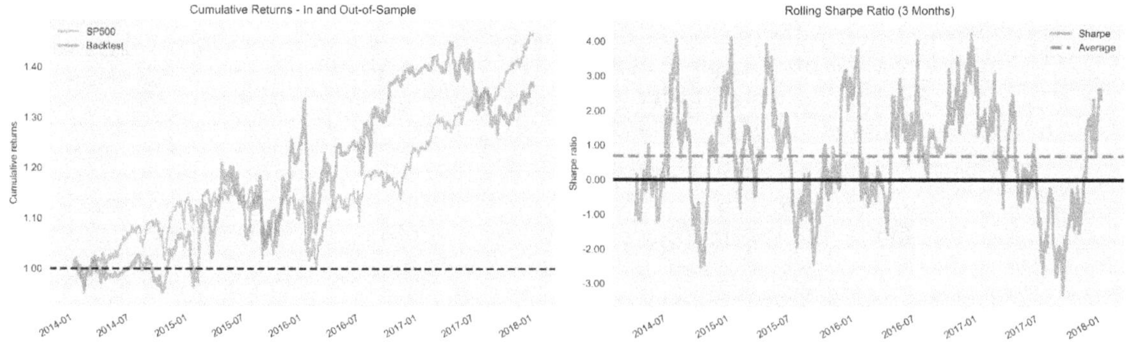

Figure 18.20: Backtest performance in- and out-of-sample

Summary and lessons learned

It appears that the CNN is able to extract meaningful information from the time series of alpha factors converted into a two-dimensional grid. Experimentation with different architectures and training parameters shows that the result is not very robust and slight modifications can yield significantly worse performance.

Tuning attempts also surface the notorious difficulties in successfully training a deep NN, especially when the signal-to-noise ratio is low: too complex a network or the wrong optimizer can lead the CNN to a local optimum where it always predicts a constant value.

The most important step to improve the results and obtain a performance closer to that achieved by the authors (using different outcomes) would be to revisit the features. There are many alternatives to different intervals of a limited set of technical indicators. Any appropriate number of time-series features could be arranged in a rectangular $n \times m$ format and benefit from the CNN's ability to learn local patterns. The choice of n indicators and m intervals just makes it easier to organize the rows and the columns of the two-dimensional grid. Give it a shot!

Furthermore, the authors take a classification approach to the algorithmically labeled buy, hold, and sell outcomes (see the paper for an outline of the computation), whereas our experiment applied regression to the daily returns. The Alphalens chart in *Figure 18.18* suggests that longer holding periods (especially 10 days) might work better, so there is also scope for adjusting the strategy accordingly or switching to a classification approach.

Summary

In this chapter, we introduced CNNs, a specialized NN architecture that has taken cues from our (limited) understanding of human vision and performs particularly well on grid-like data. We covered the central operation of convolution or cross-correlation that drives the discovery of filters that in turn detect features useful to solve the task at hand.

We reviewed several state-of-the-art architectures that are good starting points, especially because transfer learning enables us to reuse pretrained weights and reduce the otherwise rather computationally and data-intensive training effort. We also saw that Keras makes it relatively straightforward to implement and train a diverse set of deep CNN architectures.

In the next chapter, we turn our attention to recurrent neural networks that are designed specifically for sequential data, such as time-series data, which is central to investment and trading.

19

RNNs for Multivariate Time Series and Sentiment Analysis

The previous chapter showed how **convolutional neural networks** (**CNNs**) are designed to learn features that represent the spatial structure of grid-like data, especially images, but also time series. This chapter introduces **recurrent neural networks** (**RNNs**) that specialize in sequential data where patterns evolve over time and learning typically requires memory of preceding data points.

Feedforward neural networks (**FFNNs**) treat the feature vectors for each sample as independent and identically distributed. Consequently, they do not take prior data points into account when evaluating the current observation. In other words, they have no memory.

The one- and two-dimensional convolutional filters used by CNNs can extract features that are a function of what is typically a small number of neighboring data points. However, they only allow shallow parameter-sharing: each output results from applying the same filter to the relevant time steps and features.

The major innovation of the RNN model is that each output is a function of both the previous output and new information. RNNs can thus incorporate information on prior observations into the computation they perform using the current feature vector. This recurrent formulation enables parameter-sharing across a much deeper computational graph (Goodfellow, Bengio, and Courville, 2016). In this chapter, you will encounter **long short-term memory** (**LSTM**) units and **gated recurrent units** (**GRUs**), which aim to overcome the challenge of vanishing gradients associated with learning long-range dependencies, where errors need to be propagated over many connections.

Successful RNN use cases include various tasks that require mapping one or more input sequences to one or more output sequences and prominently feature natural language applications. We will explore how RNNs can be applied to univariate and multivariate time series to predict asset prices using market or fundamental data. We will also cover how RNNs can leverage alternative text data using word embeddings, which we covered in *Chapter 16*, *Word Embeddings for Earnings Calls and SEC Filings*, to classify the sentiment expressed in documents. Finally, we will use the most informative sections of SEC filings to learn word embeddings and predict returns around filing dates.

More specifically, in this chapter, you will learn about the following:

- How recurrent connections allow RNNs to memorize patterns and model a hidden state
- Unrolling and analyzing the computational graph of RNNs
- How gated units learn to regulate RNN memory from data to enable long-range dependencies
- Designing and training RNNs for univariate and multivariate time series in Python
- How to learn word embeddings or use pretrained word vectors for sentiment analysis with RNNs
- Building a bidirectional RNN to predict stock returns using custom word embeddings

You can find the code examples and additional resources in the GitHub repository's directory for this chapter.

How recurrent neural nets work

RNNs assume that the input data has been generated as a sequence such that previous data points impact the current observation and are relevant for predicting subsequent values. Thus, they allow more complex input-output relationships than FFNNs and CNNs, which are designed to map one input vector to one output vector using a given number of computational steps. RNNs, in contrast, can model data for tasks where the input, the output, or both, are best represented as a sequence of vectors. For a good overview, refer to *Chapter 10* in Goodfellow, Bengio, and Courville (2016).

The diagram in *Figure 19.1*, inspired by Andrew Karpathy's 2015 blog post *The Unreasonable Effectiveness of Recurrent Neural Networks* (see GitHub for a link), illustrates mappings from input to output vectors using nonlinear transformations carried out by one or more neural network layers:

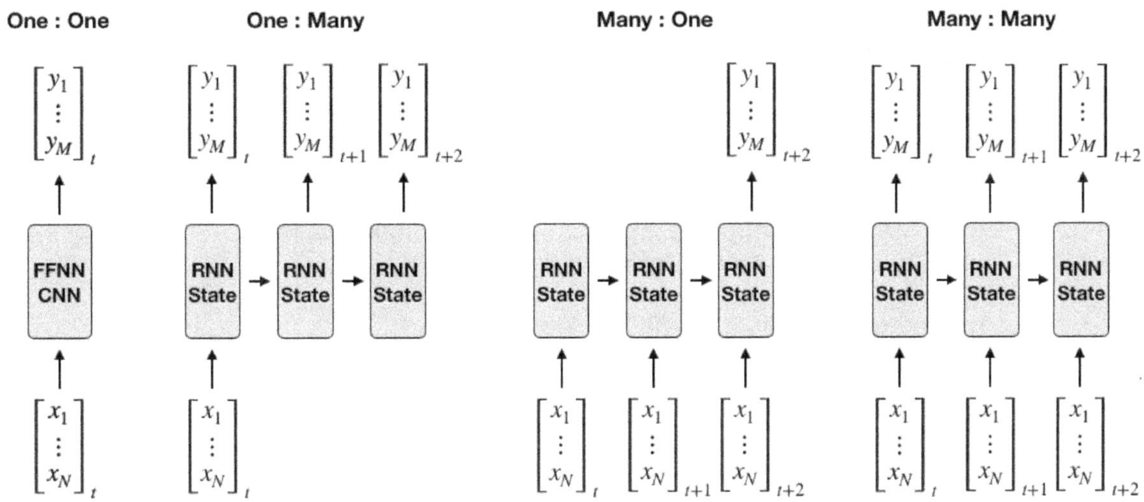

Figure 19.1: Various types of sequence-to-sequence models

The left panel shows a one-to-one mapping between vectors of fixed sizes, typical for FFNs and CNNs covered in the last two chapters. The other three panels show various RNN applications that map input vectors to output vectors by applying a recurrent transformation to the new input and the state produced by the previous iteration. The x input vectors to an RNN are also called **context**.

The vectors are time-indexed, as usually required by trading-related applications, but they could also be labeled by a different set of sequential values. Generic sequence-to-sequence mapping tasks and sample applications include:

- **One-to-many**: Image captioning, for example, takes a single vector of pixels (as in the previous chapter) and maps it to a sequence of words.
- **Many-to-one**: Sentiment analysis takes a sequence of words or tokens (see *Chapter 14, Text Data for Trading – Sentiment Analysis*) and maps it to an output scalar or vector.
- **Many-to-many**: Machine translation or labeling of video frame map sequences of input vectors to sequences of output vectors, either in a synchronized (as shown) or asynchronous fashion. Multistep prediction of multivariate time series also maps several input vectors to several output vectors.

Note that input and output sequences can be of arbitrary lengths because the recurrent transformation that is fixed but learned from the data can be applied as many times as needed.

Just as CNNs easily scale to large images and some CNNs can process images of variable size, RNNs scale to much longer sequences than networks not tailored to sequence-based tasks. Most RNNs can also process sequences of variable length.

Unfolding a computational graph with cycles

RNNs are called recurrent because they apply the same transformations to every element of a sequence in a way that the RNN's output depends on the outcomes of prior iterations. As a result, RNNs maintain an **internal state** that captures information about previous elements in the sequence, just like memory.

Figure 19.2 shows the **computational graph** implied by a single hidden RNN unit that learns two weight matrices during training:

- W_{hh}: applied to the previous hidden state, h_{t-1}
- W_{hx}: applied to the current input, x_t

The RNN's output, y_t, is a nonlinear transformation of the sum of the two matrix multiplications using, for example, the tanh or ReLU activation functions:

$$y_t = g(W_{hh}h_{t-1} + W_{xh}x_t)$$

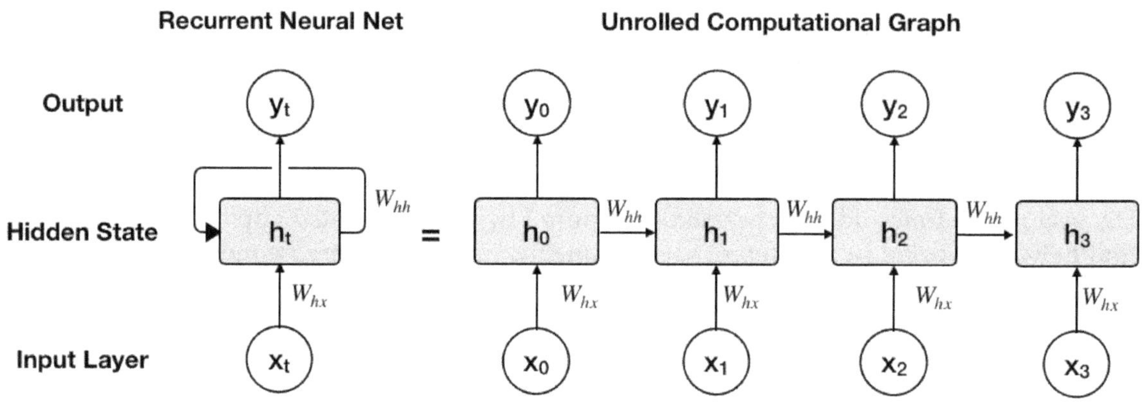

Figure 19.2: Recurrent and unrolled view of the computational graph of an RNN with a single hidden unit

The right side of the equation shows the effect of unrolling the recurrent relationship depicted in the right panel of the figure. It highlights the repeated linear algebra transformations and the resulting hidden state that combines information from past sequence elements with the current input, or context. An alternative formulation connects the context vector to the first hidden state only; we will outline additional options to modify this baseline architecture in the subsequent section.

Backpropagation through time

The unrolled computational graph in the preceding figure highlights that the learning process necessarily encompasses all time steps of the given input sequence. The backpropagation algorithm that updates the weights during training involves a forward pass from left to right along with the unrolled computational graph, followed by a backward pass in the opposite direction.

As discussed in *Chapter 17, Deep Learning for Trading*, the backpropagation algorithm evaluates a loss function and computes its gradient with respect to the parameters to update the weights accordingly. In the RNN context, backpropagation runs from right to left in the computational graph, updating the parameters from the final time step all the way to the initial time step. Therefore, the algorithm is called **backpropagation through time** (Werbos 1990).

It highlights both the power of an RNN to model long-range dependencies by sharing parameters across an arbitrary number of sequence elements while maintaining a corresponding state. On the other hand, it is computationally quite expensive, and the computations for each time step cannot be parallelized due to its inherently sequential nature.

Alternative RNN architectures

Just like the FFNN and CNN architectures we covered in the previous two chapters, RNNs can be optimized in a variety of ways to capture the dynamic relationship between input and output data.

In addition to modifying the recurrent connections between the hidden states, alternative approaches include recurrent output relationships, bidirectional RNNs, and encoder-decoder architectures. Refer to GitHub for background references to complement this brief summary.

Output recurrence and teacher forcing

One way to reduce the computational complexity of hidden state recurrences is to connect a unit's hidden state to the prior unit's output rather than its hidden state. The resulting RNN has a lower capacity than the architecture discussed previously, but different time steps are now decoupled and can be trained in parallel.

However, to successfully learn relevant past information, the training output samples need to reflect this information so that backpropagation can adjust the network parameters accordingly. To the extent that asset returns are independent of their lagged values, financial data may not meet this requirement. The use of previous outcome values alongside the input vectors is called **teacher forcing** (Williams and Zipser, 1989).

Connections from the output to the subsequent hidden state can also be used in combination with hidden recurrence. However, training requires backpropagation through time and cannot be run in parallel.

Bidirectional RNNs

For some tasks, it can be realistic and beneficial for the output to depend not only on past sequence elements, but also on future elements (Schuster and Paliwal, 1997). Machine translation or speech and handwriting recognition are examples where subsequent sequence elements are both informative and realistically available to disambiguate competing outputs.

For a one-dimensional sequence, **bidirectional RNNs** combine an RNN that moves forward with another RNN that scans the sequence in the opposite direction. As a result, the output comes to depend on both the future and the past of the sequence. Applications in the natural language and music domains (Sigtia et al., 2014) have been very successful (see *Chapter 16, Word Embeddings for Earnings Calls and SEC Filings*, and the last example in this chapter using SEC filings).

Bidirectional RNNs can also be used with two-dimensional image data. In this case, one pair of RNNs performs the forward and backward processing of the sequence in each dimension.

Encoder-decoder architectures, attention, and transformers

The architectures discussed so far assumed that the input and output sequences have equal length. Encoder-decoder architectures, also called **sequence-to-sequence** (**seq2seq**) architectures, relax this assumption and have become very popular for machine translation and other applications with this characteristic (Prabhavalkar et al., 2017).

The **encoder** is an RNN that maps the input space to a different space, also called **latent space**, whereas the **decoder** function is a complementary RNN that maps the encoded input to the target space (Cho et al., 2014). In the next chapter, we will cover autoencoders that learn a feature representation in an unsupervised setting using a variety of deep learning architectures.

Encoder and decoder RNNs are trained jointly so that the input of the final encoder hidden state becomes the input to the decoder, which, in turn, learns to match the training samples.

The **attention mechanism** addresses a limitation of using fixed-size encoder inputs when input sequences themselves vary in size. The mechanism converts raw text data into a distributed representation (see *Chapter 16, Word Embeddings for Earnings Calls and SEC Filings*), stores the result, and uses a weighted average of these feature vectors as context. The weights are learned by the model and alternate between putting more weight or attention to different elements of the input.

A recent **transformer** architecture dispenses with recurrence and convolutions and exclusively relies on this attention mechanism to learn input-output mappings. It has achieved superior quality on machine translation tasks while requiring much less time for training, not least because it can be parallelized (Vaswani et al., 2017).

How to design deep RNNs

The **unrolled computational graph** in *Figure 19.2* shows that each transformation involves a linear matrix operation followed by a nonlinear transformation that could be jointly represented by a single network layer.

In the two preceding chapters, we saw how adding depth allows FFNNs, and CNNs in particular, to learn more useful hierarchical representations. RNNs also benefit from decomposing the input-output mapping into multiple layers. For RNNs, this mapping typically transforms:

- The input and the prior hidden state into the current hidden state
- The hidden state into the output

A common approach is to **stack recurrent layers** on top of each other so that they learn a hierarchical temporal representation of the input data. This means that a lower layer may capture higher-frequency patterns, synthesized by a higher layer into lower-frequency characteristics that prove useful for the classification or regression task. We will demonstrate this approach in the next section.

Less popular alternatives include adding layers to the connections from input to the hidden state, between hidden states, or from the hidden state to the output. These designs employ skip connections to avoid a situation where the shortest path between time steps increases and training becomes more difficult.

The challenge of learning long-range dependencies

In theory, RNNs can make use of information in arbitrarily long sequences. However, in practice, they are limited to looking back only a few steps. More specifically, RNNs struggle to derive useful context information from time steps far apart from the current observation (Hochreiter et al., 2001).

The fundamental problem is the impact of repeated multiplication on gradients during backpropagation over many time steps. As a result, the **gradients tend to either vanish** and decrease toward zero (the typical case), **or explode** and grow toward infinity (less frequent, but rendering optimization very difficult).

Even if parameters allow stability and the network is able to store memories, long-term interactions will receive exponentially smaller weights due to the multiplication of many Jacobians, the matrices containing the gradient information. Experiments have shown that stochastic gradient descent faces serious challenges in training RNNs for sequences with only 10 or 20 elements.

Several RNN design techniques have been introduced to address this challenge, including **echo state networks** (Jaeger, 2001) and **leaky units** (Hihi and Bengio, 1996). The latter operate at different time scales, focusing part of the model on higher-frequency and other parts on lower-frequency representations to deliberately learn and combine different aspects from the data. Other strategies include connections that skip time steps or units that integrate signals from different frequencies.

The most successful approaches use gated units that are trained to regulate how much past information a unit maintains in its current state and when to reset or forget this information. As a result, they are able to learn dependencies over hundreds of time steps. The most popular examples include **long short-term memory** (**LSTM**) units and **gated recurrent units** (**GRUs**). An empirical comparison by Chung et al. (2014) finds both units superior to simpler recurrent units such as tanh units, while performing equally well on various speech and music modeling tasks.

Long short-term memory – learning how much to forget

RNNs with an LSTM architecture have more complex units that maintain an internal state. They contain gates to keep track of dependencies between elements of the input sequence and regulate the cell's state accordingly. These gates recurrently connect to each other instead of the hidden units we encountered earlier. They aim to address the problem of vanishing and exploding gradients due to the repeated multiplication of possibly very small or very large values by letting gradients pass through unchanged (Hochreiter and Schmidhuber, 1996).

The diagram in *Figure 19.3* shows the information flow for an unrolled LSTM unit and outlines its typical gating mechanism:

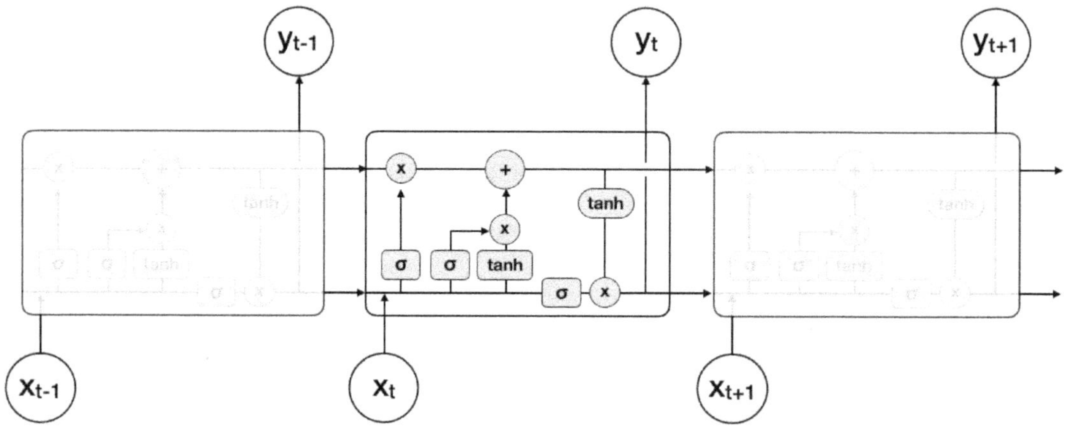

Figure 19.3: Information flow through an unrolled LSTM cell

A typical LSTM unit combines **four parameterized layers** that interact with each other and the cell state by transforming and passing along vectors. These layers usually involve an input gate, an output gate, and a forget gate, but there are variations that may have additional gates or lack some of these mechanisms. The white nodes in *Figure 19.4* identify element-wise operations, and the gray elements represent layers with weight and bias parameters learned during training:

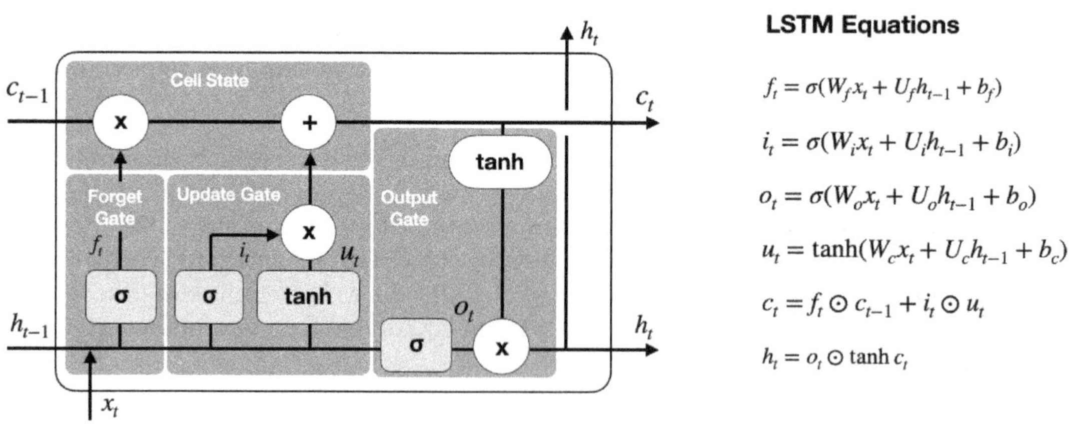

Figure 19.4: The logic of, and math behind, an LSTM cell

The **cell state**, c, passes along the horizontal connection at the top of the cell. The cell state's interaction with the various gates leads to a series of recurrent decisions:

1. The **forget gate** controls how much of the cell's state should be voided to regulate the network's memory. It receives the prior hidden state, h_{t-1}, and the current input, x_t, as inputs, computes a sigmoid activation, and multiplies the resulting value, f_t, which has been normalized to the [0, 1] range, by the cell state, reducing or keeping it accordingly.
2. The **input gate** also computes a sigmoid activation from h_{t-1} and x_t that produces update candidates. A tan_h activation in the range from [-1, 1] multiplies the update candidates, u_t, and, depending on the resulting sign, adds or subtracts the result from the cell state.
3. The **output gate** filters the updated cell state using a sigmoid activation, o_t, and multiplies it by the cell state normalized to the range [-1, 1] using a tan_h activation.

Gated recurrent units

GRUs simplify LSTM units by omitting the output gate. They have been shown to achieve similar performance on certain language modeling tasks, but do better on smaller datasets.

GRUs aim for each recurrent unit to adaptively capture dependencies of different time scales. Similar to the LSTM unit, the GRU has gating units that modulate the flow of information inside the unit but discard separate memory cells (see references on GitHub for additional details).

RNNs for time series with TensorFlow 2

In this section, we illustrate how to build recurrent neural nets using the TensorFlow 2 library for various scenarios. The first set of models includes the regression and classification of univariate and multivariate time series. The second set of tasks focuses on text data for sentiment analysis using text data converted to word embeddings (see *Chapter 16, Word Embeddings for Earnings Calls and SEC Filings*).

More specifically, we'll first demonstrate how to prepare time-series data to predict the next value for **univariate time series** with a single LSTM layer to predict stock index values.

Next, we'll build a **deep RNN** with three distinct inputs to classify asset price movements. To this end, we'll combine a two-layer, **stacked LSTM** with learned **embeddings** and one-hot encoded categorical data. Finally, we will demonstrate how to model **multivariate time series** using an RNN.

Univariate regression – predicting the S&P 500

In this subsection, we will forecast the S&P 500 index values (refer to the `univariate_time_series_regression` notebook for implementation details).

We'll obtain data for 2010-2019 from the Federal Reserve Bank's Data Service (FRED; see *Chapter 2, Market and Fundamental Data – Sources and Techniques*):

```
sp500 = web.DataReader('SP500', 'fred', start='2010', end='2020').dropna()
sp500.info()
DatetimeIndex: 2463 entries, 2010-03-22 to 2019-12-31
Data columns (total 1 columns):
 #   Column  Non-Null Count  Dtype
---  ------  --------------  -----
 0   SP500   2463 non-null   float64
```

We preprocess the data by scaling it to the [0, 1] interval using scikit-learn's `MinMaxScaler()` class:

```
from sklearn.preprocessing import MinMaxScaler
scaler = MinMaxScaler()
sp500_scaled = pd.Series(scaler.fit_transform(sp500).squeeze(),
                         index=sp500.index)
```

How to get time series data into shape for an RNN

We generate sequences of 63 consecutive trading days, approximately three months, and use a single LSTM layer with 20 hidden units to predict the scaled index value one time step ahead.

The input to every LSTM layer must have three dimensions, namely:

- **Batch size**: One sequence is one sample. A batch contains one or more samples.
- **Time steps**: One time step is a single observation in the sample.
- **Features**: One feature is one observation at a time step.

The following figure visualizes the shape of the input tensor:

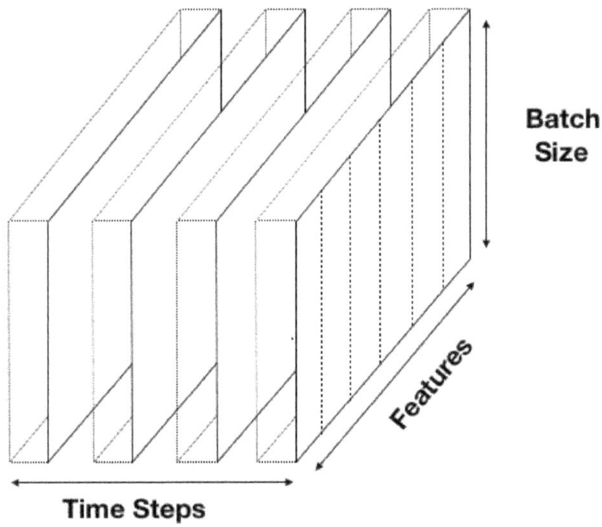

Figure 19.5: The three dimensions of an RNN input tensor

Our S&P 500 sample has 2,463 observations or time steps. We will create overlapping sequences using a window of 63 observations each. Using a simpler window of size $T = 5$ to illustrate this autoregressive sequence pattern, we obtain input-output pairs where each output is associated with its first five lags, as shown in the following table:

Input	Output
$\langle x_1, x_2, x_3, x_4, x_5 \rangle$	x_6
$\langle x_2, x_3, x_4, x_5, x_6 \rangle$	x_7
$\vdots$	$\vdots$
$\langle x_{T-5}, x_{T-4}, x_{T-3}, x_{T-2}, x_{T-1} \rangle$	x_T

Figure 19.6: Input-output pairs with a T=5 size window

We can use the `create_univariate_rnn_data()` function to stack the overlapping sequences that we select using a rolling window:

```
def create_univariate_rnn_data(data, window_size):
    y = data[window_size:]
    data = data.values.reshape(-1, 1) # make 2D
    n = data.shape[0]
    X = np.hstack(tuple([data[i: n-j, :] for i, j in enumerate(range(
                                                     window_size, 0, -1))]))
    return pd.DataFrame(X, index=y.index), y
```

We apply this function to the rescaled stock index using `window_size=63` to obtain a two-dimensional dataset with a shape of the number of samples x the number of time steps:

```
X, y = create_univariate_rnn_data(sp500_scaled, window_size=63)
X.shape
(2356, 63)
```

We will use data from 2019 as our test set and reshape the features to add a requisite third dimension:

```
X_train = X[:'2018'].values.reshape(-1, window_size, 1)
y_train = y[:'2018']

# keep the last year for testing
X_test = X['2019'].values.reshape(-1, window_size, 1)
y_test = y['2019']
```

How to define a two-layer RNN with a single LSTM layer

Now that we have created autoregressive input/output pairs from our time series and split the pairs into training and test sets, we can define our RNN architecture. The Keras interface of TensorFlow 2 makes it very straightforward to build an RNN with two hidden layers with the following specifications:

- **Layer 1**: An LSTM module with 10 hidden units (with `input_shape = (window_size,1)`; we will define `batch_size` in the omitted first dimension during training)
- **Layer 2**: A fully connected module with a single unit and linear activation
- **Loss**: `mean_squared_error` to match the regression objective

Just a few lines of code create the computational graph:

```
rnn = Sequential([
    LSTM(units=10,
         input_shape=(window_size, n_features), name='LSTM'),
    Dense(1, name='Output')
])
```

The summary shows that the model has 491 parameters:

```
rnn.summary()
Layer (type)                  Output Shape              Param #
LSTM (LSTM)                   (None, 10)                480
Output (Dense)                (None, 1)                 11
Total params: 491
Trainable params: 491
```

Training and evaluating the model

We train the model using the RMSProp optimizer recommended for RNN with default settings and compile the model with `mean_squared_error` for this regression problem:

```
optimizer = keras.optimizers.RMSprop(lr=0.001,
                                     rho=0.9,
                                     epsilon=1e-08,
                                     decay=0.0)
rnn.compile(loss='mean_squared_error', optimizer=optimizer)
```

We define an `EarlyStopping` callback and train the model for 500 episodes:

```
early_stopping = EarlyStopping(monitor='val_loss',
                               patience=50,
                               restore_best_weights=True)

lstm_training = rnn.fit(X_train,
                        y_train,
                        epochs=500,
                        batch_size=20,
                        validation_data=(X_test, y_test),
                        callbacks=[checkpointer, early_stopping],
                        verbose=1)
```

Training stops after 138 epochs. The loss history in *Figure 19.7* shows the 5-epoch rolling average of the training and validation RMSE, highlights the best epoch, and shows that the loss is 0.998 percent:

```
loss_history = pd.DataFrame(lstm_training.history).pow(.5)
loss_history.index += 1
best_rmse = loss_history.val_loss.min()
best_epoch = loss_history.val_loss.idxmin()
loss_history.columns=['Training RMSE', 'Validation RMSE']
title = f'Best Validation RMSE: {best_rmse:.4%}'
loss_history.rolling(5).mean().plot(logy=True, lw=2, title=title, ax=ax)
```

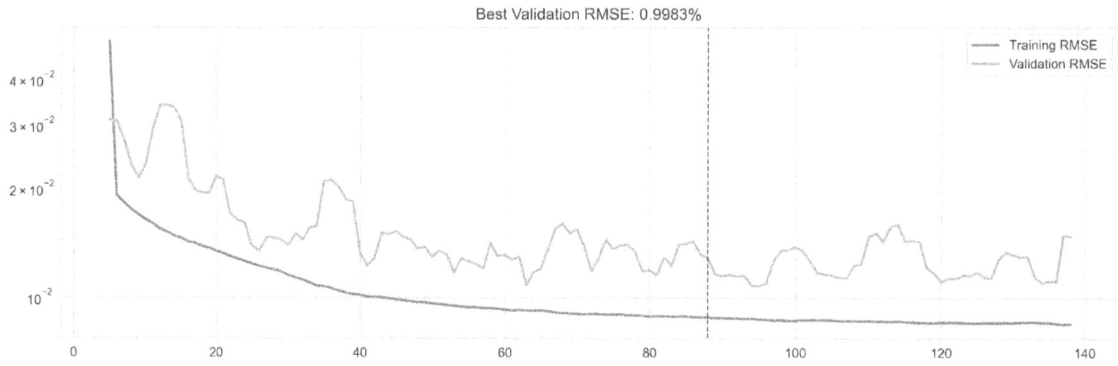

Figure 19.7: Cross-validation performance

Re-scaling the predictions

We use the `inverse_transform()` method of `MinMaxScaler()` to rescale the model predictions to the original S&P 500 range of values:

```
test_predict_scaled = rnn.predict(X_test)
test_predict = (pd.Series(scaler.inverse_transform(test_predict_scaled)
                          .squeeze(),
                          index=y_test.index))
```

The four plots in *Figure 19.8* illustrate the forecast performance based on the rescaled predictions that track the 2019 out-of-sample S&P 500 data with a test **information coefficient** (**IC**) of 0.9889:

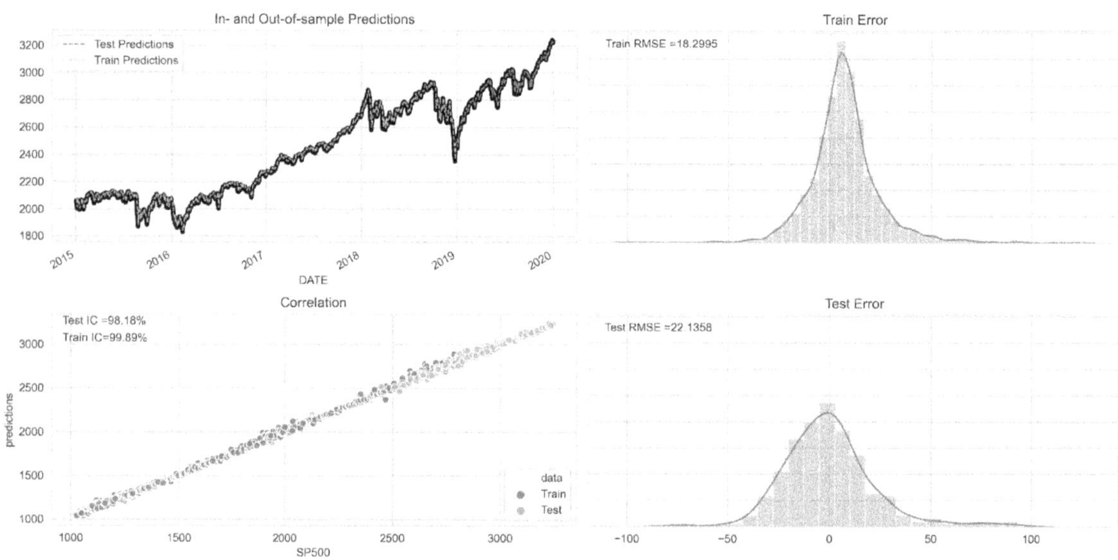

Figure 19.8: RNN performance on S&P 500 predictions

Stacked LSTM – predicting price moves and returns

We'll now build a deeper model by stacking two LSTM layers using the `Quandl` stock price data (see the `stacked_lstm_with_feature_embeddings.ipynb` notebook for implementation details). Furthermore, we will include features that are not sequential in nature, namely, indicator variables identifying the equity and the month.

Figure 19.9 outlines the architecture that illustrates how to combine different data sources in a single deep neural network. For example, instead of, or in addition to, one-hot encoded months, you could add technical or fundamental features:

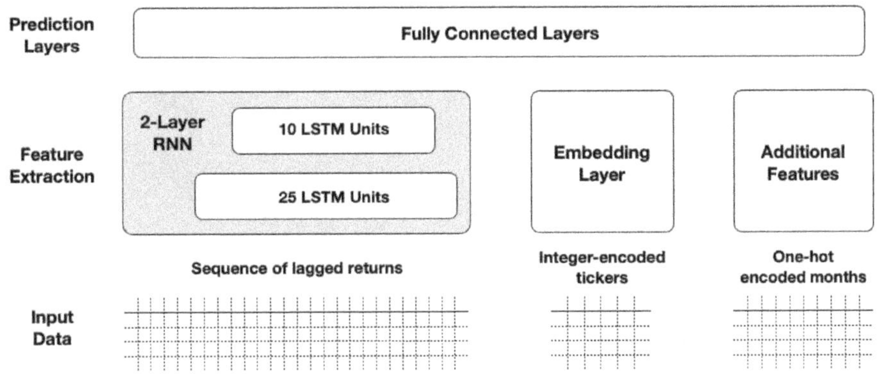

Figure 19.9: Stacked LSTM architecture with additional features

Preparing the data – how to create weekly stock returns

We load the Quandl adjusted stock price data (see instructions on GitHub on how to obtain the source data) as follows (refer to the `build_dataset.ipynb` notebook):

```
prices = (pd.read_hdf('../data/assets.h5', 'quandl/wiki/prices')
          .adj_close
          .unstack().loc['2007':])
prices.info()
DatetimeIndex: 2896 entries, 2007-01-01 to 2018-03-27
Columns: 3199 entries, A to ZUMZ
```

We start by generating weekly returns for close to 2,500 stocks with complete data for the 2008-17 period:

```
returns = (prices
           .resample('W')
           .last()
           .pct_change()
           .loc['2008': '2017']
           .dropna(axis=1)
           .sort_index(ascending=False))
```

```
returns.info()
DatetimeIndex: 2576 entries, 2017-12-29 to 2008-01-01
Columns: 2489 entries, A to ZUMZ
```

We create and stack rolling sequences of 52 weekly returns for each ticker and week as follows:

```
n = len(returns)
T = 52
tcols = list(range(T))
tickers = returns.columns

data = pd.DataFrame()
for i in range(n-T-1):
    df = returns.iloc[i:i+T+1]
    date = df.index.max()
    data = pd.concat([data, (df.reset_index(drop=True).T
                             .assign(date=date, ticker=tickers)
                             .set_index(['ticker', 'date']))])
```

We winsorize outliers at the 1 and 99 percentile level and create a binary label that indicates whether the weekly return was positive:

```
data[tcols] = (data[tcols].apply(lambda x: x.clip(lower=x.quantile(.01),
                                                   upper=x.quantile(.99))))
data['label'] = (data['fwd_returns'] > 0).astype(int)
```

As a result, we obtain 1.16 million observations on over 2,400 stocks with 52 weeks of lagged returns each (plus the label):

```
data.shape
(1167341, 53)
```

Now we are ready to create the additional features, split the data into training and test sets, and bring them into the three-dimensional format required for the LSTM.

How to create multiple inputs in RNN format

This example illustrates how to combine several input data sources, namely:

- Rolling sequences of 52 weeks of lagged returns
- One-hot encoded indicator variables for each of the 12 months
- Integer-encoded values for the tickers

The following code generates the two additional features:

```
data['month'] = data.index.get_level_values('date').month
data = pd.get_dummies(data, columns=['month'], prefix='month')
data['ticker'] = pd.factorize(data.index.get_level_values('ticker'))[0]
```

Next, we create a training set covering the 2009-2016 period and a separate test set with data for 2017, the last full year with data:

```
train_data = data[:'2016']
test_data = data['2017']
```

For training and test datasets, we generate a list containing the three input arrays as shown in *Figure 19.9*:

- The lagged return series (using the format described in *Figure 19.5*)
- The integer-encoded stock ticker as a one-dimensional array
- The month dummies as a two-dimensional array with one column per month

```
window_size=52
sequence = list(range(1, window_size+1))

X_train = [
    train_data.loc[:, sequence].values.reshape(-1, window_size , 1),
    train_data.ticker,
    train_data.filter(like='month')
]
y_train = train_data.label
[x.shape for x in X_train], y_train.shape
[(1035424, 52, 1), (1035424,), (1035424, 12)], (1035424,)
```

How to define the architecture using Keras' Functional API

Keras' Functional API makes it easy to design an architecture like the one outlined at the beginning of this section with multiple inputs (or several outputs, as in the SVHN example in *Chapter 18, CNNs for Financial Time Series and Satellite Images*). This example illustrates a network with three inputs:

1. **Two stacked LSTM layers** with 25 and 10 units, respectively
2. An **embedding layer** that learns a 10-dimensional real-valued representation of the equities
3. A **one-hot encoded** representation of the month

We begin by defining the three inputs with their respective shapes:

```
n_features = 1
returns = Input(shape=(window_size, n_features), name='Returns')
tickers = Input(shape=(1,), name='Tickers')
months = Input(shape=(12,), name='Months')
```

To define **stacked LSTM layers**, we set the `return_sequences` keyword for the first layer to `True`. This ensures that the first layer produces an output in the expected three-dimensional input format. Note that we also use dropout regularization and how the Functional API passes the tensor outputs from one layer to the subsequent layer's input:

```
lstm1 = LSTM(units=lstm1_units,
             input_shape=(window_size, n_features),
             name='LSTM1',
             dropout=.2,
             return_sequences=True)(returns)
lstm_model = LSTM(units=lstm2_units,
             dropout=.2,
             name='LSTM2')(lstm1)
```

The TensorFlow 2 guide for RNNs highlights the fact that GPU support is only available when using the default values for most LSTM settings (`https://www.tensorflow.org/guide/keras/rnn`).

The **embedding layer** requires:

- The `input_dim` keyword, which defines how many embeddings the layer will learn
- The `output_dim` keyword, which defines the size of the embedding
- The `input_length` parameter, which sets the number of elements passed to the layer (here, only one ticker per sample)

The goal of the embedding layer is to learn vector representations that capture the relative locations of the feature values to one another with respect to the outcome. We'll choose a five-dimensional embedding for the roughly 2,500 ticker values to combine the embedding layer with the LSTM layer and the month dummies we need to reshape (or flatten) it:

```
ticker_embedding = Embedding(input_dim=n_tickers,
                             output_dim=5,
                             input_length=1)(tickers)
ticker_embedding = Reshape(target_shape=(5,))(ticker_embedding)
```

Now we can concatenate the three tensors, followed by `BatchNormalization`:

```
merged = concatenate([lstm_model, ticker_embedding, months], name='Merged')
bn = BatchNormalization()(merged)
```

The fully connected final layers learn a mapping from these stacked LSTM layers, ticker embeddings, and month indicators to the binary outcome that reflects a positive or negative return over the following week. We formulate the complete RNN by defining its inputs and outputs with the implicit data flow we just defined:

```
hidden_dense = Dense(10, name='FC1')(bn)
output = Dense(1, name='Output', activation='sigmoid')(hidden_dense)

rnn = Model(inputs=[returns, tickers, months], outputs=output)
```

The summary lays out this slightly more sophisticated architecture with 16,984 parameters:

```
Layer (type)                    Output Shape         Param #     Connected to
Returns (InputLayer)            [(None, 52, 1)]      0
Tickers (InputLayer)            [(None, 1)]          0
LSTM1 (LSTM)                    (None, 52, 25)       2700        Returns[0]
[0]
embedding (Embedding)           (None, 1, 5)         12445       Tickers[0]
[0]
LSTM2 (LSTM)                    (None, 10)           1440        LSTM1[0][0]
reshape (Reshape)               (None, 5)          0           embedding[0]
[0]
Months (InputLayer)             [(None, 12)]         0
Merged (Concatenate)            (None, 27)           0           LSTM2[0][0]
                                                                 reshape[0]
[0]
                                                                 Months[0][0]
batch_normalization (BatchNorma (None, 27)           108         Merged[0][0]
FC1 (Dense)                     (None, 10)           280
atch_normalization[0][0]
Output (Dense)                  (None, 1)            11          FC1[0][0]
Total params: 16,984
Trainable params: 16,930
Non-trainable params: 54
```

We compile the model using the recommended RMSProp optimizer with default settings and compute the AUC metric that we'll use for early stopping:

```
optimizer = tf.keras.optimizers.RMSprop(lr=0.001,
                                        rho=0.9,
                                        epsilon=1e-08,
                                        decay=0.0)

rnn.compile(loss='binary_crossentropy',
            optimizer=optimizer,
            metrics=['accuracy',
                     tf.keras.metrics.AUC(name='AUC')])
```

We train the model for 50 epochs by using early stopping:

```
result = rnn.fit(X_train,
                 y_train,
                 epochs=50,
                 batch_size=32,
                 validation_data=(X_test, y_test),
                 callbacks=[early_stopping])
```

The following plots show that training stops after 8 epochs, each of which takes around three minutes on a single GPU. It results in a test AUC of 0.6816 and a test accuracy of 0.6193 for the best model:

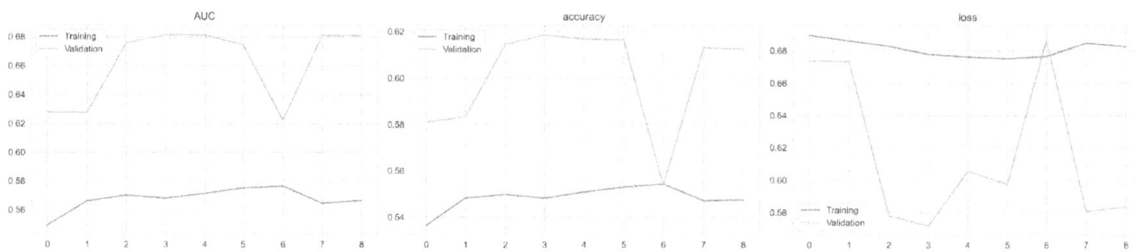

Figure 19.10: Stacked LSTM classification—cross-validation performance

The IC for the test prediction and actual weekly returns is 0.32.

Predicting returns instead of directional price moves

The `stacked_lstm_with_feature_embeddings_regression.ipynb` notebook illustrates how to adapt the model to the regression task of predicting returns rather than binary price changes.

The required changes are minor; just do the following:

1. Select the `fwd_returns` outcome instead of the binary `label`.
2. Convert the model output to linear (the default) instead of `sigmoid`.
3. Update the loss to mean squared error (and early stopping references).
4. Remove or update optional metrics to match the regression task.

Using otherwise the same training parameters (except that the Adam optimizer with default settings yields a better result in this case), the validation loss improves for nine epochs. The average weekly IC is 3.32, and 6.68 for the entire period while significant at the 1 percent level. The average weekly return differential between the equities in the top and bottom quintiles of predicted returns is slightly above 20 basis points:

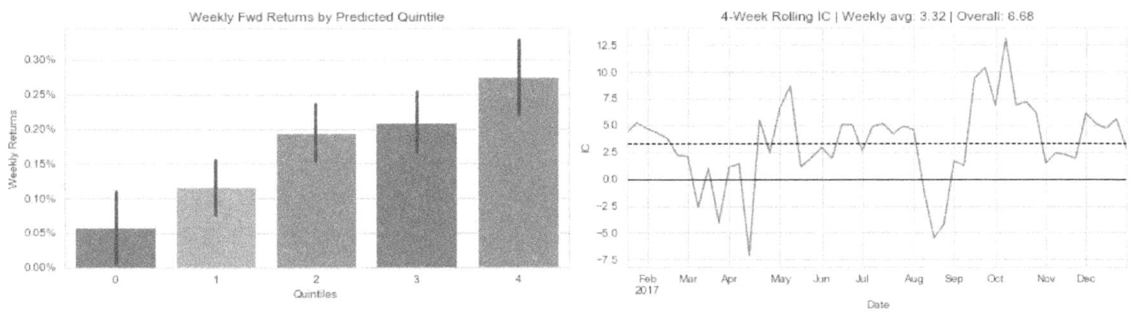

Figure 19.11: Stacked LSTM regression—out-of-sample performance

Multivariate time-series regression for macro data

So far, we have limited our modeling efforts to a single time series. RNNs are well-suited to multivariate time series and represent a nonlinear alternative to the **vector autoregressive** (**VAR**) models we covered in *Chapter 9, Time-Series Models for Volatility Forecasts and Statistical Arbitrage*. Refer to the `multivariate_timeseries` notebook for implementation details.

Loading sentiment and industrial production data

We'll show how to model and forecast multiple time series using RNNs with the same dataset we used for the VAR example. It has monthly observations over 40 years on consumer sentiment and industrial production from the Federal Reserve's FRED service:

```
df = web.DataReader(['UMCSENT', 'IPGMFN'], 'fred', '1980', '2019-12').
dropna()
df.columns = ['sentiment', 'ip']
df.info()
DatetimeIndex: 480 entries, 1980-01-01 to 2019-12-01
Data columns (total 2 columns):
sentiment     480 non-null float64
ip            480 non-null float64
```

Making the data stationary and adjusting the scale

We apply the same transformation—annual difference for both series, prior log-transform for industrial production—to achieve stationarity (see *Chapter 9, Time-Series Models for Volatility Forecasts and Statistical Arbitrage* for details). We also rescale it to the [0, 1] range to ensure that the network gives both series equal weight during training:

```
df_transformed = (pd.DataFrame({'ip': np.log(df.ip).diff(12),
                               'sentiment': df.sentiment.diff(12)}).dropna())
df_transformed = df_transformed.apply(minmax_scale)
```

Figure 19.12 displays the original and transformed macro time series:

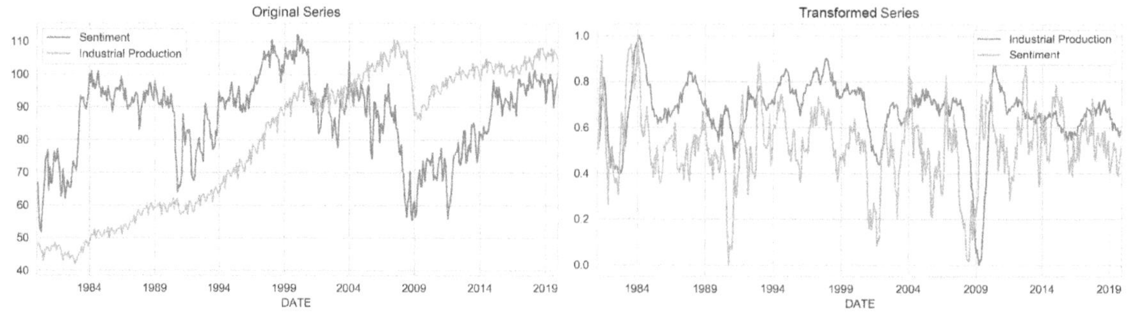

Figure 19.12: Original and transformed time series

Creating multivariate RNN inputs

The `create_multivariate_rnn_data()` function transforms a dataset of several time series into the three-dimensional shape required by TensorFlow's RNN layers, formed as `n_samples × window_size × n_series`:

```
def create_multivariate_rnn_data(data, window_size):
    y = data[window_size:]
    n = data.shape[0]
    X = np.stack([data[i: j] for i, j in enumerate(range(window_size, n))],
                 axis=0)
    return X, y
```

A `window_size` value of 18 ensures that the entries in the second dimension are the lagged 18 months of the respective output variable. We thus obtain the RNN model inputs for each of the two features as follows:

```
X, y = create_multivariate_rnn_data(df_transformed, window_size=window_size)
X.shape, y.shape
((450, 18, 2), (450, 2))
```

Finally, we split our data into a training and a test set, using the last 24 months to test the out-of-sample performance:

```
test_size = 24
train_size = X.shape[0]-test_size

X_train, y_train = X[:train_size], y[:train_size]
X_test, y_test = X[train_size:], y[train_size:]

X_train.shape, X_test.shape
((426, 18, 2), (24, 18, 2))
```

Defining and training the model

Given the relatively small dataset, we use a simpler RNN architecture than in the previous example. It has a single LSTM layer with 12 units, followed by a fully connected layer with 6 units. The output layer has two units, one for each time series.

We compile using mean absolute loss and the recommended RMSProp optimizer:

```
n_features = output_size = 2
lstm_units = 12
dense_units = 6

rnn = Sequential([
    LSTM(units=lstm_units,
         dropout=.1,
         recurrent_dropout=.1,
         input_shape=(window_size, n_features), name='LSTM',
         return_sequences=False),
    Dense(dense_units, name='FC'),
    Dense(output_size, name='Output')
])
rnn.compile(loss='mae', optimizer='RMSProp')
```

The model still has 812 parameters, compared to 10 for the `VAR(1, 1)` model from *Chapter 9, Time-Series Models for Volatility Forecasts and Statistical Arbitrage*:

```
Layer (type)                 Output Shape              Param #
LSTM (LSTM)                  (None, 12)                720
FC (Dense)                   (None, 6)                 78
Output (Dense)               (None, 2)                 14
Total params: 812
Trainable params: 812
```

We train for 100 epochs with a `batch_size` of 20 using early stopping:

```
result = rnn.fit(X_train,
                 y_train,
                 epochs=100,
                 batch_size=20,
                 shuffle=False,
                 validation_data=(X_test, y_test),
                 callbacks=[checkpointer, early_stopping],
                 verbose=1)
```

Training stops early after 62 epochs, yielding a test MAE of 0.034, an almost 25 percent improvement over the test MAE for the VAR model of 0.043 on the same task.

However, the two results are not fully comparable because the RNN produces 18 1-step-ahead forecasts whereas the VAR model uses its own predictions as input for its out-of-sample forecast. You may want to tweak the VAR setup to obtain comparable forecasts and compare the performance.

Figure 19.13 highlights training and validation errors, and the out-of-sample predictions for both series:

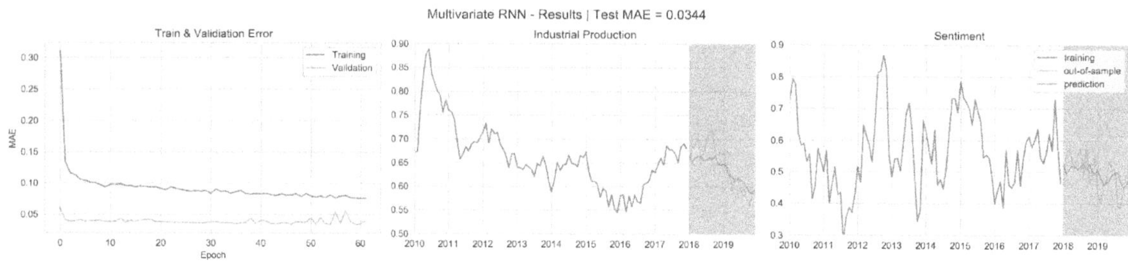

Figure 19.13: Cross-validation and test results for RNNs with multiple macro series

RNNs for text data

RNNs are commonly applied to various natural language processing tasks, from machine translation to sentiment analysis, that we already encountered in Part 3 of this book. In this section, we will illustrate how to apply an RNN to text data to detect positive or negative sentiment (easily extensible to a finer-grained sentiment scale) and to predict stock returns.

More specifically, we'll use word embeddings to represent the tokens in the documents. We covered word embeddings in *Chapter 16, Word Embeddings for Earnings Calls and SEC Filings*. They are an excellent technique for converting a token into a dense, real-value vector because the relative location of words in the embedding space encodes useful semantic aspects of how they are used in the training documents.

We saw in the previous stacked RNN example that TensorFlow has a built-in embedding layer that allows us to train vector representations specific to the task at hand. Alternatively, we can use pretrained vectors. We'll demonstrate both approaches in the following three sections.

LSTM with embeddings for sentiment classification

This example shows how to learn custom embedding vectors while training an RNN on the classification task. This differs from the word2vec model that learns vectors while optimizing predictions of neighboring tokens, resulting in their ability to capture certain semantic relationships among words (see *Chapter 16, Word Embeddings for Earnings Calls and SEC Filings*). Learning word vectors with the goal of predicting sentiment implies that embeddings will reflect how a token relates to the outcomes it is associated with.

Loading the IMDB movie review data

To keep the data manageable, we will illustrate this use case with the IMDB reviews dataset, which contains 50,000 positive and negative movie reviews, evenly split into a training set and a test set, with balanced labels in each dataset. The vocabulary consists of 88,586 tokens. Alternatively, you could use the much larger Yelp review data (after converting the text into numerical sequences; see the next section on using pretrained embeddings or TensorFlow 2 docs).

The dataset is bundled into TensorFlow and can be loaded so that each review is represented as an integer-encoded sequence. We can limit the vocabulary to `num_words` while filtering out frequent and likely less informative words using `skip_top` as well as sentences longer than `maxlen`. We can also choose the `oov_char` value, which represents tokens we chose to exclude from the vocabulary on frequency grounds:

```
from tensorflow.keras.datasets import imdb
vocab_size = 20000
(X_train, y_train), (X_test, y_test) = imdb.load_data(seed=42,
                                                      skip_top=0,
                                                      maxlen=None,
                                                      oov_char=2,
                                                      index_from=3,
                                                      num_words=vocab_size)
```

In the second step, convert the lists of integers into fixed-size arrays that we can stack and provide as an input to our RNN. The `pad_sequence` function produces arrays of equal length, truncated and padded to conform to `maxlen`:

```
maxlen = 100
X_train_padded = pad_sequences(X_train,
                               truncating='pre',
                               padding='pre',
                               maxlen=maxlen)
```

Defining embedding and the RNN architecture

Now we can set up our RNN architecture. The first layer learns the word embeddings. We define the embedding dimensions as before, using the following:

- The `input_dim` keyword, which sets the number of tokens that we need to embed
- The `output_dim` keyword, which defines the size of each embedding
- The `input_len` parameter, which specifies how long each input sequence is going to be

Note that we are using GRU units this time that train faster and perform better on smaller amounts of data. We are also using recurrent dropout for regularization:

```
embedding_size = 100
rnn = Sequential([
```

```
    Embedding(input_dim=vocab_size,
              output_dim= embedding_size,
              input_length=maxlen),
    GRU(units=32,
        dropout=0.2, # comment out to use optimized GPU implementation
        recurrent_dropout=0.2),
    Dense(1, activation='sigmoid')
])
```

The resulting model has over 2 million trainable parameters:

```
Layer (type)                 Output Shape              Param #
embedding (Embedding)        (None, 100, 100)          2000000
gru (GRU)                    (None, 32)                12864
dense (Dense)                (None, 1)                 33
Total params: 2,012,897
Trainable params: 2,012,897
```

We compile the model to use the AUC metric and train with early stopping:

```
rnn.fit(X_train_padded,
        y_train,
        batch_size=32,
        epochs=25,
        validation_data=(X_test_padded, y_test),
        callbacks=[early_stopping],
        verbose=1)
```

Training stops after 12 epochs, and we recover the weights for the best models to find a high test AUC of 0.9393:

```
y_score = rnn.predict(X_test_padded)
roc_auc_score(y_score=y_score.squeeze(), y_true=y_test)
0.9393289376
```

Figure 19.14 displays the cross-validation performance in terms of accuracy and AUC:

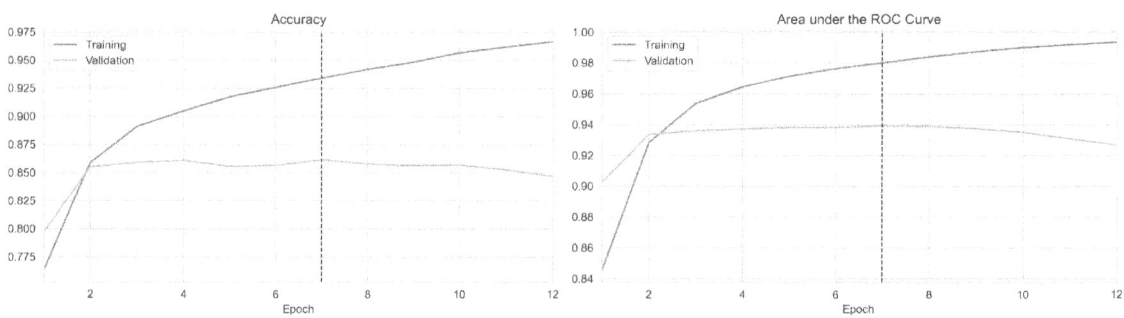

Figure 19.14: Cross-validation for RNN using IMDB data with custom embeddings

Sentiment analysis with pretrained word vectors

In *Chapter 16, Word Embeddings for Earnings Calls and SEC Filings*, we discussed how to learn domain-specific word embeddings. Word2vec and related learning algorithms produce high-quality word vectors but require large datasets. Hence, it is common that research groups share word vectors trained on large datasets, similar to the weights for pretrained deep learning models that we encountered in the section on transfer learning in the previous chapter.

We are now going to illustrate how to use pretrained **global vectors for word representation** (**GloVe**) provided by the Stanford NLP group with the IMDB review dataset (refer to GitHub for references and the `sentiment_analysis_pretrained_embeddings` notebook for implementation details).

Preprocessing the text data

We are going to load the IMDB dataset from the source to manually preprocess it (see the notebook). TensorFlow provides a `Tokenizer`, which we'll use to convert the text documents to integer-encoded sequences:

```
num_words = 10000
t = Tokenizer(num_words=num_words,
              lower=True,
              oov_token=2)
t.fit_on_texts(train_data.review)
vocab_size = len(t.word_index) + 1
train_data_encoded = t.texts_to_sequences(train_data.review)
test_data_encoded = t.texts_to_sequences(test_data.review)
```

We also use the `pad_sequences` function to convert the list of lists (of unequal length) to stacked sets of padded and truncated arrays for both the training and test data:

```
max_length = 100
X_train_padded = pad_sequences(train_data_encoded,
                               maxlen=max_length,
                               padding='post',
                               truncating='post')
y_train = train_data['label']
X_train_padded.shape
(25000, 100)
```

Loading the pretrained GloVe embeddings

We downloaded and unzipped the GloVe data to the location indicated in the code and will now create a dictionary that maps GloVe tokens to 100-dimensional, real-valued vectors:

```
glove_path = Path('data/glove/glove.6B.100d.txt')
embeddings_index = dict()
```

```
for line in glove_path.open(encoding='latin1'):
    values = line.split()
    word = values[0]
    coefs = np.asarray(values[1:], dtype='float32')
    embeddings_index[word] = coefs
```

There are around 340,000 word vectors that we use to create an embedding matrix that matches the vocabulary so that the RNN can access embeddings by the token index:

```
embedding_matrix = np.zeros((vocab_size, 100))
for word, i in t.word_index.items():
    embedding_vector = embeddings_index.get(word)
    if embedding_vector is not None:
        embedding_matrix[i] = embedding_vector
```

Defining the architecture with frozen weights

The difference with the RNN setup in the previous example is that we are going to pass the embedding matrix to the embedding layer and set it to *not trainable* so that the weights remain fixed during training:

```
rnn = Sequential([
    Embedding(input_dim=vocab_size,
              output_dim=embedding_size,
              input_length=max_length,
              weights=[embedding_matrix],
              trainable=False),
    GRU(units=32,  dropout=0.2, recurrent_dropout=0.2),
    Dense(1, activation='sigmoid')])
```

From here on, we proceed as before. Training continues for 32 epochs, as shown in *Figure 19.15*, and we obtain a test AUC score of 0.9106. This is slightly worse than our result in the previous sections where we learned custom embedding for this domain, underscoring the value of training your own word embeddings:

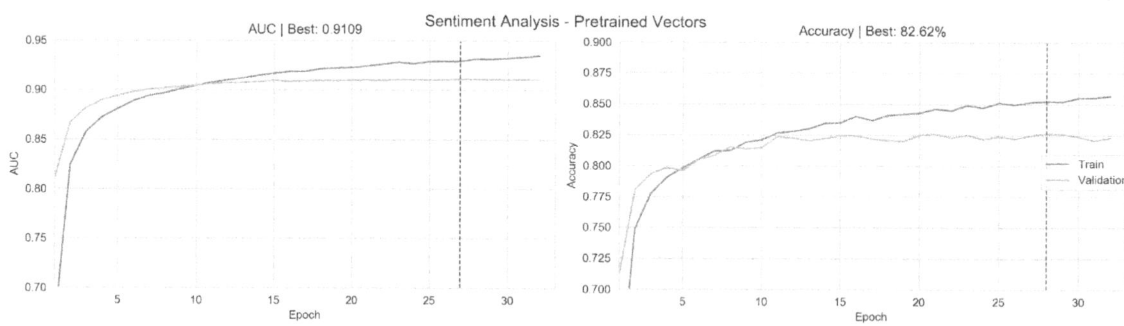

Figure 19.15: Cross-validation and test results for RNNs with multiple macro series

You may want to apply these techniques to the larger financial text datasets that we used in Part 3.

Predicting returns from SEC filing embeddings

In *Chapter 16, Word Embeddings for Earnings Calls and SEC Filings,* we discussed important differences between product reviews and financial text data. While the former was useful to illustrate important workflows, in this section, we will tackle more challenging but also more relevant financial documents. More specifically, we will use the SEC filings data introduced in *Chapter 16, Word Embeddings for Earnings Calls and SEC Filings,* to learn word embeddings tailored to predicting the return of the ticker associated with the disclosures from before publication to one week after.

The `sec_filings_return_prediction` notebook contains the code examples for this section. See the `sec_preprocessing` notebook in *Chapter 16, Word Embeddings for Earnings Calls and SEC Filings,* and instructions in the data folder on GitHub on how to obtain the data.

Source stock price data using yfinance

There are 22,631 filings for the period 2013-16. We use yfinance to obtain stock price data for the related 6,630 tickers because it achieves higher coverage than Quandl's WIKI Data. We use the ticker symbol and filing date from the filing index (see *Chapter 16, Word Embeddings for Earnings Calls and SEC Filings*) to download daily adjusted stock prices for three months before and one month after the filing data as follows, capturing both the price data and unsuccessful tickers in the process:

```
yf_data, missing = [], []
for i, (symbol, dates) in enumerate(filing_index.groupby('ticker').date_filed,
                                    1):
    ticker = yf.Ticker(symbol)
    for idx, date in dates.to_dict().items():
        start = date - timedelta(days=93)
        end = date + timedelta(days=31)
        df = ticker.history(start=start, end=end)
        if df.empty:
            missing.append(symbol)
        else:
            yf_data.append(df.assign(ticker=symbol, filing=idx))
```

We obtain data on 3,954 tickers and source prices for a few hundred missing tickers using the Quandl Wiki data (see the notebook) and end up with 16,758 filings for 4,762 symbols.

Preprocessing SEC filing data

Compared to product reviews, financial text documents tend to be longer and have a more formal structure. In addition, in this case, we rely on data sourced from EDGAR that requires parsing of the XBRL source (see *Chapter 2, Market and Fundamental Data - Sources and Techniques*) and may have errors such as including material other than the desired sections. We take several steps during preprocessing to address outliers and format the text data as integer sequences of equal length, as required by the model that we will build in the next section:

1. Remove all sentences that contain fewer than 5 or more than 50 tokens; this affects approximately. 5 percent of sentences.
2. Create 28,599 bigrams, 10,032 trigrams, and 2,372 n-grams with 4 elements.
3. Convert filings to a sequence of integers that represent the token frequency rank, removing filings with fewer than 100 tokens and truncating sequences at 20,000 elements.

Figure 19.16 highlights some corpus statistics for the remaining 16,538 filings with 179,214,369 tokens, around 204,206 of which are unique. The left panel shows the token frequency distribution on a log-log scale; the most frequent terms, "million," "business," "company," and "products" occur more than 1 million times each. As usual, there is a very long tail, with 60 percent of tokens occurring fewer than 25 times.

The central panel shows the distribution of the sentence lengths with a mode of around 10 tokens. Finally, the right panel shows the distribution of the filing length with a peak at 20,000 due to truncation:

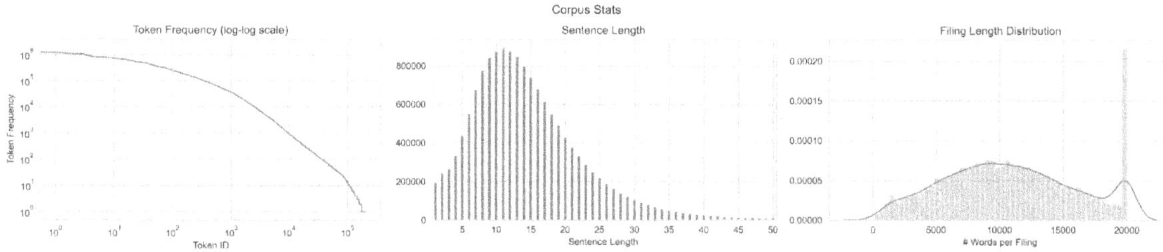

Figure 19.16: Cross-validation and test results for RNNs with multiple macro series

Preparing data for the RNN model

Now we need an outcome for our model to predict. We'll compute (somewhat arbitrarily) five-day forward returns for the day of filing (or the day before if there are no prices for that date), assuming that filing occurred after market hours. Clearly, this assumption could be wrong, underscoring the need for **point-in-time data** emphasized in *Chapter 2, Market and Fundamental Data – Sources and Techniques*, and *Chapter 3, Alternative Data for Finance – Categories and Use Cases*. We'll ignore this issue as the hidden cost of using free data.

We compute the forward returns as follows, removing outliers with weekly returns below 50 or above 100 percent:

```
fwd_return = {}
for filing in filings:
    date_filed = filing_index.at[filing, 'date_filed']
    price_data = prices[prices.filing==filing].close.sort_index()

    try:
        r = (price_data
             .pct_change(periods=5)
             .shift(-5)
             .loc[:date_filed]
             .iloc[-1])
    except:
        continue
    if not np.isnan(r) and -.5 < r < 1:
        fwd_return[filing] = r
```

This leaves us with 16,355 data points. Now we combine these outcomes with their matching filing sequences and convert the list of returns to a NumPy array:

```
y, X = [], []
for filing_id, fwd_ret in fwd_return.items():
    X.append(np.load(vector_path / f'{filing_id}.npy') + 2)
    y.append(fwd_ret)
y = np.array(y)
```

Finally, we create a 90:10 training/test split and use the `pad_sequences` function introduced in the first example in this section to generate fixed-length sequences of 20,000 elements each:

```
X_train, X_test, y_train, y_test = train_test_split(X, y, test_size=.1)
X_train = pad_sequences(X_train,
                        truncating='pre',
                        padding='pre',
                        maxlen=maxlen)
X_test = pad_sequences(X_test,
                       truncating='pre',
                       padding='pre',
                       maxlen=maxlen)
X_train.shape, X_test.shape
((14719, 20000), (1636, 20000))
```

Building, training, and evaluating the RNN model

Now we can define our RNN architecture. The first layer learns the word embeddings. We define the embedding dimensions as previously, setting the following:

- The `input_dim` keyword to the size of the vocabulary
- The `output_dim` keyword to the size of each embedding
- The `input_length` parameter to how long each input sequence is going to be

For the recurrent layer, we use a bidirectional GRU unit that scans the text both forward and backward and concatenates the resulting output. We also add batch normalization and dropout for regularization with a five-unit dense layer before the linear output:

```
embedding_size = 100
input_dim = X_train.max() + 1
rnn = Sequential([
    Embedding(input_dim=input_dim,
              output_dim=embedding_size,
              input_length=maxlen,
             name='EMB'),
    BatchNormalization(name='BN1'),
    Bidirectional(GRU(32), name='BD1'),
    BatchNormalization(name='BN2'),
    Dropout(.1, name='DO1'),
    Dense(5, name='D'),
    Dense(1, activation='linear', name='OUT')])
```

The resulting model has over 2.5 million trainable parameters:

```
rnn.summary()
Layer (type)                 Output Shape              Param #
EMB (Embedding)              (None, 20000, 100)        2500000
BN1 (BatchNormalization)     (None, 20000, 100)        400
BD1 (Bidirectional)          (None, 64)                25728
BN2 (BatchNormalization)     (None, 64)                256
DO1 (Dropout)                (None, 64)                0
D (Dense)                    (None, 5)                 325
OUT (Dense)                  (None, 1)                 6
Total params: 2,526,715
Trainable params: 2,526,387
Non-trainable params: 328
```

We compile using the Adam optimizer, targeting the mean squared loss for this regression task while also tracking the square root of the loss and the mean absolute error as optional metrics:

```
rnn.compile(loss='mse',
```

```
            optimizer='Adam',
            metrics=[RootMeanSquaredError(name='RMSE'),
                     MeanAbsoluteError(name='MAE')])
```

With early stopping, we train for up to 100 epochs on batches of 32 observations each:

```
early_stopping = EarlyStopping(monitor='val_MAE',
                               patience=5,
                               restore_best_weights=True)
training = rnn.fit(X_train,
                   y_train,
                   batch_size=32,
                   epochs=100,
                   validation_data=(X_test, y_test),
                   callbacks=[early_stopping],
                   verbose=1)
```

The mean absolute error improves for only 4 epochs, as shown in the left panel of *Figure 19.17:*

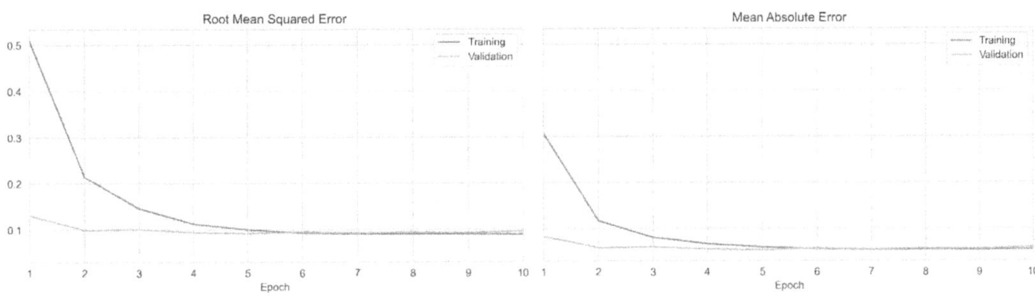

Figure 19.17: Cross-validation test results for RNNs using SEC filings to predict weekly returns

On the test set, the best model achieves a highly significant IC of 6.02:

```
y_score = rnn.predict(X_test)
rho, p = spearmanr(y_score.squeeze(), y_test)
print(f'{rho*100:.2f} ({p:.2%})')
6.02 (1.48%)
```

Lessons learned and next steps

The model is capable of generating return predictions that are significantly better than chance using only text data. There are both caveats that suggest taking the results with a grain of salt and reasons to believe we could improve on the result of this experiment.

On the one hand, the quality of both the stock price data and the parsed SEC filings is far from perfect. It's unclear whether price data issues bias the results positively or negatively, but they certainly increase the margin of error. More careful parsing and cleaning of the SEC filings would most likely improve the results by removing noise.

On the other hand, there are numerous optimizations that may well improve the result. Starting with the text input, we did not attempt to parse the filing content beyond selecting certain sections; there may be value in removing boilerplate language or otherwise trying to pick the most meaningful statements. We also made somewhat arbitrary choices about the maximum length of filings and the size of the vocabulary that we could revisit. We could also shorten or lengthen the weekly prediction horizon. Furthermore, there are multiple aspects of the model architecture that we could refine, from the size of the embeddings to the number and size of layers and the degree of regularization.

Most fundamentally, we could combine the text input with a richer set of complementary features, as demonstrated in the previous section, using stacked LSTM with multiple inputs. Finally, we would certainly want a larger set of filings.

Summary

In this chapter, we presented the specialized RNN architecture that is tailored to sequential data. We covered how RNNs work, analyzed the computational graph, and saw how RNNs enable parameter-sharing over numerous steps to capture long-range dependencies that FFNNs and CNNs are not well suited for.

We also reviewed the challenges of vanishing and exploding gradients and saw how gated units like long short-term memory cells enable RNNs to learn dependencies over hundreds of time steps. Finally, we applied RNNs to challenges common in algorithmic trading, such as predicting univariate and multivariate time series and sentiment analysis using SEC filings.

In the next chapter, we will introduce unsupervised deep learning techniques like autoencoders and generative adversarial networks and their applications to investment and trading strategies.

20

Autoencoders for Conditional Risk Factors and Asset Pricing

This chapter shows how unsupervised learning can leverage deep learning for trading. More specifically, we'll discuss **autoencoders** that have been around for decades but have recently attracted fresh interest.

Unsupervised learning addresses practical ML challenges such as the limited availability of labeled data and the curse of dimensionality, which requires exponentially more samples for successful learning from complex, real-life data with many features. At a conceptual level, unsupervised learning resembles human learning and the development of common sense much more closely than supervised and reinforcement learning, which we'll cover in the next chapter. It is also called **predictive learning** because it aims to discover structure and regularities from data so that it can predict missing inputs, that is, fill in the blanks from the observed parts.

An **autoencoder** is a **neural network** (**NN**) trained to reproduce the input while learning a new representation of the data, encoded by the parameters of a hidden layer. Autoencoders have long been used for nonlinear dimensionality reduction and manifold learning (see *Chapter 13, Data-Driven Risk Factors and Asset Allocation with Unsupervised Learning*). A variety of designs leverage the feedforward, convolutional, and recurrent network architectures we covered in the last three chapters. We will see how autoencoders can underpin a **trading strategy**: we will build a deep neural network that uses an autoencoder to extract risk factors and predict equity returns, conditioned on a range of equity attributes (Gu, Kelly, and Xiu 2020).

More specifically, in this chapter you will learn about:

- Which types of autoencoders are of practical use and how they work
- Building and training autoencoders using Python
- Using autoencoders to extract data-driven risk factors that take into account asset characteristics to predict returns

> You can find the code samples for this chapter and links to additional resources in the corresponding directory of the GitHub repository. The notebooks include color versions of the images.

Autoencoders for nonlinear feature extraction

In *Chapter 17, Deep Learning for Trading*, we saw how neural networks succeed at supervised learning by extracting a hierarchical feature representation useful for the given task. **Convolutional neural networks** (**CNNs**), for example, learn and synthesize increasingly complex patterns from grid-like data, for example, to identify or detect objects in an image or to classify time series.

An autoencoder, in contrast, is a neural network designed exclusively to learn a **new representation** that encodes the input in a way that helps solve another task. To this end, the training forces the network to reproduce the input. Since autoencoders typically use the same data as input and output, they are also considered an instance of **self-supervised learning**. In the process, the parameters of a hidden layer h become the code that represents the input, similar to the word2vec model covered in *Chapter 16, Word Embeddings for Earnings Calls and SEC Filings*.

More specifically, the network can be viewed as consisting of an encoder function $h=f(x)$ that learns the hidden layer's parameters from input x, and a decoder function g that learns to reconstruct the input from the encoding h. Rather than learning the identity function:

$$x = g(f(x))$$

which simply copies the input, autoencoders use **constraints** that force the hidden layer to **prioritize which aspects of the data to encod**e. The goal is to obtain a representation of practical value.

Autoencoders can also be viewed as a **special case of a feedforward neural network** (see *Chapter 17, Deep Learning for Trading*) and can be trained using the same techniques. Just as with other models, excess capacity will lead to overfitting, preventing the autoencoder from producing an informative encoding that generalizes beyond the training samples. See *Chapters 14* and *15* of Goodfellow, Bengio, and Courville (2016) for additional background.

Generalizing linear dimensionality reduction

A traditional use case includes dimensionality reduction, achieved by limiting the size of the hidden layer and thus creating a "bottleneck" so that it performs lossy compression. Such an autoencoder is called **undercomplete**, and the purpose is to learn the most salient properties of the data by minimizing a loss function L of the form:

$$L(x, g(f(x)))$$

An example loss function that we will explore in the next section is simply the mean squared error evaluated on the pixel values of the input images and their reconstruction. We will also use this loss function to extract risk factors from time series of financial features when we build a conditional autoencoder for trading.

Undercomplete autoencoders differ from linear dimensionality reduction methods like **principal component analysis** (**PCA**; see *Chapter 13*, *Data-Driven Risk Factors and Asset Allocation with Unsupervised Learning*) when they use **nonlinear activation functions**; otherwise, they learn the same subspace as PCA. They can thus be viewed as a nonlinear generalization of PCA capable of learning a wider range of encodings.

Figure 20.1 illustrates the encoder-decoder logic of an undercomplete feedforward autoencoder with three hidden layers: the encoder and decoder have one hidden layer each plus a shared encoder output/decoder input layer containing the encoding. The three hidden layers use nonlinear activation functions, like **rectified linear units** (**ReLU**), *sigmoid*, or *tanh* (see *Chapter 17*, *Deep Learning for Trading*) and have fewer units than the input that the network aims to reconstruct.

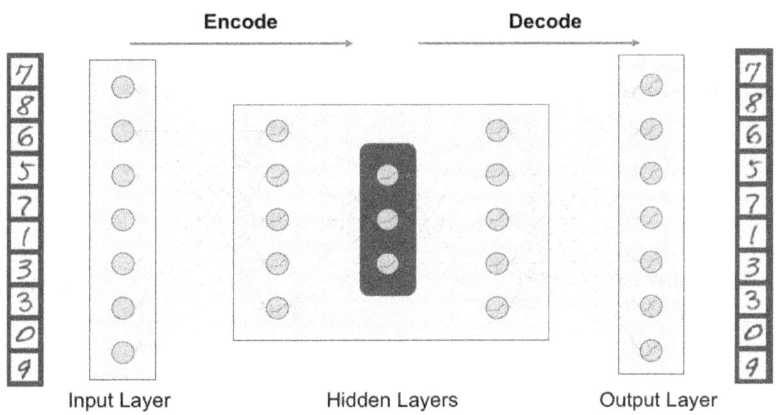

Figure 20.1: Undercomplete encoder-decoder architecture

Depending on the task, a simple autoencoder with a single encoder and decoder layer may be adequate. However, **deeper autoencoders** with additional layers can have several advantages, just as for other neural networks. These advantages include the ability to learn more complex encodings, achieve better compression, and do so with less computational effort and fewer training samples, subject to the perennial risk of overfitting.

Convolutional autoencoders for image compression

As discussed in *Chapter 18*, *CNNs for Financial Time Series and Satellite Images*, fully connected feedforward architectures are not well suited to capture local correlations typical to data with a grid-like structure. Instead, autoencoders can also use convolutional layers to learn a hierarchical feature representation. Convolutional autoencoders leverage convolutions and parameter sharing to learn hierarchical patterns and features irrespective of their location, translation, or changes in size.

We will illustrate different implementations of convolutional autoencoders for image data below. Alternatively, convolutional autoencoders could be applied to multivariate time series data arranged in a grid-like format as illustrated in *Chapter 18, CNNs for Financial Time Series and Satellite Images*.

Managing overfitting with regularized autoencoders

The powerful capabilities of neural networks to represent complex functions require tight controls of the capacity of encoders and decoders to extract signals rather than noise so that the encoding is more useful for a downstream task. In other words, when it is too easy for the network to recreate the input, it fails to learn only the most interesting aspects of the data and improve the performance of a machine learning model that uses the encoding as inputs.

Just as for other models with excessive capacity for the given task, **regularization** can help to address the **overfitting** challenge by constraining the autoencoder's learning process and forcing it to produce a useful representation (see, for instance, *Chapter 7, Linear Models – From Risk Factors to Return Forecasts*, on regularization for linear models, and *Chapter 17, Deep Learning for Trading*, for neural networks). Ideally, we could precisely match the model's capacity to the complexity of the distribution of the data. In practice, the optimal model often combines (limited) excess capacity with appropriate regularization. To this end, we add a sparsity penalty $\Omega(h)$ that depends on the weights of the encoding layer h to the training objective:

$$L\left(x, g\big(f(x)\big)\right) + \Omega(h)$$

A common approach that we explore later in this chapter is the use of **L1 regularization**, which adds a penalty to the loss function in the form of the sum of the absolute values of the weights. The L1 norm results in sparse encodings because it forces the values of parameters to zero if they do not capture independent variation in the data (see *Chapter 7, Linear Models – From Risk Factors to Return Forecasts*). As a result, even overcomplete autoencoders with hidden layers of a higher dimension than the input may be able to learn signal content.

Fixing corrupted data with denoising autoencoders

The autoencoders we have discussed so far are designed to reproduce the input despite capacity constraints. An alternative approach trains autoencoders with corrupted inputs $\tilde{x}$ to output the desired, original data points. In this case, the autoencoder minimizes a loss L:

$$L\left(x, g\big(f(\tilde{x})\big)\right)$$

Corrupted inputs are a different way of preventing the network from learning the identity function and rather extracting the signal or salient features from the data. Denoising autoencoders have been shown to learn the data generating process of the original data and have become popular in generative modeling where the goal is **to learn the probability distribution** that gives rise to the input (Vincent et al., 2008).

Seq2seq autoencoders for time series features

Recurrent neural networks (**RNNs**) have been developed for sequential data characterized by longitudinal dependencies between data points, potentially over long ranges (*Chapter 19, RNNs for Multivariate Time Series and Sentiment Analysis*). Similarly, sequence-to-sequence (seq2seq) autoencoders aim to learn representations attuned to the nature of data generated in sequence (Srivastava, Mansimov, and Salakhutdinov, 2016).

Seq2seq autoencoders are based on RNN components like **long short-term memory** (**LSTM**) or gated recurrent unit. They learn a representation of sequential data and have been successfully applied to video, text, audio, and time series data.

As mentioned in the last chapter, encoder-decoder architectures allow RNNs to process input and output sequences with variable length. These architectures underpin many advances in complex sequence prediction tasks, like speech recognition and text translation, and are being increasingly applied to (financial) time series. At a high level, they work as follows:

1. The LSTM encoder processes the input sequence step by step to learn a hidden state.
2. This state becomes a learned representation of the sequence in the form of a fixed-length vector.
3. The LSTM decoder receives this state as input and uses it to generate the output sequence.

See references linked on GitHub for examples on building sequence-to-sequence autoencoders to **compress time series data** and **detect anomalies** in time series to allow, for example, regulators to uncover potentially illegal trading activity.

Generative modeling with variational autoencoders

Variational autoencoders (**VAE**) were developed more recently (Kingma and Welling, 2014) and focus on generative modeling. In contrast to a discriminative model that learns a predictor given data, a generative model aims to solve the more general problem of learning a joint probability distribution over all variables. If successful, it could simulate how the data is produced in the first place. Learning the data-generating process is very valuable: it reveals underlying causal relationships and supports semi-supervised learning to effectively generalize from a small labeled dataset to a large unlabeled one.

More specifically, VAEs are designed to learn the latent (meaning *unobserved*) variables of the model responsible for the input data. Note that we encountered latent variables in *Chapter 15, Topic Modeling – Summarizing Financial News*, and *Chapter 16, Word Embeddings for Earnings Calls and SEC Filings*.

Just like the autoencoders discussed so far, VAEs do not let the network learn arbitrary functions as long as it faithfully reproduces the input. Instead, they aim to learn the parameters of a probability distribution that generates the input data.

In other words, VAEs are generative models because, if successful, you can generate new data points by sampling from the distribution learned by the VAE.

The operation of a VAE is more complex than the autoencoders discussed so far because it involves stochastic backpropagation, that is, taking derivatives of stochastic variables, and the details are beyond the scope of this book. They are able to learn high-capacity input encodings without regularization that are useful because the models aim to maximize the probability of the training data rather than to reproduce the input. For a detailed introduction, see Kingma and Welling (2019).

The `variational_autoencoder.ipynb` notebook includes a sample VAE implementation applied to the Fashion MNIST data, adapted from a Keras tutorial by Francois Chollet to work with TensorFlow 2. The resources linked on GitHub contain a VAE tutorial with references to PyTorch and TensorFlow 2 implementations and many additional references. See Wang et al. (2019) for an application that combines a VAE with an RNN using LSTM and outperforms various benchmark models in futures markets.

Implementing autoencoders with TensorFlow 2

In this section, we'll illustrate how to implement several of the autoencoder models introduced in the previous section using the Keras interface of TensorFlow 2. We'll first load and prepare an image dataset that we'll use throughout this section. We will use images instead of financial time series because it makes it easier to visualize the results of the encoding process. The next section shows how to use an autoencoder with financial data as part of a more complex architecture that can serve as the basis for a trading strategy.

After preparing the data, we'll proceed to build autoencoders using deep feedforward nets, sparsity constraints, and convolutions and apply the latter to denoise images.

How to prepare the data

For illustration, we'll use the Fashion MNIST dataset, a modern drop-in replacement for the classic MNIST handwritten digit dataset popularized by Lecun et al. (1998) with LeNet. We also relied on this dataset in *Chapter 13, Data-Driven Risk Factors and Asset Allocation with Unsupervised Learning*, on unsupervised learning.

Keras makes it easy to access the 60,000 training and 10,000 test grayscale samples with a resolution of 28 × 28 pixels:

```
from tensorflow.keras.datasets import fashion_mnist
(X_train, y_train), (X_test, y_test) = fashion_mnist.load_data()
X_train.shape, X_test.shape
((60000, 28, 28), (10000, 28, 28))
```

The data contains clothing items from 10 classes. *Figure 20.2* plots a sample image for each class:

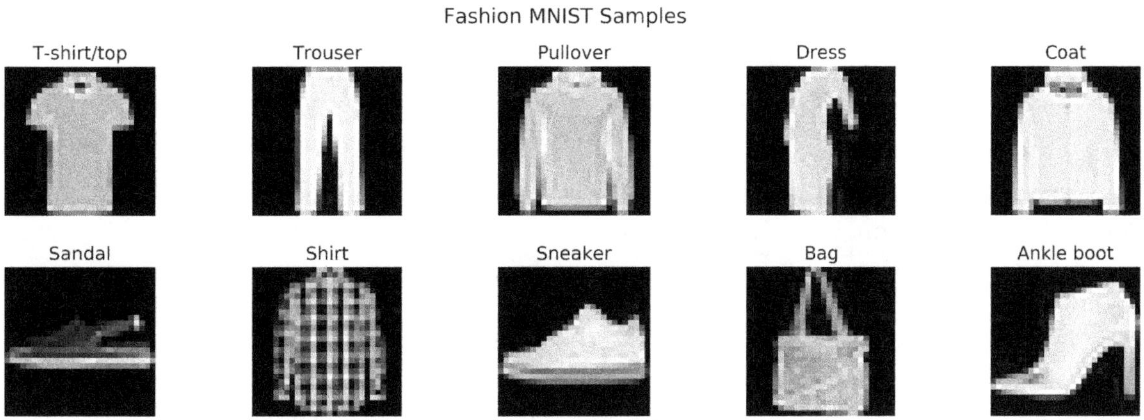

Figure 20.2: Fashion MNIST sample images

We reshape the data so that each image is represented by a flat one-dimensional pixel vector with 28 × 28 = 784 elements normalized to the range [0, 1]:

```
image_size = 28              # pixels per side
input_size = image_size ** 2 # 784

def data_prep(x, size=input_size):
    return x.reshape(-1, size).astype('float32')/255

X_train_scaled = data_prep(X_train)
X_test_scaled = data_prep(X_test)
X_train_scaled.shape, X_test_scaled.shape
((60000, 784), (10000, 784))
```

One-layer feedforward autoencoder

We start with a vanilla feedforward autoencoder with a single hidden layer to illustrate the general design approach using the Functional Keras API and establish a performance baseline.

The first step is a placeholder for the flattened image vectors with 784 elements:

```
input_ = Input(shape=(input_size,), name='Input')
```

The encoder part of the model consists of a fully connected layer that learns the new, compressed representation of the input. We use 32 units for a compression ratio of 24.5:

```
encoding_size = 32 # compression factor: 784 / 32 = 24.5
encoding = Dense(units=encoding_size,
                 activation='relu',
                 name='Encoder')(input_)
```

The decoding part reconstructs the compressed data to its original size in a single step:

```
decoding = Dense(units=input_size,
                 activation='sigmoid',
                 name='Decoder')(encoding)
```

We instantiate the `Model` class with the chained input and output elements that implicitly define the computational graph as follows:

```
autoencoder = Model(inputs=input_,
                    outputs=decoding,
                    name='Autoencoder')
```

The encoder-decoder computation thus defined uses almost 51,000 parameters:

```
Layer (type)                 Output Shape              Param #
Input (InputLayer)           (None, 784)               0
Encoder (Dense)              (None, 32)                25120
Decoder (Dense)              (None, 784)               25872
Total params: 50,992
Trainable params: 50,992
Non-trainable params: 0
```

The Functional API allows us to use parts of the model's chain as separate encoder and decoder models that use the autoencoder's parameters learned during training.

Defining the encoder

The encoder just uses the input and hidden layer with about half the total parameters:

```
encoder = Model(inputs=input_, outputs=encoding, name='Encoder')
encoder.summary()
Layer (type)                 Output Shape              Param #
Input (InputLayer)           (None, 784)               0
Encoder (Dense)              (None, 32)                25120
Total params: 25,120
Trainable params: 25,120
Non-trainable params: 0
```

We will see shortly that, once we train the autoencoder, we can use the encoder to compress the data.

Defining the decoder

The decoder consists of the last autoencoder layer, fed by a placeholder for the encoded data:

```
encoded_input = Input(shape=(encoding_size,), name='Decoder_Input')
decoder_layer = autoencoder.layers[-1](encoded_input)
decoder = Model(inputs=encoded_input, outputs=decoder_layer)
decoder.summary()
Layer (type)                 Output Shape              Param #
Decoder_Input (InputLayer)   (None, 32)                0
Decoder (Dense)              (None, 784)               25872
Total params: 25,872
Trainable params: 25,872
Non-trainable params: 0
```

Training the model

We compile the model to use the Adam optimizer (see *Chapter 17, Deep Learning for Trading*) to minimize the mean squared error between the input data and the reproduction achieved by the autoencoder. To ensure that the autoencoder learns to reproduce the input, we train the model using the same input and output data:

```
autoencoder.compile(optimizer='adam', loss='mse')
autoencoder.fit(x=X_train_scaled, y=X_train_scaled,
                epochs=100, batch_size=32,
                shuffle=True, validation_split=.1,
                callbacks=[tb_callback, early_stopping, checkpointer])
```

Evaluating the results

Training stops after some 20 epochs with a test RMSE of 0.1121:

```
mse = autoencoder.evaluate(x=X_test_scaled, y=X_test_scaled)
f'MSE: {mse:.4f} | RMSE {mse**.5:.4f}'
'MSE: 0.0126 | RMSE 0.1121'
```

To encode data, we use the encoder we just defined like so:

```
encoded_test_img = encoder.predict(X_test_scaled)
Encoded_test_img.shape
(10000, 32)
```

The decoder takes the compressed data and reproduces the output according to the autoencoder training results:

```
decoded_test_img = decoder.predict(encoded_test_img)
decoded_test_img.shape
(10000, 784)
```

Figure 20.3 shows 10 original images and their reconstruction by the autoencoder and illustrates the loss after compression:

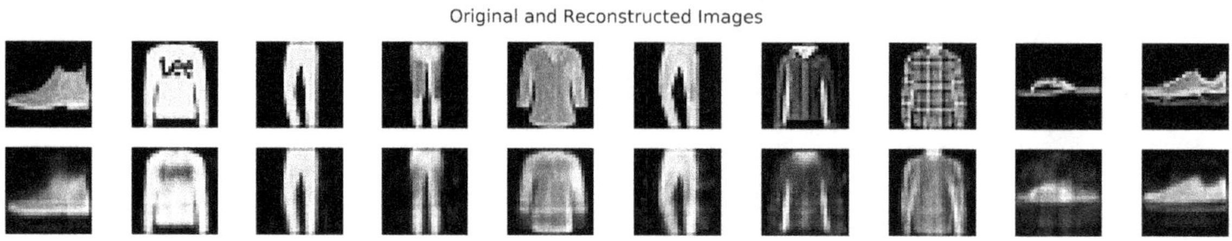

Figure 20.3: Sample Fashion MNIST images, original and reconstructed

Feedforward autoencoder with sparsity constraints

The addition of regularization is fairly straightforward. We can apply it to the dense encoder layer using Keras' `activity_regularizer` as follows:

```
encoding_l1 = Dense(units=encoding_size,
                    activation='relu',
                    activity_regularizer=regularizers.l1(10e-5),
                    name='Encoder_L1')(input_)
```

The input and decoding layers remain unchanged. In this example with compression of factor 24.5, regularization negatively affects performance with a test RMSE of 0.1229.

Deep feedforward autoencoder

To illustrate the benefit of adding depth to the autoencoder, we will build a three-layer feedforward model that successively compresses the input from 784 to 128, 64, and 32 units, respectively:

```
input_ = Input(shape=(input_size,))
x = Dense(128, activation='relu', name='Encoding1')(input_)
x = Dense(64, activation='relu', name='Encoding2')(x)
encoding_deep = Dense(32, activation='relu', name='Encoding3')(x)

x = Dense(64, activation='relu', name='Decoding1')(encoding_deep)
x = Dense(128, activation='relu', name='Decoding2')(x)
decoding_deep = Dense(input_size, activation='sigmoid', name='Decoding3')(x)

autoencoder_deep = Model(input_, decoding_deep)
```

The resulting model has over 222,000 parameters, more than four times the capacity of the previous single-layer model:

```
Layer (type)                 Output Shape              Param #
=================================================================
input_1 (InputLayer)         (None, 784)               0
_________________________________________________________________
Encoding1 (Dense)            (None, 128)               100480
_________________________________________________________________
Encoding2 (Dense)            (None, 64)                8256
_________________________________________________________________
Encoding3 (Dense)            (None, 32)                2080
_________________________________________________________________
Decoding1 (Dense)            (None, 64)                2112
_________________________________________________________________
Decoding2 (Dense)            (None, 128)               8320
_________________________________________________________________
Decoding3 (Dense)            (None, 784)               101136
=================================================================
Total params: 222,384
Trainable params: 222,384
Non-trainable params: 0
```

Training stops after 45 epochs and results in a 14 percent reduction of the test RMSE to 0.097. Due to the low resolution, it is difficult to visually note the better reconstruction.

Visualizing the encoding

We can use the manifold learning technique **t-distributed Stochastic Neighbor Embedding** (**t-SNE**; see *Chapter 13, Data-Driven Risk Factors and Asset Allocation with Unsupervised Learning*) to visualize and assess the quality of the encoding learned by the autoencoder's hidden layer.

If the encoding is successful in capturing the salient features of the data, then the compressed representation of the data should still reveal a structure aligned with the 10 classes that differentiate the observations. We use the output of the deep encoder we just trained to obtain the 32-dimensional representation of the test set:

```
tsne = TSNE(perplexity=25, n_iter=5000)
train_embed = tsne.fit_transform(encoder_deep.predict(X_train_scaled))
```

Figure 20.4 shows that the 10 classes are well separated, suggesting that the encoding is useful as a lower-dimensional representation that preserves the key characteristics of the data (see the `variational_autoencoder.ipynb` notebook for a color version):

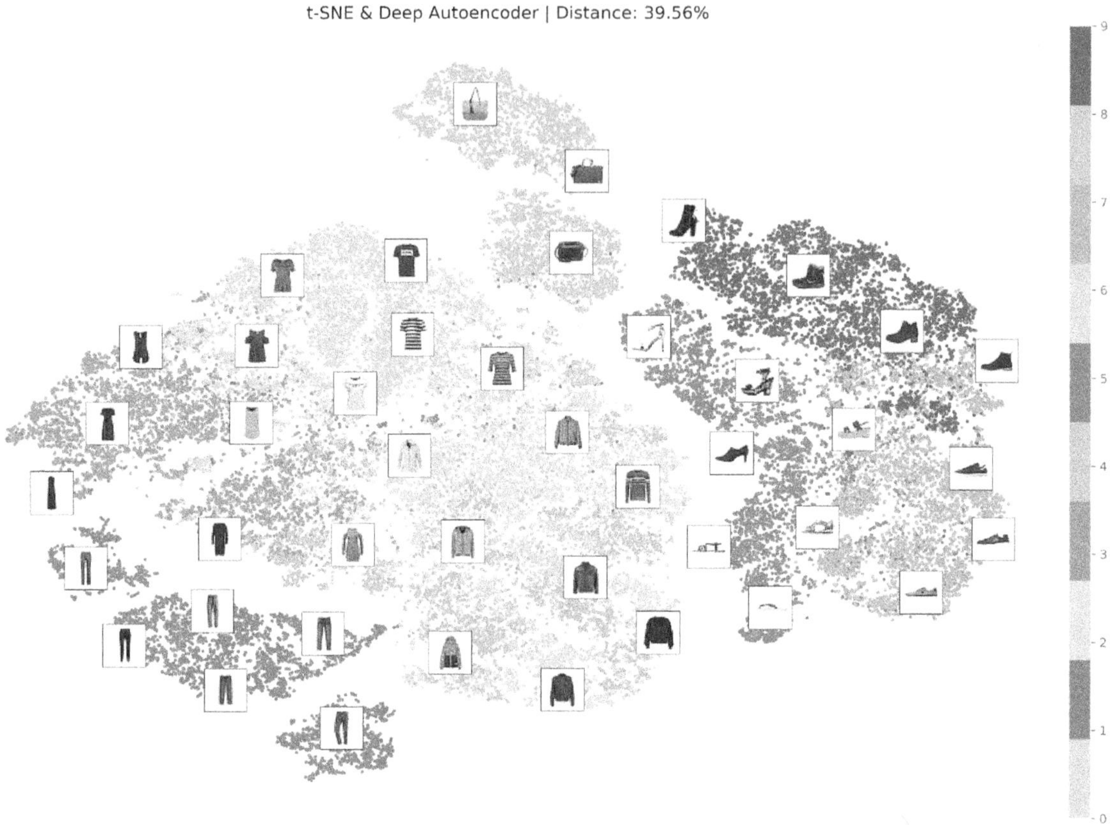

Figure 20.4: t-SNE visualization of the Fashion MNIST autoencoder embedding

Convolutional autoencoders

The insights from *Chapter 18, CNNs for Financial Time Series and Satellite Images*, on CNNs suggest we incorporate convolutional layers into the autoencoder to extract information characteristic of the grid-like structure of image data.

We define a three-layer encoder that uses 2D convolutions with 32, 16, and 8 filters, respectively, ReLU activations, and `'same'` padding to maintain the input size. The resulting encoding size at the third layer is $4 \times 4 \times 8 = 128$, higher than for the previous examples:

```
x = Conv2D(filters=32,
           kernel_size=(3, 3),
           activation='relu',
           padding='same',
           name='Encoding_Conv_1')(input_)
```

```
x = MaxPooling2D(pool_size=(2, 2), padding='same', name='Encoding_Max_1')(x)
x = Conv2D(filters=16,
           kernel_size=(3, 3),
           activation='relu',
           padding='same',
           name='Encoding_Conv_2')(x)
x = MaxPooling2D(pool_size=(2, 2), padding='same', name='Encoding_Max_2')(x)
x = Conv2D(filters=8,
           kernel_size=(3, 3),
           activation='relu',
           padding='same',
           name='Encoding_Conv_3')(x)
encoded_conv = MaxPooling2D(pool_size=(2, 2),
                            padding='same',
                            name='Encoding_Max_3')(x)
```

We also define a matching decoder that reverses the number of filters and uses 2D upsampling instead of max pooling to reverse the reduction of the filter sizes. The three-layer autoencoder has 12,785 parameters, a little more than 5 percent of the capacity of the deep autoencoder.

Training stops after 67 epochs and results in a further 9 percent reduction in the test RMSE, due to a combination of the ability of convolutional filters to learn more efficiently from image data and the larger encoding size.

Denoising autoencoders

The application of an autoencoder to a denoising task only affects the training stage. In this example, we add noise from a standard normal distribution to the Fashion MNIST data while maintaining the pixel values in the range [0, 1] as follows:

```
def add_noise(x, noise_factor=.3):
    return np.clip(x  + noise_factor * np.random.normal(size=x.shape), 0, 1)
X_train_noisy = add_noise(X_train_scaled)
X_test_noisy = add_noise(X_test_scaled)
```

We then proceed to train the convolutional autoencoder on noisy inputs, the objective being to learn how to generate the uncorrupted originals:

```
autoencoder_denoise.fit(x=X_train_noisy,
                        y=X_train_scaled,
                        ...)
```

The test RMSE after 60 epochs is 0.0931, unsurprisingly higher than before. *Figure 20.5* shows, from top to bottom, the original images as well as the noisy and denoised versions. It illustrates that the autoencoder is successful in producing compressed encodings from the noisy images that are quite similar to those produced from the original images:

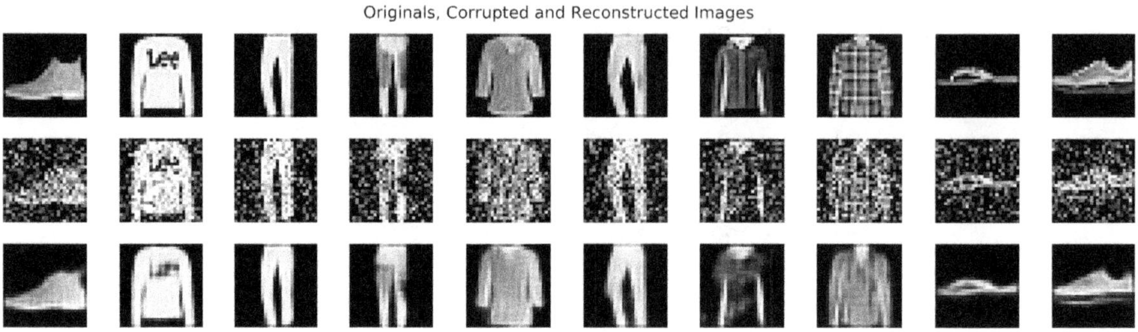

Figure 20.5: Denoising input and output examples

A conditional autoencoder for trading

Recent research by Gu, Kelly, and Xiu (GKX, 2019) developed an asset pricing model based on the exposure of securities to risk factors. It builds on the concept of **data-driven risk factors** that we discussed in *Chapter 13, Data-Driven Risk Factors and Asset Allocation with Unsupervised Learning*, when introducing PCA as well as the risk factor models covered in *Chapter 4, Financial Feature Engineering – How to Research Alpha Factors*. They aim to show that the asset characteristics used by factor models to capture the systematic drivers of "anomalies" are just proxies for the time-varying exposure to risk factors that cannot be directly measured. In this context, anomalies are returns in excess of those explained by the exposure to aggregate market risk (see the discussion of the capital asset pricing model in *Chapter 5, Portfolio Optimization and Performance Evaluation*).

The **Fama-French factor models** discussed in *Chapter 4* and *Chapter 7* explain returns by specifying risk factors like firm size based on empirical observations of differences in average stock returns beyond those due to aggregate market risk. Given such **specific risk factors**, these models are able to measure the reward an investor receives for taking on factor risk using portfolios designed accordingly: sort stocks by size, buy the smallest quintile, sell the largest quintile, and compute the return. The observed risk factor return then allows linear regression to estimate the sensitivity of assets to these factors (called **factor loadings**), which in turn helps to predict the returns of (many) assets based on forecasts of (far fewer) factor returns.

In contrast, GKX treat **risk factors as latent, or non-observable**, drivers of covariance among a number of assets large enough to prevent investors from avoiding exposure through diversification. Therefore, investors require a reward that adjusts like any price to achieve equilibrium, providing in turn an economic rationale for return differences that are no longer anomalous. In this view, risk factors are purely statistical in nature while the underlying economic forces can be of arbitrary and varying origin.

In another recent paper (Kelly, Pruitt, and Su, 2019), Kelly—who teaches finance at Yale, works with AQR, and is one of the pioneers in applying ML to trading—and his coauthors developed a linear model dubbed **Instrumented Principal Component Analysis** (IPCA) to **estimate latent risk factors and the assets' factor loadings from data**. IPCA extends PCA to include asset characteristics as covariates and produce time-varying factor loadings. (See *Chapter 13, Data-Driven Risk Factors and Asset Allocation with Unsupervised Learning*, for coverage of PCA.) By conditioning asset exposure to factors on observable asset characteristics, IPCA aims to answer whether there is a set of common latent risk factors that explain an observed anomaly rather than whether there is a specific observable factor that can do so.

GKX creates a **conditional autoencoder architecture** to reflect the nonlinear nature of return dynamics ignored by the linear Fama-French models and the IPCA approach. The result is a deep neural network that simultaneously learns the premia on a given number of unobservable factors using an autoencoder, and the factor loadings for a large universe of equities based on a broad range of time-varying asset characteristics using a feedforward network. The model succeeds in explaining and predicting asset returns. It demonstrates a relationship that is both statistically and economically significant, yielding an attractive Sharpe ratio when translated into a long-short decile spread strategy similar to the examples we have used throughout this book.

In this section, we'll create a simplified version of this model to demonstrate how you can **leverage autoencoders to generate tradeable signals**. To this end, we'll build a new dataset of close to 4,000 US stocks over the 1990-2019 period using yfinance, because it provides some additional information that facilitates the computation of the asset characteristics. We'll take a few shortcuts, such as using fewer assets and only the most important characteristics. We'll also omit some implementation details to simplify the exposition. We'll highlight the most important differences so that you can enhance the model accordingly.

We'll first show how to prepare the data before we explain, build, and train the model and evaluate its predictive performance. Please see the above references for additional background on the theory and implementation.

Sourcing stock prices and metadata information

The GKX reference implementation uses stock price and firm characteristic data for over 30,000 US equities from the Center for Research in Security Prices (CRSP) from 1957-2016 at a monthly frequency. It computes 94 metrics that include a broad range of asset attributes suggested as predictive of returns in previous academic research and listed in Green, Hand, and Zhang (2017), who set out to verify these claims.

Since we do not have access to the high-quality but costly CRSP data, we leverage yfinance (see *Chapter 2, Market and Fundamental Data - Sources and Techniques*) to download price and metadata from Yahoo Finance. There are downsides to choosing free data, including:

- The lack of quality control regarding adjustments
- Survivorship bias because we cannot get data for stocks that are no longer listed
- A smaller scope in terms of both the number of equities and the length of their history

The `build_us_stock_dataset.ipynb` notebook contains the relevant code examples for this section.

To obtain the data, we get a list of the 8,882 currently traded symbols from NASDAQ using pandas-datareader (see *Chapter 2, Market and Fundamental Data – Sources and Techniques*):

```
from pandas_datareader.nasdaq_trader import get_nasdaq_symbols
traded_symbols = get_nasdaq_symbols()
```

We remove ETFs and create yfinance `Ticker()` objects for the remainder:

```
import yfinance as yf
tickers = yf.Tickers(traded_symbols[~traded_symbols.ETF].index.to_list())
```

Each ticker's `.info` attribute contains data points scraped from Yahoo Finance, ranging from the outstanding number of shares and other fundamentals to the latest market capitalization; coverage varies by security:

```
info = []
for ticker in tickers.tickers:
    info.append(pd.Series(ticker.info).to_frame(ticker.ticker))
info = pd.concat(info, axis=1).dropna(how='all').T
info = info.apply(pd.to_numeric, errors='ignore')
```

For the tickers with metadata, we download both adjusted and unadjusted prices, the latter including corporate actions like stock splits and dividend payments that we could use to create a Zipline bundle for strategy backtesting (see *Chapter 8, The ML4T Workflow – From Model to Strategy Backtesting*).

We get adjusted OHLCV data on 4,314 stocks as follows:

```
prices_adj = []
with pd.HDFStore('chunks.h5') as store:
    for i, chunk in enumerate(chunks(tickers, 100)):
        print(i, end=' ', flush=True)
        prices_adj.append(yf.download(chunk,
                                      period='max',
                                      auto_adjust=True).stack(-1))
prices_adj = (pd.concat(prices_adj)
              .dropna(how='all', axis=1)
              .rename(columns=str.lower)
              .swaplevel())
prices_adj.index.names = ['ticker', 'date']
```

Absent any quality control regarding the underlying price data and the adjustments for stock splits, we remove equities with suspicious values such as daily returns above 100 percent or below -100 percent:

```
df = prices_adj.close.unstack('ticker')
pmax = df.pct_change().max()
pmin = df.pct_change().min()
to_drop = pmax[pmax > 1].index.union(pmin[pmin<-1].index)
```

This removes around 10 percent of the tickers, leaving us with close to 3,900 assets for the 1990-2019 period.

Computing predictive asset characteristics

GKX tested 94 asset attributes based on Green et al. (2017) and identified the 20 most influential metrics while asserting that feature importance drops off quickly thereafter. The top 20 stock characteristics fall into three categories, namely:

- **Price trend**, including (industry) momentum, short- and long-term reversal, or the recent maximum return
- **Liquidity,** such as turnover, dollar volume, or market capitalization
- **Risk measures**, for instance, total and idiosyncratic return volatility or market beta

Of these 20, we limit the analysis to 16 for which we have or can approximate the relevant inputs. The `conditional_autoencoder_for_trading_data.ipynb` notebook demonstrates how to calculate the relevant metrics. We highlight a few examples in this section; see also the *Appendix, Alpha Factor Library*.

Some metrics require information like sector, market cap, and outstanding shares, so we limit our stock price dataset to the securities with relevant metadata:

```
tickers_with_metadata = (metadata[metadata.sector.isin(sectors) &
                                   metadata.marketcap.notnull() &
                                   metadata.sharesoutstanding.notnull() &
                                  (metadata.sharesoutstanding > 0)]
                                   .index.drop(tickers_with_errors))
```

We run our analysis at a weekly instead of monthly return frequency to compensate for the 50 percent shorter time period and around 80 percent lower number of stocks. We obtain weekly returns as follows:

```
returns = (prices.close
           .unstack('ticker')
           .resample('W-FRI').last()
           .sort_index().pct_change().iloc[1:])
```

Most metrics are fairly straightforward to compute. **Stock momentum**, the 11-month cumulative stock returns ending 1 month before the current date, can be derived as follows:

```
MONTH = 21
mom12m = (close
            .pct_change(periods=11 * MONTH)
            .shift(MONTH)
            .resample('W-FRI')
            .last()
            .stack()
            .to_frame('mom12m'))
```

The **Amihud Illiquidity** measure is the ratio of a stock's absolute returns relative to its dollar volume, measured as a rolling 21-day average:

```
dv = close.mul(volume)
ill = (close.pct_change().abs()
        .div(dv)
        .rolling(21)
        .mean()
        .resample('W-FRI').last()
        .stack()
        .to_frame('ill'))
```

Idiosyncratic volatility is measured as the standard deviation of a regression of residuals of weekly returns on the returns of equally weighted market index returns for the prior three years. We compute this computationally intensive metric using `statsmodels`:

```
index = close.resample('W-FRI').last().pct_change().mean(1).to_frame('x')
def get_ols_residuals(y, x=index):
    df = x.join(y.to_frame('y')).dropna()
    model = sm.OLS(endog=df.y, exog=sm.add_constant(df[['x']]))
    result = model.fit()
    return result.resid.std()
idiovol = (returns.apply(lambda x: x.rolling(3 * 52)
                         .apply(get_ols_residuals)))
```

For the **market beta**, we can use statsmodels' `RollingOLS` class with the weekly asset returns as outcome and the equal-weighted index as input:

```
def get_market_beta(y, x=index):
    df = x.join(y.to_frame('y')).dropna()
    model = RollingOLS(endog=df.y,
                       exog=sm.add_constant(df[['x']]),
                       window=3*52)
    return model.fit(params_only=True).params['x']
```

```
beta = (returns.dropna(thresh=3*52, axis=1)
        .apply(get_market_beta).stack().to_frame('beta'))
```

We end up with around 3 million observations on 16 metrics for some 3,800 securities over the 1990-2019 period. *Figure 20.6* displays a histogram of the number of stock returns per week (the left panel) and boxplots outlining the distribution of the number of observations for each characteristic:

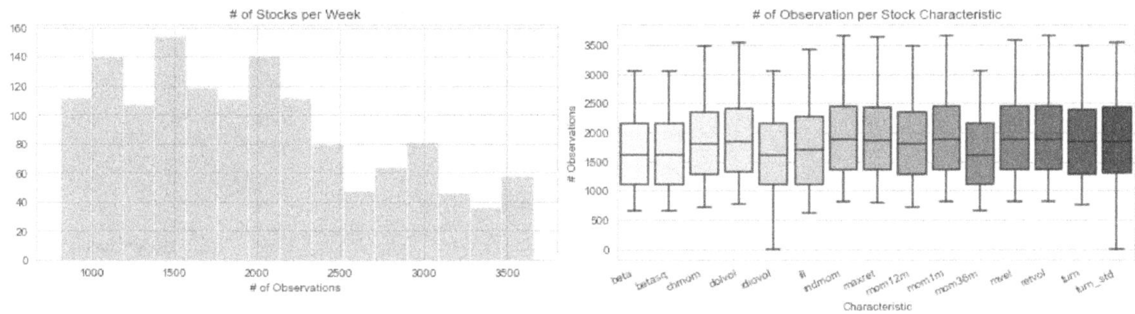

Figure 20.6: Number of tickers over time and per - stock characteristic

To limit the influence of outliers, we follow GKX and rank-normalize the characteristics to the [-1, 1] interval:

```
data.loc[:, characteristics] = (data.loc[:, characteristics]
                                .groupby(level='date')
                                .apply(lambda x:
                                       pd.DataFrame(quantile_transform(
                                       x,
                                       copy=True,
                                       n_quantiles=x.shape[0]),
                                       columns=characteristics,
                                       index=x.index.get_level_values('ticker'))
                                       )
                               .mul(2).sub(1))
```

Since the neural network cannot handle missing data, we set missing values to -2, which lies outside the range for both weekly returns and the characteristics.

The authors apply additional methods to avoid overweighting microcap stocks like market-value-weighted least-squares regression. They also adjust for data-snooping biases by factoring in conservative reporting lags for the characteristics.

Creating the conditional autoencoder architecture

The conditional autoencoder proposed by GKX allows for time-varying return distributions that take into account changing asset characteristics. To this end, the authors extend standard autoencoder architectures that we discussed in the first section of this chapter to allow for features to shape the encoding.

Figure 20.7 illustrates the architecture that models the outcome (asset returns, top) as a function of both asset characteristics (left input) and, again, individual asset returns (right input). The authors allow for asset returns to be individual stock returns or portfolios that are formed from the stocks in the sample based on the asset characteristics, similar to the Fama-French factor portfolios we discussed in *Chapter 4, Financial Feature Engineering – How to Research Alpha Factors*, and summarized in the introduction to this section (hence the dotted lines from stocks to portfolios in the lower-right box). We will use individual stock returns; see GKX for details on how and why to use portfolios instead.

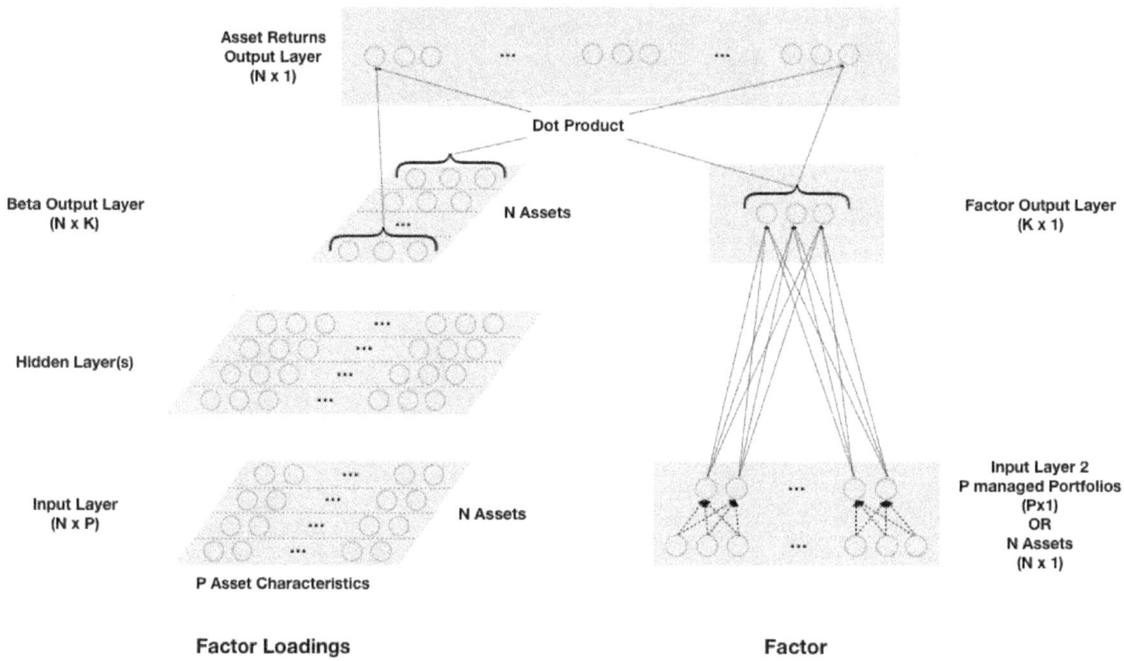

Figure 20.7: Conditional autoencoder architecture designed by GKX

The **feedforward neural network** on the left side of the conditional autoencoder models the *K* factor loadings (beta output) of *N* individual stocks as a function of their *P* characteristics (input). In our case, *N* is around 3,800 and *P* equals 16. The authors experiment with up to three hidden layers with 32, 16, and 8 units, respectively, and find two layers to perform best. Due to the smaller number of characteristics, we only use a similar layer and find 8 units most effective.

The right side of this architecture is a traditional autoencoder when used with individual asset returns as inputs because it maps *N* asset returns onto themselves. The authors use it in this way to measure how well the derived factors explain contemporaneous returns. In addition, they use the autoencoder to predict future returns by using input returns from period *t*-1 with output returns from period t. We will focus on the use of the architecture for prediction, underlining that autoencoders are a special case of a feedforward neural network as mentioned in the first section of this chapter.

The model output is the dot product of the $N \times K$ factor loadings on the left with the $K \times 1$ factor premia on the right. The authors experiment with values of K in the range 2-6, similar to established factor models.

To create this architecture using TensorFlow 2, we use the Functional Keras API and define a `make_model()` function that automates the model compilation process as follows:

```
def make_model(hidden_units=8, n_factors=3):
    input_beta = Input((n_tickers, n_characteristics), name='input_beta')
    input_factor = Input((n_tickers,), name='input_factor')

    hidden_layer = Dense(units=hidden_units,
                         activation='relu',
                         name='hidden_layer')(input_beta)
    batch_norm = BatchNormalization(name='batch_norm')(hidden_layer)

    output_beta = Dense(units=n_factors, name='output_beta')(batch_norm)

    output_factor = Dense(units=n_factors,
                          name='output_factor')(input_factor)

    output = Dot(axes=(2,1),
                 name='output_layer')([output_beta, output_factor])

    model = Model(inputs=[input_beta, input_factor], outputs=output)
    model.compile(loss='mse', optimizer='adam')
    return model
```

We follow the authors in using batch normalization and compile the model to use mean squared error for this regression task and the Adam optimizer. This model has 12,418 parameters (see the notebook).

The authors use additional regularization techniques such as L1 penalties on network weights and combine the results of various networks with the same architecture but using different random seeds. They also use early stopping.

We cross-validate using 20 years for training and predict the following year of weekly returns with five folds corresponding to the years 2015-2019. We evaluate combinations of numbers of factors K from 2 to 6 and 8, 16, or 32 hidden layer units by computing the **information coefficient** (IC) for the validation set as follows:

```
factor_opts = [2, 3, 4, 5, 6]
unit_opts = [8, 16, 32]
param_grid = list(product(unit_opts, factor_opts))

for units, n_factors in param_grid:
    scores = []
    model = make_model(hidden_units=units, n_factors=n_factors)
    for fold, (train_idx, val_idx) in enumerate(cv.split(data)):
        X1_train, X2_train, y_train, X1_val, X2_val, y_val = \
            get_train_valid_data(data, train_idx, val_idx)
```

```
    for epoch in range(250):
        model.fit([X1_train, X2_train], y_train,
                  batch_size=batch_size,
                  validation_data=([X1_val, X2_val], y_val),
                  epochs=epoch + 1,
                  initial_epoch=epoch,
                  verbose=0, shuffle=True)
        result = (pd.DataFrame({'y_pred': model.predict([X1_val,
                                                          X2_val])
                               .reshape(-1),
                                'y_true': y_val.stack().values},
                               index=y_val.stack().index)
                  .replace(-2, np.nan).dropna())
        r0 = spearmanr(result.y_true, result.y_pred)[0]
        r1 = result.groupby(level='date').apply(lambda x:
                                                 spearmanr(x.y_pred,
                                                           x.y_true)[0])
        scores.append([units, n_factors, fold, epoch, r0, r1.mean(),
                       r1.std(), r1.median()])
```

Figure 20.8 plots the validation IC averaged over the five annual folds by epoch for the five-factor count and three hidden-layer size combinations. The upper panel shows the IC across the 52 weeks and the lower panel shows the average weekly IC (see the notebook for the color version):

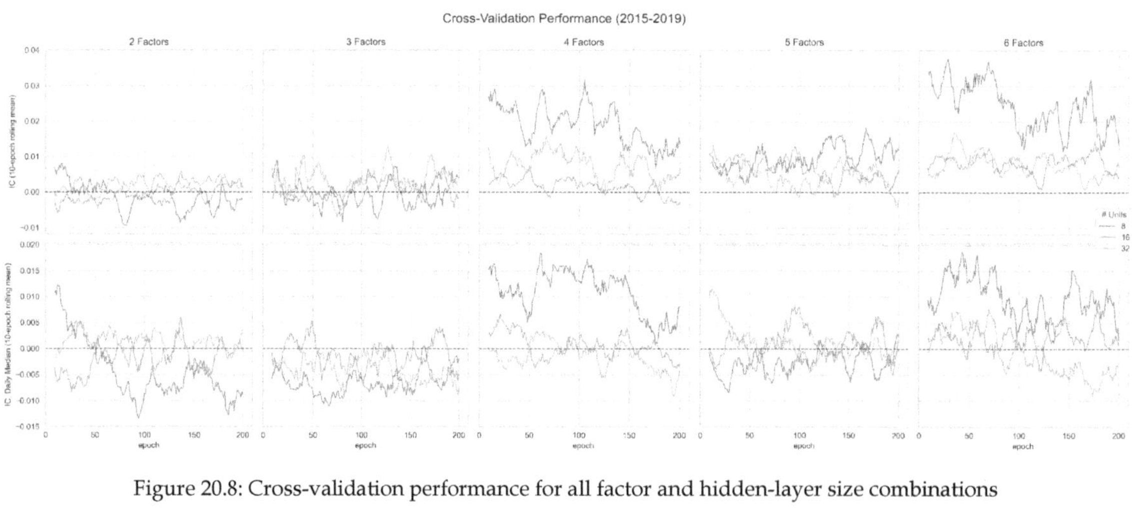

Figure 20.8: Cross-validation performance for all factor and hidden-layer size combinations

The results suggest that more factors and fewer hidden layer units work better; in particular, four and six factors with eight units perform best with overall IC values in the range of 0.02-0.03.

To evaluate the economic significance of the model's predictive performance, we generate predictions for a four-factor model with eight units trained for 15 epochs. Then we use Alphalens to compute the spreads between equal-weighted portfolios invested by a quintile of the predictions for each point in time, while ignoring transaction costs (see the `alphalens_analysis.ipynb` notebook).

Figure 20.9 shows the mean spread for holding periods from 5 to 21 days. For the shorter end that also reflects the prediction horizon, the spread between the bottom and the top decile is around 10 basis points:

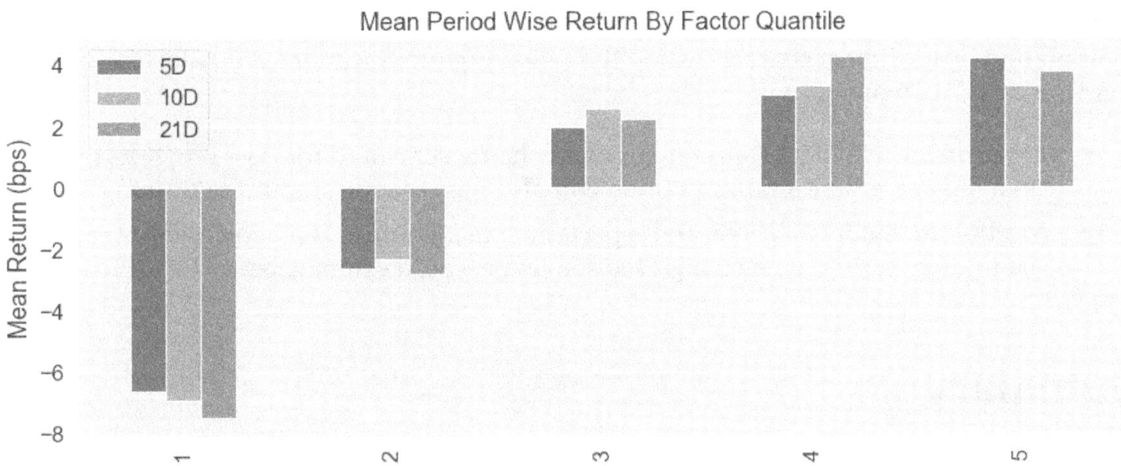

Figure 20.9: Mean period-wise spread by prediction quintile

To evaluate how the predictive performance might translate into returns over time, we lot the cumulative returns of similarly invested portfolios, as well as the cumulative return for a long-short portfolio invested in the top and bottom half, respectively:

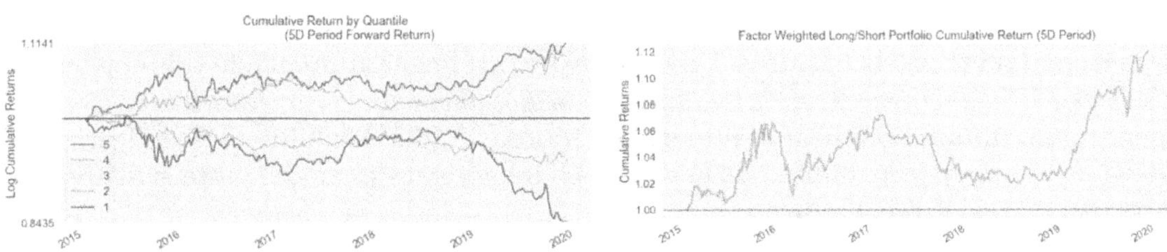

Figure 20.10: Cumulative returns of quintile-based and long-short portfolios

The results show significant spreads between quintile portfolios and positive cumulative returns for the broader-based long-short portfolio over time. This supports the hypothesis that the conditional autoencoder model could contribute to a profitable trading strategy.

Lessons learned and next steps

The conditional autoencoder combines a nonlinear version of the data-driven risk factors we explored using PCA in *Chapter 13, Data-Driven Risk Factors and Asset Allocation with Unsupervised Learning*, with the risk factor approach to modeling returns discussed in *Chapter 4* and *Chapter 7*. It illustrates how deep neural network architectures can be flexibly adapted to various tasks as well as the fluid boundary between autoencoders and feedforward neural networks.

The numerous simplifications from the data source to the architecture point to several avenues for improvements. Besides sourcing more data of better quality that also allows the computation of additional characteristics, the following modifications are a starting point—there are certainly many more:

- Experiment with **data frequencies** other than weekly and forecast horizons other than annual, where shorter periods will also increase the amount of training data
- Modify the **model architecture**, especially if using more data, which might reverse the finding that an even smaller hidden layer would estimate better factor loadings

Summary

In this chapter, we introduced how unsupervised learning leverages deep learning. Autoencoders learn sophisticated, nonlinear feature representations that are capable of significantly compressing complex data while losing little information. As a result, they are very useful to counter the curse of dimensionality associated with rich datasets that have many features, especially common datasets with alternative data. We also saw how to implement various types of autoencoders using TensorFlow 2.

Most importantly, we implemented recent academic research that extracts data-driven risk factors from data to predict returns. Different from our linear approach to this challenge in *Chapter 13, Data-Driven Risk Factors and Asset Allocation with Unsupervised Learning,* autoencoders capture nonlinear relationships. Moreover, the flexibility of deep learning allowed us to incorporate numerous key asset characteristics to model more sensitive factors that helped predict returns.

In the next chapter, we focus on generative adversarial networks, which have often been called one of the most exciting recent developments in artificial intelligence, and see how they are capable of creating synthetic training data.

21

Generative Adversarial Networks for Synthetic Time-Series Data

Following the coverage of autoencoders in the previous chapter, this chapter introduces a second unsupervised deep learning technique: **generative adversarial networks** (**GANs**). As with autoencoders, GANs complement the methods for dimensionality reduction and clustering introduced in *Chapter 13*, *Data-Driven Risk Factors and Asset Allocation with Unsupervised Learning*.

GANs were invented by Goodfellow et al. in 2014. Yann LeCun has called GANs the "most exciting idea in AI in the last ten years." A **GAN** trains two neural networks, called the **generator** and **discriminator**, in a competitive setting. The generator aims to produce samples that the discriminator is unable to distinguish from a given class of training data. The result is a generative model capable of producing synthetic samples representative of a certain target distribution but artificially and, thus, inexpensively created.

GANs have produced an avalanche of research and successful applications in many domains. While originally applied to images, Esteban, Hyland, and Rätsch (2017) applied GANs to the medical domain to generate **synthetic time-series data**. Experiments with financial data ensued (Koshiyama, Firoozye, and Treleaven 2019; Wiese et al. 2019; Zhou et al. 2018; Fu et al. 2019) to explore whether GANs can generate data that simulates alternative asset price trajectories to train supervised or reinforcement algorithms, or to backtest trading strategies. We will replicate the Time-Series GAN presented at the 2019 NeurIPS by Yoon, Jarrett, and van der Schaar (2019) to illustrate the approach and demonstrate the results.

More specifically, in this chapter you will learn about the following:

- How GANs work, why they are useful, and how they can be applied to trading
- Designing and training GANs using TensorFlow 2
- Generating synthetic financial data to expand the inputs available for training ML models and backtesting

> You can find the code samples for this chapter and links to additional resources in the corresponding directory of the GitHub repository. The notebooks include color versions of the images.

Creating synthetic data with GANs

This book mostly focuses on supervised learning algorithms that receive input data and predict an outcome, which we can compare to the ground truth to evaluate their performance. Such algorithms are also called **discriminative models** because they learn to differentiate between different output values.

GANs are an instance of **generative models** like the variational autoencoder we encountered in the previous chapter. As described there, a generative model takes a training set with samples drawn from some distribution p_{data} and learns to represent an estimate p_{model} of that data-generating distribution.

As mentioned in the introduction, GANs are considered one of the most exciting recent machine learning innovations because they appear capable of generating high-quality samples that faithfully mimic a range of input data. This is very attractive given the absence or high cost of labeled data required for supervised learning.

GANs have triggered a wave of research that initially focused on the generation of surprisingly realistic images. More recently, GAN instances have emerged that produce synthetic time series with significant potential for trading since the limited availability of historical market data is a key driver of the risk of backtest overfitting.

In this section, we explain in more detail how generative models and adversarial training work and review various GAN architectures. In the next section, we will demonstrate how to design and train a GAN using TensorFlow 2. In the last section, we will describe how to adapt a GAN so that it creates synthetic time-series data.

Comparing generative and discriminative models

Discriminative models learn how to differentiate among outcomes y, given input data X. In other words, they learn the probability of the outcome given the data: $p(y \mid X)$. Generative models, on the other hand, learn the joint distribution of inputs and outcome $p(y, X)$. While generative models can be used as discriminative models using Bayes' rule to compute which class is most likely (see *Chapter 10, Bayesian ML – Dynamic Sharpe Ratios and Pairs Trading*), it often seems preferable to solve the prediction problem directly rather than by solving the more general generative challenge first (Ng and Jordan 2002).

GANs have a generative objective: they produce complex outputs, such as realistic images, given simple inputs that can even be random numbers. They achieve this by modeling a probability distribution over the possible outputs. This probability distribution can have many dimensions, for example, one for each pixel in an image, each character or token in a document, or each value in a time series. As a result, the model can generate outputs that are very likely representative of the class of outputs.

Richard Feynman's quote "**What I cannot create, I do not understand**" emphasizes that modeling generative distributions is an important step towards more general AI and resembles human learning, which succeeds using much fewer samples.

Generative models have several **use cases** beyond their ability to generate additional samples from a given distribution. For example, they can be incorporated into model-based **reinforcement learning** (**RL**) algorithms (see the next chapter). Generative models can also be applied to time-series data to simulate alternative past or possible future trajectories that can be used for planning in RL or supervised learning more generally, including for the design of trading algorithms. Other use cases include semi-supervised learning where GANs facilitate feature matching to assign missing labels with much fewer training samples than current approaches.

Adversarial training – a zero-sum game of trickery

The key innovation of GANs is a new way of learning the data-generating probability distribution. The algorithm sets up a competitive, or adversarial game between two neural networks called the **generator** and the **discriminator**.

The generator's goal is to convert random noise input into fake instances of a specific class of objects, such as images of faces or stock price time series. The discriminator, in turn, aims to differentiate the generator's deceptive output from a set of training data containing true samples of the target objects. The overall GAN objective is for both networks to get better at their respective tasks so that the generator produces outputs that a machine can no longer distinguish from the originals (at which point we don't need the discriminator, which is no longer necessary, and can discard it).

Figure 21.1 illustrates adversarial training using a generic GAN architecture designed to generate images. We assume the generator uses a deep CNN architecture (such as the VGG16 example from *Chapter 18, CNNs for Financial Time Series and Satellite Images*) that is reversed just like the decoder part of the convolutional autoencoder we discussed in the previous chapter. The generator receives an input image with random pixel values and produces a *fake* output image that is passed on to the discriminator network, which uses a mirrored CNN architecture. The discriminator network also receives *real* samples that represent the target distribution and predicts the probability that the input is *real*, as opposed to *fake*. Learning takes place by backpropagating the gradients of the discriminator and generator losses to the respective network's parameters:

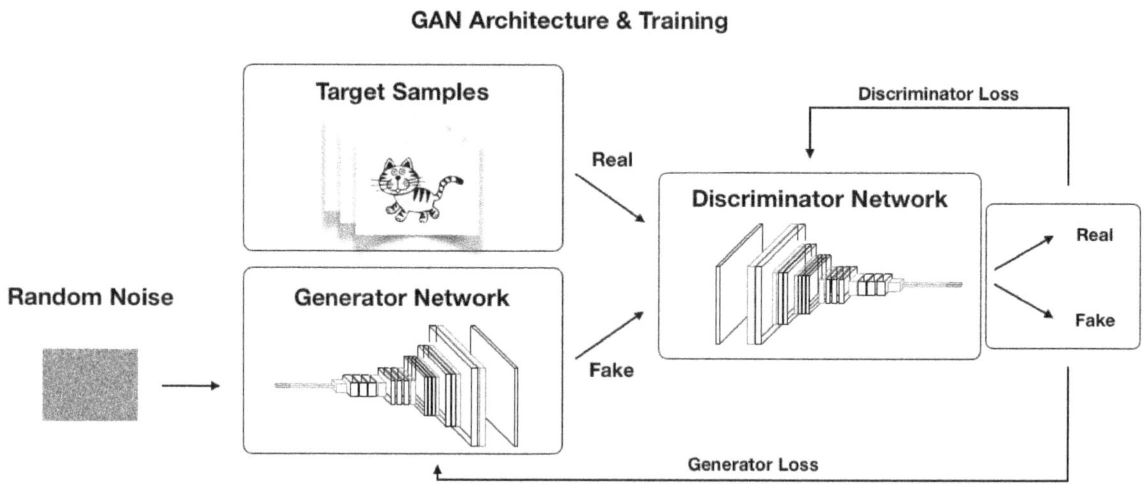

Figure 21.1: GAN architecture

The recent GAN Lab is a great interactive tool inspired by TensorFlow Playground, which allows the user to design GANs and visualize various aspects of the learning process and performance over time (see resource links on GitHub).

The rapid evolution of the GAN architecture zoo

Since the publication of the paper by Goodfellow et al. in 2014, GANs have attracted an enormous amount of interest and triggered a corresponding flurry of research.

The bulk of this work has refined the original architecture to adapt it to different domains and tasks, as well as expanding it to include additional information and create conditional GANs. Additional research has focused on improving methods for the challenging training process, which requires achieving a stable game-theoretic equilibrium between two networks, each of which can be tricky to train on its own.

The GAN landscape has become more diverse than we can cover here; see Creswell et al. (2018) and Pan et al. (2019) for recent surveys, and Odena (2019) for a list of open questions.

Deep convolutional GANs for representation learning

Deep convolutional GANs (**DCGANs**) were motivated by the successful application of CNNs to supervised learning for grid-like data (Radford, Metz, and Chintala 2016). The architecture pioneered the use of GANs for unsupervised learning by developing a feature extractor based on adversarial training. It is also easier to train and generates higher-quality images. It is now considered a baseline implementation, with numerous open source examples available (see references on GitHub).

A DCGAN network takes uniformly distributed random numbers as input and outputs a color image with a resolution of 64×64 pixels. As the input changes incrementally, so do the generated images. The network consists of standard CNN components, including deconvolutional layers that reverse convolutional layers as in the convolutional autoencoder example in the previous chapter, or fully connected layers.

The authors experimented exhaustively and made several recommendations, such as the use of batch normalization and ReLU activations in both networks. We will explore a TensorFlow implementation later in this chapter.

Conditional GANs for image-to-image translation

Conditional GANs (**cGANs**) introduce additional label information into the training process, resulting in better quality and some control over the output.

cGANs alter the baseline architecture displayed previously in *Figure 21.1* by adding a third input to the discriminator that contains class labels. These labels, for example, could convey gender or hair color information when generating images.

Extensions include the **generative adversarial what-where network** (**GAWWN**; Reed et al. 2016), which uses bounding box information not only to generate synthetic images but also to place objects at a given location.

GAN applications to images and time-series data

Alongside a large variety of extensions and modifications of the original architecture, numerous applications to images, as well as sequential data like speech and music, have emerged. Image applications are particularly diverse, ranging from image blending and super-resolution to video generation and human pose identification. Furthermore, GANs have been used to improve supervised learning performance.

We will look at a few salient examples and then take a closer look at applications to time-series data that may become particularly relevant to algorithmic trading and investment. See Alqahtani, Kavakli-Thorne, and Kumar (2019) for a recent survey and GitHub references for additional resources.

CycleGAN – unpaired image-to-image translation

Supervised image-to-image translation aims to learn a mapping between aligned input and output images. CycleGAN solves this task when paired images are not available and transforms images from one domain to match another.

Popular examples include the synthetic "painting" of horses as zebras and vice versa. It also includes the transfer of styles, by generating a realistic sample of an impressionistic print from an arbitrary landscape photo (Zhu et al. 2018).

StackGAN – text-to-photo image synthesis

One of the earlier applications of GANs to domain-transfer is the generation of images based on text. **Stacked GAN**, often shortened to **StackGAN**, uses a sentence as input and generates multiple images that match the description.

The architecture operates in two stages, where the first stage yields a low-resolution sketch of shape and colors, and the second stage enhances the result to a high-resolution image with photorealistic details (Zhang et al. 2017).

SRGAN – photorealistic single image super-resolution

Super-resolution aims at producing higher-resolution photorealistic images from low-resolution input. GANs applied to this task have deep CNN architectures that use batch normalization, ReLU, and skip connection as encountered in ResNet (see *Chapter 18, CNNs for Financial Time Series and Satellite Images*) to produce impressive results that are already finding commercial applications (Ledig et al. 2017).

Synthetic time series with recurrent conditional GANs

Recurrent GANs (**RGANs**) and **recurrent conditional GANs** (**RCGANs**) are two model architectures that aim to synthesize realistic real-valued multivariate time series (Esteban, Hyland, and Rätsch 2017). The authors target applications in the medical domain, but the approach could be highly valuable to overcome the limitations of historical market data.

RGANs rely on **recurrent neural networks** (**RNNs**) for the generator and the discriminator. RCGANs add auxiliary information in the spirit of cGANs (see the previous *Conditional GANs for image-to-image translation* section).

The authors succeed in generating visually and quantitatively compelling realistic samples. Furthermore, they evaluate the quality of the synthetic data, including synthetic labels, by using it to train a model with only minor degradation of the predictive performance on a real test set. The authors also demonstrate the successful application of RCGANs to an early warning system using a medical dataset of 17,000 patients from an intensive care unit. Hence, the authors illustrate that RCGANs are capable of generating time-series data useful for supervised training. We will apply this approach to financial market data this chapter in the *TimeGAN – adversarial training for synthetic financial data* section.

How to build a GAN using TensorFlow 2

To illustrate the implementation of a GAN using Python, we will use the DCGAN example discussed earlier in this section to synthesize images from the Fashion-MNIST dataset that we first encountered in *Chapter 13, Data-Driven Risk Factors and Asset Allocation with Unsupervised Learning*.

See the notebook `deep_convolutional_generative_adversarial_network` for implementation details and references.

Building the generator network

Both generator and discriminator use a deep CNN architecture along the lines illustrated in *Figure 20.1*, but with fewer layers. The generator uses a fully connected input layer, followed by three convolutional layers, as defined in the following `build_generator()` function, which returns a Keras model instance:

```
def build_generator():
    return Sequential([Dense(7 * 7 * 256,
                             use_bias=False,
                             input_shape=(100,),
                             name='IN'),
                       BatchNormalization(name='BN1'),
                       LeakyReLU(name='RELU1'),
                       Reshape((7, 7, 256), name='SHAPE1'),
                       Conv2DTranspose(128, (5, 5),
                                       strides=(1, 1),
                                       padding='same',
                                       use_bias=False,
                                       name='CONV1'),
                       BatchNormalization(name='BN2'),
                       LeakyReLU(name='RELU2'),
                       Conv2DTranspose(64, (5, 5),
                                       strides=(2, 2),
                                       padding='same',
                                       use_bias=False,
                                       name='CONV2'),
                       BatchNormalization(name='BN3'),
                       LeakyReLU(name='RELU3'),
                       Conv2DTranspose(1, (5, 5),
                                       strides=(2, 2),
                                       padding='same',
                                       use_bias=False,
                                       activation='tanh',
                                       name='CONV3')],
                      name='Generator')
```

The generator accepts 100 one-dimensional random values as input, and it produces images that are 28 pixels wide and high and, thus, contain 784 data points.

A call to the `.summary()` method of the model returned by this function shows that this network has over 2.3 million parameters (see the notebook for details, including a visualization of the generator output prior to training).

Creating the discriminator network

The discriminator network uses two convolutional layers that translate the input received from the generator into a single output value. The model has around 212,000 parameters:

```
def build_discriminator():
    return Sequential([Conv2D(64, (5, 5),
                              strides=(2, 2),
                              padding='same',
                              input_shape=[28, 28, 1],
                              name='CONV1'),
                       LeakyReLU(name='RELU1'),
                       Dropout(0.3, name='DO1'),
                       Conv2D(128, (5, 5),
                              strides=(2, 2),
                              padding='same',
                              name='CONV2'),
                       LeakyReLU(name='RELU2'),
                       Dropout(0.3, name='DO2'),
                       Flatten(name='FLAT'),
                       Dense(1, name='OUT')],
                      name='Discriminator')
```

Figure 21.2 depicts how the random input flows from the generator to the discriminator, as well as the input and output shapes of the various network components:

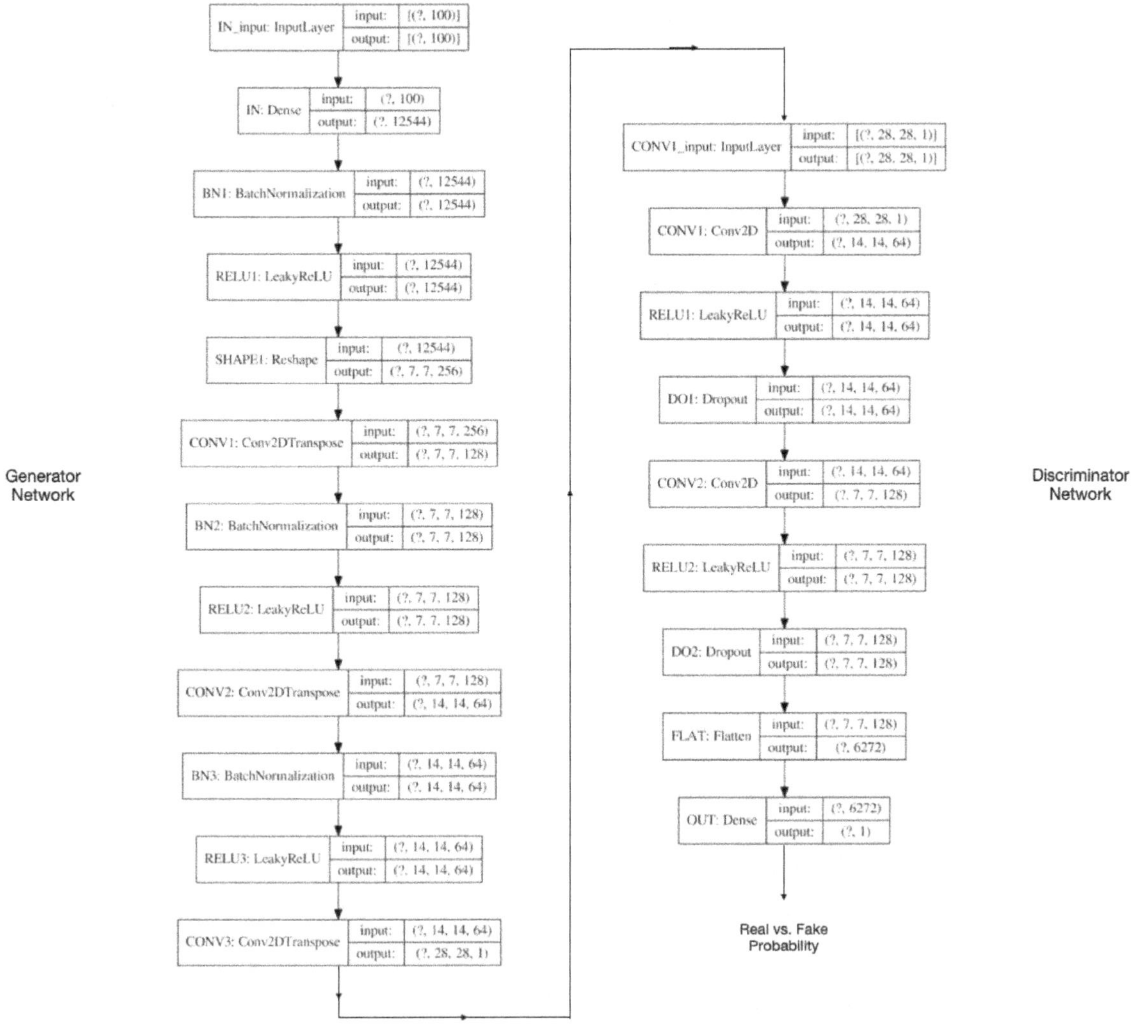

Figure 21.2: DCGAN TensorFlow 2 model architecture

Setting up the adversarial training process

Now that we have built the generator and the discriminator models, we will design and execute the adversarial training process. To this end, we will define the following:

- The loss functions for both models that reflect their competitive interaction
- A single training step that runs the backpropagation algorithm
- The training loop that repeats the training step until the model performance meets our expectations

Defining the generator and discriminator loss functions

The generator loss reflects the discriminator's decision regarding the fake input. It will be low if the discriminator mistakes an image produced by the generator for a real image, and high otherwise; we will define the interaction between both models when we create the training step.

The generator loss is measured by the binary cross-entropy loss function as follows:

```
cross_entropy = BinaryCrossentropy(from_logits=True)
def generator_loss(fake_output):
    return cross_entropy(tf.ones_like(fake_output), fake_output)
```

The discriminator receives both real and fake images as input. It computes a loss for each and attempts to minimize the sum with the goal of accurately recognizing both types of inputs:

```
def discriminator_loss(true_output, fake_output):
    true_loss = cross_entropy(tf.ones_like(true_output), true_output)
    fake_loss = cross_entropy(tf.zeros_like(fake_output), fake_output)
    return true_loss + fake_loss
```

To train both models, we assign each an Adam optimizer with a learning rate lower than the default:

```
gen_optimizer = Adam(1e-4)
dis_optimizer = Adam(1e-4)
```

The core – designing the training step

Each training step implements one round of stochastic gradient descent using the Adam optimizer. It consists of five steps:

1. Providing the minibatch inputs to each model
2. Getting the models' outputs for the current weights
3. Computing the loss given the models' objective and output
4. Obtaining the gradients for the loss with respect to each model's weights
5. Applying the gradients according to the optimizer's algorithm

The function `train_step()` carries out these five steps. We use the `@tf.function` decorator to speed up execution by compiling it to a TensorFlow operation rather than relying on eager execution (see the TensorFlow documentation for details):

```
@tf.function
def train_step(images):
    # generate the random input for the generator
    noise = tf.random.normal([BATCH_SIZE, noise_dim])
    with tf.GradientTape() as gen_tape, tf.GradientTape() as disc_tape:
        # get the generator output
        generated_img = generator(noise, training=True)
```

```
        # collect discriminator decisions regarding real and fake input
        true_output = discriminator(images, training=True)
        fake_output = discriminator(generated_img, training=True)
        # compute the loss for each model
        gen_loss = generator_loss(fake_output)
        disc_loss = discriminator_loss(true_output, fake_output)
    # compute the gradients for each loss with respect to the model variables
    grad_generator = gen_tape.gradient(gen_loss,
                                       generator.trainable_variables)
    grad_discriminator = disc_tape.gradient(disc_loss,
                                            discriminator.trainable_variables)
    # apply the gradient to complete the backpropagation step
    gen_optimizer.apply_gradients(zip(grad_generator,
                                      generator.trainable_variables))
    dis_optimizer.apply_gradients(zip(grad_discriminator,
                                      discriminator.trainable_variables))
```

Putting it together – the training loop

The training loop is very straightforward to implement once we have the training step properly defined. It consists of a simple `for` loop, and during each iteration, we pass a new batch of real images to the training step. We also will sample some synthetic images and occasionally save the model weights.

Note that we track progress using the `tqdm` package, which shows the percentage complete during training:

```
def train(dataset, epochs, save_every=10):
    for epoch in tqdm(range(epochs)):
        for img_batch in dataset:
            train_step(img_batch)
        # produce images for the GIF as we go
        display.clear_output(wait=True)
        generate_and_save_images(generator, epoch + 1, seed)
        # Save the model every 10 EPOCHS
        if (epoch + 1) % save_every == 0:
            checkpoint.save(file_prefix=checkpoint_prefix)
        # Generator after final epoch
    display.clear_output(wait=True)
    generate_and_save_images(generator, epochs, seed)

train(train_set, EPOCHS)
```

Evaluating the results

After 100 epochs that only take a few minutes, the synthetic images created from random noise clearly begin to resemble the originals, as you can see in *Figure 21.3* (see the notebook for the best visual quality):

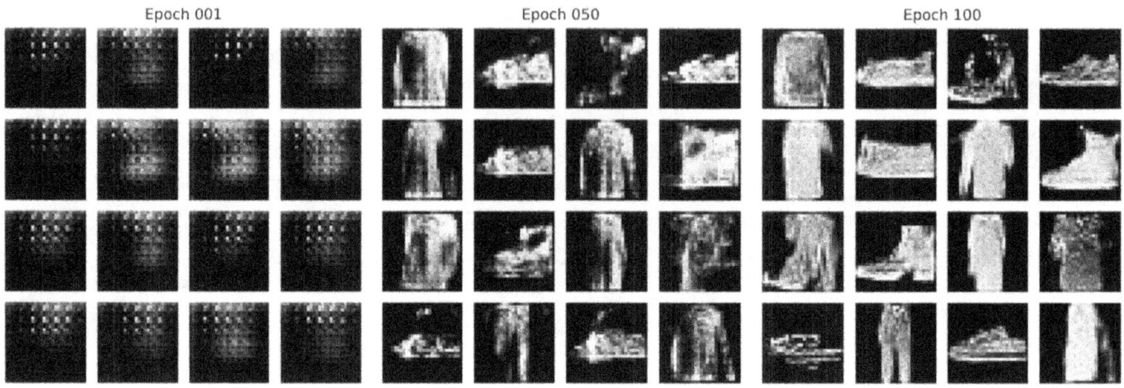

Figure 21.3: A sample of synthetic Fashion-MNIST images

The notebook also creates a dynamic GIF image that visualizes how the quality of the synthetic images improves during training.

Now that we understand how to build and train a GAN using TensorFlow 2, we will move on to a more complex example that produces synthetic time series from stock price data.

TimeGAN for synthetic financial data

Generating synthetic time-series data poses specific challenges above and beyond those encountered when designing GANs for images. In addition to the distribution over variables at any given point, such as pixel values or the prices of numerous stocks, a generative model for time-series data should also learn the temporal dynamics that shape how one sequence of observations follows another. (Refer also to the discussion in *Chapter 9*, *Time-Series Models for Volatility Forecasts and Statistical Arbitrage*).

Very recent and promising research by Yoon, Jarrett, and van der Schaar, presented at NeurIPS in December 2019, introduces a novel **time-series generative adversarial network (TimeGAN)** framework that aims to account for temporal correlations by combining supervised and unsupervised training. The model learns a time-series embedding space while optimizing both supervised and adversarial objectives, which encourage it to adhere to the dynamics observed while sampling from historical data during training. The authors test the model on various time series, including historical stock prices, and find that the quality of the synthetic data significantly outperforms that of available alternatives.

In this section, we will outline how this sophisticated model works, highlight key implementation steps that build on the previous DCGAN example, and show how to evaluate the quality of the resulting time series. Please see the paper for additional information.

Learning to generate data across features and time

A successful generative model for time-series data needs to capture both the cross-sectional distribution of features at each point in time and the longitudinal relationships among these features over time. Expressed in the image context we just discussed, the model needs to learn not only what a realistic image looks like, but also how one image evolves from the previous as in a video.

Combining adversarial and supervised training

As mentioned in the first section, prior attempts at generating time-series data, like RGANs and RCGANs, relied on RNNs (see *Chapter 19, RNNs for Multivariate Time Series and Sentiment Analysis*) in the roles of generator and discriminator. TimeGAN explicitly incorporates the autoregressive nature of time series by combining the **unsupervised adversarial loss** on both real and synthetic sequences familiar from the DCGAN example with a **stepwise supervised loss** with respect to the original data. The goal is to reward the model for learning the **distribution over transitions** from one point in time to the next that are present in the historical data.

Furthermore, TimeGAN includes an embedding network that maps the time-series features to a lower-dimensional latent space to reduce the complexity of the adversarial space. The motivation is to capture the drivers of temporal dynamics that often have lower dimensionality. (Refer also to the discussions of manifold learning in *Chapter 13, Data-Driven Risk Factors and Asset Allocation with Unsupervised Learning* and nonlinear dimensionality reduction in *Chapter 20, Autoencoders for Conditional Risk Factors and Asset Pricing*).

A key element of the TimeGAN architecture is that both the generator and the embedding (or autoencoder) network are responsible for minimizing the supervised loss that measures how well the model learns the dynamic relationship. As a result, the model learns a latent space conditioned on facilitating the generator's task to faithfully reproduce the temporal relationships observed in the historical data. In addition to time-series data, the model can also process static data that does not change or changes less frequently over time.

The four components of the TimeGAN architecture

The TimeGAN architecture combines an adversarial network with an autoencoder and thus has four network components, as depicted in *Figure 21.4*:

1. **Autoencoder**: embedding and recovery networks
2. **Adversarial network**: sequence generator and sequence discriminator components

The authors emphasize the **joint training** of the autoencoder and the adversarial networks by means of **three different loss functions**. The **reconstruction loss** optimizes the autoencoder, the **unsupervised loss** trains the adversarial net, and the **supervised loss** enforces the temporal dynamics. As a result of this key insight, the TimeGAN simultaneously learns to encode features, generate representations, and iterate across time. More specifically, the embedding network creates the latent space, the adversarial network operates within this space, and supervised loss synchronizes the latent dynamics of both real and synthetic data.

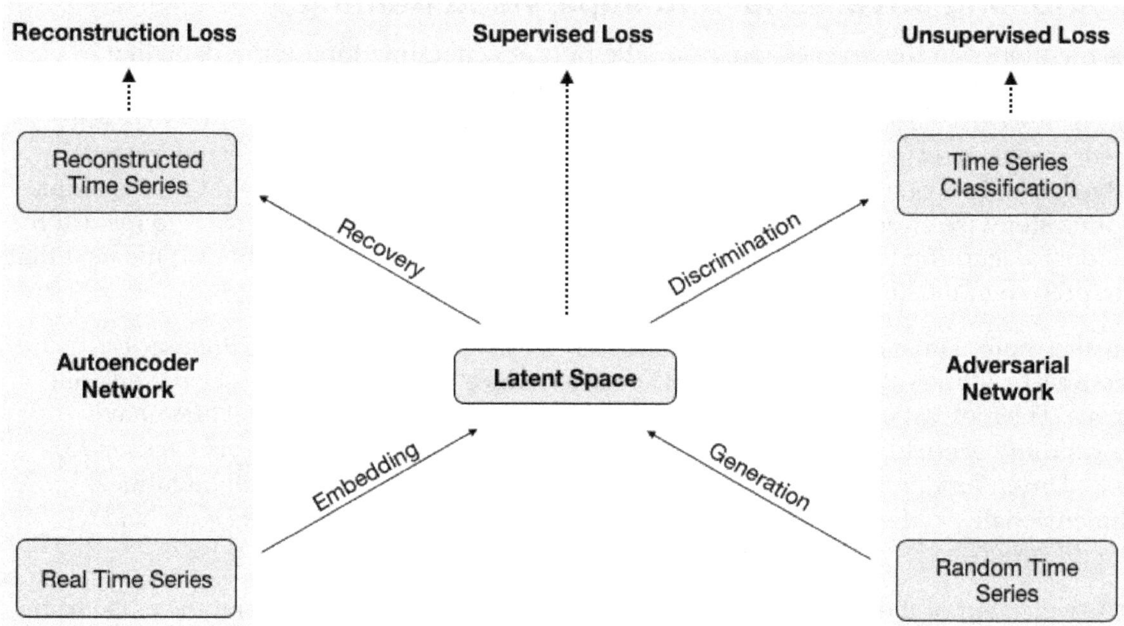

Figure 21.4: The components of the TimeGAN architecture

The **embedding and recovery** components of the autoencoder map the feature space into the latent space and vice versa. This facilitates the learning of the temporal dynamics by the adversarial network, which learns in a lower-dimensional space. The authors implement the embedding and recovery network using a stacked RNN and a feedforward network. However, these choices can be flexibly adapted to the task at hand as long as they are autoregressive and respect the temporal order of the data.

The **generator and the discriminator** elements of the adversarial network differ from the DCGAN not only because they operate on sequential data but also because the synthetic features are generated in the latent space that the model learns simultaneously. The authors chose an RNN as the generator and a bidirectional RNN with a feedforward output layer for the discriminator.

Joint training of an autoencoder and adversarial network

The three loss functions displayed in *Figure 21.4* drive the joint optimization of the network elements just described while training on real and randomly generated time series. In more detail, they aim to accomplish the following:

- The **reconstruction loss** is familiar from our discussion of autoencoders in *Chapter 20, Autoencoders for Conditional Risk Factors and Asset Pricing*; it compares how well the reconstruction of the encoded data resembles the original.
- The **unsupervised loss** reflects the competitive interaction between the generator and the discriminator described in the DCGAN example; while the generator aims to minimize the probability that the discriminator classifies its output as fake, the discriminator aims to optimize the correct classification or real and fake inputs.
- The **supervised loss** captures how well the generator approximates the actual next time step in latent space when receiving encoded real data for the prior sequence.

Training takes place in **three phases**:

1. Training the autoencoder on real time series to optimize reconstruction
2. Optimizing the supervised loss using real time series to capture the temporal dynamics of the historical data
3. Jointly training the four components while minimizing all three loss functions

TimeGAN includes several **hyperparameters** used to weigh the components of composite loss functions; however, the authors find the network to be less sensitive to these settings than one might expect given the notorious difficulties of GAN training. In fact, they **do not discover significant challenges during training** and suggest that the embedding task serves to regularize adversarial learning because it reduces its dimensionality while the supervised loss constrains the stepwise dynamics of the generator.

We now turn to the TimeGAN implementation using TensorFlow 2; see the paper for an in-depth explanation of the math and methodology of the approach.

Implementing TimeGAN using TensorFlow 2

In this section, we will implement the TimeGAN architecture just described. The authors provide sample code using TensorFlow 1 that we will port to TensorFlow 2. Building and training TimeGAN requires several steps:

1. Selecting and preparing real and random time series inputs
2. Creating the key TimeGAN model components
3. Defining the various loss functions and training steps used during the three training phases
4. Running the training loops and logging the results
5. Generating synthetic time series and evaluating the results

We'll walk through the key items for each of these steps; please refer to the notebook `TimeGAN_TF2` for the code examples in this section (unless otherwise noted), as well as additional implementation details.

Preparing the real and random input series

The authors demonstrate the applicability of TimeGAN to financial data using 15 years of daily Google stock prices downloaded from Yahoo Finance with six features, namely open, high, low, close and adjusted close price, and volume. We'll instead use close to 20 years of adjusted close prices for six different tickers because it introduces somewhat higher variability. We will follow the original paper in targeting synthetic series with 24 time steps.

Among the stocks with the longest history in the Quandl Wiki dataset are those displayed in normalized format, that is, starting at 1.0, in *Figure 21.5*. We retrieve the adjusted close from 2000-2017 and obtain over 4,000 observations. The correlation coefficient among the series ranges from 0.01 for GE and CAT to 0.94 for DIS and KO.

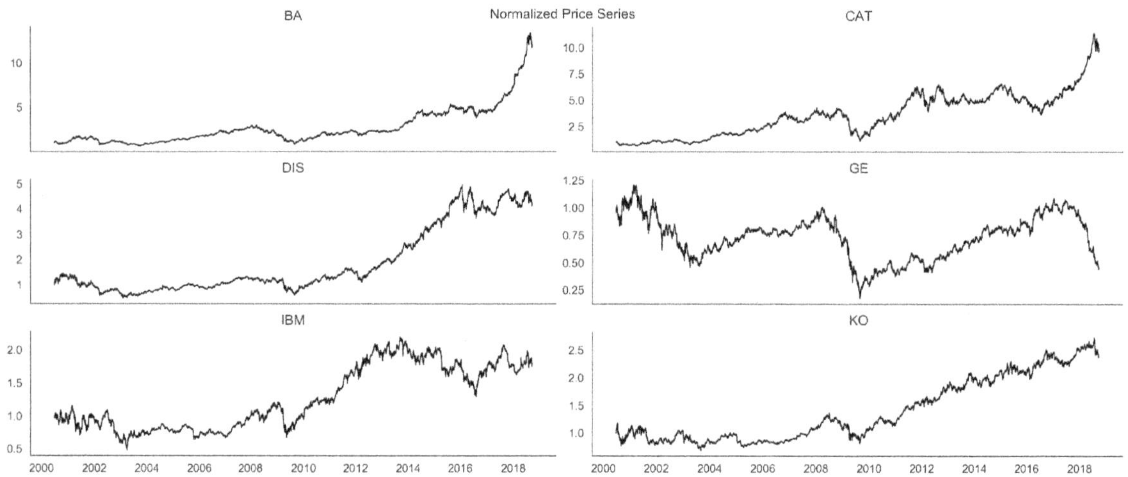

Figure 21.5: The TimeGAN input—six real stock prices series

We scale each series to the range [0, 1] using scikit-learn's `MinMaxScaler` class, which we will later use to rescale the synthetic data:

```
df = pd.read_hdf(hdf_store, 'data/real')
scaler = MinMaxScaler()
scaled_data = scaler.fit_transform(df).astype(np.float32)
```

In the next step, we create rolling windows containing overlapping sequences of 24 consecutive data points for the six series:

```
data = []
for i in range(len(df) - seq_len):
    data.append(scaled_data[i:i + seq_len])
n_series = len(data)
```

We then create a `tf.data.Dataset` instance from the list of `NumPy` arrays, ensure the data gets shuffled while training, and set a batch size of 128:

```
real_series = (tf.data.Dataset
               .from_tensor_slices(data)
               .shuffle(buffer_size=n_windows)
               .batch(batch_size))
real_series_iter = iter(real_series.repeat())
```

We also need a random time-series generator that produces simulated data with 24 observations on the six series for as long as the training continues.

To this end, we will create a generator that draws the requisite data uniform at random and feeds the result into a second `tf.data.Dataset` instance. We set this dataset to produce batches of the desired size and to repeat the process for as long as necessary:

```
def make_random_data():
    while True:
        yield np.random.uniform(low=0, high=1, size=(seq_len, n_seq))

random_series = iter(tf.data.Dataset
                     .from_generator(make_random_data,
                                     output_types=tf.float32)
                     .batch(batch_size)
                     .repeat())
```

We'll now proceed to define and instantiate the TimeGAN model components.

Creating the TimeGAN model components

We'll now create the two autoencoder components and the two adversarial network elements, as well as the supervisor that encourages the generator to learn the temporal dynamic of the historical price series.

We will follow the authors' sample code in creating RNNs with three hidden layers, each with 24 GRU units, except for the supervisor, which uses only two hidden layers. The following `make_rnn` function automates the network creation:

```
def make_rnn(n_layers, hidden_units, output_units, name):
    return Sequential([GRU(units=hidden_units,
                          return_sequences=True,
                          name=f'GRU_{i + 1}') for i in range(n_layers)] +
                     [Dense(units=output_units,
                            activation='sigmoid',
                            name='OUT')], name=name)
```

The `autoencoder` consists of the `embedder` and the recovery networks that we instantiate here:

```
embedder = make_rnn(n_layers=3,
                    hidden_units=hidden_dim,
                    output_units=hidden_dim,
                    name='Embedder')
recovery = make_rnn(n_layers=3,
                    hidden_units=hidden_dim,
                    output_units=n_seq,
                    name='Recovery')
```

We then create the generator, the discriminator, and the supervisor like so:

```
generator = make_rnn(n_layers=3,
                     hidden_units=hidden_dim,
                     output_units=hidden_dim,
                     name='Generator')
discriminator = make_rnn(n_layers=3,
                         hidden_units=hidden_dim,
                         output_units=1,
                         name='Discriminator')
supervisor = make_rnn(n_layers=2,
                      hidden_units=hidden_dim,
                      output_units=hidden_dim,
                      name='Supervisor')
```

We also define two generic loss functions, namely `MeanSquaredError` and `BinaryCrossEntropy`, which we will use later to create the various specific loss functions during the three phases:

```
mse = MeanSquaredError()
bce = BinaryCrossentropy()
```

Now it's time to start the training process.

Training phase 1 – autoencoder with real data

The autoencoder integrates the embedder and the recovery functions, as we saw in the previous chapter:

```
H = embedder(X)
X_tilde = recovery(H)

autoencoder = Model(inputs=X,
                    outputs=X_tilde,
```

```
                    name='Autoencoder')
autoencoder.summary()
Model: "Autoencoder"
_________________________________________________________________
Layer (type)                 Output Shape              Param #
=================================================================
RealData (InputLayer)        [(None, 24, 6)]           0
_________________________________________________________________
Embedder (Sequential)        (None, 24, 24)            10104
_________________________________________________________________
Recovery (Sequential)        (None, 24, 6)             10950
=================================================================
Trainable params: 21,054
```

It has 21,054 parameters. We will now instantiate the optimizer for this training phase and define the training step. It follows the pattern introduced with the DCGAN example, using `tf.GradientTape` to record the operations that generate the reconstruction loss. This allows us to rely on the automatic differentiation engine to obtain the gradients with respect to the trainable embedder and recovery network weights that drive `backpropagation`:

```
autoencoder_optimizer = Adam()
@tf.function
def train_autoencoder_init(x):
    with tf.GradientTape() as tape:
        x_tilde = autoencoder(x)
        embedding_loss_t0 = mse(x, x_tilde)
        e_loss_0 = 10 * tf.sqrt(embedding_loss_t0)

    var_list = embedder.trainable_variables + recovery.trainable_variables
    gradients = tape.gradient(e_loss_0, var_list)
    autoencoder_optimizer.apply_gradients(zip(gradients, var_list))
    return tf.sqrt(embedding_loss_t0)
```

The reconstruction loss simply compares the autoencoder outputs with its inputs. We train for 10,000 steps in a little over one minute using this training loop that records the step loss for monitoring with TensorBoard:

```
for step in tqdm(range(train_steps)):
    X_ = next(real_series_iter)
    step_e_loss_t0 = train_autoencoder_init(X_)
    with writer.as_default():
        tf.summary.scalar('Loss Autoencoder Init', step_e_loss_t0, step=step)
```

Training phase 2 – supervised learning with real data

We already created the supervisor model so we just need to instantiate the optimizer and define the train step as follows:

```
supervisor_optimizer = Adam()
@tf.function
def train_supervisor(x):
    with tf.GradientTape() as tape:
        h = embedder(x)
        h_hat_supervised = supervisor(h)
        g_loss_s = mse(h[:, 1:, :], h_hat_supervised[:, 1:, :])

    var_list = supervisor.trainable_variables
    gradients = tape.gradient(g_loss_s, var_list)
    supervisor_optimizer.apply_gradients(zip(gradients, var_list))
    return g_loss_s
```

In this case, the loss compares the output of the supervisor with the next timestep for the embedded sequence so that it learns the temporal dynamics of the historical price sequences; the training loop works similarly to the autoencoder example in the previous chapter.

Training phase 3 – joint training with real and random data

The joint training involves all four network components, as well as the supervisor. It uses multiple loss functions and combinations of the base components to achieve the simultaneous learning of latent space embeddings, transition dynamics, and synthetic data generation.

We will highlight a few salient examples; please see the notebook for the full implementation that includes some repetitive steps that we will omit here.

To ensure that the generator faithfully reproduces the time series, TimeGAN includes a moment loss that penalizes when the mean and variance of the synthetic data deviate from the real version:

```
def get_generator_moment_loss(y_true, y_pred):
    y_true_mean, y_true_var = tf.nn.moments(x=y_true, axes=[0])
    y_pred_mean, y_pred_var = tf.nn.moments(x=y_pred, axes=[0])
    g_loss_mean = tf.reduce_mean(tf.abs(y_true_mean - y_pred_mean))
    g_loss_var = tf.reduce_mean(tf.abs(tf.sqrt(y_true_var + 1e-6) -
                                       tf.sqrt(y_pred_var + 1e-6)))
    return g_loss_mean + g_loss_var
```

The end-to-end model that produces synthetic data involves the generator, supervisor, and recovery components. It is defined as follows and has close to 30,000 trainable parameters:

```
E_hat = generator(Z)
H_hat = supervisor(E_hat)
X_hat = recovery(H_hat)
synthetic_data = Model(inputs=Z,
                       outputs=X_hat,
                       name='SyntheticData')

Model: "SyntheticData"
_________________________________________________________________
Layer (type)                 Output Shape              Param #
=================================================================
RandomData (InputLayer)      [(None, 24, 6)]           0
_________________________________________________________________
Generator (Sequential)       (None, 24, 24)            10104
_________________________________________________________________
Supervisor (Sequential)      (None, 24, 24)            7800
_________________________________________________________________
Recovery (Sequential)        (None, 24, 6)             10950
=================================================================
Trainable params: 28,854
```

The joint training involves three optimizers for the autoencoder, the generator, and the discriminator:

```
generator_optimizer = Adam()
discriminator_optimizer = Adam()
embedding_optimizer = Adam()
```

The train step for the generator illustrates the use of four loss functions and corresponding combinations of network components to achieve the desired learning outlined at the beginning of this section:

```
@tf.function
def train_generator(x, z):
    with tf.GradientTape() as tape:
        y_fake = adversarial_supervised(z)
        generator_loss_unsupervised = bce(y_true=tf.ones_like(y_fake),
                                          y_pred=y_fake)

        y_fake_e = adversarial_emb(z)
        generator_loss_unsupervised_e = bce(y_true=tf.ones_like(y_fake_e),
                                            y_pred=y_fake_e)
        h = embedder(x)
        h_hat_supervised = supervisor(h)
        generator_loss_supervised = mse(h[:, 1:, :],
                                        h_hat_supervised[:, 1:, :])
```

```
        x_hat = synthetic_data(z)
        generator_moment_loss = get_generator_moment_loss(x, x_hat)

        generator_loss = (generator_loss_unsupervised +
                          generator_loss_unsupervised_e +
                          100 * tf.sqrt(generator_loss_supervised) +
                          100 * generator_moment_loss)

    var_list = generator.trainable_variables + supervisor.trainable_variables
    gradients = tape.gradient(generator_loss, var_list)
    generator_optimizer.apply_gradients(zip(gradients, var_list))
    return (generator_loss_unsupervised, generator_loss_supervised,
            generator_moment_loss)
```

Finally, the joint training loop pulls the various training steps together and builds on the learning from phase 1 and 2 to train the TimeGAN components on both real and random data. We run the loop for 10,000 iterations in under 40 minutes:

```
for step in range(train_steps):
    # Train generator (twice as often as discriminator)
    for kk in range(2):
        X_ = next(real_series_iter)
        Z_ = next(random_series)

        # Train generator
        step_g_loss_u, step_g_loss_s, step_g_loss_v = train_generator(X_, Z_)
        # Train embedder
        step_e_loss_t0 = train_embedder(X_)
    X_ = next(real_series_iter)
    Z_ = next(random_series)
    step_d_loss = get_discriminator_loss(X_, Z_)
    if step_d_loss > 0.15:
        step_d_loss = train_discriminator(X_, Z_)

    if step % 1000 == 0:
        print(f'{step:6,.0f} | d_loss: {step_d_loss:6.4f} | '
              f'g_loss_u: {step_g_loss_u:6.4f} | '
              f'g_loss_s: {step_g_loss_s:6.4f} | '
              f'g_loss_v: {step_g_loss_v:6.4f} | '
              f'e_loss_t0: {step_e_loss_t0:6.4f}')
```

```
    with writer.as_default():
        tf.summary.scalar('G Loss S', step_g_loss_s, step=step)
        tf.summary.scalar('G Loss U', step_g_loss_u, step=step)
        tf.summary.scalar('G Loss V', step_g_loss_v, step=step)
        tf.summary.scalar('E Loss T0', step_e_loss_t0, step=step)
        tf.summary.scalar('D Loss', step_d_loss, step=step)
```

Now we can finally generate synthetic time series!

Generating synthetic time series

To evaluate the `TimeGAN` results, we will generate synthetic time series by drawing random inputs and feeding them to the `synthetic_data` network just described in the preceding section. More specifically, we'll create roughly as many artificial series with 24 observations on the six tickers as there are overlapping windows in the real dataset:

```
generated_data = []
for i in range(int(n_windows / batch_size)):
    Z_ = next(random_series)
    d = synthetic_data(Z_)
    generated_data.append(d)
len(generated_data)
35
```

The result is 35 batches containing 128 samples, each with the dimensions 24×6, that we stack like so:

```
generated_data = np.array(np.vstack(generated_data))
generated_data.shape
(4480, 24, 6)
```

We can use the trained `MinMaxScaler` to revert the synthetic output to the scale of the input series:

```
generated_data = (scaler.inverse_transform(generated_data
                                           .reshape(-1, n_seq))
                  .reshape(-1, seq_len, n_seq))
```

Figure 21.6 displays samples of the six synthetic series and the corresponding real series. The synthetic data generally reflects a variation of behavior not unlike its real counterparts and, after rescaling, roughly (due to the random input) matches its range:

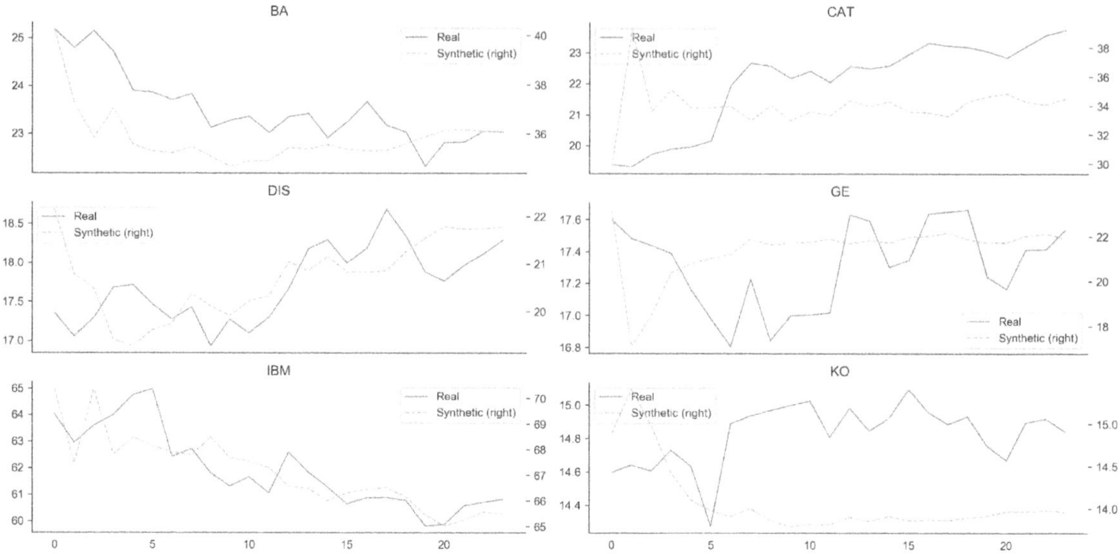

Figure 21.6: TimeGAN output—six synthetic prices series and their real counterparts

Now it's time to take a closer look at how to more thoroughly evaluate the quality of the synthetic data.

Evaluating the quality of synthetic time-series data

The TimeGAN authors assess the quality of the generated data with respect to three practical criteria:

- **Diversity**: The distribution of the synthetic samples should roughly match that of the real data.
- **Fidelity**: The sample series should be indistinguishable from the real data.
- **Usefulness**: The synthetic data should be as useful as its real counterparts for solving a predictive task.

They apply three methods to evaluate whether the synthetic data actually exhibits these characteristics:

- **Visualization**: For a qualitative diversity assessment of diversity, we use dimensionality reduction—**principal component analysis** (**PCA**) and **t-SNE** (see *Chapter 13, Data-Driven Risk Factors and Asset Allocation with Unsupervised Learning*)—to visually inspect how closely the distribution of the synthetic samples resembles that of the original data.
- **Discriminative score**: For a quantitative assessment of fidelity, the test error of a time-series classifier, such as a two-layer LSTM (see *Chapter 18, CNNs for Financial Time Series and Satellite Images*), lets us evaluate whether real and synthetic time series can be differentiated or are, in fact, indistinguishable.

- **Predictive score**: For a quantitative measure of usefulness, we can compare the test errors of a sequence prediction model trained on, alternatively, real or synthetic data to predict the next time step for the real data.

We'll apply and discuss the results of each method in the following sections. See the notebook `evaluating_synthetic_data` for the code samples and additional details.

Assessing diversity – visualization using PCA and t-SNE

To visualize the real and synthetic series with 24 time steps and six features, we will reduce their dimensionality so that we can plot them in two dimensions. To this end, we will sample 250 normalized sequences with six features each and reshape them to obtain data with the dimensionality 1,500×24 (showing only the steps for real data; see the notebook for the synthetic data):

```
# same steps to create real sequences for training
real_data = get_real_data()
# reload synthetic data
synthetic_data = np.load('generated_data.npy')
synthetic_data.shape
(4480, 24, 6)
# ensure same number of sequences
real_data = real_data[:synthetic_data.shape[0]]

sample_size = 250
idx = np.random.permutation(len(real_data))[:sample_size]
real_sample = np.asarray(real_data)[idx]
real_sample_2d = real_sample.reshape(-1, seq_len)
real_sample_2d.shape
(1500, 24)
```

PCA is a linear method that identifies a new basis with mutually orthogonal vectors that, successively, capture the directions of maximum variance in the data. We will compute the first two components using the real data and then project both real and synthetic samples onto the new coordinate system:

```
pca = PCA(n_components=2)
pca.fit(real_sample_2d)
pca_real = (pd.DataFrame(pca.transform(real_sample_2d))
            .assign(Data='Real'))
pca_synthetic = (pd.DataFrame(pca.transform(synthetic_sample_2d))
                 .assign(Data='Synthetic'))
```

t-SNE is a nonlinear manifold learning method for the visualization of high-dimensional data. It converts similarities between data points to joint probabilities and aims to minimize the Kullback-Leibler divergence between the joint probabilities of the low-dimensional embedding and the high-dimensional data (see *Chapter 13, Data-Driven Risk Factors and*

Asset Allocation with Unsupervised Learning). We compute t-SNE for the combined real and synthetic data as follows:

```
tsne_data = np.concatenate((real_sample_2d,
                            synthetic_sample_2d), axis=0)
tsne = TSNE(n_components=2, perplexity=40)
tsne_result = tsne.fit_transform(tsne_data)
```

Figure 21.7 displays the PCA and t-SNE results for a qualitative assessment of the similarity of the real and synthetic data distributions. Both methods reveal strikingly similar patterns and significant overlap, suggesting that the synthetic data captures important aspects of the real data characteristics.

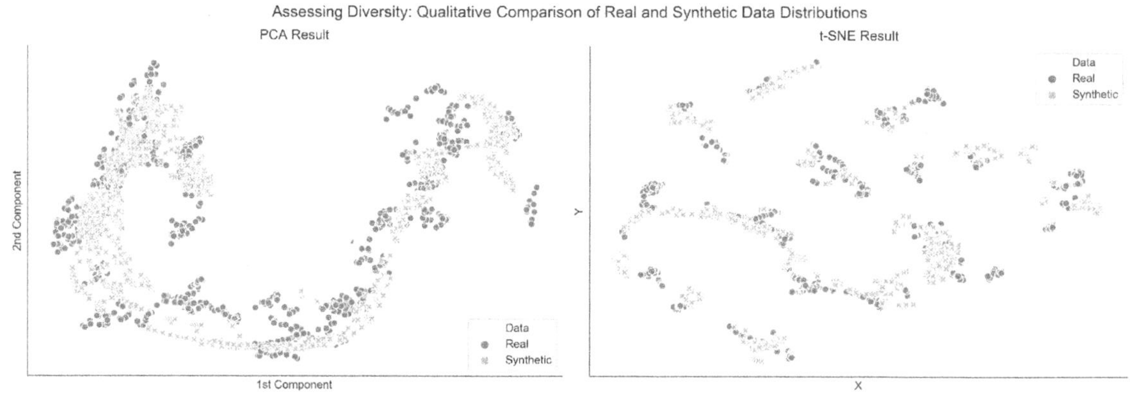

Figure 21.7: 250 samples of real and synthetic data in two dimensions

Assessing fidelity – time-series classification performance

The visualization only provides a qualitative impression. For a quantitative assessment of the fidelity of the synthetic data, we will train a time-series classifier to distinguish between real and fake data and evaluate its performance on a held-out test set.

More specifically, we will select the first 80 percent of the rolling sequences for training and the last 20 percent as a test set, as follows:

```
synthetic_data.shape
(4480, 24, 6)
n_series = synthetic_data.shape[0]
idx = np.arange(n_series)

n_train = int(.8*n_series)
train_idx, test_idx = idx[:n_train], idx[n_train:]

train_data = np.vstack((real_data[train_idx],
                        synthetic_data[train_idx]))
test_data = np.vstack((real_data[test_idx],
```

```
                                synthetic_data[test_idx]))
n_train, n_test = len(train_idx), len(test_idx)
train_labels = np.concatenate((np.ones(n_train),
                               np.zeros(n_train)))
test_labels = np.concatenate((np.ones(n_test),
                              np.zeros(n_test)))
```

Then we will create a simple RNN with six units that receives mini batches of real and synthetic series with the shape 24×6 and uses a sigmoid activation. We will optimize it using binary cross-entropy loss and the Adam optimizer, while tracking the AUC and accuracy metrics:

```
ts_classifier = Sequential([GRU(6, input_shape=(24, 6), name='GRU'),
                            Dense(1, activation='sigmoid', name='OUT')])
ts_classifier.compile(loss='binary_crossentropy',
                      optimizer='adam',
                      metrics=[AUC(name='AUC'), 'accuracy'])
```

```
Model: "Time Series Classifier"
_________________________________________________________________
Layer (type)                 Output Shape              Param #
=================================================================
GRU (GRU)                    (None, 6)                 252
_________________________________________________________________
OUT (Dense)                  (None, 1)                 7
=================================================================
Total params: 259
Trainable params: 259
```

The model has 259 trainable parameters. We will train it for 250 epochs on batches of 128 randomly selected samples and track the validation performance:

```
result = ts_classifier.fit(x=train_data,
                           y=train_labels,
                           validation_data=(test_data, test_labels),
                           epochs=250, batch_size=128)
```

Once the training completes, evaluation of the test set yields a classification error of almost 56 percent on the balanced test set and a very low AUC of 0.15:

```
ts_classifier.evaluate(x=test_data, y=test_labels)
56/56 [==============================] - 0s 2ms/step - loss: 3.7510 - AUC:
0.1596 - accuracy: 0.4403
```

Figure 21.8 plots the accuracy and AUC performance metrics for both train and test data over the 250 training epochs:

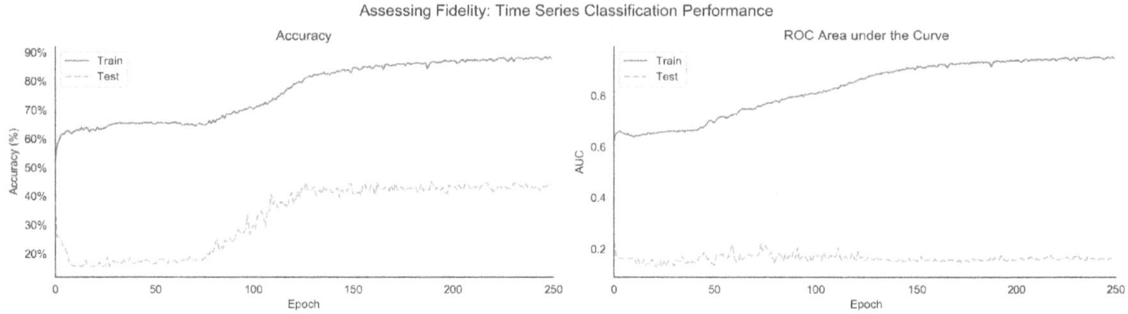

Figure 21.8: Train and test performance of the time-series classifier over 250 epochs

The plot shows that that model is not able to learn the difference between the real and synthetic data in a way that generalizes to the test set. This result suggests that the quality of the synthetic data meets the fidelity standard.

Assessing usefulness – train on synthetic, test on real

Finally, we want to know how useful synthetic data is when it comes to solving a prediction problem. To this end, we will train a time-series prediction model alternatively on the synthetic and the real data to predict the next time step and compare the performance on a test set created from the real data.

More specifically, we will select the first 23 time steps of each sequence as input, and the final time step as output. At the same time, we will split the real data into train and test sets using the same temporal split as in the previous classification example:

```
real_data.shape, synthetic_data.shape
((4480, 24, 6), (4480, 24, 6))
real_train_data = real_data[train_idx, :23, :]
real_train_label = real_data[train_idx, -1, :]

real_test_data = real_data[test_idx, :23, :]
real_test_label = real_data[test_idx, -1, :]
real_train_data.shape, real_train_label.shape
((3584, 23, 6), (3584, 6))
```

We will select the complete synthetic data for training since abundance is one of the reasons we generated it in the first place:

```
synthetic_train = synthetic_data[:, :23, :]
synthetic_label = synthetic_data[:, -1, :]
synthetic_train.shape, synthetic_label.shape
((4480, 23, 6), (4480, 6))
```

We will create a one-layer RNN with 12 GRU units that predicts the last time steps for the six stock price series and, thus, has six linear output units. The model uses the Adam optimizer to minimize the mean absolute error (MAE):

```
def get_model():
    model = Sequential([GRU(12, input_shape=(seq_len-1, n_seq)),
                        Dense(6)])

    model.compile(optimizer=Adam(),
                  loss=MeanAbsoluteError(name='MAE'))
    return model
```

We will train the model twice using the synthetic and real data for training, respectively, and the real test set to evaluate the out-of-sample performance. Training on synthetic data works as follows; training on real data works analogously (see the notebook):

```
ts_regression = get_model()
synthetic_result = ts_regression.fit(x=synthetic_train,
                                     y=synthetic_label,
                                     validation_data=(
                                         real_test_data,
                                         real_test_label),
                                     epochs=100,
                                     batch_size=128)
```

Figure 21.9 plots the MAE on the train and test sets (on a log scale so we can spot the differences) for both models. It turns out that the MAE is slightly lower after training on the synthetic dataset:

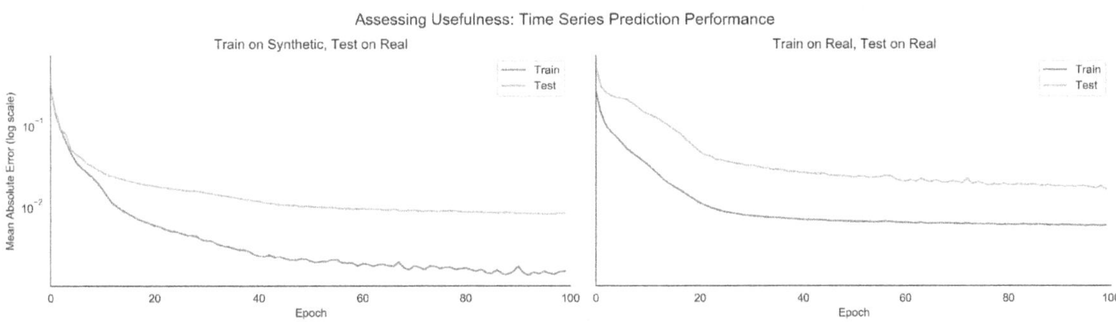

Figure 21.9: Train and test performance of the time-series prediction model over 100 epochs

The result shows that synthetic training data may indeed be useful. On the specific predictive task of predicting the next daily stock price for six tickers, a simple model trained on synthetic TimeGAN data delivers equal or better performance than training on real data.

Lessons learned and next steps

The perennial problem of overfitting that we encountered throughout this book implies that the ability to generate useful synthetic data would be quite valuable. The TimeGAN example justifies cautious optimism in this regard. At the same time, there are some **caveats**: we generated price data for a small number of assets at a daily frequency. In reality, we are probably interested in returns for a much larger number of assets, possibly at a higher frequency. The **cross-sectional and temporal dynamics** will certainly become more complex and may require adjustments to the TimeGAN architecture and training process.

These limitations of the experiment, however promising, imply natural next steps: we need to expand the scope to higher-dimensional time series containing information other than prices and also need to test their usefulness in the context of more complex models, including for feature engineering. These are very early days for synthetic training data, but this example should equip you to pursue your own research agenda towards more realistic solutions.

Summary

In this chapter, we introduced GANs that learn a probability distribution over the input data and are thus capable of generating synthetic samples that are representative of the target data.

While there are many practical applications for this very recent innovation, they could be particularly valuable for algorithmic trading if the success in generating time-series training data in the medical domain can be transferred to financial market data. We learned how to set up adversarial training using TensorFlow. We also explored TimeGAN, a recent example of such a model, tailored to generating synthetic time-series data.

In the next chapter, we focus on reinforcement learning where we will build agents that interactively learn from their (market) environment.

22

Deep Reinforcement Learning – Building a Trading Agent

In this chapter, we'll introduce **reinforcement learning** (**RL**), which takes a different approach to **machine learning** (**ML**) than the supervised and unsupervised algorithms we have covered so far. RL has attracted enormous attention as it has been the main driver behind some of the most exciting AI breakthroughs, like AlphaGo. David Silver, AlphaGo's creator and the lead RL researcher at Google-owned DeepMind, recently won the prestigious 2019 ACM Prize in Computing "for breakthrough advances in computer game-playing." We will see that the interactive and online nature of RL makes it particularly well-suited to the trading and investment domain.

RL models **goal-directed learning by an agent** that interacts with a typically stochastic environment that the agent has incomplete information about. RL aims to automate how the agent makes decisions to achieve a long-term objective by learning the value of states and actions from a reward signal. The ultimate goal is to derive a policy that encodes behavioral rules and maps states to actions.

RL is considered **most similar to human learning** that results from taking actions in the real world and observing the consequences. It differs from supervised learning because it optimizes the agent's behavior one trial-and-error experience at a time based on a scalar reward signal, rather than by generalizing from correctly labeled, representative samples of the target concept. Moreover, RL does not stop at making predictions. Instead, it takes an end-to-end perspective on goal-oriented decision-making by including actions and their consequences.

In this chapter, you will learn how to formulate an RL problem and apply various solution methods. We will cover model-based and model-free methods, introduce the OpenAI Gym environment, and combine deep learning with RL to train an agent that navigates a complex environment. Finally, we'll show you how to adapt RL to algorithmic trading by modeling an agent that interacts with the financial market to optimize its profit objective.

More specifically, after reading this chapter, you will be able to:

- Define a **Markov decision problem** (**MDP**)
- Use value and policy iteration to solve an MDP
- Apply Q-learning in an environment with discrete states and actions
- Build and train a deep Q-learning agent in a continuous environment
- Use OpenAI Gym to train an RL trading agent

> You can find the code samples for this chapter and links to additional resources in the corresponding directory of the GitHub repository. The notebooks include color versions of the images.

Elements of a reinforcement learning system

RL problems feature several elements that set them apart from the ML settings we have covered so far. The following two sections outline the key features required for defining and solving an RL problem by learning a policy that automates decisions. We'll use the notation and generally follow *Reinforcement Learning: An Introduction* (Sutton and Barto 2018) and David Silver's UCL Courses on RL (`https://www.davidsilver.uk/teaching/`), which are recommended for further study beyond the brief summary that the scope of this chapter permits.

RL problems aim to solve for actions that **optimize the agent's objective, given some observations about the environment**. The environment presents information about its state to the agent, assigns rewards for actions, and transitions the agent to new states, subject to probability distributions the agent may or may not know. It may be fully or partially observable, and it may also contain other agents. The structure of the environment has a strong impact on the agent's ability to learn a given task, and typically requires significant up-front design effort to facilitate the training process.

RL problems differ based on the complexity of the environment's state and agent's action spaces, which can be either discrete or continuous. Continuous actions and states, unless discretized, require machine learning to approximate a functional relationship between states, actions, and their values. They also require generalization because the agent almost certainly experiences only a subset of the potentially infinite number of states and actions during training.

Solving complex decision problems usually requires a simplified model that isolates the key aspects. *Figure 22.1* highlights the **salient features of an RL problem**. These typically include:

- Observations by the agent on the state of the environment
- A set of actions available to the agent
- A policy that governs the agent's decisions

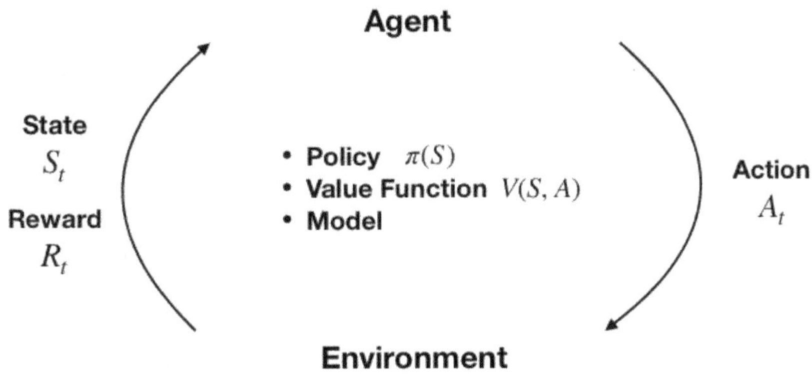

Figure 22.1: Components of an RL system

In addition, the environment emits a **reward signal** (that may be negative) as the agent's action leads to a transition to a new state. At its core, the agent usually learns a **value function** that informs its judgment of the available actions. The agent's objective function processes the reward signal and translates the value judgments into an optimal policy.

The policy – translating states into actions

At any point in time, **the policy defines the agent's behavior**. It maps any state the agent may encounter to one or several actions. In an environment with a limited number of states and actions, the policy can be a simple lookup table that's filled in during training.

With continuous states and actions, the policy takes the form of a function that machine learning can help to approximate. The policy may also involve significant computation, as in the case of AlphaZero, which uses tree search to decide on the best action for a given game state. The policy may also be stochastic and assign probabilities to actions, given a state.

Rewards – learning from actions

The reward signal is a single value that the environment sends to the agent at each time step. The agent's objective is typically to **maximize the total reward received over time**. Rewards can also be a stochastic function of the state and the actions. They are typically discounted to facilitate convergence and reflect the time decay of value.

Rewards are the **only way for the agent to learn** about the value of its decisions in a given state and to modify the policy accordingly. Due to its critical impact on the agent's learning, the reward signal is often the most challenging part of designing an RL system.

Rewards need to clearly communicate what the agent should accomplish (as opposed to how it should do so) and may require domain knowledge to properly encode this information. For example, the development of a trading agent may need to define rewards for buy, hold, and sell decisions. These may be limited to profit and loss, but also may need to include volatility and risk considerations, such as drawdown.

The value function – optimal choice for the long run

The reward provides immediate feedback on actions. However, solving an RL problem requires decisions that create value in the long run. This is where the value function comes in: it summarizes the utility of states or of actions in a given state in terms of their long-term reward.

In other words, the value of a state is the total reward an agent can expect to obtain in the future when starting in that state. The immediate reward may be a good proxy of future rewards, but the agent also needs to account for cases where low rewards are followed by much better outcomes that are likely to follow (or the reverse).

Hence, **value estimates aim to predict future rewards**. Rewards are the key inputs, and the goal of making value estimates is to achieve more rewards. However, RL methods focus on learning accurate values that enable good decisions while efficiently leveraging the (often limited) experience.

There are also RL approaches that do not rely on value functions, such as randomized optimization methods like genetic algorithms or simulated annealing, which aim to find optimal behaviors by efficiently exploring the policy space. The current interest in RL, however, is mostly driven by methods that directly or indirectly estimate the value of states and actions.

Policy gradient methods are a new development that relies on a parameterized, differentiable policy that can be directly optimized with respect to the objective using gradient descent (Sutton et al. 2000). See the resources on GitHub that include abstracts of key papers and algorithms beyond the scope of this chapter.

With or without a model – look before you leap?

Model-based RL approaches learn a model of the environment to allow the agent to plan ahead by predicting the consequences of its actions. Such a model may be used, for example, to predict the next state and reward based on the current state and action. This is the **basis for planning**, that is, deciding on the best course of action by considering possible futures before they materialize.

Simpler **model-free methods**, in contrast, learn from **trial and error**. Modern RL methods span the gamut from low-level trial-and-error methods to high-level, deliberative planning. The right approach depends on the complexity and learnability of the environment.

How to solve reinforcement learning problems

RL methods aim to learn from experience how to take actions that achieve a long-term goal. To this end, the agent and the environment interact over a sequence of discrete time steps via the interface of actions, state observations, and rewards described in the previous section.

Key challenges in solving RL problems

Solving RL problems requires addressing two unique challenges: the credit-assignment problem and the exploration-exploitation trade-off.

Credit assignment

In RL, reward signals can occur significantly later than actions that contributed to the result, complicating the association of actions with their consequences. For example, when an agent takes 100 different positions and trades repeatedly, how does it realize that certain holdings performed much better than others if it only learns about the portfolio return?

The **credit-assignment problem** is the challenge of accurately estimating the benefits and costs of actions in a given state, despite these delays. RL algorithms need to find a way to distribute the credit for positive and negative outcomes among the many decisions that may have been involved in producing it.

Exploration versus exploitation

The dynamic and interactive nature of RL implies that the agent needs to estimate the value of the states and actions before it has experienced all relevant trajectories. While it is able to select an action at any stage, these decisions are based on incomplete learning, yet generate the agent's first insights into the optimal choices of its behavior.

Partial visibility into the value of actions creates the risk of decisions that only exploit past (successful) experience rather than exploring uncharted territory. Such choices limit the agent's exposure and prevent it from learning an optimal policy.

An RL algorithm needs to balance this **exploration-exploitation trade-off**—too little exploration will likely produce biased value estimates and suboptimal policies, whereas too little exploitation prevents learning from taking place in the first place.

Fundamental approaches to solving RL problems

There are numerous approaches to solving RL problems, all of which involve finding rules for the agent's optimal behavior:

- **Dynamic programming** (**DP**) methods make the often unrealistic assumption of complete knowledge of the environment, but they are the conceptual foundation for most other approaches.
- **Monte Carlo** (**MC**) methods learn about the environment and the costs and benefits of different decisions by sampling entire state-action-reward sequences.
- **Temporal difference** (**TD**) learning significantly improves sample efficiency by learning from shorter sequences. To this end, it relies on **bootstrapping**, which is defined as refining its estimates based on its own prior estimates.

When an RL problem includes well-defined transition probabilities and a limited number of states and actions, it can be framed as a finite **Markov decision process** (**MDP**) for which DP can compute an exact solution. Much of the current RL theory focuses on finite MDPs, but practical applications are used for (and require) more general settings. Unknown transition probabilities require efficient sampling to learn about their distribution.

Approaches to continuous state and/or action spaces often leverage **machine learning** to approximate a value or policy function. They integrate supervised learning and, in particular, deep learning methods like those discussed in the previous four chapters. However, these methods face **distinct challenges** in the RL context:

- The **reward signal** does not directly reflect the target concept, like a labeled training sample.
- The **distribution of the observations** depends on the agent's actions and the policy, which is itself the subject of the learning process.

The following sections will introduce and demonstrate various solution methods. We'll start with the DP methods value iteration and policy iteration, which are limited to finite MDP with known transition probabilities. As we will see in the following section, they are the foundation for Q-learning, which is based on TD learning and does not require information about transition probabilities. It aims for similar outcomes as DP but with less computation and without assuming a perfect model of the environment. Finally, we'll expand the scope to continuous states and introduce deep Q-learning.

Solving dynamic programming problems

Finite MDPs are a simple yet fundamental framework. We will introduce the trajectories of rewards that the agent aims to optimize, define the policy and value functions used to formulate the optimization problem, and the Bellman equations that form the basis for the solution methods.

Finite Markov decision problems

MDPs frame the agent-environment interaction as a sequential decision problem over a series of time steps $t = 1, \ldots, T$ that constitute an episode. Time steps are assumed as discrete, but the framework can be extended to continuous time.

The abstraction afforded by MDPs makes its application easily adaptable to many contexts. The time steps can be at arbitrary intervals, and actions and states can take any form that can be expressed numerically.

The Markov property implies that the current state completely describes the process, that is, the process has no memory. Information from past states adds no value when trying to predict the process's future. Due to these properties, the framework has been used to model asset prices subject to the efficient market hypothesis discussed in *Chapter 5, Portfolio Optimization and Performance Evaluation*.

Sequences of states, actions, and rewards

MDPs proceed in the following fashion: at each step t, the agent observes the environment's state $S_t \in S$ and selects an action $A_t \in A$, where S and A are the sets of states and actions, respectively. At the next time step $t+1$, the agent receives a reward $R_{t+1} \in R$ and transitions to state S_{t+1}. Over time, the MDP gives rise to a trajectory $S_0, A_0, R_1, S_1, A_1, R_1, \ldots$ that continues until the agent reaches a terminal state and the episode ends.

Finite MDPs with a limited number of actions A, states S, and rewards R include well-defined discrete probability distributions over these elements. Due to the Markov property, these distributions only depend on the previous state and action.

The probabilistic nature of trajectories implies that the agent maximizes the expected sum of future rewards. Furthermore, rewards are typically discounted using a factor $0 \leq \gamma \leq 1$ to reflect their time value. In the case of tasks that are not episodic but continue indefinitely, a discount factor strictly less than 1 is necessary to avoid infinite rewards and ensure convergence. Therefore, the agent maximizes the discounted, expected sum of future returns R_t, denoted as G_t:

$$G_t = \mathbf{E}[R_{t+1} + \gamma R_{t+2} + \gamma^2 R_{t+3} + \ldots] = \sum_{s=0}^{T} \gamma^s \mathbf{E}[R_{t+s}]$$

This relationship can also be defined recursively because the sum starting at the second step is the same as G_{t+1} discounted once:

$$G_t = R_{t+1} + \gamma G_{t+1}$$

We will see later that this type of recursive relationship is frequently used to formulate RL algorithms.

Value functions – how to estimate the long-run reward

As introduced previously, a policy π maps all states to probability distributions over actions so that the probability of choosing action A_t in state S_t can be expressed as $\pi(a|s) = P(A_t = a|S_t = s)$. The value function estimates the long-run return for each state or state-action pair. It is fundamental to find the policy that is the optimal mapping of states to actions.

The state-value function $v_\pi(s)$ for policy π gives the long-term value v of a specific state s as the expected return G for an agent that starts in s and then always follows policy π. It is defined as follows, where E_π refers to the expected value when the agent follows policy π:

$$v_\pi(s) = \mathbf{E}_\pi[G_t|S_t = s] = \mathbf{E}_\pi\left[\sum_{k=0}^{\infty} \gamma^k R_{t+k+1}|S_t = s\right]$$

Similarly, we can compute the **state-action value function** $q(s,a)$ as the expected return of starting in state s, taking action, and then always following the policy π:

$$q_\pi(s,a) = \mathbf{E}_\pi[G_t|S_t = s, A_t = a] = \mathbf{E}_\pi\left[\sum_{k=0}^{\infty}\gamma^k R_{t+k+1}|S_t = s, A_t = a\right]$$

The Bellman equations

The Bellman equations define a recursive relationship between the value functions for all states s in S and any of their successor states s' under a policy π. They do so by decomposing the value function into the immediate reward and the discounted value of the next state:

$$\begin{aligned} v_\pi(s) &\doteq \mathbf{E}[G_t|S_t = s] \\ &= \mathbf{E}\left[\underbrace{R_{t+1}}_{\text{reward}} + \underbrace{\gamma v(S_{t+1})}_{\text{discounted value}}\right] \\ &= \sum_a \pi(a|s) \sum_{s'}\sum_r p(s',r|s,a)\,[r + \gamma\, v_\pi(s')] \quad \forall_s \end{aligned}$$

This equation says that for a given policy, the value of a state must equal the expected value of its successor states under the policy, plus the expected reward earned from arriving at that successor state.

This implies that, if we know the values of the successor states for the currently available actions, we can look ahead one step and compute the expected value of the current state. Since it holds for all states S, the expression defines a set of $n = |S|$ equations. An analogous relationship holds for $q(s,a)$.

Figure 22.2 summarizes this recursive relationship: in the current state, the agent selects an action a based on the policy π. The environment responds by assigning a reward that depends on the resulting new state s':

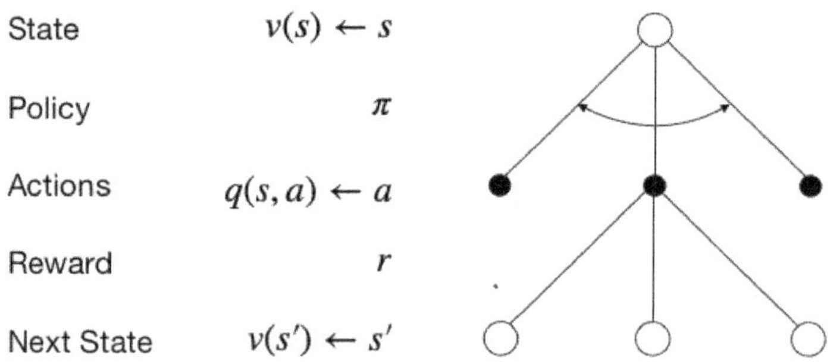

Figure 22.2: The recursive relationship expressed by the Bellman equation

From a value function to an optimal policy

The solution to an RL problem is a policy that optimizes the cumulative reward. Policies and value functions are closely connected: an optimal policy yields a value estimate for each state $v_\pi(s)$ or state-action pair $q_\pi(s,a)$ that is at least as high as for any other policy since the value is the cumulative reward under the given policy. Hence, the optimal value functions $v^*(s) = max_\pi v_\pi(s)$ and $q^*(s,a) = max_\pi q_\pi(s,a)$ implicitly define optimal policies and solve the MDP.

The optimal value functions v^* and q^* also satisfy the Bellman equations from the previous section. These Bellman optimality equations can omit the explicit reference to a policy as it is implied by v^* and q^*. For $v^*(s)$, the recursive relationship equates the current value to the sum of the immediate reward from choosing the best action in the current state, as well as the expected discounted value of the successor states:

$$v^*(s) = \max_a q^*(s,a) = \max_a R_t + \gamma \sum_{s'} p(s'|s,a) v^*(s')$$

For the optimal state-action value function $q^*(s,a)$, the Bellman optimality equation decomposes the current state-action value into the sum of the reward for the implied current action and the discounted expected value of the best action in all successor states:

$$q^*(s) = R_t + \gamma \sum_{s'} p(s'|s,a) v^*(s) = R_t + \gamma \sum_{s'} p(s'|s,a) \max_a q^*(s,a)$$

The optimality conditions imply that the best policy is to always select the action that maximizes the expected value in a greedy fashion, that is, to only consider the result of a single time step.

The optimality conditions defined by the two previous expressions are nonlinear due to the max operator and lack a closed-form solution. Instead, MDP solutions rely on an iterative solution - like policy and value iteration or Q-learning, which we will cover next.

Policy iteration

DP is a general method for solving problems that can be decomposed into smaller, overlapping subproblems with a recursive structure that permit the reuse of intermediate results. MDPs fit the bill due to the recursive Bellman optimality equations and the cumulative nature of the value function. More specifically, the **principle of optimality** applies because an optimal policy consists of picking an optimal action and then following an optimal policy.

DP requires knowledge of the MDP's transition probabilities. This is often not the case, but many methods for more general cases follow an approach similar to DP and learn the missing information from the data.

DP is useful for **prediction tasks** that estimate the value function and the control task that focuses on optimal decisions and outputs a policy (while also estimating a value function in the process).

The policy iteration algorithm to find an optimal policy repeats the following two steps until the policy has converged, that is, no longer changes more than a given threshold:

1. **Policy evaluation**: Update the value function based on the current policy.
2. **Policy improvement**: Update the policy so that actions maximize the expected one-step value.

Policy evaluation relies on the Bellman equation to estimate the value function. More specifically, it selects the action determined by the current policy and sums the resulting reward, as well as the discounted value of the next state, to update the value for the current state.

Policy improvement, in turn, alters the policy so that for each state, the policy produces the action that produces the highest value in the next state. This improvement is called greedy because it only considers the return of a single time step. Policy iteration always converges to an optimal policy and often does so in relatively few iterations.

Value iteration

Policy iteration requires the evaluation of the policy for all states after each iteration. The evaluation can be costly, as discussed previously, for search-tree-based policies, for example.

Value iteration simplifies this process by collapsing the policy evaluation and improvement step. At each time step, it iterates over all states and selects the best greedy action based on the current value estimate for the next state. Then, it uses the one-step lookahead implied by the Bellman optimality equation to update the value function for the current state.

The corresponding update rule for the value function $v_{k+1}(s)$ is almost identical to the policy evaluation update; it just adds the maximization over the available actions:

$$v_{k+1}(s) \leftarrow \max_a \sum_{s'} \sum_r p(s',r|s,a)\,[r + \gamma v_k(s')]$$

The algorithm stops when the value function has converged and outputs the greedy policy derived from its value function estimate. It is also guaranteed to converge to an optimal policy.

Generalized policy iteration

In practice, there are several ways to truncate policy iteration; for example, by evaluating the policy k times before improving it. This just means that the *max* operator will only be applied at every k^{th} iteration.

Most RL algorithms estimate value and policy functions and rely on the interaction of policy evaluation and improvement to converge to a solution, as illustrated in *Figure 22.3*. The general approach improves the policy with respect to the value function while adjusting the value function so that it matches the policy:

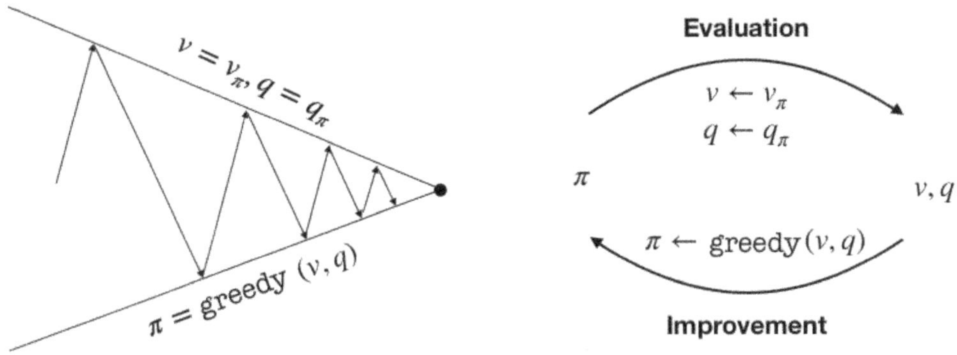

Figure 22.3: Convergence of policy evaluation and improvement

Convergence requires that the value function be consistent with the policy, which, in turn, needs to stabilize while acting greedily with respect to the value function. Thus, both processes stabilize only when a policy has been found that is greedy with respect to its own evaluation function. This implies that the Bellman optimality equation holds, and thus that the policy and the value function are optimal.

Dynamic programming in Python

In this section, we'll apply value and policy iteration to a toy environment that consists of a 3 × 4 grid, as depicted in *Figure 22.4*, with the following features:

- **States**: 11 states represented as two-dimensional coordinates. One field is not accessible and the top two states in the right-most column are terminal, that is, they end the episode.
- **Actions**: Movements of one step up, down, left, or right. The environment is randomized so that actions can have unintended outcomes. For each action, there is an 80 percent probability of moving to the expected state, and 10 percent each of moving in an adjacent direction (for example, right or left instead of up, or up/down instead of right).
- **Rewards**: As depicted in the left panel, each state results in -.02 except the +1/-1 rewards in the terminal states.

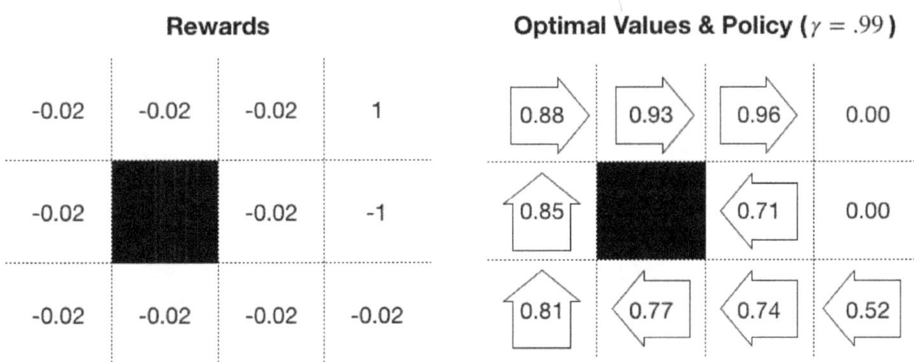

Figure 22.4: 3×4 gridworld rewards, value function, and optimal policy

Setting up the gridworld

We will begin by defining the environment parameters:

```
grid_size = (3, 4)
blocked_cell = (1, 1)
baseline_reward = -0.02
absorbing_cells = {(0, 3): 1, (1, 3): -1}
actions = ['L', 'U', 'R', 'D']
num_actions = len(actions)
probs = [.1, .8, .1, 0]
```

We will frequently need to convert between 1D and 2D representations, so we will define two helper functions for this purpose; states are one-dimensional, and cells are the corresponding 2D coordinates:

```
to_1d = lambda x: np.ravel_multi_index(x, grid_size)
to_2d = lambda x: np.unravel_index(x, grid_size)
```

Furthermore, we will precompute some data points to make the code more concise:

```
num_states = np.product(grid_size)
cells = list(np.ndindex(grid_size))
states = list(range(len(cells)))
cell_state = dict(zip(cells, states))
state_cell= dict(zip(states, cells))
absorbing_states = {to_1d(s):r for s, r in absorbing_cells.items()}
blocked_state = to_1d(blocked_cell)
```

We store the rewards for each state:

```
state_rewards = np.full(num_states, baseline_reward)
state_rewards[blocked_state] = 0
for state, reward in absorbing_states.items():
    state_rewards[state] = reward

state_rewards
array([-0.02, -0.02, -0.02,  1.  , -0.02,  0.  , -0.02, -1.  , -0.02,
       -0.02, -0.02, -0.02])
```

To account for the probabilistic environment, we also need to compute the probability distribution over the actual move for a given action:

```
action_outcomes = {}
for i, action in enumerate(actions):
    probs_ = dict(zip([actions[j % 4] for j in range(i,
                                           num_actions + i)], probs))
    action_outcomes[actions[(i + 1) % 4]] = probs_
```

```
Action_outcomes
{'U': {'L': 0.1, 'U': 0.8, 'R': 0.1, 'D': 0},
 'R': {'U': 0.1, 'R': 0.8, 'D': 0.1, 'L': 0},
 'D': {'R': 0.1, 'D': 0.8, 'L': 0.1, 'U': 0},
 'L': {'D': 0.1, 'L': 0.8, 'U': 0.1, 'R': 0}}
```

Now, we are ready to compute the transition matrix, which is the key input to the MDP.

Computing the transition matrix

The **transition matrix** defines the probability of ending up in a certain state S for each previous state and action A $P(s'|s,a)$. We will demonstrate `pymdptoolbox` and use one of the formats available to specify transitions and rewards. For both transition probabilities, we will create a NumPy array with dimensions $A \times S \times S$.

We first compute the target cell for each starting cell and move:

```
def get_new_cell(state, move):
    cell = to_2d(state)
    if actions[move] == 'U':
        return cell[0] - 1, cell[1]
    elif actions[move] == 'D':
        return cell[0] + 1, cell[1]
    elif actions[move] == 'R':
        return cell[0], cell[1] + 1
    elif actions[move] == 'L':
        return cell[0], cell[1] - 1
```

The following function uses the arguments starting `state`, `action`, and `outcome` to fill in the transition probabilities and rewards:

```
def update_transitions_and_rewards(state, action, outcome):
    if state in absorbing_states.keys() or state == blocked_state:
        transitions[action, state, state] = 1
    else:
        new_cell = get_new_cell(state, outcome)
        p = action_outcomes[actions[action]][actions[outcome]]
        if new_cell not in cells or new_cell == blocked_cell:
            transitions[action, state, state] += p
            rewards[action, state, state] = baseline_reward
        else:
            new_state= to_1d(new_cell)
            transitions[action, state, new_state] = p
            rewards[action, state, new_state] = state_rewards[new_state]
```

We generate the transition and reward values by creating placeholder data structures and iterating over the Cartesian product of $A \times S \times S$, as follows:

```
rewards = np.zeros(shape=(num_actions, num_states, num_states))
transitions = np.zeros((num_actions, num_states, num_states))
actions_ = list(range(num_actions))
for action, outcome, state in product(actions_, actions_, states):
    update_transitions_and_rewards(state, action, outcome)

rewards.shape, transitions.shape
((4,12,12), (4,12,12))
```

Implementing the value iteration algorithm

We first create the value iteration algorithm, which is slightly simpler because it implements policy evaluation and improvement in a single step. We capture the states for which we need to update the value function, excluding terminal states that have a value of 0 for lack of rewards (+1/-1 are assigned to the starting state), and skip the blocked cell:

```
skip_states = list(absorbing_states.keys())+[blocked_state]
states_to_update = [s for s in states if s not in skip_states]
```

Then, we initialize the value function and set the discount factor gamma and the convergence threshold `epsilon`:

```
V = np.random.rand(num_states)
V[skip_states] = 0

gamma = .99
epsilon = 1e-5
```

The algorithm updates the value function using the Bellman optimality equation, as described previously, and terminates when the L1 norm of V changes to less than epsilon in absolute terms:

```
while True:
    V_ = np.copy(V)
    for state in states_to_update:
        q_sa = np.sum(transitions[:, state] * (rewards[:, state] + gamma* V),
                      axis=1)
        V[state] = np.max(q_sa)
    if np.sum(np.fabs(V - V_)) < epsilon:
        break
```

The algorithm converges in 16 iterations and 0.0117s. It produces the following optimal value estimate, which, together with the implied optimal policy, is depicted in the right panel of *Figure 22.4*, earlier in this section:

```
pd.DataFrame(V.reshape(grid_size))
         0         1         2         3
0.884143  0.925054  0.961986  0.000000
1  0.848181  0.000000  0.714643  0.000000
2  0.808344  0.773327  0.736099  0.516082
```

Defining and running policy iteration

Policy iterations involve separate evaluation and improvement steps. We define the improvement part by selecting the action that maximizes the sum of the expected reward and next-state value. Note that we temporarily fill in the rewards for the terminal states to avoid ignoring actions that would lead us there:

```
def policy_improvement(value, transitions):
    for state, reward in absorbing_states.items():
        value[state] = reward
    return np.argmax(np.sum(transitions * value, 2),0)
```

We initialize the value function as before and also include a random starting policy:

```
pi = np.random.choice(list(range(num_actions)), size=num_states)
```

The algorithm alternates between policy evaluation for a greedily selected action and policy improvement until the policy stabilizes:

```
iterations = 0
converged = False
while not converged:
    pi_ = np.copy(pi)
    for state in states_to_update:
        action = policy[state]
        V[state] = np.dot(transitions[action, state],
                                        rewards[action, state] + gamma* V)
        pi = policy_improvement(V.copy(), transitions)
    if np.array_equal(pi_, pi):
        converged = True
    iterations += 1
```

Policy iteration converges after only three iterations. The policy stabilizes before the algorithm finds the optimal value function, and the optimal policy differs slightly, most notably by suggesting "up" instead of the safer "left" for the field next to the negative terminal state. This can be avoided by tightening the convergence criteria, for example, by requiring a stable policy of several rounds or by adding a threshold for the value function.

Solving MDPs using pymdptoolbox

We can also solve MDPs using the Python library `pymdptoolbox`, which includes a few other algorithms, including Q-learning.

To run value iteration, just instantiate the corresponding object with the desired configuration options, rewards, and transition matrices before calling the `.run()` method:

```
vi = mdp.ValueIteration(transitions=transitions,
                        reward=rewards,
                        discount=gamma,
                        epsilon=epsilon)

vi.run()
```

The value function estimate matches the result in the previous section:

```
np.allclose(V.reshape(grid_size), np.asarray(vi.V).reshape(grid_size))
```

Policy iteration works similarly:

```
pi = mdp.PolicyIteration(transitions=transitions,
                        reward=rewards,
                        discount=gamma,
                        max_iter=1000)

pi.run()
```

It also yields the same policy, but the value function varies by run and does not need to achieve the optimal value before the policy converges.

Lessons learned

The right panel we saw earlier in *Figure 22.4* shows the optimal value estimate produced by value iteration and the corresponding greedy policy. The negative rewards, combined with the uncertainty in the environment, produce an optimal policy that involves moving away from the negative terminal state.

The results are sensitive to both the rewards and the discount factor. The cost of the negative state affects the policy in the surrounding fields, and you should modify the example in the corresponding notebook to identify threshold levels that alter the optimal action selection.

Q-learning – finding an optimal policy on the go

Q-learning was an early RL breakthrough when developed by Chris Watkins for his PhD thesis (`http://www.cs.rhul.ac.uk/~chrisw/new_thesis.pdf`) (1989). It introduces incremental dynamic programming to learn to control an MDP without knowing or modeling the transition and reward matrices that we used for value and policy iteration in the previous section. A convergence proof followed 3 years later (Christopher J. C. H. Watkins and Dayan 1992).

Q-learning directly optimizes the action-value function q to approximate q^*. The learning proceeds "off-policy," that is, the algorithm does not need to select actions based on the policy implied by the value function alone. However, convergence requires that all state-action pairs continue to be updated throughout the training process. A straightforward way to ensure this is through an ε-greedy policy.

Exploration versus exploitation – ε-greedy policy

An **ε-greedy policy** is a simple policy that ensures the exploration of new actions in a given state while also exploiting the learning experience . It does this by randomizing the selection of actions. An ε-greedy policy selects an action randomly with a probability of ε, and the best action according to the value function otherwise.

The Q-learning algorithm

The algorithm keeps improving a state-action value function after random initialization for a given number of episodes. At each time step, it chooses an action based on an ε-greedy policy, and uses a learning rate α to update the value function, as follows:

$$Q(S_t, A_t) \longleftarrow Q(S_t, A_t) + \alpha \overbrace{\left[\underbrace{R_t + \gamma \max_a Q(S_{t+1}, a)}_{\text{TD Target}} - \underbrace{Q(S_t, A_t)}_{\text{Current Q-value}} \right]}^{\text{Temporal Difference}}$$

Note that the algorithm does not compute expected values based on the transition probabilities. Instead, it learns the Q function from the rewards R_t produced by the ε-greedy policy and its current estimate of the discounted value function for the next state.

The use of the estimated value function to improve this very estimate is called **bootstrapping**. The Q-learning algorithm is part of the **temporal difference** (**TD**) **learning** algorithms. TD learning does not wait until receiving the final reward for an episode. Instead, it updates its estimates using the values of intermediate states that are closer to the final reward. In this case, the intermediate state is one time step ahead.

How to train a Q-learning agent using Python

In this section, we will demonstrate how to build a Q-learning agent using the 3×4 grid of states from the previous section. We will train the agent for 2,500 episodes, using a learning rate of $\alpha = 0.1$ and $\varepsilon = 0.05$ for the ε-greedy policy (see the notebook `gridworld_q_learning.ipynb` for details):

```
max_episodes = 2500
alpha = .1
epsilon = .05
```

Then, we will randomly initialize the state-action value function as a NumPy array with dimensions *number of states* × *number of actions*:

```
Q = np.random.rand(num_states, num_actions)
Q[skip_states] = 0
```

The algorithm generates 2,500 episodes that start at a random location and proceed according to the ε-greedy policy until termination, updating the value function according to the Q-learning rule:

```
for episode in range(max_episodes):
    state = np.random.choice([s for s in states if s not in skip_states])
    while not state in absorbing_states.keys():
        if np.random.rand() < epsilon:
            action = np.random.choice(num_actions)
        else:
            action = np.argmax(Q[state])
        next_state = np.random.choice(states, p=transitions[action, state])
        reward = rewards[action, state, next_state]
        Q[state, action] += alpha * (reward +
                            gamma * np.max(Q[next_state])-Q[state, action])
        state = next_state
```

The episodes take 0.6 seconds and converge to a value function fairly close to the result of the value iteration example from the previous section. The `pymdptoolbox` implementation works analogously to previous examples (see the notebook for details).

Deep RL for trading with the OpenAI Gym

In the previous section, we saw how Q-learning allows us to learn the optimal state-action value function q^* in an environment with discrete states and discrete actions using iterative updates based on the Bellman equation.

In this section, we will take RL one step closer to the real world and upgrade the algorithm to **continuous states** (while keeping actions discrete). This implies that we can no longer use a tabular solution that simply fills an array with state-action values. Instead, we will see how to **approximate q* using a neural network** (**NN**), which results in a deep Q-network. We will first discuss how deep learning integrates with RL before presenting the deep Q-learning algorithm, as well as various refinements that accelerate its convergence and make it more robust.

Continuous states also imply a **more complex environment**. We will demonstrate how to work with OpenAI Gym, a toolkit for designing and comparing RL algorithms. First, we'll illustrate the workflow by training a deep Q-learning agent to navigate a toy spaceship in the Lunar Lander environment. Then, we'll proceed to **customize OpenAI Gym** to design an environment that simulates a trading context where an agent can buy and sell a stock while competing against the market.

Value function approximation with neural networks

Continuous state and/or action spaces imply an **infinite number of transitions** that make it impossible to tabulate the state-action values, as in the previous section. Rather, we approximate the Q function by learning a continuous, parameterized mapping from training samples.

Motivated by the success of NNs in other domains, which we discussed in the previous chapters in *Part 4*, deep NNs have also become popular for approximating value functions. However, **machine learning in the RL context**, where the data is generated by the interaction of the model with the environment using a (possibly randomized) policy, **faces distinct challenges**:

- With continuous states, the agent will fail to visit most states and thus needs to generalize.
- Whereas supervised learning aims to generalize from a sample of independently and identically distributed samples that are representative and correctly labeled, in the RL context, there is only one sample per time step, so learning needs to occur online.
- Furthermore, samples can be highly correlated when sequential states are similar and the behavior distribution over states and actions is not stationary, but rather changes as a result of the agent's learning.

We will look at several techniques that have been developed to address these additional challenges.

The Deep Q-learning algorithm and extensions

Deep Q-learning estimates the value of the available actions for a given state using a deep neural network. DeepMind introduced this technique in *Playing Atari with Deep Reinforcement Learning* (Mnih et al. 2013), where agents learned to play games solely from pixel input.

The Deep Q-learning algorithm approximates the action-value function q by learning a set of weights θ of a multilayered **deep Q-network** (**DQN**) that maps states to actions so that $q(s, a, \theta) \approx q^*(s, a)$.

The algorithm applies gradient descent based on a loss function that computes the squared difference between the DQN's estimate of the target:

$$y_i = \mathbb{E}\left[r + \gamma \max_{a'} Q(s', a'; \theta_{i-1} | s, a)\right]$$

and its estimate of the action-value of the current state-action pair $Q(s, a; \theta)$ to learn the network parameters:

$$L_i(\theta_i) = \left(\overbrace{\underbrace{y_i}_{\text{Q Target}} - \underbrace{Q(s, a; \theta)}_{\text{Current Prediction}}}^{\text{TD Error}} \right)^2$$

Both **the target and the current estimate depend on the DQN weights**, underlining the distinction from supervised learning where targets are fixed prior to training.

Rather than computing the full gradient, the Q-learning algorithm uses **stochastic gradient descent** (**SGD**) and updates the weights θ_i after each time step i. To explore the state-action space, the agent uses an ϵ-greedy policy that selects a random action with probability ϵ and follows a greedy policy that selects the action with the highest predicted q-value otherwise.

The basic **DQN architecture has been refined** in several directions to make the learning process more efficient and improve the final result; Hessel et al. (2017) combined these innovations in the **Rainbow agent** and demonstrated how each contributes to significantly higher performance across the Atari benchmarks. The following subsections summarize some of these innovations.

(Prioritized) Experience replay – focusing on past mistakes

Experience replay stores a history of the state, action, reward, and next state transitions experienced by the agent. It randomly samples mini-batches from this experience to update the network weights at each time step before the agent selects an ε-greedy action.

Experience replay increases sample efficiency, reduces the autocorrelation of samples collected during online learning, and limits the feedback due to current weights producing training samples that can lead to local minima or divergence (Lin and Mitchell 1992).

This technique was later refined to prioritize experience that is more important from a learning perspective. Schaul et al. (2015) approximated the value of a transition by the size of the TD error that captures how "surprising" the event was for the agent. In practice, it samples historical state transitions using their associated TD error rather than uniform probabilities.

The target network – decorrelating the learning process

To further weaken the feedback loop from the current network parameters on the NN weight updates, the algorithm was extended by DeepMind in *Human-level control through deep reinforcement learning* (Mnih et al. 2015) to use a slowly-changing target network.

The target network has the same architecture as the Q-network, but its weights θ^- are only updated periodically after τ steps when they are copied from the Q-network and held constant otherwise. The target network **generates the TD target predictions**, that is, it takes the place of the Q-network to estimate:

$$y_i = \mathbb{E}\left[r + \gamma \max_{a'} Q(s', a'; \theta^- | s, a)\right]$$

Double deep Q-learning – decoupling action and prediction

Q-learning has been shown to overestimate the action values because it purposely samples maximal estimated action values.

This bias can negatively affect the learning process and the resulting policy if it does not apply uniformly and alters action preferences, as shown in *Deep Reinforcement Learning with Double Q-learning* (van Hasselt, Guez, and Silver 2015).

To decouple the estimation of action values from the selection of actions, the **Double DQN** (**DDQN**) algorithm uses the weights θ of one network to select the best action given the next state, as well as the weights θ' of another network, to provide the corresponding action value estimate:

$$y_i = \mathbb{E}\left[r + \gamma Q\left(s', \arg\max_{a'} Q(S_{t+1}, a, \theta_t); \theta'_t\right)\right].$$

One option is to randomly select one of two identical networks for training at each iteration so that their weights will differ. A more efficient alternative is to rely on the target network to provide θ' instead.

Introducing the OpenAI Gym

OpenAI Gym is an RL platform that provides standardized environments to test and benchmark RL algorithms using Python. It is also possible to extend the platform and register custom environments.

The **Lunar Lander v2** (**LL**) environment requires the agent to control its motion in two dimensions based on a discrete action space and low-dimensional state observations that include position, orientation, and velocity. At each time step, the environment provides an observation of the new state and a positive or negative reward. Each episode consists of up to 1,000 time steps. *Figure 22.5* shows selected frames from a successful landing after 250 episodes by the agent we will train later:

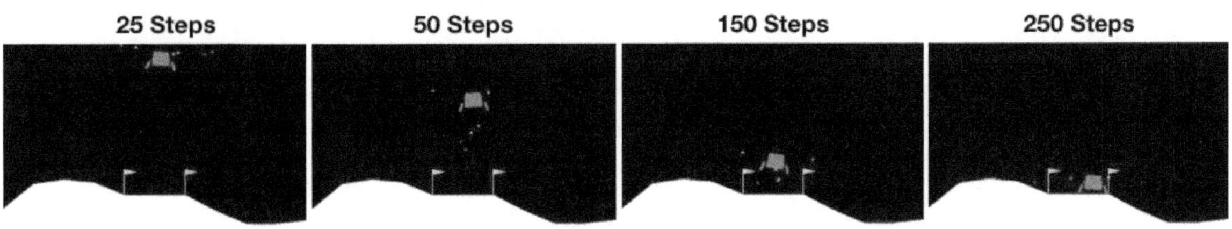

Figure 22.5: RL agent's behavior during the Lunar Lander episode

More specifically, the **agent observes eight aspects of the state**, including six continuous and two discrete elements. Based on the observed elements, the agent knows its location, direction, and speed of movement and whether it has (partially) landed. However, it does not know in which direction it should move, nor can it observe the inner state of the environment to understand the rules that govern its motion.

At each time step, the agent controls its motion using one of **four discrete actions**. It can do nothing (and continue on its current path), fire its main engine (to reduce downward motion), or steer toward the left or right using the respective orientation engines. There are no fuel limitations.

The goal is to land the agent between two flags on a landing pad at coordinates (0, 0), but landing outside of the pad is possible. The agent accumulates rewards in the range of 100-140 for moving toward the pad, depending on the exact landing spot. However, a move away from the target negates the reward the agent would have gained by moving toward the pad. Ground contact by each leg adds 10 points, while using the main engine costs -0.3 points.

An episode terminates if the agent lands or crashes, adding or subtracting 100 points, respectively, or after 1,000 time steps. Solving LL requires achieving a cumulative reward of at least 200 on average over 100 consecutive episodes.

How to implement DDQN using TensorFlow 2

The notebook `03_lunar_lander_deep_q_learning` implements a DDQN agent using TensorFlow 2 that learns to solve OpenAI Gym's **Lunar Lander** 2.0 (**LL**) environment. The notebook `03_lunar_lander_deep_q_learning` contains a TensorFlow 1 implementation that was discussed in the first edition and runs significantly faster because it does not rely on eager execution and also converges sooner. This section highlights key elements of the implementation; please see the notebook for much more extensive details.

Creating the DDQN agent

We create our `DDQNAgent` as a Python class to integrate the learning and execution logic with the key configuration parameters and performance tracking.

The agent's `__init__()` method takes, as arguments, information on:

- The **environment characteristics**, like the number of dimensions for the state observations and the number of actions available to the agent.
- The decay of the randomized exploration for the **ε-greedy policy**.
- The **neural network architecture** and the parameters for **training** and target network updates.

```
class DDQNAgent:
    def __init__(self, state_dim, num_actions, gamma,
                 epsilon_start, epsilon_end, epsilon_decay_steps,
                 epsilon_exp_decay,replay_capacity, learning_rate,
                 architecture, l2_reg, tau, batch_size,
                 log_dir='results'):
```

Adapting the DDQN architecture to the Lunar Lander

The DDQN architecture was first applied to the Atari domain with high-dimensional image observations and relied on convolutional layers. The LL's lower-dimensional state representation makes fully connected layers a better choice (see *Chapter 17, Deep Learning for Trading*).

More specifically, the network maps eight inputs to four outputs, representing the Q values for each action, so that it only takes a single forward pass to compute the action values. The DQN is trained on the previous loss function using the Adam optimizer. The agent's DQN uses three densely connected layers with 256 units each and L2 activity regularization. Using a GPU via the TensorFlow Docker image can significantly speed up NN training performance (see *Chapter 17* and *Chapter 18, CNNs for Financial Time Series and Satellite Images*).

The `DDQNAgent` class's `build_model()` method creates the primary online and slow-moving target networks based on the `architecture` parameter, which specifies the number of layers and their number of units.

We set `trainable` to `True` for the primary online network and to `False` for the target network. This is because we simply periodically copy the online NN weights to update the target network:

```
def build_model(self, trainable=True):
    layers = []
    for i, units in enumerate(self.architecture, 1):
        layers.append(Dense(units=units,
                            input_dim=self.state_dim if i == 1 else None,
                            activation='relu',
                            kernel_regularizer=l2(self.l2_reg),
                            trainable=trainable))
    layers.append(Dense(units=self.num_actions,
                        trainable=trainable))
    model = Sequential(layers)
    model.compile(loss='mean_squared_error',
                  optimizer=Adam(lr=self.learning_rate))
    return model
```

Memorizing transitions and replaying the experience

To enable experience replay, the agent memorizes each state transition so it can randomly sample a mini-batch during training. The `memorize_transition()` method receives the observation on the current and next state provided by the environment, as well as the agent's action, the reward, and a flag that indicates whether the episode is completed.

It tracks the reward history and length of each episode, applies exponential decay to epsilon at the end of each period, and stores the state transition information in a buffer:

```
def memorize_transition(self, s, a, r, s_prime, not_done):
    if not_done:
        self.episode_reward += r
        self.episode_length += 1
    else:
        self.episodes += 1
        self.rewards_history.append(self.episode_reward)
        self.steps_per_episode.append(self.episode_length)
```

```
            self.episode_reward, self.episode_length = 0, 0

        self.experience.append((s, a, r, s_prime, not_done))
```

The replay of the memorized experience begins as soon as there are enough samples to create a full batch. The `experience_replay()` method predicts the Q values for the next states using the online network and selects the best action. It then selects the predicted *q* values for these actions from the target network to arrive at the TD `targets`.

Next, it trains the primary network using a single batch of current state observations as input, the TD targets as the outcome, and the mean-squared error as the loss function. Finally, it updates the target network weights every τ steps:

```
    def experience_replay(self):
        if self.batch_size > len(self.experience):
            return
        # sample minibatch from experience
        minibatch = map(np.array, zip(*sample(self.experience,
                                              self.batch_size)))
        states, actions, rewards, next_states, not_done = minibatch

        # predict next Q values to select best action
        next_q_values = self.online_network.predict_on_batch(next_states)
        best_actions = tf.argmax(next_q_values, axis=1)

        # predict the TD target
        next_q_values_target = self.target_network.predict_on_batch(
            next_states)
        target_q_values = tf.gather_nd(next_q_values_target,
                                       tf.stack((self.idx, tf.cast(
                                           best_actions, tf.int32)), axis=1))
        targets = rewards + not_done * self.gamma * target_q_values

        # predict q values
        q_values = self.online_network.predict_on_batch(states)
        q_values[[self.idx, actions]] = targets

        # train model
        loss = self.online_network.train_on_batch(x=states, y=q_values)
        self.losses.append(loss)

        if self.total_steps % self.tau == 0:
            self.update_target()

    def update_target(self):
        self.target_network.set_weights(self.online_network.get_weights())
```

The notebook contains additional implementation details for the ε-greedy policy and the target network weight updates.

Setting up the OpenAI environment

We will begin by instantiating and extracting key parameters from the LL environment:

```
env = gym.make('LunarLander-v2')
state_dim = env.observation_space.shape[0]  # number of dimensions in state
num_actions = env.action_space.n  # number of actions
max_episode_steps = env.spec.max_episode_steps  # max number of steps per
episode
env.seed(42)
```

We will also use the built-in wrappers that permit the periodic storing of videos that display the agent's performance:

```
from gym import wrappers
env = wrappers.Monitor(env,
                       directory=monitor_path.as_posix(),
                       video_callable=lambda count: count % video_freq == 0,
                      force=True)
```

When running on a server or Docker container without a display, you can use `pyvirtualdisplay`.

Key hyperparameter choices

The agent's performance is quite sensitive to several hyperparameters. We will start with the discount and learning rates:

```
gamma=.99,  # discount factor
learning_rate=1e-4  # learning rate
```

We will update the target network every 100 time steps, store up to 1 million past episodes in the replay memory, and sample mini-batches of 1,024 from memory to train the agent:

```
tau=100  # target network update frequency
replay_capacity=int(1e6)
batch_size = 1024
```

The ε-greedy policy starts with pure exploration at $\varepsilon = 1$, linear decay to 0.01 over 250 episodes, and exponential decay thereafter:

```
epsilon_start=1.0
epsilon_end=0.01
epsilon_linear_steps=250
epsilon_exp_decay=0.99
```

The notebook contains the training loop, including experience replay, SGD, and slow target network updates.

Lunar Lander learning performance

The preceding hyperparameter settings enable the agent to solve the environment in around 300 episodes using the TensorFlow 1 implementation.

The left panel of *Figure 22.6* shows the episode rewards and their moving average over 100 periods. The right panel shows the decay of exploration and the number of steps per episode. There is a stretch of some 100 episodes that often take 1,000 time steps each while the agent reduces exploration and "learns how to fly" before starting to land fairly consistently:

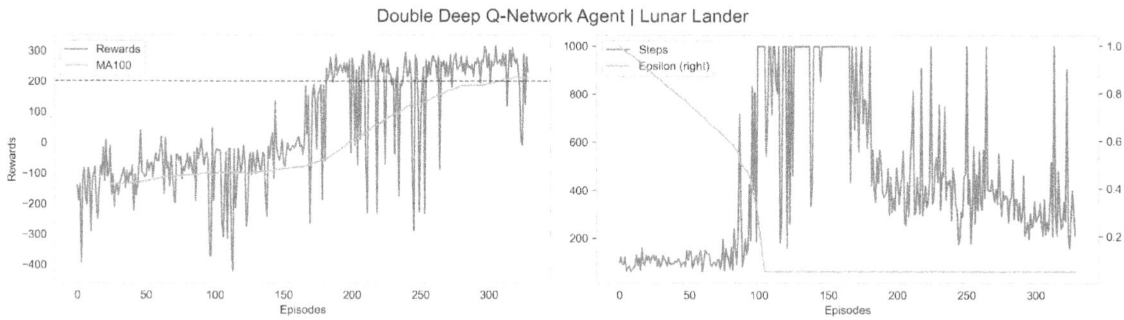

Figure 22.6: The DDQN agent's performance in the Lunar Lander environment

Creating a simple trading agent

In this and the following sections, we will adapt the deep RL approach to design an agent that learns how to trade a single asset. To train the agent, we will set up a simple environment with a limited set of actions, a relatively low-dimensional state with continuous observations, and other parameters.

More specifically, the **environment** samples a stock price time series for a single ticker using a random start date to simulate a trading period that, by default, contains 252 days or 1 year. Each **state observation** provides the agent with the historical returns for various lags and some technical indicators, like the **relative strength index** (**RSI**).

The agent can choose from three **actions**:

- **Buy**: Invest all capital for a long position in the stock.
- **Flat**: Hold cash only.
- **Sell short**: Take a short position equal to the amount of capital.

The environment accounts for **trading cost**, set to 10 basis points by default, and deducts one basis point per period without trades. The **reward** of the agent consists of the daily return minus trading costs.

The environment tracks the **net asset value** (**NAV**) of the agent's portfolio (consisting of a single stock) and compares it against the market portfolio, which trades frictionless to raise the bar for the agent.

An episode begins with a starting NAV of 1 unit of cash:

- If the NAV drops to 0, the episode ends with a loss.
- If the NAV hits 2.0, the agent wins.

This setting limits complexity as it focuses on a single stock and abstracts from position sizing to avoid the need for continuous actions or a larger number of discrete actions, as well as more sophisticated bookkeeping. However, it is useful to demonstrate how to customize an environment and permits for extensions.

How to design a custom OpenAI trading environment

To build an agent that learns how to trade, we need to create a market environment that provides price and other information, offers relevant actions, and tracks the portfolio to reward the agent accordingly. For a description of the efforts to build a large-scale, real-world simulation environment, see Byrd, Hybinette, and Balch (2019).

OpenAI Gym allows for the design, registration, and utilization of environments that adhere to its architecture, as described in the documentation. The file `trading_env.py` contains the following code examples, which illustrate the process unless noted otherwise.

The trading environment consists of three classes that interact to facilitate the agent's activities. The `DataSource` class loads a time series, generates a few features, and provides the latest observation to the agent at each time step. `TradingSimulator` tracks the positions, trades and cost, and the performance. It also implements and records the results of a buy-and-hold benchmark strategy. `TradingEnvironment` itself orchestrates the process. We will briefly describe each in turn; see the script for implementation details.

Designing a DataSource class

First, we code up a `DataSource` class to load and preprocess historical stock data to create the information used for state observations and rewards. In this example, we will keep it very simple and provide the agent with historical data on a single stock. Alternatively, you could combine many stocks into a single time series, for example, to train the agent on trading the S&P 500 constituents.

We will load the adjusted price and volume information for one ticker from the Quandl dataset, in this case for AAPL with data from the early 1980s until 2018:

```
class DataSource:
    """Data source for TradingEnvironment

    Loads & preprocesses daily price & volume data
    Provides data for each new episode.
    """

    def __init__(self, trading_days=252, ticker='AAPL'):
```

```
        self.ticker = ticker
        self.trading_days = trading_days

    def load_data(self):
        idx = pd.IndexSlice
        with pd.HDFStore('../data/assets.h5') as store:
            df = (store['quandl/wiki/prices']
                  .loc[idx[:, self.ticker],
                       ['adj_close', 'adj_volume', 'adj_low', 'adj_high']])
        df.columns = ['close', 'volume', 'low', 'high']
        return df
```

The `preprocess_data()` method creates several features and normalizes them. The most recent daily returns play two roles:

- An element of the observations for the current state
- The net of trading costs and, depending on the position size, the reward for the last period

The method takes the following steps, among others (refer to the *Appendix* for details on the technical indicators):

```
def preprocess_data(self):
"""calculate returns and percentiles, then removes missing values"""

   self.data['returns'] = self.data.close.pct_change()
   self.data['ret_2'] = self.data.close.pct_change(2)
   self.data['ret_5'] = self.data.close.pct_change(5)
   self.data['rsi'] = talib.STOCHRSI(self.data.close)[1]
   self.data['atr'] = talib.ATR(self.data.high,
                                self.data.low, self.data.close)
   self.data = (self.data.replace((np.inf, -np.inf), np.nan)
                .drop(['high', 'low', 'close'], axis=1)
                .dropna())

   if self.normalize:
       self.data = pd.DataFrame(scale(self.data),
                                columns=self.data.columns,
                                index=self.data.index)
```

The `DataSource` class keeps track of episode progress, provides fresh data to `TradingEnvironment` at each time step, and signals the end of the episodes:

```
def take_step(self):
    """Returns data for current trading day and done signal"""
    obs = self.data.iloc[self.offset + self.step].values
    self.step += 1
```

```
    done = self.step > self.trading_days
    return obs, done
```

The TradingSimulator class

The trading simulator computes the agent's reward and tracks the net asset values of the agent and "the market," which executes a buy-and-hold strategy with reinvestment. It also tracks the positions and the market return, computes trading costs, and logs the results.

The most important method of this class is the `take_step` method, which computes the agent's reward based on its current position, the latest stock return, and the trading costs (slightly simplified; see the script for full details):

```
def take_step(self, action, market_return):
    """ Calculates NAVs, trading costs and reward
        based on an action and latest market return
        returns the reward and an activity summary"""

    start_position = self.positions[max(0, self.step - 1)]
    start_nav = self.navs[max(0, self.step - 1)]
    start_market_nav = self.market_navs[max(0, self.step - 1)]
    self.market_returns[self.step] = market_return
    self.actions[self.step] = action

    end_position = action - 1 # short, neutral, long
    n_trades = end_position - start_position
    self.positions[self.step] = end_position
    self.trades[self.step] = n_trades

    time_cost = 0 if n_trades else self.time_cost_bps
    self.costs[self.step] = abs(n_trades) * self.trading_cost_bps + time_cost

    if self.step > 0:
        reward = start_position * market_return - self.costs[self.step-1]
        self.strategy_returns[self.step] = reward
        self.navs[self.step] = start_nav * (1 +
                                   self.strategy_returns[self.step])
        self.market_navs[self.step] = start_market_nav * (1 +
                                   self.market_returns[self.step])

    self.step += 1
    return reward
```

The TradingEnvironment class

The `TradingEnvironment` class subclasses `gym.Env` and drives the environment dynamics. It instantiates the `DataSource` and `TradingSimulator` objects and sets the action and state-space dimensionality, with the latter depending on the ranges of the features defined by `DataSource`:

```
class TradingEnvironment(gym.Env):
    """A simple trading environment for reinforcement learning.

    Provides daily observations for a stock price series
    An episode is defined as a sequence of 252 trading days with random start
    Each day is a 'step' that allows the agent to choose one of three
actions.
    """

    def __init__(self, trading_days=252, trading_cost_bps=1e-3,
                 time_cost_bps=1e-4, ticker='AAPL'):
        self.data_source = DataSource(trading_days=self.trading_days,
                                      ticker=ticker)
        self.simulator = TradingSimulator(
                steps=self.trading_days,
                trading_cost_bps=self.trading_cost_bps,
                time_cost_bps=self.time_cost_bps)
        self.action_space = spaces.Discrete(3)
        self.observation_space = spaces.Box(self.data_source.min_values,
                                            self.data_source.max_values)
```

The two key methods of `TradingEnvironment` are `.reset()` and `.step()`. The former initializes the `DataSource` and `TradingSimulator` instances, as follows:

```
def reset(self):
    """Resets DataSource and TradingSimulator; returns first observation"""
    self.data_source.reset()
    self.simulator.reset()
    return self.data_source.take_step()[0]
```

Each time step relies on `DataSource` and `TradingSimulator` to provide a state observation and reward the most recent action:

```
def step(self, action):
    """Returns state observation, reward, done and info"""
    assert self.action_space.contains(action),
      '{} {} invalid'.format(action, type(action))
    observation, done = self.data_source.take_step()
    reward, info = self.simulator.take_step(action=action,
                                            market_return=observation[0])
```

```
    return observation, reward, done, info
```

Registering and parameterizing the custom environment

Before using the custom environment, just as for the Lunar Lander environment, we need to register it with the gym package, provide information about the entry_point in terms of module and class, and define the maximum number of steps per episode (the following steps occur in the q_learning_for_trading notebook):

```
from gym.envs.registration import register
register(
        id='trading-v0',
        entry_point='trading_env:TradingEnvironment',
        max_episode_steps=252)
```

We can instantiate the environment using the desired trading costs and ticker:

```
trading_environment = gym.make('trading-v0')
trading_environment.env.trading_cost_bps = 1e-3
trading_environment.env.time_cost_bps = 1e-4
trading_environment.env.ticker = 'AAPL'
trading_environment.seed(42)
```

Deep Q-learning on the stock market

The notebook q_learning_for_trading contains the DDQN agent training code; we will only highlight noteworthy differences from the previous example.

Adapting and training the DDQN agent

We will use the same DDQN agent but simplify the NN architecture to two layers of 64 units each and add dropout for regularization. The online network has 5,059 trainable parameters:

```
Layer (type)                Output Shape             Param #
Dense_1 (Dense)             (None, 64)               704
Dense_2 (Dense)             (None, 64)               4160
dropout (Dropout)           (None, 64)               0
Output (Dense)              (None, 3)                195
Total params: 5,059
Trainable params: 5,059
```

The training loop interacts with the custom environment in a manner very similar to the Lunar Lander case. While the episode is active, the agent takes the action recommended by its current policy and trains the online network using experience replay after memorizing the current transition. The following code highlights the key steps:

```
for episode in range(1, max_episodes + 1):
```

```
    this_state = trading_environment.reset()
    for episode_step in range(max_episode_steps):
        action = ddqn.epsilon_greedy_policy(this_state.reshape(-1,
                                                                state_dim))
        next_state, reward, done, _ = trading_environment.step(action)

        ddqn.memorize_transition(this_state, action,
                                 reward, next_state,
                                 0.0 if done else 1.0)
        ddqn.experience_replay()
        if done:
            break
        this_state = next_state

trading_environment.close()
```

We let exploration continue for 2,000 1-year trading episodes, corresponding to about 500,000 time steps; we use linear decay of ε from 1.0 to 0.1 over 500 periods with exponential decay at a factor of 0.995 thereafter.

Benchmarking DDQN agent performance

To compare the DDQN agent's performance, we not only track the buy-and-hold strategy but also generate the performance of a random agent.

Figure 22.7 shows the rolling averages over the last 100 episodes of three cumulative return values for the 2,000 training periods (left panel), as well as the share of the last 100 episodes when the agent outperformed the buy-and-hold period (right panel). It uses AAPL stock data, for which there are some 9,000 daily price and volume observations:

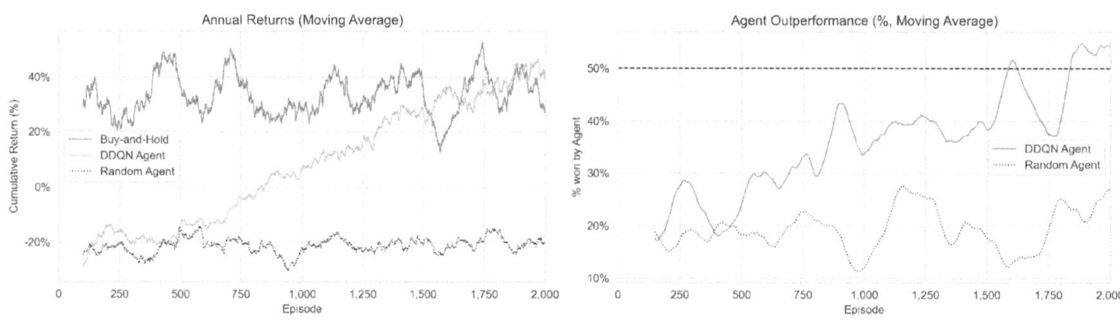

Figure 22.7: Trading agent performance relative to the market

This shows how the agent's performance improves steadily after 500 episodes, from the level of a random agent, and starts to outperform the buy-and-hold strategy toward the end of the experiment more than half of the time.

Lessons learned

This relatively simple agent uses no information beyond the latest market data and the reward signal compared to the machine learning models we covered elsewhere in this book. Nonetheless, it learns to make a profit and achieve performance similar to that of the market (after training on 2,000 years' worth of data, which takes only a fraction of the time on a GPU).

Keep in mind that using a single stock also increases the risk of overfitting to the data—by a lot. You can test your trained agent on new data using the saved model (see the notebook for Lunar Lander).

In summary, we have demonstrated the mechanics of setting up an RL trading environment and experimented with a basic agent that uses a small number of technical indicators. You should try to extend both the environment and the agent, for example, to choose from several assets, size the positions, and manage risks.

Reinforcement learning is often considered the **most promising approach to algorithmic trading** because it most accurately models the task an investor is facing. However, our dramatically simplified examples illustrate that creating a realistic environment poses a considerable challenge. Moreover, deep reinforcement learning that has achieved impressive breakthroughs in other domains may face greater obstacles given the noisy nature of financial data, which makes it even harder to learn a value function based on delayed rewards.

Nonetheless, the substantial interest in this subject makes it likely that institutional investors are working on larger-scale experiments that may yield tangible results. An interesting complementary approach beyond the scope of this book is **Inverse Reinforcement Learning**, which aims to identify the reward function of an agent (for example, a human trader) given its observed behavior; see Arora and Doshi (2019) for a survey and Roa-Vicens et al. (2019) for an application on trading in the limit-order book context.

Summary

In this chapter, we introduced a different class of machine learning problems that focus on automating decisions by agents that interact with an environment. We covered the key features required to define an RL problem and various solution methods.

We saw how to frame and analyze an RL problem as a finite Markov decision problem, as well as how to compute a solution using value and policy iteration. We then moved on to more realistic situations, where the transition probabilities and rewards are unknown to the agent, and saw how Q-learning builds on the key recursive relationship defined by the Bellman optimality equation in the MDP case. We saw how to solve RL problems using Python for simple MDPs and more complex environments with Q-learning.

We then expanded our scope to continuous states and applied the Deep Q-learning algorithm to the more complex Lunar Lander environment. Finally, we designed a simple trading environment using the OpenAI Gym platform, and also demonstrated how to train an agent to learn how to make a profit while trading a single stock.

In the next and final chapter, we'll present a few conclusions and key takeaways from our journey through this book and lay out some steps for you to consider as you continue building your skills to use machine learning for trading.

23
Conclusions and Next Steps

Our goal for this book was to enable you to apply **machine learning** (**ML**) to a variety of data sources and extract signals that add value to a trading strategy. To this end, we took a more comprehensive view of the investment process, from idea generation to strategy evaluation, and introduced ML as an important element of this process in the form of the **ML4T workflow**.

While demonstrating the use of a broad range of ML algorithms, from the fundamental to the advanced, we saw how ML can add value at multiple steps in the process of designing, testing, and executing a strategy. For the most part, however, we focused on the **core ML value proposition**, which consists of the ability to extract actionable information from much larger amounts of data more systematically than human experts would ever be able to.

This value proposition has really gained currency with the explosion of digital data that made it both more promising and necessary to leverage computing power to extract value from ever more diverse sets of information. However, the application of ML still requires significant human intervention and domain expertise to define objectives, select and curate data, design and optimize a model, and make appropriate use of the results.

Domain-specific aspects of using ML for trading include the nature of financial data and the environment of financial markets. The use of powerful models with a high capacity to learn patterns requires particular care to avoid overfitting when the signal-to-noise ratio is as low as is often the case with financial data. Furthermore, the competitive nature of trading implies that patterns evolve quickly as signals decay, requiring additional attention to performance monitoring and model maintenance.

In this concluding chapter, we will briefly summarize the key tools, applications, and lessons learned throughout the book to avoid losing sight of the big picture after so much detail. We will then identify areas that we did not cover but would be worthwhile to focus on as you expand on the many ML techniques we introduced and become productive in their daily use.

In sum, in this chapter, we will:

- Review key takeaways and lessons learned
- Point out the next steps to build on the techniques in this book
- Suggest ways to incorporate ML into your investment process

Key takeaways and lessons learned

A central goal of the book was to demonstrate the workflow of extracting signals from data using ML to inform a trading strategy. *Figure 23.1* outlines this ML-for-trading workflow. The key takeaways summarized in this section relate to specific challenges we encounter when building sophisticated predictive models for large datasets in the context of financial markets:

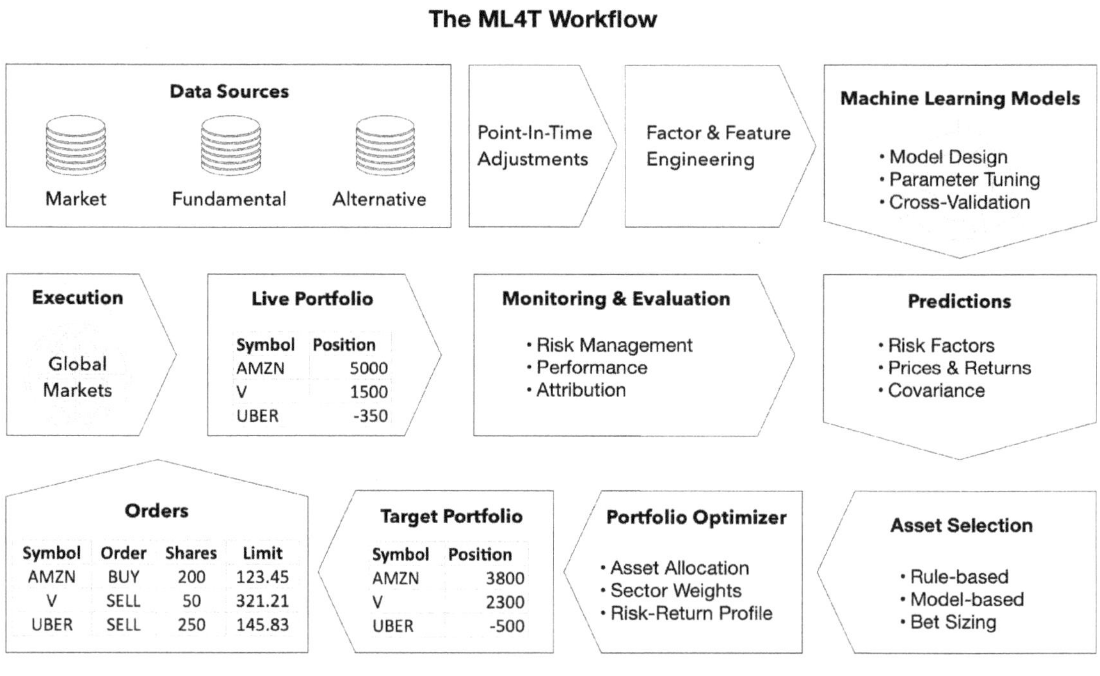

Figure 23.1: Key elements of using ML for trading

Important insights to keep in mind as you proceed to the practice of ML for trading include the following:

- **Data** is the single most important ingredient that requires careful sourcing and handling.
- **Domain expertise** is key to realizing the value contained in data and avoiding some of the pitfalls of using ML.
- ML offers **tools** that you can adapt and combine to create solutions for your use case.

- The choices of **model objectives and performance diagnostics** are key to productive iterations toward an optimal system.
- **Backtest overfitting** is a huge challenge that requires significant attention.
- **Transparency of black-box models** can help build confidence and facilitate the adoption of ML by skeptics.

We will elaborate a bit more on each of these ideas.

Data is the single most important ingredient

The rise of ML in trading and everywhere else largely complements the data explosion that we covered in great detail. We illustrated in *Chapter 2, Market and Fundamental Data – Sources and Techniques*, how to access and work with these data sources, historically the mainstay of quantitative investment. In *Chapter 3, Alternative Data for Finance – Categories and Use Cases*, we laid out a framework with criteria to assess the potential value of alternative datasets.

A key insight is that state-of-the-art ML techniques like deep neural networks are successful because their predictive performance continues to improve with more data. On the flip side, model and data complexity need to match to balance the bias-variance trade-off, which becomes more challenging the higher the noise-to-signal ratio of the data is. Managing data quality and integrating datasets are key steps in realizing the potential value.

The new oil? Quality control for raw and intermediate data

Just like oil, a popular comparison these days, data passes through a **pipeline with several stages** from its raw form to a refined product that can fuel a trading strategy. Careful attention to the quality of the final product is critical to getting the desired mileage out of it.

Sometimes, you get **data in its raw form** and control the numerous transformations required for your purposes. More often, you deal with an **intermediate product** and should get clarity about what exactly the data measures at this point.

Different from oil, there is often **no objective quality standard** as data sources continue to proliferate. Instead, the quality depends on its signal content, which in turn depends on your investment objectives. The cost-effective evaluation of new datasets requires a productive workflow, including appropriate infrastructure that we will address later in this chapter.

Data integration – the whole exceeds the sum of its parts

The value of data for an investment strategy often depends on combining complementary sources of market, fundamental, and alternative data. We saw that the predictive power of ML algorithms, like tree-based ensembles or neural networks, is in part due to their ability to detect nonlinear relationships, in particular **interaction effects among variables**.

The ability to modulate the impact of a variable as a function of other model features thrives on data inputs that capture different aspects of a target outcome. The combination of asset prices with macro fundamentals, social sentiment, credit card payment, and satellite data will likely yield significantly more reliable predictions throughout different economic and market regimes than each source on its own (provided the amount of data is large enough to learn the hidden relationships).

Working with data from multiple sources increases the **challenges of proper labeling.** It is vital to assign accurate timestamps that accurately reflect historical publication. Otherwise, we introduce lookahead bias by testing an algorithm with data before it actually becomes available. For example, third-party data may have timestamps that require adjustments to reflect the point in time when the information would have been available for a live algorithm.

Domain expertise – telling the signal from the noise

We emphasized that informative data is a necessary condition for successful ML applications. However, domain expertise is equally essential to define the strategic direction, select relevant data, engineer informative features, and design robust models.

In any domain, practitioners have theories about the drivers of key outcomes and relationships among them. Finance is characterized by a **large amount of available quantitative research**, both theoretical and empirical. However, Marcos López de Prado and others (Cochrane 2011) criticize most empirical results: claims of predictive signals found in hundreds of variables are often based on pervasive data mining and are not robust to changes in the experimental setup. In other words, statistical significance often results from large-scale trial-and-error rather than a true systematic relationship, along the lines of "if you torture the data long enough, it will confess."

On the one hand, there exists a robust understanding of how financial markets work. This should inform the selection and use of data as well as the justification of strategies that rely on ML. An important reason is to prioritize ideas that are more likely to be successful and avoid the multiple testing trap that leads to unreliable results. We outlined key ideas in *Chapter 4, Financial Feature Engineering – How to Research Alpha Factors*, and *Chapter 5, Portfolio Optimization and Performance Evaluation*.

On the other hand, novel ML techniques will likely uncover new hypotheses about drivers of financial outcomes that will inform theory and should then be independently tested.

More than the raw data, feature engineering is often the key to making signals useful for an algorithm. Leveraging decades of research into risk factors that drive returns on theoretical and empirical grounds is a good starting point to prioritize data transformations that are more likely to reflect relevant information.

However, only creative feature engineering will lead to innovative strategies that can compete in the market over time. Even for new alpha factors, a compelling narrative that explains how they work given established ideas on market dynamics and investor behavior will provide more confidence to allocate capital.

The risks of false discoveries and overfitting to historical data make it even more necessary to prioritize strategies prior to testing rather than "letting the data speak." We covered how to deflate the Sharpe ratio in *Chapter 7, Linear Models – From Risk Factors to Return Forecasts*, to account for the number of experiments.

ML is a toolkit for solving problems with data

ML offers algorithmic solutions and techniques that can be applied to many use cases. *Parts 2, 3,* and *4* of this book have presented ML as a diverse set of tools that can add value to various steps of the strategy process, including:

- Idea generation and alpha factor research
- Signal aggregation and portfolio optimization
- Strategy testing
- Trade execution
- Strategy evaluation

Moreover, ML algorithms are designed to be further developed, adapted, and combined to solve new problems in different contexts. For these reasons, it is important to understand key concepts and ideas underlying these algorithms, in addition to being able to apply them to data for productive experimentation and research as outlined in *Chapter 6, The Machine Learning Process*, and summarized in *Figure 23.2*:

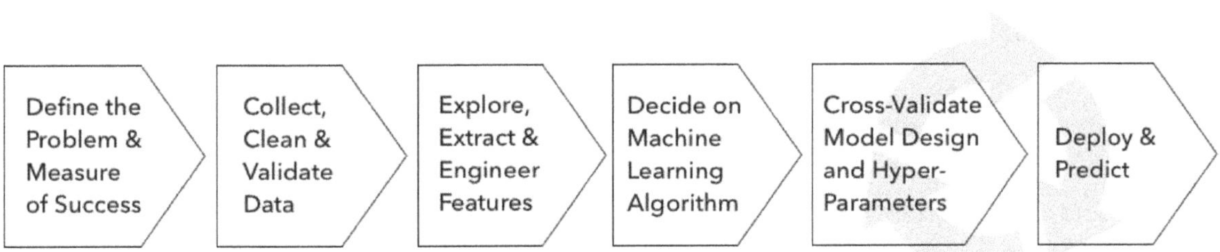

Figure 23.2: The ML workflow

Furthermore, the best results are often achieved by **human-in-the-loop solutions** that combine humans with ML tools. In *Chapter 1, Machine Learning for Trading – From Idea to Execution*, we covered the quantamental investment style where discretionary and algorithmic trading converge. This approach will likely further grow in importance and depends on the flexible and creative application of the fundamental tools that we covered and their extensions to a variety of datasets.

Model diagnostics help speed up optimization

In *Chapter 6, The Machine Learning Process*, we outlined the most important ML-specific concepts. ML algorithms learn relationships between input data and a target by making assumptions about the functional form. If the learning is based on noise rather than signal, predictive performance will suffer.

Of course, we do not know today how to separate signal and noise from the perspective of tomorrow's outcomes. Careful cross-validation that avoids lookahead bias and robust model diagnostics, such as learning curves and the optimization verification test, can help alleviate this fundamental challenge and calibrate the choice or configuration of an algorithm. This task can be made easier by defining focused model objectives and, for complex models, distinguishing between performance shortcomings due to issues with the optimization algorithm and those with the objective itself.

Making do without a free lunch

No system, whether a computer program or a human, can reliably predict outcomes for new examples beyond those it has observed during training. The only way out is to have some additional prior knowledge or make assumptions that go beyond the training examples. We covered a broad range of algorithms from linear models in *Chapter 7, Linear Models – From Risk Factors to Return Forecasts*, to nonlinear ensembles in *Chapter 11, Random Forests – A Long-Short Strategy for Japanese Stocks*, and *Chapter 12, Boosting Your Trading Strategy*, as well as neural networks in various chapters of *Part 4* of this book.

We saw that a linear model makes the strong assumption that the relationship between inputs and outputs has a very simple form, whereas nonlinear models like gradient boosting or neural networks aim to learn more complex functions. While it's probably obvious that a simple model will fail in most circumstances, a complex model is not always better. If the true relationship is linear but the data is noisy, the complex model will learn the noise as part of the complex relationship that it assumes to exist. This is the basic idea behind the **"no free lunch" theorem**, which states that no algorithm is universally superior for all tasks. Good fit in some instances comes at the cost of poor performance elsewhere.

The key tools to tailor the choice of the algorithm to the data are data exploration and experiments based on an understanding of the assumptions the model makes.

Managing the bias-variance trade-off

A key challenge in adapting an algorithm to data is the trade-off between bias and variance, which both increase prediction errors beyond the natural noisiness of the data. A simple model that does not adequately capture the relationships in the data will underfit and exhibit bias, that is, make systematically wrong predictions. A model that is too complex will overfit and learn the noise in addition to any signal so that the result will show a lot of variance for different samples.

The key tool to diagnose this trade-off at any given iteration of the model selection and optimization process is the **learning curve**. It shows how training and validation errors depend on the sample size. This allows us to decide between different options to improve performance: adjust the complexity of the model or get more data points.

The closer the training error is to human performance or another benchmark, the more likely the model will overfit. A low validation error tells us that we are lucky and found a good model. If the validation error is high, we are not. If it continues to decline with the training size, however, more data may help. If the training error is high, more data is unlikely to help, and we should instead add features or use a more flexible algorithm.

Defining targeted model objectives

One of the first steps in the ML process is the definition of an objective for the algorithm to optimize. Sometimes, the choice is simple, such as in a regression problem. A classification task can be more difficult, for example, when we care about precision and recall. Consolidating conflicting objectives into a single metric like the F1 score helps to focus optimization efforts. We can also include conditions that need to be met rather than optimized for. We also saw that reinforcement learning is all about defining the right reward function to guide the agent's learning process.

The optimization verification test

Andrew Ng emphasizes the distinction between performance shortcomings due to a problem with the learning algorithm or the optimization algorithm. Complex models like neural networks assume nonlinear relationships, and the search process of the optimization algorithm may end up in a local rather than a global optimum.

If a model fails to correctly translate a phrase, for example, the test compares the scores for the correct prediction and the solution discovered by the search algorithm. If the learning algorithm scores the correct solution higher, the search algorithm requires improvements. Otherwise, the learning algorithm is optimizing for the wrong objective.

Beware of backtest overfitting

We covered the risks of false discoveries due to overfitting to historical data repeatedly throughout the book. *Chapter 5, Portfolio Optimization and Performance Evaluation*, on strategy evaluation, lays out the main drivers and potential remedies. The low noise-to-signal ratio and relatively small datasets (compared to web-scale image or text data) make this challenge particularly serious in the trading domain. Awareness is critical since the ease of access to data and tools to apply ML increases the risks significantly.

There are no easy answers because the risks are inevitable. However, we presented methods to adjust backtest metrics to account for repeated trials, such as the deflated Sharpe ratio. When working toward a live trading strategy, staged paper-trading and closely monitored performance during execution in the market need to be part of the implementation process.

How to gain insights from black-box models

Deep neural networks and complex ensembles can raise suspicion when they are considered impenetrable black-box models, particularly in light of the risks of backtest overfitting. We introduced several methods to gain insights into how these models make predictions in *Chapter 12, Boosting Your Trading Strategy*.

In addition to conventional measures of feature importance, the recent game-theoretic innovation of **SHapley Additive exPlanations** (**SHAP**) is a significant step toward understanding the mechanics of complex models. SHAP values allow the exact attribution of features and their values to predictions so that it becomes easier to validate the logic of a model in the light of specific theories about market behavior for a given investment target. Besides justification, exact feature importance scores and attribution of predictions allow deeper insights into the drivers of the investment outcome of interest.

On the other hand, there is some controversy over how important transparency around model predictions should be. Geoffrey Hinton, one of the inventors of deep learning, argues that the reasons for human decisions are often obscure. Perhaps machines should be evaluated by their results, just as we do with investment managers.

ML for trading in practice

As you proceed to integrate the numerous tools and techniques into your investment and trading process, there are numerous things you can focus your efforts on. If your goal is to make better decisions, you should select projects that are realistic yet ambitious given your current skill set. This will help you to develop an efficient workflow underpinned by productive tools and gain practical experience.

We will briefly list some of the tools that are useful to expand on the Python ecosystem covered in this book. They include big data technologies that will eventually be necessary to implement ML-driven trading strategies at scale. We will also list some of the platforms that allow you to implement trading strategies using Python, possibly with access to data sources, and ML algorithms and libraries. Finally, we will point out good practices for adopting ML as an organization.

Data management technologies

The central role of data in the ML4T process requires familiarity with a range of technologies to store, transform, and analyze data at scale, including the use of cloud-based services like Amazon Web Services, Microsoft Azure, and Google Cloud.

Database systems

Data storage implies the use of databases. Historically, these have typically been **relational database management systems** (**RDBMSes**) that use SQL to store and retrieve data in a well-defined table format. These have included databases from commercial providers like Oracle and Microsoft and open-source implementations like PostgreSQL and MySQL. More recently, non-relational alternatives have emerged that are often collectively labeled NoSQL but are quite diverse, namely:

- **Key-value storage**: Fast read/write access to objects. We covered the HDF5 format in *Chapter 2, Market and Fundamental Data – Sources and Techniques*, which facilitates fast access to a pandas DataFrame.

- **Columnar storage**: Capitalizes on the homogeneity of data in a column to facilitate compression and faster column-based operations like aggregation. This is used in the popular Amazon Redshift data warehouse solution, Apache Parquet, Cassandra, and Google's Big Table.
- **Document store**: Designed to store data that defies the rigid schema definition required by an RDBMS. This has been popularized by web applications that use JSON or XML format, which we encountered in *Chapter 4, Financial Feature Engineering – How to Research Alpha Factors*. It is used, for example, in MongoDB.
- **Graph database**: Designed to store networks that have nodes and edges and specializes in queries about network metrics and relationships. It is used in Neo4J and Apache Giraph.

There has been some convergence toward the conventions established by the relational database systems. The Python ecosystem facilitates the interaction with many standard data sources and provides the fast HDF5 and Parquet formats, as demonstrated throughout the book.

Big data technologies – from Hadoop to Spark

Data management at scale for hundreds of gigabytes and beyond requires the use of multiple machines that form a cluster to conduct read, write, and compute operations in parallel. In other words, you need a distributed system that operates on multiple machines in an integrated way.

The **Hadoop ecosystem** has emerged as an open-source software framework for distributed storage and processing of big data using the MapReduce programming model developed by Google. The ecosystem has diversified under the roof of the Apache Foundation and today includes numerous projects that cover different aspects of data management at scale.

Key tools within Hadoop include:

- **Apache Pig**: A data processing language, developed at Yahoo, for implementing large-scale **extract-transform-load** (**ETL**) pipelines using MapReduce.
- **Apache Hive**: The de facto standard for interactive SQL queries over petabytes of data. It was developed at Facebook.
- **Apache HBASE**: A NoSQL database for real-time read/write access that scales linearly to billions of rows and millions of columns. It can combine data sources using a variety of different schemas.

Apache Spark has become the most popular platform for interactive analytics on a cluster. The MapReduce framework allowed parallel computation but required repeated read/write operations from disk to ensure data redundancy. Spark has dramatically accelerated computation at scale due to the **resilient distributed data** (**RDD**) structure, which allows highly optimized in-memory computation. This includes iterative computation as required for optimization, for example, gradient descent for numerous ML algorithms. Fortunately, the Spark DataFrame interface has been designed with pandas in mind so that your skills transfer relatively smoothly.

ML tools

We covered many libraries of the Python ecosystem in this book. Python has evolved to become the language of choice for data science and ML. The set of open-source libraries continues to both diversify and mature, and is built on the robust core of scientific computing libraries NumPy and SciPy.

The popular pandas library has contributed significantly to popularizing the use of Python for data science and has matured with its 1.0 release in January 2020. The scikit-learn interface has become the standard for modern, specialized ML libraries like XGBoost or LightGBM that often interface with the workflow automation tools like GridSearchCV and Pipeline that we have used repeatedly throughout the book.

There are several providers that aim to facilitate the ML workflow:

- **H2O.ai** offers the H2O platform, which integrates cloud computing with ML automation. It allows users to fit thousands of potential models to their data to explore patterns in the data. It has interfaces in Python as well as R and Java.
- **Datarobot** aims to automate the model development process by providing a platform to rapidly build and deploy predictive models in the cloud or on-premises.
- **Dataiku** is a collaborative data science platform designed to help analysts and engineers explore, prototype, build, and deliver their own data products.

There are also several open-source initiatives led by companies that build on and expand the Python ecosystem:

- The quantitative hedge fund **TwoSigma** contributes quantitative analysis tools to the Jupyter Notebook environment under the BeakerX project.
- **Bloomberg** has integrated the Jupyter Notebook into its terminal to facilitate the interactive analysis of its financial data.

Online trading platforms

The main options to develop trading strategies that use ML are online platforms, which often look for and allocate capital to successful trading strategies. Popular solutions include Quantopian, Quantconnect, and QuantRocket. The more recent Alpha Trading Labs focuses on high-frequency trading. In addition, **Interactive Brokers (IB)** offers a Python API that you can use to develop your own trading solution.

Quantopian

We introduced the Quantopian platform and demonstrated the use of its research and trading environment to analyze and test trading strategies against historical data. Quantopian uses Python and offers a lot of educational material.

Quantopian hosts competitions to recruit algorithms for its crowd-sourced hedge fund portfolio. It provides capital to the winning algorithm. Live trading was discontinued in September 2017, but the platform still provides a large range of historical data and attracts an active community of developers and traders. It is a good starting point to discuss ideas and learn from others.

QuantConnect

QuantConnect is another open-source, community-driven algorithmic trading platform that competes with Quantopian. It also provides an IDE to backtest and live trade algorithmic strategies using Python and other languages.

QuantConnect also has a dynamic, global community from all over the world, and provides access to numerous asset classes, including equities, futures, FOREX, and cryptocurrency. It offers live trading integration with various brokers, such as IB, OANDA, and GDAX.

QuantRocket

QuantRocket is a Python-based platform for researching, backtesting, and running automated quantitative trading strategies. It provides data collection tools, multiple data vendors, a research environment, multiple backtest engines, and live and paper trading through IB. It prides itself on support for international equity trading and sets itself apart with its flexibility (but Quantopian is working toward this as well).

QuantRocket supports multiple engines – its own Moonshot, as well as third-party engines as chosen by the user. While QuantRocket doesn't have a traditional IDE, it is integrated well with Jupyter to produce something similar. QuantRocket offers a free version with access to sample data, but access to a wider set of capabilities starts at $29 per month at the time of writing in early 2020.

Conclusion

We started by highlighting the explosion of digital data and the emergence of ML as a strategic capability for investment and trading strategies. This dynamic reflects global business and technology trends beyond finance and is much more likely to continue than to stall or reverse. Many investment firms are just getting started to leverage the range of artificial intelligence tools, just as individuals are acquiring the relevant skills and business processes are adapting to these new opportunities for value creation, as outlined in the introductory chapter.

There are also numerous exciting developments for the application of ML to trading on the horizon that are likely to propel the current momentum. They are likely to become relevant in the coming years and include the automation of the ML process, the generation of synthetic training data, and the emergence of quantum computing. The extraordinary vibrancy of the field implies that this alone could fill a book and the journey will continue to remain exciting.

Alpha Factor Library

Throughout this book, we've described how to engineer features from market, fundamental, and alternative data to build **machine learning** (**ML**) models that yield signals for a trading strategy. The smart design of features, including appropriate preprocessing and denoising, is what typically leads to an effective strategy. This appendix synthesizes some of the lessons learned on feature engineering and provides additional information on this important topic.

Chapter 4, Financial Feature Engineering – How to Research Alpha Factors, summarized the long-standing efforts of academics and practitioners to identify information or variables that help reliably predict asset returns. This research led from the single-factor capital asset pricing model to a "zoo of new factors" (Cochrane, 2011). This *factor zoo* contains hundreds of firm characteristics and security price metrics presented as statistically significant predictors of equity returns in the anomalies literature since 1970 (see a summary in Green, Hand, and Zhang, 2017).

Chapter 4, Financial Feature Engineering – How to Research Alpha Factors, categorized factors by the underlying risk they represent and for which an investor would earn a reward above and beyond the market return. These categories include value versus growth, quality, and sentiment, as well as volatility, momentum, and liquidity. Throughout this book, we used numerous metrics to capture these risk factors. This appendix expands on those examples and collects popular indicators so you can use it as a reference or inspiration for your own strategy development. It also shows you how to compute them and includes some steps to evaluate these indicators.

To this end, we'll focus on the broad range of indicators implemented by TA-Lib (see *Chapter 4, Financial Feature Engineering – How to Research Alpha Factors*) and the *101 Formulaic Alphas* paper (Kakushadze 2016), which presents real-life quantitative trading factors used in production with an average holding period of 0.6-6.4 days. To facilitate replication, we'll limit this review to indicators that rely on readily available market data. This restriction notwithstanding, the vast and rapidly evolving scope of potentially useful data sources and features implies that this overview is far from comprehensive.

Throughout this chapter, we will use P_t for the closing price and V_t for the trading volume of an asset at time *t*. Where necessary, superscripts like P_t^{high} or P_t^{H} differentiate between open, high, low, or close prices. r_t denotes the simple return for the period return at time *t*.

$P_{t-d,t} = \{p_{t-d}, p_{t-d+1}, \dots, p_t\}$ and $R_{t-d,t} = \{r_{t-d}, r_{t-d+1}, \dots, r_t\}$ refer to a time series of prices and returns, respectively, from *t-d* to *t*.

Common alpha factors implemented in TA-Lib

The TA-Lib library is widely used to perform technical analysis of financial market data by trading software developers. It includes over 150 popular indicators from multiple categories that range from overlap studies, including moving averages and Bollinger Bands, to statistic functions such as linear regression. The following table summarizes the main categories:

Function Group	# Indicators
Overlap Studies	17
Momentum Indicators	30
Volume Indicators	3
Volatility Indicators	3
Price Transform	4
Cycle Indicators	5
Math Operators	11
Math Transform	15
Statistic Functions	9

There are also over 60 functions that aim to recognize candlestick patterns popular with traders that rely on the visual inspection of charts. Given the mixed evidence on their predictive ability (Horton 2009; Marshall, Young, and Rose 2006), and the goal of learning such patterns from data using the ML algorithms covered in this book, we will focus on the categories listed in the preceding table. Specifically, we will focus on moving averages, overlap studies, momentum, volume and liquidity, volatility, and fundamental risk factors in this section.

See the notebook `common_alpha_factors` for the code examples in this section and additional implementation details regarding TA-Lib indicators. We'll demonstrate how to compute selected indicators for an individual stock, as well as a sample of the 500 most-traded US stocks over the 2007-2016 period (see the notebook `sample_selection` for the preparation of this larger dataset).

A key building block – moving averages

Numerous indicators allow for calculation using different types of **moving averages** (**MAs**). They make different tradeoffs between smoothing a series and reacting to new developments. You can use them as building blocks for your own indicators or modify the behavior of existing indicators by altering the type of MA used in its construction, as we'll demonstrate in the next section. The following table lists the available types of MAs, the TA-Lib function to compute them, and the code you can pass to other indicators to select the given type:

Moving Average	Function	Code
Simple	SMA	0
Exponential	EMA	1
Weighted	WMA	2

Double Exponential	DEMA	3
Triple Exponential	TEMA	4
Triangular	TRIMA	5
Kaufman Adaptive	KAMA	6
MESA Adaptive	MAMA	7

In the remainder of this section, we'll briefly outline their definitions and visualize their different behavior.

Simple moving average

For price series P_t with a window of length N, the **simple moving average (SMA)** at time t weighs each data point within the window equally:

$$\text{SMA}(N)_t = \frac{P_{t-N+1} + P_{t-N+2} + P_{t-N+3} + P_t}{N} = \frac{1}{N}\sum_{i=1}^{N} P_{t-N+i}$$

Exponential moving average

For price series P_t with a window of length N, the **exponential moving average (EMA)** at time t, EMA_t, is recursively defined as the weighted average of the current price and the most recent previous EMA_{t-1}, where the weights α and $1 - \alpha$ are defined as follows:

$$\text{EMA}(N)_t = \alpha P_t + (1 - \alpha)\text{EMA}(N)_{t-1}$$

$$\alpha = \frac{2}{N + 1}$$

Weighted moving average

For price series P_t with a window of length N, the **weighted moving average (WMA)** at time t is computed such that the weight of each data point corresponds to its index within the window:

$$\text{WMA}(N)_t = \frac{P_{t-N+1} + 2P_{t-N+2} + 3P_{t-N+3} + NP_t}{N(N + 1)/2}$$

Double exponential moving average

The **double exponential moving average (DEMA)** for a price series P_t at time t, DEMA_t, is based on the EMA designed to react faster to changes in price. It is computed as the difference between twice the current EMA and the EMA applied to the current EMA, labeled $\text{EMA}_2(N)_t$:

$$\text{DEMA}(N)_t = 2 \times \text{EMA}(N)_t - \text{EMA}_2(N)_t$$

Since the calculation uses EMA_2, DEMA needs $2 \times N - 1$ samples to start producing values.

Triple exponential moving average

The **triple exponential moving average** (**TEMA**) for a price series P_t at time t, $TEMA_t$, is also based on the EMA, yet designed to react even faster to changes in price and indicate short-term price direction. It is computed as the difference between three times the difference between the current EMA and the EMA applied to the current EMA, EMA_2, with the addition of the EMA applied to the EMA_2, labeled EMA_3:

$$\text{TEMA}(N)_t = 3 \times [\text{EMA}(N)_t - \text{EMA}_2(N)_t] + \text{EMA}_3(N)_t$$

Since the calculation uses EMA_3, DEMA needs $3 \times N - 2$ samples to start producing values.

Triangular moving average

The **triangular moving average** (**TRIMA**) with window length N for a price series P_t at time t, $\text{TRIMA}(N)_t$, is a weighted average of the last N $\text{SMA}(N)_t$ values. In other words, it applies the SMA to a time series of SMA values:

$$\text{TRIMA}(N)_t = \frac{1}{N}\sum_{i=1}^{N} \text{SMA}(N)_{t-N+i}$$

Kaufman adaptive moving average

The computation of the **Kaufman adaptive moving average** (**KAMA**) aims to take into account changes in market volatility. See the notebook for links to resources that explain the details of this slightly more involved computation.

MESA adaptive moving average

The **MESA adaptive moving average** (**MAMA**) is an exponential moving average that adapts to price movement based on the rate change of phase, as measured by the **Hilbert Transform discriminator** (see TA-Lib documentation). In addition to the price series, MAMA accepts two additional parameters, *fastlimit* and *slowlimit*, that control the maximum and minimum alpha values that should be applied to the EMA when calculating MAMA.

Visual comparison of moving averages

Figure A.1 illustrates how the behavior of the different MAs differs in terms of smoothing the time series and adapting to recent changes. All the time series are calculated for a 21-day moving window (see the notebook for details and color images):

Figure A.1: Comparison of MAs for AAPL closing price

Overlap studies – price and volatility trends

TA-Lib includes several indicators aimed at capturing recent trends, as listed in the following table:

Function	Name
BBANDS	Bollinger Bands
HT_TRENDLINE	Hilbert Transform - Instantaneous Trendline
MAVP	Moving average with variable period
MA	Moving average
SAR	Parabolic SAR
SAREXT	Parabolic SAR - Extended

The `MA` and `MAVP` functions are wrappers for the various MAs described in the previous section. We will highlight a few examples in this section; see the notebook for additional information and visualizations.

Bollinger Bands

Bollinger Bands combine an MA with an upper band and a lower band representing the moving standard deviation. We can obtain the three time series by providing an input price series, the length of the moving window, the multiplier for the upper and lower bands, and the type of MA, as follows:

```
s = talib.BBANDS(df.close,     # No. of periods (2 to 100000)
                 timeperiod=20,
                 nbdevup=2,    # Deviation multiplier for lower band
                 nbdevdn=2,    # Deviation multiplier for upper band
                 matype=1)     # default: SMA
```

For a sample of AAPL closing prices for 2012, we can plot the result like so:

```
bb_bands = ['upper', 'middle', 'lower']
df = price_sample.loc['2012', ['close']]
df = df.assign(**dict(zip(bb_bands, s)))
ax = df.loc[:, ['close'] + bb_bands].plot(figsize=(16, 5), lw=1);
```

The preceding code results in the following plot:

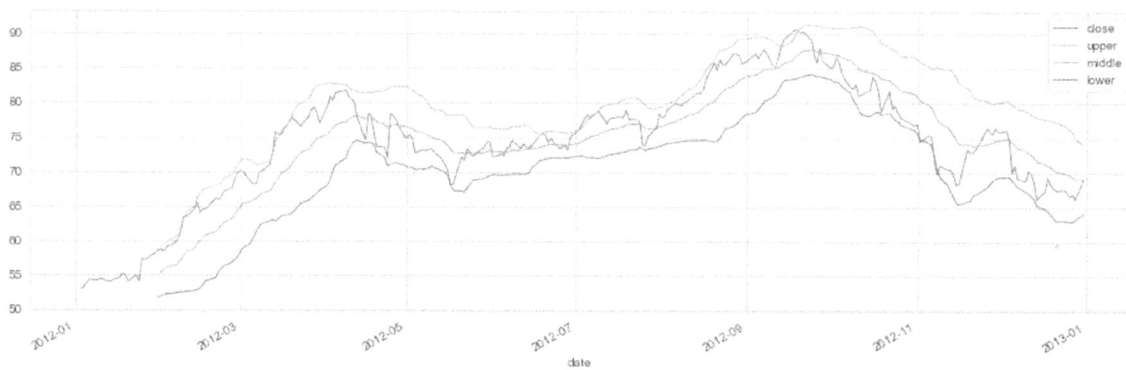

Figure A.2: Bollinger Bands for AAPL close price in 2012

John Bollinger, who invented the concept, also defined over 20 trading rules based on the relationships between the three lines and the current price (see *Chapter 4, Financial Feature Engineering – How to Research Alpha Factors*). For example, a smaller distance between the outer bands implies reduced recent price volatility, which, in turn, is interpreted as greater volatility and price change going forward.

We can standardize the security-specific values of the Bollinger Bands by forming ratios between the upper and lower bands, as well as between each of them and the close price, as follows:

```
fig, ax = plt.subplots(figsize=(16,5))
df.upper.div(df.close).plot(ax=ax, label='bb_up')
df.lower.div(df.close).plot(ax=ax, label='bb_low')
df.upper.div(df.lower).plot(ax=ax, label='bb_squeeze')
plt.legend()
fig.tight_layout();
```

The following plot displays the resulting normalized time series:

Figure A.3: Normalized Bollinger Band indicators

The following function can be used with the pandas `.groupby()` and `.apply()` methods to compute the indicators for a larger sample of 500 stocks, as shown here:

```
def compute_bb_indicators(close, timeperiod=20, matype=0):
    high, mid, low = talib.BBANDS(close,
                                  timeperiod=20,
                                  matype=matype)
    bb_up = high / close -1
    bb_low = low / close -1
    squeeze = (high - low) / close
    return pd.DataFrame({'BB_UP': bb_up,
                         'BB_LOW': bb_low,
                         'BB_SQUEEZE': squeeze},
                        index=close.index)
data = (data.join(data
                  .groupby(level='ticker')
                  .close
                  .apply(compute_bb_indicators)))
```

Figure A.4 plots the distribution of values for each indicator across the 500 stocks (clipped at the 1st and 99th percentiles, hence the spikes in the plots):

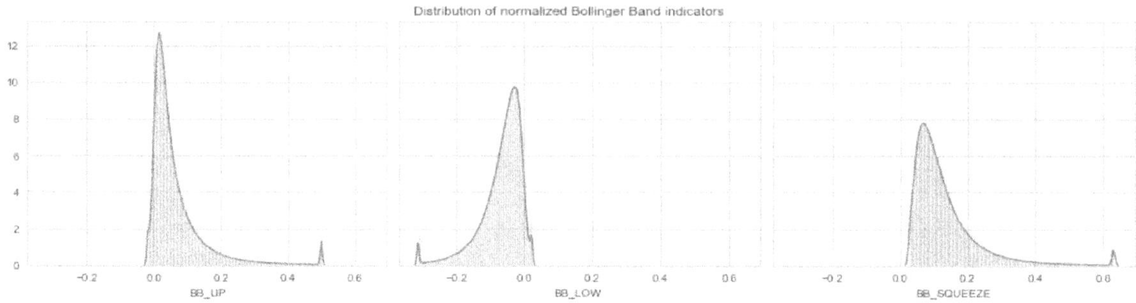

Figure A.4: Distribution of normalized Bollinger Band indicators

Parabolic SAR

The **parabolic SAR** aims to identify trend reversals. It is a trend-following (lagging) indicator that can be used to set a trailing stop loss or determine entry or exit points. It is usually represented in a price chart as a set of dots near the price bars. Generally, when these dots are above the price, it signals a downward trend; it signals an upward trend when the dots are below the price. The change in the direction of the dots can be interpreted as a trade signal. However, the indicator is less reliable in a flat or range-bound market. It is computed as follows:

$$\text{SAR}_t = \text{SAR}_{t-1} + \alpha(\text{EP} - \text{SAR}_{t-1})$$

The **extreme point** (**EP**) is a record that's kept during each trend that represents the highest value reached by the price during the current uptrend—or lowest value during a downtrend. During each period, if a new maximum (or minimum) is observed, the EP is updated with that value.

The α value represents the acceleration factor and is typically set initially to a value of 0.02. This factor increases by α each time a new EP is recorded. The rate will then quicken to a point where the SAR converges toward the price. To prevent it from getting too large, a maximum value for the acceleration factor is normally set to 0.20.

We can compute and plot it for our sample close price series as follows:

```
df = price_sample.loc['2012', ['close', 'high', 'low']]
df['SAR'] = talib.SAR(df.high, df.low,
                      acceleration=0.02, # common value
                      maximum=0.2)
df[['close', 'SAR']].plot(figsize=(16, 4), style=['-', '--']);
```

The preceding code produces the following plot:

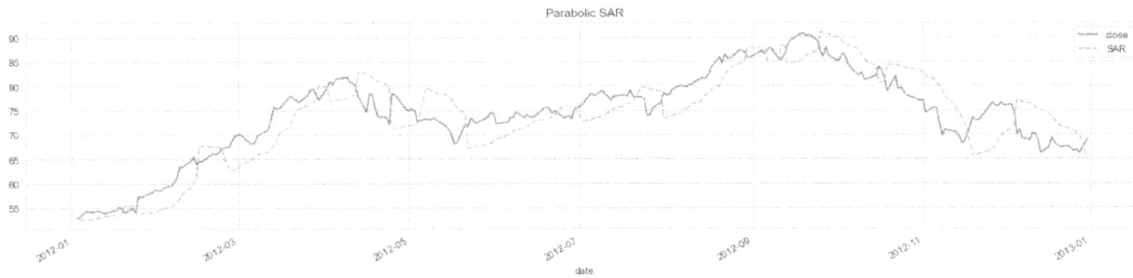

Figure A.5: Parabolic SAR for AAPL stock price

Momentum indicators

Chapter 4, Financial Feature Engineering – How to Research Alpha Factors, introduced **momentum** as one of the best-performing risk factors historically and listed several indicators designed to identify the corresponding price trends. These indicators include the **relative strength index (RSI)**, as well as **price momentum** and **price acceleration**:

Factor	Description	Calculation
Relative strength index (RSI)	RSI compares the magnitude of recent price changes across stocks to identify stocks as overbought or oversold. A high RSI (usually above 70) indicates overbought and a low RSI (typically below 30) indicates oversold. It first computes the average price change for a given number (often 14) of prior trading days with rising (Δ_p^{up}) and falling prices (Δ_p^{down}), respectively.	$\text{RSI} = 100 - \frac{100}{1 + \frac{\Delta_p^{up}}{\Delta_p^{down}}}$
Price momentum	This factor computes the total return for a given number of prior trading days d. In the academic literature, it is common to use the last 12 months except for the most recent month due to a short-term reversal effect frequently observed. However, shorter periods have also been widely used.	$\text{Mom}^d = \frac{P_t}{P_{t-1}} - 1$
Price acceleration	Price acceleration calculates the gradient of the price trend using the linear regression coefficient β of a time trend on daily prices for a longer and a shorter period, for example, 1 year and 3 months of trading days, and compares the change in the slope as a measure of price acceleration.	$\frac{\beta_{63}}{\beta_{252}}$

TA-Lib implements 30 momentum indicators; the most important ones are listed in the following table. We will introduce a few selected examples; please see the notebook `common_alpha_factors` for additional information:

Function	Name
PLUS_DM/MINUS_DM	Plus/Minus Directional Movement
PLUS_DI/MINUS_DI	Plus/Minus Directional Indicator
DX	Directional Movement Index
ADX	Average Directional Movement Index
ADXR	Average Directional Movement Index Rating
APO/PPO	Absolute/Percentage Price Oscillator
AROON/AROONOSC	Aroon/Aroon Oscillator
BOP	Balance of Power
CCI	Commodity Channel Index
CMO	Chande Momentum Oscillator
MACD	Moving Average Convergence/Divergence
MFI	Money Flow Index
MOM	Momentum
RSI	Relative Strength Index
STOCH	Stochastic
ULTOSC	Ultimate Oscillator
WILLR	Williams' %R

Several of these indicators are closely related and build on each other, as the following example demonstrates.

Average directional movement indicators

The **average directional movement index** (**ADX**) combines two other indicators, namely the positive and negative directional indicators (`PLUS_DI` and `MINUS_DI`), which, in turn, build on the positive and negative directional movement (`PLUS_DM` and `MINUS_DM`). See the notebook for additional details.

Plus/minus directional movement

For a price series P_t with daily highs P_t^H and daily lows P_t^L, the directional movement tracks the absolute size of price moves over a time period T, as follows:

$$\text{Up}_t = P_t^H - P_{t-T}^H$$

$$\text{Down}_t = P_{t-T}^L - P_t^L$$

$$\text{PLUS\_DM}_t = \begin{cases} \text{Up}_t & \text{if } \text{Up}_t > \text{Down}_t \text{ and } \text{Up}_t > 0 \\ 0 & \text{otherwise} \end{cases}$$

$$\text{MINUS\_DM}_t = \begin{cases} \text{Down}_t & \text{if Down}_t > \text{Up}_t \text{ and Down}_t < 0 \\ 0 & \text{otherwise} \end{cases}$$

We can compute and plot this indicator for a 2-year price series of the AAPL stock in 2012-13:

```
df = price_sample.loc['2012': '2013', ['high', 'low', 'close']]
df['PLUS_DM'] = talib.PLUS_DM(df.high, df.low, timeperiod=10)
df['MINUS_DM'] = talib.MINUS_DM(df.high, df.low, timeperiod=10)
```

The following plot visualizes the resulting time series:

Figure A.6: PLUS_DM/MINUS_DM for AAPL stock price

Plus/minus directional index

`PLUS_DI` and `MINUS_DI` are the simple MAs of `PLUS_DM` and `MINUS_DM`, respectively, each divided by the **average true range** (**ATR**). See the *Volatility indicators* section later in this chapter for more details.

The simple MA is calculated over the given number of periods. The ATR is a smoothed average of the true ranges.

Average directional index

Finally, the **average directional index** (**ADX**) is the (simple) MA of the absolute value of the difference between `PLUS_DI` and `MINUS_DI`, divided by their sum:

$$\text{ADX} = 100 \times \text{SMA}(N)_t \left| \frac{\text{PLUS}_\text{D}I_t - \text{MINUS}_\text{D}\text{I}_t}{\text{PLUS}_\text{D}I_t + \text{MINUS}_\text{D}\text{I}_t} \right|$$

Its values oscillate in the 0-100 range and are often interpreted as follows:

ADX Value	Trend Strength
0-25	Absent or weak trend
25-50	Strong trend
50-75	Very strong trend
75-100	Extremely strong trend

We compute the ADX time series for our AAPL sample series similar to the previous examples, as follows:

```
df['ADX'] = talib.ADX(df.high,
                      df.low,
                      df.close,
                      timeperiod=14)
```

The following plot visualizes the result over the 2007-2016 period:

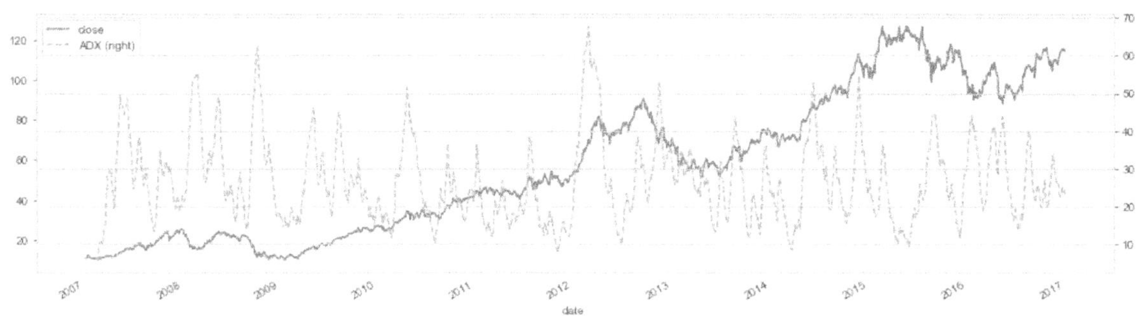

Figure A.7: ADX for the AAPL stock price series

Aroon Oscillator

The Aroon indicator measures the time between highs and the time between lows over a time period. It computes an `AROON_UP` and an `AROON_DWN` indicator, as follows:

$$\text{AROON\_UP} = \frac{T - \text{Periods since T period High}}{T} \times 100$$

$$\text{AROON\_DOWN} = \frac{T - \text{Periods since T period Low}}{T} \times 100$$

The Aroon Oscillator is simply the difference between the `AROON_UP` and `AROON_DOWN` indicators and moves within the range from -100 to 100, as shown here for the AAPL price series:

Figure A.8: Aroon Oscillator for the AAPL stock price series

Balance of power

The **balance of power** (**BOP**) intends to measure the strength of buyers relative to sellers in the market by assessing the influence of each side on the price. It is computed as the difference between the close and the open price, divided by the difference between the high and the low price:

$$\text{BOP}_t = \frac{P_t^{\text{Close}} - P_t^{\text{Open}}}{P_t^{\text{High}} - P_t^{\text{Low}}}$$

Commodity channel index

The **commodity channel index** (**CCI**) measures the difference between the current *typical* price, computed as the average of current low, high, and close price and the historical average price. A positive (negative) CCI indicates that the price is above (below) the historic average. It is computed as follows:

$$\bar{P}_t = \frac{P_t^H + P_t^L + P_t^C}{3}$$

$$\text{CCI}_t = \frac{\bar{P}_t - \text{SMA}(N)_t}{0.15 \sum_{t=i}^{T} |\bar{P}_t - \text{SMA}(N)_t| / T}$$

Moving average convergence divergence

Moving average convergence divergence (**MACD**) is a very popular trend-following (lagging) momentum indicator that shows the relationship between two MAs of a security's price. It is calculated by subtracting the 26-period EMA from the 12-period EMA.

The TA-Lib implementation returns the MACD value and its signal line, which is the 9-day EMA of the MACD. In addition, the MACD-Histogram measures the distance between the indicator and its signal line. The following charts show the results:

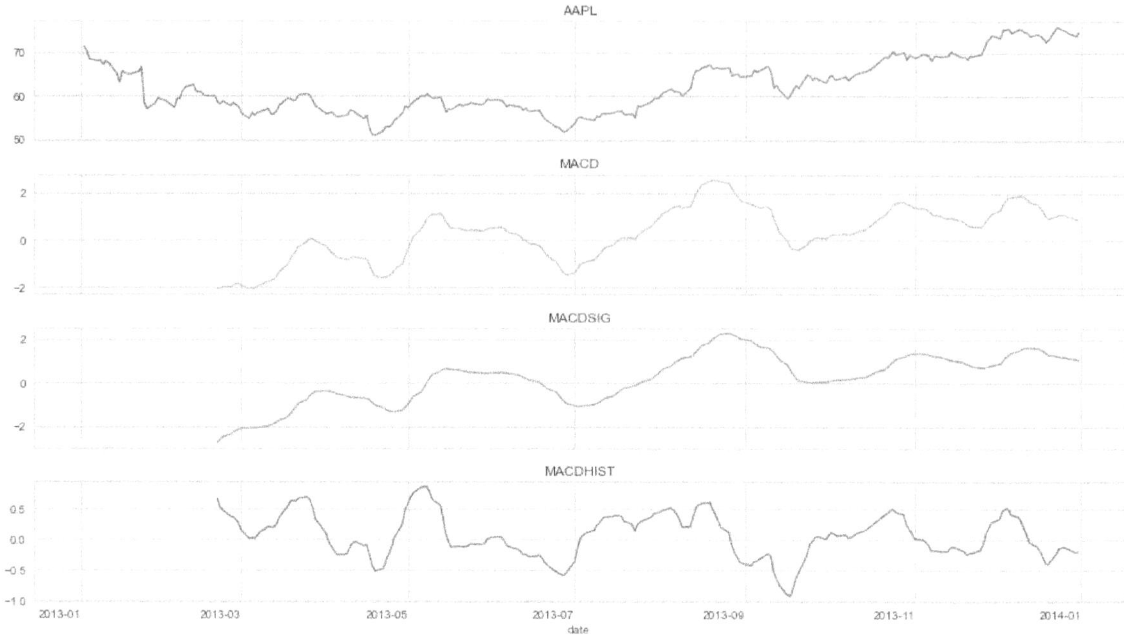

Figure A.9: The three MACD series for the AAPL stock price series

Stochastic relative strength index

The **stochastic relative strength index** (**StochRSI**) is based on the RSI described at the beginning of this section and intends to identify crossovers, as well as overbought and oversold conditions. It compares the distance of the current RSI to the lowest RSI over a given time period T to the maximum range of values the RSI has assumed for this period. It is computed as follows:

$$\text{STOCHRSI}_t = \frac{\text{RSI}_t - \text{RSI}_t^L(T)}{\text{RSI}_t^H(T) - \text{RSI}_t^L(T)}$$

The TA-Lib implementation offers more flexibility than the original unsmoothed stochastic RSI version by Chande and Kroll (1993). To calculate the original indicator, keep `timeperiod` and `fastk_period` equal.

The return value `fastk` is the unsmoothed RSI. `fastd_period` is used to compute a smoothed StochRSI, which is returned as `fastd`. If you do not care about StochRSI smoothing, just set `fastd_period` to 1 and ignore the `fasytd` output:

```
fastk, fastd = talib.STOCHRSI(df.close,
                              timeperiod=14,
                              fastk_period=14,
                              fastd_period=3,
                              fastd_matype=0)
df['fastk'] = fastk
df['fastd'] = fastd
```

Figure A.10 plots the closing price and both the smoothed and unsmoothed stochastic RSI:

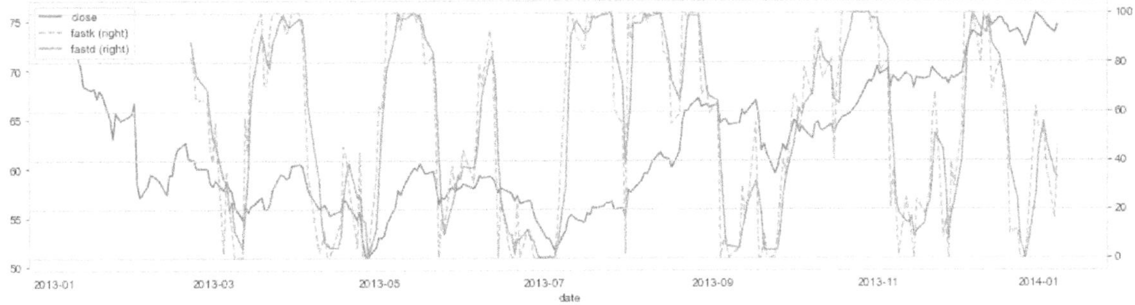

Figure A.10: Smoothed and unsmoothed StochRSI series for the AAPL stock price

Stochastic oscillator

A stochastic oscillator is a momentum indicator that compares a particular closing price of a security to a range of its prices over a certain period of time. Stochastic oscillators are based on the idea that closing prices should confirm the trend. For Stochastic (STOCH), there are four different lines: K^{Fast}, D^{Fast}, K^{Slow}, and D^{Slow}. D is the signal line usually drawn over its corresponding K function:

$$K^{\text{Fast}}(T_K) = \frac{P_t - P^L_{T_K}}{P^H_{T_K} - P^L_{T_K}} * 100$$

$$D^{\text{Fast}}(T_{\text{FastD}}) = \text{MA}(T_{\text{FastD}})[K^{\text{Fast}}]$$

$$K^{\text{Slow}}(T_{\text{SlowK}}) = \text{MA}(T_{\text{SlowK}})[K^{\text{Fast}}]$$

$$D^{\text{Slow}}(T_{\text{SlowD}}) = \text{MA}(T_{\text{SlowD}})[K^{\text{Slow}}]$$

$P^L_{T_K}$, $P^H_{T_K}$, and $P^L_{T_K}$ are the extreme values of the last T_K period. K^{Slow} and D^{Fast} are equivalent when using the same period. We obtain the series shown in *Figure A.11*, as follows:

```
slowk, slowd = talib.STOCH(df.high,
                           df.low,
                           df.close,
                           fastk_period=14,
                           slowk_period=3,
                           slowk_matype=0,
                           slowd_period=3,
                           slowd_matype=0)
df['STOCH'] = slowd / slowk
```

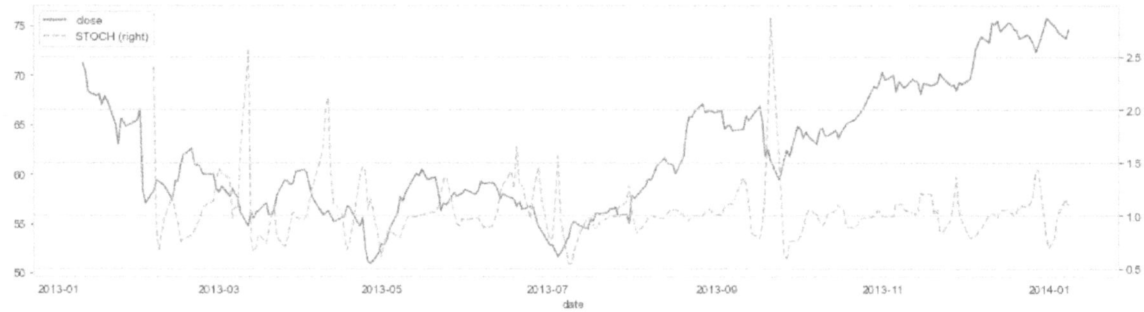

Figure A.11: STOCH series for the AAPL stock price

Ultimate oscillator

The **ultimate oscillator** (**ULTOSC**) measures the average difference between the current close and the previous lowest price over three timeframes—with the default values 7, 14, and 28—to avoid overreacting to short-term price changes and incorporate short-, medium-, and long-term market trends.

It first computes the buying pressure, BP_t, then sums it over the three periods T_1, T_2, and T_3, normalized by the true range (TR_t):

$$\mathrm{BP}_t = P_t^{\mathrm{Close}} - \min\left(P_{t-1}^{\mathrm{Close}}, P_t^{\mathrm{Low}}\right)$$

$$\mathrm{TR}_t = \max\left(P_{t-1}^{\mathrm{Close}}, P_t^{\mathrm{High}}\right) - \min\left(P_{t-1}^{\mathrm{Close}}, P_t^{\mathrm{Low}}\right)$$

ULTOSC is then computed as a weighted average over the three periods, as follows:

$$\mathrm{Avg}_t(T) = \frac{\sum_{i=0}^{T-1} \mathrm{BP}_{t-i}}{\sum_{i=0}^{T-1} \mathrm{TR}_{t-i}}$$

$$\mathrm{ULTOSC}_t = 100 * \frac{4\mathrm{Avg}_t(7) + 2\mathrm{Avg}_t(14) + \mathrm{Avg}_t(28)}{4 + 2 + 1}$$

The following plot shows the result of this:

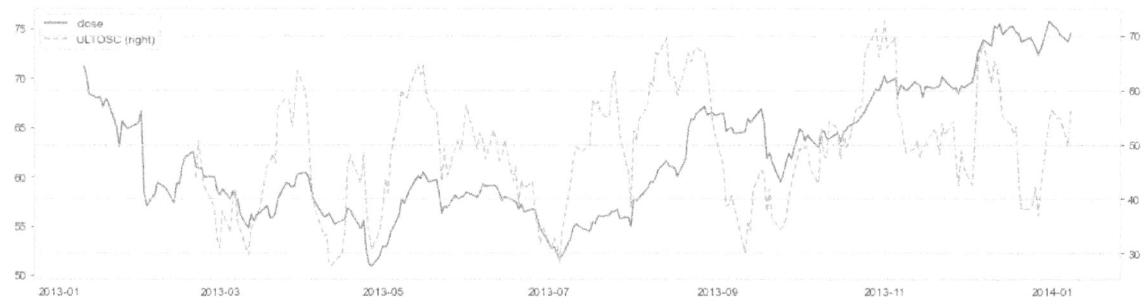

Figure A.12: ULTOSC series for the AAPL stock price

Williams %R

Williams %R, also known as the **Williams Percent Range**, is a momentum indicator that moves between 0 and -100 and measures overbought and oversold levels to identify entry and exit points. It is similar to the stochastic oscillator and compares the current closing price P_t^{Close} to the range of highest (P_T^{High}) and lowest (P_T^{Low}) prices over the last T periods (typically 14). The indicators are computed as follows, and the result is shown in the following chart:

$$\text{WILLR}_t = \frac{P_T^{\text{High}} - P_t^{\text{Close}}}{P_T^{\text{High}} - P_T^{\text{Low}}}$$

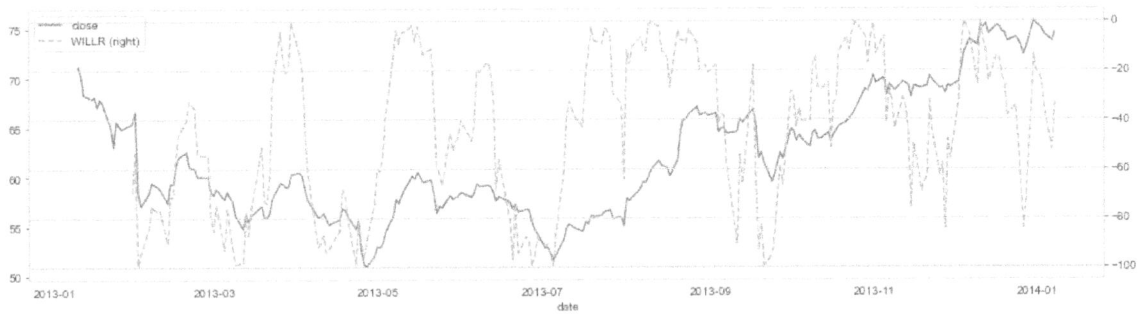

Figure A.13: WILLR series for the AAPL stock price

Volume and liquidity indicators

Risk factors that focus on volume and liquidity incorporate metrics like turnover, dollar volume, or market capitalization. TA-Lib implements three indicators, the first two of which are closely related:

Function	Name
AD	Chaikin A/D Line
ADOSC	Chaikin A/D Oscillator
OBV	On Balance Volume

Also see *Chapter 20, Autoencoders for Conditional Risk Factors and Asset Pricing,* where we use the Amihud Illiquidity indicator to measure a rolling average ratio between absolute returns and the dollar volume.

Chaikin accumulation/distribution line and oscillator

The **Chaikin advance/decline** (**AD**) or **accumulation/distribution** (**AD**) line is a volume-based indicator designed to measure the cumulative flow of money into and out of an asset. The indicator assumes that the degree of buying or selling pressure can be determined by the location of the close, relative to the high and low for the period. There is buying (selling) pressure when a stock closes in the upper (lower) half of a period's range. The intention is to signal a change in direction when the indicator diverges from the security price.

The A/D line is a running total of each period's **money flow volume** (**MFV**). It is calculated as follows:

1. Compute the **money flow index** (**MFI**) as the relationship of the close to the high-low range
2. Multiply the MFI by the period's volume V_t to come up with the MFV
3. Obtain the AD line as the running total of the MFV:

$$\text{MFI}_t = \frac{P_t^{\text{Close}} - P_t^{\text{Low}}}{P_t^{\text{High}} - P_t^{\text{Low}}}$$

$$\text{MFV}_t = \text{MFI}_t \times V_t$$

$$\text{AD}_t = \text{AD}_{t-1} + \text{MFV}_t$$

The **Chaikin A/D oscillator** (**ADOSC**) is the MACD indicator that's applied to the Chaikin AD line. The Chaikin oscillator intends to predict changes in the AD line.

It is computed as the difference between the 3-day EMA and the 10-day EMA of the AD line. The following chart shows the ADOSC series:

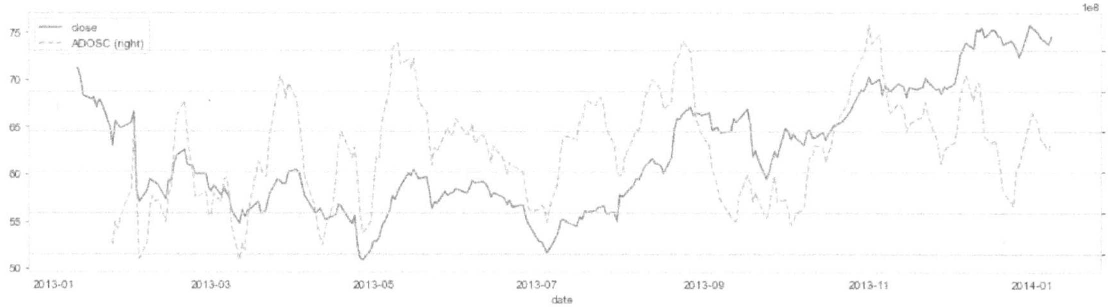

Figure A.14: ADOSC series for the AAPL stock price

On-balance volume

The **on-balance volume** (**OBV**) indicator is a cumulative momentum indicator that relates volume to price change. It assumes that OBV changes precede price changes because smart money can be seen flowing into the security by a rising OBV. When the public then follows, both the security and OBV will rise.

The current OBV_t is computed by adding (subtracting) the current volume to (from) the last OBV_{t-1} if the security closes higher (lower) than the previous close:

$$\mathrm{OBV}_t = \begin{cases} \mathrm{OBV}_{t-1} + V_t & \text{if } P_t > P_t \\ \mathrm{OBV}_{t-1} - V_t & \text{if } P_t < P_{t-1} \\ \mathrm{OBV}_{t-1} & \text{otherwise} \end{cases}$$

Volatility indicators

Volatility indicators include stock-specific measures like the rolling (normalized) standard deviation of asset prices and returns. It also includes broader market measures like the Chicago Board Options Exchange's CBOE **volatility index (VIX)**, which is based on the implied volatility of S&P 500 options.

TA-Lib implements both normalized and averaged versions of the true range indicator.

Average true range

The **average true range (ATR)** indicator shows the volatility of the market. It was introduced by Wilder (1978) and has been used as a component of numerous other indicators since. It aims to anticipate changes in trend such that the higher its value, the higher the probability of a trend change; the lower the indicator's value, the weaker the current trend.

ATR is computed as the simple moving average for a period T of the **true range (TRANGE)**, which measures volatility as the absolute value of the largest recent trading range:

$$\mathrm{TRANGE}_t = \max\left[P_t^{\mathrm{High}} - P_t^{\mathrm{low}}, \left|P_t^{\mathrm{High}} - P_{t-1}^{\mathrm{Close}}\right|, \left|P_t^{\mathrm{low}} - P_{t-1}^{\mathrm{Close}}\right|\right]$$

The resulting series is shown in the following plot:

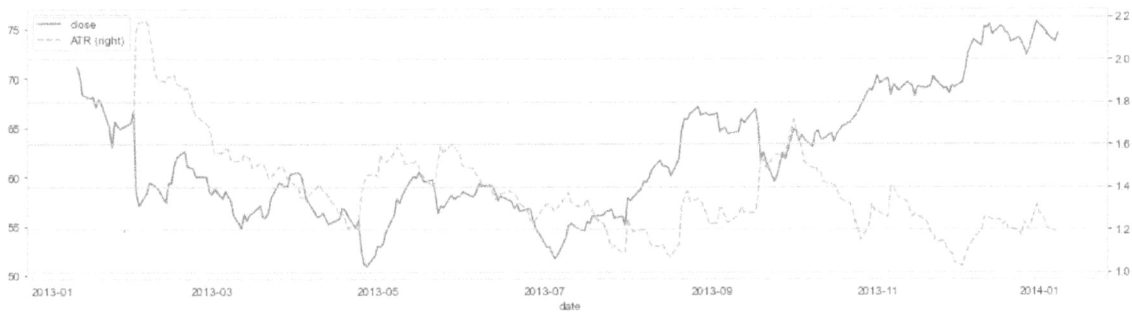

Figure A.15: ATR series for the AAPL stock price

Normalized average true range

TA-Lib also offers a normalized ATR that permits comparisons across assets. The **normalized average true range (NATR)** is computed as follows:

$$\mathrm{NATR}_t = \frac{\mathrm{ATR}_t(T)}{P_t^{\mathrm{Close}}} * 100$$

Normalization makes the ATR more relevant for long-term analysis where the price changes substantially and for cross-market or cross-security comparisons.

Fundamental risk factors

Commonly used measures of risk include the exposure of asset returns to the returns of portfolios designed to represent fundamental factors. We introduced the five-factor model by Fama and French (2015) and showed how to estimate factor loadings and risk factor premia using two-state Fama-Macbeth regressions in *Chapter 7, Linear Models – From Risk Factors to Return Forecasts*.

To estimate the relationship between the price of security and the forces included in the five-factor model such as firm size, value-versus-growth dynamic, investment policy and profitability, in addition to the broad market, we can use the portfolio returns provided by Kenneth French's data library as exogenous variables in a rolling linear regression.

The following example accesses the data using the `pandas_datareader` module (see *Chapter 2, Market and Fundamental Data – Sources and Techniques*). It then computes the regression coefficients for windows of 21, 63, and 252 trading days:

```
factor_data = (web.DataReader('F-F_Research_Data_5_Factors_2x3_daily',
'famafrench',
                              start=2005)[0].rename(columns={'Mkt-RF':
'MARKET'}))
factor_data.index.names = ['date']
factors = factor_data.columns[:-1]
t = 1
ret = f'ret_{t:02}'

windows = [21, 63, 252]
for window in windows:
    print(window)
    betas = []
    for ticker, df in data.groupby('ticker', group_keys=False):
        model_data = df[[ret]].merge(factor_data, on='date').dropna()
        model_data[ret] -= model_data.RF

        rolling_ols = RollingOLS(endog=model_data[ret],
                                 exog=sm.add_constant(model_data[factors]),
                                 window=window)
        factor_model = rolling_ols.fit(params_only=True).params.rename(
            columns={'const':'ALPHA'})
        result = factor_model.assign(ticker=ticker).set_index(
            'ticker', append=True).swaplevel()
        betas.append(result)
    betas = pd.concat(betas).rename(columns=lambda x: f'{x}_{window:02}')
    data = data.join(betas)
```

The risk factors just described are commonly used and also known as **smart beta factors** (see *Chapter 1, Machine Learning for Trading – From Idea to Execution*). In addition, hedge funds have started to resort to alpha factors derived from large-scale data mining exercises, which we'll turn to now.

WorldQuant's quest for formulaic alphas

We introduced WorldQuant in *Chapter 1, Machine Learning for Trading – From Idea to Execution,* as part of a trend toward crowd-sourcing investment strategies. WorldQuant maintains a virtual research center where quants worldwide compete to identify **alphas**. These alphas are trading signals in the form of computational expressions that help predict price movements, just like the common factors described in the previous section.

These **formulaic alphas** translate the mechanism to extract the signal from data into code, and they can be developed and tested individually with the goal to integrate their information into a broader automated strategy (Tulchinsky 2019). As stated repeatedly throughout this book, mining for signals in large datasets is prone to multiple testing bias and false discoveries. Regardless of these important caveats, this approach represents a modern alternative to the more conventional features presented in the previous section.

Kakushadze (2016) presents 101 examples of such alphas, 80 percent of which were used in a real-world trading system at the time. It defines a range of functions that operate on cross-sectional or time-series data and can be combined, for example, in nested form.

The notebook `101_formulaic_alphas` shows how to implement these functions using pandas and NumPy, and also illustrates how to compute around 80 of these formulaic alphas for which we have input data (we lack, for example, accurate historical sector information).

Cross-sectional and time-series functions

The building blocks of the formulaic alphas proposed by Kakushadze (2016) are relatively simple expressions that compute over longitudinal or cross-sectional data that are readily implemented using pandas and NumPy.

The cross-sectional functions include ranking and scaling, as well as the group-wise normalization of returns, where the groups are intended to represent sector information at different levels of granularity:

We can directly translate the ranking function into a pandas expression, using a DataFrame as an argument in the format *number of period* × *number of tickers*, as follows:

```
def rank(df):
    """Return the cross-sectional percentile rank

     Args:
         :param df: tickers in columns, sorted dates in rows.

     Returns:
         pd.DataFrame: the ranked values
     """
    return df.rank(axis=1, pct=True)
```

There are also several time-series functions that will likely be familiar:

Function	Definition
`ts_{O}(x, d)`	Operator *O* applied to the time series for the past *d* days; non-integer number of days *d* converted to floor(*d*).
`ts_lag(x, d)`	Value of *x*, *d* days ago.
`ts_delta(x, d)`	Difference between the value of *x* today and *d* days ago.
`ts_rank(x, d)`	Rank over the past *d* days.
`ts_mean(x, d)`	Simple moving average over the past *d* days.
`ts_weighted_mean(x, d)`	Weighted moving average over the past *d* days with linearly decaying weights *d*, *d* - 1, …, 1 (rescaled to sum up to 1).
`ts_sum(x, d)`	Rolling sum over the past *d* days.
`ts_product(x, d)`	Rolling product over the past *d* days.
`ts_stddev(x, d)`	Moving standard deviation over the past *d* days.
`ts_max(x, d), ts_min(x, d)`	Rolling maximum/minimum over the past *d* days.
`ts_argmax(x, d), ts_argmin(x, d)`	Day of ts*_max(x, d), ts_min*(*x*, *c*).
`ts_correlation(x, y, d)`	Correlation of *x* and *y* for the past *d* days.

These time-series functions are also straightforward to implement using pandas' rolling window functionality. For the rolling weighted mean, for example, we can combine pandas with TA-Lib, as demonstrated in the previous section:

```
def ts_weighted_mean(df, period=10):
    """
    Linear weighted moving average implementation.
    :param df: a pandas DataFrame.
    :param period: the LWMA period
    :return: a pandas DataFrame with the LWMA.
    """
    return (df.apply(lambda x: WMA(x, timeperiod=period)))
```

To create the rolling correlation function, we provide two DataFrames containing time series for different tickers in the columns:

```
def ts_corr(x, y, window=10):
    """
    Wrapper function to estimate rolling correlations.
    :param x, y: pandas DataFrames.
    :param window: the rolling window.
    :return: DataFrame with time-series min for past 'window' days.
    """
    return x.rolling(window).corr(y)
```

In addition, the expressions use common operators, as we will see as we turn to the formulaic alphas that each combine several of the preceding functions.

Formulaic alpha expressions

To illustrate the computation of the alpha expressions, we need to create the following input tables using the sample of the 500 most-traded stocks from 2007-2016 from the previous section (see the notebook `sample_selection` for details on data preparation). Each table contains columns of time series for individual tickers:

Variable	Description
`returns`	Daily close-to-close returns
`open`, `close`, `high`, `low`, `volume`	Standard definitions for daily price and volume data
`vwap`	Daily volume-weighted average price
adv(d)	Average daily dollar volume for the past *d* days

Our data does not include the daily volume-weighted average price required by many alpha expressions. To be able to demonstrate their computation, we very roughly approximate this value using the simple average of the daily open, high, low, and close prices.

Contrary to the common alphas presented in the previous section, the formulaic alphas do not come with an economic interpretation of the risk exposure they represent. We will now demonstrate a few simply numbered instances.

Alpha 001

The first alpha expression is formulated as follows:

```
rank(ts_argmax(power(((returns < 0) ? ts_std(returns, 20) : close), 2.), 5))
```

The ternary operator `a ? b : c` executes *b* if *a* evaluates to `true`, and *c* otherwise. Thus, if the daily returns are positive, it squares the 20-day rolling standard deviation; otherwise, it squares the current close price. It then proceeds to rank the assets by the index of the day that shows the maximum for this value.

Using *c* and *r* to represent the close and return inputs, the alpha translates into Python using the previous functions and pandas methods, like so:

```
def alpha001(c, r):
    """(rank(ts_argmax(power(((returns < 0)
        ? ts_std(returns, 20)
        : close), 2.), 5)) -0.5)"""
    c[r < 0] = ts_std(r, 20)
    return (rank(ts_argmax(power(c, 2), 5)).mul(-.5)
            .stack().swaplevel())
```

For the 10-year sample of 500 stocks, the distribution of Alpha 001 values and its relationship with one-day forward returns looks as follows:

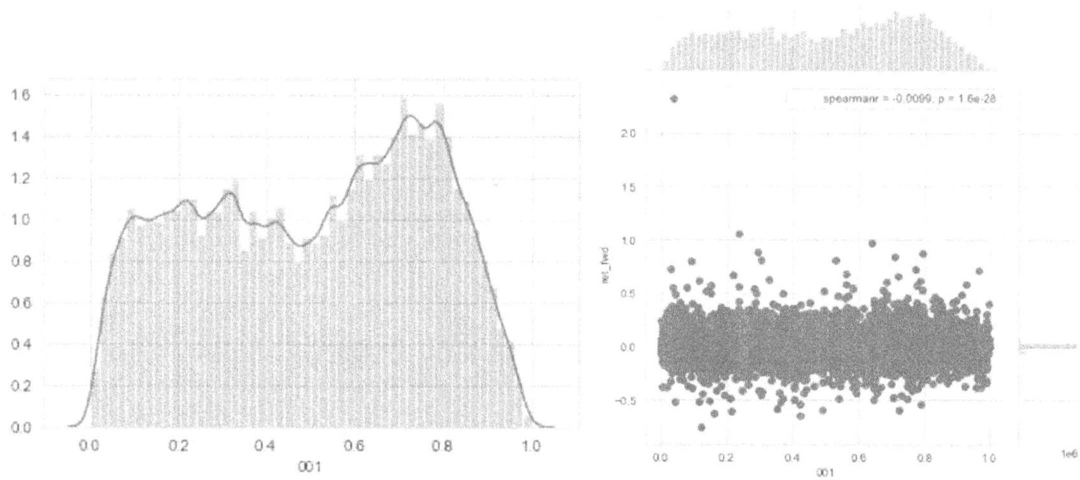

Figure A.16: Alpha 001 histogram and scatter plot

The **information coefficient** (**IC**) is fairly low, yet it is statistically significant at -0.0099 and the **mutual information** (**MI**) estimate yields 0.0129 (see *Chapter 4, Financial Feature Engineering – How to Research Alpha Factors*, and the notebook `101_formulaic_alphas`, for implementation details).

Alpha 054

Our second expression is the ratio of the difference between the low and the close price and the low and the high price, each multiplied by the open and close, respectively, raised to the fifth power:

```
-(low - close) * power(open, 5) / ((low - high) * power(close, 5))
```

Similarly, the translation into pandas is straightforward. We use `o`, `h`, `l`, and `c` to represent the DataFrames containing the respective price series for each ticker in the 500 columns:

```
def alpha054(o, h, l, c):
    """-(low - close) * power(open, 5) / ((low - high) * power(close, 5))"""
    return (l.sub(c).mul(o.pow(5)).mul(-1)
            .div(l.sub(h).replace(0, -0.0001).mul(c ** 5))
            .stack('ticker')
            .swaplevel())
```

In this case, the IC is significant at 0.025, while the MI score is lower at 0.005.

We will now take a look at how these different types of alpha factors compare from a univariate and a multivariate perspective.

Bivariate and multivariate factor evaluation

To evaluate the numerous factors, we rely on the various performance measures introduced in this book, including the following:

- Bivariate measures of the signal content of a factor with respect to the one-day forward returns
- Multivariate measures of feature importance for a gradient boosting model trained to predict the one-day forward returns using all factors
- Financial performance of portfolios invested according to factor quantiles using Alphalens

We will first discuss the bivariate metrics and then turn to the multivariate metrics; we will conclude by comparing the results. See the notebook `factor_evaluation` for the relevant code examples and additional exploratory analysis, such as the correlation among the factors, which we'll omit here.

Information coefficient and mutual information

We will use the following bivariate metrics, which we introduced in *Chapter 4, Financial Feature Engineering – How to Research Alpha Factors*:

- The IC measured as the Spearman rank correlation
- The MI score computed using `mutual_info_regression`, provided by scikit-learn

The MI score uses a sample of 100,000 observations to limit the computational cost of the nearest neighbor computations. Both metrics are otherwise easy to compute and have been used repeatedly; see the notebook for implementation details. We will see, however, that they can yield quite different results.

Feature importance and SHAP values

To measure the predictive relevance of a feature given all other available factors, we can train a LightGBM gradient boosting model with default settings to predict the forward returns using all of the (approximately) 130 factors. The model uses 8.5 years of data to train 104 trees using early stopping. We will obtain test predictions for the last year of data, which yield a global IC of 3.40 and a daily average of 2.01.

We will then proceed to compute the feature importance and **SHapley Additive exPlanation** (**SHAP**) values, as described in *Chapter 12, Boosting Your Trading Strategy*; see the notebook for details. The influence plot in *Figure A.17* highlights how the values of the 20 most important features impact the model's predictions positively or negatively relative to the model's default output. In SHAP value terms, alphas 054 and 001 are among the top five factors:

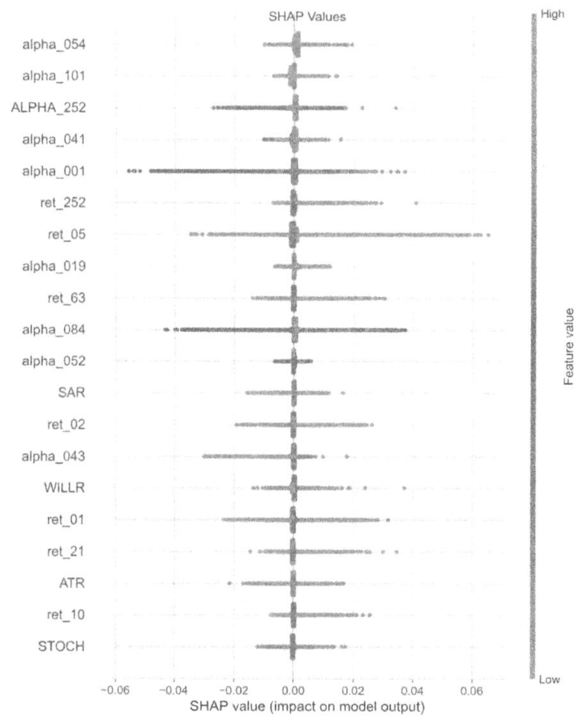

Figure A.17: SHAP values for common and formulaic alphas

Now, let's compare how the different metrics rate our factors.

Comparison – the top 25 features for each metric

The rank correlation among SHAP values and conventional feature importance measured as the weighted contribution of a feature to the reduction of the model's loss function is high at 0.89. It is also substantial between SHAP values and both univariate metrics at around 0.5.

Interestingly, though, MI and IC disagree significantly in their feature rankings with a correlation of only 0.16, as shown in the following diagram:

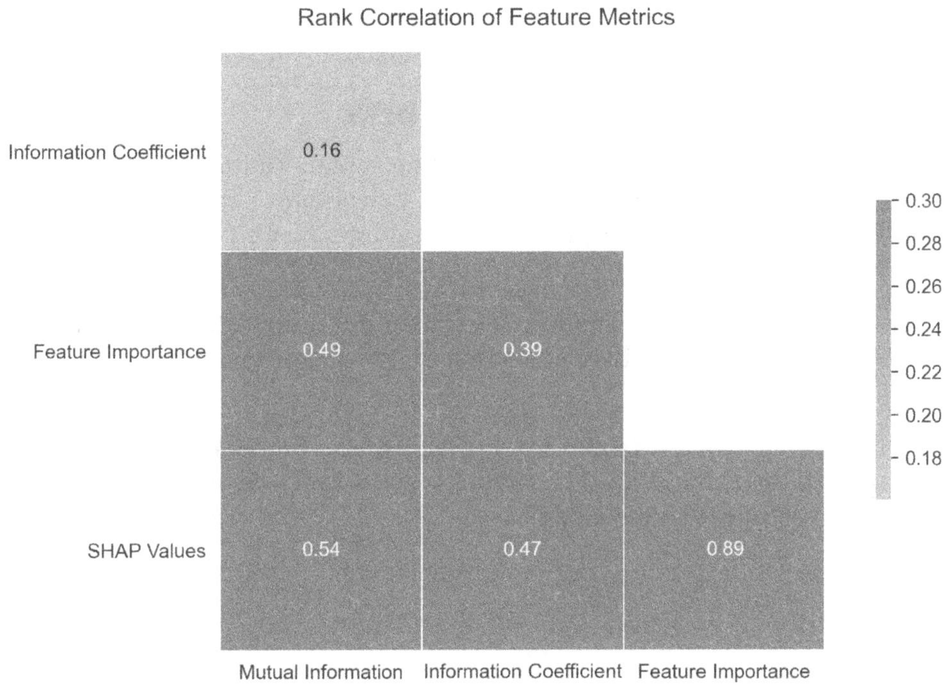

Figure A.18: Rank correlation of performance metrics

Figure A.19 displays the top 25 features according to each metric. Except for the MI score, which prefers the "common" alpha factors, features from both sources are ranked highly:

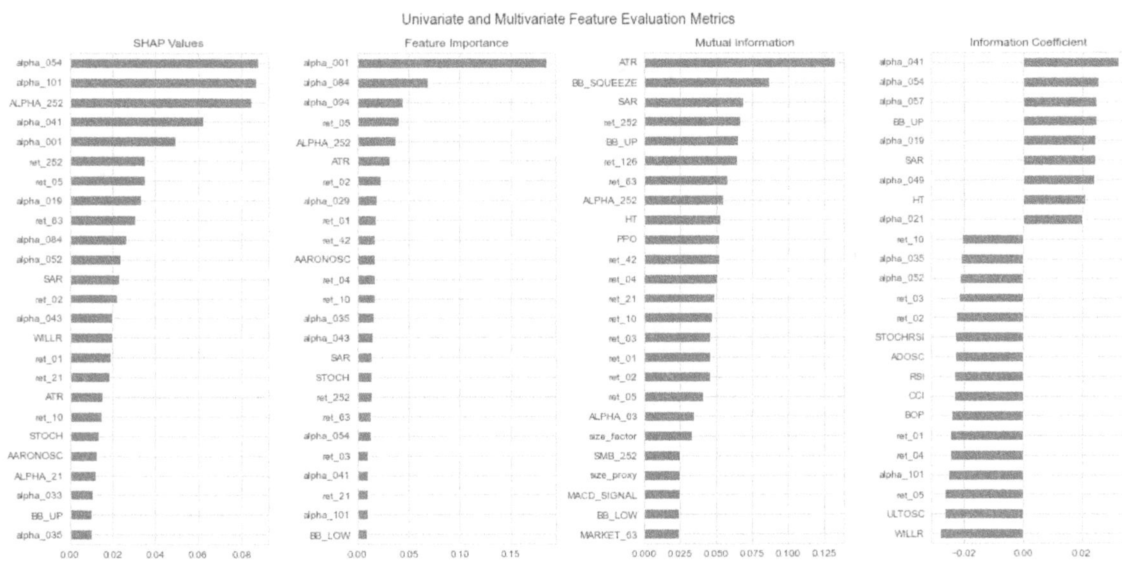

Figure A.19: Top 25 features for each performance metric

It is not immediately apparent why MI disagrees with the other metrics and why few of the features it assigns a high score play a significant role in the gradient boosting model. A possible explanation is that the computation uses only a 10 percent sample and the scores appear sensitive to the sample size.

Financial performance – Alphalens

Finally, we mostly care about the value of the trading signals emitted by an alpha factor. As introduced in *Chapter 4, Financial Feature Engineering – How to Research Alpha Factors*, and demonstrated repeatedly, Alphalens evaluates factor performance on a standalone basis.

The notebook `alphalens_analysis` lets you select an individual factor and compute how portfolios invested for a given horizon according to how factor quantile values would have performed.

The example in *Figure A.20* shows the result for Alpha 54; while portfolios in the top and bottom quintiles did achieve a 1.5 bps average spread on a daily basis, the cumulative returns of a long-short portfolio were negative:

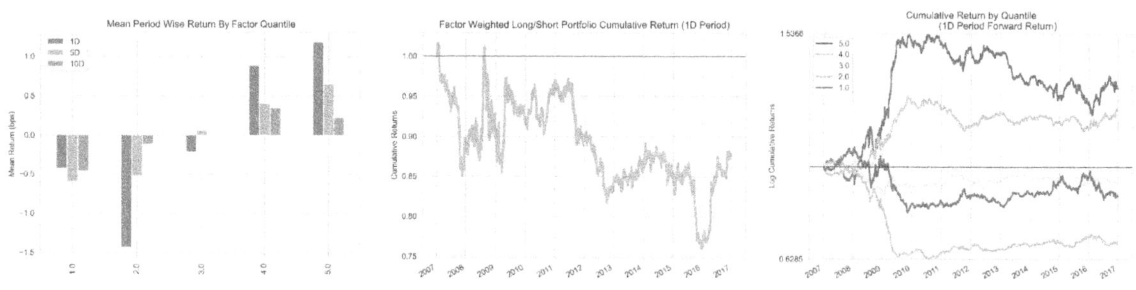

Figure A.20: Alphalens performance metric for Alpha 54

Feel free to use the notebook as a template to evaluate the sample factors or others of your own choosing more systematically.

References

Abdel-Hamid, Ossama, Abdel-rahman Mohamed, Hui Jiang, Li Deng, Gerald Penn, and Dong Yu. 2014. "Convolutional Neural Networks for Speech Recognition." *IEEE/ACM Transactions on Audio, Speech, and Language Processing* 22 (10): 1533–45. `https://doi.org/10.1109/TASLP.2014.2339736`.

Alqahtani, Hamed, Manolya Kavakli-Thorne, and Gulshan Kumar. 2019. "Applications of Generative Adversarial Networks (GANs): An Updated Review." *Archives of Computational Methods in Engineering*, December. `https://doi.org/10.1007/s11831-019-09388-y`.

Ang, Andrew, Robert J Hodrick, Yuhang Xing, and Xiaoyan Zhang. 2006. "The Cross-Section of Volatility and Expected Returns." *The Journal of Finance* 61 (1): 259–99.

Ang, Andrew. 2014. *Asset Management: A Systematic Approach to Factor Investing*. 1 edition. Oxford: Oxford University Press.

Araci, Dogu. 2019. "FinBERT: Financial Sentiment Analysis with Pre-Trained Language Models." *ArXiv:1908.10063 [Cs]*, August. `http://arxiv.org/abs/1908.10063`.

Arora, Saurabh, and Prashant Doshi. 2019. "A Survey of Inverse Reinforcement Learning: Challenges, Methods and Progress." *ArXiv:1806.06877 [Cs, Stat]*, August. `http://arxiv.org/abs/1806.06877`.

Asness, Clifford S., Tobias J. Moskowitz, and Lasse Heje Pedersen. 2013. "Value and Momentum Everywhere." *The Journal of Finance* 68 (3): 929–85. `https://www.jstor.org/stable/42002613`.

Bahdanau, Dzmitry, Kyunghyun Cho, and Yoshua Bengio. 2016. "Neural Machine Translation by Jointly Learning to Align and Translate." *ArXiv:1409.0473 [Cs, Stat]*, May. `http://arxiv.org/abs/1409.0473`.

Bailey, David H., Jonathan M. Borwein, and Marcos Lopez de Prado. 2016. *The Probability of Backtest Overfitting*. Journal of Computational Finance, September. `https://www.risk.net/node/2471206`.

Banz, Rolf W. 1981. "The Relationship between Return and Market Value of Common Stocks." *Journal of Financial Economics* 9 (1): 3–18.

Barberis, Nicholas, Andrei Shleifer, and Robert Vishny. 1998. "A Model of Investor Sentiment." *Journal of Financial Economics* 49 (3): 307–43.

Basu, Sanjoy, and others. 1981. "The Relationship between Earnings' Yield, Market Value and Return for NYSE Common Stocks: Further Evidence."

Bengio, Y., A. Courville, and P. Vincent. 2013. "Representation Learning: A Review and New Perspectives." *IEEE Transactions on Pattern Analysis and Machine Intelligence* 35 (8): 1798–1828. `https://doi.org/10.1109/TPAMI.2013.50`.

Betancourt, Michael. 2018. "A Conceptual Introduction to Hamiltonian Monte Carlo." *ArXiv:1701.02434 [Stat]*, July. `http://arxiv.org/abs/1701.02434`.

Bishop, Christopher. 2006. *Pattern Recognition and Machine Learning*. Information Science and Statistics. New York: Springer-Verlag. `https://www.springer.com/gp/book/9780387310732`.

Blei, David M., Andrew Y. Ng, and Michael I. Jordan. 2003. "Latent Dirichlet Allocation." *Journal of Machine Learning Research* 3 (Jan): 993–1022. `http://jmlr.csail.mit.edu/papers/v3/blei03a.html`.

Burges, Chris J. C. 2010. "Dimension Reduction: A Guided Tour." *Foundations and Trends in Machine Learning*, January. `https://www.microsoft.com/en-us/research/publication/dimension-reduction-a-guided-tour-2/`.

Byrd, David, Maria Hybinette, and Tucker Hybinette Balch. 2019. "ABIDES: Towards High-Fidelity Market Simulation for AI Research." `ArXiv:1904.12066 [Cs]`, April. `http://arxiv.org/abs/1904.12066`.

Casella, George, and Edward I. George. 1992. "Explaining the Gibbs Sampler." *The American Statistician* 46 (3): 167–74. `https://doi.org/10.2307/2685208`.

Chan, Ernie., 2008. *Quantitative Trading: How to Build Your Own Algorithmic Trading Business*, 1 edition. ed. Wiley, Hoboken, N.J.

Chan, Ernie. 2013. *Algorithmic Trading: Winning Strategies and Their Rationale*. 1st ed. Wiley Publishing.

Chen, Tianqi, and Carlos Guestrin. 2016. "XGBoost: A Scalable Tree Boosting System." *Proceedings of the 22nd ACM SIGKDD International Conference on Knowledge Discovery and Data Mining - KDD '16*, 785–94. `https://doi.org/10.1145/2939672.2939785`.

Chen, Wei, Tie-yan Liu, Yanyan Lan, Zhi-ming Ma, and Hang Li. 2009. "Ranking Measures and Loss Functions in Learning to Rank." *In Advances in Neural Information Processing Systems* 22, edited by Y. Bengio, D. Schuurmans, J. D. Lafferty, C. K. I. Williams, and A. Culotta, 315–323. Curran Associates, Inc. `http://papers.nips.cc/paper/3708-ranking-measures-and-loss-functions-in-learning-to-rank.pdf`.

Cheung, W., 2010. *The Black–Litterman model explained*. J Asset Manag 11, 229–243. `https://doi.org/10.1057/jam.2009.28`.

Chib, Siddhartha, and Edward Greenberg. 1995. "Understanding the Metropolis-Hastings Algorithm." *The American Statistician* 49 (4): 327–35. `https://doi.org/10.1080/00031305.1995.10476177`.

Cho, Kyunghyun, Bart van Merriënboer, Caglar Gulcehre, Dzmitry Bahdanau, Fethi Bougares, Holger Schwenk, and Yoshua Bengio. 2014. "Learning Phrase Representations Using RNN Encoder–Decoder for Statistical Machine Translation." *In Proceedings of the 2014 Conference on Empirical Methods in Natural Language Processing (EMNLP)*, 1724–1734. Doha, Qatar: Association for Computational Linguistics. `https://doi.org/10.3115/v1/D14-1179`.

Chung, Junyoung, Caglar Gulcehre, Kyunghyun Cho, and Yoshua Bengio. 2014. "Empirical Evaluation of Gated Recurrent Neural Networks on Sequence Modeling." *NIPS 2014 Workshop on Deep Learning*, December 2014. `https://nyuscholars.nyu.edu/en/publications/empirical-evaluation-of-gated-recurrent-neural-networks-on-sequen`.

Clarke, R., Silva, H. de, Thorley, S., 2002. *Portfolio Constraints and the Fundamental Law of Active Management*. Financial Analysts Journal 58, 48–66.

Creswell, Antonia, Tom White, Vincent Dumoulin, Kai Arulkumaran, Biswa Sengupta, and Anil A. Bharath. 2018. "Generative Adversarial Networks: An Overview." *IEEE Signal Processing Magazine* 35 (1): 53–65. `https://doi.org/10.1109/MSP.2017.2765202`.

Cubuk, Ekin D. 2019. "AutoAugment: Learning Augmentation Strategies From Data." *CVFPR*, 11.

Cummins, Mark, and Andrea Bucca. 2012. "Quantitative Spread Trading on Crude Oil and Refined Products Markets." *Quantitative Finance* 12 (12): 1857–75. `https://doi.org/10.1080/14697688.2012.715749`.

Cybenko, G. 1989. "Approximation by Superpositions of a Sigmoidal Function." *Mathematics of Control, Signals and Systems* 2 (4): 303–14. `https://doi.org/10.1007/BF02551274`.

David H. Bailey et al. (2015), *Backtest Overfitting: An Interactive Example*. `http://datagrid.lbl.gov/backtest/`.

De Prado, Marcos Lopez. 2018. *Advances in Financial Machine Learning*. John Wiley & Sons.

DeMiguel, V., Garlappi, L., Uppal, R., 2009. *Optimal Versus Naive Diversification: How Inefficient is the 1/N Portfolio Strategy?* Rev Financ Stud 22, 1915–1953. `https://doi.org/10.1093/rfs/hhm075`.

Devlin, Jacob, Ming-Wei Chang, Kenton Lee, and Kristina Toutanova. 2019. "BERT: Pre-Training of Deep Bidirectional Transformers for Language Understanding." In *Proceedings of the 2019 Conference of the North American Chapter of the Association for Computational Linguistics: Human Language Technologies, Volume 1* (Long and Short Papers), 4171–4186. Minneapolis, Minnesota: Association for Computational Linguistics. `https://doi.org/10.18653/v1/N19-1423`.

Dumais, S. T., G. W. Furnas, T. K. Landauer, S. Deerwester, and R. Harshman. 1988. "Using Latent Semantic Analysis to Improve Access to Textual Information." In *Proceedings of the SIGCHI Conference on Human Factors in Computing Systems*, 281-285. CHI '88. Washington, D.C., USA: Association for Computing Machinery. `https://doi.org/10.1145/57167.57214`.

Elliott, Robert J., John Van Der Hoek, and William P. Malcolm. 2005. "Pairs Trading." *Quantitative Finance* 5 (3): 271–76. `https://doi.org/10.1080/14697680500149370`.

Esposito, F., D. Malerba, G. Semeraro, and J. Kay. 1997. "A Comparative Analysis of Methods for Pruning Decision Trees." *IEEE Transactions on Pattern Analysis and Machine Intelligence* 19 (5): 476–91. `https://doi.org/10.1109/34.589207`.

Esteban, Cristóbal, Stephanie L. Hyland, and Gunnar Rätsch. 2017. "Real-Valued (Medical) Time Series Generation with Recurrent Conditional GANs." *ArXiv:1706.02633 [Cs, Stat]*, December. `http://arxiv.org/abs/1706.02633`.

Fabozzi, Frank J, Sergio M Focardi, and Petter N Kolm. 2010. *Quantitative Equity Investing: Techniques and Strategies*. John Wiley & Sons.

Fama, E.F., French, K.R., 2004. *The Capital Asset Pricing Model: Theory and Evidence.* Journal of Economic Perspectives 18, 25–46. `https://doi.org/10.1257/0895330042162430`.

Fama, Eugene F, and James D MacBeth. 1973. "Risk, Return, and Equilibrium: Empirical Tests." *Journal of Political Economy* 81 (3): 607–36.

Fama, Eugene F, and Kenneth R French. 1993. "Common Risk Factors in the Returns on Stocks and Bonds." *Journal of Financial Economics* 33: 3–56.

Fama, Eugene F, and Kenneth R French. 1998. "Value versus Growth: The *International Evidence." The Journal of Finance* 53 (6): 1975–99.

Fama, Eugene F., and Kenneth R. French. 2015. "A Five-Factor Asset Pricing Model." *Journal of Financial Economics* 116 (1): 1–22. `https://doi.org/10.1016/j.jfineco.2014.10.010`.

Fawcett, Tom. 2006. "An Introduction to ROC Analysis." *Pattern Recognition Letters*, ROC Analysis in Pattern Recognition, 27 (8): 861–74. `https://doi.org/10.1016/j.patrec.2005.10.010`.

Fefferman, Charles, Sanjoy Mitter, and Hariharan Narayanan. 2016. "Testing the Manifold Hypothesis." *Journal of the American Mathematical Society* 29 (4): 983–1049. `https://doi.org/10.1090/jams/852`.

Fei-Fei, Li. 2015. "ImageNet Large Scale Visual Recognition Challenge." *International Journal of Computer Vision* 115 (3): 211–52. `https://doi.org/10.1007/s11263-015-0816-y`.

Fisher, Walter D. 1958. "On Grouping for Maximum Homogeneity." *Journal of the American Statistical Association* 53 (284): 789–98. `https://doi.org/10.2307/2281952`.

Freund, Yoav, and Robert E Schapire. 1997. "A Decision-Theoretic Generalization of On-Line Learning and an Application to Boosting." *Journal of Computer and System Sciences* 55 (1): 119–39. `https://doi.org/10.1006/jcss.1997.1504`.

Friedman, Jerome H. 2001. "Greedy Function Approximation: A Gradient Boosting Machine." *The Annals of Statistics* 29 (5): 1189–1232. `https://www.jstor.org/stable/2699986`.

Fu, Rao, Jie Chen, Shutian Zeng, Yiping Zhuang, and Agus Sudjianto. 2019. "Time Series Simulation by Conditional Generative Adversarial Net." *ArXiv:1904.11419 [Cs, Eess, Stat]*, April. `http://arxiv.org/abs/1904.11419`.

Gatev, Evan, William N. Goetzmann, and K. Geert Rouwenhorst. 2006. "Pairs Trading: Performance of a Relative-Value Arbitrage Rule." *The Review of Financial Studies* 19 (3): 797–827. `https://doi.org/10.1093/rfs/hhj020`.

Gelman, Andrew, John B. Carlin, Hal S. Stern, David B. Dunson, Aki Vehtari, and Donald B. Rubin. 2013. *Bayesian Data Analysis, Third Edition*. CRC Press.

Gómez, David, and Alfonso Rojas. 2015. "An Empirical Overview of the No Free Lunch Theorem and Its Effect on Real-World Machine Learning Classification." *Neural Computation* 28 (1): 216–28. `https://doi.org/10.1162/NECO_a_00793`.

Gonzalo, Jesús, and Tae-Hwy Lee. 1998. "Pitfalls in Testing for Long-Run Relationships." *Journal of Econometrics* 86 (1): 129–54. `https://doi.org/10.1016/S0304-4076(97)00111-5`.

Goodfellow, Ian, Jean Pouget-Abadie, Mehdi Mirza, Bing Xu, David Warde-Farley, Sherjil Ozair, Aaron Courville, and Yoshua Bengio. 2014. "Generative Adversarial Nets." In *Advances in Neural Information Processing Systems* 27, edited by Z. Ghahramani, M. Welling, C. Cortes, N. D. Lawrence, and K. Q. Weinberger, 2672–2680. Curran Associates, Inc. `http://papers.nips.cc/paper/5423-generative-adversarial-nets.pdf`.

Goodfellow, Ian, Yoshua Bengio, and Aaron Courville. 2016. *Deep Learning*. MIT press.

Goodfellow, Ian. 2014. "Multi-Digit Number Recognition from Street View Imagery Using Deep Convolutional Neural Networks." In *ICLR2014*.

Goyal, Amit. 2012. "Empirical Cross-Sectional Asset Pricing: A Survey." *Financial Markets and Portfolio Management* 26 (1): 3–38. `https://doi.org/10.1007/s11408-011-0177-7`.

Graham, Benjamin, David Dodd, and David Le Fevre Dodd. 1934. *Security Analysis: The Classic 1934 Edition*. McGraw Hill Professional.

Green, Jeremiah, John R. M. Hand, and X. Frank Zhang. 2017. "The Characteristics That Provide Independent Information about Average U.S. Monthly Stock Returns." *The Review of Financial Studies* 30 (12): 4389–4436. `https://doi.org/10.1093/rfs/hhx019`.

Grinold, R.C., 1989. *The fundamental law of active management*. The Journal of Portfolio Management 15, 30–37. `https://doi.org/10.3905/jpm.1989.409211`.

Gu, S., Kelly, B., and Xu, D. 2020 "Autoencoder Asset Pricing Models." *Journal of Econometrics* (forthcoming).

Gu, Shihao, Bryan Kelly, and Dacheng Xiu. 2020. "Empirical Asset Pricing via Machine Learning." *The Review of Financial Studies*, no. hhaa009 (February). `https://doi.org/10.1093/rfs/hhaa009`.

Harris, Larry. 2003. *Trading and Exchanges: Market Microstructure for Practitioners*. Oxford University Press.

Hasselt, Hado van, Arthur Guez, and David Silver. 2015. "Deep Reinforcement Learning with Double Q-Learning." *ArXiv:1509.06461 [Cs]*, September. `http://arxiv.org/abs/1509.06461`.

Hastie, Trevor, Robert Tibshirani, and Jerome Friedman. 2009. *The Elements of Statistical Learning: Data Mining, Inference, and Prediction, Second Edition*. 2nd ed. Springer Series in Statistics. New York: Springer-Verlag. `https://doi.org/10.1007/978-0-387-84858-7`.

Hastie, Trevor, Robert Tibshirani, and Martin Wainwright. 2015. *Statistical Learning with Sparsity: The Lasso and Generalizations*. CRC press.

He, Kaiming, Xiangyu Zhang, Shaoqing Ren, and Jian Sun. 2015. "Deep Residual Learning for Image Recognition." *ArXiv:1512.03385 [Cs]*, December. `http://arxiv.org/abs/1512.03385`.

Hendricks, Dieter, and Diane Wilcox. 2014. "A Reinforcement Learning Extension to the Almgren-Chriss Framework for Optimal Trade Execution." In 2014 *IEEE Conference on Computational Intelligence for Financial Engineering Economics (CIFEr)*, 457–64. `https://doi.org/10.1109/CIFEr.2014.6924109`.

Hessel, Matteo, Joseph Modayil, Hado van Hasselt, Tom Schaul, Georg Ostrovski, Will Dabney, Dan Horgan, Bilal Piot, Mohammad Azar, and David Silver. 2017. "Rainbow: Combining Improvements in Deep Reinforcement Learning." *ArXiv:1710.02298 [Cs]*, October. `http://arxiv.org/abs/1710.02298`.

Hihi, Salah El, and Yoshua Bengio. 1996. "Hierarchical Recurrent Neural Networks for Long-Term Dependencies." In *Advances in Neural Information Processing Systems* 8, edited by D. S. Touretzky, M. C. Mozer, and M. E. Hasselmo, 493–499. MIT Press. `http://papers.nips.cc/paper/1102-hierarchical-recurrent-neural-networks-for-long-term-dependencies.pdf`.

Hochreiter, Sepp, and Jürgen Schmidhuber. 1996. "LSTM Can Solve Hard Long Time Lag Problems." In *Proceedings of the 9th International Conference on Neural Information Processing Systems*, 473–479. NIPS'96. Denver, Colorado: MIT Press.

Hochreiter, Sepp, Yoshua Bengio, Paolo Frasconi, Jürgen Schmidhuber, and others. 2001. "Gradient Flow in Recurrent Nets: The Difficulty of Learning Long-Term Dependencies."

Hoerl, Arthur E, and Robert W Kennard. 1970. "Ridge Regression: Biased Estimation for Nonorthogonal Problems." *Technometrics* 12 (1): 55–67.

Hoffman, Matthew D., and Andrew Gelman. 2011. "The No-U-Turn Sampler: Adaptively Setting Path Lengths in Hamiltonian Monte Carlo." *ArXiv:1111.4246 [Cs, Stat]*, November. `http://arxiv.org/abs/1111.4246`.

Hofmann, Thomas. 2001. "Unsupervised Learning by Probabilistic Latent Semantic Analysis." *Machine Learning* 42 (1): 177–96. `https://doi.org/10.1023/A:1007617005950`.

Hong, Harrison, Terence Lim, and Jeremy C. Stein. 2000. "Bad News Travels Slowly: Size, Analyst Coverage, and the Profitability of Momentum Strategies." *The Journal of Finance* 55 (1): 265–95. `https://doi.org/10.1111/0022-1082.00206`.

Hornik, Kurt. 1991. "Approximation Capabilities of Multilayer Feedforward Networks." *Neural Networks* 4 (2): 251–57. https://doi.org/10.1016/0893-6080(91)90009-T.

Hou, Kewei, Chen Xue, and Lu Zhang. 2015. "Digesting Anomalies: An Investment Approach." *The Review of Financial Studies* 28 (3): 650–705. https://doi.org/10.1093/rfs/hhu068.

Hou, K., Xue, C., Zhang, L., 2017. *Replicating Anomalies* (SSRN Scholarly Paper No. ID 2961979). Social Science Research Network, Rochester, NY.

Huang, Gao, Zhuang Liu, Laurens van der Maaten, and Kilian Q. Weinberger. 2018. "Densely Connected Convolutional Networks." *ArXiv:1608.06993 [Cs]*, January. http://arxiv.org/abs/1608.06993.

Ismail Fawaz, Hassan, Germain Forestier, Jonathan Weber, Lhassane Idoumghar, and Pierre-Alain Muller. 2019. "Deep Learning for Time Series Classification: A Review." *Data Mining and Knowledge Discovery* 33 (4): 917–63. https://doi.org/10.1007/s10618-019-00619-1.

Jaeger, Herbert. 2001. "The 'Echo State' Approach to Analysing and Training Recurrent Neural Networks with an Erratum Note." *Bonn, Germany: German National Research Center for Information Technology GMD Technical Report* 148 (34): 13.

James, Gareth, Daniela Witten, Trevor Hastie, and Robert Tibshirani. 2013. *An Introduction to Statistical Learning*. Vol. 112. Springer.

Jegadeesh, Narasimhan, and Sheridan Titman. 1993. "Returns to Buying Winners and Selling Losers: Implications for Stock Market Efficiency." *The Journal of Finance* 48 (1): 65–91.

Jones, Charles. 2018. "Understanding the Market for Us Equity Market Data." *NYSE*. https://www0.gsb.columbia.edu/faculty/cjones/papers/2018.08.31%20US%20Equity%20Market%20Data%20Paper.pdf.

JP Morgan, 2012. *Improving on risk parity – Hedging Forecast Uncertainty*. https://am.jpmorgan.com/blobcontent/1378404528937/83456/11_77%20Risk%20Parity.pdf.

Ke, Guolin, Qi Meng, Thomas Finley, Taifeng Wang, Wei Chen, Weidong Ma, Qiwei Ye, and Tie-Yan Liu. 2017. "LightGBM: A Highly Efficient Gradient Boosting Decision Tree." In *Advances in Neural Information Processing Systems* 30, edited by I. Guyon, U. V. Luxburg, S. Bengio, H. Wallach, R. Fergus, S. Vishwanathan, and R. Garnett, 3146–3154. Curran Associates, Inc. http://papers.nips.cc/paper/6907-lightgbm-a-highly-efficient-gradient-boosting-decision-tree.pdf.

Kearns, Michael, and Yuriy Nevmyvaka. 2013. "Machine Learning for Market Microstructure and High Frequency Trading." *High Frequency Trading: New Realities for Traders, Markets, and Regulators*.

Kelley, David. 2019. "Which Leading Indicators Have Done Better at Signaling Past Recessions?" *Chicago Fed Letter*, no. 425: 1.

Kelly, Bryan T., Seth Pruitt, and Yinan Su. 2019. "Characteristics Are Covariances: A Unified Model of Risk and Return." *Journal of Financial Economics* 134 (3): 501–24. https://doi.org/10.1016/j.jfineco.2019.05.001.

Kelly, J.L., 2011. *A New Interpretation of Information Rate*, in: The Kelly Capital Growth Investment Criterion, World Scientific Handbook in Financial Economics Series. WORLD SCIENTIFIC, pp. 25–34. `https://doi.org/10.1142/9789814293501_0003`.

Kingma, Diederik P., and Max Welling. 2014. "Auto-Encoding Variational Bayes." *ArXiv:1312.6114 [Cs, Stat]*, May. `http://arxiv.org/abs/1312.6114`.

Kingma, Diederik, and Jimmy Ba. 2014. "Adam: A Method for Stochastic Optimization," December. `https://arxiv.org/abs/1412.6980v8`.

Kingma, Diederik P., and Max Welling. 2019. "An Introduction to Variational Autoencoders." *Foundations and Trends® in Machine Learning* 12 (4): 307–92. `https://doi.org/10.1561/2200000056`.

Kolanovic, Marko, and Rajesh Krishnamachari. 2017. "Big Data and AI Strategies - Machine Learning and Alternative Data Approach to Investing." White Paper. JP Morgan. `http://www.fullertreacymoney.com/system/data/files/PDFs/2017/October/18th/Big%20Data%20and%20AI%20Strategies%20-%20Machine%20Learning%20and%20Alternative%20Data%20Approach%20to%20Investing.pdf`.

Koshiyama, Adriano, Nick Firoozye, and Philip Treleaven. 2019. "Generative Adversarial Networks for Financial Trading Strategies Fine-Tuning and Combination." *ArXiv:1901.01751 [Cs, q-Fin, Stat]*, March. `http://arxiv.org/abs/1901.01751`.

Krauss, Christopher, Xuan Anh Do, and Nicolas Huck. 2017. "Deep Neural Networks, Gradient-Boosted Trees, Random Forests: Statistical Arbitrage on the S&P 500." *European Journal of Operational Research* 259 (2): 689–702. `https://doi.org/10.1016/j.ejor.2016.10.031`.

Krizhevsky, Alex, Ilya Sutskever, and Geoffrey E Hinton. 2012. "ImageNet Classification with Deep Convolutional Neural Networks." In *Advances in Neural Information Processing Systems* 25, edited by F. Pereira, C. J. C. Burges, L. Bottou, and K. Q. Weinberger, 1097–1105. Curran Associates, Inc. `http://papers.nips.cc/paper/4824-imagenet-classification-with-deep-convolutional-neural-networks.pdf`.

Lecun, Y., L. Bottou, Y. Bengio, and P. Haffner. 1998. "Gradient-Based Learning Applied to Document Recognition." *Proceedings of the IEEE* 86 (11): 2278–2324. `https://doi.org/10.1109/5.726791`.

LeCun, Yann, Bernhard Boser, John S Denker, Donnie Henderson, Richard E Howard, Wayne Hubbard, and Lawrence D Jackel. 1989. "Backpropagation Applied to Handwritten Zip Code Recognition." *Neural Computation* 1 (4): 541–51.

LeCun, Yann, Yoshua Bengio, and Geoffrey Hinton. 2015. "Deep Learning." *Nature* 521 (7553): 436–44. `https://doi.org/10.1038/nature14539`.

Ledig, Christian, Lucas Theis, Ferenc Huszar, Jose Caballero, Andrew Cunningham, Alejandro Acosta, Andrew Aitken, et al. 2017. "Photo-Realistic Single Image Super-Resolution Using a Generative Adversarial Network." In , 4681–90. `http://openaccess.thecvf.com/content_cvpr_2017/html/Ledig_Photo-Realistic_Single_Image_CVPR_2017_paper.html`.

Ledoit, O., Wolf, M., 2003. *Improved estimation of the covariance matrix of stock returns with an application to portfolio selection*. Journal of Empirical Finance 10, 603–621. https://doi.org/10.1016/S0927-5398(03)00007-0.

Levy, Omer, and Yoav Goldberg. 2014. "Neural Word Embedding as Implicit Matrix Factorization." In *Advances in Neural Information Processing Systems* 27, edited by Z. Ghahramani, M. Welling, C. Cortes, N. D. Lawrence, and K. Q. Weinberger, 2177–2185. Curran Associates, Inc. http://papers.nips.cc/paper/5477-neural-word-embedding-as-implicit-matrix-factorization.pdf.

Lin, Long-Ji, and Tom M Mitchell. 1992. *Memory Approaches to Reinforcement Learning in Non-Markovian Domains*. Citeseer.

Liu, Yinhan, Myle Ott, Naman Goyal, Jingfei Du, Mandar Joshi, Danqi Chen, Omer Levy, Mike Lewis, Luke Zettlemoyer, and Veselin Stoyanov. 2019. "RoBERTa: A Robustly Optimized BERT Pretraining Approach." *ArXiv:1907.11692 [Cs]*, July. http://arxiv.org/abs/1907.11692.

Lo, A.W., 2002. *The Statistics of Sharpe Ratios*. https://doi.org/10.2469/faj.v58.n4.2453.

Maaten, Laurens van der, and Geoffrey Hinton. 2008. "Visualizing Data Using T-SNE." *Journal of Machine Learning Research* 9 (Nov): 2579–2605. http://www.jmlr.org/papers/v9/vandermaaten08a.html.

Madhavan, Ananth. 2002. "Market Microstructure: A Practitioner's Guide." *Financial Analysts Journal* 58 (5): 28–42. www.jstor.org/stable/4480415.

Madhavan, Ananth. 2000. "Market Microstructure: A Survey." *Journal of Financial Markets* 3 (3): 205–58. https://doi.org/10.1016/S1386-4181(00)00007-0.

Malkiel, Burton G. 2003. "The Efficient Market Hypothesis and Its Critics." *Journal of Economic Perspectives* 17 (1): 59–82. https://doi.org/10.1257/089533003321164958.

Man, Xiliu, Tong Luo, and Jianwu Lin. 2019. "Financial Sentiment Analysis(FSA): A Survey." In 2019 *IEEE International Conference on Industrial Cyber Physical Systems (ICPS)*, 617–22. https://doi.org/10.1109/ICPHYS.2019.8780312.

Markowitz, H., 1952. *Portfolio Selection*. The Journal of Finance 7, 77–91. https://doi.org/10.2307/2975974.

Meredith, Mike, and John Kruschke. 2018. "Bayesian Estimation Supersedes the T-Test," 14.

Michaud, Richard O., Esch, D.N., Michaud, Robert O., 2017. *The "Fundamental Law of Active Management" is No Law of Anything*. https://doi.org/10.2139/ssrn.2834020.

Mikolov, Tomas, Ilya Sutskever, Kai Chen, Greg Corrado, and Jeffrey Dean. 2013. "Distributed Representations of Words and Phrases and Their Compositionality." In *Proceedings of the 26th International Conference on Neural Information Processing Systems – Volume 2*, 3111–3119. NIPS'13. USA: Curran Associates Inc. http://dl.acm.org/citation.cfm?id=2999792.2999959.

Miller, Rena S. 2016. "High Frequency Trading: Overview of Recent Developments." *High Frequency Trading*, 19.

Mimno, David, Hanna M. Wallach, Edmund Talley, Miriam Leenders, and Andrew McCallum. 2011. "Optimizing Semantic Coherence in Topic Models." In *Proceedings of the Conference on Empirical Methods in Natural Language Processing*, 262–272. EMNLP '11. Edinburgh, United Kingdom: Association for Computational Linguistics.

Mitchell, Tom M. 1997. "Machine Learning."

Mnih, Andriy, and Koray Kavukcuoglu. 2013. "Learning Word Embeddings Efficiently with Noise-Contrastive Estimation." In *Advances in Neural Information Processing Systems* 26, edited by C. J. C. Burges, L. Bottou, M. Welling, Z. Ghahramani, and K. Q. Weinberger, 2265–2273. Curran Associates, Inc. `http://papers.nips.cc/paper/5165-learning-word-embeddings-efficiently-with-noise-contrastive-estimation.pdf`.

Mnih, Volodymyr, Koray Kavukcuoglu, David Silver, Alex Graves, Ioannis Antonoglou, Daan Wierstra, and Martin Riedmiller. 2013. "Playing Atari with Deep Reinforcement Learning." *ArXiv:1312.5602 [Cs]*, December. `http://arxiv.org/abs/1312.5602`.

Mnih, Volodymyr, Koray Kavukcuoglu, David Silver, Andrei A. Rusu, Joel Veness, Marc G. Bellemare, Alex Graves, et al. 2015. "Human-Level Control through Deep Reinforcement Learning." *Nature* 518 (7540): 529–33. `https://doi.org/10.1038/nature14236`.

Morin, Frederic, and Yoshua Bengio. 2005. "Hierarchical Probabilistic Neural Network Language Model." In *Aistats*, 5:246–52.

Nakamoto, Yukikazu. 2011. "A Short Introduction to Learning to Rank." *IEICE Transactions on Information and Systems* E94-D (1): 1–2. `https://doi.org/10.1587/transinf.E94.D.1`.

Nasseri, Alya Al, Allan Tucker, and Sergio de Cesare. 2015. "Quantifying StockTwits Semantic Terms' Trading Behavior in Financial Markets: An Effective Application of Decision Tree Algorithms." *Expert Systems with Applications* 42 (23): 9192–9210. `https://doi.org/10.1016/j.eswa.2015.08.008`.

Netzer, Yuval. 2011. "Reading Digits in Natural Images with Unsupervised Feature Learning." In *NIPS Workshop on Deep Learning*.

Nevmyvaka, Yuriy, Yi Feng, and Michael Kearns. 2006. "Reinforcement Learning for Optimized Trade Execution." In *Proceedings of the 23rd International Conference on Machine Learning*, 673–680. ICML '06. Pittsburgh, Pennsylvania, USA: Association for Computing Machinery. `https://doi.org/10.1145/1143844.1143929`.

Ng, Andrew Y., and Michael I. Jordan. 2002. "On Discriminative vs. Generative Classifiers: A Comparison of Logistic Regression and Naive Bayes." In *Advances in Neural Information Processing Systems* 14, edited by T. G. Dietterich, S. Becker, and Z. Ghahramani, 841–848. MIT Press. `http://papers.nips.cc/paper/2020-on-discriminative-vs-generative-classifiers-a-comparison-of-logistic-regression-and-naive-bayes.pdf`.

Nilsson, Nils J. 2009. *The Quest for Artificial Intelligence*. Cambridge University Press.

Novy-Marx, R., 2015. *Backtesting Strategies Based on Multiple Signals (Working Paper No. 21329)*. National Bureau of Economic Research. https://doi.org/10.3386/w21329.

Odena, Augustus. 2019. "Open Questions about Generative Adversarial Networks." *Distill* 4 (4): e18. https://doi.org/10.23915/distill.00018.

Pan, Zhaoqing, Weijie Yu, Xiaokai Yi, Asifullah Khan, Feng Yuan, and Yuhui Zheng. 2019. "Recent Progress on Generative Adversarial Networks (GANs): A Survey." *IEEE Access* 7: 36322–33. https://doi.org/10.1109/ACCESS.2019.2905015.

Pennington, Jeffrey, Richard Socher, and Christoper Manning. 2014. "Glove: Global Vectors for Word Representation." In *EMNLP*, 14:1532–43. https://doi.org/10.3115/v1/D14-1162.

Perold, A.F., 2004. *The Capital Asset Pricing Model*. Journal of Economic Perspectives 18, 3–24. https://doi.org/10.1257/0895330042162340.

Prabhavalkar, Rohit, Kanishka Rao, Tara N. Sainath, Bo Li, Leif Johnson, and Navdeep Jaitly. 2017. "A Comparison of Sequence-to-Sequence Models for Speech Recognition." In *Interspeech* 2017, 939–43. ISCA. https://doi.org/10.21437/Interspeech.2017-233.

Prado, M.L. de, 2016. "Building Diversified Portfolios that Outperform Out of Sample." *The Journal of Portfolio Management* 42, 59–69. https://doi.org/10.3905/jpm.2016.42.4.059.

Preis, Tobias, Helen Susannah Moat, and H. Eugene Stanley. 2013. "Quantifying Trading Behavior in Financial Markets Using Google Trends." *Scientific Reports* 3 (1): 1–6. https://doi.org/10.1038/srep01684.

Prokhorenkova, Liudmila, Gleb Gusev, Aleksandr Vorobev, Anna Veronika Dorogush, and Andrey Gulin. 2019. "CatBoost: Unbiased Boosting with Categorical Features." *ArXiv:1706.09516 [Cs]*, January. http://arxiv.org/abs/1706.09516.

Radford, Alec, Luke Metz, and Soumith Chintala. 2016. "Unsupervised Representation Learning with Deep Convolutional Generative Adversarial Networks." *ArXiv:1511.06434 [Cs]*, January. http://arxiv.org/abs/1511.06434.

Raffinot, T., 2017. *Hierarchical Clustering-Based Asset Allocation*. The Journal of Portfolio Management 44, 89–99. https://doi.org/10.3905/jpm.2018.44.2.089.

Rasekhschaffe, Keywan Christian, and Robert C. Jones. 2019. "Machine Learning for Stock Selection." *Financial Analysts Journal* 75 (3): 70–88. https://doi.org/10.1080/0015198X.2019.1596678.

Redmon, Joseph. 2016. "You Only Look Once: Unified, Real-Time Object Detection." *ArXiv:1506.02640 [Cs]*, May.

Reed, Scott, Zeynep Akata, Santosh Mohan, Samuel Tenka, Bernt Schiele, and Honglak Lee. 2016. "Learning What and Where to Draw." *ArXiv:1610.02454 [Cs]*, October. http://arxiv.org/abs/1610.02454.

Reinganum, Marc R. 1981. "Misspecification of Capital Asset Pricing: Empirical Anomalies Based on Earnings' Yields and Market Values." *Journal of Financial Economics* 9 (1): 19–46.

Ren, Shaoqing, Kaiming He, Ross Girshick, and Jian Sun. 2015. "Faster R-CNN: Towards Real-Time Object Detection with Region Proposal Networks." In *Advances in Neural Information Processing Systems* 28, edited by C. Cortes, N. D. Lawrence, D. D. Lee, M. Sugiyama, and R. Garnett, 91–99. Curran Associates, Inc. http://papers.nips.cc/paper/5638-faster-r-cnn-towards-real-time-object-detection-with-region-proposal-networks.pdf.

Roa-Vicens, Jacobo, Cyrine Chtourou, Angelos Filos, Francisco Rullan, Yarin Gal, and Ricardo Silva. 2019. "Towards Inverse Reinforcement Learning for Limit Order Book Dynamics." *ArXiv:1906.04813 [Cs, q-Fin, Stat]*, June. http://arxiv.org/abs/1906.04813.

Röder, Michael, Andreas Both, and Alexander Hinneburg. 2015. "Exploring the Space of Topic Coherence Measures." In *Proceedings of the Eighth ACM International Conference on Web Search and Data Mining*, 399–408. WSDM '15. Shanghai, China: Association for Computing Machinery. https://doi.org/10.1145/2684822.2685324.

Rokach, Lior, and Oded Z. Maimon. 2008. *Data Mining with Decision Trees: Theory and Applications*. World Scientific.

Roll, Richard, and Stephen A. Ross. 1984. "The Arbitrage Pricing Theory Approach to Strategic Portfolio Planning." *Financial Analysts Journal* 40 (3): 14–26. https://doi.org/10.2469/faj.v40.n3.14.

Romero, P.J., Balch, T., 2014. *What Hedge Funds Really Do: An Introduction to Portfolio Management*. Business Expert Press.

Ruder, Sebastian. 2017. "An Overview of Gradient Descent Optimization Algorithms." *ArXiv:1609.04747 [Cs]*, June. http://arxiv.org/abs/1609.04747.

Salimans, Tim, Diederik P. Kingma, and Max Welling. 2015. "Markov Chain Monte Carlo and Variational Inference: Bridging the Gap." *ArXiv:1410.6460 [Stat]*, May. http://arxiv.org/abs/1410.6460.

Samuelson, P., Thorp, E., T. Kassouf, S., 1968. *Beat the Market: A Scientific Stock Market System*. Journal of the American Statistical Association 63, 1049. https://doi.org/10.2307/2283900.

Saul, Lawrence K, and Sam T Roweis. 2000. "An Introduction to Locally Linear Embedding." Unpublished. Available at: https://cs.nyu.edu/~roweis/lle/papers/lleintro.pdf.

Schapire, Robert E., and Yoav Freund. 2012. *Boosting: Foundations and Algorithms*. MIT Press.

Schaul, Tom, John Quan, Ioannis Antonoglou, and David Silver. 2015. "Prioritized Experience Replay." *ArXiv:1511.05952 [Cs]*, November. http://arxiv.org/abs/1511.05952.

Schuster, M., and K.K. Paliwal. 1997. "Bidirectional Recurrent Neural Networks." *IEEE Transactions on Signal Processing* 45 (11): 2673–81. `https://doi.org/10.1109/78.650093`.

Sezer, Omer Berat, and Ahmet Murat Ozbayoglu. 2018. "Algorithmic Financial Trading with Deep Convolutional Neural Networks: Time Series to Image Conversion Approach." *Applied Soft Computing* 70 (September): 525–38. `https://doi.org/10.1016/j.asoc.2018.04.024`.

Sievert, Carson, and Kenneth Shirley. 2014. "LDAvis: A Method for Visualizing and Interpreting Topics." In *Proceedings of the Workshop on Interactive Language Learning, Visualization, and Interfaces*, 63–70.

Sigtia, Siddharth, Emmanouil Benetos, Srikanth Cherla, Tillman Weyde, A. Garcez, and Simon Dixon. 2014. "RNN-Based Music Language Models for Improving Automatic Music Transcription."

Simonyan, Karen. 2015. "Very Deep Convolutional Networks for Large-Scale Image Recognition." *ArXiv:1409.1556 [Cs]*, April.

Srivastava, Nitish, Elman Mansimov, and Ruslan Salakhutdinov. 2016. "Unsupervised Learning of Video Representations Using LSTMs," 10.

Stevens, Keith, Philip Kegelmeyer, David Andrzejewski, and David Buttler. 2012. "Exploring Topic Coherence over Many Models and Many Topics."

Strumeyer, Gary. 2017. *The Capital Markets: Evolution of the Financial Ecosystem.* John Wiley & Sons.

Sutskever, Ilya, James Martens, George Dahl, and Geoffrey Hinton. 2013. "On the Importance of Initialization and Momentum in Deep Learning." In *International Conference on Machine Learning*, 1139–47. `http://proceedings.mlr.press/v28/sutskever13.html`.

Sutton, Richard S, and Andrew G Barto. 2018. *Reinforcement Learning: An Introduction.* MIT press.

Sutton, Richard S, David A. McAllester, Satinder P. Singh, and Yishay Mansour. 2000. "Policy Gradient Methods for Reinforcement Learning with Function Approximation." In *Advances in Neural Information Processing Systems* 12, edited by S. A. Solla, T. K. Leen, and K. Müller, 1057–1063. MIT Press. `http://papers.nips.cc/paper/1713-policy-gradient-methods-for-reinforcement-learning-with-function-approximation.pdf`.

Szegedy, Christian, Wei Liu, Yangqing Jia, Pierre Sermanet, Scott Reed, Dragomir Anguelov, Dumitru Erhan, Vincent Vanhoucke, and Andrew Rabinovich. 2015. "Going Deeper with Convolutions." In 2015 *IEEE Conference on Computer Vision and Pattern Recognition (CVPR)*, 1–9. `https://doi.org/10.1109/CVPR.2015.7298594`.

Trichilo, D., Braun, J.L., 2005. *Extending the Fundamental Law of Investment Management.*

Vaswani, Ashish, Noam Shazeer, Niki Parmar, Jakob Uszkoreit, Llion Jones, Aidan N Gomez, Łukasz Kaiser, and Illia Polosukhin. 2017. "Attention Is All You Need." In *Advances in Neural Information Processing Systems* 30, edited by I. Guyon, U. V. Luxburg, S. Bengio, H. Wallach, R. Fergus, S. Vishwanathan, and R. Garnett, 5998–6008. Curran Associates, Inc. `http://papers.nips.cc/paper/7181-attention-is-all-you-need.pdf`.

Vincent, Pascal, Hugo Larochelle, Yoshua Bengio, and Pierre-Antoine Manzagol. 2008. "Extracting and Composing Robust Features with Denoising Autoencoders." In *Proceedings of the 25th International Conference on Machine Learning*, 1096–1103. ICML '08. Helsinki, Finland: Association for Computing Machinery. `https://doi.org/10.1145/1390156.1390294`.

Wang, Alex, Yada Pruksachatkun, Nikita Nangia, Amanpreet Singh, Julian Michael, Felix Hill, Omer Levy, and Samuel R. Bowman. 2019. "SuperGLUE: A Stickier Benchmark for General-Purpose Language Understanding Systems." *ArXiv:1905.00537 [Cs]*, May. `http://arxiv.org/abs/1905.00537`.

Wang, Jia, Tong Sun, Benyuan Liu, Yu Cao, and Hongwei Zhu. 2019. "CLVSA: A Convolutional LSTM Based Variational Sequence-to-Sequence Model with Attention for Predicting Trends of Financial Markets." In *Proceedings of the Twenty-Eighth International Joint Conference on Artificial Intelligence*, 3705–11. Macao, China: International Joint Conferences on Artificial Intelligence Organization. `https://doi.org/10.24963/ijcai.2019/514`.

Watkins, Christopher J. C. H., and Peter Dayan. 1992. "Q-Learning." In *Machine Learning*, 279–292.

Watkins, Christopher John Cornish Hellaby. 1989. "Learning from Delayed Rewards.", `http://www.cs.rhul.ac.uk/~chrisw/new_thesis.pdf`.

Werbos, P.J. 1990. "Backpropagation through Time: What It Does and How to Do It." *Proceedings of the IEEE 78 (10)*: 1550–60. `https://doi.org/10.1109/5.58337`.

Wiese, Magnus, Robert Knobloch, Ralf Korn, and Peter Kretschmer. 2019. "Quant GANs: Deep Generation of Financial Time Series." *ArXiv:1907.06673 [Cs, q-Fin, Stat]*, December. `http://arxiv.org/abs/1907.06673`.

Williams, Ronald J, and David Zipser. 1989. "A Learning Algorithm for Continually Running Fully Recurrent Neural Networks." *Neural Computation* 1 (2): 270–80.

Wooldridge, Jeffrey M. 2002. "Econometric Analysis of Cross Section and Panel Data MIT Press." *Cambridge*, MA 108.

Wooldridge, Jeffrey M. 2008. *Introductory Econometrics: A Modern Approach. Cengage Learning*.

Yoon, Jinsung, Daniel Jarrett, and Mihaela van der Schaar. 2019. "Time-Series Generative Adversarial Networks." In *Advances in Neural Information Processing Systems* 32, edited by H. Wallach, H. Larochelle, A. Beygelzimer, F. d\textquotesingle Alché-Buc, E. Fox, and R. Garnett, 5508–5518. Curran Associates, Inc. `http://papers.nips.cc/paper/8789-time-series-generative-adversarial-networks.pdf`.

Zhang, Han, Tao Xu, Hongsheng Li, Shaoting Zhang, Xiaogang Wang, Xiaolei Huang, and Dimitris Metaxas. 2017. "StackGAN: Text to Photo-Realistic Image Synthesis with Stacked Generative Adversarial Networks." *ArXiv:1612.03242 [Cs, Stat]*, August. `http://arxiv.org/abs/1612.03242`.

Zhou, Xingyu, Zhisong Pan, Guyu Hu, Siqi Tang, and Cheng Zhao. 2018. "Stock Market Prediction on High-Frequency Data Using Generative Adversarial Nets." *Research Article: Mathematical Problems in Engineering. Hindawi*. 2018. `https://doi.org/10.1155/2018/4907423`.

Zhu, Jun-Yan, Taesung Park, Phillip Isola, and Alexei A. Efros. 2018. "Unpaired Image-to-Image Translation Using Cycle-Consistent Adversarial Networks." *ArXiv:1703.10593 [Cs]*, November. `http://arxiv.org/abs/1703.10593`.

Index

Symbols

A

B

C

D

E

F

G

H

I

J

K

L

M

N

O

P

Q

R

T

U

V

W

X

Y

Z

Download a free PDF copy of this book

Thanks for purchasing this book!

Do you like to read on the go but are unable to carry your print books everywhere?
Is your eBook purchase not compatible with the device of your choice?

Don't worry, now with every Packt book you get a DRM-free PDF version of that book at no cost.

Read anywhere, any place, on any device. Search, copy, and paste code from your favorite technical books directly into your application.

The perks don't stop there, you can get exclusive access to discounts, newsletters, and great free content in your inbox daily

Follow these simple steps to get the benefits:

1. Scan the QR code or visit the link below

   `https://packt.link/free-ebook/9781839217715`

2. Submit your proof of purchase
3. That's it! We'll send your free PDF and other benefits to your email directly

www.ingramcontent.com/pod-product-compliance
Lightning Source LLC
Chambersburg PA
CBHW080731150926
51501CB00006B/179